1860

The German physiologist Gustav Fechner publishes *Elements of Psychophysics,* in which he explores the way people respond to stimuli such as light and sound. The work prompts thought and experimentation in the area of human and animal perception.

1869

Sir Francis Galton, half cousin to Charles Darwin, publishes a study of heredity and genius, pioneering a statistical technique that Karl Pearson would later call *correlation.* Subsequently, Galton makes numerous contributions to measurement with various inventions and innovations.

1879

Wilhelm Max Wundt founds the first experimental psychology laboratory, in Leipzig, Germany. The event is momentous because psychology is now being treated as a science and not just a branch of philosophy. Wundt, a structuralist, relies heavily on a tool of assessment called *introspection,* wherein subjects try to faithfully describe their conscious experience of a stimulus. The researchers at Leipzig and their disciples concentrate on the measurement of sensory-related abilities, reaction time, and the like, but they tended to not measure things like cognitive ability or social judgment.

1890

American psychologist James McKeen Cattell coins the term *mental test* in a publication. Cattell studied with Wundt at Leipzig and was inspired by Galton at Cambridge. Returning to the United States, Cattell was very instrumental in launching mental testing. He founded a number of publications (notably *Science* and *Psychological Review*) and in 1921 started Psychological Corporation, a company with the goal of "useful applications of psychology."

1892

Psychiatrist Emil Kraeplin, who studied with Wundt, publishes his work regarding the use of a test that involves word association.

1895

Alfred Binet and Victor Henri publish articles calling for the measurement of cognitive abilities such as memory, as well as other human abilities such as social comprehension. Interestingly, Binet also wonders aloud about the possible use of inkblots to study personality.

1896

Lightner Witmer establishes the first psychological clinic in the United States, at the University of Pennsylvania. Subsequently, in 1907, Witmer would found a journal called *Psychological Clinic.* The first article in that journal would be written by Witmer and entitled "Clinical Psychology." In it, Witmer does *not* anticipate managed care.

1904

Charles Spearman, a student of Wundt at Leipzig, begins to lay the foundation for the concept of test reliability. He also begins building the mathematical framework for factor analysis.

1905

Alfred Binet and Theodore Simon publish a 30-item "measuring scale of intelligence" designed to help identify mentally retarded Paris schoolchildren. The notion of measuring intelligence has great intuitive appeal worldwide, and the Binet-Simon Intelligence Scale launches a new era in measurement.

1913

Swiss psychiatrist Hermann Rorschach, the son of an art teacher, publishes papers on how analysis of patients' artwork can provide insights into personality. In 1921, his now famous monograph, *Psychodiagnostics,* would evolve into a test that has become almost synonymous with psychological testing in the public eye, the Rorschach Inkblot Test.

1913

John Watson publishes *Psychology as the Behaviorist Views It,* which becomes known as the "behaviorist manifesto." And as the behaviorist views it, behavioral observation becomes a key tool of assessment.

1914

World War I serves as a boon to the testing movement since thousands of recruits must be quickly screened for intellectual functioning, as well as emotional fitness.

1916

After years of research, Lewis M. Terman, working at Stanford University, publishes the Stanford Revision of the Binet-Simon Intelligence Scale. This American adaptation and revision of the test first developed in France would become widely known as the Stanford-Binet.

1926

The College Board sponsors the development of the Scholastic Aptitude Test (SAT) and administers the test for the first time this year. About 15 years later, a fixed reference group scoring system for this test would be put in place as the scores of the 11,000 SAT test takers in 1941 become immortalized as a standard to be used in the conversion of raw scores on future administrations of the test. Years later, data from the more than 2 million test takers who would take the SAT in 1990 would be used to create a new fixed reference group data base, which would go into service in 1995.

1927

Carl Spearman publishes a two-factor theory of intelligence in which he postulates the existence of a general intellectual ability factor (g) and specific (s) components of that general ability. Also this year, German neurologist Kurt Goldstein begins to develop neurodiagnostic tests on the basis of research with soldiers who suffered brain injury during World War I.

(continued on inside back cover)

This is the property of the Office of the SVP of R+D. Please Return to Margaret Sudhakar at the end of the Semester.

Psychological Testing and Assessment

Psychological Testing and Assessment

An Introduction to Tests and Measurement

SIXTH EDITION

Ronald Jay Cohen

Mark E. Swerdlik
ILLINOIS STATE UNIVERSITY

ONLINE LEARNING CENTER
www.mhhe.com/cohentesting6

Boston   Burr Ridge, IL   Dubuque, IA   Madison, WI   New York   San Francisco   St. Louis
Bangkok   Bogotá   Caracas   Kuala Lumpur   Lisbon   London   Madrid   Mexico City
Milan   Montreal   New Delhi   Santiago   Seoul   Singapore   Sydney   Taipei   Toronto

The McGraw·Hill Companies

Higher Education

PSYCHOLOGICAL TESTING AND ASSESSMENT: AN INTRODUCTION TO
TESTS AND MEASUREMENT, SIXTH EDITION

Published by McGraw-Hill, a business unit of The McGraw-Hill Companies, Inc.,
1221 Avenue of the Americas, New York, NY 10020. Copyright © 2005, 2002, 1999,
1996, 1992, 1988 by The McGraw-Hill Companies, Inc. All rights reserved. No part
of this publication may be reproduced or distributed in any form or by any means,
or stored in a database or retrieval system, without the prior written consent of The
McGraw-Hill Companies, Inc., including, but not limited to, any network or other
electronic storage or transmission, or broadcast for distance learning.

Some ancillaries, including electronic and print components, may not be available
to customers outside the United States.

ISBN-13: 978-0-07-288767-9
ISBN-10: 0-07-288767-2

5 6 7 8 9 0 C CI/CCI 0 9 8 7 6

Editor-in-chief: *Emily Barrosse*
Publisher: *Stephen D. Rutter*
Sponsoring editor: *John Wannemacher*
Marketing manager: *Melissa Caughlin*
Production services manager: *Jennifer Mills*
Production service: *Fairplay Publishing Services*
Manuscript editor: *April Wells-Hayes*
Art director: *Jeanne M. Schreiber*

Design manager and cover designer: *Violeta
Diaz*
Interior designer: *Michael Remener*
Art manager: *Robin Mouat*
Photo researcher: *LouAnn Wilson*
Illustrators: *Judith Ogus, Robin Mouat*
Production supervisor: *Tandra Jorgensen*

The text was set in 10/12 Palatino by G&S Typesetters, Inc., and printed on
acid-free, 45# New Era Matte by Courier Kendallville, Inc.

Cover image: *Naomi Shea*

The credits for this book begin on page C-1, a continuation of the copyright page.

Library of Congress Cataloging-in-Publication Data

Cohen, Ronald Jay.
    Psychological testing and assessment : an introduction to tests and
measurement / Ronald Jay Cohen, Mark E. Swerdlik. — 6th ed.
        p. cm.
    Includes bibliographical references and index.
    ISBN 0-07-288767-2
    1. Psychological tests—Textbooks.   2. Psychometrics—Textbooks.
I. Swerdlik, Mark E.   II. Title.

BF176.C63   2004
150'.28'7—dc22   2004040325

www.mhhe.com

This book is dedicated with love to the memory of Edith and Harold Cohen.

Contents

7   Test Development   190

PART IV *The Assessment of Personality*

12   Personality Assessment Methods   376

PART **V** *Testing and Assessment in Action*

13   Clinical and Counseling Assessment   419

Preface

I remember walking with some of my fellow clinical psychology interns at Bellevue Hospital, entering a building in the NYU-Bellevue Medical Center complex, and hearing someone—pointing to a man in the distance—say, "There's David Wechsler!" Indeed, there stood one of the living legends in the field of psychology. As a graduate student, I had learned to administer each of the Wechsler intelligence tests and had even been privileged enough to serve as an examiner in the restandardization of one of them. Seeing this psychologist in person, for the first time, as a fellow employee at Bellevue, inspired a sense of awe.

It was during my internship year at Bellevue that I first began to think about writing a textbook on testing, assessment, and measurement in psychology. I was gaining a great deal of clinical experience in the area of assessment, was completing a doctoral dissertation involving assessment and impression management, and had access to some of the most renowned human resources in the field of clinical psychology. In settings as diverse as the Bellevue child/adolescent/adult in-patient services, psychiatric emergency room, prison service, adult out-patient clinic, and in-hospital courtroom, academic instruction was complemented by supervised experience with a wide variety of assessment-related dilemmas and solutions. This growing body of knowledge and experience reinforced my developing views about the need for a new measurement textbook. This new textbook would be authored by people who actually used tests with real people. It would address not only psychometric essentials but various areas of interest to students of assessment who have wondered about sundry aspects of the enterprise.

My education and experience in the area of testing and assessment continued after my internship year with my appointment as senior psychologist on the NYU-Bellevue staff. I handled a regular stream of assessment cases and instructed and supervised clinical psychology interns. The work entailed daily immersion in all phases of clinical assessment, including routine case presentations to colleagues. One day, while chatting informally with David Wechsler—the luminary I had come to know as a colleague—he related a story about the time Dan Rather and a CBS camera crew had set up shop in his Upper East Side apartment. They had come to conduct an in-depth interview with him on the subject of intelligence, for use on *CBS Reports*. Dr. Wechsler quipped that it wasn't until that day that the people in his building got an inkling that he must be kind of an important person; he had to be, if Dan Rather was coming to interview him! Even as Dr. Wechsler spoke, I envisioned a time when I, too, would request a formal interview with him, the better to provide some "insider" insights for this book. But the interview was not to be. Dr. Wechsler's death preceded that request.

Although we did not have the benefit of Dr. Wechsler's personal input for the first edition of this textbook, we have been—through the more than quarter-century in which the present edition of this textbook has evolved—fortunate enough to obtain the input of dozens of other authorities in areas such as intelligence, personality, statistics, and culture. During that period, the authors collectively gained not only greater knowledge about how to effectively convey essential measurement principles in a textbook but also greater personal experience using tests and applying measurement principles in a truly wide array of clinical, school, and organizational settings. In these pages, you have the opportunity to reap the benefit of this accumulated experience and knowledge as well as countless hours of diligent research to make this work as current as possible.

Reviewers of previous editions of this work have tended to praise its breadth and depth—which I dare say has only improved with age. Beyond coverage, I believe you will find the writing style and level of this book to be somewhere between "most accessible" and "highly appealing." As has been our custom, we have interspersed elements of humor in various forms (original cartoons, examples, and vignettes) throughout the text. The judicious use of humorous examples to engage and maintain student interest is something of a novelty among measurement textbooks. Where else would one turn for pedagogy that employs an example involving a bimodal distribution of test scores from a new trade school called *The Home Study School of Elvis Presley Impersonators*? What about the use of regression equations to predict prospective grade-point averages at the *DeSade School of Dentistry*? As readers learn about face validity, they discover why it "gets no respect" and how it has been characterized as "the Rodney Dangerfield of psychometric variables." We could list more examples, but let's reserve those smiles for a pleasant surprise when you come upon them in the text.

Also in the interest of engaging and maintaining student interest, we draw heavily on various examples from popular culture, including popular media. Take note, for example, when you find mention of programs such as *Trading Spaces, Wild On . . . , Iron Chef, South Park,* and *Survivor.* These are television shows that students watch, and a (surprise) reference to one of them in order to illustrate an assessment-related point is designed to elicit a pleasant feeling of recognition—all in the context of involving students in the material. In the course of learning how to write a good matching-type item, for example, students are challenged to identify what actors Pierce Brosnan, Sean Connery, Timothy Dalton, George Lazenby, David Niven, and Roger Moore all have in common.

Throughout, we have tried to incorporate timely, relevant, and intriguing illustrations of assessment-related material. For example, in the new *Everyday Psychometrics* box in Chapter 1, we introduce the subject of evaluation and ratings in the context of the Motion Picture Association of America's film rating system. In the new *Close-up* box in Chapter 2, we take a detailed look at the Supreme Court case *Grutter v. Bollinger et al.* (2003). In that case, the Court grappled with issues of diversity as they affect the evaluation and selection of applicants for admission to public universities.

Novel, thought-provoking, assessment-related material has been something of a tradition in each edition of this book. Intriguing discussion has been presented on topics as diverse as the Szondi Pictures Test (first edition), marital and family assessment (second edition), in-home evaluation of consumer response to television commercials (third edition), computer-assisted behavioral assessment in institutional settings (fourth edition), and "life-or-death" psychological assessment (fifth edition). The tradition continues in the present work. For example, in Chapter 12, many readers will be surprised to learn of B. F. Skinner's flirtation with projective testing (yes, *that* B. F. Skinner).

Beyond intriguing assessment-related sidebars, there is a great deal that is new to this edition, and new about it. Of course, we have updated the text with regard to new tests that have been published since our last edition. This updating includes descriptions of the new Wechsler, Stanford-Binet, Bender-Gestalt, GRE, and SAT tests, among others. Of course, we have updated the text with new test-related legislation, judicial decisions, and administrative regulations that have gone into effect since our last edition. Expanded and updated coverage is presented on a wide variety of topic areas, including

- culture-related issues, including specific recommendations for culturally informed psychological assessment
- the medical model of disability as compared to the new paradigm of disability
- test-item writing, including item writing for item-branched and item-banked tests
- geriatric assessment

- assessment in the military
- assessment for career change and career transition
- dynamic assessment
- biopsychosocial assessment
- the Big Five, Cattell's "Big Five," and Tellegen's "Big Three"
- recent critiques of projective methods, along with rebuttals to those critiques
- quality assurance methods during the test revision process, including the introduction of new terms such as *anchor protocol* and *scoring drift*

In the interest of conserving space while providing students with a quick and easy way to reference information, we have placed more material in tabular form. New tables in this edition include information regarding

- pros and cons of various sources of information about tests
- advantages and disadvantages of various item formats
- pros and cons of traditional group testing
- important legislation, litigation, and administrative regulations
- major entrance examinations for professional or occupational training
- essential "dos" and "don'ts" of cultural sensitivity in assessment

Complementing all of the new material is an expanded glossary. More than 100 new terms have been added to the glossary in this edition. With all of the new and enhanced coverage, the length of this book could easily have been increased significantly over previous editions. Instead, through thoughtful writing and rewriting, careful editing, and the liberal use of tables to summarize information, the book's size is about the same as previous editions'. The initial, introductory material has been reduced in length so that students can obtain a general overview of the field relatively quickly. Throughout the book, the size of most of the paragraphs has been reduced compared to previous editions. Essential material from the former Chapter 17, "Computer-Assisted Psychological Testing and Assessment," was transferred as appropriate into other chapters throughout the book. Indeed, *less can be more.*

One thing that has *not* changed in this edition is our dedicated resolve to develop a leading-edge, much-emulated-but-never-duplicated, measurement textbook that

- introduces students to the assessment enterprise and overviews the wide range of instruments and procedures they may encounter
- familiarizes students with the reasoning behind the construction of tests and the rationale of various approaches to assessment
- leaves students with a sense of the appropriate uses of tests
- leaves students with a sense of the inappropriate uses of tests
- compels students to think actively about issues related to testing and assessment

Along the way, there has been a concerted effort to *humanize* the material, the better to involve students with it. Such humanizing of the material can be seen in the writing and in the illustrations, as when we include interesting biographical facts on historical figures in assessment. See, for example, the new photo and brief biographical statement of MMPI senior author James Butcher (Figure 11-4). Throughout the text, an attempt has been made to truly involve students via intriguing, real-life illustrations of points. Some examples:

- life-or-death psychological assessment and the ethical issues involved (pages 55–56)
- human emotion in the context of categorical cutoffs (page 7)
- the breathalyzer as a point of departure to discuss reliability (page 147)
- the confessions of a behavior rater (pages 408–409)
- assessment through means such as evaluation of college yearbook photos (page 415)
- the utility of tests to measure aggressiveness (page 338) and dangerousness (pages 440–441)

The first proposal for this book was sent to a publisher in the mid-1970s. In that document, I envisioned a measurement text that was different in key ways from any existing book. As it happened, the first edition of this text would begin a tradition in terms of setting the standard and then raising the bar for measurement textbooks to follow. It would be a textbook that stood in stark contrast to any other of the day in terms of content, organization, style, originality, and pedagogy, among other variables. With regard to content, for example, it contained material not seen before—but now rather standard—in measurement textbooks. Contrary to prevailing beliefs, I believed that topics such as forensic assessment, neuropsychological assessment, and assessment for custody evaluations merited coverage in a measurement textbook. Having acted as a consultant to businesses and commercial test development firms such as Educational Testing Service, I appreciated how valuable it would be to cover business-related applications, including consumer assessment. Having been employed full-time as a clinician who regularly administered tests, I wanted to write a chapter on clinical assessment that imparted a firsthand sense of what clinical assessment is about. Having taught testing and assessment, I knew that many students entered the course "rusty" or downright unsure of themselves with regard to basic statistics—hence the development of the "Statistics Refresher" chapter.

The style of the book—somewhat informal in tone—complemented the new content well. Because I found my sense of humor to be a valuable asset in the classroom, I attempted to intersperse some "personality" and humorous illustrations in the writing. Because I always enjoyed reading about historical aspects of the enterprise, I included photos of historical figures in assessment, complete with interesting biographical facts. In these and other ways, the first edition of this book represented a major departure from what was then available in measurement textbooks. Our new way of defining what a measurement textbook could be might best be characterized as *magical*, judging from the overwhelmingly positive response it elicited from instructors who taught measurement courses.

Upon publication of the first edition, I learned that many people in the field found the unique aspects of the book most appealing. One of those people was Lee J. Cronbach, who shared with me, when we met at an APA meeting, how very much he enjoyed the book. I was so grateful to Lee for his encouragement, and felt so uplifted by our meeting, that I subsequently requested a photo from him for use in the second edition. The photo he sent me was indeed published in the second edition of this book—in spite of the fact that Lee had out at the time a measurement book that could be viewed as a direct competitor in the textbook marketplace. Regardless, I wanted Lee's place in history acknowledged, and I wanted to thank him in my own way for his kind words and "seal of approval."

Beyond content and style, the first edition of this book was unique in terms of its organization. Here, there really was no magic involved, only logic. We started with a few chapters to overview the field, gave some historical perspective, and provided important background related to legal, ethical, and cultural issues. After the statistics refresher, we proceeded with several chapters designed to impart the essential basics of measurement. Logic dictated that prior to any discussion of the assessment of intelligence, personality, or whatever, some preliminary information regarding definitional and related issues must precede it. What followed next were several chapters designed to illustrate sundry aspects of measurement in various applied contexts. Having served as a consultant to many businesses and organizations, and being the founder and editor-in-chief of a scholarly journal (*Psychology & Marketing*) that regularly features articles detailing business applications of assessment, I felt I had unique and valuable information to offer students taking a course in measurement.

As it turns out, the organization of our book has been so appealing that almost every major textbook on the subject published since we first submitted our proposal follows the same or a similar formula. In fact, reviewers have sometimes referred to these similar books as "Cohen clones" or "Cohen wannabes." My own characterization would lean more toward "wannabes" than "clones," as a *clone* is an exact replica; all of the "wannabe" measurement textbooks are but pale copies.

Imitation is the sincerest form of flattery, and we look on with some sense of gratification as others try to capitalize on our success. But while the wannabes may copy our organization, and even some of the illustrations and features, there is so much that they cannot copy. They do not (and seem unable to) copy our style. They do not humanize the material in the way that we do. They cannot copy our leading-edge content because they are, by their self-evident nature, followers. It will take them an edition or two, for example, to incorporate some of the new material in this edition. For some topics, such as culture-related issues in assessment, the wannabes have a particularly long way to go to catch up. Some of the wannabes depart from our chapter organization by covering legal/ethical issues near the end of the book rather than at the beginning. Personally, I view such placement as ill-advised. Legal and ethical issues set a context for the assessment enterprise. Discussion of legal and ethical issues helps place the discussion of measurement, assessment, and testing in perspective. Also, unless chapters are assigned from the rear of such books early on, the possibility exists that some students will receive no exposure at all to this most important information.

Another key way in which this book parts company with comparable books is in the way that issues of testing and assessment are distinguished. In a bygone era, we believe every reason existed to entitle a book such as this *Psychological Testing* and then proceed to clump issues of testing with issues of assessment in all discussion. Today, in an era when it is important to distinguish between *testing* and *assessment*, we believe a title such as *Psychological Testing* can be anachronistic, if not misleading, in terms of the material that is actually being covered. We believe that it is incumbent upon contemporary textbook authors to make a clear distinction between *testing* and *assessment*. We do that in the first few pages in an effort to orient the student to all that follows. We also believe that it is a sound teaching practice to maintain the definitional distinction between *testing* and *assessment* throughout the book. We heartily encourage instructors to exercise some critical thinking with regard to how well many of the competing measurement textbooks make a distinction between testing and assessment—beginning with the book's title—and then maintain that distinction in their writing. And speaking of critical thinking . . .

Critical thinking may be defined as "the active employment of judgment capabilities and evaluative skills in the thought process" (Cohen, 1994, p. 12). *Generative thinking* may be defined as "the goal-oriented intellectual production of new or creative ideas" (Cohen, 1994, p. 13). The exercise of both of these processes, I believe, helps optimize one's chances for success in the academic world as well as in more applied pursuits. In previous editions, questions to stimulate critical and generative thinking were raised "the old-fashioned way." That is, they were right in the text, and usually part of a paragraph.

Acting on the advice of reviewers, we have made this special feature of our writing even more special by writing more questions and setting them in the margins. Now it is up to motivated students to do their part and actually *think* about the *Just Think* questions. In this context, instructors, too, may consider thinking about one question related to student motivation: Will awarding extra credit for writing responses to selected *Just Think* exercises further motivate students?

In addition to critical thinking and generative thinking questions called out in the text, other pedagogical aids in this book include original cartoons created by the authors, original illustrations created by the authors (including the model of memory in the neuropsychological assessment chapter), and original acronyms created by the authors.

We have offered a student workbook, an instructor's manual, and a test item bank as part of the teaching package with every edition of this book since the very first. Recent editions have further supplemented this excellent teaching package with Internet-based study aids for students, as well as teaching tips and a discussion forum for instructors.

The authors have been very focused and very diligent in their efforts to bring you a leading-edge measurement textbook that involves students in the subject matter and imparts a wealth of academic and applied information essential to understanding psychological testing and assessment. Mark Swerdlik persevered in these objectives under very challenging conditions since the last edition. During that time period, Mark lost his mother, Edna (1912–2003); his father, Al (1910–2002); and his uncle, Aaron Swerdlik (1917–2002), who holds the distinction of being a layperson with no background in psychology who actually read our book cover to cover. Mark dedicates his contributions to this edition to the memory of these cherished family members.

As we were completing work on this edition, I received the most unexpected news that my mother had suffered a massive stroke. She did not survive. It is impossible to express the sense of sadness and loss experienced by myself, my brother, and my sister, as well as the countless other people who knew this gentle, loving, and much loved person. We will miss her counsel, her sense of humor, and just knowing that she's there for us. We will miss her genuine exhilaration, which in turn exhilarated us, and the image of her welcoming, outstretched arms whenever we came to visit. Her children were her life, and the memory of her smiling face, making each of us feel so special, survives as a private source of peace and comfort for us all. She kept a copy of this book proudly displayed on her coffee table; one need not be an expert in evaluation to understand the significance of that. My dedication of this book is only one small way I can acknowledge how very special she was to me. In looking through family albums for a photo to include, it was perhaps not surprising that few photos existed of Mom by herself. For this reason, I decided to use my parents' wedding photo in the dedication. They were so good together. And so there she is, reunited with Dad. Now, that is something that would make her very happy.

Our thanks go out to the wonderfully professional editorial, production, and marketing staff at McGraw-Hill, including John Wannemacher, Jane Acheson, Jen Mills, Melissa Caughlin, Courtney Cooney, and the always-great-to-work-with freelancer April Wells-Hayes. Thanks to graduate assistant Adam Godfrey for careful library research that exceeded expectations. Thanks to Rajan Nataraajan for impromptu quantitative consultations whenever there was a plethora of Greek letters in reference sources. Finally, the authors thank their family members—I thank my wife, Susan, and son, Harrison; Mark thanks his wife, Peggy, his son, Danny, and his daughter, Jenny, along with her husband, John—for their support during the many hours, days, months, and years we devoted to this labor of love.

Ronald Jay Cohen, Ph.D., ABAP

1

Psychological Testing and Assessment

ll fields of human endeavor use measurement in some form, and each field has its own set of measuring tools and measuring units. If you're recently engaged or thinking about becoming engaged, you may have learned about a unit of measure called the *carat*. If you've been shopping for a computer, you may have learned something about a unit of measurement called a *byte*. And if you're in need of an air conditioner, you'll no doubt want to know about the *Btu* (British thermal unit). Other units of measure you may or may not be familiar with include a *mile*, a *nautical mile, miles per hour,* and *cycles per second.* Professionals in the fields that employ these units know the potential uses, benefits, and limitations of such units in the measurements they make. So, too, users and potential users of psychological measurements need a working familiarity with the commonly used units of measure, the theoretical underpinnings of the enterprise, and the tools employed.

Testing and Assessment

The roots of contemporary psychological testing and assessment can be found in early twentieth-century France. In 1905, Alfred Binet and a colleague published a test designed to help place Paris schoolchildren in appropriate classes. Binet's test would have consequences well beyond the Paris school district. Within a decade, an English-language version of Binet's test was prepared for use in schools in the United States. When the United States declared war on Germany and entered World War I in 1917, the military needed a way to screen large numbers of recruits quickly for intellectual as well as emotional problems. Psychological testing provided this methodology. During World War II, the military would depend even more on psychological tests to screen recruits for service. Following the war, more and more tests purporting to measure an ever-widening array of psychological variables were developed and used.

Psychological Testing and Assessment Defined

The world's receptivity to Binet's test in the early twentieth century spawned not only more tests but more test developers, more test publishers, more test users, and the emergence of what, logically enough, has become known as a testing industry. *Testing* was the term used to refer to everything from the administration of a test (as in "Testing in progress") to the interpretation of a test score ("The testing indicated that . . ."). During World War I, the process of testing aptly described the group screening of thousands of military recruits. We suspect it was at that time that *testing* gained a powerful foothold in the vocabulary of professionals and lay people. The use of *testing* to denote everything from test administration to test interpretation can be found not only in postwar textbooks (such as Chapman, 1921; Hull, 1922; Spearman, 1927) but in varied test-related writings for decades thereafter. However, by World War II a semantic distinction between *testing* and a more inclusive term, *assessment,* began to emerge.

During World War II, the United States Office of Strategic Services (OSS) used a variety of procedures and measurement tools—psychological tests among them—in selecting military personnel for highly specialized positions involving espionage, intelligence gathering, and the like. As summarized in *Assessment of Men* (OSS, 1948) and elsewhere (Murray & MacKinnon, 1946), the assessment data generated were subjected to thoughtful integration and evaluation by highly trained assessment center staff. The OSS model—using an innovative variety of evaluative tools along with data from the evaluations of highly trained assessors—would later inspire what is now referred to as the **assessment center approach** to personnel evaluation (Bray, 1982).

Military, clinical, educational, and business settings are but a few of the many contexts that entail behavioral observation and active integration by assessors of test scores and other data. In such situations, the term *assessment* may be preferable to *testing.* The term *assessment* acknowledges that tests are only one type of tool used by professional assessors, and that a test's value is intimately linked to the knowledge, skill, and experience of the assessor. As Sundberg and Tyler (1962) observed, *"Tests are tools. In the hands of a fool or an unscrupulous person they become pseudoscientific perversion"* (p. 131, emphasis in the original). In most evaluation contexts, it is the process of assessment that breathes life and meaning into test scores.

Psychological Assessment, a measurement textbook by Maloney and Ward (1976), echoed the uneasiness of psychologists with the anachronistic use of "psychological testing" to describe their many varied assessment-related activities. By articulating several differences between testing and assessment, Maloney and Ward clarified the rich texture of the thoughtful, problem-solving processes of psychological assessment— "unclumping" it from the more technician-like tasks of psychological testing.

Maloney and Ward conceived of assessment as a problem-solving process that could take many different forms. How an assessment proceeds depends on many factors, not the least of which is the reason for assessing. Different tools of evaluation—psychological tests among them—might be marshaled in the process of assessment, depending on the particular objectives, people, and circumstances involved as well as on other variables unique to the particular situation. By contrast, psychological testing was seen as much narrower in scope, referring only to "the process of administering, scoring, and interpreting psychological tests" (Maloney & Ward, 1976, p. 9). The examiner is more key to the process of assessment, in which decisions, predictions, or both are made on the basis of many possible sources of data (including tests).

Maloney and Ward also distinguished testing from assessment in regard to their respective objectives. In testing, a typical objective is to measure the magnitude of some psychological trait or attribute. For example, one might speak of *intelligence testing* if the purpose of administering a test was confined to obtaining a numerical gauge of the intelligence of a testee or group of testees. In assessment, which is always conducted on a one-to-one basis, the objective more typically extends beyond obtaining a number. In this context, it should not come as a surprise that the use of the term *intelligence test* may be out of vogue. Certainly this seems the trend among the folks who create and develop the major instruments to measure intelligence.

Published in 2002, the third edition of the Wechsler Preschool and Primary Scale of Intelligence (*WPPSI-III*, Wechsler, 2002) was introduced in its manual as "an individually administered clinical instrument for assessing the intelligence of children" (p. 1). The fifth edition of the Stanford-Binet (*SB5*, Roid, 2003a) was introduced by its author, Gale H. Roid (2003b, p. 2) as "an individually administered assessment of intelligence and cognitive abilities." The fourth edition of the Wechsler Intelligence Scale for Children (*WISC-IV*, Wechsler, 2003) was introduced as "an individually administered, comprehensive clinical instrument for assessing the intelligence of children" (p. 1). In each of these three introductory self-descriptions, *assessment* or *assessing* is a key word, and the word *test* is notable for its absence.

The term *assessment* is preferable to *testing* for various evaluation situations. Consider, for example, an evaluation of a student's intelligence designed to answer referral questions about the student's ability to function in a regular classroom. Such an evaluation might explore not only the student's intellectual strengths and weaknesses but also social skills and judgment. By contrast, testing "could take place without being directed at answering a specific referral question and even without the tester actually seeing the client or testee" (Maloney & Ward, 1976, p. 9).

In testing, a tester will typically add up "the number of correct answers or the number of certain types of responses . . . with little if any regard for the how or mechanics of such content" (Maloney & Ward, 1976, p. 39). Assessment is more apt to focus on *how* the individual processes rather than the *results* of that processing. Thus, very different goals and purposes are served.

Regarding the collection of psychological assessment data, Maloney and Ward (1976) urged that, far beyond the use of psychological tests alone, "literally, any method the examiner can use to make relevant observations is appropriate" (p. 7). Years later, Roberts and Magrab (1991) argued that assessment was not an activity to be confined to the consulting room. For them, assessment involved less emphasis on the measurement of the strength of traits and more emphasis on the understanding of problems in their social contexts. To achieve such understanding, assessment might entail routine home visits or other community observations.

The semantic distinction between *psychological testing* and *psychological assessment* is blurred in everyday conversation, even in many published textbooks that make little distinction between the two terms. Yet the distinction is important. Society at large is best served by clear definition of and differentiation between these two terms as well as related terms such as *psychological test user* and *psychological assessor*. In the section "Test-User Qualifications" in Chapter 2, the point is made that clear distinctions between such terms not only serves the public good but might also help avoid the turf wars now brewing between psychology and various users of psychological tests. Admittedly, the line between what constitutes testing and what constitutes assessment is not always as clear as we might like it to be. However, by acknowledging that such ambiguity exists, we can work to sharpen our definition and use of these terms; denying or ignoring their distinctiveness provides no hope of a satisfactory remedy.

> **JUST THINK . . .**
>
> Describe a situation in which testing is more appropriate than assessment. Then describe a situation in which assessment is more appropriate than testing.

We define **psychological assessment** as the gathering and integration of psychology-related data for the purpose of making a psychological evaluation, accomplished through the use of tools such as tests, interviews, case studies, behavioral observation, and specially designed apparatuses and measurement procedures. We define **psychological testing** as the process of measuring psychology-related variables by means of devices or procedures designed to obtain a sample of behavior.

The process of assessment   In general, the process of assessment begins with a referral for assessment from a source such as a teacher, a school psychologist, a counselor, a judge, a clinician, or a corporate human resources specialist. Typically, one or more referral questions are put to the assessor about the assessee. Some examples of referral questions are "Can this child function in a regular classroom?" "Is this defendant competent to stand trial?" and "How well can this employee be expected to perform if promoted to an executive position?"

The assessor may meet with the assessee or others before the formal assessment to clarify aspects of the reason for referral. Then comes the formal assessment, during which tests and other tools will typically be employed by the assessor to help answer the referral question(s). After the assessment, the assessor writes a report of the findings. More personal feedback sessions with the assessee and/or interested third parties (such as the assessee's parents and the referring professional) may also be scheduled.

Different assessors may approach the assessment task in different ways. Some assessors approach the assessment with minimal input from assessees themselves. In this approach to assessment, the assessor's primary focus is on test scores, interview data, case history data, and other available data derived from the formal assessment. Other assessors view the process of assessment as more of a collaboration between the assessor and the assessee. For example, in the process of **collaborative psychological assessment** described by Constance Fischer (1978), the assessor and assessee may work as "partners" from initial contact through final feedback. In this approach, the assessee is viewed as "an expert about his or her current views and remembered life events" (Fischer, 2004, p. 14).

Another variety of collaborative assessment may include an element of therapy as part of the process. Stephen Finn and his colleagues (Finn, 2003; Finn & Martin, 1997; Finn & Tonsager, 2002) have described **therapeutic psychological assessment** as an approach that encourages therapeutic self-discovery and new understandings through the assessment process. A term increasingly used with regard to testing and assessment in the schools is *dynamic assessment.* **Dynamic psychological assessment** may be defined as a model and philosophy of interactive evaluation involving various types of assessor intervention during the assessment process. For example, an assessor may intervene with increasingly more explicit prompts, feedback, or hints in order to not only evaluate what the assessee knows but to effectively modify and improve the way the assessee thinks about the problem or subject matter. Although aspects of the dynamic assessment model have been written about at least since the 1920s (Lidz, 1987), it was not until the 1970s and 1980s that a number of tools incorporating this approach were published (Lidz, 1991, 1996).

Alternate assessment   The Individuals with Disabilities Education Act (IDEA) Amendments, PL 105-17, became law in 1997. Many of the provisions of the IDEA amendments are discussed elsewhere in this book. For now, let's focus on a section of this law that introduces the term *alternate assessment.* Specifically, this section provides that the State or local educational agency "(i) develops guidelines for the participation of children with disabilities in alternate assessments for those children who cannot participate in State and district-wide assessment programs; and (ii) develops and . . . conducts those alternate assessments."

PL 105-17 does not define "alternate assessments." However, a look at past practice by assessors involved in evaluating students with special needs will illustrate the concept. For example, the student who has difficulty reading the small print of a particular test may be accommodated with a large-print version of the same test or with a specially lit test environment. A student with a hearing impairment may be administered the test in sign language. A child with attention deficit disorder (ADD) might have an extended evaluation time, with frequent breaks during periods of evaluation.

So far, the process of alternate assessment may seem fairly simple and straightforward; in practice, however, it may be anything but. Consider, for example, the case of a student with a vision impairment who is scheduled to be given a written, multiple-choice test using an alternate procedure. There are several possible alternate procedures. For instance, the test could be translated into Braille and administered in that form, or it could be administered by means of audiotape. Whether the test is administered by Braille or audiotape may affect the test scores; some students may do better with a Braille administration and others with audiotape. Students with superior short-term attention and memory skills for auditory stimuli would seem to have an advantage with the audiotaped administration. Students with superior haptic (sense of touch) and perceptual-motor skills might have an advantage with the Braille administration.

Some alternative methods may take the form of performance-based tasks rather than paper-and-pencil tasks. For example, students whose math skills cannot be assessed by the administration of paper-and-pencil questions might be evaluated through tasks such as making change or making purchases in a "real-life" context. Another alternative method of assessment entails the evaluation of a collection of the assessee's work samples over time.

A number of important questions can be raised about the equivalence of various alternate and traditional assessments. To what extent does each method really measure the same thing? How equivalent is the alternate test to the original test? How does modifying the format of a test, the time limits of a test, or any other aspect of the way a test was originally designed to be administered, affect test scores? And taking a step back from such complex issues, how shall we define *alternate assessment*?

Keeping in mind the complexities involved, we propose this definition of this somewhat elusive process: **Alternate assessment** is an evaluative or diagnostic procedure or process that varies from the usual, customary, or standardized way a measurement is derived, either by virtue of some special accommodation made to the assessee or by means of alternative methods designed to measure the same variable(s). This definition avoids the thorny issue of equivalence of methods. Unless the alternate procedures have been thoroughly researched, there is no reason to expect them to be equivalent. In most cases, because the alternate procedures have been individually tailored, there is seldom compelling research to support equivalence. Governmental guidelines for alternate assessment will evolve to include ways of translating measurement procedures from one format to another. Other guidelines may suggest substituting one tool of assessment for another.

All this talk about assessment might lead one to wonder how assessments are typically conducted and what tools are used. Before reading on, however, try the "Just Think" exercise.

JUST THINK . . .

Besides tests, what are some other tools of psychological assessment? For each tool, describe an assessment situation for which it is ideally suited.

The Tools of Psychological Assessment

The test   A **test** may be defined simply as a measuring device or procedure. When the word *test* is prefaced with a modifier, it refers to a device or procedure designed to measure a variable related to that modifier. Consider, for example, the term *medical test*, which refers to a device or procedure designed to measure some variable related to the practice of medicine (including a wide range of tools and procedures such as X-rays, blood tests, and testing of reflexes). In a like manner, the term **psychological test** refers to a device or procedure designed to measure variables related to psychology (for example, intelligence, personality, aptitude, interests, attitudes, and values). And whereas a medical test might involve the analysis of a sample of blood, tissue, or the like, a psychological test almost always involves the analysis of a sample of behavior. The behavior sample could range from responses to a pencil-and-paper questionnaire to oral responses to questions to performance of some task. The behavior sample could be elicited by the stimulus of the test itself, or it could be naturally occurring behavior (under observation).

Psychological tests and other tools of assessment may differ on a number of variables such as content, format, administration procedures, scoring and interpretation procedures, and technical quality. The *content* (subject matter) of the test will, of course, vary with the focus of the particular test. But even two psychological tests purporting to measure the same thing—for example, *personality*—may differ widely in item content because of factors such as the test developer's definition of personality and the theoretical orientation of the test. For example, items on a psychoanalytically oriented personality test may have little resemblance to those on an existentially oriented personality test, yet both are personality tests.

The term **format** pertains to the form, plan, structure, arrangement, and layout of test items as well as to related considerations such as time limits. *Format* is also used to refer to the form in which a test is administered: computerized, pencil-and-paper, or some other form. When making specific reference to a computerized test, *format* may further refer to the form of the software: IBM- or Apple-compatible. The term *format* is not confined to tests; it is also used to denote the form or structure of other evaluative tools and processes, such as the specific procedures used in obtaining a particular type of work sample.

Tests differ in their *administration procedures*. Some tests, particularly those designed for administration on a one-to-one basis, may require a very active and knowledgeable test administrator. The test administration may involve demonstration of various kinds of tasks on the part of the assessee as well as trained observation of an assessee's performance. Alternatively, some tests, particularly those designed for administration to groups, may not even require the test administrator to be present while the testtakers independently do whatever it is the test requires.

Tests differ in their *scoring and interpretation procedures*. To better understand how and why, let's define *score* and *scoring*. Sports enthusiasts are no strangers to these terms. For them, these terms refer to the number of points accumulated by competitors and the process of accumulating those points. In testing and assessment, we may formally define **score** as a code or summary statement, usually but not necessarily numerical in nature, that reflects an evaluation of performance on a test, task, interview, or some other sample of behavior. **Scoring** is the process of assigning such evaluative codes or statements to performance on tests, tasks, interviews, or other behavior samples. As we will see in the chapters that follow, there are many different types of scores. Some scores result from the simple summing of responses (such as the summing of correct/incorrect or agree/disagree responses), and some scores result from the application of more elaborate procedures.

Scores themselves can be described and categorized in many different ways. Here, let's consider one such category of scores, the *cut score*. A **cut score** (also referred to as a *cutoff score* or simply a *cutoff*) is a reference point, usually numerical, derived by judgment and used to divide a set of data into two or more classifications. Some action will be taken or some inference will be made on the basis of these classifications. Cut scores on tests, usually in combination with other data, are used in schools in many contexts, such as grading and making decisions about the class or program to which a particular child will be assigned. Cut scores are used by employers as aids to decision making

Figure 1–1
Emotion Engendered by Categorical Cutoffs

According to research by Victoria Husted Medvec and her colleagues (Medvec et al., 1995; Medvec & Savitsky, 1997), people who just make some categorical cutoff may feel better about their accomplishment than those who make the cutoff by a substantial margin. But those who just miss the cutoff may feel worse than those who miss it by a substantial margin. Evidence consistent with this view was presented in research with Olympic athletes. Bronze medalists were—somewhat paradoxically—happier with the outcome than silver medalists. Bronze medalists might say to themselves, "At least I won a medal" and be happy about it. By contrast, silver medalists might feel frustrated about having gone for the gold and missed winning it.

about personnel hiring and advancement. State agencies use cut scores to help determine who shall be licensed as a professional in a given field. There are probably upwards of 20 different methods that can be used to formally derive cut scores (Dwyer, 1996).

Sometimes, no formal method is used to arrive at a cut score. Some teachers use an informal, "eyeball" method to proclaim, for example, that a score of 65 or more on a test means "pass" and a score of 64 or below means "fail." Whether formally or informally derived, cut scores typically take into account, to at least some degree, the values of those who set them. Further, there is another side to the human equation as it relates to cut scores, one seldom written about in measurement texts. Human judgment is very much a part not only of setting cut scores but of reacting to them. Some consequences of being "cut" by cut scores have been explored in innovative research; see Figure 1-1.

Tests differ widely in terms of their guidelines for scoring and interpretation. Some tests are designed to be scored by testtakers themselves, and others are designed to be scored by trained examiners. Still other tests may be scored and fully interpreted in seconds by computer. Some tests, such as most tests of intelligence, come with test manuals that are very explicit not only about scoring criteria but also about the nature of the interpretations that can be made from the calculated score. Other tests, such as the Rorschach Inkblot Test (discussed in Chapter 12), are sold with no manual at all. The (qualified) purchaser buys the stimulus materials and then selects and uses one of many available guides for administration, scoring, and interpretation.

Tests differ with respect to their *technical quality.* More commonly, reference is made to what is called the *psychometric soundness* of a test. Synonymous with the antiquated term *psychometry,* **psychometrics** may be defined as the science of psychological measurement.[1] The adjective *psychometric* refers to measurement of a psychological nature. And the *psychometric soundness* of a test is a reference to how consistently and how accurately a psychological test measures what it purports to measure.

We have much more to say about what constitutes quality in a test or other tool of assessment. Throughout this book, consistent with common practice, we sometimes use the word *test* (as well as related terms such as *test score*) in a generic sense when discussing general principles applicable to various measurement procedures. These measurement procedures range from those widely labeled as tests (such as paper-and-pencil examinations) to procedures that measurement experts might label with more specific terms (such as *situational performance measures*). But now let's get back to the tools of assessment and introduce one that probably, as they say, "needs no introduction."

The interview   Another widely used tool in psychological assessment is the interview, a word that may conjure images of face-to-face talk. But the interview as a tool of psychological assessment involves more than talk. If the interview is conducted face to face, the interviewer probably notes nonverbal as well as verbal behavior, such as the interviewee's dress, manner, and eye contact. An interview may be conducted over the telephone, in which case the interviewer might make inferences about what is said as a function of changes in the interviewee's voice quality. Interviews need not involve speech, as when they are conducted in sign language. Interviews may be conducted by means of electronic media, such as e-mail. In its broadest sense, then, we can define an **interview** as a method of gathering information through direct communication involving reciprocal exchange.

JUST THINK . . .

What are the strengths of the interview as a tool of assessment? What are the weaknesses of the interview as a tool of assessment?

Interviews differ with regard to many variables, such as their purpose, their length, or other restrictions under which they are conducted, and the willingness of the interviewee to provide information candidly. Interviews may be used by psychologists and others in clinical, counseling, forensic, or neuropsychological settings to help make diagnostic or treatment decisions. School psychologists and others in educational settings may use interviews to help make decisions about the appropriateness of various educational interventions or class placements. An interview may be used to help human resources professionals make more informed recommendations about the hiring, firing, and advancement of personnel. In some instances, the process takes the form of a **panel interview,** wherein more than one interviewer participates in the assessment of personnel. A presumed advantage of the panel interview (also sometimes referred to as a *board interview*) is that any idiosyncratic biases of a lone interviewer will be minimized by the use of two or more interviewers (Dipboye, 1992). A disadvantage of the panel interview

---

1. Variants of these words include the adjective *psychometric* and the nouns *psychometrist* and *psychometrician.* Traditionally, a **psychometrist** holds a master's degree and is qualified to administer specific tests. A **psychometrician** holds a doctoral degree in psychology or some related field (such as education) and specializes in areas such as individual differences, quantitative psychology, or theory of assessment.

Figure 1–2
On Interviewing and Being Interviewed

Different interviewers have different styles of interviewing. How would you characterize the interview style of Howard Stern versus that of Jay Leno?

is the additional cost of using multiple interviewers, especially when the return on this investment is questionable (Dixon et al., 2002).

Interviews are used by psychologists who study consumer behavior to answer corporate America's questions about the market for various products and services and how best to advertise and promote them. Researchers in psychology and related fields use interviews to explore myriad other topics. A casual survey of the literature reveals recent research employing the interview to explore topics as diverse as food choice negotiation by newly married couples (Bove et al., 2003), the experience of hearing voices from the perspective of those who hear them (Jones et al., 2003), and a conception of what constitutes "masculinity" from the perspective of teenage boys (Pascoe, 2003).

The popularity of the interview as a method of gathering information extends far beyond psychology. Just try to think of one day when you were *not* exposed to an interview on television, radio, or the Internet! Regardless of the forum, the quality, if not the quantity, of useful information produced by an interview depends to some degree on the interviewer. An interview is a reciprocal affair. The interviewee reacts to the interviewer, and the interviewer reacts to the interviewee. Interviewers differ in many ways; for example, their pacing of interviews, their rapport with interviewees, and their ability to convey genuineness, empathy, and humor. With these differences between interviewers in mind, look at Figure 1-2. Think about how attributes of these well-known celebrities might affect responses of interviewees. More generally, think about other dimensions on

> **JUST THINK . . .**
>
> What types of interviewing skills must the host of a talk show possess to be considered an effective interviewer? Do these skills differ from those needed by a professional in the field of psychological assessment?

which you might characterize interviewers you have seen and come to know in the media. "Juvenile versus adult" and "eager-to-speak versus eager-to-listen" are two such dimensions that may come to mind.

The portfolio   In recent years, the popularity of **portfolio** (work sample) assessment in many fields, including education, has been rising. Some have argued, for example, that the best evaluation of a student's writing skills can be accomplished not by the administration of a test but by asking the student to compile a selection of writing samples. From the perspective of education administrators, portfolio assessment also has distinct advantages in assessing the effectiveness of teachers. By examining teachers' portfolios and seeing how teachers approach their coverage of various topics, educational evaluators have another tool to help anchor judgments to work samples.

JUST THINK . . .

What are the strengths of the portfolio as a tool of assessment? What are the weaknesses of the portfolio as a tool of assessment?

Case history data   In a general sense, **case history data** refers to records, transcripts, and other accounts in written, pictorial, or other form, in any media, that preserve archival information, official and informal accounts, and other data and items relevant to an assessee. Case history data may include files or excerpts from files maintained at institutions and agencies such as schools, hospitals, employers, religious institutions, and criminal justice agencies. Other examples of case history data are letters and written correspondence; photos and family albums; newspaper and magazine clippings; and home videos, movies, and audiotapes. Work samples, artwork, doodlings, and accounts and pictures pertaining to interests and hobbies are yet other examples.

Case history data can be a very useful tool in a wide variety of assessment contexts. In a clinical evaluation, for example, case history data can shed light on an individual's past and current adjustment, as well as the events and circumstances that may have contributed to any changes in adjustment. Case history data can be of critical value in neuropsychological evaluations, where it often provides information about neuropsychological functioning prior to the occurrence of a trauma or other event that results in a deficit. School psychologists rely on case history data to, among other things, answer questions about the course of a student's developmental history.

Another use of the term *case history*, one synonymous with *case study*, has to do with the assembly of case history data into an illustrative account. For example, a case study might detail how a number of aspects of an individual's personality combined with environmental conditions to produce a successful world leader. A case study of an individual who attempted to assassinate a high-ranking political figure might shed light on what types of individuals and conditions might lead to similar attempts in the future. A now classic work on the subject of **groupthink** contains rich case history material on collective decision making that did not always result in the best decisions (Janis, 1972).

JUST THINK . . .

What are the strengths of the case study as a tool of assessment? What are the weaknesses of the case study as a tool of assessment?

Behavioral observation   If you want to know how someone behaves in a particular situation, observe his or her behavior in that situation. Such "down-home" wisdom underlies at least one approach to evaluation. **Behavioral observation** as it is employed by assessment professionals may be defined as monitoring the actions of others or oneself by visual or electronic means while recording quantitative and/or qualitative information regarding the actions. Behavioral observation may be used in a variety of settings for a

Figure 1–3
Price (and Judgment) Check in Aisle 5

Hamera and Brown (2000) described the development of a context-based Test of Grocery Shopping Skills. Designed primarily for use with persons with psychiatric disorders, this assessment tool may be useful in evaluating a skill necessary for independent living.

variety of assessment objectives. It may be used, for example, as a diagnostic aid in a clinical setting or as a means of data collection in basic research. Observations may be made in laboratory or otherwise structured settings. An example of this is a researcher's observation of a child who is asked to perform some task as part of an experiment. Observation may also occur in the natural setting in which the behavior would typically be elicited or expected to occur. This variety of behavioral observation is referred to as **naturalistic observation.**

Behavioral observation as an aid to designing therapeutic intervention has proven extremely useful in institutional settings such as schools, hospitals, prisons, and group homes. Using published or self-constructed lists of targeted behaviors, staff can observe firsthand the behavior of the person under observation and design interventions accordingly. In a school situation, for example, naturalistic observation on the playground of a culturally different child suspected to have linguistic problems might reveal that the child does have English language skills but is unwilling—for reasons of shyness, cultural upbringing, or whatever—to demonstrate those abilities to adults.

Despite the potential value of behavioral observation, it tends to be used infrequently outside institutional settings. For private practitioners, it is typically not economically feasible to spend hours out of the consulting room observing clients. Just think about the time it would take to administer a test of grocery-shopping skills if the assessee/shopper required a couple of price checks (see Figure 1-3).

JUST THINK . . .

What are the strengths of behavioral observation as a tool of assessment? What are the weaknesses of behavioral observation as a tool of assessment?

Role-play tests If you have ever enjoyed the television program *Whose Line Is It Anyway*, you may appreciate just how entertaining improvisation can be. Beyond entertainment, however, improvisational acting has a place in the context of psychological assessment. In this context, **role play** may be defined as acting an improvised or partially improvised part in a simulated situation. A **role-play test** is a tool of assessment wherein assessees are directed to act as if they were in a particular situation. Assessees may then be evaluated with regard to their expressed thoughts, behaviors, abilities, and other variables. (Note that *role play* is hyphenated when used as an adjective or a verb but not as a noun.)

An individual being evaluated in a corporate, industrial, organizational, or military context for managerial or leadership ability, for example, might be asked to mediate a hypothetical dispute between personnel at a work site. The context of the role play may be created by various techniques ranging from live actors to computer-generated simulation. Outcome measures for such an assessment might include ratings related to various aspects of the individual's ability to resolve the conflict, such as effectiveness of approach, quality of resolution, and number of minutes to resolution.

JUST THINK . . .

What are the strengths of role play as a tool of assessment? What are the weaknesses of role play as a tool of assessment?

Role play as a tool of assessment may be used in various clinical contexts. For example, it is routinely employed in many interventions with substance abusers. Clinicians may attempt to obtain a baseline measure of abuse, cravings, or coping skills by administering a role-play test prior to therapeutic intervention and then again at the completion of a course of treatment.

Computers as tools Professionals who specialize in psychological and educational assessment have long recognized the value of computers in administering, scoring, and interpreting tests. As early as 1930, electromechanical scoring was available for at least one psychological test, the Strong Vocational Interest Blank (SVIB) (Campbell, 1971). By 1946, thanks to the efforts of a Minneapolis engineer named Elmer Hankes, profiling of the SVIB could be done by machine. And by the late 1950s, computers were used not only for scoring and profiling but also for test interpretation (Rome et al., 1965). With the advent of the personal computer in the 1970s, office-based test administration, scoring, and interpretation became reality. As technology has flourished, the use of computers has burgeoned.

Today, computers, whether desktop, laptop, or palm-held, are a part of the essential office of clinicians, consultants, and other test users. From the standpoint of test users, **computer-assisted psychological assessment (CAPA)** refers to the convenience and economy of time in administering, scoring, and interpreting tests. Thus, the "assistance" in the term *computer-assisted* is assistance to test users, not testtakers. CAPA allows testtakers to work independently, responding to items presented on a video screen. The computer may then score the test, analyze response patterns, and even provide some sort of report (see *Close-up*).

For many test users, CAPA represents a great advance over the not-too-distant past when they had to personally administer tests and possibly even place the responses in some other form for analysis (manually using a scoring template or other device) before beginning the often laborious tasks of scoring and interpreting the resulting data. CAPA opened a world of possibilities for test users, enabling the building into tests of complex scoring and data combination strategies that would not otherwise be practical. CAPA has also enabled the measurement of abilities that could not be measured by more

Types of Computer-Generated Psychological Reports

Have you ever taken a test and had the results given in a computer-generated report? What type of report was it? And how did it get there?

Computer-generated psychological reports may be categorized as scoring reports, interpretive reports, or integrative reports. Here we define each of these types of reports and describe the type of information that might be found in them.

Scoring Reports

In general, a **scoring report** may be defined as a formal or official computer-generated account of test performance, usually presented in numeric form. One type of scoring report, a **simple scoring report,** simply lists test scores. Another type of scoring report is an **extended scoring report.** Beyond a simple listing of test scores, an extended scoring report may contain more detailed information, such as a statistical analysis of how testtakers performed on individual items.

Interpretive Reports

In general, an **interpretive report** is a computer-generated account of test performance, presented in numeric as well as narrative form, including an explanation of the findings. There are three varieties of interpretive report: a descriptive report, a screening report, and a consultative report.

A **descriptive report** is a type of interpretive report that features brief narrative summaries. In fact, the "description" in a descriptive report may be so brief as to amount to a one-sentence comment regarding where a particular score stands from a normative perspective. Descriptive reports can help a test user determine which of many scores on a test need to be focused on.

A **screening report** provides more information than a descriptive report but less than a consultative report. It provides narrative information as well as analysis or commentary regarding relationships between the scores. As its name implies, a screening report is particularly useful for screening purposes. Programmed into the software are various criteria that must be met before the software causes a line of narrative text to be automatically printed on the report.

More than a bare-bones descriptive report and less tentative in its conclusions than a screening report is a consultative report. A **consultative report** provides a detailed analysis of test data in language appropriate for communication between assessment professionals. It provides the expert opinion of an individual or group of individuals who may have devoted years of study to the interpretation of a particular instrument.

Integrative Reports

An **integrative report** provides a level of description and analysis found in interpretive reports but integrates into the report data from other sources such as behavioral observations or medication records. From a report that integrates behavioral observation data with medication records, for example, a clinician might receive valuable assistance concerning optimal medications and dosages for a client.

CAPA Processing

Regardless of its nature, a report may be created in different ways at different sites. Here is a "short course" in CAPA processing.

The term **central processing** is used to refer to the sending of test protocols completed on paper or some other form at one location to some other central location for scoring or interpretation. The results may then be returned to the test user by e-mail, disk, mail, fax, or telephone.

One variety of central processing is *teleprocessing.* **Teleprocessing** refers to the computerized scoring, interpretation, or other conversion of raw test data that have been sent for processing over telephone or wireless lines from the test site to a central facility.

Local processing may be defined simply as on-site computerized scoring, interpretation, or other conversion of raw test data. With the appropriate hardware and software, the test user may use the same computer to administer a test and then score it. In an era of relatively inexpensive computer hardware, most tests today are locally processed.

What are the pros and cons of the various types of CAPA processing?

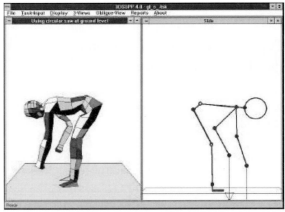

Figure 1–4
A Method of Quantifying Back Stress

The innovative application of computer technology has facilitated the measurement of traits or abilities by techniques that could not be measured by more traditional methods. For example, Mirka et al. (2000) described an assessment methodology that employs video, computer, and other components to obtain continuous assessment of back stress. It involves capturing an image with a video camera (in this illustration, the act of sawing at ground level), computerized representation of the action, and laboratory simulation.

traditional methods (Figure 1-4). Of course, every rose has its thorns; some of the pros and cons of CAPA are presented in Table 1-1.

Other tools Varied instruments can be applied as tools of assessment. Psychologists and others who devise tools to assess people with disabilities and members of other special populations have been most innovative. For example, Wilson et al. (1982) developed a mechanism for test response involving a dental plate activated by the tongue. Useful to testtakers who lack the capacity for speech or control of their limbs, the device permits five kinds of response.

On your next trip to the video store to rent a DVD, take a moment to consider the role that video can play in assessment. In fact, specially created videos are widely used in training and evaluation contexts. For example, corporate personnel may be asked to respond to a variety of video-presented incidents of sexual harassment in the workplace. Police personnel may be asked about how they would respond to various types of emergencies, which are presented either as reenactments or as video recordings of actual occurrences. Psychotherapists may be asked to respond with a diagnosis and a treatment plan for each of several clients presented to them on videotape. The list of potential applications of video to assessment is endless.

JUST THINK . . .

In general, when is assessment using videotape a good idea? What are the drawbacks, if any, to using videotape in assessment?

Table 1-1
CAPA: Some Pros and Cons

Pros	Cons
CAPA saves professional time in test administration, scoring, and interpretation.	Professionals must still spend significant time reading software and hardware documentation and even ancillary books on the test and its interpretation.
CAPA results in minimal scoring errors resulting from human error or lapses of attention or judgment.	With CAPA, the possibility of software or hardware error is ever present, from difficult-to-pinpoint sources such as software glitches or hardware malfunction.
CAPA assures standardized test administration to all testtakers with little, if any, variation in test administration procedures.	CAPA leaves those testtakers at a disadvantage who are unable to employ familiar test-taking strategies (previewing test, skipping questions, going back to previous question, etc.).
CAPA yields standardized interpretation of findings due to elimination of unreliability traceable to differing points of view in professional judgment.	CAPA's standardized interpretation of findings based on a set, unitary perspective may not be optimal; interpretation could profit from alternative viewpoints.
Computers' capacity to combine data according to rules is more accurate than that of humans.	Computers lack the flexibility of humans to recognize the exception to a rule in the context of the "big picture."
Nonprofessional assistants can be used in the test administration process, and the test can typically be administered to groups of testtakers in one sitting.	Use of nonprofessionals leaves diminished, if any, opportunity for the professional to observe the assessee's testtaking behavior and note any unusual extra-test conditions that may have affected responses.
Professional groups such as APA develop guidelines and standards for use of CAPA products.	Profit-driven nonprofessionals may also create and distribute tests with little regard for professional guidelines and standards.
Paper-and-pencil tests may be converted to CAPA products with consequential advantages, such as a shorter time between the administration of the test and its scoring and interpretation.	The use of paper-and-pencil tests that have been converted for computer administration raises questions about the equivalence of the original test and its converted form.
Security of CAPA products can be maintained not only by traditional means (such as locked filing cabinets) but by high-tech electronic products (such as firewalls).	Security of CAPA products can be breached by computer hackers, and integrity of data can be altered or destroyed by untoward events such as introduction of computer viruses.
Computers can automatically tailor test content and length based on responses of testtakers.	Not all testtakers take the same test or have the same test-taking experience.

The list of tools used in the service of psychological assessment includes, for example, many tools traditionally associated with medical health, such as thermometers to measure body temperature and gauges to measure blood pressure. Biofeedback equipment is sometimes used to obtain measures of bodily reactions (such as muscular tension or galvanic skin response) to various sorts of stimuli. An instrument called a penile plethysmograph, which gauges male sexual arousal, may be very helpful in the diagnosis and treatment of sexual predators. Impaired ability to identify odors is common in many disorders in which there is central nervous system involvement, and simple tests of smell may be administered to help determine if such impairment is present. In general, there has been no shortage of innovation on the part of psychologists in devising measurement tools, or adapting existing tools, for use in psychological assessment.

To this point, our introduction has focused on some basic definitions and a look at some of the "tools of the trade." We now raise some very fundamental questions regarding the who, what, why, and where of testing and assessment.

Who, What, Why, and Where?

Who are the parties in the assessment enterprise? In what types of settings are assessments conducted? Why is assessment conducted? Where does one go for authoritative information about tests? Think about the answer to each of these important questions before reading on. Then check your own ideas against those that follow.

Who Are the Parties?

Parties in the assessment enterprise include developers and publishers of tests, users of tests, and people who are evaluated by means of tests. A fourth and frequently overlooked party is society at large.

The test developer   Test developers and publishers create tests or other methods of assessment. The **American Psychological Association (APA)** estimates that more than 20,000 new psychological tests are developed each year (APA, 1993). Among these new tests are some that were created for a specific research study, some that were created in the hope that they would be published, and some that represent refinements or modifications of existing tests. Test creators bring a wide array of backgrounds and interests to the test development process. For an intriguing glimpse at biographical information on a sampling of test developers, visit the "Test Developer Profiles" section of our Web site: www.mhhe.com/cohentesting6.

Test developers and publishers appreciate the significant impact that test results can have on people's lives. Accordingly, a number of professional organizations have published standards of ethical behavior that specifically address aspects of responsible test development and use. Perhaps the most detailed document addressing such issues is one jointly written by the American Educational Research Association, the American Psychological Association, and the National Council on Measurement in Education (NCME). Referred to by many psychologists simply as "the *Standards*," *Standards for Educational and Psychological Testing* covers issues related to test construction and evaluation, test administration and use, and special applications of tests, such as special considerations when testing linguistic minorities. Initially published in 1954, revisions of the *Standards* were published in 1966, 1974, 1985, and 1999. The *Standards* is an indispensable reference work not only for test developers but for test users as well.

The test user   Tests are used by a wide range of professionals, including clinicians, counselors, human resources personnel, teachers, and other school personnel. The *Standards*, as well as the official guidelines of various other professional organizations, have much to impart to test users about how, why, and under what conditions tests should be used. For example, the principles of professional ethics promulgated by the National Association of School Psychologists (Jacob-Timm & Hartshorne, 1998) stress that school psychologists should select and use the test or tests that are most appropriate for each individual student. NASP (2000) further emphasizes that any questions that serve to prompt the psychological assessment of students should be answered in as comprehensive a manner as possible—that is, with as much background information and other data as possible, including data from behavioral observation.

No matter how sound a test is, its purpose will be defeated if the test user fails to competently manage all phases of the testing or assessment process. For this reason, a responsible test user has obligations before, during, and after a test is administered. Ethical guidelines dictate that before a test is administered, it should be stored in a way that

Figure 1–5
Less-Than-Optimal Testing Conditions

In 1917, new Army recruits sat on the floor as they were administered the first group tests of intelligence—not ideal testing conditions by current standards.

reasonably ensures that its specific contents will not be made known in advance. Another obligation of the test user before the test's administration is to ensure that a prepared and suitably trained person administers the test properly. The test administrator (or examiner) must be familiar with the test materials and procedures and must have at the test site all the materials needed to properly administer the test. Materials needed might include a stopwatch, a supply of pencils, and a sufficient number of test *protocols*.[2]

In addition to having sufficient supplies, the examiner also ensures that the room in which the test will be conducted is suitable and conducive to the testing (Figure 1-5). To the extent that it is possible, distracting conditions such as excessive noise, heat, cold, interruptions, glaring sunlight, crowding, inadequate ventilation, and so forth should be avoided.

During test administration, and especially in one-on-one or small-group testing, rapport between the examiner and the examinee can be critically important. In the

---

2. In everyday, nontest-related conversation, *protocol* refers to diplomatic etiquette. A less common use of the word is as a synonym for the first copy or rough draft of a treaty or other official document before its ratification. This second meaning comes closer to the way the word is used with reference to psychological tests. **Protocol** refers to the form or sheet on which the testtaker's responses have been entered. Protocols are typically single sheets of paper or booklets.

context of the testing situation, **rapport** may be defined as a working relationship between the examiner and the examinee. Such a working relationship can sometimes be achieved with a few words of small talk when examiner and examinee are introduced. If appropriate, some words about the nature of the test and why it is important for examinees to do their best may also be helpful. In other instances, for example, with a frightened child, the achievement of rapport might involve more elaborate techniques such as engaging the child in play or some other activity until the child has acclimated to the examiner and the surroundings. It is important that attempts to establish rapport with the testtaker not compromise any rules of the test administration instructions.

After a test administration, test users have many obligations as well. These obligations may range from safeguarding the test protocols to conveying the test results in a clearly understandable fashion. In between, there are other obligations such as those related to scoring the test. If a test is to be scored by people, scorers need to be in agreement about scoring criteria—even if that is not always the case in everyday, nontest, evaluation situations (see *Everyday Psychometrics*). Interpreting the test results and seeing to it that the test data are used in accordance with established procedures and ethical guidelines are additional obligations of test users.

The testtaker Testtakers approach an assessment situation in different ways, and test users must be sensitive to the diversity of possible responses to a testing situation. On the day of test administration, testtakers may vary on a continuum with respect to numerous variables, including:

- The amount of test anxiety they are experiencing and the degree to which that test anxiety might significantly affect the test results
- Their capacity and willingness to cooperate with the examiner or to comprehend written test instructions
- The amount of physical pain or emotional distress they are experiencing
- The amount of physical discomfort brought on by not having had enough to eat, having had too much to eat, or other physical conditions
- The extent to which they are alert and wide-awake as opposed to nodding off
- The extent to which they are predisposed to agreeing or disagreeing when presented with stimulus statements
- The extent to which they have received prior coaching
- The importance they may attribute to portraying themselves in a good (or bad) light
- The extent to which they are, for lack of a better term, "lucky" and can "beat the odds" on a multiple-choice achievement test (even though they may not have learned the subject matter).

In the broad sense in which we are using the term "testtaker," anyone who is the subject of an assessment or an evaluation can be a testtaker or an assessee. As amazing as it sounds, this means that even a deceased individual can be considered an assessee. True, it's the exception to the rule, but there is such a thing as a *psychological autopsy*. A **psychological autopsy** may be defined as a reconstruction of a deceased individual's psychological profile on the basis of archival records, artifacts, and interviews previously conducted with the deceased assessee or people who knew him or her. For interested readers, a fascinating case study that employed the technique of psychological autopsy is presented by Neagoe (2000).

"The Following Film Is Rated *PG-13*" . . . But Whodunnit? How? And Why?

PG-13 | PARENTS STRONGLY CAUTIONED
Some Material May Be Inappropriate For Children Under 13

The Motion Picture Association of America (MPAA) ratings— we have all heard them: "The following film is rated *PG-13*." The *PG-13* stands for "parents strongly cautioned" with respect to allowing children younger than 13 to see the movie. There's also *G* for "general audiences," *PG* for "parental guidance suggested," and *NC-17* for "no one 17 and under admitted."

Have you ever wondered who actually evaluates movies and gives them one of these five age-based ratings? It is actually a group of 8 to 13 parents who are employed full-time by MPAA to watch and evaluate movies. Some criteria used for rating films PG through NC-17 are published on the MPAA Web site, http://www.mpaa.org. There you will find, for example, that "an R-rated film may include hard language or tough violence, or nudity within sensual scenes, or drug abuse or other elements, or a combination of some of the above, so that parents are counseled, in advance, to take this advisory rating very seriously."

The group of parents who do the rating sees a film submitted by a producer, discusses the film, and then votes on a rating. A majority vote wins. Beyond that description, few details regarding the actual rating process are provided on the Web site. We do know that regardless how the board of paid parents votes, their rating can be overturned by the two-thirds vote of an appeals board that is made up of 14 to 18 entertainment industry members.

If there is mystery about the process of rating movies, it is only the tip of the iceberg with regard to mystery about ratings in the entertainment industry in general. There are television rating systems presented with age-range recommendations and content summaries in icon form. There are rating systems for music, electronic software, and coin-operated video games. There is even a rat-

ing system for Internet content promulgated by the Internet Content Rating Association. Reviewing these systems and the literature available on them, one research team concluded:

> The efforts of a variety of independent media industries have resulted in a dizzying array of ratings, icons, definitions, and procedures that are, in many cases, difficult to understand and remember. Almost all of these rating systems have been prompted by the threat of government intervention, and each industry has attempted to balance the provision of information against its own economic concerns. Although creating a rating system that works well for parents is not an easy task, it is clear that the preferences of parents have not often prevailed. (Bushman & Cantor, 2003, pp. 138–139)

As you learn more about psychological testing and assessment, think back on occasion to this description of evaluation in the entertainment industry. Contrast evaluation in that industry with evaluation in psychology. Think about *issues*. For example, think about issues regarding the definition of terms in psychological evaluation. How clearly is whatever is being measured by a psychological test defined? Think about the *process* of evaluation. For example, think about differences among raters or scorers and how these differences might figure into an ultimate rating or score. And think about the *utility* of the evaluations. In the entertainment industry, the "end user" is a parent or guardian making a decision regarding an entertainment-related choice for a minor. Who are the potential "end users" when it comes to psychological and educational evaluations? What types of decisions may have to be made on the basis of such information? How useful is the information developed in making these decisions?

Society at large

> The uniqueness of individuals is one of the most fundamental characteristic facts of life. . . . At all periods of human history men have observed and described differences between individuals. . . . But educators, politicians, and administrators have felt a need for some way of organizing or systematizing the many-faceted complexity of individual differences. (Tyler, 1965, p. 3)

The societal need for "organizing" and "systematizing" has historically manifested itself in such varied questions as "Who is a witch?" "Who is schizophrenic?" and "Who is qualified?" The specific questions asked have shifted with societal concerns. The methods used to determine the answers have varied throughout history as a function of factors such as intellectual sophistication and religious preoccupation. Palmistry, podoscopy, astrology, and phrenology, among other pursuits, have had proponents who argued that the best means of understanding and predicting human behavior was through the study of the palms of the hand, the feet, the stars, bumps on the head, tea leaves, and so on. Unlike such pursuits, the assessment enterprise has roots in science. Through systematic and replicable means that can produce compelling evidence, the assessment enterprise responds to what Tyler (1965, p. 3) referred to as the societal "need for some way of organizing or systematizing the many-faceted complexity of individual differences."

Other parties   Beyond the four primary parties we have focused on here, let's briefly make note of others who may participate in varied ways in the testing and assessment enterprise. Organizations, companies, and governmental agencies sponsor the development of tests for various reasons, such as to certify personnel. Companies and services offer test scoring or interpretation services. In some cases, these companies and services are simply extensions of test publishers, and in other cases they are independent. There are people whose sole responsibility is the marketing and sales of tests. Sometimes these people are employed by the test publisher; sometimes they are not. There are academicians who review tests and evaluate their psychometric soundness. All of these people, as well as many others, are also parties to a greater or lesser extent in the assessment enterprise, an enterprise that clearly has few boundaries in terms of the settings in which it can be found.

In What Types of Settings Are Assessments Conducted, and Why?

Educational settings   You are probably no stranger to the many types of tests administered in the classroom. As mandated by law, tests are administered early in school life to help identify children who may need special services or accommodations. In addition to **school ability tests,** you are by now no stranger to **achievement tests:** evaluations of accomplishment or the degree of learning that has taken place. Some of the achievement tests you have taken in school were constructed by your teachers; others were constructed for more widespread use by other educators and measurement professionals. In the latter category, acronyms such as SAT and GRE may ring a bell (and if they do not, they will after you have read Chapter 10).

You know from your own experience that a **diagnosis** may be defined as a description or conclusion reached on the basis of evidence and opinion. Typically, this conclusion is reached through a process of distinguishing the nature of something and ruling out alternative conclusions. As its name implies, a **diagnostic test** is a tool of assessment used to help narrow down and identify areas of deficit to be targeted for intervention. Diagnostic tests of reading, mathematics, and other academic subjects may be administered in educational settings by teachers, school counselors, and school psychologists to assess the need for educational interventions as well as eligibility for special education programs.

Schoolchildren receive grades on their report cards that are not based on any formal assessment. For example, the grade next to "Works and plays well with others" is probably based more on the teacher's *informal evaluation* in the classroom than on scores on any published measure of social interaction. We may define **informal evaluation** as a typically nonsystematic assessment that leads to the formation of an opinion or attitude.

Informal evaluation is, of course, not limited to educational settings; it is very much a part of everyday life. In fact, many of the types of tests we have listed as being administered in educational settings (achievement tests, diagnostic tests, etc.) are also administered in various other settings. And some of the types of tests we discuss in the context of the settings that follow are also administered in educational settings. Thus, it is important to remember that the tools discussed in one context may overlap tools discussed in another. At this point we are simply introducing a sampling of the types of tests used in different settings, not providing a comprehensive list.

Geriatric settings   In the United States, more than 12 million adults are currently in the age range of 75 to 84; that is about 16 times more people in this age range than there were in 1900. Four million adults in the United States are currently 85 years old or older; that is a 33-fold increase in the number of people in that age range in 1900 (Administration on Aging, 1999). Clearly, people in the United States are living longer, and the population as a whole is getting older.

Older Americans may live at home, in special housing designed for independent living, in housing designed for assisted living, or in long-term care facilities such as hospitals and hospices. Wherever older individuals reside, they may at some point require psychological assessment to evaluate cognitive, psychological, adaptive, or other functioning.

Counseling settings   Assessment in a counseling context may occur in environments as diverse as schools, prisons, and government- or privately-owned institutions. Regardless of the particular tools used, the ultimate objective of many such assessments is the improvement of the assessee in terms of adjustment, productivity, quality of life, or some related variable. Measures of social and academic skills and measures of personality, interest, attitudes, and values are among the many types of tests that a counselor might administer to a client. Referral questions to be answered range from "How can this child better focus on tasks?" to "For what career is the client best suited?" to "What activities are recommended for retirement?" Because the testtaker is in many instances the primary recipient and user of the data from a test administered by a counselor, it is imperative that the counselor understand the strengths and limitations of the findings and be able to competently convey the test results to the client.

> **JUST THINK . . .**
>
> Tests are used in clinical and counseling settings to help improve quality of life. But are there some things a psychological test just can't measure?

Clinical settings   Tests and many other tools of assessment are widely used in clinical settings such as public, private, and military hospitals, inpatient and outpatient clinics, private-practice consulting rooms, schools, and other institutions. These tools are used to help screen for or diagnose behavior problems. What types of situations might prompt the employment of such tools? Here's a small sample.

- A private psychotherapy client wishes to be evaluated to see if the assessment can provide any nonobvious clues regarding his maladjustment.

- A school psychologist clinically evaluates a child experiencing learning difficulties to determine what factors are primarily responsible for it.

- A psychotherapy researcher uses assessment procedures to determine if a particular method of psychotherapy is effective in treating a particular problem.

- A psychologist-consultant retained by an insurance company is called on to give an opinion as to the reality of a client's psychological problems; is the client really experiencing such problems, or just malingering?

- A court-appointed psychologist is asked to give an opinion as to a defendant's competency to stand trial.

- A prison psychologist is called on to give an opinion regarding the extent of a convicted violent prisoner's rehabilitation.

The tests employed in clinical settings may be intelligence tests, personality tests, neuropsychological tests, or other specialized instruments, depending on the presenting or suspected problem area. The hallmark of testing in clinical settings is that the test or measurement technique is employed with only one individual at a time. Group testing is used primarily for screening; that is, identifying those individuals who require further diagnostic evaluation. In Chapter 13 and elsewhere, we will look at the nature, uses, and benefits of assessment in both clinical and counseling settings.

Business and military settings   In business, as in the military, tests are used in many ways, perhaps most notably in decision making about the careers of personnel. As we will see in Chapter 16, a wide range of achievement, aptitude, interest, motivational, and other tests may be employed in the decision to hire, as well as in related decisions regarding promotions, transfer, job satisfaction, and eligibility for further training. For a prospective air traffic controller, successful performance on a test of sustained attention to detail may be one requirement of employment. For promotion to the rank of officer in the military, successful performance on a series of leadership tasks may be essential.

Another application of psychological tests involves the engineering and design of products and environments. Engineering psychologists employ a variety of existing and specially devised tests in research designed to help people at home, in the workplace, and in the military. Products ranging from home computers to office furniture to jet cockpit control panels benefit from the work of such research efforts.

Using tests, interviews, and other tools of assessment, psychologists who specialize in the marketing and sale of products are involved in taking the pulse of consumers—helping to predict the public's receptivity to a new product, a new brand, or a new advertising or marketing campaign.

Governmental and organizational credentialing   One of the many applications of measurement is in governmental licensing, certification, or general credentialing of professionals. Before they are legally entitled to practice medicine, physicians must pass an examination. Law school graduates cannot hold themselves out to the public as attorneys until they pass their state's bar examination. Psychologists, too, must pass an examination entitling them to present themselves to the public with the title "psychologist."

Members of some professions have formed organizations with requirements for membership that go beyond those of licensing or certification requirements. For example, physicians can take further specialized training and a specialty examination to earn the distinction of being "board certified" in a particular specialty area of medicine. Psychologists specializing in certain areas may be evaluated for a diploma from the **American Board of Professional Psychology (ABPP)** to recognize excellence in the practice of psychology. Another organization, the **American Board of Assessment Psychology (ABAP),** awards its diploma on the basis of an examination to test users, test developers, and others who have distinguished themselves in the field of testing and assessment.

Other settings Many different kinds of measurement procedures find application in a wide variety of settings. For example, the courts rely on psychological test data and related expert testimony as one source of information to help answer important questions such as "Is this defendant competent to stand trial?" and "Did this defendant know right from wrong at the time the criminal act was committed?"

Measurement may play an important part in program evaluation, be it a large-scale government program or a small-scale, privately funded one. Is the program working? How can the program be improved? Are funds being spent in the areas where they ought to be spent? How sound is the theory on which the program is based? These are the types of general questions that tests and measurement procedures used in program evaluation are designed to answer.

Tools of assessment can be found in use in research and practice in every specialty area within psychology. For example, consider **health psychology,** a specialty area that focuses on understanding the role of psychological variables in the onset, course, treatment, and prevention of illness, disease, and disability (Cohen, 1994). Health psychologists are involved in teaching, research, or direct-service activities designed to promote good health. Individual interviews, surveys, and paper-and-pencil tests are some of the tools that may be employed to help assess a current state of affairs with regard to some disease or condition, gauge treatment progress, and evaluate outcome of intervention.

One research approach in health psychology entails reporting on the nature of the psychological adjustment, the nature of coping measures, or the nature of the quality of life of members of targeted groups. Various measures of adjustment, coping, and quality of life may be employed in research with a wide variety of populations ranging from middle-aged women who have just given birth to elderly men afflicted with debilitating medical conditions. Another general line of research in health psychology focuses on aspects of personality, behavior, or lifestyle as they relate to variables ranging from good physical health and longevity to sudden death by heart attack. For example, Hill and Pargament (2003) reviewed advances in the measurement of spirituality and the possible implications of those advancements for physical and mental health. Using a test called the Drinking Motives Measure (DMM), Martens et al. (2003) studied college athletes' motivations for alcohol use. Consistent with prior research, these investigators concluded that athletes involved in intercollegiate sports may be particularly susceptible to using alcohol as well as other drugs as a coping mechanism, due to elevated stressors. The researchers concluded that the DMM was effective in predicting alcohol consumption and might therefore have an application in prevention or intervention programs.

What personality traits, if any, are predictive of smoking initiation and cessation? Compliance or noncompliance with physicians' instructions? Strengthened or compromised immune functioning in AIDS patients? These questions are representative of many asked by health psychologists. All such questions require sound techniques of evaluation if answers are to be forthcoming.

Of course, psychological testing and assessment is not confined to health psychology. It is very much a part of *all* specialty areas within psychology and education. Further, what constitutes a "test" may take many different forms ranging from paper-and-pencil form to . . . well, just take a look at Figure 1-6. There you will find a very small sample of the tens of thousands of measurement methods that have been used in one situation or another. They are not presented here to illustrate the most typical kinds of assessment procedures, but rather to illustrate the diversity of measuring tools that have

At least since the beginning of the nineteenth century, military units throughout the world have relied on psychological and other tests for personnel selection, program validation, and related reasons (Hartmann et al., 2003). In some cultures, where military service is highly valued, students take preparatory courses with hopes of being accepted into elite military units. This is the case in Israel, where rigorous training such as that pictured here prepares high school students for physical and related tests that only 1 in 60 military recruits will pass.

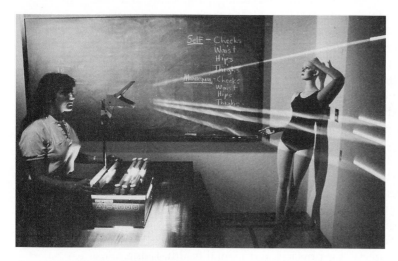

Evidence suggests that some people with eating disorders may actually have a self-perception disorder; that is, they see themselves as heavier than they really are (Thompson & Smolak, 2001). J. Kevin Thompson and his associates devised the adjustable light beam apparatus to measure body image distortion. Assessees adjust four beams of light to indicate what they believe is the width of their cheeks, waist, hips, and thighs. A measure of accuracy of these estimates is then obtained.

Herman Witkin and his associates (Witkin & Goodenough, 1977) studied personality-related variables in some very innovative ways. For example, they identified field (or context) dependent and field independent people by means of this specially constructed tilting room/tilting chair device. Assessees were asked questions designed to evaluate their dependence or independence of visual cues.

Figure 1–6
The Wide World of Measurement

Pictures such as these sample items from the Meier Art Judgment Test might be used to evaluate people's aesthetic perception. Which of these two renderings do you find more aesthetically pleasing? The difference between the two pictures has to do with the positioning of the objects on the shelf.

Impairment of certain sensory functions can indicate neurological deficit. For purposes of diagnosis, as well as in measuring progress in remediation, the neurodevelopment training ball can be useful in evaluating one's sense of balance.

been created for varied uses. In short, if a need exists to measure a particular variable, a way to measure that variable will be devised.

Having considered some of the *who, what,* and *why* of assessment, it remains for us to raise the question of *where* to go for more information. Actually, we think you will find this book to be most useful when future questions arise.[3] But in addition to a book such as this one, where does one go for up-to-date information about tests, testing, and assessment?

Where to Go for Authoritative Information: Reference Sources

Many reference sources exist for learning more about published tests and assessment-related issues. These sources vary with respect to detail. Some merely provide descriptions of tests, whereas others provide very detailed information regarding technical aspects.

Test catalogues Perhaps one of the most readily accessible sources of information about a test is a catalogue distributed by the publisher of the test. Because most test publishers make available catalogues of their offerings, this source of test information can be tapped by a simple telephone call, e-mail, or note. As you might expect, however, publishers' catalogues usually contain only a brief description of the test and seldom contain the kind of detailed technical information that a prospective user of the test might require. Further, the objective of the catalogue is to sell the test. For this reason, highly critical reviews of a test are seldom, if ever, found in a publisher's test catalogue.

Test manuals Detailed information concerning the development of a particular test and technical information relating to it should be found in the manual for the test itself. Test manuals are usually available from test publishers. However, for security purposes, the test publisher will typically require documentation of professional training before filling an order for a test manual. Beyond purchasing a manual from the publisher, the chances are good that somewhere within your university (be it the library or the counseling center), a collection of popular test manuals is maintained. If the test manual you are interested in looking at is not available there, ask your instructor about how best to obtain a reference copy.

Reference volumes The Buros Institute of Mental Measurements provides "one-stop shopping" for a great deal of test-related information. The initial version of what would evolve into the *Mental Measurements Yearbook* (*MMY*) was compiled by Oscar Buros (Figure 1-7) in 1933. At this writing, the latest edition of this authoritative compilation of test reviews is the *15th Mental Measurements Yearbook* (Plake et al., 2003), although the *16th* cannot be far behind. The Buros Institute also publishes *Tests in Print* (Murphy et al., 2002) as well as a number of other test-related reference works. For a list of its latest offerings, as well as links to a number of other useful test-related test databases, visit the Institute's Web site at http://www.unl.edu/buros/index/simm.html.

Journal articles Articles in current journals may contain reviews of the test, updated or independent studies of its psychometric soundness, or examples of how the instrument

---

3. We sincerely hope this thought occurs to you when you have completed your coursework and find yourself in line at the bookstore to sell used textbooks.

Figure 1–7
Oscar Krisen Buros (1906–1978)

Buros is best remembered as the creator of the
Mental Measurements Yearbook (MMY), *a
kind of* Consumer Reports *for tests and a much-
needed source of "psychometric policing" (Peterson, 1997, p. 718). His work lives on at the Buros
Institute of Mental Measurements at the University of Nebraska, Lincoln. In addition to the
MMY, which is updated periodically, the institute publishes a variety of other test-related
publications.*

was used in either research or an applied context. Such articles may appear in a wide
array of behavioral science journals such as *Psychological Bulletin, Psychological Review,
Professional Psychology: Research and Practice, Journal of Personality and Social Psychology,
Psychology & Marketing, Psychology in the Schools, School Psychology Quarterly,* and *School
Psychology Review.* There are also journals that focus more specifically on matters related
to testing and assessment. For example, take a look at journals such as the *Journal of
Psychoeducational Assessment, Psychological Assessment, Educational and Psychological Mea-
surement, Applied Measurement in Education,* and the *Journal of Personality Assessment.*
Journals such as *Psychology, Public Policy, and Law* and *Law and Human Behavior* frequently contain highly informative articles on legal and ethical issues and controversies
as they relate to psychological testing and assessment.

In addition to articles relevant to specific tests, journals are a rich source of information on important trends in testing and assessment. For example, with reference to
clinical psychological assessment, the negative impact of managed health care and the
reluctance or refusal of insurers to pay for assessment services have spurred a great deal
of self-evaluation on the part of those in the business of evaluation (Camara et al., 2000;
Sanchez & Turner, 2003). While critics of clinical assessment argue that testing and assessment is too expensive, too time consuming, and of too little value (Griffith, 1997),
more informed reviews of the issues find abundant empirical support for the value of
the enterprise (Kubiszyn et al., 2000).

Online databases One of the most widely used bibliographic databases for test-related
publications is that maintained by the Educational Resources Information Center
(ERIC). Funded by the United States Department of Education and operated out of the
University of Maryland, the ERIC Web site at www.eric.ed.gov/searchdb/index.html
contains a wealth of resources and news about tests, testing, and assessment. There are
abstracts of articles, original articles, and links to other useful Web sites. ERIC strives to
provide balanced information concerning educational assessment and to provide resources to encourage responsible test use.

The American Psychological Association (APA) maintains a number of databases
useful in locating psychology-related information in journal articles, book chapters,
and doctoral dissertations. **PsycINFO** is a database of abstracts dating back to 1887.

Table 1-2
Some Web Sites of Test Publishers

Academic Therapy www.academictherapy.com	Lafayette Instruments www.lafayetteinstrument.com	Scholastic Testing Service www.ststesting.com
American Guidance Service www.agsnet.com	Multi-Health Systems www.mhs.com	Slosson Educational Publications www.slosson.com
CPP www.cpp.com	Pearson Assessments www.pearsonassessments.com	Sopris West www.sopriswest.com
CTB McGraw-Hill www.ctb.com	Pro-Ed www.proedinc.com	Stoelting www.stoeltingco.com
Educator Publishing Service www.epsbooks.com	Psychological Assessment Resources www.parinc.com	Vort www.vort.com
Harcourt Assessment, Inc. www.hbem.com	The Psychological Corporation www.psychcorp.com.au	
James Stanfield Company www.stanfield.com	Riverside Publishing www.riverpub.com	

ClinPSYC is a database derived from PsycINFO that focuses on abstracts of a clinical nature. PsycSCAN: Psychopharmacology contains abstracts of articles having to do with psychopharmacology. PsycARTICLES is a database of full-length articles dating back to 1988. Health and Psychosocial Instruments (HAPI) contains a listing of measures created or modified for specific research studies but not commercially available. It is available at many college libraries through BRS Information Technologies, and also available on CD-ROM (updated twice a year). PsycLAW is a free database available to everyone that contains discussions of selected topics having to do with psychology and law. It can be accessed at http://www.apa.org/psyclaw. For more information on any of these databases, visit APA's Web site at http://www.apa.org.

Educational Testing Service (ETS), "the world's largest and most influential testing organization" (Frantz & Nordheimer, 1997), maintains its own Web site at http://www.ets.org. The site contains a wealth of information about college and graduate school admission and placement tests, as well as many related resources. If you wanted to try your hand at some practice questions for a test such as the Graduate Record Examination (GRE), for example, this is the place to go. For more information, ETS can be contacted by e-mail at etsinfo@ets.org. A list of Web sites for publishers of other educational and psychological tests is presented in Table 1-2. A number of other Web sites may be of interest to students of assessment, and we have listed a sample of them in Table 1-3.

Other sources　Your school library contains a number of other sources that may be used to acquire information about tests and test-related topics. For example, two sources for exploring the world of unpublished tests and measures are the *Directory of Unpublished Experimental Measures* (Goldman & Mitchell, 1997) and *Tests in Microfiche*, available from Test Collections. APA makes available *Finding Information About Psychological Tests* (1995), its own guide to locating test-related information. And now for one source of information about these various sources of information . . . see Table 1-4.

Armed with a wealth of background information about tests and other tools of assessment, we'll explore historical, cultural, and legal/ethical aspects of the assessment enterprise in the following chapter.

Table 1-3
Web Sites Having To Do With Testing and Assessment

Web Site Address	Reason to Visit
http://edres.org/scripts/cat	To obtain some firsthand experience with computerized assessment, learn its logic, and take a "behind-the-scenes" look at it
www.apa.org/science/faq-findtests.html	A wealth of general information about finding information on published and unpublished psychological tests
www.apa.org/journals/pas.html	This is the home page of the APA journal *Psychological Assessment*. There you will find a table of contents for the current issue and even be able to access the articles.
www.gre.org	The Graduate Record Exam (GRE) is a test in the future of many readers of this book. This is the official site for GRE authoritative information about this test.
http://edres.org/irt	After you have read Chapter 7 of this book, you may wish to read this advanced, in-depth material on an approach to measurement called *item response theory*.
http://edres.org/mdt	After you have read Chapter 7 of this book, you may wish to read this advanced, in-depth material on an approach to classifying examinees on the basis of statistical decision theory.

Table 1-4
Sources of Information About Tests: Some Pros and Cons

Information Source	Pros	Cons
Test catalogues available from the publisher of the test as well as affiliated distributors of the test	Contains general description of test, including what it is designed to do and who it is designed to be used with. Readily available to most anyone who requests a catalogue.	Primarily designed to sell the test to test users and seldom contains any critical reviews. Information not detailed enough for basing a decision to use the test.
Test manual	Usually the most detailed source available for information regarding the standardization sample and test administration instructions. May also contain useful information regarding the theory the test is based on, if that is the case. Typically contains at least some information regarding psychometric soundness of the test.	Details regarding the test's psychometric soundness are usually self-serving and written on the basis of studies conducted by the test author and/or test publisher. Test manual itself may be difficult to obtain by students, as its distribution may be restricted to qualified professionals.
Reference volumes such as the *Mental Measurements Yearbook,* available in bound book form or online	Much like a *Consumer Reports* for tests, contains descriptions and critical reviews of test written by third parties who presumably have nothing to gain or lose by praising or criticizing the instrument, its standardization sample, and its psychometric soundness.	Few disadvantages if reviewer is genuinely trying to be objective and is knowledgeable, but as with any review, can provide a misleading picture if this is not the case. Also, for very detailed accounts of the standardization sample and related matters, it is best to consult the test manual itself.
Journal articles	Up-to-date source of reviews and studies of psychometric soundness. Can provide practical examples of how an instrument is used in research or applied contexts.	As with reference volumes, reviews are valuable to the extent they are informed and, to the extent that is possible, unbiased. Reader should research as many articles as possible when attempting to learn how the instrument is actually used; any one article alone may provide an atypical picture.
Online databases	Widely known and respected online databases such as the ERIC database are virtual "gold mines" of useful information containing varying amounts of detail. Although some legitimate psychological tests may be available for self-administration and scoring online, the vast majority are not.	Consumer beware! Some sites masquerading as databases for psychological tests are designed more to entertain or to sell something than to inform. These sites frequently offer tests you can take online. As you learn more about tests, you will probably become more critical of the value of these self-administered and self-scored "psychological tests."

Self-Assessment

Test your understanding of elements of this chapter by seeing if you can explain each of the following terms, expressions, and abbreviations:

American Board of Assessment Psychology (ABAP)
American Board of Professional Psychology (ABPP)
achievement test
alternate assessment
American Psychological Association (APA)
assessment center approach
behavioral observation
case history data
central processing
collaborative psychological assessment
computer-assisted psychological assessment (CAPA)
consultative report
cut score
descriptive report
diagnosis
diagnostic test
dynamic psychological assessment

extended scoring report
format
groupthink
health psychology
informal evaluation
integrative report
interpretive report
interview
local processing
measurement
naturalistic observation
panel interview
portfolio
protocol
psychological assessment
psychological autopsy
psychological test
psychological testing
psychometrician
psychometrics
psychometrist
psychometry
PsycINFO

Public Law 94-142
Public Law 99-457
rapport
role play
role-play test
school ability test
score
scoring
scoring report
screening report
simple scoring report
teleprocessing
test
test catalogue
test developer
test manual
testtaker
test user
therapeutic psychological assessment

Web Watch

Check out the following Web sites for more information about topics in this chapter:

Standards for Educational and Psychological Testing
www.apa.org/science/standards.html

National Council on Measurement in Education
www.ncme.org

American Educational Research Association (AERA)
www.aera.net

Illinois State Board of Education-Alternative Assessment
www.isbe.net/assessment/IAA.htm

www.isbe.net/assessment/default.htm

IDEA
www.ed.gov/offices/OSERS/Policy/IDEA/index.html

www.ideapractices.org/law/index.php

American Board of Professional Psychology (ABPP)
www.abpp.org

American Board of Assessment Psychology (ABAP)
www.assessmentpsychologyboard.org

American Academy of School Psychology
http://espse.ed.psu.edu/spsy/aasp/aasp.ssi

National Association of School Psychologists (NASP)
www.nasponline.org/index2.html

PsycLAW
www.apa.org/psyclaw

2

Historical, Cultural, and Legal/Ethical Considerations

We continue our broad overview of the field of psychological testing and assessment with a look backward, the better to appreciate the historical context of the enterprise. We also present food for thought regarding cultural and legal/ethical matters. Consider this "food" only as an appetizer; material on historical, cultural, and legal/ethical considerations is interwoven where appropriate throughout this book.

A Historical Perspective

Antiquity to the Nineteenth Century

A primitive form of proficiency testing existed in China as early as 2200 B.C.E. (DuBois, 1966, 1970), where some form of examination of public officials by the Chinese emperor was conducted every third year. Civil service examinations began in China during the Chan Dynasty in 1115 B.C.E. and ended in 1905 when a reform measure abolished the system. For three thousand years, the open and competitive system of examinations in China provided for evaluation of proficiency in areas such as music, archery, horsemanship, writing, and arithmetic. Proficiency was also examined with respect to skill in the rites and ceremonies of public and social life, civil law, military affairs, agriculture, revenue, and geography (Figure 2-1).

Why were the civil service examinations first introduced? It may well have been as the result of the influential teachings of Confucius, who taught that self-perfection is something to strive for. Using examinations to select government employees may have been an extension of the "be all you can be" philosophy to government; government, too, should strive to be all it can be. When Confucius spoke about civil service, he did so in the context of a moral and social duty to ensure striving for perfection in government (Li, 2003).

The historical significance of the testing program in ancient China is that thousands of years ago there existed a civilization concerned with some of the same basic principles of psychometrics that we are concerned with today. In a period of history when nepotism was no doubt rampant, it is admirable that employment was based on open,

> **JUST THINK . . .**
>
> How might the teachings of Confucius be incorporated in this country in the evaluation of applicants for employment at the post office?

Figure 2–1
Testing Booths in China

Pictured here are hundreds of civil service examination cubicles in Nanking. Testing would go on for days, and some applicants even died of the strain. This photograph was taken about twenty years after the cessation of such testing in 1905.

competitive examinations. Modern readers might note with fascination that activities such as archery and horsemanship were included among the tests. However, the test users of the day felt that civil servants should be proficient in those skills.

Fascinating from a historical perspective are Greco-Roman writings that proposed various physiological bases for personality and temperament. Also intriguing are accounts of attempts during the Middle Ages to answer diagnostic questions of critical importance to society at the time, such as "Who is in league with the Devil?" However, it was not until the Renaissance that measurement in the modern sense began to emerge. By the eighteenth century, Christian von Wolff (1732, 1734) had anticipated psychology as a science and psychological measurement as a specialty within that science.

The Nineteenth Century

In 1859, a book was published entitled *On the Origin of Species by Means of Natural Selection* by **Charles Darwin** (1809–1882). In this important, far-reaching work, Darwin argued that chance variation in species would be selected or rejected by nature according to adaptivity and survival value. He further argued that humans had descended from the ape as a result of such chance genetic variations. This revolutionary notion aroused interest, admiration, and a good deal of enmity. The enmity arose primarily from members of the religious community who interpreted Darwin's ideas as an affront to the biblical account of creation in Genesis. Still, the notion of an evolutionary link between human beings and animals conferred a new scientific respectability on experimentation with animals. It also raised questions about how animals and humans compare with respect to states of consciousness—questions that would beg for answers in laboratories of future behavioral scientists.[1]

History records that it was Darwin who spurred scientific interest in individual differences. Darwin (1859) wrote:

> The many slight differences which appear in the offspring from the same parents . . . may be called individual differences. . . . These individual differences are of the highest importance . . . [for they] afford materials for natural selection to act on. (p. 125)

Indeed, Darwin's writing on individual differences kindled interest in research on heredity in his half cousin, **Francis Galton.** In the course of his efforts to explore and quantify individual differences between people, Galton became an extremely influential contributor to the field of measurement (Forrest, 1974). Galton (1869) aspired to classify people "according to their natural gifts" (p. 1) and to ascertain their "deviation from an average" (p. 11). Along the way, Galton would be credited with devising or contributing to the development of many contemporary tools of psychological assessment including questionnaires, rating scales, and self-report inventories.

Galton's initial work on heredity was done with sweet peas, in part because there tended to be fewer variations among the peas in a single pod. In this work, Galton pioneered the use of a statistical concept central to psychological experimentation and testing: the coefficient of correlation. Although **Karl Pearson** (1857–1936) developed the product-moment correlation technique, the roots of this technique can be traced directly to the work of Galton (Magnello & Spies, 1984). From heredity in peas, Galton's interest turned to heredity in humans and various ways of measuring aspects of people and their abilities.

At an exhibition in London in 1884, Galton displayed his Anthropometric Laboratory where, for three or four pence, depending on whether you were already registered or not, you could be measured on variables such as height (standing), height (sitting), arm span, weight, breathing capacity, strength of pull, strength of squeeze, swiftness of blow, keenness of sight, memory of form, discrimination of color, and steadiness of hand. Through his own efforts and his urging of educational institutions to keep anthropometric records on their students, Galton excited widespread interest in the measurement of psychology-related variables.

Assessment was also an important activity at the first experimental psychology laboratory, founded at the University of Leipzig in Germany by **Wilhelm Max Wundt** (1832–1920), a medical doctor whose title at the university was professor of philosophy. Wundt and his students tried to formulate a general description of human abilities with respect to variables such as reaction time, perception, and attention span. In contrast to Galton, Wundt focused on questions relating to how people were similar, not different. In fact, individual differences were viewed by Wundt as a frustrating source of error in experimentation. Wundt attempted to control all extraneous variables in an effort to reduce error to a minimum. As we will see, attempting to control extraneous variables to minimize the role

JUST THINK . . .

Which orientation in assessment research appeals to you more, the Galtonian orientation (researching how individuals differ) or the Wundtian one (researching how individuals are the same)? Why?

---

1. The influence of Darwin's thinking is also apparent in the theory of personality formulated by Sigmund Freud. From a Darwinian perspective, the strongest people with the most efficient sex drives would have been most responsible for contributing to the human gene pool. In this context, Freud's notion of the primary importance of instinctual sexual and aggressive urges can be better understood.

Figure 2–2
The Cattells, James McKeen and Psyche

The psychologist who coined the term mental test, *James McKeen Cattell (1860–1944), has often been mistakenly credited (along with another psychologist, Raymond B. Cattell, no relation) with the authorship of a measure of infant intelligence called the Cattell Infant Intelligence Scale (CIIS). Actually, it was Psyche (1893–1989), the third of seven children of Cattell and his wife, Josephine Owen, who created the CIIS. From 1919 through 1921, Psyche assisted her famous father in statistical analyses for the third edition of* American Men of Science. *In 1927, she earned a doctor of education degree at Harvard. In 1931, she adopted a son, becoming one of the first unmarried women to do so (Sokal, 1991). Later in the decade she adopted a daughter. Her book* The Measurement of Intelligence in Infants and Young Children *was published in 1940, and it was in that book that the CIIS was introduced. Later in her career, she would write a popular book,* Raising Children with Love and Limits, *which refuted the permissiveness advocated by child-rearing authorities such as Benjamin Spock.*

of extraneous variables is fairly routine in contemporary assessment. The idea is to ensure that any observed differences between people are indeed due to differences between people and not to any extraneous variables. Standardized conditions are used to help ensure that differences in scores are the result of true differences among individuals.

In spite of the prevailing research focus on people's similarities, one of Wundt's students at Leipzig, an American named **James McKeen Cattell** (Figure 2-2), completed a doctoral dissertation that dealt with individual differences, specifically individual differences in reaction time. After receiving his doctoral degree from Leipzig, Cattell returned to the United States and taught at Bryn Mawr and then at the University of Pennsylvania before leaving for Europe to teach at Cambridge. At Cambridge, Cattell came in contact with Galton, whom he later described as "the greatest man I have known" (Roback, 1961, p. 96).

Inspired by his contact with Galton, Cattell returned to the University of Pennsylvania in 1888 and coined the term *mental test* in an 1890 publication. Boring (1950, p. 283) has noted that "Cattell more than any other person was in this fashion responsible for getting mental testing underway in America, and it is plain that his motivation was similar to Galton's and that he was influenced, or at least reinforced, by Galton." Cattell went on to become professor and chair of the psychology department at Columbia University. For the next 26 years, he not only trained many psychologists but also founded a number of publications (such as *Psychological Review, Science,* and *American Men of Science*). In 1921, Cattell was instrumental in founding the Psychological Corporation, which named 20 of the country's leading psychologists as its directors. The goal of the corporation was the "advancement of psychology and the promotion of the useful applications of psychology." Today the Psychological Corporation is still very active in providing services related to psychological testing and assessment.

Other students of Wundt at Leipzig included Charles Spearman, Victor Henri, Emil Kraepelin, E. B. Titchener, G. Stanley Hall, and Lightner Witmer. Spearman is credited with originating the concept of test reliability as well as building the mathematical framework for factor analysis. Victor Henri is the Frenchman who would collaborate with Alfred Binet on papers suggesting how mental tests could be used to measure higher mental processes (for example, Binet & Henri, 1895a, 1895b, 1895c). Psychiatrist Emil Kraepelin was an early experimenter with the word association technique as a formal test (Kraepelin, 1892, 1895). **Lightner Witmer** received his Ph.D. from Leipzig and went on to succeed Cattell as director of the psychology laboratory at the University of Pennsylvania. Witmer has been cited as the "little-known founder of clinical psychology" (McReynolds, 1987), owing at least in part to his being challenged to treat a "chronic bad speller" in March of 1896 (Brotemarkle, 1947). Later that year, Witmer founded the first psychological clinic in the United States at the University of Pennsylvania. In 1907, Witmer founded the journal *Psychological Clinic* with the first article entitled "Clinical Psychology" (Witmer, 1907).

The Twentieth Century

The early 1900s witnessed the birth of the first formal tests of intelligence. As we will see in the rest of this section, there was initially great receptivity to instruments that could purportedly measure mental characteristics—at first intelligence and later other characteristics, such as those related to personality, interests, attitudes, and values.

The measurement of intelligence   Much of the nineteenth-century testing that could be described as psychological in nature involved the measurement of sensory abilities, reaction time, and the like. One person who had a vision of broadening testing to include the measurement of cognitive abilities was **Alfred Binet** (1857–1911). As early as 1895, Binet and his colleague Victor Henri published several articles in which they argued for the measurement of abilities such as memory and social comprehension. Ten years later, Binet and collaborator Theodore Simon published a 30-item "measuring scale of intelligence" designed to help identify mentally retarded Paris schoolchildren (Binet & Simon, 1905). The Binet test would go through many revisions and translations—and in the process launch both the intelligence testing movement and the clinical testing movement. Before long, psychological tests were used in settings as diverse as juvenile courts, reformatories, prisons, children's homes, and schools (Pintner, 1931).

In 1939, **David Wechsler,** a clinical psychologist at Bellevue Hospital in New York City, introduced a test designed to measure adult intelligence—defined as "the aggregate or global capacity of the individual to act purposefully, to think rationally, and to deal effectively with his environment" (p. 3). The test, originally called the Wechsler-Bellevue Intelligence Scale, was revised and renamed the Wechsler Adult Intelligence Scale (WAIS). The WAIS has since been periodically revised.

> **JUST THINK . . .**
>
> In the early 1900s, the Binet test was being used worldwide for various purposes far beyond identifying exceptional Paris schoolchildren. What do you think were some of the other uses of the test? How appropriate do you think it was to use this test for these other purposes?

In subsequent chapters, we will examine Wechsler's definition of intelligence as it was reflected in the series of adults', children's, and young children's intelligence tests that bear his name.

A natural outgrowth of the individually administered intelligence test devised by Binet was the *group* intelligence test. Group intelligence tests came into being in the United States in response to the military's need for an efficient method of screening the intellectual ability of World War I recruits. Because of military manpower needs during World War II, psychologists were enlisted into government service to develop, administer, and interpret group psychological test data.

◆
JUST THINK . . .

What do you think are the advantages of group intelligence testing? What do you think are the disadvantages of group intelligence testing?

After the war, psychologists returning from military service brought back a wealth of applied testing skills that would be useful not only in government service but also in settings as diverse as private industry, hospitals, and schools. Tests would be developed to measure not only various abilities and interests but personality as well.

The measurement of personality   The general receptivity to tests of intellectual ability spurred the development of a wide variety of other types of tests (Garrett & Schneck, 1933; Pintner, 1931), Only eight years after the publication of Binet's scale, the field of psychology was being criticized for being too test oriented (Sylvester, 1913). By the late 1930s, approximately four thousand different psychological tests were in print (Buros, 1938), and "clinical psychology" was synonymous with "mental testing" (Institute for Juvenile Research, 1937; Tulchin, 1939).

World War I had brought with it not only the need to screen the intellectual functioning of recruits but the need to screen for recruits' general adjustment. A government Committee on Emotional Fitness chaired by psychologist **Robert S. Woodworth** was assigned the task of developing a measure of adjustment and emotional stability that could be administered quickly and efficiently to groups of recruits. The committee developed several experimental versions of what in essence were paper-and-pencil psychiatric interviews. To disguise the true purpose of the test, the questionnaire was labeled and referred to as a Personal Data Sheet. Draftees and volunteers were asked to indicate *yes* or *no* to a series of questions that probed for the existence of various kinds of psychopathology. For example, one of the test questions was "Are you troubled with the idea that people are watching you on the street?"

The Personal Data Sheet developed by Woodworth and his colleagues never went beyond the experimental stages. The treaty of peace rendered the development of this and other tests less urgent. After the war, Woodworth developed a personality test for civilian use that was based on the Personal Data Sheet. He called it the Woodworth Psychoneurotic Inventory. This inventory was the first widely used **self-report test** of personality—a method of assessment that would soon be employed in a long line of succeeding personality tests.

◆
JUST THINK . . .

Describe the ideal candidate for personality assessment by means of self-report.

Personality tests that employ self-report methodologies have both advantages and disadvantages. On the face of it, the respondent is arguably the best-qualified person to provide answers about himself or herself. However, there are also compelling arguments against respondents themselves supplying such information. For example, respondents may have poor insight into themselves. That is, one might honestly believe something about oneself that in reality is not true. Regardless of the quality of insight, some respondents are unwilling to reveal anything about themselves that is very personal or that could put them in a negative light. Given these shortcomings of the self-report method of personality assessment, a need existed for alternative types of personality tests.

Filling the need for measures of personality that did not rely on self-report were various methods. One such method or approach to personality assessment came to be described as *projective* in nature. As we will see later in this book, a **projective test** is one in which an individual is assumed to "project" onto some ambiguous stimulus his or her own unique needs, fears, hopes, and motivation. The ambiguous stimulus might be an inkblot, a drawing, a photograph, or something else.

JUST THINK . . .

What potential problems do you think might attend the use of projective methods to assess personality?

Perhaps the best known of all projective tests is the Rorschach, a series of inkblots developed by the Swiss psychiatrist **Hermann Rorschach.** The use of pictures as projective stimuli was popularized in the late 1930s by **Henry A. Murray, Christiana D. Morgan,** and their colleagues at the Harvard Psychological Clinic. In addition to projective tests, other alternatives to self-report for personality assessment have been developed. A sampling of these instruments and a general discussion of personality assessment are presented in Chapters 11 and 12.

The academic and applied traditions   Like the development of the parent field of psychology, the development of psychological measurement can be traced along two distinct threads: the academic and the applied. In the tradition of Galton, Wundt, and other scholars, psychological testing and assessment are practiced today in university psychology laboratories as a means of furthering knowledge about the nature of the human experience. There is also a very strong applied tradition—one that dates back in modern times to the work of people like Binet and in ancient times to China and the administration of competitive civil service examinations. Which child should be placed in which class? Which person is best suited for the job? Society requires answers to questions such as these, and tests and measures used in a competent manner can help provide answers.

Perhaps more today than ever before, there is a great appreciation for the role of culture in the human experience. So, whether in academic or applied settings, assessment professionals recognize the need for cultural sensitivity in the development and use of psychological tests. Let's briefly look at some of the major issues that such sensitivity entails. These and related issues are elaborated and expanded on throughout this book as they relate to specific aspects of testing and assessment.

Culture and Assessment

Culture may be defined as "the socially transmitted behavior patterns, beliefs, and products of work of a particular population, community, or group of people" (Cohen, 1994, p. 5). As taught to us by parents, peers, and societal institutions such as schools, culture prescribes many behaviors and ways of thinking. Spoken language, attitudes toward elders, and techniques of child rearing are but a few critical manifestations of culture. Culture teaches specific rituals to be performed at birth, marriage, death, and other momentous occasions. Culture imparts much about what is to be valued or prized, as well as what is to be rejected or despised. Culture teaches a point of view about what it means to be born of one or another gender, race, or ethnic background. Culture teaches us something about what we

JUST THINK . . .

Can you think of one or two ways in which you are a product of your culture? How about one or two ways this fact might come through on a psychological test?

can expect from other people and what we can expect from ourselves. Indeed, the influence of culture on an individual's thoughts and behavior may be a great deal stronger than most of us would acknowledge at first blush.

Professionals involved in the assessment enterprise have shown increasing sensitivity to the role of culture in many different aspects of measurement. This sensitivity is manifested in greater consideration of cultural issues with respect to every aspect of test development and use, including decision making on the basis of test data. Unfortunately, it was not always that way.

Evolving Interest in Culture-Related Issues

Soon after Alfred Binet introduced intelligence testing in France, the United States Public Health Service began using such tests to measure the intelligence of people seeking to immigrate to the United States (Figure 2-3). **Henry H. Goddard** was the chief researcher assigned to the project and a specialist in the field of mental retardation. Previously he had opened a psychological laboratory at the training school in Vineland, New Jersey, and championed the use of the Binet-Simon intelligence test for special class placement in the schools. Early on, he raised questions about how meaningful such tests are when used with people from various cultural and language backgrounds. Goddard (1913) used interpreters in test administration, employed a bilingual psychologist, and administered mental tests to selected immigrants who appeared mentally retarded to trained observers (Goddard, 1917). In 1914, Goddard introduced intelligence tests to the courts for the purpose of arguing against the death penalty for the "feebleminded." But although he argued against the death penalty, Goddard was at the time a believer in **eugenics.** He advocated institutionalization or sterilization of the feebleminded to prevent future generations of impaired individuals. Goddard's reputation would eventually be tarnished by the publication of a book in 1912 that employed poor research methods and made the case that mental defect was hereditary.

The impact of language and culture on mental ability test scores was recognized by psychologists even in the early 1900s. One way for the early test developers to deal with this psychometric fact of life was to develop **culture-specific tests,** that is, tests designed for use with people from one culture but not from another. Representative of the culture-specific approach to test development were early versions of some of the best-known tests of intelligence. For example, the 1937 revision of the Stanford-Binet Intelligence Scale, which enjoyed widespread use until it was revised in 1960, included no minority children in its standardization sample. Similarly, the Wechsler-Bellevue Intelligence Scale, a forerunner of a widely used measure of adult intelligence, contained no minority members in its published standardization sample data. The test's author, David Wechsler (1944), noted that "a large number" of Blacks were tested during the standardization trials but that those data were omitted from the final test manual "because we did not feel that norms derived by mixing the populations could be interpreted without special provisos and reservations." Hence, Wechsler (1944) stated at the outset that the Wechsler-Bellevue norms could not be used for "the colored populations of the United States." Similarly, the inaugural edition of the Wechsler Intelligence Scale for Children (WISC), first published in 1949 and not revised until 1974, contained no minority children in its standardization sample.

Even though many published tests were in essence culture-specific, it soon became apparent that the tests were being administered—improperly—to people from differ-

JUST THINK . . .

Try your hand at creating one culture-specific test item on any subject. Testtakers from what culture would probably succeed in responding correctly to the item? Testtakers from what culture would not?

Figure 2–3
Psychological Testing at Ellis Island

Immigrants coming to America via Ellis Island were greeted not only by the Statue of Liberty but also by immigration officials ready to evaluate them with respect to physical, mental, and other variables. Here, a block design test, one measure of intelligence, is administered to a would-be American. Immigrants who failed physical, mental, or other tests were returned to their country of origin at the expense of the shipping company that had brought them. Critics would later charge that at least some of the immigrants who had fared poorly on mental tests were sent away from our shores not because they were indeed mentally deficient but simply because they did not understand English well enough to execute instructions. Additionally, the criterion against which these immigrants from many lands were being evaluated was questioned.

ent cultures. Perhaps not surprisingly, testtakers from minority cultures tended to score lower as a group than people from the group for whom the test was developed and standardized. As a specific example, consider this item from the 1949 WISC: "If your mother sends you to the store for a loaf of bread and there is none, what do you do?" Whether or not you perceive any problem with this item may depend on your own cultural background. In fact, the item could be problematic for Hispanic children, many of whom had routinely been sent to the store for tortillas. Accordingly, many of these children may not have been routinely exposed to the phrase "a loaf of bread."

Translation of test materials for people who speak a language different from the one in which the test was initially written typically poses several problems. Some items may be easier or more difficult than originally intended when translated directly into another language. For example, the old Stanford-Binet vocabulary item *skunk* would have to be changed for administration in Puerto Rico, where skunks are nonexistent. Some vocabulary items may change meanings or have dual meanings when translated. For example, consider the WISC item "Why should most government positions be filled through examinations?" In some languages and cultures the word *examinations* most typically refers to medical examinations. In such instances, a better wording of the item might be "Why should most government positions be filled through civil service examinations?"

Today, test developers typically take many steps to ensure that a major test developed for national use is indeed suitable for such use. Those steps might involve administering a preliminary version of the test to a tryout sample of testtakers. The data from the tryout sample are typically analyzed in many ways. Test items deemed to be biased with regard to race, gender, or other factors will be eliminated. Further, a panel of independent reviewers may be asked to go through the test items and screen them for possible bias. Examiners who administer the test may be asked to describe their impressions of various aspects of the test administration. For example, subjective impressions may be noted, such as the examiner's impressions of the testtaker's reaction to the test materials or opinions regarding the clarity of instructions and the design of the materials. The test may be administered to a large sample of testtakers that is representative of key variables of the latest U.S. Census data (such as age, gender, ethnic background, and socioeconomic status). Information from this large-scale test administration will be used to root out any identifiable sources of bias. More details regarding the contemporary process of test development will be presented in Chapter 7.

Some Issues Regarding Culture and Assessment

Communication between assessor and assessee is a most basic part of assessment. Assessors must be sensitive to any differences between the language or dialect familiar to assessees and the language in which the assessment is conducted. Assessors must also be sensitive to the degree to which assessees have been exposed to the dominant culture and the extent to which they have made a conscious choice to become assimilated. Below, we briefly consider issues of assessment and communication—both verbal and nonverbal—in a cultural context.

Verbal communication Language, the means by which information is communicated, is a key yet sometimes overlooked variable in the assessment process. Most obviously, the examiner and the examinee must speak the same language. This is necessary not only for the assessment to proceed but for the assessor's conclusions regarding the assessment to be reasonably accurate. If a test is in written form, complete with written instructions, the testtaker must be able to read and comprehend what is written. When the language in which the assessment is conducted is not the assessee's primary language, he or she may not fully comprehend the instructions or the test items. The danger of such misunderstanding may increase as infrequently used vocabulary or unusual idioms are employed in the assessment. Even when an assessment is conducted with the aid of a translator, subtle nuances of meaning may become lost in the translation. In some instances, assessees may purposely attempt to use a language deficit to frustrate evaluation efforts (Stephens, 1992).

The spoken dialect of a language may also influence test results. Although Standard American English is the established language in the United States, many variants and dialects of Standard American English are routinely spoken in various communities throughout the country (Wolfram, 1971). In interviews or other situations in which an evaluation is made on the basis of an oral exchange between two parties, a trained examiner may detect through verbal or nonverbal means that the examinee's grasp of a language or a dialect is too deficient to proceed. Such is not the case when the evaluation is being made in written form. In the case of written tests, it is clearly essential that the examinee be able to read and comprehend what is written. Otherwise, the evaluation may be more about language or dialect competency than whatever the test purports to measure.

In the assessment of an individual whose proficiency in the English language is limited or nonexistent, some very basic questions may need to be raised: What level of proficiency in English is required on the part of the testtaker, and does the testtaker have that proficiency? Can a meaningful assessment take place through a trained interpreter? Can an alternative and more appropriate assessment procedure be devised to meet the objectives of the assessment?

Nonverbal communication and behavior   Humans communicate not only through verbal means but also through nonverbal means. Facial expressions, finger and hand signs, and shifts in one's position in space may all convey messages. Of course, the messages conveyed by such body language may be different from culture to culture. For example, in American culture, one who fails to look another person in the eye when speaking may be viewed as deceitful or having something to hide. However, in other cultures, failure to make eye contact when speaking may be a sign of respect.

Having gone on or conducted a job interview, you may have developed a firsthand appreciation of the value of nonverbal communication in an evaluative setting. Interviewees who show enthusiasm and interest have the edge over interviewees who appear to be drowsy or bored. In clinical settings, an experienced evaluator may develop hypotheses to be tested from the nonverbal behavior of the interviewee. For example, a person who is slouching, moving slowly, and exhibiting a sad facial expression may be depressed. Then again, such an individual may be experiencing physical discomfort from a muscle spasm or an arthritis attack. It remains for the assessor to determine which hypothesis best accounts for the observed behavior.

Certain theories and systems in the mental health field go beyond more traditional interpretations of body language. For example, in **psychoanalysis,** a theory of personality and psychological treatment developed by Sigmund Freud, symbolic significance is assigned to many nonverbal acts. From a psychoanalytic perspective, an interviewee's fidgeting with a wedding band during an interview may be interpreted as a message regarding an unstable marriage. As evidenced by his thoughts on "the first chance actions" of a patient during a therapy session, Sigmund Freud believed he could tell much about motivation from nonverbal behavior:

> The first . . . chance actions of the patient . . . will betray one of the governing complexes of the neurosis. . . . A young girl . . . hurriedly pulls the hem of her skirt over her exposed ankle; she has betrayed the kernel of what analysis will discover later; her narcissistic pride in her bodily beauty and her tendencies to exhibitionism. (Freud, 1913, p. 359)

By the way, this quote from Freud is also useful in illustrating the influence of culture on diagnostic and therapeutic views. Freud lived in Victorian Vienna. In that time and in that place, sex was not a subject for public discussion. In many ways, Freud's views regarding a sexual basis for various thoughts and behaviors were a product of the sexually repressed culture in which he lived.

An example of a nonverbal behavior in which people differ is the speed at which they characteristically move to complete tasks. The overall pace of life in one geographic area, for example, may tend to be faster than in another. In a similar vein, differences in pace of life across cultures may enhance or detract from test scores on tests involving timed items (Gopaul-McNicol, 1993; Knapp, 1960). In a more general sense, Hoffman (1962) questioned the value of timed tests of ability, particularly those tests that employed multiple-choice items. He believed such tests relied too heavily on testtakers' quickness of response and as such discriminated against the individual who is characteristically a "deep, brooding

JUST THINK . . .

Play the role of Sigmund Freud as illustrated in the verbatim extract and cite one example of behavior that you believe may be quite telling about an individual's motivation.

thinker." By the way, as we will see in Chapter 9, the trend in the assessment of intelligence is away from timed tasks.

Examiners ideally must be knowledgeable about relevant aspects of the testtakers' cultures. For example, a child may present as noncommunicative and having only minimal language skills when verbally examined. This finding may be due to the fact that the child is from a culture where elders are revered, where children speak to adults only when they are spoken to and then only in as short a phrase as possible. In addition to linguistic barriers, the contents of tests from a particular culture are typically laden with items and material—some obvious, some very subtle—that draw heavily from that culture. Test performance may, at least in part, reflect not only whatever variables the test purports to measure but also one additional variable—the degree to which the testtaker has assimilated the culture.

JUST THINK . . .

What type of test is best suited for administration to people who are "deep, brooding thinkers"? How practical for group administration would such tests be?

Standards of evaluation Suppose that master chefs from more than a hundred nations entered a contest to discover the best chicken soup in the world. Who do you think would win? The answer to that question hinges on the evaluative standard to be employed. If the sole judge of the contest was the owner of a kosher delicatessen on the Lower East Side of Manhattan, the entry that came closest to the "Jewish mother homemade" variety might well be declared the winner. However, other judges might have other standards and preferences. For example, soup connoisseurs from Arabic cultures might prefer chicken soup with fresh lemon juice in the recipe. Judges from India might be inclined to give their vote to a chicken soup flavored with curry and other exotic spices. For other Asian judges, soy sauce might be viewed as an indispensable ingredient, and any chicken soup prepared without it might lose by default. Ultimately, it probably is not the case that one soup is truly better than all the rest; judging which soup is best will be very much a matter of personal preference and the standard of evaluation employed.

Similarly, judgments related to certain psychological traits can also be culturally relative. For example, whether specific patterns of behavior are considered to be male- or female-appropriate will depend on the prevailing societal standards regarding masculinity and femininity. In some societies, for example, it is role-appropriate for women to fight wars and put food on the table while the men are occupied in more domestic activities. Whether specific patterns of behavior are considered to be psychopathological also depends on the prevailing societal standards. In Sudan, for example, there are tribes that live among cattle because they regard the animals as sacred. Judgments as to who might be the best employee, manager, or leader may differ as a function of culture, as might judgments regarding intelligence, wisdom, courage, and other psychological variables.

A challenge inherent in the assessment enterprise has to do with tempering test- and assessment-related outcomes with good judgment regarding the cultural relativity of those outcomes. In practice, this means raising questions about the applicability of assessment-related findings to specific individuals. Thus, in addition to attempting to answer questions such as "How intelligent is this person?" or "How assertive is this individual?", some additional questions must also be raised. How appropriate are the norms or other standards that will be used to make the evaluation? To what extent has the individual been assimilated by the culture from which the test is drawn, and what influence might such assimilation (or lack of it) have on the test results? What research has been done on the test to support its applicability for use in evaluating this particular individual? Increasingly, these questions are being raised not only by careful test users but by the courts as well.

Tests and Group Membership

Tests and other evaluative measures administered in vocational, education, counseling, and other settings leave little doubt that people differ—not only from one another on an individual basis but from group to group on a collective basis. On the face of it, questions such as "What student is best qualified to be admitted to this school?" or "Which job candidate should get the job?" are rather straightforward. On the other hand, societal concerns about fairness not only to individuals but to groups of individuals have made the answers to such questions matters of heated debate, if not lawsuits and civil disobedience.

In vocational assessment, test users are sensitive to legal and ethical mandates concerning the use of tests with regard to hiring, firing, and related decision making. If a test is used to evaluate a candidate's ability to do a job, one point of view is that the test should do just that—regardless of the group membership of the testtaker. According to this view, scores on a test of job ability should be influenced only by job-related variables. That is, scores should not be affected by variables such as hair length, eye color, group membership, or any other variable extraneous to the ability to perform the job. Although this rather straightforward view of the role of tests in personnel selection may seem consistent with principles of equal opportunity, it has attracted charges of unfairness and claims of discrimination. Why?

Claims of test-related discrimination made against major test publishers may be best understood as evidence of the great complexity of the assessment enterprise rather than as a conspiracy to use tests to discriminate. In vocational assessment, for example, conflicts may arise from disagreements about the criteria for performing a particular job. The potential for controversy looms over almost all selection criteria an employer sets, regardless of whether the criteria are physical, educational, psychological, or experiential.

The critical question with regard to hiring, promotion, and other selection decisions in almost any work setting is "What criteria must be met to do this job?" A state police department may require all applicants for the position of police officer to meet certain physical requirements, including a minimum height of 5 feet 4 inches. A person who is 5 feet 2 inches tall and from a cultural background where the average height of adults is less than 5 feet 4 inches is effectively barred from applying. Because the police force evaluation policies have the effect of systematically excluding members of a specific cultural group, the result may be a class action lawsuit charging discrimination. Whether the police department's height requirement is reasonable and job related, and whether discrimination in fact occurred, are very complex questions that will have to be considered by a court. Compelling arguments may be presented on both sides, as benevolent, fair-minded, knowledgeable, and well-intentioned people may have honest differences about the necessity of the prevailing height requirement for the job of police officer in this state.

> **JUST THINK . . .**
>
> Devise your own version of a fair and equitable process to determine the minimum required height, if any, for police officers in your community.

Beyond the variable of height, it would seem that variables such as appearance and religion should have little to do with what job one is qualified to perform. However, it is precisely such factors that keep some group members from entry into many jobs and careers. Consider in this context observant Jews. Their appearance and dress is not mainstream. The food they eat must be kosher. They are unable to work or travel on weekends. Given the established selection criteria for many positions in corporate America, candidates who are members of the group known as observant Jews are effectively excluded regardless of their ability to perform the work (Korman, 1988; Mael, 1991; Zweigenhaft, 1984).

General differences among groups of people also extend to psychological attributes such as measured intelligence. Unfortunately, the mere suggestion that such differences in psychological variables exist arouses skepticism, if not charges of discrimination, bias, or worse. This is especially true when the observed group differences are deemed responsible for blocking one or another group from job or educational opportunities.

What if systematic differences as a function of group membership are found to exist on job ability test scores? What, if anything, should be done? One view is that nothing needs to be done. According to this view, the test was designed to measure job ability, and it does what it was designed to do. In support of this view is evidence suggesting that group differences in scores on professionally developed tests do reflect differences in real-world performance (Gottfredson, 2000; Halpern, 2000; Hartigan & Wigdor, 1989; Kubiszyn et al., 2000; Neisser et al., 1996; Schmidt, 1988; Schmidt & Hunter, 1992).

A contrasting view is that efforts should be made to "level the playing field" between groups of people. The term **affirmative action** is used to refer to voluntary and mandatory efforts undertaken by federal, state, and local governments, private employers, and schools to combat discrimination and to promote equal opportunity in education and employment for all (APA, 1996, p. 2). Affirmative action seeks to create equal opportunity actively, not passively; inherent in it is the view that "policies that appear to be neutral with regard to ethnicity or gender can operate in ways that advantage individuals from one group over individuals from another group" (Crosby et al., 2003, p. 95).

JUST THINK . . .

What are your thoughts on the manipulation of test scores as a function of group membership to advance certain social goals?

In assessment, one way of implementing affirmative action is by altering test scoring procedures according to set guidelines. For example, an individual's score on a test could be revised according to the individual's group membership (McNemar, 1975). While proponents of such remedies see them as necessary to address past inequities, others condemn such manipulation of test scores as introducing "inequity in equity" (Benbow & Stanley, 1996).

As sincerely committed as they may be to principles of egalitarianism and fair play, test developers and test users must ultimately look to society at large—and more specifically to laws, administrative regulations, and other rules and professional codes of conduct—for guidance in the use of tests and test scores.

Psychology, tests, and public policy Few people would object to using psychological tests in academic and applied contexts that obviously benefit human welfare. Then again, few people are aware of the everyday use of psychological tests in such ways. More typically, members of the general public become acquainted with the use of psychological tests in high-profile contexts, as when an individual or a group has a great deal to gain or to lose as a result of a test score. In such situations, tests and other tools of assessment are portrayed as instruments that can have a momentous and immediate impact on one's life. In such situations, tests may be perceived by the everyday person as tools used to deny people things they very much want or need. Denial of educational advancement, job opportunity, parole, or custody are some of the more threatening consequences that the public may associate with psychological tests and assessment procedures.

Members of the public call upon government policy-makers to protect them from perceived threats. Legislators pass laws, administrative agencies make regulations, judges hand down rulings, and citizens call for referenda to reflect and enforce prevailing public policy or to modify it. In the section that follows, we broaden our view of the assessment enterprise to include not only the concerns of the profession but the concerns of the public.

Legal and Ethical Considerations

Laws are rules that individuals must obey for the good of the society as a whole—or rules thought to be for the good of society as a whole. Some laws are and have been relatively uncontroversial. For example, the law that mandates driving on the right side of the road has not been a subject of debate, a source of emotional soul-searching, or a stimulus to civil disobedience. For safety and the common good, most people are willing to relinquish their freedom to drive all over the road. But what about laws pertaining to abortion? To busing? To capital punishment? To euthanasia? To deprogramming of religious cult members? To affirmative action in employment? Exactly how laws regulating matters such as these should be written and interpreted are issues of heated controversy, as are some of the laws that impact the way that psychological testing and assessment are conducted.

Whereas a body of laws is a body of rules, a body of **ethics** is a body of principles of right, proper, or good conduct. Thus, for example, an ethic of the Old West was "Never shoot 'em in the back." Two well-known principles subscribed to by seafarers are "Women and children leave first in an emergency" and "A captain goes down with his ship."[2] The ethics of journalism dictate that reporters present all sides of a controversial issue. A principle of ethical research is that the researcher should never fudge data; all data must be reported accurately. What ethical guidelines do you think should govern the professional behavior of psychologists involved in psychological testing and assessment? To the extent that a **code of professional ethics** is recognized and accepted by members of a profession, it defines the standard of care expected of members of that profession.

Members of the public and members of the profession have in recent times been on different sides of the fence with respect to issues of ethics and law. Let's review how and why this has been the case.

The Concerns of the Public

The assessment enterprise has never been very well understood by the public. Even today, it is unfortunate that we may hear statements symptomatic of misunderstanding with regard to tests (for example, "The only thing tests measure is the ability to take tests"). Possible consequences of public misunderstanding include fear, anger, legislation, litigation, and administrative regulations.

Perhaps the first time the American public evinced widespread concern about psychological testing came in the aftermath of World War I. At that time, various professionals (as well as nonprofessionals) sought to adapt group tests developed by the military for civilian use in schools and industry. Reflecting growing public discomfort with the burgeoning assessment industry were popular magazine articles featuring stories with titles such as "The Abuse of Tests" (see Haney, 1981). Less well known were voices of reason who offered constructive ways to correct what was wrong with assessment practices.

Anticipating the present-day *Standards*, Ruch (1925), a measurement specialist, proposed a number of standards for tests and guidelines for test development. He also wrote of "the urgent need for a fact-finding organization which will undertake impartial, experimental, and statistical evaluations of tests" (Ruch, 1933). History records that one team of measurement experts even took on the (overly) ambitious task of attempting

---

2. We leave the question of what to do when the captain of the ship is a woman to a volume dedicated to an in-depth exploration of seafaring ethics.

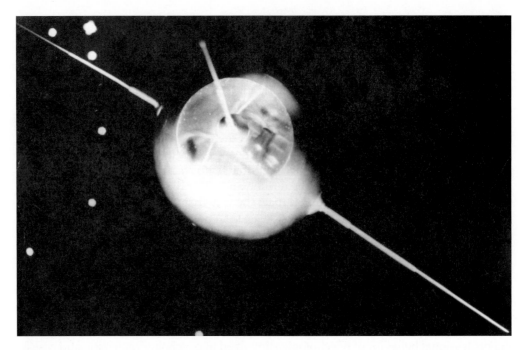

Figure 2–4
The Launch of a Satellite . . . and Renewed Interest in Testing

On October 4, 1957, scientists in the country then known as the Union of Soviet Socialist Republics launched a satellite (they called it Sputnik) into space. The event was greeted with surprise if not shock by most Americans. The prospect of a cold war enemy having a satellite orbiting Earth twenty-four hours a day was very unsettling. The launch caused widespread concern about the ability of the United States to compete in the new frontier of space. More emphasis would have to be placed on education, particularly in subjects such as math, science, engineering, and physics. And greater efforts would have to be made to identify the gifted children who would one day apply such knowledge in the race to space.

to rank all published tests designed for use in educational settings. The result was a pioneering book (Kelley, 1927) that provided test users with information needed to compare the merits of published tests. However, given the pace at which test instruments were being published, this resource required regular updating. And so, Oscar Buros was not the first measurement professional to undertake a comprehensive testing of the tests. He was, however, the most tenacious in updating and revising the information.

The widespread military testing during the 1940s as a result of World War II did not attract as much popular attention as the testing undertaken during World War I. Rather, it was an event in a faraway land that would have a momentous effect on testing in the United States: the launching of a satellite into space (see Figure 2-4).

About a year after the Soviet Union's launch of *Sputnik*, Congress passed the National Defense Education Act, which provided federal money to local schools for the purpose of ability and aptitude testing to identify gifted and academically talented students. This event triggered the proliferation of large-scale testing programs in the schools. At the same time, the use of ability tests and personality tests for personnel selection increased in government, the military, and business. The wide and growing use of tests led to renewed public concern, reflected in magazine articles such as "Testing: Can Everyone Be Pigeonholed?" (*Newsweek,* July 20, 1959) and "What the Tests Do Not

Test" (*New York Times Magazine,* October 2, 1960). The upshot of such concern was congressional hearings on the subject of testing (Amrine, 1965).

The fires of public concern about testing were again fanned in 1969, when widespread media attention was given to the publication of an article in the prestigious *Harvard Educational Review*. The article was entitled "How Much Can We Boost IQ and Scholastic Achievement?" and its author, Arthur Jensen, argued that "genetic factors are strongly implicated in the average Negro-white intelligence difference" (1969, p. 82). What followed was an outpouring of public and professional attention to nature-versus-nurture issues, as well as widespread skepticism about what intelligence tests were really measuring. By 1972, the United States Select Committee on Equal Education Opportunity was preparing for hearings on the matter. However, according to Haney (1981), the hearings "were canceled because they promised to be too controversial" (p. 1026).

The extent of public concern about psychological assessment is reflected in the extensive involvement of the government in many aspects of the assessment process in recent decades. Assessment has been affected in numerous and important ways by activities of the legislative, executive, and judicial branches of federal and state governments. Table 2-1 summarizes some landmark legislation and litigation.

Legislation Although the legislation summarized in Table 2-1 was enacted at the federal level, states too have passed legislation that affects the assessment enterprise. In the 1970s, numerous states enacted **minimum competency testing programs**—formal testing programs designed to be used in decisions regarding various aspects of students' education. The data from such programs was used in decision making about grade promotions, awarding of diplomas, and identification of areas for remedial instruction. These laws grew out of grassroots support for the idea that high school graduates should have, at the very least, "minimal competencies" in areas such as reading, writing, and arithmetic.

Truth-in-testing legislation was also passed at the state level beginning in the 1980s. The primary objective of these laws was to provide testtakers with a means of learning the criteria by which they are being judged. To meet that objective, some laws mandate the disclosure of answers to postsecondary and professional school admissions tests within 30 days of the publication of test scores. Some laws require that information relevant to a test's development and technical soundness be kept on file. Some truth-in-testing laws require providing descriptions of (1) the test's purpose and its subject matter, (2) the knowledge and skills the test purports to measure, (3) procedures for ensuring accuracy in scoring, (4) procedures for notifying testtakers of errors in scoring, and (5) procedures for ensuring the testtaker's confidentiality. Truth-in-testing laws create special difficulties for test developers and publishers, who argue that it is essential for them to keep the test items secret. They note that there may be a limited item pool for some tests and that the cost of developing an entirely new set of items for each succeeding administration of a test is prohibitive.

Some laws mandate the involvement of the executive branch of government in their application. For example, Title VII of the Civil Rights Act of 1964 created the Equal Employment Opportunity Commission (EEOC) to enforce the act. EEOC has published sets of guidelines concerning standards to be met in constructing and using employment tests. In 1978, the EEOC, the Civil Service Commission, the Department of Labor, and the Justice Department jointly published the *Uniform Guidelines on Employee Selection Procedures.* Here is a sample guideline:

> The use of any test which adversely affects hiring, promotion, transfer or any other employment or membership opportunity of classes protected by Title VII constitutes

Table 2-1
Some Significant Legislation and Litigation

Legislation	Significance
Americans with Disabilities Act of 1990	Employment testing materials and procedures must be essential to the job and not discriminate against persons with handicaps.
Civil Rights Act of 1964 (amended in 1991), also known as the Equal Opportunity Employment Act	It is an unlawful employment practice to adjust the scores of, use different cutoff scores for, or otherwise alter the results of, employment-related tests on the basis of race, religion, sex, or national origin.
Family Education Rights and Privacy Act (1974)	Mandated that parents and eligible students be given access to school records. Also granted right to challenge findings in records by a hearing.
Health Insurance Portability and Account-ability Act of 1996 (HIPAA)	Provided for federal privacy standards that limit the way that health care providers and others can use patients' personal information.
Education for All Handicapped Children (PL 94-142) (1975 and then amended several times thereafter, including IDEA of 1997)	Mandated screening of children with suspected mental or physical handicaps. Once identified, individual child must be evaluated by a professional team qualified to determine that child's special educational needs. Child must be reevaluated periodically. Amended in 1986 to extend disability-related protections downward to infants and toddlers.
Individuals with Disabilities Education Act (IDEA) Amendments of 1997 (PL 105-17)	Deterred inappropriate placement in special education programs due to cultural differences. Encouraged accommodation of existing test instruments and other alternate means of assessment for the purpose of gauging the progress of special education students as measured by state- and district-wide assessments.
The No Child Left Behind (NCLB) Act of 2001	Known as the NCLB, the reauthorization of the Elementary and Secondary Education Act of 2001 was de-signed to "close the achievement gaps between minority and nonminority students and between disadvantaged children and their more advantaged peers" by, among other things, setting strict standards for school accountability and establishing periodic assessments to gauge the progress of school districts in improving academic achievement. The "battle cry" driving this legislation was "Demographics are not destiny!"

Litigation	
Hobson v. Hanson (1967)	Supreme Court ruled that ability tests developed on Whites could not lawfully be used to track Black students in the school system. To do so could result in resegregation of desegregated schools.
Tarasoff v. Regents of the University of California (1974)	Therapists (and presumably psychological assessors) must reveal privileged information if a third party is endangered. In the words of the Court, "Protective privilege ends where the public peril begins."
Larry P. v. Riles (1979 and reaffirmed by the same judge in 1986)	California judge ruled that the use of intelligence tests to place Black children in special classes had a discriminatory impact because the tests were "racially and culturally biased."
Debra P. v. Turlington (1981)	Federal court ruled that minimum competency testing in Florida was unconstitutional because it perpetuated the effects of past discrimination.
Griggs v. Duke Power Company (1971)	Black employees brought suit against a private company for discriminatory hiring practices. The Supreme Court found problems with "broad and general testing devices" and ruled that tests must "fairly measure the knowledge or skills required by a particular job."
Albemarle Paper Company v. Moody (1976)	An industrial psychologist at a paper mill found that scores on a general ability test predicted measures of job performance. However, as a group, Whites scored better than Blacks on the test. The U.S. District Court found the use of the test to be sufficiently job related. An appeals court did not. It ruled that discrimination had occurred, however unintended.
Regents of the University of California v. Bakke (1978)	When Alan Bakke learned that his test scores were higher than those of some minority students who had gained admission to the University of California, Davis, medical school, he sued. A highly divided Supreme Court agreed that Bakke should be admitted, but it did not preclude the use of diversity considerations in admission decisions.
Allen v. District of Columbia (1993)	Blacks scored lower than Whites on a city fire department promotion test based on specific aspects of fire-fighting. The court found in favor of the fire department, ruling that "the promotional examination . . . was a valid measure of the abilities and probable future success of those individuals taking the test. . . ."
Adarand Constructors, Inc. v. Pena et al. (1995)	A construction firm competing for a federal contract brought suit against the federal government for losing a bid to a minority-controlled competitor which the government had retained instead in the interest of affirm-ative action. The Supreme Court, in a close (5−4) decision, found in favor of the plaintiff, ruling that the government's affirmative action policy violated the equal protection clause of the 14th Amendment. The Court ruled, "Government may treat people differently because of their race only for the most compelling reasons."
Jaffee v. Redmond (1996)	Communication between a psychotherapist and a patient (and presumably a psychological assessor and a client) is privileged in federal courts.
Grutter v. Bollinger (2003)	In a highly divided decision, the Supreme Court approved the use of race in admissions decisions on a time-limited basis to further the educational benefits that flow from a diverse student body (see *Close-Up*).

discrimination unless (a) the test has been validated and evidences a high degree of util-ity as hereinafter described, and (b) the person giving or acting upon the results of the particular test can demonstrate that alternative suitable hiring, transfer or promotion procedures are unavailable for . . . use.

Note that in this excerpted guideline a definition of discrimination as exclusionary co-exists with the proviso that a valid test that evidences "a high degree of utility" (among other criteria) will not be considered discriminatory. Generally, however, the public has been quick to label a test as unfair and discriminatory regardless of its utility. As a con-sequence, a great public demand for proportionality by group membership in hiring and college admissions now coexists with a great lack of proportionality by group mem-bership in skills. Gottfredson (2000) noted that while selection standards can often be improved, the manipulation of such standards "will produce only lasting frustration, not enduring solutions." She recommended that enduring solutions be sought by ad-dressing the problem related to gaps in skills between groups. She recommended against addressing the problem by lowering hiring and admission standards or by leg-islation designed to make hiring and admissions decisions matters of group quotas. Yet it is in the latter direction that the tide seems to be turning, at least according to recent legislation and court decisions.

In Texas, state law now mandates that the top 10% of graduating seniors from all Texas high schools be admitted to a state university regardless of SAT scores. This means that regardless of the quality of education in any particular Texas high school, a senior in the top 10% of the graduating class is guaranteed college admission regardless of how he or she might score on a nationally standardized measure. There have been reports that in some Texas high schools as many as 25% of the students are in the top 10% of their class (Kronholz, 1998). In California, the use of skills tests in the public sector has de-creased as a result of the passage of Proposition 209, which banned racial preferences (Rosen, 1998). One consequence has been the deemphasis of the Law School Admissions Test (LSAT) as an admission criterion to the University of California, Berkeley, law school. Additionally, the law school has stopped weighing grade point averages from undergraduate schools in their admission criteria, so that "a 4.0 from California State is now worth as much as a 4.0 from Harvard" (Rosen, 1998, p. 62).

Gottfredson (2000) argued that those who advocate reversal of achievement stan-dards obtain "nothing of lasting value by eliminating valid tests." For her, lowering stan-dards amounts to hindering process "while providing only the illusion of progress." Rather than reversing achievement standards, society is best served by action to reverse unfortunate trends in family structure. In the face of consistent gaps between members of various groups, Gottfredson emphasized the need for skills training, not a lowering of achievement standards or an unfounded attack on tests.

State and federal legislatures, executive bodies, and courts have been involved in many aspects of testing and assessment. There has been little consensus about whether validated tests on which there are racial differences can be used to assist with employment-related decisions. Courts have also been grappling with the role of diver-sity in criteria for admission to colleges, universities, and professional schools (see *Close-Up*). Of course, the public has no monopoly on concern about issues related to test-ing and assessment.

The Concerns of the Profession

As early as 1895, the infant American Psychological Association (APA) formed its first committee on mental measurement. The committee was charged with investigating various aspects of the relatively new practice of testing. Another APA committee on

Assessment, Admissions, and Affirmative Action: *Grutter v. Bollinger et al.* (2003)

Barbara Grutter, a White resident of Michigan, applied to the University of Michigan Law School (UML) in 1996. She had a 3.8 grade point average, among other requisite credentials. In response to her application, UML first notified her that she was being placed on a waiting list. However, when she was subsequently denied admission, she filed a lawsuit against Lee Bollinger (then dean of the law school) and others, alleging that UML had discriminated against her on the basis of race. The lawsuit claimed that UML gave applicants who belong to certain minority groups *a significantly greater chance of admission than students with similar credentials from disfavored racial groups.* * The trial court found in favor of the plaintiff, Grutter. An appeals court reversed the ruling of the trial court and found for the defendant, UML. An appeal was made to the Supreme Court to hear and decide the case.

The last time the Supreme Court dealt with a similar issue was more than twenty-five years ago, in the case of *Regents of the University of California v. Bakke.* In *Bakke,* a sharply divided Supreme Court ruled that *a State has a substantial interest that legitimately may be served by a properly devised admissions program involving the competitive consideration of race and ethnic origin.* A "properly devised admissions program" was one that, in part, allowed for truly individualized assessment of applicants while employing race criteria in a flexible, nonmechanical way. Even so, Justice Powell, writing the opinion in *Bakke,* had cautioned: *The guarantee of equal protection cannot mean one thing when applied to one individual and something else when applied to a person of another color. If both are not accorded the same protection, then it is not equal* (*Bakke,* 438 U.S., at 289).

The Supreme Court agreed to hear *Grutter.* Before presenting the decision, here is some background based on the evidence presented. UML receives about 3,500 applications for only about 350 places. Like other institutions of higher learning, UML has developed assessment procedures to determine who among the applicants will be accepted and who will not. The university uses a number of criteria in evaluation, such as undergraduate grade point average, scores on the Law School Admission Test (LSAT), the enthusiasm of those writing letters in support of the application, and the applicant's own essay outlining how she or he will contribute

to the life and diversity of the law school. Although no accepted applicant is expected to have difficulty academically, high grade point average and test scores alone are insufficient to secure admission. The school's policy dictates that other criteria, including an assessment of *an applicant's likely contributions to the intellectual and social life of the institution* must be taken into account in an admissions decision.

The UML policy aspired to enroll a *critical mass* of underrepresented minority students. "Critical mass" referred not to any particular number or percentage of students but rather to meaningful numbers so that minority students would not feel isolated or made to feel like spokespersons for their race. A UML witness testified that *when a critical mass of underrepresented minority students is present, racial stereotypes lose their force because nonminority students learn there is no "minority viewpoint" but rather a variety of viewpoints among minority students.* Other testimony suggested that UML's admission had the effect of making classroom discussions livelier, more spirited, and more enlightening because students hailed from a variety of backgrounds. Companies such as 3M and General Motors filed briefs in support of UML, arguing that skills needed in today's global marketplace required exposure to diverse people and cultures.

UML witnesses never quantified what was meant by a "critical mass" of enrollment of minority students. These witnesses denied that they maintained, in any form, what could be characterized as a **quota system.** In this context, a quota system may be defined as a selection procedure in which a fixed number or percentage of applicants from certain backgrounds must be selected. UML did, however, admit to monitoring daily reports that kept track of the racial and ethnic composition of the class.

Echoing the sharply divided opinions and lack of general consensus last seen in *Bakke,* the Supreme Court ruled in favor of UML. Dissenters questioned whether the State indeed had a compelling interest to protect diversity and whether the UML policy concealed an attempt to achieve racial balancing. One of the dissenters made reference to UML's consultation of daily reports regarding the "critical mass" and wrote that during the final stages of the admission process, *there was no further attempt at individual review save for race itself.* This dissenting Justice further speculated that race was likely the determining factor *for many members*

---

*All italicized text represents verbatim text from the transcript of the opinion written for the Supreme Court majority by Justice O'Connor dated June 23, 2003.

The Justices of the United States Supreme Court agreed to hear the Grutter *case, framing the question before them in terms of "whether diversity is a compelling interest that can justify the narrowly tailored use of race in selecting applicants for admission to public universities."*

of minority groups who do not fall within the upper range of LSAT scores and grades.

Still, the Court stated flatly, *Today, we hold that the Law School has a compelling interest in attaining a diverse student body.* The Court accepted UML's arguments, including their argument that no quota system was used. The Court noted that between 1993 and 2000 the number of African American, Latino, and Native American students in each class had varied from 13.5% to 20.1%, a range the Court found inconsistent with a quota. The Court rejected Grutter's argument that race-neutral means existed to create the diversity sought by UML. The Court did acknowledge, as it had acknowledged in *Bakke*, that *there are serious problems of justice connected with the idea of preference itself.* Still, as the majority concluded in *Bakke*, *so long as a race-conscious admissions program uses race as a "plus" factor in the context of individualized consideration, a rejected applicant*

will not have been foreclosed from all consideration for that seat simply because he was not the right color or had the wrong surname. . . . His qualifications would have been weighed fairly and competitively, and he would have no basis to complain of unequal treatment under the Fourteenth Amendment. (438 U.S., at 318)

The Court cautioned that race-conscious admission programs must be time limited. *Enshrining a permanent justification for racial preferences would offend [the] fundamental equal protection principle.* The requirement of time limitation could be met either by "sunset" provisions (guidelines for when they will be phased out) or by periodic reviews to determine *whether racial preferences are still necessary to achieve student body diversity.* Citing earlier decisions and law review articles, the Court observed,

It would be a sad day indeed, were America to become a quota-ridden society, with each identifiable minority assigned proportional representation in every desirable walk of life. But that is not the rationale for programs of preferential treatment; the acid test of their justification will be their efficacy in eliminating the need for any racial or ethnic preferences at all.

In summary, the Supreme Court ruled in *Grutter* that the Equal Protection Clause *does not prohibit the Law School's narrowly tailored* [and time-limited] *use of race in admissions decisions to further a compelling interest in obtaining the educational benefits that flow from a diverse student body.*

measurements was formed in 1906 to further study various testing-related issues and problems. In 1916 and again in 1921, symposia dealing with various issues surrounding the expanding uses of tests were sponsored (*Mentality Tests*, 1916; *Intelligence and Its Measurement*, 1921). In 1954, APA published its *Technical Recommendations for Psychological Tests and Diagnostic Tests*, a document that set forth testing standards and technical recommendations. The following year, another professional organization, the National Educational Association (working in collaboration with the National Council on Measurements Used in Education—now known as the National Council on Measurement) published its *Technical Recommendations for Achievement Tests*. Collaboration between these professional organizations led to the development of rather detailed testing standards and guidelines that would be periodically updated in future years.

Currently, APA and related professional organizations in the United States have made available numerous reference works and publications, all designed to delineate ethical, sound practice in the field of psychological testing and assessment.[3] Along the way, these professional organizations have tackled a variety of thorny questions, such as: Who should be privy to test data? Who should be able to purchase psychological test materials? Who is qualified to administer, score, and interpret psychological tests? What level of expertise in psychometrics qualifies someone to administer which type of test? Let's take a closer look at the issues.

Test-user qualifications   Should just anyone be allowed to purchase and use psychological test materials? If not, who should be permitted to use psychological tests? As early as 1950, an APA Committee on Ethical Standards for Psychology published a report called *Ethical Standards for the Distribution of Psychological Tests and Diagnostic Aids*. This report defined three levels of tests in terms of the degree to which the test's use required knowledge of testing and psychology:

Level A: Tests or aids that can adequately be administered, scored, and interpreted with the aid of the manual and a general orientation to the kind of institution or organization in which one is working (for instance, achievement or proficiency tests).

Level B: Tests or aids that require some technical knowledge of test construction and use and of supporting psychological and educational fields such as statistics, individual differences, psychology of adjustment, personnel psychology, and guidance (for example, aptitude tests, adjustment inventories applicable to normal populations).

Level C: Tests and aids that require substantial understanding of testing and supporting psychological fields, together with supervised experience in the use of these devices (for instance, projective tests, individual mental tests).

The report included descriptions of the general levels of training corresponding to each of the three levels of tests. Although many test publishers continue to use this three-level classification, some do not. In general, professional standards promulgated by APA (AERA, 1999), NASP (2000; Jacob-Timm & Hartshorne, 1998), and other professional organizations state that psychological tests should be used only by qualified persons. Further, there is an ethical mandate to take reasonable steps to prevent the misuse of the tests and the information they provide. The obligations of professionals to testtakers are set forth in a document called the *Code of Fair Testing Practices in Education*. Jointly authored and/or sponsored by the Joint Committee of Testing Practices (a coalition of APA, AERA,

---

3. Unfortunately, although organizations in many other countries have verbalized concern about ethics and standards in testing and assessment, relatively few organizations outside North America have actually taken meaningful and effective action (Gregoire, 1999).

NCME, the American Association for Measurement and Evaluation in Counseling and Development, and the American Speech-Language-Hearing Association), this document presents standards for educational test developers in four areas: (1) developing/ selecting tests, (2) interpreting scores, (3) striving for fairness, and (4) informing testtakers. This document is presented for reference on the companion Web site to this textbook at www.mhhe.com/cohentesting6.

Beyond promoting high standards in testing and assessment among professionals, APA has initiated or assisted in litigation to limit the use of psychological tests to qualified personnel. Skeptics label such measurement-related legal action as a kind of jockeying for turf, done solely for financial gain. A more charitable, perhaps more realistic view is that such actions benefit society at large. It is essential to the survival of the assessment enterprise that certain assessments be conducted by people qualified to conduct them by virtue of their education, training, and experience.

A psychologist licensing law designed to serve as a model for state legislatures has been available from APA since 1987. The law contains no definition of psychological testing. In the interest of the public, the profession of psychology, and other professions that employ psychological tests, it may now be time for that model legislation to be rewritten, with terms such as "psychological testing" and "psychological assessment" clearly defined and differentiated. Terms such as "test-user qualifications" and "psychological assessor qualifications" must also be clearly defined and differentiated. It seems that part of the problem surrounding legal conflicts regarding psychological test usage stems from confusion of the terms *psychological testing* and *psychological assessment.* People who are not considered professionals by society may be qualified to use psychological tests (psychological testers). However, these same people may not be qualified to engage in psychological assessment. As we argued in the previous chapter, psychological assessment requires certain skills, talents, expertise, and training in psychology and measurement over and above that required to engage in psychological testing. In the past, psychologists have been lax in differentiating psychological testing from psychological assessment. However, continued laxity may prove to be a costly indulgence, given current legislative and judicial trends.

Amid the legal battles, turf wars, and other potential conflicts over testing and assessment, there is at least one development that many measurement experts in the field of psychology have found gratifying. In 1993 the American Board of Assessment Psychology (ABAP) was founded with a mandate to identify highly competent assessment psychologists. Applicants for ABAP's Diplomate in Assessment Psychology must meet ABAP's standards in terms of general qualifications (including academic excellence, moral character, and relevant training and experience) and applied knowledge (as evidenced by a work product such as a published test, and a formal oral or written examination). Assessment professionals who are awarded the ABAP Diplomate become members of the American Academy of Assessment Psychology, the education and training arm of ABAP.[4]

Testing people with disabilities   Difficulties analogous to those concerning testtakers from linguistic and cultural minorities are present when testing people with disabling conditions. Specifically, these difficulties may include (1) transforming the test into a form that can be taken by the testtaker, (2) transforming the responses of the testtaker so that they are scorable, and (3) meaningfully interpreting the test data.

---

4. For more information on ABAP, write to this organization at 1000 Brickell Avenue, Suite 910, Miami, Florida 33131.

The nature of the transformation of the test into a form ready for administration to the individual with disabling conditions will, of course, depend on the nature of the disability. Then, too, some test stimuli do not translate easily. For example, if a critical aspect of a test item contains artwork to be analyzed, there may be no meaningful way to translate this item for use with testtakers who are blind. With respect to any test converted for use with a population for which the test was not originally intended, choices must inevitably be made regarding exactly how the test materials will be modified, what standards of evaluation will be applied, and how the results will be interpreted. As you might expect, professional assessors do not always agree on the answers to such questions.

Another issue on which there is little consensus among professional assessors has to do with a request by a terminally ill individual for aid in dying. Because such a request may only be granted contingent on the findings of a psychological evaluation, life or death literally hangs in the balance of such assessments. Presently, only Oregon has a law on the books dealing with this complex scenario. However, if other states adopt similar legislation, such scenarios will no doubt become more common, and many more psychological assessors will be called upon to be a part of them. Some ethical and related issues surrounding this phenomenon are discussed in this chapter's *Everyday Psychometrics.*

Computerized test administration, scoring, and interpretation The widespread availability of inexpensive computers has had a great impact, and computer-assisted psychological assessment (CAPA) is commonplace. An ever-growing number of psychological tests can be purchased on disk, and their administration, scoring, and interpretation are as simple as pressing keys on a keyboard. In many respects, the relative simplicity, convenience, and range of potential testing activities that computer technology brings to the testing industry have been a great boon. Test users have under one roof the means by which they can quickly administer, score, and interpret a wide range of tests. However, if the prospect of test by computer looks rosy at first, a more careful look reveals a welter of thorns.

For assessment professionals, some major issues with regard to CAPA are:

- *Access to test administration, scoring, and interpretation software*
  Despite purchase restrictions on software and technological safeguards to guard against unauthorized copying, software may still be copied. Unlike test kits, which may contain manipulatable objects, manuals, and other things, a computer-administered test may be easily copied onto one CD.

- *Comparability of pencil-and-paper and computerized versions of tests*
  Many tests once available only in a paper-and-pencil format are now available in computerized form as well. In many instances, the comparability of the traditional and the computerized forms of the test has not been researched, or has only insufficiently been researched.

- *The value of computerized test interpretations*
  Many tests available for computerized administration also come with computerized scoring and interpretation procedures. Thousands of words are spewed out every day in the form of test interpretation results, but the value of these words in many cases is questionable.

- *Unprofessional, unregulated "psychological testing" online*
  A growing number of Internet sites purport to provide, usually for a fee, online psychological tests. Yet the vast majority of the tests offered would not meet a psychologist's standards. Assessment professionals wonder about the long-term effect

Life-or-Death Psychological Assessment

The state of Oregon has the distinction—dubious to some people, depending on one's values—of having enacted the nation's first aid-in-dying law. Oregon's Death with Dignity Act (ODDA) provides that a patient with a medical condition thought to give that patient six months or less to live may end his or her own life by voluntarily requesting a lethal dose of medication. The law requires that two physicians corroborate the terminal diagnosis, and that either may request a psychological evaluation of the patient by a state-licensed psychologist or psychiatrist to ensure that the patient is competent to make the life-ending decision and to rule out impaired judgment due to psychiatric disorder. Aid-in-dying will be denied to persons "suffering from a psychiatric or psychological disorder, or depression causing impaired judgement" (ODDA, 1997).

The ODDA was hotly debated prior to its passage by referendum, and it remains controversial today. Critics of the law question whether suicide is ever a rational choice under any circumstances, and they fear that such aid-in-dying condoned by the state will serve to destigmatize suicide in general (Callahan, 1994; see also Richman, 1988). It is argued that the first duty of health and mental health professionals is to do no harm (Jennings, 1991). Some fear that professionals willing to testify to almost anything (so-called **hired guns**) will corrupt the process and accommodate those who can pay their fees with any professional opinion desired. Critics also point with concern to the experience of the Dutch death-with-dignity legislation. In the Netherlands, relatively few individuals requesting physician-assisted suicide are referred for psychological assessment. Further, the highest court of that land ruled that "in rare cases, physician-assisted suicide is possible even for individuals suffering only from mental problems rather than from physical illnesses" (Abeles & Barleve, 1999, p. 233). On moral and religious grounds, it has been argued that death should be viewed as the sole province of divine, not human, intervention.

Supporters of death-with-dignity legislation argue that life-sustaining equipment and methods can extend life beyond a time when it is meaningful, and that the first obligation of health and mental health professionals is to relieve suffering (Latimer, 1991; Quill et al., 1992; Weir, 1992). Additionally, they may point to the dogged determination of people intent on dying and to stories of how many terminally ill people have struggled to end their lives using all kinds of less-than-sure methods, enduring even greater suffering in the process. In marked contrast to such horror stories, the

Sigmund Freud (1856–1939)

It has been said that Sigmund Freud made a "rational decision" to end his life. Suffering from terminal throat cancer, having great difficulty in speaking, and experiencing increasing difficulty in breathing, the founder of psychoanalysis asked his physician for a lethal dose of morphine. For years it has been debated whether a decision to die, even on the part of a terminally ill patient, can ever truly be "rational." Today, in accordance with death-with-dignity legislation, the responsibility for evaluating just how rational such a choice is falls on mental health professionals.

first patient to die under the ODDA is said to have described how the family "could relax and say what a wonderful life we had. We could look back at all the lovely things because we knew we finally had an answer" (cited in Farrenkopf & Bryan, 1999, p. 246).

Professional associations such as the American Psychological Association and the American Psychiatric Association have long promulgated codes of ethics requiring the prevention of suicide. The enactment of the law in Oregon has

(continued)

Life-or-Death Psychological Assessment
(continued)

placed clinicians in that state in a unique, if not awkward, position. For years, many of these same clinicians have devoted their efforts to suicide prevention. Currently, they have been thrust into the position of being a potential party to, if not a facilitator of, physician-assisted suicide—regardless of how the aid-in-dying process is referred to in the legislation. Note that the Oregon law scrupulously denies that its objective is the legalization of physician-assisted suicide. In fact, the language of the act mandates that action taken under it "shall not, for any purpose, constitute suicide, assisted suicide, mercy killing or homicide, under the law." The framers of the legislation perceived it as a means by which a terminally ill individual could exercise some control over the dying process. Couched in these terms, the sober duty of the clinician drawn into the process may be made more palatable, if not ennobled.

Psychologists and psychiatrists called upon to make death-with-dignity competency evaluations may accept or decline the responsibility (Haley & Lee, 1998). Judging from one survey of 423 psychologists in clinical practice in Oregon (Fenn & Ganzini, 1999), many of the psychologists who could be asked to make such a life-or-death assessment might decline to do so. About one-third of the sample responded that an ODDA assessment would be outside the scope of their practice. Another 53% of the sample said they would either refuse to perform the assessment and take no further action or refuse to perform the assessment themselves and refer the patient to a colleague.

Although firm guidelines as to what an ODDA assessment should entail have yet to be established, Farrenkopf and Bryan (1999) offered several useful suggestions (summarized in the accompanying table).

The ODDA Assessment Process

1. Review of Records and Case History
With the patient's consent, the assessor will gather records from all relevant sources, including medical and mental health records. A goal is to understand the patient's current functioning in the context of many factors, ranging from the current medical condition and prognosis to the effects of medication and substance use.

2. Consultation with Treating Professionals
With the patient's consent, the assessor may consult with the patient's physician and other professionals involved in the case to better understand the patient's current functioning and current situation.

3. Patient Interviews
Sensitive but thorough interviews with the patient will explore the reasons for the aid-in-dying request, including the pressures and values motivating the request. Other areas to explore include: (a) the patient's understanding of his or her medical condition, the prognosis, and the treatment alternatives; (b) the patient's experience of physical pain, limitations of functioning, and changes over time in cognitive, emotional, and perceptual functioning; (c) the patient's characterization of his or her quality of life, including exploration of related factors including personal identity, role functioning, and self-esteem; and (d) external pressures on the patient, such as personal or familial financial inability to pay for continued treatment.

4. Interviews with Family Members and Significant Others
With the permission of the patient, separate interviews should be conducted with the patient's family and significant others. One objective is to explore from their perspective how the patient has adjusted in the past to adversity and how the patient has changed and adjusted to his or her current situation.

5. Assessment of Competence
Like the other elements of this overview, this aspect of the assessment is complicated, and only the barest of guidelines can be presented here. In general, the assessor seeks to understand the patient's reasoning and decision-making process, including all information relevant to the decision and its consequences. Some formal tests of competency are available (Appelbaum & Grisso, 1995a, 1995b; Lavin, 1992), but the clinical and legal applicability of such tests to an ODDA assessment has yet to be established.

6. Assessment of Psychopathology
To what extent is the decision to end one's life a function of pathological depression, anxiety, dementia, delirium, psychosis, or some other pathological condition? This is a question the assessor addresses using not only interviews but formal tests. Examples of the many possible instruments the assessor might employ include intelligence tests, personality tests, neuropsychological tests, symptom checklists, and depression and anxiety scales; refer to the Appendix in Farrenkopf and Bryan (1999) for a complete list of these tests.

7. Reporting Findings and Recommendations
Findings, including those related to the patient's mental status and competence, family support and pressures, and anything else relevant to the patient's aid-in-dying request, should be reported. If treatable conditions were found, treatment recommendations relevant to those conditions may be made. Nontreatment types of recommendations may include recommendations for legal advice, estate planning, or other resources. In Oregon, a Psychiatric/Psychological Consultant's Compliance Form with the consultant's recommendations should be completed and sent to the Oregon Health Division.

Adapted from Farrenkopf and Bryan, 1999.

of the largely unprofessional and unregulated "psy-chological testing" sites. Might they, for example, con-tribute to more public skepticism about psychological tests?

Perhaps the most basic right of testtakers is to know that the psychological test they are taking is one that most psy-chologists would agree *is* a psychological test. Let's look at some of the other rights of testtakers.

JUST THINK . . .

Use any search engine to find some Web sites purporting to administer quick and easy psychological tests. See if you can tell why a psychologist might consider the test to be more for entertainment purposes than for psychological insight. Repeat the exercise af-ter you have read Chapter 7 of this book.

The Rights of Testtakers

As prescribed by the *Standards* and in some cases by law, some of the rights test users accord to testtakers are the right of informed consent, the right to be informed of test findings, the right to privacy and confidentiality, and the right to the least stigmatizing label.

The right of informed consent   Testtakers have a right to know why they are being eval-uated, how the test data will be used, and what, if any, information will be released to whom. With full knowledge of such information, testtakers give their **informed consent** to be tested. The disclosure of the information needed for consent, of course, must be in language the testtaker can understand. Thus, for a testtaker as young as 2 or 3 years of age or an individual who is mentally retarded with limited language ability, a disclosure before testing might be worded as follows: "I'm going to ask you to try to do some things so that I can see what you know how to do and what things you could use some more help with" (APA, 1985, p. 85).

If a testtaker is incapable of providing an informed consent to testing, such consent may be obtained from a parent or a legal representative. Consent must be in written rather than oral form. The written form should specify (1) the general purpose of the testing, (2) the specific reason it is being undertaken in the present case, and (3) the gen-eral type of instruments to be administered. Many school districts now routinely send home such forms before testing children. Such forms typically include the option to have the child assessed privately if the parent so desires. In instances where testing is legally mandated (as in a court-ordered situation), obtaining informed consent to test may be considered more a courtesy (undertaken in part for reasons of establishing good rap-port) than a necessity.

One gray area with respect to the testtaker's right of fully informed consent before testing involves research and experimental situations wherein the examiner's complete disclosure of all facts pertinent to the testing (including the experimenter's hypothesis and so forth) might irrevocably contaminate the test data. In some instances, deception is used to create situations that occur relatively rarely. For example, a deception might be created to evaluate how an emergency worker might react under emergency condi-tions. Sometimes deception involves the use of confederates to simulate social condi-tions that are likely or unlikely to occur in a particular situation.

In situations in which it is deemed advisable not to obtain fully informed consent to evaluation, professional discretion is in order. Testtakers might be given a minimum amount of information before the testing. For example, "This testing is being undertaken as part of an experiment on obedience to authority." A full disclosure and debriefing would be made after the testing. Various professional organizations have created poli-cies and guidelines regarding deception in research. For example, the APA *Ethical Prin-ciples of Psychologists and Code of Conduct* (2002) provides that psychologists (a) do not use deception unless it is absolutely necessary, (b) do not use deception at all if it will cause participants emotional distress, and (c) fully debrief participants.

The right to be informed of test findings   In a bygone era, the inclination of many psychological assessors, particularly many clinicians, was to tell testtakers as little as possible about the nature of their performance on a particular test or test battery. In no case would they disclose diagnostic conclusions that could arouse anxiety or precipitate a crisis. This orientation was reflected in at least one authoritative text that advised testers to keep information about test results superficial and focus only on "positive" findings. This was done so that the examinee would leave the test session feeling "pleased and satisfied" (Klopfer et al., 1954, p. 15). But all that has changed, and giving realistic information about test performance to examinees is not only ethically and legally mandated but may be useful from a therapeutic perspective as well. Testtakers have a right to be informed, in language they can understand, of the nature of the findings with respect to a test they have taken. They are also entitled to know what recommendations are being made as a consequence of the test data. If the test results, findings, or recommendations made on the basis of test data are voided for any reason (such as irregularities in the test administration), testtakers have a right to know that as well.

Because of the possibility of untoward consequences of providing individuals with information about themselves—ability, lack of ability, personality, values—the communication of results of a psychological test is a most important part of the evaluation process. With sensitivity to the situation, the test user will inform the testtaker (and the parent or the legal representative or both) of the purpose of the test, the meaning of the score relative to those of other testtakers, and the possible limitations and margins of error of the test. And regardless of whether such reporting is done in person or in writing, a qualified professional should be available to answer any further questions testtakers (or their parents) have about the test scores. Ideally, counseling resources will be available for those who react adversely to the information presented.

The right to privacy and confidentiality   The concept of the **privacy right** "recognizes the freedom of the individual to pick and choose for himself the time, circumstances, and particularly the extent to which he wishes to share or withhold from others his attitudes, beliefs, behavior, and opinions" (Shah, 1969, p. 57). When people in court proceedings "take the Fifth" and refuse to answer a question put to them on the grounds that the answer might be self-incriminating, they are asserting a right to privacy provided by the Fifth Amendment to the Constitution. The information withheld in such a manner is termed *privileged;* it is information that is protected by law from disclosure in a legal proceeding. State statutes have extended the concept of **privileged information** to parties who communicate with each other in the context of certain relationships, including the lawyer-client relationship, the doctor-patient relationship, the priest-penitent relationship, and the husband-wife relationship. In most states, privilege is also accorded to the psychologist-client relationship.

Privilege is extended to parties in various relationships because it has been deemed that the parties' right to privacy serves a greater public interest than would be served if their communications were vulnerable to revelation during legal proceedings. Stated another way, it is for society's good if people feel confident that they can talk freely to their attorneys, clergy, physicians, psychologists, and spouses. Professionals such as psychologists who are parties to such special relationships have a legal and ethical duty to keep their clients' communications confidential.

Confidentiality may be distinguished from *privilege* in that whereas "confidentiality concerns matters of communication outside the courtroom, privilege protects clients from disclosure in judicial proceedings" (Jagim et al., 1978, p. 459). Privilege is not absolute. There are occasions when a court can deem the disclosure of certain information necessary and can order the disclosure of that information. Should the psychologist or other professional so ordered refuse, he or she does so under the threat of going to jail, being fined, or both.

Privilege in the psychologist-client relationship belongs to the client, not the psychologist. The competent client can direct the psychologist to disclose information to some third party (such as an attorney or an insurance carrier), and the psychologist is obligated to make the disclosure. In some rare instances, the psychologist may be ethically (if not legally) compelled to disclose information if that information will prevent harm to either the client or some endangered third party. An illustrative case would be the situation where a client details a plan to commit suicide or homicide. In such an instance, the psychologist would be legally and ethically compelled to take reasonable action to prevent such an occurrence. Here, the preservation of life would be deemed an objective more important than the nonrevelation of privileged information.

A wrong judgment on the part of the clinician regarding the revelation of confidential communication may lead to a lawsuit or worse. A landmark Court case in this area was the 1974 case of *Tarasoff v. Regents of the University of California.* In that case, a therapy patient had made known to his psychologist his intention to kill an unnamed but readily identifiable girl two months before the murder. The Court held that "protective privilege ends where the public peril begins," and so the therapist had a duty to warn the endangered girl of her peril. Clinicians may have a duty to warn endangered third parties not only of potential violence but of potential AIDS infection from an HIV-positive client (Buckner & Firestone, 2000; Melchert & Patterson, 1999).

Test users must take reasonable precautions to safeguard test records. If these data are stored in a filing cabinet, the cabinet should be locked and preferably made of steel. If these data are stored in a computer, electronic safeguards must be taken to ensure only authorized access. We might also mention here that it is not a good idea for individuals and institutions to store records in perpetuity. Rather, the individual or institution should have a reasonable policy covering (1) the storage of test data—when, if at any time, these records will be deemed to be outdated, invalid, or useful only from an academic perspective—and (2) the conditions under which requests for release of records to a third party will be honored.

Relevant to the release of assessment-related information is the Health Insurance Portability and Accountability Act of 1996 (HIPAA) which took effect in April 2003. These federal privacy standards limited the ways that health care providers, health plans, pharmacies, and hospitals can use patients' personal medical information. For example, personal health information may not be used for purposes unrelated to health care.

In part due to the decision of the United States Supreme Court in the case of *Jaffee v. Redmond* (1996), HIPAA singled out "psychotherapy notes" as requiring even more stringent protection than other records. The ruling in *Jaffee* affirmed that communications between a psychotherapist and a patient were privileged in federal courts. The HIPAA privacy rule cited *Jaffee* and defined privacy notes as "notes recorded (in any medium) by a health care provider who is a mental health professional documenting or analyzing the contents of conversation during a private counseling session or a group, joint, or family counseling session and that are separated from the rest of the individual's medical record." Although "results of clinical tests" were specifically *excluded* in this definition, we would caution assessment professionals to obtain specific consent from assessees in releasing assessment-related information. This is particularly essential with respect to data gathered using assessment tools such as the interview, behavioral observation, and role play.

The right to the least stigmatizing label   The *Standards* advise that the least stigmatizing labels should always be assigned when reporting test results. To better appreciate the need for this standard, consider the case of Jo Ann Iverson.[5] Jo Ann was 9 years old and suffering from claustrophobia when her mother brought her to a state hospital in Blackfoot, Idaho, for a psychological evaluation. Arden Frandsen, a psychologist employed part-time at the hospital, conducted an evaluation of Jo Ann, during the course of which he administered a Stanford-Binet Intelligence Test. In his report, Frandsen classified Jo Ann as "feeble-minded, at the high-grade moron level of general mental ability." Following a request from Jo Ann's school guidance counselor, a copy of the psychological report was forwarded to the school—and embarrassing rumors concerning Jo Ann's mental condition began to circulate.

Jo Ann's mother, Carmel Iverson, brought a libel (defamation) suit against Frandsen on behalf of her daughter.[6] Mrs. Iverson lost the lawsuit. The court ruled in part that the psychological evaluation "was a professional report made by a public servant in good faith, representing his best judgment." But although Mrs. Iverson did not prevail in her lawsuit, we can certainly sympathize with her anguish at the thought of her daughter going through life with a label such as "high-grade moron"—this despite the fact that the psychologist had probably merely copied that designation from the test manual. We would also add that, in retrospect, it might have been possible to prevail in a suit against the guidance counselor for breach of confidentiality, because there appeared to be uncontested testimony that it was from the guidance counselor's office that rumors concerning Jo Ann first emanated.

On the subject of the rights of testtakers, let's not forget about the rights—of sorts—of students of testing and assessment. Having been introduced to various aspects of the assessment enterprise, you have the right to learn more about technical aspects of measurement. Exercise that right in the succeeding chapters.

Self-Assessment

Test your understanding of elements of this chapter by seeing if you can explain each of the following terms, expressions, abbreviations, events, or names in terms of their significance in the context of psychological testing and assessment:

affirmative action	Darwin, Charles	informed consent
Albemarle Paper Company v. Moody	*Debra P. v. Turlington*	*Jaffee v. Redmond*
Binet, Alfred	ethics	*Larry P. v. Riles*
Cattell, James McKeen	eugenics	laws
Code of Fair Testing Practices in Education	Galton, Francis	minimum competency testing programs
	Goddard, Henry H.	
code of professional ethics	*Griggs v. Duke Power Company*	Morgan, Christiana D.
confidentiality	HIPAA	Murray, Henry A.
culture	hired gun	ODDA
culture-specific test	*Hobson v. Hansen*	Pearson, Karl

---

5. See *Iverson v. Frandsen*, 237 F. 2d 898 (Idaho, 1956) or Cohen (1979, pp. 149–150).

6. An interesting though tangential aspect of this case was the argument advanced by Iverson that she had brought her child in for claustrophobia and, given that fact, the administration of an intelligence test was unauthorized and beyond the scope of the consultation. However, the defendant proved to the satisfaction of the court that the administration of the Stanford-Binet was necessary to determine whether Jo Ann had the mental capacity to respond to psychotherapy.

privacy right	Rorschach, Hermann	Witmer, Lightner
privileged information	self-report test	Woodworth, Robert S.
projective test	Sputnik	World War I
psychoanalysis	*Tarasoff v. Regents of California*	World War II
Public Law 105-17	truth-in-testing legislation	Wundt, Wilhelm Max
quota system	Wechsler, David	

Web Watch

Check out the following Web sites for more information about topics discussed in this chapter.

Affirmative Action
www.affirmativeaction.org

Eugenics
www.pbs.org/wgbh/aso/databank/entries/
dh23eu.html

HIPAA
www.hhs.gov/ocr/hipaa

www.hhs.gov/ocr/hipaa/privacy.html

www.hipaa.com

3

A Statistics Refresher

From the red-pencil number circled at the top of your first spelling test to the computer printout of your college entrance examination scores, tests and test scores touch your life. They seem to reach out from the paper and shake your hand when you do well and punch you in the face when you do poorly. They can point you toward or away from a particular school or curriculum. They can help you to identify strengths and weaknesses in your physical and mental abilities. They can accompany you on job interviews and influence a job or career choice.

In your role as a student, you have probably found that your relationship to tests has been primarily that of a testtaker. But as a psychologist, teacher, researcher, or employer, you may find that your relationship with tests is primarily that of a test user—the person who breathes life and meaning into test scores by applying the knowledge and skill to interpret them appropriately. You may one day create a test, whether in an academic or a business setting, and then have the responsibility for scoring and interpreting it. In that situation, or even from the perspective of a testtaker, it's essential to understand the theory underlying test use and the principles of test score interpretation.

Test scores are frequently expressed as numbers, and statistical tools are used to describe, make inferences from, and draw conclusions about numbers.[1] In this statistics refresher, we cover scales of measurement, tabular and graphic presentations of data, measures of central tendency, correlation and regression, measures of variability, and standard scores. If these statistics-related terms look painfully familiar to you, we ask your indulgence and ask you to remember that overlearning is the key to retention. Of course, if these terms are unfamiliar, we urge you to obtain and spend ample time reviewing a good elementary statistics text. The brief review of statistical concepts that follows is designed to supplement, not replace, an introductory course in statistics.

---

1. Of course, a test score may be expressed in other forms, such as a letter grade or a pass/fail designation. Unless stated otherwise, terms such as *test score, test data, test results,* and *test scores* are used throughout this book to refer to numeric descriptions of test performance.

Scales of Measurement

We may formally define **measurement** as the act of assigning numbers or symbols to characteristics of things (people, events, whatever) according to rules. The rules used in assigning numbers are guidelines for representing the magnitude (or some other characteristic) of the object being measured. An example of a measurement rule is: *Assign the number 12 to all lengths that are exactly the same length as a 12-inch ruler.* A **scale** is a set of numbers (or other symbols) whose properties model empirical properties of the objects to which the numbers are assigned.[2] There are various ways of categorizing scales.

One way of categorizing a scale is according to the type of variable being measured. Thus, a scale used to measure a continuous variable might be referred to as a *continuous scale,* whereas a scale used to measure a discrete variable might be referred to as a *discrete scale.* If, for example, research subjects were to be categorized as either female or male, the categorization scale would be said to be discrete because it would not be meaningful to categorize a subject as anything other than female or male.[3] By contrast, a continuous scale exists when it is possible theoretically to divide any of the values of the scale. A distinction must be made, however, between what is theoretically possible and what is practically desirable. The units into which a continuous scale will actually be divided may depend on factors such as the purpose of the measurement and practicality. In measurement to install venetian blinds, for example, it is theoretically possible to measure by the millimeter or even the micrometer. But is such precision necessary? Most installers do just fine with measurement by the inch.

> **JUST THINK . . .**
>
> The *scale* with which we are all perhaps most familiar is the common bathroom scale. How are a psychological test and a bathroom scale alike? How are they different? Your answer may change as you read this chapter as well as succeeding ones.

Measurement always involves **error.** In the language of assessment, error refers to the collective influence of all of the factors on a test score or measurement beyond those specifically measured by the test or measurement. As we will see, there are many different sources of error in measurement. Consider, for example, the score someone received on a test in American history. We might conceive of part of the score as reflecting the testtaker's knowledge of American history and part of the score as reflecting error. The error part of the test score may be due to many different factors. One source of error might have been a distracting thunderstorm going on outside at the time the test was administered. Another source of error was the particular selection of test items the instructor chose to use for the test. Had a different item or two been used in the test, the testtaker's score on the test might have been higher or lower.

> **JUST THINK . . .**
>
> Assume the role of a test creator. Now write some instructions to users of your test designed to reduce error associated with test scores to the absolute minimum. Be sure to include instructions regarding the preparation of the site where the test will be administered.

---

2. David L. Streiner recently reflected, "Many terms have been used to describe a collection of items or questions—*scale, test, questionnaire, index, inventory,* and a host of others—with no consistency from one author to another" (2003a, p. 217, emphasis in the original). Streiner proposed to refer to questionnaires of theoretically like or related items as *scales* and theoretically unrelated items as *indexes.* He readily acknowledged that as it stands now, counterexamples of each term could readily be found.

3. We acknowledge that if all females were labeled "1" and all males were labeled "2," some people, for example individuals born with a gender-related genetic abnormality, might seem to qualify as "1.5." Such exceptions aside, however, all cases on a discrete scale must lie on a point on the scale, and it is theoretically impossible for a case to lie between two points on the scale.

Error is very much an element of all measurement. And it is an element for which any theory of measurement must surely account.

Measurement using continuous scales always involves error. To illustrate why, let's go back to the scenario involving venetian blinds. The length of the window measured to be 35.5 inches could, in reality, be 35.7 inches. The measuring scale is conveniently marked off in grosser gradations of measurement. Most scales used in psychological and educational assessment are continuous and therefore can be expected to contain this sort of error. The number or score used to characterize the trait being measured on a continuous scale should be thought of as an approximation of the "real" number. Thus, for example, a score of 25 on some test of anxiety should not be thought of as a precise measure of anxiety. Rather, it should be thought of as an approximation of the real anxiety score had the measuring instrument been calibrated to yield such a score. In such a case, perhaps the score of 25 is an approximation of a real score of 24.7 or 25.44.

It is generally agreed that there are four different levels or scales of measurement. Within these different levels or scales of measurement, assigned numbers convey different kinds of information. Accordingly, certain statistical manipulations may or may not be appropriate, depending upon the level or scale of measurement.[4]

The French word for black is *noir* (pronounced "n'wăre"). We bring this up here only to call attention to the fact that this French word is a useful acronym for remembering the four levels or scales of measurement. Each letter in *noir* is the first letter of each of the succeedingly more rigorous levels. *N* stands for *nominal, o* for *ordinal, i* for *interval,* and *r* for *ratio* scales.

Nominal Scales

Nominal scales are the simplest form of measurement. These scales involve classification or categorization based on one or more distinguishing characteristics where all things measured must be placed into mutually exclusive and exhaustive categories. For example, people may be characterized by gender in a study designed to compare performance of men and women on some test. In such a study, all males might be labeled "men," "1," "B," or some other symbol, and all females might be labeled "women," "2," or "A." In the specialty area of clinical psychology, one often-used nominal scale is the American Psychiatric Association's *Diagnostic and Statistical Manual of Mental Disorders IV (DSM-IV)*. Each disorder listed in the manual is assigned its own number. Thus, for example, the number 303.00 identifies alcohol intoxication, and the number 307.00 identifies stuttering. But these numbers are used exclusively for classification purposes and cannot be meaningfully added, subtracted, ranked, or averaged. So, no, the number 305 does *not* equal an intoxicated stutterer.

Individual test items may also employ nominal scaling, including *yes/no* responses. For example:

Instructions: Answer either *yes* or *no.*

Are you actively contemplating suicide? _____

---

4. For the purposes of our statistics refresher, we present what Nunnally (1978) called the "fundamentalist" view of measurement scales—a view that "... holds that 1. there are distinct types of measurement scales into which all possible measures of attributes can be classified, 2. each measure has some 'real' characteristics that permit its proper classification, and 3. once a measure is classified, the classification specifies the types of mathematical analyses that can be employed with the measure" (p. 24). Nunnally and others have acknowledged that alternatives to the "fundamentalist" view may also be viable.

Are you currently under professional care for a psychiatric disorder? _____

Have you ever been convicted of a felony? _____

In each case, a *yes* or *no* response results in the placement into one of a set of mutually exclusive groups: suicidal or not, under care for psychiatric disorder or not, and felon or not. Arithmetic operations that can legitimately be performed with nominal data include counting for the purpose of determining how many cases fall into each category and some consequential determination of proportion or percentages.[5]

Ordinal Scales

Like nominal scales, **ordinal scales** permit classification. However, in addition to classification, rank-ordering on some characteristic is also permissible with ordinal scales. In business and organizational settings, job applicants may be rank-ordered according to their desirability for a position. In clinical settings, people on a waiting list for psychotherapy may be rank-ordered according to their need for treatment. In these examples, individuals are compared with others and assigned a rank (perhaps 1 to the best applicant or the most needy wait-listed client, 2 to the next, and so forth).

Although he may have never used the term *ordinal scale*, Alfred Binet, a developer of the intelligence test that today bears his name, believed strongly that the data derived from an intelligence test are ordinal in nature. He emphasized that what he tried to do in the test was not to *measure* people, as one might measure a person's height, but merely to *classify* (and rank) people on the basis of their performance on the tasks. He wrote:

> I have not sought . . . to sketch a method of measuring, in the physical sense of the word, but only a method of classification of individuals. The procedures which I have indicated will, if perfected, come to classify a person before or after such another person, or such another series of persons; but I do not believe that one may measure one of the intellectual aptitudes in the sense that one measures a length or a capacity. Thus, when a person studied can retain seven figures after a single audition, one can class him, from the point of his memory for figures, after the individual who retains eight figures under the same conditions, and before those who retain six. It is a classification, not a measurement . . . we do not measure, we classify. (Binet, cited in Varon, 1936, p. 41)

Assessment instruments applied to the individual subject may also use an ordinal form of measurement. The Rokeach Value Survey uses such an approach. In that test, a list of personal values, such as freedom, happiness, and wisdom, are put in order according to their perceived importance to the testtaker (Rokeach, 1973). If a set of ten values is rank-ordered, the testtaker may assign a value of "1" to the most important and "10" to the least important.

Ordinal scales imply nothing about how much greater one ranking is than another. Even though ordinal scales may employ numbers or "scores" to represent the rank ordering, the numbers do not indicate units of measurement. So, for example, the performance difference between the first-ranked job applicant and the second-ranked applicant may be very small, while the difference between the second- and third-ranked applicants might be huge. On the Rokeach Value Survey, the value ranked "1" may be handily the most important in the mind of the testtaker. However, ordering the values that follow may be difficult to the point of being almost arbitrary.

---

5. There are other ways to analyze nominal data (Gokhale & Kullback, 1978; Kranzler & Moursund, 1999). However, these methods are beyond the scope of this book.

Ordinal scales have no absolute zero point. In the case of a test of job performance ability, every testtaker, regardless of standing on the test, is presumed to have *some* ability. No testtaker is presumed to have zero ability. Zero is without meaning in such a test because the number of units that separate one testtaker's score from another's is simply not known. The scores are ranked, but the actual number of units separating one score from the next may be many, just a few, or practically none. Because there is no zero point on an ordinal scale, the ways in which data from such scales can be analyzed statistically are limited. One cannot average the qualifications of the first- and third-ranked job applicants, for example, and expect to come out with the qualifications of the second-ranked applicant.

Interval Scales

In addition to the features of nominal and ordinal scales, **interval scales** contain equal intervals between numbers. Each unit on the scale is exactly equal to any other unit on the scale. But, like ordinal scales, interval scales contain no absolute zero point. With interval scales, we have reached a level of measurement at which it *is* possible to average a set of measurements and get a meaningful result.

Scores on many tests, such as tests of intelligence, are analyzed statistically in ways appropriate for data at the interval level of measurement. The difference in intellectual ability represented by IQs of 80 and 100, for example, is thought to be similar to that existing between IQs of 100 and 120. However, if an individual were to achieve an IQ of 0 (something that is not even possible given the way that many intelligence tests are structured), that would not be an indication of zero (the total absence of) intelligence. Because interval scales contain no absolute zero point, a presumption inherent in their use is that no testtaker possesses zero of the ability or trait (or whatever) being measured.

Ratio Scales

In addition to all the properties of nominal, ordinal, and interval measurement, a **ratio scale** has a true zero point. All mathematical operations can meaningfully be performed, because there exist equal intervals between the numbers on the scale as well as a true or absolute zero point.

In psychology, ratio-level measurement is employed in some types of tests and test items, perhaps most notably those having to do with assessment of neurological functioning. One example is a test of hand grip, in which the variable measured is the amount of pressure one can exert with one hand (see Figure 3–1). Another example is a timed test of perceptual-motor ability that requires the testtaker to assemble a jigsaw-like puzzle. In such an instance, the time taken to successfully complete the puzzle is the measure that is recorded. Because there is a true zero point on this scale (that is, 0 seconds), it is meaningful to say that a testtaker who completes the assembly in 30 seconds has taken half the time of a testtaker who completed it in 60 seconds. In this example, it is meaningful to speak of a true zero point on the scale—but in theory only. Why? *Just think . . .*

No testtaker could ever obtain a score of zero on this assembly task. Stated another way, no testtaker, not even The Flash (a comic book superhero whose superpower is the ability to move at superhuman speed) could assemble the puzzle in zero seconds.

Measurement Scales in Psychology

The ordinal level of measurement is most frequently used in psychology. As Kerlinger (1973, p. 439) put it, "Intelligence, aptitude, and personality test scores are, *basically and strictly speaking*, ordinal. These tests indicate with more or less accuracy not the

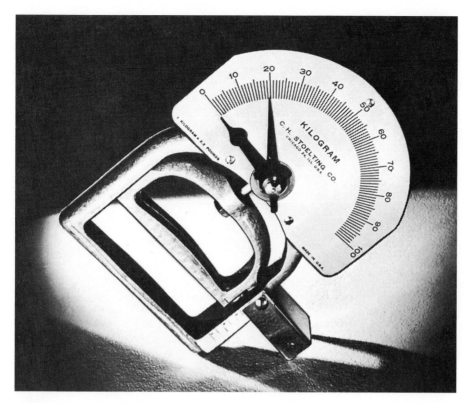

Figure 3–1
Ratio Level Measurement in the Palm of One's Hand

*Pictured above is a **dynamometer**, an instrument used to measure strength of hand grip. The examinee is instructed to squeeze the grips as hard as possible. The squeezing of the grips causes the gauge needle to move and reflect the number of pounds of pressure exerted. The highest point reached by the needle is the score. This measure employs ratio level measurement. Someone who can exert 10 pounds of pressure (and earns a score of 10) exerts twice as much pressure as a person who exerts 5 pounds of pressure (and earns a score of 5). On this test it is possible to achieve a score of zero, indicating a complete lack of exerted pressure. But while it is meaningful to speak of a score of zero on this test, we have to wonder about its meaning. Is such a score indicative of a total incapability of exerting any hand grip pressure? Such a score would be expected from an assessee who suffers from a condition such as paralysis of the hand. Alternatively, is a score of zero indicative of something else, such as an unwillingness to cooperate with the examiner or an attempt to malinger or "fake bad" on the test? Ratio scales may provide us with "solid" numbers to work with, but assessors may still have to do the math before drawing conclusions.*

amount of intelligence, aptitude, and personality traits of individuals, but rather the rank-order positions of the individuals." Kerlinger allowed that "most psychological and educational scales approximate interval equality fairly well," though he cautioned that if ordinal measurements were treated as if they were interval measurements, the test user must "be constantly alert to the possibility of *gross* inequality of intervals" (pp. 440–441).

Why would psychologists want to treat their assessment data as interval when those data would be better described as ordinal? Why not just say that they are ordinal? The attraction of interval measurement for users of psychological tests is the flexibility with

	Student	Score (number correct)
Table 3–1	Judy	78
Data From Your Measurement Course Test	Joe	67
	Lee-Wu	69
	Miriam	63
	Valerie	85
	Diane	72
	Henry	92
	Esperanza	67
	Paula	94
	Martha	62
	Bill	61
	Homer	44
	Robert	66
	Michael	87
	Jorge	76
	Mary	83
	"Mousey"	42
	Barbara	82
	John	84
	Donna	51
	Uriah	69
	Leroy	61
	Ronald	96
	Vinnie	73
	Bianca	79

which such data can be manipulated statistically. What kinds of statistical manipulation, you may ask.

In this chapter we discuss the various ways in which test data can be described or converted to make those data more manageable and understandable. Some of the techniques we'll describe, such as the computation of an average, can be used if data are assumed to be interval or ratio level in nature but not if they are ordinal or nominal. Other techniques, such as those involving the creation of graphs or tables, may be used with ordinal or even nominal level data.

Describing Data

Suppose you have magically changed places with the professor teaching this course, and you have just administered an examination that consists of 100 multiple-choice items (where one point is awarded for each correct answer). The distribution of scores for the 25 students enrolled in your class could theoretically range from 0 (none correct) to 100 (all correct). A **distribution** may be defined as a set of test scores arrayed for recording or study. The 25 scores in this distribution are referred to as *raw scores*. As its name implies, a **raw score** is a straightforward, unmodified accounting of performance, usually numerical. A raw score may reflect a simple tally, as in *number of items responded to correctly on an achievement test*. As we will see later in this chapter, raw scores can be converted into other types of scores. For now, let's assume it's the day after the examination, and you are sitting in your office looking at the raw scores listed in Table 3–1. What do you do next?

Table 3–2
Frequency Distribution of Scores From Your Test

Score	f (frequency)
96	1
94	1
92	1
87	1
85	1
84	1
83	1
82	1
79	1
78	1
76	1
73	1
72	1
69	2
67	2
66	1
63	1
62	1
61	2
51	1
44	1
42	1

One task at hand is to communicate the test results to your class. You want to do that in a way that will help students understand how their performance on the test compared to the performance of other students. Perhaps the first step is to organize the data. Transform it from a random listing of raw scores into something that immediately conveys a bit more information. Later, as we will see, you may wish to transform the data in other ways.

Frequency Distributions

The data from the test could be organized into a distribution of the raw scores. One way the scores could be distributed is by the frequency with which they occur. In a **frequency distribution,** all scores are listed alongside the number of times each score occurred. The scores might be listed in tabular or graphic form. Table 3–2 lists the frequency of occurrence of each score in one column and the score itself in the other column.

Often, a frequency distribution is referred to as a *simple frequency distribution* to indicate that individual scores have been used and the data have not been grouped. Another kind of frequency distribution used to summarize data is a *grouped frequency distribution*. In a **grouped frequency distribution,** test-score intervals, also called *class intervals*, replace the actual test scores. The number of class intervals used and the size or *width* of each class interval (that is, the range of test scores contained in each class interval) are for the test user to decide. But how?

In most instances, a decision as to the size of a class interval in a grouped frequency distribution is made on the basis of convenience. Of course, virtually any decision will represent a trade-off of sorts. A convenient, easy-to-read summary of the data is the trade-off for the loss of detail. To what extent must the data be summarized? How important is detail? These types of questions must be considered. In the grouped frequency

Table 3–3
A Grouped Frequency Distribution

Class Interval	f (frequency)
95–99	1
90–94	2
85–89	2
80–84	3
75–79	3
70–74	2
65–69	5
60–64	4
55–59	0
50–54	1
45–49	0
40–44	2

distribution in Table 3–3, the test scores have been grouped into 12 class intervals with each class interval being equal to 5 points.[6] The highest class interval (95 to 99) and the lowest class interval (40 to 44) are referred to respectively as the upper and lower limits of the distribution. Here, the need for convenience in reading the data outweighs the need for great detail, so such groupings of data seem logical.

Frequency distributions of test scores can also be illustrated graphically. A **graph** is a diagram or chart composed of lines, points, bars, or other symbols that describe and illustrate data. With a good graph, the place of a single score in relation to a distribution of test scores can be understood easily. Three kinds of graphs used to illustrate frequency distributions are the histogram, the bar graph, and the frequency polygon (Figure 3–2). A **histogram** is a graph with vertical lines drawn at the true limits of each test score (or class interval), forming a series of contiguous rectangles. It is customary for the test scores (either the single scores or the midpoints of the class intervals) to be placed along the graph's horizontal axis (also referred to as the *abscissa* or X-axis), and numbers indicative of the frequency of occurrence are placed along the graph's vertical axis (also referred to as the *ordinate* or Y-axis). In a **bar graph,** numbers indicative of frequency also appear on the Y-axis, and reference to some categorization (such as yes/no/maybe, male/female, and so forth) appears on the X-axis. Here the rectangular bars typically are not contiguous. Data illustrated in a **frequency polygon** are expressed by a continuous line connecting the points where test scores or class intervals (as indicated on the X-axis) meet frequencies (as indicated on the Y-axis).

Graphic representations of frequency distributions may assume any of a number of different shapes (Figure 3–3). Regardless of the shape of graphed data, it is a good idea for the consumer of the information contained in the graph to examine it carefully—and if need be, critically. Consider in this context our *Everyday Psychometrics.*

As we discuss in detail later in this chapter, one graphic representation of data is of particular interest to measurement professionals: the *normal* or *bell-shaped curve.* Before getting to that, however, let's get back to the subject of distributions—how we can describe and characterize them. One way to describe a distribution of test scores is by a measure of central tendency.

---

6. Technically, each number on such a scale would be viewed as ranging from as much as 0.5 below it to as much as 0.5 above it. For example, the "real" but hypothetical width of the class interval ranging from 95 to 99 would be the difference between 99.5 and 94.5, or 5. The true upper and lower limits of the class intervals presented in the table would be 99.5 and 39.5 respectively.

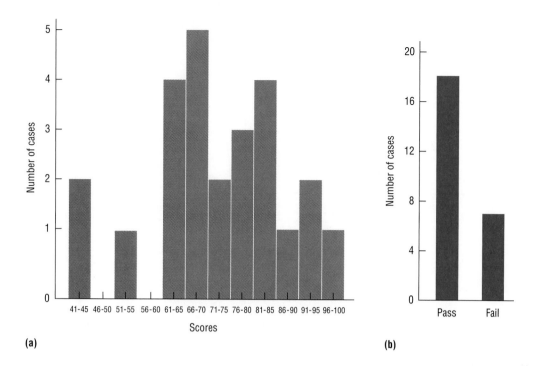

(a)

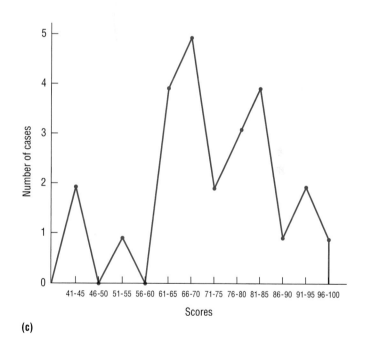

(b)

Figure 3–2
Graphic Illustrations of Data From Table 3–3

A histogram (a), a bar graph (b), and a frequency polygon (c) all may be used to graphically convey information about test performance. Of course, the labeling of the bar graph and the specific nature of the data conveyed by it depend on the variables of interest; in (b) the variable of interest is the number of students who passed the test (assuming for the purpose of this illustration that a raw score of 65 or higher had been arbitrarily designated in advance as a passing grade).

Returning to the question posed earlier—the one in which you play the role of instructor and must communicate the test results to your students—which type of graph would best serve your purpose? Why?

As we continue our review of descriptive statistics, you may wish to return to your role of professor and formulate your response to challenging related questions, such as "Which measure(s) of central tendency shall I use to convey this information?" and "Which measure(s) of variability would convey the information best?"

(c)

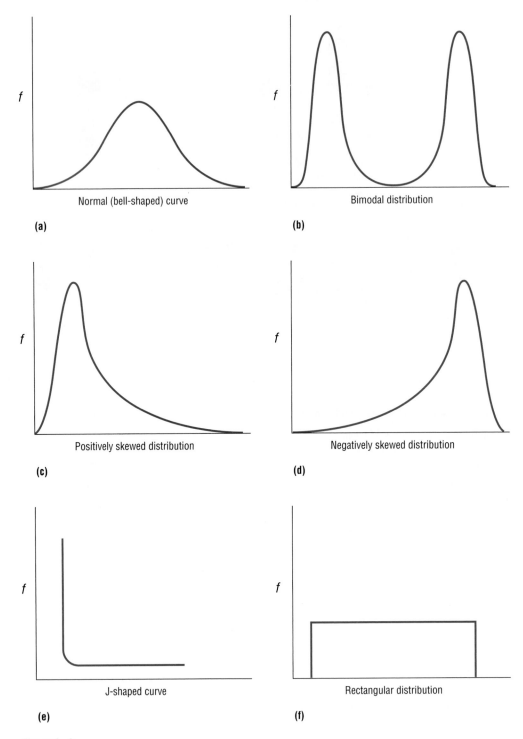

Figure 3–3
Shapes Frequency Distributions Can Take

Consumer (of Graphed Data), Beware!

One picture is worth a thousand words, and one purpose of representing data in graphic form is to convey information at a glance. However, although two graphs may be accurate with respect to the data they represent, their pictures—and the impression drawn from a glance at them—may be vastly different. As an example, consider the following hypothetical scenario involving a hamburger restaurant chain we'll call "The Charred House."

The Charred House chain serves very charbroiled, microscopically thin hamburgers formed in the shape of little triangular houses. In the ten-year period since its founding in 1993, the company has sold, on average, 100 million burgers per year. On the chain's tenth anniversary, The Charred House distributes a press release proudly announcing "Over a Billion Served."

Reporters from two business publications set out to research and write a feature article on this hamburger restaurant chain. Working solely from sales figures as compiled from annual reports to the shareholders, Reporter 1 focuses her story on the differences in yearly sales. Her article is entitled "A Billion Served—But Charred House Sales Fluctuate From Year to Year," and its graphic illustration is reprinted here.

Quite a different picture of the company emerges from Reporter 2's story, entitled "A Billion Served—And Charred House Sales Are as Steady as Ever," and its accompanying graph. The latter story is based on a diligent analysis of comparable data for the same number of hamburger chains in the same areas of the country over the same time period. While researching the story, Reporter 2 learned that yearly fluctuations in sales are common to the entire industry and that the annual fluctuations observed in the Charred House figures were—relative to other chains—insignificant.

Compare the graphs that accompanied each story. Although both are accurate insofar as they are based on the correct numbers, the impressions they are likely to leave are quite different.

Incidentally, custom dictates that the intersection of the two axes of a graph be at 0 and that all the points on the Y-axis be in equal and proportional intervals from 0. This custom is followed in Reporter 2's story, where the first point on the ordinate is 10 units more than 0, and each succeeding point is also 10 more units away from 0. However,

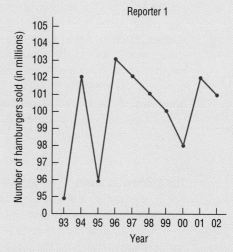

(a) The Charred House Sales Over a 10-Year Period

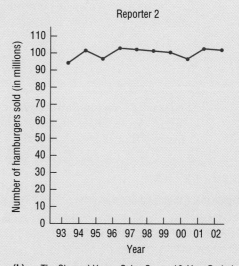

(b) The Charred House Sales Over a 10-Year Period

the custom is violated in Reporter 1's story, where the first point on the ordinate is 95 units more than 0, and each succeeding point increases only by 1. The fact that the custom is violated in Reporter 1's story should serve as a warning to evaluate pictorial representations of data all the more critically.

Measures of Central Tendency

A **measure of central tendency** is a statistic that indicates the average or midmost score between the extreme scores in a distribution. The center of a distribution can be defined in different ways. Perhaps the most commonly used measure of central tendency is the *arithmetic mean* (or simply, **mean**), referred to in everyday language as the "average." The mean takes into account the actual numerical value of every score. In special instances, such as when there are only a few scores and one or two of the scores are extreme in relation to the remaining ones, a measure of central tendency other than the mean may be desirable. Other measures of central tendency we review include the *median* and the *mode.* Note that in the formulas that follow, the standard statistical shorthand called "summation notation" (*summation* meaning "the sum of") is used. The Greek uppercase letter sigma, Σ, is the symbol used to signify "sum"; if X represents a test score, then the symbol ΣX means "add all the test scores."

The arithmetic mean   The **arithmetic mean,** denoted by the symbol $\overline{X}$ (pronounced "X bar") is equal to the sum of the observations (or test scores in this case) divided by the number of observations. Symbolically written, the formula for the arithmetic mean is $\overline{X} = \Sigma X/n$, where n equals the number of observations or test scores. The arithmetic mean is typically the most appropriate measure of central tendency for interval or ratio data when the distributions are believed to be approximately normal. An arithmetic mean can also be computed from a frequency distribution. The formula for doing this is

$$\overline{X} = \frac{\Sigma f X}{n}$$

where $\Sigma f X$ means "multiply the frequency of each score by its corresponding score and sum." An estimate of the arithmetic mean may also be obtained from a grouped frequency distribution using the same formula, where X is equal to the midpoint of the class interval. Table 3–4 illustrates a calculation of the mean from a grouped frequency distribution. Do the math, and you will find that using the grouped data, a mean of 71.8 (which may be rounded to 72) is calculated. Using the raw scores, a mean of 72.12 (which also may be rounded to 72) is calculated. Frequently, the choice of statistic will depend on the degree of precision in measurement that is required.

JUST THINK . . .

Imagine that a thousand or so engineers took an extremely difficult pre-employment test. A handful of the engineers earned very high scores, but the vast majority did poorly, earning extremely low scores. Given this scenario, what are the pros and cons of using the mean as a measure of central tendency?

The median   The **median,** defined as the middle score in a distribution, is another commonly used measure of central tendency. Determine the median of a distribution of scores by ordering the scores in a list by magnitude, in either ascending or descending order. When the total number of scores ordered is an odd number, the median will be the score that is exactly in the middle, with one-half of the remaining scores lying above it and the other half of the remaining scores lying below it. When the total number of scores ordered is an even number, the median can be calculated by determining the arithmetic mean of the two middle scores. For example, suppose that ten people took a pre-employment word processing

Table 3–4
Calculating the Arithmetic Mean From a Grouped Frequency Distribution

Class Interval	f	X (midpoint of class interval)	fX
95–99	1	97	97
90–94	2	92	184
85–89	2	87	174
80–84	3	82	246
75–79	3	77	231
70–74	2	72	144
65–69	5	67	335
60–64	4	62	248
55–59	0	57	000
50–54	1	52	52
45–49	0	47	000
40–44	2	42	84
	$\Sigma f = 25$		$\Sigma (fX) = 1{,}795$

To estimate the arithmetic mean of this grouped frequency distribution,

$$\overline{X} = \frac{\Sigma (fX)}{n} = \frac{1795}{25} = 71.80$$

To calculate the mean of this distribution using raw scores,

$$\overline{X} = \frac{\Sigma X}{n} = \frac{1803}{25} = 72.12$$

test at The Rochester Wrenchworks (TRW) Corporation. They obtained the following scores, presented here in descending order:

66

65

61

59

53

52

41

36

35

32

The median in these data would be calculated by obtaining the average (that is, the arithmetic mean) of the two middle scores, 53 and 52 (which would be equal to 52.5). The median is an appropriate measure of central tendency for ordinal, interval, and ratio data. The median may be a particularly useful measure of central tendency in cases where relatively few scores fall at the high end of the distribution or relatively few scores fall at the low end of the distribution.

Suppose not ten but tens of thousands of people had applied for jobs at the Rochester Wrenchworks? It would be impractical to find the median by simply ordering the data and finding the midmost scores. So, how would the median score be identified? For our purposes, the answer is simply that there are advanced methods for doing so. There are also techniques for identifying the median in other sorts of distributions, such as a grouped frequency distribution and a distribution wherein various scores are identical. However, instead of delving into such new and complex territory, let's go back to our discussion of measures of central tendency and consider another such measure.

The mode The most frequently occurring score in a distribution of scores is the **mode.**[7] As an example, determine the mode for the following scores obtained by another TRW job applicant, Bruce. The scores reflect the number of words Bruce word-processed in seven one-minute trials:

43   34   45   51   42   31   51

TRW policy is that new hires must be able to word-process at least 50 words per minute. Now, place yourself in the role of the corporate personnel officer. Would you hire Bruce? The most frequently occurring score in this distribution of scores is 51. If hiring guidelines gave you the freedom to use any measure of central tendency in your personnel decision-making, it would be your choice as whether or not to hire him. You could hire him and justify this decision on the basis of his modal score (51). You could not hire him and justify this decision on the basis of his mean score (below the required 50 words per minute). Ultimately, whether Rochester Wrenchworks will be Bruce's new home away from home will depend on other job-related factors, such as the nature of the job market in Rochester and the qualifications of competing applicants. Of course, if company guidelines dictated that only the mean score be used in hiring decisions, a career at TRW would not be in Bruce's immediate future.

Distributions that contain a tie for the designation "most frequently occurring score" can have more than one mode. Consider the following scores—arranged in no particular order—obtained by 20 students on the final exam of a new trade school called the Home Study School of Elvis Presley Impersonators:

51   49   51   50   66   52   53   38   17   66

33   44   73   13   21   91   87   92   47   3

The distribution of these scores is said to be **bimodal** because it contains two scores (51 and 66) that occur with the highest frequency (a frequency of two). Except with nominal data, the mode tends not to be a very commonly used measure of central tendency. Unlike the arithmetic mean, which has to be calculated, the value of the modal score is not calculated; one simply counts and determines which score occurs most frequently. Because the mode is arrived at in this manner, the modal score may be a totally atypical score—one at an extreme end of the distribution—which nonetheless occurs with the greatest frequency. In fact, it is theoretically possible for a bimodal distribution to have two modes that each fall at the high or the low end of the distribution—thus violating the expectation that a measure of central tendency should be . . . well, central (or indicative of a point at the middle of the distribution).

---

7. If adjacent scores occur equally often and more often than other scores, custom dictates that the mode be referred to as the *average.*

Even though the mode is not calculated in the sense that the mean is calculated, and even though the mode is not necessarily a unique point in a distribution (a distribution can have two, three, or even more modes), the mode can still be quite useful in conveying certain types of information. The mode is useful in analyses of a qualitative or verbal nature. For example, when assessing consumers' recall of a commercial by means of interviews, a researcher might be interested in which word or words were mentioned most by interviewees.

The mode can convey a wealth of information *in addition to* the mean. As an example, suppose you wanted an estimate of the number of journal articles published by clinical psychologists in the United States in the past year. To arrive at this figure, you might total the number of journal articles accepted for publication written by each clinical psychologist in the United States, divide by the number of psychologists, and arrive at the arithmetic mean. This calculation would yield an indication of the average number of journal articles published. Whatever that number would be, we can say with certainty that it would be more than the mode. It is well known that most clinical psychologists do not write journal articles. The mode for publications by clinical psychologists in any given year is zero. In this example, the arithmetic mean would provide us with a precise measure of the average number of articles published by clinicians. What might be lost in that measure of central tendency, however, is the fact

JUST THINK . . .

Devise your own example to illustrate how the mode, and not the mean, can be the most useful measure of central tendency.

that, proportionately, very few of all clinicians do most of the publishing. The mode (in this case, a mode of zero) would provide us with a great deal of information at a glance. It would tell us that regardless of the mean, most clinicians do not publish.

Because the mode is not calculated in a true sense, it is a nominal statistic and cannot legitimately be used in further calculations. The median is a statistic that takes into account the order of scores and is itself ordinal in nature. The mean, an interval level statistic, is the most stable and useful (in most cases) measure of central tendency.

Measures of Variability

Variability is an indication of how scores in a distribution are scattered or dispersed. As Figure 3–4 illustrates, two or more distributions of test scores can have the same mean, though differences in the scatter or dispersion of scores around the mean can be wide. In both distributions A and B, test scores could range from 0 to 100. In distribution A, we see that the mean score was 50 and the remaining scores were widely distributed

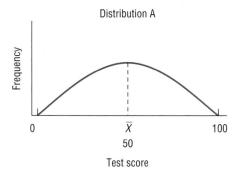
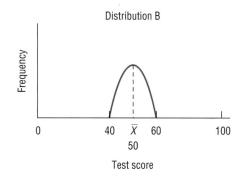

Figure 3–4
Two Distributions with Differences in Variability

around the mean. In distribution B, the mean was also 50, though few if any people scored higher than 60 or lower than 40.

Measures of variability—statistics that describe the amount of variation in a distribution—include the range, the interquartile range, the semi-interquartile range, the average deviation, the standard deviation, and the variance.

The range The **range** of a distribution is equal to the difference between the highest and the lowest scores. We could describe distribution B of Figure 3–3, for example, as having a range of 20 if we knew that the highest score in this distribution was 60 and the lowest score was 40 (60 − 40 = 20). With respect to distribution A, if we knew that the lowest score was 0 and the highest score was 100, the range would be equal to 100 − 0, or 100. The range is the simplest measure of variability to calculate, but its potential use is limited. Because the range is based entirely on the value of the two extreme scores, one extreme score can radically alter the value of the range. For example, suppose that there was one score in distribution B equal to 90. The range of this distribution would now be equal to 90 − 40, or 50. Yet, in looking at the data in the graph for distribution B, it is clear that the vast majority of scores tend to be between 40 and 60.

JUST THINK . . .

Devise two distributions of test scores to illustrate how the range can overstate or understate the degree of variability in the scores.

As a descriptive statistic of variation, the range provides a quick but gross description of the spread of scores. When its value is based on extreme scores in a distribution, the resulting description of variation may be understated or overstated. Better measures of variation include the interquartile range and the semi-interquartile range.

The interquartile and semi-interquartile ranges A distribution of test scores (or any other data for that matter) can be divided into four parts such that 25% of the test scores occur in each quarter. As illustrated in Figure 3–5, the dividing points between the four quarters in the distribution are the **quartiles.** There are three of them, respectively labeled "Q_1," "Q_2," and "Q_3." Note that *quartile* refers to a specific point, whereas *quarter* refers to an interval. An individual score may, for example, fall *at* the third quartile or *in* the third quarter (but *not* "in" the third quartile or "at" the third quarter). It should not come as a surprise to you that Q_2 and the median are exactly the same. And just as the median is the midpoint in a distribution of scores, so quartiles Q_1 and Q_3 are *quarter-points* in a distribution of scores. Formulas may be employed to determine the exact value of these points.

The **interquartile range** is a measure of variability equal to the difference between Q_3 and Q_1. Like the median, it is an ordinal statistic. A related measure of variability is the **semi-interquartile range,** which is equal to the interquartile range divided by two. Knowledge of the relative distances of Q_1 and Q_3 from Q_2 (the median) provides the seasoned test interpreter with immediate information as to the shape of the distribution of scores. In a perfectly symmetrical distribution, Q_1 and Q_3 will be exactly the same distance from the median. If these distances are unequal, there will be a lack of symmetry. This lack of symmetry is referred to as *skewness,* and we will have more to say about that shortly.

The average deviation Another tool that could be used to describe the amount of variability in a distribution is the **average deviation,** or *AD* for short. Its formula is

$$AD = \frac{\Sigma |x|}{n}$$

The lowercase italic x in the formula signifies a score's deviation from the mean. The value of x is obtained by subtracting the mean from the score (X − mean = x). The bars

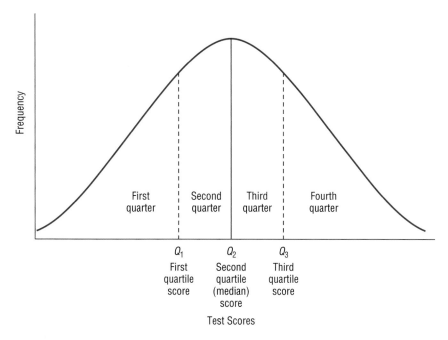

Figure 3–5
A Quartered Distribution

on each side of x indicate that it is the absolute value of the deviation score (ignoring the positive or negative sign and treating all deviation scores as positive). All the deviation scores are then summed and divided by the total number of scores (n) to arrive at the average deviation. As an exercise, calculate the average deviation for the following distribution of test scores:

$$85 \quad 100 \quad 90 \quad 95 \quad 80$$

Begin by calculating the arithmetic mean. Next, obtain the absolute value of each of the five deviation scores and sum them. As you sum them, note what would happen if you did not ignore algebraic signs: all the deviation scores would sum to 0. Divide the sum of the deviation scores by the number of measurements (5). Did you obtain an AD of 6? The AD tells us that the five scores in this distribution varied, on average, 6 points from the mean.

The average deviation is rarely used. Perhaps this is so because the deletion of algebraic signs renders it a useless measure for purposes of any further operations. Why then discuss it here? A clear understanding of what an average deviation measures provides a solid foundation for understanding the conceptual basis of another, more widely used measure, the *standard deviation*. Keeping in mind what an average deviation is, what it tells us, and how it is derived, let's consider the average deviation's much more widely used "cousin," the standard deviation.

The standard deviation Recall that in calculating the average deviation, the problem of the sum of all deviation scores around the mean equaling zero was solved by employing only the absolute value of the deviation scores. In calculating the standard deviation, the same problem needs to be dealt with. Here it is dealt with in a different way. Instead of using the absolute value of each of the deviation scores, each score is squared. With each score squared, the sign of the negative deviations becomes positive. Because all the deviation scores are squared, we know that before we are finished with our calculations, we must go back and obtain the square root of whatever number we reach.

We may define the **standard deviation** as a measure of variability equal to the square root of the average squared deviations about the mean. More succinctly, it is equal to the square root of the *variance*. The **variance** is equal to the arithmetic mean of the squares of the differences between the scores in a distribution and their mean. The formula used to calculate the variance (s^2) using deviation scores is

$$s^2 = \frac{\Sigma\, x^2}{n}$$

Simply stated, the variance is calculated by squaring and summing all the deviation scores and dividing by the total number of scores. The variance can also be calculated in other ways. For example, from raw scores, first calculate the summation of the raw scores squared, divide by the number of scores, and then subtract the mean squared:

$$s^2 = \frac{\Sigma\, X^2}{n} - \overline{X}^2$$

The variance is a widely used measure in psychological research. To make meaningful interpretations, the test-score distribution should be approximately normal. We'll have more to say about "normal" distributions later in this chapter. At this point, think of it as a distribution with the greatest frequency of scores occurring near the arithmetic mean. Correspondingly fewer and fewer scores relative to the mean occur on both sides of it.

For some hands-on experience with—as well as a sense of mastery of—the concepts of variance and standard deviation, why not allot the next 10 or 15 minutes to calculating the standard deviation for the test scores originally contained in Table 3–1? Use both formulas to verify that they produce the same results. Using deviation scores, your calculations should look similar to these:

$$s^2 = \frac{\Sigma\, x^2}{n}$$

$$s^2 = \frac{\Sigma\, (X - \text{mean})^2}{n}$$

$$s^2 = \frac{[(78 - 72.12)^2 + (67 - 72.12)^2 + \cdots (79 - 72.12)^2]}{25}$$

$$s^2 = \frac{4972.64}{25}$$

$$s^2 = 198.91$$

Using the raw-scores formula, your calculations should look similar to these:

$$s^2 = \frac{\Sigma\, X^2}{n} - \overline{X}^2$$

$$s^2 = \frac{[(78)^2 + (67)^2 + \cdots (79)^2]}{25} - 5201.29$$

$$s^2 = \frac{135005}{25} - 5201.29$$

$$s^2 = 5400.20 - 5201.29$$

$$s^2 = 198.91$$

In both cases, the standard deviation is the square root of the variance (s^2). According to our calculations, the standard deviation of the test scores is 14.10. If $s = 14.10$, 1 standard deviation unit is approximately equal to 14 units of measurement, or with reference to our example and rounded to a whole number, 14 test-score points. The test data did not provide a good normal curve approximation. Test professionals would describe these data as "positively skewed." *Skewness,* as well as related terms such as *negatively skewed* and *positively skewed* are covered in the next section. Once you are "positively familiar" with terms like *positively skewed,* you'll appreciate all the more the section later in this chapter entitled "The Area Under the Normal Curve." There you will find a wealth of information about test-score interpretation in the case when the scores are *not* skewed—that is, when the test scores are approximately normal in distribution.

The symbol for standard deviation has variously been represented as *s, S,* SD, and the lowercase Greek letter sigma (σ). One custom (the one we adhere to) has it that *s* refers to the sample standard deviation and σ refers to the population standard deviation. The number of observations in the sample is *n,* and the denominator $n - 1$ is sometimes used to calculate what is referred to as an "unbiased estimate" of the population value—it's actually only *less* biased (see Hopkins & Glass, 1978). Unless *n* is 10 or less, the use of *n* or $n - 1$ tends not to make a meaningful difference.

Whether the denominator is more properly *n* or $n - 1$ has been a matter of debate. Lindgren (1983) has argued for the use of $n - 1$, in part because this denominator tends to make correlation formulas simpler. By contrast, most texts recommend the use of $n - 1$ only when the data constitute a sample; when the data constitute a population, *n* is preferable. For Lindgren (1983), it matters not whether the data are from a sample or a population. Perhaps the most reasonable convention is to use *n* either when the entire population has been assessed or when no inferences to the population are intended. So, when considering the examination scores of one class of students—including all the people about whom we're going to make inferences—it seems appropriate to use *n*.

Having cleared the air (we hope) with regard to the *n* versus $n - 1$ controversy, our formula for the population standard deviation follows below. In this formula, $\overline{X}$ represents a sample mean and *M* (mu) a population mean:

$$\sigma = \sqrt{\frac{\Sigma (X - M)^2}{n}}$$

The standard deviation is a very useful measure of variation, since each individual score's distance from the mean of the distribution is employed in its computation. You will come across it frequently in the study of measurement.

Skewness

Distributions can be characterized by their **skewness,** or the nature and extent to which symmetry is absent. Skewness is an indication of how the measurements in a distribution are distributed. A distribution has a **positive skew** when relatively few of the scores fall at the high end of the distribution. Positively skewed examination results may indicate that the test was too difficult. More items that were easier would have been desirable, to discriminate better at the lower end of the distribution of test scores. A distribution has a **negative skew** when relatively few of the scores fall at the low end of the distribution. Negatively skewed examination results may indicate that the test was too easy. In such an instance, more items of a higher level of difficulty would have been desirable to better discriminate between scores at the upper end of the distribution. (Turn back to Figure 3–3 for graphic examples of skewed distributions.)

The term *skewed* carries with it negative implications for many students. We suspect that *skewed* is associated with *abnormal,* perhaps because the skewed distribution deviates from the symmetrical or so-called normal distribution. However, the presence or absence of symmetry in a distribution (skewness) is simply one characteristic by which a distribution can be described. In and of itself, skewness is not inherently good or bad, normal or abnormal. Consider in this context a hypothetical Marine Corps Ability and Endurance Screening Test administered to all civilians seeking to enlist to become United States Marines. Now look again at the graphs in Figure 3–3. Which graph do you think would best describe the resulting distribution of test scores? No peeking at the next paragraph before you respond.

No one can say with certainty, but if we had to guess, we would say that the Marine Corps Ability and Endurance Screening Test data would look like graph C, the positively skewed distribution in Figure 3–3. We say this assuming that a level of difficulty would have been built into the test to ensure that relatively few assessees would score at the high end of the distribution. Most of the applicants would probably score at the low end of the distribution. All of this is quite consistent with the advertised objective of the Marines. According to their advertising, they are not looking for a lot of good men. Rather, they are only looking for a *few* good men. Now, a question regarding this positively skewed distribution: Is the skewness a good thing? A bad thing? An abnormal thing? In truth, it is probably none of these things—it just *is*. By the way, they don't advertise this fact, but the Marines are also looking for (an unknown quantity of) good women. But here we are straying a bit too far from skewness.

Various formulas exist for measuring skewness. One way of gauging the skewness of a distribution is through examination of the relative distances of quartiles from the median. In a positively skewed distribution, $Q_3 - Q_2$ will be greater than the distance of $Q_2 - Q_1$. In a negatively skewed distribution, $Q_3 - Q_2$ will be less than the distance of $Q_2 - Q_1$. In a distribution that is symmetrical, the distances from Q_1 and Q_3 to the median are the same.

Kurtosis

The term testing professionals use to refer to the steepness of a distribution in its center is **kurtosis.** To the root *kurtic* is added one of the prefixes *platy-*, *lepto-*, or *meso-* to describe the peakedness/flatness of three general types of curves (Figure 3–6). Distributions are generally described as **platykurtic** (relatively flat), **leptokurtic** (relatively

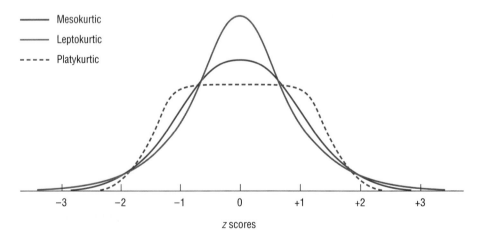

Figure 3–6
The Kurtosis of Curves

peaked), or—somewhere in the middle—**mesokurtic.** Many methods exist for measuring kurtosis. Some computer programs feature an index of skewness that ranges from −3.00 to +3.00. In many ways, however, technical matters related to the measurement and interpretation of kurtosis are controversial among measurement specialists. So let's move on to a discussion of a distribution that happens to be the standard against which all other distributions, including all of the kurtic ones, are compared: the normal distribution.

JUST THINK . . .

Like skewness, reference to the kurtosis of a distribution can provide a kind of "shorthand" description of a distribution of test scores. Imagine and describe the kind of test that might yield a distribution of scores that form a platykurtic curve.

The Normal Curve

Before delving into the statistical, a little bit of the historical is in order. Development of the concept of a normal curve began in the middle of the eighteenth century with the work of Abraham DeMoivre and, later, the Marquis de Laplace. At the beginning of the nineteenth century, Karl Friedrich Gauss made some substantial contributions. Through the early nineteenth century, scientists referred to it as the "Laplace-Gaussian curve." Karl Pearson is credited with being the first to refer to the curve as the *normal curve,* perhaps in an effort to be diplomatic to all of the people who helped develop it. Somehow, the term *normal curve* stuck—but don't be surprised if you're sitting at some scientific meeting one day and you hear this distribution or curve referred to as *Gaussian.*

Theoretically, the **normal curve** is a bell-shaped, smooth, mathematically defined curve that is highest at its center. From the center it tapers on both sides approaching the X-axis *asymptotically* (meaning that it approaches, but never touches, the axis). In theory, the distribution of the normal curve ranges from negative infinity to positive infinity. The curve is perfectly symmetrical, with no skewness. If you folded it in half at the mean, one side would lie exactly on top of the other. Because it is symmetrical, the mean, the median, and the mode all have the same exact value.

Why is the normal curve important in understanding the characteristics of psychological tests? Our *Close-up* provides some answers.

The Area Under the Normal Curve

The normal curve can be conveniently divided into areas defined in standard deviation units. A hypothetical distribution of National Spelling Test scores with a mean of 50 and a standard deviation of 15 is illustrated in Figure 3–7. In this example, a score equal to 1 standard deviation above the mean would be equal to 65 ($\overline{X} + 1s = 50 + 15 = 65$).

Before reading on, take a minute or two to calculate what a score exactly at 3 standard deviations below the mean would be equal to. How about a score exactly at 3 standard deviations above the mean? Were your answers 5 and 95, respectively? The graph tells us that 99.74% of all scores in these normally distributed spelling test data lie between ±3 standard deviations. Stated another way, 99.74% of all spelling test scores lie between 5 and 95. This graph also illustrates other characteristics of all normal distributions:

- 50% of the scores occur above the mean, and 50% of the scores occur below the mean.

- Approximately 34% of all scores occur between the mean and 1 standard deviation above the mean.

The Normal Curve and Psychological Tests

Scores on many psychological tests are often approximately normally distributed, particularly when the tests are administered to large numbers of subjects. Few if any psychological tests yield precisely normal distributions of test scores (Micceri, 1989). As a general rule, with ample exceptions, the larger the sample size and the wider the range of abilities measured by a particular test, the more the graph of the test scores will approximate the normal curve. A classic illustration of this was provided by E. L. Thorndike and his colleagues (1927). They compiled intelligence test scores from several large samples of students. As you can see in Figure 1, the distribution of scores closely approximated the normal curve.

Following is a sample of more varied examples of the wide range of characteristics that psychologists have found to be approximately normal in distribution:

- The strength of handedness in right-handed individuals, as measured by the Waterloo Handedness Questionnaire (Tan, 1993).

- Scores on the Women's Health Questionnaire, a scale measuring a variety of health problems in women across a wide age range (Hunter, 1992).

- Responses of both college students and working adults to a measure of intrinsic and extrinsic work motivation (Amabile et al., 1994).

- The intelligence scale scores of girls and women with eating disorders, as measured by the Wechsler Adult Intelligence Scale-Revised and the Wechsler Intelligence Scale for Children-Revised (Ranseen & Humphries, 1992).

- The intellectual functioning of children and adolescents with cystic fibrosis (Thompson et al., 1992).

- Decline in cognitive abilities over a one-year period in people with Alzheimer's disease (Burns et al., 1991).

- The rate of motor-skill development in developmentally delayed preschoolers, as measured by the Vineland Adaptive Behavior Scale (Davies & Gavin, 1994).

- Scores on the Swedish translation of the Positive and Negative Syndrome Scale, which assesses the presence of positive and negative symptoms in people with schizophrenia (von Knorring & Lindstrom, 1992).

- The scores of psychiatrists on the Scale for Treatment Integration of the Dually Diagnosed (people with both a drug problem and another mental disorder). The scale examines opinions about drug treatment for this group of patients (Adelman et al., 1991).

- Responses to the Tridimensional Personality Questionnaire, a measure of three distinct personality features (Cloninger et al., 1991).

- Scores on a self-esteem measure among undergraduates (Addeo et al., 1994).

In each case, the researchers made a special point of stating that the scale under investigation yielded something close to a normal distribution of scores. Why? One benefit of a normal distribution of scores is that it simplifies the interpretation of individual scores on the test. In a normal distribution, the mean, the median, and the mode take on the same value. For example, if we know that the average score for intellectual ability of children with cystic fibrosis is a particular value, and that the scores are normally distributed, we know quite a bit more. We know that the average is the most com-

- Approximately 34% of all scores occur between the mean and 1 standard deviation below the mean.

- Approximately 68% of all scores occur between the mean and ±1 standard deviation.

- Approximately 95% of all scores occur between the mean and ±2 standard deviations.

A normal curve has two *tails*. The area on the normal curve between 2 and 3 standard deviations above the mean is referred to as a **tail.** The area between −2 and −3 standard deviations below the mean is also referred to as a tail. Let's digress here mo-

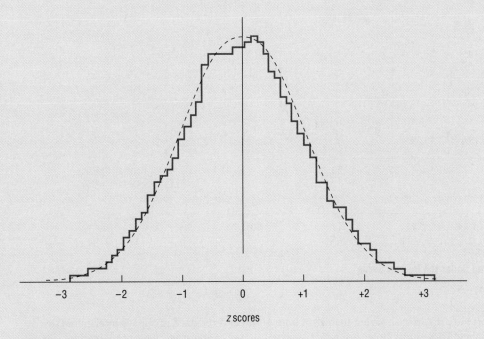

z scores

Figure 1
Graphic Representation of Thorndike et al. Data

mon score and the score below and above which half of all the scores fall. Knowing the mean and the standard deviation of a scale and that it is approximately normally distributed tells us that approximately two-thirds of all testtakers' scores are within a standard deviation of the mean. Approxi-mately 95% of the scores fall within 2 standard deviations of the mean.

The characteristics of the normal curve provide a ready model for score interpretation that can be applied to a wide range of test results.

mentarily for a "real-life" tale of the tails to consider along with our rather abstract discussion of statistical concepts.

As observed in a thought-provoking article entitled "Two Tails of the Normal Curve," an intelligence test score that falls within the limits of either tail can have momentous consequences in terms of the tale of one's life:

> Individuals who are mentally retarded or gifted share the burden of deviance from the norm, in both a developmental and a statistical sense. In terms of mental ability as operationalized by tests of intelligence, performance that is approximately two standard deviations from the mean (i.e., IQ of 70–75 or lower or IQ of 125–130 or higher) is one key element in identification. Success at life's tasks, or its absence, also plays a defining role,

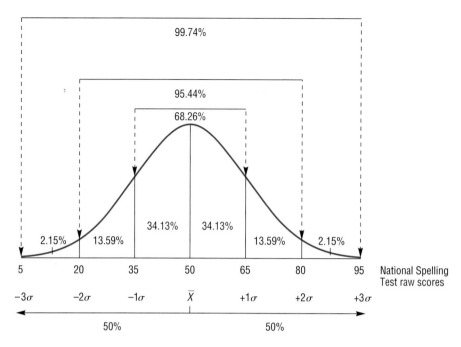

Figure 3–7
The Area Under the Normal Curve

but the primary classifying feature of both gifted and retarded groups is intellectual deviance. These individuals are out of sync with more average people, simply by their difference from what is expected for their age and circumstance. This asynchrony results in highly significant consequences for them and for those who share their lives. None of the familiar norms apply, and substantial adjustments are needed in parental expectations, educational settings, and social and leisure activities. (Robinson et al., 2000, p. 1413)

As illustrated by Robinson et al. (quite dramatically, we think), knowledge of the areas under the normal curve can be quite useful to the interpreter of test data. This knowledge can tell us not only something about where the score falls among a distribution of scores, but something about a *person,* maybe even something about the people who share that person's life. This knowledge might also convey something about how impressive, average, or lackluster the individual is with respect to a particular discipline or ability. For example, consider a high school student whose score on a national, well-reputed spelling test is close to 3 standard deviations above the mean. It's a good bet that the student would know how to spell words like *asymptotic* and *leptokurtic.*

Just as knowledge of the areas under the normal curve can instantly convey useful information about a test score in relation to other test scores, so can knowledge of standard scores.

Standard Scores

Simply stated, a **standard score** is a raw score that has been converted from one scale to another scale, the latter scale having some arbitrarily set mean and standard deviation. Why convert raw scores to standard scores?

Raw scores may be converted to standard scores because standard scores are more readily interpretable than raw scores. With a standard score, the position of a testtaker's performance relative to other testtakers is readily apparent.

Different systems for standard scores exist, each unique as regards its respective mean and standard deviations. We will briefly describe z scores, T scores, stanines, and some other standard scores. First for consideration is the type of standard score scale that may be thought of as the *zero plus or minus one scale.* This is so because it has a mean set at zero and a standard deviation set at one. Raw scores converted into standard scores on the *zero plus or minus one scale* are more popularly referred to as z scores.

z *Scores*

A **z score** results from the conversion of a raw score into a number indicating how many standard deviation units the raw score is below or above the mean of the distribution. Let's use an example from the normally distributed "National Spelling Test" data in Figure 3–7 to demonstrate how a raw score is converted to a z score. Let's convert a raw score of 65 to a z score. To do so, we use the following formula:

$$z = \frac{X - \overline{X}}{s} = \frac{65 - 50}{15} = \frac{15}{15} = 1$$

In essense, a z score is equal to the difference between a particular raw score and the mean divided by the standard deviation. In the example above, a raw score of 65 was found to be equal to a z score of +1. Knowing that someone obtained a z score of 1 on a spelling test provides context and meaning for the score. Drawing on our knowledge of areas under the normal curve, for example, we would know that only about 16% of the other testtakers obtained higher scores. By contrast, knowing simply that someone obtained a raw score of 65 on a spelling test conveys virtually no usable information, because information about the context of this score is lacking.

In addition to providing a convenient context for comparing scores on the same test, standard scores provide a convenient context for comparing scores on different tests. As an example, consider that Crystal's raw score on the hypothetical Main Street Reading Test was 24 and that her raw score on the (equally hypothetical) Main Street Arithmetic Test was 42. Without knowing anything other than these raw scores, one might conclude that Crystal did better on the arithmetic test as compared to the reading test. More informative than the two raw scores would be the two z scores.

Converting Crystal's raw scores to z scores based on the performance of other students in her class, suppose we find that her z score on the reading test was 1.32 and her z score on the arithmetic test was −0.75. Thus, although her raw score in arithmetic was higher than in reading, the z scores paint a different picture. The z scores tell us that relative to the other students in her class (and assuming that the distribution of scores is relatively normal), Crystal performed above average on the reading test and below average on the arithmetic test. An interpretation of exactly how much better she performed could be obtained by reference to tables detailing distances under the normal curve as well as the resulting percentage of cases that could be expected to fall above or below a particular standard deviation point (or z score).

T *Scores*

If the scale used in the computation of z scores is called a *zero plus or minus one scale,* then the scale used in the computation of **T scores** is called a *fifty plus or minus ten scale;* that is, a scale with a mean set at 50 and a standard deviation set at 10. Devised by W. A.

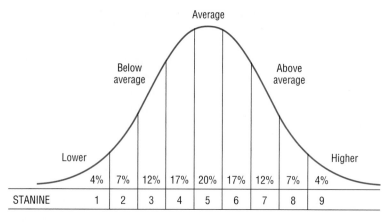

Figure 3–8
Stanines and the Normal Curve

McCall (1922, 1939) and named a *T* score in honor of his professor E. L. Thorndike, this standard score system is composed of a scale that ranges from 5 standard deviations below the mean to 5 standard deviations above the mean. Thus, for example, a raw score that fell exactly at 5 standard deviations below the mean would be equal to a *T* score of 0, a raw score that fell at the mean would be equal to a *T* of 50, and a raw score 5 standard deviations above the mean would be equal to a *T* of 100. An advantage in using *T* scores is that none of the scores is negative. By contrast, in a *z* score distribution, scores can be positive and negative, making further computation cumbersome in some instances.

Other Standard Scores

Numerous other standard scoring systems exist. Researchers during World War II developed a standard score with a mean of 5 and a standard deviation of approximately 2. Divided into nine units, the scale was christened a **stanine**, deriving from a contraction of the words *standard* and *nine.*

Stanine scoring may be familiar to many students from achievement tests administered in elementary and secondary school, where test scores are often represented as stanines. Stanines are different from other standard scores in that they take on whole values from 1 to 9, which represent a range of performance that is ½ standard deviation in width (Figure 3–8.) The 5th stanine indicates performance in the average range, from ¼ standard deviation below the mean to ¼ standard deviation above the mean, capturing the middle 20% of the scores in a normal distribution. The 4th and 6th stanines are also ½ standard deviation wide and capture the 17% of cases below and above the 5th stanine respectively.

Another type of standard score is employed on tests such as the Scholastic Aptitude Test (SAT) and the Graduate Record Examination (GRE). Raw scores on those tests are converted to standard scores such that the resulting distribution has a mean of 500 and a standard deviation of 100. If the letter *A* is used to represent a standard score from a college or graduate school admissions test whose distribution has a mean of 500 and a standard deviation of 100, then the following is true:

$$(A = 600) = (z = 1) = (T = 60)$$

Have you ever heard the term *IQ* used as a synonym for one's score on an intelligence test? Of course you have. What you may not know is that what is referred to var-

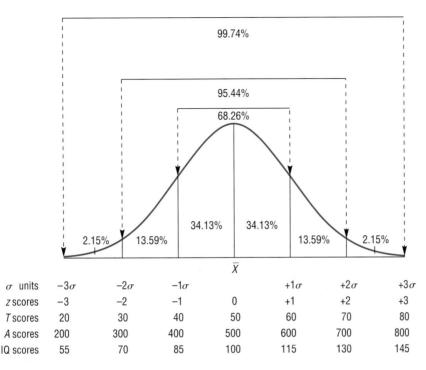

σ units	-3σ	-2σ	-1σ		$+1\sigma$	$+2\sigma$	$+3\sigma$
z scores	-3	-2	-1	0	$+1$	$+2$	$+3$
T scores	20	30	40	50	60	70	80
A scores	200	300	400	500	600	700	800
IQ scores	55	70	85	100	115	130	145

Figure 3–9
Some Standard Score Equivalents

Note that the values presented here for the IQ scores assume that the intelligence test scores have a mean of 100 and a standard deviation of 15. This is true for many but not all intelligence tests. If a particular test of intelligence yielded scores with a mean other than 100 and/or a standard deviation other than 15, the values shown for IQ scores would have to be adjusted accordingly.

iously as IQ, deviation IQ, or deviation intelligence quotient is yet another kind of standard score. For most IQ tests, the distribution of raw scores is converted to IQ scores, whose distribution typically has a mean set at 100 and a standard deviation set at 15. Let's emphasize *typically* because there is some variation in standard scoring systems depending on the test used. The typical mean and standard deviation for IQ tests results in approximately 95% of deviation IQs ranging from 70 to 130. That's 2 standard deviations below and above the mean, respectively. In the context of a normal distribution, the relationship of deviation IQ scores to the other standard scores we have discussed so far (*z*, *T*, and *A* scores) is illustrated in Figure 3–9.

Standard scores converted from raw scores may involve either linear or nonlinear transformations. A standard score obtained by a **linear transformation** is one that retains a direct numerical relationship to the original raw score. The magnitude of differences between such standard scores exactly parallels the differences between corresponding raw scores. Sometimes scores may undergo more than one transformation. For example, the creators of the SAT did a second linear transformation on their data to convert *z* scores into a new scale that has a mean of 500 and a standard deviation of 100.

A **nonlinear transformation** may be required when the data under consideration are not normally distributed and comparisons with normal distributions need to be made. In a nonlinear transformation, the resulting standard score does not necessarily have a direct numerical relationship to the original, raw score. As the result of a nonlinear transformation, the original distribution is said to have been *normalized*.

Normalized standard scores   Many test developers hope that the test they are working on will yield a normal distribution of scores. Yet even after very large samples have been tested with the instrument under development, skewed distributions result. What should be done?

One alternative available to the test developer is to normalize the distribution. Conceptually, **normalizing a distribution** involves "stretching" the skewed curve into a shape of a normal curve and creating a corresponding scale of standard scores—a scale that is technically referred to as a **normalized standard score scale.**

Normalization of a skewed distribution of scores may also be desirable for purposes of comparability. One of the primary advantages of a standard score on one test is that it can readily be compared with a standard score on another test. However, such comparisons are appropriate only when the distributions from which they derived are the same. In most instances, they are the same because the two distributions are approximately normal. But if, for example, distribution A was normal and distribution B was highly skewed, z scores in these respective distributions would represent different amounts of area subsumed under the curve. A z score of -1 with respect to normally distributed data tells us, among other things, that about 84% of the scores in this distribution were higher than this score. A z score of -1 with respect to data that were very positively skewed might mean, for example, that only 62% of the scores were higher.

For test developers intent on creating tests that yield normally distributed measurements, it is generally preferable to fine-tune the test according to difficulty or other relevant variables so that the resulting distribution will approximate the normal curve. That usually is a better bet than attempting to normalize skewed distributions. This is so because there are technical cautions to be observed before attempting normalization. For example, transformations should be made only when there is good reason to believe that the test sample was large and representative enough and that the failure to obtain normally distributed scores was due to the measuring instrument.

Speaking of transformations, it's about time to make one to Chapter 4. It may be helpful at this time to review this statistics refresher to make certain that you indeed feel "refreshed" and ready to continue. We will build on your knowledge of basic statistical principles in the chapters to come, and it is important to build on a rock-solid foundation.

◆

JUST THINK . . .

Apply what you have learned about frequency distributions, graphing frequency distributions, measures of central tendency, measures of variability, and the normal curve and standard scores to the question of the data listed in Table 3–1. How would you communicate the data from Table 3–1 to the class? Which type of frequency distribution might you use? Which type of graph? Which measure of central tendency? Which measure of variability? Might reference to a normal curve or to standard scores be helpful? Why or why not?

Self-Assessment

Test your understanding of elements of this chapter by seeing if you can explain each of the following terms, expressions, and abbreviations:

arithmetic mean	error	interquartile range
average deviation	frequency distribution	interval scale
bar graph	frequency polygon	kurtosis
bimodal distribution	graph	leptokurtic
distribution	grouped frequency distribution	linear transformation
dynamometer	histogram	mean

measure of central tendency
measure of variability
measurement
median
mesokurtic
mode
negative skew
nominal scale
nonlinear transformation
normal curve

normalized standard score scale
ordinal scale
platykurtic
positive skew
quartile
range
ratio scale
raw score
scale
semi-interquartile range

skewness
standard deviation
standard score
stanine
tail
T score
variability
variance
z score

Web Watch

Check out the following Web sites for more information about topics discussed in this chapter.

Statistics review
www.statsoftinc.com/textbook/stathome.html

Measures of central tendency
http://simon.cs.vt.edu/SoSci/Site/MMM/mmm.html

http://davidmlane.com/hyperstat/A5185.html

Normal distribution
http://davidmlane.com/hyperstat/normal_distribution.html

Bar graphs, histograms, and charts
www.visualmining.com/examples/styles

"Real-life" statistics
www.fedstats.gov/qf/states/17000.html

4

Of Tests and Testing

Is this person competent to stand trial?

Who should be hired, transferred, promoted, or fired?

Who should gain entry to this special program or be awarded a scholarship?

Which parent shall have custody of the children?

Every day, throughout the world, critically important questions like these are addressed through the use of tests. The answers to these kinds of questions are likely to have a significant impact on many lives.

> **JUST THINK . . .**
>
> What's a "good test"? Outline some elements or features that you believe are essential to a good test before reading on.

If they are to sleep comfortably at night, assessment professionals must have confidence in the tests and other tools of assessment they employ. They need to know, for example, what does and does not constitute a "good test."

Our objective in this chapter is to overview the elements of a good test. As background, we begin by listing some basic assumptions about assessment. Aspects of these fundamental assumptions will be elaborated later in this chapter as well as in subsequent chapters.

Some Assumptions About Psychological Testing and Assessment

Assumption 1: Psychological Traits and States Exist

A **trait** has been defined as "any distinguishable, relatively enduring way in which one individual varies from another" (Guilford, 1959, p. 6). **States** also distinguish one person from another but are relatively less enduring (Chaplin et al., 1988). The trait term that an observer applies, as well as the strength or magnitude of the trait presumed to be present, is based on observing a sample of behavior. Samples of behavior may be obtained in a number of ways, ranging from direct observation to the analysis of self-report statements or pencil-and-paper test answers.

The term *psychological trait*, much like the term *trait* alone, covers a very wide range of possible characteristics. Thousands of psychological trait terms can be found in the English language (Allport & Odbert, 1936). Among them are psychological traits that re-

Figure 4–1
Measuring Sensation Seeking

The psychological trait of sensation seeking *has been defined as "the need for varied, novel, and complex sensations and experiences and the willingness to take physical and social risks for the sake of such experiences" (Zuckerman, 1979, p. 10). A 22-item Sensation-Seeking Scale (SSS) seeks to identify people who are high or low on this trait. Assuming the SSS actually measures what it purports to measure, how would you expect a random sample of people lining up to bungee jump to score on the test, as compared with another age-matched sample of people shopping at the local mall? What are the comparative advantages of using paper-and-pencil measures, such as the SSS, and using more performance-based measures, such as the one pictured here?*

late to intelligence, specific intellectual abilities, cognitive style, adjustment, interests, attitudes, sexual orientation and preferences, psychopathology, personality in general, and specific personality traits. New concepts or discoveries in research may bring new trait terms to the fore. For example, a trait term seen with increasing frequency in the professional literature on human sexuality is *androgynous* (referring to an absence of primacy of male or female characteristics). Cultural evolution may bring new trait terms into common usage, as it did in the 1960s when people began speaking of the degree to which women were *liberated* (or freed from the constraints of gender-dependent social expectations). A more recent example is the trait term *New Age*, used in the popular culture to refer to a particular nonmainstream orientation to spirituality and health.

Few people deny that psychological traits exist. Yet there has been a fair amount of controversy regarding just *how* they exist. For example, do traits have a physical existence, perhaps as a circuit in the brain? Although some have argued in favor of such a conception of psychological traits (Allport, 1937; Holt, 1971), compelling evidence to support such a view has been difficult to obtain. For our purposes, a psychological trait exists only as a **construct**—an informed, scientific concept developed or *constructed* to describe or explain behavior. We can't see, hear, or touch constructs, but we can infer their existence from *overt behavior*. In this context, **overt behavior** refers to an observable action or the product of an observable action, including test- or assessment-related responses. A challenge facing test developers is to construct tests that are at least as telling as observable behavior like that illustrated in Figure 4–1.

The phrase *relatively enduring* in our definition of *trait* is a reminder that a trait is not expected to be manifested in behavior 100% of the time. Thus, it is important to be aware of the context or situation in which a particular behavior is displayed. Whether a trait manifests itself in observable behavior, and to what degree it manifests, is presumed to depend not only on the strength of the trait in the individual but also on the nature of the situation. Stated another way, exactly how a particular trait manifests itself is, at least to some extent, situation dependent. For example, a violent parolee may be prone to behave in a rather subdued way with her parole officer and much more violently in the presence of her family and friends. John may be viewed as dull and cheap by his wife but charming and extravagant by his business associates, whom he keenly wants to impress.

The context within which behavior occurs also plays a role in helping us select appropriate trait terms for observed behavior. Consider how we might label the behavior of someone who is kneeling and talking to God. Such behavior might be viewed as either religious or deviant, depending on the context in which it occurs. A person who is kneeling and talking to God inside a church or upon a prayer rug may be described as *religious,* whereas another person engaged in the exact same behavior in a public restroom might be viewed as deviant or *paranoid.*

JUST THINK . . .

Give another example of how the same behavior in two different contexts may be viewed in terms of two different traits.

The definitions of *trait* and *state* we are using also refer to *a way in which one individual varies from another.* The attribution of a trait or state term is a relative phenomenon. For example, in describing one person as *shy,* or even in using terms such as *very shy* or *not shy,* most people are making an unstated comparison with the degree of shyness they could reasonably expect the average person to emit under the same or similar circumstances. In psychological assessment, assessors may also make such comparisons with respect to the hypothetical average person. Alternatively, assessors may make comparisons among people who, because of their membership in some group or for any number of other reasons, are decidedly not average.

JUST THINK . . .

Is the strength of a particular psychological trait the same across all situations or environments? What are the implications of one's answer to this question for assessment?

As you might expect, the reference group with which comparisons are made can greatly influence one's conclusions or judgments. For example, suppose a psychologist administers a test of shyness to a 22-year-old male who earns his living as an exotic dancer. The interpretation of the test data will almost surely differ as a function of the reference group with which the testtaker is compared; that is, other males in his age group, or other male exotic dancers in his age group.

Assumption 2: Psychological Traits and States Can Be Quantified and Measured

Having acknowledged that psychological traits and states do exist, the specific traits and states to be measured and quantified first need to be carefully defined. Test developers and researchers, much like people in general, have many different ways of looking at and defining the same phenomenon. Just think, for example, of the different ways a term such as *aggressive* is used. We speak of an aggressive salesperson, an aggressive killer, and an aggressive dancer, to name but a few contexts. In each of these different contexts, *aggressive* carries with it a different meaning. If a personality test yields a score purporting to provide information about how aggressive a testtaker is, a first step in understanding the meaning of that score is understanding how *aggressive* was defined by the test developer. More specifically, what types of behaviors are presumed to be indicative of someone who is aggressive as defined by the test?

Once having defined the trait, state, or other construct to be measured, a test developer considers the types of item content that would provide insight into it. From a world of behaviors presumed to be indicative of the targeted trait, a test developer has a world of possible items that can be written to gauge the strength of that trait in testtakers.[1] For example, if the test developer deems knowledge of American history to be one component of adult intelligence, then the item *Who was the second president of the United States?* may appear on the test. Similarly, if social judgment is deemed to be indicative of adult intelligence, then it might be reasonable to include the item *Why should guns in the home always be inaccessible to children?*

Suppose we agree that an item tapping knowledge of American history and an item tapping social judgment are both appropriate for an adult intelligence test. Another question arises: Should both items be given equal weight? That is, should we place more importance on—and award more points for—an answer keyed "correct" to one or the other of these two items? Perhaps a correct response to the social judgment question should earn more credit than a correct response to the American history question. Weighting the comparative value of a test's items comes about as the result of a complex interplay among many factors, including technical considerations, the way a construct has been defined for the purposes of the test, and the value society attaches to the behaviors evaluated.

> **JUST THINK . . .**
>
> On an adult intelligence test, what type of item should be given the most weight? What type of item should be given the least weight?

Measuring traits and states by means of a test entails developing not only appropriate test items but also appropriate ways to score the test and interpret the results. For many varieties of psychological tests, some number representing the score on the test is derived from the examinee's responses. The test score is presumed to represent the strength of the targeted ability or trait or state and is frequently based on **cumulative scoring.**[2] Inherent in cumulative scoring is the assumption that the more the testtaker responds in a particular direction as keyed by the test manual as correct or consistent with a particular trait, the higher that testtaker is presumed to be on the targeted ability or trait. You were probably first introduced to cumulative scoring early in elementary school when you observed that your score on a weekly spelling test had everything to do with how many words you spelled correctly or incorrectly. The score reflected the extent to which you had successfully mastered the spelling assignment for the week. On the basis of that score, we might predict that you would spell those words correctly if called upon to do so. This brings us to our next assumption.

Assumption 3: Test-Related Behavior Predicts Non-Test-Related Behavior

Many tests involve tasks such as blackening little grids with a number two pencil or simply pressing keys on a computer keyboard. The objective of such tests typically has little to do with predicting future grid-blackening or key-pressing behavior. Rather, the objective of the test is typically to provide some indication of other aspects of the examinee's behavior. For example, patterns of answers to true/false questions on one widely used test of personality are used in decision making regarding mental disorders.

---

1. In the language of psychological testing and assessment, the word *domain* is substituted for *world* in this context. Assessment professionals speak, for example, of **domain sampling,** which may refer to either (1) a sample of behaviors from all possible behaviors that could conceivably be indicative of a particular construct, or (2) a sample of test items from all possible items that could conceivably be used to measure a particular construct.

2. Other models of scoring are discussed in Chapter 7.

The tasks in some tests mimic the actual behaviors that the test user is attempting to understand. By their nature, however, such tests yield only a sample of the behavior that can be expected to be emitted under nontest conditions. The obtained sample of behavior is typically used to make predictions about future behavior, such as work performance of a job applicant. In some forensic (legal) matters, psychological tests may be used not to predict behavior but to postdict it—that is, to aid in the understanding of behavior that has already taken place. For example, there may be a need to understand a criminal defendant's state of mind at the time of the commission of a crime. It is beyond the capability of any known testing or assessment procedure to reconstruct someone's state of mind. Still, behavior samples taken at one point may shed light, under certain circumstances, on someone's state of mind at some point in the past. Additionally, other tools of assessment, such as case history data or the defendant's personal diary during the period in question, might all be of great value in such an evaluation.

JUST THINK . . .

In practice, tests have proven to be better predictors of some types of behaviors as opposed to others. For examples, tests have *not* proven to be as good at predicting violence as had been hoped. Why do you think that might be the case?

Assumption 4: Tests and Other Measurement Techniques Have Strengths and Weaknesses

Competent test users understand a great deal about the tests they use. They understand, among other things, how a test was developed, the circumstances under which it is appropriate to administer the test, how the test should be administered and to whom, and how the test results should be interpreted. Competent test users understand and appreciate the limitations of the tests they use as well as how those limitations might be compensated for by data from other sources. All of this may sound quite commonsensical. It probably is. Yet this deceptively simple assumption—that test users know the tests they use and are aware of the tests' limitations—is emphasized repeatedly in the codes of ethics of associations of assessment professionals.

Assumption 5: Various Sources of Error Are Part of the Assessment Process

In everyday conversation, we use the word *error* to refer to mistakes, miscalculations, and the like. In the context of assessment, error need not refer to a deviation, an oversight, or something that otherwise violates expectations. To the contrary, *error* traditionally refers to something that is more than expected; it is actually a component of the measurement process. More specifically, *error* refers to a long-standing assumption that factors other than what a test attempts to measure will influence performance on the test. Test scores are always subject to questions about the degree to which the measurement process includes error. For example, an intelligence test score could be subject to debate concerning the degree to which the obtained score truly reflects the examinee's intelligence and the degree to which it was due to factors other than intelligence. Because error is a variable that must be taken account of in any assessment, we often speak of **error variance;** that is, the component of a test score attributable to sources other than the trait or ability measured.

There are many potential sources of error variance. Whether or not an assessee has the flu when taking a test is a source of error variance. In a more general sense, then, assessees themselves are sources of error variance. Assessors, too, are sources of error variance. For example, some assessors are more professional than others in the extent to which they follow the instructions governing how and under what conditions a test should be administered. In addition to assessors and assessees, measuring instruments themselves are another source of error variance. Some tests are simply better than others in measuring what they purport to measure.

Instructors who teach the undergraduate measurement course will occasionally hear a student refer to error as "creeping into" or "contaminating" the measurement process. Yet measurement professionals tend to view error as simply an element in the process of measurement, one for which any theory of measurement must surely account. In what is referred to as **classical** or **true score theory** of measurement, an assumption is made that each testtaker has a *true* score on a test that would be obtained but for the random action of measurement error.

Assumption 6: Testing and Assessment Can Be Conducted in a Fair and Unbiased Manner

If we had to pick the one of these seven assumptions that is more controversial than the remaining six, this one is it. Decades of court challenges to various tests and testing programs have sensitized test developers and users to the societal demand for fair tests used in a fair manner. Today, all major test publishers strive to develop instruments that are fair when used in strict accordance with guidelines in the test manual. One source of fairness-related problems is the test user who attempts to use a particular test with people whose background and experience are different from the background and experience of people for whom the test was intended. In such instances, it is useful to emphasize that tests are tools. And just like other, more familiar tools (hammers, ice picks, wrenches, and so on), they can be used properly or abused.

> **JUST THINK . . .**
> Do you believe that testing can be conducted in a fair and unbiased manner?

Some potential problems related to test fairness are more political than psychometric. For example, heated debate on selection, hiring, and access or denial of access to various opportunities often surrounds affirmative action programs. In many cases, the real question for debate is not, "Is this test or assessment procedure fair?" but rather, "What do we as a society wish to accomplish by the use of this test or assessment procedure?"

Assumption 7: Testing and Assessment Benefit Society

At first glance, the prospect of a world devoid of testing and assessment might seem very appealing, especially from the perspective of a harried student preparing for a week of midterm examinations. Yet a world without tests would most likely be more a nightmare than a dream. In such a world, people present themselves as surgeons, bridge builders, or airline pilots, regardless of their background, ability, or professional credentials. In a world without tests or other assessment procedures, personnel might be hired on the basis of nepotism rather than documented merit. In a world without tests, teachers and school administrators could arbitrarily place

> **JUST THINK . . .**
> How else might a world without tests or other assessment procedures be different from the world today?

children in different types of special classes simply because that is where they believed the children belonged. In a world without tests, there would be a great need for instruments to diagnose educational difficulties in reading and math and point the way to remediation. In a world without tests, there would be no instruments to diagnose and pinpoint for treatment areas of neuropsychological impairment. In a world without tests, there would be no practical way for the military to screen thousands of recruits with regard to many key variables.

Considering the many critical decisions that are based on testing and assessment procedures, we can readily appreciate the need for tests, especially good tests. And that, of course, raises one critically important question . . .

What's a "Good Test"?

Logically, the criteria for a good test would include clear instructions for administration, scoring, and interpretation. It would also seem to be a plus if a test offered economy in the time it takes to administer, score, and interpret it. Most of all, a good test would seem to be one that measures what it purports to measure.

Beyond simple logic, there are technical criteria that assessment professionals use to evaluate the quality of tests and other measurement procedures. Test users often speak of the *psychometric soundness* of tests, two key aspects of which are *reliability* and *validity*.

Reliability

A good test or, more generally, a good measuring tool or procedure, is *reliable*. As we will explain in Chapter 5, the criterion of reliability has to do with the *consistency* of the measuring tool: that is, the precision with which the test measures and the extent to which error is present in measurements. In theory, the perfectly reliable measuring tool consistently measures in the same way.

To exemplify reliability, visualize three digital scales labeled A, B, and C. To determine if they are reliable measuring tools, we will use a standard 1-pound gold bar that has been certified by experts to indeed weigh one pound and not a fraction of an ounce more or less. Now, let the testing begin.

Repeated weighings of the 1-pound bar on Scale A register a reading of 1 pound every time. No doubt about it, Scale A is a reliable tool of measurement. On to Scale B. Repeated weighings of the bar on Scale B yield a reading of 1.3 pounds. Is this scale reliable? It sure is! It may be consistently inaccurate by three-tenths of a pound, but there's no taking away the fact that it is reliable. Finally, Scale C. Repeated weighings of the bar on Scale C register a different weight every time. On one weighing, the gold bar weighs in at 1.7 pounds. On the next weighing, the weight registered is 0.9 pound. In short, the weights registered are all over the map. Is this scale reliable? Hardly. This scale is neither reliable nor accurate. Contrast it to Scale B, which was also inaccurate. Although inaccurate, Scale B was very consistent in terms of how much the registered weight deviated from the true weight. By contrast, the weight registered by Scale C deviated from the true weight of the bar in seemingly random fashion.

Whether we are measuring gold bars, behavior, or anything else, unreliable measurement is to be avoided. We want to be reasonably certain that the measuring tool or test that we are using is consistent. That is, we want to know that it yields the same numerical measurement every time it measures the same thing under the same conditions. Psychological tests, like other tests and instruments, are reliable to varying degrees. Much more on the subject of reliability in Chapter 5; for now, know that reliability is a necessary but not sufficient element of a good test. In addition to being reliable, tests must be reasonably accurate. In the language of psychometrics, tests must be *valid*.

Validity

A test is considered valid for a particular purpose if it in fact measures what it purports to measure. In the gold bar example cited earlier, the scale that consistently indicated that the 1-pound gold bar weighed 1 pound is a valid scale. Likewise, a test of reaction time is a valid test if it accurately measures reaction time. A test of intelligence is a valid test if it truly measures intelligence. Well, yes, but . . .

Although there is relatively little controversy about the definition of a term such as reaction time, a great deal of controversy exists about the definition of intelligence. Because there is controversy surrounding the definition of intelligence, the validity of any test purporting to measure this variable is sure to come under close scrutiny by critics. If the definition of intelligence on which the test is based is sufficiently different from the definition of intelligence on other accepted tests, then the test may be condemned as not measuring what it purports to measure.

Questions regarding a test's validity may focus on the items that collectively make up the test. Do the items adequately sample the range of areas that must be sampled to adequately measure the construct? Individual items will also come under scrutiny in an investigation of a test's validity. How do individual items contribute to or take away from the test's validity? The validity of a test may also be questioned on grounds related to the interpretation of resulting test scores. What do these scores really tell us about the targeted construct? How are high scores on the test related to testtakers' behavior? How are low scores on the test related to testtakers' behavior? How do scores on this test relate to scores on other tests purporting to measure the same construct? How do scores on this test relate to scores on other tests purporting to measure opposite types of constructs?

JUST THINK . . .

Why might a test shown to be valid for use for a particular purpose with members of one population not be valid for use for that same purpose with members of another population?

We might expect one person's score on a valid test of introversion to be inversely related to that same person's score on a valid test of extraversion; that is, the higher the introversion test score, the lower the extraversion test score, and vice versa. As we will see when we discuss validity in greater detail in Chapter 6, questions concerning the validity of a particular test may be raised at every stage in the life of a test. From its initial development through the life of its use with members of different populations, assessment professionals may raise questions regarding the extent to which a test is measuring what it purports to measure.

Other Considerations

A good test is one that trained examiners can administer, score, and interpret with a minimum of difficulty. A good test is a useful test, one that yields actionable results that will ultimately benefit individual testtakers or society at large. In "putting a test to the test," there are a number of different ways to evaluate just how good it really is (see *Everyday Psychometrics*).

If the purpose of a test is to compare the performance of the testtaker with the performance of other testtakers, a good test is one that contains adequate *norms*. Also referred to as *normative data*, norms provide a standard with which the results of measurement can be compared. Let's explore the important subject of norms in a bit more detail.

Norms

We may define **norm-referenced testing and assessment** as a method of evaluation and a way of deriving meaning from test scores by evaluating an individual testtaker's score and comparing it to scores of a group of testtakers. In this approach, the meaning of an individual test score is understood relative to other test scores on the same test. A

Putting Tests to the Test

For experts in the field of testing and assessment, certain questions occur almost reflexively in evaluating a test or measurement technique. You may not be an assessment expert yet, but your consideration of the following questions is a significant first step in that direction. Try to think of these questions when you come across mention of various tests in this book, in other books and journal articles, and in life. These questions will help you evaluate the psychometric soundness of tests and other measurement methods.

Why Use This Particular Instrument or Method?

A choice of measuring instruments typically exists when it comes to measuring a particular psychological or educational variable, and the test user must therefore choose from many available tools. Published information, such as test catalogues, test manuals, and published test reviews, can be of great value in deciding to use a particular test. Unpublished sources of information, such as that obtained by writing directly to the test developer or test publisher, may also be a possibility. Some of the prospective test user's questions relate to the objectives of the test and the goodness of fit between those objectives and the objectives of the testing or assessment. What type of information will result from an administration of this test? Do alternate forms of this test exist and, if so, how might they be used? How long does it take to administer this test? What is the recommended age range for testtakers, and what reading level is required? How will this resulting information be applied to answer the test referral question? What types of decisions can or cannot be made on the basis of information from the use of this test? What other information will be required to adequately answer the test referral question?

Are There Any Published Guidelines for the Use of This Test?

Measurement professionals make it their business to be aware of published guidelines from professional associations and related organizations for the use of tests and measurement techniques. For example, suppose you are a psychologist called upon to provide input to a court in the matter of a child custody decision. More specifically, the court has asked your professional opinion of the parenting capacity of one parent. How would you proceed? Many psychologists who perform such evaluations use a psychological test as part of the evaluation process. However, the psychologist performing such an evaluation is—or should

be—aware of the guidelines promulgated by the American Psychological Association's Committee on Professional Practice and Standards (1994a). These guidelines describe three types of assessments relevant to a child custody decision: (1) the assessment of parenting capacity, (2) the assessment of psychological and developmental needs of the child, and (3) the assessment of the goodness of fit between the parent's capacity and the child's needs. Clearly, an evaluation of a parent, or even two parents, does not provide the evaluator with sufficient information to express an opinion as to custody. Rather, only an evaluation of the parents (or others seeking custody), the child, and the goodness of fit between the needs and capacity of each of the parties can provide information relevant to an educated opinion about child custody.

There are many psychological tests and measurement procedures used to obtain information about parenting capacity (Holden & Edwards, 1989; Lovejoy et al., 1999; Touliatos et al., 1991). Some commonly used instruments are the Ackerman-Schoendorf Scales for Parent Evaluation of Custody, the Bricklin Perceptual Scales, the Bricklin Perception of Relationships Test, the Child Abuse Potential Inventory (CAP), the Parent-Child Relationship Inventory, and the Parenting Stress Index (PSI). Regardless of the test employed, the psychologist will use other sources of data, such as interviews, behavioral observation, and document analysis, in the evaluation of parenting capacity. This is consistent both with accepted professional practice and with the published guideline that encourages psychologists to "use multiple methods of data gathering" (APA, 1994a, p. 679). Data from multiple sources can provide varied support for a professional opinion, conclusion, or recommendation.

The area of child custody evaluation provides a useful illustration of why mere knowledge of assessment or of a test may not adequately equip an assessor to assess. Assessors who undertake child custody evaluations must have working familiarity not only with the specific tools they use and the current literature in psychological assessment in general, but with the ever-changing laws and professional guidelines applicable to such evaluations, as well as the current literature in areas such as child development, family dynamics, and divorce. Executing a competent child custody evaluation is no simple matter, and there are many published resources designed to assist professionals who wish to become involved in this type of work (for example, Ackerman, 1995; Bushard & Howard, 1994; Schultz et al., 1989; Stahl, 1995).

Is This Instrument Reliable?

Earlier, we introduced you to the psychometric concept of reliability and noted that it had to do with the consistency of measurement. Measuring reliability is not always a straightforward matter. As an example, consider one of the tests that might be used in the evaluation of parenting capacity, the Bricklin Perceptual Scales (BPS; Bricklin, 1984). The BPS was designed to explore a child's perception of father and mother. A measure of one type of reliability, referred to as *test-retest reliability,* would indicate how consistent a child's perception of father and mother is over time. However, the BPS test manual contains no reliability data because, as Bricklin (1984, p. 42) put it, "there are no reasons to expect the measurements reported here to exhibit any particular degree of stability, since they should vary in accordance with changes in the child's perceptions." Such an assertion has not stopped others (such as Speth, 1992) from exploring the test-retest reliability of the BPS. But whether or not one accepts Bricklin's assertion regarding the need for reliability data, such opinions illustrate the complexity of reliability questions—as well as the need for multiple sources of data to strengthen arguments regarding the confirmation or rejection of a hypothesis.

Is This Instrument Valid?

Validity, as you have learned, refers to the extent that a test measures what it purports to measure. Like reliability, questions related to the validity of a test can be complex and colored more in shades of gray than black or white. For example, even if data from a test such as the BPS were valid for the purpose of gauging children's perceptions of their parents, the data would not necessarily be valid as the sole source on which to base an opinion regarding child custody (Brodzinsky, 1993). In this context, Heinze and Grisso (1996) bemoaned what they saw as a trend by experts to rely on data concerning perceptions of the desirability of parents:

> Questions of parental desirability cannot be answered without reference to the characteristics, needs, and demands of the specific child who is in need of parenting. We suspect that no instrument that only assesses parents (e.g., whether through children's perceptions or direct observations of parents themselves) can ever meet basic scientific standards for making judgments about "preferred parents," or for making comparisons between parents that would justify suggesting that one parent's abilities are more desirable than the other's. (p. 310)

Instruments designed to measure variables such as stressful reactions to parenting (such as the PSI) and the potential for child abuse (such as the CAP) have yielded valuable data that could be very useful to courts as they evaluate all of the elements necessary for an informed judgment in child custody matters (Heinze & Grisso, 1996). However, in the courtroom and beyond, questions concerning which test or combination of tests is valid for what purpose under what conditions sometimes stimulate heated debate and controversy.

What Inferences May Reasonably Be Made From This Test Score, and How Generalizable Are the Findings?

The *raison d'être* (or "reason for being") of many psychological tests and other tools of psychological assessment is to make inferences about behavior. In evaluating a test, it is therefore critical to consider the inferences that may reasonably be made as a result of administering that test. Will we learn something about a child's readiness to begin first grade? How prepared a student is for the first year of college at a particular institution? Whether one is harmful to oneself or others? These represent but a small sampling of critical questions for which answers must be inferred on the basis of test scores and other data derived from various tools of assessment.

Intimately related to considerations regarding the inferences that can be made are considerations regarding the generalizability of the findings. From your reading of our discussion of norms, you know that normative data provide a context in which to interpret and generalize from test results. With that as background, consider that the normative sample for the Parenting Stress Index (PSI) consisted of 2,633 parents drawn primarily from the state of Virginia. The majority of the children in the sample were under 5 years of age and Caucasian. How generalizable would you say the findings from an administration of the PSI are to non-Caucasian parents? If this question occurred to you, you are in good company (see, for example, Krauss, 1993; McBride, 1989; Teplin et al., 1991; Younger, 1991). By the way, since its publication the PSI has been adapted to include parents from different cultures (Abidin, 1990; Beebe et al., 1993; Black et al., 1993).

In addition to applicability of the norms, a number of other factors may give rise to questions about the generalizability of a test or a particular administration of a test. The

(continued)

Putting Tests to the Test *(continued)*

wording of test items, for example, may bias scores in some way. For example, all other things being equal, the BPS may be biased toward more favorable perceptions of mothers. Mothers and fathers may score similarly on all of the sub-tests except the Supportiveness subscale, on which mothers tend to score higher (Heinze & Grisso, 1996).

The question of generalizability of findings may also be raised concerning a particular administration of a test. Most published tests have very explicit directions that test administrators—or a computer, if the test is computer-administered—must follow to the letter. If test administration is compromised in any way, whether by design, negligence, or any other reason, the generalizability of the data derived from the testing has also been compromised.

And so, although you may not yet be an expert in measurement, you are now armed with a working knowledge of the types of questions experts ask when evaluating any test or measurement technique.

common goal of norm-referenced tests is to yield information on a testtaker's standing or ranking relative to some comparison group of testtakers.

Norm in the singular is used in the scholarly literature to refer to behavior that is usual, average, normal, standard, expected, or typical. Reference to a particular variety of norm may be specified by means of modifiers such as *age,* as in the term *age norm. Norms* is the plural form of norm, as in the term *gender norms.* In a psychometric context, **norms** are the test performance data of a particular group of testtakers that are designed for use as a reference for evaluating or interpreting individual test scores. As used in this definition, the "particular group of testtakers" may be defined broadly (for example, "a sample representative of the adult population of the United States") or narrowly (for example, "female inpatients at the Bronx Community Hospital with a primary diagnosis of depression"). A **normative sample** is that group of people whose performance on a particular test is analyzed for reference in evaluating the performance of individual testtakers.

Whether broad or narrow in scope, members of the normative sample will all be typical with respect to some characteristic(s) of the people for whom the particular test was designed. A test administration to this representative sample of testtakers yields a distribution (or distributions) of scores. These data constitute the norms for the test and typically are used as a reference source for evaluating and placing into context test scores obtained by individual testtakers. The data may be in the form of raw scores or converted scores.

The verb *to norm,* as well as related terms such as **norming,** refer to the process of deriving norms. *Norming* may be modified to describe a particular type of norm derivation. For example, **race norming** is the controversial practice of norming on the basis of race or ethnic background. Race norming was once engaged in by some government agencies and private organizations, and the practice resulted in the establishment of different cut scores for hiring by cultural group. Members of one cultural group would have to attain one score to be hired, whereas members of another cultural group would have to attain a different score. Although initially instituted in the service of affirmative action objectives (Greenlaw & Jensen, 1996), the practice was outlawed by the Civil Rights Act of 1991. The law left unclear a number of issues, however, including "whether, or under what circumstances, in the development of an assessment procedure, it is lawful to adjust item content to minimize group differences" (Kehoe & Tenopyr, 1994, p. 291).

Norming a test, especially with the participation of a nationally representative normative sample, can be a very expensive proposition. For this reason, some test manuals provide what are variously known as **user norms** or **program norms,** which "consist of descriptive statistics based on a group of testtakers in a given period of time rather than norms obtained by formal sampling methods" (Nelson, 1994, p. 283).

Standardization, Sampling, and Norming

Standardization   The process of administering a test to a representative sample of test-takers for the purpose of establishing norms is referred to as **standardization.** A test is said to be *standardized* when it has clearly specified procedures for administration and scoring, including normative data. But to understand how norms are derived, an understanding of sampling is necessary.

Sampling   In the process of developing a test, a test developer has targeted some defined group as the population for which the test is designed. This population is the complete universe or set of individuals with at least one common, observable characteristic. The common observable characteristic(s) could be just about anything. For example, it might be *high school seniors who aspire to go to college,* or the *16 boys and girls in Mrs. Perez's day-care center,* or *all housewives with primary responsibility for household shopping who have purchased over-the-counter headache remedies within the last two months.*

To obtain a distribution of scores, the test developer could have the test administered to every person in the targeted population. If the total targeted population consists of something like the 16 boys and girls in Mrs. Perez's day-care center, it may well be possible and feasible to administer the test to each member of the targeted population. However, with tests developed for use with large or wide-ranging populations, it is usually impossible, impractical, or simply too expensive to administer the test to everyone, nor is it necessary.

The test developer can obtain a distribution of test responses by administering the test to a **sample** of the population—a portion of the universe of people deemed to be representative of the whole population. The size of the sample could be as small as one person, though as the size of the sample approaches the size of the population, possible sources of error as a result of insufficient sample size diminish. The process of selecting the portion of the universe deemed to be representative of the whole population is referred to as **sampling.**

Subgroups within a defined population may differ with respect to some characteristics, and it is sometimes essential to have these differences proportionately represented in the sample. Thus, for example, if you devised a public opinion test, and you wanted to sample the opinions of Manhattan residents with this instrument, it would be desirable to include in your sample people representing different subgroups (or strata) of the population, such as Blacks, Whites, Asians, other non-Whites, males, females, the poor, the middle class, the rich, professional people, business people, office workers, skilled and unskilled laborers, the unemployed, homemakers, Catholics, Jews, members of

JUST THINK . . .

Truly random sampling is relatively rare. Why do you think this is so?

other religions, and so forth—all in proportion to the current occurrence of these strata in the population of people who reside on the island of Manhattan. Such sampling, termed **stratified sampling,** would help prevent sampling bias and ultimately aid in the interpretation of the findings. If such sampling were *random* (that is, if every member of the population had the same chance of being included in the sample), then the procedure would be termed **stratified-random sampling.**

Two other types of sampling procedures are *purposive sampling* and *incidental sampling*. If we arbitrarily select some sample because we believe it to be representative of the population, the sample we have selected is referred to as **purposive.** Manufacturers of products frequently use purposive sampling when they test the appeal of a new product in one city or market and then make assumptions about how that product would sell nationally. For example, the manufacturer might test a product in a market such as Cleveland because, on the basis of experience with this particular product, "how goes Cleveland, so goes the nation." The danger in using such a purposive sample is that the sample, in this case Cleveland residents, may no longer be representative of the nation. Alternatively, this sample may simply not be representative of national preferences with regard to the particular product being test-marketed.

Often, a test user's decisions regarding sampling wind up pitting what is ideal against what is practical. It may be ideal, for example, to use as a sample in an experiment, 50 chief executive officers from any of the *Fortune 500* companies (that is, the top 500 companies in terms of income). Conditions may dictate, however, that it is only practical for the experimenter to use 50 volunteers recruited from the local Chamber of Commerce. This important distinction between what is *ideal* and what is *practical* in sampling brings us to a discussion of what has been referred to variously as an *incidental sample* or a *convenience sample.*

When the authors think of this type of an incidental sample, we think of the old joke about the drunk searching for some money he lost under the lamppost. He may not have lost his money there, but that is where the light is. Like the drunk searching for money under the lamppost, a researcher may sometimes employ a sample that is not necessarily the most appropriate but, rather, the most convenient. Unlike the drunk, the researcher employing this type of sample is not doing it as a result of poor judgment but because of budgetary limitations or other constraints. An **incidental sample** or **convenience sample** is one that is convenient or available for use. You may have been a party to incidental sampling if you have ever been placed in a subject pool for experimentation with introductory psychology students. It's not that the students in such subject pools are necessarily the most appropriate subjects for the experiments, it's just that they are the most available. Generalization of findings from incidental samples must be made with caution.

If incidental or convenience samples were clubs, they would not be considered very exclusive clubs. By contrast, there are many samples that are exclusive, in a sense, since they contain many exclusionary criteria. Consider, for example, the group of children and adolescents who served as the normative sample for the Wechsler Intelligence Scale for Children-IV (WISC-IV; Wechsler, 2003). The sample was selected to reflect key demographic variables representative of the United States population according to the latest available census data. Still, some persons were excluded from participation. For example, persons tested on any intelligence measure in the six months prior to the standardization were excluded. Persons not fluent in English or primarily nonverbal or uncommunicative were excluded, as were persons with certain handicapping conditions. More specifically, members of the following groups were excluded:

- Persons with uncorrected visual impairment or hearing loss
- Persons with upper-extremity disability that affects motor performance
- Persons currently admitted to a hospital or mental or psychiatric facility
- Persons currently taking medication that might depress test performance
- Persons previously diagnosed with any physical condition or illness that might depress test performance (such as stroke, epilepsy, or meningitis)

The developers of the WISC-IV reported that "a representative proportion of children from the special group studies were added to the normative sample (approximately 5.7%) to accurately represent the population of children attending school" (Wechsler, 2003, p. 23). More details on how this and other widely used intelligence tests were normed are presented in Chapter 9.

Developing norms for a standardized test   Having obtained a sample, the test developer administers the test according to the standard set of instructions that will be used with the test. The test developer also provides a setting for the testtakers that will be the recommended setting for giving the test. This may be as simple as making sure that the room is quiet and well lit or as complex as providing a specific set of toys to test an infant's cognitive skills. Establishing a standard set of instructions and conditions under which the test is given makes the test scores of the normative sample more comparable with the scores of future testtakers. For example, if a test of concentration ability is given to a normative sample in the summer with the windows open and people mowing the grass and arguing about whether the hedges need trimming, the normative sample probably won't concentrate well. If a testtaker then completes the concentration test under quiet, comfortable conditions, that person may well do much better than the normative group, resulting in a high standard score. That high score would not be very helpful in understanding the testtaker's concentration abilities, because it would reflect the differing conditions under which the test was taken. This example illustrates how important it is that the normative sample take the test under a standard set of conditions, which are then repeated as closely as possible each time the test is given.

After all the test data have been collected and analyzed, the test developer will describe the data using descriptive statistics, including measures of central tendency and variability. In addition, it is incumbent on the test developer to provide a precise description of the standardization sample itself. Good practice dictates that the norms be developed with data derived from a group of people who are presumed to be representative of the people who will take the test in the future. In order to best assist future users of the test, test developers are encouraged to "describe the population(s) represented by any norms or comparison group(s), the dates the data were gathered, and the process used to select the samples of testtakers" (*Code of Fair Testing Practices in Education*, 1988, p. 3).

In practice, descriptions of normative samples vary widely in detail. Not surprisingly, test authors wish to present their tests in the most favorable light possible. Accordingly, shortcomings in the standardization procedure or elsewhere in the process of the test's development may be given short shrift or totally overlooked in a test's manual. Sometimes, although the sample is scrupulously defined, the generalizability of the norms to a particular group or individual is questionable. For example, a test carefully normed on school-age children who reside within the Los Angeles school district may be relevant only to some lesser degree to school-age children who reside within the Dubuque, Iowa, school district. How many children in the standardization sample were English speaking? How many were of Hispanic origin? How does the elementary school curriculum in Los Angeles differ from the curriculum in Dubuque? These are the types of questions that must be raised before the Los Angeles norms are judged to be generalizable to the children of Dubuque. Test manuals sometimes supply prospective test users with guidelines for establishing *local norms* (discussed below), one of many different ways norms can be categorized.

One note on terminology is in order before moving on. When the people in the normative sample are the same people on whom the test was standardized, the phrases *normative sample* and *standardization sample* are often used interchangeably. Increasingly, however, new norms for standardized tests for specific groups of testtakers are developed some time after the original standardization. That is, the test remains standardized based on data from the original standardization sample; it's just that new normative data are developed based on an administration of the test to a new normative sample. Included in this new normative sample may be groups of people who may have been underrepresented or not represented in the original standardization sample data. For example, if there had been a great influx of potential testtakers from the Czech Republic since original standardization, the new normative sample might well include a sample of Czech Republic nationals. In such a scenario, the normative sample for the new norms clearly would not be identical to the standardization sample, and it would be inaccurate to use the terms *standardization sample* and *normative sample* interchangeably.

Types of Norms

Some of the many different ways we can classify norms are as follows: *age norms, grade norms, national norms, national anchor norms, local norms, norms from a fixed reference group, subgroup norms,* and *percentile norms.* We begin with a detailed explanation of the term *percentile* because the norms for many tests are expressed as percentile norms. *Percentile norms* are the raw data from a test's standardization sample converted to percentile form.

Percentiles   In our discussion of the median, we saw that a distribution could be divided into quartiles where the median was the second quartile (Q_2), the point at or below which 50% of the scores fell and above which the remaining 50% fell. Instead of dividing a distribution of scores into quartiles, we might wish to divide the distribution into *deciles,* or ten equal parts. Alternatively, we could divide a distribution into 100 equal parts—100 *percentiles.* In such a distribution, the xth percentile is equal to the score at or below which x% of scores fall. Thus, the 15th percentile is the score at or below which 15% of the scores in the distribution fall. The 99th percentile is the score at or below which 99% of the scores in the distribution fall. If 99% of a particular standardization sample answered fewer than 47 questions on a test correctly, then we could say that a raw score of 47 corresponds to the 99th percentile on this test. It can be seen that a percentile is a ranking that conveys information about the relative position of a score within a distribution of scores.

A **percentile** is an expression of the percentage of people whose score on a test or measure falls below a particular raw score. A more familiar description of test performance, the concept of *percentage correct,* must be distinguished from the concept of a percentile. A percentile is a converted score that refers to a percentage of testtakers. **Percentage correct** refers to the distribution of raw scores—more specifically, to the number of items that were answered correctly multiplied by 100 and divided by the total number of items.

Because percentiles are easily calculated, they are a popular way of organizing test data, be they data from the standardization sample or otherwise. Additionally, percentiles are very adaptable to a wide range of tests. A problem with using percentiles with normally distributed scores is that real differences between raw scores may be minimized near the ends of the distribution and exaggerated in the middle of the distribution. This distortion may even be worse with highly skewed data. In the normal distribution, the highest frequency of raw scores occurs in the middle. That being the case, the differences between all those scores that cluster in the middle might be quite small, yet even the smallest differences will appear as differences in percentiles. The reverse is true at the extremes of the distributions, where differences between raw scores may be great, though we would have no way of knowing that from the relatively small differences in percentiles.

Age norms   Also known as **age-equivalent scores, age norms** indicate the average performance of different samples of testtakers who were at various ages at the time the test was administered. If the measurement under consideration is height in inches, for example, we know that scores (heights) for children will gradually increase at various rates as a function of age up to the middle to late teens. With the graying of America, there has been increased interest in performance on various types of psychological tests, particularly neuropsychological tests, as a function of advancing age.

Carefully constructed age-norm tables for physical characteristics such as height enjoy widespread acceptance and are virtually noncontroversial. This is not the case, however, with respect to age-norm tables for psychological characteristics such as intelligence. For many years, psychologists have referred to the "mental age" of testtakers. The child of any chronological age whose performance on a valid test of intellectual ability indicated that he or she had intellectual ability similar to that of the average child of some other age was said to have the mental age of the norm group in which his or her test score fell. The reasoning here was that irrespective of chronological age, children with the same mental age could be expected to read the same level of material, solve the same kinds of math problems, reason with a similar level of judgment, and so forth. But some have complained that the concept of mental age is too broad and that although a 6-year-old might, for example, perform intellectually like a 12-year-old, the 6-year-old might not be very similar at all to the average 12-year-old socially, psychologically, and otherwise. In addition to such intuitive considerations, the mental age concept has also been criticized on technical grounds.[3]

Grade norms   Designed to indicate the average test performance of testtakers in a given school grade, **grade norms** are developed by administering the test to representative samples of children over a range of consecutive grade levels (such as first through sixth grades). Next, the mean or median score for children at each grade level is computed. Because the school year typically runs from September to June—ten months—fractions in the mean or median are easily expressed as decimals. Thus, for example, a sixth-grader performing exactly at the average on a grade-normed test administered during the fourth month of the school year (December) would achieve a grade-equivalent score of 6.4. Like age norms, grade norms have widespread application with children of elementary school age, the thought here being that children learn and develop at varying rates but in ways that are in some aspects predictable.

A student in twelfth grade scores 6 on a grade-normed spelling test. Does this mean that the student has the same spelling abilities as the average sixth-grader? The answer is no. Accurately interpreted, all this finding means is that this student and a hypothetical average sixth-grader answered the same fraction of items correctly on that test. Grade norms do not provide information as to the content or type of items that a student could or could not answer correctly. Perhaps the primary use of grade norms is as a

> **JUST THINK . . .**
>
> Some experts in testing have called for a moratorium on the use of grade-equivalent as well as age-equivalent scores because such scores may so easily be misinterpreted. What is your opinion on this issue?

---

3. For many years, IQ (intelligence quotient) scores on tests such as the Stanford-Binet were calculated by dividing mental age (as indicated by the test) by chronological age. The quotient would then be multiplied by 100 to eliminate the fraction. The distribution of IQ scores had a mean set at 100 and a standard deviation of approximately 16. A child of 12 with a mental age of 12 had an IQ of 100 ($12/12 \times 100 = 100$). The technical problem here is that IQ standard deviations were not constant with age. At one age, an IQ of 116 might be indicative of performance at 1 standard deviation above the mean, whereas at another age an IQ of 121 might be indicative of performance at 1 standard deviation above the mean.

convenient, readily understandable gauge of how one student's performance compares with that of fellow students in the same grade.

One drawback of grade norms is that they are useful only with respect to years and months of schooling completed. They have little or no applicability to children who are not yet in school or who are out of school. Age norms are also limited in this regard, since for many tests the value of such norms is limited with an adult population.

National norms   As the name implies, **national norms** are derived from a normative sample that was nationally representative of the population at the time the norming study was conducted. In the fields of psychology and education, for example, national norms may be obtained by testing large numbers of people representative of different variables of interest such as age, gender, racial/ethnic background, socioeconomic strata, geographical location (such as North, East, South, West, Midwest), and different types of communities within the various parts of the country (such as rural, urban, suburban).

If the test was designed for use in the schools, norms might be obtained for students in every grade to which the test sought to be applicable. Factors related to the representativeness of the school from which members of the norming sample were drawn might also be criteria for inclusion in or exclusion from the sample. For example, is the school the student attends publicly funded, privately funded, religiously oriented, military, or something else? How representative are the pupil–teacher ratios in the school under consideration? Does the school have a library, and if so, how many books are in it? These are only a sample of the types of questions that could be raised in assembling a normative sample to be used in the establishment of national norms. The precise nature of the questions raised when developing national norms will depend on whom the test is designed for and what the test is designed to do.

Norms from many different tests may all claim to have nationally representative samples. Still, close scrutiny of the description of the sample employed may reveal that the sample differs in many important respects from similar tests also claiming to be based on a nationally representative sample. For this reason, it is always a good idea to check the manual of the tests under consideration to see exactly how comparable the tests are. Two important questions test users must raise as consumers of test-related information are "What are the differences between the tests I am considering for use in terms of their normative samples?" and "How comparable are these normative samples to the sample of testtakers with whom I will be using the test?"

National anchor norms   Even the most casual survey of catalogues from various test publishers will reveal that, with respect to almost any human characteristic or ability, there exist many different tests purporting to measure the characteristic or ability. Dozens of tests, for example, purport to measure reading. Suppose we select a reading test designed for use in grades 3 to 6, which, for the purposes of this hypothetical example, we call the Best Reading Test (BRT). Suppose further that we now want to be able to compare findings obtained on another national reading test designed for use with grades 3 to 6, the hypothetical XYZ Reading Test, with the BRT. An equivalency table for scores on the two tests, or **national anchor norms,** could provide the tool for such a comparison. Just as an anchor provides some stability to a vessel, so national anchor norms provide some stability to test scores by anchoring them to other test scores.

The method by which such equivalency tables or national anchor norms are established typically begins with the computation of percentile norms for each of the tests to be compared. Using the **equipercentile method,** the equivalency of scores on different tests is calculated with reference to corresponding percentile scores. Thus, if the 96th percentile corresponds to a score of 69 on the BRT, and if the 96th percentile corresponds to a score of 14 on the XYZ, we can say that a BRT score of 69 is equivalent to an XYZ score of 14. We should note that the national anchor norms for our hypothetical BRT and XYZ tests must have been obtained on the same sample—each member of the sample took both tests, and the equivalency tables were then calculated on the basis of these data.[4] Although national anchor norms provide an indication of the equivalency of scores on various tests, it would be a mistake, because of technical considerations, to treat these equivalencies as precise equalities (Angoff, 1964, 1966, 1971).

Subgroup norms A normative sample can be segmented by any of the criteria initially used in selecting subjects for the sample. What results from such segmentation are more narrowly defined **subgroup norms.** Thus, for example, suppose criteria used in selecting children for inclusion in the XYZ Reading Test normative sample were age, educational level, socioeconomic level, geographic region, community type, and handedness (whether the child was right-handed or left-handed). The test manual or a supplement to it might report normative information by each of these subgroups. A community school board member might find the regional norms to be most useful, whereas a psychologist doing exploratory research in the area of brain lateralization and reading scores might find the handedness norms most useful.

Local norms Typically developed by test users themselves, **local norms** provide normative information with respect to the local population's performance on some test. A local company personnel director might find some nationally standardized test useful in making selection decisions but might deem the norms published in the test manual to be far afield of local job applicants' score distributions. Individual high schools may wish to develop their own school norms (local norms) for student scores on some examination that is administered statewide. A school guidance center may find that locally derived norms for a particular test—say, a survey of personal values—are more useful in counseling students than the national norms printed in the manual.

Fixed Reference Group Scoring Systems

Norms provide a context for interpreting the meaning of a test score. Another type of aid in providing a context for interpretation is termed a **fixed reference group scoring system.** Here, the distribution of scores obtained on the test from one group of testtakers— referred to as the *fixed reference group*—is used as the basis for the calculation of test scores for future administrations of the test. Perhaps the test most familiar to college students that exemplifies the use of a fixed reference group scoring system is the SAT. This test was first administered in 1926. Its norms were then based on the mean and standard deviation of the people who took the test at the time. With passing years, more colleges became members of the College Board, the sponsoring organization for the test. It soon became evident that SAT scores tended to vary somewhat as a function of the time of year the test was administered. In an effort to ensure perpetual comparability and continuity of scores, a fixed reference group scoring system was put into place in 1941.

The distribution of scores from the 11,000 people who took the SAT in 1941 was immortalized as a standard to be used in the conversion of raw scores on future administrations of the test.[5] A new fixed reference group, the more than 2 million testtakers who

---

4. When two tests are normed from the same sample, the norming process is referred to as *co-norming.*

5. Conceptually, the idea of a *fixed reference group* is analogous to the idea of a *fixed reference foot,* the foot of the English king that also became immortalized as a measurement standard (Angoff, 1962).

completed the SAT in 1990, began to be used in 1995. A score of 500 on the SAT corresponds to the mean obtained by the 1990 sample, a score of 400 corresponds to a score that is 1 standard deviation below the 1990 mean, and so forth. As an example, suppose John took the SAT in 1995 and answered 50 items correctly on a particular scale. And let's say Mary took the test in 1996 and, just like John, answered 50 items correctly. Although John and Mary may have achieved the same raw score, they would not necessarily achieve the same scaled score. If, for example, the 1996 version of the test under discussion was judged to be somewhat easier than the 1995 version, scaled scores for the 1996 testtakers would be calibrated downward. This would be done so as to make scores achieved in 1996 comparable to scores earned in 1995.

Test items common to each new version of the SAT and each previous version of it are employed in a procedure (termed *anchoring*) that permits the conversion of raw scores on the new version of the test into *fixed reference group scores.* Like other fixed reference group scores, including Graduate Record Examination scores (see the *Close-up*), SAT scores are most typically interpreted with respect to local norms. Thus, for example, college admissions officers usually rely on their own independently collected norms to make selection decisions. They will compare applicants' SAT scores to the SAT scores of students in their school who completed and failed to complete the program. Of course, admissions decisions are seldom made on the basis of the SAT (or any other single test) alone. Various criteria are typically evaluated in admissions decisions.

Norm-Referenced Versus Criterion-Referenced Evaluation

One way to derive meaning from a test score is to evaluate the test score in relation to other scores on the same test. As we have pointed out, this approach to evaluation is norm-referenced. Another way to derive meaning from a test score is to evaluate it on the basis of whether or not some criterion has been met. We may define a **criterion** as a standard on which a judgment or decision may be based. **Criterion-referenced testing and assessment** may be defined as a method of evaluation and a way of deriving meaning from test scores by evaluating an individual's score with reference to a set standard. Some examples:

- To be eligible for a high school diploma, students must demonstrate at least a sixth-grade reading level.

- To earn the privilege of driving an automobile, would-be drivers must take a road test and demonstrate their driving skill to the satisfaction of a state-appointed examiner.

- To be licensed as a psychologist, the applicant must achieve a score that meets or exceeds the score mandated by the state on the licensing test.

The criterion in criterion-referenced assessments typically derives from the values or standards of an individual or organization. For example, in order to earn a black belt in karate, students must demonstrate a black-belt level of proficiency in karate and meet related criteria such as those related to self-discipline and focus. Each student is evaluated individually to see if all of these criteria are met. Regardless of the level of performance of all the testtakers, only students who meet all the criteria will leave the *dojo* (training room) with a brand-new black belt.

Criterion-referenced testing and assessment goes by other names. Because the focus in this approach is on how scores relate to a particular content area or domain, the

Good Ol' Norms and the GRE

Some time before or after you graduate from college, the Graduate Record Exam (GRE) may be on your "to do" list. Knowing that the GRE test scores may influence the choices of graduate school open to you and, by extension, your graduate career and your life in general, you are likely to read the test results eagerly but a bit fearfully as well. Assuming you have taken the GRE General Test, you will have three scores, one each for verbal ability, quantitative ability, and analytical ability. How do you understand those scores?

You know something about norms, and you know that the GRE has a mean of 500 and a standard deviation of 100. But here is something that you may not know: That mean of 500 and standard deviation of 100 apply to scores obtained by people who took the GRE in 1952. Their scores were immortalized as a normative or fixed reference group. To understand the meaning of a score earned today requires current normative tables supplied by the test's developer, Educational Testing Service (ETS).

By way of explanation, consider the case of Dexter, an English literature major. Just last week, Dexter received the following GRE scores: 640 on verbal ability, 700 on quantitative ability, and 520 on analytical ability. Knowing that the GRE has a mean of 500 and a standard deviation of 100, and not taking the time to learn much more about the actual meaning of the scores, Dexter made some immediate conclusions about his abilities.

Dexter concluded that quantitative ability was his strong suit. After all, his quantitative score was 2 standard deviations above the mean—a score that exceeded the scores of more than 97% of his fellow testtakers. "Perhaps English literature was the wrong major," he thought aloud. He then went on to analyze his analytic ability score. "Average to slightly above average compared with those I will be competing with for entrance to graduate school." So far, is Dexter's analysis accurate?

In a word, no. Dexter is wrongly assuming that the GRE among current testtakers has a mean of 500 and a standard deviation of 100. He obviously is not aware that the GRE uses a fixed reference group scoring system. The reference group for the verbal and quantitative portions of the test comprised people who took the GRE in 1952. On that occasion, the mean score of the people who took the test was set at 500, with a standard deviation at 100. In the 50-plus years since the fixed reference group was tested, there have been significant changes in the population taking the GRE. These changes in the population of testtakers have necessitated changes in the way a contemporary GRE score report is interpreted.

ETS makes available the current norms of the GRE to individual students and institutions. The information is presented in terms of percentiles, with the percentage of examinees scoring below a particular score reported across the distribution of GRE scores. The report of scores sent to testtakers includes such percentile information for the scores earned by that testtaker. Had Dexter taken the time to read this information, he could have more accurately interpreted his scores relative to the college seniors and college graduates who took the test in the same period of time as he. In this hypothetical example, we will refer to this time period simply as "now."

Suppose, for the sake of this example, that verbal ability scores of 640 are at the 87th percentile, quantitative ability scores of 700 are at the 79th percentile, and analytical ability scores of 520 are at the 35th percentile. With that information, a different picture of Dexter and his abilities emerges.

Relative to testtakers "now," Dexter does best in the verbal ability area, scoring better than 87% of other testtakers. His quantitative ability performance, better than 79% of others, is clearly above the median but not as outstanding as his verbal performance. Dexter's analytical performance is actually below the median, with only 35% of testtakers scoring lower than he did. After reviewing his score report with a staff member in his school's counseling center, Dexter is reassured that English literature was a good choice of major after all.

Learning about the derivation and interpretation of GRE scores, you may wonder about the benefits of perpetuating what may seem to be a needlessly complicated and outdated system. Why retain decades-old data as a fixed reference norm group? Why the necessity for changing percentile values corresponding to specific GRE scores? Why hasn't ETS reset the GRE mean at 500 and its standard deviation at 100 for each new year, if not for each administration of the test? Certainly such a resetting would simplify interpretation of individual scores.

Frequent renorming of the GRE would make meaningful comparisons between people who sat for the examination at different times extremely difficult, if not impossible. By contrast, the system that is in place guarantees that meaningful comparisons between people and across time can be made. Indeed, the GRE exists for the purpose of assisting institutions in making decisions about matters such as graduate school admission and the awarding of scholarships. The test's ability to make meaningful comparisons

(continued)

Good Ol' Norms and the GRE
(continued)

is retained under the current system. A GRE score of 500 on the quantitative (or verbal) test means that the testtaker has performed at the average level of people who took the GRE in 1952. For this or any other specific score, the score represents a set level of performance regardless of when the test was taken.

When members of the fixed reference group took the test in 1952, the GRE scores were set with a mean of 500 and a standard deviation of 100. Assuming a normal distribution of scores, percentile values for a sampling of specific scores would be as follows:

GRE Score	Percentile Value in 1952
700	98
600	84
500	50
400	16
300	2

In our hypothetical example for "now," the patterns of test scores have changed somewhat:

GRE Score	Percentile Value in 1952	Percentile Value "Now"	
		Verbal	Quantitative
700	98	95	79
600	84	79	56
500	50	51	31
400	16	19	11
300	2	3	2

As compared with 1952, the distribution of scores on the verbal ability test is not vastly different. Although the scores seem to have spread out a bit more in recent years, the median is essentially the same. A slightly larger proportion of people score both at the lower and at the higher ends of the scale. For example, 16% of students scored over 600 in 1952, and 21% of students scored over 600 in 1989 to 1992.

The distribution of scores on the quantitative ability test is considerably different for the two time periods. In this case, a greater proportion of people are getting higher scores than in 1952. In 1952, students scoring over 700 constituted only about 2% of the population of testtakers.

In the "now" sample, such students constituted fully 21% of the group.

A factor contributing to the change in the distribution of quantitative scores is that more international students now take the GRE than in 1952. Many of these students have better math ability than do U.S. students, causing a rise in the median ability level among all testtakers.

Returning to the issue of renorming the GRE more frequently, can you imagine how things would be different if that were the case? If the level of ability being tested in the population were to change, as it seems to have done for quantitative ability, then the meaning of specific scores would also change. This can be illustrated by the case of two students taking the GRE five years apart. The two students are applying for admission to the same competitive graduate program. During the five-year period separating the testings, an increasing proportion of people with good quantitative ability entered the population and took the GRE. The first student took the GRE with relatively few highly quantitatively skilled people and got a score of 660 on the quantitative test. The second student took the GRE with many highly quantitatively skilled people and also got a score of 660 on the quantitative test.

Under the current system, in which the test is not renormed annually, we would conclude that two students with similar scores have similar levels of quantitative performance; a direct comparison would be valid. However, if the test were renormed annually, the second student's score described above would actually represent better quantitative skill because that student was compared with more quantitatively skilled people. Clearly, renorming would diminish comparability of scores across different testings.

In this discussion, we have touched on issues related to the GRE verbal and quantitative test scores. As you might suspect, there are additional issues related to norms concerning the analytical ability scores and Subject Test scores. A consideration of these more complex norm-related issues awaits you after you have taken the GRE and earned a place in a graduate psychometrics program. Alternatively, you can contact ETS at their Web site or write to them at Educational Testing Service, P.O. Box 6000, Princeton, NJ 08541-6000, for more information about the GRE or any of its other tests. Interested students may also wish to write to obtain current percentile values that correspond to GRE scores, as the "now" data presented here were only hypothetical.

approach is also referred to as **domain-** or **content-referenced testing and assessment.**[6] While norm-referenced interpretations of test data provide information about an individual's performance relative to other people, criterion-referenced interpretations provide information about what people can do. Because criterion-referenced tests are frequently used to gauge achievement or mastery, they are sometimes referred to as *mastery tests*. The criterion-referenced approach has enjoyed widespread acceptance in the field of computer-assisted education programs. In such programs, mastery of segments of materials is assessed before the program user can proceed to the next level.

"Has this flight trainee mastered the material she needs to be an airline pilot?" This is the type of question that an airline personnel office might seek to address with a mastery test on a flight simulator. If a standard, or criterion, for passing a hypothetical "Airline Pilot Test" (APT) has been set at 85% correct, then trainees who score 84% correct or less will not pass. It matters not whether they scored 84% or 42%. Conversely, trainees who score 85% or better on the test will pass whether they scored 85% or 100%. All who score 85% or better are said to have mastered the skills and knowledge necessary to be an airline pilot. Taking this example one step further, another airline might find it useful to set up three categories of findings based on criterion-referenced interpretation of test scores:

85% or better correct = pass

75% to 84% correct = retest after a two-month refresher course

74% or less = fail

How should cut scores in mastery testing be determined? How many and what kinds of test items are needed to demonstrate mastery in a given field? The answers to these and related questions have been tackled in diverse ways (Ferguson & Novick, 1973; Glaser & Nitko, 1971; Panell & Laabs, 1979), all beyond the scope of this book.

Critics of the criterion-referenced approach argue that if it is strictly followed, potentially important information about an individual's performance relative to other test-takers is lost. Another criticism is that although this approach may have value with respect to the assessment of mastery of basic knowledge, skills, or both, it has little or no meaningful application at the upper end of the knowledge/skill continuum. Thus, the approach is clearly meaningful in evaluating whether pupils have mastered basic reading, writing, and arithmetic. But how useful is it in evaluating doctoral-level writing or math? Identifying stand-alone originality or brilliant analytic ability is *not* the stuff of which criterion-oriented tests are made. By contrast, brilliance and superior abilities are recognizable in tests that employ norm-referenced interpretations. They are the scores that trail off all the way to the right on the normal curve, past the third standard deviation.

> **JUST THINK . . .**
>
> For licensing of physicians, psychologists, engineers, and other professionals, would you advocate that your state use criterion- or norm-referenced assessment? Why?

In a sense, all testing is ultimately normative, even if the scores are as seemingly criterion-referenced as pass/fail. This is so because even in a pass/fail score, there is an

---

6. Although acknowledging that content-referenced interpretations can be referred to as criterion-referenced interpretations, the 1974 edition of *Standards* also noted a technical distinction between interpretations so designated: "*Content-referenced* interpretations are those where the score is directly interpreted in terms of performance at each point on the achievement continuum being measured. *Criterion-referenced* interpretations are those where the score is directly interpreted in terms of performance at any given point on the continuum of an *external* variable. An external criterion variable might be grade averages or levels of job performance" (p. 19; footnote in original omitted).

inherent acknowledgment of a continuum of abilities. At some point in that continuum, a dichotomizing cutoff point has been applied.

We now proceed to a discussion of another word that—along with *impeach* and *percentile*—would easily make a national list of Frequently Used but Little Understood Terminology. The word is *correlation*—a word that enjoys widespread confusion with the concept of causation. Let's state at the outset that correlation is *not* synonymous with causation. But what does *correlation* mean? And what is meant by *regression*? Read on.

Correlation and Inference

Central to psychological testing and assessment are inferences (deduced conclusions) about how some things (such as traits, abilities, or interests) are related to other things (such as behavior). A **coefficient of correlation** (or **correlation coefficient**) is a number that provides us with an index of the strength of the relationship between two things. An understanding of the concept of correlation and an ability to compute a coefficient of correlation is therefore central to the study of tests and measurement.

The Concept of Correlation

Simply stated, **correlation** is an expression of the degree and direction of correspondence between two things. A coefficient of correlation (r) expresses a linear relationship between two (and only two) variables, usually continuous in nature. It reflects the degree of concomitant variation between variable X and variable Y. The *coefficient of correlation* is the numerical index that expresses this relationship. It tells us the extent to which X and Y are "co-related."

The meaning of a correlation coefficient is interpreted by its sign and magnitude. If a correlation coefficient were a person asked "What's your sign?" it wouldn't answer anything like "Leo" or "Pisces." It would answer "Plus" (for a positive correlation), "Minus" (for a negative correlation), or "None" (in the rare instance that the correlation coefficient was exactly equal to zero). If asked to supply information about its magnitude, it would respond with a number anywhere at all between -1 and $+1$. And here is a rather intriguing fact about the magnitude of a correlation coefficient: it is judged by its absolute value. This means that to the extent that we are impressed by correlation coefficients, a correlation of $-.99$ is every bit as impressive as a correlation of $+.99$. To understand why, you need to know a bit more about correlation.

"Ahh . . . a perfect correlation! Let me count the ways." Well, actually there are only *two*. The two ways to describe a perfect correlation between two variables can be summed up as either $+1$ or -1. If a correlation coefficient has a value of $+1$ or -1, the relationship between the two variables being correlated is perfect, without error in the statistical sense. And just as perfection in almost anything is difficult to find, so too are perfect correlations. It's challenging to try to think of any two variables in psychological work that are perfectly correlated. Perhaps that is why we raise that very question in the margin.

JUST THINK . . .

What two psychological variables are perfectly correlated? How about two psychological variables that just come close to being perfectly correlated?

If two variables simultaneously increase or simultaneously decrease, then those two variables are said to be *positively* (or directly) correlated. The height and weight of normal, healthy children ranging in age from birth to 10 years tend to be positively or directly correlated. As children get older, their height and their weight generally increase simultaneously. A positive correlation also exists when two variables simultaneously decrease. For example, the less preparation a student does for an examination, the lower the score on the examination. A *negative* (or inverse) correlation occurs when one variable increases while the other variable decreases. For example, there tends to be an inverse relationship between the number of miles on your car's odometer (mileage indicator) and the number of dollars a car dealer is willing to give you on a trade-in allowance; all other things being equal, as the mileage increases, the number of dollars offered on trade-in decreases.

If a correlation is zero, then absolutely no relationship exists between the two variables. And just as it is nearly impossible in psychological work to identify two variables that have a perfect correlation, so it is nearly impossible to identify two variables that have a zero correlation. Most of the time, two variables will be fractionally correlated. The fractional correlation will often be small but seldom zero.

As we stated in our introduction to this topic, correlation is often confused with causation. It must be emphasized that a correlation coefficient is merely an index of the relationship between two variables, *not* an index of the causal relationship between two variables. If you were told, for example, that from birth to age 9 there is a high positive correlation between hat size and spelling ability, would it be appropriate to conclude that hat size causes spelling ability? Of course not. The period from birth to age 9 is a time of maturation in *all* areas, including physical size and cognitive abilities such as spelling. Intellectual development parallels physical development during these years, and a relationship clearly exists between physical and mental growth. Still, the relationship between hat size and spelling ability is not necessarily causal.

Although correlation does not imply causation, there *is* an implication of prediction. Stated another way, if we know that there is a high correlation between X and Y, we should be able to predict—with various degrees of accuracy, depending on other factors—the value of one of these variables if we know the value of the other.

> **JUST THINK . . .**
>
> What two psychological variables have a correlation of zero? How about two psychological variables that just come close to having a zero correlation?

The Pearson r

Many techniques have been devised to measure correlation. The most widely used of all is the **Pearson r,** also known as the *Pearson correlation coefficient* and the *Pearson product-moment coefficient of correlation.* Devised by Karl Pearson (Figure 4–2), *r* can be the statistical tool of choice when the relationship between the variables is linear and when the two variables being correlated are continuous (that is, they can theoretically take any value). Other correlational techniques can be employed with data that are discontinuous and where the relationship is nonlinear. The formula for the Pearson *r* takes into account the relative position of each test score or measurement with respect to the mean of the distribution.

A number of formulas can be used to calculate a Pearson *r.* One formula necessitates converting each raw score to a standard score and then multiplying each pair of standard scores. A mean for the sum of the products is calculated, and that mean is the value of the Pearson *r.* Even from this simple verbal conceptualization of the Pearson *r,* it can be seen that the sign of the resulting *r* would be a function of the sign and the magnitude of the standard scores used. If, for example, negative standard score values for measurements of X always corresponded with negative standard score values for Y scores, the resulting *r* would be positive (because the product of two negative values is positive).

Figure 4–2
Karl Pearson (1857–1936)

Pictured here with his daughter is Karl Pearson, whose name has become synonymous with correlation. History records, however, that it was actually Sir Francis Galton who should be credited with developing the concept of correlation (Magnello & Spies, 1984). Galton experimented with many formulas to measure correlation, including one he labeled r. Pearson, a contemporary of Galton's, modified Galton's r, and the rest, as they say, is history. The Pearson r eventually became the most widely used measure of correlation.

Similarly, if positive standard score values on X always corresponded with positive standard score values on Y, the resulting correlation would also be positive. However, if positive standard score values for X corresponded with negative standard score values for Y and vice versa, an inverse relationship would exist, and a negative correlation would result. A zero or near-zero correlation could result when some products are positive and some are negative.

The formula used to calculate a Pearson r from raw scores is

$$r = \frac{\Sigma (X - \overline{X})(Y - \overline{Y})}{\sqrt{[\Sigma (X - \overline{X})^2][\Sigma (Y - \overline{Y})^2]}}$$

This formula has been simplified for shortcut purposes. One such shortcut is a deviation formula employing "little x," or x in place of $X - \overline{X}$, and "little y," or y in place of $Y - \overline{Y}$:

$$r = \frac{\Sigma xy}{\sqrt{(\Sigma x^2)(\Sigma y^2)}}$$

Another formula for calculating a Pearson r is

$$r = \frac{N \Sigma XY - (\Sigma X)(\Sigma Y)}{\sqrt{N \Sigma X^2 - (\Sigma X)^2} \sqrt{N \Sigma Y^2 - (\Sigma Y)^2}}$$

Although this formula looks more complicated than the previous deviation formula, it is easier to use. N represents the number of paired scores; ΣXY is the sum of the product of the paired X and Y scores; ΣX is the sum of the X scores; ΣY is the sum of the Y scores; ΣX^2 is the sum of the squared X scores; and ΣY^2 is the sum of the squared Y scores. Similar results are obtained with the use of each formula.

The next logical question concerns what to do with the number obtained for the value of r. The answer is that you ask even more questions, such as "Is this number statistically significant given the size and nature of the sample?" or "Could this result have occurred by chance?" At this point, you will need to consult tables of significance for Pearson r—tables that are probably in the back of your old statistics textbook. In those tables you will find, for example, that a Pearson r of .899 with an $N = 10$ is significant at the .01 level (using a two-tailed test). You will recall from your statistics course that significance at the .01 level tells you, with reference to these data, that a correlation such as this could have been expected to occur by chance alone one time or less in a hundred if X and Y are not correlated in the population. You will also recall that significance at either the .01 level or the (somewhat less rigorous) .05 level provides a basis to conclude that a correlation does indeed exist. Significance at the .05 level means that the result could have been expected to occur by chance alone five times or less in a hundred.

The value obtained for the coefficient of correlation can be further interpreted by deriving from it what is called a **coefficient of determination,** or r^2. The coefficient of determination is an indication of how much variance is shared by the X and the Y variables. The calculation of r^2 is quite straightforward. Simply square the correlation coefficient, multiply by 100, and express the result equal to the percentage of the variance accounted for. If, for example, you calculated r to be .9, then r^2 would be equal to .81. The remaining variance, equal to 100 $(1 - r^2)$, or 19%, could presumably be accounted for by chance, error, or otherwise unmeasured or unexplainable factors.[7]

Before moving on to consider another index of correlation, let's address a very logical question sometimes raised by students when they hear the Pearson r referred to as the *product-moment coefficient of correlation.* Why is it called that? The answer is a little complicated, but here goes.

In the language of psychometrics, a *moment* describes a deviation about a mean of a distribution. Individual deviations about the mean of a distribution are referred to as *deviates.* Deviates are referred to as the *first moments* of the distribution. The *second moments* of the distribution are the moments squared. The *third moments* of the distribution are the moments cubed, and so forth. The computation of the Pearson r in one of its many formulas entails multiplying corresponding standard scores on two measures. One way of conceptualizing standard scores is as the first moments of a distribution. This is because standard scores are deviates about a mean of zero. A formula that entails the multiplication of two corresponding standard scores can therefore be conceptualized as one that entails the computation of the *product* of corresponding *moments.* And there you have the reason r is called *product-moment correlation.* It's probably all more a matter of psychometric trivia than anything else, but we think it's cool to know.

The Spearman Rho

The Pearson r enjoys such widespread use and acceptance as an index of correlation that if for some reason it is not used to compute a correlation coefficient, mention is made of the statistic that was used. There are many alternative ways to derive a coefficient of correlation. One commonly used alternative statistic is variously called a **rank-order correlation coefficient,** a **rank-difference correlation coefficient,** or simply **Spearman's rho.**

---

7. On a technical note, Ozer (1985) cautioned that the actual estimation of a coefficient of determination must be made with scrupulous regard to the assumptions operative in the particular case. Evaluating a coefficient of determination solely in terms of the variance accounted for may lead to interpretations that underestimate the magnitude of a relation.

YOU STANDARD SCORES ARE A BUNCH OF
DEVIATES ABOUT A MEAN OF ZERO!

Developed by Charles Spearman, a British psychologist (Figure 4–3), this coefficient of correlation is frequently used when the sample size is small (fewer than 30 pairs of measurements) and especially when both sets of measurements are in ordinal (or rank-order) form. Special tables are used to determine if an obtained rho coefficient is or is not significant.

Graphic Representations of Correlation

One type of graphic description of correlation is the **scatterplot** or **scatter diagram.** A scatterplot is a simple graphing of the coordinate points for values of the X variable (placed along the graph's horizontal axis) and the Y variable (placed along the graph's vertical axis). Scatterplots are useful because they provide a quick indication of the direction and magnitude of the relationship, if any, between the two variables. Figures 4–4 and 4–5 offer a quick course in eyeballing the nature and degree of correlation by means of scatterplots. In distinguishing positive from negative correlations, note the direction of the curve. And in estimating the strength of magnitude of the correlation, note the degree to which the points form a straight line.

Scatterplots are useful in revealing the presence of curvilinearity in a relationship. Remember that a Pearson r should be used only if the relationship between the variables is linear. If the graph does not appear to take the form of a straight line, the chances are good that the relationship is not linear (Figure 4–6). When the relationship is nonlinear, other statistical tools and techniques may be employed.[8]

---

8. The specific statistic to be employed will depend at least in part on the suspected reason for the nonlinearity. For example, if it is believed that the nonlinearity is due to one distribution being highly skewed because of a poor measuring instrument, the skewed distribution may be statistically normalized, and the result may be a correction of the curvilinearity. If even after graphing the data a question remains concerning the linearity of the correlation, a statistic called "eta squared" (η^2) can be used to compute the exact degree of curvilinearity.

Figure 4–3
Charles Spearman (1863–1945)

Charles Spearman is best known as the developer of the Spearman rho statistic and the Spearman-Brown prophecy formula, which is used to "prophesize" the accuracy of tests of different sizes. Spearman is also credited with being the father of a statistical method called factor analysis, discussed later in this text.

A graph also makes the spotting of outliers relatively easy. An **outlier** is an extremely atypical point located at a relatively long distance—an outlying distance—from the rest of the coordinate points in a scatterplot (Figure 4–7). Outliers stimulate interpreters of test data to speculate about the reason for the atypical score. For example, consider an outlier on a scatterplot that reflects a correlation between hours each member of a fifth-grade class spent studying and their grades on a 20-item spelling test. And let's say one student studied for 10 hours and received a failing grade. This outlier on the scatterplot might raise a red flag and compel the test user to raise some important questions, such as "How effective are this student's study skills and habits?" or "What was this student's state of mind during the test?"

In some cases, outliers are simply the result of administering a test to a very small sample of testtakers. In the example cited above, if the test were given statewide to fifth-graders and the sample size were much larger, perhaps many more low-scorers who put in large amounts of study time would be identified.

As is the case with very low raw scores or raw scores of zero, outliers can sometimes help identify a testtaker who did not understand the instructions, was not able to follow the instructions, or was simply oppositional and did not follow the instructions. In other cases, an outlier can provide a hint of some deficiency in the testing or scoring procedures.

People who have occasion to use or make interpretations from graphed data need to know if the range of scores has been restricted in any way. To understand why this is so necessary to know, consider Figure 4–8. Let's say that graph A describes the relationship between Public University entrance test scores for 600 applicants (all of whom were later admitted) and their grade-point averages at the end of the first semester. The scatterplot indicates that the relationship between entrance test scores and grade-point average is both linear and positive. But what if the admissions officer had accepted only

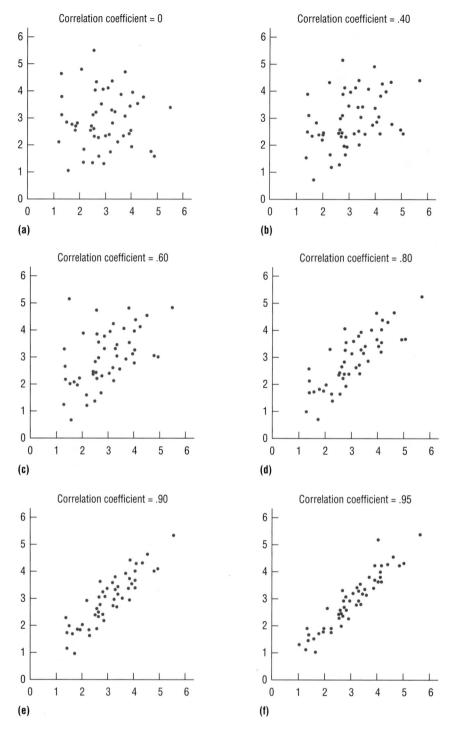

Figure 4–4
Scatterplots and Correlations for Positive Values of _r_

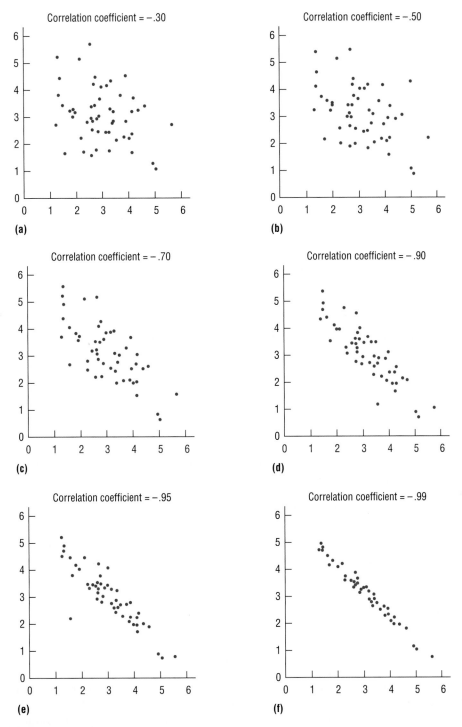

Figure 4–5
Scatterplots and Correlations for Negative Values of _r_

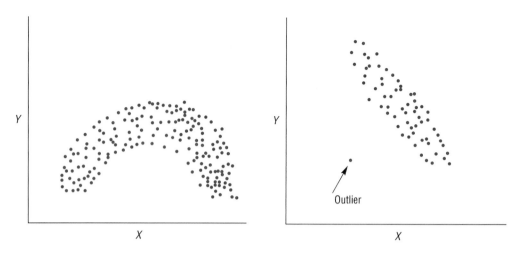

Figure 4–6
Scatterplot Showing a Nonlinear Correlation

Figure 4–7
Scatterplot Showing an Outlier

the applications of the students who scored within the top half or so on the entrance exam? To a trained eye, this scatterplot (graph B) appears to indicate a weaker correlation than that indicated in graph A—an effect attributable exclusively to the restriction of range. Graph B is less a straight line than graph A, and its direction is not as obvious.

Regression

In everyday language, the word *regression* is synonymous with "reversion to some previous state." In the language of statistics, *regression* also describes a kind of reversion—a reversion to the mean over time or generations (or at least that is what it meant originally).

Regression may be defined broadly as the analysis of relationships among variables for the purpose of understanding how one variable may predict another. **Simple regression** involves one independent variable (X), typically referred to as the *predictor variable*, and one dependent variable (Y), typically referred to as the *outcome variable*. Simple regression analysis results in an equation for a regression line. The **regression line** is the *line of best fit*, the straight line that, in one sense, comes closest to the greatest number of points on the scatterplot of X and Y.

Does the following equation look familiar?

$$Y = a + bX$$

In high school algebra, you were probably taught that this is the equation for a straight line. It's also the equation for a regression line. In the formula, a and b are **regression coefficients;** b is equal to the slope of the line, and a is the **intercept,** a constant indicating where the line crosses the Y-axis. The regression line represented by specific values of a and b is fitted precisely to the points on the scatterplot, such that the sum of the squared vertical distances from the points to the line will be smaller than for any other line that could be drawn through the same scatterplot. Although finding the equation for the regression line might seem difficult, the values of a and b can be determined through simple algebraic calculations.

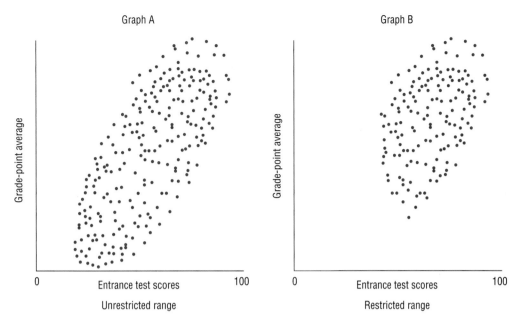

Figure 4–8
Two Scatterplots Illustrating Unrestricted and Restricted Ranges

The primary use of a regression equation in testing is to predict one score or variable from another. For example, suppose a dean at the De Sade School of Dentistry wishes to predict what grade-point average (GPA) an applicant might have after the first year at De Sade. The dean would accumulate data about current students' scores on the dental college entrance examination and end-of-the-first-year GPA. These data would then be used to help predict the GPA (Y) from the score on the dental college admissions test (X). Individual dental students are represented by points in the scatterplot in Figure 4–9. The equation for the regression line is computed from these data. This means that the values of a and b are calculated. In this hypothetical case:

$$GPA = 0.82 + 0.03 \text{ (entrance exam)}$$

This line has been drawn onto the scatterplot in Figure 4–9.

Using the regression line, the likely value of Y (the GPA) can be predicted based on specific values of X (the entrance exam) by plugging the X-value into the equation. A student with an entrance exam score of 50 would be expected to have a GPA of 2.3. A student with an entrance exam score of 85 would be expected to earn a GPA of 3.7. This prediction could also be done graphically by tracing a particular value on the X-axis (the entrance exam score) up to the regression line, then straight across to the Y-axis, reading off the predicted GPA.

Of course, all students who get an entrance exam score of 50 do not earn the same GPA. This can be seen in Figure 4–8 by tracing from any specific entrance exam score on the X-axis up to the cloud of points surrounding the regression line. This is what is meant by error in prediction: Each of these students would be predicted to get the same GPA based on the entrance exam, but in fact they earned different GPAs. This error in the prediction of Y from X is represented by the **standard error of the estimate.** As you

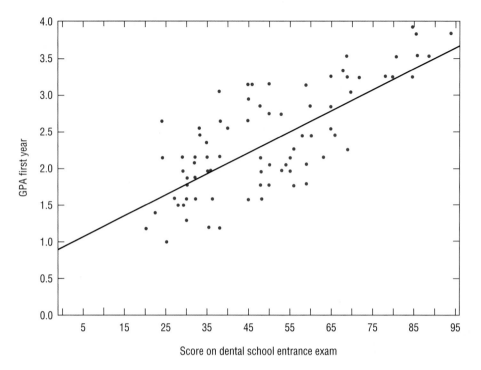

Figure 4–9
Graphic Representation of Regression Line

The correlation between X and Y is 0.76. The equation for this regression line is Y = 0.82 + 0.03(X); for each unit increase on X (the dental school entrance examination score), the predicted value of Y (the first-year grade-point average) is expected to increase by .03 unit. The standard error of the estimate for this prediction is 0.49.

might expect, the higher the correlation between *X* and *Y*, the greater the accuracy of the prediction and the smaller the standard error of the estimate.

Multiple regression   Suppose that the dean suspects that the prediction of GPA will be enhanced if another test score—say, a score on a test of fine motor skills—is also used as a predictor. The use of more than one score to predict *Y* requires the use of a *multiple regression* equation.

The **multiple regression** equation takes into account the intercorrelations among all the variables involved. The correlation between each of the predictor scores and what is being predicted is reflected in the weight given to each predictor. In this case, what is being predicted is the correlation of the entrance exam and the fine motor skills test with the GPA in the first year of dental school. Predictors that correlate highly with the predicted variable are generally given more weight. This means that their regression coefficients (referred to as *b*-values) are larger. No surprise there. We would expect test users to pay the most attention to predictors that predict (*Y*) best.

The multiple regression equation also takes into account the correlations among the predictor scores. In this case, it takes into account the correlation between the dental college admissions test scores and scores on the fine motor skills test. If many predictors are used, and one is not correlated with any of the other predictors but is correlated with the predicted score, then that predictor may be given relatively more weight because it is providing unique information. In contrast, if two predictor scores are highly correlated with each other, they could be providing redundant information. If both were kept in the regression equation, each might get less weight so that they would "share" the prediction of Y.

More predictors are not necessarily better. If two predictors are providing the same information, the person using the regression equation may decide to use only one of them for the sake of efficiency. If the De Sade dean observed that dental school admission test scores and scores on the test of fine motor skills were highly correlated with each other and that each of these scores correlated about the same with GPA, the dean might decide to use only one predictor because nothing was gained by the addition of the second predictor.

Inference from Measurement

Correlation, regression, and multiple regression are all statistical tools used to help ensure that predictions or inferences drawn from test data are reasonable and, to the extent that it is technically possible, accurate. Another statistical tool that can be helpful in achieving such objectives is meta-analysis.

Meta-Analysis

Generally, the best estimate of the correlation between two variables is most likely to come not from a single study alone but from analysis of the data from several studies. However, the data from several studies are likely to contain correlation coefficients as well as other statistics that differ for each study. One option to facilitate understanding of the research across a number of studies is to present the range of statistical values that appear in various studies: "The correlation between variable X and variable Y ranges from .73 to .91." Another option is to combine statistically the information across the various studies. This statistical combination of information across studies is termed **meta-analysis.** Meta-analysis produces single estimates of the statistics being studied. See, for example, Kuncel et al.'s (2001) meta-analysis of the Graduate Record Examination (GRE). Using a number of published studies, these researchers explored the predictive value of the GRE and undergraduate grade-point average for performance in graduate school.

A key advantage of meta-analysis over simply reporting a range of findings is that in meta-analysis more weight can be given to studies that have larger numbers of subjects. This weighting process results in more accurate estimates (Hunter & Schmidt, 1990). Despite this fact as well as other advantages (Hall & Rosenthal, 1995), meta-analysis remains, to some degree, art as well as science. The value of any meta-analytic investigation is very much a matter of the skill and ability of the meta-analyst (Kavale, 1995).

Culture and Inference

In a series of experiments on conformity, Solomon Asch (1951, 1955, 1957a, 1957b) demonstrated the profound influence of the opinions of group members on an individual. In one version of the experiment, subjects were seated around a table and told that their task would be to select verbally one of three lines that was the same length as a stimulus line. Actually, only one of the group members was a bona fide subject, the other group members were confederates of the experimenter who would, on cue, unanimously name the same, wrong line.

Asch found that under such circumstances 76% of the subjects conformed to the obviously wrong choice of the group at least once. Since the mid-1950s, 133 studies in 17 countries have employed the Asch line judgment paradigm to study conformity. A meta-analysis of such studies brought to light differences in the results as a function of whether the culture in which the study was conducted was collectivistic or individualistic. Bond and Smith (1996) concluded that collectivistic countries evidenced higher levels of conformity than countries identified as more individualistic.

The Bond and Smith meta-analysis of international research employing Asch-type line judgment tasks provides a useful point of departure for emphasizing the roles of culture and context in measurement and the process of making inferences. In describing people with the use of trait terms such as, for example, *conformist* versus *nonconformist*, we need to be clear about standards of comparison. In this case, conforming or nonconforming with reference to whom?

Consider an individual born and raised in a collectivistic country such as China. The individual relocates to the United States, a country that is strongly individualistic by contrast. In China, the person may have been viewed as a nonconformist given the norm of conformity in China. However, in the United States, this person's behavior might be viewed as conformist. In all likelihood, the conformity-related trait of this individual's personality did not reverse itself as a result of boarding a jet for the United States. What changed was the background or context that framed the behavior under scrutiny. In the figure-ground relationship, we know that changing the ground can markedly affect one's perception of the figure.

In addition to culture, we may look to other variables for useful contextual cues in which to interpret and analyze assessment data. One such contextual cue is what is variously referred to as the era, the generation, or the "times" in which an individual was born and raised. Recalling her own youth, anthropologist Margaret Mead (1978, p. 71) wrote, "We grew up under skies across which no satellite had flashed." In interpreting assessment data from assessees from different generations, it would seem useful to keep in mind whether satellites had or had not flashed in the sky. More generally, Rogler (2002) has brought much needed attention to the relevance of historical context in evaluation.

JUST THINK . . .

What event in recent history may have relevance when interpreting data from a psychological assessment?

Moving from a focus on assessees to broader, methodological issues in everyday testing and assessment, let's briefly revisit the subject of norms. Norms typically provide the background and context for the test behavior under scrutiny. In most instances, as in the case of the vast majority of standardized tests, the test norms come in the form of tables published in the test manual.[9] Test users and assessment professionals have an obligation to use the appropriate norms when attempting to derive meaning and make inferences from data derived from tests, interviews, and other tools of psychological assessment. In recognition of this professional mandate, it is increasingly common to read of published evaluations of existing norms for use with particular populations. Additionally, we increasingly read of norming projects conducted after the publication of a particular test, typically with groups that either were not included in the original nor-

---

9. Less frequently, as in the case of a projective test used by a clinician in idiosyncratic fashion, the norms are more subjective and intuitive. That is, they are the product not of formal normative research but of the test user's own education, training, and clinical experience.

Table 4–1
Culturally Informed Assessment: Some "Do's" and "Don'ts"

Do	Do *Not*
Be aware of the cultural assumptions on which a test is based	Take for granted that a test is based on assumptions that impact all groups in much the same way
Consider consulting with members of particular cultural communities regarding the appropriateness of particular assessment techniques, tests, or test items	Take for granted that members of all cultural communities will automatically deem particular techniques, tests, or test items appropriate for use
Strive to incorporate assessment methods that complement the worldview and lifestyle of assessees who come from a specific cultural and linguistic population	Take a "one-size-fits-all" view of assessment when it comes to evaluation of persons from various cultural and linguistic populations
Be knowledgeable about the many alternative tests or measurement procedures that may be used to fulfill the assessment objectives	Select tests or other tools of assessment with little or no regard for the extent to which such tools are appropriate for use with the assessees
Be aware of equivalence issues across cultures, including equivalence of language used and the constructs measured	Simply assume that a test that has been translated into another language is automatically equivalent in every way to the original
Score, interpret, and analyze assessment data in its cultural context with due consideration of cultural hypotheses as possible explanations for findings	Score, interpret, and analyze assessment in a cultural vacuum

mative sample or were believed to be underrepresented in that sample.[10] Also, in recent years increasing attention has been given to the technical and multifaceted issues regarding the adaptation of a test standardized and normed with members of one culture for use with members of another culture.

Interwoven throughout this book is discussion of culture in the assessment enterprise. At this point, it is appropriate to introduce some "do's" and "don'ts" with regard to *culturally informed assessment* (a term we elaborate on in Chapter 11). Think of the guidelines presented in Table 4–1 as a list of themes that may be repeated in different ways as you continue to learn about the assessment enterprise. To supplement this list, the interested reader is referred to guidelines published by the American Psychological Association (2003). For now, let's continue to build a sound foundation in testing and assessment with a discussion of the psychometric concept of *reliability* in the next chapter.

Self-Assessment

Test your understanding of elements of this chapter by seeing if you can explain each of the following terms, expressions, and abbreviations:

age-equivalent scores
age norms
coefficient of correlation
coefficient of determination

construct
content-referenced testing and assessment
convenience sample

correlation
criterion
criterion-referenced testing and assessment

---

10. Other situations may prompt an evaluation of the adequacy of existing norms or stimulate the development of new norms. These situations include substituting one subtest for another subtest, abbreviating a test in some way, or making any deviation from the test administration instructions in the test's manual (Lyons & Scotti, 1994; McCusker, 1994; Reynolds et al., 1996).

cumulative scoring
domain sampling
equipercentile method
error variance
fixed reference group scoring
grade norms
incidental sample
intercept
local norms
meta-analysis
multiple regression
national anchor norms
national norms
norm
normative sample
norming

norm-referenced testing and
   assessment
outlier
Pearson *r*
percentage correct
percentile
program norms
purposive sampling
race norming
rank-order/rank-difference
   correlation coefficient
regression
regression coefficient
regression line
sample
sampling

scatterplot
simple regression
Spearman's rho
standard error of the estimate
standardization
state
stratified-random sampling
stratified sampling
subgroup norms
trait
true score theory
user norms
$Y = a + bX$

Web Watch

Check out the following Web sites for more information about topics discussed in this chapter.

Assumption 7: testing and assessment is beneficial for society
http://chiron.valdosta.edu/mawhatley/3900/testmeas.htm

APA Web site: How to find information about "good" psychological tests
www.apa.org/science/faq-findtests.html

Norm-referenced vs. criterion-referenced tests (basic chart)
http://chiron.valdosta.edu/whuitt/col/measeval/crnmref.html

The Pearson correlation coefficient
www.texasoft.com/winkpear.html

Reliability and validity
www.sportsci.org/resource/stats/precision.html

Correlation
www.stat.uiuc.edu/courses/stat100//java/guess/GCApplet.html

http://noppa5.pc.helsinki.fi/koe/corr/cor7.html

http://stat-www.berkeley.edu/users/stark/Java/Correlation.htm

Regression
www.stat.sc.edu/~west/javahtml/Regression.html

www.math.csusb.edu/faculty/stanton/m262/regress/regress.html

www.stat.uiuc.edu/courses/stat100//java/guess/PPApplet.html

5

Reliability

In everyday conversation, *reliability* is a synonym for *dependability* or *consistency.* We speak of the train that is so reliable you can set your watch by it. If we are lucky, we have a reliable friend who is always there for us in a time of need.

Broadly speaking, in the language of psychometrics *reliability* refers to consistency in measurement. And whereas in everyday conversation *reliability* always connotes something positive, in the psychometric sense it really only refers to something that is consistent—not necessarily consistently good or bad, but simply consistent.

It is important for us, as users of tests and consumers of information about tests, to know how reliable tests and other measurement procedures are. But reliability is not an all-or-none matter. A test may be reliable in one context and unreliable in another. There are different types and degrees of reliability. A **reliability coefficient** is an index of reliability, a proportion that indicates the ratio between the true score variance on a test and the total variance. In this chapter, we explore different kinds of reliability coefficients, including those for measuring test-retest reliability, alternate-forms reliability, split-half reliability, and inter-scorer reliability.

The Concept of Reliability

Recall from our discussion of classical test theory that a score on an ability test is presumed to reflect the testtaker's true score on the ability being measured, as well as error.[1] In its broadest sense, *error* refers to the component of the observed test score that does *not* have to do with the testtaker's ability. If we use X to represent an observed score, T to represent a true score, and E to represent error, then the fact that an observed score equals the true score plus error may be expressed as follows:

$$X = T + E$$

---

1. For illustration purposes, ability as a trait being measured is frequently used. However, unless stated otherwise, the principles to which we refer with respect to ability tests also hold true with respect to other types of tests, such as tests for personality. Thus, according to the true score model, it is also true that the magnitude of the presence of a certain psychological trait (such as extraversion) as measured by a test of extraversion will be due to (1) the "true" amount of extraversion and (2) other factors.

A statistic useful in describing sources of test score variability is the **variance** (σ^2)—the standard deviation squared. This statistic is useful because it can be broken into components. Variance from true differences is **true variance,** and variance from irrelevant, random sources is **error variance.** If (σ^2) represents the total variance, (σ_{tr}^2) the true variance, and (σ_e^2), the error variance, then the relationship of the variances can be expressed as

$$\sigma^2 = \sigma_{tr}^2 + \sigma_e^2$$

In this equation, the total variance in an observed distribution of test scores (σ^2) equals the sum of the true variance (σ_{tr}^2) plus the error variance (σ_e^2). The term **reliability** refers to the proportion of the total variance attributed to true variance. The greater the proportion of the total variance attributed to true variance, the more reliable the test. Because true differences are assumed to be stable, they are presumed to yield consistent scores on repeated administrations of the same test as well as on equivalent forms of tests. Because error variance may increase or decrease a test score by varying amounts, consistency of the test score—and thus the reliability—would be affected.

♦
JUST THINK . . .

What might be a source of systematic error inherent in all the tests an assessor administers in his or her private office?

Let's emphasize here that a systematic source of error would *not* affect score consistency. If a measuring instrument such as a weight scale consistently underweighed everyone who stepped on it by 5 pounds, then the relative standings of the people would remain unchanged. Of course, the recorded weights themselves would consistently vary from the true weight by 5 pounds. A scale underweighing all comers by 5 pounds is analogous to a constant being subtracted from (or added to) every test score. A systematic error source does not change the variability of the distribution or affect reliability.

Sources of Error Variance

Sources of error variance include test construction, administration, scoring, and/or interpretation.

Test construction   One source of variance during test construction is **item sampling** or **content sampling,** terms that refer to variation among items within a test as well as to variation among items between tests. Consider two or more tests designed to measure a specific skill, personality attribute, or body of knowledge. Differences are sure to be found in the way the items are worded and in the exact content sampled. Each of us has probably walked into an achievement test setting thinking, "I hope they ask this question," or "I hope they don't ask that question." With luck, only the questions we wanted to be asked appeared on the examination. In such situations, a testtaker would achieve a higher score on one as opposed to another test purporting to measure the same thing. The higher score would be due to the specific content sampled, the way the items were worded, and so on. The extent to which a testtaker's score is affected solely by the content sampled on the test as well as the way the content is sampled (that is, the way in which the item is constructed) is a source of error variance. From the perspective of a test creator, a challenge in test development is to maximize the proportion of the total variance that is true variance and minimize the proportion of the total variance that is error variance.

Test administration   Sources of error variance that occur during test administration may influence the testtaker's attention or motivation. The testtaker's reactions to those influences are the source of one kind of error variance. Examples of untoward influences during administration of a test include factors related to the *test environment:* the room temperature, the level of lighting, and the amount of ventilation and noise, for instance. A relentless fly may develop a tenacious attraction to an examinee's face. A wad of gum on the seat of the chair may make itself known only after the testtaker sits down on it. Other environment-related variables include the instrument used to enter responses, even the writing surface on which responses are entered. A pencil with a dull or broken point can hamper the blackening of little grids. The writing surface on a school desk may be riddled with heart carvings, the legacy of past years' students who felt compelled to express their eternal devotion to someone now long forgotten.

Other potential sources of error variance during test administration are *testtaker variables.* Pressing emotional problems, physical discomfort, lack of sleep, and the effects of drugs or medication can all be sources of error variance. A testtaker may, for whatever reason, make a mistake in entering a test response. For example, the examinee might blacken a "b" grid when he or she meant to blacken the "d" grid. An examinee may simply misread a test item. For example, an examinee might read "Which is not a source of error variance?" as "Which is a source of error variance?" Other simple mistakes can have score-depleting consequences. Responding to the fifth item on a multiple-choice test, for example, the testtaker might blacken the grid for the sixth item. Just one skipped question will result in every subsequent test response being out of sync. Formal learning experiences, casual life experiences, therapy, illness, and changes in mood or mental state are other potential sources of testtaker-related error variance.

Examiner-related variables are potential sources of error variance. The examiner's physical appearance and demeanor, even the presence or absence of an examiner, are some factors for consideration here. Some examiners in some testing situations might knowingly or unwittingly depart from the procedure prescribed for a particular test. On an oral examination, some examiners might unwittingly provide clues by emphasizing key words as they pose questions. They may convey information about the correctness of a response through head nodding, eye movements, or other nonverbal gestures. Clearly, the level of professionalism exhibited by examiners is a source of error variance.

Test scoring and interpretation   The advent of computer scoring and a growing reliance on objective, computer-scorable items virtually have eliminated error variance caused by scorer differences in many tests. However, not all tests can be scored from grids blackened by number two pencils. Individually administered intelligence tests, some tests of personality, tests of creativity, various behavioral measures, and countless other tests still require hand scoring by trained personnel.

Manuals for individual intelligence tests tend to be very explicit about scoring criteria lest examinees' measured intelligence vary as a function of who is doing the testing and scoring. In some tests of personality, examinees are asked to supply open-ended responses to stimuli such as pictures, words, sentences, and inkblots, and it is the examiner who must then quantify or qualitatively evaluate responses. In one test of creativity, examinees might be given the task of creating as many things as they can out of a set of blocks. Here, it is the examiner's task to determine which block constructions will be awarded credit and which will not. For a behavioral measure of social skills in an inpatient psychiatric service, the scorers or raters might be asked to rate patients with respect to the variable "social relatedness." Such a behavioral measure might require the rater to check *yes* or *no* to items like *Patient says "Good morning" to at least two staff members.*

Scorers and scoring systems are potential sources of error variance. A test may employ objective-type items amenable to computer scoring of well-documented reliability.

> **JUST THINK . . .**
>
> Can you conceive of a test item on a rating scale requiring human judgment that all raters will score the same 100% of the time?

Yet even then, the possibility of a technical glitch contaminating the data is possible. If subjectivity is involved in scoring, the scorer (or rater) can be a source of error variance. Indeed, despite very rigorous scoring criteria set forth in many of the better-known tests of intelligence, examiner/scorers occasionally still are confronted by situations where an examinee's response lies in a gray area. The element of subjectivity in scoring may be much greater in the administration of certain nonobjective-type personality tests, tests of creativity (such as the block test described above), and certain academic tests (such as essay examinations). Subjectivity in scoring can even enter into behavioral assessment. Consider the case of two behavior observers given the task of rating one psychiatric in-patient on the variable of "social relatedness." On an item that asks simply whether two staff members were greeted in the morning, one rater might judge the patient's eye contact and mumbling of something to two staff members to qualify as a *yes* response. The other observer might feel strongly that a *no* response to the item is appropriate. Such problems in scoring agreement can be addressed through rigorous training designed to make the consistency—or reliability—of various scorers as nearly perfect as can be.

Other sources of error   Certain types of assessment situations lend themselves to particular varieties of systematic and nonsystematic error. For example, consider assessing the degree of agreement between partners regarding the quality and quantity of physical and psychological abuse in their relationship. As Moffitt et al. (1997) observed, "Because partner abuse usually occurs in private, there are only two persons who 'really' know what goes on behind closed doors: the two members of the couple" (p. 47). Potential sources of nonsystematic error in such an assessment situation include forgetting, failing to notice abusive behavior, and misunderstanding instructions regarding reporting. A number of studies (O'Leary & Arias, 1988; Riggs et al., 1989; Straus, 1979) have suggested underreporting or overreporting of perpetration of abuse also may contribute to systematic error. Females, for example, may underreport abuse due to fear, shame, or social desirability factors and overreport abuse if they are seeking help. Males may underreport abuse due to embarrassment and social desirability factors and overreport abuse if they are attempting to justify the report.

> **JUST THINK . . .**
>
> Recall your score on the most recent test you took. What percentage of that score do you think represented your "true" ability, and what percentage of that score was represented by error? Now, hazard a guess as to what type(s) of error.

Just as the amount of abuse one partner suffers at the hands of the other may never be known, so the amount of test variance that is true relative to error may never be known. A so-called true score, as Stanley (1971, p. 361) put it, is "not the ultimate fact in the book of the recording angel." Further, the utility of the methods used for estimating true versus error variance is a hotly debated matter (see, for example, Collins, 1996; Humphreys, 1996; Williams & Zimmerman, 1996a, 1996b). Let's take a closer look at such estimates and how they are derived.

Reliability Estimates

Test-Retest Reliability Estimates

A ruler made from the highest-quality steel can be a very reliable instrument of measurement. Every time you measure something that is exactly 12 inches long, for example, your ruler will tell you that what you are measuring is exactly 12 inches long. The reliability of this instrument of measurement may also be said to be stable over time. Whether you measure the 12 inches today, tomorrow, or next year, the ruler is still going to measure 12 inches as 12 inches. By contrast, a ruler constructed of putty might be a very unreliable instrument of measurement. One minute it could measure some known 12-inch standard as 12 inches, the next minute it could measure it as 14 inches, and a week later it could measure it as 18 inches. One way of estimating the reliability of a measuring instrument is by using the same instrument to measure the same thing at two points in time. In psychometric parlance, this approach to reliability evaluation is called the *test-retest method,* and the result of such an evaluation is an estimate of *test-retest reliability.*

Test-retest reliability is an estimate of reliability obtained by correlating pairs of scores from the same people on two different administrations of the same test. The test-retest measure is appropriate when evaluating the reliability of a test that purports to measure something that is relatively stable over time, such as a personality trait. If the characteristic being measured is assumed to fluctuate over time, there would be little sense in assessing the reliability of the test using the test-retest method.

As time passes, people change. For example, people may learn new things, forget some things, and acquire new skills. It is generally the case, although there are exceptions, that as the time interval between administrations of the same test increases, the correlation between the scores obtained on each testing decreases. The passage of time can be a source of error variance. The longer the time that passes, the greater the likelihood that the reliability coefficient will be lower. When the interval between testing is greater than six months, the estimate of test-retest reliability is often referred to as the **coefficient of stability.**

An estimate of test-retest reliability from a math test might be low if the testtakers took a math tutorial before the second test was administered. An estimate of test-retest reliability from a personality profile might be low if the testtaker suffered some emotional trauma or received counseling during the intervening period. A low estimate of test-retest reliability might be found even when the interval between testings is relatively brief. This may well be the case when the testings occur during a time of great developmental change with respect to the variables they are designed to assess. An evaluation of a test-retest reliability coefficient must therefore extend beyond the magnitude of the obtained coefficient. If we are to come to proper conclusions about the reliability of the measuring instrument, evaluation of a test-retest reliability estimate must extend to a consideration of possible intervening factors between test administrations.

An estimate of test-retest reliability may be most appropriate in gauging the reliability of tests that employ outcome measures such as reaction time or perceptual judgments (including discriminations of brightness, loudness, or taste). However, even in measuring variables such as these, and even when the time period between the two administrations of the test is relatively small, various factors (such as experience, practice, memory, fatigue, and motivation) may intervene and confound an obtained measure of reliability.[2]

Parallel-Forms and Alternate-Forms Reliability Estimates

If you have ever taken a makeup exam in which the questions were not all the same as on the test initially given, you have had experience with different forms of a test. And if you have ever wondered whether the two forms of the test were really equivalent, you

---

2. Although we may refer to a number as the summary statement of the reliability of individual tools of measurement, any such index of reliability can be meaningfully interpreted only in the context of the process of measurement—the unique circumstances surrounding the use of the ruler, the test, or some other measuring instrument in a particular application or situation. More on that later.

have wondered about the *alternate-forms* or *parallel-forms* reliability of the test. The degree of the relationship between various forms of a test can be evaluated by means of an alternate-forms or parallel-forms coefficient of reliability, which is often termed the **coefficient of equivalence.**

Although frequently used interchangeably, there is a difference between the terms *alternate forms* and *parallel forms.* **Parallel forms** of a test exist when, for each form of the test, the means and the variances of observed test scores are equal. In theory, the means of scores obtained on parallel forms correlate equally with the true score. More practically, scores obtained on parallel tests correlate equally with other measures.

Alternate forms are simply different versions of a test that have been constructed so as to be parallel. Although they do not meet the requirements for the legitimate designation "parallel," alternate forms of a test are typically designed to be equivalent with respect to variables such as content and level of difficulty.

JUST THINK . . .

You missed the midterm examination and have to take a make-up exam. Your classmates tell you that they found the midterm impossibly difficult. Your instructor tells you that you will be taking an alternate form, not a parallel form, of the original test. How do you feel about that?

Obtaining estimates of **alternate-forms reliability** and **parallel-forms reliability** is similar in two ways to obtaining an estimate of test-retest reliability: (1) Two test administrations with the same group are required, and (2) test scores may be affected by factors such as motivation, fatigue, or intervening events such as practice, learning, or therapy (although not as much as when the same test is administered twice). An additional source of error variance, item sampling, is inherent in the computation of an alternate- or parallel-forms reliability coefficient. Testtakers may do better or worse on a specific form of the test not as a function of their true ability but simply because of the particular items that were selected for inclusion in the test.[3]

Developing alternate forms of tests can be time-consuming and expensive. Imagine what might be involved in trying to create sets of equivalent items and then getting the same people to sit for repeated administrations of an experimental test! On the other hand, once an alternate or parallel form of a test has been developed, it is advantageous to the test user in several ways. For example, it minimizes the effect of memory for the content of a previously administered form of the test.

JUST THINK . . .

From the perspective of the test user, what are other possible advantages of having alternate or parallel forms of the same test?

Certain traits are presumed to be relatively stable in people over time, and we would expect tests measuring those traits—alternate forms, parallel forms, or otherwise—to reflect that stability. As an example, we expect that there will be, and in fact there is, a reasonable degree of stability in scores on intelligence tests. Conversely, we might expect relatively little stability in scores obtained on a measure of state anxiety (anxiety felt at the moment).

An estimate of the reliability of a test can be obtained without developing an alternate form of the test and without having to administer the test twice to the same people. Deriving this type of estimate entails an evaluation of the *internal consistency* of the test items. Logically enough, it is referred to as an **internal consistency estimate of reliability** or as an **estimate of inter-item consistency.** There are different methods of obtaining internal consistency estimates of reliability. One such method is the *split-half estimate.*

---

3. According to the classical true score model, the effect of such factors on test scores is indeed presumed to be measurement error. There are alternative models in which the effect of such factors on fluctuating test scores would not be considered error (Atkinson, 1981).

Split-Half Reliability Estimates

An estimate of **split-half reliability** is obtained by correlating two pairs of scores obtained from equivalent halves of a single test administered once. It is a useful measure of reliability when it is impractical or undesirable to assess reliability with two tests or to have two test administrations (because of factors such as time or expense). The computation of a coefficient of split-half reliability generally entails three steps:

Step 1: Divide the test into equivalent halves.

Step 2: Compute a Pearson r between scores on the two halves of the test.

Step 3: Adjust the half-test reliability using the Spearman-Brown formula (discussed shortly).

When it comes to calculating split-half reliability coefficients, there's more than one way to split a test—but there are some ways you should *never* split a test. Simply dividing the test in the middle is not recommended, because this procedure would probably spuriously raise or lower the reliability coefficient. Different amounts of fatigue for the first as opposed to the second part of the test, different amounts of test anxiety, and differences in item difficulty as a function of placement in the test are all factors to consider.

One acceptable way to split a test is to randomly assign items to one or the other half of the test. Another acceptable way to split a test is to assign odd-numbered items to one-half of the test and even-numbered items to the other half. This method yields an estimate of split-half reliability that is also referred to as **odd-even reliability**.[4] Yet another way to split a test is to divide the test by content so that each half contains items equivalent with respect to content and difficulty. In general, a primary objective in splitting a test in half for the purpose of obtaining a split-half reliability estimate is to create what might be called "mini-parallel-forms," with each half equal to the other—or as nearly equal as humanly possible—in format, stylistic, statistical, and related aspects.

Step 2 in the procedure entails the computation of a Pearson r, which requires little explanation at this point. However, the third step requires the use of the Spearman-Brown formula.

The Spearman-Brown formula   The **Spearman-Brown formula** allows a test developer or user to estimate internal consistency reliability from a correlation of two halves of a test. It is a specific application of a more general formula to estimate the reliability of a test that is lengthened or shortened by any number of items. Because the reliability of a test is affected by its length, a formula is necessary for estimating the reliability of a test that has been shortened or lengthened. The general Spearman-Brown (r_{SB}) formula is

$$r_{SB} = \frac{nr_{xy}}{1 + (n-1)r_{xy}}$$

where r_{SB} is equal to the reliability adjusted by the Spearman-Brown formula, r_{xy} is equal to the Pearson r in the original-length test, and n is equal to the number of items in the revised version divided by the number of items in the original version.

---

4. One precaution here: With respect to a group of items on an achievement test that deals with a single problem, it is usually desirable to assign the whole group of items to one half of the test. Otherwise—if part of the group were in one half and another part in the other half—the similarity of the half scores would be spuriously inflated. In this instance, a single error in understanding, for example, might affect items in both halves of the test.

Table 5–1 Odd-Even Reliability Coefficients Before and After the Spearman-Brown Adjustment*	Grade	Half-Test Correlation (unadjusted r)	Whole-Test Estimate (r_{SB})
	K	.718	.836
	1	.807	.893
	2	.777	.875

*For scores on a test of mental ability.

By determining the reliability of one half of a test, a test developer can then use the Spearman-Brown formula to estimate the reliability of a whole test. Because a whole test is two times longer than half a test, n becomes 2 in the Spearman-Brown formula for the adjustment of split-half reliability. The symbol r_{hh} stands for the Pearson r of scores in the two half tests:

$$r_{SB} = \frac{2r_{hh}}{1 + r_{hh}}$$

Usually, but not always, reliability increases as test length increases. Ideally, the additional test items are equivalent with respect to the content and the range of difficulty of the original items. Estimates of reliability based on consideration of the entire test therefore tend to be higher than those based on half of a test. Table 5–1 shows half-test correlations presented alongside adjusted reliability estimates for the whole test. You can see that all the adjusted correlations are higher than the unadjusted correlations. This is so because Spearman-Brown estimates are based on a test that is twice as long as the original half test. For the data from the kindergarten pupils, for example, a half-test reliability of .718 can be estimated to be equivalent to a whole-test reliability of .836.

If test developers or users wish to shorten a test, the Spearman-Brown formula may be used to estimate the effect of the shortening on the test's reliability. Reduction in test size for the purpose of reducing test administration time is a common practice in certain situations. For example, the test administrator may have only limited time with a particular testtaker or group of testtakers. Reduction in test size may be indicated in situations where boredom or fatigue could produce responses of questionable meaningfulness.

JUST THINK . . .

What are other situations in which a reduction in test size or the time it takes to administer a test might be desirable? What are the arguments against reducing test size?

A Spearman-Brown formula could also be used to determine the number of items needed to attain a desired level of reliability. In adding items to increase test reliability to a desired level, the rule is that the new items must be equivalent in content and difficulty so that the longer test still measures what the original test measured. If the reliability of the original test is relatively low, it may be impractical to increase the number of items to reach an acceptable level of reliability. Another alternative would be to abandon this relatively unreliable instrument and locate—or develop—a suitable alternative. The reliability of the instrument could also be raised in some way. For example, the reliability of the instrument might be raised by creating new items, clarifying the test's instructions, or simplifying the scoring rules.

Internal consistency estimates of reliability, such as that obtained by use of the Spearman-Brown formula, are inappropriate for measuring the reliability of heterogeneous tests and speed tests. The impact of test characteristics on reliability is discussed in detail later in this chapter.

Other Methods of Estimating Internal Consistency

In addition to the Spearman-Brown formula, other methods in use to obtain estimates of internal consistency reliability include formulas developed by Kuder and Richardson (1937) and Cronbach (1951). **Inter-item consistency** refers to the degree of correlation among all the items on a scale. A measure of inter-item consistency is calculated from a single administration of a single form of a test. An index of inter-item consistency in turn is useful in assessing the **homogeneity** of the test. Tests are said to be *homogeneous* if they contain items that measure a single trait. As an adjective used to describe test items, *homogeneity* (derived from the Greek words *homos*, meaning "same," and *genos*, meaning "kind") is the degree to which a test measures a single factor. In other words, homogeneity is the extent to which items in a scale are unifactorial.

In contrast to test homogeneity, **heterogeneity** describes the degree to which a test measures different factors. A *heterogeneous* (or *nonhomogeneous*) test is composed of items that measure more than one trait. A test that assesses knowledge only of color television repair skills could be expected to be more homogeneous in content than a test of electronic repair. The former test assesses only one area, and the latter assesses several, such as knowledge not only of televisions but also of DVD players, digital cameras, video recorders, compact disc players, car satellite radio, and so forth.

The more homogeneous a test is, the more inter-item consistency it can be expected to have. Because a homogeneous test samples a relatively narrow content area, it is to be expected to contain more inter-item consistency than a heterogeneous test. Test homogeneity is desirable because it allows relatively straightforward test-score interpretation. Testtakers with the same score on a homogeneous test probably have similar abilities in the area tested. Testtakers with the same score on a more heterogeneous test may have quite different abilities.

Although a homogeneous test is desirable because it so readily lends itself to clear interpretation, it is often an insufficient tool for measuring multifaceted psychological variables such as intelligence or personality. One way to circumvent this potential source of difficulty has been to administer a series of homogeneous tests, each designed to measure some component of a heterogeneous variable.[5]

The Kuder-Richardson formulas   Dissatisfaction with existing split-half methods of estimating reliability compelled G. Frederic Kuder and M. W. Richardson (1937; Richardson & Kuder, 1939) to develop their own measures for estimating reliability. The most widely known of the many formulas they collaborated on is their **Kuder-Richardson formula 20,** or *KR-20,* so named because it was the twentieth formula developed in a series. Where test items are highly homogeneous, KR-20 and split-half reliability estimates will be similar. However, KR-20 is the statistic of choice for determining the inter-item consistency of dichotomous items, primarily those items that can be scored right or wrong (such as multiple-choice items). If test items are more heterogeneous, KR-20 will yield lower reliability estimates than the split-half method. Table 5–2 summarizes items on a sample heterogeneous test. Assuming the difficulty level of all the items on the test to be about the same, would you expect a split-half (odd-even) estimate of reliability to

---

5. As we will see elsewhere throughout this textbook, important decisions are seldom made on the basis of one test only. Psychologists frequently rely on a **test battery**—a selected assortment of tests and assessment procedures—in the process of evaluation. A test battery is typically composed of tests designed to measure different variables.

Table 5–2
Content Areas Sampled for 18 Items of the
Hypothetical Electronics Repair Test (HERT)

Item Number	Content Area
1	Color television
2	Color television
3	Black-and-white television
4	Black-and-white television
5	Radio
6	Radio
7	Video recorder
8	Video recorder
9	Computer
10	Computer
11	Compact disc player
12	Compact disc player
13	Stereo receiver
14	Stereo receiver
15	Video camera
16	Video camera
17	DVD player
18	DVD player

be fairly high or low? How would the KR-20 reliability estimate compare with the odd-even estimate of reliability—would it be higher or lower?

We might guess that because the content areas sampled for the 18 items from this "Hypothetical Electronics Repair Test" are ordered in a manner whereby odd and even items tap the same content area, the odd-even reliability estimate will probably be quite high. Because of the great heterogeneity of content areas when taken as a whole, it could reasonably be predicted that the KR-20 estimate of reliability will be lower than the odd-even one. How can KR-20 be computed? The following formula may be used:

$$r_{KR20} = \left(\frac{k}{k-1} \right) \left(1 - \frac{\Sigma\,pq}{\sigma^2} \right)$$

where r_{KR20} stands for the Kuder-Richardson formula 20 reliability coefficient, k is the number of test items, σ^2 is the variance of total test scores, p is the proportion of test-takers who pass the item, q is the proportion of people who fail the item, and $\Sigma\,pq$ is the sum of the pq products over all items. For this particular example, k equals 18. Based on the data in Table 5–3, $\Sigma\,pq$ can be computed to be 3.975. The variance of total test scores is 5.26. Thus, $r_{KR20} = .259$.

An approximation of KR-20 can be obtained by the use of the twenty-first formula in the series developed by Kuder and Richardson, a formula known as—you guessed it—*KR-21*. KR-21 may be used if there is reason to assume that all the test items have approximately the same degree of difficulty. Let's add that this assumption is seldom justified. Formula KR-21 has become outdated in an era of calculators and computers. Way back when, KR-21 was sometimes used to estimate KR-20 only because it required many fewer calculations.

Numerous modifications of Kuder-Richardson formulas have been proposed through the years. The one variant of the KR-20 formula that has received the most acceptance and is in widest use today is a statistic called *coefficient alpha*. You may even hear it referred to as *coefficient α-20*. This expression incorporates both the Greek letter alpha (α) and the number twenty, the latter being a reference to KR-20.

Table 5-3

HERT Performance by Item for 20 Testtakers

Item Number	Number of Testtakers Correct
1	14
2	12
3	9
4	18
5	8
6	5
7	6
8	9
9	10
10	10
11	8
12	6
13	15
14	9
15	12
16	12
17	14
18	7

Coefficient alpha Developed by Cronbach (1951) and subsequently elaborated on by others (such as Kaiser & Michael, 1975; Novick & Lewis, 1967), **coefficient alpha** may be thought of as the mean of all possible split-half correlations, corrected by the Spearman-Brown formula. In contrast to KR-20, which is appropriately used only on tests with dichotomous items, coefficient alpha is appropriate for use on tests containing non-dichotomous items. The formula for coefficient alpha is

$$r_\alpha = \left(\frac{k}{k-1} \right) \left(1 - \frac{\Sigma\, \sigma_i^2}{\sigma^2} \right)$$

where r_α is coefficient alpha, k is the number of items, σ_i^2 is the variance of one item, $\Sigma\, \sigma_i^2$ is the sum of variances of each item, and σ^2 is the variance of the total test scores.

Coefficient alpha is the preferred statistic for obtaining an estimate of internal consistency reliability. A variation of the formula has been developed for use in obtaining an estimate of test-retest reliability (Green, 2003). Essentially, this formula yields an estimate of the mean of all possible test-retest, split-half coefficients. Coefficient alpha is widely used as a measure of reliability, owing in part to the fact that it requires only one administration of the test.

Unlike a Pearson r, which may range in value from -1 to $+1$, coefficient alpha typically ranges in value from 0 to 1. This is so because conceptually coefficient alpha, much like other coefficients of reliability, is calculated to help answer questions about how *similar* sets of data are. Here, similarity is gauged, in essence, on a scale from 0 (absolutely no similarity) to 1 (perfectly identical). It is possible, however, to conceive of data sets that would yield a negative value of alpha (Streiner, 2003b). Still, because negative values of alpha are theoretically impossible, it is recommended under such rare circumstances that the alpha coefficient be reported as zero (Henson, 2001). Also, a myth about alpha is that "bigger is always better." As Streiner (2003b) pointed out, a value of alpha above .90 may be "too high" and indicate redundancy in the items.

In contrast to coefficient alpha, a Pearson r may be thought of as dealing conceptually with both dissimilarity and similarity. Accordingly, an r with a value of -1 may be conceived as indicative of "perfect dissimilarity." In practice, most reliability coefficients, regardless of the specific type of reliability they are measuring, range in value from 0 to 1. This is generally true, although it is possible to conceive of exceptional cases, with data sets that would yield an *r* with a value in the negative range.

Before proceeding, let's emphasize that all indexes of reliability, coefficient alpha among them, provide an index that is a characteristic of a particular group of test scores, *not* the test itself (Caruso, 2000; Yin & Fan, 2000). Measures of reliability are estimates, and estimates are subject to error. The precise amount of error inherent in a reliability estimate will vary with the sample of testtakers from which the data were drawn. A reliability index published in a test manual might be very impressive. However, it should be kept in mind that the reported reliability was achieved with a particular group of testtakers. If a new group of testtakers is sufficiently different from the group of testtakers on whom the reliability studies were done, the reliability coefficient may not be as impressive—and even may be unacceptable.

Measures of Inter-Scorer Reliability

When we are being evaluated, we usually would like to believe that no matter who is doing the evaluating, we would be evaluated in the same way.[6] For example, if you take a road test for a driver's license, you would like to believe that whether you pass or fail is solely a matter of your performance behind the wheel and not a function of who is sitting in the passenger's seat. Unfortunately, in some types of tests under some conditions, the score may be more a function of the scorer than anything else. This was demonstrated back in 1912 when researchers presented one pupil's English composition to a convention of teachers, and volunteers graded the papers. The grades ranged from a low of 50% to a high of 98% (Starch & Elliott, 1912).

Variously referred to as *scorer reliability, judge reliability, observer reliability,* and *inter-rater reliability,* **inter-scorer reliability** is the degree of agreement or consistency between two or more scorers (or judges or raters). Reference to levels of inter-scorer reliability for a particular test may be published in the test's manual or elsewhere. If the reliability coefficient is very high, the prospective test user knows that test scores can be derived in a systematic, consistent way by various scorers with sufficient training. A responsible test developer who is unable to create a test that can be scored with a reasonable degree of consistency by trained scorers will go back to the drawing board to discover the reason for this problem. If, for example, the problem is a lack of clarity in scoring criteria, then the remedy might be to rewrite the scoring criteria section of the manual to include clearly written scoring rules. Inter-rater consistency may be promoted by providing raters with the opportunity for group discussion along with practice exercises and information on rater accuracy (Smith, 1986).

Perhaps the simplest way of determining the degree of consistency among scorers in the scoring of a test is to calculate a coefficient of correlation. This correlation coefficient is referred to as a **coefficient of inter-scorer reliability.**

JUST THINK . . .

Can you think of a measure in which it might be desirable for different judges, scorers, or raters to have *different* views on what is being judged, scored, or rated?

---

6. We say "usually" because exceptions do exist. Thus, for example, if you go on a job interview and the employer/interviewer is a parent or other loving relative, you might reasonably expect that the evaluation you receive would *not* be the same were the evaluator someone else. On the other hand, if the employer/interviewer is someone with whom you have had a run-in, it may be time to revisit the want ads.

Using and Interpreting a Coefficient of Reliability

We have seen that with respect to the test itself, there are basically three approaches to the estimation of reliability: (1) test-retest, (2) alternate or parallel forms, and (3) internal or inter-item consistency. The method or methods employed will depend on a number of factors, such as the purpose of obtaining a measure of reliability.

Another question that is linked in no trivial way to the purpose of the test is, "How high should the coefficient of reliability be?" Perhaps the best "short answer" to this question is, "On a continuum relative to the purpose and importance of the decisions to be made on the basis of scores on the test." Reliability is a mandatory attribute in all tests we use. However, we need more of it in some tests, and we will admittedly allow for less of it in others. If a test score carries with it life-or-death implications, we need to hold that test to some high standards—as well as to relatively high standards with regard to coefficients of reliability. If a test score is routinely used in combination with many other test scores and typically accounts for only a small part of the decision process, the test will not be held to the highest standards of reliability. As a rule of thumb, it may be useful to think of reliability coefficients in a way that parallels many grading systems: In the .90s rates a grade of A, in the .80s rates a B, and from about .65 through the .70s we are talking C, still in passing territory at the lower end but closely bordering on unacceptable and failing. Now, let's get a bit more technical with regard to the purpose of the reliability coefficient.

The Purpose of the Reliability Coefficient

If a specific test of employee performance is designed for use at various times over the course of the employment period, it would be reasonable to expect the test to demonstrate reliability across time. It would be desirable to have an estimate of the instrument's test-retest reliability. For a test designed for a single administration only, an estimate of internal consistency would be the reliability measure of choice. If the purpose of determining reliability is to break down the error variance into its parts, as shown in Figure 5–1, then a number of reliability coefficients would have to be calculated.

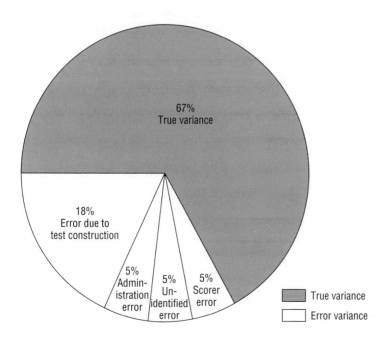

Figure 5–1
Sources of Variance in a Hypothetical Test

*In this hypothetical situation, 5% of the variance has not been identified by the test user. It is possible, for example, that this portion of the variance could be accounted for by **transient error,** a source of error attributable to variations in the testtaker's feelings, moods, or mental state over time. Then again, this 5% of the error may be due to other factors that are yet to be identified.*

Table 5–4
Summary of Reliability Types

Type of Reliability	Number of Testing Sessions	Number of Test Forms	Sources of Error Variance	Statistical Procedures
Test-retest	2	1	Administration	Pearson *r* or Spearman rho
Alternate-forms	1 or 2	2	Test construction or administration	Pearson *r* or Spearman rho
Internal consistency	1	1	Test construction	Pearson *r* between equivalent test halves with Spearman-Brown correction or Kuder-Richardson for dichotomous items, or coefficient alpha for multipoint items
Inter-scorer	1	1	Scoring and interpretation	Pearson *r* or Spearman rho

Note that the various reliability coefficients do not all reflect the same sources of error variance. Thus, an individual reliability coefficient may provide an index of error from test construction, test administration, or test scoring and interpretation. A coefficient of inter-rater reliability, for example, provides information about error as a result of test scoring. Specifically, it can be used to answer questions about how consistently two scorers score the same test items. Table 5–4 summarizes the different kinds of error variance that are reflected in different reliability coefficients.

The Nature of the Test

Closely related to considerations concerning the purpose and use of a reliability coefficient are considerations concerning the nature of the test itself. Included here are considerations such as whether (1) the test items are homogeneous or heterogeneous in nature; (2) the characteristic, ability, or trait being measured is presumed to be dynamic or static; (3) the range of test scores is or is not restricted; (4) the test is a speed or a power test; and (5) the test is or is not criterion-referenced. Some tests present special problems regarding the measurement of their reliability (see this chapter's *Close-up*).

Homogeneity versus heterogeneity of test items   Recall that a test is said to be *homogeneous* in items if it is functionally uniform throughout. Tests designed to measure one factor, such as one ability or one trait, are expected to be homogeneous in items. For such tests, it is reasonable to expect a high degree of internal consistency. By contrast, if the test is *heterogeneous* in items, an estimate of internal consistency might be low relative to a more appropriate estimate of test-retest reliability.

Dynamic versus static characteristics   Whether what is being measured by the test is *dynamic* or *static* is also a consideration in obtaining an estimate of reliability. A **dynamic characteristic** is a trait, state, or ability presumed to be ever changing as a function of situational and cognitive experiences. If, for example, one were to take hourly measurements of the dynamic characteristic of anxiety as manifested by a stockbroker throughout a business day, one might find the measured level of this characteristic to change from hour to hour. Such changes might even be related to the magnitude of the Dow Jones average. Because the true amount of anxiety presumed to exist would vary with each assessment, a test-retest measure would be of little help in gauging the reliability of the measuring instrument. The best estimate of reliability could be obtained from an

The Reliability of the Bayley-II

The Bayley Scales of Infant Development (BSID; Bayley, 1969) were designed to sample for measurement aspects of the mental, motor, and behavioral development of infants. Bayley scores tended to drift upward over the course of some two decades of use (Schuler et al., 2003), and the test was revised in 1993.

Much like the original test, the Bayley Scales of Infant Development, second edition (BSID-II; Bayley, 1993), was designed to assess the developmental level of children between 1 month and 3½ years old. It is used primarily to help identify children who are developing slowly and might benefit from cognitive intervention. The BSID-II includes three scales. Items on the Motor Scale focus on the control and skill employed in bodily movements. Items on the Mental Scale focus on cognitive abilities. The Behavior Rating Scale assesses behavior problems, such as lack of attention.

Is the BSID-II a reliable measure? Because the Mental, Motor, and Behavior Rating Scales are each expected to measure a homogeneous set of abilities, internal consistency reliability for each of these scales is an appropriate measure of reliability. Bayley (1993) reported coefficient alphas ranging from .78 to .93 for the Mental Scale (variations exist across the age groups), .75 to .91 for the Motor Scale, and .64 to .92 for the Behavior Rating Scale. From these reliability studies, Bayley (1993) concluded that the BSID-II is internally consistent.

Consider, however, an issue unique to instruments used in assessing infants. We know that cognitive development during the first months and years of life is uneven and fast. Children often grow in spurts, changing dramatically over a few days (Hetherington & Parke, 1993). The child tested just before and again just after a developmental advance may perform very differently on the BSID-II at the two testings. In such cases, a change in test score would not be the result of error in the test itself or in test administration. Instead, such changes in the test score could reflect an actual change in the child's skills. Of course, not all differences between the child's test performance at two test administrations need to result from changes in skills. The challenge in gauging the test-retest reliability of the BSID-II is to do it in such a way that it is not spuriously lowered by the test-taker's actual developmental changes between testings.

Bayley's solution to this dilemma entailed examining test-retest reliability over short periods of time. The median interval between testings was just four days. Correlations between the results of the two testing sessions were strong

Nancy Bayley, Ph.D.

for both the Mental (.83 to .91) and the Motor (.77 to .79) Scales. The Behavior Rating Scale demonstrated lower test-retest reliability: .48 to .70 at 1 month of age, .57 to .90 at 12 months of age, and .60 to .71 at 24 to 36 months of age (Bayley, 1993).

Inter-scorer reliability is an important concern for the BSID-II because many items require judgment on the part of the examiner. The test manual provides clear criteria for scoring the infant's performance. However, by their nature, many of the tasks involve some subjectivity in scoring. For example, one of the Motor Scale items is "Keeps hands open . . . Scoring: Give credit if the child holds his hands open most of the time when he is free to follow his own interests" (Bayley, 1993, p. 147). Sources of examiner error on this item can arise from a variety of sources. Different examiners may note the position of the child's hands at different times. Examiners may define differently when the

(continued)

The Reliability of the Bayley-II
(continued)

child is "free to follow his own interests." And examiners may disagree about what constitutes "most of the time."

An alternate or parallel form of the BSID-II does not exist, so alternate-forms reliability cannot be assessed. An alternate form of the test would be useful, especially in cases in which the examiner makes a mistake in administering the first version of it. Still, the creation of an alternate form of this test would almost surely entail a great investment of time, money, and effort. If you were the test's publisher, would you make that investment? In considering the answer to that question, don't forget that the ability level of the test-taker is changing rapidly.

Nellis and Gridley (1994) noted that a primary goal of revision was to strengthen the test psychometrically. Based on the data provided in the test manual, Nellis and Gridley concluded that this goal was accomplished: The BSID-II

does seem to be more reliable than the original Bayley Scales. However, there are still some important weaknesses. For example, the manual focuses on the psychometric quality of the BSID-II as administered to children without significant developmental problems. Whether the same levels of reliability would be obtained with children who are developmentally delayed is unknown. Perhaps a more intriguing unknown is the question of why there was drift in the scores upward over the course of about two decades in which the first edition was in use. Will this phenomenon of upward score-drift repeat itself in two decades or so of use of the second edition? Time will tell.

For a glimpse of how the Bayley test has been used by practitioners and researchers, interested readers may review Alessandri et al. (1998), Drotar et al. (1999), Levy-Shiff et al. (1998), Nelson et al. (2000), and Raz et al. (1998).

---

internal-consistency measure. Contrast this situation to one in which hourly assessments of this same stockbroker are made on a trait, state, or ability presumed to be relatively unchanging (a **static characteristic**) such as intelligence. In this instance, obtained measurement would not be expected to vary significantly as a function of time, and either the test-retest or the alternate-forms method would be appropriate.

JUST THINK . . .

Provide another example of a dynamic characteristic that a psychological test could measure as well as a static characteristic.

Restriction or inflation of range In using and interpreting a coefficient of reliability, the issue variously referred to as **restriction of range** or **restriction of variance** (or, conversely, **inflation of range** or **inflation of variance**) is important. If the variance of either variable in a correlational analysis is restricted by the sampling procedure used, then the resulting correlation coefficient tends to be lower. If the variance of either variable in a correlational analysis is inflated by the sampling procedure, then the resulting correlation coefficient tends to be higher. Refer back to Figure 4–8 (page 123) in the previous chapter (Two Scatterplots Illustrating Unrestricted and Restricted Ranges) for a graphic illustration.

Also of critical importance is whether the range of variances employed is appropriate to the objective of the correlational analysis. Consider in the latter context, for example, a published educational test designed for use with children in grades 1 through 6. Ideally, the manual for this test should contain not one reliability value covering all the testtakers in grades 1 through 6 but reliability values for testtakers at each grade level. A corporate personnel officer who employs a certain screening test in the hiring process must maintain reliability data with respect to scores achieved by job applicants—as opposed to hired employees—if the range of measurements is not to be restricted. This is so because the people who were hired typically scored higher on the test than any comparable group of applicants.

Speed tests versus power tests   When a time limit is long enough to allow testtakers to attempt all items, and if some items are so difficult that no testtaker is able to obtain a perfect score, then the test is a **power test.** By contrast, a **speed test** generally contains items of uniform level of difficulty (typically uniformly low) so that when given generous time limits, all testtakers should be able to complete all the test items correctly. In practice, however, the time limit on a speed test is established so that few if any of the testtakers will be able to complete the entire test. Score differences on a speed test are therefore based on performance speed because items attempted tend to be correct.

A reliability estimate of a speed test should be based on performance from two independent testing periods using one of the following: (1) test-retest reliability, (2) alternate-forms reliability, or (3) split-half reliability from *two separately timed* half tests. If a split-half procedure is used, the obtained reliability coefficient is for a half test and should be adjusted using the Spearman-Brown formula.

Because a measure of the reliability of a speed test should reflect the consistency of response speed, the reliability of a speed test should not be computed from a single administration of the test with a single time limit. If a speed test is administered once and some measure of internal consistency is computed, like the Kuder-Richardson or a split-half correlation, the result will be a spuriously high reliability coefficient. To understand why the KR-20 or split-half reliability coefficient will be spuriously high, consider the following example.

When a group of testtakers completes a speed test, almost all the items completed will be correct. If reliability is examined using an odd-even split, and if the testtakers completed the items in order, testtakers will get close to the same number of odd as even items correct. A testtaker completing 82 items can be expected to get approximately 41 odd and 41 even items correct. A testtaker completing 61 items may get 31 odd and 30 even items correct. When the numbers of odd and even items correct are correlated across a group of testtakers, the correlation will be close to 1.00. This impressive correlation coefficient actually tells us nothing about response consistency.

Using the same scenario described above, a Kuder-Richardson reliability coefficient would yield a similar coefficient that would also be, well, equally useless. Recall that KR-20 reliability is based on the proportion of testtakers correct (p) and the proportion of testtakers incorrect (q) on each item. In the case of a speed test, it is conceivable that p would equal 1.0 and q would equal 0 for many of the items. Toward the end of the test— when many items would not even be attempted because of the time limit—p might equal 0 and q might equal 1.0. For many if not a majority of the items, then, the product of pq would equal or approximate 0. When 0 is substituted in the KR-20 formula for $\Sigma\, pq$, the reliability coefficient is 1.0 (a meaningless coefficient in this instance).

Criterion-referenced tests   A **criterion-referenced** test is designed to provide an indication of where a testtaker stands with respect to some criterion such as an educational or a vocational objective. Unlike norm-referenced tests, criterion-referenced tests tend to contain material that has been mastered in hierarchical fashion. For example, the would-be pilot masters on-ground skills before attempting to master in-flight skills. Scores on criterion-referenced tests tend to be interpreted in pass/fail (or, perhaps more accurately, "master/failed-to-master") terms, and any scrutiny of performance on individual items tends to be for diagnostic and remedial purposes.

Traditional techniques of estimating reliability employ measures that take into account scores on the entire test. Recall that a test-retest reliability estimate is based on the correlation between the total scores on two administrations of the same test. In alternate-forms reliability, a reliability estimate is based on the correlation between the two total scores on the forms. In split-half reliability, a reliability estimate is based on the correlation between scores on two halves of the test and then adjusted using the Spearman-Brown formula to obtain a reliability estimate of the whole test. Although there are exceptions, such traditional procedures of estimating reliability are usually not appropriate for use with criterion-referenced tests. To understand why, recall that reliability is defined as the proportion of total variance (σ^2) attributable to true variance (σ_{tr}^2). Total variance in a test score distribution equals the sum of the true variance plus the error variance (σ_e^2):

$$\sigma^2 = \sigma_{tr}^2 + \sigma_e^2$$

A measure of reliability, therefore, depends on the variability of the test scores: how different the scores are from one another. In criterion-referenced testing, and particularly in mastery testing, how different the scores are from one another is seldom a focus of interest. In fact, individual differences between examinees on total test scores may be minimal. The critical issue for the user of a mastery test is whether or not a certain criterion score has been achieved.

As individual differences (and the variability) decrease, a traditional measure of reliability would also decrease, regardless of the stability of individual performance. Traditional ways of estimating reliability are therefore not always appropriate for criterion-referenced tests, though there may be instances in which traditional estimates can be adopted. An example might be a situation in which the same test is being used at different stages in some program—training, therapy, or the like—and variability in scores could reasonably be expected. Statistical techniques useful in determining the reliability of criterion-referenced tests have been discussed in detail elsewhere (for example, Hambleton & Jurgensen, 1990) and are beyond the scope of an introductory measurement text.

Are there models of measurement other than the true score model? As we will see in what follows, the answer to that question is yes. Before proceeding, however, take a moment to review a "real-life" application of reliability in measurement in this chapter's *Everyday Psychometrics*.

Alternatives to the True Score Model

Thus far, and throughout this book unless specifically stated otherwise, the model we have assumed to be operative is the true score or classical model. This is the most widely used and accepted model in the psychometric literature today. Historically, the true score model of the reliability of measurement enjoyed a virtually unchallenged reign of acceptance from the early 1900s through the 1940s. The 1950s saw the development of an alternative theoretical model, one originally referred to as the *domain sampling theory*, and better known today in one of its many modified forms as *generalizability theory*.

As set forth by Tryon (1957), the theory of domain sampling rebels against the concept of a true score existing with respect to the measurement of psychological constructs. Whereas those who subscribe to **true score theory** seek to estimate the portion of a test score that is attributable to error, proponents of domain sampling theory seek to estimate the extent to which specific sources of variation under defined conditions are contributing to the test score. In domain sampling theory, a test's reliability is conceived of as an objective measure of how precisely the test score assesses the domain from which the test draws a sample (Thorndike, 1985). A *domain* of behavior, or the universe of items that could conceivably measure that behavior, can be thought of as a hypothetical construct: one that shares certain characteristics with (and is measured by) the sample

The Reliability Defense and the Breathalyzer Test

*B*reathalyzer is the generic name for a number of different instruments used by law enforcement agencies to determine if a suspect, most typically the operator of a motor vehicle, is legally drunk. The driver is required to blow into a tube attached to the breathalyzer. The breath sample then mixes with a chemical that is added to the machine for each new test. The resulting mixture is automatically analyzed for alcohol content in the breath. The value for the alcohol content in the breath is then converted to a value for blood alcohol level. Whether the testtaker is deemed to be legally drunk will vary from state to state as a function of the state law regarding the blood alcohol level necessary for a person to be declared intoxicated.

In New Jersey, the blood alcohol level required for a person to be declared legally drunk is one-tenth of 1 percent (.10%). Drivers in New Jersey found guilty of a first drunk-driving offense face fines and surcharges amounting to about $3,500, mandatory detainment in an Intoxicated Driver Resource Center, suspension of driving privileges for a minimum of six months, and a maximum of 30 days' imprisonment. Two models of a breathalyzer (Models 900 and 900A made by National Draeger, Inc.) have been used in New Jersey since the 1950s. Well-documented test-retest reliability regarding the 900 and 900A breathalyzers indicate that the instruments have a margin of error of about one-100th of a percentage point. This means that an administration of the test to a testtaker who in reality has a blood alcohol level of .10% (a "true score," if you will) might yield a test score anywhere from a low of .09% to a high of .11%.

A driver in New Jersey who was convicted of driving drunk appealed the decision on grounds relating to the test-retest reliability of the breathalyzer. The breathalyzer had indicated that the driver's blood alcohol level was .10%. The driver argued that the law did not take into account the margin of error inherent in the measuring instrument. However, the state supreme court ruled against the driver, finding that the legislature must have taken into consideration such error when it wrote the law.

Another issue related to the use of breathalyzers has to do with where and when they are administered. In some states, the test is most typically administered at police headquarters, not at the scene of the arrest. Expert witnesses were once retained on behalf of defendants to calculate what the defendant's blood alcohol was at the actual time of the arrest. Working backward from the time the test was admin-

A suspect being administered a breathalyzer test

istered, and figuring in values for variables such as what the defendant had to drink and when, as well as the defendant's weight, they could calculate a blood alcohol level at the time of arrest. If that level was lower than the level required for a person to be declared legally drunk, the case might be dismissed. However, in some states, such as New Jersey, this defense would not be entertained. In these states, higher courts have ruled that because it was aware that breathalyzer tests would not be administered at the arrest scene, the legislature had intended the measured blood alcohol level to apply at the time of the test's administration at police headquarters.

One final reliability-related issue regarding breathalyzers has to do with inter-scorer reliability. When using the 900 and 900A models, the police officer who makes the arrest also records the measured blood alcohol level. Although the vast majority of police officers are honest when it comes to such recording, there is potential for abuse. A police officer who wished to save face on a drunk-driving arrest, or even a police officer who simply wanted to add to a record of drunk-driving arrests, could record an incorrect breathalyzer value to ensure a conviction. In 1993, one police officer in Camden County, New Jersey, was convicted of and sent to prison for recording incorrect breathalyzer readings (Romano, 1994). Such an incident is representative of extremely atypical "error" entering into the assessment process.

of items that make up the test. In theory, the items in the domain are thought to have the same means and variances of those in the test that samples from the domain. Of the three types of estimates of reliability, measures of internal consistency are perhaps the most compatible with domain sampling theory.

Generalizability theory may be viewed as an extension of true score theory wherein the concept of a universe score replaces that of a true score (Shavelson et al., 1989). Developed by Lee J. Cronbach (1970) and his colleagues (Cronbach et al., 1972), this theory is based on the idea that a person's test scores vary from testing to testing because of variables in the testing situation. Instead of conceiving of all variability in a person's scores as error, Cronbach encouraged test developers and researchers to describe the details of the particular test situation or **universe** leading to a specific test score. This universe is described in terms of its **facets,** which include things like the number of items in the test, the amount of training the test scorers have had, and the purpose of the test administration. According to generalizability theory, given the exact same conditions of all the facets in the universe, the exact same test score should be obtained. This test score is the **universe score,** and it is, as Cronbach noted, analogous to a true score in the true score model. Here Cronbach explains in his own words:

> "What is Mary's typing ability?" This must be interpreted as "What would Mary's word processing score on this be if a large number of measurements on the test were collected and averaged?" The particular test score Mary earned is just one out of a *universe* of possible observations. If one of these scores is as acceptable as the next, then the mean, called the *universe score* and symbolized here by M_p (mean for person p), would be the most appropriate statement of Mary's performance in the type of situation the test represents.
>
> The universe is a collection of possible measures "of the same kind," but the limits of the collection are determined by the investigator's purpose. If he needs to know Mary's typing ability on May 5 (for example, so that he can plot a learning curve that includes one point for that day), the universe would include observations on that day and on that day only. He probably does want to generalize over passages, testers, and scorers—that is to say, he would like to know Mary's ability on May 5 without reference to any particular passage, tester, or scorer. . . .
>
> The person will ordinarily have a different universe score for each universe. Mary's universe score covering tests on May 5 will not agree perfectly with her universe score for the whole month of May. . . . Some testers call the average over a large number of comparable observations a "true score"; e.g., "Mary's true typing rate on 3-minute tests." Instead, we speak of a "universe score" to emphasize that what score is desired depends on the universe being considered. For any measure there are many "true scores," each corresponding to a different universe.
>
> When we use a single observation as if it represented the universe, we are generalizing. We generalize over scorers, over selections typed, perhaps over days. If the observed scores from a procedure agree closely with the universe score, we can say that the observation is "accurate," or "reliable," or "generalizable." And since the observations then also agree with each other, we say that they are "consistent" and "have little error variance." To have so many terms is confusing, but not seriously so. The term most often used in the literature is "reliability." The author prefers "generalizability" because that term immediately implies "generalization to what?" . . . There is a different degree of generalizability for each universe. The older methods of analysis do not separate the sources of variation. They deal with a single source of variance, or leave two or more sources entangled. (Cronbach, 1970, pp. 153–154)

How can these ideas be applied? Cronbach and his colleagues suggested that tests be developed with the aid of a **generalizability study** followed by a **decision study.** A generalizability study examines how generalizable scores from a particular test are if the test is administered in different situations. Stated in the language of generalizability theory, a generalizability study examines how much of an impact different facets of the universe have on the test score. Is the test score affected by group as opposed to individual administration? Is the test score affected by the time of day in which the test is administered? The influence of particular facets on the test score is represented by **coefficients of generalizability.** These coefficients are similar to reliability coefficients in the true score model.

After the generalizability study is done, Cronbach et al. recommended that test developers do a decision study, which involves the application of information from the generalizability study. In the decision study, developers examine the usefulness of test scores in helping the test user make decisions. In practice, test scores are used to guide a variety of decisions, from placing a child in special education to hiring new employees to discharging mental patients from the hospital. The decision study is designed to tell the test user how test scores should be used and how dependable those scores are as a basis for decisions, depending on the context of their use. Why is this so important? Cronbach (1970) explained:

> The decision that a student has completed a course or that a patient is ready for termination of therapy must not be seriously influenced by chance errors, temporary variations in performance, or the tester's choice of questions. An erroneous favorable decision may be irreversible and may harm the person or the community. Even when reversible, an erroneous unfavorable decision is unjust, disrupts the person's morale, and perhaps retards his development. Research, too, requires dependable measurement. An experiment is not very informative if an observed difference could be accounted for by chance variation. Large error variance is likely to mask a scientifically important outcome. Taking a better measure improves the sensitivity of an experiment in the same way that increasing the number of subjects does. (p. 152)

Generalizability has not replaced the true score model. Still, it has great appeal owing to its message that a test's reliability does not reside within the test itself. Rather, a test's reliability is very much a function of the circumstances under which the test is developed, administered, and interpreted.

Another alternative to the true score model is **item response theory** (Lord, 1980), also referred to by the acronym *IRT* or the term *latent trait theory.* This model focuses on the extent to which individual test items are useful in evaluating individuals presumed to possess various amounts of a particular trait or ability. IRT is increasingly used by commercial test developers and large-scale test publishers in test development.

Reliability and Individual Scores

The reliability coefficient helps the test developer build an adequate measuring instrument, and it helps the test user select a suitable test. However, the usefulness of the reliability coefficient does not end with test construction and selection. By employing the reliability coefficient in the formula for the standard error of measurement, the test user now has another descriptive statistic relevant to test interpretation, this one useful in estimating the precision of a particular test score.

The Standard Error of Measurement

The *standard error of measurement,* abbreviated variously as *SEM* or SE_M provides a measure of the precision of an observed test score. Stated another way, it provides an estimate of the amount of error inherent in an observed score or measurement. In general, the relationship between the *SEM* and the reliability of a test is inverse; the higher the reliability of a test (or individual subtest within a test), the lower the *SEM*.

To illustrate the utility of the *SEM*, let's revisit The Rochester Wrenchworks (TRW) and reintroduce Mary (from Cronbach's excerpt earlier in this chapter), who is now applying for a job as a word processor. To be hired at TRW as a word processor, a candidate must be able to word-process accurately at the rate of 50 words per minute. The personnel office administers a total of seven brief word-processing tests to Mary over the course of seven business days. In words per minute, Mary's scores on each of the seven tests are as follows:

52   55   39   56   35   50   54

If you were in charge of hiring at TRW and you looked at these seven scores, you might logically ask, "Which of these scores is the best measure of Mary's 'true' word-processing ability?" And more to the point, "Which is her 'true' score?"

The "true" answer to the question posed above is that we cannot conclude with absolute certainty from the data we have exactly what Mary's true word-processing ability is. We *can* make an educated guess. Our educated guess would be that her true word processing ability is equal to the mean of the distribution of her word-processing scores plus or minus a number of points accounted for by error in the measurement process. We do not know how many points are accounted for by error in the measurement process. The best we can do is estimate how much error entered into a particular test score.

The **standard error of measurement** is the tool used to estimate or infer the extent to which an observed score deviates from a true score. We may define the standard error of measurement as the standard deviation of a theoretically normal distribution of test scores obtained by one person on equivalent tests. Also known as the **standard error of a score** and denoted by the symbol σ_{meas}, the standard error of measurement is an index of the extent to which one individual's scores vary over tests presumed to be parallel. In accordance with the true score model, an obtained test score represents one point in the theoretical distribution of scores the testtaker could have obtained. But where on the continuum of possible scores is this obtained score? If the standard deviation for the distribution of test scores is known (or can be calculated), and if an estimate of the reliability of the test is known (or can be calculated), an estimate of the standard error of a particular score (that is, the standard error of measurement) can be determined with the following formula:

$$\sigma_{meas} = \sigma\sqrt{1 - r_{xx}}$$

where σ_{meas} is equal to the standard error of measurement, σ is equal to the standard deviation of test scores by the group of testtakers, and r_{xx} is equal to the reliability coefficient of the test. The standard error of measurement allows us to estimate the range in which the true score is likely to exist, with a specific level of confidence.

If, for example, a spelling test has a reliability coefficient of .84 and a standard deviation of 10, then

$$\sigma_{meas} = 10\sqrt{1 - .84} = 4$$

To use the standard error of measurement to estimate the range of the true score, we make an assumption: If the individual were to take a large number of equivalent tests, scores on those tests would tend to be normally distributed with the individual's true score as the mean. Because the standard error of measurement functions like a standard deviation in this context, we can use it to predict what would happen if an individual took additional equivalent tests:

- Approximately 68% (actually, 68.26%) of the scores would be expected to occur within $\pm 1\sigma_{meas}$ of the true score.
- Approximately 95% (actually, 95.44%) of the scores would be expected to occur within $\pm 2\sigma_{meas}$ of the true score.
- Approximately 99% (actually, 99.74%) of the scores would be expected to occur within $\pm 3\sigma_{meas}$ of the true score.

Of course, we don't know the true score for any individual testtaker, and so we must estimate it. The best estimate available of the individual's true score on the test is the test score already obtained. Thus, if a student achieved a score of 50 on one spelling test, and if the test had a standard error of measurement of 4, then using 50 as the point estimate, we can be

- 68% (actually, 68.26%) confident that the true score falls within $50 \pm 1\sigma_{meas}$ (or between 46 and 54, including 46 and 54).
- 95% (actually, 95.44%) confident that the true score falls within $50 \pm 2\sigma_{meas}$ (or between 42 and 58, including 42 and 58).
- 99% (actually, 99.74%) confident that the true score falls within $50 \pm 3\sigma_{meas}$ (or between 38 and 62, including 38 and 62).

The standard error of measurement, like the reliability coefficient, is one way of expressing test reliability. If the standard deviation of a test is held constant, the smaller the σ_{meas}, the more reliable the test will be; as r_{xx} increases, the σ_{meas} decreases. For example, when a reliability coefficient equals .64 and σ equals 15, the standard error of measurement equals 9:

$$\sigma_{meas} = 15\sqrt{1 - .64} = 9$$

With a reliability coefficient equal to .96 and σ still equal to 15, the standard error of measurement decreases to 3:

$$\sigma_{meas} = 15\sqrt{1 - .96} = 3$$

In practice, the standard error of measurement is most frequently used in the interpretation of individual test scores. For example, intelligence tests are given as part of the assessment of individuals for mental retardation. One of the criteria for mental retardation is an IQ score of 70 or below (when the mean is 100 and the standard deviation is 15) on an individually administered intelligence test (American Psychiatric Association, 1994). One question that could be asked about these tests is how scores that are close to the cutoff value of 70 should be treated. Specifically, how high above 70 must a score be for us to conclude confidently that the individual is unlikely to be retarded? Is 72 clearly above the retarded range, so that if the person were to take a parallel form of the test, we could be confident that the second score would be above 70? What about a score of 75? A score of 79?

Useful in answering such questions is an estimate of the amount of error in an observed test score. The standard error of measurement provides such an estimate. Further, the standard error of measurement is useful in establishing what is called a **confidence interval;** that is, a range or band of test scores that is likely to contain the true score.

Here is a "real-life" application of a confidence interval with the Wechsler Adult Intelligence Scale-III (WAIS-III), a widely used test designed to measure adult intelligence (see Chapter 9). The technical manual for the WAIS-III provides a great deal of information relevant to the reliability of the test as a whole, as well as more specific

Table 5–5
Standard Errors of Measurement of SB5 IQ Scores at Ages 5, 10, 15, and 80+

IQ Type	Age (in years)			
	5	10	15	80+
Full Scale IQ	2.12	2.60	2.12	2.12
Nonverbal IQ	3.35	2.67	3.00	3.00
Verbal IQ	3.00	3.35	3.00	2.60
Abbreviated Battery IQ	4.24	5.20	4.50	3.00

reliability-related information for each of its subtests. As reported in the manual, the standard deviation is 3 for the subtest scaled scores and 15 for the IQ and Index scores. Across all of the age groups in the normative sample, the average reliability coefficient for the Full Scale IQ (FSIQ) is .98, and the average standard error of measurement for the FSIQ is 2.3. The manual also provides much more specific information, including standard error of measurement data by individual subtest and age group.

Knowing an individual testtaker's FSIQ score and his or her age, we can calculate a confidence interval. For example, suppose a 22-year-old testtaker obtained a WAIS-III FSIQ of 75. The test user can be 95% confident that this testtaker's true FSIQ falls in the range of 70 to 80. This is so because the 95% confidence interval is set by taking the observed score of 75, plus or minus 1.96, multiplied by the standard error of measurement. As reported on page 54 of the WAIS-III manual, the standard error of measurement of the FSIQ for a 22-year-old testtaker is 2.37. With this information in hand, the 95% confidence interval is calculated as follows:

$$75 \pm 1.96\sigma_{\text{meas}} = 75 \pm 1.96(2.37) = 75 \pm 4.645$$

The calculated interval of 4.645 is rounded to the nearest whole number, 5. We can therefore be 95% confident that this testtaker's true FSIQ on the WAIS-III lies somewhere in the range of the observed score of 75 plus or minus 5, or somewhere in the range of 70 to 80.

In the interests of increasing your *SEM* "comfort level," consider the data presented in Table 5–5. These are *SEM*s for selected age ranges and selected types of IQ measurements as reported in the Technical Manual for the Stanford Binet Intelligence Scales, Fifth Edition (SB5). When presenting these and related data, Roid (2003b, p. 65) noted: "Scores that are more precise and consistent have smaller differences between true and observed scores, resulting in lower *SEM*s." Given this, *just think:* What hypotheses come to mind regarding SB5 IQ scores at ages 5, 10, 15, and 80+?

The standard error of measurement can be used to set the confidence interval for a particular score or to determine whether a score is significantly different from a criterion (such as the cutoff score of 70 described above). The standard error of measurement *cannot* be used to compare scores. So, how do test users compare scores?

The Standard Error of the Difference Between Two Scores

Error related to any of the number of possible variables operative in a testing situation can contribute to a change in a score achieved on the same test, or a parallel test, from one administration of the test to the next. The amount of error in a specific test score is embodied in the standard error of measurement. But scores can change from one testing to the next for reasons other than error.

True differences in the characteristic being measured can also affect test scores. These differences may be of great interest, as in the case of a personnel officer who must decide which of many applicants to hire. Indeed, such differences may be hoped for, as in the case of a psychotherapy researcher who hopes to prove the effectiveness of a particular approach to therapy. Comparisons between scores are made using the **standard error of the difference,** a statistical measure that can aid a test user in determining how large a difference should be before it is considered statistically significant. As you are probably aware from your course in statistics, custom in the field of psychology dictates that if the probability is more than 5% that the difference occurred by chance, then for all intents and purposes it is presumed that there was no difference. A more rigorous standard is the 1% standard. Applying the 1% standard, no statistically significant difference would be deemed to exist unless the observed difference could have occurred by chance alone less than one time in a hundred.

The standard error of the difference between two scores can be the appropriate statistical tool to address three types of questions:

1. How did this individual's performance on test 1 compare with his or her performance on test 2?

2. How did this individual's performance on test 1 compare with someone else's performance on test 1?

3. How did this individual's performance on test 1 compare with someone else's performance on test 2?

As you might have expected, when comparing scores achieved on the different tests, it is essential that the scores be converted to the same scale. The formula for the standard error of the difference between two scores is

$$\sigma_{\text{diff}} = \sqrt{\sigma^2_{\text{meas 1}} + \sigma^2_{\text{meas 2}}}$$

where σ_{diff} is the standard error of the difference between two scores, $\sigma^2_{\text{meas 1}}$ is the squared standard error of measurement for test 1, and $\sigma^2_{\text{meas 2}}$ is the squared standard error of measurement for test 2. If we substitute reliability coefficients for the standard errors of measurement of the separate scores, the formula becomes

$$\sigma_{\text{diff}} = \sigma\sqrt{2 - r_1 - r_2}$$

where r_1 is the reliability coefficient of test 1, r_2 is the reliability coefficient of test 2, and σ is the standard deviation. Note that both tests would have the same standard deviation, because they would have had to have been on the same scale (or converted to the same scale) before a comparison could be made.

The standard error of the difference between two scores will be larger than the standard error of measurement for either score alone because the former is affected by measurement error in both scores. This also makes good sense: If two scores *each* contain error, such that in each case the true score could be higher or lower, we would want the two scores to be further apart before we conclude that there is a significant difference between them.

The value obtained when the standard error of the difference is calculated is used in much the same way as the standard error of the mean. If we wish to be 95% confident that the two scores are different, we would want them to be separated by two standard errors of the difference. A separation of only one standard error of the difference would give us 68% confidence that the two true scores are different.

As an illustration of the use of the standard error of the difference between two scores, consider the situation of a corporate personnel manager who is seeking a highly responsible person for the position of vice president of safety. The personnel officer in this hypothetical situation decides to use a new published test we will call the Safety-Mindedness Test (S-MT) to screen applicants for the position. After placing an ad in the employment section of the local newspaper, the personnel officer tests 100 applicants for the position, using the S-MT. The personnel officer narrows the search for the vice president to the two highest scorers on the S-MT: Moe, who scored 125, and Larry, who scored 134. Assuming the measured reliability of this test to be .92 and its standard deviation to be 14, should the personnel officer conclude that Larry performed significantly better than Moe? To answer this question, first calculate the standard error of the difference:

$$\sigma_{\text{diff}} = 14\sqrt{2 - .92 - .92} = 14\sqrt{.16} = 5.6$$

Note that in this application of the formula, the two test reliability coefficients are the same because the two scores being compared are derived from the same test.

What does this standard error of the difference mean? For any standard error of the difference, we can be

- 68% confident that two scores differing by 1 σ_{diff} represent true score differences.
- 95% confident that two scores differing by 2 σ_{diff} represent true score differences.
- 99.7% confident that two scores differing by 3 σ_{diff} represent true score differences.

Applying this information to the standard error of the difference just computed for the S-MT, we see that the personnel officer can be

- 68% confident that two scores differing by 5.6 represent true score differences.
- 95% confident that two scores differing by 11.2 represent true score differences.
- 99.7% confident that two scores differing by 16.8 represent true score differences.

The difference between Larry's and Moe's scores is only 9 points, not a large enough difference for the personnel officer to conclude with 95% confidence that the two individuals actually have true scores that differ on this test. Stated another way, if Larry and Moe were to take a parallel form of the S-MT, the personnel officer could not be 95% confident that, at the next testing, Larry would again outperform Moe. The personnel officer in this example would have to resort to other means to decide whether Moe, Larry, or someone else would be the best candidate for the position (Curly has been patiently waiting in the wings).

As a postscript to the preceding example, suppose Larry got the job primarily on the basis of data from our hypothetical S-MT. And let's further suppose that it soon became all too clear that Larry turned out to be the hands-down, absolute worst vice president of safety that the company had ever seen. Larry spent much of his time playing practical jokes on fellow corporate officers, and he spent many of his off-hours engaged in his favorite pastime, flagpole sitting. The personnel officer might then have very good reason to question how well the instrument called the Safety-Mindedness Test truly measured safety-mindedness. Or, to put it another way, the personnel officer might question the *validity* of the test. Not coincidentally, the subject of test validity is taken up in the next chapter.

JUST THINK . . .

Please tell us that you have not forgotten about Mary. You know, *Mary* from the Cronbach quote on page 148; yes, *that* Mary. Should she get the job at TRW? If your instructor thinks it would be useful to do so, do the math before responding.

Self-Assessment

Test your understanding of elements of this chapter by seeing if you can explain each of the following terms, expressions, and abbreviations:

alternate forms
alternate-forms reliability
coefficient alpha
coefficient of equivalence
coefficient of generalizability
coefficient of interscorer reliability
coefficient of stability
confidence interval
content sampling
criterion-referenced test
decision study
dynamic characteristic
error variance
facet
generalizability study
generalizability theory

heterogeneity
homogeneity
inflation of range
inter-item consistency
internal consistency
inter-scorer reliability
IRT
item sampling
Kuder-Richardson formula
odd-even reliability
parallel forms
parallel-forms reliability
power test
reliability
reliability coefficient

restriction of range
Spearman-Brown formula
speed test
split-half reliability
standard error of the difference
standard error of measurement
standard error of a score
static characteristics
test-retest reliability
transient error
true score theory
true variance
universe
universe score
variance

Web Watch

Check out the following Web sites for more information about topics discussed in this chapter.

Coefficient alpha
www.geolog.com/msmnt/malpha.htm

Reliability interactive quiz
http://chiron.valdosta.edu/mawhatley/3900/reliablec.htm

Generalizability theory
www.psychology.sdsu.edu/faculty/matt/Pubs/GThtml/GTheory_GEMatt.html

Reliability
www.socialresearchmethods.net/kb/reltypes.htm

6

Validity

In everyday language, we say that something is valid if it is sound, meaningful, or well grounded on principles or evidence. For example, we speak of a valid theory, a valid argument, or a valid reason. In legal terminology, lawyers say that something is valid if it is "executed with the proper formalities" (Black, 1979), such as a valid contract and a valid will. In each of these instances, people make judgments based on evidence of the meaningfulness or the veracity of something. Similarly, in the language of psychological assessment, *validity* is a term used in conjunction with the meaningfulness of a test score—what the test score truly means.

The Concept of Validity

Validity, as applied to a test, is a judgment or estimate of how well a test measures what it purports to measure in a particular context. More specifically, it is a judgment based on evidence about the appropriateness of inferences drawn from test scores.[1] An **inference** is a logical result or deduction. Characterizations of the validity of tests and test scores are frequently phrased in terms such as "acceptable" or "weak." These terms reflect a judgment about how adequately the test measures what it purports to measure.

Inherent in a judgment of an instrument's validity is a judgment of how useful it is for a particular purpose with a particular population of people. As a shorthand, assessors may refer to a particular test as a "valid test." However, what is really meant is that the test has been shown to be valid for a particular use with a particular population of testtakers at a particular time. No test or measurement technique is 'universally valid' for all time, for all uses, with all types of testtaker populations. Rather, tests may be shown to be valid within what we would characterize as *reasonable boundaries* of a contemplated usage. If those boundaries are exceeded, the validity of the test may be called

◆
JUST THINK . . .

Why is the phrase *valid test* sometimes misleading?

---

1. Recall from Chapter 1 that the word *test* is used in the broadest possible sense. It may therefore also apply to measurement procedures and processes that, strictly speaking, would not be referred to colloquially as "tests."

into question. Further, to the extent that the validity of a test may diminish as the culture or the times change, the validity of a test must be proven again from time to time.

Validation is the process of gathering and evaluating validity evidence. Both the test developer and the test user may play a role in the validation of a test for a specific purpose. It is the test developer's responsibility to supply validity evidence in the test manual. It may sometimes be appropriate for test users to conduct their own **validation studies** with their own groups of testtakers. Such *local validation studies* may yield insights regarding a particular population of testtakers as compared to the norming sample described in a test manual. **Local validation studies** are absolutely necessary when the test user plans to alter in some way the format, instructions, language, or content of the test. For example, a local validation study would be necessary if the test user sought to transform a nationally standardized test into Braille for administration to blind and visually impaired testtakers. Local validation studies would also be necessary if a test user sought to use a test with a population of testtakers that differed in some significant way from the population on which the test was standardized.

JUST THINK . . .

Local validation studies require professional time and know-how, and they may be costly. For these reasons, they may not be done even if they are desirable or necessary. What would you recommend to a test user who is in no position to conduct such a local validation study but who nonetheless is contemplating the use of a test that really requires one?

One way measurement specialists have traditionally conceptualized validity is according to three categories:

- content validity
- criterion-related validity
- construct validity

In this classic conception of validity, referred to as the *trinitarian* view (Guion, 1980), it might be useful to visualize construct validity as being "umbrella validity," since every other variety of validity falls under it. Why construct validity is the overriding variety of validity will become clear as we discuss what makes a test valid and the methods and procedures used in validation. Indeed, there are many different ways of approaching the process of test validation, and these different plans of attack are often referred to as *strategies*. We speak, for example, of *content validation strategies, criterion-related validation strategies*, and *construct validation strategies*.

Three approaches to assessing validity associated respectively with content validity, criterion-related validity, and construct validity are

1. scrutinizing the test's content
2. relating scores obtained on the test to other test scores or other measures
3. executing a comprehensive analysis of
   a. how scores on the test relate to other test scores and measures
   b. how scores on the test can be understood within some theoretical framework for understanding the construct that the test was designed to measure

These three approaches to validity assessment are not mutually exclusive. Each should be thought of as one type of evidence that, with others, contributes to a judgment concerning the validity of the test. All three types of validity evidence contribute to a unified picture of a test's validity, though a test user may not need to know about all three. Depending on the use to which a test is being put, all three types of validity evidence may not be equally relevant.

The trinitarian model of validity is not without its critics (Landy, 1986). Messick (1995), for example, condemned this approach as fragmented and incomplete. He called for a unitary view of validity, one that takes into account everything from the implications of test scores in terms of societal values to the consequences of test use. Few people would deny that a unitary view of validity is probably preferable to the three-part view. However, even in the so-called unitary view, different elements of validity may come to the fore for scrutiny, and so an understanding of those elements in isolation is necessary.

In this chapter, we discuss content validity, criterion-related validity, and construct validity. As you learn more about *classical criterion-related validity, traditional content validity,* and other age-old conceptions of validity, you will be in a better position to evaluate their stand-alone utility, even within the overall context of a unitary conceptualization.

Let's note at the outset that although the trinitarian model focuses on three types of validity, you are likely to come across other varieties of validity in your readings. For example, you may see terms such as *predictive validity* and *concurrent validity*. In fact, you will see these terms again later in this chapter when we discuss *criterion-related validity.* Another term you may come across in the literature is *face validity.* This variety of validity has been described as the "Rodney Dangerfield of psychometric variables" because it has "received little attention—and even less respect—from researchers examining the construct validity of psychological tests and measures" (Bornstein et al., 1994, p. 363). Without further ado, we give you . . .

Face Validity

Face validity relates more to what a test appears to measure to the person being tested than to what the test actually measures. Face validity is a judgment concerning how relevant the test items appear to be. Stated another way, if a test definitely appears to measure what it purports to measure "on the face of it," it could be said to be high in face validity. A paper-and-pencil personality test labeled The Introversion/Extraversion Test, with items that ask respondents whether they have acted in an introverted or an extraverted way in particular situations, may be perceived by respondents as a highly face-valid test. On the other hand, a personality test in which respondents are asked to report what they see in inkblots may be perceived as a test with low face validity. Many respondents would be left wondering how what they said they saw in the inkblots really had anything at all to do with personality.

In contrast to judgments about the reliability of a test and judgments about the content, construct, or criterion-related validity of a test, judgments about face validity are frequently thought of from the perspective of the testtaker, not the test user. A test's *lack* of face validity could contribute to a lack of confidence in the perceived effectiveness of the test—with a consequential decrease in the testtaker's cooperation or motivation to do his or her best. In a similar vein, parents may object to having their children tested with instruments that lack ostensible validity. Such concern might stem from a belief that the use of such tests will result in invalid conclusions.

In reality, a test that lacks face validity may be very relevant and useful. However, if it is not perceived as such by testtakers, parents, legislators, and others, negative consequences may result. These consequences may range from a poor attitude on the part of the testtaker to lawsuits filed by disgruntled parties against a test user and test publisher. Ultimately, face validity may be more a matter of public relations than psychometric soundness, but it seems important nonetheless.

JUST THINK . . .

What is the value of face validity from the perspective of the test user?

Content Validity

Content validity describes a judgment of how adequately a test samples behavior representative of the universe of behavior that the test was designed to sample. For example, the universe of behavior referred to as *assertive* is very wide-ranging. A content-valid, paper-and-pencil test of assertiveness would be one that is adequately representative of this wide range. We might expect that such a test would contain items sampling from hypothetical situations at home (such as whether the respondent has difficulty in making her or his views known to fellow family members), on the job (such as whether the respondent has difficulty in asking subordinates to do what is required of them), and in social situations (such as whether the respondent would send back a steak not done to order in a fancy restaurant).

With respect to educational achievement tests, it is customary to consider a test a content-valid measure when the proportion of material covered by the test approximates the proportion of material covered in the course. A cumulative final exam in introductory statistics would be considered content valid if the proportion and type of introductory statistics problems on the test approximates the proportion and type of introductory statistics problems presented in the course.

The early stages of a test being developed for use in the classroom—be it one classroom or those throughout the state or the nation—typically entail research exploring the universe of possible instructional objectives for the course. Included among the many possible sources of information on such objectives are course syllabi, course textbooks, teachers of the course, specialists who develop curricula, and professors and supervisors who train teachers in the particular subject area. From the pooled information (along with the judgment of the test developer), a blueprint for the structure of the test will emerge. This blueprint represents the culmination of efforts to adequately sample the universe of content areas that conceivably could be sampled in such a test.[2]

For an employment test to be content valid, its content must be a representative sample of the job-related skills required for employment. Behavioral observation is one technique frequently used in blueprinting the content areas to be covered in certain types of employment tests. The test developer will observe successful veterans on that job, note the behaviors necessary for success on the job, and design the test to include a representative sample of those behaviors. Those same workers (as well as their supervisors and others) may subsequently be called on to act as experts or judges in rating the degree to which the content of the test is a representative sample of the required job-related skills. At that point, the test developer will want to know about the extent to which the experts or judges agree. Here is one method for quantifying the degree of agreement between such raters.

> **JUST THINK . . .**
>
> A test developer is working on a brief screening instrument designed to predict student success in a psychological testing and assessment course. You are the consultant called upon to blueprint the content areas covered. Your recommendations?

The Quantification of Content Validity

The measurement of content validity is important in employment settings, where tests used to hire and promote people are carefully scrutinized for their relevance to the job.

---

2. The application of the concept of *blueprint* and of *blueprinting* is, of course, not limited to achievement tests. Blueprinting may be used in the design of a personality test, an attitude measure, or any other test, sometimes employing the judgments of experts in the field.

Courts often require evidence that employment tests are work related. Several methods for quantifying content validity have been created (for example, James et al., 1984; Lindell et al., 1999; Tinsley & Weiss, 1975). One method of measuring content validity, developed by C. H. Lawshe, is essentially a method for gauging agreement among raters or judges regarding how essential a particular item is. Lawshe (1975) proposed that each rater respond to the following question for each item: "Is the skill or knowledge measured by this item

- essential
- useful but not essential
- not necessary

to the performance of the job?" (p. 567). For each item, the number of panelists stating that the item is essential is noted. According to Lawshe, if more than half the panelists indicate that an item is essential, that item has at least some content validity. Greater levels of content validity exist as larger numbers of panelists agree that a particular item is essential. Using these assumptions, Lawshe developed a formula termed the **content validity ratio (CVR):**

$$CVR = \frac{n_e - (N/2)}{N/2}$$

where CVR = content validity ratio, n_e = number of panelists indicating "essential," and N = total number of panelists. Assuming a panel of ten experts, the following three examples illustrate the meaning of the CVR when it is negative, zero, and positive:

1. *Negative CVR:* When fewer than half the panelists indicate "essential," the CVR is negative. Assume four of ten panelists indicated "essential":

$$CVR = \frac{4 - (10/2)}{10/2} = -0.2$$

2. *Zero CVR:* When exactly half the panelists indicate "essential," the CVR is zero:

$$CVR = \frac{5 - (10/2)}{10/2} = .00$$

3. *Positive CVR:* When more than half but not all the panelists indicate "essential," the CVR ranges between .00 and .99. Assume nine of ten indicated "essential":

$$CVR = \frac{9 - (10/2)}{10/2} = .80$$

In validating a test, the content validity ratio is calculated for each item. Lawshe recommended that if the amount of agreement observed has more than a 5% chance of occurring by chance, the item should be eliminated. The minimal CVR values corresponding to this 5% level are presented in Table 6–1. In the case of ten panelists, an item would need a minimum CVR of .62. In our third example (in which nine of ten panelists agreed), the CVR of .80 is significant; the item could therefore be retained. Subsequently, in our discussion of criterion-related validity, our attention shifts from an index of validity based not on test content but on test scores. First, some perspective on culture as it relates to a test's validity.

Table 6–1

Minimum Values of the Content Validity Ratio to Ensure That Agreement Is Unlikely to Be Due to Chance

Number of Panelists	Minimum Value
5	.99
6	.99
7	.99
8	.75
9	.78
10	.62
11	.59
12	.56
13	.54
14	.51
15	.49
20	.42
25	.37
30	.33
35	.31
40	.29

Source: Lawshe (1975)

Culture and the Relativity of Content Validity

Tests are often thought of as either valid or not valid. A history test, for example, either does or does not accurately measure one's knowledge of historical fact. However, it is also true that what constitutes historical fact depends in some cases on who is writing the history. Consider, for example, a momentous event in the history of the world, one that served as a catalyst for World War I. Archduke Franz Ferdinand was assassinated on June 28, 1914, by a Serb named Gavrilo Princip (Figure 6–1). Now think about how you would answer the following multiple-choice item on a history test:

Gavrilo Princip was

    a. a poet.

    b. a hero.

    c. a terrorist.

    d. a nationalist.

    e. all of the above.

For various textbooks in the Bosnian region of the world, choice "e"—that's right, "all of the above"—is the "correct" answer. According to Hedges (1997), textbooks in areas of Bosnia and Herzegovina that are controlled by different ethnic groups impart widely varying characterizations of the assassin. In the Serb-controlled region of the country, history textbooks, and presumably the tests constructed to measure students' learning, regard Princip as a "hero and poet." By contrast, Croatian students read that Princip was an assassin trained to commit a terrorist act. Muslims in the region are taught that Princip was a nationalist whose deed sparked anti-Serbian rioting.

As incredible as it may sound to Westerners, students in Bosnia and Herzegovina today are taught different versions of history, art, and language depending upon their ethnic background. Such a situation illustrates in stark relief the influence of culture on what is taught to students, as well as aspects of test construction, scoring, interpretation, and validation. The influence of culture thus extends to judgments concerning validity of tests and test items. Differences in judgments concerning the validity of

Figure 6–1
Cultural Relativity, History, and Test Validity

Austro-Hungarian Archduke Franz Ferdinand and his wife Sophia are pictured (left) as they left Sarajevo's City Hall on June 28, 1914. Moments later, Ferdinand would be assassinated by Gavrilo Princip, shown in custody at right. The killing served as a catalyst for World War I and is discussed and analyzed in history textbooks in every language around the world. Yet descriptions of the assassin Princip in those textbooks—and ability test items based on those descriptions—vary as a function of culture.

tests and test items may be observed from country to country throughout the world, even from classroom to classroom. A history test considered valid in one classroom will not be considered so in another classroom. Moreover, interpretations made on the basis of testtaker responses will vary as a function of culture. So, for example, Croatian students in Bosnia who select choice "b" ("hero") for the test item about Gavrilo Princip may do more than depress their scores on the history test: They may draw unwanted scrutiny, if not a formal investigation, of their political loyalties. Such scenarios bring new meaning to the term *politically correct* as it applies to tests, test items, and testtaker responses.

The Bosnian region is hardly unique in this regard. Consider in this context a *60 Minutes* segment entitled "Brother Against Brother," first aired December 7, 1997. Correspondent Ed Bradley reported on the case of a Palestinian professor who included questions regarding governmental corruption on an examination. The Palestinian Authority responded by interrogating, confining, and torturing the professor—all in the interest of maintaining governmentally approved "content validity" of university examinations.

◆

JUST THINK . . .

National, commercial test developers who publish widely used tests of intelligence must maintain the content validity of their tests. How would you imagine they do that?

Criterion-Related Validity

Criterion-related validity is a judgment of how adequately a test score can be used to infer an individual's most probable standing on some measure of interest—the measure of interest being the criterion. Two types of validity evidence are subsumed under the heading *criterion-related validity.* **Concurrent validity** is an index of the degree to which a test score is related to some criterion measure obtained at the same time (concurrently). **Predictive validity** is an index of the degree to which a test score predicts some criterion measure. Before we discuss each of these types of validity evidence in detail, it seems appropriate to raise (and answer) an important question.

What Is a Criterion?

A **criterion** may be broadly defined as the standard against which a test or a test score is evaluated. Operationally, a criterion can be most anything: *pilot performance in flying a Boeing 767, grade on examination in Advanced Hairweaving, number of days spent in psychiatric hospitalization;* the list is endless. There are no hard-and-fast rules for what constitutes a criterion. It can be a test score, a specific behavior or group of behaviors, an amount of time, a rating, a psychiatric diagnosis, a training cost, an index of absenteeism, an index of alcohol intoxication, and so on. Whatever the criterion, ideally it is relevant, valid, and uncontaminated.

Characteristics of a criterion   An adequate criterion is *relevant.* By this we mean that it is pertinent or applicable to the matter at hand. We would expect, for example, that a test purporting to advise testtakers whether they share the same interests of successful actors to have been validated using the interests of successful actors as a criterion.

An adequate criterion measure must also be *valid* for the purpose for which it is being used. If one test (X) is being used as the criterion to validate a second test (Y), then evidence should exist that test X is valid. If the criterion used is a rating made by a judge or a panel, then evidence should exist that the rating is valid. Suppose, for example, that a test purporting to measure depression is said to have been validated using as a criterion the diagnoses made by a blue-ribbon panel of psychodiagnosticians. A test user might wish to probe further regarding variables such as the credentials of the "blue-ribbon panel" (that is, their educational background, training, and experience) and the actual procedures used to validate a diagnosis of depression. Answers to such questions would help address the issue of whether the criterion (in this case, the diagnoses made by panel members) was indeed valid.

Ideally, a criterion is also *uncontaminated.* **Criterion contamination** is the term applied to a criterion measure that has been based, at least in part, on predictor measures. Suppose that a team of researchers from a company called Ventura International Psychiatric Research (VIPR) just completed a study of how accurately a test called the MMPI-2 predicted psychiatric diagnosis in the psychiatric population of the Minnesota state hospital system. As we will see in Chapter 11, the MMPI-2 is, in fact, a widely used test. In this study, the predictor is the MMPI-2, and the criterion is the psychiatric diagnosis that exists in the patient's record. Further, let's suppose that while all the data are being analyzed at VIPR headquarters, someone informs these researchers that the diagnosis for every patient in the Minnesota state hospital system was determined, at least in part, by an MMPI-2 test score. Should they still proceed with their analysis? The answer is no. Because the predictor measure has contaminated the criterion measure, it would be of little value to find, in essence, that the predictor can indeed predict itself.

Now, let's take a closer look at concurrent validity and predictive validity.

Concurrent Validity

If test scores are obtained at about the same time that the criterion measures are obtained, measures of the relationship between the test scores and the criterion provide evidence of *concurrent validity*. Statements of concurrent validity indicate the extent to which test scores may be used to estimate an individual's present standing on a criterion. If, for example, scores (or classifications) made on the basis of a psychodiagnostic test were to be validated against a criterion of already diagnosed psychiatric patients, the process would be one of concurrent validation. In general, once the validity of the inference from the test scores is established, the test may provide a faster, less expensive way to offer a diagnosis or a classification decision. A test with satisfactorily demonstrated concurrent validity may therefore be very appealing to prospective users because it holds out the potential of savings of money and professional time.

Sometimes the concurrent validity of a particular test (let's call it Test A) is explored with respect to another test (we'll call Test B). In such studies, prior research has satisfactorily demonstrated the validity of Test B, and the question becomes "How well does Test A compare with Test B?" Here, Test B is used as the *validating criterion*. In some studies, Test A is either a brand-new test or a test being used for some new purpose, perhaps with a new population.

Here is a 'real-life' example of a concurrent validity study in which a group of researchers explored whether a test validated for use with adults could be used with adolescents. The Beck Depression Inventory (BDI, Beck et al., 1961, 1979; Beck & Steer, 1993) and its revision, the Beck Depression Inventory-II (BDI-II, Beck et al., 1996) are self-report measures used to identify symptoms of depression and quantify their severity. Although the BDI had been widely used with adults, questions were raised regarding its appropriateness for use with adolescents. Ambrosini et al. (1991) conducted a concurrent validity study to explore the utility of the BDI with adolescents. They also sought to determine if the test could successfully differentiate patients with depression from those without depression in a population of adolescent outpatients. Diagnoses generated from the concurrent administration of an instrument previously validated for use with adolescents were used as the criterion validators. The findings suggested that the BDI is valid for use with adolescents.

> **JUST THINK . . .**
>
> What else might these researchers have done to explore the utility of the BDI with adolescents?

We now turn our attention to another form of criterion validity, one in which the criterion measure is obtained not concurrently but at some future time.

Predictive Validity

Test scores may be obtained at one time and the criterion measures obtained at a future time, usually after some intervening event has taken place. The intervening event may take varied forms, such as training, experience, therapy, medication, or simply the passage of time. Measures of the relationship between the test scores and a criterion measure obtained at a future time provide an indication of the *predictive validity* of the test; that is, how accurately scores on the test predict some criterion measure. Measures of the relationship between college admissions tests and freshman grade-point averages, for example, provide evidence of the predictive validity of the admissions tests.

In settings where tests might be employed, such as a personnel agency, a college admissions office, or a warden's office, a test's high predictive validity can be a very useful aid to decision makers who must select successful students, productive workers, or good parole risks. Whether a test result is valuable in decision making depends on how well the test results improve selection decisions over decisions made without knowledge of test results. In an industrial setting where volume turnout is important, if the use of a personnel selection test can enhance productivity to even a small degree, the enhanced productivity will pay off year after year and may translate into millions of dollars of increased revenue. And in a clinical context, no price could be placed on a test that could save more lives from suicide or by providing predictive accuracy over and above existing tests with respect to such acts. Unfortunately, the difficulties inherent in developing such tests are numerous and multifaceted (Mulvey & Lidz, 1984; Murphy, 1984; Petrie & Chamberlain, 1985).

Judgments of criterion-related validity, whether concurrent or predictive, are based on two types of statistical evidence: the validity coefficient and expectancy data.

The validity coefficient The **validity coefficient** is a correlation coefficient that provides a measure of the relationship between test scores and scores on the criterion measure. The correlation coefficient computed from a score (or classification) on a psychodiagnostic test and the criterion score (or classification) assigned by psychodiagnosticians is one example of a validity coefficient. Typically, the Pearson correlation coefficient is used to determine the validity between the two measures. However, depending on variables such as the type of data, the sample size, and the shape of the distribution, other correlation coefficients could be used. For example, in correlating self-rankings of performance on some job with rankings made by job supervisors, the formula for the Spearman rho rank-order correlation would be employed.

Like the reliability coefficient and other correlational measures, the validity coefficient is affected by restriction or inflation of range. And as in other correlational studies, a key issue is whether the range of scores employed is appropriate to the objective of the correlational analysis. In situations where, for example, attrition in the number of subjects has occurred over the course of the study, the validity coefficient may be adversely affected.

The problem of restricted range can also occur through a self-selection process in the sample employed for the validation study. Thus, for example, if the test purports to measure something as technical or as dangerous as oil barge fire-fighting skills, it may well be that the only people who reply to an ad for the position of oil barge firefighter are people who are actually highly qualified for the position. Accordingly, the range of the distribution of scores on this test of oil barge fire-fighting skills would be restricted. For less technical or dangerous positions, a self-selection factor might be operative if the test developer selects a group of newly hired employees to test (with the expectation that criterion measures will be available for this group at some subsequent date). However, because the newly hired employees have probably already passed some formal or informal evaluation in the process of being hired, there is a good chance that ability to do the job will be higher among this group than among a random sample of ordinary job applicants. Consequently, scores on the criterion measure that is later administered will tend to be higher than scores on the criterion measure obtained from a random sample of ordinary job applicants. Stated another way, the scores will be restricted in range.

Whereas it is the responsibility of the test developer to report validation data in the test manual, it is the responsibility of test users to read carefully the description of the validation study and evaluate the suitability of the test for their specific purposes. What were the characteristics of the sample used in the validation study? How matched are those characteristics to the people for whom an administration of the test is contemplated? For a specific test purpose, are some subtests of a test more appropriate than the entire test?

How high should a validity coefficient be for a user or a test developer to infer that the test is valid? There are no rules for determining the minimum acceptable size of a validity coefficient. In fact, Cronbach and Gleser (1965) cautioned against the establishment of such rules. They argued that validity coefficients need to be large enough to enable the test user to make accurate decisions within the unique context in which a test is being used. Essentially, the validity coefficient should be high enough to result in the identification and differentiation of testtakers with respect to target attribute(s), such as employees who are likely to be more productive, police officers who are less likely to misuse their weapons, and students who are more likely to be successful in a particular course of study.

Incremental validity   Test users involved in predicting some criterion from test scores are often interested in the utility of multiple predictors. The value of including more than one predictor depends on a couple of factors. First, of course, each measure used as a predictor should have criterion-related predictive validity. Second, additional predictors should possess **incremental validity,** defined here as the degree to which an additional predictor explains something about the criterion measure that is not explained by predictors already in use.

Incremental validity may be used when predicting something like academic success in college. Grade-point average (GPA) at the end of the first year may be used as a measure of academic success. A study of potential predictors of GPA may reveal that time spent in the library and time spent studying are highly correlated with GPA. How much sleep a student's roommate allows the student to have during exam periods correlates with GPA to a smaller extent. What is the most accurate but most efficient way to predict GPA? One approach, employing the principles of incremental validity, is to start with the best predictor, the predictor that is most highly correlated with GPA. This may be time spent studying. Then, using multiple regression techniques, one would examine the usefulness of the other predictors.

Even though time in the library is highly correlated with GPA, it may not possess incremental validity if it overlaps too much with the first predictor, time spent studying. Said another way, if time spent studying and time in the library are so highly correlated with each other that they reflect essentially the same thing, then only one of them needs to be included as a predictor. Including both predictors will provide little new information. By contrast, the variable of how much sleep a student's roomate allows the student to have during exams may have good incremental validity. This is so because it reflects a different aspect of preparing for exams (resting) from the first predictor (studying). Incremental validity has been used to improve the prediction of job performance for Marine Corps mechanics (Carey, 1994) and the prediction of child abuse (Murphy-Berman, 1994). In both instances, predictor measures were included only if they demonstrated that they could explain something about the criterion measure that was not already known from the other predictors.

JUST THINK . . .

From your own personal experience, what is a nonobvious predictor of GPA that is probably not correlated with time spent studying?

Expectancy data   **Expectancy data** provide information that can be used in evaluating the criterion-related validity of a test. Using a score obtained on some test(s) or measure(s), expectancy tables illustrate the likelihood that the testtaker will score within some interval of scores on a criterion measure—an interval that may be seen as "passing," "acceptable," and so on. An **expectancy table** shows the percentage of people within specified test-score intervals who subsequently were placed in various categories of the criterion (for example, placed in "passed" category or "failed" category). An expectancy table may be created from a scatterplot according to the steps listed in Figure 6–2. An expectancy table showing the relationship between scores on a subtest of the Differential Aptitude Test (DAT) and course grades in American history for eleventh-grade boys is presented in Table 6–2. You can see that of the students who scored between 40 and 60, 83% scored 80 or above in their American history course.

To illustrate how an expectancy table might be used by a corporate personnel office, suppose that on the basis of various test scores and personal interviews, personnel experts rated all applicants for a manual labor position entailing piecework as *excellent, very good, average, below average,* or *poor.* In this example, then, the test score is actually a rating made by personnel experts on the basis of a number of test scores and a personal interview. Let's further suppose that because of a severe labor scarcity at the time, all the applicants were hired—which, by the way, is a dream come true for a researcher interested in conducting a validation study of the assessment procedure. Floor supervisors were not informed of the composite score obtained by the newly hired workers. The floor supervisors provided the criterion measure by rating each employee's performance *satisfactory* or *unsatisfactory.* Figure 6–3 is the resulting **expectancy chart,** or graphic representation of an expectancy table.

As illustrated in the expectancy chart, of all applicants originally rated *excellent,* 94% were rated *satisfactory* on the job. By contrast, among applicants originally rated *poor,* only 17% were rated *satisfactory* on the job. In general, this expectancy chart tells us that the higher the initial rating, the greater the probability of job success. Stated another way, it tells us that the lower the initial rating, the greater the probability of job failure. The company experimenting with such a rating system could reasonably expect to improve its productivity by using this rating system. Specifically, job applicants who obtained ratings of *average* or higher would be the only applicants hired.

Tables that could be used as an aid for personnel directors in their decision-making chores were published by H. C. Taylor and J. T. Russell in the *Journal of Applied Psychology* in 1939. Referred to by the names of their authors, the **Taylor-Russell tables** provide an estimate of the extent to which inclusion of a particular test in the selection system will actually improve selection. More specifically, the tables provide an estimate of the percentage of employees hired by the use of a particular test who will be successful at their jobs, given different combinations of three variables: the test's validity, the selection ratio used, and the base rate.

The value assigned for the test's validity is the computed validity coefficient. The *selection ratio* is a numerical value that reflects the relationship between the number of people to be hired and the number of people available to be hired. For instance, if there are 50 positions and 100 applicants, the selection ratio is 50/100, or .50. As used here, *base rate* refers to the percentage of people hired under the existing system for a particular position. If, for example, a firm employs 25 computer programmers and 20 are considered successful, the base rate would be .80. With knowledge of the validity coefficient of a particular test along with the selection ratio, reference to the Taylor-Russell tables provides the personnel officer with an estimate of how much using the test would improve selection over existing methods.

A sample Taylor-Russell table is presented in Table 6–3 (page 170). This table is for the base rate of .60, meaning that 60% of those hired under the existing system are successful in their work. Down the left-hand side are validity coefficients for a test that

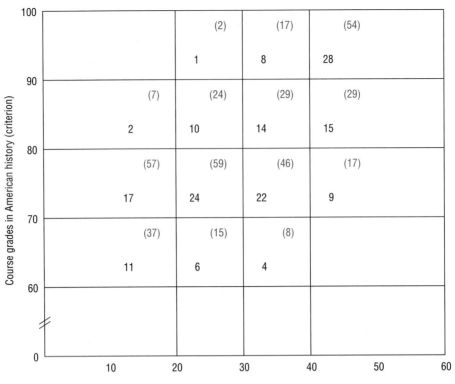

Language usage raw scores from the Differential Aptitude Tests
( ) percentage of points per cell

Figure 6–2
Seven Steps to an Expectancy Table

1. *Draw a scatterplot such that each point in the plot represents a particular test score–criterion score combination. The criterion should be on the Y-axis.*

2. *Draw grid lines in such a way as to summarize the number of people who scored within a particular interval.*

3. *Count the number of points in each cell (n_i) as shown in the figure.*

4. *Count the total number of points within each vertical interval (N_v). This number represents the number of people scoring within a particular test score interval.*

5. *Convert each cell frequency to a percentage (n_i/N_v). This represents the percentage of people obtaining a particular test score–criterion score combination. Write the percentages in the cells. Enclose the percentages in parentheses to distinguish them from the frequencies.*

6. *On a separate sheet, create table headings and subheadings and copy the percentages into the appropriate cell tables as shown in Table 6–2. Be careful to put the percentages in the correct cell tables. (Note that it's easy to make a mistake at this stage because the percentages of people within particular score intervals are written horizontally in the table and vertically in the scatterplot.)*

7. *If desired, write the number and percentage of cases per test-score interval. If the number of cases in any one cell is very small, it is more likely to fluctuate in subsequent charts. If cell sizes are small, the user could create fewer cells or accumulate data over several years.*

Table 6–2

DAT Language Usage Subtest Scores and American History Grade for 171 Eleventh-Grade Boys (Showing Percentage of Students Obtaining Course Grades in the Interval Shown)

Test Score	Course Grade Interval				Cases per Test-Score Interval	
	0–69	70–79	80–89	90–100	N_v	%
40 and above	0	17	29	54	52	100
30–39	8	46	29	17	48	100
0–29	15	59	24	2	41	100
Below 20	37	57	7	0	30	101*

*Total sums to more than 100% because of rounding.

Source: From the *Manual of Differential Aptitude Tests,* Fifth Edition. Copyright © 1973, 1974 by The Psychological Corporation, a Harcourt Assessment Company. Reproduced by permission. All rights reserved. "Differential Aptitude Tests" and "DAT" are trademarks of The Psychological Corporation, registered in the United States of America and/or other jurisdictions.

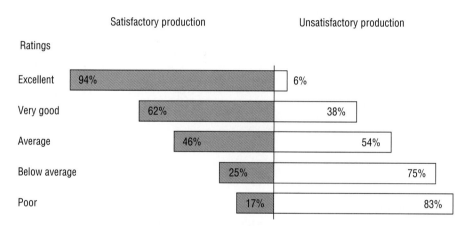

Figure 6–3
Expectancy Chart for Test Ratings and Job Performance

Source: From Test Service Bulletin, "How Effective Are Your Tests?" The Psychological Corporation, San Antonio, Texas. Reproduced by permission of the publisher.

could be used to help select employees. Across the top are the various selection ratios. They reflect the proportion of the people applying for the jobs who will be hired. If a new test is introduced to help select employees in a situation with a selection ratio of .20, and if the new test has a predictive validity coefficient of .55, the table shows that the base rate will increase to .88. This means that, rather than 60% of the hired employees being expected to perform successfully, a full 88% can be expected to do so. When selection ratios are low, as when only 5% of the applicants will be hired, even tests with low validity coefficients, such as .15, can result in improved base rates.

One limitation of the Taylor-Russell tables is that the relationship between the predictor (the test) and the criterion (rating of performance on the job) must be linear. If, for example, there is some point at which job performance levels off, no matter how high the score on the test gets, use of the Taylor-Russell tables would be inappropriate. Another limitation of the Taylor-Russell tables is the potential difficulty of identifying a criterion score that separates "successful" from "unsuccessful" employees.

Table 6-3
Taylor-Russell Table for a Base Rate of .60

Validity (ρ_{xy})	Selection Ratio										
	.05	.10	.20	.30	.40	.50	.60	.70	.80	.90	.95
.00	.60	.60	.60	.60	.60	.60	.60	.60	.60	.60	.60
.05	.64	.63	.63	.62	.62	.62	.61	.61	.61	.60	.60
.10	.68	.67	.65	.64	.64	.63	.63	.62	.61	.61	.60
.15	.71	.70	.68	.67	.66	.65	.64	.63	.62	.61	.61
.20	.75	.73	.71	.69	.67	.66	.65	.64	.63	.62	.61
.25	.78	.76	.73	.71	.69	.68	.66	.65	.63	.62	.61
.30	.82	.79	.76	.73	.71	.69	.68	.66	.64	.62	.61
.35	.85	.82	.78	.75	.73	.71	.69	.67	.65	.63	.62
.40	.88	.85	.81	.78	.75	.73	.70	.68	.66	.63	.62
.45	.90	.87	.83	.80	.77	.74	.72	.69	.66	.64	.62
.50	.93	.90	.86	.82	.79	.76	.73	.70	.67	.64	.62
.55	.95	.92	.88	.84	.81	.78	.75	.71	.68	.64	.62
.60	.96	.94	.90	.87	.83	.80	.76	.73	.69	.65	.63
.65	.98	.96	.92	.89	.85	.82	.78	.74	.70	.65	.63
.70	.99	.97	.94	.91	.87	.84	.80	.75	.71	.66	.63
.75	.99	.99	.96	.93	.90	.86	.81	.77	.71	.66	.63
.80	1.00	.99	.98	.95	.92	.88	.83	.78	.72	.66	.63
.85	1.00	1.00	.99	.97	.95	.91	.86	.80	.73	.66	.63
.90	1.00	1.00	1.00	.99	.97	.94	.88	.82	.74	.67	.63
.95	1.00	1.00	1.00	1.00	.99	.97	.92	.84	.75	.67	.63
1.00	1.00	1.00	1.00	1.00	1.00	1.00	1.00	.86	.75	.67	.63

Source: Taylor and Russell (1939)

The potential problems of the Taylor-Russell tables were avoided by an alternative set of tables (Naylor & Shine, 1965) that provided an indication of the difference in average criterion scores for the selected group as compared with the original group. Use of the **Naylor-Shine tables** entails obtaining the difference between the means of the selected and unselected groups to obtain an index of what the test (or some other tool of assessment) is adding to already established procedures. Both the Taylor-Russell and the Naylor-Shine tables can assist in judging the utility of a particular test, the former by determining the increase over current procedures and the latter by determining the increase in average score on some criterion measure. With both tables, the validity coefficient used must be one obtained by concurrent validation procedures—a fact that should not be surprising, because it is obtained with respect to current employees hired by the selection process in effect at the time of the study.

If hiring decisions were made solely on the basis of variables such as the validity of an employment test and the prevailing selection ratio, then tables such as those offered by Taylor and Russell and Naylor and Shine would be in wide use today. The fact is that many other kinds of variables might enter into hiring and other sorts of personnel selection decisions (including decisions relating to promotion, transfer, layoff, and firing). Some additional variables might include, for example, applicants' minority status, general physical or mental health, or drug use. Given that many variables may affect a personnel selection decision (including, for example, hiring), of what use is a given test in the decision process?

JUST THINK . . .

In addition to testing, what types of assessment procedures might employers use to help them make judicious personnel selection decisions?

After publication of the Taylor-Russell tables, a number of articles began to appear probing ways to determine the appropriateness of a given test with respect to different types of assessment procedures (Brogden, 1946, 1949; Smith, 1948), and a literature dealing with **test utility theory** began to grow. Also during this period, statisticians such as Wald (1947, 1950) were involved in identifying statistical rules for developing a sequential analysis of a problem that would lead to an optimal decision. Decision theory had been born, and it would be applied to answering questions about the utility of psychological tests.

Decision theory and test utility   Perhaps the most oft-cited application of statistical decision theory to the field of psychological testing is Cronbach and Gleser's *Psychological Tests and Personnel Decisions* (1957, 1965). The idea of applying statistical decision theory to questions of test utility was conceptually appealing and promising, and an authoritative textbook of the day reflects the great enthusiasm with which this marriage of enterprises was greeted:

> The basic decision-theory approach to selection and placement . . . has a number of advantages over the more classical approach based upon the correlation model. . . . There is no question but that it is a more general and better model for handling this kind of decision task, and we predict that in the future problems of selection and placement will be treated in this context more frequently—perhaps to eventual exclusion of the more stereotyped correlational model. (Blum & Naylor, 1968, p. 58)

Stated generally, Cronbach and Gleser (1965) presented (1) a classification of decision problems, (2) various selection strategies ranging from single-stage processes to sequential analyses, (3) a quantitative analysis of the relationship between test utility, the selection ratio, cost of the testing program, and expected value of the outcome, and (4) a recommendation that in some instances job requirements be tailored to the applicant's ability instead of the other way around (a concept they refer to as *adaptive treatment*).

Before we illustrate decision theory in action, let us briefly (and somewhat loosely) define five terms frequently encountered in discussions of decision theory as applied to psychological testing and measurement: *base rate, hit rate, miss rate, false positive,* and *false negative.*

Generally, a **base rate** is the extent to which a particular trait, behavior, characteristic, or attribute exists in the population (expressed as a proportion). As illustrated in this chapter's *Close-up,* due consideration must be given to the base rate of a targeted attribute in the sample of people being studied in predictive validity research, versus the base rate of that same attribute in the population at large. In psychometric parlance, a **hit rate** may be defined as the proportion of people a test accurately identifies as possessing or exhibiting a particular trait, behavior, characteristic, or attribute. For example, *hit rate* could refer to the proportion of people accurately predicted to be able to perform work at the graduate school-level, or the proportion of neurological patients accurately identified as having a brain tumor. In like fashion, a **miss rate** may be defined as the proportion of people the test fails to identify as having, or not having, a particular characteristic or attribute. Here, a *miss* amounts to an inaccurate prediction. The category of *misses* may be further subdivided. A **false positive** is a miss wherein the test predicted that the testtaker did possess the particular characteristic or attribute being measured when the testtaker did not. A **false negative** is a miss wherein the test predicted that the testtaker did not possess the particular characteristic or attribute being measured when the testtaker did.

Suppose you developed a measurement procedure you called the Vapor Test (VT), which was designed to determine if alive-and-well subjects are indeed breathing. The

Base Rates and Predictive Validity

To evaluate the predictive validity of a test, a test targeting a particular attribute may be administered to a sample of research subjects in which approximately half of the subjects possess or exhibit the targeted attribute and the other half do not. Questions may subsequently arise about the appropriateness of the use of such a test in which the base rate of the occurrence of the targeted attribute in the population being tested is substantially less than 50%. Such questions arose, for example, with regard to the use of a test called the Child Abuse Potential Inventory (CAP; Milner, 1986).

The CAP was designed to be a screening aid in the identification of adults at high risk for physically abusing children. A high score on the CAP, especially in combination with confirmatory evidence from other sources, might prompt the test user to probe further with regard to the testtaker's history of, or present intentions regarding, child abuse. Another use of the CAP is as an outcome measure in programs designed to prevent physical abuse of children (Milner, 1989). Participants would be administered the CAP upon entry to the program and again upon exit.

Predictive validity research conducted with the CAP has "demonstrated an uncanny hit rate (about 90%) in discriminating abusers from nonabusers" (Melton & Limber, 1989, p. 1231). Yet as the author of the CAP has pointed out, "the reported 90% hit rate was determined in studies using groups that consisted of equal numbers of abusers and nonabusers that by design contain base rates of 50% which are optimal for classification purposes" (Milner, 1991, p. 80). Thus, as the base rate for child abuse decreases, the number of false positives in the group indicated as abusive will increase, while the number of false negatives in the group indicated as nonabusive will decrease. If these facts related to base rates and predictive validity are not known and appreciated by the test user, a potential exists for misuse of tests such as the CAP.

Table 1
Application of the CAP in a Population With a High Base Rate of Child Abuse

	Actual Status		
	Abuser	**Nonabuser**	**Row Totals**
CAP results indicate:			
Abuser	91	13	104
Nonabuser	19	97	116
Column totals	**110**	**110**	**220**

The base rate for child abuse in the general population is about 2–3% annually (Finkelhor & Dziuba-Leatherman, 1994). This base rate is low relative to the 50% base rate that prevailed in the predictive validity studies with the CAP. This fact must therefore be considered in any use of the CAP with members of the general population.

With this background, consider a study conducted by Milner et al. (1986) with 220 adults, including 110 known abusers and 110 nonabusers. All subjects completed the CAP, and the test was scored. Fully 82.7% of the abusers and 88.2% of the nonabusers were correctly classified using the CAP (Table 1). Working down the columns of Table 1, note that of the 110 known abusers, 19 were incorrectly classified as nonabusers. Of the 110 known nonabusers, 13 were incorrectly identified as abusers. Of course, in most applications of the CAP, one would not know whether the person being tested was an actual child abuser; that would probably be the reason for administering the test. To gain an understanding of the errors that would be made, look at Table 1 again, but this time work across the rows. When the CAP indicates that a person is an abuser, the finding is correct 87.5% of the time (91 of 104 instances). When the CAP indicates that a person is not an abuser, it is correct 83.6% of the time (97 of 116 instances).

procedure for the VT entails having the examiner hold a mirror under the subject's nose and mouth for a minute or so and observing whether the subject's breath fogs the mirror. Let's say that 100 introductory psychology students are administered the VT, and it is concluded that 89 were, in fact, breathing (whereas 11 are deemed, on the basis of the VT, not to be breathing). Is the VT a good test? Obviously not. Because the base rate is 100% of the (alive-and-well) population, we really don't even need a test to measure the characteristic *breathing*. If for some reason we did need such a measurement procedure,

Table 2

Application of the CAP in a Population With a Low Base Rate of Child Abuse

	Actual Status		
	Abuser	Nonabuser	Row Totals
CAP results indicate:			
Abuser	41	112	153
Nonabuser	9	838	847
Column totals	**50**	**950**	**1000**

The picture changes dramatically, however, in a low base rate environment. For the purposes of this example, let's say that physical child abuse occurs in 5% of the population. In a hypothetical study, we test 1,000 people using the CAP. Because physical child abuse occurs in 5% of the population, we would expect 50 or so of our testtakers to be abusers. And let's say further that just as in the Milner et al. (1986) study, 82.7% of the abusers and 88.2% of the nonabusers are correctly identified in our study (Table 2). Working down the columns in Table 2, if 82.7% of the abusers are correctly identified, 41 will be identified as abusers, and the remaining 9 will be identified as nonabusers. If the test has an 88.2% accuracy rate for nonabusers, 838 of the nonabusers will be correctly identified, and the remaining 112 will be identified as abusers.

Now look at Table 2 again, this time working across the rows. If the CAP score indicates that the individual is an abuser, it is probably *in*correct. Most of the people (73.2% of them, in this example) with CAP scores indicating that they are abusers are, in reality, not abusers. This inaccuracy is entirely the product of working with a low base rate sample. Even if the CAP were more accurate, because abuse is a low base rate phenomenon, using test results to identify abusers will still result in many identified abusers being

wrongly classified. Stated another way, when the nonabusing population is much larger than the abusing population, the chances are that most of the mistakes will be made in classifying the nonabusing population.

Place yourself in the seat of the judge or the jury hearing a physical child abuse case. A psychologist testifies that the CAP, which has an accuracy rate of 85–90%, indicates that the defendant is a physical abuser. The psychologist attempts an explanation about population base rates and the possibility of error. Still, what might stick in your mind about the psychologist's testimony? Many people would reason that, if the CAP is right more than 85% of the time, and if the defendant is *identified* as a child abuser, there must be at least an 85% chance that the defendant *is* a child abuser. This conclusion, as you know now, would be incorrect and could result in justice not being served (Melton & Limber, 1989).

This example illustrates that the test developer's intended use of the test must be respected. Lacking any compelling psychometric evidence to deviate from the test developer's intended use of the test, such deviations may result in harm to the testtaker. The example further serves as a reminder that when data about the accuracy and consistency of a test are collected, the data are collected using a sampling of people from a particular population. Conclusions drawn from those psychometric data are applicable only to groups of people from a similar population.

Joel Milner, the author of the CAP, has urged test users to keep in mind that it is inappropriate to use any single psychological test as a diagnostic criterion. Milner (1991) went on to remind readers that "data from multiple sources, such as several tests, client interviews, collateral interviews, direct observations, and case histories should be used in making decisions regarding child abuse and treatment" (p. 81).

we probably wouldn't use one that was inaccurate in approximately 11% of the cases. A test is obviously of no value if the hit rate is higher *without* using it. One measure of the value of a test lies in the extent to which its use improves on the hit rate that exists without its use.

As a simple illustration of decision theory applied to testing, suppose a test is administered to a group of 100 job applicants, and some cutoff score is applied to distinguish applicants who will be hired (applicants judged to have passed the test) from applicants whose employment application will be rejected (applicants judged to have failed the test). And let's further suppose that some criterion measure will be applied some time later to ascertain whether the newly hired person was considered a success or a failure at the job. In such a situation, if the test is a perfect predictor (if its validity coefficient is equal to 1), two distinct types of outcomes can be identified: (1) Some applicants will score at or above the cutoff score on the test and be successful at the job, and (2) some applicants will score below the cutoff score and would not have been successful at the job.

In reality, few if any employment tests are perfect predictors with validity coefficients equal to 1. Consequently, two additional types of outcomes are possible: (3) Some applicants will score at or above the cutoff score, be hired, and fail at the job (the criterion), and (4) some applicants who scored below the cutoff score and were not hired could have been successful at the job. People who fall into the third category could be categorized as *false positives,* and those who fall into the fourth category could be categorized as *false negatives.*

In this illustration, logic alone tells us that if the selection ratio is, say, 90% (nine out of ten applicants will be hired), the cutoff score will probably be set lower than if the selection ratio is 5% (only five of the 100 applicants will be hired). Further, if the selection ratio is 90%, it is a good bet that the number of false positives (people hired who will fail on the criterion measure) will be greater than in a case where the selection ratio is 5%. Conversely, if the selection ratio is only 5%, it is a good bet that the number of false negatives (people not hired who could have succeeded on the criterion measure) will be greater than in a case where the selection ratio is 90%.

Decision theory provides guidelines for setting optimal cutoff scores. In setting such scores, the relative seriousness of making false-positive or false-negative selection decisions is frequently taken into account. Thus, for example, it is a prudent policy for an airline personnel office to set cutoff scores on tests for pilots that might result in a false negative (a pilot who is truly qualified being rejected) as opposed to a cutoff score that would allow a false positive (a pilot who is in reality unqualified being hired).

In the hands of highly skilled researchers, principles of decision theory applied to problems of test utility have led to some enlightening and impressive findings. For example, Schmidt, Hunter, McKenzie, and Muldrow (1979) demonstrated in dollars and cents how the utility of a company's selection program (and the validity coefficient of the tests used in that program) can play a critical role in the profitability of the company. Focusing on one employer's population of computer programmers, these researchers asked supervisors to rate, in dollars, the value of good, average, and poor programmers. This information was used in conjunction with other information, including these facts: (1) Each year the employer hired 600 new programmers, (2) the average programmer remained on the job for about ten years, (3) the Programmer Aptitude Test currently in use as part of the hiring process had a validity coefficient of .76, (4) it cost about $10 per applicant to administer the test, and (5) the company currently employed more than 4,000 programmers.

Schmidt et al. (1979) made a number of calculations using different values for some of the variables. For example, knowing that some of the tests previously used in the hiring process had validity coefficients ranging from .00 to .50, they varied the value of the test's validity coefficient (along with other factors such as different selection ratios that had been in effect) and examined the relative efficiency of the various conditions. Among their findings was the fact that the existing selection ratio and selection process provided a great gain in efficiency over a previous situation (when the selection ratio was 5% and the validity coefficient of the test used in hiring was equal to .50). The gain was equal to almost $6 million per year. Multiplied over, say, ten years, that's $60 million. The existing selection ratio and selection process provided an even greater gain in efficiency over a previously existing situation in which the test had no validity at all and the selection ratio was .80. Here, in one year, the gain in efficiency was estimated to be equal to over $97 million.

By the way, the employer in the study above was the United States government. Hunter and Schmidt (1981) applied the same type of analysis to the national workforce and made a compelling argument with respect to the critical relationship between valid tests and measurement procedures and our national productivity. In a subsequent study, Schmidt, Hunter, and their colleagues found that substantial increases in work output or reductions in payroll costs would result from using valid measures of cognitive ability as opposed to non-test procedures (Schmidt et al., 1986).

JUST THINK . . .

What must happen in society at large if the promise of decision theory in personnel selection is to be fulfilled?

Employers are reluctant to use decision theory–based strategies in their hiring practices because of the complexity of their application and the threat of legal challenges. Thus, although decision theory approaches to assessment hold great promise, this promise has yet to be fulfilled.

Construct Validity

Construct validity is a judgment about the appropriateness of inferences drawn from test scores regarding individual standings on a variable called a *construct*. A **construct** is an informed, scientific idea developed or hypothesized to describe or explain behavior. *Intelligence* is a construct that may be invoked to describe why a student performs well in school. *Anxiety* is a construct that may be invoked to describe why a psychiatric patient paces the floor. Other examples of constructs are *job satisfaction, personality, bigotry, clerical aptitude, depression, motivation, self-esteem, emotional adjustment, potential dangerousness, executive potential, creativity,* and *mechanical comprehension,* to name but a few.

Constructs are unobservable, presupposed (underlying) traits that a test developer may invoke to describe test behavior or criterion performance. The researcher investigating a test's construct validity must formulate hypotheses about the expected behavior of high scorers and low scorers on the test. These hypotheses give rise to a tentative theory about the nature of the construct the test was designed to measure. If the test is a valid measure of the construct, the high scorers and the low scorers will behave as predicted by the theory. If high scorers and low scorers on the test do not behave as predicted, the investigator will need to reexamine the nature of the construct itself or hypotheses made about it. One possible reason for obtaining results contrary to those predicted by the theory is that the test simply does not measure the construct. An alternative explanation could lie in the theory that generated hypotheses about the construct. The theory may need to be reexamined.

In some instances, the reason for obtaining contrary findings can be traced to the statistical procedures used or to the way the procedures were executed. One procedure may have been more appropriate than another, given the particular assumptions. Thus, although confirming evidence contributes to a judgment that a test is a valid measure of a construct, evidence to the contrary can also be useful. Contrary evidence can provide a stimulus for the discovery of new facets of the construct as well as alternative methods of measurement.

Increasingly, construct validity has been viewed as the unifying concept for all validity evidence (AERA, APA, & NCME, 1999). As we noted at the outset, all types of validity evidence, including evidence from the content- and criterion-related varieties of validity, come under the umbrella of construct validity. Let's look at the types of evidence that might be gathered.

Evidence of Construct Validity

A number of procedures may be used to provide different kinds of evidence that a test has construct validity. The various techniques of construct validation may provide evidence, for example, that

- The test is homogeneous, measuring a single construct.
- Test scores increase or decrease as a function of age, the passage of time, or an experimental manipulation as theoretically predicted.
- Test scores obtained after some event or the mere passage of time (that is, posttest scores) differ from pretest scores as theoretically predicted.
- Test scores obtained by people from distinct groups vary as predicted by the theory.
- Test scores correlate with scores on other tests in accordance with what would be predicted from a theory that covers the manifestation of the construct in question.

A brief discussion of each type of construct validity evidence and the procedures used to obtain it follows.

Evidence of homogeneity   When describing a test and its items, **homogeneity** refers to how uniform a test is in measuring a single concept. A test developer can increase test homogeneity in several ways. Consider, for example, a test of academic achievement that contains subtests in areas such as mathematics, spelling, and reading comprehension. The Pearson *r* could be used to correlate average subtest scores with average total test score. Subtests that in the test developer's judgment do not correlate very well with the test as a whole might have to be reconstructed (or eliminated) lest the test not measure the construct *academic achievement*. Correlations between subtest scores and total test score are generally reported in the test manual as evidence of homogeneity.

One way a test developer can improve the homogeneity of a test containing items that are scored dichotomously (for example, true/false) is by eliminating those items that do not show significant correlation coefficients with total test scores. If all test items show significant, positive correlations with total test scores, and high scorers on the test tend to pass each item more than low scorers do, then each item is probably measuring the same construct as the total test. Each item is contributing to test homogeneity.

The homogeneity of a test in which items are scored on a multipoint scale can also be improved. For example, some attitude and opinion questionnaires require respondents to indicate level of agreement with specific statements by responding, for example, *strongly agree, agree, disagree,* or *strongly disagree.* Each response is assigned a numerical score, and items that do not show significant Spearman rank-order correlation coefficients are eliminated. If all test items show significant, positive correlations with total test scores, then each item is most likely measuring the same construct that the test as a whole is measuring (and is thereby contributing to the test's homogeneity). Coefficient alpha may also be used in estimating the homogeneity of a test composed of multiple-choice items (Novick & Lewis, 1967).

As a case study illustrating how a test's homogeneity can be improved, consider the Marital Satisfaction Scale (MSS; Roach et al., 1981). Designed to assess various aspects of married people's attitudes toward their marital relationship, the MSS contains an approximately equal number of items expressing positive and negative sentiments with respect to marriage. For example, *My life would seem empty without my marriage* and *My marriage has "smothered" my personality.* In one stage of the development of this test, subjects indicated how much they agreed or disagreed with the various sentiments in each of 73 items by marking a 5-point scale that ranged from *strongly agree* to *strongly disagree.* Based on the correlations between item scores and total score, the test developers elected to retain 48 items with correlation coefficients greater than .50, thus creating a more homogeneous instrument.

Item-analysis procedures have also been employed in the quest for test homogeneity. One item-analysis procedure focuses on the relationship between testtakers' scores on individual items and their score on the entire test. Each item is analyzed with respect to how high scorers as opposed to low scorers responded to it. If it is an academic test, and high scorers on the entire test for some reason tended to get that particular item wrong while low scorers on the test as a whole tended to get the item right, the item is obviously not a good one. The item should be eliminated in the interest of test homogeneity, among other considerations. If the test is one of, say, marital satisfaction, and individuals who score high on the test as a whole respond to a particular item in a way that would indicate that they are not satisfied, whereas people who tend not to be satisfied respond to the item in a way that would indicate that they are satisfied, then again the item should probably be eliminated or at least reexamined for clarity.

JUST THINK . . .

Is it possible for a test to be *too* homogeneous in item content?

Although test homogeneity is desirable because it assures us that all the items on the test tend to be measuring the same thing, it is not the "be-all and end-all" of construct validity. Knowing that a test is homogeneous contributes no information about how the construct being measured relates to other constructs. It is therefore important to report evidence of a test's homogeneity along with other evidence of construct validity.

Evidence of changes with age   Some constructs are expected to change over time. *Reading rate,* for example, tends to increase dramatically year by year from age 6 to the early teens. If a test score purports to be a measure of a construct that could be expected to change over time, the test score too should show the same progressive changes with age to be considered a valid measure of the construct. We would expect, for example, that if children in grades 6, 7, 8, and 9 sat for a test of eighth-grade vocabulary, the total number of items scored as correct from all the test protocols would increase as a function of the higher grade level of the testtakers.

Some constructs lend themselves more readily than others to predictions of change over time. Thus, although we may be able to predict, for example, that a gifted child's scores on a test of reading skills will increase over the course of the testtaker's years of elementary and secondary education, we may not be able to predict with such confidence how a newlywed couple will score through the years on a test of marital satisfaction. This fact does not relegate a construct such as *marital satisfaction* to a lower stature than *reading ability.* Rather, it simply means that measures of marital satisfaction may be less stable over time or more vulnerable to situational events (such as in-laws coming to visit and refusing to leave for three months) than is reading ability. Evidence of change over time, like evidence of test homogeneity, does not in itself provide information about how the construct relates to other constructs.

Evidence of pretest/posttest changes   Evidence that test scores change as a result of some experience between a pretest and a posttest can be evidence of construct validity. Some of the more typical intervening experiences responsible for changes in test scores are formal education, a course of therapy or medication, and on-the-job experience. Of course, depending on the construct being measured, almost any intervening life experience could be predicted to yield changes in score from pretest to posttest. Reading an inspirational book, watching a TV talk show, undergoing surgery, serving a prison sentence, or the mere passage of time may each prove to be a potent intervening variable.

Returning to our example regarding the use of the Marital Satisfaction Scale, one investigator cited in Roach et al. (1981) compared scores on that instrument before and after a sex therapy treatment program. Scores showed a significant change between pretest and posttest. A second posttest given eight weeks later showed that scores remained stable (suggesting the instrument was reliable), whereas the pretest/posttest measures were still significantly different. Such changes in scores in the predicted direction after the treatment program contribute to evidence of the construct validity for this test.

We would expect a decline in marital satisfaction scores if a pretest were administered to a sample of couples shortly after they took their nuptial vows, and a posttest were administered shortly after members of the couples first consulted their respective divorce attorneys sometime within the first five years of marriage. The experimental group in this study would consist of couples who consulted a divorce attorney within the first five years of marriage. The design of such pretest/posttest research ideally should include a control group to rule out alternative explanations of the findings.

Evidence from distinct groups   Also referred to as the **method of contrasted groups,** one way of providing evidence for the validity of a test is to demonstrate that scores on the test vary in a predictable way as a function of membership in some group. The rationale here is that if a test is a valid measure of a particular construct, then test scores from groups of people who would be presumed to differ with respect to that construct should have correspondingly different test scores. Consider in this context a test of depression wherein the higher the test score, the more depressed the testtaker is presumed to be. We would expect individuals psychiatrically hospitalized for depression to score higher on this measure than a random sample of Wal-Mart shoppers.

Now, suppose it was your intention to provide construct validity evidence for the Marital Satisfaction Scale by showing differences in scores between distinct groups. How might you go about doing that?

Roach and colleagues (1981) proceeded by identifying two groups of married couples, one relatively satisfied in their marriage, the other not so satisfied. The groups were identified by ratings by peers and professional marriage counselors. A t test on the difference between mean score on the test was significant ($p < .01$)—evidence to support the notion that the Marital Satisfaction Scale is indeed a valid measure of the construct *marital satisfaction.*

In a bygone era, the method many test developers used to create distinct groups was deception. For example, if it had been predicted that more of the construct would be exhibited on the test in question if the subject felt highly anxious, an experimental situation might be designed to make the subject feel highly anxious. Virtually any feeling state the theory called for could be induced by an experimental scenario that typically involved giving the research subject some misinformation. However, given the ethical constraints of contemporary psychologists, combined with the fact that academic institutions and other sponsors of research tend not to condone deception in human research, the method of obtaining distinct groups by creating them through the dissemination of deceptive information is seldom allowed today.

Convergent evidence   Evidence for the construct validity of a particular test may converge from a number of sources, such as other tests or measures designed to assess the same (or a similar) construct. Thus, if scores on the test undergoing construct validation tend to correlate highly in the predicted direction with scores on older, more established, and already validated tests designed to measure the same (or a similar) construct, this would be an example of **convergent evidence.**[3]

Convergent evidence for validity may come not only from correlations with tests purporting to measure an identical construct but also from correlations with measures purporting to measure related constructs. Consider, for example, a new test designed to measure the construct *test anxiety*. Generally speaking, we might expect high positive correlations between this new test and older, more established measures of test anxiety. However, we might also expect more moderate correlations between this new test and measures of general anxiety.

Roach et al. (1981) provided convergent evidence of the construct validity of the Marital Satisfaction Scale by computing a validity coefficient between scores on it and scores on the Marital Adjustment Test (Locke & Wallace, 1959). The validity coefficient of .79 provided additional evidence of the construct validity of the instrument.

Discriminant evidence   A validity coefficient showing little (that is, a statistically insignificant) relationship between test scores and/or other variables with which scores on the test being construct-validated should *not* theoretically be correlated provides **discriminant evidence** of construct validity (also known as *discriminant validity*). In the course of developing the Marital Satisfaction Scale (MSS), its authors correlated scores on that instrument with scores on the Marlowe-Crowne Social Desirability Scale (Crowne & Marlowe, 1964). Roach et al. (1981) hypothesized that high correlations between these two instruments would suggest that respondents were probably not answering items on the MSS entirely honestly but instead were responding in socially desirable ways. But the correlation between the MSS and the social desirability measure did not prove to be significant, and the test developers concluded that social desirability could be ruled out as a primary factor in explaining the meaning of MSS test scores.

In 1959, an experimental technique useful for examining both convergent and discriminant validity evidence was presented in *Psychological Bulletin*. This rather technical procedure, called the **multitrait-multimethod matrix,** is presented in our companion workbook to this textbook. Here, let's simply point out that *multitrait* means "two or more traits" and *multimethod* means "two or more methods." The multitrait-multimethod matrix (Campbell & Fiske, 1959) is the matrix or table that results from correlating variables (traits) within and between methods. Values for any number of traits (such as aggressiveness or extraversion) as obtained by various methods (such as behavioral observation or a personality test) are inserted into the table, and the resulting matrix of correlations provides insight with respect to both the convergent and the discriminant validity of the methods used.[4]

---

3. Data indicating that a test measures the same construct as other tests purporting to measure the same construct are also referred to as evidence of **convergent validity.** One question that may be raised here concerns the necessity for the new test if it simply duplicates existing tests that measure the same construct. The answer, generally speaking, is a claim that the new test has some advantage over the more established test. For example, the new test may be shorter and capable of administration in less time without significant loss in reliability or validity. On a practical level, the new test may be less costly.

4. For an interesting, real-life application of the multitrait-multimethod technique, see Meier's (1984) examination of the validity of the construct *burnout*. In a subsequent construct validity study, Meier (1991) used an alternative to the multitrait-multimethod matrix to examine another construct, *occupational stress*.

Factor analysis   Both convergent and discriminant evidence of construct validity can be obtained by the use of factor analysis. **Factor analysis** is a singular, shorthand term for a class of mathematical procedures designed to identify *factors* or specific variables that are typically attributes, characteristics, or dimensions on which people may differ. In psychometric research, factor analysis is frequently employed as a data reduction method in which several sets of scores and the correlations between them are analyzed. In such studies, the purpose of the factor analysis may be to identify the factor or factors in common between test scores on subscales within a particular test, or the factors in common between scores on a series of tests. In general, factor analysis is conducted on either an exploratory or a confirmatory basis. **Exploratory factor analysis** typically entails "estimating, or extracting factors; deciding how many factors to retain; and rotating factors to an interpretable orientation" (Floyd & Widaman, 1995, p. 287). By contrast, in **confirmatory factor analysis,** "a factor structure is explicitly hypothesized and is tested for its fit with the observed covariance structure of the measured variables" (Floyd & Widaman, 1995, p. 287).

A term commonly employed in factor analysis is **factor loading,** which is "a sort of metaphor. Each test is thought of as a vehicle carrying a certain amount of one or more abilities" (Tyler, 1965, p. 44). Loading a factor in a test conveys information about the extent to which the factor determines the test score or scores. A new test purporting to measure bulimia, for example, can be factor-analyzed with other known measures of bulimia, as well as with other kinds of measures (such as measures of intelligence, self-esteem, general anxiety, anorexia, or perfectionism). High factor loadings by the new test on a "bulimia factor" would provide convergent evidence of construct validity. Moderate to low factor loadings by the new test with respect to measures of other eating disorders such as anorexia would provide discriminant evidence of construct validity.

Factor analysis frequently involves technical procedures so complex that few contemporary researchers would attempt to routinely conduct one without the aid of a prepackaged computer program. But although the actual data analysis has become work for computers, humans still tend to be very much involved in the *naming* of factors once the computer has identified them. Thus, for example, suppose a factor analysis identified a common factor being measured by two hypothetical instruments, a "Bulimia Test" and an "Anorexia Test." This common factor would have to be named. One factor analyst looking at the data and the items of each test might christen the common factor an *eating disorder factor*. Another factor analyst examining exactly the same materials might label the common factor a *body weight preoccupation factor*. A third analyst might name the factor a *self-perception disorder factor*. Which of these is correct?

From a statistical perspective, it is simply impossible to say what the common factor should be named. Naming factors that emerge from a factor analysis has more to do with knowledge, judgment, and verbal abstraction ability than with mathematical expertise. There are no hard-and-fast rules. Factor analysts exercise their own judgment about what factor name best communicates the meaning of the factor. Further, even the criteria used to identify a common factor, as well as related technical matters, can be a matter of debate, if not heated controversy (see, for example, Bartholomew, 1996a, 1996b; Maraun, 1996a, 1996b, 1996c; McDonald, 1996a, 1996b; Mulaik, 1996a, 1996b; Rozeboom, 1996a, 1996b; Schönemann, 1996a, 1996b; Steiger, 1996a, 1996b).

Factor analysis is a subject rich in technical complexity. Its uses and applications can vary as a function of the research objectives as well as the nature of the tests and the constructs under study. Factor analysis is the subject of our *Close-up* in Chapter 9. If you are interested in learning more about the advantages (and pitfalls) of factor analysis, visit the companion Web site to this textbook, and consult any of many instructive books (Comrey, 1992) and articles (Floyd & Widaman, 1995; Gorsuch, 1997; Panter et al., 1997) on the subject.

Validity, Bias, and Fairness

In the eyes of many laypeople, questions concerning the validity of a test are intimately tied to questions concerning the fair use of tests and the issues of bias and fairness. Let us hasten to point out that validity, fairness in test use, and test bias are three separate issues. It is possible, for example, for a valid test to be used fairly or unfairly.

Test Bias

For the general public, the term *bias* as applied to psychological and educational tests may conjure up many meanings having to do with prejudice and preferential treatment (Brown et al., 1999). For federal judges, the term *bias* as it relates to items on children's intelligence tests is synonymous with "too difficult for one group as compared to another" (Sattler, 1991). For psychometricians, **bias** is a factor inherent in a test that systematically prevents accurate, impartial measurement.

Psychometricians have developed the technical means to identify and remedy bias, at least in the mathematical sense. As a simple illustration, consider a test we will call the "flip-coin test" (FCT). The "equipment" needed to conduct this test is a two-sided coin. One side has the image of a profile ("heads"), and the other side does not ("tails"). The FCT would be considered biased if the instrument (the coin) were weighted so that either heads or tails appears more frequently than by chance alone. If the test in question were an intelligence test, the test would be considered biased if it were constructed so that people who had brown eyes consistently and systematically obtained higher scores than people with green eyes—assuming, of course, that in reality people with brown eyes are not generally more intelligent than people with green eyes. *Systematic* is a key word in our definition of test bias. We have previously looked at sources of *random* or chance variation in test scores. *Bias* implies *systematic* variation.

Another illustration: Let's suppose we need to hire 50 secretaries, and so we place an ad in the newspaper. In response to the ad, 200 people reply, including 100 people who happen to have brown eyes and 100 people who happen to have green eyes. Each of the 200 applicants is individually administered a hypothetical test we will call the "Test of Secretarial Skills" (TSS). Logic tells us that eye color is probably not a relevant variable with respect to performing the duties of a secretary. We would therefore have no reason to believe that green-eyed people are better secretaries than brown-eyed people or vice versa. We might reasonably expect that after the tests have been scored and the selection process has been completed, an approximately equivalent number of brown-eyed and green-eyed people would have been hired (that is, approximately 25 brown-eyed people and 25 green-eyed people). But what if it turned out that 48 green-eyed people were hired and only 2 brown-eyed people were hired? Is this evidence that the TSS is a biased test?

Although the answer to this question seems simple on the face of it—"Yes, the test is biased because they should have hired 25 and 25!"—a truly responsible answer to this question would entail statistically troubleshooting the test and the entire selection procedure (see Berk, 1982). To begin with, the three characteristics of the regression lines (Figure 6–4) used to predict success on the criterion would have to be scrutinized: (1) the slope, (2) the intercept, (3) the error of estimate. And because these three factors of regression are functions of two other statistics (the validity coefficient and the reliability coefficient for both the test and the criterion) that could vary with respect to the two groups in question, a total of five characteristics must be statistically examined. A test of significance could indicate that our brown-eyed and green-eyed groups are the same or different with respect to any of these five characteristics. This binary choice (that is, same or different) taken to the fifth power (meaning that there are five ways that the two groups could conceivably differ) means that a comprehensive troubleshooting would entail examination of a total of 32 ($2^5 = 32$) possible ways the test could be found to be biased.

If, for example, a test systematically underpredicts or overpredicts the performance of members of a particular group (such as people with green eyes) with respect to a criterion (such as supervisory rating), it exhibits what is known as *intercept bias*. **Intercept bias** is a term derived from the point where the regression line intersects the Y-axis. If a test systematically yields significantly different validity coefficients for members of different groups, it has what is known as **slope bias**—so named because the slope of one group's regression line is different in a statistically significant way from the regression line of another group.

Stone (1992) identified slope and intercept bias on the Differential Abilities Scale (DAS; Elliot, 1990a, 1990b). The DAS is designed to measure school-related ability and achievement in children and adolescents. The test yields a General Conceptual Ability score, which is a measure of general ability, and achievement scores in a variety of areas, including Basic Number Skills and Word Reading. Stone (1992) computed regression lines for two racial groups: Whites and Asian Americans. When Word Reading scores were predicted from General Conceptual Ability, the regression lines for the two races had different slopes, indicating slope bias. When Basic Number Skills were predicted from General Conceptual Ability, the regression lines for the two races crossed the Y-axis at different places, indicating intercept bias.

The presence of slope and intercept bias on the DAS has important practical implications for testtakers. We will look specifically at the slope bias that Stone found in relation to the Word Reading achievement test. To understand the impact of that bias, draw a graph, using Figure 6–4 as a guide. Place General Conceptual Ability on the X-axis and Word Reading on the Y-axis. Then draw two regression lines with different slopes. Both lines should have a positive slope and should cross the Y-axis in the same place. The line with the steeper slope represents the Asian American children, and the other line represents the White children.

On your drawing, examine the relative position of the regression lines on each graph for X-axis values that are in the intermediate range, representing realistic test scores. You should find that the regression line for the Asian American children is higher than the regression line for the White children. This means that Asian American children at a particular level of achievement generally have lower ability scores than White students achieving at the same level. To see how this is so, pick a point relatively high on the Y-axis, representing a high level of achievement. Then draw a horizontal line across to the two regression lines, and drop a vertical line down to the X-axis from where you cross each regression line (as was done in Figure 6–4). The resulting points on the X-axis represent the average ability levels for the level of reading achievement selected on the Y-axis. You should cross the line for the Asian American students first, meaning that those students have a lower X-value, corresponding to a lower ability level than the White students at the same level of performance.

Now let's assume that teachers nominate students to a program for gifted individuals based on classroom achievement. However, entry to the gifted program is based on ability. This is the approach that is taken in many programs for gifted students. Nominated students are given an ability test, and those above a specific score are admitted. The exercise you just completed indicates that a smaller percentage of nominated Asian American students would be accepted into the gifted program. The Asian American students in this case may well feel discriminated against. They were doing as well in the classroom as their White counterparts but were denied a place in a special program in which they might receive extra attention and more challenging work. Note further that,

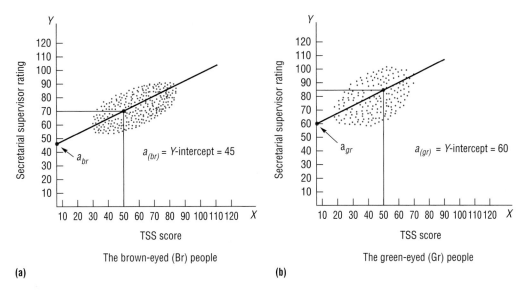

Figure 6–4
TSS Scores and Supervisor Ratings for Two Groups

Note the different points of the Y-intercept corresponding to a TSS score of 50 for the green-eyed and brown-eyed testtakers. If the TSS were an unbiased test, any given score on it would correspond to exactly the same criterion score for the two groups.

because of the nonparallel nature of the lines, this will become a greater problem at higher levels of achievement. This is just one of several results of slope and intercept bias explored by Stone (1992). We refer interested students to the original article for a more detailed discussion.

One reason some tests have been found to be biased has more to do with the design of the research study than the design of the test; if there are too few testtakers in one of the groups (such as the minority group—literally), this methodological problem will make it appear as if the test is biased when in fact it may not be. A situation in which a test may justifiably be deemed biased is one in which some portion of its variance stems from some factor(s) irrelevant to performance on the criterion measure; as a consequence, one group of testtakers will systematically perform differently from another. Prevention during test development is the best cure for test bias, though a procedure called *estimated true score transformations* represents one of many available post hoc remedies (Mueller, 1949; see also Reynolds & Brown, 1984).[5]

Rating error A **rating** is a numerical or verbal judgment (or both) that places a person or an attribute along a continuum identified by a scale of numerical or word descriptors known as a **rating scale.** Simply stated, a **rating error** is a judgment resulting from the intentional or unintentional misuse of a rating scale. Thus, for example, a **leniency error** (also known as a **generosity error**) is, as its name implies, an error in rating that arises from the tendency on the part of the rater to be lenient in scoring, marking, and/or grading. From your own experience during course registration, you might be aware that a

---

5. Lest you think that there is something not quite right about transforming data under such circumstances, we add that even though *transformation* is synonymous with *change*, the change referred to here is merely a change in form, not meaning. Data may be transformed to place them in a more useful form, not to change their meaning.

section of a particular course will fill very quickly if the section is being taught by a professor with a reputation for leniency errors in end-of-term grading.

At the other extreme is a **severity error.** Movie critics who pan just about everything they review may be guilty of severity errors. Of course, that is only true if they review a wide range of movies that might consensually be viewed as good and bad.

Another type of error might be termed a **central tendency error.** Here the rater, for whatever reason, exhibits a general and systematic reluctance to giving ratings at either the positive or the negative extreme. Consequently, all of this rater's ratings would tend to cluster in the middle of the rating continuum.

JUST THINK . . .

What factor do you think might account for the phenomenon of raters whose ratings always seem to fall victim to the central tendency error?

One way to overcome what might be termed *restriction-of-range rating errors* (central tendency, leniency, severity errors) is to use **rankings,** a procedure that requires the rater to measure individuals against one another instead of against an absolute scale. By using rankings instead of ratings, the rater (now the "ranker") is forced to select first, second, third choices and so forth.

Halo effect describes the fact that, for some raters, some ratees can do no wrong. More specifically, a halo effect may also be defined as a tendency to give a particular ratee a higher rating than he or she objectively deserves, because of the rater's failure to discriminate among conceptually distinct and potentially independent aspects of a ratee's behavior. Just for the sake of example—and not for a moment because we believe it is even in the realm of possibility—let's suppose Britney Spears consented to write and deliver a speech on multivariate analysis. Her speech probably would earn much higher all-around ratings if given before the founding chapter of the Britney Spears Fan Club than if delivered before and rated by the membership of, say, the Royal Statistical Society. This would be true even in the highly improbable case that the members of each group were equally savvy with respect to multivariate analysis. We would expect that halo effect to be operative at full power as Spears spoke before the fan club membership.

Criterion data may also be influenced by the rater's knowledge of the ratee's race or sex (Landy & Farr, 1980). Males have been shown to receive more favorable evaluations than females in traditionally masculine occupations. Except in highly integrated situations, ratees tend to receive higher ratings from raters of the same race (Landy & Farr, 1980). Returning to our TSS situation, a particular rater may have had particularly great—or particularly distressing—prior experiences with green-eyed (or brown-eyed) people and be making extraordinarily high (or low) ratings on that irrational basis.

Training programs to familiarize raters with common rating errors and sources of rater bias have shown promise in reducing rating errors and increasing measures of reliability and validity. Lecture, role playing, discussion, watching oneself on videotape, and computer simulation of different situations are some of the many techniques that could be brought to bear in such training programs. We revisit the subject of rating and rating error in our discussion of personality assessment in Chapter 11. Now, we take up issues related to test fairness.

Test Fairness

In contrast to questions of test bias, which may be thought of as technically complex statistical problems, issues of test fairness tend to be rooted more in thorny issues involving values (Halpern, 2000). Thus, while questions of test bias can sometimes be answered with mathematical precision and finality, questions of fairness can be grappled with endlessly by well-meaning people who hold opposing points of view. With that caveat in mind, and with exceptions most certainly in the offing, we will define **fairness** in a psychometric context as the extent to which a test is used in an impartial, just, and equitable way.[6]

Some uses of tests are patently unfair in the judgment of any reasonable person. During the cold war, the government in what was then called the Soviet Union used psychiatric tests to suppress political dissidents. People were imprisoned or institutionalized for verbalizing opposition to the government. Apart from such blatantly unfair uses of tests, what constitutes a fair and an unfair use of tests is a matter left to various parties in the assessment enterprise. Ideally, the test developer strives for fairness in the test development process and in the test's manual and usage guidelines. The test user strives for fairness in the way the test is actually used. Society strives for fairness in test use by means of legislation, judicial decisions, and administrative regulations.

Fairness as applied to tests is a difficult and complicated subject. However, it is possible to discuss some rather common misunderstandings regarding what are sometimes perceived as unfair or even biased tests. Some tests, for example, have been labeled "unfair" because they discriminate among groups of people.[7] The reasoning here goes something like this: "Although individual differences exist, it is a truism that all people are created equal. Accordingly, any differences found among groups of people on any psychological trait must be an artifact of an unfair or biased test." Because this belief is rooted in faith as opposed to scientific evidence—in fact, it flies in the face of scientific evidence—it is virtually impossible to refute. One either accepts it on faith or does not.

We would all like to believe that people are equal in every way and that all people are capable of rising to the same heights given equal opportunity. A more realistic view would appear to be that each person is capable of fulfilling a personal potential. Because people differ so obviously with respect to physical traits, one would be hard put to believe that psychological differences found to exist between individuals—and groups of individuals—are purely a function of inadequate tests. Again, although a test is not inherently unfair or biased simply because it is a tool by which group differences are found, the *use* of the test data, like the use of any data, can be unfair.

Another misunderstanding of what constitutes an unfair or biased test is that it is unfair to administer to a particular population a standardized test that did not include members of that population in the standardization sample. In fact, the test may well be biased, but that must be determined by statistical or other means. The sheer fact that no members of a particular group were included in the standardization sample does *not*, in and of itself, invalidate the test for use with that group.

A final source of misunderstanding is the complex problem of remedying situations where bias or unfair test usage has been found to occur. In the area of selection for jobs, positions in universities and professional schools, and the like, a number of different preventive measures and remedies have been attempted. As you read about the tools used in these attempts in this chapter's *Everyday Psychometrics*, form your own opinions regarding what constitutes a fair use of employment and other tests in a selection process.

---

6. On a somewhat more technical note, Ghiselli et al. (1981, p. 320) observed that "fairness refers to whether a difference in mean predictor scores between two groups represents a useful distinction for society, relative to a decision that must be made, or whether the difference represents a bias that is irrelevant to the objectives at hand." For more practical guidelines regarding fairness, at least as construed by legislative bodies and the courts, see Russell (1984).

7. The verb *to discriminate* here is used in the psychometric sense, meaning *to show a statistically significant difference between individuals or groups with respect to measurement.* The great difference between this statistical, scientific definition and other colloquial definitions (such as *to treat differently and/or unfairly because of group membership*) must be kept firmly in mind in discussions of bias and fairness.

Adjustment of Test Scores by Group Membership: Fairness in Testing or Foul Play?

Any test, regardless of its psychometric soundness, may be knowingly or unwittingly used in a way that has an adverse impact on one or another group. If such adverse impact is found to exist, and if social policy demands some remedy or an affirmative action program, then psychometricians have a number of techniques at their disposal to create change. The accompanying table lists some of these techniques.

Although psychometricians have the tools to institute special policies through manipulations in test development, scoring, and interpretation, there are few clear guidelines in this controversial area (Brown, 1994; Gottfredson, 1994, 2000; Sackett & Wilk, 1994). The waters are further muddied by the fact that some of the guidelines seem to have contradictory implications. For example, although racial preferment in employee selection (disparate impact) is unlawful, the use of valid and unbiased selection procedures virtually guarantees disparate impact. This state of affairs will change only when racial disparities in job-related skills and abilities are minimized (Gottfredson, 1994).

In 1991, Congress enacted legislation effectively barring employers from adjusting testtakers' scores for the purpose of making hiring or promotion decisions. Section 106 of the Civil Rights Act of 1991 made it illegal for employers "in connection with the selection or referral of applicants or candidates for employment or promotion to adjust the scores of, use different cutoffs for, or otherwise alter the results of employment-related tests on the basis of race, color, religion, sex, or national origin."

The law prompted concern on the part of many psychologists who believed it would adversely affect various societal groups and might reverse social gains. Brown (1994, p. 927) forecast that "the ramifications of the Act are more far-reaching than Congress envisioned when it considered the amendment and could mean that many personality tests and physical ability tests that rely on separate scoring for men and women are outlawed in employment selection." Arguments in favor of group-related test-score adjustment have been made on philosophical as well as technical grounds. From a philosophical perspective, increased minority representation is socially valued to the point that minority preference in test scoring is warranted. In the same vein, minority preference is viewed both as a remedy for past societal wrongs and as a contemporary guarantee of proportional workplace representation. From a more technical perspective, it is argued that some tests require adjustment in scores because (1) the tests are biased, and a given score on them does not necessarily carry the same meaning for all testtakers; and/or (2) "a particular way of using a test is at odds with an espoused position as to what constitutes fair use" (Sackett & Wilk, 1994, p. 931).

In contrast to advocates of test-score adjustment are those who view such adjustments as part of a social agenda for preferential treatment of certain groups. These opponents of test-score adjustment reject the subordination of individual effort and ability to group membership as criteria in the assignment of test scores (Gottfredson, 1988, 2000). Hunter and Schmidt (1976, p. 1069) described the unfortunate consequences for all parties involved in a college selection situation wherein poor-risk applicants were accepted on the basis of score adjustments or quotas. With reference to the employment setting, Hunter and Schmidt (1976) described one case in which entrance standards were lowered so more members of a particular group could be hired. However, many of these new hires did not pass promotion tests—with the result that the company was sued for discriminatory promotion practice. Yet another consideration has to do with the feelings of "minority applicants who are selected under a quota system but who also would have been selected under unqualified individualism and must therefore pay the price, in lowered prestige and self-esteem" (Jensen, 1980, p. 398).

A number of psychometric models of fairness in testing have been presented and debated in the scholarly literature (Hunter & Schmidt, 1976; Petersen & Novick, 1976; Schmidt & Hunter, 1974; Thorndike, 1971). Despite a wealth of research and debate, a long-standing question in the field of personnel psychology remains: "How can group differences on cognitive ability tests be reduced while retaining existing high levels of reliability and criterion-related validity?"

According to Gottfredson (1994), the answer probably will not come from measurement-related research, because differences in scores on many of the tests in question arise principally from differences in job-related abilities. For Gottfredson (1994, p. 963), "the biggest contribution personnel psychologists can make in the long run may be to insist

**Psychometric Techniques for Preventing or Remedying Adverse Impact
and/or Instituting an Affirmative Action Program**

*Some of these techniques may be preventive if employed in the test development process, and others may
be employed with already established tests. Some of these techniques entail direct score manipulation;
others, such as banding, do not. Preparation of this table benefited from Sackett and Wilk (1994), and
their work should be consulted for more detailed consideration of the complex issues involved.*

Technique	Description
Addition of Points	A constant number of points is added to the test score of members of a particular group. The purpose of the point addition is to reduce or eliminate observed differences between groups.
Differential Scoring of Items	This technique incorporates group membership information, not in adjusting a raw score on a test but in deriving the score in the first place. The application of the technique may involve the scoring of some test items for members of one group but not scoring the same test items for members of another group. This technique is also known as *empirical keying by group.*
Elimination of Items Based on Differential Item Functioning	This procedure entails removing from a test any items found to inappropriately favor one group's test performance over another's. Ideally, the intent of the elimination of certain test items is not to make the test easier for any group but simply to make the test fairer. Sackett and Wilk (1994) put it this way: "Conceptually, rather than asking 'Is this item harder for members of Group X than it is for Group Y?' these approaches ask 'Is this item harder for members of Group X with true score Z than it is for members of Group Y with true score Z?'"
Differential Cutoffs	Different cutoffs are set for members of different groups. For example, a passing score for members of one group is 65, whereas a passing score for members of another group is 70. As with the addition of points, the purpose of differential cutoffs is to reduce or eliminate observed differences between groups.
Separate Lists	Different lists of testtaker scores are established by group membership. For each list, test performance of testtakers is ranked in top-down fashion. Users of the test scores for selection purposes may alternate selections from the different lists. Depending on factors such as the allocation rules in effect and the equivalency of the standard deviation within the groups, the separate-lists technique may yield effects similar to those of other techniques, such as the addition of points and differential cutoffs. In practice, the separate list is popular in affirmative action programs where the intent is to over-select from previously excluded groups.
Within-Group Norming	Used as a remedy for adverse impact if members of different groups tend to perform differentially on a particular test, within-group norming entails the conversion of all raw scores into percentile scores or standard scores based on the test performance of one's own group. In essence, an individual testtaker is being compared only with other members of his or her own group. When race is the primary criterion of group membership and separate norms are established by race, this technique is known as *race-norming.*
Banding	The effect of banding of test scores is to make equivalent all scores that fall within a particular range or band. For example, thousands of raw scores on a test may be transformed to a stanine having a value of 1 to 9. All scores that fall within each of the stanine boundaries will be treated by the test user as either equivalent or subject to some additional selection criteria. A *sliding band* (Cascio et al., 1991) is a modified banding procedure wherein a band is adjusted ("slid") to permit the selection of more members of some group than would otherwise be selected.
Preference Policies	In the interest of affirmative action, reverse discrimination, or some other policy deemed to be in the interest of society at large, a test user might establish a policy of preference based on group membership. For example, if a municipal fire department sought to increase the representation of female personnel in its ranks, it might institute a test-related policy designed to do just that. A key provision in this policy might be that when a male and a female earn equal scores on the test used for hiring, the female will be hired.

(continued)

Adjustment of Test Scores by Group Membership: Fairness in Testing or Foul Play? *(continued)*

collectively and candidly that their measurement tools are neither the cause of nor the cure for racial differences in job skills and consequent inequalities in employment."

Beyond the workplace and personnel psychology, what role, if any, should measurement play in promoting diversity? And as Haidt et al. (2003) reflected, there are several varieties of diversity, some perceived as more valuable than others. Do we need to develop more specific measures designed, for example, to discourage "moral diversity" while encouraging "demographic diversity"? These types of questions have implications in a number of areas from academic admission policies to immigration.

JUST THINK . . .

How do *you* feel about the use of various procedures to adjust test scores on the basis of group membership? Are these types of issues best left to measurement experts?

If performance differences are found between identified groups of people on a valid and reliable test used for selection purposes, some hard questions may have to be dealt with if the test is to continue to be used. Is the problem due to some technical deficiency in the test, or is the test in reality too good at identifying people of different levels of ability? Regardless, is the test being used fairly? If so, what might society do to remedy the skill disparity between different groups as reflected on the test?

Our discussion of issues of test fairness and test bias may seem to have brought us far afield of the seemingly cut-and-dried, relatively nonemotional subject of test validity. However, the complex issues accompanying discussions of test validity, including issues of fairness and bias, must be wrestled with by us all. For further consideration of the philosophical issues involved, we refer you to the solitude of your own thoughts and the reading of your own conscience.

Self-Assessment

Test your understanding of elements of this chapter by seeing if you can explain each of the following terms, expressions, and abbreviations:

base rate	convergent validity	factor analysis
bias	criterion	factor loading
central tendency error	criterion contamination	fairness
concurrent validity	criterion-related validity	false negative
confirmatory factor analysis	discriminant evidence	false positive
construct	expectancy chart	generosity error
construct validity	expectancy data	halo effect
content validity	expectancy table	hit rate
content validity ratio (CVR)	exploratory factor analysis	homogeneity
convergent evidence	face validity	incremental validity

inference	Naylor-Shine tables	slope bias
intercept bias	predictive validity	Taylor-Russell tables
leniency error	ranking	test utility theory
local validation study	rating	validation
method of contrasted groups	rating error	validation study
miss rate	rating scale	validity
multitrait-multimethod matrix	severity error	validity coefficient

Web Watch

Check out the following Web sites for more information about topics discussed in this chapter.

Validity
www.socialresearchmethods.net/kb/measval.htm

www.psychol.ucl.ac.uk/edpsych/courses/rmstats/measurement_theory/typesofvalidity.htm

www.socialresearchmethods.net/tutorial/driebe/tweb1.htm

Is content validity valid?
www.rasch.org/rmt/rmt111j.htm

Taylor-Russell tables
http://luna.cas.usf.edu/~mbrannic/files/tnm/taylor.htm

Key events in psychological measurement
www.wku.edu/~sally.kuhlenschmidt/mttmln.htm

The halo effect
www.aft.org/parentpage/discipline/halo.html

Predictive Validity of SAT
www.fairtest.org/facts/satvalidity.html

bernard.pitzer.edu/~hfairchi/courses/Spring2001/LATonSAT022601.htm

Test bias
www.questia.com/popularSearches/test_bias.jsp

www.leadersunlimited.co.za/html/PressRoom/suntimes1.html

7

Test Development

All tests are not created equal. The creation of a good test is not a matter of chance. It is the product of the thoughtful and sound application of established principles of test construction.

In this chapter, we introduce the basics of test development and examine in detail the processes by which tests are constructed. We explore, for example, a number of techniques designed for construction and selection of good items. Although we focus on tests of the published, standardized variety, much of what we have to say also applies to custom-made tests such as those created by teachers, researchers, and employers.

The process of developing a test occurs in five stages:

1. test conceptualization
2. test construction
3. test tryout
4. item analysis
5. test revision

Once the idea for a test is conceived (test conceptualization), items for the test are drafted (test construction). This first draft of the test is then tried out on a group of sample testtakers (test tryout). Once the data from the tryout are collected, testtakers' performance on the test as a whole and on each item is analyzed. Statistical procedures, referred to as *item analysis,* are employed to assist in making judgments about which items are good as they are, which items need to be revised, and which items should be discarded. The analysis of the test's items may include analyses of item reliability, item validity, and item discrimination. Depending on the type of test, item-difficulty level may be analyzed as well. On the basis of the item analysis and related considerations, a revision or second draft of the test is created. This revised version of the test is tried out on a new sample of testtakers, the results are analyzed, and the test is further revised if necessary—and so it goes (Figure 7–1). At some point, the test developer will either finalize the form of the test or go back to the proverbial drawing board.

Test Conceptualization

The beginnings of any published test can probably be traced to thoughts—self-talk, in behavioral terms. The test developer says to himself or herself something like: "There

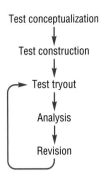

Figure 7–1
The Test Development Process

ought to be a test designed to measure [fill in the blank] in [such and such] way." The stimulus for such a thought could be almost anything. A review of the available literature on existing tests designed to measure a particular construct might indicate that such tests leave much to be desired in psychometric soundness. An emerging social phenomenon or pattern of behavior might serve as the stimulus for the development of a new test. If, for example, celibacy were to become a widely practiced lifestyle, we might witness the development of a variety of test related to celibacy. These tests might measure variables such as reasons for adopting a celibate lifestyle, commitment to a celibate lifestyle, and degree of celibacy by specific behaviors. The analogy with medicine is straightforward: Once a new disease comes to the attention of medical researchers, they attempt to develop diagnostic tests to assess its presence or absence as well as the severity of its manifestations in the body.

> **JUST THINK . . .**
>
> What is a "hot topic" today that developers of psychological tests should be working on? What aspects of this topic might be explored by means of a psychological test?

The development of a new test may be in response to a need to assess mastery in an emerging occupation or profession. For example, new tests may be developed to assess mastery in fields such as environmental engineering, wireless communications, and computer networking.

Some Preliminary Questions

Regardless of the stimulus for developing the new test, a number of questions immediately confront the prospective test developer. Here are some of those questions:

- *What is the test designed to measure?* This is a deceptively simple question. Its answer is very closely linked to how the test developer defines the construct being measured and how that definition is the same as or different from other tests purporting to measure the same construct.

- *What is the objective of the test?* In the service of what goal will the test be employed? In what way or ways is the objective of this test the same as or different from other tests with similar goals? What real-world behaviors would be anticipated to correlate with testtaker responses?

- *Is there a need for this test?* Are there any other tests purporting to measure the same thing? In what ways will the new test be better than or different from existing ones? Will there be more compelling evidence for its reliability or validity? Will it be more comprehensive? Will it take less time to administer? In what ways would this test *not* be better than existing tests?

- *Who will use this test?* Clinicians? Educators? Others? For what purpose or purposes would this test be used?

- *Who will take this test?* Who is this test for? Who needs to take it? Who would find it desirable to take it? For what age range of testtakers is the test designed? What reading level is required of a testtaker? What cultural factors might affect testtaker response?

- *What content will the test cover?* Why should it cover this content? Is this coverage different from the content coverage of existing tests with the same or similar objectives? How and why is the content area different? To what extent is this content culture-specific?

- *How will the test be administered?* Individually or in groups? Is it amenable to both group and individual administration? What differences will exist between individual and group administrations of this test? Will the test be designed for or amenable to computer administration? How might differences between versions of the test be reflected in test scores?

- *What is the ideal format of the test?* Should it be true-false, essay, multiple-choice, or in some other form? Why is the form selected the best form for this test?

- *Should more than one form of the test be developed?* On the basis of a cost/benefit analysis, should alternate or parallel forms of this test be created?

- *What special training will be required of test users for administering or interpreting the test?* What background and qualifications will a prospective user of data derived from an administration of this test need to have? What restrictions, if any, should be placed on distributors of the test and on the test's usage?

- *What types of responses will be required of testtakers?* What kind of disability might preclude someone from being able to take this test? What adaptations or accommodations are recommended for persons with disabilities?

- *Who benefits from an administration of this test?* What would the testtaker learn, or how might the testtaker benefit, from an administration of this test? What would the test user learn, or how might the test user benefit? What social benefit, if any, derives from an administration of this test?

- *Is there any potential for harm as the result of an administration of this test?* What safeguards are built into the recommended testing procedure to prevent any sort of harm to any of the parties involved in the use of this test?

- *How will meaning be attributed to scores on this test?* Will a testtaker's score be compared to others taking the test at the same time? To others in a criterion group? Will the test evaluate mastery of a particular content area?

This last question provides a point of departure to elaborate on issues related to test development with regard to norm- versus criterion-referenced tests.

Norm-referenced versus criterion-referenced tests: Item development issues　Different approaches to test development and individual item analyses are necessary, depending upon whether the finished test is designed to be norm-referenced or criterion-referenced. Generally speaking, for example, a good item on a norm-referenced achievement test is an item for which high scorers on the test respond correctly. Low scorers on the test tend to respond to that same item incorrectly. On a criterion-oriented test, this same pattern of results may occur: High scorers on the test get a particular item right, whereas low scorers on the test get that same item wrong. However, that is not what makes an item good or acceptable from a criterion-oriented perspective. Ideally, each item on a criterion-oriented test addresses the issue of whether the testtaker—a would-be physician, engineer, piano student, or whoever—has met certain criteria. In short, when it comes to criterion-oriented assessment, being "first in the class" does not count and very often is irrelevant. Although we can envision exceptions to this general rule, norm-referenced comparisons are typically insufficient and inappropriate when knowledge of mastery is what the test user requires.

Criterion-referenced testing and assessment is commonly employed in licensing contexts, be it a license to practice medicine or a license to drive a car. Criterion-referenced approaches are also employed in educational contexts in which mastery of particular material must be demonstrated before the student moves on to advanced material that conceptually builds on the existing base of knowledge, skills, or both.

In contrast to techniques and principles applicable to the development of norm-referenced tests (many of which are discussed in this chapter), the development of criterion-referenced instruments derives from a conceptualization of the knowledge or skills to be mastered. The required cognitive or motor skills may be analyzed into component parts for assessment. The test developer may attempt to sample criterion-related knowledge with regard to general principles relevant to the criterion being assessed. Experimentation with different items, tests, formats, or measurement procedures will help the test developer discover the best measure of mastery for the targeted skills or knowledge.

In general, the development of a criterion-referenced test or assessment procedure may entail exploratory work with at least two groups of testtakers: one group known to have mastered the knowledge or skill being measured and another group known not to have mastered such knowledge or skill. For example, in developing a criterion-referenced written test for a driver's license, a preliminary version of the test may be administered to one group of people who have been driving about 15,000 miles per year for ten years and who have perfect safety records (no accidents and no moving violations). The second group of testtakers might be a group of adults matched in demographic and related respects to the first group but who have never had any instruction in driving or driving experience. The items that best discriminate between these two groups would be considered "good" items. The preliminary exploratory experimentation done in test development need not have anything at all to do with flying, but you wouldn't know that from its name . . .

> **JUST THINK . . .**
>
> Suppose you were charged with developing a criterion-referenced test to measure mastery of Chapter 7 of this book. Explain, in as much detail as you think sufficient, how you would go about doing that. It's okay (in fact, you are encouraged) to read on before answering.

Pilot Work

In the context of test development, terms such as **pilot work,** *pilot study,* and *pilot research* refer, in general, to the preliminary research surrounding the creation of a prototype of the test. Test items may be pilot studied (or *piloted*) to evaluate whether they should be included in the final form of the instrument. In developing a structured interview to measure introversion/extraversion, for example, pilot research may entail open-ended interviews with research subjects believed for some reason (perhaps on the basis of an existing test) to be introverted or extraverted. Additionally, interviews with parents, teachers, friends, and others who know the subject might also be arranged. Another type of pilot study might entail physiological monitoring of the subjects (such as monitoring of heart rate) as a function of exposure to different types of stimuli.

In pilot work, the test developer typically attempts to determine how best to measure a targeted construct. The process may entail the creation, revision, and deletion of many test items, as well as literature reviews, experimentation, and related activities. Once pilot work has been completed, the process of test construction begins. Keep in mind, however, that depending on the nature of the test, particularly its need for updates and revisions, the need for additional pilot research is always a possibility.

Test Construction

Pilot work, like many of the other elements of test conceptualization and construction that we discuss in this chapter, is a necessity when constructing tests or other measuring instruments for publication and wide distribution. Of course, pilot work need not be part of the process of developing teacher-made tests for classroom use (see *Everyday Psychometrics*). As you read about more formal aspects of professional test construction, think about which, if any, technical procedures might lend itself to modification for everyday use by classroom teachers.

Scaling

We have previously defined *measurement* as the assignment of numbers according to rules. **Scaling** may be defined as the process of setting rules for assigning numbers in measurement. Stated another way, scaling is the process by which a measuring device is designed and calibrated, and the way numbers (or other indices)—scale values—are assigned to different amounts of the trait, attribute, or characteristic being measured.

Historically, the prolific L. L. Thurstone (Figure 7–2) is credited for being at the forefront of efforts to develop methodologically sound scaling methods. He adapted psychophysical scaling methods to the study of psychological variables such as attitudes and values (Thurstone, 1959; Thurstone & Chave, 1929). Thurstone's (1925) article

Figure 7–2
L. L. Thurstone (1887–1955)

Among his many achievements in the area of scaling was Thurstone's (1927) influential article on the "law of comparative judgment"—one of the few "laws" in psychology. This law was Thurstone's proudest achievement (Nunnally, 1978, pp. 60–61), but he had many achievements to choose from. Thurstone's adaptation of scaling methods for use in psychophysiological research and the study of attitudes and values has served as models for generations of researchers (Bock & Jones, 1968). He is also widely considered to be one of the primary architects of modern factor analysis.

Psychometrics in the Classroom

Many concerns of professors and students about testing are psychometric. Professors want to give, and students want to take, reliable and valid measures of student knowledge. Even students who have not taken a course in psychological testing and assessment seem to understand psychometric issues regarding the tests they are administered in the classroom. As an illustration, consider each of the following pairs of statements. The first is a criticism of a classroom test you may have heard (or said yourself). The second statement is that criticism translated into the language of psychometrics.

> "I spent all last night studying Chapter 3, and there wasn't one item on that test from that chapter!"
> *Translation:* "I question the examination's content validity!"
>
> "The instructions on that essay test weren't clear, and I think it affected my grade."
> *Translation:* "There was excessive error variance related to the test administration procedures."
>
> "I wrote the same thing my friend did for this short-answer question—how come she got full credit and the professor took three points off my answer?"
> *Translation:* "I have grave concerns about rater error affecting reliability."
>
> "I didn't have enough time to finish; this test didn't measure what I know—only how fast I could write!"
> *Translation:* "I wish the person who wrote this test had paid more attention to issues related to criterion-related validity and the comparative efficacy of speed as opposed to power tests!"

Like their students, professors have concerns about the tests they administer. They want their examination questions to be clear, relevant, and representative of the material covered. They sometimes wonder about the length of their examinations. Their concern is to cover voluminous amounts of material while still providing enough time for students to give thoughtful consideration to their answers.

For most published psychological tests, these types of psychometric concerns would be addressed in a formal way during the test development process. In the classroom, however, rigorous psychometric evaluation of the dozen or so tests that any one instructor may administer during the course of a semester is impractical. Classroom tests are typically created for the purpose of testing just one group of students during one semester. Tests change to reflect changes in lectures and readings as courses evolve. Also,

if tests are reused, they are in danger of becoming measures of who has seen or heard about the examination before taking it, rather than measures of how well the students know the course material. Of course, although formal psychometric evaluation of classroom tests may be impractical, informal methods are frequently used.

Concerns about content validity are routinely addressed, usually informally, by professors in the test development process. For example, suppose an examination containing 50 multiple-choice questions and five short essays is to cover the reading and lecture material on four broad topics. The professor might systematically include 12 or 13 multiple-choice questions and at least one short essay from each topic area. The professor might also draw a certain percentage of the questions from the readings and a certain percentage from the lectures. Such a deliberate approach to content coverage may well boost the test's content validity, although no formal evaluation of the test's content validity will be made. The professor may also make an effort to inform the students that all textbook boxes and appendices and all instructional media presented in class (such as videotapes) are fair game for evaluation.

Criterion-related validity is difficult to establish on many classroom tests because no obvious criterion reflects the level of the students' knowledge of the material. Exceptions may exist for students in a technical or applied program who take an examination for licensure or certification. Informal assessment of something akin to criterion validity may occur on an individual basis in a student-professor chat. A student who obtained the lowest score in the class may demonstrate to the professor an unambiguous lack of understanding of the material. It is also true that by the same method, the criterion validity of the test may be called into question. For example, a chat with the student who scored the highest might also reveal that the student has not a clue about the material the test was designed to tap. Such a finding would give the professor pause.

The construct validity of classroom tests is often assessed informally as well, as when an anomaly in test performance may call attention to construct validity–related issues. For example, consider a group of students who have a history of performing at an above-average level on exams. Now suppose that on one exam, all students in this group perform poorly. If all these students report not having studied for the test or just not having understood the text material, then there is an adequate explanation for their low

(continued)

Psychometrics in the Classroom
(continued)

scores. However, if the students report that they studied and understood the material as usual, then one might question the construct validity of the test as an explanation of the outcome.

Aspects of a classroom test's reliability can also be informally assessed. For example, a discussion with students can shed light on the internal consistency of the test. Then again, if the test was designed to be heterogeneous, low internal consistency ratings might be desirable. On essay tests, inter-rater reliability can be explored by providing a group of volunteers with the criteria used in grading the essays and letting them grade some. Such an exercise might clarify the scoring criteria. In the rare instance when the same classroom test, for some reason, is given twice or in an alternate form, a discussion of the test-retest or alternate-forms reliability can be conducted. In practice, however, it is rare for classroom tests to be administered twice or in alternate forms.

Have you ever taken an exam in which one student quietly asks for clarification of a specific question, and the professor then announces to the entire class the response to the student's question? This professor is attempting to reduce administration error (and increase reliability) by providing the same experience for all testtakers. When grading short-answer or essay questions, professors may try to reduce rater error by several techniques. For example, they may ask a colleague to decipher a student's poor handwriting or regrade a set of essays (blind to the original grades). Professors also try to reduce administration error and increase reliability when they eliminate items that many students misunderstand.

Tests developed for classroom use may not be perfect. Few if any tests for any purpose are. Still, most professors are always on the lookout for ways—formal and informal—to make the tests they administer as psychometrically sound as possible.

"A Method of Scaling Psychological and Educational Tests" introduced, among other things, the notion of **absolute scaling**—a procedure for obtaining a measure of item difficulty across samples of testtakers who vary in ability.

Types of scales In common parlance, scales are instruments used to measure something, such as weight. In psychometrics, scales may also be conceived of as instruments used to measure. Here, however, that *something* being measured is likely to be a trait, a state, or an ability. When we think of types of scales, we think of the different ways that scales can be categorized. In Chapter 3, for example, we saw that scales can be meaningfully categorized along a continuum of level of measurement and referred to as nominal, ordinal, interval, or ratio. But we might also characterize scales in other ways.

If the testtaker's test performance as a function of age is of critical interest, then the test might be referred to as an *age-based scale*. If the testtaker's test performance as a function of grade is of critical interest, then the test might be referred to as a *grade-based scale*. If all raw scores on the test are to be transformed into scores that can range from 1 to 9, then the test might be referred to as a *stanine scale*. A scale might be described in still other ways. For example, it may be categorized as *unidimensional* as opposed to *multidimensional*. It may be categorized as *comparative* as opposed to *categorical*. This is just a sampling of the many ways that scales can be categorized.

Given that scales can be categorized in many different ways, it would be reasonable to assume that there are many different methods of scaling. Indeed, there are; there is no one method of scaling. There is no best type of scale. Test developers scale a test in the

Rating Scale Item A
How did you feel about what you saw on television?

Rating Scale Item B
I believe I would like the work of a lighthouse keeper.
True   False   (circle one)

Rating Scale Item C
Please rate the employee on ability to cooperate and get along with fellow employees:
Excellent _____ / _____ / _____ / _____ / _____ / _____ / _____ / Unsatisfactory

Figure 7–3
The Many Faces of Rating Scales

Rating scales can take many forms. "Smiley" faces, such as those illustrated here as Item A, have been used in social-psychological research with young children and adults with limited language skills. The faces are used in lieu of words such as positive, neutral, *and* negative.

manner they believe is optimally suited to their conception of the measurement of the trait (or whatever) that is being measured.

Scaling methods   Speaking generally, a testtaker is presumed to have more or less of the characteristic measured by a (valid) test as a function of the test score. The higher or lower the score, the more or less of the characteristic he or she presumably possesses. But how are numbers assigned to responses so that a test score can be calculated? This is done through scaling the test items, using any one of several available methods.

For example, consider a moral-issues opinion measure called the Morally Debatable Behaviors Scale-Revised (MDBS-R; Katz et al., 1994). Developed to be "a practical means of assessing what people believe, the strength of their convictions, as well as individual differences in moral tolerance" (p. 15), the MDBS-R contains 30 items. Each item contains a brief description of a moral issue or behavior on which testtakers express their opinion by means of a 10-point scale that ranges from *never justified* to *always justified.* Here is a sample.

Cheating on taxes if you have a chance is:

    1   2   3   4   5   6   7   8   9   10
  never   always
justified   justified

The MDBS-R is an example of a **rating scale,** which can be defined as a grouping of words, statements, or symbols on which judgments of the strength of a particular trait, attitude, or emotion are indicated by the testtaker. Rating scales can be used to record judgments of oneself, others, experiences, or objects, and may take several forms (Figure 7–3).

On the MDBS-R, the ratings that the testtaker makes for each of the 30 test items are added together to obtain a final score. Scores range from a low of 30 (if the testtaker indicates that all 30 behaviors are never justified) to a high of 300 (if the testtaker indicates that all 30 situations are always justified). Because the final test score is obtained by summing the ratings across all the items, it is termed a **summative scale.**

One type of summative rating scale, the **Likert scale** (Likert, 1932), is used extensively in psychology, usually to scale attitudes. Likert scales are relatively easy to construct. Each item presents the testtaker with five alternative responses (sometimes seven), usually on an agree/disagree or approve/disapprove type of continuum. If Katz et al. had used a Likert scale, an item on their test might have looked like this:

Cheating on taxes if you have a chance.
    This is (check one):

_____	_____	_____	_____	_____
never	rarely	sometimes	usually	always
justified	justified	justified	justified	justified

Likert scales are usually reliable, which may account for their widespread popularity. Likert (1932) experimented with different weightings of the five categories but concluded that assigning weights of 1 (for endorsement of items at one extreme) through 5 (for endorsement of items at the other extreme) generally worked best.

JUST THINK . . .

It's debatable, but which form of the Morally Debatable Behaviors Scale worked best for you? Why?

The use of rating scales of any type results in ordinal-level data. With reference to the Likert scale item, for example, if the response *never justified* is assigned the value 1, *rarely justified* the value 2, and so on, the higher the score, the more the response is indicative of permissiveness with regard to cheating on taxes. Respondents could even be ranked with regard to such permissiveness. However, the difference in permissiveness between the opinions of a pair of people who scored 2 and 3 on this scale is not necessarily the same as the difference between the opinions of a pair of people who scored 3 and 4.

Rating scales differ in the number of dimensions underlying the ratings being made. Some rating scales are *unidimensional,* meaning that only one dimension is presumed to underlie the ratings. Other rating scales are *multidimensional,* meaning that more than one dimension is thought to guide the testtaker's responses. Consider in this context an item from the MDBS-R regarding marijuana use. Responses to this item, particularly responses in the low to middle range, may be interpreted in many different ways. Such responses may reflect the view (a) that people should not engage in illegal activities, (b) that people should not take risks with their health, or (c) that people should avoid activities that could lead to contact with a bad crowd. Responses to this item may reflect other attitudes and beliefs, such as those related to the beneficial use of marijuana as an adjunct to chemotherapy for cancer patients. When more than one dimension is tapped by an item, multidimensional scaling techniques are used to identify the dimensions.

Another scaling method that produces ordinal data is the **method of paired comparisons.** Testtakers are presented with pairs of stimuli (two photographs, two objects, two statements), which they are asked to compare. They must select one of the stimuli according to some rule; for example, the rule that they agree more with one statement than the other, or the rule that they find one stimulus more appealing than the other.

Had Katz et al. used the method of paired comparisons, an item on their scale might have looked like this:

Select the behavior that you think would be more justified:
a. cheating on taxes if one has a chance
b. accepting a bribe in the course of one's duties

For each pair of options, testtakers receive a higher score for selecting the option deemed more justifiable by the majority of a group of judges. The judges would have been asked to rate the pairs of options before the distribution of the test, and a list of the options selected by the judges would be provided along with the scoring instructions as an answer key. The test score would reflect the number of times the choices of a testtaker agreed with those of the judges. If we use Katz et al.'s (1994) standardization sample as the judges, the more justifiable option is cheating on taxes. A testtaker might receive a point toward the total score for selecting option a but no points for selecting option b. An advantage of the method of paired comparisons is that it forces testtakers to choose between items.

Another way of deriving ordinal information through a scaling system entails sorting tasks. In these approaches, printed cards, drawings, photographs, objects, or other such stimuli are typically presented to testtakers for evaluation. One method of sorting, **comparative scaling,** entails judgments of a stimulus in comparison with every other stimulus on the scale. A version of the MDBS-R that employs comparative scaling might feature 30 items, each printed on a separate index card. Testtakers would be asked to sort the cards from most justifiable to least justifiable. Comparative scaling could also be accomplished by providing testtakers with a list of 30 items on a sheet of paper and asking them to rank the justifiability of the items from 1 to 30.

Another scaling system that relies on sorting is **categorical scaling.** Stimuli are placed into one of two or more alternative categories that differ quantitatively with respect to some continuum. In our running MDBS-R example, testtakers might be given 30 index cards on each of which is printed one of the 30 items. Testtakers would be asked to sort the cards into three piles: those behaviors that are never justified, those that are sometimes justified, and those that are always justified.

A **Guttman scale** (1944, 1947) is yet another scaling method that yields ordinal-level measures. Items on it range sequentially from weaker to stronger expressions of the attitude, belief, or feeling being measured. A feature of Guttman scales is that all respondents who agree with the stronger statements of the attitude will also agree with milder statements. Using the MDBS-R scale as an example, consider the following statements that reflect attitudes toward suicide.

Do you agree or disagree with each of the following:
a. All people should have the right to decide whether they wish to end their lives.
b. People who are terminally ill and in pain should have the option to have a doctor assist them in ending their lives.
c. People should have the option to sign away the use of artificial life-support equipment before they become seriously ill.
d. People have the right to a comfortable life.

If this were a perfect Guttman scale, all respondents who agree with a (the most extreme position) should also agree with b, c, and d. All respondents who disagree with *a* but agree with *b* should also agree with *c* and *d,* and so forth. Guttman scales are developed through the administration of a number of items to a target group. The resulting data are then analyzed by means of **scalogram analysis,** an item-analysis procedure and approach to test development that entails a graphic mapping of a testtaker's responses. The objective for the developer of a measure of attitudes is to obtain an arrangement of items wherein endorsement of one item automatically connotes endorsement of less extreme positions. It is not always possible to do this. Beyond the measurement of attitudes, Guttman scaling or scalogram analysis (the two terms are used synonymously) appeals to test developers in consumer psychology, where an objective may be to learn if a consumer who will purchase one product will purchase another product.

All the foregoing methods yield ordinal data. The method of equal-appearing intervals, first described by Thurstone (1929), is one scaling method used to obtain data that are presumed to be interval. Again using the example of attitudes about the justifiability of suicide, let's outline the steps that would be involved in creating a scale using Thurstone's equal-appearing intervals method.

1. A reasonably large number of statements reflecting positive and negative attitudes toward suicide are collected, such as *Life is sacred, so people should never take their own lives,* and *A person in a great deal of physical or emotional pain may rationally decide that suicide is the best option available to him or her.*

2. Judges (or experts in some cases) evaluate each statement as to how strongly it indicates that suicide is justified. Each judge is instructed to rate each statement on a scale *as if* the scale were interval in nature. For example, the scale might range from 1 (the statement indicates that suicide is never justified) to 9 (the statement indicates that suicide is always justified). Judges are instructed that the 1-to-9 scale is being used *as if* there were equal distance between each of the values—that is, as if it were an interval scale. Judges are cautioned to focus their ratings on the statements, not on their own views on the matter.

3. A mean and a standard deviation of the judges' ratings are calculated for each statement. For example, if 15 judges rated 100 statements on a scale from 1 to 9, then for each of these 100 statements, the 15 judges' ratings would be averaged. Suppose five of the judges rated a particular item as a 1, five other judges rated it as a 2, and the remaining five judges rated it as a 3. The average rating would be 2 (with a standard deviation of 0.816).

4. Items are selected for inclusion in the final scale based on several criteria, including the degree to which the item contributes to a comprehensive measurement of the variable in question and the test developer's degree of confidence that the items have indeed been sorted into equal intervals. Item means and standard deviations are also considered. Items should represent a wide range of attitudes reflected in a variety of means. A low standard deviation is indicative of a good item; the judges agreed about the meaning of the item with respect to its reflection of attitudes toward suicide.

5. The scale is now ready for administration. The way the scale is used depends on the objectives of the test situation. Typically, respondents are asked to select those statements that most accurately reflect their own attitudes. The values of the items that the respondent selects (based on the judges' ratings) are averaged, producing a score on the test.

The method of equal-appearing intervals is an example of a scaling method of the direct estimation variety. In contrast to other methods that involve indirect estimation, there is no need to transform the testtaker's responses into some other scale.

The particular scaling method employed in the development of a new test depends on many factors, including the variables being measured, the group for whom the test is intended (children may require a less complicated scaling method than adults, for example), and the preferences of the test developer.

Writing Items

In the grand scheme of test construction, considerations related to the actual writing of the test's items go hand in hand with scaling considerations. Three questions that the prospective test developer/item writer faces immediately are:

- What range of content should the items cover?
- Which of the many different types of item formats should be employed?
- How many items should be written?

When devising a standardized test using a multiple-choice format, it is usually advisable that the first draft contain approximately twice the number of items that the final version of the test will contain.[1] If, for example, a test called "American History: 1940 to 1990" is to have 30 questions in its final version, it would be useful to have as many as 60 items in the item pool. Ideally, these items will adequately sample the domain of the test. An **item pool** is the reservoir or well from which items will be drawn or discarded for the final version of the test.

A comprehensive sampling provides a basis for content validity of the final version of the test. Because approximately half of these items will be eliminated from the test's final version, the test developer needs to ensure that the final version also contains items that adequately sample the domain. Thus, if all the questions about the Persian Gulf War from the original 60 items were determined to be poorly written, the test developer should either rewrite items sampling this period or create new items. The new or rewritten items would then be subjected to tryout as well, in order not to jeopardize the content validity of the test. As in earlier versions of the test, effort is made to ensure adequate sampling of the domain in the final version of the test. Another consideration here is whether or not alternate forms of the test will be created, and if so, how many. Multiply the number of items required in the pool for one form of the test by the number of forms planned, and you have the total number of items needed for the initial item pool.

How does one develop items for the item pool? The test developer may write a large number of items from personal experience or academic acquaintance with the subject matter. Help may also be sought from others, including experts. For psychological tests designed for use in clinical settings, clinicians, patients, patients' family members, clinical staff, and others may be interviewed for insights that could assist in the item writing. For psychological tests designed for use by personnel psychologists, interviews with members of a targeted industry or organization will likely be of great value. For psychological tests designed for use by school psychologists, interviews with teachers, administrative staff, educational psychologists, and others may be invaluable. Searches through the research literature may be fruitful, as might searches through nonresearch literature.

---

1. Common sense and the practical demands of the situation may dictate that fewer items be written for the first draft of a test. If, for example, the final draft were to contain 1,000 items, it could be an undue burden to attempt to create an item pool of 2,000 items. Or, if the test developer is a very knowledgeable and capable item writer, it might be necessary to create only about 1,200 items for the item pool.

Considerations related to variables such as the purpose of the test and the number of examinees to be tested at one time enter into decisions regarding the *format* in which items will be presented to testtakers.

Item format Variables such as the form, plan, structure, arrangement, and layout of individual test items are collectively referred to as **item format.** Two types of item format we will discuss in detail are the *selected-response format* and the *constructed-response format.* Items presented in a **selected-response format** require testtakers to select a response from a set of alternative responses. Items presented in a **constructed-response format** require testtakers to supply or to create the correct answer, not merely to select it.

If a test is designed to measure achievement, and the items are written in a selected-response format, then examinees must select the response that is keyed as correct. If the test is designed to measure the strength of a particular trait, and the items are written in a selected-response format, then examinees must select the alternative that best answers the question with respect to themselves. As we further discuss item formats, for the sake of simplicity we will confine our examples to achievement tests. The reader may wish to mentally substitute other appropriate terms for words such as *correct* for personality or other types of tests that are not achievement tests.

Three types of selected-response item formats are *multiple-choice, matching,* and *true-false.* An item written in a **multiple-choice** format has three elements: (1) a stem, (2) a correct alternative or option, and (3) several incorrect alternatives or options variously referred to as *distractors* or *foils.* Two illustrations follow (despite the fact that you are probably all too familiar with multiple-choice items).

Item A

Stem   ⟶   A psychological test, an interview, and a case study are:

Correct alt.   ⟶   a. psychological assessment tools

Distractors   ⟶   b. standardized behavioral samples
                          c. reliable assessment instruments
                          d. theory-linked measures

Now consider Item B:

Item B

A good multiple-choice item in an achievement test:

a. has one correct alternative
b. has grammatically parallel alternatives
c. has alternatives of similar length
d. has alternatives that fit grammatically with the stem
e. includes as much of the item as possible in the stem to avoid unnecessary repetition
f. avoids ridiculous distractors
g. is not excessively long
h. all of the above
i. none of the above

If you answered "h" to Item B, you are correct. As you read the list of alternatives, it may have occurred to you that Item B violated many of the rules it set forth!

In a **matching item,** the testtaker is presented with two columns, *premises* on the left and *responses* on the right. The testtaker's task is to determine which response is best associated with which premise. For very young testtakers, the instructions will direct them to draw a line from one premise to one response. Older testtakers are typically asked to write a letter or number. Here's an example of a matching item one might see on a test in a class on film history:

Directions: Match an actor's name in Column X with a film role the actor played in Column Y. Write the letter of the film role next to the number of the corresponding actor. Each film role in Column Y may be used once, more than once, or not at all.

Column X	Column Y
_____ 1. Anthony Hopkins	a. Ace Ventura
_____ 2. Jim Carrey	b. The Jackal
_____ 3. Wesley Snipes	c. Captain Jack Aubrey
_____ 4. Mike Myers	d. Hannibal Lecter
_____ 5. Dustin Hoffman	e. Austin Powers
_____ 6. Jack Black	f. Blade
_____ 7. George Lazenby	g. Yu Shu
_____ 8. Robin Williams	h. Dewey Finn
_____ 9. Sigourney Weaver	i. Professor Brainard
_____ 10. Michelle Yeoh	j. Benjamin Braddock
_____ 11. Russell Crowe	k. James Bond
	l. Ellen Ripley
	m. John Book

You may have noticed that the two columns contain different numbers of items. If the number of items in the two columns were the same, then a person unsure about one of the actor's roles could deduce it by matching all the other options first. A perfect score would then result even though the testtaker did not actually know all the answers. Providing more options than needed minimizes such a possibility. Another way to lessen the probability of chance or guessing as a factor in the test score is to state in the directions that each response may be a correct answer once, more than once, or not at all.

Some guidelines should be observed in writing matching items for classroom use. The wording of the premises and the responses should be fairly short and to the point. No more than a dozen or so premises should be included; otherwise, some students will forget what they were looking for as they go through the lists. The lists of premises and responses should both be homogeneous—that is, lists of the same sort of thing. Our film school example provides a homogeneous list of premises (all names of actors) and a homogeneous list of responses (all names of film characters). Care must be taken to ensure that one and only one premise is matched to one and only one response. For example, adding the name of actors such as Sean Connery, Roger Moore, David Niven, Timothy Dalton, or Pierce Brosnan to the premise column as it now exists would be inadvisable, regardless of what character's name was added to the response column. Do you know why?

At one time or another, Connery, Moore, Niven, Dalton, and Brosnan all played the role of James Bond (response *k*). As the list of premises and responses currently stands, the match to response *k* is premise 7 (this Australian actor played Agent 007 in the film *On Her Majesty's Secret Service*). If in the future the test developer wanted to substitute the name of another actor, say, Pierce Brosnan for George Lazenby, it would be prudent to review the columns to confirm that Brosnan did not play any of the other characters in the response list and that James Bond still was not played by any actor in the premise list besides Brosnan.[2]

A multiple-choice item that contains only two possible responses is called a **binary-choice item.** Perhaps the most familiar binary-choice item is the **true/false item.** As you know, this type of selected-response item usually takes the form of a sentence that requires the testtaker to indicate whether the statement is or is not a fact. Other varieties of binary-choice items include sentences to which the testtaker responds with one of two responses, such as *agree/disagree, yes/no, right/wrong,* or *fact/opinion.*

A good binary choice contains a single idea, is not excessively long, and is not subject to debate; the correct response must undoubtedly be one of the two choices. Like multiple-choice items, binary-choice items are readily applicable to a wide range of subjects. Unlike multiple-choice items, binary-choice items need not contain distractor alternatives. For this reason, binary-choice items are typically easier to write than multiple-choice items and can be written relatively quickly. A disadvantage of the binary-choice item is that the probability of obtaining a correct response purely on the basis of chance (guessing) on any one item is .5, or 50%.[3] In contrast, the probability of obtaining a correct response by guessing on a four-alternative multiple-choice question is .25, or 25%.

JUST THINK . . .

Respond either *true* or *false*, depending upon your opinion as a student: *In the field of education, selected-response items are preferable to constructed-response items.* Then respond again, this time from the perspective of an educator and test user. Explain your answers.

Moving from a discussion of the selected-response format to the constructed variety, three types of constructed-response items are the *completion item,* the *short answer,* and the *essay.*

A **completion item** requires the examinee to provide a word or phrase that completes a sentence, as in the following example:

The standard deviation is generally considered the most useful measure of

_____.

A good completion item should be worded so that the correct answer is specific. Completion items that can be correctly answered in many ways can lead to scoring problems. The correct completion for the item above is *variability.* An alternative way of writing this item would be as a short-answer item:

What descriptive statistic is generally considered the most useful measure of variability?

A completion item may also be referred to as a **short-answer item.** It is desirable for completion or short-answer items to be written clearly enough that the testtaker can respond succinctly—that is, with a short answer. There are no hard-and-fast rules for how short an answer must be to be considered a short answer; a word, a term, a sentence, or a paragraph may suffice. Beyond a paragraph or two, the item might more properly be

---

2. Here's the entire answer key: 1-d, 2-a, 3-f, 4-e, 5-j, 6-h, 7-k, 8-i, 9-l, 10-g, 11-c.

3. We note in passing, however, that although the probability of guessing correctly on an individual binary-choice item on the basis of chance alone may be .5, the probability of guessing correctly on a *sequence* of such items decreases as the number of items increases. The probability of guessing correctly on two such items is equal to $.5^2$, or 25%. The probability of guessing correctly on ten such items is equal to $.5^{10}$, or .001. There is therefore a one-in-a-thousand chance that a testtaker would guess correctly on ten true/false (or other binary-choice) items on the basis of chance alone.

referred to as an *essay item*. We may define an **essay item** as a test item that requires the testtaker to respond to a question by writing a composition, typically one that demonstrates recall of facts, understanding, analysis, or interpretation.

Here is an example of an essay item:

Compare and contrast definitions and techniques of classical and operant conditioning. Include examples of how principles of each have been applied in clinical as well as educational settings.

An essay item is useful when the test developer wants the examinee to demonstrate a depth of knowledge about a single topic. In contrast to selected-response items and constructed-response items such as the short-answer item, the essay question not only permits the restating of learned material but also allows for the creative integration and expression of the material in the testtaker's own words. The skills tapped by essay items are different from those tapped by true-false and matching items. Whereas an essay requires recall, organization, planning, and writing ability, the other types of items require only recognition. A drawback of the essay item is that it tends to focus on a more limited area than can be covered in the same amount of time using a series of selected-response items or completion items. Another potential problem with essays can be subjectivity in scoring and inter-scorer differences. A review of some advantages and disadvantages of these different item formats, especially as used in academic classroom settings, is presented in Table 7–1.

Writing items for computer administration   A number of widely available computer programs are designed to facilitate the construction of tests as well as their administration, scoring, and interpretation. These programs typically make use of two advantages of CAPA: the ability to store items in an *item bank* and the ability to individualize testing through a technique called *item branching.*

An **item bank** is a relatively large, easily accessible collection of test questions. Instructors who regularly teach a particular course sometimes create their own item bank of questions they have found to be useful on examinations. One of the many potential advantages of an item bank is accessibility to a large number of test items conveniently classified by subject area, item statistics, or other variables. And just as funds may be added to or withdrawn from a more traditional bank, so items may be added to, withdrawn from, and even modified in an item bank (see this chapter's *Close-up*).

> **JUST THINK . . .**
>
> If an item bank is sufficiently large, some have argued that it makes sense to publish it to the testtakers *before* the test. Your thoughts?

The term **computerized adaptive testing (CAT)** refers to an interactive, computer-administered testtaking process wherein items presented to the testtaker are based in part on the testtaker's performance on previous items. As in traditional test administration, the test might begin with some sample, practice items. However, the computer may not permit the testtaker to continue with the test until the practice items have been responded to in a satisfactory manner and the testtaker has demonstrated that he or she understands the test procedure. A test may be different for each testtaker, depending on individual performance on the items presented. Each item on an achievement test, for example, may have a known difficulty level. This fact as well as other data (such as a statistical allowance for blind guessing) may be factored in when it comes time to derive a final score on the items administered. Note that we do not say "final score on the test," because what constitutes "the test" is ultimately different for different testtakers.

The advantages of CAT have been well documented for some time (Weiss & Vale, 1987). Only a sample of the total number of items in the item pool is administered to any

Table 7–1
Some Advantages and Disadvantages of Various Item Formats

Format of Item	Advantages	Disadvantages
Multiple-choice	• Can sample a great deal of content in a relatively short time. • Allows for precise interpretation and little "bluffing" other than guessing. This, in turn, may allow for more content-valid test score interpretation than some other formats. • May be machine- or computer-scored.	• Does not allow for expression of original or creative thought. • Not all subject matter lends itself to reduction to one and only one answer keyed correct. • May be time-consuming to construct series of good items. • Advantages of this format may be nullified if item is poorly written or if a pattern of correct alternatives is discerned by the testtaker.
Binary-choice items (such as true/false)	• Can sample a great deal of content in a relatively short time. • Test consisting of such items is relatively easy to construct and score. • May be machine- or computer-scored.	• Susceptibility to guessing is high, especially for "test-wise" students who may detect cues to reject one choice or the other. • Some wordings, including use of adverbs such as *typically* or *usually,* can be interpreted differently by different students. • Can be used only when a choice of dichotomous responses can be made without qualification.
Matching	• Can effectively and efficiently be used to evaluate testtakers' recall of related facts. • Particularly useful when there are a large number of facts on a single topic. • Can be fun or game-like for testtaker (especially the well-prepared testtaker). • May be machine- or computer-scored.	• As with other items in the selected-response format, test-takers need only *recognize* a correct answer and not recall it or devise it. • One of the choices may help eliminate one of the other choices as the correct response. • Requires pools of related information and is of less utility with distinctive ideas.
Completion or short-answer (fill-in-the-blank)	• Wide content area, particularly of questions that require factual recall, can be sampled in relatively brief amount of time. • This type of test is relatively easy to construct. • Useful in obtaining picture of what testtaker is able to generate as opposed to merely recognize, since test-taker must generate response.	• Useful only with responses of one word or a few words. • May demonstrate only recall of circumscribed facts or bits of knowledge. • Potential for inter-scorer reliability problems when test is scored by more than one person. • May not be machine- or computer-scored.
Essay	• Useful in measuring responses that require complex, imaginative, or original solutions, applications, or demonstrations. • Useful in measuring how well testtaker is able to communicate ideas in writing. • Requires testtaker to generate entire response, not merely recognize it or supply a word or two.	• May not sample wide content area as well as other tests do. • Testtaker with limited knowledge can attempt to bluff with confusing, sometimes long and elaborate writing designed to be as broad and ambiguous as possible. • Scoring can be time-consuming and fraught with pitfalls. • When more than one person is scoring, inter-scorer reliability issues may be raised. • May rely too heavily on writing skills, even to the point of confounding writing ability with what is purportedly being measured. • May not be machine- or computer-scored.

one testtaker. On the basis of previous response patterns, items that have a very high probability of being answered in a particular fashion (correctly, if an ability test) are not presented, thus providing economy in terms of testing time and total number of items presented. Computer-adaptive testing has been found to reduce the number of test items that need to be administered by as much as 50% while simultaneously reducing measurement error by 50%.

The ability of the computer to tailor the content and order of presentation of test items on the basis of responses to previous items is referred to as **item branching.** A

Designing an Item Bank

Developing an item bank is more work than simply writing items for a test. Many questions and issues need to be resolved relating to the development of such a bank and to the maintenance of a satisfactory pool of items. These questions and issues relate to the items, the test, the system, the use to which the item bank will be put, and the cost.

I. Items
  A. *Acquisition and development*
    1. Develop/use your own item collection or use collections of others?
      a. If develop your own item collection, what development procedures will be followed?
      b. If use collections of others, will the items be leased or purchased? Is the classification scheme sufficiently documented, and can the item format specifications be easily transferred and used?
    2. What types of items will be permitted?
      a. Will open-ended (constructed-response) items, opinion questions, instructional objectives, or descriptions of performance tasks be included in the bank?
      b. Will all the items be made to fit a common format (for example, all multiple-choice with options "a," "b," "c," and "d")?
      c. Must the items be calibrated, or validated or otherwise carry additional information?
    3. What will be the size of the item collection?
      a. How many items per objective or subtopic (collection depth)?
      b. How many different topics (collection breadth)?
    4. What review, tryout, and editing procedures will be used?
      a. Who will perform the review and editing?
      b. Will there be a field tryout, and if so, what statistics will be gathered, and what criteria will be used for inclusion in the bank?
  B. *Classification*
    1. How will the subject matter classifications be performed?
      a. Will the classification by subject matter use fixed categories, keywords, or some combination of the two?
      b. Who will be responsible for preparing, expanding, and refining the taxonomy?

  c. How detailed will the taxonomy be? Will it be hierarchically or nonhierarchically arranged?
      d. Who will assign classification indices to each item, and how will this assignment be verified?
    2. What other assigned information about the items will be stored in the item bank?
    3. What measured information about the items will be stored in the bank? How will the item measures be calculated? *
  C. *Management*
    1. Will provision be made for updating the classification scheme and items? If so:
      a. Who will be permitted to make additions, deletions, and revisions?
      b. What review procedures will be followed?
      c. How will the changes be disseminated?
      d. How will duplicate (or near-duplicate) items be detected and eliminated?
      e. When will a revision of an item be trivial enough that item statistics from a previous version can be aggregated with revisions from the current version?
      f. Will item statistics be stored from each use, or from last use, or will they be aggregated across uses?
    2. How will items be handled that require pictures, graphs, special characters, or other types of enhanced printing?
    3. How will items that must accompany other items be handled, such as a series of questions about the same reading passage?
II. Tests
  A. *Assembly*
    1. Must the test constructor specify the specific items to appear on the test, or will the items be selected by computer?
    2. If the items are selected by computer:
      a. How will one item be selected out of several that match the search specification (randomly, time since last usage, frequency of previous use)?

*This question is the subject of considerable controversy and discussion in the technical measurement literature.

(continued)

Designing an Item Bank *(continued)*

b. What happens if no item meets the search specifications?

c. Will a test constructor have the option to reject a selected item, and if so, what will be the mechanism for doing so?

d. What precautions will be taken to ensure that examinees who are tested more than once do not receive the same items?

3. What item or test parameters can be specified for test assembly (item format restrictions, limits on difficulty levels, expected score distribution, expected test reliability, and so on)?

4. What assembly procedures will be available (options to multiple-choice items placed in random order, the test items placed in random order, different items on each test)?

5. Will the system print tests, or only specify which items to use? If the former, how will the tests be printed or duplicated, and where will the answers be displayed?

B. *Administration, scoring, and reporting*

1. Will the system be capable of online test administration? If so:

a. How will access be managed?

b. Will test administration be adaptive, and if so, using what procedures?

2. Will the system provide for test scoring? If so:

a. What scoring formula will be used (rights only, correction for guessing, partial credit for some answers, weighting by discrimination values)?

b. How will constructed responses be evaluated (offline by the instructor, online or offline by examiners comparing their answers to a key, online by computer with or without employing a spelling algorithm)?

3. Will the system provide for test reporting? If so:

a. What records will be kept (the tests themselves, individual student item responses, individual student test scores, school or other group scores) and for how long? Will new scores for individuals and groups supplement or replace old scores?

b. What reporting options (content and format) will be available?

c. To whom will the reports be sent?

C. *Evaluation*

1. Will reliability and validity data be collected? If so, what data will be collected by whom, and how will they be used?

2. Will norms be made available, and if so, based on what norm-referenced measures?

III. System

A. *Acquisition and development*

1. Who will be responsible for acquisition and development, given what resources, and operating under what constraints?

2. Will the system be transportable to others? What levels and degree of documentation will be available?

B. *Software and hardware*

1. What aspects of the system will be computer-assisted?

a. Where will the items be stored (computer, paper, card file)?

b. Will requests be filled using a batch, online, or manual mode?

2. Will a microcomputer be used, and if so, what special limits does such a choice place on item text, item bank size, and test development options?

3. Will items be stored as one large collection, or will separate files be maintained for each user?

4. How will the item banking system be constructed (from scratch; by piecing together word processing, database management, and other general-purpose programs; by adopting existing item banking systems)?

5. What specific equipment will be needed (for storage, retrieval, interactions with the system, and so on)?

6. How user- and maintenance-friendly will the equipment and support programs be?

7. Who will be responsible for equipment maintenance?

C. *Monitoring and training*

1. What system features will be monitored (number of items per classification category, usage by user group, number of revisions until a user is satisfied, distribution of test lengths or other test characteristics, and so on)?

2. Who will monitor the system, train users, and give support (initially and ongoing)?

3. How will information be disseminated about changes in system procedures?
D. *Access and security*
1. Who will have access to the items and other information in the bank (authors/owners, teachers, students)? Who can request tests?
2. Will users have direct access to the system, or must they go through an intermediary?
3. What procedures will be followed to secure the contents of the item bank (if they are to be secure)?
4. Where will the contents of the item bank be housed (centrally, or will each user also have a copy)?
5. Who will have access to score reports?

IV. Use and Acceptance
A. *General*
1. Who decides to what uses the item bank will be put? And will these uses be those the test users need and want?
2. Who will develop the tests, and who will be allowed to use the system? Will those people be acceptable to the examinees and recipients of the test information?
3. Will the system be able to handle the expected demand for use?
4. Is the output of the system likely to be used and used as intended?
5. How will user acceptance and item bank credibility be enhanced?
B. *Instructional improvement.* If this is an intended use:
1. Will the item bank be part of a larger instructional or decision-making system?
2. Which textbooks, curriculum guidelines, and other materials, if any, will be keyed to the bank's items? Who will make that decision, and how will the assignments be validated?
3. Will items be available for drill and practice as well as for testing?
4. Will information be available to users that will assist in the diagnosis of educational needs?
C. *Adaptive testing.* If this is an option:
1. How will test administrations be scheduled?
2. How will the items be selected to ensure testing efficiency yet maintain content representation and avoid duplication between successive test administrations?

3. What criteria will be used to terminate testing?
4. What scoring procedures will be followed?
D. *Certification of competence.* If this is an intended use:
1. Will the item bank contain measures that cover all the important component skills of the competence being assessed?
2. How many attempts at passing the test will be allowed? When? How will these attempts be monitored?
E. *Program and curriculum evaluation.* If this is an intended use:
1. Will it be possible to implement the system to provide reliable measures of student achievement in a large number of specific performance areas?
2. Will the item bank contain measures that cover all the important stated objectives of the curriculum? That go beyond the stated objectives of the curriculum?
3. Will the item bank yield commensurable data that permit valid comparisons over time?
F. *Testing and reporting requirements imposed by external agencies.* If meeting these requirements is an intended use:
1. Will the system be able to handle requirements for program evaluation, student selection for specially funded programs, assessing educational needs, and reporting?
2. Will the system be able to accommodate minor modifications in the testing and reporting requirements?

V. Costs
A. *Cost feasibility*
1. What are the (fixed, variable) costs (financial, time, space, equipment, and supplies) to create and support the system?
2. Are those costs affordable?
B. *Cost comparisons*
1. How do the item banking system costs compare with the present or other testing systems that achieve the same goals?
2. Do any expanded capabilities justify the extra cost? Are any restricted capabilities balanced by cost savings?

Source: Millman and Arter (1984).

computer may have a bank of achievement test items of different difficulty levels. It may be programmed to present items according to a rule. For example, a rule might be not to present an item of the next difficulty level until two consecutive items of the previous difficulty level are answered correctly. Another rule might be to terminate the test when five consecutive items of a given level of difficulty have been answered incorrectly. Alternatively, the pattern of items to which the testtaker is exposed may be based not on the testtaker's response to preceding items but on a random drawing from the total pool of test items. Random presentation of items reduces the ease with which testtakers can memorize items for future testtakers.

Item-branching technology may be applied not only in the construction of tests of achievement but in tests of personality. For example, if a respondent answers an item in a way that suggests he or she is depressed, the computer might automatically probe for depression-related symptoms and behavior. The next item presented might be designed to probe the respondents' sleep patterns or the existence of suicidal ideation.

Item-branching technology may be used in personality tests to recognize nonpurposive or inconsistent responding. For example, on a computer-based true-false test, if

JUST THINK . . .

Try your hand at writing a couple of true/false items that would be used to detect nonpurposive or random responding on a personality test.

the examinee responds *true* to an item such as *I spent Christmas in Beirut last year,* there would be reason to suspect that the examinee is responding nonpurposively, randomly, or in some way other than genuinely. And if the same respondent responds *false* to the identical item later on in the test, the respondent is being inconsistent as well. Should the computer recognize a nonpurposive response pattern, it may be programmed to respond in a prescribed way, for example, by admonishing the respondent to be more careful or even by refusing to proceed until a purposive response is given.

Scoring Items

Many different test scoring models have been devised. Perhaps the most commonly used model is the cumulative model, due in large part to its simplicity and logic. Typically, the rule in a cumulatively scored test is that the higher the score on the test, the higher the testtaker is on the ability, the trait, or some other characteristic the test purports to measure. For each testtaker response to targeted items made in a particular way, the testtaker earns cumulative credit with regard to a particular construct.

In tests that employ **class** or **category scoring,** testtaker responses earn credit toward placement in a particular class or category with other testtakers whose pattern of responses is presumably similar in some way. This approach is used in some diagnostic systems wherein individuals must exhibit a certain number of symptoms to qualify for a specific diagnosis. A third scoring model, *ipsative scoring*, departs radically in rationale from either cumulative or class models. A typical objective in **ipsative scoring** is the comparison of a testtaker's score on one scale within a test with another scale within that same test.

Consider, for example, a personality test called the Edwards Personal Preference Schedule (EPPS), which is designed to measure the relative strength of different psychological needs. The EPPS ipsative scoring system yields information on the strength of various needs in relation to the strength of other needs of the testtaker. The test does not yield information on the strength of a testtaker's need relative to the presumed strength of that need in the general population. Edwards constructed his test of 210 pairs of statements in a way such that respondents were "forced" to answer *true* or *false* or *yes* or *no* to only one of two statements. Prior research by Edwards had indicated that the two statements were equivalent in terms of how socially desirable responses were. Here is a sample of an EPPS-like forced-choice item, to which the respondents would indicate which is more true of themselves:

I feel depressed when I fail at something.

I feel nervous when giving a talk before a group.

On the basis of such an ipsatively scored personality test, it would be possible to draw only intra-individual conclusions about the testtaker. Here's an example: "John's need for achievement is higher than his need for affiliation." It would *not* be appropriate to draw inter-individual comparisons on the basis of an ipsatively scored test. It would be inappropriate, for example, to compare two testtakers with a statement like "John's need for achievement is higher than Jane's need for achievement."

Once the test developer has decided on a scoring model and has done everything else necessary to get the first draft of the test ready for administration, the next step is test tryout.

Test Tryout

Having created a pool of items from which the final version of the test will be developed, the test developer will try out the test. The test should be tried out on people similar in critical respects to the people for whom the test was designed. Thus, for example, if a test is designed to aid in decisions regarding the selection of corporate employees with management potential at a certain level, it would be appropriate to try out the test on corporate employees at the targeted level.

Equally important are questions about the number of people on whom the test should be tried out. An informal rule of thumb is that there be no fewer than five subjects and preferably as many as ten for each item on the test. In general, the more subjects in the tryout the better. The thinking here is that the more subjects employed, the weaker the role of chance in the data analysis. A definite risk in using too few subjects during test tryout comes during factor analysis of the findings, when what we might call *phantom factors*—nonexistent factors that are actually artifacts of the small sample size—may emerge.

> **JUST THINK . . .**
>
> How appropriate would it be to try out this test on a convenience sample of introductory psychology students?

The test tryout should be executed under conditions as identical as possible to the conditions under which the standardized test will be administered; all instructions, and everything from the time limits allotted for completing the test to the atmosphere at the test site, should be as similar as possible. As Nunnally (1978, p. 279) so aptly phrased it, "If items for a personality inventory are being administered in an atmosphere that encourages frankness and the eventual test is to be administered in an atmosphere where subjects will be reluctant to say bad things about themselves, the item analysis will tell a faulty story." In general, the test developer endeavors to ensure that differences in response to the test's items are due in fact to the items, not to extraneous factors.

In Chapter 4, we dealt in detail with the important question "What is a good test?" Now seems like a good time to raise a related question.

What Is a Good Item?

In the same sense that a good test is reliable and valid, a good test *item* is reliable and valid. Further, a good test item helps to discriminate testtakers. That is, a good test item is one that high scorers on the test as a whole get right. An item that high scorers on the test as a whole do not get right is probably not a good item. We may also describe a good test item as one that low scorers on the test as a whole get wrong. An item that low scorers on the test as a whole get right may not be a good item.

How does a test developer identify good items? After the first draft of the test has been administered to a representative group of examinees, the test developer analyzes test scores and responses to individual items. The different types of statistical scrutiny that the test data can potentially undergo at this point are referred to collectively as **item analysis.** Note that although item analysis tends to be regarded as a quantitative endeavor, it may be qualitative as well, as we shall see.

JUST THINK . . .

Well, do a bit more than think: *Write* one good item in any format, along with a brief explanation of why you think it is a good item. The item should be for a new test you are developing called the American History Test, to be administered to ninth-graders.

Item Analysis

Statistical procedures used to analyze items may become quite complex, and our treatment of this subject should be thought of as only introductory. We briefly survey some procedures typically used by test developers in their efforts to select the best items from a pool of tryout items. The criteria for the best items may differ as a function of the test developer's objectives. Thus, for example, one test developer might deem the best items to be those that optimally contribute to the internal reliability of the test. Another test developer might wish to design a test with the highest possible criterion-related validity—and select items accordingly. Among the tools test developers might employ to analyze and select items are

- an index of the item's difficulty
- an index of the item's reliability
- an index of the item's validity
- an index of item discrimination

JUST THINK . . .

Apply these item-analysis statistics to a test of personality. Make translations in phraseology as you think about how statistics such as an item-difficulty index or an item-validity index could be used to help identify good items, not for an achievement test but for a personality test.

Assume for the moment that you got carried away on the previous *Just Think* exercise and are now the proud author of 100 items for a ninth-grade-level American History Test (AHT). Let's further assume that this 100-item (draft) test has been administered to 100 ninth-graders. Hoping in the long run to standardize the test and have it distributed by a commercial test publisher, you have a more immediate, short-term goal: to select the 50 best of the 100 items you originally created. How might that short-term goal be achieved? As we will see, the answer lies in item-analysis procedures.

The Item-Difficulty Index

Suppose every examinee got item 1 of the AHT correct. Can we say that item 1 is a good item? What if no one got item 1 correct? In either case, item 1 is not a good item. If everyone gets the item right, the item is too easy. If everyone gets the item wrong, the item is too difficult. Just as the test as a whole is designed to provide an index of degree of knowledge about American history, so each individual item on the test should be passed (scored as correct) or failed (scored as incorrect) on the basis of testtakers' differential knowledge of American history.[4]

An index of an item's difficulty is obtained by calculating the proportion of the total number of testtakers who got the item right. A lowercase, italicized p (p) is used to denote item difficulty, and a subscript refers to the item number (p_1 is read "item-difficulty index for item 1"). The value of an item-difficulty index can theoretically range from 0 (if no one got the item right) to 1 (if everyone got the item right). If 50 of the 100 examinees got item 2 right, then the item-difficulty index for this item would be equal to 50 divided by 100, or .5 ($p_2 = .5$). If 75 of the examinees got item 3 right, p_3 would be equal to .75, and we could say that item 3 was easier than item 2. Note that the larger the item-difficulty index, the easier the item. Because p refers to the percent of people passing an item, the higher the p for an item, the easier the item. The statistic referred to as an **item-difficulty index** in the context of achievement testing may be an **item-endorsement index** in other contexts, such as personality testing. Here, the statistic provides not a measure of the percent of people passing the item but a measure of the percent of people who said yes to, agreed with, or otherwise endorsed the item.

An index of the difficulty of the average test item for a particular test can be calculated by averaging the item-difficulty indices for all the test's items. This is accomplished by summing the item-difficulty indices for all test items and dividing by the total number of items on the test. For maximum discrimination among the abilities of the test-takers, the optimal average item difficulty is approximately .5, with individual items on the test ranging in difficulty from about .3 to .8. Note, however, that the possible effect of guessing must be taken into account when considering items of the selected-response variety. With this type of item, the optimal average item difficulty is usually the midpoint between 1.00 and the chance success proportion, defined as the probability of answering correctly by random guessing. In a true-false item, the probability of guessing correctly on the basis of chance alone is 1/2, or .50. Therefore, the optimal item difficulty is halfway between .50 and 1.00, or .75. In general, the midpoint representing the optimal item difficulty is obtained by summing the chance success proportion and 1.00 and then dividing the sum by 2, or

$$.50 + 1.00 = 1.5$$

$$\frac{1.5}{2} = 7.5$$

For a five-option multiple-choice item, the probability of guessing correctly on any one item on the basis of chance alone is equal to 1/5, or .20. The optimal item difficulty is therefore .60:

$$.20 + 1.00 = 1.20$$

$$\frac{1.20}{2} = .60$$

---

4. An exception here may be a **giveaway item.** Such an item might be inserted near the beginning of an achievement test to spur motivation and a positive testtaking attitude and lessen testtakers' test-related anxiety. In general, however, if an item analysis suggests that a particular item is too easy or too difficult, the item must be either rewritten or discarded.

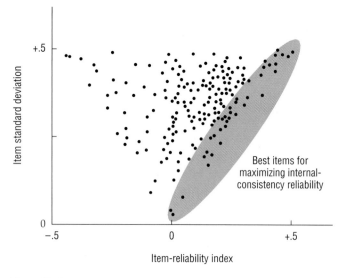

Figure 7–4
Maximizing Internal-Consistency Reliability

(Source: Allen & Yen, 1979)

The Item-Reliability Index

The **item-reliability index** provides an indication of the **internal consistency** of a test (Figure 7–4); the higher this index, the greater the test's internal consistency. This index is equal to the product of the item-score standard deviation (s) and the correlation (r) between the item score and the total test score.

Factor analysis and inter-item consistency   A statistical tool useful in determining whether items on a test appear to be measuring the same thing(s) is the technique of factor analysis. Through the judicious use of factor analysis, items that do not "load on" the factor that they were written to tap (that is, items that do not appear to be measuring what they were designed to measure) can be revised or eliminated. If too many items appear to be tapping a particular area, the weakest of such items can be eliminated. Additionally, factor analysis can be useful in the test interpretation process, especially when comparing the constellation of responses to the items from two or more groups. Thus, for example, if a particular personality test is administered to two groups of hospitalized psychiatric patients, each group with a different diagnosis, the same items may be found to load on different factors in the two groups. Such information will compel the responsible test developer to revise or eliminate certain items from the test or to describe the differential findings in the test manual.

The Item-Validity Index

The **item-validity index** is a statistic designed to provide an indication of the degree to which a test is measuring what it purports to measure; the higher the item-validity index, the greater the test's criterion-related validity. The item-validity index can be calculated once the following two statistics are known:

- the item-score standard deviation
- the correlation between the item score and the criterion score

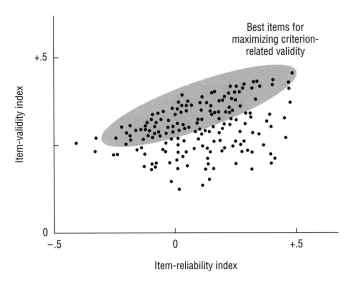

Figure 7–5
Maximizing Criterion-Related Validity

(Source: Allen & Yen, 1979)

The item-score standard deviation of item 1 (denoted by the symbol s_1) can be calculated using the index of the item's difficulty (p_1) in the following formula:

$$s_1 = \sqrt{p_1(1 - p_1)}$$

The correlation between the score on item 1 and a score on the criterion measure (denoted by the symbol r_{1C}) is multiplied by item 1's item-score standard deviation (s_1), and the product is equal to an index of an item's validity ($s_1 r_{1C}$). The calculation of the item-validity index will be important when the test developer's goal is to maximize the criterion-related validity of the test. A visual representation of the best items on a test (if the objective is to maximize criterion-related validity) can be achieved by plotting each item's item-validity index and item-reliability index (Figure 7–5).

The Item-Discrimination Index

Measures of item discrimination indicate how adequately an item separates or discriminates between high scorers and low scorers on an entire test. In this context, a multiple-choice item on an achievement test is a good item if most of the high scorers answer correctly and most of the low scorers answer incorrectly. If most of the high scorers fail a particular item, these testtakers may be making an alternative interpretation of a response intended to serve as a distractor. In such a case, the test developer should interview the examinees to understand better the basis for the choice and then appropriately revise (or eliminate) the item. Common sense dictates that an item on an achievement test is not doing its job if it is answered correctly by respondents who least understand the subject matter. Similarly, an item on a test purporting to measure a particular personality trait is not doing its job if responses indicate that people who score very low on the test as a whole (indicating absence or low levels of the trait in question) tend to score very high on the item (indicating that they are very high on the trait in question—contrary to what the test as a whole indicates).

Table 7–2
Item-Discrimination Indices for Five Hypothetical Items

Item	U	L	U − L	n	d [(U − L)/n]
1	20	16	4	32	.13
2	30	10	20	32	.63
3	32	0	32	32	1.00
4	20	20	0	32	0.00
5	0	32	−32	32	−1.00

The **item-discrimination index** is a measure of item discrimination, symbolized by a lowercase, italicized letter d (d). This estimate of item discrimination, in essence, compares performance on a particular item with performance in the upper and lower regions of a distribution of continuous test scores. The optimal boundary lines to demarcate what we are referring to as the "upper" and "lower" areas of a distribution of scores are scores within the upper and lower 27% of the distribution of scores—provided the distribution is normal (Kelley, 1939). As the distribution of test scores becomes more platykurtic (flat), the optimal boundary line for defining upper and lower gets larger and approaches 33% (Cureton, 1957). Allen and Yen (1979, p. 122) assure us that "for most applications, any percentage between 25 and 33 will yield similar estimates."

The item-discrimination index is a measure of the difference between the proportion of high scorers answering an item correctly and the proportion of low scorers answering the item correctly; the higher the value of d, the greater the number of high scorers answering the item correctly. A negative d value on a particular item is a red flag because it indicates that low-scoring examinees are more likely to answer the item correctly than high-scoring examinees. This situation calls for some action such as revision or elimination of the item.

Assume a history teacher gave the AHT to a total of 119 students who were just weeks away from completing ninth grade. The teacher isolated the upper (U) and lower (L) 27% of the test papers with a total of 32 papers in each group. Data and item-discrimination indices for items 1 through 5 are presented in Table 7–2. Note that 20 testtakers in the U group answered item 1 correctly, and 16 testtakers in the L group answered item 1 correctly. With an item-discrimination index equal to .13, item 1 is probably a reasonable item because more U group members than L group members answered it correctly. The higher the value of d, the more adequately the item discriminates the higher-scoring from the lower-scoring testtakers. For this reason, item 2 is a better item than item 1. Its item-discrimination index is .63. The highest possible value of d is +1.00. This value indicates that all members of the U group answered the item correctly, while all members of the L group answered the item incorrectly.

If the same proportion of members of the U and L groups pass the item, the item is not discriminating between testtakers at all, and d, appropriately enough, would be equal to 0. The lowest value that an index of item discrimination can take is −1. A d equal to −1 is a test developer's nightmare. It indicates that all members of the U group failed the item and all members of the L group passed it. On the face of it, such an item is the worst possible type of item and is in dire need of revision or elimination. However, through further investigation of this unanticipated finding, the test developer might learn or discover something new about the construct being measured.

Analysis of item alternatives The quality of each alternative within a multiple-choice item can be readily assessed with reference to the comparative performance of upper and lower scorers. No formulas or statistics are necessary here. By charting the number of testtakers in the U and L groups who chose each alternative, the test developer can get an idea of the effectiveness of a distractor by means of a simple eyeball test. To illustrate, let's analyze responses to five items on a hypothetical test, assuming that there were 32 scores in the upper level (U) of the distribution and 32 scores in the lower level (L) of the distribution. Let's begin by looking at the pattern of responses to item 1. In each case, ★ denotes the correct alternative.

Alternatives

Item 1		★a	b	c	d	e
	U	24	3	2	0	3
	L	10	5	6	6	5

The response pattern to item 1 indicates that the item is a good one. More U group members than L group members answered the item correctly, and each of the distractors attracted some testtakers.

Item 2		a	b	c	d	★e
	U	2	13	3	2	12
	L	6	7	5	7	7

Item 2 signals a situation in which a relatively large number of members of the U group chose a particular distractor choice (in this case, "b"). This item could probably be improved upon revision, preferably one made after an interview with some or all of the U students who chose "b."

Item 3		a	b	★c	d	e
	U	0	0	32	0	0
	L	3	2	22	2	3

Item 3 indicates a most desirable pattern of testtaker response. All members of the U group answered the item correctly, and each distractor attracted one or more members of the L group.

Item 4		a	★b	c	d	e
	U	5	15	0	5	7
	L	4	5	4	4	15

Item 4 is more difficult than item 3—fewer examinees answered it correctly. Still, this item provides useful information about discrimination because it effectively discriminates higher-scoring from lower-scoring examinees. For some reason, one of the alternatives ("e") was particularly effective—perhaps too effective—as a distractor to students in the low-scoring group. The test developer may wish to further explore why this was the case.

Item 5		a	b	c	★d	e
	U	14	0	0	5	13
	L	7	0	0	16	9

Item 5 is a poor item because more L group members than U group members answered the item correctly. Furthermore, none of the examinees chose the "b" or "c" distractors.

Item-Characteristic Curves

A graphic representation of item difficulty and discrimination can be made in an **item-characteristic curve (ICC)**. As shown in Figure 7–6, an ICC is a graph on which ability is plotted on the horizontal axis and probability of correct response is plotted on the

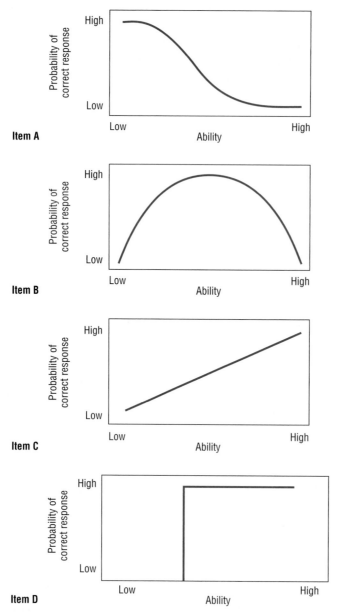

Figure 7–6
Some Sample Item-Characteristic Curves

(Source: Ghiselli et al., 1981)

For simplicity, we have omitted scale values for the axes. The vertical axis in such a graph lists probability of correct response in values ranging from 0 to 1. Values for the horizontal axis, which we have simply labeled "ability," are total scores on the test. In other sources, you may find the vertical axis of an item-characteristic curve labeled something like "proportion of examinees who respond correctly to the item" and the horizontal axis labeled "total test score."

vertical axis. Note that the extent to which an item discriminates high- from low-scoring examinees is apparent from the slope of the curve. The steeper the slope, the greater the item discrimination. Also note that if the slope is positive, more high scorers are getting the item correct than low scorers. If the slope is negative, the reverse is true.

Now focus on the item-characteristic curve for item A. Do you think this is a good item? The answer is that it is not. The probability of a testtaker's responding correctly is high for testtakers of low ability and low for testtakers of high ability. What about item B; is that a good item? Again, the answer is no. The curve tells us that testtakers of moderate ability have the highest probability of answering this item correctly. Testtakers with the greatest amount of ability—as well as their counterparts at the other end of the ability spectrum—are unlikely to respond correctly to this item. Item B may be one of those items to which people who know too much or think too much are likely to respond incorrectly.

Item C is a good item. The probability of responding correctly to it increases with ability. What about item D? This item-characteristic curve profiles an item that discriminates at only one point on the continuum of ability. The probability is very high that all testtakers at or above this point will respond correctly to the item. We can also say that the probability of an incorrect response is very high for testtakers who fall below that particular point in ability. An item such as D has excellent discriminative ability and would be useful in a test designed, for example, to select applicants on the basis of some cutoff score. However, such an item might not be desirable in a test designed to provide detailed information on testtaker ability across all ability levels. This might be the case, for example, in a diagnostic reading or arithmetic test.

Item response theory You may recall our mention of item response theory (IRT) in Chapter 5. Actually, IRT is not a single theory; rather, IRT refers to a number of test development models that are collectively referred to by names (besides *item response theory*) such as *latent-trait theory,* the *latent-trait model,* and the *Rasch model,* among others. This family of test development models and procedures relies on complex mathematical models to evaluate how a testtaker's performance on a test is interpreted relative to predicted test performance. For example, one variety of IRT was developed by the Danish mathematician, Georg Rasch. Now widely used in educational assessment, the **Rasch model** offers a way to model the probability that a person with X ability will be able to perform at a level of Y. Stated in terms of personality assessment, it models the probability that a person with X amount of a particular personality trait will exhibit Y amount of that trait on a personality test designed to measure it. Although generally viewed as a more sophisticated model of test development than classical test theory (Mitchell, 1999), latent-trait models seem to have garnered more use from large-scale users of tests than from everyday, mom-and-pop researchers and clinicians. Perhaps the most compelling reason latent-trait theory is not more widely used in everyday applications has to do with the very technical and complex issues that must be addressed in order to determine whether the test data accumulated will fit the mathematics of the model (see, for example, Chapter 12 in Bond & Fox, 2001).

Issues of usage aside for the moment, a frequently asked question concerns why the model is referred to as *latent-trait*. To understand why, consider that a test is typically designed to provide an estimate of the amount of knowledge or ability, or strength of a particular trait,[5] possessed by the testtaker. The variable on which performance on the test is presumed to depend—be it knowledge, ability, a personality trait, or something

---

5. See Chapter 12 in Bond & Fox (2001).

else—is never directly measurable itself. An estimate of the amount of the variable is obtained through the test. In this way, *latent traits* are like the factors in factor analysis, which are not directly measured but are reflected in the test items. According to **latent-trait theory,** this underlying, unobservable variable—this latent trait—is unidimensional. Presumably, all the items on a test measure this trait.

An application of the latent-trait model can be found in the Illness Causality Scale, a measure of children's understanding of illness (Sayer et al., 1993). Researching the validity of the test, the authors expected that three latent traits would be found. These three latent traits were labeled *verbal intelligence, level of cognitive development,* and *understanding of illness.* The test authors sought to demonstrate the presence of each of these latent traits by a correlational study. The Illness Causality Scale was correlated with other scales, each of which represented a measure of one of the latent traits. For example, the authors found that the Illness Causality Scale was moderately correlated with a scale measuring verbal intelligence, presumably because the two scales share the latent trait of verbal intelligence.

Latent-trait models differ in some important ways from classical "true score" test theory. For example, in classical true score test theory, no assumptions are made about the frequency distribution of test scores. By contrast, such assumptions are inherent in latent-trait models. As Allen and Yen (1979, p. 240) put it, "Latent-trait theories propose models that describe how the latent trait influences performance on each test item. Unlike test scores or true scores, latent traits theoretically can take on values from $-\infty$ to $+\infty$ [minus to plus infinity]."

The widespread applicability of latent-trait models to psychological tests has been questioned by some theoreticians. It has been argued, for example, that the assumption of test unidimensionality is violated when many psychological tests are considered. It has been further argued that even the same item on a psychological test may be tapping different abilities from the same testtaker, depending on the life experiences of the testtaker. Despite lingering theoretical questions, latent-trait models appear to be playing an increasingly dominant role in the design and development of new tests and testing programs. This is particularly the case with respect to large testing firms, state agencies, and school districts as they rely on IRT methods to construct, analyze, and score major achievement, proficiency, entrance, and professional licensure examinations.[6]

Other Considerations in Item Analysis

Guessing   In achievement testing, the problem of how to handle testtaker **guessing** is one that has eluded any universally acceptable solution. It is true that a number of different procedures purporting to be corrections for guessing have been published, but none has proven to be entirely satisfactory. The reason is that the problem of guessing is more complex than it first appears. To understand why, consider the following three criteria that any correction for guessing must meet, as well as the interacting problems that must be addressed:

1.   A correction for guessing must recognize that when a respondent guesses at an answer on an achievement test, the guess is not typically made on a totally random basis. It is more reasonable to assume that the testtaker's guess is based on some knowledge of the subject matter and the ability to rule out one or more of the dis-

---

6. Obstacles to the use of these techniques in more "everyday" assessment applications have been discussed by Reise and Henson (2003).

tractor alternatives. However, the individual testtaker's amount of knowledge of the subject matter will vary from one item to the next.

2. A correction for guessing must also deal with the problem of omitted items. Sometimes, instead of guessing, the testtaker will simply omit a response to an item. Should the omitted item be scored "wrong"? Should the omitted item be excluded from the item analysis? Should the omitted item be scored as if the testtaker had made a random guess? Exactly how should the omitted item be handled?

3. Just as some people may be luckier than others in front of a Las Vegas slot machine, so some testtakers may be luckier than others in guessing the choices that are keyed correct. Any correction for guessing may seriously underestimate or overestimate the effects of guessing for lucky and unlucky testtakers.

A number of different solutions to the problem of guessing have been proposed. In addition to proposed interventions at the level of test scoring through the use of corrections for guessing (referred to as *formula scores*), intervention has also been proposed at the level of test instructions. Testtakers may be instructed to provide an answer only when they are certain (no guessing) or to complete all items and guess when in doubt. Individual differences in testtakers' willingness to take risks result in problems for this approach to guessing (Slakter et al., 1975). Some people who don't mind taking risks may guess even when instructed not to do so. Others who tend to be reluctant to take risks refuse to guess under any circumstances. This creates a situation in which one's predisposition to take risks can affect one's test score.

To date, no solution to the problem of guessing has been deemed entirely satisfactory. The responsible test developer addresses the problem of guessing by including in the test manual (1) explicit instructions regarding this point for the examiner to convey to the examinees, and (2) specific instructions for scoring and interpreting omitted items.

Guessing on responses to personality and related psychological tests is not thought of as a great problem. Although it may sometimes be difficult to choose the most appropriate alternative on a selected-response format personality test (particularly one with forced-choice items), the presumption is that the testtaker does indeed make the best choice.

> **JUST THINK . . .**
>
> The prevailing logic among measurement professionals is that when testtakers guess at an answer on a personality test in a selected-response format, the testtaker is making the best choice. Why should professionals continue to believe this? Alternatively, why might they modify their view?

Item fairness Just as we may speak of biased tests, we may speak of biased test items. A **biased test item** is an item that favors one particular group of examinees in relation to another when differences in group ability are controlled (Camilli & Shepard, 1985). Many different methods may be used to identify biased test items. In fact, evidence suggests that the choice of item-analysis method may affect determinations of item bias (Ironson & Subkoviak, 1979).

Item-characteristic curves may be used to identify biased items. Specific items are identified as biased in a statistical sense if they exhibit differential item functioning. Differential item functioning is exemplified by different shapes of item-characteristic curves for different groups (say, men and women) even though the two groups do not differ in total test score (Mellenbergh, 1994). If an item is to be considered fair to different groups of testtakers, the item-characteristic curves for the different groups should not be significantly different:

> The essential rationale of this ICC criterion of item bias is that any persons showing the same ability as measured by the whole test should have the same probability of passing

any given item that measures that ability, regardless of the person's race, social class, sex, or any other background characteristics. In other words, the same proportion of persons from each group should pass any given item of the test, provided that the persons all earned the same total score on the test. (Jensen, 1980, p. 444)

A determination of the presence of differential item functioning requires a statistical test of the null hypothesis of no difference between the item-characteristic curves of the two groups. Advantages and problems of different statistical tests for detecting differential item functioning continue to be debated (Raju et al., 1993). Items that show significant difference in item-characteristic curves should be either revised or eliminated from the test. If a relatively large number of items biased in favor of one group coexist with approximately the same number of items biased in favor of another group, it cannot be claimed that the test measures the same abilities in the two groups. This is true even though overall test scores of the individuals in the two groups may not be significantly different (Jensen, 1980).

Speed tests   Item analyses of tests taken under speed conditions yield misleading or uninterpretable results. The closer an item is to the end of the test, the more difficult it may appear to be. This is the case because testtakers simply may not get to items near the end of the test before time runs out.

In a similar vein, measures of item discrimination may be artificially high for late-appearing items. This is so because testtakers who know the material better may work faster and are thus more likely to answer the later items. Items appearing late in a speed test are consequently more likely to show positive item-total correlations because of the select group of examinees reaching those items.

Given these problems, how can items on a speed test be analyzed? Perhaps the most obvious solution is to restrict the item analysis of items on a speed test only to the items completed by the testtaker. However, this solution is *not* recommended, for at least three reasons: (1) Item analyses of the later items would be based on a progressively smaller number of testtakers, yielding progressively less reliable results; (2) if the more knowledgeable examinees reach the later items, part of the analysis is based on all testtakers and part of the analysis is based on a selected sample; and (3) because the more knowledgeable testtakers are more likely to score correctly, their performance will make items occurring toward the end of the test appear easier than they are.

If speed is not an important element of the ability being measured by the test, and because speed as a variable may produce misleading information about item performance, the test developer ideally should administer the test to be item-analyzed with generous time limits to complete the test. Once the item analysis is completed, norms should be established using the speed conditions intended for use with the test in actual practice.

Qualitative Item Analysis

Test users have had a long-standing interest in understanding test performance from the perspective of testtakers (Fiske, 1967; Mosier, 1947). The calculation of item-validity, item-reliability, and other such quantitative indices represents one approach to understanding testtakers. Another general class of research methods is referred to as *qualitative*. In contrast to quantitative methods, **qualitative methods** are techniques of data generation and analysis that rely primarily on verbal rather than mathematical or statistical procedures. Encouraging testtakers on a group or individual basis to discuss aspects of their testtaking experience is, in essence, eliciting or generating "data" (words). These data may then be used by test developers, users, and publishers to improve various aspects of the test.

Table 7–3
Potential Areas of Exploration by Means of Qualitative Item Analysis

This table lists sample topics and questions of possible interest to test users. The questions could be raised either orally or in writing shortly after a test's administration. Additionally, depending upon the objectives of the test user, the questions could be placed into other formats, such as true-false or multiple choice. Depending upon the specific questions to be asked and the number of testtakers being sampled, the test user may wish to guarantee the anonymity of the respondents.

Topic	Sample Question
Cultural Sensitivity	Did you feel that any item or aspect of this test was discriminatory with respect to any group of people? If so, why?
Face Validity	Did the test appear to measure what you expected it would measure? If not, what was contrary to your expectations?
Test Administrator	Did the behavior of the test administrator affect your performance on this test in any way? If so, how?
Test Environment	Did any conditions in the room affect your performance on this test in any way? If so, how?
Test Fairness	Do you think the test was a fair test of what it sought to measure? Why or why not?
Test Language	Were there any instructions or other written aspects of the test that you had difficulty understanding?
Test Length	How did you feel about the length of the test with respect to (a) the time it took to complete and (b) the number of items?
Testtaker's Guessing	Did you guess on any of the test items? What percentage of the items would you estimate you guessed on? Did you employ any particular strategy for guessing, or was it basically random?
Testtaker's Integrity	Do you think that there was any cheating during this test? If so, please describe the methods you think may have been used.
Testtaker's Mental/Physical State Upon Entry	How would you describe your mental state going into this test? Do you think that your mental state in any way affected the test outcome? If so, how? How would you describe your physical state going into this test? Do you think that your physical state in any way affected the test outcome? If so, how?
Testtaker's Mental/Physical State During the Test	How would you describe your mental state as you took this test? Do you think that your mental state in any way affected the test outcome? If so, how? How would you describe your physical state as you took this test? Do you think that your physical state in any way affected the test outcome? If so, how?
Testtaker's Overall Impressions	What is your overall impression of this test? What suggestions would you offer the test developer for improvement?
Testtaker's Preferences	Did you find any part of the test educational, entertaining, or otherwise rewarding? What, specifically, did you like or dislike about the test? Did you find any part of the test anxiety-provoking, condescending, or otherwise upsetting? Why?
Testtaker's Preparation	How did you prepare for this test? If you were going to advise others how to prepare for it, what would you tell them?

Qualitative item analysis is a general term for various nonstatistical procedures designed to explore how individual test items work. The analysis compares individual test items to each other and to the test as a whole. In contrast to statistically based procedures, qualitative methods involve exploration of the issues through verbal means such as interviews and group discussions conducted with testtakers and other relevant parties. Some of the topics researchers may wish to explore qualitatively are summarized in Table 7–3.

On a cautionary note, it is true that in some instances, providing testtakers with the opportunity to describe a test is like providing students with the opportunity to describe their instructors. In both cases, there can be abuse of the process, especially by respondents who have extra-test (or extra-instructor) axes to grind. Respondents may be disgruntled for any number of reasons, from failure to prepare adequately for the test to disappointment in their test performance. In such cases, the opportunity to evaluate the test is an opportunity to lash out. The test, the administrator of the test, and the institution, agency, or corporation responsible for the test administration may all become objects of criticism. Testtaker questionnaires, much like other qualitative research tools, must be interpreted with an eye toward the full context of the experience for the respondent(s).

"Think aloud" test administration   An innovative approach to cognitive assessment entails having respondents verbalize thoughts as they occur. Although different researchers use different procedures (Davison et al., 1997; Hurlburt, 1997; Klinger, 1978), this general approach has been employed in a variety of research contexts, including studies of adjustment (Kendall et al., 1979; Sutton-Simon & Goldfried, 1979), problem solving (Duncker, 1945; Montague, 1993), educational remediation (Randall et al., 1986), and clinical intervention (Gann & Davison, 1997; Haaga et al., 1993; White et al., 1992).

Cohen et al. (1988) proposed the use of **"think aloud" test administration** as a qualitative research tool designed to shed light on the testtaker's thought processes during the administration of a test. On a one-to-one basis with an examiner, examinees are asked to take a test, thinking aloud as they respond to each item. If the test is designed to measure achievement, such verbalizations may be useful in assessing not only if certain students (such as low or high scorers on previous examinations) are misinterpreting a particular item but also why and how they are misinterpreting the item. If the test is designed to measure personality or some aspect of it, the "think aloud" technique may also yield valuable insights regarding the way individuals perceive, interpret, and respond to the items.

Expert panels   In addition to interviewing testtakers individually or in groups, **expert panels** may also provide qualitative analyses of test items. A **sensitivity review** is a study of test items typically conducted during the test development process, in which items are examined for fairness to all prospective testtakers and for the presence of offensive language, stereotypes, or situations. Sensitivity reviews have become a standard part of contemporary test development (Reckase, 1996). For example, in an effort to root out any possible bias in the Stanford Achievement Test Series, the test publisher formed an advisory panel of 12 minority group members, each a prominent member of the educational community. Panel members met with the publisher to obtain an understanding of the history and philosophy of the test battery and to discuss and define the problem of bias (Stanford Special Report, 1992). Some of the possible forms of content bias that may find their way into any achievement test were identified as follows:

> *Status:* Are the members of a particular group shown in situations that do not involve authority or leadership?
>
> *Stereotype:* Are the members of a particular group portrayed as uniformly having certain: (1) aptitudes, (2) interests, (3) occupations, or (4) personality characteristics?
>
> *Familiarity:* Is there greater opportunity on the part of one group to: (1) be acquainted with the vocabulary, or (2) experience the situation presented by an item?
>
> *Offensive Choice of Words:* (1) Has a demeaning label been applied, or (2) has a male term been used where a neutral term could be substituted?
>
> *Other:* Panel members were asked to be specific regarding any other indication of bias they detected. (Stanford Special Report, 1992, pp. 3–4)

On the basis of qualitative information from an expert panel or testtakers themselves, a test user or developer may elect to modify or revise the test. In this sense, revision typically entails rewording items, deleting items, or creating new items. Note that there is another meaning of *test revision* beyond that associated with a stage in the development of a new test. After a period of time, many existing tests are scheduled for republication in new versions or editions. The development process that the test undergoes as it is modified and revised is called, not surprisingly, *test revision*. The time, effort, and expense entailed by this latter variety of test revision may be quite extensive. For example, the revision may involve an age extension of the population for which the test is designed for use—upward for older testtakers and/or downward for younger testtakers—and corresponding new validation studies.

Test Revision

We now consider aspects of test revision as a stage in the development of a new test. Next, we consider aspects of test revision in the context of modifying an existing test to create a new edition. Much of our discussion of test revision in the development of a brand-new test may also apply to the development of subsequent editions of existing tests, depending on just how revised the revision really is.

Test Revision as a Stage in New Test Development

Having conceptualized the new test, constructed it, tried it out, and item-analyzed it both quantitatively and qualitatively, what remains is to act judiciously on all the information and mold the test into its final form. A tremendous amount of information is generated at the item-analysis stage, particularly given that a developing test may have hundreds of items. On the basis of that information, some items from the original item pool will be eliminated and others will be rewritten. How is information about the difficulty, validity, reliability, discrimination, and bias of test items, along with information from the item-characteristic curves, integrated and used to revise the test?

There are probably as many ways of approaching test revision as there are test developers. One approach is to characterize each item according to its strengths and weaknesses. Some items may be highly reliable but lack criterion validity, whereas other items may be purely unbiased but too easy. Some items will be found to have many weaknesses, making them prime candidates for deletion or revision. For example, very difficult items have a restricted range; all or almost all testtakers get them wrong. Very difficult items will tend to lack reliability and validity because of their restricted range. The same is true of very easy items.

Test developers may find that they must balance various strengths and weaknesses across items. For example, if many otherwise good items tend to be somewhat easy, the test developer may purposefully include some more difficult items, even if the items have other problems. Those more difficult items may be specifically targeted for rewriting. The purpose of the test also influences revising; for example, if the test will be used to influence major decisions about educational placement or employment, the test developer should be scrupulously concerned with item bias. If there is a need to identify the most highly skilled individuals among those being tested, items demonstrating excellent item discrimination, leading to the best possible test discrimination, will be made a priority.

As revision proceeds, the advantage of writing a large item pool becomes more and more apparent. Poor items can be eliminated in favor of those that were shown on the test tryout to be good items. Even when working with a large item pool, the revising test developer must be aware of the domain the test should sample. For some aspects of the domain, it may be particularly difficult to write good items, and blind deletion of all poorly functioning items could cause those aspects of the domain to remain untested.

Having balanced all these concerns, the test developer comes out of the revision stage with a better test. The next step is to administer the revised test under standardized conditions to a second appropriate sample of examinees. On the basis of an item analysis of data derived from this administration of the second draft of the test, the test developer may deem the test to be in its finished form. Once the test is in finished form, the test's norms may be developed from the data, and the test will be said to have been "standardized" on this (second) sample.

Standardization can be viewed as "the process employed to introduce objectivity and uniformity into test administration, scoring and interpretation" (Robertson, 1990, p. 75). A standardization sample represents the group(s) of individuals with whom examinees' performance will be compared. For norm-referenced tests, it is important that this sample be representative of the population on those variables that might affect performance. Ability tests, for example, are developed so that the standardization group is representative of the population on such characteristics as age, gender, geographic region, type of community, ethnic group, and parent education. The latest census data are usually utilized to ensure that the standardization sample closely matches the population on these demographic characteristics.

JUST THINK . . .

Surprise! An international publisher is interested in publishing your American History Test. You've just been asked what population demographic characteristics you think it is most important to have represented in your international standardization sample. Your response?

When the item analysis of data derived from a test administration indicates that the test is not yet in finished form, the steps of revision, tryout, and item analysis are repeated until the test is satisfactory and standardization can occur. Once the test items have been finalized, professional test development procedures dictate that conclusions about the test's validity await a *cross-validation* of findings. We'll discuss cross-validation shortly; for now, let's briefly consider some of the issues surrounding the development of a new edition of an existing test.

Test Revision in the Life Cycle of an Existing Test

Time waits for no person. We all get old, and tests get old too. Just like people, some tests seem to age more gracefully than others. For example, as we will see when we study projective techniques in Chapter 12, the Rorschach Inkblots seem to have held up quite well over the years. By contrast, the stimulus materials for another projective technique, the Thematic Apperception Test (TAT), are showing their age. There comes a time in the life of most tests when the test will be revised in some way or its publication will be discontinued. When is that time?

No hard-and-fast rules exist for when to revise a test. APA (1996, Standard 3.18) offered the general suggestion that an existing test be kept in its present form as long as it remains "useful," and that it be revised "when significant changes in the domain represented, or new conditions of test use and interpretation, make the test inappropriate for its intended use."

Practically speaking, many tests are deemed to be due for revision when any of the following conditions exist:

1. The stimulus materials look dated and current testtakers cannot relate to them.

2. The verbal content of the test, including the administration instructions and the test items, contains dated vocabulary that is not readily understood by current testtakers.

3. As popular culture changes and words take on new meanings, certain words or expressions in the test items or directions may be perceived as inappropriate or even offensive to a particular group and must therefore be changed.

4. The test norms are no longer adequate as a result of group membership changes in the population of potential testtakers.

5. The test norms are no longer adequate as a result of age-related shifts in the abilities measured over time, and an age extension of the norms (upward, downward, or in both directions) is necessary.

6. The reliability or the validity of the test, as well as the effectiveness of individual test items, can be significantly improved by a revision.

7. The theory on which the test was originally based has been improved significantly, and the changes should be reflected in the design and content of the test.

The steps to revise an existing test parallel those to create a brand-new one. In the test conceptualization phase, the test developer must think through the objectives of the revision and how they can best be met. In the test construction phase, the proposed changes are made. Test tryout, item analysis, and test revision (in the sense of making final refinements) follow. While all this sounds relatively easy and straightforward, creating a revised edition of an existing test can be a most ambitious undertaking. For example, recalling the revision of a test called the Strong Vocational Interest Blank, Campbell (1972) reflected that the process of conceiving the revision started about ten years prior to actual revision work, and the revision work itself ran for another ten years. Butcher (2000) echoed these thoughts in an article that provided a detailed "inside view" of the process of revising a widely used personality test called the MMPI. Others have also noted the sundry considerations that must be kept in mind when contemplating the revision of an existing instrument (Adams, 2000; Okazaki & Sue, 2000; Reise et al., 2000; Silverstein & Nelson, 2000).

Once the successor to an established test is published, there are inevitably questions about the equivalence of the two editions. For example, does a measured full-scale IQ of 110 on the first edition of an intelligence test mean exactly the same thing as a full-scale IQ of 110 on the second edition? A number of researchers have advised caution in making interpretations from an original and a revised edition of a test, despite similarities in appearance (Reitan & Wolfson, 1990; Strauss et al., 2000). Even if the content of individual items does not change, the context in which the items appear may change, thus opening up the possibility of significant differences in testtakers' interpretation of the meaning of the items. Simply developing a computerized version of a test may make a difference, at least in terms of test scores achieved by members of different populations (Ozonoff, 1995).

Formal item-analysis methods must be employed to evaluate the stability of items between revisions of the same test (Knowles & Condon, 2000). Ultimately, scores on a test and on its updated version may not be directly comparable. As Tulsky and Ledbetter (2000) summed it up in the context of original and revised versions of tests of cognitive ability, "Any improvement or decrement in performance between the two cannot automatically be viewed as a change in examinee performance" (p. 260).

A key step in the development of all tests—brand-new or revised editions—is cross-validation. Next we discuss that important process as well as a more recent trend in test publishing, *co-validation.*

Cross-validation and co-validation   The term **cross-validation** refers to the revalidation of a test on a sample of testtakers other than those on whom test performance was originally found to be a valid predictor of some criterion. We expect that items selected for the final version of the test (in part because of their high correlations with a criterion measure) will have smaller item validities when administered to a second sample of testtakers. This is so because of the operation of chance. The decrease in item validities that inevitably occurs after cross-validation of findings is referred to as **validity shrinkage.** Such shrinkage is expected and is viewed as integral to the test development process. Further, such shrinkage is infinitely preferable to a scenario wherein (spuriously) high item validities are published in a test manual as a result of the inappropriate use of the identical sample of testtakers for test standardization and cross-validation of findings. When such scenarios occur, test users will typically be let down by lower-than-expected test validity. The test manual accompanying commercially prepared tests should outline the test development procedures used. Reliability information, including test-retest reliability and internal consistency estimates, should be reported along with evidence of the test's validity. Articles discussing cross-validation of tests are often published in scholarly journals. For example, Bank et al. (2000) provided a detailed account of the cross-validation of an instrument used to screen for cognitive impairment in older adults.

Not to be confused with "cross-validation," **co-validation** may be defined as a test validation process conducted on two or more tests using the same sample of testtakers. When used in conjunction with the creation of norms or the revision of existing norms, this process may also be referred to as **co-norming.** A current trend among test publishers who publish more than one test designed for use with the same population is to co-validate and/or co-norm tests. Co-validation of new tests and revisions of existing tests can be beneficial in various ways to all parties in the assessment enterprise. Co-validation is beneficial to test publishers because it is economical. During the process of validating a test, many prospective testtakers must first be identified. In many instances, after being identified as a possible participant in the validation study, a person will be prescreened for suitability by means of a face-to-face or telephone interview. This costs money, which is charged to the budget for developing the test. Both money and time are saved if the same person is deemed suitable in the validation studies for multiple tests and can be scheduled to participate with a minimum of administrative preliminaries. Qualified examiners to administer the test and other personnel to assist in scoring, interpretation, and statistical analysis must also be identified, retained, and scheduled to participate in the project. The cost of retaining such professional personnel on a per-test basis is kept down when the work is done for multiple tests simultaneously.

Beyond benefits to the publisher, co-validation can hold potentially important benefits for test users and testtakers. Many tests that tend to be used together are published by the same publisher. For example, the third edition of the Wechsler Adult Intelligence Scale (WAIS-III) and the third edition of the Wechsler Memory Scale (WMS-III) might be used together in the clinical evaluation of an adult. And let's suppose that after an evaluation using these two tests, differences in measured memory ability emerged as a function of the test used. Had these two tests been normed on different samples, then sampling error would be one possible reason for the observed differences in measured memory. However, because the two tests were normed on the same population, sampling error as a causative factor has been greatly minimized, if not eliminated completely. A clinician might look to factors such as differences in the way that the two tests measure memory. One test, for example, might measure short-term memory using the recall of number sequences. The other test might measure the same variable using recalled comprehension of short reading passages. How each test measures the variable under study may yield important diagnostic insights.

On the other hand, consider two co-normed tests that are almost identical in how they measure the variable under study. With sampling error minimized by the co-norming process, a test user can be that much more confident that the scores on the two tests are comparable.

Quality assurance during test revision   Once upon a time, a long time ago in Manhattan, the senior author of this text (Cohen) held the title of senior psychologist at Bellevue Hospital. Among other duties, senior psychologists supervised clinical psychology interns in all phases of their professional development, including the administration of psychological tests:

> One day, in the course of reviewing a test protocol handed in by an intern, something very peculiar caught my eye. On a subtest that had several tasks scored on the basis of number of seconds to completion, all of the recorded times on the protocol were in multiples of 5 (as in 10 seconds, 15 seconds, etc.). I had never seen a protocol like that. All of the completed protocols I had seen previously had recorded completion times with no identifiable pattern or multiple (like 12 seconds, 17 seconds, 9 seconds, etc.). Curious about the way that the protocol had been scored, I called in the intern to discuss it.
>
> As it turned out, the intern had not equipped herself with either a stopwatch or a watch with a second-hand before administering this test. She had ignored this mandatory bit of preparation prior to test administration. Lacking any way to record the exact number of seconds it took to complete each task, the intern said she had "estimated" the number of seconds. Estimating under such circumstances is not permitted, because it violates the standardized procedure set forth in the manual. Beyond that, estimating could easily result in the testtaker either earning or failing to earn bonus points for (inaccurately) timed scores. The intern was advised of the error of her ways, and the patient was retested.

Well, that's one "up close and personal" example of quality control in psychological testing at a large municipal hospital. But what mechanisms of quality assurance are put into place by test publishers in the course of standardizing a new test or restandardizing an existing test? Let's take a brief look at some quality control mechanisms for examiners, protocol scoring, and data entry. For the purpose of illustration, we draw some examples from procedures followed by the developers of the Wechsler Intelligence Scale for Children-Fourth Edition, or WISC-IV (Wechsler, 2003), a test that is discussed in greater detail in Chapter 9.

The examiner is the front-line person in test development, and it is critically important that examiners adhere to standardized procedures. In developing a new test, or in restandardizing or renorming an existing test, test developers seek to employ examiners who have experience testing members of the population targeted for the test. For example, the developers of the WISC-IV sought to

> . . . recruit examiners with extensive experience testing children and adolescents. Potential examiners completed a questionnaire by supplying information about their educational and professional experience, administration experience with various intellectual

measures, certification, and licensing status. Those selected as potential standardization examiners were very familiar with childhood assessment practices. (Wechsler, 2003, p. 22)

Although it might be desirable for every examiner to hold a doctoral degree, this simply is not feasible, given that many thousands of tests may have to be individually administered. The professional time of doctoral-level examiners tends to be at a premium—not to mention their fees. Regardless of education or experience, all examiners will be trained to administer the instrument. Training will typically take the form of written guidelines for test administration and may entail everything from classroom instruction to practice test administrations on site to videotaped demonstrations to be reviewed at home. Publishers may evaluate potential examiners by a quiz or other means to determine how well they have learned what they need to know. During the standardization of the WISC-IV, examiners were required to submit a review case prior to testing additional children. And during the course of the test's standardization, all persons selected as examiners received a periodic newsletter advising them of potential problems in test administration. The newsletter was designed to provide an ongoing way to maintain quality assurance in test administration.

In the course of test development, examiners may be involved to greater or lesser degrees in the final scoring of protocols. Regardless of whether it is the examiner or a "dedicated scorer," all persons who have responsibility for scoring protocols will typically undergo training. As with examiner training, the training for scorers may take many forms, from classroom instruction to videotaped demonstrations.

Quality assurance in the restandardization of the WISC-IV was in part maintained by having two qualified scorers rescore each protocol collected during the national tryout and standardization stages of test development. If there were discrepancies in scoring, the discrepancies were resolved by yet another scorer, referred to as a *resolver*. According to the manual, "The resolvers were selected based on their demonstration of exceptional scoring accuracy and previous scoring experience" (Wechsler, 2003, p. 22).

Another mechanism for ensuring consistency in scoring is the *anchor protocol.* An **anchor protocol** is a test protocol scored by a highly authoritative scorer, designed as a model for scoring and a mechanism for resolving scoring discrepancies. A term used to reflect a discrepancy between scoring in an anchor protocol and the scoring of another protocol is **scoring drift.** Anchor protocols were used for quality assurance in the development of the WISC-IV:

> If two independent scorers made the same scoring error on a protocol, comparison to the anchor score revealed the scoring drift. Scorers received feedback immediately to prevent repetition of the error and to correct for scoring drift. (Wechsler, 2003, p. 23)

Once protocols are scored, the data from them must be entered into a database. For quality assurance during the data entry phase of test development, test developers may employ computer programs to seek out and identify any irregularities in score reporting. For example, if a score on a particular subtest can range from a low of 1 to a high of 10, any score reported out of that range would be flagged by the computer. Additionally, a proportion of protocols can be randomly selected to make certain that the data entered from them faithfully match the data they originally contained.

And now for some "personal quality control" for students of assessment. Quiz yourself on the words contained in this chapter's *Self-Assessment* before moving on to the following chapter.

Self-Assessment

Test your understanding of elements of this chapter by seeing if you can explain each of the following terms, expressions, and abbreviations:

absolute scaling
anchor protocol
biased test item
binary-choice item
categorical scaling
class scoring (category scoring)
comparative scaling
completion item
computerized adaptive testing (CAT)
co-norming
constructed-response format
co-validation
cross-validation
essay item
expert panel
guessing
Guttman scale
ipsative scoring

internal consistency
item analysis
item bank
item branching
item-characteristic curve (ICC)
item-difficulty index
item-discrimination index
item-endorsement index
item fairness
item format
item pool
item-reliability index
item-validity index
latent-trait theory (latent-trait model)
Likert scale
matching item
multiple-choice item
pilot work

qualitative item analysis
qualitative methods
Rasch model
rating scale
scales
scaling
scalogram analysis
scoring drift
selected-response format
sensitivity review
short-answer item
summative scale
test conceptualization
test construction
test revision
test tryout
"think aloud" test administration
true/false item
validity shrinkage

Web Watch

Check out the following Web sites for more information about topics discussed in this chapter.

Likert scales
http://education.uncc.edu/rfalgozz/ADMN8699/likerttips.pdf

www.socialresearchmethods.net/kb/scallik.htm

Test items
http://siop.org/workplace/employment%20testing/testformats.htm

www.edtech.vt.edu/edtech/id/assess/items.html

Item analysis
www.statsoftinc.com/textbook/streliab.html

www.ericfacility.net/databases/ERIC_Digests/ed398237.html

Michigan State's item analysis
www.msu.edu/dept/soweb/itanhand.html#guide

Guttman scoring and scalogram analysis
www.socialresearchmethods.net/scalgutt.htm

Penn State's test design and construction
www.uts.psu.edu/Test_construction_frame.htm

Helpful PDF field guide of test approach and format
www.aea11.k12.ia.us/assessment/docs/dwafieldguide.pdf

PDF relating to computer adaptive testing
www.teamrees.com/training/comptia_adaptive.pdf

Item response theory
http://edres.org/irt/

Qualitative item analysis: professor's perspective
http://faculty.mansfield.edu/rfeil/201/item-analysis-explained.htm

Validity shrinkage
www.testconstruction.com/comp_28.htm

Test construction Web site (from the above link)
www.testconstruction.com/contents.htm

8

Intelligence and Its Measurement

As long as there has been a discipline of psychology, psychologists have had differing definitions of intelligence and how best to measure it.

In this chapter, we look at the varied ways intelligence has been defined and survey the ways it has been measured. We conclude with a discussion of a few major issues surrounding the practice of measuring intelligence, including the relationship between culture and intelligence. In Chapter 9, we look more closely at the "nuts and bolts" of intelligence tests and focus on some representative tests. The measurement of intelligence and other ability- and achievement-related constructs in preschool and educational settings is the subject of Chapter 10. We begin, however, by raising a question that logically precedes consideration of intelligence measurement issues.

JUST THINK . . .

How do *you* define intelligence?

What Is Intelligence?

We may define **intelligence** as a multifaceted capacity that manifests itself in different ways across the lifespan. In general, intelligence includes the abilities to

- acquire and apply knowledge
- reason logically
- plan effectively
- infer perceptively
- make sound judgments and solve problems
- grasp and visualize concepts
- pay attention
- be intuitive
- find the right words and thoughts with facility
- cope, adjust, and make the most of new situations

And with all of that having been said, please do not interpret this as the last word defining intelligence. Rather, think of this description of intelligence as a point of departure for reflection on the meaning of a most intriguing term, one that, as we will see, is paradoxically both simple and complex.

Most people believe they can recognize intelligence when it is expressed in observable behavior; yet a widely accepted definition has remained elusive (Neisser, 1979). It really should be defined (Neisser et al., 1996) if we are going to use the construct, design tests to measure it, and act on the basis of the test results. Beyond attempts to create a definition that incorporates "all the right words," the search for an adequate and widely acceptable definition has inspired cerebral glucose metabolism studies (Haier, 1993) and other such research on brain physiology (Vernon, 1993). Still, devising a widely acceptable definition of intelligence remains a challenge.

How do laypeople define intelligence? And how do lay definitions of intelligence contrast with those of scholars who have studied intelligence? Let's consider these questions now.

Intelligence Defined: Views of the Lay Public

Research conducted by Sternberg and his associates (Sternberg, 1981, 1982; Sternberg & Detterman, 1986; Sternberg et al., 1981) sought to shed light on how intelligence is defined by laypeople and psychologists. In one study, a total of 476 people (students, commuters, supermarket shoppers, people who answered newspaper ads, and people randomly selected from phone books) were asked to list behaviors they associated with "intelligence," "academic intelligence," "everyday intelligence," and "unintelligence." After a list of various behaviors characterizing intelligence was generated, 28 nonpsychologists in the New Haven area were asked to rate on a scale of 1 (low) to 9 (high) how characteristic each of the behaviors was for the ideal "intelligent" person, the ideal "academically intelligent" person, and the ideal "everyday intelligent" person. The views of 140 doctoral-level research psychologists who were experts in the area of intelligence were also solicited. These experts were themselves involved in research on intelligence in major universities and research centers around the United States.

All people polled in Sternberg's study had definite ideas about intelligence and the lack of it. For the nonpsychologists, the behaviors most commonly associated with intelligence were "reasons logically and well," "reads widely," "displays common sense," "keeps an open mind," and "reads with high comprehension." Leading the list of most frequently mentioned behaviors associated with unintelligence were "does not tolerate diversity of views," "does not display curiosity," and "behaves with insufficient consideration of others."

Sternberg and his colleagues grouped the list of 250 behaviors characterizing intelligence and unintelligence into subsets that were most strongly related to each other. The analysis indicated that the nonpsychologists and the experts conceived of intelligence in general as practical problem-solving ability (such as "listens to all sides of an argument"), verbal ability ("displays a good vocabulary"), and social competence ("is on time for appointments"). Each specific type of intelligence was characterized by various descriptors. "Academic intelligence" included verbal ability, problem-solving ability, and social competence, as well as specific behaviors associated with acquiring academic skills (such as "studying hard"). "Everyday intelligence" included practical problem-solving ability, social competence, character, and interest in learning and culture. In general, the researchers found a surprising degree of similarity between the experts' and laypeople's conceptions of intelligence. With respect to academic intelligence, however, the experts tended to stress motivation ("is persistent," "highly dedicated and motivated in chosen pursuits"), whereas laypeople stressed the interpersonal and social aspects of intelligence ("sensitivity to other people's needs and desires," "is frank and honest with self and others").

In another study (Siegler & Richards, 1980), students enrolled in college developmental psychology classes were asked to list behaviors associated with intelligence in infancy, childhood, and adulthood. Perhaps not surprisingly, different conceptions of intelligence as a function of developmental stage were noted. In infancy, intelligence was associated with physical coordination, awareness of people, verbal output, and attachment. In childhood, verbal facility, understanding, and characteristics of learning were most often listed. Verbal facility, use of logic, and problem solving were most frequently associated with adult intelligence.

A study conducted with first-, third-, and sixth-graders (Yussen & Kane, 1980) suggested that children also have notions about intelligence as early as first grade. Younger children's conceptions tended to emphasize interpersonal skills (acting nice, being helpful, being polite), whereas older children emphasized academic skills (reading well).

Intelligence Defined: Views of Scholars and Test Professionals

In a symposium published in the *Journal of Educational Psychology* in 1921, seventeen of the country's leading psychologists addressed the following questions: (1) What is intelligence? (2) How can it best be measured in group tests? and (3) What should be the next steps in the research? No two psychologists agreed (Thorndike et al., 1921). Six years later, Spearman (1927, p. 14) would reflect, "In truth, intelligence has become . . . a word with so many meanings that finally it has none." And decades after the symposium was first held, Wesman (1968, p. 267) concluded that there appeared to be "no more general agreement as to the nature of intelligence or the most valid means of measuring intelligence today than was the case 50 years ago."

JUST THINK . . .

Must professionals agree on a definition of intelligence?

As Neisser (1979) observed, although the *Journal* felt that the symposium would generate vigorous discussion, it generated more heat than light and led to a general increase in exasperation with discussion on the subject. Symptomatic of that exasperation was an unfortunate statement by a historian of psychology and—nonpsychometrician—experimental psychologist, Edwin G. Boring. Boring (1923, p. 5) attempted to quell the argument by pronouncing that "intelligence is what the tests test." Although such a view is not entirely devoid of merit (see Neisser, 1979, p. 225), it is an unsatisfactory, incomplete, and circular definition. The thoughts of some other behavioral scientists throughout history follow, as well as more contemporary views.

Francis Galton Among other accomplishments, Sir Francis Galton is remembered as the first person to publish on the heritability of intelligence, thus framing the contemporary nature/nurture debate (McGue, 1997). Galton (1883) believed that the most intelligent persons were those equipped with the best sensory abilities. This position was intuitively appealing because, as Galton observed, "The only information that reaches us concerning outward events appears to pass through the avenues of our senses; and the more perceptive the senses are of difference, the larger is the field upon which our judgment and intelligence can act" (p. 27). Following this logic, tests of visual acuity or hearing ability are, in a sense, tests of intelligence. Galton attempted to measure this sort of intelligence in many of the sensorimotor and other perception-related tests he devised. In this respect, he anticipated more contemporary physiological research that examines,

JUST THINK . . .

What was wrong with Galton's logic defining the most intelligent people?

for example, the relationship between intelligence and speed of neural conductivity (Reed & Jensen, 1992, 1993).

Alfred Binet   Although his test at the turn of the century had the effect of launching the testing movement, intelligence and otherwise, Alfred Binet did not leave us an explicit definition of intelligence. He did write that the components of intelligence included reasoning, judgment, memory, and abstraction (Varon, 1936). In papers critical of Galton's approach to intellectual assessment, Binet and a colleague called for more complex measurements of intellectual ability (Binet & Henri, 1895a, 1895b, 1895c). Unlike Galton, Binet was motivated by the very demanding and challenging task of developing a procedure for identifying intellectually limited Parisian schoolchildren who could not benefit from a regular instructional program and required special educational experiences. Galton viewed intelligence as a number of distinct processes or abilities that could be assessed only by separate tests. By contrast, Binet argued that when one solves a particular problem, the abilities used cannot be separated but rather interact to produce the solution. For example, memory and concentration interact when a subject is asked to repeat digits presented orally. When analyzing a testtaker's response to such a task, it is difficult to determine the relative contribution of memory and concentration to the successful solution. This difficulty is the reason that Binet called for more complex measurements of intellectual ability.

David Wechsler   David Wechsler's conceptualization of intelligence can perhaps best be summed up in his own words:

> Intelligence, operationally defined, is the aggregate or global capacity of the individual to act purposefully, to think rationally and to deal effectively with his environment. It is aggregate or global because it is composed of elements or abilities which, though not entirely independent, are qualitatively differentiable. By measurement of these abilities, we ultimately evaluate intelligence. But intelligence is not identical with the mere sum of these abilities, however inclusive. . . . The only way we can evaluate it quantitatively is by the measurement of the various aspects of these abilities. (1958, p. 7)

Elsewhere, Wechsler added that there are nonintellective factors that must be taken into account when assessing intelligence (Kaufman, 1990). Included among those factors are "capabilities more of the nature of conative, affective, or personality traits (which) include such traits as drive, persistence, and goal awareness (as well as) an individual's potential to perceive and respond to social, moral and aesthetic values" (Wechsler, 1975, p. 136). Binet also had observed that a comprehensive study of intelligence involved the study of personality as well.

JUST THINK . . .

What is the role of personality in measured intelligence?

Jean Piaget   Since the early 1960s, the theoretical research of the Swiss developmental psychologist Jean Piaget (1954, 1971) has received increasing attention. Piaget's research focused on the development of cognition in children: how children think, how they understand themselves and the world around them, and how they reason and solve problems. For Piaget, intelligence may be conceived of as a kind of evolving biological adaptation to the outside world. As cognitive skills are gained, adaptation (at a symbolic level) increases, and mental trial and error replaces actual physical trial and error. Yet, according to Piaget, the process of cognitive development is thought to occur neither solely through maturation nor solely through learning. He believed that as a consequence of interaction with the environment, psychological structures become reorganized.

Piaget described four stages of cognitive development through which, he theorized, all of us pass during our lifetimes. Although individuals can move through these stages at different rates and ages, he believed that their order was unchangeable. Piaget viewed the unfolding of these stages of cognitive development as the result of the interaction of biological factors and learning.

According to this theory, biological aspects of mental development are governed by inherent maturational mechanisms. As individual stages are reached and passed through, the child also has experiences within the environment. Each new experience, according to Piaget, requires some form of cognitive organization or reorganization in a mental structure called a *schema*. More specifically, Piaget used the term **schema** to refer to an organized action or mental structure that, when applied to the world, leads to knowing or understanding. Infants are born with several simple **schemata** (the plural of schema), including sucking and grasping. Learning initially by grasping and by putting almost anything in their mouths, infants use these schemata to understand and appreciate their world. As the infant grows older, schemata become more complicated and are tied less to overt action than to mental transformations. For example, adding a series of numbers requires mental transformation of numbers to arrive at the correct sum. Infants, children, and adults continue to apply schemata to objects and events to achieve understanding, and these schemata are constantly adjusted.

Piaget hypothesized that learning occurs through two basic mental operations: **assimilation** (actively organizing new information so that it fits in with what already is perceived and thought) and **accommodation** (changing what is already perceived or thought, to fit in with new information). For example, a child who sees a butterfly and calls it a "bird" has assimilated the idea of butterfly into an already existing mental structure, "bird." However, when the new concept of "butterfly," separate from "bird," has also been formed, the mental operation of *accommodation* has been employed. Piaget also stressed the importance of physical activities and social peer interaction in promoting a disequilibrium that represents the process by which mental structures change. Disequilibrium causes the individual to discover new information, perceptions, and communication skills.

The four periods of cognitive development, each representing a more complex form of cognitive organization, are outlined in Table 8–1. The stages range from the sensorimotor period, wherein infants' thoughts are dominated by their perceptions, to the formal operations period, wherein an individual has the ability to construct theories and make logical deductions without direct experience.

A major thread running through the theories of Binet, Wechsler, and Piaget is a focus on interactionism. **Interactionism** refers to the complex concept by which heredity and environment are presumed to interact to influence the development of one's intelligence. As we will see, other theorists have focused on other aspects of intelligence. In **factor-analytic theories,** the focus is squarely on identifying the ability or groups of abilities deemed to constitute intelligence. In **information-processing theories,** the focus is on identifying the specific mental processes that constitute intelligence.

Factor-Analytic Theories of Intelligence

Factor analysis is a group of statistical techniques designed to determine the existence of underlying relationships between sets of variables, including test scores. In search of a definition of intelligence, theorists have used factor analysis to study correlations between tests measuring varied abilities presumed to reflect the underlying attribute of in-

Table 8–1
Piaget's Stages of Cognitive Development

Stage	Age Span	Characteristics of Thought
Sensorimotor Period	Birth–2 years of age	Child develops ability to exhibit goal-directed, intentional behavior; develops the capacity to coordinate and integrate input from the five senses; acquires the capacity to recognize the world and its objects as permanent entities (that is, the infant develops "object permanence").
Preoperational Period	2–6 years of age	Child's understanding of concepts is based largely on what is seen; the child's comprehension of a situation, an event, or an object is typically based on a single, usually the most obvious, perceptual aspect of the stimulus; thought is irreversible (child focuses on static states of reality and cannot understand relations between states; for example, child believes the quantities of a set of beads change if the beads are pushed together or spread apart); animistic thinking (attributing human qualities to nonhuman objects and events).
Concrete Operations Period	7–12 years of age	Reversibility of thought now appears; conservation of thought (certain attributes of the world remain stable despite some modification in appearance); part-whole problems and serial ordering tasks can now be solved (able to put ideas in rank order); can deal only with relationships and things with which he or she has direct experience; able to look at more than one aspect of a problem and able to clearly differentiate between present and historical time.
Formal Operations Period	12 years of age and older	Increased ability to abstract and to deal with ideas independent of his or her own experience; greater capacity to generate hypotheses and test them in a systematic fashion ("if-then" statements, more alternatives); able to think about several variables acting together and their combined effects; can evaluate own thought; applies learning to new problems in a deductive way.

telligence. As early as 1904, the British psychologist Charles Spearman pioneered new techniques to measure intercorrelations between tests. He found that measures of intelligence tended to correlate to various degrees with each other. Spearman (1927) formalized these observations into an influential theory of general intelligence that postulated the existence of a general intellectual ability factor (referred to with an italicized, lowercase *g*), which is partially tapped by all other mental abilities. This theory is sometimes referred to as a **two-factor theory of intelligence,** with *g* representing the portion of the variance that all intelligence tests have in common, and the remaining portions of the variance being accounted for either by specific components (*s*), or by error components (*e*) of this general factor (Figure 8–1). Tests that exhibited high, positive correlations with other intelligence tests were thought to be highly saturated with *g*, while tests with low or moderate correlations with other intelligence tests were thought of as possible measures of specific factors (such as visual or motor ability). The greater the magnitude of *g* in a test of intelligence, the better the test was thought to predict overall intelligence.

Spearman (1927) conceived of the basis of the *g* factor as some type of general electrochemical mental energy available to the brain for problem solving. In addition, it was associated with facility in thinking of one's own experience and in making observations and extracting principles. It was *g* rather than *s* that was assumed to afford the best prediction of overall intelligence. Abstract-reasoning problems were thought to be the best measures of *g* in formal tests. As Spearman and his students continued their research, they acknowledged the existence of an intermediate class of factors common to a group of activities but not to all. This class of factors, called **group factors,** is neither as general

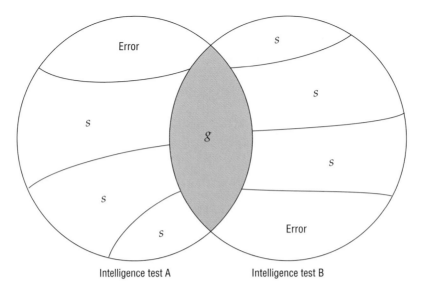

Figure 8–1
Spearman's Two-Factor Theory of Intelligence

Here, g *stands for a general intelligence factor, and* s *stands for a specific factor of intelligence (specific to a single intellectual activity only).*

as g nor as specific as s. Examples of these broad group factors include linguistic, mechanical, and arithmetical abilities.

Other theorists attempted to "dig deeper," to be even more specific about identifying and describing factors other than g in intelligence. The number of factors listed to define intelligence in a factor-analytic theory of intelligence may depend, in part, on just how specific the theory is in terms of defining discrete cognitive abilities. These abilities may be conceived of in many ways, from very broad to highly specific. As an example, consider that one researcher has identified an ability "to repeat a chain of verbally presented numbers" that he labels "Factor R." Another researcher analyzes Factor R into three "facilitating abilities" or subfactors, which she labels "ability to process sound" ("R1"), "ability to retain verbally presented stimuli" ("R2"), and "speed of processing verbally presented stimuli" ("R3"). Both researchers present factor-analytic evidence to support their respective positions.[1] Which of these two models will prevail? All other things being equal, it will probably be the model that is perceived as having the greater real-world application, the greater intuitive appeal in terms of how intelligence should be defined, and the greater amount of empirical support.

Many multiple-factor models of intelligence have been proposed. Some of these models, such as that developed by Guilford (1967), have sought to explain mental activ-

JUST THINK . . .

Is it possible to develop an intelligence test that does not tap *g*?

---

1. Recall that factor analysis may take many forms. In exploratory factor analysis, the researcher essentially explores what relationships exist. In confirmatory factor analysis, the researcher is typically testing the viability of a proposed model or theory. Some factor-analytic studies are conducted on the subtests of a single test (such as a Wechsler test), while other studies are conducted on subtests from two (or more) tests (such as the current versions of a Wechsler test and the Binet test). The type of factor analysis employed by a theorist may well be the tool that will present that theorist's conclusions in the best possible light.

ities by deemphasizing, if not eliminating, any reference to g. Thurstone (1938) initially conceived of intelligence as being composed of seven "primary abilities." However, after designing tests to measure these abilities and noting a moderate correlation between the tests, Thurstone became convinced it was difficult if not impossible to develop an intelligence test that did not tap g. Gardner (1983, 1994) developed a theory of multiple (seven, actually) intelligences: logical-mathematical, bodily-kinesthetic, linguistic, musical, spatial, interpersonal, and intrapersonal. Gardner (1983) described the last two as follows:

> Interpersonal intelligence is the ability to understand other people: what motivates them, how they work, how to work cooperatively with them. Successful sales people, politicians, teachers, clinicians, and religious leaders are all likely to be individuals with high degrees of interpersonal intelligence. Intrapersonal intelligence, a seventh kind of intelligence, is a correlative ability, turned inward. It is a capacity to form an accurate, veridical model of oneself and to be able to use that model to operate effectively in life. (p. 9)

Aspects of Gardner's writings, particularly his descriptions of **interpersonal intelligence** and **intrapersonal intelligence,** have found expression in popular books written by others on the subject of so-called **emotional intelligence.** But whether or not constructs related to empathy and self-understanding qualify more for the study of emotion and personality than the study of intelligence has been a subject of debate (Davies et al., 1998).

In recent years, a theory of intelligence first proposed by Raymond B. Cattell (1941, 1971) and subsequently modified by Horn (Cattell & Horn, 1978; Horn & Cattell, 1966, 1967) has received increasing attention from test developers and test users. As originally conceived by Cattell, the theory postulated the existence of two major types of cognitive abilities: crystallized intelligence and fluid intelligence. The abilities that make up **crystallized intelligence** (symbolized Gc) include acquired skills and knowledge that are dependent on exposure to a particular culture as well as formal and informal education (vocabulary, for example). Retrieval of information and application of general knowledge are conceived of as elements of crystallized intelligence. The abilities that make up **fluid intelligence** (symbolized Gf) are nonverbal, relatively culture-free, and independent of specific instruction (such as memory for digits). Through the years, Horn (1968, 1985, 1988, 1991, 1994) proposed the addition of several factors: visual processing (Gv), auditory processing (Ga), quantitative processing (Gq), speed of processing (Gs), facility with reading and writing (Grw), short-term memory (Gsm), and long-term storage and retrieval (Glr). According to Horn (1989; Horn & Hofer, 1992), some of the abilities (such as Gv) are **vulnerable abilities** in that they decline with age and tend not to return to preinjury levels following brain damage. Others of these abilities (such as Gq) are **maintained abilities;** they tend not to decline with age and may return to pre-injury levels following brain damage.

Another influential multiple intelligences model based on factor-analytic studies is the **three-stratum theory of cognitive abilities** (Carroll, 1997). In geology, a stratum is a layer of rock formation having the same composition throughout. Strata (the plural of *stratum*) are illustrated in Figure 8–2, along with a representation of each of the three strata in Carroll's theory. The top stratum or level in Carroll's model is g, or general intelligence. The second stratum is composed of eight abilities and processes: fluid intelligence (Gf), crystallized intelligence (Gc), general memory and learning (Y), broad visual perception (V), broad auditory perception (U), broad retrieval capacity (R), broad cognitive speediness (S), and processing/decision speed (T). Below each of the abilities in the second stratum are many "level factors" and/or "speed factors," each different, depending on the second-level stratum to which they are linked. For example, three level

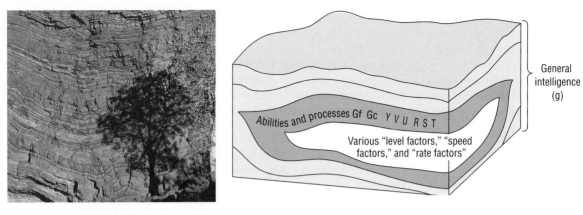

Figure 8–2
Strata in Geology and Carroll's Three-Stratum Theory

Erosion can bare multiple levels of strata on a cliff. In psychology, theory can bare the strata of hypothe-sized mental structure and function. In Carroll's three-stratum theory of cognitive ability, the first level is g, followed by a stratum made up of eight abilities and processes, followed by a stratum containing what Carroll refers to as varying "level factors" and "speed factors."

factors linked to *Gf* are general reasoning, quantitative reasoning, and Piagetian reason-ing. A speed factor linked to *Gf* is speed of reasoning. Four level factors linked to *Gc* are language development, comprehension, spelling ability, and communication ability. Two speed factors linked to *Gc* are oral fluency and writing ability. The three-stratum theory is a **hierarchical model,** meaning that all of the abil-ities listed in a stratum are subsumed by or incorporated in the strata above.

Desire for a comprehensive, agreed-upon conceptual-ization of human cognitive abilities has led some research-ers to try to extract elements of existing models to create a new, more complete model. Using factor analysis as well as other statistical tools, these researchers have attempted to modify and reconfigure existing models to better fit empir-ical evidence. One such modification that has gained in-creasing attention blends the Cattell-Horn theory with Carroll's three-stratum theory. Although this blending was not initiated by Cattell, or Horn or Carroll, it is nonetheless referred to as the Cattell-Horn-Carroll **(CHC) model** of cognitive abilities.

> **JUST THINK . . .**
>
> Moving from an analogy based on geology to one based on chemistry, think of the periodic table, which lists all known elements. Will it ever be possible to develop a comparable, generally agreed-upon "periodic table" of human abilities?

The CHC model   The Cattell-Horn and Carroll models are similar in several respects, among them the designation of broad abilities (second-stratum level in Carroll's theory), which subsume several narrow abilities (first-stratum level in Carroll's theory). Still, any prospective integration of the Cattell-Horn and Carroll models must somehow account for the differences between these two models. One difference has to do with the exis-tence of a general intellectual (*g*) factor. For Carroll, *g* is the third-stratum factor, sub-suming *Gf, Gc,* and the remaining six other broad, second-stratum abilities. By contrast, *g* has no place in the Cattell-Horn model. Another difference between the two models has to do with whether or not abilities labeled "quantitative knowledge" and "reading/ writing ability" should each be considered a distinct, broad ability as they are in the Cattell-Horn model. For Carroll, all of these abilities are first-stratum, narrow abilities.

Other differences between the two models have to do with the notation, the specific definitions of abilities, and the grouping of narrow factors related to memory.

An integration of the Cattell-Horn and Carroll models was proposed by Kevin S. McGrew (1997). On the basis of additional factor-analytic work, McGrew and Flanagan (1998) subsequently modified McGrew's initial CHC model. In its current form, the McGrew-Flanagan CHC model features ten "broad-stratum" abilities and over seventy "narrow-stratum" abilities, with each broad-stratum ability subsuming two or more narrow-stratum abilities. The ten broad-stratum abilities, with their "code names" in parentheses, are labeled as follows: Fluid Intelligence (*Gf*), Crystallized Intelligence (*Gc*), Quantitative Knowledge (*Gq*), Reading/Writing Ability (*Grw*), Short-Term Memory (*Gsm*), Visual Processing (*Gv*), Auditory Processing (*Ga*), Long-Term Storage and Retrieval (*Glr*), Processing Speed (*Gs*), and Decision/Reaction Time or Speed (*Gt*).

The McGrew-Flanagan CHC model makes no provision for the general intellectual ability factor (*g*). To understand the reason for this omission, it is important to understand why the authors undertook to create the model in the first place. The model was the product of efforts designed to improve the practice of psychological assessment in education (sometimes referred to as **psychoeducational assessment**) by identifying tests from different batteries that could be used to provide a comprehensive assessment of a student's abilities. Having identified key abilities, the authors made recommendations for **cross-battery assessment** of students, or assessment that employs tests from different test batteries and entails interpretation of data from specified subtests to provide a comprehensive assessment. According to these authors, *g* was not employed in their CHC model because it lacked utility in psychoeducational evaluations. They explained:

> The exclusion of *g* does not mean that the integrated model does not subscribe to a separate general human ability or that *g* does not exist. Rather, it was omitted by McGrew (1997) (and is similarly omitted in the current integrated model) since it has little practical relevance to cross-battery assessment and interpretation. (McGrew & Flanagan, 1998, p. 14)

Other differences between the Cattell-Horn and Carroll models were resolved more on the basis of factor-analytic studies than judgments regarding practical relevance to cross-battery assessment. The abilities labeled "quantitative knowledge" and "reading/writing" were conceived of as distinct broad abilities, much as they were by Horn and Cattell. McGrew and Flanagan drew heavily on Carroll's (1993) writings for definitions of many of the broad and narrow abilities listed, as well as the codes for these abilities.

> **JUST THINK . . .**
>
> Do you agree that *g* has little practical relevance in educational settings?

At the very least, CHC theory as formulated by McGrew and Flanagan has great value from a heuristic standpoint. It compels practitioners and researchers alike to think about exactly how many human abilities really need to be measured, and how narrow or broad an approach is optimal in terms of being clinically useful. Further, it stimulates researchers to revisit other existing theories, which may also be ripe for reexamination by means of statistical methods like factor analysis. The best features of such theories might then be combined with the goal of developing a clinically useful and actionable model of human abilities.

The Information-Processing View

Another approach to conceptualizing intelligence derives from the work of the Russian neuropsychologist Aleksandr Luria (1966a, 1966b, 1970, 1973, 1980). This approach focuses on the mechanisms by which information is processed—*how* information is processed, rather than *what* is processed. Two basic types of information-processing styles, simultaneous and successive, have been distinguished (Das et al., 1975; Luria, 1966a, 1966b). In **simultaneous** (or **parallel**) **processing,** information is integrated all at one time. In **successive** (or **sequential**) **processing,** each bit of information is individually processed in sequence. As its name implies, sequential processing is logical and analytic in nature; piece by piece and one piece after the other, information is arranged and rearranged so that it makes sense. In trying to anticipate who the murderer is while watching *Law & Order,* for example, one's thinking could be characterized as sequential. The viewer constantly integrates bits of information that will lead to a solution of the problem "Whodunnit?" Memorizing a telephone number or learning the spelling of a new word is typical of the types of tasks that involve acquisition of information through successive processing.

In contrast, *simultaneous* processing may be described as "synthesized." Information is integrated and synthesized at once and as a whole. As you stand before and appreciate a painting in an art museum, the information conveyed by the painting is processed in a manner that, at least for most of us, could reasonably be described as simultaneous. Of course, art critics and connoisseurs may be exceptions to this general rule. In general, tasks that involve the simultaneous mental representations of images or information involve simultaneous processing. Map reading is another task that is typical of such processing.

Some tests, such as the Kaufman Assessment Battery for Children (Kaufman & Kaufman, 1983a, 1983b), which will be discussed in Chapter 10, rely heavily on this concept of a distinction between successive and simultaneous information processing. The strong influence of an information-processing perspective is also evident in the work of others (Das, 1972; Das et al., 1975; Naglieri, 1989, 1990; Naglieri & Das, 1988) who have developed the **PASS model** of intellectual functioning—PASS being an acronym for planning, attention, simultaneous, and successive. In this model, *planning* refers to strategy development for problem solving; *attention* (also referred to as *arousal*) refers to receptivity to information; and *simultaneous* and *successive* refer to the type of information processing employed. Proponents of the PASS model have argued that existing tests of intelligence do not adequately assess planning. Naglieri and Das (1997) developed the Cognitive Assessment System (CAS), a cognitive ability test expressly designed to tap PASS factors. Although these test authors presented evidence to support the construct validity of the CAS, other researchers have questioned whether the test is actually measuring what it purports to measure (Keith & Kranzler, 1999; Kranzler & Keith, 1999).

Robert Sternberg proposed another information-processing approach to intelligence, arguing that "the essence of intelligence is that it provides a means to govern ourselves so that our thoughts and actions are organized, coherent, and responsive to both our internally driven needs and to the needs of the environment" (Sternberg, 1986, p. 141). He proposed a triarchic theory of intelligence with three principal elements: metacomponents, performance components, and knowledge-acquisition components. Metacomponents are involved in planning what one is going to do, monitoring what one is doing, and evaluating what one has done upon completion. Performance components administer the instructions of metacomponents. Knowledge-acquisition components are involved in "learning how to do something in the first place" (Sternberg, 1994, p. 221).

Now that you have some background on the various ways that intelligence has been conceptualized, let's briefly look at some of the ways in which test developers have endeavored to measure it. In the following two chapters, we look more closely at specific tests.

Measuring Intelligence

The measurement of intelligence entails sampling an examinee's performance on different types of tests and tasks as a function of developmental level. At all developmental levels, the intellectual assessment process also provides a standardized situation from which the examinee's approach to the various tasks can be closely observed. It therefore provides an opportunity for an assessment that in itself can have great clinical utility.

Types of Tasks Used in Intelligence Tests

In infancy (the period from birth through 18 months), intellectual assessment consists primarily of measurement of sensorimotor development. This includes, for example, the measurement of nonverbal, motor responses such as turning over, lifting the head, sitting up, following a moving object with the eyes, imitating gestures, and reaching for a group of objects (Figure 8–3). The examiner who attempts to assess the intellectual and related abilities of infants must be skillful in establishing and maintaining rapport with examinees who do not yet know the meaning of words like *cooperation* and *patience*. Typically, measures of infant intelligence rely to a great degree on information obtained from a structured interview with the examinee's parents, guardians, or other caretakers.

The focus in evaluation of the older child shifts to verbal and performance abilities. More specifically, the child may be called on to perform tasks designed to yield a measure of general fund of information, vocabulary, social judgment, language, reasoning, numerical concepts, auditory and visual memory, attention, concentration, and spatial

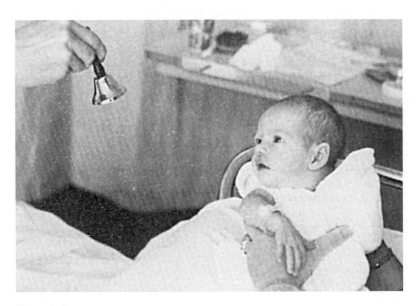

Figure 8–3
Testing the Alerting Response

One assessment technique common to infant development tests is a test of the alerting response. The **alerting response** *indicates an infant's capacity for responsiveness. It is deemed to be present when the infant's eyes brighten and widen—in contrast to the* **orienting response,** *which defines the response of turning in the direction of a stimulus. Here, the child is exhibiting an alerting response to the sound of the bell.*

visualization. The administration of many of the items may be preceded, as prescribed by the test manual, with teaching items designed to provide the examinee with practice in what is required by a particular test item.

In a bygone era, many intelligence tests were scored and interpreted with reference to the concept of mental age. **Mental age** is an index that refers to the chronological age equivalent of one's performance on a test or a subtest. This index was typically derived by reference to norms that indicate the age at which most testtakers are able to pass or otherwise meet some criterion performance.

Especially when individually administered by a trained professional, tests administered to children, much like tests individually administered to adults, afford the examiner a unique opportunity to observe an examinee's reactions to success, failure, and frustration. The examiner can see, up close, the examinee's general approach to problem solving and the test situation with its varied demands. Keen observation of such verbal and nonverbal behavior can yield a wealth of insights that in many cases will help to bring to light hitherto unidentified assets and deficits, and help to clarify ambiguities that arise in the test data. For schoolchildren, such observation may be useful with regard to a variety of objectives ranging from the individual tailoring of teaching agendas to class placement decisions.

According to Wechsler (1958), adult intelligence scales should tap such abilities as retention of general information, quantitative reasoning, expressive language and memory, and social judgment. The types of tasks used to reach these measurement objectives on the Wechsler scale for adults are the same as many of the tasks used on the Wechsler scales for children, although the content of specific items may vary. The fact that similar stimulus materials are used with children and adults has caused some to question whether children tend to be more motivated when presented with such materials (Marquette, 1976; Schaie, 1978), and whether the tasks fail to capture an adequate sampling of skills acquired by adults (Wesman, 1968). Publishers of intelligence tests have made available series of tests that can be used through a period that not quite, but almost, spans cradle to grave.

Tests of intelligence are seldom administered to adults for purposes of educational placement. Rather, they may be given to obtain clinically relevant information or some measure of learning potential and skill acquisition.

More basic than age as a factor to consider when developing a test of intelligence is the foundation or theory of the test. Let's consider the role of theory in the development and the interpretation of data from intelligence tests.

Theory in Intelligence Test Development and Interpretation

How one measures intelligence has to do in large part with what one conceives intelligence to be. A chapter in Galton's (1869) *Hereditary Genius* entitled "Classification of Men According to Their Natural Gifts" discussed sensory and other differences between people, which he believed were inherited. Perhaps not surprisingly, many Galtonian measures of cognitive ability were perceptual or sensorimotor in nature. Alfred Binet wrote extensively on what intelligence is, although the formal theory with which the original Binet test is perhaps best associated is Carl Spearman's (1904) "universal unity of the intellective function," with *g* as its centerpiece.

David Wechsler also wrote extensively on what intelligence is and usually emphasized that intelligence is multifaceted, consisting not only of cognitive abilities but personality-related factors as well. Still, because his original test, the Wechsler-Bellevue (W-B) Scale (as well as all subsequent Wechsler tests), provided for the calculation of a Verbal IQ and a Performance IQ, some have misinterpreted his position as representing a two-factor theory of intelligence: verbal abilities and performance abilities. Commenting on the development of the W-B and on the Verbal subtests (numbered 1 through 6) and the Performance subtests (numbered 7 through 11), Matarazzo explained:

> The grouping of the subtests into Verbal (1 to 6) and Performance (7 to 11), while intending to emphasize a dichotomy as regards possible types of ability called for by the individual tests, does *not* imply that these are the only abilities involved in the tests. Nor does it presume that there are different kinds of intelligence, e.g., verbal, manipulative, etc. It merely implies that these are different ways in which intelligence may manifest itself. The subtests are different measures of intelligence, not measures of different kinds of intelligence, and the dichotomy into Verbal and Performance areas is only one of several ways in which the tests could be grouped. (Matarazzo, 1972, p. 196, emphasis in the original)

In a footnote accompanying the extracted text, Matarazzo pointed out that the verbal and performance areas presumably coincided with the so-called primary factors of mental ability first postulated by Thurstone (1938). Regardless, decades of factor-analytic research on the Wechsler tests have pointed to the existence of more than two factors being tapped. Exactly how many factors are tapped by the various Wechsler tests and what they should be called have been matters of heated debate. And that brings us to an important point about theory and intelligence tests: Different theorists with different ideas about what factors are key in a theory of intelligence can look for (and probably find) their preferred factors in most widely used tests of intelligence.

A Wechsler intelligence test or any other such major test could be factor-analyzed with an eye toward identifying subtests that tap the cognitive abilities deemed to be dominant in a particular theory. As a consequence, practitioners and researchers who find the Cattell-Horn model of intelligence most appealing may make interpretations from Wechsler test data (or other intelligence test data) with reference to that model. Practitioners and researchers who find Carroll's three-stratum theory most appealing may make interpretations with reference to that model. Practitioners and researchers who find an integration of the Cattell-Horn and Carroll models to be most appealing may make interpretations with reference to a Cattell-Horn-Carrol (CHC) model, such as that proposed by McGrew & Flanagan (1998).

JUST THINK . . .

Name one factor that you believe is common to all intelligence tests. Explain why it is a common factor.

Beyond putting new interpretation-related templates over existing tests, new tests may be developed to measure the abilities and related factors described in a theory. Imagine what it might be like to develop a test of intelligence from a theory of intelligence. In fact, don't imagine it; try your hand at it! As an exercise in converting a theory of intelligence into a test of intelligence, consider the multifactor theory of intelligence developed by a pioneer in psychometrics, E. L. Thorndike. According to Thorndike (Thorndike et al., 1909; Thorndike et al., 1921), intelligence can be conceived in terms of three clusters of ability: social intelligence (dealing with people), concrete intelligence (dealing with objects), and abstract intelligence (dealing with verbal and mathematical symbols). Thorndike also incorporated a general mental ability factor (g) into the theory, defining g as the total number of modifiable neural connections or "bonds" available in the brain. For Thorndike, one's ability to learn is determined by the number and speed of the bonds that can be marshaled. No major test of intelligence was ever developed based on Thorndike's multifactor theory. *This is your moment!* Complete the *Just Think* exercise on this page before reading on.

JUST THINK . . .

Outline notes for your very own version of a "Thorndike Test of Intelligence." How will test items be grouped? What types of items would be found in each grouping? What types of summary scores might be reported for each testtaker? What types of interpretations would be made from the test data?

Even in the course of completing this *Just Think* exercise, you may have encountered some questions or issues about how a theory about intelligence can actually be applied in the development of an intelligence test. Well, welcome to the "real world," where test developers have long grappled with many questions and issues regarding intelligence in theory and intelligence in practice.

Intelligence: Some Issues

Nature Versus Nurture

Although most behavioral scientists today believe that measured intellectual ability represents an interaction between (1) innate ability and (2) environmental influences, such a belief was not always popular. As early as the seventeenth century, *preformationism* began to gain a foothold, as scientists of the day made discoveries that seemed to support this doctrine. **Preformationism** holds that all living organisms are preformed at birth: All of an organism's structures, including intelligence, are preformed at birth and therefore unable to be improved upon. In 1672, one scientist reported that butterflies were preformed inside their cocoons and that their maturation was a result of an unfolding. In that same year, another scientist, this one studying chick embryos, generalized from his studies to draw a similar conclusion about humans (Malphigi, *De Formatione Pulli in Ovo,* 1672; cited in Needham, 1959, p. 167).

The invention of the compound microscope in the late seventeenth century provided a new tool with which preformationists could attempt to gather supportive evidence. Scientists confirmed their expectations by observing semen under the microscope. Various investigators "claimed to have seen a microscopic horse in the semen of a horse, an animalcule with very large ears in the semen of a donkey, and minute roosters in the semen of a rooster" (Hunt, 1961, p. 38; Figure 8–4).

The influence of preformationist theory waned slowly as evidence inconsistent with it was brought forth. For example, the theory could not explain the regeneration of limbs by crayfish and other organisms. With the progression of work in the area of genetics, preformationism as the dominant theory of development was slowly replaced by *predeterminism.* **Predeterminism** is the doctrine that holds that one's abilities are predetermined by genetic inheritance and that no amount of learning or other intervention can enhance what has been genetically encoded to unfold in time.

Experimental work with animals was often cited in support of the predeterminist position. For example, a study by Carmichael (1927) showed that newborn salamanders and frogs that had been anesthetized and deprived of an opportunity to swim swam at about the same time as unanesthetized controls. Carmichael's work did not take into consideration the influence of the environment in the swimming behavior of salamanders and frogs. In parallel studies with humans, Dennis and Dennis (1940) observed the development of walking behavior in Hopi Indian children. Comparisons were made between children who spent much of their first year of life bound to a cradle board and children who had spent no such time constricted. Their conclusion was that there was no significant difference between the two groups of children at time of onset of walking and that walking was not a skill that could be enhanced by practice. Walking had been "proven" to be a human activity that unfolded with maturation.

Another proponent of the predeterminist view was Arnold Gesell. Generalizing from early twin studies that showed that practice had little effect on tasks such as climb-

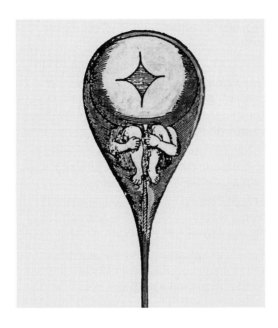

Figure 8–4
A Human Sperm Cell According to a Preformationist

This is how one scientist drew a human sperm cell as he saw it through a microscope—dramatic testimony to the way in which one's beliefs can affect perception (from Hartsoeker, 1694, cited in Needham, 1959, p. 20).

ing stairs, cutting with scissors, building with cubes, and buttoning buttons, Gesell (with Helen Thompson, 1929) concluded that "training does not transcend maturation." For Gesell, it was primarily the maturation of neural mechanisms and not learning or experience that was most important in the development of what might be referred to as intelligence. Gesell described mental development as a "progressive morphogenesis of patterns of behavior" (Gesell et al., 1940, p. 7) and argued that behavior patterns are determined by "innate processes of growth" that he viewed as synonymous with maturation (Gesell, 1945). Gesell (1954, p. 335) described infancy as "the period in which the individual realizes his racial inheritance" and has argued that this inheritance "is the end product of evolutionary processes that trace back to an extremely remote antiquity."

Is intelligence genetically encoded, unfolding with maturation? Or does the learning environment account for our intelligence? Nature/nurture questions like these have been raised for as long as there have been concepts of intelligence and tests to measure those concepts—sometimes amid great publicity and controversy. Galton firmly believed that genius was hereditary, a belief that was expressed in works such as *Hereditary Genius* (1869) and *English Men of Science* (1874). Galton came to these conclusions not on the basis of intelligence tests (which had not yet been devised), but rather on the basis of family histories of eminent people. In doing so, he greatly minimized the role of environmental enrichment.

Richard Dugdale, another predeterminist, argued that degeneracy, like genius, was also inherited. Dugdale (1877) traced the immoral, lecherous lineage of the infamous Jukes family and hypothesized that the observed trail of poverty, harlotry, and laziness was a matter of heredity. Complementing the work of Dugdale was Henry Goddard's book, *The Kallikak Family* (1912). Goddard traced the family lineage resulting from the legitimate and illegitimate unions of a man given the pseudonym "Martin Kallikak" (the last name was a combination of the Greek words for "good" and "bad"). Kallikak had fathered children with a mentally defective waitress and with the reportedly normal woman he married. Goddard documented how Kallikak's illegitimate descendants were far less socially desirable than the legitimate ones.

Goddard's research was attacked as faulty and eventually thoroughly discredited for several reasons:

- The accuracy of the diagnoses of the descendants was called into question. The family members had been diagnosed as feebleminded or not from a variety of sources, from medical records to conversations with neighbors. Field workers with relatively little training made those diagnostic decisions. Yet it was on these diagnoses that the conclusions of the study would stand or fall.

- Geneticists of the day refuted the idea that feeblemindedness was the product of a single gene. Experimentation with simple organisms such as fruit flies had suggested that inheritance of even simple traits was a very complex matter.

- A very basic flaw in Goddard's argument lay in the fact that he conceptualized feeblemindedness as a recessive gene. Even if this were true, a feebleminded son or daughter would have had to inherit the gene from *both* parents.

- Psychiatrist Abraham Myerson attacked the Kallikak study, and the eugenics movement in general, as pseudoscience. He reanalyzed data from studies purporting to support the idea that various physical and mental conditions could be inherited, and criticized those studies on statistical grounds. He especially criticized Goddard for making sweeping and unfounded generalizations from questionable data.

By the mid-1920s, Goddard himself moved away from theories of mental defect based on heredity and gravitated toward a view that focused on the environment. Still, he was haunted by his work, which ardent eugenicists continued to cite in support of their causes.

Based on his testing of a sample of Mexican and Native American children, the father of the American version of Binet's test, Lewis M. Terman, concluded that people from these cultures were genetically inferior. The noted English statistician Karl Pearson wrote that as compared with the native British, immigrating Jews were "somewhat inferior physiologically and mentally" (Pearson & Moul, 1925, p. 126). Such observations seem flawed, even prejudiced—if not racist—by current standards, yet they tended to reflect the prevailing beliefs of the day.

Although a scholarly consideration of the role of environmental and cultural factors (not to mention language barriers) is lacking in the writings of many behavioral scientists of the early twentieth century, a research literature that shed light on the environment side of the hereditary/environment issue subsequently began to mount. It was found, for example, that when identical twins are reared apart, they still show remarkably similar intelligence test scores, though not as similar as if they had been reared together (Johnson, 1963; Newman et al., 1937). Children born to poverty-stricken parents, but adopted at an early age by better-educated, middle-class families, tend to have higher intelligence test scores than their counterparts who are not adopted by families of higher socioeconomic status—though the natural mothers with the higher IQs tend to have the children with the higher IQs, irrespective of the family in which the adopted child is raised (Leahy, 1932, 1935).

In general, proponents of the "nurture" side of the nature/nurture controversy emphasize the crucial importance of factors such as prenatal and postnatal environment, socioeconomic status, educational opportunities, and parental modeling with respect to intellectual development. Proponents of this view characteristically suspect that oppos-

JUST THINK . . .

Eugenics remains very much alive in the twenty-first century. What accounts for its appeal? How can assessment professionals shed light on the issues?

Figure 8–5
What Does It Take to Win?

During the 1998 Winter Olympics in Nagano, Japan, the world looked on as Tara Lipinski became the youngest figure skater in Olympic history to win the gold. What does it take to do that? To what extent is such an accomplishment a matter of genes, training, motivation, and other factors?

ing arguments that champion the role of nature in the controversy are based more on factors like political leanings than on sound, impartial scientific inquiry and analysis. Somewhere between the rhetoric arguing that heredity plays *no* part in intelligence (Kamin, 1974) and assertions such as "Nature has color-coded groups of individuals so that statistically reliable predictions of their adaptability to intellectually rewarding and effective lives can easily be made and profitably be used by the pragmatic man-in-the-street" (Shockley, 1971, p. 375) lies the middle ground of the interactionist position: that intelligence, as measured by intelligence tests, is the result of the interaction between heredity and environment.

Inheritance and interactionism   People differ in intelligence levels just as they differ in blood pressure levels, cerebrospinal fluid levels, sensitivity to pain (Sheffield et al., 2000), and many other characteristics. Once that is understood, it is natural to wonder *why* people differ in intellectual abilities. According to the interactionist view, people inherit a certain intellectual potential. Exactly how much of that genetic potential is realized depends partially on the nature of the environment in which it is nurtured. No one to date has inherited X-ray vision or the ability to fly. You might spend your entire life in libraries or on mountaintops visiting gurus, but all your studies cannot result in acquiring the ability to fly or to see through things, because those abilities have not been encoded in your genetic makeup.

The interactionist perspective on intellectual development can be conceived as a very optimistic one. According to it, we are free to become all that we can be. The notion that we can use the environment to push our genetic potential to the limit can be illustrated most graphically by reference to dedicated athletes (Figure 8–5).

The Stability of Intelligence

Although research on the stability of measured intelligence in young children has yielded mixed findings (Dougherty & Haith, 1997; Lamp & Krohn, 1990; Smith, Bolin, & Stovall, 1988; Wesman, 1968), intelligence does seem to be stable for much of one's adult life (Birren & Schaie, 1985; Shock et al., 1984; Youngjohn & Crook, 1993). Using archival intelligence test data from World War II, Gold et al. (1995) administered the same intelligence test to a sample of 326 veterans some 40 years later. In general, the data pointed to stability in measured intelligence over time. Increases in vocabulary were noted, as were decreases in arithmetic, verbal analogies, and other nonverbal skills. The researchers concluded that young adult intelligence was the most important determinant of cognitive performance as an older adult.

Longitudinal research on adult intelligence, especially with older subjects, can be complicated by many factors, such as the extent to which one remains mentally active (Kaufman, 1990), physical health (Birren, 1968; Palmore, 1970), and myriad other potentially confounding factors (ranging from medication to personality). It is also important to distinguish between *group* similarities and differences in cognitive abilities over time and *intraindividual* similarities and differences. Full-scale IQs may seem to remain the same over time, although the individual abilities assessed may change significantly (Smith et al., 2000).

Ivnik and colleagues (Ivnik et al., 1995; Malec et al., 1993) noted that in many studies conducted over time, group means and standard deviations would seem to point to the conclusion that cognitive abilities are remarkably stable over the course of adult life. However, in a sample of normal adults, a focus on aging-related, within-individual variability in cognitive abilities may lead to a different conclusion. Ivnik et al. (1995) found verbal intellectual skills to be highly stable over time, with delayed free recall of newly learned information being the least stable of the cognitive abilities they surveyed. The researchers concluded, "These data challenge the assumption that normal persons' cognitive abilities are stable over long periods of time. In actuality, none of the general cognitive abilities measured in this study is absolutely stable, although some are more stable than others" (p. 160).

In later adulthood, especially after age 75, a decline in cognitive abilities has been noted (Nettelbeck & Rabbit, 1992; Ryan et al., 1990; Storandt, 1994). One study compared the performance of medical doctors over the age of 75 to the performance of younger colleagues on measures of cognitive ability. The performance of the elder physicians was about 26% lower than that of the younger group (Powell, 1994).

A popular stereotype that once existed about very bright children was "early ripe, early rot." A longitudinal study initiated by Terman at Stanford University in 1921 would subsequently expose this belief as myth. Terman and his colleagues identified 1,528 children (with an average age of 11) whose measured intelligence placed them within the top 1% in the country in intellectual functioning.[2] Terman followed these children for the remainder of his own life, taking measures of achievement, physical and social development, books read, character traits, and recreational interests. He conducted

---

2. The children followed in the Terman study were humorously referred to as **"Termites."** One Termite, Lee Cronbach, would himself later earn his place as a luminary in the field of psychometrics. However, as Hirsch (1997) reported, Cronbach believed that serious errors were made in the scoring of the Termites' intelligence test protocols. Cronbach (cited in Hirsch, 1997, p. 214) reflected that "Terman was looking for high IQs and his assistants provided them. . . . Sears [a Stanford colleague of Terman] has found and recalculated my own IQ and it turns out that I have lived my life with an IQ that was 10 points too high."

interviews with parents, teachers, and the subjects themselves. Some of the findings were published four years after the study had begun (Terman et al., 1925), although other researchers continued to collect and analyze data (Oden, 1968; Sears, 1977; Holahan & Sears, 1995). In general, the Terman studies suggested that gifted children tended to maintain their superior intellectual ability.

In contrast to Terman's conclusion is more recent work that suggests there may be a point at which gifted children cease to pursue or exploit their gift. Winner (2000) writes that child prodigies may become "frozen into expertise." By this is meant that the public acclaim garnered by these prodigies may make it increasingly difficult for them to break away from their acknowledged expertise. Also, after having been pushed so hard by family or others to achieve at an early age, gifted children may lose motivation as adults (Winner, 1996).

From the Terman studies, we also know that the gifted tend to have lower mortality rates and to be in better physical and mental health than their nongifted counterparts. They tend to hold moderate political and social views and tend to be successful in educational and vocational pursuits. They commit less crime than the nongifted. This all sounds fine. But there is another side to being gifted—see *Everyday Psychometrics*.

> **JUST THINK . . .**
>
> How might life be different for you if you believed your measured IQ was significantly higher than it actually is? By the way, for the stimulus for this exercise, read footnote 2.

Other Issues

Measured intelligence may vary as a result of factors related to the measurement process. Just a few of the many factors that may affect measured intelligence are a test author's definition of intelligence, the diligence of the examiner, the amount of feedback the examiner gives the examinee (Vygotsky, 1978), the amount of previous practice or coaching the examinee has had, and the competence of the person interpreting the test data.

Another possible factor in measured intelligence is what is called the **Flynn effect.** James R. Flynn, of the Department of Political Studies at the University of Otago in Dunedin, New Zealand, published findings that caused those who study and use intelligence tests in the United States to take notice. In his article entitled "The Mean IQ of Americans: Massive Gains 1932 to 1978," Flynn (1984) presented compelling evidence of what might be termed "intelligence inflation." He found that measured intelligence seems to rise on average, year by year, starting with the year that the test is normed. The rise in measured IQ is not accompanied by any academic dividend, and so it is not thought to be due to any actual rise in "true intelligence." The phenomenon has since been well documented not only in the United States but other countries as well (Flynn, 1988). The exact amount of the rise in IQ will vary as a function of a number of factors, such as how culture-specific the items are and whether the measure used is one of fluid or crystallized intelligence (Flynn, 2000).

The Flynn effect is of more than academic interest; it has real-world implications and consequences. Flynn (2000) sarcastically observed that the present state of affairs is empowering to psychologists and educators who examine children for placement in special classes. He advised examiners who want the children they test to be eligible for special services to use the most recently normed version of an intelligence test. On the other hand, examiners who want the children they test to escape the stigma of any labeling were advised to use "the oldest test they can get away

> **JUST THINK . . .**
>
> What is your opinion regarding the ethics of Flynn's advice to psychologists and educators who examine children for placement in special classes?

Being Gifted

Who Is Gifted?

An informal answer to this question might be "one whose performance is consistently remarkable in any positively valued area" (Witty, 1940, p. 516). Criteria for **giftedness** cited in legislation such as PL 95-561 include intellectual ability ("consistently superior"), creative thinking, leadership ability, ability in performing arts, and mechanical or other psychomotor aptitudes. To that list, others have added many other variables ranging from diversity of interests to love of metaphors, abstract ideas, and novelty. The origin of giftedness is a matter of debate, but factors such as heredity, atypical brain organization (O'Boyle et al., 1994; Hassler & Gupta, 1993), and environmental influences, including family environment (Gottfried et al., 1994), are frequently cited.

Identifying the Gifted

Tests of intelligence may aid in the identification of members of special populations at all points in the possible range of human abilities—including that group of exceptional people collectively referred to as "the gifted." As you may suspect, exactly who is identified as gifted may sometimes vary as a function of the measuring instrument. Wechsler tests of intelligence are commonly used. They contain subtests that are labeled "Verbal" and subtests that are labeled "Performance." A composite or Full Scale score thought to reflect overall intelligence has in some cases been used (sometimes along with other measures) to identify the gifted.

The Wechsler Full Scale score has been questioned because it obscures superior performance on individual subtests if the record as a whole is not superior. The Full Scale score further obscures a significant discrepancy, if one exists, between the Verbal and Performance scores. Additionally, each of the subtests does not contribute equally to overall intelligence. In one study that employed gifted students as subjects, Malone et al. (1991) cautioned that their findings might be affected by a **ceiling effect.** That is, some of the test items were not sufficiently challenging—had too low a "ceiling"—to accurately gauge the gifted students' ability. A greater range of items at the high end of the difficulty continuum would have been preferable. Malone

Anyone who has ever watched the E! *television program* Mysteries and Scandals *knows that fame isn't always all that it seems to be. In each episode of that series, host A. J. Benza takes viewers on a journey through what he refers to as the "flip side of Hollywood's walk of fame." The inevitable moral of each story is that a gift can come with a price. Here, after some background about what giftedness is and how it is identified, we consider its price.*

et al. (1991, p. 26) cautioned that "the use of the overall IQ score to classify students as gifted, or as a criterion for acceptance into special advanced programs, may contribute to the lack of recognition of the ability of some students."

Identification of the gifted should ideally be made not simply on the basis of an intelligence test but also on the basis of the goals of the program for which the test is being conducted. Thus, for example, if an assessment program is undertaken to identify gifted writers, common sense indicates that a component of the assessment program should be a writing sample taken from the examinee and evaluated by an authority. It is true, however, that the most effective and most frequently used instrument for identifying gifted children is an intelligence test.

School systems screening for candidates for gifted programs might employ a group test for the sake of economy. A group test frequently employed for this purpose is the Otis-Lennon School Ability Test. To screen for social abilities or aptitudes, tests such as the Differential Aptitude Test or Guilford et al.'s (1974) Structure of Intellect (SOI) test may be administered. Creativity might be assessed through the use of the SOI, through personality and biographical inventories (Davis, 1989), or through other measures of creative thinking.

Other tools of assessment to identify the gifted include case studies, behavior rating scales, and nominating techniques. A **nominating technique** is a method of peer appraisal in which members of a class, team, work unit, or other type of group are asked to select (or nominate) people in response to a question or statement. Class members, parents, or teachers might be asked questions such as "Who has the most leadership ability?" "Who has the most original ideas?" and "Who would you most like to help you with this project?" Although teacher nomination is a widely used method of identifying gifted children, it is not necessarily the most reliable one (French, 1964; Gallagher, 1966; Jacobs, 1970; Tuttle & Becker, 1980). The gifted child may be a misbehaving child in the classroom, whose misbehavior may be due to boredom with the low level of the material presented. The gifted child may ask questions of or make comments to the teacher that the teacher doesn't understand or misconstrues as smart-alecky. Clark (1988) outlined specific behaviors that gifted children may display in the classroom.

The Pros and Cons of Giftedness

Most people can readily appreciate and list many benefits of being gifted. Depending on the nature of their gifts, gifted children may, for example, read at an age when their nongifted peers are learning the alphabet, do algebra at an age when their nongifted peers are learning addition, or play a musical instrument with expert proficiency at an age when their nongifted peers are struggling with introductory lessons. The gifted child can earn admiration and respect, and the gifted adult may add to that a certain level of financial freedom.

The downside of being gifted is not as readily apparent. As Plucker and Levy (2001) remind us,

> . . . many talented people are not happy, regardless of whether they become experts in their fields. The literature contains a growing number of studies of underachievers who fail to develop their talents and achieve personal fulfillment. Furthermore, even the happiest, most talented individuals must face considerable personal and professional roadblocks emanating from their talent. The process of achieving professional success and personal happiness and adjustment involves overcoming many common, interrelated challenges. (p. 75)

Plucker and Levy (2001) cited the widely held assumption that "the gifted will do just fine" as a challenge to be overcome. Other challenges that must frequently be overcome by gifted individuals include depression and feelings of isolation (Jacobsen, 1999), sometimes to the point of suicidal ideation, gestures, or action (Weisse, 1990). Such negative feeling states may arise, at least in part, as a result of cultural pressure to be average or "normal" and even from stigma associated with talent and giftedness (Cross et al., 1991, 1993). Plucker and Levy add that there are self-imposed pressures, which often lead to long hours of study or practice—not without consequence:

> Being talented, or exceptional in almost any other way, entails a number of personal sacrifices. These sacrifices are not easy, especially when the issue is maintaining relationships, having a family, or maintaining a desirable quality of life. We would all like to believe that a person can work hard and develop his or her talent with few ramifications, but this is simply not realistic. (Plucker & Levy, 2001, p. 75)

with," which should, according to Flynn, allow at least 10 points leeway in measured intelligence. Because of the well-documented Flynn effect, it is advisable to use extra caution with regard to important decisions when employing an intelligence test at the beginning or end of its norming cycle (Kanaya et al., 2003).

Let's briefly consider some other factors that to a greater or lesser degree may play a role in measured intelligence: personality, gender, family environment, and culture.

Personality Sensitive to the manifestations of intelligence in *all* human behavior, Alfred Binet had conceived of the study of intelligence as being synonymous with the study of personality. David Wechsler (1958) also believed that all tests of intelligence measure traits of temperament and personality, such as drive, energy level, impulsiveness, persistence, and goal awareness. More contemporary researchers have expressed similar opinions regarding the great overlap of intelligence and personality (Ackerman & Heggestad, 1997; Sternberg et al., 2003).

Longitudinal and cross-sectional studies of children have explored the relationship between various personality characteristics and measured intelligence. Aggressiveness with peers, initiative, high need for achievement, competitive striving, curiosity, self-confidence, and emotional stability are some personality factors associated with gains in measured intelligence over time. Passivity, dependence, and maladjustment are some of the factors present in children whose measured intellectual ability has not increased over time.

In discussions of the role of personality in the measured intelligence of infants, the term *temperament* (rather than *personality*) is typically employed. In this context, **temperament** may be defined as the distinguishing manner of the child's observable actions and reactions. Evidence suggests that infants differ quite markedly in temperament with respect to a number of dimensions, including vigor of responding, general activity rate, restlessness during sleep, irritability, and "cuddliness" (Chess & Thomas, 1973). An infant's temperament can affect his or her measured intellectual ability in that irritable, restless children who do not enjoy being held have a negative reciprocal influence on their parents—and perhaps on test administrators as well. Parents are less likely to want to pick such children up and spend more time with them. They may therefore be less likely to engage in activities with them that are known to stimulate intellectual development, such as talking to them (White, 1971). One longitudinal study that began with assessment of temperament at age 3 and followed subjects through a personality assessment at age 21 concluded that differences in temperament were associated with differences in health risk–related behaviors such as dangerous driving, alcohol dependence, unsafe sex, and violent crime (Caspi et al., 1997).

Gender A great deal of research has been conducted on the cognitive differences between males and females. Although some differences have been found consistently, their exact significance has been a matter of controversy. Concluding her comprehensive review of the literature in this area, Halpern (1997) attempted to place the issue in perspective: "It is about as meaningful to ask 'Which is the smarter sex?' or 'Which has the better brain?' as it is to ask 'Which has the better genitals?'" (p. 1092). Reasons advanced to account for observed gender differences have been psychosocial (Eccles, 1987) as well as physiological (Hines et al., 1992; Shaywitz et al., 1995).

Family environment To what extent does family environment contribute to measured intelligence? The answer to this relatively straightforward question is complicated, in part because of the intrusion of nature/nurture, or issues of family environment versus genetic inheritance (Baumrind, 1993; Jackson, 1993; Scarr, 1992, 1993). Yet a new wrinkle in the controversy comes with the assertion that "family environment" begins in the womb and that a "maternal effects model" may more satisfactorily integrate data than a family effects model (Devlin et al., 1997). In this regard, it has been reported that "twins, and especially monozygotic twins, can experience radically different intrauterine environments even though they share the womb at the same time" (B. Price, cited in McGue, 1997, p. 417).

At a minimum, we can begin by stating what we hope is the obvious: Children thrive in a loving home where their safety and welfare are of the utmost concern and where they are given ample opportunity for learning and growth. Beyond that, other environmental factors may affect measured intelligence, such as the presence of resources (Gottfried, 1984), parental use of language (Hart & Risley, 1992), parental expression of concern about achievement (Honzik, 1967), and parental explanation of discipline policies in a warm, democratic home environment (Baldwin et al., 1945; Kent & Davis, 1957; Sontag et al., 1958).

JUST THINK . . .

What role would you attribute to your own family environment with regard to your own intellectual abilities?

Culture   Much of our discussion of the relationship between culture and psychological assessment in general applies to any consideration of the role of culture in measured intelligence. A culture provides specific models for thinking, acting, and feeling. Culture enables people to survive both physically and socially and to master and control the world around them (Chinoy, 1967). Because values may differ radically between cultural and subcultural groups, people from different cultural groups can have radically different views about what constitutes intelligence (Super, 1983; Wober, 1974). Because different cultural groups value and promote different types of abilities and pursuits, testtakers from different cultural groups can be expected to bring to a test situation differential levels of ability, achievement, and motivation. These differential levels may even find expression in measured perception and perceptual-motor skills. For example, working with children who were members of a rural community in eastern Zambia, Serpell (1979) tested Zambian and English research subjects on a task involving the reconstruction of models using pencil and paper, clay, or wire. The English children did best on the paper-and-pencil reconstructions because those were the materials with which they were most familiar. By contrast, the Zambian children did best using wire, because that was the medium with which they were most familiar. Both groups of children did about equally well using clay.

Items on a test of intelligence tend to reflect the culture of the society where the test is employed. To the extent that a score on such a test reflects the degree to which testtakers have been integrated into the society and the culture, it would be expected that members of subcultures (as well as others who, for whatever reason, choose not to identify themselves with the mainstream society) would score lower. In fact, Blacks (Baughman & Dahlstrom, 1968; Dreger & Miller, 1960; Lesser et al., 1965; Shuey, 1966), Hispanics (Gerry, 1973; Holland, 1960; Lesser et al., 1965; Mercer, 1976; Simpson, 1970), and Native Americans (Cundick, 1976) tend to score lower on intelligence tests than Whites or Asians (Flynn, 1991). These findings are controversial on many counts—ranging from the great diversity of the people who are grouped under each of these categories to sampling differences (Zuckerman, 1990). The meaningfulness of such findings can be questioned further when claims of genetic difference are made, because of the complexity of separating the effects of genes from effects of the environment. For an authoritative and readable account of the complex issues involved in making such separations, see Neisser et al. (1996).

Alfred Binet shared with many others the desire to develop a measure of intelligence as untainted as possible by factors such as prior education and economic advantages. The Binet-Simon test was designed to separate "natural intelligence from instruction" by "disregarding, insofar as possible, the degree of instruction which the subject possesses" (Binet & Simon, 1908, p. 93, Kite translation). This desire to create what might be termed a **culture-free** intelligence test has resurfaced with various degrees of fervor throughout history. One assumption inherent in the development of such tests is that if cultural factors can be controlled, differences between cultural groups will be lessened. A related assumption is that the effect of culture can be controlled through the elimination of verbal items and the exclusive reliance on nonverbal, performance items. Nonverbal items were thought to represent the best available means for determining the cognitive ability of minority group children and adults. However logical this assumption may seem on its face, it has not been borne out in practice (see, for example, Cole & Hunter, 1971, and McGurk, 1975).

JUST THINK . . .

Is it possible to create a culture-free test of intelligence? Is it desirable to create one?

Exclusively nonverbal tests of intelligence have not lived up to the high expectations of their developers. They have not been found to have the same high level of predictive validity as more verbally loaded tests. This may be due to the fact that nonverbal items do not sample the same psychological processes as do the more verbally loaded, conventional tests of intelligence. Whatever the reason, nonverbal tests tend not to be very good at predicting success in various academic and business settings. Perhaps this is so because such settings require at least some verbal facility.

The idea of developing a truly culture-free test has had great intuitive appeal but has proven to be a practical impossibility. All tests of intelligence, to a greater or lesser degree, reflect the culture in which they were devised and will be used. Stated another way, intelligence tests differ in the extent to which they are *culture loaded.*

Culture loading may be defined as the extent to which a test incorporates the vocabulary, concepts, traditions, knowledge, and feelings associated with a particular culture. A test item such as "Name three words for snow" is a highly culture-loaded item—one that draws heavily from the Eskimo culture, where many words exist for snow. Testtakers from Brooklyn would be hard put to come up with more than one word for snow (well, maybe two, if you count *slush*).

Soon after it became evident that no test could legitimately be called "culture free," a number of tests referred to as *culture fair* began to be published. We may define a **culture-fair** test as a test or assessment process designed to minimize the influence of culture with regard to various aspects of the evaluation procedures, such as administration instructions, item content, responses required of testtakers, and interpretations made from the resulting data. Table 8–2 lists techniques used to reduce the culture loading of tests. Note that in contrast to the factor-analytic concept of *factor loading,* which can be quantified, the *culture loading* of a test tends to be more of a subjective, qualitative, non-numerical judgment.

In general, the rationale for culture-fair test items was to include only those tasks that seemed to reflect experiences, knowledge, and skills common to all different cultures. In addition, all the tasks were designed to be motivating to all groups (Samuda, 1982). An attempt was made to minimize the importance of factors such as verbal skills

Table 8–2
Ways of Reducing the Culture Loading of Tests

Culture Loaded	Culture Loading Reduced
Paper-and-pencil tasks	Performance tests
Printed instructions	Oral instructions
Oral instructions	Pantomime instructions
No preliminary practice	Preliminary practice items
Reading required	Purely pictorial
Pictorial (objects)	Abstract figural
Written response	Oral response
Separate answer sheet	Answers written on test itself
Language	Nonlanguage
Speed tests	Power tests
Verbal content	Nonverbal content
Specific factual knowledge	Abstract reasoning
Scholastic skills	Nonscholastic skills
Recall of past-learned information	Solving novel problems
Content graded from familiar to rote	All item content highly familiar
Difficulty based on rarity of content	Difficulty based on complexity of relation education

Source: Jensen (1980)

thought to be responsible for the lower mean scores of various minority groups. Therefore, the culture-fair tests tended to be nonverbal, with simple, clear directions administered orally by the examiner. The nonverbal tasks typically consisted of assembling, classifying, selecting, or manipulating objects and drawing or identifying geometric designs. Some sample items from the Cattell Culture Fair Test are illustrated in this chapter's *Close-up.*

In general, although the culture loading of culture-fair intelligence tests has been reduced, so has their value as tests of intelligence. Culture-fair tests were found to lack the hallmark of traditional tests of intelligence: predictive validity. And still minority group members tended to score lower on these tests than did majority group members. Various subcultural characteristics have been presumed to penalize unfairly some minority group members who take intelligence tests that are culturally loaded with American White, middle-class values. Some have argued, for example, that Americans living in urban ghettos share common beliefs and values quite different from those of mainstream America. Included among these common beliefs and values, for example, are a "live for today" orientation and a reliance on slang in verbal communication. Native Americans also share a common subculture with core values that may negatively influence their measured intelligence. Central to these values is the belief that individuals should be judged for their relative contribution to the group, not for their individual accomplishments. Native Americans also value their relatively unhurried, present–time-oriented lifestyle (Foerster & Little Soldier, 1974).

Frustrated by their seeming inability to develop culture-fair equivalents of traditional intelligence tests, some test developers attempted to develop equivalents of traditional intelligence tests that were culture specific. Expressly developed for members of a particular cultural group or subculture, such tests were thought to be able to yield a more valid measure of mental development. One culture-specific intelligence test developed expressly for use with Blacks was the Black Intelligence Test of Cultural

Culture Fair/Culture Loaded

What types of test items are thought to be "culture fair"—or at least more culture fair than other, more culture-loaded items? The items reprinted below from the Culture Fair Test of Intelligence (Cattell, 1940) are a sample. As you look at them, think about how culture fair they really are.

Mazes

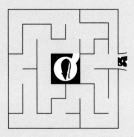

Classification

Pick out the two odd items in each row of figures.

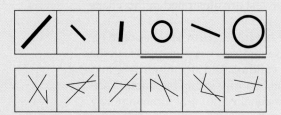

Figure Matrices

Choose from among the six alternatives the one that most logically completes the matrix pattern above it.

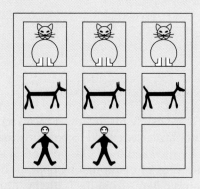

Series

Choose one figure from the six on the right that logically continues the series of three figures at the left.

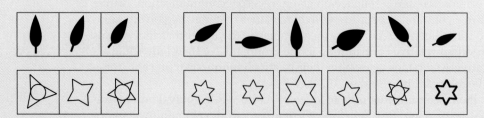

Items from the Culture Fair Test of Intelligence (Cattell, 1940)

In contrast to items designed to be culture fair, consider the items on the Cultural/Regional Uppercrust Savvy Test (CRUST; Herlihy, 1977). This tongue-in-cheek test of intelligence was intentionally designed for illustrative purposes to be culture loaded. Members of society's upper crust should have no problem at all achieving a perfect score.

1. When you are "posted" at the country club, (a) you ride horses with skill, (b) you are elected to the governance board, (c) you are publicly announced as not having paid your dues, (d) a table is reserved for you in the dining room whether you use it or not.

2. An arabesque in ballet is (a) an intricate leap, (b) a posture in which the dancer stands on one leg, the other extended backward, (c) a series of steps performed by a male and a female dancer, (d) a bow similar to a curtsy.

3. The *Blue Book* is (a) the income tax guidelines, (b) a guide to pricing used cars, (c) a booklet used for writing essay exams, (d) a social register listing 400 prominent families.

4. Brookline is located (a) in suburban Boston, (b) on Cape Cod, (c) between Miami Beach and Fort Lauderdale, (d) on the north shore of Chicago.

5. Beef Wellington is (a) the king's cut of roast beef, (b) tenderloin in a pastry crust lined with pâté, (c) an hors d'oeuvre flavored with sherry, (d) roast beef with béarnaise sauce.

6. Choate is (a) a gelded colt used in fox hunts, (b) a prep school, (c) an imported brandy, (d) the curator of the Metropolitan Museum of Art.

7. The most formal dress for men is (a) white tie, (b) black tie, (c) tuxedo, (d) décolletage.

8. *The Stranger* is (a) the . . . family who moved into the neighborhood, (b) Howard Hughes, (c) a book by Camus, (d) an elegant restaurant in San Francisco.

9. Waterford is (a) a health spa for the hep set, (b) a "fat farm," (c) hand-cut crystal from Ireland, (d) the Rockefeller family estate in upper New York.

10. Dining *alfresco* means (a) by candlelight, (b) a buffet supper, (c) at a sidewalk cafe, (d) outdoors.

According to Herlihy (1977), the answers keyed correct are 1(c), 2(b), 3(d), 4(a), 5(b), 6(b), 7(a), 8(c), 9(c), 10(d).

Homogeneity (Williams, 1975), a 100-item multiple-choice test. Keeping in mind that many of the items on this test are now dated, here are three samples:[3]

1. *Mother's Day* means
    a. Black independence day.
    b. a day when mothers are honored.
    c. a day the welfare checks come in.
    d. every first Sunday in church.
2. *Blood* means
    a. a vampire.
    b. a dependent individual.
    c. an injured person.
    d. a brother of color.
3. The following are popular brand names. Which one does not belong?
    a. Murray's
    b. Dixie Peach
    c. Royal Crown
    d. Preparation H

As you read the items above, you may be asking yourself, "Is this really an intelligence test? Should I be taking this seriously?" If you were thinking such questions, you are in good company. Many psychologists probably asked themselves the same questions. In fact, a kind of parody of the BITCH (the acronym for the test) was published in the May 1974 issue of *Psychology Today* (p. 101), and it was called the "S.O.B. (Son of the Original BITCH) Test." However, the Williams (1975) test was purported to be a genuine culture-specific test of intelligence standardized on 100 Black high school students in the St. Louis area. Williams was awarded $153,000 by the National Institute of Mental Health to develop the BITCH.

In what was probably one of the few published studies designed to explore the test's validity, the Wechsler Adult Intelligence Scale (WAIS) and the BITCH were both administered to Black ($n = 17$) and White ($n = 116$) applicants for a job with the Portland, Oregon, police department. The Black subjects performed much better on the test than did the White subjects, with a mean score that exceeded the White mean score by 2.83 standard deviations. The White mean IQ as measured by the WAIS exceeded the Black mean IQ by about 1.5 standard deviations. None of the correlations between the BITCH score and any of the following variables for either the Black or the White testtakers differed significantly from zero: WAIS Verbal IQ, WAIS Performance IQ, WAIS Full Scale IQ, and years of education. Even though the Black sample in this study had an average of more than 2½ years of college education, and even though their overall mean on the WAIS was about 20 points higher than for Blacks in general, their scores on the BITCH fell below the average of the standardization sample (high school pupils ranging in age from 16 to 18). What, then, is the BITCH measuring? The study authors, Matarazzo and Wiens (1977), concluded that the test was measuring "street wiseness."

Although many of the culture-specific tests did yield higher mean scores for the minority group for which they were specifically designed, they lacked predictive validity

---

3. The answers keyed correct are as follows: 1(c), 2(d), and 3(d).

and provided little useful, practical information.[4] The knowledge required to score high on all of the culture-specific and culture-reduced tests has not been seen as relevant for educational purposes within our pluralistic society. Such tests have low predictive validity for the criterion of success in academic as well as vocational settings.

At various phases in the life history of the development of an intelligence test, a number of approaches to reduce cultural bias may be employed. Panels of experts may evaluate the potential bias inherent in a newly developed test, and those items judged to be biased may be eliminated. The test may be devised so that relatively few verbal instructions are needed to administer it or demonstrate how to respond. Related efforts can be made to minimize any possible language bias. A tryout or pilot testing with ethnically mixed samples of testtakers may be undertaken. If differences in scores emerge solely as a function of ethnic group membership, individual items may be studied further for possible bias.

Major tests of intelligence have undergone a great deal of scrutiny for bias in many investigations. Procedures range from analysis of individual items to analysis of the test's predictive validity. Only when it can be reasonably concluded that a test is as free as it can be of systematic bias is it made available for use. Of course, even if a test is free of bias, other potential sources of bias still exist. These sources range from the criterion for referral for assessment, to the conduct of the assessment, to the scoring of items (particularly those items that are somewhat subjective), and, finally, to the interpretation of the findings.

A Perspective

So many decades after the publication of the 1921 Symposium, professionals still debate the nature of intelligence and how it should be measured. In the wake of the controversial book *The Bell Curve* (Herrnstein & Murray, 1994), the American Psychological Association commissioned a panel to write a report on intelligence that would carry psychology's official imprimatur. The panel's report reflected wide disagreement with regard to the definition of intelligence but noted that "such disagreements are not cause for dismay. Scientific research rarely begins with fully agreed definitions, though it may eventually lead to them" (Neisser et al., 1996, p. 77). The panel apparently ignored the fact that, in terms of the relative youth of psychology as a discipline (in contrast to, for example, geology, archaeology, or physics), research on intelligence may have only just begun. The panel also overlooked a number of newer approaches to intelligence as well as some controversial evidence and viewpoints regarding differences between groups in measured intelligence (Frumkin, 1997; Lynn, 1997; Reed, 1997; Velden, 1997).

There has been no shortage of controversy when it comes to the subject of intelligence, beginning with how that word is defined. A trend in recent years has been to be much more liberal when defining and allowing for behavior presumed to be indicative of intelligence in the real world (Detterman, 1986). So, for example, we read discussions of "managerial intelligence" by no less an authority than Robert Sternberg (1997). Such work also reflects a trend toward context orientation in terms of defining intelligence.

---

4. Perhaps the most psychometrically sound of the instruments designed especially for use with Black subjects was the Listening Comprehension Test (Carver, 1968–1969, 1969; Orr & Graham, 1968). On this test, however, Blacks tended to score lower than Whites even when the groups were matched with respect to socioeconomic status.

There seems to be more interest in specific types of intelligence, as opposed to *g*. Still, disagreement over "the issue of the one versus the many" (Sternberg & Berg, 1986, p. 157) shows no sign of abatement.

Another issue that is not going to go away has to do with group differences in measured intelligence. Although human beings do certainly differ in size, shape, and color—and it is therefore reasonable to consider that there is also a physical basis for differences in intellectual ability—discerning where and how nature can be differentiated from nurture is a laudable academic pursuit. Still, such differentiation remains not only a very complex business but one potentially fraught with social, political, and even legal consequences. Claims about group differences can and have been used as political and social tools to oppress religious, ethnic, or other minority group members. This is most unfortunate, because as Jensen (1980) observed, variance attributable to group differences is far less than variance attributable to individual differences. Echoing this sentiment is the view that "what matters for the next person you meet (to the extent that test scores matter at all) is that person's own particular score, not the mean of some reference group to which he or she happens to belong" (Neisser et al., 1996, p. 90).

JUST THINK . . .

In a "real-life" competitive job market, what part, if any, does the "mean of the reference group" play in employment decisions?

The relationship between intelligence and a wide range of social outcomes has been well documented. Scores on intelligence tests, especially when used with other indicators, have value in predicting outcomes such as school performance, years of education, even social status and income. Measured intelligence is negatively correlated with socially undesirable outcomes such as juvenile crime (Moffitt et al., 1981). For these and related reasons, we would do well to concentrate research attention on the environmental end of the heredity-versus-environment spectrum. We need to find ways to effectively boost measured intelligence through environmental interventions, the better to engender hope and optimism.

Unfairly maligned by some and unduly worshiped by others, intelligence has endured, and will continue to endure, as a key construct in psychology and psychological assessment. For this reason, professionals who administer intelligence tests have a great responsibility, one for which thorough preparation is a necessity. That being said, we press on to the following chapter and a look at some widely used tests of intelligence.

Self-Assessment

Test your understanding of elements of this chapter by seeing if you can explain each of the following terms, expressions, and abbreviations:

accommodation	factor-analytic theories of	intelligence
alerting response	intelligence	interactionism
assimilation	fluid intelligence	interpersonal intelligence
ceiling effect	Flynn effect	intrapersonal intelligence
CHC theory	*g* factor	maintained abilities
cross-battery assessment	*Gf-Gc*	mental age
crystallized intelligence	giftedness	nominating technique
culture-fair test	group factors	orienting response
culture-free test	hierarchical model	parallel processing
culture loading	information-processing theories	PASS model
emotional intelligence	of intelligence	predeterminism

preformationism
psychoeducational assessment
s factor
schema
schemata

sequential processing
simultaneous processing
successive processing
temperament
"Termites"

three-stratum theory of cognitive
   abilities
two-factor theory of intelligence
vulnerable abilities

Web Watch

Check out the following Web sites for more information about topics discussed in this chapter.

Defining intelligence
www.wilderdom.com/personality/
L1-6StudentDefinitions.html

Intelligence
http://nicologic.free.fr/GeneralIntelligence.htm

Piaget's assimilation and accommodation
www.dmu.ac.uk/~jamesa/learning/assimacc.htm

CHC theory
www.iapsych.com/CHCPP/map.htm

http://media.wiley.com/product_data/
excerpt/47/04713826/0471382647.pdf

Terman and his studies
www.indiana.edu/%7Eintell/terman.shtml

The Flynn effect
www.indiana.edu/%7Eintell/flynneffect.shtml

http://pespmc1.vub.ac.be/FLYNNEFF.html

http://home.online.no/~itlandm/Flynn.html

Charles Spearman and the two-factor (*g*) theory
www.indiana.edu/~intell/spearman.shtml

Viewpoints on intelligence
http://socsci.uwosh.edu/IntroPsych/Ansfield/
Sessions/Index/index8.htm

http://sq.4mg.com/IQbasics.htm

www.angelfire.com/hi/psychoedservices/page6.
html

Alfred Binet
www.indiana.edu/~intell/binet.shtml

David Wechsler
www.indiana.edu/~intell/wechsler.shtml

Gardner's theory of multiple intelligences
www.ericfacility.net/ericdigests/ed410226.html

www.pz.harvard.edu/PIs/HG.htm

www.thomasarmstrong.com/multiple
_intelligences.htm

www.swopnet.com/ed/TAG/7_Intelligences.html

www.cio.com/archive/031596_qa.html

Article on "intelligent" intelligence
www.apa.org/monitor/feb03/intelligent.html

Online IQ tests (for possible use in an exercise on how *not* to construct an intelligence test)
www.queendom.org/tests/iq/classical_iq_r2
_access.html

www.iqtest.com/iq-test.html#TEST

Culture-fair intelligence tests
www.findarticles.com/cf_dls/g2699/0004/
2699000434/p1/article.jhtml

9

Tests of Intelligence

A test developer's conception of intelligence is, in a sense, both the starting point and the ending point in the development of a test of intelligence. To the extent that a test developer conceives of intelligence in terms of mental structures, the test will be designed to shed light on those structures. To the extent that a test developer conceives of intelligence in terms of processes, the test will be designed to shed light on those processes.

Beginning with initial considerations of item content and item format, continuing with considerations of scoring and interpretation, and following with plans for revising the test, the conception of intelligence at the test's foundation remains a guiding force—one that is reflected in decisions about almost every aspect of the test. It is evident in the final form of the test and in the uses to which the test will be put.

In this chapter, we look at a sampling of individual and group tests of intelligence.[1] As attested to by reference volumes such as *Tests in Print,* many different intelligence tests exist. From the test user's standpoint, several considerations figure into a test's appeal:

- the theory on which the test is based (if any)
- the ease with which the test can be administered
- the ease with which the test can be scored
- the ease with which results can be interpreted for a particular purpose
- the adequacy and appropriateness of the norms
- the acceptability of the published reliability and validity indices

Some tests of intelligence were constructed on the basis of a theory. For example, Louis L. Thurstone conceived of intelligence as composed of what he termed *primary mental abilities* (PMAs). Thurstone (1938) developed and published the Primary Mental Abilities test, which consisted of separate tests, each designed to measure one PMA: verbal meaning, perceptual speed, reasoning, number facility, rote memory, word fluency, and spatial relations. Although the test was not widely used, this early model of mul-

---

1. Our objective in this and succeeding chapters is to provide a brief description of a small but representative sample of tests in various categories. We selected for discussion only a few tests for illustrative purposes. Readers are asked not to draw any conclusions about the value of any particular test from its inclusion in or omission from our discussion.

tiple abilities inspired other theorists and test developers to explore various components of intelligence and ways to measure them.

An intelligence test may be developed on the basis of one theory but reconceptualized in terms of another theory. For example, much has been written about a theory of intelligence that contains features of the Cattell-Horn model and the Carroll three-stratum model. This theory is becoming known as the Cattell-Horn-Carroll (CHC) theory. As receptivity to the Cattell-Horn-Carroll model has grown, books and manuals have been published illustrating how this model can be used to supplement findings from other well-known ability tests.

JUST THINK . . .

In everyday living, mental abilities tend to operate in unison rather than in isolation. How useful is it, therefore, to attempt to isolate and measure "primary mental abilities"?

Through history, some tests seem to have been developed more as a matter of necessity than anything else. In the early 1900s, for example, Alfred Binet was charged with the responsibility of developing a test to screen for developmentally disabled children in the Paris schools. Binet collaborated with Theodore Simon to create the world's first formal test of intelligence in 1905. Adaptations and translations of Binet's work soon appeared in many countries throughout the world. The original Binet-Simon Scale was in use in the United States as early as 1908 (Goddard, 1908, 1910). By 1912 a modified version had been published that extended the age range of the test downward to 3 months (Kuhlmann, 1912). However, it was the work of Lewis Madison Terman at Stanford University that culminated in the ancestor of what we know now as the Stanford-Binet Intelligence Scale.

In 1916, Terman published a translation and "extension" of the Binet-Simon Intelligence Scale. The publication included new items he had devised on the basis of years of research, as well as a methodological approach that included normative studies. Terman's efforts helped garner worldwide recognition and success for Binet's test (Minton, 1988). Below we take a closer look at the test over time (see Table 9–1) and in its current version.

The Stanford-Binet Intelligence Scales

Although the first edition of the **Stanford-Binet** was certainly not without major flaws (such as lack of representativeness of the standardization sample), it also contained some important innovations. It was the first published intelligence test to provide organized and detailed administration and scoring instructions. It was also the first American test to employ the concept of IQ. And it was the first test to introduce the concept of an **alternate item,** an item to be used only under certain conditions. For example, an alternate item might be used if the regular item had not been administered properly by the examiner.

In 1926, Lewis Terman began a collaboration with a Stanford colleague, Maude Merrill, in a project to revise the test. The project would take 11 years to complete. Innovations in the 1937 scale included the development of two equivalent forms, labeled *L* (for Lewis) and *M* (for Maude, according to Becker, 2003), as well as new types of tasks for use with preschool-level and adult-level testtakers.[2] The manual contained many examples to aid the examiner in scoring. The test authors went to then-unprecedented

---

2. L. M. Terman left no clue to what initials would have been used for Forms *L* and *M* if his co-author's name had not begun with the letter *M*.

Table 9–1
Features and Possible Limitations of the Stanford-Binet Over Time

Year	Advantages	Limitations
1916	Contains alternate items at most age levels Shares items to maintain continuity with earlier versions Emphasizes abstraction and novel problem solving Extends range of items relative to Binet-Simon Based on extensive research literature Extensive standardization performed	Inadequately measures adult mental capacity Has inadequate scoring and administrative procedures at some points Measures only single factor (g) Has nonuniform IQ standard deviation Has single test form Is verbally loaded
1937	Contains alternate items at most levels Shares items to maintain continuity with earlier versions Extends range of items Based on extensive research literature Contains more performance tests at earlier age levels Contains more representative norms Includes parallel form Uses toys to make test more engaging for young children Verbal items allow subjects to display fluency, imagination, unusual or advanced concepts, and complex linguistic usage	Some items have ambiguous scoring rules Form M lacks vocabulary Has longer administration time than 1916 version Measures only single factor (g) Has nonuniform IQ standard deviation IQs not comparable across ages Sample had higher SES and higher percentage of urban children than general population Has unequal coverage of different abilities at different levels Is verbally loaded
1960/1973	Administers several varied tests to each examinee to keep children interested Retains best items from Forms L and M Has better layout than previous versions Manual presents clear scoring rules Contains alternate items at each age level Shares items to maintain continuity with earlier versions Eliminates items that are no longer appropriate Based on extensive research literature Presents stimulus material in spiral-bound book Has uniform IQ standard deviation Uses toys to make test more engaging for young children	Has inadequate ceiling for adolescents and highly gifted examinees Measures only single factor (g) Separates scoring standards from items Is verbally loaded
1986	Contains both a general composite score and several factor scores Shares items to maintain continuity with earlier versions Easel format with directions, scoring criteria, and stimuli makes administration easier Emphasizes abstraction and novel problem solving; emphasizes verbal reasoning less compared with prior versions Technical Manual reports extensive validity studies Has flexible administration procedures Contains higher ceilings for advanced adolescents than Form L-M Number of basic concepts in preschool-level tests compares favorably with other tests for that age range Contains understandable age-level instructions for young children Uses adaptive testing (routing) to economize on administration time and reduce examinee frustration Uses explicit theoretical framework as guide for item development and alignment of subtests within modeled hierarchy Has wider age range than prior versions (2-0 through 23) Creatively extends many classic item types	Less gamelike than earlier versions; yields less information from styles and strategies due to decreased examiner/examinee interaction Contains no toys Norming sample overrepresents managerial / professional and college-educated adults and their children Has possible lack of comparability in the content of area scores at different ages due to variability of subtests used in their computation Has psychometric rather than developmental emphasis Has standard deviation of 16 rather than 15 for composite scores; $M = 50$, $SD = 8$ for subtests Contains subjectivity (examiner preference) when determining subtests used to compute composite score Unable to diagnose mild retardation before age 4 and moderate retardation before age 5

Table 9–1
(continued)

Year	Advantages	Limitations
2003	More gamelike than earlier versions with colorful artwork, toys, and manipulatives Matches norms to 2000 U.S. Census Contains nonverbal as well as verbal routing test Contains both a general composite score and several factor scores Shares items to maintain continuity with earlier versions Covers age range of 2-0 through 85+ Change-sensitive scores allow for evaluation of extreme performance Has easel format with directions, scoring criteria, and stimuli, for easy administration Has equal balance of verbal and nonverbal content in all factors Contains Nonverbal IQ Has standard deviation of 15 for composite scores, allowing easy comparison with other tests; $M = 10$, $SD = 3$ for subtests Uses adaptive testing (routing) to economize on administration time and reduce examinee frustration Uses explicit theoretical framework as guide for item development and alignment of subtests within modeled hierarchy Extends low-end items, allowing earlier identification of individuals with delays or cognitive difficulties Extends high-end items to measure gifted adolescents and adults	Not cited

Source: Becker, K. A. (2003). *History of the Stanford-Binet Intelligence Scales: Content and Psychometrics* (Stanford-Binet Intelligence Scales, Fifth Edition Assessment Service Bulletin No. 1). Itasca, IL: Riverside Publishing. Used by permission.

lengths to achieve an adequate standardization sample (Flanagan, 1938), and the test was praised for its technical achievement in the areas of validity and especially reliability. A serious criticism of the test remained: lack of representation of minority groups during the test's development.

Another revision of the Stanford-Binet was well under way at the time of Terman's death in 1956 at age 79. This edition of the Stanford-Binet, the 1960 revision, consisted of only a single form (labeled *L-M*), composed of the items considered to be the best from the two forms of the 1937 test, with no new items added to the test. A major innovation, however, was the use of the **deviation IQ** tables in place of the ratio IQ tables. Earlier versions of the Stanford-Binet had employed the *ratio IQ*, which was based on the concept of mental age (the age level at which an individual appears to be functioning intellectually). The **ratio IQ** is the ratio of the testtaker's mental age divided by his or her chronological age, multiplied by 100 to eliminate decimals. As illustrated by the formula for its computation, those were the days, now long gone, when an **IQ** (for **intelligence quotient**) really was a quotient:

$$\text{ratio IQ} = \frac{\text{mental age}}{\text{chronological age}} \times 100$$

If the child's mental age was equal to his or her chronological age, the IQ would equal 100. Beginning with the third edition of the Stanford-Binet, the deviation IQ was used in place of the ratio IQ. The deviation IQ reflects a comparison of the performance of the individual with the performance of others of the same age in the standardization sample. Essentially, test performance is converted into a standard score with a mean of 100 and a standard deviation of 16. If an individual performs at the same level as the average person of the same age, the deviation IQ is 100. If performance is a standard deviation above the mean for the examinee's age group, the deviation IQ is 116.

Another revision of the Stanford-Binet was published in 1972. As with previous revisions, the quality of the standardization sample was criticized. Specifically, the manual was vague about the number of minority individuals in the standardization sample, stating only that a "substantial portion" of Black and Spanish-surnamed individuals was included. The 1972 norms may also have overrepresented the West and large, urban communities (Waddell, 1980).

The fourth edition of the Stanford-Binet Intelligence Scale (SB:FE; Thorndike et al., 1986) represented a significant departure from previous versions of the Stanford-Binet in theoretical organization, test organization, test administration, test scoring, and test interpretation. Previously, different items were grouped by age and the test was referred to as an **age scale.** The Stanford-Binet: Fourth Edition (SB:FE) was a *point scale.* In contrast to an age scale, a **point scale** is a test organized into subtests by category of item, not by age at which most testtakers are presumed capable of responding in the way keyed correct. The SB:FE manual contained an explicit exposition of the theoretical model of intelligence that guided the revision. The model was one based on the Cattell-Horn (1966) model of intelligence. A *test composite*—formerly described as a deviation IQ score—could also be obtained. In general, a **test composite** may be defined as a test score or index derived from the combination of, and/or mathematical transformation of, one or more subtest scores. This brief review brings us to the point at which the current edition was published. Let's take a closer look at it.

The Stanford-Binet Intelligence Scales: Fifth Edition

The fifth edition of the Stanford-Binet (SB5; Roid, 2003a) was designed for administration to assessees as young as 2 and as old as 85 (or older). The test yields a number of composite scores, including a Full Scale IQ derived from the administration of 10 subtests. Subtest scores all have a mean of 10 and a standard deviation of 3. Other composite scores are an Abbreviated Battery IQ score, a Verbal IQ score, and a Nonverbal IQ score. All composite scores have a mean set at 100 and a standard deviation of 15. In addition, the test yields five Factor Index scores corresponding to each of the five factors that the test is presumed to measure (see Table 9–2).

The SB5 was based on the Cattell-Horn-Carroll (CHC) theory of intellectual abilities. In fact, according to Roid (2003b), on the basis of a factor analysis of the early Forms L and M, "the CHC factors were clearly recognizable in the early editions of the Binet scales" (Roid et al., 1997, p. 8). The SB5 measures five CHC factors by different types of tasks and subtests at different levels. Table 9–2 summarizes the five CHC factor names and abbreviation along with their SB5 equivalents. It also provides a brief definition of the cognitive ability being measured by the SB5, as well as illustrative SB5 verbal and nonverbal subtests designed to measure the ability.

JUST THINK . . .

A critic of such equal balancing might claim that we live in a society where ability to express oneself in language is highly prized and therefore should be given more weight on any measure of general ability. Your response?

In designing the SB5, an attempt was made to strike an equal balance between tasks requiring facility with language (both expressive and receptive) and tasks that minimize demands on facility with language. In the latter category are subtests that use pictorial items with brief vocal directions administered by the examiner. The examinee response to such items may be made in the form of nonvocal pointing, gesturing, or manipulating.

Standardization After about five years in development and extensive item analysis to address possible objections on the grounds of gender, racial/ethnic, cultural, or religious bias, the final standardization edition of the test was developed. Some 500 examiners

Table 9–2
CHC and Corresponding SB5 Factors

CHC Factor Name	SB5 Factor Name	Brief Definition	Sample SB5 Subtest
Fluid Intelligence (*Gf*)	Fluid Reasoning (FR)	Novel problem solving; understanding of relationships that are not culturally bound	Object Series/Matrices (nonverbal) Verbal Analogies (verbal)
Crystallized Knowledge (*Gc*)	Knowledge (KN)	Skills and knowledge acquired by formal and informal education	Picture Absurdities (nonverbal) Vocabulary (verbal)
Quantitative Knowledge (*Gq*)	Quantitative Reasoning (QR)	Knowledge of mathematical thinking including number concepts, estimation, problem solving, and measurement	Verbal Quantitative Reasoning (verbal) Nonverbal Quantitative Reasoning (nonverbal)
Visual Processing (*Gv*)	Visual-Spatial Processing (VS)	Ability to see patterns and relationships and spatial orientation as well as the gestalt among diverse visual stimuli	Position and Direction (verbal) Form Board (nonverbal)
Short-Term Memory (*Gsm*)	Working Memory (WM)	Cognitive process of temporarily storing and then transforming or sorting information in memory	Memory for Sentences (verbal) Delayed Response (nonverbal)

from all 50 states were trained to administer the test. Examinees in the norming sample were 4,800 subjects from age 2 to over 85. The sample was nationally representative according to year 2000 United States Census data, stratified with regard to age, race/ethnicity, geographic region, and socioeconomic level. No accommodations were made for persons with special needs in the standardization sample, although such accommodations were made in separate studies. Persons were excluded from the standardization sample (although included in separate validity studies) if they had limited English proficiency, severe medical conditions, severe sensory or communication deficits, or severe emotional/behavior disturbance (Roid, 2003b).

Psychometric soundness   To determine the reliability of the SB5 Full Scale IQ with the norming sample, an internal-consistency reliability formula designed for the sum of multiple tests (Nunnally, 1967, p. 229) was employed. The calculated coefficients for the SB5 Full Scale IQ were consistently high (.97 to .98) across age groups, as was the reliability for the Abbreviated Battery IQ (average of .91). Test-retest reliability coefficients reported in the manual were also high. The test-retest interval was only 5 to 8 days—shorter by some 20 to 25 days than the interval employed on other, comparable tests. Interscorer reliability coefficients reported in the SB5 Technical Manual ranged from .74 to .97 with an overall median of .90. Items showing especially poor interscorer agreement had been deleted during the test development process.

Content-related evidence of validity for SB5 items was established in various ways, ranging from expert input to empirical item analysis. Criterion-related evidence was presented in the form of both concurrent and predictive data. For the concurrent studies, Roid (2003b) studied correlations between the SB5 and the SB:FE, as well as the SB5 and all three of the then-current major Wechsler batteries (WPPSI-R, WISC-III, and WAIS-III). The correlations were high when comparing the SB5 to the SB:FE and, perhaps as expected, less on average with the Wechsler tests. Roid (2003b) attributed the difference in part to the varying extents to which the SB5 and the Wechsler tests were presumed to tap *g*. To establish predictive validity evidence, correlations with measures of achievement (the Woodcock Johnson III Test of Achievement and the Wechsler Individual Achievement Test, among other tests) were employed and the detailed findings reported in the manual. Roid (2003b) also presented a number of factor-analytic studies in support of the construct validity of the SB5.

Test administration   Developers of intelligence tests, particularly tests designed for use with children, have traditionally been sensitive to the need for **adaptive testing,** testing individually tailored to the testtaker. Other terms used to refer to adaptive testing include *tailored testing, sequential testing, branched testing,* and *response-contingent testing.* As employed in intelligence tests, adaptive testing might entail beginning a subtest with a question in the middle range of difficulty. If the testtaker responds correctly to the item, an item of greater difficulty is posed next. If the testtaker responds incorrectly to the item, an item of lesser difficulty is posed. Adaptive testing is in essence designed "to mimic automatically what a wise examiner would do" (Wainer, 1990, p. 10).

Adaptive testing helps ensure that the early test or subtest items are not so difficult as to frustrate the testtaker and not so easy as to lull the testtaker into a false sense of security or a state of mind in which the task will not be taken seriously enough. Three other advantages of beginning an intelligence test or subtest at an optimal level of difficulty are that (1) it allows the test user to collect the maximum amount of information in the minimum amount of time, (2) it facilitates rapport, and (3) it minimizes the potential for examinee fatigue from being administered too many items.

After the examiner has established a rapport with the testtaker, the examination formally begins with an item from what is called a *routing test.* A **routing test** may be defined as a task used to direct or route the examinee to a particular level of questions. A purpose of the routing test, then, is to direct an examinee to test items that have a high probability of being at an optimal level of difficulty. There are two routing tests on the SB5, each of which may be referred to by either their activity names (Object Series/Matrices and Vocabulary) or their factor-related names (Nonverbal Fluid Reasoning and Verbal Knowledge). By the way, these same two subtests, and only these, are administered for the purpose of obtaining the Abbreviated Battery IQ score.

The routing tests, as well as many of the other subtests, contain **teaching items,** which are designed to illustrate the task required and assure the examiner that the examinee understands. Qualitative aspects of an examinee's performance on teaching items may be recorded as examiner observations on the test protocol. However, performance on teaching items is not formally scored, and performance on such items in no way enters into calculations of any other scores.

Now for a sampling of "nuts-and-bolts" information on administering the SB5. All of the test items for the SB5 are contained in three item books. Item Book 1 contains the first two (routing) subtests. After the second subtest has been administered, the examiner has recorded estimated ability scores designed to identify an appropriate start point in Item Books 2 and 3. The examiner administers the next four nonverbal subtests of an appropriate level from Item Book 2. These subtests are labeled Knowledge, Quantitative Reasoning, Visual-Spatial Processing, and Working Memory. The examiner then administers the final four verbal subtests from Item Book 3, again starting at an appropriate level. The four verbal subtests are labeled Fluid Reasoning, Quantitative Reasoning, Visual-Spatial Processing, and Working Memory.

Although many of the subtests for the verbal and nonverbal tests share the same name, they involve different tasks. For example, a *verbal measure* of Working Memory is a test called Memory for Sentences, in which the examinee's task is to repeat brief phrases and sentences. A *nonverbal measure* of Working Memory, Delayed Response, entails a totally different task, one reminiscent of the shell game or three-card monte (when played with cards) wagered on by passersby on many city streets (see Figure 9–1). Such street games, as well as the more standardized SB5 task, draw on visual memory and

Figure 9–1
Keep Your Eye on the Prize

Players of shell games know they must follow the hidden object as its position is changed under one of three shells or cups. In the new SB5 subtest called Delayed Response, *the examiner places objects under cups and then manipulates the position of the cups. The examinee's task is to locate the hidden object after a brief delay. On the SB5, the "prize" for successful performance comes in the form of raw score points that figure into the calculation of one's measured intelligence,* not—*as above*—*a monetary return on a wager.*

possibly verbal mediation. The latter process is presumed to occur as during the delay, the examinee (or onlooker of the game) *subvocalizes* (verbalizes in thought, not aloud) the name of the hidden object and the path it takes while being manipulated.

Some of the ways that the items of a subtest in intelligence and other ability tests are described by assessment professionals have parallels in your home. For example, there is the *floor.* In intelligence testing parlance, the **floor** refers to the lowest level of the items on a subtest. So, for example, if the items on a particular subtest run the gamut of ability from *developmentally delayed,* at one end of the spectrum, to *intellectually gifted,* at the other, the lowest-level item at the former end would be considered the *floor* of the subtest. The highest-level item of the subtest is the **ceiling.** On the Binet, another useful term, this one to describe a subtest with reference to a specific testtaker's performance, is *basal level.* Many Binet subtests have rules for establishing a **basal level,** or a base-level criterion that must be met for testing on the subtest to continue. For example, a rule for establishing a basal level might be "Examinee answers two consecutive items correctly." When and if examinees fail a certain number of items in a row, a **ceiling level** is said to have been reached, and testing is discontinued.[3]

---

3. Experienced clinicians who have had occasion to test the limits of an examinee will tell you that this assumption is not always correct. **Testing the limits** is a procedure that entails the administration of test items beyond the level at which the test manual dictates discontinuance. The procedure may be employed when an examiner has reason to believe that an examinee can respond correctly to items at the higher level. On a standardized ability test such as the SB:FE, the discontinue guidelines must be respected, at least in terms of scoring. Testtakers do not earn formal credit for passing the more difficult items. Rather, the examiner would simply note on the protocol that testing of the limits was conducted with regard to a particular subtest and then record the findings.

For each subtest on the SB5, there are explicit rules for where to *start*, where to *reverse*, and where to *stop* (or *discontinue*). For example, an examiner might start at the examinee's estimated present ability level. The examiner might reverse if the examinee scores 0 on the first two items from the start point. The examiner would discontinue testing (stop) after a certain number of item failures after reversing. The manual also provides explicit rules for prompting examinees. If a vague or ambiguous response is given on some verbal items in subtests such as Vocabulary, Verbal Absurdities, or Verbal Analogies, the examiner is encouraged to give the examinee a prompt such as "Tell me more."

JUST THINK . . .

In what way(s) might an examiner misuse or abuse the obligation to prompt examinees? How could such misuse or abuse be prevented?

Although a few of the subtests are timed, most of the SB5 items are not. The test was constructed this way to accommodate testtakers with special needs and to fit the item response theory model used to calibrate the difficulty of items.

Scoring and interpretation   The test manual contains explicit directions for administering, scoring, and interpreting the test, as well as numerous examples of correct and incorrect responses useful in the scoring of individual items. Scores on the individual items of the various subtests are tallied to yield raw scores on each of the various subtests. The scorer then employs tables found in the manual to convert each of the subtest scores into a standard score. From these standard scores, composite scores are derived.

When scored by a knowledge test user, an administration of the SB5 may yield much more than a number for a Full Scale IQ and related composite scores. The test may yield a wealth of valuable information regarding the testtaker's strengths and weaknesses with respect to cognitive functioning. This information may be used by clinical and academic professionals in interventions designed to make a meaningful difference in the quality of examinees' lives. Various methods of profile analysis have been described for use with all major tests of cognitive ability (see, for example, Kaufman & Lichtenberger, 1999). These methods tend to have in common the identification of significant differences between subtest, composite, or other types of index scores, and a detailed analysis of the factors analyzing those differences. In identifying these significant differences, the test user relies not only on statistical calculations (or tables, if they are provided in the test manual) but also on the normative data described in the test manual. The magnitude of the differences between the scores under analysis should be uncommon or infrequent. The SB5 Technical Manual contains various tables designed to assist the test user in analysis. For example, one such table is "Differences Between SB5 IQ Scores and Between SB5 Factor Index Scores Required for Statistical Significance at .05 Level by Age."

In addition to formal scoring and analysis of significant difference scores, the occasion of an individually administered test affords the examiner an opportunity for behavioral observation. More specifically, the assessor is alert to the assessee's **extra-test behavior.** The way the examinee copes with frustration; how the examinee reacts to items considered very easy; the amount of support the examinee seems to require; the general approach to the task; how anxious, fatigued, cooperative, distractable, or compulsive the examinee appears to be—these are the types of behavioral observations that will supplement formal scores. The SB5 record form includes a checklist form of notable examinee behaviors. Included is a brief, yes/no questionnaire with items such as *Examinee's English usage was adequate for testing* and *Examinee was adequately cooperative*. There is also space to record notes and observations regarding the examinee's physical appearance, mood, and activity level, current medications, and related variables. Examiners may also note specific observations during the assessment. For example, when administering Memory for Sentences, there is usually no need to record an examinee's verbatim response. However, if the examinee produced unusual elaborations on the stimulus sentences, good judgment on the part of the examiner dictates that verbatim responses be recorded. Unusual responses on this subtest may also cue the examiner to possible hearing or speech problems.

A long-standing custom with regard to Stanford-Binet Full Scale scores is to convert them into nominal categories designated by certain cutoff boundaries for quick reference. Through the years, these categories have had different names. For the SB5, here are the cutoff boundaries with their corresponding nominal categories:

Measured IQ Range	Category
145–160	Very gifted or highly advanced
130–144	Gifted or very advanced
120–129	Superior
110–119	High average
90–109	Average
80–89	Low average
70–79	Borderline impaired or delayed
55–69	Mildly impaired or delayed
40–54	Moderately impaired or delayed

With reference to this list, Roid (2003c) cautioned that "the important concern is to describe the examinee's skills and abilities in detail, going beyond the label itself" (p. 150). The primary value of such labels is as a shorthand reference in some psychological reports. For example, in a summary statement at the end of a detailed SB5 report, a school psychologist might write, "In summary, Theodore presents as a well-groomed, engaging, and witty fifth-grader who is functioning in the high average range of intellectual ability."

JUST THINK . . .

Not that very long ago, *moron*, a word with pejorative connotations, was one of the categories in use. What, if anything, can test developers do to guard against the use of classification categories with pejorative connotations?

The Wechsler Tests

David Wechsler designed a series of individually administered intelligence tests to assess the intellectual abilities of people from preschool through adulthood. A general description of the various types of tasks measured in current as well as past revisions of these tests is presented in Table 9–3.

Traditionally, whether it was the Wechsler adult scale, the child scale, or the preschool scale, an examiner familiar with one Wechsler test would not have a great deal of difficulty navigating any other Wechsler test. Although this is probably still true, the Wechsler tests have shown a clear trend away from such uniformity. For example, until recently all Wechsler scales yielded, among other possible composite scores, a Full Scale IQ (a measure of general intelligence), a Verbal IQ (calculated on the basis of scores on subtests categorized as verbal), and a Performance IQ (calculated on the basis of scores on subtests categorized as nonverbal). All of that changed in 2003 with the publication

Table 9–3
General Types of Items Used in Wechsler Tests

A listing of the subtests specific to individual Wechsler scales is presented in Table 9–6.

Subtest	Description
Information	*In what continent is Brazil?* Questions such as these, which are wide-ranging and tap general knowledge, learning, and memory, are asked. Interests, education, cultural background, and reading skills are some influencing factors in the score achieved.
Comprehension	In general, these questions tap social comprehension, the ability to organize and apply knowledge, and what is colloquially referred to as "common sense." An illustrative question is *Why should children be cautious in speaking to strangers?*
Similarities	*How are a pen and a pencil alike?* This is the general type of question that appears in this subtest. Pairs of words are presented to the examinee, and the task is to determine how they are alike. The ability to analyze relationships and engage in logical, abstract thinking are two cognitive abilities tapped by this type of test.
Arithmetic	Arithmetic problems are presented and solved verbally. At lower levels, the task may involve simple counting. Learning of arithmetic, alertness and concentration, and short-term auditory memory are some of the intellectual abilities tapped by this test.
Vocabulary	The task is to define words. This test is thought to be a good measure of general intelligence, although education and cultural opportunity clearly contribute to success on it.
Receptive Vocabulary	The task is to select from four pictures what the examiner has said aloud. This tests taps auditory discrimination and processing, auditory memory, and the integration of visual perception and auditory input.
Picture Naming	The task is to name a picture displayed in a book of stimulus pictures. This test taps expressive language and word retrieval ability.
Digit Span	The examiner verbally presents a series of numbers, and the examinee's task is to repeat the numbers in the same sequence or backwards. This subtest taps auditory short-term memory, encoding, and attention.
Letter-Number Sequencing	Letters and numbers are orally presented in a mixed-up order. The task is to repeat the list with numbers in ascending order and letters in alphabetical order. Success on this subtest requires attention, sequencing ability, mental manipulation, and processing speed.
Picture Completion	The subject's task here is to identify what important part is missing from a picture. For example, the testtaker might be shown a picture of a chair with one leg missing. This subtest draws on visual perception abilities, alertness, memory, concentration, attention to detail, and ability to differentiate essential from nonessential detail. Because respondents may point to the missing part, this test provides a good nonverbal estimate of intelligence. However, successful performance on a test such as this still tends to be highly influenced by cultural factors.
Picture Arrangement	In the genre of a comic-strip panel, this subtest requires the testtaker to re-sort a scrambled set of cards with pictures on them into a story that makes sense. Because the testtaker must understand the whole story before a successful re-sorting will occur, this subtest is thought to tap the ability to comprehend or "size up" a situation. Additionally, attention, concentration, and ability to see temporal and cause-and-effect relationships are tapped.
Block Design	A design with colored blocks is illustrated either with blocks themselves or with a picture of the finished design, and the examinee's task is to reproduce the design. This test draws on perceptual-motor skills, psychomotor speed, and the ability to analyze and synthesize. Factors that may influence performance on this test include the examinee's color vision, frustration tolerance, and flexibility or rigidity in problem solving.
Object Assembly	The task here is to assemble, as quickly as possible, a cut-up picture of a familiar object. Some of the abilities called on here include pattern recognition, assembly skills, and psychomotor speed. Useful qualitative information pertinent to the examinee's work habits may also be obtained here by careful observation of the approach to the task. For example, does the examinee give up easily or persist in the face of difficulty?
Coding	If you were given the dot-and-dash equivalents of several letters in Morse code and then had to write out letters in Morse code as quickly as you could, you would be completing a coding task. The Wechsler coding task involves using a code from a printed key. The test is thought to draw on factors such as attention, learning ability, psychomotor speed, and concentration ability.
Symbol Search	The task is to visually scan two groups of symbols, one search group and one target group, and determine whether the target symbol appears in the search group. The test is presumed to tap cognitive processing speed.
Matrix Reasoning	A nonverbal analogy-like task involving an incomplete matrix designed to tap perceptual organizing abilities and reasoning.
Word Reasoning	The task is to identify the common concept being described with a series of clues. This test taps verbal abstraction ability and the ability to generate alternative concepts.
Picture Concepts	The task is to select one picture from two or three rows of pictures to form a group with a common characteristic. It is designed to tap the ability to abstract as well as categorical reasoning ability.
Cancellation	The task is to scan either a structured or an unstructured arrangement of visual stimuli and mark targeted images within a specified time limit. This subtest taps visual selective attention and related abilities.

of the fourth edition of the children's scale (discussed in greater detail below), a test that dispensed with the long-standing Wechsler dichotomy of Verbal and Performance subtests. We expect more changes in future editions of these tests.

Regardless of the changes instituted to date, there remains a great deal of commonality between the scales. The Wechsler tests are all point scales that yield deviation IQs with a mean of 100 (interpreted as average) and a standard deviation of 15. On each of the Wechsler tests, a testtaker's performance is compared with scores earned by others in that age group. The tests have in common clearly written manuals that provide descriptions of each of the subtests, including the rationale for their inclusion. The manuals also contain clear, explicit directions for administering subtests, as well as a number of standard prompts for dealing with a variety of questions, comments, or other contingencies. There are similar starting, stopping, and discontinue guidelines and explicit scoring instructions with clear examples. For test interpretation, all the Wechsler manuals come with myriad statistical charts which can prove very useful when it comes time for the assessor to make recommendations on the basis of the assessment. In addition, a number of aftermarket publications authored by various assessment professionals are also available to supplement guidelines presented in the test manuals.

In general, the Wechsler tests have been evaluated favorably from a psychometric standpoint. Although the coefficients of reliability will predictably vary as a function of the specific type of reliability assessed, reported reliability estimates for the Wechsler tests in various categories (internal consistency, test-retest reliability, interscorer reliability) tend to be satisfactory, even more than satisfactory in many cases. Wechsler manuals also typically contain a great deal of information on validity studies, usually in the form of correlational studies or factor-analytic studies.

The three Wechsler intelligence tests in use at this writing are the Wechsler Adult Intelligence Scale-Third Edition (WAIS-III), for ages 16 through 89; the Wechsler Intelligence Scale for Children-Fourth Edition (WISC-IV), for ages 6 through 16 years 11 months; and the Wechsler Pre-school and Primary Scale of Intelligence-Third Edition (WPPSI-III), for ages 3 years to 7 years 3 months. We briefly describe each of these tests here. As you will see in our discussion of the adult scale, long before "the W-B" had become a television network, this abbreviation was used to refer to the first in what would evolve into a long line of Wechsler tests.

The Wechsler Adult Intelligence Scale-Third Edition (WAIS-III)

The **WAIS-III** was designed to measure the intelligence of adults. The predecessors of this test, from the most recent on back, were the WAIS-R, the WAIS, the W-B II (Wechsler-Bellevue II), and the W-B I (Wechsler-Bellevue I). Now, some history.

In the early 1930s, Wechsler's employer, Bellevue Hospital in Manhattan, needed an instrument for evaluating the intellectual capacity of its multilingual, multinational, and multicultural clients. Dissatisfied with existing intelligence tests, Wechsler began to experiment. The eventual result was a test of his own, the W-B I, which he published in 1939. This new test borrowed from existing tests in format, though not in content.

Unlike the most popular individually administered intelligence test of the time, the Stanford-Binet, the W-B I was a point scale, not an age scale. The items were classified by subtests rather than by age. The test was organized into six verbal subtests and five performance subtests, and all the items in each test were arranged in order of increasing difficulty. An equivalent alternate form of the test, the W-B II, was published in 1942, but was never thoroughly standardized (Rapaport et al., 1968). Unless a specific reference is made to the W-B II, references here (and in the literature in general) to the Wechsler-Bellevue or the W-B are referring to the Wechsler-Bellevue I (W-B I).

Although research suggested that the W-B was indeed measuring something comparable to what other intelligence tests were measuring, the test had these problems: (1) The standardization sample was rather restricted; (2) some subtests lacked sufficient inter-item reliability; (3) some of the subtests were made up of items that were too easy; (4) and the scoring criteria for certain items were too ambiguous. Sixteen years after the publication of the W-B, a revision was published: the Wechsler Adult Intelligence Scale (WAIS; Wechsler, 1955).

Like its predecessor, the WAIS was organized into Verbal and Performance scales. Scoring yielded a Verbal IQ, a Performance IQ, and a Full Scale IQ. The test was carefully constructed and standardized and quickly became "the standard against which other adult tests can be compared" (Lyman, 1972, p. 429). The need for a more contemporary norm group soon became evident, and a revision of the test, the WAIS-R, was published in 1981 shortly after Wechsler's death. In addition to new norms and updated materials, the administration instructions were changed to mandate alternation between verbal and performance tests. In 1997, the third edition of the test (the WAIS-III) was published, with authorship credited to David Wechsler.

The WAIS-III contained updated and colorized materials. Due to greater life expectancies, norms were expanded to include testtakers in the age range of 74 to 89. In some cases, test materials were made physically larger to facilitate viewing by older adults. Some items were added to each of the subtests to extend the test's floor (more than 3 standard deviations below average) and to make the test more useful for evaluating people with extreme intellectual deficits. Analyses were undertaken to detect and replace any WAIS-R items found to be biased. The test was co-normed with another new edition of another Wechsler test, the Wechsler Memory Scale-Third Edition (WMS-III). The technical manual, which contained data for both the WAIS-III and the WMS-III (Tulsky et al., 1997), facilitated comparisons of memory with other indices of intellectual functioning when both the WAIS-III and the WMS-III were administered.

Three new subtests were added to the WAIS-III, primarily to address concerns about the limited domains of cognitive functioning tapped in many intelligence tests. Sample items from two of these new subtests, Symbol Search and Letter-Number Sequencing, are illustrated and explained in Figure 9–2. Symbol Search is a performance subtest designed to measure processing speed. Letter-Number Sequencing is a verbal subtest designed to measure attention and working memory. The third new subtest is Matrix Reasoning, a nonverbal, analogy-like task designed to tap perceptual organizing abilities and reasoning. Because it is an untimed performance test, it reduces the contribution of perceptual speed to performance test scores.

A comprehensive guide to administration is presented in the *WAIS-III Administration and Scoring Manual.* Additionally, the test is packaged with a video that gives an overview of changes in the test, reviews new features, and illustrates various aspects of test administration, scoring, and interpretation.

Standardization and norms The WAIS-III standardization sample consisted of 2,450 adults aged 16 to 89 years, divided into 13 age bands, from 16 to 17 years at one end of the spectrum to 85 to 89 years at the other. The sample was stratified on the basis of 1995 U.S. Census data with regard to variables such as age, sex, race/ethnicity, educational level, and geographic region. Consistent with census data, there were more females than males in the older age bands.

Following a Wechsler tradition, most subtest raw scores for each age group were converted to percentiles and then to a scale with a mean of 10 and a standard deviation of 3. There was, however, a break with tradition in terms of the derivation of the scaled

Symbol Search

Letter-Number Sequencing

Item	Response
Q-3	3-Q
T-9-1	1-9-T
M-3-P-6	3-6-M-P
F-7-K-2-8	2-7-8-F-K
5-J-4-A-1-S	1-4-5-A-J-S
C-6-4-W-O-7-D	4-6-7-C-D-O-W

Figure 9–2
Sample Items From the WAIS-III

In the Symbol Search subtest, testtakers are presented with paired groups of stimuli, a target group (two symbols), and a search group. The testtaker marks a box to indicate whether either of the two target symbols appears in the search group. In the Letter-Number Sequencing subtest, the examiner verbalizes a list of letters and numbers. The testtaker's task is to repeat the list in reordered fashion—numbers in ascending order first, followed by letters in alphabetical order.

scores. On the WAIS-R, scaled scores for each subtest had been based on the performance of a nonimpaired reference group of testtakers who were 20 to 34 years old. This was done because Wechsler believed that "optimal performance tended to occur at these ages" (Tulsky et al., 1997, p. 40). However, this belief had been challenged (Kaufman et al., 1989), and the use of the reference group for calculation of scaled scores contributed to a number of problems in WAIS-R interpretation, especially with older testtakers (Ivnik et al., 1992; Ryan et al., 1990; Tulsky et al., 1997). On the WAIS-III, scores obtained by the testtaker's same-age normative group serve as the basis for the testtaker's scaled score.

> **JUST THINK . . .**
> Which do you think is more useful, comparing a testtaker's test performance to optimal or to someone in their own age group? Why?

Psychometric issues   The *WAIS-III Technical Manual* presents data from a number of studies attesting to the reliability, validity, and overall psychometric soundness of the test. A bit surprising, however, is the relatively small sample sizes used in some of the studies. For example, to help document the criterion-related validity of the WAIS-III, correlations between scores on that test and the SB:FE were analyzed in a study that employed only 26 adults. Those same 26 adults served as the sample for a similar criterion-related validity study that compared WAIS-III scores with scores on Raven's (1976) Standard Progressive Matrices. Use of the same relatively small group of subjects in test validation research raises questions about the effect of practice on test performance. Larger samples were employed in similar criterion-related validity studies for the WISC-III ($n=184$ 16-year-olds) and the WAIS-R ($n=192$ adults aged 16 to 74).

The evaluation of the construct validity of a test proceeds on the assumption that one knows in advance exactly what the test is supposed to measure. For intelligence tests, it is essential to know in advance how the test developer defined intelligence. If in a specific test intelligence was defined as Spearman's g, for example, then we would expect a factor analysis of such a test to yield a single large common factor. The single large common factor would indicate that the different questions or tasks on the test largely reflected the same underlying characteristic (intelligence, or g). By contrast, if intelligence were defined by a test developer in accordance with Guilford's theory, no one factor would be expected to dominate. Instead, one would anticipate many different factors reflecting a diverse set of abilities. Recall that from Guilford's perspective, there is no single underlying intelligence for the different test items to reflect. Therefore, there would be no basis for a large common factor.

In a sense, a compromise between Spearman and Guilford is Thorndike. Thorndike's theory of intelligence leads us to look for one central factor reflecting g, along with three additional factors representing social, concrete, and abstract intelligences. In this case, analysis would suggest that testtakers' responses to specific items reflected a general intelligence in part, but also different types of intelligence: social, concrete, and abstract.

Wechsler defined intelligence as general ("the global capacity of the individual") but originating in distinct components ("composed of . . . abilities which . . . are quantitatively differentiable"). Recall that Wechsler (1974) said there were two such components, verbal and performance. Historically, users of Wechsler tests have interpreted test data with reference to individual subtest scores as well as the Verbal, Performance, and Full Scale scores, with the IQ calculated on the basis of these indices. Clinicians were trained to look for diagnostically significant discrepancies within and between these many indices—yet all within the Verbal/Performance framework. However, as early as the 1950s, alternative, multifactor models of what the Wechsler-Bellevue (Cohen, 1952a, 1952b) and the WAIS (Cohen, 1957a, 1957b) seemed to be measuring were in evidence.

In the years that followed, test users and theorists would wonder whether data derived from Wechsler tests might fit better conceptually with alternative, factorially derived models of cognitive ability (Hishinuma & Yamakawa, 1993; Kaufman, 1990, 1994; Sattler, 1992; Shaw et al., 1993; Smith et al., 1993). The question "How many factors are there *really* on the Wechsler tests?" seemed to have been transformed from a passing academic interest to a pressing user obsession. The issue was addressed in the WAIS-III development, as evidenced by extensive exploratory and confirmatory factor-analytic investigations described in the test's technical manual. A result of these investigations was that in addition to the traditional Verbal/Performance dichotomy, WAIS-III users would be able to group test data by four factors: Verbal Comprehension, Working Memory, Perceptual Organization, and Processing Speed. Based on these four factors, four *index scores*, each with a mean set at 100 and a standard deviation set at 15, could be derived from the test data. A listing of the subtests used to derive each of these index scores is presented in Table 9–4.

The appeal of the Wechsler test for adults prompted a "brand extension" of sorts, the Wechsler test for children.

Table 9–4
WAIS-III Subtests Grouped According to Indices

Verbal Comprehension	Working Memory	Perceptual Organization	Processing Speed
Vocabulary	Arithmetic Picture	Completion	Digit Symbol
Similarities	Digit Span	Block Design	Symbol Search
Information	Letter-Number Sequencing	Matrix Reasoning	

Source: The Psychological Corporation

The Wechsler Intelligence Scale for Children-Fourth Edition (WISC-IV)

Background   The Wechsler Intelligence Scale for Children (WISC) was first published in 1949. It represented a downward extension of the W-B and actually incorporated many items contemplated for use in the (never-published) W-B II. "A well-standardized, stable instrument correlating well with other tests of intelligence" (Burstein, 1972, p. 844), the WISC was not without its flaws, however. The standardization sample contained only White children, and some of the test items were viewed as perpetuating gender and cultural stereotypes. Further, parts of the test manual were so unclear as to lead to ambiguities in the administration and scoring of the test. A revision of the WISC, called the Wechsler Intelligence Scale for Children-Revised (WISC-R), was published in 1974. The WISC-R included non-Whites in the standardization sample. Test material pictures were also more balanced culturally. The test's language was modernized and "child-ized"; the word *cigars* in an arithmetic item, for example, was replaced with *candy bars*. There were also innovations in the administration and scoring of the test. For example, Verbal and Performance tests were administered in alternating fashion, a practice that would also be extended to the WAIS-III and the WPPSI-R.

The revision of the WISC-R yielded the Wechsler Intelligence Scale for Children-III, published in 1991. This revision was undertaken to update and improve test items as well as the norms. For example, easier items were added to the Arithmetic scale to assess counting ability. At the other end of the Arithmetic scale, relatively difficult, multi-step word problems were added. A Symbol Search subtest (similar to that described in our discussion of the WAIS-III) was introduced in the WISC-III. The test was added as the result of research on controlled attention, and it was thought to tap *freedom from distractibility*.

The test today   Published in 2003, the WISC-IV represents the culmination of a five-year research program involving several research stages from conceptual development through final assembly and evaluation. Perhaps most noteworthy in the introduction to the fourth edition is a noticeable "warming" to the CHC model of intelligence—qualified by a reminder that Carroll (1997), much like Wechsler and others, believed *g* to be very much alive and well in the major instruments designed to measure intelligence:

> Based on the most comprehensive factor-analytic investigation of cognitive ability measures to date, Carroll (1993, 1997) concluded that evidence for a general factor of intelligence was overwhelming. Thus, the trend toward an emphasis on multiple, more narrowly defined cognitive abilities has not resulted in rejection of an underlying, global aspect of

JUST THINK . . .

The last *C* in the CHC model belongs to Carroll, and Carroll is a firm believer in *g*. Cattell and Horn, the first *C* and the *H* in CHC, are no fans of *g*. It goes to show the strange bedfellows that can come together when a theory named for three people was not developed by the three people. Your thoughts?

general intelligence. Despite continuing debate over the existence of a single, underlying construct of intelligence, the results of factor-analytic research converge in the identification of 8 to 10 broad domains of intelligence. . . . (Wechsler, 2003, p. 2)

Also emphasized in the manual is the fact that cognitive functions are interrelated, making it difficult if not impossible to obtain a "pure" measure of a function. A test purporting to measure *processing speed,* for example, may involve multiple abilities, such as visual discrimination ability and motor ability. Further, questions were raised regarding the desirability of even trying to isolate specific abilities for measurement, because in "real life" cognitive tasks are rarely performed in isolation. This point was made by Wechsler (1975) himself:

> . . . the attributes and factors of intelligence, like the elementary particles in physics, have at once collective and individual properties; that is, they appear to behave differently when alone from what they do when operating in concert. (p. 138)

Consistent with the foregoing, the developers of the WISC-IV revised the test so that it now yields a measure of general intellectual functioning (a Full Scale IQ, or FSIQ) as well as four index scores: a Verbal Comprehension Index, a Perceptual Reasoning Index, a Working Memory Index, and a Processing Speed Index. Each of these indexes is based on scores on three to five subtests. It is the scores from each index, based on the core subtests only, that combine to yield the Full Scale IQ. It is also possible to derive up to seven *process scores* using tables supplied in the Administration and Scoring Manual. A **process score** may be generally defined as an index designed to help understand the way the testtaker processes various kinds of information. In what many would view as a momentous departure from previous versions of the test, the WISC-IV does *not* yield separate Verbal and Performance IQ scores.

Examiners familiar with previous versions of the WISC may be surprised by some of the other changes instituted in this edition. The subtests known as Picture Arrangement, Object Assembly, and Mazes have all been eliminated. Separate norms are now presented for Block Design, with and without time bonuses. In part, these separate norms represent an acknowledgment that certain cultures value speeded tasks more than others. The subtests Information, Arithmetic, and Picture Completion, all once *core subtests,* are now *supplementary subtests.* On the WISC-IV and other tests, a **core subtest** measures ability that contributes to a composite score such as the Full Scale IQ or an index score. A **supplemental subtest** is used either to extend the range of abilities measured or to substitute for a core subtest when necessary. On the WISC-IV, there are 10 core subtests and five supplemental subtests.

After pilot work and national tryouts using preliminary versions of the new scale, a standardization edition of the WISC-IV was created and administered to a stratified sample of 2,200 subjects ranging in age from 6 years old to 16 years 11 months old. The sample was stratified to be representative of U.S. Census data for the year 2000 with regard to key variables such as age, gender, race/ethnicity, parent education level, and geographic region (Figure 9–3). Persons who were not fluent in English or who suffered from a variety of physical or mental conditions that might depress test performance were excluded from participation in the standardization sample (see Wechsler, 2003, p. 24, for a complete list of exclusionary criteria). Quality assurance procedures were put in place for qualifying examiners, scoring procedures, and data entry. All items were reviewed qualitatively for possible bias by reviewers as well as quantitatively by means of IRT bias analysis methodologies.

The manual for the WISC-IV presents a number of studies as evidence of the psychometric soundness of the test. In terms of reliability, evidence is presented to support the test's internal consistency and its test-retest stability. Additionally, evidence of excellent interscorer agreement (low to high .90s) is presented. Evidence for the validity

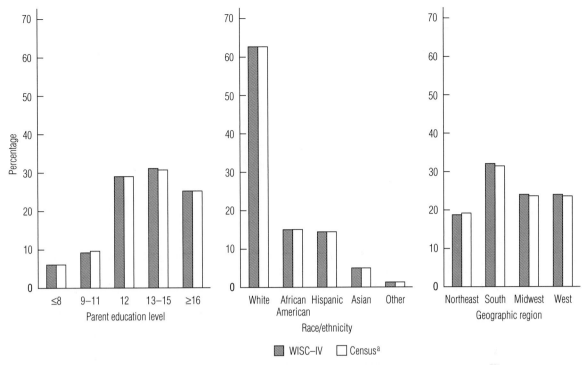

ªU.S. Population data are from Current Population Survey, March 2000: School Enrollment Supplemental File [CD-ROM] by U.S. Bureau of the Census, 2000, Washington, DC: U.S. Bureau of the Census (Producer/Distributor).

Figure 9–3
Demographic Characteristics of the WISC-IV Standardization Sample Compared to the U.S. Population

These graphs, reprinted from the test's technical manual, illustrate the close correspondence between WISC-IV standardization sample demographic characteristics and those of the 2000 U.S. Census.

of the test came in the form of a number of correlational studies which focused on WISC-IV scores as compared to scores achieved on other tests, as well as a series of factor-analytic studies. Detailed data are presented in the test manual.

The WISC-IV compared to the SB5   Although the SB5 can be used with testtakers who are both much younger and much older than the testtakers who can be tested with the WISC-IV, comparisons between the Binet and the WISC have become something akin to a tradition among assessors who test children. Both tests were published in 2003, and formal reviews were not available at the time of this writing. However, it is useful to see how these two major tests match up with regard to several variables.

Both are individually administered instruments that take about an hour or so of test administration time to yield a Full Scale IQ composite score based on the administration of 10 subtests. The WISC-IV also contains five supplemental tests (add about 30 minutes for the administration of the "extended battery"); the SB5 contains none. With the SB5, an Abbreviated Battery IQ can be obtained from the administration of two subtests. The WISC-IV formally contains no such short forms, although this fact has not stopped many assessors from devising their own "short form" or finding a way to construct one from some aftermarket publication. Both tests contain child-friendly materials, and both tests have optional available software for scoring and report writing.

The norming sample for testtakers aged 6 through 16 was 2,200 for both tests. The WISC-IV included parent education as one stratifying variable that the SB5 did not. The

Table 9–5
Cognitive and Nonverbal Factors on the WISC-IV Compared to the Stanford-Binet 5

	WISC-IV	SB5
Cognitive Factors	Working Memory Processing Speed Verbal Comprehension Perceptual Reasoning	Working Memory Visual-Spatial Processing Knowledge Fluid Reasoning Quantitative Reasoning
Nonverbal Factors	Working Memory Processing Speed Perceptual Reasoning	Working Memory Visual-Spatial Processing Fluid Reasoning Quantitative Reasoning Knowledge

SB5 included socioeconomic status and testtaker education as stratifying variables that the WISC-IV did not. The test developers for both tests included exclusionary criteria in the norming sample, and separate validity studies with some of these exceptional samples were conducted in both tests. Consult the respective manuals for differences between the two tests in terms of these separate validity studies because they did, in fact, employ different kinds of samples for these validity studies.

The developers of both the WISC-IV and the SB5 were obvious fans of the CHC model of intelligence. Still, both seemed to accept the model only to the extent that they could still find a place for *g* at the top of the hierarchy. The two tests employ some similar and some dissimilar kinds of subtests. As a whole, both tests may be interpreted with respect to several cognitive and nonverbal indices that are drawn, to greater or lesser degrees, from the CHC model. However, it is here that some interesting differences emerge (see Table 9–5). Future researchers may explore further the extent to which these two tests are indeed measuring different variables.

JUST THINK . . .

The SB5 and the WISC-IV are similar in many respects except with regard to exclusionary criteria and the populations on which separate validity studies were conducted. Why do you think that is? What are the implications of these differences for test users who test members of exceptional populations?

The Wechsler Preschool and Primary Scale of Intelligence-Third Edition (WPPSI-III)

Project Head Start, as well as other 1960s programs for preschool children who were culturally different or exceptional (defined in this context as atypical in ability—gifted or developmentally delayed), fostered interest in the development of new tests for preschoolers (Zimmerman & Woo-Sam, 1978). The Stanford-Binet traditionally had been the test of choice for use with preschoolers. Should the WISC be restandardized for children under 6, or should an entirely new test be developed? Wechsler (1967) decided that a new scale should be developed and standardized especially for children under age 6. The new test was the WPPSI (the Wechsler Preschool and Primary Scale of Intelligence), usually pronounced "whipsy." Its publication in 1967 extended the age range of the Wechsler series of intelligence tests downward to age 4.

The WPPSI was the first major intelligence test that "adequately sampled the total population of the United States, including racial minorities" (Zimmerman & Woo-Sam, 1978, p. 10). This advantage contributed greatly to the success of the WPPSI, especially in an era when standardized tests were under attack for inadequate minority represen-

Table 9–6
The Wechsler Tests at a Glance*

	WPPSI-III	WISC-IV	WAIS-III
Information	X	X	X
Comprehension	X	X	X
Similarities	X	X	X
Arithmetic	—	X	X
Vocabulary	X	X	X
Receptive Vocabulary	X	—	—
Picture Naming	X	—	—
Digit Span	—	X	X
Letter-Number Sequencing	—	X	X
Picture Completion	X	X	X
Picture Arrangement	—	—	X
Block Design	X	X	X
Object Assembly	X	—	X
Coding	X	X	—
Symbol Search	X	X	X
Matrix Reasoning	X	X	X
Digit Symbol	—	—	X
Word Reasoning	X	X	—
Picture Concepts	X	X	—
Cancellation	—	X	—

*Consult the individual test manuals to see whether a particular subtest is a core subtest, a supplemental subtest, or an optional subtest. On the WPPSI-III, some subtests function as one type of test at one age level and as another type of test at another age level. For example, Receptive Vocabulary is a *core* verbal subtest for testtakers up to 3 years 11 months, and an *optional* verbal subtest for ages 4 years and over. Picture Naming is a *supplemental* verbal subtest for testtakers up to 3 years 11 months, and an *optional* verbal subtest for ages 4 years and over.

tation in standardization samples. A revision of the WPPSI, the WPPSI-R, was published in 1989. It was designed to assess the intelligence of children from ages 3 years through 7 years 3 months. New items were developed to extend the range of the test both upward and downward.

Published in 2002, the WPPSI-III extended the age range of children who could be tested with this instrument downward to 2 years 6 months. The technical manual for this instrument contained the same sort of historical introduction to intelligence testing as the WISC-IV. However, instead of arriving at the conclusion that it was time to drop Wechsler's traditional Verbal/Performance dichotomy, as was done with the WISC-IV, the utility of the dichotomy was reaffirmed in the WPPSI-III manual. Accordingly, three composite scores may be obtained: Verbal IQ, Performance IQ, and Full Scale IQ.

The WPPSI-III was changed in many ways from its previous edition. Five subtests (Arithmetic, Animal Pegs, Geometric Design, Mazes, and Sentences) were dropped. Seven new subtests were added: Matrix Reasoning, Picture Concepts, Word Reasoning, Coding, Symbol Search, Receptive Vocabulary, and Picture Naming. On the WPPSI-III, subtests are labeled *core, supplemental,* or *optional,* and some tests have different labels at different age levels (for example, *supplemental* at one age level and *optional* at another age level). Core subtests are required for the calculation of composite scores. Supplemental subtests are used to provide a broader sampling of intellectual functioning. Supplemental subtests may also substitute for a core subtest if a core subtest for some reason was not administered or was administered but is not usable. Supplemental subtests are also used to derive additional scores, such as a *Processing Speed Quotient.* **Optional subtests** may not be used to substitute for core subtests but may be used in the derivation of optional scores such as a *General Language Composite.* A complete list of all the subtests on all of the Weschsler scales, including the WPPSI-III, the WISC-IV, and the WAIS-III, is presented in Table 9–6.

The structure of the WPPSI-III reflects the interest of the test developers in enhancing measures of fluid reasoning and processing speed. Three of the new tests (Matrix Reasoning, Picture Concepts, and Word Reasoning) were designed to tap fluid reasoning, and two of the new tests (Coding and Symbol Search) were designed to tap processing speed. In an effort to reduce the confounding effects of speed on cognitive ability, the test developers discontinued the practice of awarding bonus points to Block Design and Object Assembly scores for quick, successful performance. The test developers hoped that the incorporation of the Symbol Search and Coding subtests would provide a less confounded measure of processing speed.

If you have ever watched *Trading Spaces, While You Were Out, This Old House,* or any other television show that deals with home renovation, you know that attention is always given to the floors and ceilings. Well, it's that way when renovating intelligence tests, too. The designers of the WPPSI-III added easier items as well as more difficult ones to each of the retained subtests. They concluded that the improved subtest floors and ceilings made the WPPSI-III "a more accurate measure of cognitive functioning for children with significant developmental delays, as well as for children suspected of being intellectually gifted" (Wechsler, 2002, p. 17).

JUST THINK . . .

David Wechsler believed that the factors of intelligence, much like elementary particles in physics, have both collective and individual properties. Most of the time, Wechsler tests seem to have as their goal the measurement of the collective properties "acting in concert." However, with the incorporation of Symbol Search and Coding on the WPPSI-III, the test developers seem to be striving for a "purer" measure of processing speed. What are your thoughts on the apparent mixing of the measurement of the collective and individual properties of factors in intellectual ability?

After pilot work and a national tryout of the WPPSI-III in development, a standardization edition of the test was created. The test was administered to a stratified sample of 1,700 children between the ages of 2 years 6 months and 7 years 3 months, as well as samples of children from special groups. The sample was selected in proportion to year 2000 U. S. Census data, stratified on the variables of age, sex, race/ethnicity, parent education level, and geographic region. As has become custom when revising major intelligence scales, a number of steps were taken to guard against item bias. Included were statistical methods as well as reviews by bias experts. A number of quality assurance procedures were put in place, including anchor protocols, to ensure that tests were scored

JUST THINK . . .

Why is it important for independent researchers to attempt to verify some of the findings regarding the psychometric soundness of major tests?

and that data were entered properly. As has become custom as well, a number of studies attesting to the psychometric soundness of the scale are presented in the technical manual.

Wechsler, Binet, and the Short Form

An issue related to Wechsler tests but certainly not exclusive to them is the development and use of short forms. The term **short form** refers to a test that has been abbreviated in length, typically to reduce the time needed for test administration, scoring, and interpretation. Sometimes, particularly when the testtaker is believed to have an atypically short attention span or other problems that would make administration of the complete test impossible, a sampling of representative subtests is administered. Arguments for such use of Wechsler scales have been made with reference to testtakers from the general population (Kaufman et al., 1991), the elderly (Paolo & Ryan, 1991), and others (Benedict et al., 1992; Boone, 1991; Grossman et al., 1993; Hayes, 1999; Randolph et al.,

1993; Sweet et al., 1990). A seven-subtest short form of the WAIS-III is sometimes used by clinicians, and it seems to demonstrate acceptable psychometric characteristics (Ryan & Ward, 1999; Schoop et al., 2001).

Short forms of intelligence tests are nothing new. In fact, they have been around almost as long as the long forms. Soon after the Binet-Simon reached the United States, a short form of it was proposed (Doll, 1917). Today, school psychologists with long waiting lists for assessment appointments, forensic psychologists working in an overburdened criminal justice system, and health insurers seeking to pay less for assessment services are some of the groups to whom the short form appeals.

In 1958, David Wechsler endorsed the use of short forms but only for screening purposes. Years later, perhaps in response to the potential for abuse of short forms, he took a much dimmer view of reducing the number of subtests just to save time. He advised those claiming that they did not have the time to administer the entire test to "find the time" (Wechsler, 1967, p. 37).

Some literature reviews on the validity of short forms have tended to support Wechsler's admonition to "find the time." Watkins (1986) concluded that short forms may be used for screening purposes only, not to make placement or educational decisions. From a historical perspective, Smith et al. (2000) characterized views on the transfer of validity from the parent form to the short form as "overly optimistic." In contrast to some critics who have called for the abolishment of short forms altogether, Smith et al. (2000) argued that the standards for the validity of a short form must be high. They suggested a series of procedures to be used in the development of valid short forms. Silverstein (1990) provided an incisive review of the history of short forms, focusing on four issues: (1) how to abbreviate the original test; (2) how to select subjects; (3) how to estimate scores on the original test; and (4) the criteria to apply when comparing the short form with the original. Ryan and Ward (1999) advised that anytime a short form is used, the score should be reported on the official record with the abbreviation "Est" next to it, to indicate that the reported value is only an estimate.

From a psychometric standpoint, the validity of a test is affected by and is somewhat dependent on the test's reliability. Changes in a test that lessen its reliability may also lessen its validity. Reducing the number of items in a test typically reduces the test's reliability and hence its validity. For that reason, decisions made on the basis of data derived from administrations of a test's short form must, in general, be made with caution (Nagle & Bell, 1993). In fact, when data from the administration of a short form clearly suggest the need for intervention or placement, the best practice may be to "find the time" to administer the full form of the test.

The Wechsler Abbreviated Scale of Intelligence   Against a backdrop in which many practitioners view short forms as desirable and many psychometricians urge caution in their use, the Wechsler Abbreviated Scale of Intelligence (WASI) was published in 1999. Because many test users find the appeal of a short form irresistible, many different short forms have been devised informally from longer forms of tests—short forms with varying degrees of psychometric soundness and seldom with any normative data. The WASI was designed to answer the need for a short instrument to screen intellectual ability in testtakers from 6 to 89 years of age. The test comes in a two-subtest form (consisting of Vocabulary and Block Design) that takes about 15 minutes to administer and a four-subtest form that takes about 30 minutes to administer. The four subtests (Vocabulary, Block Design, Similarities, and Matrix Reasoning) are WISC- and WAIS-type subtests that had high correlations with Full Scale IQ on those tests. They are thought to tap a wide range of cognitive abilities. The WASI yields measures of Verbal IQ, Performance IQ, and Full

Scale IQ. Consistent with many other intelligence tests, the Full Scale IQ was set at 100 and a standard deviation at 15.

The WASI was standardized with 2,245 cases including 1,100 children and 1,145 adults. The manual presents evidence for satisfactory psychometric soundness, although some reviewers of this test were not completely satisfied with the way the validity research was conducted and reported (Keith et al., 2001). Other reviewers, however, found the psychometric qualities of the WASI, as well as its overall usefulness, to far exceed that of comparable, brief measures of intelligence (Lindskog & Smith, 2001).

The Wechsler Tests in Perspective

Read the manual for a recently developed Wechsler intelligence test, and the chances are good that you will find illustrations of exemplary practices in test development. Qualified examiners can learn to administer the tests relatively quickly, and examinees tend to find the test materials engaging. A number of computer-assisted scoring and interpretive aids are available for each of the tests, as are a number of manuals and guides. Moreover, the test developers are evidently making efforts to keep the scoring and interpretation of the tests fresh. Witness the efforts of the developers of the WISC-IV as they have reexamined the traditional Wechsler verbal/performance dichotomy and transformed it into a model that is more conducive to analysis by means of the more contemporary, multiple-factor conceptualization of intelligence.

In becoming acquainted with the Wechsler tests as well as the SB5, you have probably noticed that the statistical technique of factor analysis plays a key role in the test development process. To increase your understanding of this important though sometimes complicated statistical technique, we asked a "factor analyst-type colleague" to prepare a description that was "as uncomplicated as possible." That description is this chapter's *Close-up.* For yet more on factor analysis, see Cohen (2005), the companion workbook to this text.

Other Measures of Intelligence

Tests Designed for Individual Administration

In recent years, a growing number of tests purporting to measure intelligence have become available to test users. Some of these tests were developed by Alan and Nadeen Kaufman. This husband-wife team developed the Kaufman Adolescent and Adult Intelligence Test (KAIT; Kaufman & Kaufman, 1993) and the Kaufman Brief Intelligence Test (K-BIT; Kaufman & Kaufman, 1990). Their first flagship test was the Kaufman Assessment Battery for Children (K-ABC; Kaufman & Kaufman, 1983a, 1983b). The K-ABC departed conceptually from previously published intelligence tests with its focus on information processing and, more specifically, with its distinction between sequential and simultaneous processing. The Kaufmans drew on the theoretical writings of A. R. Luria (1966a) in the design of the K-ABC, as did J. P. Das and Jack Naglieri in the development of their test called the Cognitive Assessment System. Another test battery that deviated in many ways from prior measures of cognitive ability is the Differential Ability Scales (DAS). Widely used in educational settings, the DAS is discussed in more detail in Chapter 10.

Factor Analysis*

To measure characteristics of physical objects, there may be some disagreement about the best methods to use, but there is little disagreement about which dimensions are being measured. We know, for example, that we are measuring length when we use a ruler, and we know that we are measuring temperature when we use a thermometer. Such certainty is not always present in measuring psychological dimensions such as personality traits, attitudes, and cognitive abilities.

Psychologists may disagree about what to name the dimensions being measured and about the number of dimensions being measured. Consider a personality trait one researcher refers to as *niceness.* Another researcher views *niceness* as a vague term that lumps together two related but independent traits called *friendliness* and *kindness.* Yet another researcher claims that *kindness* is too general and that it must be dichotomized into *kindness to friends* and *kindness to strangers.* Who is right? Is everybody right? If researchers are ever going to build on each others' findings, there needs to be some way of reaching consensus about what is being measured. Towards that end, factor analysis can be helpful.

An assumption of factor analysis is that things that co-occur tend to have a common cause. Note here that "tend to" does *not* mean "always." Fevers, sore throats, stuffy noses, coughs, and sneezes may *tend to* occur at the same time in the same person, but they do not always co-occur. When these symptoms do co-occur, they may be caused by one thing: the virus that causes the common cold. Although the virus is one thing, its manifestations are quite diverse.

In psychological assessment research, we measure a diverse set of abilities, behaviors, and symptoms and attempt to deduce which underlying dimensions cause or account for the variations in behavior and symptoms we observe in large groups of people. We measure the relations among various behaviors, symptoms, and test scores with correlation coefficients. We then use factor analysis to discover patterns of correlation coefficients that suggest the existence of underlying psychological dimensions.

All else being equal, a simple theory is better than a complicated theory. Factor analysis helps us discover the smallest number of psychological dimensions (or factors) that

*Prepared by W. Joel Schneider

can account for the various behaviors, symptoms, and test scores we observe. For example, imagine that we create four different tests to measure people's knowledge of vocabulary, grammar, multiplication, and geometry. If the correlations between all of these tests were zero (i.e., high scorers on one test are no more likely than low scorers to score high on the other tests), then the factor analysis would suggest to us that we have measured four distinct abilities.

Of course, you probably recognize that it is very unlikely that the correlations between these tests would be zero. Therefore, imagine that the correlation between the vocabulary and grammar tests was quite high (i.e., high scorers on vocabulary were likely also to score high on grammar, and low scorers on vocabulary were likely to score low on grammar). The correlation between multiplication and geometry was high also. Furthermore, the correlations between the verbal tests and the mathematics tests were zero. Factor analysis would suggest that we have measured not four distinct abilities but two. The researcher interpreting the results of the factor analysis would have to use his or her best judgment to decide what to call these two abilities. In this case, it would seem reasonable to call them *language ability* and *mathematical ability.*

Now imagine that the correlations between all four tests were equally high—for example, that vocabulary was as strongly correlated with geometry as it was with grammar. In this case, factor analysis suggests that the simplest explanation for this pattern of correlations is that there is just one factor that causes all these tests to be equally correlated. We might call this factor *general academic ability.*

In reality, if you were to actually measure these four abilities, the results would not be so clear. It is likely that all of the correlations would be positive and substantially above zero. It is likely that the verbal subtests would correlate more strongly with each other than with the mathematical subtests. It is likely that factor analysis would suggest that language and mathematical abilities are distinct from but not entirely independent of each other—that is, that language abilities and mathematics abilities are substantially correlated, suggesting that a general academic (or intellectual) ability influences performance in all academic areas.

Factor analysis can help researchers decide how best to summarize large amounts of information about people by using just a few scores. For example, when we ask parents to complete questionnaires about their children's behavior

(continued)

Factor Analysis (*continued*)

problems, the questionnaires can have hundreds of items. It would take too long and would be too confusing to review every item. Factor analysis can simplify the information while minimizing the loss of detail. Here is an example of a short questionnaire that factor analysis can be used to summarize.

On a scale of 1 to 5, compared to other children his or her age, my child:

1. gets in fights frequently at school
2. is defiant to adults
3. is very impulsive
4. has stomachaches frequently
5. is anxious about many things
6. appears sad much of the time

If we give this questionnaire to a large, representative sample of parents, we can calculate the correlations between the items. Table 1 illustrates what we might find.

Note that all of the perfect 1.00 correlations in this table are used to emphasize the fact that each item correlates perfectly with itself. In the analysis of the data, the software would ignore these correlations and analyze only all of the correlations below this diagonal "line of demarcation" of 1.00 correlations.

Using the set of correlation coefficients presented in Table 1, factor analysis suggests that there are two factors measured by this behavior rating scale. The logic of factor analysis suggests that the reason Items 1 through 3 have high correlations with each other is that each has a high correlation with the first factor. Similarly, Items 4 through 6 have high correlations with each other because they have high correlations with the second factor. The correlations of the items with the hypothesized factors are called *factor loadings.* The factor loadings for this hypothetical example are presented in Table 2.

Factor analysis tells us which items *load* on which factors, but it cannot interpret the meaning of the factors. Researchers usually look at all the items that load on a factor and use their intuition or knowledge of theory to identify what the items have in common. In this case, Factor 1 could receive any number of names, such as *Conduct Problems, Acting Out,* or *Externalizing Behaviors.* Factor 2 might

Table 1
A Sample Table of Correlations

	1	2	3	4	5	6
1. gets in fights frequently at school	1.00					
2. is defiant to adults	.81	1.00				
3. is very impulsive	.79	.75	1.00			
4. has stomachaches frequently	.42	.38	.36	1.00		
5. is anxious about many things	.39	.34	.34	.77	1.00	
6. appears sad much of the times	.37	.34	.32	.77	.74	1.00

Table 2
Factor Loadings for Our Hypothetical Example

	Factor 1	Factor 2
1. gets in fights frequently at school	.91	.03
2. is defiant to adults	.88	−.01
3. is very impulsive	.86	−.01
4. has stomachaches frequently	.02	.89
5. is anxious about many things	.01	.86
6. appears sad much of the time	−.02	.87

also go by various names, such as *Mood Problems, Negative Affectivity,* or *Internalizing Behaviors.* Thus, the problems on this behavior rating scale can be summarized fairly efficiently with just two scores. In this example, a reduction of six scores to two scores may not seem terribly useful. In actual behavior rating scales, factor analysis can reduce the overwhelming complexity of hundreds of different behavior problems to a more manageable number of scores that help professionals more easily conceptualize individual cases.

Factor analysis also calculates the correlation among factors. If a large number of factors are identified and there are substantial correlations among factors, this new correlation matrix too can be factor-analyzed to obtain *second-order factors.* These factors, in turn, can be analyzed to obtain *third-order factors.* Theoretically, it is possible to have even higher order factors, but most researchers rarely find it necessary to go beyond third-order factors. The *g*-factor from intelligence test data is an example of a third-order factor that emerges because all tests of cognitive abilities are positively correlated. In our example above, the two factors have a correlation of .46, suggesting that children who have externalizing problems are also at risk of having internalizing problems. It is therefore reasonable to calculate a second-order factor score that measures the overall level of behavior problems.

This example illustrates the most commonly used type of factor analysis: *exploratory factor analysis.* Exploratory factor analysis is helpful when we wish to summarize data efficiently, when we are not sure how many factors are present in our data, or when we are not sure which items load on which factors. In short, when we are exploring or looking for factors, we may use exploratory factor analysis. When we think we have found factors and seek to *confirm* this, we may use another variety of factor analysis.

Researchers can use *confirmatory factor analysis* to test highly specific hypotheses. For example, a researcher might want to know if the two different types of items on the WISC-IV Digit Span subtest measure the same ability or two different abilities. On the Digits Forward type of item, the child must repeat a string of digits in the same order in which they were heard. On the Digits Backward type of item, the child must repeat the string of digits in reverse order. Some researchers believe that repeating numbers verbatim measures auditory short-term memory and that repeating numbers in reverse order measures executive control, the ability to allocate attentional resources efficiently to solve multistep problems. Typically, clinicians add the raw scores of both types of items to produce a single score. If the two item types measure different abilities, adding the raw scores together is kind of like adding apples and oranges, peaches and pears . . . you get the idea. If, however, the two items measure the same ability, adding the scores together may yield a more reliable score than the separate scores.

Confirmatory factor analysis may be used to determine whether the two item types measure different abilities. We would need to identify or invent several additional tests

that are likely to measure the two separate abilities we believe are measured by the two types of Digit Span items. Usually, three tests per factor is sufficient. Let's call the short-term memory tests STM1, STM2, and STM3. Likewise, we can call the executive control tests EC1, EC2, and EC3.

Next, we specify the hypotheses, or models, we wish to test. There are three of them:

1. *All of the tests measure the same ability.* A graphical representation of a hypothesis in confirmatory factor analysis is called a *path diagram.* Tests are drawn with rectangles, and hypothetical factors are drawn with ovals. The correlations between tests and factors are drawn with arrows. The path diagram for this hypothesis is presented in Figure 1.

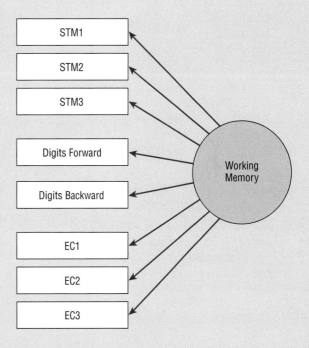

Figure 1
This path diagram is a graphical representation of the hypothesis that All of the tests measure the same ability.

(*continued*)

Factor Analysis (*continued*)

2. *Both Digits Forward and Digits Backward measure short-term memory and are distinct from executive control.* The path diagram for this hypothesis is presented in Figure 2.

3. *Digits Forward and Digits Backward measure different abilities.* The path diagram for this hypothesis is presented in Figure 3.

Confirmatory factor analysis produces a number of statistics, called *fit statistics,* that tell us which of the models or hypotheses we tested are most in agreement with the data. Studying the results, we can select the model that provides the best fit with the data or perhaps even generate a new model. Actually, factor analysis can quickly become a lot more complicated than described here, but for now, let's hope this is helpful.

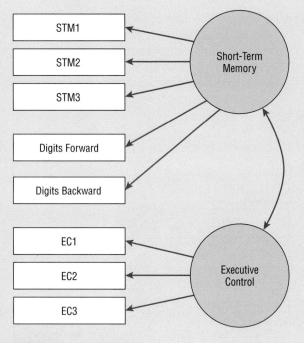

Figure 2
This path diagram is a graphical representation of the hypothesis that Both Digits Forward and Digits Backward measure short-term memory and are distinct from executive control. *Note that the curved arrow indicates the possibility that the two factors might be correlated.*

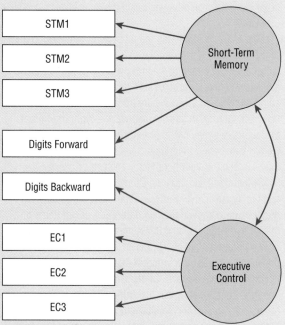

Figure 3
This path diagram is a graphical representation of the hypothesis that Digits Forward and Digits Backward measure different abilities.

An estimate of intelligence can be derived from an assessee's paper-and-pencil rendering of a human figure and other drawings, according to some researchers and clinicians (Bardos, 1993; Buck, 1948; Holtzman, 1993; Naglieri, 1993). Many methods have been proposed for obtaining such estimates, the best-known of these being the Goodenough-Harris scoring system (Harris, 1963). A long-standing controversy, however, is whether the Goodenough system is indeed good enough. Although there is evidence that the system is reliable (Kamphaus & Pleiss, 1993; Scott, 1981), questions remain about its validity (Aikman et al., 1992; Motta et al., 1993a, 1993b; Sattler, 1992). Figure drawings hold out the promise of less time needed for evaluation, especially when the same drawings may be used for personality assessment. However, their use to assess intelligence—even as a screening device—remains controversial.

JUST THINK . . .

Using a drawing of a human figure to gauge intelligence has been controversial on many counts. Comment on the practice with regard to the face validity of such a measure (all puns aside).

Tests Designed for Group Administration

The Stanford revision of the Binet-Simon test was published in 1916, and only one year later, many psychologists were compelled to start thinking about how such a test could be adapted for group administration. To understand why, we need to take a brief historical look at testing in the military.

Group tests in the military On April 6, 1917, the United States entered World War I. On April 7th, the president of the American Psychological Association, Robert M. Yerkes, began efforts to mobilize psychologists to help in the war effort. By late May, the APA committee that would develop group tests for the military had their first meeting. There was little debate among the participants about the nature of intelligence, only a clear sense of urgency about developing instruments for the military to identify both the "unfit" and those of "exceptionally superior ability."

Whereas the development of a major intelligence or ability test today might take three to five years, the committee had two tests ready in a matter of weeks and a final form of those tests ready for the printer on July 7th. One test became known as the **Army Alpha test.** This test would be administered to Army recruits who could read. It contained tasks such as general information questions, analogies, and scrambled sentences to reassemble. The other test was the **Army Beta test,** designed for administration to foreign-born recruits with poor knowledge of English or to illiterate recruits (defined as "someone who could not read a newspaper or write a letter home"). It contained tasks such as mazes, coding, and picture completion (wherein the examinee's task was to draw in the missing element of the picture). Both tests were soon administered in army camps by teams of officers and enlisted men. By 1919, nearly two million recruits had been tested, eight thousand of whom had been recommended for immediate discharge on the basis of the test results. Other recruits had been assigned to various units in the Army based on their Alpha or Beta test results. For example, recruits who scored in the low but acceptable range were likely to draw duty that involved digging ditches or similar kinds of assignments.

If one dream drove the development of the Army Alpha and Beta tests, it was for the Army, other organizations, and society as a whole to run smoothly and efficiently as a result of the proper allocation of human resources—all thanks to tests. Some psychometric scrutiny of the Alpha and Beta tests supported their use. The tests were reliable enough, and they seemed to correlate acceptably with external criteria such as Stanford-Binet Full Scale IQ scores and officers' ratings of men on "practical soldier value." Yerkes (1921) provided this explanation of what he thought the test actually measured:

> The tests give a reliable index of a man's ability to learn, to think quickly and accurately, and to comprehend instructions. They do not measure loyalty, bravery, dependability, or the emotional traits that make a man "carry on." A man's value to the service is measured by his intelligence plus other necessary qualifications. (p. 424)

An original objective of the Alpha and Beta tests was to measure the ability to be a good soldier. However, after the war, that objective seemed to get lost in the shuffle as the tests were used in various aspects of civilian life to measure general intelligence. An Army Alpha or Beta test was much easier to obtain, administer, and interpret than a Stanford-Binet test and much cheaper as well. Thousands of unused Alpha and Beta booklets became government surplus that almost anyone could buy. The tests were administered, scored, and interpreted by many who lacked the background and training to use them properly. The utopian vision of a society in which individuals contributed according to their abilities as determined by tests would never materialize. To the contrary, the misuse of tests soured many members of the public and the profession on the use of tests, particularly group tests.

The military's interest in psychological testing during the 1920s and 1930s was minimal. It was only when the threat of a second world war loomed that interest in group intelligence testing reemerged. The Army General Classification Test (AGCT) was developed. During the course of World War II, the AGCT would be administered to more than 12 million recruits. Other, more specialized tests were also developed by military psychologists. An assessment unit discretely named the Office of Strategic Services developed innovative measures for selecting spies and secret agents to work abroad.

> **JUST THINK . . .**
>
> James Bond aside, what qualities do you think a real secret agent needs to have? How might you measure these qualities in an applicant?

Today, group tests are still administered to prospective recruits, primarily for screening purposes. In general, we may define a **screening tool** as an instrument or procedure used to identify a particular trait or constellation of traits at a gross or imprecise level. Data derived from the process of screening may be explored in more depth by more individualized methods of assessment. Various types of screening instruments are used in many different settings. For example, in the following chapter we see how screening tools such as behavior checklists are used in preschool settings to identify young children to be evaluated with more individualized, in-depth procedures.

In the military, the long tradition of using data from screening tools as an aid to duty and training assignments continues to this day. Such data also serve to mold the nature of training experiences. For example, data from group testing have indicated a downward trend in the mean intelligence level of recruits since the inception of an all-volunteer army. In response to such findings, the military has developed new weapons training programs incorporating, for example, simpler vocabulary in programmed instruction.

Included among many group tests used today by the armed forces are the Officer Qualifying Test (a 115-item multiple-choice test used by the U.S. Navy as an admissions test to Officer Candidate School), the Airman Qualifying Exam (a 200-item multiple-choice test given to all U.S. Air Force volunteers), and the Armed Services Vocational Aptitude Battery (ASVAB). The ASVAB is administered to prospective new recruits in all the armed services. It is also made available to high school students and other young adults who seek guidance and counseling about their future education and career plans.

Annually, hundreds of thousands of people take the ASVAB, making it perhaps the most widely used multiple aptitude test in the United States. It is administered by school counselors as well as at various walk-in centers at no cost to the testtakers. In the context of a career exploration program, the ASVAB is designed to help testtakers learn about their interests, abilities, and personal preferences in relation to career opportunities in military and civilian settings. Illustrative items from each of the ten subtests are presented in this chapter's *Everyday Psychometrics*.

The Armed Services Vocational Aptitude Battery (ASVAB): A Test You Can Take

If you would like firsthand experience in taking an ability test that can be useful in vocational guidance, do what about 900,000 other people do each year and take the Armed Services Vocational Aptitude Battery (ASVAB). Uncle Sam makes this test available to you free of charge—along with other elements of a career guidance package, including a workbook and other printed materials and test scoring and interpretation. Although an objective is to get testtakers "into boots" (that is, into the military), taking the test entails no obligation of military service. For more information about how you can take the ASVAB, contact your school's counseling office or a military recruiter. Meanwhile, you may wish to warm up with the following ten sample items representing each of the ten ASVAB subtests.

I. General Science

Included here are general science questions, including questions from the areas of biology and physics.

   1. An eclipse of the sun throws the shadow of the
- a. moon on the sun.
- b. moon on the earth.
- c. earth on the sun.
- d. earth on the moon.

II. Arithmetic Reasoning

The task here is to solve arithmetic problems. Testtakers are permitted to use (government-supplied) scratch paper.

   2. It costs $0.50 per square yard to waterproof canvas. What will it cost to waterproof a canvas truck that is 15′ × 24′?
- a. $ 6.67
- b. $18.00
- c. $ 20.00
- d. $180.00

III. Word Knowledge

Which of four possible definitions best defines the underlined word?

   3. Rudiments most nearly means
- a. politics.
- b. minute details.
- c. promotion opportunities.
- d. basic methods and procedures.

IV. Paragraph Comprehension

A test of reading comprehension and reasoning.

   4. Twenty-five percent of all household burglaries can be attributed to unlocked windows or doors. Crime is the result of opportunity plus desire. To prevent crime, it is each individual's responsibility to
- a. provide the desire.
- b. provide the opportunity.
- c. prevent the desire.
- d. prevent the opportunity.

V. Numerical Operations

This speeded test contains simple arithmetic problems that the testtaker must do quickly; it is one of two speeded tests on the ASVAB.

   5. $6 - 5 =$
- a. 1
- b. 4
- c. 2
- d. 3

VI. Coding Speed

This subtest contains coding items that measure perceptual / motor speed among other factors.

KEY

green . . . 2715	man . . . 3451	salt . . . 4586
hat . . . 1413	room . . . 2864	tree . . . 5927

	a.	b.	c.	d.	e.
6. room	1413	2715	2864	3451	4586

(continued)

The Armed Services Vocational Aptitude Battery (ASVAB): A Test You Can Take

(continued)

VII. Auto and Shop Information
This test assesses knowledge of automobile shop practice and the use of tools.

7. What tool is shown above?
   a. hole saw
   b. keyhole saw
   c. counter saw
   d. grinding saw

VIII. Mathematics Knowledge
This is a test of ability to solve problems using high school–level mathematics. Use of scratch paper is permitted.

8. If $3X = -5$, then $X =$
   a. -2
   b. $-5/3$
   c. $-3/5$
   d. $3/5$

IX. Mechanical Comprehension
Knowledge and understanding of general mechanical and physical principles are probed by this test.

9. Liquid is being transferred from the barrel to the bucket by
   a. capillary action.
   b. gravitational forces.
   c. fluid pressure in the hose.
   d. water pressure in the barrel.

X. Electronics Information
Here, knowledge of electrical, radio, and electronics information is assessed.

10. Which of the above is the symbol for a transformer?
    a. A
    b. B
    c. C
    d. D

Answer Key	
1. b	6. c
2. c	7. a
3. d	8. b
4. d	9. b
5. Why are you looking this one up?	10. a

Through the years, various forms of the ASVAB have been produced, some for exclusive use in schools and some for exclusive use in the military. A set of 100 selected items included in the subtests of Arithmetic Reasoning, Numerical Operations, Word Knowledge, and Paragraph Comprehension make up a measure within the ASVAB called the Armed Forces Qualification Test (AFQT). The AFQT is a measure of general ability used in the selection of recruits. The different armed services employ different cutoff scores in making accept/reject determinations for service, based on considerations such as their preset quotas for particular demographic groups. In addition to the AFQT score, ten aptitude areas are also tapped on the ASVAB, including general technical, general mechanics, electrical, motor-mechanics, science, combat operations, and skill-technical. These are combined to assess aptitude in five separate career areas, including clerical, electronics, mechanics, skill-technical (medical, computers), and combat operations.

The test battery is continually reviewed and improved on the basis of data on how predictive scores are of actual performance in various occupations and military training programs. The ASVAB has been found to predict success in computer programming and computer operating roles (Besetsny et al., 1993) and grades in military technical schools across a variety of fields (Earles & Ree, 1992; Ree & Earles, 1990). A review of validity studies supports the construct, content, and criterion-related validity of the ASVAB as a device to guide training and selection decisions (Welsh et al., 1990). In general, the test has been deemed quite useful for selection and placement decisions regarding personnel in the armed forces (Chan et al., 1999).

Group tests in the schools Perhaps no more than a decade or two ago, approximately two-thirds of all school districts in the United States used group intelligence tests on a routine basis to screen 90% of their students. The other 10% were administered individual intelligence tests. Litigation and legislation surrounding the routine use of group intelligence tests have altered this picture somewhat. Still, the group intelligence test, now also referred to as a *school ability test,* is by no means extinct. In many states, legal mandates prohibit the use of group intelligence data alone for class assignment purposes. However, group intelligence test data, combined with other data, can be extremely useful in developing a profile of a child's intellectual assets.

Group intelligence test results provide school personnel with valuable information for instruction-related activities and increased understanding of the individual pupil. One primary function of data from a group intelligence test is to alert educators to students who might profit from more extensive assessment with individually administered ability tests. The individually administered intelligence test, along with other tests, may point the way to placement in a special class, a program for the gifted, or some other program. Group intelligence test data can also help a school district plan educational goals for all children.

Group intelligence tests in the schools are used in special forms as early as the kindergarten level. The tests are administered to groups of 10 to 15 children, each of whom receives a test booklet that includes printed pictures and diagrams. For the most part, simple motor responses are required to answer items. Oversized alternatives in the form of pictures in a multiple-choice test might appear on the pages, and it is the child's job to circle or place an X on the picture that represents the correct answer to the item presented orally by the examiner. During such testing in small groups, the testtakers will be carefully monitored to make certain they are following the directions.

The California Test of Mental Maturity, the Kuhlmann-Anderson Intelligence Tests, the Henmon-Nelson Tests of Mental Ability, and the Cognitive Abilities Test are some of the many group intelligence tests available for use in school settings. The first group intelligence test to be used in U.S. schools was the Otis-Lennon School Ability Test, formerly the Otis Mental Ability Test. In its current edition, the test is designed to measure abstract thinking and reasoning ability and to assist in school evaluation and placement decision-making. This nationally standardized test yields Verbal and Nonverbal score indexes as well as an overall School Ability Index (SAI).

In general, group tests are useful screening tools when large numbers of examinees must be evaluated either simultaneously or within a limited time frame. More specific

Table 9–7
The Pros and Cons of Traditional Group Testing

Advantages of Group Tests	Disadvantages of Group Tests
Large numbers of testtakers can be tested at one time, offering efficient use of time and resources.	All testtakers, regardless of ability, typically must start on the same item, end on the same item, and be exposed to every item on the test. Opportunity for adaptive testing is minimized.
Testtakers work independently at their own pace.	Testtakers must be able to work independently and understand what is expected of them, with little or no opportunity for questions or clarification once testing has begun.
Test items are typically in a format easily scored by computer or machine.	Test items may not be in more innovative formats or any format involving examiner manipulation of materials or examiner–examinee interaction.
The test administrator need not be highly trained, as task may require little beyond reading instructions, keeping time, and supervising testtakers.	Opportunity for assessor observation of testtaker's extra-test behavior is lost.
Test administrator may have less effect on the examinee's score than a test administrator in a one-on-one situation.	Opportunity for learning about assessee through assessor–assessee interaction is lost.
Group testing is less expensive than individual testing on a per-testtaker basis.	The information from a group test may not be as detailed and actionable as information from an individual test administration.
Group testing has proven value for screening purposes.	Instruments designed expressly for screening are occasionally used for making momentous decisions.
Group tests may be normed on large numbers of people more easily than an individual test.	In any testtaking situation, testtakers are assumed to be motivated to perform and following directions. The opportunity to verify these assumptions may be minimized in large-scale testing programs. The testtaker who "marches to the beat of a different drummer" is at a greater risk of obtaining a score that does not accurately approximate his or her hypothetical true score.
Group tests work well with people who can read, follow directions, grip a pencil, and do not require a great deal of assistance.	Group tests may not work very well with people who cannot read, who cannot grip a pencil (such as very young children), who "march to the beat of a different drummer," or who have exceptional needs or requirements.

advantages—and disadvantages—of traditional group testing are listed in Table 9–7. We qualify group testing with *traditional* because more contemporary forms of group testing, especially testing with all testtakers seated at a computer station, might more aptly be termed *individual assessment simultaneously administered in a group* rather than *group testing*.

> **JUST THINK . . .**
>
> After reading Table 9–7, construct your own two-column table, label one column Individual Tests and the other column Group Tests. Then, write some of your own thoughts comparing individual and group tests. Feel free to draw on your own experiences taking both kinds of tests.

Measures of Specific Intellectual Abilities

Widely used measures of general intelligence of necessity sample only a small realm of the many human abilities that may be conceived of as contributing to an individual's intelligence. There are many intellectual abilities and talents that are not—or are only indirectly—assessed by the more widely used tests of intellectual functioning. There are, for example, tests available to measure very specific abilities such as critical thinking, music, or art appreciation. One area that understandably has received a great deal of attention is creativity. Interestingly, although most intelligence tests do not measure creativity, tests designed to measure creativity may well measure variables related to intelligence. For example, some component abilities of creativity are thought to be originality in problem solving, originality in perception, and originality in abstraction. To the extent that tests of intelligence tap these components, measures of creativity may also be thought of as tools for assessing intelligence.

A number of tests and test batteries are available to measure creativity in children and adults. In fact, some universities, such as the University of Georgia and the State University College of New York at Buffalo, maintain libraries containing several hundred of these tests. What types of tasks are featured on these tests? And what do these tests really measure?

Four terms common to many measures of creativity are *originality, fluency, flexibility,* and *elaboration. Originality* refers to the ability to produce something that is innovative or nonobvious. It may be something abstract like an idea or something tangible and visible like artwork or a poem. *Fluency* refers to the ease with which responses are reproduced and is usually measured by the total number of responses produced. For example, an item in a test of word fluency might be *In the next thirty seconds, name as many words as you can that begin with the letter w. Flexibility* refers to the variety of ideas presented and the ability to shift from one approach to another. *Elaboration* refers to the richness of detail in a verbal explanation or pictorial display.

A criticism frequently leveled at group standardized intelligence tests (as well as at other ability and achievement tests) is that evaluation of test performance is too heavily focused on whether the answer is correct. The heavy emphasis on correct response leaves little room for the evaluation of processes such as originality, fluency, flexibility, and elaboration. Stated another way, on most achievement tests the thought process typically required is *convergent thinking.* **Convergent thinking** is a deductive reasoning process that entails recall and consideration of facts as well as a series of logical judgments to narrow down solutions and eventually arrive at one solution. In his structure-of-intellect model, Guilford (1967) drew a distinction between the intellectual processes of *convergent* and *divergent* thinking. **Divergent thinking** is a reasoning process in which thought is free to move in many different directions, making several solutions possible. Divergent thinking requires flexibility of thought, originality, and imagination. There is much less emphasis on recall of facts than in convergent thinking. Guilford's model has served to focus research attention not only on the products of creative thought but on the process as well.

Guilford (1954) described several tasks designed to measure creativity, such as Consequences ("Imagine what would happen if . . .") and Unusual Uses (for example, "Name as many uses as you can think of for a rubber band"). Included in Guilford et al.'s (1974) test battery, the Structure-of-Intellect Abilities, are verbally oriented tasks (such as Word Fluency) as well as nonverbally oriented (such as Sketches).

A number of other tests are available to tap various aspects of creativity. For example, based on the work of Mednick (1962), the Remote Associates Test (RAT) presents the testtaker with three words, and the task is to find a fourth word associated with the other three. The Torrance (1966, 1987a, 1987b) Tests of Creative Thinking consist of word-based, picture-based, and sound-based test materials. In a subtest of different sounds, for example, the examinee's task is to respond with the thoughts each sound conjures up. Each subtest is designed to measure various characteristics deemed important in the process of creative thought.

JUST THINK . . .

Based on this brief description of the RAT and the Torrance Tests, demonstrate your own creativity by creating a new RAT or Torrance Test item that is unmistakably one from the twenty-first century.

Interestingly, many tests of creativity do not fare well when evaluated by traditional psychometric procedures. For example, the test-retest reliability estimates for some of these tests tend to border on the unacceptable range. Some have wondered aloud whether tests of creativity should be judged by different standards from other tests.

After all, creativity may differ from other abilities in that it may be highly susceptible to emotional or physical health, motivation, and related factors—even more so than other abilities. This fact would explain tenuous reliability and validity estimates.

JUST THINK . . .

Should tests of creativity be held to different psychometric standards from other ability tests?

As you read about various human abilities and how they all might be related to that intangible construct *intelligence*, you may have said to yourself, Why doesn't anyone create a test that measures all these diverse aspects of intelligence?

Although no one has undertaken that ambitious project, in recent years test packages have been developed to test not only intelligence but also related abilities in educational settings. These test packages, called *psychoeducational batteries*, are discussed in Chapter 10, along with other tests used to measure academic abilities.

Self-Assessment

Test your understanding of elements of this chapter by seeing if you can explain each of the following terms, expressions, and abbreviations:

adaptive testing	deviation IQ	short form
AFQT	divergent thinking	Stanford-Binet
alternate item	extra-test behavior	supplemental subtest
Army Alpha test	floor	Terman, Lewis
Army Beta test	IQ	teaching item
ASVAB	optional subtest	test composite
basal level	point scale	testing the limits
Binet, Alfred	process score	WAIS-III
ceiling	RAT	Wechsler, David
ceiling level	ratio IQ	WISC-IV
convergent thinking	routing test	WPPSI-III
core subtest	screening tool	

Web Watch

Check out the following Web sites for more information about topics discussed in this chapter.

The Stanford Binet, 5th Edition
www.riverpub.com/products/clinical/sbis5/home.html

http://assess.nelson.com/test-ind/stan-b5.html

www.nelson.com/nelson/assess/test-ind/stan-b5.html

http://alpha.fdu.edu/psychology/SB5_index.htm

TheWISC-IV
http://marketplace.psychcorp.com/PsychCorp.com/Cultures/en-US/dotCom/WISC-IV.com.htm

http://alpha.fdu.edu/psychology/WISCIV_Substitution.htm

http://marketplace.psychcorp.com/PsychCorp.com/Cultures/en-US/dotCom/WISC-IV.com/Product+Information.htm

Test blueprints—WISC-IV
www.psychcorp.com.au/WISC-IV%20report%201.pdf

The WISC-IV—psychometric properties
www.psychcorp.com.au/WISC-IV%20report%202.pdf

The WISC-IV
http://marketplace.psychcorp.com/PsychCorp.com/Cultures/en-US/dotCom/WISC-IV.com.htm

Dumont/Willis on the WISC-IV
http://alpha.fdu.edu/psychology/WISCIV_Index.htm

Buros on the WISC-IV
www.unl.edu/buros/

The WAIS-III
http://marketplace.psychcorp.com/PsychCorp/Images/resource/library/ppt/waispres.ppt

The WPPSI-III
http://marketplace.psychcorp.com/PsychCorp.com/Cultures/en-US/dotCom/WPPSI-III.com.htm

http://alpha.fdu.edu/psychology/WPPSIIII.htm

The WASI
www.psychcorp.com.au/wasi.html

Army Alpha and Beta tests and adult literacy
www.nald.ca/fulltext/adlitUS/Index.htm

10

Preschool and Educational Assessment

What are some of the things you associate with the word *school*? If the word *test* comes to mind, you probably have lots of company; many different tests are administered in public and private schools. Educators are interested in answers to questions as diverse as *How good is your reading ability?* and *How far can you broad jump?* In this chapter, we consider tests designed to facilitate education, such as achievement and aptitude tests as well as diagnostic tests. We begin, however, with a brief look at some education-related tests that may be administered long before a child sets foot in a classroom.

Preschool Assessment

The first five years of life—the span of time referred to as the *preschool period*—is a time of profound change. Basic reflexes develop, and the child passes a number of sensorimotor milestones, such as crawling, sitting, standing, walking, running, and grasping. Usually between 18 and 24 months, the child becomes capable of symbolic thought and develops language skills. By age 2, the average child has a vocabulary of more than 200 words. Of course, all such observations about the development of children are of more than mere academic interest to professionals legally charged with the responsibility of assessment.

In the mid-1970s, Congress enacted Public Law (PL) 94-142, which mandated the professional evaluation of children age 3 and older suspected of having physical or mental disabilities, to determine their special educational needs. The law also provides federal funds to help states meet those needs. In 1986, a set of amendments to PL 94-142 known as PL 99-457 extended downward to birth the obligation of states toward children with disabilities. It further mandates that beginning with the school year 1990–1991, all disabled children from ages 3 to 5 be provided with a free, appropriate education. The law was expanded in scope in 1997 with the passage of PL 105-17. Among other things, PL 105-17 is intended to give greater attention to diversity issues, especially as a factor in evaluation and assignment of special services. The law also mandates that infants and toddlers with disabilities must receive services in the home or in other natural settings and that such services are to continue in preschool programs. In 1999, attention deficit hyperactivity disorder (ADHD) was officially added to the list of disabling conditions that can qualify a child for special services. This, combined with other federal legislation and a growing movement toward "full-service schools" that dispense health and psychological services in addition to education (Reeder et al., 1997), all signal a growing societal reliance on infant and preschool assessment techniques.

Tools of Preschool Assessment

The tools of preschool assessment are, with age-appropriate variations built into them, the same types of tools used to assess school-age children and adults. These tools include, among others, checklists and rating scales, tests, and interviews.

Checklists and rating scales Checklists and rating scales are tools of assessment commonly used with preschoolers, although their use is certainly not exclusive to this population. In general, a **checklist** is a questionnaire on which a person marks items to indicate the presence or absence of a specified behavior, thought, event, or circumstance. Checklists can cover broad areas and still be relatively economical and quick to administer. These attributes can make them appealing to busy clinicians (Kamphaus et al., 2000). A rating scale is quite similar in definition and sometimes even identical in form. In general, a **rating scale** is a form completed by an evaluator (a rater, judge, or examiner) to make a judgment of relative standing with regard to a specified variable or variables. As with a checklist, the variables may reflect, for example, the frequency, magnitude, or presence/absence of an observable behavior or event or a verbalized thought. Today, newborns are likely to be greeted by hospital delivery room staff equipped with a checklist or rating scale (see *Everyday Psychometrics*).

Two commonly used checklists and rating scales are the Achenbach Child Behavior Checklist (CBCL) and the Connors Rating Scales-Revised (CRS-R). The CBCL comes in versions appropriate for use with children from ages 1½ to 5 years (CBCL/1½–5), as well as for use with children through young adults, ages 4 through 18 (CBCL/4–18). Parents and others with a close relationship to the subject provide information for competence items covering the subject's activities, social relations, and school performance. The checklist also contains items that describe specific behavioral and emotional problems, as well as open-ended items for reporting additional problems. The protocols are hand scored, machine scored, or computer scored, yielding scores on competence as well as clinical scales. The CRS-R is designed primarily to help assess attention deficit hyperactivity disorder and to screen for other behavior problems. The instrument comes in various versions, each of which has a long form (15 to 20 minutes administration time) and a short form (5 to 10 minutes administration time). There is a parent version and a teacher version for use with children ages 3 to 17. An adolescent self-report version is for use by respondents ages 12 to 17. The instrument is hand scored and has norms based on more than eight thousand children ages 3 to 17.

Most checklists and rating scales serve the purpose of screening tools. In preschool assessment, screening tools may be used as a first step in identifying children who are said to be *at risk*. This term came into vogue as an alternative to diagnostic labels that might have a detrimental effect (Smith & Knudtson, 1990). Today, what a child is actually at risk *for* may vary in terms of not only the context of the discussion, but the state in which the child resides. *At risk* has been used to refer to preschool children who may not be ready for first grade and to children who are not functioning within normal limits. In a most general sense, **at risk** refers to children who have documented difficulties in one or more psychological, social, or academic areas and for whom intervention is or may be required. The need for intervention may be decided on the basis of a more complete evaluation, often involving psychological tests.

First Impressions

It's been said that every person in contemporary society is a number. We are represented by a Social Security number, a driver's license number, and myriad others. Before these, however, we are represented by what is called an **Apgar number.** The Apgar number is actually a score on a rating scale developed by physician Virginia Apgar (1909–1974), an obstetrical anesthesiologist who saw a need for a simple, rapid method of evaluating newborn infants and determining what immediate action, if any, is necessary.

As first presented in the early 1950s, the Apgar evaluation is conducted at one minute after birth to assess how well the infant tolerated the birthing process. The evaluation is conducted again at five minutes after birth to assess how well the infant is adapting to the environment. Each evaluation is made with respect to the same five variables; each variable can be scored on a range from 0 to 2; and each score (at 1 minute and 5 minutes) can range from 0 to 10. The five variables are heart rate, respiration, color, muscle tone, and reflex irritability, the last measure being obtained by response to a stimulus such as a mild pinch. For example, with respect to the variable of reflex irritability, the infant will earn a score of 2 for a vigorous cry in response to the stimulus, a score of 1 for a grimace, and a score of 0 if it shows no reflex irritability. Few babies are "perfect 10s" on their 1-minute Apgar; many are 7s, 8s, and 9s. An Apgar score below 7 or 8 may indicate the need for assistance in being stabilized. A very low Apgar score, in the 0-to-3 range, may signal a more enduring problem such as neurological deficit. By the way, a useful acronym for remembering the five variables is the name "APGAR" itself: A stands for activity (or muscle tone), P for pulse (or heart rate), G for grimace (or reflex irritability), A for appearance (or color), and R for respiration.

Moving from the realm of the medical to the realm of the psychological, another evaluation takes place shortly after birth, one far less formal, by the child's mother. Judith

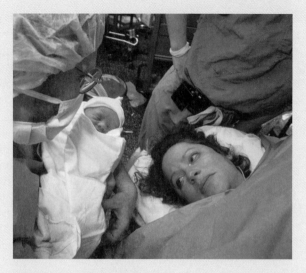

Welcome to the World of Evaluation

Only seconds after birth, a newborn infant is given its first formal evaluation by the hospital staff. The infant's next evaluation, conducted by the mother, may be no less momentous in its consequences.

Langlois and colleagues (1995) studied the relationship between infant attractiveness and maternal behavior and attitudes using a sample of 173 mothers and their firstborn infants (86 girls and 87 boys). Approximately one-third of the sample was identified as White, one-third was African American, and one-third was Mexican American. For the record, the mean first Apgar score for the infants in the study was 8.36, and the mean second Apgar score was 9.04.

To gauge attractiveness, the investigators used judges' ratings of photographs taken a standard distance from each infant's face while the child was either sleeping or had an otherwise neutral expression. Maternal behavior during feed-

Psychological tests   Tests such as the WPPSI-III, the SB5, and others may be used to gauge developmental strengths and weaknesses by sampling children's performance in cognitive, motor, and social/behavioral content areas.

At the earliest levels, cognitive and social abilities are gauged by scales that assess the presence or absence of various developmental achievements through such means as observation and parental (or caretaker) interviews. By age 2, the child enters a challenging period for psychological assessors. Language and conceptual skills are beginning to

ing and play was directly observed by trained raters in the hospital. A second set of observations was recorded around the time of the infant's three-month birthday. A measure developed by Parke and Sawin (1975) called the Parent Attitude Questionnaire was used to assess maternal attitudes both in the hospital and approximately three months later out of the hospital. The researchers found that although all of the infants studied received adequate care, the attractive infants received more positive treatment and attitudes from their mothers than did the unattractive infants. The mothers of the attractive infants were more affectionate and playful. The mothers of less attractive infants were more likely to be attentive to other people rather than to their infant. These mothers were also more likely to engage in routine caregiving than in affectionate behavior. The attitudes of the mothers of less attractive infants, particularly during the first assessment, were also more negative than those of mothers of more attractive infants. At the time of the first assessment, the mothers of the less attractive infants were more likely than the mothers of more attractive infants to endorse the belief that their infant was interfering with their lives. Approximately three months later, the mothers of the less attractive infants, as compared with the mothers of more attractive infants, were more likely to endorse the belief that their infants needed more stimulation, although they no longer differed in beliefs regarding interference with their lives.

These findings are consistent with prior research suggesting that attractive children are treated less harshly by adults than unattractive children are (Berkowitz & Frodi, 1979; Dion, 1979; Elder et al., 1985) and that mothers of children with physical anomalies may behave less desirably toward their children than mothers whose children had no such anomalies (Allen et al., 1990; Barden et al., 1989; Field & Vega-Lahr, 1984). Fathers, too, may behave differently as a function of the attractiveness of their offspring. Parke et al.

(1977) found quality of paternal caregiving to 3-month-old infants to be significantly and positively correlated with infant attractiveness.

Langlois et al. (1995) cautioned that their correlational findings should not be interpreted as indicative of cause and effect; the results cannot be used to support statements indicating that attractiveness causes or affects maternal behavior and attitudes. It does seem the case, however, that for whatever reason, infant attractiveness tends to predict maternal behavior and attitudes. The researchers also wondered whether the results of their study would generalize to families of other income levels, or what effect the birth of additional children might have on the main findings. It may be that the mothers' relative inexperience with the range of infant behaviors led them to be more influenced by appearance than mothers who have had other children.

From moments after birth and onward, evaluation—both formal and informal—is very much a fact of life. We may define **informal evaluation** as a typically nonsystematic, relatively brief, and "off-the-record" assessment leading to the formation of an opinion or attitude conducted by any person, in any way, for any reason, in an unofficial context that is not subject to the ethics or other standards of an evaluation by a professional. The process of informal evaluation has not received a great deal of attention in the psychological assessment literature. Accordingly, the nature and extent of the influence of informal evaluations by people (such as parents, teachers, supervisors, personnel in the criminal justice system, and others) is largely unknown. On the one hand, considering the need for privacy, perhaps it is best that such private evaluations remain that way. On the other hand, research such as that conducted by Langlois and her colleagues brings to light the everyday implications of such informal evaluations—implications that may ultimately help to improve the quality of life for many people.

emerge, yet the kinds of verbal and performance tests traditionally used with older children and adults are inappropriate. The attention span of the preschooler is short. Ideally, test materials are colorful, engaging, and hold the attention. Approximately one hour is a good rule-of-thumb limit for an entire test session with a preschooler; less time is preferable. As testing time increases, so does the possibility of fatigue and distraction. And with assessee fatigue and distraction comes a higher potential for an underestimation of the assessee's ability. Motivation of the young child may vary from one

Figure 10–1
A Dual-Easel Format in Test Administration

Easel format *in the context of test administration refers to test materials, usually some sort of book that contains test-stimulus materials and that can be folded and placed on a desk; the examiner turns the pages to reveal to the examinee, for example, objects to identify or designs to copy. When corresponding test administration instructions or notes are printed on the reverse side of the test-stimulus pages for the examiner's convenience during test administration, the format is sometimes referred to as* dual easel.

test session to the next, and this is something of which the examiner must be aware. Most welcomed by examiners who regularly work with preschoolers are tests that are relatively easy to administer, have simple start/discontinue rules, and allow the examiner ample opportunity to make behavioral observations of the child. Dual-easel test administration format (Figure 10–1), sample and teaching items for each subtest, and dichotomous scoring (for example, right/wrong) all facilitate test administration.

JUST THINK . . .

"Especially for very young children, establishing test-retest reliability with an intervening interval of as little as a month or so can be a problem." Do you agree? Why or why not?

Data from infant intelligence tests, especially when combined with other information (such as birth history, emotional and social history, health history, data on the quality of the physical and emotional environment, and measures of adaptive behavior) have proved useful to health professionals when suspicions about developmental disability and related deficits have been raised. The tests have also proved useful in helping to define the abilities, as well as the extent of disability, in older, psychotic children. Furthermore, the tests have been in use for a number of years by many adoption agencies that will disclose and interpret such information to prospective adoptive parents. Infant tests also have wide application in the area of research and can play a part in selecting infants for specialized early educational experiences or in measuring the outcome of educational, therapeutic, or prenatal care interventions.

What is the meaning of a score on an infant intelligence test? Whereas some of the developers of infant tests (such as Cattell, 1940; Gesell et al., 1940) claimed that such tests can predict future intellectual ability because they measure the developmental precursors to such ability, others have insisted that performance on such tests at best reflects the infant's physical and neuropsychological intactness. The research literature supports a middle ground between these extreme positions. In general, the tests have not been found to predict performance on child or adult intelligence tests—tests that tap vastly different types of abilities and thought processes. The predictive ability of infant intelligence tests does tend to increase with the extremes of the infant's performance. The test interpreter can say with authority more about the future performance of an infant whose performance was either profoundly below age expectancy or significantly precocious. Still, infancy is a developmental period of many spurts and lags, and infants who are slow or precocious at this age might catch up or fall back in later years. Perhaps the great value of preschool tests lies in their ability to help in the identification of children who are in a very low range of functioning and in need of intervention.

Other measures   Many other instruments and assessment techniques are available for use with preschoolers, including interviews, case history methods, portfolio evaluation, and role-play methods. There are instruments, for example, to measure temperament (Fullard et al., 1984; McDevitt & Carey, 1978), language skills (Smith et al., 2000), the family environment in general (Moos & Moos, 1994), and specific aspects of parenting and caregiving (Arnold et al., 1993; Lovejoy et al., 1999). Some techniques, such as figure drawings to assess personality, are covered in Chapter 12. Some techniques are very specialized and would be used only under rather extraordinary conditions or in the context of research focused on a specific subject matter. An example of the latter is the Child Sexual Behavior Inventory (Friedrich et al., 2001), a 38-item behavior checklist that may be helpful in identifying sexually abused children as young as 2 years. In sum, a growing number of instruments is available for use with preschoolers to help evaluate, better understand, and address with appropriate intervention (if possible) a wide variety of areas related to personal, social, and academic development.

From here on in this chapter, we focus on school-age children and young adults and on various types of testing and assessment conducted with them in educational contexts. We begin with achievement tests, a topic with which many students report that they are (all too) familiar.

Achievement Tests

Achievement tests are designed to measure accomplishment. An achievement test for a first-grader might have as its subject matter the English language alphabet, whereas an achievement test for someone else might contain questions relating to principles of psychological assessment. In short, achievement tests are designed to measure the degree of learning that has taken place as a result of exposure to a relatively defined learning experience. "Relatively defined learning experience" may be as broad as *what was learned from four years of college*. It may be much narrower, such as *preparing dough for use in making pizza*. A test of achievement may be standardized nationally, regionally, or locally, or it may not be standardized at all. The pop quiz on the anatomy of a frog given by your high school biology teacher qualifies as an achievement test every bit as much as a statewide examination in biology.

Like other tests, achievement tests vary widely with respect to their psychometric soundness. A sound achievement test is one that adequately samples the targeted subject matter and reliably gauges the extent to which all the examinees learned it.

Scores on achievement tests may be put to varied uses. They may help school personnel make decisions about a student's placement in a particular class, acceptance into a program, or advancement to a higher grade level. Achievement test data can be helpful in gauging the quality of instruction in a particular class, school, school district, or state. Achievement tests are sometimes used to screen for difficulties, and in such instances they may precede the administration of more specific diagnostic tests designed to identify areas for remediation.

Achievement tests play an essential role in identifying children with learning disabilities. Although a definition in federal law was published over a quarter-century ago (see the Education for All Handicapped Children Act of 1975, Public Law 94-142, at Section 5b, 4), as were procedures for evaluation (Procedures for Evaluating Specific Learning Disabilities, 1977), consensus among professionals regarding a definition of *learning disability* has been elusive. Consequently, a wide variety of assessment methods have been employed in an effort to comply with the law. For our purposes, we will define a **learning disability** as a disorder involving a discrepancy between ability and achievement that may manifest itself in attentional, emotional, perceptual, and/or motor deficits, and/or in problems related to doing mathematical calculations, reading, writing, spelling, or in using or understanding language, spoken or written. The term does not apply to persons who have academic problems that are cultural or economic in origin, nor to persons who have learning problems arising primarily from visual, hearing, or motor handicaps, or mental retardation.

JUST THINK . . .

What do you think accounts for the fact that there have been so much disagreement and controversy over the definition of the term *learning disability*?

Given a federal mandate to identify children with a "severe discrepancy between achievement and intellectual ability" (Procedures for Evaluating Specific Learning Disabilities, 1977, p. 65083), it can readily be appreciated how achievement tests, as well as intelligence tests and other measures of cognitive ability and aptitude, could play a role in the diagnosis of a learning disability (or a *specific learning disability* as it is referred to in the legislation). A common approach to diagnosis is to administer tests of achievement and cognitive ability and then determine by means of some formula whether a significant discrepancy exists. By law, a child will be diagnosed as learning disabled and therefore entitled to special school services only if a significant discrepancy exists between the child's achievement and his or her expected level of achievement in one or more of the following areas: oral expression, listening comprehension, written expression, basic reading skills, reading comprehension, mathematics calculation, or mathematics reasoning. As we will see, in recent years test publishers have sought to provide "all-in-one" tests that provide means for determining whether a child should be diagnosed as learning disabled.

Measures of General Achievement

Measures of general achievement may survey learning in one or more academic areas. Tests that cover a number of academic areas are typically divided into several subtests and are referred to as *achievement batteries*. Such batteries may be individually administered or group administered. They may consist of a few subtests, as does the Wide Range Achievement Test-3 (Wilkinson, 1993) with its measures of reading, spelling, and arithmetic. They may be as comprehensive as the STEP Series, which includes subtests in reading, vocabulary, mathematics, writing skills, study skills, science, and social studies; a behavior inventory; an educational environment questionnaire; and an activities inventory.

Some batteries, such as the SRA California Achievement Tests, span kindergarten through grade 12, whereas others are grade- or course-specific. Some batteries are constructed to provide both norm-referenced and criterion-referenced analyses. Others are concurrently normed with scholastic aptitude tests to enable a comparison between achievement and aptitude. Some batteries are constructed with practice tests that may be administered several days before actual testing to help students familiarize themselves with testtaking procedures. Other batteries contain **locator** or routing tests, pretests administered to determine the level of the actual test most appropriate for administration.

One popular instrument appropriate for use with persons age 4 through adult is the Wechsler Individual Achievement Test-Second Edition, otherwise known as the WIAT-II (Psychological Corporation, 2001). This instrument is used not only to gauge achievement but also to develop hypotheses about achievement versus ability. It features nine subtests that sample content in each of the seven areas required by the Individuals with Disabilities Education Act: oral expression, listening comprehension, written expression, basic reading skill, reading comprehension, mathematics calculation, and mathematics reasoning. The test was designed to facilitate understanding of the problem-solving processes and strategies that testtakers use in these areas. The manual provides age- and grade-based standard score information. Test scores allow for detailed skill analysis and specification of intervention targets for individualized education plans. Scoring is done either manually or by means of optional software capable of creating a basic report exportable to a word processor.

Of the many available achievement batteries, the test most appropriate for use is the one most consistent with the educational objectives of the individual teacher or school system. For a particular purpose, a battery that focuses on achievement in a few select areas may be preferable to one that attempts to sample achievement in several areas. On the other hand, a test that samples many areas may be advantageous when an individual comparison of performance across subject areas is desirable. If a school or a local school district undertakes to follow the progress of a group of students as measured by a particular achievement battery, the battery of choice will be one that spans the targeted subject areas in all the grades to be tested. If ability to distinguish individual areas of difficulty is of primary concern, achievement tests with strong diagnostic features will be chosen.

Although achievement batteries sampling a wide range of areas, across grades, and standardized on large, national samples of students have much to recommend them, they also have certain drawbacks. For example, such tests usually take years to develop; in the interim the items, especially in fields such as social studies and science, may become outdated. Further, any nationally standardized instrument is only as good as the extent to which it meets the (local) test user's objectives.

Measures of Achievement in Specific Subject Areas

Whereas achievement batteries tend to be standardized instruments, most measures of achievement in specific subject areas are teacher-made tests. Every time a teacher gives a quiz, a test, or a final examination in a course, a test in a specific subject area has been created. Still, there are a number of standardized instruments designed to gauge achievement in specific areas.

At the elementary school level, the acquisition of basic skills such as reading, writing, and arithmetic is emphasized. Tests to measure achievement in reading come in many different forms. For example, there are tests for individual or group administration or silent or oral reading. The tests may vary in the theory of cognitive ability on which they are based (see, for example, Vanderwood et al., 2001) and the type of subtest data they yield. In general, the tests present the examinee with words, sentences, or paragraphs to be read silently or aloud, and reading ability is assessed by variables such as comprehension and vocabulary. When the material is read aloud, accuracy and speed are measured. Tests of reading comprehension also vary with respect to the intellectual demands placed on the examinee over and above mere comprehension of the words read. Thus, some tests might require the examinee to simply recall facts from a passage, whereas others might require interpretation and making inferences.

At the secondary school level, one popular battery is the Cooperative Achievement Test. It consists of a series of separate achievement tests in areas as diverse as English, mathematics, literature, social studies, science, and foreign languages. Each test was standardized on different populations appropriate to the grade level, and in general the tests tend to be technically sound instruments. For example, the American History component of the Social Studies series was standardized on seventh- and eighth-graders who represented 44 junior and 73 senior high schools. The sample was randomly selected and stratified according to public, parochial, and private schools. Assessment of achievement in high school students may involve evaluation of minimum competencies, often as a requirement for a high school diploma (see this chapter's *Close-up*).

At the college level, there has been growing interest on the part of state legislatures to mandate end-of-major outcomes assessment in state colleges and universities. Apparently, taxpayers want confirmation that their education tax dollars are being well spent. Thus, for example, undergraduate psychology students attending a state-run institution could be required in their senior year to sit for a final—in the literal sense— examination encompassing a range of subject matter that could be described as "everything that an undergraduate psychology major should know." And if that sounds formidable to you, trust us when we advise you that the task of developing such examinations will be all the more formidable.

Another use for achievement tests at the college as well as the adult level is placement. The advanced placement program developed by the College Entrance Examination Board offers high school students the opportunity to achieve college credit for work completed in high school. Successful completion of the advanced placement test may result in advanced standing, advanced course credit, or both, depending on the college policy. Since its inception, the advanced placement program has resulted in advanced credit or standing for more than 100,000 high school students in approximately 2,000 colleges.

Another type of test that has application for placement purposes, particularly in areas of the country where English may be spoken as a second language by a relatively large segment of the population (such as parts of California, Florida, and Texas) is a test of English proficiency. Data from English proficiency tests are currently used in the placement of college program applicants in appropriate levels of English as a Second Language (ESL) programs. However, other uses of data from measures of English proficiency can be foreseen. In an era of growing numbers of native and immigrant Americans with limited English proficiency, and in a social climate that has legislators writing bills proclaiming English to be the official language of the state, one can foresee the increasing importance of issues related to the testing of English proficiency.

Achievement tests at the college or adult level may also assess whether college credit should be awarded for learning acquired outside a college classroom. Numerous programs are designed to systematically assess whether sufficient knowledge has been acquired to qualify for course credit. The College Level Examination Program (CLEP) is based on the premise that knowledge may be obtained through independent study and

Tests of Minimum Competency

Soon after the United States became an independent nation, one citizen commented in a book entitled *Letters from an American Farmer* that a "pleasing uniformity of decent competence appears throughout our habitations" (Crèvecoeur, 1782, cited in Lerner, 1981). Over two hundred years later, widespread dissatisfaction with the *lack* of competence in this country has become evident. At about the time of the nation's bicentennial celebration, a grassroots movement aimed at eradicating illiteracy and anumeracy began taking shape. By 1980, 38 states had passed legislation requiring the schools to administer a test to determine whether secondary school graduates had developed "minimum competence." Exactly what constituted minimum competence varied from one jurisdiction to the next, but it generally referred to some basic knowledge of reading, writing, and arithmetic. The movement has gained momentum with the realization that the illiterate and anumerate often wind up not just unemployed but unemployable. The unfortunate consequence is that too many of these individuals require public assistance or, alternatively, turn to crime—some finding their way to jail.

A minimum-competency testing program is designed to ensure that a student who is awarded a high school diploma has at least acquired the minimal skills to become a productive member of society. Such minimal skills include filling out an employment application, writing checks, balancing a checkbook, and interpreting a bank statement.

As an example of one test of minimum competency, we focus attention on the Alabama High School Graduation Exam (AHSGE). A publication of the Alabama State Department of Education (Teague, 1983) sets forth very detailed specifications for items to be used in the AHSGE. The skills that are tested are based on ninth-grade minimum competencies in the areas of Reading, Language, and Mathematics. Some of the skills listed in the area of Language are

- *Observe pronoun-antecedent agreement.* The student chooses the pronoun that agrees with its antecedent.

- *Use correct forms of nouns and verbs.* The student chooses the correct form of nouns (singular and/or plural) and verbs (regular and/or irregular) and selects verbs that agree with the subjects.

- *Include in a message or request all necessary information (who, what, when, where, how, or why).* The student demonstrates knowledge about the information necessary in a message or request.

- *Determine what information is missing from a message, an announcement, or a process explanation; or what information is irrelevant.*

- *Identify question marks, periods, and exclamation points to punctuate sentences.*

- *Identify words frequently used in daily activities.* The student recognizes frequently used words that are spelled incorrectly.

- *Complete a common form, such as a driver's license application or change of address form.*

- *Identify the proper format of a friendly letter.*

- *Identify the proper format of a business letter.* The student demonstrates knowledge of the proper format of a business letter, which includes punctuation and capitalization. Test questions refer to business letters reproduced in the test booklet. An example appears at the end of this Close-up.

Although minimum competency may seem like a good idea, it has not gone unchallenged in the courts. Who should determine the skills involved in minimum competence and the lack of it? What consequence should result from being found not minimally competent? Will a minimum competence requirement for a high school diploma motivate the academically unmotivated? In 1979, a federal judge in Florida found the scheduled application of that state's minimum competency law unconstitutional. Condemning the judge's decision, Lerner (1981) wrote that "disputes over empirical questions cannot be resolved by judicial fiat," and she went on to document that (1) substantial numbers of Americans are failing to master basic skills, such as reading; (2) the consequences of such deficits warrant action, and (3) the actions recommended by minimum competence advocates offer reasonable hope of bringing about the desired change (see also Lerner, 1980). Critics (such as Airasian et al., 1979; Haney & Madaus, 1978; Tyler, 1978) object primarily on the grounds of the potential for abuse inherent in such programs, though some criticisms have also been voiced regarding the psychometric soundness of the instruments.

(continued)

Tests of Minimum Competency
(*continued*)

---

120 Drewry Road
Monroeville Alabama 36460

Miss Ann Andrews, Director
Parks and Recreation
Monroeville, Alabama 36460

Dear Miss Andrews:

Our class would like to use the Community House for our senior prom. The tentative date for the prom is April 30, 2005. Please let me know if the ballroom is available on this date and the charges for the use of this facility.

yours truly,

Jan Austin

---

1. What part of the letter is the salutation?

   a. Jan Austin
   *b. Dear Miss Andrews:
   c. yours truly,
   d. Miss Ann Andrews

2. Which part of the letter has an error in punctuation?

   a. The salutation
   b. The closing
   c. The signature
   *d. The heading

3. Which part of the letter has an error in capitalization?

   *a. The closing
   b. The body
   c. The inside address
   d. The heading

4. Which part of this business letter has been omitted?

   *a. The date of the letter
   b. The salutation
   c. The closing
   d. The inside address

Sample Items Designed to Evaluate the Testtaker's Knowledge of the Format for a Business Letter

sources other than formal schooling. The program includes exams in subjects ranging from African American history to tests and measurement. The Proficiency Examination Program (PEP) offered by the American College Testing Program is another service designed to assess achievement and skills learned outside the classroom.

The special needs of adults with a wide variety of educational backgrounds are addressed in tests such as the Adult Basic Learning Examination (ABLE), a test intended for use with examinees age 17 and older who have not completed eight years of formalized schooling. The

JUST THINK . . .

For what extracurricular life experience should you be given college credit? What would a test to measure what you learned from that experience look like?

test is designed to assess achievement in the areas of vocabulary, reading, spelling, and arithmetic; it was developed in consultation with experts in the field of adult education.

Achievement tests in nationwide use may test for information or concepts that are not taught within a specific school's curriculum. Some children will do well on such items anyway, having been exposed to the concepts or information independently. Performance on a school achievement test therefore does not depend entirely on school achievement. Concern about such issues has led to an interest in **curriculum-based assessment (CBA),** a term used to refer to assessment of information acquired from teachings at school. **Curriculum-based measurement (CBM),** a type of CBA, is characterized by the use of standardized measurement procedures to derive local norms to be used in the evaluation of student performance on curriculum-based tasks.

Before leaving the topic of achievement tests, we will briefly point out that there are at least two distinctly different types of achievement test items. One type demands only rote memory. Such an item on an examination designed to measure mastery of the material in this chapter might look like this:

1. One type of item that could be used in an achievement test is an item that requires

    a. remote memory.

    b. rote memory.

    c. memory loss.

    d. mnemonic loss.

Alternatively, items in achievement tests could require the testtaker not only to know and understand the material but also to be able to apply it. In a test of English proficiency, for example, it might be important for the examinee to know more than vocabulary or rules of grammar. Items that gauge the ability of the examinee to understand or speak conversational English might be of far greater importance.

Let's move—but not very far—from the subject of achievement tests to the subject of aptitude tests. Before doing so, try your hand (and mind) on the *Just Think . . .* exercise.

> **JUST THINK . . .**
>
> "Achievement tests measure learned knowledge, whereas aptitude tests measure innate potential." Why is this belief a myth?

Aptitude Tests

We are all constantly acquiring information through everyday life experiences and formal learning experiences (such as course work in school). The primary difference between achievement tests and aptitude tests is that **aptitude tests** tend to focus more on informal learning or life experiences, whereas achievement tests tend to focus on the learning that has occurred as a result of relatively structured input. Keeping this distinction in mind, consider the following two items, the first from a hypothetical achievement test and the second from a hypothetical aptitude test.

1. A correlation of .7 between variables X and Y in a predictive validity study accounts for what percentage of the variance?

    a. 7%

    b. 70%

    c. .7%

    d. 49%

    e. 25%

2. o is to O as x is to

    a.   /

    b.   %

    c.   X

    d.   Y

At least on the face of it, Item 1 appears to be more dependent on formal learning experiences than does Item 2. The successful completion of Item 1 hinges on familiarity with the concept of correlation and the knowledge that the variance accounted for by a correlation coefficient is equal to the square of the coefficient (in this case, $.7^2$, or $.49$—choice *d*). The successful completion of Item 2 requires experience with the concept of size as well as the ability to grasp the concept of analogies. The latter abilities tend to be gleaned from life experiences (witness how quickly you determined that the correct answer was choice *c*).

It must also be kept in mind that the label *achievement* or *aptitude* for a test is very much dependent on the intended *use* of the test, not just on the type of items contained in it. It is possible for two tests to contain some of the same items and for one of the tests to be called an aptitude test, whereas the other is referred to as an achievement test. Although we chose a nonverbal analogy item to represent an aptitude test item, it could very well have been an achievement test item—one administered to test knowledge acquired, for example, at a seminar on conceptual thinking. Similarly, the first item, presented as an illustrative achievement test item, might well be used to assess aptitude (in statistics or psychology, for example) were it included in a test not expressly designed to measure achievement in this area.

JUST THINK . . .

Create an item for an aptitude test that will compel testtakers to draw on life experience rather than classroom learning for a response.

Aptitude tests, also referred to as **prognostic tests,** are typically used to make predictions. Some aptitude tests have been used to measure readiness:

- to enter elementary school
- to successfully complete a challenging course of study in secondary school
- to do college-level work
- to do graduate-level work, including a course of study at a professional or trade school

Achievement tests may also be used for predictive purposes. For example, an individual who performs well on a first-semester foreign-language achievement test might be considered a good candidate for the second term's work. The operative assumption here is that because an individual was able to master certain basic skills, he or she will be able to master more advanced skills. When such assumptions are operative, achievement tests, as well as test items that tap achievement, are used in ways akin to aptitude tests.

Typically, when measures of achievement tests are used to make predictions, the measures tend to draw on narrower and more formal learning experiences than aptitude tests do. For example, a measure of achievement in a course entitled Basic Conversational French might be used as a predictor of achievement for a course entitled Advanced Conversational French. Aptitude tests tend to draw on a broader fund of information and abilities and may be used to predict a wider variety of variables.

In the following sections, we survey some aptitude tests used in schools from entry level through graduate and professional institutions. Note that at the entry level, an "unwritten rule" known to assessment professionals is to refer to what is essentially an aptitude test by another name: a **readiness test.** Perhaps this is because the primary purpose of such tests is to assess a child's readiness for learning. As the level of education climbs, however, the term *readiness* is dropped in favor of the term *aptitude,* although readiness is very much implied at all levels. So, for example, the Graduate Record Examination (GRE), given in college and used as a predictor of ability to do graduate-level work, might have been called the "GSRE" or "Graduate School Readiness Examination."

The Elementary School Level

The age at which a child is mandated by law to enter school varies from state to state. Yet, individual children of the same chronological age may vary widely in how ready they are to separate from their parents and begin academic learning. Children entering the educational system come from a wide range of backgrounds and experiences, and their rates of physiological, psychological, and social development also vary widely. School readiness tests provide educators with a yardstick by which to assess pupils' abilities in areas as diverse as general information and sensorimotor skills. One of many instruments designed to assess children's readiness and aptitude for formal education is the Metropolitan Readiness Tests (MRT).

The Metropolitan Readiness Tests (MRT)   The MRT are a group-administered battery that assesses the development of reading and mathematics skills important in the early stages of formal school learning. The test is divided into two levels: Level I, to be used with beginning and middle kindergarteners, and Level II, which spans the end of kindergarten through first grade (Table 10–1). There are two forms of the test at each level.

Table 10–1
The Metropolitan Readiness Tests

Level I
  Auditory Memory: Four pictures containing familiar objects are presented. The examiner reads aloud several words. The child must select the picture that corresponds to the same sequence of words that were presented orally.
  Rhyming: The examiner supplies the names of each of the pictures presented and then gives a fifth word that rhymes with one of them. The child must select the picture that rhymes with the examiner's word.
  Letter Recognition: The examiner names different letters, and the child must identify each from the series presented in the test booklet.
  Visual Matching: A sample is presented, and the child must select the choice that matches the sample.
  School Language and Listening: The examiner reads a sentence, and the child selects the picture that describes what was read. The task involves some inference-making and awareness of relevancy of detail.
  Quantitative Language: The test assesses comprehension of quantitative terms and knowledge of ordinal numbers and simple mathematical operations.

Level II
  Beginning Consonants: Four pictures representing familiar objects are presented in the test booklet and are named by the examiner. The examiner then supplies a fifth word (not presented), and the child must select the picture that begins with the same sound.
  Sound-Letter Correspondence: A picture is presented, followed by a series of letters. The examiner names the picture, and the child selects the choice that corresponds to the beginning sound of the pictured item.
  Visual Matching: As in the corresponding subtest at Level I, a model is presented, and the child must select the choice that matches the model.
  Finding Patterns: A stimulus consisting of several symbols is presented, followed by a series of representative options. The child must select the option that contains the same sequence of symbols, even though they are presented in a larger grouping with more distractions.
  School Language: As in the School Language and Listening Test at Level I, the child must select the picture that corresponds to an orally presented sentence.
  Listening: Material is orally presented, and the child must select the picture that reflects comprehension of and drawing conclusions about the stimulus material.

  Quantitative Concepts ⎱ Both are optional tests that, like the Quantitative Language of Level I, assess comprehension of basic mathematical concepts
  Quantitative Operations ⎰ and operations.

The tests are orally administered in several sessions and are untimed, though they typically require about 90 minutes to administer. A practice test (especially useful with young children who have had minimal or no prior testtaking experience) may be administered several days before the actual testing to help familiarize students with the procedures and format.

Normative data for the current edition of the MRT are based on a national sample of approximately 30,000 children. The standardization sample was stratified according to geographic regions, socioeconomic factors, prior school experience, and ethnic background. Data were obtained from both public and parochial schools and from both large and small schools. Split-half reliability coefficients for both forms of both levels of the MRT as well as Kuder-Richardson measures of internal consistency were in the acceptably high range. Content validity was developed through an extensive review of the literature, analysis of the skills involved in the reading process, and the development of test items that reflected those skills. Items were reviewed by minority consultants in an attempt to reduce, if not eliminate, any potential ethnic bias. The predictive validity of MRT scores has been examined with reference to later school achievement indices, and the obtained validity coefficients have been acceptably high.

The Secondary School Level

Perhaps the most obvious example of an aptitude test widely used in the schools at the secondary level is the SAT, which up until 1993 went by the name Scholastic Aptitude Test. The test has been of value not only in the college selection process but also as an aid to high school guidance and job placement counselors in advising students about what course of action might be best for them. In addition to the SAT, the ACT Assessment (formerly known as the American College Testing Program) serves similar purposes.

How much do colleges really rely on criteria such as SAT or ACT scores in making college entrance decisions? Probably less than most people believe. Institutions of higher learning in this country differ widely with respect to their admission criteria. Even among schools that require SAT or ACT test scores, varying weights are accorded to the scores with respect to admission decisions. Highly selective institutions may admit large numbers of students with lower test scores and reject large numbers of students with high test scores. With that preface, we briefly describe the SAT and the ACT Assessment.

The Scholastic Assessment Test (SAT) The SAT was first introduced as an objective exam in 1926. Until 1995, the SAT was a three-hour test divided into two parts: Verbal and Mathematics. The Verbal part consisted of sections that included Analogies, Reading Comprehension, Antonyms, and Sentence Completion. The Reading Comprehension section consisted of reading passages containing subject material from a variety of academic areas, such as science, social studies, and the humanities. The Sentence Completion section consisted of single sentences or paragraphs in which one or two words had been omitted, and the examinee's task was to select the choice that best completed the written thought. Vocabulary knowledge was measured by performance on the Antonyms and Analogies items.

In 1974, a Test of Standard Written English was introduced for the first time to assess the student's ability to comprehend the type of language utilized in most college textbooks. It consisted of 50 multiple-choice questions and required 30 minutes to complete. A Reading Comprehension score was also computed based on the Sentence Completion and Reading Comprehension sections. The Mathematics part of the SAT assessed the understanding and application of mathematical principles as well as numerical reasoning ability. The subject matter of the test questions in this section assumed knowledge of the basic arithmetic operations, such as addition, subtraction, multiplication, division, averages, percentages, odd-even integers, and geometric and algebraic concepts, including linear and quadratic equations, exponents, and factoring.

Major changes in the SAT's format and normative base were instituted in the early 1990s. The format changes were designed to make the test more "educationally relevant" with respect to its objective of predicting college performance (Moses, 1991). Essentially, the format change involved dichotomizing the SAT into two major components and renaming the components of the test. The SAT I (Reasoning) was a three-hour test that measured verbal and mathematical skills. The SAT II (Subject Tests) was a one-hour test that measured knowledge in a particular subject area as well as the testtaker's ability to apply that knowledge. Subject Tests are more directly related to high school course work and are given in various subject areas, such as world history, biology, and chemistry.

Test items for the SAT are constructed by experts in the field and pretested on national samples during the actual examination. The experimental items are placed in separately timed sections of the examination. Such a pretesting procedure on a sample of examinees who are representative of the group that will be taking future forms of the test provides the test constructors with useful information regarding the value of proposed new items. The responses of students are statistically analyzed to determine the percent answering each question correctly, the percent choosing each of the distractor items, and the percent who omit the item. An index of the response to each item with the total score on the test (that is, a difficulty rating for each item) is computed. The test is under continual revision, and the total time to develop an item may exceed 18 months.

The technical quality of the SAT is good. Reliability of recent forms of the test as measured by internal-consistency estimates has resulted in reliability coefficients in the .90s for both the Verbal and the Mathematics scales. Research concerning the validity of the SAT has focused mostly on correlations between SAT scores and college grades, or on a combination of SAT scores and high school grades with college grades. In general, high school grades have been found to correlate higher with college grades than do SAT scores. When SAT scores and high school grade-point average are combined, the correlation with college performance increases. For example, in one study, grades in the first year of college correlated .20 with SAT scores and .30 with high school class rank. Together, SAT scores and high school class rank correlated .34 with college grades, accounting for 11.3% of the variance in college grades (Baron & Norman, 1992). Correlations between the Verbal and Mathematics parts of the SAT have been in the high .60s, a finding that suggests that overlapping skills, probably verbal in nature, are tapped on both parts of the exam.

When the SAT was standardized in 1941, the average performance was reflected in a score of 500. In the years since 1941, SAT scores have declined, such that the average testtaker in 1993 received a verbal SAT score of 424 and a mathematics score of 478. Because the norms were anchored, the scores retained the same meaning in 1993 as they had in 1941. That is, a score of 500 in 1993 meant that the testtaker performed at the average level of testtakers in 1941. This made possible the comparison of students taking the test during different years. A similar shift in GRE scores had taken place (see *Everyday Psychometrics* in Chapter 4).

As of April 1995, the SAT norms were "recentered" so that a score of 500 indicated average performance among testtakers in 1995. Test users, like college admissions offices, have been provided with tables to convert old SAT scores (based on the 1941 norms) to scores based on the 1995 norms for comparison purposes (*Q and A,* 1994). Unless recentering occurs in the meantime, an SAT score of 500 indicates an average level of performance relative to the immortalized performance of people who took the test in 1995.

The SAT is administered several times a year under carefully controlled conditions in cities throughout the United States and in foreign countries. Foreign-language editions of the test have been made available, as have special editions for students with disabilities. A special form (the Preliminary SAT, or PSAT) is available for administration as a practice exam and as a tool for counselors. Because the PSAT is cosponsored by the National Merit Scholarship Corporation, it is now formally referred to as the Preliminary SAT/National Merit Scholarship Qualifying Test (PSAT/NMSQT). Taking this test makes students eligible for National Merit scholarships. Other reasons students take the PSAT/NMSQT include to obtain feedback on skills they will need for the SAT and to see how their scores compare to those of other students who take the test.

Both the PSAT and the SAT underwent change recently in an effort to better align the test with contemporary high school curricula and practices. The PSAT was changed in the fall of 2004, and the SAT was changed in the spring of 2005. A new writing section was added, including multiple-choice grammar and usage questions and a student essay. In the Critical Reading section (formally called Verbal), the analogy items have been eliminated, and short reading passages have been added to long reading passages. In the Math section, quantitative comparisons have been eliminated, and content has been expanded to include topics from third-year preparatory math. In general, what is measured by the revised SAT is more achievement oriented; that is, the test content has shifted to be more in line with what students are expected to learn from formal classroom instruction. A chief competitor of the SAT, the ACT Assessment, has from its inception been more achievement oriented.

The ACT Assessment (ACT)   Commonly referred to by saying its three letters (*the A-C-T*) rather than rhyming it with *fact*, the ACT was developed at the University of Iowa. This college entrance examination was an outgrowth of the Iowa Tests of Educational Development. The test is curriculum-based, with questions directly based on typical high school teachings in English, science, and mathematics. The test is divided into four sections: Writing, Reading, Math, and Science Reasoning. Additionally, there is a measure designed to explore areas of the testtaker's interest. Scores are calculated on each of the four tests, and the average of those scores rounded to the nearest whole number is the test Composite. Actual testing time is about three hours, although the session typically runs for about three and one-half hours with breaks. All colleges and universities in the United States accept ACT results.

> **JUST THINK . . .**
>
> *An ACT Composite, much like all the other test scores discussed in this book, might best be thought of as a range of scores rather than a precise point in the universe of possible scores.* Explain why this statement is true with reference to the standard error of measurement.

The College Level and Beyond

If you are a college student planning to pursue further education after graduation, you are probably familiar with the letters G, R, and E (which together form an acronym that is very much on the minds of many graduate-school-bound students).

The Graduate Record Examinations (GRE)   This long-standing rite of passage for students seeking admission to graduate school has a General Test form as well as specific subject tests. The General Test contains verbal and quantitative sections as well as analytical writing sections. The verbal subtest taps, among other things, the ability to analyze and evaluate written materials, as well as the ability to recognize relationships between concepts. The quantitative subtest taps, among other things, knowledge of basic mathematical concepts and the ability to reason quantitatively. The analytical writing subtest taps, among other things, the ability to articulate and argue ideas effectively in standard written English, as well as critical thinking. The General Test may be taken by paper and pencil or by computer at a test center. If it is taken by computer, testtakers use an "elementary word processor" devised by the test developer so that persons familiar with one or another commercially available word-processing programs will not have an advantage. Essays written by respondents may be sent in their entirety to graduate institutions receiving GRE test reports.

Perhaps because of the potentially momentous importance of GRE test results, a number of independent researchers have critically examined the test with regard to various psychometric variables. One comprehensive meta-analysis of the relevant literature focused on the use of the GRE along with undergraduate grade-point average as predictors of graduate success. The researchers concluded that the GRE was a valid predictor of several important criterion measures (ranging from graduate grade-point average to faculty ratings) across disciplines (Kuncel et al., 2001).

Experience tells us that many readers of this book have a very focused interest in one specific GRE subject test: Psychology. "How do I prepare for it?" is a common question. Here is a three-step preparation program you may wish to consider:

- *Step 1:* Visit the official GRE Web site at http://www.gre.org. Click on *Subject Tests,* and then click on *Psychology.* Use this resource to get all the information you can about the current form of the test, even a practice sample of the test.

- *Step 2:* Dust off your introductory psychology textbook and then reread it, review it, do whatever you need to in order to relearn it. If for some reason you no longer have that textbook, or if you took introductory psychology ages ago, ask your instructor to recommend a current text that provides a comprehensive review of the field. Then, read that textbook diligently from cover to cover.

- *Step 3:* Many students have praise for some commercially available review books. Typically, these books contain a number of sample tests that may be very helpful in pinpointing areas requiring extra study. Two review books you may want to check out are *Cracking the GRE Psychology* (Jay, 2002) and *Graduate Record Examination Psychology* (Raphael & Halpert, 1999).

After you have made your best effort to prepare for the test, know that you have the authors' best wishes for luck with it. Or, in psychological and psychometric terms, may the content sampled on the test match the content you have learned in preparing to take it, and may that information be readily accessed!

The Miller Analogies Test (MAT)   Another widely used examination is the Miller Analogies Test. This is a 100-item, multiple-choice analogy test that draws not only on the examinee's ability to perceive relationships but also on general intelligence, vocabulary, and academic learning. As an example, complete the following analogy:

Classical conditioning is to *Pavlov* as *operant conditioning* is to

   a. Freud.

   b. Rogers.

   c. Skinner.

   d. Jung.

   e. Westheimer.

Successful completion of this item demands not only the ability to understand the relationship between classical conditioning and Pavlov but also the knowledge that it was B. F. Skinner (choice *c*) whose name—of those listed—is best associated with operant conditioning.

Other aptitude tests   Applicants for training in certain professions and occupations may be required to take specialized entrance examinations (see Table 10–2). For example, undergraduate students interested in pursuing a career in medicine, including podiatry or osteopathy, will probably be required to sit for the Medical College Admission Test (MCAT). A high rate of attrition among students studying to become physicians in the 1920s was the stimulus for the development of this test in 1928. Since that time, the test has gone through a number of revisions. The various versions of the test "demonstrate that the definition of aptitude for medical education reflects the professional and social mores and values of the time" (McGaghie, 2002, p. 1085). In its present form, the MCAT consists of four sections: Verbal Reasoning, Physical Sciences, Writing Sample, and Biological Sciences.

Numerous other aptitude tests have been developed to assess specific kinds of academic, professional, and/or occupational aptitudes. Some of the more widely used tests are described briefly in Table 10–2. There are also a number of lesser known (and less widely used) aptitude tests. For example, the Seashore Measures of Musical Talents (Seashore, 1938) is a now-classic measure of musical aptitude administered with the aid of a record (if you can find a record player) or pre-recorded tape. The six subtests measure specific aspects of musical talent (for example, comparing different notes and rhythms on variables such as loudness, pitch, time, and timbre). The Horn Art Aptitude Inventory is a measure of art aptitude that is divided into two sections. Items in the Scribbles and Doodles section are thought to measure variables such as clarity of thought and originality. Items in the Imagery section contain key lines or "springboards" from art masterpieces to be incorporated in the examinee's artistic production. Scoring categories for the Imagery section include Design, Imagination, and Scope of Interests.

JUST THINK . . .

A really "offbeat" (for lack of a better term) artist takes the Imagery subtest of the Horn Art Aptitude Inventory as an admission requirement for an art school. Simon, the admissions officer for the school, finds the testtaker's productions to be "off the norm charts" and so abstract so as to be beyond his comprehension. Does the artist have an aptitude for art?

Diagnostic Tests

By the early twentieth century, it was recognized that tests of intelligence could be used to do more than simply measure cognitive ability. Binet and Simon (1908) wrote of their concept of "mental orthopedics," whereby intelligence test data could be used to improve learning. Today, a distinction is made between tests and test data used primarily for *evaluative* purposes and tests and test data used primarily for *diagnostic* purposes. The term **evaluative,** as used in phrases such as *evaluative purposes* or *evaluative information,* is typically applied to tests or test data that are used to make judgments (such as pass/fail and admit/reject decisions). By contrast, the term **diagnostic,** as used in educational contexts and phrases such as *diagnostic purposes* or *diagnostic information,* is typically applied to tests or test data used to pinpoint a student's difficulty, usually for remedial purposes.

A diagnostic reading test may, for example, contain a number of subtests. Each subtest is designed to analyze a specific knowledge or skill required for reading and to bring

Table 10-2
Some Entrance Examinations for Professional or Occupational Training

Entrance Examination and Web Site for More Information	Brief Description
Medical College Admission Test (MCAT) www.aamc.org	Designed to assess problem solving, critical thinking, and writing skills, as well as knowledge of science concepts prerequisite to the study of medicine.
Law School Admission Test (LSAT) www.lsac.org	A standardized measure of acquired reading and verbal reasoning skills. Includes measures of reading comprehension, analytical reasoning, and logical reasoning, as well as a writing sample.
Veterinary College Admission Test (VCAT) www.tpcweb.com (follow links)	Assesses five content areas: biology, chemistry, verbal ability, quantitative ability, and reading comprehension.
Dental Admission Test (DAT) www.ada.org	Conducted by the American Dental Association, this test may be computer administered almost any day of the year. Includes four sections: Natural Sciences (biology, general chemistry, organic chemistry), Perceptual Ability (including angle discrimination tasks), Reading Comprehension, and Quantitative Reasoning (including algebra, various conversions, probability and statistics, geometry, trigonometry, and applied mathematics).
Pharmacy College Admission Test (PCAT) http://marketplace.psychcorp.com (follow links)	Contains five subtests: Verbal (including vocabulary with analogies and antonyms), Quantitative (arithmetic, fractions, decimals, percentages, algebra, and reasoning), Biology, Chemistry (basic organic and inorganic), Reading Comprehension (analyze and interpret passages).
Optometry Admission Test (OAT) www.opted.org	Contains four subtests: Natural Sciences (tapping knowledge of biology, general chemistry, and organic chemistry), Reading Comprehension, Physics, and Quantitative Reasoning.
Allied Health Professions Admission Test (AHPAT) www.tpcweb.com (follow links)	Assesses ability in five content areas: biology, chemistry, verbal ability, quantitative ability, and reading comprehension. Designed for use with aspiring physical and occupational therapists, physician's assistants, and other members of allied health professions.
Entrance Examination for Schools of Nursing (RNEE) www.tpcweb.com (follow links)	Voted by the authors of this textbook as "Test with Trickiest Acronym," the RNEE assesses ability in five content areas: physical sciences, numerical ability, life sciences, verbal ability, and reading comprehension.
Accounting Program Admission Test (APAT) www.tpcweb.com (follow links)	Measures student achievement in elementary accounting by means of 75 multiple-choice questions, 60% of which deal with financial accounting and the remaining 40% of which deal with managerial accounting.
Graduate Management Admission Test www.mba.com	Measures basic verbal and mathematical and analytical writing skills through three subtests: Analytical Writing Assessment, the Quantitative section, and the Verbal section.

into full relief the specific problems, if any, that need to be addressed if the testtaker is to read at an appropriate grade level. By the way, diagnostic information can also be used for evaluative purposes. On the basis of a child's performance on a diagnostic reading test, for example, a teacher or an administrator might make a class placement decision. Also, diagnostic tests do not necessarily provide information that will answer questions concerning *why* the learning difficulty exists. Other educational, psychological, and perhaps medical examinations are needed to answer that question. In general, diagnostic tests are administered to students who have already demonstrated their problem with a particular subject area through their poor performance either in the classroom or on some achievement test. It is therefore understandable that diagnostic tests tend to contain simpler items than achievement tests designed for use with members of the same grade.

Reading Tests

The ability to read is integral to virtually all classroom learning, and so it is not surprising that a number of diagnostic tests are available to help pinpoint difficulties in acquiring this skill. Some of the many tests available to help pinpoint reading difficulties include the Stanford Diagnostic Reading Test, the Metropolitan Reading Instructional Tests, the Diagnostic Reading Scales, and the Durrell Analysis of Reading Test. For illustrative purposes we briefly describe one such diagnostic battery, the Woodcock Reading Mastery Tests.

The Woodcock Reading Mastery Tests-Revised (WRMT-R)   This test battery is suitable for children age 5 and older and adults to age 75 and beyond. In short, it seems to be one of those tests that we characterize as being rated *E* for *Everyone* (to borrow from *X-Box* and *Playstation* parlance). Here is a listing of this test's subtests, including a brief description of the kinds of tasks on each:

Letter Identification: Items that measure the ability to name letters presented in different forms. Both cursive/manuscript and uppercase/lowercase letters are presented.

Word Identification: Words in isolation arranged in order of increasing difficulty. The student is asked to read each word aloud.

Word Attack: Nonsense syllables that incorporate phonetic as well as structural analysis skills. The student is asked to pronounce each nonsense syllable.

Word Comprehension: Items that assess word meaning by using a four-part analogy format.

Passage Comprehension: Phrases, sentences, or short paragraphs, read silently, in which a word is missing. The student must supply the missing word.

The tests are individually administered and are designed to measure skills inherent in reading. The tests come in two forms, *G* and *H,* and each form contains the five subtests listed above. Form *G* also contains a test labeled Visual-Auditory Learning. A cassette tape is packaged with the tests and serves as a guide to the proper pronunciation of the Word Attack items and the Word Identification items.

Test scores may be combined to form what are referred to as *clusters,* such as a Readiness cluster (the Visual-Auditory Learning and Letter Identification tests), a Basic Skills cluster (the Word Identification and Word Attack tests), a Reading Comprehension cluster (the Word Comprehension and Passage Comprehension tests), a Total Reading–Full Scale cluster (the Word Identification, Word Attack, Word Comprehension, and Passage Comprehension tests), and a Total Reading–Short Scale (the Word Identification and Passage Comprehension tests). Each cluster of tests typically takes between 10 and 30 minutes to administer. The last scale may be used for quick screening and takes about 15 minutes to administer. Computer software is available for score conversion and storage of pre- and post-test scores.

The test manual for the WRMT-R suggests that the test measures two factors with regard to reading: Basic Skills and Reading Comprehension. Factor-analytic research conducted by independent researchers was unable to confirm this two-factor structure. Rather, the factor analysis suggested that the WRMT-R measures only a single, "total reading" factor as reflected by the Full Scale score on the test.

Math Tests

The Stanford Diagnostic Mathematics Test, the Metropolitan Mathematics Instructional Tests, the Diagnostic Mathematics Inventory, and the KeyMath Revised: A Diagnostic Inventory of Essential Mathematics are some of the many tests that have been developed to help diagnose difficulties with arithmetic and mathematical concepts. Items on such tests typically analyze the skills and knowledge necessary for segregating the parts of mathematical operations. The KeyMath Revised test, for example, contains 13 subtests designed to assess areas such as basic concepts (including knowledge of symbols, numbers, and fractions), operations (including skill in addition, subtraction, multiplication, division, and mental computation), and applications (numerical problems employing variables such as money and time).

Diagnostic information is obtained from an evaluation of the examinee's performance in the various areas, subtests, and items. Total test scores are translated into grade equivalents. Area performance may be translated into a general pattern of mathematical functioning. Subtest performance may be translated into a profile illustrating strengths and weaknesses. For each item on the test, the manual lists a description of the skill involved and a corresponding behavior objective—information useful in determining the skills to be included in a remedial program. A computerized scoring program converts raw scores into derived scores, summarizes the examinee's performance, and offers suggestions for remedial instruction.

Other Diagnostic Tests

In addition to individually administered diagnostic tests such as the KeyMath Revised, a number of diagnostic tests designed for group administration have been developed. Two examples of group diagnostic tests are the Stanford Diagnostic Reading Test (SDRT) and the Stanford Diagnostic Mathematics Test (SDMT). Although developed independently and standardized on separate populations, the two instruments share certain characteristics of test design and format. Both instruments are available in two forms, and both are divided into four overlapping levels that assess performance from grade 1 through high school. Both are considered useful screening instruments in identifying children who require more detailed and individualized assessment.

The SDRT consists of ten subtests that reflect skills required in three major areas of reading: decoding, vocabulary, and comprehension. The SDMT consists of three subtests administered at all levels. Norm-referenced as well as criterion-referenced information is provided in the test manual for each of these tests. Norms were last updated in 2002 and are presented as percentile ranks, stanines, grade equivalents, and scaled scores. Criterion-referenced information is provided for each skill through the use of a "progress indicator," a cutoff score that shows whether the student is sufficiently competent in that skill to progress to the next stage of the instructional program. The manuals for both instruments include an index of behavioral objectives useful in prescriptive teaching strategies. The SDRT also contains informal measures designed to probe students' attitudes toward reading, reading interests and habits, and ability to retell a read story.

Psychoeducational Test Batteries

Psychoeducational test batteries are test kits that generally contain two types of tests: those that measure abilities related to academic success and those that measure educational achievement in areas such as reading and arithmetic. Data derived from these batteries allow for normative comparisons (how the student compares with other students within the same age group), as well as an evaluation of the testtaker's own strengths and weaknesses—all the better to plan educational interventions.

One psychoeducational battery is the Kaufman Assessment Battery for Children (K-ABC).

The Kaufman Assessment Battery for Children (K-ABC)

Developed by a husband-wife team of psychologists, the K-ABC was designed for use with testtakers from age 2½ through age 12½. Subtests measuring both intelligence and achievement are included. The K-ABC intelligence subtests are divided into two groups reflecting the two kinds of information-processing skills identified by Luria and his students (Das et al., 1975; Luria, 1966a, 1966b): *simultaneous skills* and *sequential skills* (see page 242). Table 10–3 presents the particular learning and teaching styles that reflect the two types of intelligence measured by the K-ABC. Scores on the simultaneous and sequential subtests are combined into a Mental Processing Composite, which is analogous to the IQ measure calculated on other tests.

Factor-analytic studies of the K-ABC have confirmed the presence of a factor researchers label *simultaneous processing* and a factor labeled *sequential processing*. Perhaps surprisingly, it is an achievement factor that researchers have had difficulty finding. Kaufman (1993) found evidence for the presence of an achievement factor, but independent researchers have different ideas about what that third factor is. Good and Lane (1988) identified the third factor of the K-ABC as *verbal comprehension and reading achievement*. Kaufman and McLean (1986) identified it as *achievement and reading ability*. Keith and Novak (1987) identified it as *reading achievement and verbal reasoning*. Whatever the factor is, the K-ABC Achievement Scale has been shown to predict achievement (Lamp & Krohn, 2001). In addition to questions about what the elusive third factor actually measures, questions have also been raised about whether or not sequential and simultaneous learning are entirely independent (Bracken, 1985; Keith, 1985).

Recommendations for teaching based on Kaufman and Kaufman's (1983a, 1983b) concept of *processing strength* can be derived from the K-ABC test findings. It may be recommended, for example, that a student whose strength is processing sequentially should be taught using the teaching guidelines for sequential learners. Students who do not have any particular processing strength may be taught using a combination of methods. This model of test interpretation and consequential intervention may engender great enthusiasm on the basis of its intuitive appeal. However, research findings related to this approach have been mixed (Ayres & Cooley, 1986; Good et al., 1989; McCloskey, 1989; Salvia & Hritcko, 1984). Good et al. (1993) concluded that educational decisions based on a child's processing style as defined by the K-ABC did not improve the quality of these decisions.

> **JUST THINK . . .**
>
> How realistic is it to expect that children can be taught a variety of subjects by classroom teachers in a way that is individually tailored to each child's unique processing strength as measured by a test?

The second edition of the K-ABC was published in 2004 with an age range extended upward (ages 3 to 18) in order to expand the possibility of making ability/achievement comparisons with the same test through high school. The KABC-II has been promoted as the most flexible psychoeducational test because results may be interpreted using the Luria or CHC model. Exactly how results are interpreted in practice depend on different variables such as the preferences of the test user and the reason for referral. The KABC-II was co-normed with the second edition of the Kaufman Test of Educational Achievement (KTEA-II). At the time of press for this textbook, both tests were too new for extended description and evaluation. However, the interested reader will find detailed information about both of these instruments on the Internet site of the test publisher, American Guidance Service (www.agsnet.com).

Two other widely known psychoeducational test batteries we briefly discuss for contrast purposes are the Differential Abilities Scales and the Woodcock-Johnson III.

Table 10–3

Characteristics and Teaching Guidelines for Sequential and Simultaneous Learners

Learner Characteristics

The Sequential Learner	The Simultaneous Learner
The sequential learner solves problems best by mentally arranging small amounts of information in consecutive, linear, step-by-step order. He/she is most at home with verbal instructions and cues because the ability to interpret spoken language depends to a great extent on the sequence of words.	The simultaneous learner solves problems best by mentally integrating and synthesizing many parallel pieces of information at the same time. He/she is most at home with visual instructions and cues because the ability to interpret the environment visually depends on perceiving and integrating many details at once.

Sequential processing is especially important in

- learning and retaining basic arithmetic facts
- memorizing lists of spelling words
- making associations between letters and their sounds
- learning the rules of grammar, the chronology of historical events
- remembering details
- following a set of rules, directions, steps
- solving problems by breaking them down into their components or steps

Simultaneous processing is especially important in

- recognizing the shape and physical appearance of letters and numbers
- interpreting the overall effect or meaning of pictures and other visual stimuli, such as maps and charts
- understanding the overall meaning of a story or poem
- summarizing, comparing, evaluating
- comprehending mathematical or scientific principles
- solving problems by visualizing them in their entirety

Sequential learners who are weak in simultaneous processing may have difficulty with

- sight word recognition
- reading comprehension
- understanding mathematical or scientific principles
- using concrete, hands-on materials
- using diagrams, charts, maps
- summarizing, comparing, evaluating

Simultaneous learners who are weak in sequential processing may have difficulty with

- word attack, decoding, phonics
- breaking down science or arithmetic problems into parts
- interpreting the parts and features of a design or drawing
- understanding the rules of games
- understanding and following oral instructions
- remembering specific details and sequence of a story

Teaching Guidelines

For the Sequential Learner	For the Simultaneous Learner

1. Present material step by step, gradually approaching the overall concept or skill. Lead up to the big question with a series of smaller ones. Break the task into parts.
2. Get the child to verbalize what is to be learned. When you teach a new word, have the child say it, aloud or silently. Emphasize verbal cues, directions, and memory strategies.
3. Teach and rehearse the steps required to do a problem or complete a task. Continue to refer back to the details or steps already mentioned or mastered. Offer a logical structure or procedure by appealing to the child's verbal/temporal orientation.

For example, the sequential learner may look at one or two details of a picture but miss the visual image as a whole. To help such a student toward an overall appreciation of the picture, start with the parts and work up to the whole. Rather than beginning with "What does the picture show?" or "How does the picture make you feel?" first ask about details:

"What is the little boy in the corner doing?"
"Where is the dog?"
"What expression do you see on the woman's face?"
"What colors are used in the sky?"

Lead up to questions about the overall interpretation or appreciation:

"How do all these details give you clues about what is happening in this picture?"
"How does this picture make you feel?"

The sequential learner prefers a step-by-step teaching approach, one that may emphasize the gradual accumulation of details.

1. Present the overall concept or question before asking the child to solve the problem. Continue to refer back to the task, question, or desired outcome.
2. Get the child to visualize what is to be learned. When you teach a new word, have the child write it and picture it mentally, see it on the page in the mind's eye. Emphasize visual cues, directions, and memory strategies.
3. Make tasks concrete wherever possible by providing manipulative materials, pictures, models, diagrams, graphs. Offer a sense of the whole by appealing to the child's visual/spatial orientation.

The simultaneous learner may react to a picture as a whole but may miss details. To help such a student notice the parts that contribute to the total visual image, begin by establishing an overall interpretation or reaction:

"What does the picture show?"
"How does the picture make you feel?"

Then consider the details:

"What is the expression on the woman's face?"
"What is the little boy in the corner doing?"
"What colors are used in the sky?"

Relate the details to the student's initial interpretation:

"How do these details explain why the picture made you feel the way it did?"

The simultaneous learner responds best to a holistic teaching approach that focuses on groups of details or images and stresses the overall meaning or configuration of the task.

Source: Kaufman, A. S., Kaufman, N. L., & Goldsmith, B. (1984). *Kaufman Sequential or Simultaneous (K-SOS)*. Circle Pines, MN: American Guidance Service. Used by permission.

The Differential Ability Scales (DAS)

The Differential Ability Scales (DAS; Elliott, 1990a, 1990b) is actually an American adaptation of the BAS (British Ability Scales), which, in turn, was a descendant of a test called the BIT (British Intelligence Test). The BAS was first published in Great Britain in 1979, and a revision was published in 1983. Development of the American version of the DAS began in 1984, and the test was published about six years later (Elliott 1990a, 1990b). Appropriate for use with individuals from 2 years 6 months of age through 17 years 11 months, the DAS is a measure not only of ability (as one might expect from its name) but of achievement as well. As summarized in Table 10–4, the total battery consists of 17 cognitive subtests and 3 achievement subtests (tapping achievement in basic number skills, spelling, and word reading), although no more than 12 subtests are ever administered to any one testtaker. In the words of the test's developer, school psychologist Colin Elliott (1990b), the DAS was developed "to obtain and evaluate profiles of strengths and weaknesses. The achievement tests were co-normed with the cognitive battery to make direct ability-achievement discrepancy analyses possible" (p. 1).

The conception of intelligence (a term Elliott assiduously avoids) underlying the DAS can best be described as a developmental, hierarchical model of cognitive abilities with three levels: general conceptual ability (GCA, also known as *g*) at the top of this hierarchy, followed by general verbal and nonverbal abilities (as measured by cluster scores for clusters of subtests), followed by individual, specific verbal and nonverbal abilities as measured by individual subtests (Figure 10–2). GCA is a composite measure of intelligence, that is, a composite measure of conceptual and reasoning abilities derived from the scores on core subtests forming the foundation of the battery. Additionally, diagnostic subtests measure specific cognitive skills, such as short-term auditory memory and visual discrimination. Developmentally, it is presumed that only certain abilities are present at certain ages, and the actual structure of the battery varies by age.

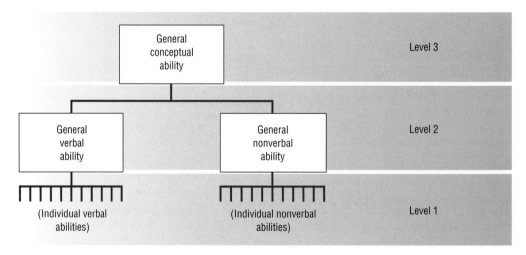

Figure 10–2
A Three-Level Hierarchical Model of Cognitive Abilities

The theory on which the DAS is based posits that individual abilities are at the first level, and clusters of individual abilities are at the second level. At the third and highest level in this model is general conceptual ability (GCA).

Table 10–4
The Subtests of the DAS

Subtest	Description	Abilities Measured
Core Subtests		
Block Building (ages 2–6 through 3–5)	Copying a two- or three-dimensional design with blocks.	Perceptual-motor ability
Verbal Comprehension (ages 2–6 through 5–11)	Pointing to pictures and manipulating toys or objects in response to examiner instructions.	Receptive verbal knowledge
Picture Similarities (ages 2–6 through 5–11)	The child is shown a row of four pictures (such as geometric designs, or everyday objects) and is given a card with a fifth picture, which is to be placed under the picture sharing an element or concept.	Nonverbal reasoning
Naming Vocabulary (ages 2–6 through 5–11)	Naming objects and pictures.	Expressive verbal knowledge
Pattern Construction (ages 3–6 through 17–11)	Constructing a design with foam-rubber squares or plastic blocks to match patterns depicted on cards.	Nonverbal, spatial reasoning
Early Number Concepts (ages 3–6 through 5–11)	Responding to questions about number, size, and other numerical concepts using colored chips or pictures.	Nonverbal and verbal knowledge
Copying (ages 3–6 through 5–11)	Copying drawings made by the examiner or displayed in a picture.	Perceptual-motor ability
Recall of Designs (ages 6–0 through 17–11)	Reproducing an abstract geometric design after being exposed to it.	Short-term visual spatial memory
Word Definitions (ages 6–0 through 17–11)	Defining words presented orally or visually.	Expressive verbal knowledge
Matrices (ages 6–0 through 17–11)	The testtaker is shown an incomplete matrix of abstract figures and selects the figure (from four or six choices) that completes the matrix.	Nonverbal reasoning
Similarities (ages 6–0 through 17–11)	Stating how things are similar or go together.	Verbal reasoning
Sequential and Quantitative Reasoning (ages 6–0 through 17–11)	The subtest is presented in two parts. The testtaker is first shown a series of abstract figures and must complete it. In the second part, the testtaker identifies a relationship within each pair of two pairs of numbers and then provides the missing number in an incomplete pair.	Detection of sequential patterns in figures or numbers
Diagnostic Subtests		
Recall of Objects—Immediate (ages 4–0 through 17–11)	Three immediate recall trials in which the testtaker views a card with pictures of 20 objects for 20 to 60 seconds and then tries to recall as many objects as possible.	Short-term verbal memory
Recall of Objects—Delayed (ages 4–0 through 17–11)	The testtaker recalls as many objects as possible from Recall of Ojects—Immediate subtest. Administration occurs 10 to 30 minutes after initial presentation of the objects.	Intermediate verbal memory
Matching Letterlike Forms (ages 4–6 through 5–11)	Choosing a figure (from six choices) that matches an abstract figure.	Visual perceptual matching
Recall of Digits (ages 3–0 through 17–11)	Repeating a sequence of digits presented orally at the rate of two digits per second.	Short-term auditory memory
Recognition of Pictures (ages 3–0 through 7–11)	After being shown black-and-white pictures of common objects for 5 or 10 seconds, a second picture with the same objects as well as distractors (objects not in the first picture) is shown, the task being to point to the object(s) that were in the first picture.	Short-term visual memory
Speed of Information Processing (ages 6–0 through 17–11)	The testtaker is presented with items consisting of rows of figures (circles containing small boxes or numbers). In each row the task is to mark the circle with the most boxes or highest number.	Quickness in performing mental operations
Achievement Subtests		
Basic Number Skills (ages 6–0 through 17–11)	Basic arithmetic skills, ranging from identifying numbers to problems requiring addition, subtraction, multiplication, or division. At upper age levels, word problems.	Numerical computation
Spelling (ages 6–0 through 17–11)	Writing words dictated by the examiner.	Spelling
Word Reading (ages 6–0 through 17–11)	Reading aloud words presented on a card.	Reading decoding skills

The DAS standardization sample consisted of 3,475 subjects, with 175 subjects for each six-month age group from 2 years 6 months through 4 years 11 months and 200 subjects per age-group year in age-group years 5 through 17. The sample was stratified at each level on the basis of sex, race/ethnicity, parent education, geographic region, and preschool enrollment using 1988 Census data as a criterion. Children enrolled in special education classes were included in the standardization sample. Children from smaller metropolitan and nonmetropolitan areas were underrepresented.

◆
JUST THINK . . .

What are the practical implications of certain populations being underrepresented in a nationally standardized test?

Generally satisfactory estimates of internal consistency and test-retest reliability are reported in the test manual. Test-retest reliability coefficients for the GCA range from .85 to .94. Test-retest reliability coefficients for the clusters range from .79 to .90 for 393 children randomly selected from three age levels and tested twice at intervals of two to seven weeks. Internal consistency was established through a procedure which, in the words of the test developer, "is based purely on the items expected to be taken by an individual and makes no assumptions about the person's performance on unadministered items" (Elliott, 1990b, p. 175). For subtests that entail subjective scoring (Copying, Recall of Designs, Similarities, and Word Definitions), mean inter-rater reliability estimates for each subtest were quite high, ranging from .90 to .96.

On the basis of factor-analytic research reported in the test's manual, the test taps one factor (GCA) at ages 2 years 6 months through 3 years 5 months and two factors (a verbal and a nonverbal factor) at ages 3 years 6 months through 5 years 11 months. The DAS taps three factors (a verbal, a nonverbal reasoning, and a spatial ability factor) at ages 6 years 0 months through 17 years 11 months.

Several validity studies comparing the DAS to other measures of ability and achievement using nonhandicapped as well as exceptional children are reported in the test manual. Although the studies are limited in terms of sample size and region of the country, they tend to support the validity of the DAS as a measure of ability and achievement.

Administration instructions are presented clearly in the manual, with starting and stopping points based on the testtaker's chronological age and number of successes and failures. The core subtests are administered in a prescribed order, whereas the examiner has some discretion with regard to the sequence of administration of diagnostic and achievement subtests. Some subtests (1) make provision for sample items, teaching items, and examiner demonstration of items; (2) may be administered through gestures rather than verbal instructions to produce a Nonverbal Composite score; and/or (3) have an "out of level range" permitting their administration to high-ability or low-ability children—the net effect being an extension of the age and ability range of these subtests. Independent research suggests that the test can be translated into Spanish and yield data comparable to a nontranslated version (Sandoval et al., 2002).

Scoring is done on two record forms provided, one for the preschool level and one for the school-age level. The record forms are user friendly, with clearly marked starting/stopping points and instructions for scoring. Most test items are scored correct (1 point) or incorrect (0 points), though some provide for 0, 1, or 2 scoring. Bonus points are awarded for rapid, successful completion of timed items. Raw scores are tallied and converted to subtest scores, which in turn are converted into standard scores (having a mean of 50 and a standard deviation of 10 for the cognitive subtests, and a mean of 100 and a standard deviation of 15 for the achievement subtests). From these standard scores, the GCA and cluster scores are derived, both of which have a mean of 100 and a standard deviation of 15.

Interpreting the DAS is similar in many ways to interpreting other ability-achievement batteries. Composite and cluster scores are compared and evaluated, as are individual subtest scores—all in an effort to profile the testtaker's strengths and weaknesses. Additionally, extra-test behavior and other test-related findings may be included in the experienced examiner's interpretation of the testing.

For preschool and school-age children alike, the DAS materials tend to be engaging. A variety of colorful objects that the testtaker can manipulate aid in maintaining interest and keeping testtakers task oriented. Because the assessment is tailored or adaptive, overall testing time is reduced. Administration time for the complete battery ranges from about 35 minutes at age 2 years 6 months to about 90 minutes for the school-age testtaker.

Children within a broad ability range can be evaluated with the DAS, owing to the extended range of the norms that were developed. In general, the psychometric properties of the battery are in the acceptable range. Reliability and validity data are in the acceptable range, and the battery's factor structure has been confirmed in studies reported in the test manual. We would caution, however, that the samples with which the validity research was conducted tended to be relatively small and not geographically diverse. During the test's development, procedures were employed to reduce or eliminate any possible race or gender bias, though the manual does not report any comparative data for White, Black, and Hispanic testtakers.

> **JUST THINK . . .**
>
> On the basis of what you have just read and may know from other sources about the DAS, describe the testtaker you think could profit most from taking this battery.

The Woodcock-Johnson III (WJ III)

The WJ III (Woodcock et al., 2000) is a psychoeducational test package consisting of two co-normed batteries: Tests of Achievement and Tests of Cognitive Abilities, both of which are based on the Cattell-Horn-Carroll (CHC) theory of cognitive abilities. The WJ III was designed for use with persons as young as 2 and as old as "90+," according to the test manual. The WJ III yields a measure of general intellectual ability (g), as well as measures of specific cognitive abilities, achievement, scholastic aptitude, and oral language. It may be used to diagnose learning disabilities, determine discrepancies between ability and achievement, and plan educational programs and interventions. The Tests of Achievement are packaged in parallel forms designated A and B, each of which are divided into a standard battery (12 subtests) and an extended battery (10 additional subtests). As illustrated in Table 10–5, interpretation of an achievement test is based on the testtaker's performance on clusters of tests in specific curricular areas.

The Tests of Cognitive Abilities may also be divided into a standard battery (10 subtests) and an extended battery (10 additional subtests). As illustrated in Table 10–6, the subtests tapping cognitive abilities are conceptualized in terms of broad cognitive factors, primary narrow abilities, and cognitive performance clusters.

When using either the achievement or cognitive abilities tests, the standard battery might be appropriate for screenings or brief reevaluations. The extended battery would likely be used to provide a more comprehensive and detailed assessment, complete with diagnostic information. In any case, cluster scores are used to help evaluate performance level, gauge educational progress, and identify individual strengths and weaknesses.

According to the test manual, the WJ III was normed on a sample of 8,818 subjects from ages 24 months to "90+" years who were representative of the population of the United States. Age-based norms are provided from ages 24 months to 19 years by

Table 10–5
WJ III Tests of Achievement

Curricular Area	Cluster	Standard Battery—Forms A & B	Extended Battery—Forms A & B
Reading	Basic Skills	Test 1 Letter-Word Identification	Test 13 Word Attack
	Fluency	Test 2 Reading Fluency	
	Comprehension	Test 9 Passage Comprehension	Test 17 Reading Vocabulary
	Broad	Tests 1, 2, 9	
Oral Language	Oral Expression	Test 3 Story Recall	Test 14 Picture Vocabulary
	Listening Comprehension	Test 4 Understanding Directions	Test 15 Oral Comprehension
Mathematics	Calculation Skills	Test 5 Calculation	
	Fluency	Test 6 Math Fluency	
	Reasoning	Test 10 Applied Problems	Test 18 Quantitative Concepts
	Broad	Tests 5, 6, 10	
Written Language	Basic Skills	Test 7 Spelling	Test 16 Editing
	Fluency	Test 8 Writing Fluency	
	Expression	Test 11 Writing Samples	
	Broad	Tests 7, 8, 11	
Knowledge			Test 19 Academic Knowledge
Supplemental		Test 12 Story Recall-Delayed	Test 20 Spelling of Sounds
		Handwriting Legibility Scale	Test 21 Sound Awareness
			Test 22 Punctuation & Capitalization

Table 10–6
WJ III Tests of Cognitive Abilities*

Broad Cognitive Factor	Test (Standard & Extended)	Primary Narrow Ability	Cognitive Performance
Comprehension-Knowledge (Gc)	Test 1 Verbal Comprehension	Lexical knowledge, language development	Verbal ability
	Test 11 General Information	General (verbal) information	
Long-Term Retrieval (Glr)	Test 2 Visual-Auditory Learning	Associate memory	Thinking ability
	Test 12 Retrieval Fluency	Ideational fluency	
	Test 10 Visual-Auditory Learning—Delayed	*Associative memory*	
Visual-Spatial Thinking (Gv)	Test 3 Spatial Relations	Visualization, spatial relations	Thinking ability
	Test 13 Picture Recognition	Visual memory	
	Test 19 Planning (Gv/Gf)	*Spatial scanning, general sequential reasoning*	
Auditory Processing (Ga)	Test 4 Sound Blending	Phonetic coding, synthesis	Thinking ability
	Test 14 Auditory Attention	Speech-sound discrimination, resistance to auditory stimulus distortion	
	Test 8 Incomplete Words	*Phonetic coding, analysis*	
Fluid Reasoning (Gf)	Test 5 Concept Formation	Induction	Thinking ability
	Test 15 Analysis-Synthesis	General sequential reasoning	
	Test 19 Planning (Gv/Gf)	*Spatial scanning, general sequential reasoning*	
Processing Speed (Gs)	Test 6 Visual Matching	Perceptual speed	Cognitive efficiency
	Test 16 Decision Speed	Semantic processing speed	
	Test 18 Rapid Picture Naming	*Naming facility*	
	Test 20 Pair Cancellation	*Attention and concentration*	
Short-Term Memory (Gsm)	Test 7 Numbers Reversed	Working memory	Cognitive efficiency
	Test 17 Memory for Words	Memory span	
	Test 9 Auditory Working Memory	*Working memory*	

*Tests shown in italics are not part of the factor or cognitive performance cluster.

month, and by year after that. Grade-based norms are provided for kindergarten through grade 12, two-year college, and four-year college, including graduate school. Procedures for analysis of reliabilities for each subtest were appropriate, depending upon the nature of the tests. For example, the reliability of tests that were not speeded and that did not have multiple-point scoring systems was analyzed by means of the split-half method, corrected for length using the Spearman-Brown correction formula. The test manual also presents concurrent validity data. Support for the validity of various aspects of the test has also come from independent researchers. For example, Floyd et al. (2003) found that certain cognitive clusters were significantly related to mathematics achievement in a large, nationally representative sample of children and adolescents.

Scoring of the WJ III is accomplished with the aid of software provided in the test kit. Data from the raw scores are entered, and the program produces a summary report (in English or Spanish) and a table of scores, including all derived scores for tests administered as well as clusters of tests. The program also provides age/grade profiles and standard score/percentile rank profiles. Optional interpretive software is also available (Riverside Publishing, 2001). This software features checklist protocols (a teacher checklist, a parent checklist, a self-report checklist, and a classroom observation form) in a form that integrates the checklist data into the report. The test publisher has also made available optional training materials, including CD-ROMs and videos, for assistance in administering and using the battery.

Other Tools of Assessment in Educational Settings

Beyond traditional achievement, aptitude, and diagnostic instruments lies a wide universe of other instruments and techniques of assessment that may be used in the service of students and society at large. Let's take a look at a sampling of these approaches, beginning with performance, portfolio, and authentic assessment.

Performance, Portfolio, and Authentic Assessment

For many years, the very broad label *performance assessment* has vaguely referred to any type of assessment that requires the examinee to do more than choose the correct response from a small group of alternatives. Thus, for example, essay questions and the development of an art project are examples of performance tasks. By contrast, true/false questions and multiple-choice test items would not be considered performance tasks.

Among testing and assessment professionals, contemporary usage of performance-related terms focuses less on the type of item or task involved and more on the knowledge, skills, and values that the examinee must marshal and exhibit. Additionally, there is a growing tendency to speak of performance tasks and performance assessment in the context of a particular domain of study, with experts in that particular domain of study typically required to set the evaluation standards. For example, a performance task for an architecture student might be to construct a blueprint of a contemporary home. The overall quality of the student's work, as well as the knowledge, skill, and values inherent in it, will be judged according to standards set by architects acknowledged by the community of architects to have expertise in the construction of contemporary homes. In keeping with contemporary trends, particularly in educational and work settings, we will define a **performance task** as a work sample designed to elicit representative knowledge, skills, and values from a particular domain of study. **Performance assessment** will be defined as an evaluation of performance tasks according to criteria developed by experts from the domain of study tapped by those tasks.

One of many possible types of performance assessment is portfolio assessment. *Portfolio* has many meanings in different contexts. It may refer to a portable carrying case, most typically used to carry artwork, drawings, maps, and the like. Bankers and investors use it as a shorthand reference to one's financial holdings. In the language of psychological and educational assessment, **portfolio** is synonymous with *work sample*. **Portfolio assessment** refers to the evaluation of one's work samples. In many educational settings, dissatisfaction with some more traditional methods of assessment has led to calls for more performance-based evaluations. *Authentic assessment* (discussed subsequently) is one name given to this trend toward more performance-based assessment. When used in the context of like-minded educational programs, portfolio assessment and authentic assessment are techniques designed to target academic teachings to real-world settings external to the classroom.

Consider, for example, how students could use portfolios to gauge their progress in a high school algebra course. They could be instructed to devise their own personal portfolios to illustrate all they have learned about algebra. An important aspect of portfolio assessment is the freedom of the person being evaluated to select the content of the portfolio. Some students might include narrative accounts of their understanding of various algebraic principles. Other students might reflect in writing on the ways algebra can be used in daily life. Still other students might attempt to make a convincing case that they can do some types of algebra problems that they could not do before taking the course. Throughout, the portfolio may be illustrated with items such as gas receipts (complete with algebraic formulas for calculating mileage), paychecks (complete with formulas used to calculate an hourly wage and taxes), and other items limited only by the student's imagination. The illustrations might go from simple to increasingly complex—providing compelling evidence for the student's grasp of the material.

JUST THINK . . .

What might your personal portfolio, detailing all that you have learned about psychological testing and assessment to date, look like?

Innovative use of the portfolio method to assess giftedness (Hadaway & Marek-Schroer, 1992) and reading (Henk, 1993), among many other characteristics, can be found in the scholarly literature. Portfolios have also been applied at the college and graduate level as devices to assist students with career decisions (Bernhardt et al., 1993). Benefits of the portfolio approach include engaging students in the assessment process, giving them the opportunity to think generatively, and encouraging them to think about learning as an ongoing and integrated process. A key drawback, however, is the penalty such a technique may levy on the noncreative student. Typically, exceptional portfolios are creative efforts. A person whose strengths do not lie in creativity may have learned the course material but be unable to adequately demonstrate that learning in such a medium. Another drawback, this one from the other side of the instructor's desk, concerns the evaluation of portfolios. Typically, a great deal of time and thought must be devoted to their evaluation. In a lecture class of 300 people, for example, portfolio assessment would be impractical. Also, it is difficult to develop reliable criteria for portfolio assessment, given the great diversity of work products. Hence, inter-rater reliability in portfolio assessment can become a problem.

A related form of assessment is **authentic assessment,** also known as *performance-based assessment* (Baker et al., 1993) as well as other names. We may define authentic assessment in educational contexts as evaluation of relevant, meaningful tasks that may be conducted to examine learning of academic subject matter but that demonstrate the student's transfer of that study to real-world activities. Authentic assessment of students' writing skills, for example, would therefore be based on writing samples rather than on responses to multiple-choice tests. Authentic assessment of students' reading would be based on tasks that have to do with reading—preferably "authentic" reading, such as an article in a local newspaper as opposed to a piece contrived especially for the purposes of assessment. Students in a college-level psychopathology course might be asked to identify patients' psychiatric diagnoses on the basis of videotaped interviews with the patients.

Authentic assessment is thought to increase student interest and the transfer of knowledge to settings outside the classroom. A drawback is that the assessment might assess prior knowledge and experience, not simply what was learned in the classroom. For example, students from homes where there has been a long-standing interest in legislative activities may well do better on an authentic assessment of reading skills using an article on legislative activity. Additionally, authentic skill may inadvertently entail the assessment of some skills that have little to do with classroom learning. For example, authentic assessment of learning a cooking school lesson on fileting fish may be confounded with an assessment of the would-be chef's perceptual-motor skills.

Peer Appraisal Techniques

One method of obtaining information about an individual is by asking that individual's peer group to make the evaluation. Techniques employed to obtain such information are termed **peer appraisal** methods. A teacher, a supervisor, or some other group leader may be interested in peer appraisals for a variety of reasons. Peer appraisals can help call needed attention to an individual who is experiencing academic, personal, social, or work-related difficulties—difficulties that for whatever reason have not come to the attention of the person in charge. Peer appraisals allow the individual in charge to view members of a group from a different perspective, the perspective of people who work, play, socialize, eat lunch, and walk home with the person being evaluated. In addition to providing information about behavior that is rarely observable, peer appraisals supply information about the group's dynamics: who takes which roles under what conditions. Knowledge of an individual's place within the group is an important aid in guiding the group to optimal efficiency.

Peer appraisal techniques may be used in university settings as well as in grade school, industrial, and military settings. Such techniques tend to be most useful in settings where the individuals doing the rating have functioned as a group long enough to be able to evaluate each other on specific variables. The nature of peer appraisals may change as a function of changes in the assessment situation and the membership of the group. Thus, for example, an individual who is rated as the shyest in the classroom can theoretically be quite gregarious—and perhaps even be rated the rowdiest—in a peer appraisal undertaken at an after-school center.

One method of peer appraisal that can be employed in elementary school (as well as other) settings is called the Guess Who? technique. Brief descriptive sentences (such as "This person is the most friendly") are read or handed out in the form of questionnaires to the class, and the children are instructed to guess who. Whether negative attributes should be included in the peer appraisal (for example, "This person is the least friendly") must be decided on an individual basis, considering the potential negative consequences such an appraisal could have on a member of the group.

The nominating technique is a method of peer appraisal in which individuals are asked to select or nominate other individuals for various types of activities. A child being interviewed in a psychiatric clinic may be asked, "Who would you most like to go to the moon with?" as a means of determining which parent or other individual is most important to the child. Members of a police department might be asked, "Who would you most like as your partner for your next tour of duty and why?" as a means of finding out which police officers are seen by their peers as especially competent or incompetent.

The results of a peer appraisal can be graphically illustrated. One graphic method of organizing such data is the **sociogram.** Figures such as circles or squares are drawn to represent different individuals, and lines and arrows are drawn to indicate various types of interaction. At a glance, the sociogram can provide information such as who is popular in the group, who tends to be rejected by the group, and who is relatively neutral in the opinion of the group. Nominating techniques have been the most widely researched of the peer appraisal techniques, and they have generally been found to be highly reliable and valid. Still, the careful user of such techniques must be aware that an individual's perceptions within a group are constantly changing. Anyone who has ever watched any of the so-called reality television shows such as *Survivor* certainly is aware of such group dynamics. As some members leave the group and others join it, the positions and roles the members hold within the group change. New alliances form, and as a result, all group members may be looked at in a new light. It is therefore important to periodically update and verify information.

Measuring Study Habits, Interests, and Attitudes

Academic performance is the result of a complex interplay of a number of factors. Ability and motivation are inseparable partners in the pursuit of academic success. A number of instruments designed to look beyond ability and toward factors such as study habits, interests, and attitudes have been published. For example, the Study Habits Checklist, designed for use with students in grades 9 through 14, consists of 37 items that assess study habits with respect to note taking, reading material, and general study practices. In the development of the test, potential items were presented for screening to 136 Phi Beta Kappa members at three colleges. This procedure was based on the premise that good students are the best judges of important and effective study techniques (Preston, 1961). The judges were asked to evaluate the items according to their usefulness to students having difficulty with college course material. Although the judges conceded that they did not always engage in these practices themselves, they identified the techniques they deemed the most useful in study activities. Standardization for the Checklist took place in 1966, and percentile norms were based on a sample of several thousand high school and college students residing in Pennsylvania. In one validity study, 302 college freshmen who had demonstrated learning difficulties and had been referred to a learning skills center were evaluated with the Checklist. As predicted, it was found that these students demonstrated poor study practices, particularly in the areas of note taking and proper use of study time (Bucofsky, 1971).

If a teacher knows a child's areas of interest, instructional activities engaging those interests can be employed. The What I Like to Do Interest Inventory consists of 150 forced-choice items that assess four areas of interests: academic interests, artistic interests, occupational interests, and interests in leisure time (play) activities. Included in the test materials are suggestions for designing instructional activities that are consonant with the designated areas of interest.

Attitude inventories used in educational settings assess student attitudes toward a variety of school-related factors. Interest in student attitudes is based on the premise that "positive reactions to school may increase the likelihood that students will stay in school, develop a lasting commitment to learning, and use the school setting to advantage" (Epstein & McPartland, 1978, p. 2). Some instruments assess attitudes in specific subject areas, while others, such as the Survey of School Attitudes and the Quality of School Life Scales, are more general in scope.

The Survey of Study Habits and Attitudes (SSHA) and the Study Attitudes and Methods Survey combine the assessment of attitudes with the assessment of study methods. The SSHA, intended for use in grades 7 through college, consists of 100 items tapping poor study skills and attitudes that could affect academic performance. Two forms are available, Form H for grades 7 to 12 and Form C for college, each requiring 20 to 25 minutes to complete. Students respond to items on the following 5-point scale: *rarely, sometimes, frequently, generally,* or *almost always.* Test items are divided into six areas: Delay Avoidance, Work Methods, Study Habits, Teacher Approval, Education Acceptance, and Study Attitudes. The test yields a study skills score, an attitude score, and a total orientation score.

As you *just think* about the questions raised regarding study and personality, *just know* that you will learn about personality and its assessment in the next two chapters.

> **JUST THINK . . .**
>
> While we're on the subject of study habits, skills, and attitudes, this seems an appropriate time to raise a question about how these variables are related to another, more global variable: *personality.* Are one's study habits, skills, and attitudes a part of one's personality? Why might it be useful to think about them as such?

Self-Assessment

Test your understanding of elements of this chapter by seeing if you can explain each of the following terms, expressions, and abbreviations:

achievement test
Apgar number
aptitude test
at risk
authentic assessment
checklist
curriculum-based assessment (CBA)
curriculum-based measurement (CBM)

DAS
diagnostic information
evaluative information
informal evaluation
K-ABC
learning disability
locator test
peer appraisal
performance assessment
performance task

portfolio
portfolio assessment
prognostic test
psychoeducational test battery
rating scale
readiness test
sociogram
WJ III

Web Watch

Check out the following Web sites for more information about topics discussed in this chapter.

Public Law 94-142
www.scn.org/~bk269/94-142.html

Conners Rating Scale
www.widerange.com/conners.html

Curriculum-based measurement
http://education.umn.edu/research/ResearchWorks/CBM.htm

www.interventioncentral.org/htmdocs/interventions/cbmwarehouse.shtml

www.lefthandlogic.com/htmdocs/tools/cbaprobe/
cba.shtml

www.nasponline.org/publications/cq276cba.html

www.nasponline.org/certification/ss_module6
.html

http://alpha.fdu.edu/psychology/extended_links
.htm

Educational Testing Service
www.ets.org

College Board (SAT)
www.collegeboard.com

The PSAT
www.collegeboard.com/student/testing/psat/
about.html

GRE
www.gre.org/splash.html

American College Testing Program (ACT)
www.act.org/aap/

The Miller Analogies Test (MAT)
http://marketplace.psychcorp.com/PsychCorp
.com/Cultures/en-US/dotCom/milleranalogies
.com.htm

The Medical College Admissions Test (MCAT)
www.aamc.org/students/mcat/start.htm

The WRMT-R
www.thecoo.edu/~jknutson/woodcock_reading
_mastery_tests.htm

The K-ABC II
www.agsnet.com/group.asp?nGroupInfoID=
a21000

The DAS
www.psychcorp.com.au/das.html

http://alpha.fdu.edu/psychology/DAS.html

The WJ III
http://alpha.fdu.edu/psychology/woodcock
_index.htm

www.riverpub.com/products/clinical/wj3/
home.html

http://assess.nelson.com/test-ind/wj-3.html

Portfolio assessment
www.eduplace.com/rdg/res/literacy/assess6.html

Sociograms
http://maxweber.hunter.cuny.edu/pub/eres/
EDSPC715_MCINTYRE/Sociogram.html

11

Personality Assessment: An Overview

In a 1950s rock 'n' roll tune called "Personality," singer Lloyd Price described the subject of his song with the words *walk, talk, smile,* and *charm.* In so doing, Price used the term *personality* the way most people tend to use it. For laypeople, *personality* refers to components of an individual's makeup that can elicit positive or negative reactions from others. Someone who consistently tends to elicit positive reactions from others is thought to have a "good personality." Someone who consistently tends to elicit not-so-good reactions from others is thought to have a "bad personality" or, perhaps worse yet, "no personality." We also hear of people described in other ways, with adjectives such as *aggressive, warm,* or *cold.* For professionals in the field of behavioral science, the terms tend to be more well-defined, if not more descriptive.

JUST THINK . . .

Despite great effort, a definition of personality itself, much like a definition of intelligence, has been somewhat elusive. Why do you think this is so?

Personality and Personality Assessment Defined

Personality

Dozens of different definitions of personality exist in the psychology literature. Some definitions appear to be all-inclusive. For example, McClelland (1951, p. 69) defined personality as "the most adequate conceptualization of a person's behavior in all its detail." Menninger (1953, p. 23) defined it as "the individual as a whole, his height and weight and love and hates and blood pressure and reflexes; his smiles and hopes and bowed legs and enlarged tonsils. It means all that anyone is and that he is trying to become." Some definitions focus narrowly on a particular aspect of the individual (Goldstein, 1963a), while others view the individual in the context of society (Sullivan, 1953). Some theorists avoid any definition at all. For example, Byrne (1974, p. 26) characterized the entire area of personality psychology as "psychology's garbage bin in that any research which doesn't fit other existing categories can be labeled 'personality.'"

In their widely read and authoritative textbook *Theories of Personality,* Hall and Lindzey (1970, p. 9) wrote, "It is our conviction that *no substantive definition of personality can be applied with any generality*" and "*Personality is defined by the particular empirical concepts which are a part of the theory of personality employed by the observer*" [emphasis in the original]. Noting that there were important theoretical differences in many theories of personality, Hall and Lindzey encouraged their readers to select a definition of personality from the many presented and adopt it as their own.

You may well ask, "If venerable authorities on personality such as Hall and Lindzey do not define personality, who are Cohen and Swerdlik to think that they can do it?" In response, we humbly offer our definition of **personality** as an individual's unique constellation of psychological traits and states. We view this definition as one that has the advantage of parsimony yet still is flexible enough to incorporate a wide variety of variables. Included in our definition, then, are variables on which individuals may differ, such as values, interests, attitudes, worldview, acculturation, personal identity, sense of humor, and cognitive and behavioral styles.

Personality Assessment

Personality assessment may be defined as the measurement and evaluation of psychological traits, states, values, interests, attitudes, worldview, acculturation, personal identity, sense of humor, cognitive and behavioral styles, and/or related individual characteristics. In this chapter we overview the process of personality assessment, including different approaches to the construction of personality tests. In the following chapter, we focus on various methods of personality assessment, including objective, projective, and behavioral methods. Before all that, however, some background is needed regarding the use of the terms *trait, type,* and *state.*

Traits, Types, and States

Personality traits   Just as no consensus exists regarding the definition of personality, there is none regarding the definition of *trait.* Theorists such as Gordon Allport (1937) have tended to view personality traits as real physical entities that are "bona fide mental structures in each personality" (p. 289). For Allport, a trait is a "generalized and focalized neuropsychic system (peculiar to the individual) with the capacity to render many stimuli functionally equivalent, and to initiate and guide consistent (equivalent) forms of adaptive and expressive behavior" (p. 295). Robert Holt (1971) noted that there "*are* real structures inside people that determine their behavior in lawful ways" (p. 6), and he went on to conceptualize these structures as changes in brain chemistry that might occur as a result of learning: "Learning causes submicroscopic structural changes in the brain, probably in the organization of its biochemical substance" (p. 7). Raymond Cattell (1950) also conceptualized traits as mental structures, but for him *structure* did not necessarily imply actual physical status.

Our own preference is to shy away from definitions that elevate *trait* to the status of physical existence. We view psychological traits as attributions made in an effort to identify threads of consistency in behavioral patterns. In this context, a definition of **personality trait** offered by Guilford (1959, p. 6) has great appeal: "Any distinguishable, relatively enduring way in which one individual varies from another."

This relatively simple definition has some aspects in common with the writings of other personality theorists such as Allport (1937), Cattell (1950, 1965), and Eysenck (1961). The word *distinguishable* indicates that behaviors labeled with different trait terms are actually different from one another. For example, a behavior labeled "friendly" should be distinguishable from a behavior labeled "rude." The *context,* or the situation in which the behavior is displayed, is important in applying trait terms to behaviors. A behavior present in one context may be labeled with one trait term, but the same behavior exhibited in another context may be better described using another trait term. For example, if we observe someone involved in a lengthy, apparently interesting conversation, we would observe the context before drawing any conclusions about the person's traits. A person talking with a friend over lunch may be demonstrating friendliness, whereas that same person talking to that same friend during a wedding ceremony may be considered rude. Thus, the trait term selected by an observer is dependent both on the behavior itself and on the context in which it appears.

A measure of behavior in a particular context may be obtained using varied tools of psychological assessment. For example, using naturalistic observation, an observer could watch the assessee interact with co-workers during break time. Alternatively, the assessee could be administered a self-report questionnaire that probes various aspects of the assessee's interaction with co-workers during break time.

In his definition of trait, Guilford did not assert that traits represent enduring ways in which individuals vary from one another. Rather, he said *relatively enduring. Relatively* emphasizes that exactly how a particular trait manifests itself is situation dependent, at least to some extent. For example, a "violent" parolee generally may be prone to behave in a rather subdued way with her parole officer and much more violently in the presence of her family and friends. Allport (1937) addressed the issue of cross-situational consistency of traits—or lack of it—as follows:

> Perfect consistency will never be found and must not be expected. . . . People may be ascendant and submissive, perhaps submissive only towards those individuals bearing traditional symbols of authority and prestige; and towards everyone else aggressive and domineering. . . . The ever-changing environment raises now one trait and now another to a state of active tension. (p. 330)

For years, personality theorists and assessors have assumed that personality traits are relatively enduring over the course of one's life. Roberts and DelVecchio (2000) explored the endurance of traits by means of a meta-analysis of 152 longitudinal studies. These researchers concluded that trait consistency increases in a steplike pattern until one is 50 to 59 years old, at which time such consistency peaks. Their findings may be interpreted as compelling testimony to the relatively enduring nature of personality traits over the course of one's life. Do you think the physically aggressive high school students pictured in Figure 11–1 will still be physically aggressive when they approach retirement age?

Returning to our elaboration of Guilford's definition, note that *trait* is described as a way in which one individual varies from another. Let's emphasize here that the attribution of a trait term is always a *relative* phenomenon. For instance, some behavior described as "patriotic" may differ greatly from other behavior also described as "patriotic." There are no absolute standards. In describing an individual as patriotic, we are, in essence, making an unstated comparison with the degree of patriotic behavior that could reasonably be expected to be emitted under the same or similar circumstances.

Classic research on the subject of cross-situational consistency in traits has pointed to a lack of consistency with regard to traits such as honesty (Hartshorne & May, 1928), punctuality (Dudycha, 1936), conformity (Hollander & Willis, 1967), attitude toward authority (Burwen & Campbell, 1957), and introversion/extraversion (Newcomb, 1929). These are the types of studies cited by Mischel (1968, 1973, 1977, 1979) and others who have been critical of the predominance of the concept of traits in personality theory. Such critics may also allude to the fact that some undetermined portion of behavior exhibited in public may be governed more by societal expectations and cultural role restrictions than by an individual's personality traits (Barker, 1963; Goffman, 1963). Research designed to shed light on the primacy of individual differences, as opposed to situational factors in behavior, is methodologically complex (Golding, 1975), and a definitive verdict as to the primacy of the trait or the situation is simply not in.

Figure 11–1
Trait Aggressiveness and Flare-ups on the Ice

Bushman and Wells (1998) administered a self-report measure of trait aggressiveness (the Physical Aggression subscale of the Aggression Questionnaire) to 91 high school team hockey players before the start of the season. The players responded to items such as "Once in a while I cannot control my urge to strike another person" presented in Likert scale format ranging from 1 to 5 (where 1 corresponded to "extremely uncharacteristic of me" and 5 corresponded to "extremely characteristic of me"). At the end of the season, trait aggressiveness scores were examined with respect to minutes served in the penalty box for aggressive penalties such as fighting, slashing, and tripping. The preseason measure of trait aggressiveness predicted aggressive penalty minutes served. The study is particularly noteworthy because the test data were used to predict real-life aggression, not a laboratory analogue of aggression such as the administration of electric shock. The authors recommended that the possible applications of the Aggression Questionnaire be explored in other settings where aggression is a problematic behavior.

Personality types   Having defined personality as a unique constellation of traits and states, we might define a **personality type** as a constellation of traits and states that is similar in pattern to one identified category of personality within a taxonomy of personalities. Whereas traits are frequently discussed as if they were *characteristics* possessed by an individual, types are more clearly *descriptions* of people. So, for example, describing an individual as "depressed" is different from describing that individual as a "depressed type." The latter term has more far-reaching implications regarding characteristic aspects of the individual, such as the person's worldview, activity level, capacity to enjoy life, and level of social interest.

At least since Hippocrates' classification of people into four types (melancholic, phlegmatic, choleric, and sanguine), there has been no shortage of personality typolo-

◆ **JUST THINK . . .**

What are the possible benefits of classifying people into types? What possible problems may arise from doing so?

gies through the ages. A typology devised by Carl Jung (1923) became the basis for the Myers-Briggs Type Indicator (MBTI; Myers & Briggs, 1943/1962). An assumption guiding the development of this test was that people exhibit definite preferences in the way that they perceive or become aware of, and judge or arrive at conclusions about, people, events, situations, and ideas. According to Myers (1962, p. 1), these differences in perception and judging result in "corresponding differences in their reactions, in their interests, values, needs, and motivations, in what they do best, and in what they like to do." For example, in one study designed to better understand the personality of chess players, the Myers-Briggs Type Indicator was administered to 2,165 chess players, including players at the masters and senior masters level. The chess players were found to be significantly more introverted, intuitive, and thinking (as opposed to feeling) than members of the general population. The investigator also found masters to be more judgmatic than the general population (Kelly, 1985).

John Holland (1973, 1985, 1999) argued that most people can be categorized as one of the following six personality types: Artistic, Enterprising, Investigative, Social, Realistic, or Conventional. His Self-Directed Search test (SDS; Holland et al., 1994) is a self-administered, self-scored, and self-interpreted aid used to type people according to this system and to offer vocational guidance. Another personality typology, this one having only two categories, was devised by cardiologists Meyer Friedman and Ray Rosenman (1974; Rosenman et al., 1975). They conceived of a **Type A personality,** characterized by competitiveness, haste, restlessness, impatience, feelings of being time-pressured, and strong needs for achievement and dominance. A **Type B personality** has the opposite of the Type A's traits: mellow or laid-back. A 52-item self-report inventory called the Jenkins Activity Survey (JAS; Jenkins et al., 1979) has been used to type respondents as Type A or Type B personalities.

The personality typology that has attracted the most attention from researchers and practitioners alike is associated with scores on a test called the MMPI, and its successor, the MMPI-2 (both to be discussed shortly). Data from the administration of these tests, as with others, are frequently discussed in terms of the patterns of scores that emerge on the subtests. The pattern is referred to as a *profile.* In general, a **profile** is a narrative description, graph, table, or other representation of the extent to which a person has demonstrated certain targeted characteristics as a result of the administration or application of tools(s) of assessment.[1] In the term **personality profile,** the targeted characteristics are typically traits, states, or types. With specific reference to the MMPI, different profiles of scores are associated with different patterns of behavior. So, for example, a particular MMPI profile designated as "2-4-7" is associated with a type of individual who has a history of alcohol abuse alternating with sobriety and self-recrimination (Dahlstrom, 1995).

Personality states   The word **state** has been used in at least two distinctly different ways in the personality assessment literature. In one usage, a personality state is an inferred psychodynamic disposition designed to convey the dynamic quality of id, ego, and superego in perpetual conflict. Assessment of these psychodynamic dispositions may be made through the use of various psychoanalytic techniques such as free association, word association, symbolic analysis of interview material, dream analysis, and analysis of slips of the tongue, accidents, jokes, and forgetting.

---

1. The verb *to profile* refers to the creation of such a description. The term **profile analysis** refers to the interpretation of patterns of scores on a test or test battery. Profile analysis is frequently used to generate diagnostic hypotheses from intelligence test data. The noun **profiler** refers to an occupation: one who creates personality profiles of crime suspects to assist law enforcement personnel in capturing the profiled suspects.

Presently, a more popular usage of the *state*—and the one we use in the discussion that follows—refers to the transitory exhibition of some personality trait. Put another way, the use of the word *trait* presupposes a relatively enduring behavioral predisposition, whereas the term *state* is indicative of a relatively temporary predisposition (Chaplin et al., 1988). Thus, for example, Sally may be described as being "in an anxious state" before her midterms, though no one who knows Sally well would describe her as "an anxious person."

Measuring personality states amounts, in essence, to a search for and an assessment of the strength of traits that are relatively transitory or fairly situation specific. Relatively few existing personality tests seek to distinguish traits from states. Seminal work in this area was done by Charles D. Spielberger and his associates (Spielberger et al., 1980).

◆
JUST THINK . . .

Do you view traits and states as two distinctly different entities, or do you view states as "mini-manifestations" of traits?

These researchers developed a number of personality inventories designed to distinguish various states from traits. In the manual for the State-Trait Anxiety Inventory (STAI), for example, we find that *state anxiety* refers to a transitory experience of tension because of a particular situation. By contrast, *trait anxiety* or *anxiety proneness* refers to a relatively stable or enduring personality characteristic. The STAI test items consist of short descriptive statements, and subjects are instructed to indicate either (1) how they feel right now or at this moment (and to indicate the intensity of the feeling), or (2) how they generally feel (and to record the frequency of the feeling). The test-retest reliability coefficients reported in the manual are consistent with the theoretical premise that trait anxiety is the more enduring characteristic, whereas state anxiety is transitory.

Personality Assessment: Some Basic Questions

For what type of employment is a person with this type of personality best suited?

Is this individual sufficiently well adjusted for military service?

What emotional and other adjustment-related factors may be responsible for this student's level of academic achievement?

What pattern of traits and states does this psychotherapy client evince, and to what extent may this pattern be deemed pathological?

How has this patient's personality been affected by neurological trauma?

These questions are a sampling of the kind that might lead to a referral for personality assessment. Collectively, these types of referral questions provide insight into a more general question in a clinical context, Why assess personality?

We might raise the same question in the context of basic research and find another, very wide world of potential applications for personality assessment. For example, aspects of personality could be explored in identifying determinants of knowledge about health (Beier & Ackerman, 2003), in categorizing different types of commitment in intimate relationships (Frank & Brandstaetter, 2002), or in determining peer response to a team's weakest link (Jackson & LePine, 2003). Personality assessment is a staple in developmental research, be it tracking trait development over time (McCrae et al., 2002) or studying some uniquely human characteristic such as moral judgment (Eisenberg et al., 2002). In the corporate world, personality assessment is a key tool of the human resources department, relied on to aid in hiring, firing, promoting, transferring, and related decision. Perhaps as long as there have been tests to measure people's interests, there have been questions regarding how those interests relate to personality (Larson et al., 2002). In military organizations around the world, leadership is a sought-after trait, and personality tests help identify who has it (see, for example, Bradley et al., 2002; Handler, 2001). In the most general sense, basic research involving personality assessment helps to validate or invalidate theories of behavior and to generate new hypotheses.

Beyond the *why* of personality assessment are several other questions that must be addressed in any overview of the enterprise. Approaches to personality assessment differ in terms of *who* is being assessed, *what* is being assessed, *where* the assessment is conducted, and *how* the assessment is conducted. Let's take a closer look at each of these and related issues.

Who?

Who is actually being assessed? Can the testtaker be someone other than the subject of the assessment?

Some methods of personality assessment rely on the assessee's own self-report. Assessees may respond to interview questions, answer questionnaires in writing, blacken squares on computer answer forms, or sort cards with various terms on them—all with the ultimate objective of providing the assessor with personality-related self-description. By contrast, other methods of personality assessment rely on informants other than the person being assessed to provide personality-related information. So, for example, parents or teachers may be asked to participate in the personality assessment of a child by providing ratings, judgments, opinions, and impressions relevant to the child's personality. These two different approaches to personality assessment vary in terms of the respondent's primary referent. In the self-report situation, the self is the primary referent.

The self as the primary referent   People typically undergo personality assessment so that they, as well as the assessor, can learn something about who they are. In many instances, the assessment or some aspect of it requires **self-report,** or a process wherein information about assessees is supplied by the assessees themselves. Self-reported information may be obtained in the form of diaries kept by assessees or in the form of responses to oral or written questions or test items. In some cases, the information sought by the assessor is so private that only the individual assessees themselves are capable of providing it. For example, when researchers investigated the psychometric soundness of the Sexual Sensation Seeking Scale with a sample of college students, only the students themselves could provide the highly personal information needed. The researchers viewed their reliance on self-report as a possible limitation of the study, but noted that this methodology "has been the standard practice in this area of research because no gold standard exists for verifying participants' reports of sexual behaviors" (Gaither & Sellbom, 2003, p. 165).

Self-report methods are very commonly used to explore an assessee's *self-concept.* **Self-concept** may be defined as one's attitudes, beliefs, opinions, and related thoughts about oneself. Inferences about an assessee's self-concept may be derived from many tools of assessment. However, the tool of choice is typically a **self-concept measure,** an instrument designed to yield information relevant to how an individual sees him- or herself with regard to selected psychological variables. Data from such an instrument are usually interpreted in the context of how others may see themselves on the same or similar variables. On the Beck Self-Concept Test (BST; Beck & Stein, 1961), for example, respondents are asked to compare themselves to other people on variables such as looks, knowledge, and the ability to tell jokes.

A number of self-concept measures for children have been developed. Some representative tests include the Tennessee Self-Concept Scale and the Piers-Harris Self-Concept Scale. The latter test contains 80 self-statements (such as "I don't have any friends") to which respondents from grades 3 to 12 respond either yes or no as the statement applies to them. Factor analysis has suggested that the items cover six general areas of self-concept: behavior, intellectual and school status, physical appearance and attributes, anxiety, popularity, and happiness and satisfaction.

Some measures of self-concept are based on the notion that states and traits related to self-concept are to a large degree context dependent—that is, ever-changing as a result of the particular situation (Callero, 1992). The term **self-concept differentiation** refers to the degree to which a person has different self-concepts in different roles (Donahue et al., 1993). People characterized as *highly differentiated* are likely to perceive themselves quite differently in various roles. For example, a highly differentiated businessman in his forties may perceive himself as motivated and hard driving in his role at work, conforming and people pleasing in his role as son, and emotional and passionate

JUST THINK . . .

Highly differentiated or not very differentiated in self-concept . . . Which do *you* think is preferable? Why?

in his role as husband. By contrast, people whose concept of self is not very differentiated tend to perceive themselves similarly across their social roles. According to Donahue et al. (1993), people with low levels of self-concept differentiation tend to be healthier psychologically, perhaps because of their more unified and coherent sense of self.

Assuming that assessees have reasonably accurate insight into their own thinking and behavior, and assuming that they are motivated to respond to test items honestly, self-report measures can be extremely valuable. An assessee's candid and accurate self-report can illustrate what that individual is thinking, feeling, and doing. Unfortunately, some assessees may intentionally or unintentionally paint distorted pictures of themselves in self-report measures.

Consider what would happen if employers were to rely on job applicants' representations concerning their personality and their suitability for a particular job. Employers might be led to believe they have found a slew of perfect applicants. Many job applicants—as well as people in contexts as diverse as high school reunions, singles bars, and child custody hearings—attempt to "fake good" in their presentation of themselves to other people.

JUST THINK . . .

Have you ever engaged in "faking good" behavior, in or out of an assessment context?

The other side of the "faking good" coin is "faking bad." Litigants in civil actions who claim injury may seek high awards as compensation for their alleged pain, suffering, and emotional distress—all of which may be exaggerated and dramatized for the benefit of a judge and jury. The accused in a criminal action may view time in a mental institution as preferable to time in prison (or capital punishment) and strategically choose an insanity defense—with accompanying behavior and claims to make such a defense as believable as possible. A homeless person who prefers the environs of a mental hospital to that of the street may attempt to fake bad on tests and in interviews if failure to do so will result in discharge. In the days of the military draft, it was not uncommon for draft resisters to fake bad on psychiatric examinations in their efforts to be deferred.

Some testtakers truly may be impaired with regard to their ability to respond accurately to self-report questions. They may lack insight, for example, because of certain medical or psychological conditions at the time of assessment. By contrast, other testtakers seem blessed with an abundance of self-insight that they can convey with ease and expertise on self-report measures. It is for this latter group of individuals that self-report measures, according to Burisch (1984), will not reveal anything the testtaker does not already know. Of course, Burisch may have overstated the case. Even people with an abundance of self-insight can profit from learning about themselves from the perspective of others.

Another person as the referent   In some situations, the best available method for the assessment of personality, behavior, or both entails reporting by a third party such as a parent, teacher, peer, supervisor, spouse, or trained observer. Consider, for example, the assessment of a child for emotional difficulties. The child may be unable or unwilling to complete any measure (self-report, performance, or whatever) that will be of value in making a valid determination as to that child's emotional status. Even case history data may be of minimal value because the problems may be so subtle as to become evident only after careful and sustained observation. In such cases, the use of a test in which the testtaker is an informant but not the subject of study may be valuable.

The Personality Inventory for Children (PIC), as well as its revision, the PIC-2, are examples of a kind of standardized interview of a child's parent. Although the child is the subject of the test, the respondent is the parent (usually the mother), guardian, or other adult qualified to respond with reference to the child's characteristic behavior.[2] The test consists of a series of true/false items designed to be free of racial and gender bias. The items may be administered by computer or paper and pencil. Test results yield scores that shed light on the validity of the testtaker's response patterns, as well as clinical information. A number of studies attest to the validity of the PIC for its intended purpose (Kline et al., 1992, 1993; Lachar & Wirt, 1981; Lachar et al., 1985; Wirt et al., 1984). However, as with any test that relies on the observations and judgment of a rater, some concerns about this instrument have also been expressed (Achenbach, 1981; Cornell, 1985).

In general, there are many cautions to consider when one person undertakes to evaluate another. These cautions are by no means limited to the area of personality assessment. Rather, in any situation when one individual undertakes to rate another individual, it is important to understand the dynamics of the situation. Although a rater's report can provide a wealth of information about an assessee, it may also be instructive to look at the source of that information.

Some raters may tend to be favorably lenient and generous, harshly severe, or relatively neutral in their ratings. Generalized biases to rate in a particular direction are referred to in terms such as **leniency** or **generosity error** and **severity error.** A general tendency to rate everyone near the midpoint of a rating scale is termed an **error of central tendency.** In some situations, a particular set of circumstances may create a certain bias. For example, a teacher might be disposed to judging one pupil very favorably because that pupil's older sister was teacher's pet in a prior class. This variety of favorable response bias is sometimes referred to as a **halo effect.**

---

2. The PIC was originally published in 1958, although a formal test manual was not published until 1977. Five years later, a revised-format manual supplement (Lachar, 1982) was published. Since that time, the test has continually been referred to as the PIC. This footnote is intended to address the confusion created by erroneous references to the PIC as the "PIC-R" and "PIC-Revised" (Kline et al., 1985, 1993; Kline & Lachar, 1992; Lachar et al., 1985, 1986; LaCombe et al., 1991; Wirt et al., 1984) prior to the publication of the Personality Inventory for Children, Second Edition (PIC-2) in 2001. By the way, in the course of a phone call to the test's publisher we learned that the test is referred to around the office as the PIC, pronounced like the word *pick.*

Figure 11–2
Ratings in One's
Own Self-Interest

"Monsters and screamers have always worked for me; I give it 'thumbs up,' Roger."

Raters may make biased judgments, consciously or unconsciously, simply because it is in their own self-interest to do so (see Figure 11–2). Therapists who passionately believe in the efficacy of a particular therapeutic approach may be more disposed than others to see the benefits of that approach. Proponents of alternative approaches may be more disposed to see the negative aspects of that same treatment.

Numerous other factors may contribute to bias in a rater's ratings. The rater may feel competitive with, physically attracted to, or physically repelled by the subject of the ratings. The rater may not have the proper background, experience, and trained eye needed for the particular task. The rater's judgments may be limited by his or her general level of conscientiousness and willingness to devote the time and effort required to do the job properly. The rater may harbor biases concerning various stereotypes. Subjectivity based on the rater's own subjective preferences and taste may also enter into judgments. Features that rate a "perfect 10" in one person's opinion may represent more like a "mediocre 5" in the eyes of another person. If such marked diversity of opinion occurs frequently with regard to a particular instrument, we would expect it to be reflected in low inter-rater reliability coefficients. It would probably be desirable to take another look at the criteria used to make ratings and how specific they are.

Another factor to consider with regard to ratings when another is the referent is the *context* of the evaluation. Different raters may have different perspectives on the individual they are rating by virtue of the context in which they typically view that person.

A parent may indicate on a rating scale that a child is hyperactive, whereas that same child's teacher may indicate on that same rating scale that the child's activity level is within normal limits. Can they both be right?

The answer is yes, according to one meta-analysis of 119 articles in the scholarly literature (Achenbach et al., 1987). Different informants may have different perspectives on the subjects being evaluated. These different perspectives derive from observing and interacting with the subjects in different contexts. The study also noted that raters tended to agree more about the difficulties of young children (ages 6 to 11) than about those of older children and adolescents. Raters also tended to show more agreement about a child exhibiting self-control problems (such as hyperactivity and mistreating other children) in contrast to "overcontrol" problems (such as anxiety or depression). The researchers urged professionals to view the differences in evaluation that arise from different perspectives as something more than error in the evaluation process. They urged professionals to employ context-specific differences in treatment plans. Many of their ideas regarding context-dependent evaluation and treatment were incorporated into Achenbach's (1993) Multiaxial Empirically Based Assessment system. The system is an approach to the assessment of children and adolescents that incorporates cognitive and physical assessments of the subject, self-report of the subject, and ratings by parents and teachers. Additionally, performance measures of the child alone, with the family, or in the classroom may be included.

> **JUST THINK . . .**
>
> How might you be rated differently on the same variable in different contexts?

Regardless whether the self or another person is the subject of study, one context of the evaluation that must be kept in mind by the assessor is the cultural context.

The cultural background of assessees In recent years, test developers and users have shown increased sensitivity to issues of cultural diversity. A number of concerns have been raised regarding the use of personality tests and other tools of assessment with members of culturally and linguistically diverse populations (Anderson, 1995; Campos, 1989; Greene, 1987; Hinkle, 1994; Irvine & Berry, 1983; Lonner, 1985; López & Hernandez, 1987; Sundberg & Gonzales, 1981). How fair or generalizable is a particular instrument or measurement technique with a member of a particular cultural group? How a test was developed, how it is administered, and how scores on it are interpreted are all questions to be raised when considering the appropriateness of administering a particular personality test to members of culturally and linguistically diverse populations. We continue to explore these and related questions later in this chapter and throughout this book. In Chapter 13, for example, we consider in detail what is meant by *culturally informed psychological assessment.*

What?

What is assessed when a personality assessment is conducted? For many personality tests, it is meaningful to answer this question with reference to the primary content area sampled by the test, as well as that portion of the test devoted to measuring aspects of the testtaker's general response style.

Primary content area sampled Personality measures are tools used to gain insight into a wide array of thoughts, feelings, and behaviors associated with all aspects of the human experience. Some tests are designed to measure particular traits (such as introversion) or states (such as test anxiety), whereas others focus on descriptions of behavior, usually in particular contexts. For example, an observational checklist may concentrate

Table 11–1
A Sampling of Test Response Styles

Response Style Name	Explanation: A Tendency To . . .
Socially desirable responding	present oneself in a favorable (socially acceptable or desirable) light
Acquiescence	agree with whatever is presented
Nonacquiescence	disagree with whatever is presented
Deviance	make unusual or uncommon responses
Extreme	make extreme, as opposed to middle, ratings on a rating scale
Gambling/cautiousness	guess—or not guess—when in doubt
Overly positive	Claim extreme virtue through self-presentation in a superlative manner (Butcher & Han, 1995)

on classroom behaviors associated with movement in order to assess a child's hyperactivity. Extended discussion of behavioral measures is presented in the following chapter.

Many contemporary personality tests, especially tests that can be computer scored and interpreted, are designed to measure not only some targeted trait or other personality variable, but some aspect of the testtaker's response style. For example, in addition to scales labeled *Introversion* and *Extraversion,* a test of introversion/extraversion might contain other scales. These other scales could be designed to shed light on how honestly testtakers responded to the test, how consistently they answered the questions, and other matters related to the validity of the test findings. These measures of response pattern are also known as *measures of response set* or *response style.* Let's take a look at some different testtaker response styles as well as the scales used to identify them.

Testtaker response styles **Response style** refers to a tendency to respond to a test item or interview question in some characteristic manner regardless of the content of the item or question. For example, an individual may be more apt to respond *yes* or *true* than *no* or *false* on a short-answer test. This particular pattern of responding is characterized as **acquiescent.** Table 11–1 shows a listing of other identified response styles.

Impression management is a term used to describe the attempt to manipulate others' impressions through "the selective exposure of some information (it may be false information) . . . coupled with suppression of [other] information" (Braginsky et al., 1969, p. 51). In the process of personality assessment, assessees might employ any number of impression management strategies for any number of reasons. Paulhus (1984, 1986, 1990; Paulhus & Levitt, 1987) and his colleagues have explored impression management in testtaking as well as the related phenomena of enhancement (the claiming of positive attributes), denial (the repudiation of negative attributes), and self-deception ("the tendency to give favorably biased but honestly held self-descriptions" (Paulhus & Reid, 1991, p. 307). Testtakers who engage in impression management are exhibiting, in the broadest sense, a response style (Jackson & Messick, 1962).

Some personality tests contain items designed to detect different types of response styles. So, for example, a *true* response to an item like "I summer in Baghdad" would raise a number of questions, such as: Did the testtaker understand the instructions? Take the test seriously? Respond *true* to all items? Respond randomly? Endorse other infrequently endorsed items? Analysis of the entire protocol will help answer such questions.

Responding to a personality test in an inconsistent, contrary, or random way, or attempting to fake good or bad, may affect the validity of the interpretations of the test data. Because a response style can affect the validity of the outcome, one particular type of response style measure is referred to as a *validity scale*. We may define a **validity scale** as a subscale of a test designed to assist in judgments regarding how honestly the test-taker responded and whether observed responses were products of response sets, carelessness, deliberate efforts to deceive, or unintentional misunderstanding. Validity scales can provide a kind of shorthand indication of how honestly, diligently, and carefully a testtaker responded to test items. Some tests, such as the MMPI and its revision (to be discussed shortly), contain multiple validity scales. Although there are those who question the utility of formally assessing response styles (Costa & McCrae, 1997; Rorer, 1965), perhaps the more common view is that response styles are themselves important for what they reveal about testtakers. As Nunnally (1978, p. 660) observed, "To the extent that such stylistic variables can be measured independently of content relating to nonstylistic variables or to the extent that they can somehow be separated from the variance of other traits, they might prove useful as measures of personality traits."

Where?

Where are personality assessments conducted? Traditionally, personality assessment, as well as other varieties of assessment, has been conducted in schools, clinics, hospitals, academic research laboratories, employment counseling and vocational selection centers, and the offices of psychologists and counselors. In addition to such traditional venues, contemporary assessors may be found observing behavior and making assessments in natural settings ranging from the assessee's own home (Marx, 1998; McElwain, 1998; Polizzi, 1998) to the incarcerated assessee's prison cell (Glassbrenner, 1998). As we will see in the discussion of behavioral assessment in the following chapter, behavioral observation may be undertaken just about anywhere.

How?

How are personality assessments structured and conducted? Let's look at various facets of this multidimensional question, beginning with issues of scope and theory. We then discuss procedures and item formats that may be employed, the frame of reference of the assessment, and scoring and interpretation.

Scope and theory   One dimension of the *how* of personality assessment concerns its scope. The scope of an evaluation may be very wide, seeking to take a kind of general inventory of an individual's personality. The California Psychological Inventory (CPI) is an example of an instrument with a relatively wide scope. This test contains 434 true/false items and is designed to yield information on many personality-related variables such as responsibility, self-acceptance, and dominance.

In contrast to instruments and procedures designed to inventory various aspects of personality are those with a much narrower scope. These instruments may be designed to focus narrowly, on as little as one particular aspect of personality. As an example, consider tests designed to measure a personality variable called *locus of control* (Rotter, 1966; Wallston et al., 1978). **Locus** (meaning "place" or "site") **of control** is a person's perception about the source of things that happen to him or her. In general, people who see themselves as largely responsible for what happens to them are said to have an *internal* locus of control. People who are prone to attribute what happens to them to external factors (such as fate or the actions of others) are said to have an *external* locus of control. For example, a person who believes in the value of seatbelts, as opposed to a nonbuckling counterpart, would be expected to score closer to the internal than to the external end of the continuum on a valid measure of locus of control. Research with different measures of locus of control has yielded intriguing implications regarding the utility of this construct, especially with regard to health and lifestyle.

◆
JUST THINK . . .

Suppose you would like to learn as much as you can about the personality of an assessee from one personality test that is narrow in scope. On what single aspect of personality do you believe it would be most important to focus?

To what extent is a personality test theory based or relatively atheoretical? Instruments used in personality testing and assessment vary in the extent to which they are based on a theory of personality. Some are based entirely on a theory, and some are relatively atheoretical. An example of a theory-based instrument is the Blacky Pictures Test (Blum, 1950). This test consists of cartoon-like pictures of Blacky, a dog, in various situations, each image designed to elicit fantasies associated with various psychoanalytic themes. For example, one card depicts Blacky with a knife hovering over his tail, a scene (according to the test's author) designed to elicit material related to the psychoanalytic concept of castration anxiety. The respondent's task is to make up stories in response to such cards, and the stories are then analyzed according to the guidelines set forth by Blum (1950). The test is seldom used today; we cite it here as a particularly dramatic and graphic illustration of how a personality theory (in this case, psychoanalytic theory) can saturate a test.

The other side of the theory saturation coin is the personality test that is relatively atheoretical. The single most popular personality test in use today is atheoretical: the Minnesota Multiphasic Personality Inventory (MMPI), in both its original and revised forms. We will discuss it at length later in this chapter. Streiner (2003a) referred to this test as "the epitome of an atheoretical, 'dust bowl empiricism' approach to the development of a tool to measure personality traits" (p. 218). You will see why shortly. For now, let's simply point out one advantage of an atheoretical tool of personality assessment: It allows test users, should they so desire, to impose their own theoretical preferences on the interpretation of the findings.

Pursuing another aspect of the *how* of personality assessment, let's turn to a nuts-and-bolts look at the methods used.

Procedures and item formats Personality may be assessed by many different methods, such as face-to-face interviews, computer-administered tests, behavioral observation, paper-and-pencil tests, evaluation of case history data, evaluation of portfolio data, and recording of physiological responses. The equipment required for assessment varies greatly, depending upon the method employed. In one technique, for example, all that may be required is a blank sheet of paper and a pencil. The assessee is asked to draw a person, and the assessor makes inferences about the assessee's personality from the drawing. Other approaches to assessment, whether in the interest of basic research or for more applied purposes, may be far more elaborate in terms of the equipment they require (Figure 11–3).

Measures of personality vary in terms of the degree of *structure* built into them. For example, personality may be assessed by means of an interview, but it may also be assessed by a **structured interview.** In the latter method, the interviewer must typically follow an interview guide and has little leeway in terms of posing questions not in that guide. The variable of structure is also applicable to the tasks assessees are instructed to perform. In some approaches to personality assessment, the tasks are straightforward, highly structured, and unambiguous. Here is one example of such a task: *Respond* yes *or* no *to the following questions.*

In other approaches to personality, what is required of the assessee is not so straightforward, not very structured, and intentionally ambiguous. Here is one example of a

Figure 11–3
Learning About Personality in the Field—Literally

During World War II, the assessment staff of the Office of Strategic Services (OSS) selected American secret agents using a variety of measures. One measure used to assess leadership ability and emotional stability in the field entailed a simulation that involved rebuilding a blown bridge. Candidates were deliberately supplied with insufficient materials for rebuilding the bridge. In some instances, "assistants" who were actually confederates of the experimenter further frustrated the efforts of the candidates.

highly unstructured task: Hand the assessee one of a series of inkblots and ask, *What might this be?*

The same personality trait or construct may be measured with different instruments in different ways. Consider the many possible ways of determining how aggressive a person is. Measurement of this trait could be made in different ways, including a paper-and-pencil test, a computerized test, an interview with the assessee, an interview with family, friends, and associates of the assessee, analysis of official records and other case history data, behavioral observation, and laboratory experimentation. Of course, criteria for what constitutes the trait measured, in

JUST THINK . . .

Straightforward or ambiguous? Which approach to personality assessment has more appeal for you as an assessor? Why?

this case aggression, would have to be rigorously defined in advance. After all, psychological traits and constructs can and have been defined in many different ways, and virtually all such definitions tend to be context dependent. For example, *aggressive* may be defined in ways ranging from hostile and assaultive (as in the "aggressive inmate") to bold and enterprising (as in the "aggressive salesperson"). This personality trait, like many others, may or may not be socially desirable; it depends entirely on its context.

In personality assessment, as well as assessment in other areas, information may be gathered and questions answered in a variety of ways. For example, a researcher or practitioner interested in learning about the degree to which respondents are field dependent may construct an elaborate tilting chair/tilting room device—the same one you may recall from Chapter 1 (Figure 1–6). In the interests of time and expense, an equivalent process administered by paper and pencil or computer may be more practical for everyday use. In this chapter's *Everyday Psychometrics*, we illustrate some of the more common item formats employed in the study of personality and related psychological variables. Keep in mind that although we are using these formats to illustrate different ways that personality has been studied, some are employed in other areas of assessment as well.

Frame of reference Another variable relevant to the *how* of personality measurement has to do with the *frame of reference* of the assessment. In the context of item format and assessment in general, **frame of reference** may be defined as aspects of the focus of exploration such as the time frame (the past, the present, or the future), as well as other

Some Common Item Formats

How may personality be assessed? Here are some of the more typical types of item formats.

ITEM 1

I enjoy being out and among other people.   TRUE   FALSE

This item illustrates the true/false format. Was your reaction something like "been there, done that" when you saw this item?

ITEM 2

Working with fellow community members
on organizing and staging a blood drive.   LIKE   DISLIKE

This two-choice item is designed to elicit information about the respondents' likes and dislikes. It is a common format in interest inventories, particularly those used in vocational counseling.

ITEM 3

How I feel when I am out and among other people

Warm	_:_:_:_:_:_	Cold
Tense	_:_:_:_:_:_	Relaxed
Weak	_:_:_:_:_:_	Strong
Brooks Brothers suit	_:_:_:_:_:_	Hawaiian shirt

This item format, called a **semantic differential** (Osgood et al., 1957), is characterized by bipolar adjectives separated by a 7-point rating scale on which respondents select one point to indicate their response. This type of item is useful for gauging the strength, degree, or magnitude of the direction of a particular response and has applications ranging from self-concept descriptions to opinion surveys.

ITEM 4

I enjoy being out and among other people.

or

I have an interest in learning about art.

ITEM 5

I am depressed too much of the time.

or

I am anxious too much of the time.

These are two examples of items written in a **forced-choice format,** where ideally each of the two choices (there may be more than two choices) is equal in social desirability. The Edwards Personal Preference Schedule (Edwards, 1953) is a classic forced-choice test. Edwards (1957a, 1957b, 1966) described in detail how he determined the items in this test to be equivalent in social desirability.

ITEM 6

naughty

needy

negativistic

new age

nerdy

nimble

nonproductive

numb

This illustrates an item written in an adjective checklist format. Respondents check the traits that apply to them.

contextual issues having to do with people, places, and events. Perhaps for most measures of personality, the frame of reference for the assessee may be described in phrases such as *what is* or *how I am right now.* However, some techniques of measurement are easily adapted to tap alternative frames of reference, such as *what I could be ideally, how I am in the office, how others see me, how I see others,* and so forth. Obtaining self-reported information from different frames of reference is, in itself, a way of developing information related to states and traits. For example, in comparing self-perception in the present versus what is anticipated for the future, assessees who report that they will become better

ITEM 7

Complete this sentence.

I feel as if I _____ .

Respondents are typically instructed to finish the sentence with their "real feelings" in what is called a sentence completion item. The Rotter Incomplete Sentence Blank (Rotter & Rafferty, 1950) is a standardized test that employs such items, and the manual features normative data (Rotter et al., 1992).

ITEM 8

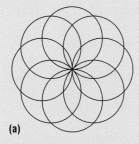 

(a)   **(b)**

Can you distinguish the figure labeled *b* in the figure labeled *a*? This type of item is found in embedded-figures tests. Identifying hidden figures is a skill thought to tap the same field dependence/independence variable tapped by more elaborate apparatuses such as the tilting chair/tilting room illustrated in Figure 1–6.

ITEM 9

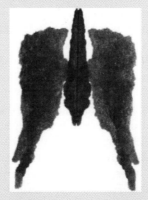

This is an item reminiscent of one of the Rorschach inkblots. We will have much more to say about the Rorschach in the following chapter.

ITEM 10

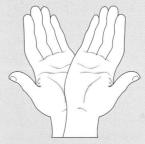

Much like the Rorschach test, which uses inkblots as ambiguous stimuli, many other tests ask the respondent to "project" onto an ambiguous stimulus. This item is reminiscent of one such projective technique called the Hand Test. Respondents are asked to tell the examiner what they think the hands might be doing.

people may be presumed to be more optimistic than assessees who report a reverse trend.

Representative of methodologies that can be readily applied in the exploration of varied frames of reference is the **Q-sort** technique. Originally developed by Stephenson (1953), the Q-sort is an assessment technique in which the task is to sort a group of statements, usually in perceived rank order ranging from *most descriptive* to *least descriptive*. The statements, traditionally presented on index cards, may be sorted in ways designed to reflect various perceptions. They may, for example, reflect how respondents see themselves or how they would like to see themselves. Illustrative statements are *I am confident, I try hard to please others,* and *I am uncomfortable in social situations.*

One of the best-known applications of Q-sort methodology in clinical and counseling settings was advocated by the personality theorist and psychotherapist Carl Rogers. Rogers (1959) used the Q-sort to evaluate the discrepancy between the perceived actual self and the ideal self. At the beginning of psychotherapy, clients might be asked to sort cards twice, once according to how they perceived themselves to be and then according to how they would ultimately like to be. The larger the discrepancy between the sortings, the more goals would have to be set in therapy. Presumably the retesting of the client who successfully completed a course of therapy would reveal much less discrepancy between the present and idealized selves.

Beyond its application in initial assessment and reevaluation of a therapy client, the Q-sort technique has also been used extensively in basic research in the area of personality and other areas. Some highly specialized Q-sorts include the Leadership Q-Test (Cassel, 1958) and the Tyler Vocational Classification System (Tyler, 1961). The former test was designed for use in military settings and contains cards with statements the assessee is instructed to sort with respect to their perceived importance to effective leadership. The Tyler Q-sort contains cards on which occupations are listed; the cards are sorted in terms of the perceived desirability of each occupation. A desirable feature of Q-sort methodology is the ease with which it can be adapted for use with a wide population range for varied clinical and research purposes. DeMulder et al. (2000) described how Q-sort methodology was used with preschoolers to measure the variable of attachment security.

Two other item presentation formats readily adaptable to different frames of reference are the *adjective checklist* format and the *sentence completion* format (both discussed in Chapter 12). With the adjective checklist method, respondents simply check off on a list of adjectives those that apply to themselves (or to people they are rating). With the same list of adjectives, the frame of reference can easily be changed by changing the instructions. For example, to gauge various states, respondents can be asked to check off adjectives indicating how they feel *right now.* Alternatively, to gauge various traits, they may be asked to check off adjectives indicative of how they have felt for the last year or so. A test called, simply enough, the Adjective Check List (Gough, 1960; Gough & Heilbrun, 1980) has been used in a wide range of research studies to study assessees' perceptions of themselves or others. For example, the instrument has been used to study managers' self-perceptions (Hills, 1985), parents' perceptions of their children (Brown, 1972), and clients' perceptions of their therapists (Reinehr, 1969).

JUST THINK . . .

Envision and describe an assessment scenario in which it would be very important to obtain the assessee's perception of others.

As its name implies, the testtaker's task in responding to an item written in a sentence completion format is to complete an incomplete sentence. Items may tap how assessees feel about themselves, as in *I would describe my feeling about myself* _____ . Items may tap how assessees feel about others, as in *My classmates* _____ . More on sentence completion methods in the following chapter; right now, let's briefly overview *how* personality tests are scored and interpreted.

Scoring and interpretation Personality measures differ with respect to the way conclusions are drawn from the data they provide. For some paper-and-pencil measures, a simple tally of responses to targeted items is presumed to provide a measure of the strength of a particular trait. For other measures, a computer programmed to apply highly technical manipulations of the data is required for purposes of scoring and interpretation. Yet other measures may require a highly trained clinician reviewing a verbatim transcript of what the assessee said in response to certain stimuli such as inkblots or pictures.

It is also meaningful to dichotomize measures with respect to the *nomothetic/idiographic* variable. The **nomothetic approach** to assessment is characterized by efforts to learn how a limited number of personality traits can be applied to all people. By contrast, the **idiographic approach** is characterized by efforts to learn about each individual's unique constellation of personality traits, with no attempt to characterize each person according to any particular set of traits. A test such as the 16 PF (Cattell et al., 1993), which seeks to measure testtakers on 16 *personality factors* (which is what "PF" stands for), is representative of the nomothetic orientation. The idiographic orientation is evident in assessment procedures that are more flexible not only in terms of listing the observed traits but also in naming new trait terms.[3] The idiographic approach to personality assessment was described in detail by Allport (1937; Allport & Odbert, 1936).

Another dimension related to how meaning is attached to test scores has to do with whether interindividual or intraindividual comparisons are made with respect to test scores. Most common in personality assessment is the normative approach, whereby a testtaker's responses and the presumed strength of a measured trait are interpreted relative to the strength of that trait in a sample of a larger population. However, you may recall from Chapter 7 an alternative to the normative approach in test interpretation. In the ipsative approach, a testtaker's responses, as well as the presumed strength of measured traits, are interpreted relative to the strength of measured traits for that same individual. On a test that employs ipsative scoring procedures, two people with the same score for a particular trait or personality characteristic may differ markedly with regard to the magnitude of that trait or characteristic relative to members of a larger population.

Concluding our overview of the *how* of personality assessment, and in preparation to discuss the ways personality tests are developed, let's review some issues in personality test development and use.

> **JUST THINK . . .**
>
> Place yourself in the role of a human resources executive for a large airline. As part of the evaluation process, all new pilots will be given a personality test. You are asked whether the test should be ipsative or normative in nature. Your response?

Issues in personality test development and use   Many of the issues inherent in the test development process mirror the basic questions just discussed about personality assessment in general. With whom will this test be designed for use? Will the test entail self-report? Or will it require the use of raters or judges? If raters or judges are needed, what special training or other qualifications must they have? How will a reasonable level of inter-rater reliability be assured? What content area will be sampled by the test? How will issues of testtaker response sets be dealt with? What item format should be employed, and what is the optimal frame of reference? How will the test be scored and interpreted?

---

3. Consider in this context the adjective *new age* used as a personality trait (referring to a belief in spirituality). A personality assessment conducted with an idiographic orientation would be flexible enough to characterize the assessee as "new age" should this trait be judged applicable. Nomothetic instruments developed prior to the usage of such a new trait term would subsume cognitive and behavioral characteristics of the new trait term under whatever existing trait or traits in the nomothetic system were judged appropriate. So, for example, a nomothetic system that included *spiritual* as one of its core traits might subsume "new age" under "spiritual." At some point, if trends and usage warrant it, an existing nomothetic instrument could be revised to include a new trait term.

As previously noted, personality assessment that relies exclusively on self-report is a two-edged sword. On the one hand, the information is from "the source." Respondents are in most instances presumed to know themselves better than anyone else does and therefore should be able to supply accurate responses about themselves. On the other hand, the consumer of such information has no way of knowing with certainty which self-reported information is entirely true, partly true, not really true, or an outright lie. Consider a response to a single item on a personality inventory written in a true/false format. The item reads: *I tend to enjoy meeting new people.* A respondent indicates *true*. In reality, we do not know whether the respondent (1) enjoys meeting new people; (2) honestly believes that he or she enjoys meeting new people but really does not (in which case, the response is more the product of a lack of insight than a report of reality); (3) does not enjoy meeting new people but would like people to think that he or she does; or (4) did not even bother to read the item, is not taking the test seriously, and is responding *true* or *false* randomly to each item.

One way developers of personality inventories have attempted to deal with the problems of self-report is by building into their tests so-called validity scales. In recent years, there has been some debate about whether validity scales should be included in personality tests. Arguing the case for the inclusion of validity scales, it has been asserted that "detection of an attempt to provide misleading information is a vital and absolutely necessary component of the clinical interpretation of test results" and that using any instrument without validity scales "runs counter to the basic tenets of clinical assessment" (Ben-Porath & Waller, 1992, p. 24). By contrast, the authors of the widely used Revised NEO Personality Inventory (NEO PI-R), Paul T. Costa, Jr., and Robert R. McCrae, perceived no need to include any validity scales in their instrument and have been less enthusiastic about the use of such scales in other tests (McCrae & Costa, 1983; McCrae et al., 1989; Piedmont & McCrae, 1996; Piedmont et al., 2000). Referring to validity scales as SD (social desirability) scales, Costa and McCrae (1997) opined:

> SD scales typically consist of items that have a clearly desirable response. We know that people who are trying falsely to appear to have good qualities will endorse many such items, and the creators of SD scales wish to infer from this that people who endorse many SD items are trying to create a good impression. That argument is formally identical to asserting that presidential candidates shake hands, and therefore people who shake hands are probably running for president. In fact, there are many more common reasons for shaking hands, and there is also a more common reason than impression management for endorsing SD items—namely, because the items are reasonably accurate self-descriptions. (p. 89)

According to Costa and McCrae, assessors can affirm that self-reported information is reasonably accurate by consulting external sources such as peer raters. Of course, the use of raters necessitates certain other precautions to guard against rater error and bias. Education regarding the nature of various types of rater error and bias has been a key weapon in the fight against intentional or unintentional inaccuracies in ratings. Training sessions may be designed to accomplish several objectives, such as clarifying terminology to increase the reliability of ratings. A term like *satisfactory*, for example, may have different meanings to different raters. During training, new raters can observe and work with more experienced raters to become acquainted with aspects of the task that may not be described in the rater's manual, to compare ratings with more experienced raters, and to discuss the thinking that went into the ratings.

JUST THINK . . .

Having read about some of the pros and cons of using validity scales in personality assessment, where do you come out on the issue? Feel free to revise your opinion as you learn more.

To include or not include a validity scale in a personality test is definitely an issue that must be dealt with. What about the language in which the assessment is conducted? At first blush, this would appear to be a nonissue. Well, yes and no. If an assessee is from a culture different from the culture for use in which the test was developed, or if the assessee is fluent in one or more languages, language may well become an issue. Words tend to lose—or gain—something in translation, and some words and expressions are not readily translatable into other languages. Consider the following true/false item from a popular personality test: *I am known for my prudence and common sense.* If you are a bilingual student, translate that statement now as an exercise in test item translation before reading on.

A French translation of this item is quite close, adding only an extra first-person possessive pronoun ("par ma prudence et *mon* bon sens"; McCrae et al., 1998, p. 176). However, the Filipino translation of this item would read, *I can be relied on to decide carefully and well on matters* (McCrae et al., 1998, p. 176).

In addition to sometimes significant differences in the meaning of individual items, the traits measured by personality tests sometimes have different meanings as well. Acknowledging this fact, McCrae et al. (1998, p. 183) cautioned that "personality-trait relations reported in Western studies should be considered promising hypotheses to be tested in new cultures."

The broader issue relevant to the development and use of personality tests with members of a culture different from the culture in which the test was normed concerns the applicability of the norms. For example, a number of MMPI studies conducted with members of groups from diverse backgrounds yield findings in which minority group members tend to present with more psychopathology than majority group members (see, for example, Montgomery & Orozco, 1985; Whitworth & Unterbrink, 1994). Such differences have elicited questions regarding the appropriateness of the use of the test with members of different populations (Dana, 1995; Dana & Whatley, 1991; Malgady et al., 1987).

A test may well be appropriate for use with members of culturally different populations. As Lopez (1988, p. 1096) observed, "To argue that the MMPI is culturally biased, one needs to go beyond reporting that ethnic groups differ in their group profiles." Lopez noted that many of the studies showing differences between the groups did not control for psychopathology. Accordingly, there may well have been veritable differences across the groups in psychopathology. The size of the sample used in the research, as well as the appropriateness of the statistical analysis, are other extracultural factors to consider when evaluating cross-cultural research. Of course, if culture and "learned meanings" (Rohner, 1984, pp. 119–120), as opposed to psychopathology, are found to account for differences in measured psychopathology with members of a particular cultural group, the continued use of the measures with members of that cultural group must be questioned.

Armed with some background information regarding the nature of personality and its assessment, let's take a closer look at the process of developing instruments designed to assess personality.

Developing Instruments to Assess Personality

Tools such as *logic, theory,* and *data reduction methods* (such as factor analysis) are frequently used in the process of developing personality tests. Another tool in the test development process may be a *criterion group.* As we will see, most personality tests employ two or more of these of these tools in the course of their development.

Logic and Reason

Notwithstanding the grumblings of skeptics, there is a place for logic and reason in psychology, at least when it comes to writing items for a personality test. Logic and reason may dictate what content is covered by the items. Indeed, the use of logic and reason in the development of test items is sometimes referred to as the *content* or *content-oriented* approach to test development.

As an example of the content approach to test development, let's suppose you wished to create a new test, the purpose of which is to identify people who are at high risk for developing anorexia nervosa. Let's call this new test the "Evaluation of Anorexic Tendencies Test" (EATT). Logically, the content of the test items would relate to what is known about this eating disorder. In writing the items for the test, you might rely on what you know about anorexia nervosa from reading, personal experience, and the accounts of others. The fruit of your efforts might be a list of yes/no questions, a sample of which might look something like this:

1. Is your current weight at least 85% of expected body weight for your age and height?
2. Do you fear gaining weight?
3. Do you perceive your body as abnormal in any way?

The portion of the EATT presented above contains items based on the American Psychiatric Association's *Diagnostic and Statistical Manual* criteria for a diagnosis of anorexia nervosa. Whether or not your content-oriented test ever enjoys widespread usage will depend on a number of factors, not the least of which is how well it measures anorexic tendencies (or whatever it is that it purports to measure).

Efforts to develop such content-oriented, face-valid items can be traced at least as far back as an instrument used to screen World War I recruits for personality and adjustment problems. The Personal Data Sheet (Woodworth, 1917), later known as the Woodworth Psychoneurotic Inventory, contained items designed to elicit self-report of fears, sleep disorders, and other problems deemed symptomatic of psychoneuroticism. The greater the number of problems reported, the more psychoneurotic the respondent was presumed to be.

A great deal of clinically actionable information can be collected in relatively little time using such self-report instruments—provided, of course, that the testtaker has the requisite insight and responds with candor. A highly trained professional is not required for administration of the test, and a computerized report of the findings can be available in minutes. Moreover, such instruments are particularly well suited to clinical settings in managed care environments, where drastic cost cutting has led to reductions in orders for assessment, and insurers are reluctant to authorize assessments. In such environments, the preferred use of psychological tests is to identify conditions of "medical necessity" (Glazer et al., 1991), and the quicker and less expensive the test, the better the insurer likes it.

Typical companions to logic, reason, and intuition in item development are research and clinical experience. Another possible aid in the test development process is correspondence with experts on the subject matter of the test. And yet another possible tool—sometimes even the guiding force—is psychological theory.

Theory

As we noted earlier, personality measures differ in the extent to which they rely on a particular theory of personality in their development as well as their interpretation. For example, if, instead of logic and reason, psychoanalytic theory was the guiding force behind the development of the hypothetical "EATT," the items might be quite different. For example, based on the psychoanalytic notion that people with anorexia nervosa are unconsciously attempting to fade away into obscurity, EATT items might attempt to evaluate this possibility. Given that dreams are thought to reveal unconscious motivation, here's an example of a yes/no item that might be found on a version of the EATT derived from psychoanalytic theory:

1. Have you ever dreamed that you were fading away?

One theory-based test in current usage today is the Self-Directed Search (SDS), which is a measure of one's interests as well as one's perceived abilities. Authored by John Holland and his associates, the test is based on Holland's theory of *vocational per-sonality*. At the heart of this theory is the view that occupational choice has a great deal to do with one's personality and self-perception of abilities. The SDS is a rarity among widely used tests in many respects. This is so because it is self-administered, self-scored, and self-interpreted. Test scores point testtakers in the direction of specific occupational themes. From there, testtakers follow instructions to learn about various occupations that are consistent with their expressed pattern of interests and abilities.

> **JUST THINK . . .**
>
> Self-administered, self-scored, and self-interpreted tests like the SDS have their advantages. But such tests may have disadvantages too. What are some disadvantages of largely self-directed tests?

Data Reduction Methods

Data reduction methods represent another class of widely used tool in contemporary test development. Data reduction methods include several types of statistical techniques collectively known as factor analysis or cluster analysis. One use of data reduction methods in the design of personality measures is to aid in the identification of the minimum number of variables or factors that account for the intercorrelations in observed phenomena.

Let's illustrate the process of data reduction with a simple example related to painting your apartment. You may not have a strong sense of the exact color that best complements your "early undergraduate" decor. Your investment in a subscription to *Architectural Digest* proved to be no help at all. You go to the local paint store and obtain free card samples of every shade of paint known to humanity—thousands of color samples. Next, you undertake an informal factor analysis of these thousands of color samples. You attempt to identify the minimum number of variables or factors that account for the intercorrelations among all of these colors. You discover that there are three factors (which might be labeled "primary" factors) and four more factors (which might be labeled "secondary" or "second-order" factors), the latter set of factors being combinations of the first set of factors. Because all colors can be reduced to three primary colors and their combinations, the three primary factors would correspond to the three primary colors, red, yellow, and blue (which you might christen factor *R*, factor *Y*, and factor *B*), and the four secondary or second-order factors would correspond to all the possible combinations that could be made from the primary factors (factors *RY*, *RB*, *YB*, and *RYB*).

The paint sample illustration might be helpful to keep in mind as we review how factor analysis is used in test construction and personality assessment. In a way analogous to the factoring of all those shades of paint into three primary colors, think of all personality traits being factored into what one psychologist referred to as "the most important individual differences in human transactions" (Goldberg, 1993, p. 26). After all the factoring is over and the dust has settled, how many personality-related terms do you think would remain? Stated another way, just how many *primary* factors of personality are there?

As the result of a pioneering research program in the 1940s, Raymond Bernard Cattell's answer to the question posed above was "16." Cattell (1946, 1947, 1948a, 1948b) reviewed previous research by Allport and Odbert (1936), which suggested that there were more than 18,000 personality trait names and terms in the English language. Of these, however, only about a quarter were "real traits of personality" or words and terms that designated "generalized and personalized determining tendencies— consistent and stable modes of an individual's adjustment to his environment . . . not . . . merely temporary and specific behavior" (Allport, 1937, p. 306).

Cattell added to the list some trait names and terms employed in the professional psychology and psychiatric literature and then had judges rate "just distinguishable" differences between all the words (Cattell, 1957). The result was a reduction in the size of the list to 171 trait names and terms. College students were asked to rate their friends with respect to these trait names and terms, and the factor-analyzed results of that rating further reduced the number of names and terms to 36, which Cattell referred to as *surface traits*. Still more research indicated that 16 basic dimensions or *source traits* could be distilled. In 1949, Cattell's research culminated in the publication of a test called the Sixteen Personality Factor (16 PF) Questionnaire. Revisions of the test were published in 1956, 1962, 1968, and 1993. In 2002, supplemental updated norms were published (Maraist & Russell, 2002).

Over the years, many questions have been raised regarding (1) whether the 16 factors identified by Cattell do indeed merit the description as the "source traits" of personality, and (2) whether, in fact, the 16 PF measures 16 distinct factors. Although some research supports Cattell's claims, give or take a factor or two depending on the sample (Cattell & Krug, 1986; Lichtenstein et al., 1986), serious reservations regarding these assertions have also been expressed (Eysenck, 1985, 1991; Goldberg, 1993). Some have argued that the 16 PF may be measuring fewer than 16 factors, because several of the factors are substantially intercorrelated.

With colors in the paint store, we can be certain that there are three that are primary. But with regard to personality factors, certainty doesn't seem to be in the cards. Some theorists have argued that the primary factors of personality can be narrowed down to three (Eysenck, 1991), or maybe four, five, or six (Church & Burke, 1994). At least four different five-factor models exist (Johnson & Ostendorf, 1993; Costa & McCrae, 1992a), and Waller and Zavala (1993) made a case for a seven-factor model. Costa and McCrae's five-factor model (with factors that have come to be known simply as the "Big Five") has gained the greatest following. Interestingly, using factor analysis in the 1960s, Raymond Cattell had also derived five factors from his "primary 16" (H. Cattell, 1996). A side-by-side comparison of "Cattell's five" with the Big Five shows strong similarity between the two sets of derived factors (Table 11–2). But Cattell believed strongly in the primacy of the 16 factors he originally identified.

The Big Five   The Revised NEO Personality Inventory (NEO PI-R; Costa & McCrae, 1992a) is widely used in both clinical applications and a wide range of research that involves personality assessment. Based on a five-dimension (or factor) model of personality, the NEO PI-R is a measure of five major dimensions (or "domains") of personality and a total of 30 elements or *facets* that define each domain.

The original version of the test was called the NEO Personality Inventory (NEO-PI; Costa & McCrae, 1985), where NEO was an acronym for the first three domains measured: Neuroticism, Extraversion, and Openness. The NEO PI-R provides for the measurement of two additional domains: Agreeableness and Conscientiousness. Stated briefly, the Neuroticism domain taps aspects of adjustment and emotional stability. The Extraversion domain taps aspects of sociability and assertiveness. Openness refers to

Table 11-2
The Big Five Compared to Cattell's Five

The Big Five	Cattell's Five (circa 1960)
Extraversion	Introversion/Extraversion
Neuroticism	Low Anxiety/High Anxiety
Openness	Tough-Mindedness/Receptivity
Agreeableness	Independence/Accommodation
Conscientiousness	Low Self-Control/High Self-Control

Cattell expressed what he viewed as the source traits of personality in terms of bipolar dimensions. The 16 personality factors measured by the test today are: Warmth (Reserved vs. Warm), Reasoning (Concrete vs. Abstract), Emotional Stability (Reactive vs. Emotionally Stable), Dominance (Deferential vs. Dominant), Liveliness (Serious vs. Lively), Rule-Consciousness (Expedient vs. Rule-Conscious), Social Boldness (Shy vs. Socially Bold), Sensitivity (Utilitarian vs. Sensitive), Vigilance (Trusting vs. Vigilant), Abstractedness (Grounded vs. Abstracted), Privateness (Forthright vs. Private), Apprehension (Self-Assured vs. Apprehensive), Openness to Change (Traditional vs. Open to Change), Self-Reliance (Group-Oriented vs. Self-Reliant), Perfectionism (Tolerates Disorder vs. Perfectionistic), and Tension (Relaxed vs. Tense).

openness to experience as well as active imagination, aesthetic sensitivity, attentiveness to inner feelings, preference for variety, intellectual curiosity, and independence of judgment. Agreeableness is primarily a dimension of interpersonal tendencies that include altruism, sympathy toward others, and the belief that others are similarly inclined. Conscientiousness is a dimension of personality that has to do with the active processes of planning, organizing, and following through. Each of these major dimensions or domains of personality may be subdivided into individual traits or facets measured by the NEO PI-R.

The NEO PI-R is designed for use with persons 17 years of age and older and is essentially self-administered. Computerized scoring and interpretation are available. Validity and reliability data are presented in the manual. A more detailed description of this test prepared by the test authors (Costa and McCrae) is presented in the companion workbook to this text, *Exercises in Psychological Testing and Assessment*, 6th edition Cohen (2005).

We began our discussion of the tools of test development with a note that many personality tests have used two or more of these tools in the process of their development. At this point you may begin to appreciate how, as well as why, two or more tools might be used. A pool of items for an objective personality measure could be created, for example, on the basis of logic or theory, or both logic and theory. The items might then be arranged into scales on the basis of factor analysis. The draft version of the test could be administered to a criterion group and to a control group to see if responses to the items differ as a function of group membership. But here we are getting just a bit ahead of ourselves. We need to define, discuss, and illustrate what is meant by *criterion group* in the context of personality test development.

Criterion Groups

A **criterion** may be defined as a standard on which a judgment or decision can be made. With regard to scale development, a **criterion group** is a reference group of testtakers who share specific characteristics and whose responses to test items serve as a standard according to which items will be included in or discarded from the final version of a scale. The process of using criterion groups to develop test items is referred to as **empirical criterion keying** because the scoring or keying of items has been demonstrated empirically to differentiate among groups of testtakers. The shared characteristic of the criterion group to be researched—a psychiatric diagnosis, a unique skill or ability, a genetic aberration, or whatever—will vary as a function of the nature and scope of the test. Development of a test by means of empirical criterion keying may be summed up as follows:

1. Create a large, preliminary pool of test items from which the test items for the final form of the test will be selected.

2. Administer the preliminary pool of items to at least two groups of people:

   Group 1: A criterion group composed of people known to possess the trait being measured.

   Group 2: A randomly selected group of people (who may or may not possess the trait being measured)

3. Conduct an item analysis to select items indicative of membership in the criterion group. Items in the preliminary pool that discriminate between membership in the two groups in a statistically significant fashion will be retained and incorporated in the final form of the test.

4. Obtain data on test performance from a standardization sample of testtakers who are representative of the population from which future testtakers will come. The test performance data for Group 2 members on items incorporated into the final form of the test may be used for this purpose if deemed appropriate. The performance of Group 2 members on the test would then become the standard against which future testtakers will be evaluated. After the mean performance of Group 2 members on the individual items (or scales) of the test has been identified, future testtakers will be evaluated in terms of the extent to which their scores deviate in either direction from the Group 2 mean.

At this point you may ask, "But what about that initial pool of items? How is it created?" The answer is that the test developer may have found inspiration for each of the items from reviews of journals and books, interviews with patients, or consultations with colleagues. The test developer may have relied on logic or reason alone to write the items, or on other tests. Alternatively, the test developer may have relied on none of these and simply let imagination loose and committed to paper whatever emerged. An interesting aspect of test development by means of empirical criterion keying is that the content of the test items does not have to relate in a logical, rational, direct, or face-valid way to the measurement objective. Burisch (1984, p. 218) captured the essence of empirical criterion keying when he stated flatly, "If shoe size as a predictor improves your ability to predict performance as an airplane pilot, use it."[4] Burisch went on to offer this tongue-in-cheek description of how criterion groups could be used to develop an "M-F" test to differentiate males from females:

> Allegedly not knowing where the differences were, he or she would never dream of using an item such as "I can grow a beard if I want to" or "In a restaurant I tend to prefer the ladies' room to the men's room." Rather, a heterogeneous pool of items would be assembled and administered to a sample of men and women. Next, samples would be compared item by item. Any item discriminating sufficiently well would qualify for inclusion in the M-F test. (p. 214)

Now imagine that it is the 1930s. A team of researchers is keenly interested in devising a paper-and-pencil test that will improve reliability in psychiatric diagnosis.

---

4. It should come as no surprise, however, that any scale that is the product of such wildly empirical procedures would be expected to be extremely high in heterogeneity of item content and profoundly low in internal consistency measures.

Their idea is to use empirical criterion keying to create the instrument. A preliminary version of the test will be administered (1) to several criterion groups of adult inpatients, each group homogeneous with respect to psychiatric diagnosis, and (2) to a group of randomly selected normal adults. Using item analysis, items useful in differentiating members of the various clinical groups from members of the normal group will be retained to make up the final form of the test. The researchers envision that future users of the published test will be able to derive diagnostic insights by comparing a testtaker's response pattern to that of testtakers in the normal group.

And there you have the beginnings of a relatively simple idea that would, in time, win widespread approval from clinicians around the world. It is an idea for a test that stimulated the publication of thousands of research studies, an idea that led to the development of a test that would serve as a model for countless other instruments devised through the use of criterion group research. The test, originally called the Medical and Psychiatric Inventory (Dahlstrom & Dahlstrom, 1980), is the MMPI. Years after its tentative beginnings, the test's senior author recalled that "it was difficult to persuade a publisher to accept the MMPI" (Hathaway, cited in Dahlstrom & Welsh, 1960, p. vii). However, the University of Minnesota Press was obviously persuaded because in 1943 it published the test under a new name, the Minnesota Multiphasic Personality Inventory (MMPI). The rest, as they say, is history.

In the next few pages, we describe the development of the original MMPI as well as its more contemporary progeny, the MMPI-2 and the MMPI-A. Let's note at the outset that this test occupies a prominent place in psychometrics, having served as a model for so many other tests and having earned the distinction of being the most widely used psychological test in the world.

The MMPI The MMPI was the product of a collaboration between psychologist Starke R. Hathaway and psychiatrist/neurologist John Charnley McKinley (Hathaway & McKinley, 1940, 1942, 1943, 1951; McKinley & Hathaway, 1940, 1944). It contained 566 true/false items and was designed as an aid to psychiatric diagnosis with adolescents and adults 14 years of age and older. Research preceding the selection of test items included review of textbooks, psychiatric reports, and previously published personality test items. In this sense, the beginnings of the MMPI can be traced to an approach based on logic and reason with an emphasis on item content.

A listing of the ten clinical scales of the MMPI is presented in Table 11–3 along with a description of the corresponding criterion group. Each of the diagnostic categories listed for the ten clinical scales were popular diagnostic categories in the 1930s. Members of the clinical criterion group for each scale were presumed to have met the criteria for inclusion in the category named in the scale. MMPI clinical scale items were derived empirically by administration to clinical criterion groups and normal control groups. The items that successfully differentiated between the two groups were retained in the final version of the test (Welsh & Dahlstrom, 1956). Well, it's actually a bit more complicated than that, and you really should know some of the details . . .

To understand the meaning of *normal control group* in this context, think of an experiment. In experimental research, an experimenter manipulates the situation so that the experimental group is exposed to something (the independent variable) and the control group is not. In the development of the MMPI, members of the criterion groups were drawn from a population of people presumed to be members of a group with a shared diagnostic label. Analogizing an experiment to this test development situation, it is as if the experimental treatment for the criterion group members was membership in the category named. By contrast, members of the **control group** were normal (nondiagnosed) people who ostensibly received no such experimental treatment.

Table 11–3
The Clinical Criterion Groups for MMPI Scales

Scale	Clinical Criterion Group
1. Hypochondriasis (Hs)	Patients who showed exaggerated concerns about their physical health
2. Depression (D)	Clinically depressed patients; unhappy and pessimistic about their future
3. Hysteria (Hy)	Patients with conversion reactions
4. Psychopathic deviate (Pd)	Patients who had had histories of delinquency and other antisocial behavior
5. Masculinity-femininity (Mf)	Minnesota draftees, airline stewardesses, and male homosexual college students from the University of Minnesota campus community
6. Paranoia (Pa)	Patients who exhibited paranoid symptomatology such as ideas of reference, suspiciousness, delusions of persecution, and delusions of grandeur
7. Psychasthenia (Pt)	Anxious, obsessive-compulsive, guilt-ridden, and self-doubting patients
8. Schizophrenia (Sc)	Patients who were diagnosed as schizophrenic (various subtypes)
9. Hypomania (Ma)	Patients, most diagnosed as manic-depressive, who exhibited manic symptomatology such as elevated mood, excessive activity, and easy distractibility
0. Social introversion (Si)	College students who had scored at the extremes on a test of introversion/extraversion

Note that these same ten clinical scales formed the core not only of the original MMPI, but of its 1989 revision, the MMPI-2. The clinical scales did undergo some modification for the MMPI-2, such as editing and reordering, and nine items were eliminated. Still, the MMPI-2 retained the ten original clinical scale names, despite the fact that some of them (such as "Psychopathic Deviate") are relics of a bygone era. Perhaps that accounts for why convention has it that these scales be referred to by scale numbers only, not their names.

The normal control group, also referred to as the standardization sample, consisted of approximately 1,500 subjects. Included were 724 people who happen to be visiting friends or relatives at University of Minnesota hospitals, 265 high school graduates seeking precollege guidance at the University of Minnesota Testing Bureau, 265 skilled workers participating in a local Works Progress Administration program, and 243 medical (nonpsychiatric) patients.

The clinical criterion group for the MMPI was for the most part made up of psychiatric inpatients at the University of Minnesota Hospital. We say "for the most part" because Scale 5 (Masculinity-Femininity) and Scale 0 (Social Introversion) were not derived in this way. The number of people included in each diagnostic category was relatively low by contemporary standards. For example, the criterion group for Scale 7 (Psychasthenia) contained only 20 people, all diagnosed as psychasthenic. Two of the "clinical" scales (Scale 0 and Scale 5) did not even use members of a clinical population in the criterion group. The members of the Scale 0 (Social Introversion) clinical criterion group were college students who had earned extreme scores on a measure of introversion-extraversion. Scale 5 was not even originally designed to measure masculinity or femininity; rather, it was originally designed to differentiate heterosexual from homosexual males. Due to a dearth of items that effectively differentiated people on this variable, the test developers broadened the definition of Scale 5 and added items that discriminated between normal males (soldiers) and females (airline personnel). Some of the added items were obtained from the Attitude Interest Scale (Terman & Miles, 1936). Hathaway and McKinley had also attempted to develop a scale to differentiate lesbians from female heterosexuals but were unable to do so.

By the 1930s, research on the Personal Data Sheet (Woodworth, 1917) and other face-valid, logic-derived instruments had brought to light problems inherent in self-report methods. Hathaway and McKinley (1943) evinced a keen awareness of such problems. They built into the MMPI three validity scales: the L scale (the Lie scale), the F scale (the

JUST THINK . . .

Applying what you know about the standardization of tests, what are your thoughts regarding the standardization of the original MMPI? What about the composition of the clinical criterion groups? The normal control group?

Frequency, or perhaps more accurately, the Infrequency scale), and the K (Correction) scale. Note that these scales were not designed to measure validity in the technical, psychometric sense. There is, after all, something inherently self-serving, if not suspect, about a test that purports to gauge its own validity! Rather, *validity* here was a reference to a built-in indicator of the operation of testtaker response sets and related response patterns (such as carelessness, deliberate efforts to deceive, or unintentional misunderstanding) that could affect the test results.

The L scale contains 15 items that are somewhat negative but that apply to most people. Two examples: "I do not always tell the truth" and "I gossip a little at times" (Dahlstrom et al., 1972, p. 109). The preparedness of the examinee to reveal *anything* negative about himself or herself will be called into question if the score on the L scale does not fall within certain limits.

The 64 items on the F scale (1) are infrequently endorsed by members of nonpsychiatric populations (that is, normal people) and (2) do not fit into any known pattern of deviance. A response of *true* to an item such as the following would be scored on the F scale: "It would be better if almost all laws were thrown away" (Dahlstrom et al., 1972, p. 115). An elevated F score may mean that the respondent did not take the test seriously and was just responding to items randomly. Alternatively, the individual with a high F score may be a very eccentric individual or someone who was attempting to fake bad. Malingerers in the armed services, people intent on committing fraud with respect to health insurance, and criminals attempting to cop a psychiatric plea are some of the groups of people who might be expected to have elevated F scores on their profiles.

> **JUST THINK . . .**
> Try your hand at writing a good L scale item.

Like the L score and the F score, the K score is a reflection of the frankness of the test-taker's self-report. An elevated K score is associated with defensiveness and the desire to present a favorable impression. A low K score is associated with excessive self-criticism, desire to detail deviance, or desire to fake bad. A *true* response to the item "I certainly feel useless at times" and a *false* response to "At times I am all full of energy" (Dahlstrom et al., 1972, p. 125) would be scored on the K scale. The K scale is sometimes used to correct scores on five of the clinical scales. The scores are statistically corrected for an individual's overwillingness or unwillingness to admit deviancy.

Another scale that bears on the validity of a test administration is the *Cannot Say* scale, also referred to simply as the ? (question mark) scale. This scale is a simple frequency count of the number of items to which the examinee responded *cannot say* or failed to mark any response. Items may be omitted or marked *cannot say* for many reasons, including respondent indecisiveness, defensiveness, carelessness, and lack of experience relevant to the item. Traditionally, the validity of an answer sheet with a *cannot say* count of 30 or higher is called into question and deemed uninterpretable (Dahlstrom et al., 1972). Even for tests with a *Cannot Say* count of 10, caution has been urged in test interpretation. High *Cannot Say* scores may be avoided by a proctor's emphasis in the initial instructions to answer *all* items.

The MMPI contains 550 true/false items, 16 of which are repeated on some forms of the test (for a total of 566 items administered). Scores on each MMPI scale are reported in the form of *T* scores which, you may recall, have a mean set at 50 and a standard deviation set at 10. A score of 70 on any MMPI clinical scale is 2 standard deviations above the average score of members of the standardization sample, and a score of 30 is 2 standard deviations below their average score.

In addition to the clinical scales and the validity scales, there are MMPI content scales, supplementary scales, and Harris-Lingoes subscales. As its name implies, the content scales, sometimes referred to as the Wiggins Content Scales (after Wiggins,

1966), are composed of groups of test items of similar content. Examples of content scales on the MMPI include the scales labeled Depression and Family Problems.

Supplementary scales is a catch-all phrase for the hundreds of different MMPI scales that have been developed since the test's publication. These scales have been devised by different researchers using a variety of methods and statistical procedures, most notably factor analysis. There are supplementary scales that are fairly consistent with the original objectives of the MMPI, such as scales designed to shed light on alcoholism and ego strength. And then there are dozens of other supplementary scales, created by independent researchers. They range from Success in Baseball to—well, name it![5]

♦
JUST THINK . . .

If you were going to develop a supplementary MMPI scale, what would it be, and why would you want to develop it?

The publisher of the MMPI makes available for computerized scoring only a limited selection of the many hundreds of supplementary scales that have been developed and discussed in the professional literature. The Harris-Lingoes subscales, often referred to simply as the Harris scales, are a set of supplementary scales widely available to test users. The Harris scales are groupings of items into subscales (with labels such as Brooding and Social Alienation) that were designed to be more internally consistent than the umbrella scale from which the subscale was derived.

Historically administered by paper and pencil, the MMPI is today administered by many methods: online, offline on disk, or by index cards. An audio version for semiliterate testtakers is also available, with instructions recorded on audiocassette. Testtakers respond to items by answering *true* or *false*. Items left unanswered are construed as *cannot say*. In the version of the test administered using individual items printed on cards, testtakers are instructed to sort the cards into three piles labeled *true, false,* and *cannot say.* At least a sixth-grade reading level is required to understand all the items. There are no time limits, and the time required to administer 566 items is typically between 60 and 90 minutes.

It is possible to score MMPI answer sheets by hand, but the process is labor intensive and rarely done. Computer scoring of protocols is accomplished by software on personal computers, by computer transmission to a scoring service via modem, or by physically mailing the completed form to a computer scoring service. Computer output may range from a simple numerical and graphic presentation of scores to a highly detailed narrative report complete with analysis of scores on selected supplementary scales.

Soon after the MMPI was published, it became evident that the test could not be used to neatly categorize testtakers into diagnostic categories. When testtakers had elevations in the pathological range of two or more scales, diagnostic dilemmas arose. Hathaway and McKinley (1943) had urged users of their test to opt for *configural interpretation* of scores—that is, interpretation based not on scores of single scales but on the pattern, profile, or configuration of the scores. However, their proposed method for profile interpretation was extremely complicated, as were many of the proposed adjunctive and alternative procedures.

Paul Meehl (1951) proposed a 2-point code derived from the numbers of the clinical scales on which the testtaker achieved the highest (most pathological) scores. If a testtaker achieved the highest score on Scale 1 and the second highest score on Scale 2, that

---

5. Here, astute reader, you may begin to obtain an appreciation of just how far from its original intended purpose the MMPI has strayed. In fact, the MMPI, and more recently the MMPI-2, has been used for an extraordinarily wide range of adventures related to psychiatric diagnosis tangentially at best.

testtaker's 2-point code type would be 12. The 2-point code type for a highest score on Scale 2 and a second highest score on Scale 1 would be 21. Because each digit in the code is interchangeable, a code of 12 would be interpreted in exactly the same way as a code of 21. By the way, a code of 12 (or 21) is indicative of an individual in physical pain. An assumption here is that each score in the 2-point code type exceeds an elevation of $T = 70$. If the scale score does not exceed 70, this is indicated by the use of a prime (') after the scale number. Meehl's system had great appeal for many MMPI users. Before long, a wealth of research mounted on the interpretive meanings of the 40 code types that could be derived using ten scales and two interchangeable digits.[6]

Another popular approach to scoring and interpretation came in the form of **Welsh codes**—referred to as such because they were created by Welsh (1948, 1956), not because they were written in Welsh (although to the uninitiated, they may be equally incomprehensible). Here is an example of a Welsh code:

$$6*\underline{78}'''1\text{-}53/4\text{:}2\#\underline{90}\ F'L\text{-}/K.$$

To the seasoned Welsh code user, this expression provides information about a testtaker's scores on the MMPI clinical and validity scales.[7]

Students interested in learning more about the MMPI need not expend a great deal of effort in tracking down sources. Chances are your university library is teeming with books and journal articles written on or about this multiphasic (many-faceted) instrument. Of course, you may also want to go well beyond this historical introduction by becoming better acquainted with this test's more contemporary revisions, the MMPI-2 and the MMPI-A. Here is a brief overview.

The MMPI-2   Much of what has already been said about the MMPI in terms of its general structure, as well as its administration, scoring, and interpretation, is applicable to the MMPI-2. The most significant difference between the two tests is the more representative standardization sample (normal control group) used in the norming of the MMPI-2 (discussed shortly). Approximately 14% of the MMPI items were rewritten to correct grammatical errors and to make the language more contemporary, nonsexist, and readable. Items thought to be objectionable to present-day testtakers were eliminated. Added were items addressing topics such as drug abuse, suicide potential, marital adjustment, attitudes toward work, and Type A behavior patterns.[8] In all, the MMPI-2 contains a total of 567 true/false items, including 394 items that are identical to the original MMPI items, 66 items that were modified or rewritten, and 107 new items. The suggested age range of testtakers for the MMPI-2 is 18 years old and older, as compared to 14 years old and older for the MMPI. The reading level required (sixth grade) is the same as for the MMPI. The MMPI-2, like its predecessor, may be administered online, offline by paper and pencil, or by audiocassette, and takes about the same length of time to administer.

The ten clinical scales of the MMPI are identical to those on the MMPI-2, as is the policy of referring to them primarily by number. Content component scales were added to the MMPI-2 to provide more focused indices of content. For example, Family Problems

---

6. In addition to 2-point coding systems, at least one 3-point coding system has been proposed. In that system, the first number is the highest score, the second number is the second highest score, and the third number is the third highest score.

7. With the instructor's approval, the motivated student may translate this code for extra credit.

8. Recall from our discussion of psychological types earlier in this chapter (page 339) what constitutes Type A and Type B behavior.

content is now subdivided into Family Discord and Familial Alienation content. The three original validity scales of the MMPI are included in the MMPI-2, as are three additional validity scales: Back-Page Infrequency (Fb), True Response Inconsistency (TRIN), and Variable Response Inconsistency (VRIN). The Back-Page Infrequency scale contains items seldom endorsed by testtakers who are candid, deliberate, and diligent in their approach to the test. Of course, some testtakers' diligence wanes as the test wears

JUST THINK . . .

To maintain continuity with the original test, the MMPI-2 used the same names for the clinical scales. Some of these scale names, such as Psychasthenia, are no longer used. Would you have recommended updating the names of the scales? Are there any other changes you may have recommended to the revision?

on, so that by the "back pages" of the test, a random or inconsistent pattern of responses is evident. The Fb scale is designed to detect such a pattern.

The TRIN scale is designed to identify acquiescent and nonacquiescent response patterns. It contains 23 pairs of items worded in opposite forms. Consistency in responding dictates that, for example, a *true* response to the first item in the pair is followed by a *false* response to the second item in the pair.

The VRIN scale is designed to identify indiscriminate response patterns. It too is made up of item pairs, each item in the pair worded in either opposite or similar forms. The senior author of the MMPI-2, James Butcher (Figure 11–4), developed yet another validity scale after the publication of that test.[9] The *S* scale is a validity scale designed to detect self-presentation in a superlative manner (Butcher & Han, 1995; Lanyon, 1993a, 1993b; Lim & Butcher, 1996).

A nagging criticism of the original MMPI was the lack of representation of the standardization sample of the U.S. population. This criticism was addressed in the standardization of the MMPI-2. The 2,600 individuals (1,462 females, 1,138 males) from seven states who made up the MMPI-2 standardization sample had been matched to 1980 United States Census data on the variables of age, gender, minority status, social class, and education (Butcher, 1990). Whereas the original MMPI did not contain any non-Whites in the standardization sample, the MMPI-2 sample was 81% White and 19% non-White. Age of subjects in the sample ranged from 18 years to 85 years. Formal education ranged from 3 years to 20+ years, with more highly educated people and people working in the professions overrepresented in the sample. Median annual family income for females in the sample was $25,000 to $30,000. Median annual family income for males in the sample was $30,000 to $35,000.

As with the original MMPI, the standardization sample data provided the basis for transforming the raw scores obtained by respondents into *T* scores for the MMPI-2. However, a technical adjustment was deemed to be in order. The *T* scores used for standardizing the MMPI clinical scales and content scales were linear *T* scores. For the MMPI-2, linear *T* scores were also used for standardization of the validity scales, the supplementary scales, and Scales 5 and 0 of the clinical scales. However, a different *T* score was used to standardize the remaining eight clinical scales, as well as all of the content scales; these scales were standardized with uniform *T* scores (*UT* scores). The *UT* scores were used in an effort to make the *T* scores corresponding to percentile scores more comparable across the MMPI-2 scales (Graham, 1990; Tellegen & Ben-Porath, 1992).

---

9. Pictured to the right of James Butcher is his buddy, Dale Moss, who was killed in the war. The authors pause at this juncture to remember and express gratitude to all the people in all branches of the military and government who have sacrificed for this country.

Figure 11–4
James Butcher (1933–) and Friend

That's Jim, today better known as the senior author of the MMPI-2, to your right as an Army infantryman at Outpost Yoke in South Korea in 1953. Returning to civilian life, Jim tried various occupations, including salesman and private investigator. He later earned a Ph.D. at the University of North Carolina, where he had occasion to work with W. Grant Dahlstrom and George Welsh (as in MMPI "Welsh code"). Butcher's first teaching job was at the University of Minnesota, where he looked forward to working with Starke Hathaway and Paul Meehl. But he was disappointed to learn that "Hathaway had moved on to the pursuit of psychotherapy research and typically disclaimed any expertise in the test. . . . Hathaway always refused to become involved in teaching people about the test. Meehl had likewise moved on to other venues" (Butcher, 2003, p. 233).

The MMPI-A Although its developers had recommended the original MMPI for use with adolescents, test users had evinced skepticism of this recommendation through the years. Early on it was noticed that adolescents as a group tended to score somewhat higher on the clinical scales than adults, a finding that left adolescents as a group in the unenviable position of appearing to suffer from more psychopathology than adults. In part for this reason, separate MMPI norms for adolescents were developed. In the 1980s, with the MMPI revision under way, the test developers had a choice of simply renorming the MMPI-2 for adolescents or creating a new instrument. They opted to develop a new test that was in many key respects a downward extension of the MMPI-2.

The Minnesota Multiphasic Personality Inventory-Adolescent (MMPI-A; Butcher et al., 1992) is a 478-item, true/false test designed for use in clinical, counseling, and school settings for the purpose of assessing psychopathology and identifying personal, social, and behavioral problems. The individual items of the MMPI-A, much like the clinical and validity scales, largely parallel the MMPI-2, although there are 88 fewer items. Some of the MMPI-2 items were discarded, others were rewritten, and some completely new ones were added. In its written (as opposed to audiocassette) form, the test is designed for administration to testtakers in the 14- to 18-year-old age range who have at least a sixth-grade reading ability. As with the MMPI-2, versions of the test are available for administration by computer, by paper and pencil, and by audiocassette. The time required for an administration of all the items typically is between 45 and 60 minutes.

The MMPI-A contains 16 basic scales, including 10 Clinical Scales (identical in name and number to those of the MMPI-2) and six Validity Scales (actually, a total of eight Validity Scales given that the F scale is subdivided into F, F_1, and F_2 scales). The validity scales are Variable Response Inconsistency (VRIN), True Response Inconsistency (TRIN), Infrequency (F), Infrequency 1 (F_1; specifically applicable to the clinical scales), Infrequency 2 (F_2; specifically applicable to the content and supplementary scales), Lie (L), Defensiveness (K), and Cannot Say (?).

In addition to basic Clinical and Validity Scales, the MMPI-A contains six Supplementary Scales (dealing with areas such as alcohol and drug use, immaturity, anxiety, and repression), 15 Content Scales (including areas such as Conduct Problems and School Problems), 28 Harris-Lingoes scales, and three scales labeled Social Introversion. As with the MMPI-2, uniform T (UT) scales were employed for use with all the Content Scales and eight of the Clinical Scales (Scales 5 and 0 excluded), to make percentile scores comparable across scales.

The normative sample for the MMPI-A consisted of 805 adolescent males and 815 adolescent females drawn from schools in California, Minnesota, New York, North Carolina, Ohio, Pennsylvania, Virginia, and Washington. The objective was to obtain a sample that was nationally representative in terms of demographic variables such as ethnic background, geographic region of the United States, and urban/rural residence. Concurrent with the norming of the MMPI-A, a clinical sample of 713 adolescents was tested for the purpose of obtaining validity data. However, no effort was made to ensure representativeness of the clinical sample. Subjects were all drawn from the Minneapolis area, most from drug and alcohol treatment centers.

> **JUST THINK . . .**
>
> Your comments on the norming of the MMPI-A?

In general, the MMPI-A has earned high marks from test reviewers and may well have quickly become the most widely used measure of psychopathology in adolescents. The MMPI-A content scales offer incremental validity over the test's clinical scales and should therefore be used as an adjunct to the clinical scales (McGrath et al., 2002). There is some evidence to suggest that when this test is used with 18-year-old testtakers, it tends to underestimate the degree of psychopathology that may be present (Osberg & Poland, 2002).

The MMPI and its revisions in perspective We might analogize the original MMPI to a classic car. At its core is an engine (the 10 clinical scales) that, although clearly outdated, remains familiar and serviceable enough to maintain wide appeal. Many of the engine's component parts were named using a vocabulary of a bygone era. For this reason, these parts are today referred to by number rather than by name. But although its engine may be technologically anachronistic, the car is a long-respected, known quantity with a strong brand heritage. It has been the subject of thousands of research studies since its introduction in the early 1940s. Moreover, an abundance of appealing bells, whistles, and options have been added to the vehicle (in terms of additional scales and a new normative sample), which attracts buyers to the showroom.

The MMPI-2 and MMPI-A revision processes had two seemingly contrary objectives. One objective was to keep the revision as similar as possible to the original, for the purpose of retaining the applicability and relevance of the many research studies that employed the MMPI. The second objective was to change the original test to respond to the many constructive criticisms leveled at the original over the years. In most ways, the developers of the MMPI-2 and the MMPI-A achieved this delicate balance, although, as might be expected, not everyone is entirely happy about the means to the end.

The most glaring problem with the MMPI was its lack of representative norms, a criticism addressed in both the MMPI-2 and the MMPI-A. However, it was only in the MMPI-A, and not in the MMPI-2, that a clinical sample was concurrently tested for comparative and validation purposes. Comparable MMPI-2 data on a contemporary, nationally representative clinical sample would have gone a long way toward breathing new life and meaning into the tired but recycled clinical scales. Also puzzling is the fact that a nationally unrepresentative clinical sample was employed in the study of the MMPI-A. Once the decision had been made to employ a clinical sample, why wasn't the effort made to make that sample nationally representative? All the subjects in the clinical sample cited in the MMPI-A manual were from Minnesota. In this respect, the MMPI-A retained a feature of the original MMPI it would have done better to change.

In the late 1930s and early 1940s, when Hathaway and McKinley were feeling their way to develop a new diagnostic instrument, the lack of representativeness of the clinical subjects could be overlooked. Admittedly, obtaining such a sample, testing all of the subjects, and thoroughly analyzing all of the resulting data is a herculean and expensive undertaking. On the other hand, given the contemporary status of the MMPI (a veritable institution among psychological tests), and the great frequency with which it is used worldwide, why would the current test developers want to do any less? It is our opinion that the presentation of data from a nationally representative clinical sample would have been a most valuable—and eminently manageable—addition to the manuals of the two MMPI revisions.

The MMPI clinical scales each exhibit relatively low inter-item consistencies—not surprising, given the empirical nature of their development. At the same time, the intercorrelations between the clinical scales are high. This combination of facts naturally raises questions such as, What do the clinical scales really measure? Questions regarding exactly how scores on the clinical scales should be interpreted persist even with regard to the MMPI-2 and the MMPI-A. In large part, these questions have been addressed with reference to the use of other scales (such as the validity, content, Harris, and supplementary scales) as interpretive aids. Of course, scales other than the clinical scales carry their own interpretation-related baggage. For example, although an elevated F scale may reflect on the validity of the protocol, it may also reflect severe psychopathology. Here again, one needs to evaluate other scales in order to reach conclusions about the meaning of a particular scale.

In general, a wealth of reliability and validity studies support the continued use of the MMPI-2. Exactly how useful the MMPI-2 is for non-Caucasian populations is a question that has received a great deal of attention since the test's publication. The original MMPI was standardized on Caucasians, but the MMPI-2 used a broader normative sample. Research has supported the adequacy of the MMPI-2 and its norms for African Americans (Timbrook & Graham, 1994) and Hispanic Americans (Whitworth & Unterbrink, 1994). However, there is some evidence to suggest that the MMPI-2 may underpredict psychopathology in African Americans (Arbisi et al., 2002).

As we have emphasized throughout this book, assessment professionals must be sensitive to cultural differences when conducting evaluations. Tests may be profoundly influential in one cultural milieu but of questionable consequence in another. For example, although Holland's notion of a vocational personality and its associated theory of six occupational themes has been received enthusiastically in the United States, questions have been raised concerning its applicability across cultures (Fouad & Dancer, 1992; Hansen, 1987; Khan et al., 1990; Swanson, 1992). Juni (1996) characterized the five-factor model of the NEO PI-R as "intrinsically bound to the culture and language that spawned it," although McCrae et al. (1998) have challenged this assertion. Let's now take a closer look at some culture-related issues in personality assessment.

Personality Assessment and Culture

Every day, assessment professionals across the United States are routinely called on to evaluate personality and related variables of people from culturally and linguistically diverse populations. Yet personality assessment is anything but routine with children, adolescents, and adults from Native American, Hispanic, Asian, African American, and other cultures that may have been underrepresented in the development, standardization, and interpretation protocols of the measures used. Especially with members of culturally and linguistically diverse populations, a routine and business-as-usual approach to psychological testing and assessment is inappropriate, if not irresponsible. What is required is a professionally trained assessor capable of conducting a meaningful assessment, with sensitivity to how culture relates to the behaviors and cognitions being measured (López, 2000).

Before any tool of personality assessment—an interview, a test, a protocol for behavioral observation, a portfolio, or something else—can be employed, and before data derived from an attempt at measurement can be imbued with meaning, the assessor will ideally consider some important issues with regard to assessment of a particular assessee. Many of these issues relate to the level of acculturation, values, identity, worldview, and language of the assessee. Professional exploration of these areas is capable of yielding not only information necessary as a prerequisite for formal personality assessment but a wealth of personality-related information in its own right. Let's take a closer look.

Acculturation and Related Considerations

Acculturation is an ongoing process by which an individual's thoughts, behaviors, values, worldview, and identity develop in relation to the general thinking, behavior, customs, and values of a particular cultural group. The process of acculturation begins at birth, a time at which the newborn infant's family or caretakers serve as agents of the culture.[10] In the years to come, other family members, teachers, peers, books, films, theater, newspapers, television and radio programs, and other media serve as agents of acculturation. Through the process of acculturation, one develops culturally accepted ways of thinking, feeling, and behaving.

A number of tests and questionnaires have been developed in recent years to yield insights regarding assessees' level of acculturation to their native culture or the dominant culture. A sampling of these measures is presented in Table 11–4. As you survey this list, keep in mind that the amount of psychometric research done on these instruments varies. Some of these instruments may be little more than content valid, if that. In such cases, let the buyer beware. Should you wish to use any of these measures, you may wish to look up more information about it in a resource such as the *Mental Measurements*

---

10. The process of acculturation may begin before birth. It seems reasonable to assume that nutritional and other aspects of the mother's prenatal care may have implications for the newborn infant's taste and other preferences.

Table 11–4
Some Published Acculturation Measures

Source	Description
Acculturation Questionnaire (Smither & Rodriguez-Giegling, 1982)	Designed for use with members of various refugee populations, this questionnaire taps the assessee's willingness to acculturate.
Acculturation Rating Scale for Mexican Americans (Cuellar et al., 1980)	A test designed for use with Mexican Americans as a measure of Mexican acculturation.
African American Acculturation (Snowden & Hines, 1999)	Taps race-related cultural and media preferences, degree of comfort in interracial social interaction, and attitudes regarding reliance on relatives for help and desirability of interracial marriage.
African Self-Consciousness Scale (Baldwin & Bell, 1985)	A test designed for use in conjunction with an Africentric personality theory (Baldwin, 1984). Includes components designed to measure several variables, such as those related to opposition to oppression. The validity of both the theory it is derived from and the test itself remains to be documented.
Asian Indian Acculturation Measure (Sodowsky & Carey, 1988)	This questionnaire, published in the context of a journal article, may have exploratory value in terms of the insights it yields regarding Asian Indian acculturation.
Asian Values Scale (Kim et al., 1999)	Developed to assist in the provision of culturally relevant and sensitive psychological services by focusing on the assessment of values.
Assimilation Measure for Spokane Indians (Roy, 1962)	A measure designed to assess degree of assimilation, among other factors.
Children's Acculturation Scale (Franco, 1983)	Designed for use as a tool for learning about Mexican American children, this is a 10-item questionnaire completed by the child's teacher.
Chinese Acculturation Measures (Yao, 1979)	Two tests, one of traditional Chinese culture and the other of Chinese American assimilation, both of which may have value for exploratory purposes with persons who have immigrated to the United States from China.
Cuban Behavioral Identity Questionnaire (Garcia & Lega, 1979)	A brief scale to measure acculturation of Cuban Americans.
Cultural Health Attributions Questionnaire (Murguia et al., 2000)	Developed in response to a need for a measure that captures the full range of health beliefs among Latinos and the Latino worldview that includes complex beliefs about the etiology, symptom expression, and treatment of illnesses.
Cultural Life Style Inventory (Mendoza, 1989)	Developed for use with Mexican American adolescents and adults, this test measures various aspects of acculturation.
Ethnic Identity Questionnaire (Masuda et al., 1970)	A questionnaire designed for use with Japanese Americans.
Hawaiian Culture Scale-Adolescent Version (Hishinuma et al., 2000)	Measures sources of learning about the Hawaiian way of life and the extent to which Hawaiian and non-Hawaiian beliefs are valued.
Indian Assimilation Scale (Howe Chief, 1940)	Developed for use with young females, this test taps attitudes toward assimilation, Native American lineage, and related factors.
Intercultural Contact and Western Identification Scales (Chance, 1965)	Designed for use with Eskimo populations.
Multicultural Acculturation Scale (Wong-Rieger & Quintana, 1987)	Developed for use with people of various cultural backgrounds.
Multicultural Experience Inventory (Ramirez, 1984)	Developed for use with Mexican American adults, this test taps various aspects of acculturation, biculturalism, and multicultural participation.
Self-Identity Inventory (Sevig et al., 2000)	Developed to assist in the understanding of how minority group members differ within and across groups in their perceptions of and reaction to oppression.
Social, Attitudinal, Familial, and Environmental Acculturative Stress Scale (Padilla et al., 1985)	Measures stress of adapting to a new culture, including perceived discrimination and barriers to adaptation, as well as related variables. Developed for use with Japanese testtakers but can be used with a wide variety of populations (see, for example, Joiner & Walker, 2002).
Suinn-Lew Asian Self-Identity Acculturation Scale (Suinn et al., 1987)	Developed for use with people of various Asian heritages.

Assessing Acculturation
and Related Variables

A number of important questions regarding acculturation and related variables may be raised with regard to assessees from culturally diverse populations. Many general types of interview questions may yield rich insights regarding the overlapping areas of acculturation, values, worldview, and identity. A sampling of such questions follows. Before actually posing these or other questions with assessees, some caveats are in order. Keep in mind the critical importance of rapport when conducting an interview. Be sensitive to cultural differences in readiness to engage in self-disclosure about family or other matters that may be perceived as too personal to discuss with a stranger. Be ready and able to change the wording of these questions should you need to facilitate the assessee's understanding of them, and to change the order of these questions should an assessee respond to more than one question in the same response. Listen carefully and do not hesitate to probe for more information if you perceive value in doing so. Finally, note that the relevance of each of these questions will vary with the background and unique socialization experiences of each assessee.

- Describe yourself.
- Describe your family. Who lives at home?
- Describe roles in your family, such as the role of mother, the role of father, the role of grandmother, the role of child, and so forth.

- What traditions, rituals, or customs were passed down to you by family members?
- What traditions, rituals, or customs do you think it is important to pass to the next generation?
- With regard to your family situation, what obligations do you see yourself as having?
- What obligations does your family have to you?
- What role does your family play in everyday life?
- How does the role of males and females differ from your own cultural perspective?
- What kind of music do you like?
- What kinds of foods do you eat most routinely?
- What do you consider fun things to do? When do you do these things?
- Describe yourself in the way that you think most other people would describe you. How would you say your own self-description would differ from that description?
- How might you respond to the question "Who are you?" with reference to your own sense of personal identity?
- With which cultural group or groups do you identify most? Why?
- What aspect of the history of the group with which you most identify is most significant to you? Why?
- Who are some of the people who have influenced you most?

Yearbook. Perhaps the most appropriate use of many of these tests would be to derive hypotheses for future testing by means of other tools of assessment. Unless compelling evidence exists to attest to the use of a particular instrument with members of a specific population, data derived from any of these tests and questionnaires should not be used alone to make selection, treatment, placement, or other momentous decisions. Some of our own thoughts on assessing acculturation and related variables are presented in the *Close-up.*

Intimately entwined with acculturation is the learning of *values.* **Values** are that which an individual prizes or the ideals an individual believes in. An early systematic treatment of the subject of values came in a book entitled *Types of Men* (Spranger, 1928), which listed different types of people based on whether they valued things like truth, practicality, and power. The book served as an inspiration for a yet more systematic treatment of the subject (Allport et al., 1951). Before long, a number of different systems for listing and categorizing values had been published.

- What are some things that have happened to you in the past that have influenced you most?
- What sources of satisfaction are associated with being you?
- What sources of dissatisfaction or conflict are associated with being you?
- What do you call yourself when asked about your ethnicity?
- What are your feelings regarding your racial and ethnic identity?
- Describe your most pleasant memory as a child.
- Describe your least pleasant memory as a child.
- Describe the ways in which you typically learn new things. In what ways might cultural factors have influenced this learning style?
- Describe the ways you typically resolve conflicts with other people. What influence might cultural factors have on this way of resolving conflicts?
- How would you describe your general view of the world?
- How would you characterize human nature in general?
- How much control do you believe you have over the things that happen to you? Why?
- How much control do you believe you have over your health? Your mental health?
- What are your thoughts regarding the role of work in daily life? Has your cultural identity influenced your views about work in any way? If so, how?

- How would you characterize the role of doctors in the world around you?
- How would you characterize the role of lawyers in the world around you?
- How would you characterize the role of politicians in the world around you?
- How would you characterize the role of spirituality in your daily life?
- What are your feelings about the use of illegal drugs?
- What is the role of play in daily life?
- How would you characterize the ideal relationship between human beings and nature?
- What defines a person who has power?
- What happens when one dies?
- Do you tend to live your life more in the past, the present, or the future? What influences on you do you think helped shape this way of living?
- How would you characterize your attitudes and feelings about the older people in your family? Older people in society in general?
- Describe your thinking about the local police and the criminal justice system.
- How do you see yourself ten years from now?

Rokeach (1973) differentiated what he called *instrumental* from *terminal* values. **Instrumental values** are guiding principles to help one attain some objective. Honesty, imagination, ambition, and cheerfulness are examples of instrumental values. **Terminal values** are guiding principles and a mode of behavior that is an end-point objective. A *comfortable life,* an *exciting life,* a *sense of accomplishment,* and *self-respect* are some examples of terminal values. Other value-categorization systems focus on values in specific contexts, such as employment settings. Values such as financial reward, job security, or prestige may figure prominently in decisions regarding occupational choice and employment or feelings of job satisfaction.

JUST THINK . . .

What values figure prominently in your own career choice?

Writing from an anthropological/cultural perspective, Kluckhohn (1954, 1960; Kluckhohn & Strodtbeck, 1961) conceived of values as answers to key questions with which civilizations must grapple. So, for example, from questions about how the individual should relate to the group, values emerge about individual versus group priorities. In one culture, the answers to such questions might take the form of norms and sanctions that encourage strict conformity and little competition among group members. In another culture, norms and sanctions may encourage individuality and competition among group members. In this context, one can begin to appreciate how members of different cultural groups can grow up with vastly different values, ranging from views on various "isms" (such as individualism versus collectivism) to views on what is trivial and what is worth dying for. The different values people from various cultures bring to the assessment situation may translate into widely varying motivational and incentive systems. Understanding an individual's values is an integral part of understanding personality.

Also intimately tied to the concept of acculturation is the concept of personal identity. **Identity** in this context may be defined as a set of cognitive and behavioral characteristics by which individuals define themselves as members of a particular group. Stated simply, identity refers to one's sense of self. Levine and Padilla (1980) defined **identification** as a process by which an individual assumes a pattern of behavior characteristic of other people, and referred to it as one of the "central issues that ethnic minority groups must deal with" (p. 13). Echoing this sentiment, Zuniga (1988) suggested that a question such as "What do you call yourself when asked about your ethnicity?" might be used as an icebreaker when assessing identification. She went on:

> How a minority client handles their response offers evidence of their comfortableness with their identity. A Mexican-American client who responds by saying, "I am an American, and I am just like everyone else," displays a defensiveness that demands gentle probing. One client sheepishly declared that she always called herself Spanish. She used this self-designation since she felt the term "Mexican" was dirty. (p. 291)

Another key culture-related personality variable concerns how an assessee tends to view the world. As its name implies, **worldview** is the unique way people interpret and make sense of their perceptions as a consequence of their learning experiences, cultural background, and related variables.

Our overview of personality began with a consideration of some superficial, lay perspectives on this multifaceted subject. We made reference to the now-classic rock oldie "Personality" and its "definition" of personality in terms of observable variables such as *walk, talk, smile,* and *charm.* Here, at the end of the chapter, we have come a long way in considering more personal, nonobservable elements of personality in the form of constructs such as *worldview, identification, values,* and *acculturation.* In the chapter that follows, we take a closer look at the tools used to assess personality.

Self-Assessment

Test your understanding of elements of this chapter by seeing if you can explain each of the following terms, expressions, and abbreviations:

acculturation	empirical criterion keying	identification
acquiescence	error of central tendency	identity
Big Five	forced-choice format	idiographic approach
control group (for the MMPI)	frame of reference	impression management
criterion	generosity (leniency) error	instrumental values
criterion group	halo effect	locus of control

MMPI
MMPI-A
MMPI-2
NEO PI-R
nomothetic approach
personality
personality assessment
personality profile
personality type
profile

profile analysis
profiler
Q-sort technique
response style
self-concept
self-concept differentiation
self-concept measure
self-report
semantic differential
severity error

state
structured interview
terminal values
trait
Type A personality
Type B personality
validity scale
values
Welsh code
worldview

Web Watch

Check out the following Web sites for more information about topics discussed in this chapter.

The NEO PI-R
www.psychpage.com/objective/neopir.html

www.rpp.on.ca/neopir.htm

The MMPI
http://alpha.fdu.edu/psychology/horror_
evaluation.htm

www.aaml.org/MMPI.htm

www.falseallegations.com/mmpi-bw.htm

The MMPI-2
www.pearsonassessments.com/tests/mmpi_2.htm

www.falseallegations.com/mmpi-bw.htm

The MMPI-A
www.pearsonassessments.com/tests/mmpia.htm

The Self-Directed Search
www.self-directed-search.com/Holland.html

**Assorted online personality tests
(usual cautions apply)**
http://psychology.about.com/library/jv/bljv_pers
.htm?once=true&

www.od-online.com/app/profiler-intro.asp

www.outofservice.com/bigfive

12

Personality Assessment Methods

Some people see the world as filled with love and goodness, where others see hate and evil. Some people equate *living* with behavioral excess, whereas others strive for moderation in all things. Some people have relatively realistic perceptions of themselves. Others labor under grossly distorted self-images and inaccurate perceptions of family, friends, and acquaintances. For psychologists and others interested in exploring differences among people with regard to these and other dimensions, many different tools are available. In this chapter, we survey some of the tools of personality assessment, including projective methods of assessment and behavioral assessment. We begin with objective methods.

JUST THINK . . .

How objective are objective methods of assessment?

Objective Methods

Typically associated with paper-and-pencil and computer-administered personality tests, **objective methods of personality assessment** characteristically contain short-answer items for which the assessee's task is to select one response from the two or more provided, and scoring is done according to set procedures involving little, if any, judgment on the part of the scorer. As with tests of ability, objective methods of personality assessment may include items written in a multiple-choice, true/false, or matching format.

Whereas a particular response on an objective ability test may be scored *correct* or *incorrect,* a response on an objective personality test is scored with reference to either the personality characteristic(s) being measured or the validity of the respondent's pattern of responses. For example, on a personality test where a *true* response is deemed indicative of the presence of a particular trait, a number of *true* responses to *true/false* items will be interpreted with reference to the presumed strength of that trait in the testtaker. Well, maybe.

If the respondent has also responded *true* to items indicative of the *absence* of the trait as well as to items rarely endorsed as such by testtakers, the validity of the protocol will be called into question. Scrutiny of the protocol may suggest an irregularity of some sort. For example, the items may have been responded to inconsistently, in random fashion, or with a *true* response to all questions. As we saw in the previous chapter, some objective personality tests are constructed with validity scales or other devices (such as a forced-choice format), designed to detect or deter response patterns that would call into question the meaningfulness of the scores.

Objective personality tests share many advantages with objective tests of ability. The items can be answered quickly, allowing the administration of many items covering varied aspects of the trait or traits the test is designed to assess. If the items on an objective test are well written, they require little explanation; this makes them very suitable for both group and computerized administration. Objective items can usually be scored quickly and reliably by varied means, from hand-scoring (usually with the aid of a template held over the test form) to computer-scoring. Analysis and interpretation of such tests may be almost as fast as scoring, especially if conducted by computer and custom software.

Although objective personality test items share many characteristics with objective measures of ability, we hasten to add that the adjective *objective* is something of a misnomer as applied to personality testing and assessment. With reference to short-answer items on *ability* tests, the term *objective* gained favor because all items contained only one correct response. Well, that was not always true either, but that's the way they were designed.

In contrast to the scoring of, say, essay tests, the scoring of objective, multiple-choice tests of ability left little room for emotion, bias, or favoritism on the part of the test scorer. Scoring was dispassionate and—for lack of a better term—objective. But unlike objective ability tests, objective personality tests typically contain no one correct answer. Rather, the selection of a particular choice from multiple-choice items provides information relevant to something about the testtaker, such as the presence, absence, or strength of a personality-related variable. Yes, the scoring of such tests can still be dispassionate and objective. However, the "objectivity" of the score derived from a so-called objective test of personality can be a matter of debate. Consider, for example, a personality test written in an objective test format designed to detect the existence of an unresolved oedipal conflict. The extent to which these test results will be viewed as "objective" is inextricably linked to one's views about the validity of psychoanalytic theory and, more specifically, the construct *oedipal conflict*.

Another issue related to the use of the adjective *objective* to modify *personality test* has to do with self-report—and the distinct lack of objectivity that can be associated with it. Testtakers' self-reports of what they like or dislike, what they agree or disagree with, what they do or do not do, and so forth, can be anything but "objective" for many reasons. Some respondents may lack the insight to respond in what could reasonably be described as an objective manner. Some respondents respond in a manner they believe will place them in the best or worst possible light, depending on their goal. In other words, they can attempt to manage impressions by faking good or faking bad.

Ultimately, the term *objective* as applied to most personality tests may be best thought of as a shorthand description for a test format. Objective personality tests are objective in the sense that they employ a short-answer, typically multiple-choice format, one that provides little, if any, room for discretion in terms of scoring. To describe a personality test as objective serves to distinguish it from projective and other measurement methods rather than to impart information about the reality, tangibility, or objectivity of scores derived from it. However, as we will see in our discussion of projective methods, tests can be objective in format as well as projective.

Projective Methods

Suppose the lights in your classroom were dimmed and everyone was told to stare at the clean chalkboard for a minute or so. And suppose everyone was then asked to take out some paper and write down what he or she thought could be seen on the chalkboard, other than the chalkboard itself. If you examined what each of your fellow students wrote, you might find as many different things as there were students responding. You could assume that the students saw on the chalkboard—or more accurately, *projected* onto the chalkboard—something that was not really there but rather in (or on) their own minds. You might further assume that each student's response to the blank chalkboard reflected something very telling about the student's personality structure.

The **projective hypothesis** holds that an individual supplies structure to unstructured stimuli in a manner consistent with the individual's own unique pattern of conscious and unconscious needs, fears, desires, impulses, conflicts, and ways of perceiving and responding. In like manner, we may define **projective method** as a technique of personality assessment in which some judgment of the assessee's personality is made on the basis of performance on a task that involves supplying some sort of structure to relatively unstructured or incomplete stimuli. Almost any relatively unstructured stimulus will do for this purpose. In a scene in Shakespeare's play *Hamlet*, Polonius and Hamlet discuss what can be seen in clouds. Indeed, clouds could be used as a projective stimulus.[1] But psychologists, slaves to practicality (and scientific methods) as they are, have developed projective measures of personality that are more reliable than clouds and more portable than chalkboards. Inkblots, pictures, words, drawings, and other things have been used as projective stimuli.

JUST THINK . . .

Name something else that could be used as a projective stimulus for personality assessment purposes. Outline briefly how you might attempt to validate this new test.

Unlike self-report methods, projective tests are *indirect* methods of personality assessment. The examinee's task may be to talk about something or someone other than herself or himself, and inferences about the examinee's personality are made from the response. On such a task, the ability—and presumably the inclination—of examinees to fake is greatly minimized. Also somewhat minimized on some projective tasks is the testtaker's need for great proficiency in the English language. Minimal language skills are required to respond to or create a drawing. For that reason, and because some projective methods may be less linked to culture than are other measures of personality, proponents of projective testing believe that there is a promise of cross-cultural utility with these tests that has yet to be fulfilled. Proponents of projective measures also argue that a major advantage of such measures is that they tap unconscious as well as conscious material. In the words of the man who coined the term *projective methods,* "the most important things about an individual are what he cannot or will not say" (Frank, 1939, p. 395).[2]

Projective tests were born in the spirit of rebellion against normative data and through attempts by personality researchers to break down the study of personality into the study of specific traits of varying strengths. This orientation is exemplified by Frank

---

1. In fact, clouds *have* been used as projective stimuli. Wilhelm Stern's Cloud Picture Test, in which subjects were asked to tell what they saw in pictures of clouds, was one of the earliest projective measures.

2. The first published use of the term *projective methods* that we are aware of was in an article entitled "Projective Methods in the Psychological Study of Children" by Ruth Horowitz and Lois Barclay Murphy (1938). However, these authors had read Lawrence K. Frank's (1939) as-yet-unpublished manuscript and credited him for having "applied the term 'projective methods.'"

(1939), who reflected, "It is interesting to see how the students of personality have attempted to meet the problem of individuality with methods and procedures designed for study of uniformities and norms that ignore or subordinate individuality, treating it as a troublesome deviation which derogates from the real, the superior, and only important central tendency, mode, average, etc." (pp. 392–393).

In contrast to methods of personality assessment that focused on the individual from a statistics-based, normative perspective, projective techniques were once the technique of choice for focusing on the individual from a purely clinical perspective—a perspective that examined the unique way an individual projects onto an ambiguous stimulus "his way of seeing life, his meanings, significances, patterns, and especially his feelings" (Frank, 1939, p. 403). As we will see, however, years of clinical experience with these tests and a growing volume of research data have led interpretation of responses to projective stimuli to become increasingly norm referenced.

Inkblots as Projective Stimuli

Spill some ink in the center of a blank, white sheet of paper and fold it over. Allow to dry. There you have the recipe for an inkblot. Inkblots are not only used by assessment professionals as projective stimuli, they are very much associated with psychology itself in the public eye. The most famous inkblot test is, of course . . .

The Rorschach   Hermann Rorschach (Figure 12–1) developed what he called a "form interpretation test" using inkblots as the forms to be interpreted. In 1921, he published his monograph on the technique, *Psychodiagnostics.* In the last section of that monograph, Rorschach proposed applications of his test to personality assessment. He provided 28 case studies employing normal (well, undiagnosed) subjects and people with various psychiatric diagnoses (including neurosis, psychosis, and manic-depressive illness) to illustrate his test. Rorschach died suddenly and unexpectedly at the age of 38, just a year after his book was published. A paper co-authored by Rorschach and Emil Oberholzer entitled "The Application of the Form Interpretation Test" was published posthumously in 1923.

Figure 12–1
Herman Rorschach (1884–1922)

Rorschach was a Swiss psychiatrist whose father had been an art teacher and whose interests included art as well as psychoanalysis—particularly the work of Carl Jung, who had written extensively on methods of bringing unconscious material to light. In 1913 Rorschach published papers on how analysis of a patient's artwork could provide insights into personality. Rorschach's inkblot test was published in 1921, and it was not an immediate success. Rorschach died of peritonitis the following year at the age of 38, unaware of the great legacy he would leave. For more on Hermann Rorschach, read his Test Developer Profile on our companion Internet site at www.mhhe.com/cohentesting6.

Figure 12–2
A Rorschach-Like Inkblot

Like Rorschach, we will refer to his test as just that—a test. However, students should be aware of controversy about whether it is properly a test, a method, a technique, or something else. For example, Goldfried et al. (1971) view the Rorschach as a structured interview, and Korchin and Schuldberg (1981) regard it as "less of a test" and more "an open and flexible arena for studying interpersonal transactions" (p. 1151). There has also been debate about whether or not the Rorschach is properly considered a projective instrument (Acklin, 1995; Aronow et al., 1995; Moreland et al., 1995b; Ritzler, 1995). For example, John Exner, an authority on all things Rorschach, argued that the inkblots are "not completely ambiguous," that the task does not necessarily "force projection," and that "unfortunately, the Rorschach has been erroneously mislabeled a projective test for far too long" (1989, pp. 526–527; see also Exner, 1997). Regardless, *Rorschach* remains virtually synonymous with *projective test* among assessment professionals.

The Rorschach consists of ten bilaterally symmetrical (that is, mirror-imaged if folded in half) inkblots printed on separate cards. Five inkblots are achromatic (meaning without color, or black-and-white). Two inkblots are black, white, and red. The remaining three inkblots are multicolored. The test comes with the cards only; there is no test manual or any administration, scoring, or interpretation instructions. There is no rationale for why some of the inkblots are achromatic and others are chromatic (with color). Unlike most psychological test kits, which today are published complete with test manual and optional, upgradable carrying case, this test contains 10 cards packaged in a cardboard box; that's it.

To fill the need for a test manual and instructions for administration, scoring, and interpretation, a number of manuals and handbooks set forth a variety of methods (such as Aronow & Reznikoff, 1976, 1983; Beck, 1944, 1945, 1952, 1960; Exner, 1974, 1978, 1986; Exner & Weiner, 1982; Klopfer & Davidson, 1962; Lerner, 1991, 1996a, 1996b; Piotrowski, 1957). The system most widely used is the "comprehensive system" devised by Exner. We will discuss Exner's system shortly; first, here is a very general description of the process of administering, scoring, and interpreting the Rorschach.

Inkblot cards (Figure 12–2) are initially presented to the testtaker one at a time in numbered order from 1 to 10. The testtaker is instructed to tell what is on each of the cards with a question such as "What might this be?" Testtakers have a great deal of freedom with the Rorschach. They may, for example, rotate the cards and vary the number and length of their responses to each card. The examiner records all relevant information, including the testtaker's verbatim responses, nonverbal gestures, the length of time before the first response to each card, the position of the card, and so forth. The examiner does not engage in any discussion concerning the testtaker's responses during the initial administration of the cards. Every effort is made to provide the testtaker with the opportunity to *project,* free from any outside distractions.

After the entire set of cards has been administered once, a second administration, referred to as the **inquiry,** is conducted. During the inquiry, the examiner attempts to determine what features of the inkblot played a role in formulating the testtaker's **percept** (perception of an image). Questions such as "What made it look like (whatever)?" and "How do you see (whatever it is that the testtaker reported seeing)?" are asked in an attempt to clarify what was seen and which aspects of the inkblot were most influential in forming the perception. The inquiry provides information that is useful in scoring and interpreting the responses. The examiner also learns whether the testtaker remembers earlier responses, whether the original percept is still seen, and whether any new responses are now perceived.

A third component of the administration, referred to as **testing the limits,** may also be included. This procedure enables the examiner to restructure the situation by asking specific questions that provide additional information concerning personality functioning. If, for example, the testtaker has utilized the entire inkblot when forming percepts throughout the test, the examiner might want to determine if details within the inkblot could be elaborated on. Under those conditions, the examiner might say, "Sometimes people use a part of the blot to see something." Alternatively, the examiner might point to a specific area of the card and ask, "What does this look like?"

Other objectives of limit-testing procedures are (1) to identify any confusion or misunderstanding concerning the task, (2) to aid the examiner in determining if the testtaker is able to refocus percepts given a new frame of reference, and (3) to see if a testtaker made anxious by the ambiguous nature of the task is better able to perform given this added structure. At least one Rorschach researcher has advocated the technique of trying to elicit one last response from testtakers who think they have already given as many responses as they are going to give (Cerney, 1984). The rationale was that endings have many meanings, and the one last response may provide a source of questions and inferences applicable to treatment considerations.

JUST THINK . . .

The Rorschach is viewed by some as more of a structured interview than a test. What arguments could be made to support that point of view?

Hypotheses concerning personality functioning will be formed on the basis of all the variables we have outlined (such as the content of the response, the location of the response, the length of time to respond), plus many additional ones. In general, Rorschach protocols are scored according to several categories, including location, determinants, content, popularity, and form. *Location* is the part of the inkblot that was utilized in forming the percept. Individuals may use the entire inkblot, a large section, a small section, a minute detail, or white spaces. *Determinants* are the qualities of the inkblot that determine what the individual perceives. Form, color, shading, or movement that the individual attributes to the inkblot are all considered determinants. *Content* is the content category of the response. Different scoring systems vary in some of the categories scored. Some typical content areas include human figures, animal figures, anatomical parts, blood, clouds, X-rays, and sexual responses. *Popularity* refers to the frequency with which a certain response has been found to correspond with a particular inkblot or section of an inkblot. A popular response is one that has frequently been obtained from the general population. A rare response is one that has been perceived infrequently by the general population. The *form* of a response is how accurately the individual's perception matches or fits the corresponding part of the inkblot. Form level may be evaluated as being adequate or inadequate, or good or poor.

The scoring categories are considered to correspond to various aspects of personality functioning. Hypotheses concerning aspects of personality are based both on the number of responses that fall within each category and on the interrelationships among the categories. For example, the number of whole responses (using the entire inkblot) in a Rorschach record is typically associated with conceptual thought process. Form level is associated with reality testing. Accordingly, psychotic patients would be expected to achieve low scores for form level. Human movement has been associated with creative imagination. Color responses have been associated with emotional reactivity.

Patterns of response, recurrent themes, and the interrelationships among the different scoring categories are all considered in arriving at a final description of the individual from a Rorschach protocol. Data concerning the responses of various clinical and nonclinical groups of adults, adolescents, and children have been compiled in various books and research publications.

Rorschach's form interpretation test was in its infancy at the time of its developer's death. The orphaned work-in-progress found a receptive home in the United States, where it was nurtured by several different schools, each with its own vision of how the test should be administered, scored, and interpreted. In this sense, the Rorschach is, as McDowell and Acklin (1996, p. 308) characterized it, "an anomaly in the field of psychological measurement when compared to objective and other projective techniques."

Although the test is widely referred to as "the Rorschach" as though it were a standardized test, Rorschach practitioners and researchers have for many years employed a variety of Rorschach systems—on some occasions picking and choosing interpretive criteria from one or more systems. Consider in this context a study by Saunders (1991), which focused on Rorschach indicators of child abuse. Saunders (1991, p. 55) wrote, "Rorschach protocols were scored using Rapaport et al.'s (1945–46) system as the basic framework, but special scores of four different types were added. I borrowed two of these additional measures from other researchers . . . and developed the other two specifically for this study." Given the variation that existed in terminology and in administration and scoring practices, one readily appreciates how difficult it might be to muster consistent and credible evidence for the test's psychometric soundness.[3]

In a book that reviewed several Rorschach systems, Exner wrote of the advisability of approaching "the Rorschach problem through a research integration of the systems" (1969, p. 251). Exner would subsequently develop such an integration, a "comprehensive system," as he called it (Exner 1974, 1978, 1986, 1990, 1991, 1993; Exner & Weiner, 1982, 1995; see also Handler, 1996), for the test's administration, scoring, and interpretation. Exner's system has been well received by clinicians and is probably the system most used and most taught today.

Prior to the development of Exner's system and its widespread adoption by clinicians and researchers, evaluations of the Rorschach's psychometric soundness tended to be mixed at best. Exner's system brought a degree of uniformity to Rorschach use and thus facilitated "apples-to-apples" (or "bats-to-bats") comparison of research studies. Yet, regardless of the scoring system employed, there were a number of reasons why the evaluation of the psychometric soundness of the Rorschach was a tricky business. For example, because each inkblot is considered to have a unique stimulus quality, evaluation of reliability by a split-half method would be inappropriate. Of historical interest in

---

3. A test called the Holtzman Inkblot Technique (HIT; Holtzman et al., 1961) was designed to be more psychometrically sound than any existing inkblot test. A description of the HIT, as well as speculation as to why it never achieved the popularity and acceptance of the Rorschach, can be found in the companion workbook to this text, *Exercises in Psychological Testing and Assessment,* 6th Edition (Cohen, 2005).

this regard is the work of Behn, who, under Sigmund Freud's direction, attempted to develop a similar but not alternate form of the test called the Behn-Rorschach (Buckle & Holt, 1951; Eichler, 1951; Swift, 1944).

Traditional test-retest reliability procedures were also inappropriate for use with the Rorschach. This is so because of the effect of familiarity on response to the cards and because responses may reflect transient states as opposed to enduring traits. Relevant to the discussion of the Rorschach's reliability is Exner's (1983) reflection that "some Comprehensive System scores defy the axiom that something cannot be valid unless it is also reliable" (p. 411).

The widespread acceptance of Exner's system has advanced the cause of Rorschach reliability. Well, inter-scorer reliability, anyway. Exner, as well as others, have provided ample evidence that acceptable levels of inter-scorer reliability can be attained with the Rorschach. Using Exner's system, McDowell and Acklin (1996) reported an overall

JUST THINK . . .

Is it possible for scores on a test to defy the axiom that the score cannot be valid unless it is reliable?

mean percentage agreement of 87% among Rorschach scorers. Still, as these researchers cautioned, "The complex types of data developed by the Rorschach introduce formidable obstacles to the application of standard procedures and canons of test development" (pp. 308–309). Far more pessimistic about such "formidable obstacles" and far less subtle in their conclusions were Hunsley and Bailey (1999). After reviewing the literature on the clinical utility of the Rorschach, they wrote of "meager support from thousands of publications" and expressed doubt that evidence would ever be developed that the Rorschach or the Comprehensive System could "contribute, in routine clinical practice, to scientifically informed psychological assessment" (p. 274).

Countering such pessimism are other reviews of the literature that are far more favorable to this test (Bornstein, 1998, 1999; Ganellen, 1996; Meyer & Handler, 1997; Viglione, 1999). In their meta-analysis designed to compare the validity of the Rorschach with that of the MMPI, Hiller et al. (1999) concluded that "on average, both tests work about equally well when used for purposes deemed appropriate by experts" (p. 293). In a similar vein, Stricker and Gold (1999, p. 240) reflected that

> a test is not valid or invalid; rather, there are as many validity coefficients as there are purposes for which the test is used. The Rorschach can demonstrate its utility for several purposes and can be found wanting for several others.

They went on to argue for an approach to assessment that incorporated many different types of methods:

> Arguably, Walt Whitman's greatest poem was entitled "Song of Myself." We believe that everything that is done by the person being assessed is a song of the self. The Rorschach is one instrument available to the clinician, who has the task of hearing all of the music. (Stricker & Gold, 1999, p. 249)

Decades ago, Jensen (1965, p. 509) opined that "the rate of scientific progress in clinical psychology might well be measured by the speed and thoroughness with which it gets over the Rorschach." If this statement were true, then the rate of scientific progress in clinical psychology could be characterized as a crawl. The Rorschach remains one of the most frequently used and frequently taught psychological tests. It is widely used in forensic work and generally accepted by the courts. As Weiner (1997) concluded in his evaluation of the status of the Rorschach at age 75, "Widely used and highly valued by clinicians and researchers in many countries of the world, it appears despite its fame

JUST THINK . . .

"If the Rorschach has anything at all going for it, it has great intuitive appeal." Explain.

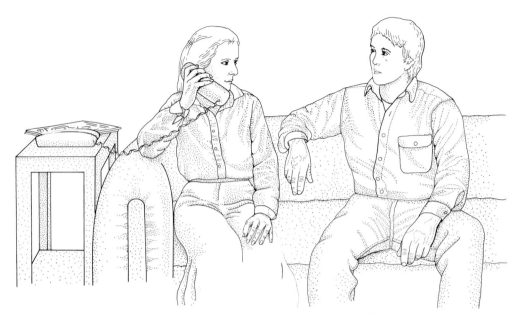

Figure 12–3
Ambiguous Picture for Use in Projective Storytelling Task

not yet to have received the academic respect it deserves and, it can be hoped, will someday enjoy" (p. 17).

Pictures as Projective Stimuli

Look at Figure 12–3. Now make up a story about it. Your story should have a beginning, a middle, and an end. Write it down, using as much paper as you need. Bring the story to class with you and compare it with some other student's story. What does the story reveal about your needs, fears, desires, impulse control, ways of viewing the world—your personality? What does the story written by your classmate reveal about her or him?

This exercise introduces you to the use of pictures as projective stimuli. Pictures used as projective stimuli may be photos of real people, animals, objects, or anything. They may be paintings, drawings, etchings, or any other variety of picture.

One of the earliest uses of pictures as projective stimuli came at the beginning of the twentieth century. Long before the men-are-from-Mars-women-are-from-Venus stuff, sex differences were reported in the stories that children gave in response to nine pictures (Brittain, 1907). The author reported that the girls were more interested in religious and moral themes than the boys were. Another early experiment using pictures and a storytelling technique investigated children's imagination. Differences in themes as a function of age were observed (Libby, 1908). In 1932, a psychiatrist working at the Clinic for Juvenile Research in Detroit developed the Social Situation Picture Test (Schwartz, 1932), a projective instrument that contained pictures relevant to juvenile delinquents. Working at the Harvard Psychological Clinic in 1935, Christiana D. Morgan (Figure 12–4) and Henry Murray (Figure 12–5) published the Thematic Apperception Test (TAT)—pronounced by saying the letters, not by rhyming with *cat*—the instrument that has come to be the most widely used of all the picture/storytelling projective tests.

Figure 12–4
Christiana D. Morgan (1897–1967)

On the box cover of the widely used TAT and in numerous other measurement-related books and articles, the authorship of the TAT is listed as "Henry A. Murray, Ph.D., and the Staff of the Harvard Psychological Clinic." However, the first articles describing the TAT were written by Christiana D. Morgan (Morgan, 1938) or Morgan and Murray with Morgan listed as senior author (Morgan & Murray, 1935, 1938). In a mimeographed manuscript in the Harvard University archives, an early version of the test was titled the "Morgan-Murray Thematic Apperception Test" (White et al., 1941). Wesley G. Morgan (1995) noted that because Christiana Morgan "had been senior author of the earlier publications, a question is raised about why her name was omitted as an author of the 1943 version" (p. 238). W. G. Morgan (1995) took up that and related questions in a brief but fascinating account of the origin and history of the TAT images. More on the life of Christiana Morgan can be found in Translate This Darkness: The Life of Christiana Morgan *(Douglas, 1993). Her Test Developer Profile can be found on our Internet site at www.mhhe.com/cohentesting6.*

The Thematic Apperception Test (TAT)   The TAT was originally designed as an aid to eliciting fantasy material from patients in psychoanalysis (Morgan & Murray, 1935). The stimulus materials consisted, as they do today, of 31 cards, one of which is blank. The 30 picture cards, all black-and-white, contain a variety of scenes designed to present the testtaker with "certain classical human situations" (Murray, 1943). Some of the pictures contain a lone individual, some contain a group of people, and some contain no people. Some of the pictures appear to be as real as a photo, and others are surrealistic drawings. Examinees are introduced to the examination with the cover story that it is a test of imagination in which it is their task to tell what events led up to the scene in the picture, what is happening at that moment, and what the outcome will be. Examinees are also asked to tell what the people depicted in the cards are thinking and feeling. If the blank card is administered, examinees are instructed to imagine that there is a picture on the card and then proceed to tell a story about it.

In the TAT Manual, Murray (1943) also advised examiners to attempt to find out the source of the examinee's story. It is noteworthy that the noun *apperception* is derived from

Figure 12–5
Henry A. Murray (1893–1988)

Henry Murray is perhaps best known for the influential theory of personality he developed, as well as for his role as author of the Thematic Apperception Test. Biographies of Murray have been written by Anderson (1990) and Robinson (1992). Murray's Test Developer Profile can be found on the Internet at www.mhhe.com/cohentesting6.

the verb **apperceive,** which may be defined as *to perceive in terms of past perceptions.* The source of a story could be a personal experience, a dream, an imagined event, a book, an episode of *South Park*—really most anything.

In clinical practice, examiners tend to take liberties with various elements pertaining to the administration, scoring, and interpretation of the TAT. For example, although 20 cards is the recommended number for presentation, in practice an examiner might administer as few as one or two cards or as many as all 31. If a clinician is assessing a patient who has a penchant for telling stories that fill reams of the clinician's notepad, it's a good bet that fewer cards will be administered. If, on the other hand, a patient tells brief, one-or two-sentence stories, more cards may be administered in an attempt to collect more raw data with which to work. Some of the cards are suggested for use with adult males, adult females, or both, and some are suggested for use with children. This is so because certain pictorial representations lend themselves more than others to identification and projection by members of these groups. In one study involving 75 males (25 each of 11-, 14-, and 17-year-olds), Cooper (1981) identified the ten most productive cards for use with adolescent males. In practice, however, any card—be it one recommended for use with males, with females, or with children—may be administered to any subject. The administering clinician selects the cards that he or she believes will elicit responses pertinent to the objective of the testing.

◆

JUST THINK . . .

And just imagine . . . describe a picture on a card that would really get *you* talking. What would you say?

The raw material used in drawing conclusions about the individual examined with the TAT are (1) the stories as they were told by the examinee, (2) the clinician's notes about the way or the manner in which the examinee responded to the cards, and (3) the clinician's notes about extra-test behavior and verbalizations. The last two categories of raw data (test and extra-test behavior) are sources of clinical interpretations for almost any individually administered test. Analysis of the story content requires special training. One illustration of how a testtaker's behavior during testing may influence the examiner's interpretations of the findings was provided by Sugarman (1991, p. 140), who

Table 12–1
A Description of the Sample TAT-Like Picture

Author's Description

A male and a female are seated in close proximity on a sofa. The female is talking on the phone. There is an end table with a magazine on it next to the sofa.

Manifest Stimulus Demand

Some explanation of the nature of the relationship between these two persons and some reason the woman is on the phone are required. Less frequently noted is the magazine on the table and its role in this scene.

Form Demand

Two large details, the woman and the man, must be integrated. Small details include the magazine and the telephone.

Latent Stimulus Demand

This picture is likely to elicit attitudes toward heterosexuality and, within that context, material relevant to the examinee's "place" on optimism-pessimism, security-insecurity, dependence-independence, passivity-assertiveness, and related continuums. Alternatively, attitudes toward family and friends may be elicited, with the two primary figures being viewed as brother and sister, the female talking on the phone to a family member, and so on.

Frequent Plots

We haven't administered this card to enough people to make judgments about what constitutes "frequent plots." We have, however, provided a sampling of plots (Table 12–2).

Significant Variations

Just as we cannot provide information on frequent plots, we cannot report data on significant variations. We would guess, however, that most college students viewing this picture would perceive the two individuals in it as being involved in a heterosexual relationship. Were that to be the case, a significant variation would be a story in which the characters are not involved in a heterosexual relationship (for example, they are employer/employee). Close clinical attention will also be paid to the nature of the relationship of the characters to any "introduced figures" (persons not pictured in the card but introduced into the story by the examinee). The "pull" of this card is to introduce the figure to whom the woman is speaking. What is the phone call about? How will the story be resolved?

---

told of a "highly narcissistic patient [who] demonstrated contempt and devaluation of the examiner (and presumably others) by dictating TAT stories complete with spelling and punctuation as though the examiner was a stenographer."

A number of systems for interpreting TAT data exist (for example, Thompson, 1986; Westen et al., 1988). Most of these interpretive systems incorporate or are to some degree based on Henry Murray's concepts of **need** (determinants of behavior arising from within the individual), **press** (determinants of behavior arising from within the environment), and **thema** (a unit of interaction between needs and press). In general, the guiding principle in interpreting TAT stories is that the testtaker is identifying with someone (the protagonist) in the story and that the needs, environmental demands, and conflicts of the protagonist in the story are in some way related to the concerns, hopes, fears, or desires of the examinee.

In his discussion of the TAT from the perspective of a clinician, William Henry (1956) examined each of the cards in the test with regard to such variables as *manifest stimulus demand, form demand, latent stimulus demand, frequent plots,* and *significant variations.* To get an idea of how some of these terms are used, look again at Figure 12–3— a picture that is *not* a TAT card—and then read Tables 12–1 and 12–2, which are descriptions of the card and some responses to the card from college-age respondents.

Table 12-2
Some Responses to the Sample Picture

Respondent	Story
1. (Male)	This guy has been involved with this girl for a few months. Things haven't been going all that well. He's suspected that she's been seeing a lot of guys. This is just one scene in a whole evening where the phone hasn't stopped ringing. Pretty soon he is just going to get up and leave.
2. (Female)	This couple is dating. They haven't made any plans for the evening, and they are wondering what they should do. She is calling up another couple to ask if they want to get together. They will go out with the other couple and have a good time.
3. (Male)	This girl thinks she is pregnant and is calling the doctor for the results of her test. This guy is pretty worried because he has plans to finish college and go to graduate school. He is afraid she will want to get married, and he doesn't want to get trapped into anything. The doctor will tell her she isn't pregnant, and he'll be really relieved.
4. (Female)	This couple has been dating for about two years, and they're very much in love. She's on the phone firming up plans for a down payment on a hall that's going to cater the wedding. That's a bridal magazine on the table over there. They look like they're really in love. I think things will work out for them even though the odds are against it—the divorce rates and all.
5. (Male)	These are two very close friends. The guy has a real problem and needs to talk to someone. He is feeling really depressed and that he is all alone in the world. Every time he starts to tell her how he feels, the phone rings. Pretty soon he will leave feeling like no one has time for him and even more alone. I don't know what will happen to him, but it doesn't look good.

Although a clinician may obtain bits of information from the stories told about every individual card, the clinician's final impressions will usually derive from a consideration of the overall patterns of themes that emerge.

As with the Rorschach and many other projective techniques, a debate between academics and practitioners regarding the psychometric soundness of the TAT has been unceasing through the years. Because of the general lack of standardization and uniformity with which administration, scoring, and interpretation procedures tend to be applied in everyday clinical practice, concern on psychometric grounds is clearly justified. However, in experimental tests where trained examiners use the same procedures and scoring systems, inter-rater reliability coefficients can range from adequate to impressive (Stricker & Healy, 1990).

JUST THINK . . .

Why are split-half, test-retest, and alternate-form reliability measures inappropriate for use with the TAT?

Research suggests that situational factors, including who the examiner is, how the test is administered, and the testtaker's experiences prior to and during the test's administration, may affect test responses. Additionally, transient internal need states such as hunger, thirst, fatigue, and higher than ordinary levels of sexual tension can affect a testtaker's responses. Different TAT cards have different stimulus "pulls" (Murstein & Mathes, 1996). Some pictures are more likely than others to elicit stories with themes of despair, for example. Given that the pictures have different stimulus "pulls" or, more technically stated, different latent stimulus demands, it becomes difficult if not impossible to determine the inter-item (read "inter-card") reliability of the test. Card 1 might reliably elicit themes of need for achievement, whereas card 16, for example, might not typically elicit any such themes. The possibility of widely variable story lengths in response to the cards presents yet another challenge to the documentation of inter-item reliability.

Conflicting opinions are presented in the scholarly literature concerning the validity of the TAT, including the validity of its assumptions and the validity of various ap-

Table 12–3
Some Picture-Story Tests

Picture-Story Test	Description
Thompson (1949) modification of the original TAT	Designed specifically for use with African American testtakers, with pictures containing both Black and White protagonists.
TEMAS (Malgady et al., 1984)	Designed for use with urban Hispanic children, with drawings of scenes relevant to their experience.
Children's Apperception Test (CAT; Bellak, 1971) (first published in 1949)	Designed for use with ages 3 to 10 and based on the idea that animals engaged in various activities were useful in stimulating projective storytelling by children.
Children's Apperception Test-Human (CAT-H; Bellak & Bellak, 1965)	A version of the CAT based on the idea that depending on the maturity of the child, a more clinically valuable response might be obtained with humans instead of animals in the pictures.
Senior Apperception Technique (SAT; Bellak & Bellak, 1973)	Picture-story test depicting themes relevant to older adults.
The Picture Story Test (Symonds, 1949)	For use with adolescents, with pictures designed to elicit adolescent-related themes such as coming home late and leaving home.
Education Apperception Test (Thompson & Sones, 1973) and the School Apperception Method (Solomon & Starr, 1968)	Two independent tests, listed here together because both were designed to tap school-related themes.
The Michigan Picture Test (Andrew et al., 1953)	For ages 8 to 14, contains pictures designed to elicit various themes ranging from conflict with authority to feelings of personal inadequacy.
Roberts Apperception Test for Children (RATC; McArthur & Roberts, 1982)	Designed to elicit a variety of developmental themes such as family confrontation, parental conflict, parental affection, attitudes toward school, and peer action.
Children's Apperceptive Story-Telling Test (CAST; Schneider, 1989)	Theory-based test based on the work of Alfred Adler.
Blacky Pictures Test (Blum, 1950)	Psychoanalytically based, cartoon-like items featuring Blacky the Dog.
Make a Picture Story Method (Shneidman, 1952)	For ages 6 and up, respondents construct their own pictures from cutout materials included in the test kit and then tell a story.

plications (Barends et al., 1990; Cramer, 1996; Gluck, 1955; Hibbard et al., 1994; Kagan, 1956; Keiser & Prather, 1990; Mussen & Naylor, 1954; Ronan et al., 1995; Worchel & Dupree, 1990). Although the relationship between expression of fantasy stories and real-life behavior is tentative at best, and although the TAT is highly susceptible to faking, the test is widely used by practitioners. Yet, in contrast to the test's apparently widespread use stand the findings of one survey of training directors of APA-approved programs in clinical psychology: The majority of these programs place very little emphasis on the test and typically rely on psychoanalytic writings in their teaching of it (Rossini & Moretti, 1997).

The rationale for the TAT and many published picture-story tests like it (Table 12–3) is that they have great intuitive appeal. It does make sense that people would project their own motivation when asked to construct a story from an ambiguous stimulus. Another appeal for users of this test is that it is the clinician who tailors the test administration by selecting the cards and the nature of the inquiry—an undoubtedly welcome feature in the era of standardization, computer-adaptive testing, and computer-generated narrative summaries. But as with many projective tests, it seems the TAT must ulti-

> **JUST THINK . . .**
>
> Should all tests be measured by the same "psychometric yardstick"?

mately be judged by a different, more clinically than psychometrically oriented standard if its contribution to personality assessment is to be fully appreciated.

Figure 12–6
Sample Item From the Rosenzweig
Picture-Frustration Study

Other tests using pictures as projective stimuli   A projective technique called the Hand Test (Wagner, 1983) consists of nine cards with pictures of hands on them and a tenth blank card. The testtaker is asked what the hands on each card might be doing. When presented with the blank card, the testtaker is instructed to imagine a pair of hands on the card and then describe what they might be doing. Testtakers may make several responses to each card, and all responses are recorded. Responses are interpreted according to 24 categories such as affection, dependence, and aggression.

Another projective technique, the Rosenzweig Picture-Frustration Study (Rosenzweig, 1945, 1978), employs cartoons depicting frustrating situations (Figure 12–6). The testtaker's task is to fill in the response of the cartoon figure being frustrated. The test, which is based on the assumption that the testtaker will identify with the person being frustrated, is available in forms for children, adolescents, and adults. Young children respond orally to the pictures, whereas older testtakers may respond either orally or in writing. An inquiry period is suggested after administration of all of the pictures in order to clarify the responses.

Test responses are scored in terms of the type of reaction elicited and the direction of the aggression expressed. The direction of the aggression may be *intropunitive* (aggression turned inward), *extrapunitive* (outwardly expressed), or *inpunitive* (aggression is evaded so as to avoid or gloss over the situation). Reactions are grouped into categories such as *obstacle dominance* (in which the response concentrates on the frustrating barrier), *ego defense* (in which attention is focused on protecting the frustrated person), and *need persistence* (in which attention is focused on solving the frustrating problem). For each scoring category, the percentage of responses is calculated and compared with normative data. A group conformity rating (GCR) is derived representing the degree to which one's responses conform to or are typical of those of the standardization group. The test has captured the imagination of researchers for decades, although questions remain concerning how reactions to cartoons depicting frustrating situations are related to real-life situations.

One variation of the picture-story method may appeal to "old school" clinicians as well as to clinicians who thrive on normative data with all of the companion statistics.

The Apperceptive Personality Test (APT; Karp et al., 1990) represents an attempt to address some long-standing criticisms of the TAT as a projective instrument while introducing objectivity into the scoring system. The test consists of eight stimulus cards "depicting recognizable people in everyday settings" (Holmstrom et al., 1990, p. 252), including males and females of different ages as well as minority group members. This, by the way, is in contrast to the TAT stimulus cards, some of which depict fantastic or unreal types of scenes.[4] Another difference between the APT and the TAT is the emotional tone and draw of the stimulus cards. A long-standing criticism of the TAT cards has been their negative or gloomy tone, which might work to restrict the range of affect projected by a testtaker (Garfield & Eron, 1948; Ritzler et al., 1980). After telling a story about each of the APT pictures orally or in writing, testtakers respond to a series of multiple-choice questions. In addition to supplying quantitative information, the questionnaire segment of the test was designed to fill in information gaps from stories that are too brief or cryptic to otherwise score. Responses are thus subjected to both clinical and actuarial interpretation and may, in fact, be scored and interpreted with computer software.

Every picture tells a story—well, hopefully for the sake of the clinician or researcher trying to collect data—otherwise it may be time to introduce another type of test, maybe even one with words themselves being used as projective stimuli.

Words as Projective Stimuli

Projective techniques that employ words or open-ended phrases and sentences are referred to as *semi-structured* techniques because, although they allow for a variety of responses, they still provide a framework within which the subject must operate. Perhaps the two best-known examples of verbal projective techniques are *word association tests* and *sentence completion tests*.

Word association tests In general, a word association test may be defined as a semi-structured, individually administered, projective technique of personality assessment that entails the presentation of a list of stimulus words, to each of which an assessee responds verbally or in writing with whatever comes to mind first upon hearing the word. Responses are then analyzed on the basis of content and other variables. The first attempt to investigate word association was made by Galton (1879). Galton's method consisted of presenting a series of unrelated stimulus words and instructing the subject to respond with the first word that came to mind. Continued interest in the phenomenon of word association resulted in additional studies. Precise methods were developed for recording the responses given and the length of time elapsed before obtaining a response (Cattell, 1887; Trautscholdt, 1883). Cattell and Bryant (1889) were the first to use cards with stimulus words printed on them. Kraepelin (1896) studied the effect of physical states such as hunger and fatigue as well as the effect of practice on word association. Mounting experimental evidence led psychologists to believe that the associations individuals made to words were not chance happenings but rather the result of the interplay between one's life experiences, one's attitudes, and one's unique personality characteristics.

Jung (1910) maintained that by selecting certain key words that represented possible areas of conflict, word association techniques could be employed for psychodiagnostic

---

4. Murray et al. (1938) believed that fantastic or unreal types of stimuli might be particularly effective in tapping unconscious processes.

purposes. Jung's experiments served as an inspiration to creators of such tests as the Word Association Test developed by Rapaport, Gill, and Schafer (1946) at the Menninger Clinic. This test consisted of three parts. In the first part, each stimulus word was administered to the examinee, who had been instructed to respond quickly with the first word that came to mind. The examiner recorded the length of time it took the subject to respond to each item. In the second part of the test, each stimulus word was again presented to the examinee. The examinee was instructed to reproduce the original responses. Any deviation between the original and this second response was recorded, as was the length of time before reacting. The third part of the test was the inquiry. Here the examiner asked questions to clarify the relationship that existed between the stimulus word and the response (for example, "What were you thinking about?" or "What was going through your mind?"). In some cases, the relationship may have been obvious; in others, however, the relationship between the two words may have been extremely idiosyncratic or even bizarre.

The test consisted of 60 words, some considered neutral by the test authors (for example, *chair, book, water, dance, taxi*) and some characterized as *traumatic*. In the latter category were "words that are likely to touch upon sensitive personal material according to clinical experience, and also words that attract associative disturbances" (Rapaport et al., 1968, p. 257). Examples of words so designated were *love, girlfriend, boyfriend, mother, father, suicide, fire, breast,* and *masturbation.*

Responses on the Word Association Test were evaluated with respect to variables such as popularity, reaction time, content, and test-retest responses. Normative data were provided regarding the percentage of occurrence of certain responses for college students and schizophrenic groups. For example, to the word *stomach,* 21% of the college group responded with "ache"; 13% with "ulcer." Ten percent of the schizophrenic group responded with "ulcer." To the word *mouth,* 20% of the college sample responded with "kiss"; 13% with "nose"; 11% with "tongue"; 11% with "lips"; and 11% with "eat." In the schizophrenic group, 19% responded with "teeth," and 10% responded with "eat." The test does not enjoy widespread clinical use today but is more apt to be found in the occasional research application.

JUST THINK . . .

As compared to the 1940s, how emotion-arousing do you think the *traumatic* stimuli on the Word Association Test are by contemporary standards? Why?

The Kent-Rosanoff Free Association Test (1910) represented one of the earliest attempts at developing a standardized test using words as projective stimuli.[5] The test consisted of 100 stimulus words, all commonly used and believed to be neutral with respect to emotional impact. The standardization sample consisted of 1,000 normal adults who varied in geographic location, educational level, occupation, age, and intellectual capacity. Frequency tables based on the responses of these 1,000 cases were developed. These tables were used to evaluate examinees' responses according to the clinical judgment of psychopathology. Psychiatric patients were found to have a lower frequency of popular responses than the normal subjects in the standardization group. However, as it became apparent that individuality of response may be influenced by many variables other than psychopathol-

---

5. The term **free association** refers to the technique of having subjects relate all their thoughts as they are occurring and is most frequently used in psychoanalysis; the only structure imposed is provided by the subjects themselves. The technique employed in the Kent-Rosanoff is that of **word association** (not free association), in which the examinee relates the first word that comes to mind in response to a stimulus word. The term *free association* in the test's title is, therefore, a misnomer.

ogy (such as creativity, age, education, and socioeconomic factors), the popularity of the Kent-Rosanoff as a differential diagnostic instrument diminished. Damaging, too, was research indicating that scores on the Kent-Rosanoff were unrelated to other measures of psychotic thought (Ward et al., 1991). Still, the test endures as a standardized instrument of word association responses, and more than ninety years after its publication, it continues to be used in experimental research and clinical practice.

Sentence completion tests   Other projective techniques that use verbal material as projective stimuli are sentence completion tests. How might you complete the following sentences?

I like to ——————————————————————.

Someday, I will ——————————————————.

I will always remember the time ——————————————.

I worry about ——————————————————.

I am most frightened when ————————————————.

My feelings are hurt ——————————————————.

My mother ————————————————————.

I wish my parents ——————————————————.

Sentence completion tests may contain items that, like the items listed, are quite general and appropriate for administration in a wide variety of settings. Alternatively, **sentence completion stems** (the first part of the item) may be developed for use in specific types of settings (such as school or business) or for specific purposes. Sentence completion tests may be relatively atheoretical or linked very closely to some theory. As an example of the latter, the Washington University Sentence Completion Test (Loevinger et al., 1970) was based on the writings of Loevinger and her colleagues in the area of ego development.

Loevinger (1966; Loevinger & Ossorio, 1958) believes that maturity brings a transformation of one's self-image from an essentially stereotypic and socially acceptable one to a more personalized and realistic one. The Washington University Sentence Completion Test was constructed to assess self-concept according to Loevinger's theory. Some evidence for the validity of this test comes from its ability to predict social attitudes in a manner consistent with Loevinger's theory (Browning, 1987). It is possible to obtain other traditional psychometric indices on this test. For example, inter-rater reliability for this test has been estimated to range from .74 to .88, internal consistency is in the high .80s, and test-retest reliability ranges from .67 to .76 or from .88 to .92, depending upon how the test is scored (Weiss et al., 1989).

A number of standardized sentence completion tests are available to the clinician. One such test, the Rotter[6] Incomplete Sentences Blank (Rotter & Rafferty, 1950) is the most popular of all. The Rotter was developed for use with populations from grade 9 through adulthood and is available in three levels: high school (grades 9 through 12), college (grades 13 through 16), and adult. Testtakers are instructed to respond to each of the 40 incomplete sentence items in a way that expresses their "real feelings." The

———————————————

6. The *o* in *Rotter* is long, as in *rote.*

manual suggests that responses on the test be interpreted according to several categories: family attitudes, social and sexual attitudes, general attitudes, and character traits. Each response is evaluated on a 7-point scale that ranges from *need for therapy* to *extremely good adjustment.*

The manual contains normative data for a sample of 85 female and 214 male college freshmen but no norms for high school and adult populations. Also presented in the test manual are sample responses of several subjects along with background information about the subjects. According to the psychometric studies quoted in the test manual, the Rotter is a reliable, valid instrument. Estimates of inter-scorer reliability were reported to be in the .90s. Independently from the original validity studies, sociometric techniques have been used to demonstrate the validity of the Rotter as a measure of adjustment (Lah, 1989).

In general, a sentence completion test may be useful for obtaining diverse information about an individual's interests, educational aspirations, future goals, fears, conflicts, needs, and so forth. The tests have a high degree of face validity. However, with this high degree of face validity comes a certain degree of transparency about the objective of the test. For this reason, sentence completion tests are perhaps the most vulnerable of all the projective methods to faking on the part of an examinee intent on making a good—or a bad—impression.

Sounds as Projective Stimuli

Let's state at the outset that this section is included more as a fascinating footnote in the history of projectives, than as a description of widely used tests. The history of the use of sound as a projective stimulus is fascinating because of its origins in the laboratory of a then-junior fellow of Harvard University. You may be surprised to learn that it was a behaviorist whose name has seldom been uttered in the same sentence as the term *projective test* by any contemporary psychologist: B. F. Skinner (Figure 12–7). The device was something "like auditory inkblots" (Skinner, 1979, p. 175).

The time was the mid-1930s. Skinner's colleagues, Henry Murray and Christiana Morgan, were working on the TAT in the Harvard Psychological Clinic. Psychoanalytic theory was very much in vogue. Even behaviorists were curious about Freud's approach, and some were even undergoing psychoanalysis themselves. Switching on the equipment in his laboratory in the biology building, the rhythmic noise served as a stimulus for Skinner to create words that went along with it. This inspired Skinner to think of an application for sound, not only in behavioral terms but in the elicitation of "latent" verbal behavior that was significant "in the Freudian sense" (Skinner, 1979, p. 175). Skinner created a series of recorded sounds much like muffled, spoken vowels, to which people would be instructed to associate. The sounds, packaged as a device he called a *verbal summator*, presumably would act as a stimulus for the person to verbalize certain unconscious material. Henry Murray, by the way, liked the idea and supplied Skinner with a room at the clinic in which to test subjects. Saul Rosenzweig also liked the idea; he and David Shakow renamed the instrument the *tautophone* (from the Greek *tauto*, meaning "repeating the same") and did research with it (Rutherford, 2003). Their instructions to subjects were as follows:

> Here is a phonograph. On it is a record of a man's voice saying different things. He speaks rather unclearly, so I'll play over what he says a number of times. You'll have to listen carefully. As soon as you have some idea of what he's saying, tell me at once. (Shakow & Rosenzweig, 1940, p. 217).

Figure 12–7
Projective Test Pioneer B. F. Skinner . . . *What?!*

Working at the Harvard Psychological Clinic with the blessing (and even some financial support) of Henry Murray, B. F. Skinner (who today is an icon of behaviorism) evinced great enthusiasm for an auditory projective test he had developed. He believed the technique had potential as "a device for snaring out complexes" (Skinner, 1979, p. 176). A number of well-known psychologists of the day apparently agreed. For example, Joseph Zubin, in correspondence with Skinner, wrote that Skinner's technique had promise "as a means for throwing light on the less objective aspects of the Rorschach experiment" (Zubin, 1939). Of course, if the test really had that much promise, Skinner would probably be getting equal billing in this chapter with Murray and Rorschach.

As recounted in detail by Rutherford (2003), there was little compelling evidence to show that the instrument could differentiate between members of clinical and non-clinical groups. Still, a number of other auditory projective techniques were developed. There was the Auditory Apperception Test (Stone, 1950), in which the subject's task was to respond by creating a story based on three sounds played on a phonograph record. Other researchers produced similar tests, one called an auditory sound association test (Wilmer & Husni, 1951) and the other referred to as an auditory apperception test (Ball & Bernardoni, 1953). Henry Murray got into the act as well with his Azzageddi test (Davids & Murray, 1955), named for a Herman Melville character. Unlike other auditory projectives, the Azzageddi presented subjects with spoken paragraphs.

So, why aren't test publishers today punching out CDs with projective sounds at a pace to match the publication of inkblots and pictures? Rutherford (2003) speculated that a combination of factors conspired to cause the demise of auditory projective methods. The tests proved not to differentiate between different groups of subjects who took it. Responses to the auditory stimuli lacked the complexity and richness of responses to inkblots, pictures, and other projective stimuli. None of the available scoring systems was very satisfactory. Except for use with the blind, auditory projective tests were seen as redundant with but not as good as the TAT.

The Production of Figure Drawings

A relatively quick, easily administered projective technique is the analysis of drawings. Drawings can provide the psychodiagnostician with a wealth of clinical hypotheses to be confirmed or discarded as the result of other findings (Figure 12–8). The use of drawings in clinical and research settings has extended beyond the area of personality assessment. Attempts have been made to use artistic productions as a source of

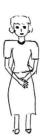 Drawing by a 25-year-old schoolteacher after becoming engaged. Previously, she had entered psychotherapy because of problems relating to men and a block against getting married. The positioning of the hands is indicative of a fear of sexual intercourse that remains.

 Drawing by a male with a "Don Juan" complex—a man who pursued one affair after another. The collar pulled up to guard the neck and the excessive shading of the buttocks is suggestive of a fear of being attacked from the rear. It is possible that this man's Don Juanism is an outward defense against the lack of masculinity—even feelings of effeminacy—he may be struggling with inside.

 Drawing by an authoritarian and sadistic male who had been head disciplinarian of a reformatory for boys before he was suspended for child abuse. His description of this picture was that it "looked like a Prussian or a Nazi General."

 The manacled hands, tied feet, exposed buttocks, and large foot drawn to the side of the drawing taken together are reflective, according to Hammer, of masochistic, homosexual, and exhibitionistic needs.

 This drawing by an acutely paranoid, psychotic man was described by Hammer (1981, p. 170) as follows: "The savage mouth expresses the rage-filled projections loose within him. The emphasized eyes and ears with the eyes almost emanating magical rays reflect the visual and auditory hallucinations the patient actually experiences. The snake in the stomach points up his delusion of a reptile within, eating away and generating venom and evil."

Figure 12–8
Some Sample Interpretations Made From Figure Drawings
Source: Hammer, 1981

information about intelligence, neurological intactness, visual-motor coordination, cognitive development, and even learning disabilities (Neale & Rosal, 1993). Figure drawings are an appealing source of diagnostic data because the instructions for them can be administered individually or in a group by nonclinicians such as teachers, and no materials other than a pencil and paper are required.

Figure-drawing tests   In general, a **figure drawing test** may be defined as a projective method of personality assessment that entails the production of a drawing by the assessee, which is analyzed on the basis of its content and related variables. The classic work on the use of figure drawings as a projective stimulus is a book entitled *Personality Projection in the Drawing of the Human Figure: A Method of Personality Investigation* by Karen Machover (1949). Machover wrote that

> . . . the human figure drawn by an individual who is directed to "draw a person" related intimately to the impulses, anxieties, conflicts, and compensations characteristic of that individual. In some sense, the figure drawn is the person, and the paper corresponds to the environment. (p. 35)

The instructions for administering the Draw A Person (DAP) test are quite straightforward. The examinee is given a pencil and a blank sheet of 8½-by-11-inch white paper and told to draw a person. Inquiries on the part of the examinee concerning how the picture is to be drawn are met with statements such as "Make it the way you think it should be" or "Do the best you can." Immediately after the first drawing is completed, the examinee is handed a second sheet of paper and instructed to draw a picture of a person of the sex opposite that of the person just drawn.[7] Subsequently, many clinicians will ask questions about the drawings, such as "Tell me a story about that figure," "Tell me about that boy/girl, man/lady," "What is the person doing?" "How is the person feeling?" "What is nice or not nice about the person?" Responses to these questions are used in forming various hypotheses and interpretations about personality functioning.

Traditionally, the drawings generated on the DAP have been formally evaluated through analysis of various characteristics of the drawing. Attention has been given to such factors as the length of time required to complete the picture, placement of the figures, the size of the figure, pencil pressure used, symmetry, line quality, shading, the presence of erasures, facial expressions, posture, clothing, and overall appearance. Various hypotheses have been generated based on these factors (Knoff, 1990a). For example, the *placement* of the figure on the paper is seen as representing how the individual functions within the environment. The person who draws a tiny figure at the bottom of the paper might have a poor self-concept or might be insecure or depressed. The individual who draws a picture that cannot be contained on one sheet of paper and goes off the page is considered to be impulsive. Unusually light pressure suggests character disturbance (Exner, 1962). According to Buck (1948, 1950), placement of drawing on the right of the page suggests orientation to the future; placement to the left suggests an orientation to the past. Placement at the upper right suggests a desire to suppress an unpleasant past, plus excessive optimism about the future. Placement to the lower left suggests depression with a desire to flee into the past.

Another variable of interest to those who analyze figure drawings is the *characteristics* of the individual drawn. For example, unusually large eyes or large ears suggest suspiciousness, ideas of reference, or other paranoid characteristics (Machover, 1949; Shneidman, 1958). Unusually large breasts drawn by a male may be interpreted as unresolved oedipal problems with maternal dependence (Jolles, 1952). Long and conspicuous ties suggest sexual aggressiveness, perhaps overcompensating for fear of impotence (Machover, 1949). Button emphasis suggests dependent, infantile, inadequate personality (Halpern, 1958).

---

7. When instructed simply to "draw a person," most people will draw a person of the same sex. It is deemed clinically significant if the person draws a person of the opposite sex when given these instructions. Rierdan and Koff (1981) found that in some cases children are uncertain of the sex of the figure drawn. They hypothesized that in such cases "the child has an indefinite or ill-defined notion of sexual identity" (p. 257).

The House-Tree-Person test (HTP; Buck, 1948) is another projective figure-drawing test. As the name of the test implies, the testtaker's task is to draw a picture of a house, a tree, and a person. In much the same way that different aspects of the human figure are presumed to be reflective of psychological functioning, the ways in which an individual represents a house and a tree are considered symbolically significant. Another test, this one thought to be of particular value in learning about the examinee in relation to her or his family, is the Kinetic Family Drawing (KFD). Derived from Hulse's (1951, 1952) Family Drawing Test, an administration of the KFD (Burns & Kaufman, 1970, 1972) begins with the presentation of an 8½-by-11-inch sheet of paper and a pencil with an eraser. The examinee, usually though not necessarily a child, is instructed as follows:

JUST THINK . . .

Draw a person. Contemplate what that drawing tells about you.

> Draw a picture of everyone in your family, including you, DOING something. Try to draw whole people, not cartoons or stick people. Remember, make everyone DOING something—some kind of actions. (Burns & Kaufman, 1972, p. 5)

In addition to yielding graphic representations of each family member for analysis, this procedure may yield a wealth of information in the form of examinee verbalizations while the drawing is being executed. After the examinee has completed the drawing, a rather detailed inquiry follows. The examinee is asked to identify each of the figures, talk about their relationship, and detail what they are doing in the picture and why. A number of formal scoring systems for the KFD are available. Related techniques include a school adaptation called the Kinetic School Drawing (KSD; Prout & Phillips, 1974); a test that combines aspects of the KFD and the KSD called the Kinetic Drawing System (KDS; Knoff & Prout, 1985); and the Collaborative Drawing Technique (Smith, 1985), a test that provides an occasion for family members to collaborate on the creation of a drawing—presumably all the better to "draw together."

The Draw A Person: Screening Procedure for Emotional Disturbance (DAP:SPED; Naglieri et al., 1991) features a standardized test administration and quantitative scoring system designed to screen testtakers (ages 6 through 17) for emotional problems. Based on the assumption that the rendering of unusual features in figure drawings signals emotional problems, one point is scored for each such feature. With age and normative information taken into account, high scores signal the need for more detailed evaluation. Validity data are presented in the test manual, but both an independent evaluation of the test (Motta et al., 1993a, 1993b) and a study by two of the test's authors (McNeish & Naglieri, 1993) raised concerns about the number of misidentifications (both false positives and false negatives) that might result from the test's use even as a screening tool.

Like other projective techniques, figure-drawing tests, although thought to be clinically useful, have had a rather embattled history in relation to their psychometric soundness (Joiner & Schmidt, 1997). In general, the techniques are vulnerable with regard to the assumptions that drawings are essentially self-representations (Tharinger & Stark, 1990) and represent something far more than drawing ability (Swensen, 1968). Although a number of systems have been devised for scoring figure drawings, solid support for the validity of such approaches has been elusive (Watson et al., 1967). Experience and expertise do not necessarily correlate with greater clinical accuracy in drawing interpretation. Karen Machover (cited in Watson, 1967) herself reportedly had "grave misgivings" (p. 145) about the misuse of her test for diagnostic purposes.

To be sure, the clinical use of figure drawings has its academic defenders (Riethmiller & Handler, 1997a, 1997b). Waehler (1997), for example, cautioned that tests are not foolproof and that a person who comes across as rife with pathology in an interview might well seem benign on a psychological test. He went on to advise that figure drawings "can be considered more than 'tests'; they involve tasks that can also serve as stepping-off points for clients and examiners to discuss and clarify the picture" (p. 486).

Projective Methods in Perspective

Used enthusiastically by many clinicians and criticized harshly by many academics, projective methods continue to occupy a rather unique habitat in the psychological landscape. Lilienfeld et al. (2000) raised serious questions regarding whether that habitat is worth maintaining. These authors focused their criticism on scoring systems for the Rorschach, the TAT, and figure drawings. They concluded that there was empirical support for only a relatively small number of Rorschach and TAT indices. They found even fewer compelling reasons to justify the continued use of figure drawings. Some of their assertions with regard to the Rorschach and the TAT, as well as the response of a projective test user and advocate, Stephen Hibbard (2003), are presented in Table 12–4. Hibbard (2003) commented only on the Rorschach and the TAT, because of his greater experience with these tests as opposed to figure drawings.

In general, critics have attacked projective methods on grounds related to the *assumptions* inherent in their use, the *situational variables* that attend their use, and several *psychometric considerations*, most notably a paucity of data to support their reliability and validity.

TABLE 12–4
The Cons and Pros (or Cons Rebutted) of Projective Methods

Lilienfeld et al. (2000) on the Cons	Hibbard (2003) in Rebuttal
Projective techniques tend not to provide incremental validity above more structured measures, as is the argument of proponents of the projective hypothesis as stated by Dosajh (1996).	Lilienfeld et al. presented an outmoded caricature of projection and then proceeded to attack it. Dosajh has not published on any of the coding systems targeted for criticism. None of the authors who developed coding systems that were attacked espouse a view of projection similar to Dosajh's. Some of the criticized authors have even positioned their systems as nonprojective.
The norms for Exner's Comprehensive System (CS) are in error. They may overpathologize normal individuals and may even harm clients.	Evidence is inconclusive as to error in the norms. Observed discrepancies may have many explanations. Overpathologization may be a result of "drift" similar to that observed in the measurement of intelligence (Flynn effect).
There is limited support for the generalizability of the CS across different cultures.	More cross-cultural studies do need to be done, but the same could be said for most major tests.
Four studies are cited to support the deficiency of the test-retest reliability of the CS.	Only three of the four studies cited are in *refereed journals* (for which submitted manuscripts undergo critical review and may be selected or rejected for publication), and none of these three studies are bona fide test-retest reliability studies.
With regard to the TAT, there is no point in aggregating scores into a scale in the absence of applying internal consistency reliability criteria.	This assertion is incorrect because "each subunit of an aggregated group of predictors of a construct could be unrelated to the other, but when found in combination, they might well predict important variance in the construct" (p. 264).
TAT test-retest reliability estimates have been "notoriously problematic" (p. 41).	". . . higher retest reliability would accrue to motive measures if the retest instructions permitted participants to tell stories with the same content as previously" (p. 265).
Various validity studies with different TAT scoring systems can be faulted on methodological grounds.	Lilienfeld et al. (2000) misinterpreted some studies they cited and did not cite other studies. For example, a number of relevant validity studies in support of Cramer's (1991) Defense Mechanism Manual coding system for the TAT were not cited.

Interested readers are encouraged to read the full text of Lilienfeld et al. (2000) and Hibbard (2003), as the arguments made by each are far more detailed than the brief samples presented here.

Assumptions Murstein (1961) examined ten assumptions of projective techniques and argued that none of them was scientifically compelling. Several assumptions concern the stimulus material. For example, it is assumed that the more ambiguous the stimuli, the more subjects reveal about their personality. However, Murstein describes the stimulus material as only one aspect of the "total stimulus situation." Environmental variables, response sets, reactions to the examiner, and related factors all contribute to response patterns. In addition, in situations where the stimulus properties of the projective material were designed to be unclear or hazy or are presented with uncompleted lines—thereby increasing ambiguity—projection on the part of the subject was not found to increase.

Another assumption concerns the supposedly idiosyncratic nature of the responses evoked by projective stimuli. In fact, similarities in the response themes of different subjects to the same stimulus cards suggest that the stimulus material may not be as ambiguous and amenable to projection as previously assumed. Some consideration of the stimulus properties and the ways they affect the subject's responses is therefore indicated. The assumption that projection is greater onto stimulus material that is similar to the subject (in physical appearance, gender, occupation, and so on) has also been found questionable.

JUST THINK . . .

Suppose a Rorschach card or a TAT card elicited much the same response from *most* people. Would that be an argument for or against the use of the card?

Murstein raised questions about the way projective tests are interpreted. He questioned numerous assumptions, including the assumptions that

- every response provides meaning for personality analysis
- a relationship exists between the strength of a need and its manifestation on projective instruments
- testtakers are unaware of what they are disclosing about themselves
- a projective protocol reflects sufficient data concerning personality functioning for formulation of judgments
- there is a parallel between behavior obtained on a projective instrument and behavior displayed in social situations

Murstein dismissed such contentions as "cherished beliefs" accepted "without the support of sufficient research validation" (p. 343).

To Murstein's list we might add one assumption that is very basic to projective assessment: that something called "the unconscious" exists. Though the term *unconscious* is widely used as if its existence were a given, some academicians have questioned whether in fact the unconscious exists in the same way that, say, the liver exists. The scientific studies typically cited to support the existence of the unconscious (or perhaps more accurately, the efficacy of the construct *unconscious*) have used a very wide array of methodologies—see, for example, Diven (1937), Erdelyi (1974), Greenspoon (1955), and Razran (1961). The conclusions of each of these types of studies are subject to alternative explanations. Also inconclusive have been conclusions about the existence of the unconscious based on experimental testing of predictions derived from hypnotic phenomena, from signal detection theory, and from specific personality theories (Brody, 1972).

Situational variables Proponents of projective techniques have claimed that such tests are capable of illuminating the recesses of the mind like X-rays illuminate the body. Frank (1939) conceptualized projective tests as tapping personality patterns without disturbing the pattern being tapped. If that were true, then variables related to the test situation should have no effect on the data obtained. However, situational variables such as the examiner's presence or absence have significantly affected the responses of experimental subjects. TAT stories written in private are likely to be less guarded, less optimistic, and more affectively involved than those written in the presence of the examiner (Bernstein, 1956). The age of the examiner is likely to affect projective protocols (Mussen & Scodel, 1955), as are the specific instructions (Henry & Rotter, 1956) and the subtle reinforcement cues provided by the examiner (Wickes, 1956).

Masling (1960) reviewed the literature on the influence of situational and interpersonal variables in projective testing and concluded that there was strong evidence for a role of situational and interpersonal influences in projection. Masling concluded that subjects utilized every available cue in the testing situation, including cues related to the actions or the appearance of the examiner. Moreover, Masling argued that examiners also relied on situational cues, in some instances over and above what they were taught. Examiners appeared to interpret projective data with regard to their own needs and expectations, their own subjective feelings about the person being tested, and their own constructions regarding the total test situation. Masling (1965) experimentally demonstrated that through postural, gestural, and facial cues, Rorschach examiners are capable of unwittingly eliciting the responses they expect.

In any given clinical situation, many variables may be placed in the mix. The interaction of these variables may influence clinical judgments. So it is that research has suggested that even in situations involving objective (not projective) tests or simple history taking, the effect of the clinician's training (Chapman & Chapman, 1967; Fitzgibbons & Shearn, 1972) and role perspective (Snyder et al., 1976), the patient's social class (Hollingshead & Redlich, 1958; Lee, 1968; Routh & King, 1972) and motivation to manage a desired impression (Edwards & Walsh, 1964; Wilcox & Krasnoff, 1967) are all capable of influencing ratings of pathology (Langer & Abelson, 1974) and related conclusions (Batson, 1975). These and other variables are given wider latitude in the projective test situation in which the examiner may be at liberty to choose not only the test and extra-test data on which interpretation will be focused but also the scoring system that will be used to arrive at that interpretation.

Psychometric considerations The psychometric soundness of many widely used projective instruments has yet to be demonstrated. Critics of projective techniques have called attention to variables such as uncontrolled variations in protocol length, inappropriate subject samples, inadequate control groups, and poor external criteria as factors contributing to spuriously increased ratings of validity. There are methodological obstacles in researching projectives, as many test-retest or split-half methods are inappropriate. It is challenging at best to design and execute validity studies that effectively rule out, limit, or statistically take into account the unique situational variables that attend the administration of such tests.

The debate between academicians who argue that projective tests are not technically sound instruments and clinicians who find such tests useful has been raging ever since projectives came into widespread use. Frank (1939) responded to those who would reject projective methods because of their lack of technical rigor:

> **JUST THINK . . .**
>
> Projective tests have been around for a long time, owing to their appeal to many clinicians. What are their advantages? Why should they be around for a long time to come?

> These leads to the study of personality have been rejected by many psychologists because they do not meet psychometric requirements for validity and reliability, but they are being employed in association with clinical and other studies of personality where they are finding increasing validation in the consistency of results for the same subject when independently assayed by each of these procedures. . . .

If we face the problem of personality, in its full complexity, as an active dynamic process to be studied as a *process* rather than as entity or aggregate of traits, factors, or as static organization, then these projective methods offer many advantages for obtaining data on the process of organizing experience which is peculiar to each personality and has a life career. (Frank, 1939, p. 408; emphasis in the original)

Behavioral Assessment Methods

Traits, states, motives, needs, drives, defenses, and related psychological constructs have no tangible existence. They are constructs whose existence must be inferred from behavior. In the traditional approach to clinical assessment, tests as well as other tools are employed to gather data. From these data, diagnoses and inferences are made concerning the existence and strength of psychological constructs. The traditional approach to assessment might therefore be labeled a *sign* approach, because test responses are deemed to be signs or clues to underlying personality or ability. In contrast to this traditional approach is an alternative philosophy of assessment that may be termed the *sample* approach. The sample approach focuses on the behavior itself. Emitted behavior is viewed not as a sign of something but rather as a sample to be interpreted in its own right.

The emphasis in **behavioral assessment** is on "what a person *does* in situations rather than on inferences about what attributes he *has* more globally" (Mischel, 1968, p. 10). Predicting what a person will do is thought to entail an understanding of the assessee with respect to both antecedent conditions and consequences of a particular situation (Smith & Iwata, 1997). Upon close scrutiny, however, the trait concept is still present in many behavioral measures, though more narrowly defined and more closely linked to specific situations (Zuckerman, 1979).

To illustrate behavioral observation as an assessment strategy, consider the plight of the single female client who presents herself at the university counseling center. She complains that even though all her friends tell her how attractive she is, she has great difficulty meeting men—so much so that she doesn't even want to try anymore. A counselor confronted with such a client might, among other things, (1) interview the client about this problem, (2) administer an appropriate test to the client, (3) ask the client to keep a detailed diary of her thoughts and behaviors related to various aspects of her efforts to meet men, including her expectations, and (4) accompany the client on a typical night out to a singles bar or similar venue and observe her behavior. The latter two strategies come under the heading of behavioral observation. With regard to the diary, the client is engaging in self-observation. In the scenario of the night out, the counselor is doing the actual observation.

The more traditional administration of a psychological test or test battery to a client such as this single woman might yield signs that then could be inferred to relate to the problem. For example, if a number of the client's TAT stories involved themes of demeaning, hostile, or otherwise unsatisfactory heterosexual encounters as a result of venturing out into the street, a counselor might make an interpretation at a deeper or second level of inference. For example, a counselor, especially one with a psychoanalytic orientation, might reach a conclusion something like this:

The client's expressed fear of going outdoors, and ultimately her fear of meeting men, might in some way be related to an unconscious fear of promiscuity—a fear of becoming a streetwalker.

Such a conclusion in turn would have implications for treatment. Many hours of treatment might be devoted to uncovering the "real" fear so that it is apparent to the client herself and ultimately dealt with effectively.

In contrast to the sign approach, the clinician employing the sample or behavioral approach to assessment might examine the behavioral diary that the client kept and design an appropriate therapy program on the basis of those records. Thus, for example, the antecedent conditions under which the client would feel most distraught and unmotivated to do anything about the problem might be delineated and worked on in counseling sessions. In going through the diary, the clinician might find, for example, that the client regularly watches the cable show *Wild On . . .* on the *E!* network. The expectations this program may have aroused could be covered in a session where the clinician reviews all of the findings.

An advantage of the sign approach over the sample approach is that in the hands of a skillful, perceptive clinician, the client might be put in touch with feelings that even she was not really aware of before the assessment. The client may have been consciously (or unconsciously) avoiding certain thoughts and images (those attendant on the expression of her sexuality, for example), and this inability to deal with those thoughts and images may indeed have been a factor contributing to her ambivalence about meeting men.

Behavioral assessors seldom make such deeper-level inferences. For example, if sexuality is not raised as an area of difficulty by the client (in an interview, a diary, a checklist, or by some other behavioral assessment technique), this problem area may well be ignored or given short shrift. Behavioral assessors do, however, tend to be more empirical in their approach, as they systematically assess the client's presenting problem from both the perspective of the client and the perspective of one observing the client in social situations and the environment in general. The behavioral assessor does not search the Rorschach or other protocols for clues to treatment. Rather, the behaviorally oriented counselor or clinician relies much more on what the client *does* and *has done* for guideposts to treatment. In a sense, the behavioral approach does not require as much clinical creativity as the sign approach. Perhaps for that reason, the behavioral approach may be considered less an art than a science.

Early on, the shift away from traditional psychological tests by behaviorally oriented clinicians compelled some to call for a way to integrate such tests in behavioral evaluations. This view is typified by the wish that "psychological tests should be able to provide the behavior therapist with information that should be of value in doing behavior therapy. This contention is based on the assumption that the behavior on any psychological test should be lawful" (Greenspoon & Gersten, 1967, p. 849). Accordingly, psychological tests could be useful, for example, in helping the behavior therapist identify the kinds of contingent stimuli that would be most effective with a given patient. For example, patients with high percentages of color or color/form responses on the Rorschach and with IQs over 90 might be most responsive to positive verbal contingencies (such as *good, excellent,* and so forth), whereas patients with high percentages of movement or vista (three-dimensional) responses on the Rorschach and IQs over 90 might be most responsive to negative verbal contingencies (such as *no* or *wrong*). Such innovative efforts to narrow a widening schism in the field of clinical assessment have failed to ignite experimental enthusiasm, perhaps because more direct ways exist to assess responsiveness to various contingencies.

> **JUST THINK . . .**
>
> Is there a way to integrate traditional psychological testing and assessment and behavioral assessment?

Differences between traditional and behavioral approaches to assessment have to do with varying assumptions about the nature of personality and the causes of behavior.

Table 12–5

Differences Between Behavioral and Traditional Approaches to Psychological Assessment

	Behavioral	Traditional
Assumptions		
Conception of personality	Personality constructs mainly employed to summarize specific behavior patterns, if at all	Personality as a reflection of enduring, underlying states or traits
Causes of behavior	Maintaining conditions sought in current environment	Intrapsychic, or within the individual
Implications		
Role of behavior	Important as a sample of person's repertoire in specific situation	Behavior assumes importance only insofar as it indexes underlying causes
Role of history	Relatively unimportant except, for example, to provide a retrospective baseline	Crucial in that present conditions seen as products of the past
Consistency of behavior	Behavior thought to be specific to the situation	Behavior expected to be consistent across time and settings
Uses of data	To describe target behaviors and maintaining conditions	To describe personality functioning and etiology
	To select the appropriate treatment	To diagnose or classify
	To evaluate and revise treatment	To make prognosis; to predict
Other characteristics		
Level of inferences	Low	Medium to high
Comparisons	More emphasis on intraindividual or idiographic	More emphasis on interindividual or nomothetic
Methods of assessment	More emphasis on direct methods (e.g., observations of behavior in natural environment)	More emphasis on indirect methods (e.g., interviews and self-report)
Timing of assessment	More ongoing; prior, during, and after treatment	Pre- and perhaps posttreatment, or strictly to diagnose
Scope of assessment	Specific measures and of more variables (e.g., of target behaviors in various situations, of side effects, context, strengths as well as deficiencies)	More global measures (e.g., of cure, or improvement) but only of the individual

Source: Hartmann, Roper, and Bradford (1979)

The data from traditional assessment are used primarily to describe, classify, or diagnose, whereas the data from a behavioral assessment are typically more directly related to the formulation of a specific treatment program. Some of the other differences between the two approaches are summarized in Table 12–5.

The Who, What, When, Where, Why, and How of It

The name says it all: *Behavior* is the focus of assessment in behavioral assessment—not traits, states, or other constructs presumed to be present in various strengths, just behavior. This will become clear as we survey the *who, what, when, where, why,* and *how* of behavioral assessment.

Who? *Who* is assessed? The person being assessed may be, for example, a patient on a closed psychiatric ward, a client seeking help at a counseling center, or a subject in an academic experiment. Regardless of whether the assessment is for research, clinical, or other purposes, the hallmark of behavioral assessment is intensive study of individuals. This is in contrast to mass testing of groups of people to obtain normative data with respect to some hypothesized trait or state.

Who is the assessor? Depending on the particular assessment, the assessor may be a highly qualified professional or a technician/assistant trained to conduct a particular assessment. Technicians are frequently employed to record the number of times a targeted behavior is emitted. In this context, the assessor may also be a classroom teacher recording, for example, the number of times a child leaves her or his seat. An assessor in behavioral assessment may also be the assessee. Assessees are frequently directed to maintain behavioral diaries, complete behavioral checklists, or engage in other activities designed to monitor their own behavior.

What? *What* is measured in behavioral assessment? Perhaps not surprisingly, the behavior or behaviors targeted for assessment will vary as a function of the objectives of the assessment. What constitutes a targeted behavior will typically be described in sufficient detail prior to any assessment. For the purposes of assessment, the targeted behavior must be measurable—quantifiable in some way. Examples of such measurable behaviors can range from the number of seconds elapsed before a child calls out in class to the number of degrees body temperature is altered. Note that descriptions of targeted behaviors in behavioral assessment typically begin with the phrase *the number of.*

When? *When* is an assessment of behavior made? One response to this question is that assessment of behavior is typically made at times when the problem behavior is most likely to be elicited. So, for example, if Valeria is most likely to get into verbal and physical altercations during lunch, a behavioral assessor would focus on lunch hour as a time to assess her behavior.

Another way to address the *when* question has to do with the various schedules with which behavioral assessments may be made. For example, one schedule of assessment is referred to as *frequency* or *event recording*. Each time the targeted behavior occurs, it is recorded. Another schedule of assessment is referred to as *interval recording*. Assessment according to this schedule occurs only during predefined intervals of time (for example, every other minute, every 48 hours, every third week). Beyond merely tallying the number of times a particular behavior is emitted, the assessor may also maintain a record of the *intensity* of the behavior. Intensity of a behavior may be gauged by observable and quantifiable events such as the *duration* of the behavior, stated in number of seconds, minutes, hours, days, weeks, months, or years. Alternatively, it may be stated in terms of some ratio or percentage of time that the behavior occurs during a specified interval of time. One widely used method of recording the frequency and intensity of target behavior is **timeline followback (TLFB) methodology** (Sobell & Sobell, 1992, 2000). An illustration of the application of TLFB with gambling behavior can be found in Weinstock (2004).

JUST THINK . . .

You are a behavior therapist with a client who is a compulsive gambler. You advise the client to keep a record of his behavior. Do you advise that this self-monitoring be kept on a frequency basis or an interval schedule?

Where? *Where* does the assessment take place? In contrast to the administration of psychological tests, behavioral assessment may take place just about anywhere—preferably in the environment where the targeted behavior is most likely to occur naturally. For example, a behavioral assessor studying the obsessive-compulsive habits of a patient might wish to visit the patient at home to see firsthand the variety and intensity of the behaviors exhibited. Does the patient check the oven for gas left on, for example? If so, how many times per hour? Does the patient engage in excessive hand-washing? If so, to what extent? These and related questions may be raised and answered effectively through firsthand observation in the patient's home.

Why? *Why* conduct behavioral assessment? In general, data derived from behavioral assessment may have several advantages over data derived by other means. Data derived from behavioral assessment can be used

- to provide behavioral baseline data with which other behavioral data (accumulated after the passage of time, after intervention, or after some other event) may be compared
- to provide a record of the assessee's behavioral strengths and weaknesses across a variety of situations
- to pinpoint environmental conditions that are acting to trigger, maintain, or extinguish certain behaviors
- to target specific behavioral patterns for modification through interventions
- to create graphic displays useful in stimulating innovative or more effective treatment approaches

In the era of managed care and frugal third-party payers, let's also note that insurance companies tend to favor behavioral assessments over more traditional assessments. This is because behavioral assessment is typically not linked to any particular theory of personality, and patient progress tends to be gauged on the basis of documented behavioral events.

How? *How* is behavioral assessment conducted? The answer to this question will vary, of course, according to the purpose of the assessment. In some situations, the only special equipment required will be a trained observer with pad and pencil. In other types of situations, highly sophisticated recording equipment may be necessary.

Another key *how* question relates to the analysis of data from behavioral assessment. The extent to which traditional psychometric standards are deemed applicable to behavioral assessment is a controversial issue, with two opposing camps. One camp may be characterized as accepting traditional psychometric assumptions about behavioral assessment, including assumptions about the measurement of reliability (Russo et al., 1980) and validity (Haynes et al., 1979, 1981). Representative of this position are statements such as that made by Bellack and Hersen (1988) that "the reliability, validity, and utility of any procedure should be paramount, regardless of its behavioral or nonbehavioral development" (p. 614).

Cone (1977) championed the traditionalist approach to behavioral assessment in an article entitled "The Relevance of Reliability and Validity for Behavioral Assessment." However, as the years passed, Cone (1986, 1987) became a leading proponent of an alternative position, one in which traditional psychometric standards are rejected as inappropriate yardsticks for behavioral assessment. Cone (1981) wrote, for example, that "a truly behavioral view of assessment is based on an approach to the study of behavior so radically different from the customary individual differences model that a correspondingly different approach must be taken in evaluating the adequacy of behavioral assessment procedures" (p. 51).

Others, too, have questioned the utility of traditional approaches to test reliability in behavioral assessment, noting that "the assessment tool may be precise, but the behavior being measured may have changed" (Nelson et al., 1977, p. 428). Based on the conceptualization of each behavioral assessment as an experiment unto itself, Dickson (1975) wrote, "If one assumes that each target for assessment represents a single experiment, then what is needed is the scientific method of experimentation and research, rather than a formalized schedule for assessment. . . . Within

JUST THINK . . .

Imagine that you are a NASA psychologist studying the psychological and behavioral effects of space travel on astronauts. What types of behavioral measures might you employ, and what special equipment would you need—or design—to obtain those measures?

JUST THINK . . .

Do traditional psychometric standards apply to behavioral assessment?

this framework, each situation is seen as unique, and the reliability of the approach is not a function of standardization techniques . . . but rather is a function of following the experimental method in evaluation" (pp. 376–377).

Approaches to Behavioral Assessment

Behavioral assessment may be accomplished through various means, including behavioral observation and behavior rating scales, analogue studies, self-monitoring, and situational performance methods. Let's briefly take a closer look at each of these as well as related methods.

Behavioral observation and rating scales *A child psychologist observes a client in a playroom through a one-way mirror. A family therapist views a videotape of a troubled family attempting to resolve a conflict. A school psychologist observes a child interacting with peers in the school cafeteria.* These are all examples of the use of an assessment technique termed **behavioral observation.** As its name implies, this technique entails watching the activities of targeted clients or research subjects and, typically, maintaining some kind of record of those activities. Researchers, clinicians, or counselors may themselves serve as observers, or they may designate trained assistants or other people (such as parents, siblings, teachers, and supervisors) as the observers. Even the observed person herself or himself can be the behavior observer, although in that instance the term *self-observation* would be more appropriate than *behavioral observation*.

In some instances, behavioral observation entails mechanical means, such as a video recording of an event. Recording behavioral events relieves the clinician, the researcher, or any other observer of the need to be physically present when the behavior occurs and allows for detailed analysis of it at a more convenient time. Factors noted in behavioral observation will typically include the presence or absence of specific, targeted behaviors, behavioral excesses, behavioral deficits, behavioral assets, and the situational antecedents and consequences of the emitted behaviors. Of course, because the people doing the observing and rating are human themselves, behavioral observation isn't always as cut and dried as it may appear (see *Everyday Psychometrics*).

Behavioral observation may take many forms. The observer may, in the tradition of the naturalist, record a running narrative of events, using tools such as pencil and paper, a video, film, or still camera, or a cassette recorder. Mehl and Pennebaker (2003), for example, used such a naturalistic approach in their study of student social life. They tracked the conversations of 52 undergraduates across 2 two-day periods by means of a computerized tape recorder.

Another form of behavioral observation employs what is called a *behavior rating scale*—a preprinted sheet on which the observer notes the presence or intensity of targeted behaviors, usually by checking boxes or filling in coded terms. Sometimes the user of a behavior rating form writes in coded descriptions of various behaviors. The code is preferable to a running narrative because it takes far less time to enter the data and frees the observer familiar with the code to enter data relating to any of hundreds of possible behaviors, not just the ones printed on the sheets. For example, a number of coding systems for observing the behavior of couples and families are available. Two such systems are the Marital Interaction Coding System (Weiss & Summers, 1983) and the Couples Interaction Scoring System (Notarius & Markman, 1981). Handheld data entry devices are frequently used today to facilitate the work of the observer.

As approaches to behavioral assessment in general, behavior rating scales and systems may be categorized in different ways. A continuum of *direct* to *indirect* has to do with the setting in which the observed behavior occurs and how closely that setting

Confessions of a Behavior Rater

In discussions of behavioral assessment, the focus is often placed squarely on the individual being evaluated. Only infrequently, if ever, is reference made to the thoughts and feelings of the person responsible for evaluating the behavior of another. What follows are the hypothetical thoughts of one behavior rater. We say hypothetical because these ideas are not really one person's thoughts, but a compilation of thoughts of many people responsible for conducting behavioral evaluations.

The behavior raters interviewed for this feature were all on the staff at a community-based inpatient/outpatient facility in Brewster, New York. An objective of this facility is to prepare its adolescent and adult members for a constructive, independent life. Members live in residences with varying degrees of supervision, and their behavior is monitored on a 24-hour basis. Each day, members are issued an eight-page behavior rating sheet referred to as a CDR (clinical data recorder), which is circulated to supervising staff for rating through the course of the day. The staff records behavioral information on variables such as activities, social skills, support needed, and dysfunctional behavior.

On the basis of behavioral data, certain medical or other interventions may be recommended. Because behavioral monitoring is daily and consistent, changes in patient behavior as a function of medication, activities, or other variables are quickly noted and intervention strategies adjusted. In short, the behavioral data may significantly affect the course of a patient's institutional stay—everything from amount of daily supervision to privileges to date of discharge is influenced by the behavioral data. Both patients and staff are aware of this fact of institutional life; therefore, both patients and staff take the completion of the CDR very seriously. With that as background, here are some private thoughts of a behavior rater:

> I record behavioral data in the presence of patients, and the patients are usually keenly aware of what I am doing. After I am through coding patients' CDRs for the time they are with me, other staff members will code them with respect to the time they spend with the patient. And so it goes. It is as if each patient is keeping a detailed diary of his or her life; only, it is we, the staff, who are keeping that diary for them.

> Sometimes, especially for new staff, it feels odd to be rating the behavior of fellow human beings. One morning, perhaps out of empathy for a patient, I tossed a blank CDR to a patient and jokingly offered to let him rate my behavior. By dinner, long after I had forgotten that incident in the morning, I realized the patient was coding me for poor table manners. Outwardly, I laughed. Inwardly, I was really a bit offended. Subsequently, I told a joke to the assembled company that in retrospect probably was not in the best of taste. The patient coded me for being socially offensive. Now, I was genuinely becoming self-conscious. Later that evening, we drove to a local video store to return a tape we had rented, and the patient coded me for reckless driving. My discomfort level rose to the point where I thought it was time to end the joke. In retrospect, I had experienced firsthand the self-consciousness and discomfort some of our patients had experienced as

approximates the setting in which the behavior naturally occurs. The more natural the setting, the more direct the measure; the more removed from the natural setting, the less direct the measure (Shapiro & Skinner, 1990). According to this categorization, for example, assessing a firefighter's actions and reactions while he or she is fighting a real fire would provide a *direct* measure of firefighting ability. Asking the firefighter to demonstrate how he or she would react to events that occur during a fire would constitute an *indirect* measure of firefighting ability. Shapiro and Skinner (1990) also distinguished between *broad-band* instruments, designed to measure a wide variety of behaviors, and *narrow-band instruments*, which may focus on behaviors related to single, specific constructs such as hyperactivity, shyness, or depression.

Self-monitoring **Self-monitoring** may be defined as the act of systematically observing and recording aspects of one's own behavior and/or events related to that behavior. Self-monitoring is different from self-report. As noted by Cone (1999, p. 411), self-monitoring

their every move was monitored on a daily basis by staff members.

Even though patients are not always comfortable having their behavior rated—and indeed many patients have outbursts with staff members that are in one way or another related to the rating system—it is also true that the system seems to work. Sometimes, self-consciousness is what is needed for people to get better. Here, I think of Sandy, a bright young man who gradually became fascinated by the CDR and soon spent much of the day asking staff members various questions about it. Before long, Sandy asked if he could be allowed to code his own CDR. No one had ever asked to do that before, and a staff meeting was held to mull over the consequences of such an action. As an experiment, it was decided that this patient would be allowed to code his own CDR. The experiment paid off. Sandy's self-coding kept him relatively "on track" with regard to his behavioral goals, and he found himself trying even harder to get better as he showed signs of improvement. Upon discharge, Sandy said he would miss tracking his progress with the CDR.

Instruments such as the CDR can and probably have been used as weapons or rewards by staff. Staff may threaten patients with a poor behavioral evaluation. Overly negative evaluations in response to dysfunctional behavior that is particularly upsetting to the staff is also an ever-present possibility. Yet all the time you are keenly aware that the system works best when staff code patients' behavior consistently and fairly.

A member receives training in kitchen skills for independent living as a staff member monitors behavior on the CDR.

. . . relies on observations of *the* behavior of clinical interest . . . at the *time* . . . and *place* . . . of its actual occurrence. In contrast, self-report uses stand-ins or surrogates (verbal descriptions, reports) of the behavior of interest that are obtained at a time and place different from the time and place of the behavior's actual occurrence [emphasis in the original].

Self-monitoring may be used to record specific thoughts, feelings, or behaviors. The utility of self-monitoring depends in large part on the competence, diligence, and motivation of the assessee, although a number of ingenious methods have been devised to assist in the process or ensure compliance (Barton et al., 1999; Bornstein et al., 1986; Wilson & Vitousek, 1999). For example, handheld computers have been programmed to beep as a cue to observe and record behavior (Shiffman et al., 1997).

Self-monitoring is both a tool of assessment and a tool of intervention. In some instances, the very act of self-monitoring (of smoking, eating, anxiety, and panic, for example) may be therapeutic. Practical issues that must be considered include the methodology employed, the targeting of specific thoughts, feelings, or behaviors, the sampling procedures put in place, the actual self-monitoring devices and procedures, and the training and preparation (Foster et al., 1999).

Psychometric issues also must be considered (Jackson, 1999), including the potential problem of *reactivity*. **Reactivity** refers to the possible changes in an assessee's behavior, thinking, or performance that may arise in response to being observed, assessed, or evaluated. For example, if you are on a weight-loss program and self-monitoring your food intake, you may be more inclined to forgo the cheesecake than to consume it. Education, training, and adequate preparation are some of the tools used to counter the effects of reactivity in self-monitoring. In addition, post-self-monitoring interviews on the effects of reactivity can provide additional insights about the emission of the targeted thoughts or behaviors.

> **JUST THINK . . .**
>
> Create an original example to illustrate how self-monitoring can be a tool of assessment as well as an intervention.

Analogue studies The behavioral approach to clinical assessment and treatment has been likened to a researcher's approach to experimentation. The behavioral assessor proceeds in many ways like a researcher; the client's problem is the dependent variable, and the factor(s) responsible for causing or maintaining the problem behavior is the independent variable(s). Behavioral assessors typically use the phrase **functional analysis** of behavior to convey the process of identifying the dependent and independent variables with respect to the presenting problem. However, just as experimenters must frequently employ independent and dependent variables that imitate those variables in the real world, so must behavioral assessors.

An **analogue study** is a research investigation in which one or more variables are similar or analogous to the real variable the investigator wishes to examine. This definition is admittedly very broad, and the term *analogue study* has been used in varied ways. It has been used, for example, to describe research conducted with white rats when the experimenter really wishes to learn about humans. It has been used to describe research conducted with full-time students when the experimenter really wishes to learn about people employed full-time in business settings. It has been used to describe research on aggression, with aggression defined as the laboratory administration of electric shock, when the experimenter really wishes to learn about real-world aggression outside the laboratory.

More specific than the term *analogue study* is **analogue behavioral observation,** which, after Haynes (2001a), may be defined as the observation of a person or persons in an environment designed to increase the chance that the assessor can observe targeted behaviors and interactions. The person or persons in this definition may be clients (including individual children and adults, families, or couples) or research subjects (including students, co-workers, or any other research sample). The targeted behavior, of course, depends on the objective of the research. For a client who avoids hiking because of a fear of snakes, the behavior targeted for assessment (and change) is the fear reaction to snakes, most typically elicited while hiking. This behavior may be assessed (and treated) in analogue fashion within the confines of a clinician's office, using photos of snakes, videos of snakes, live snakes that are caged, and live snakes that are not caged.

> **JUST THINK . . .**
>
> As a result of a car accident, a client of a behavior therapist claims not to be able to get into a car and drive again. The therapist wishes to assess this complaint by means of analogue behavioral observation. How should the therapist proceed?

A variety of environments designed to increase the chances that the assessor can observe the targeted behavior have been employed (see, for example, Heyman, 2001; Mori

& Armendariz, 2001; Norton & Hope, 2001; and Roberts, 2001). Questions about how analogous some analogue studies really are have been raised, along with questions regarding their ultimate utility (Haynes, 2001b).

Situational performance measures and role-play measures both may be thought of as analogue approaches to assessment.

Situational performance measures   If you have ever applied for a part-time clerical job and been required to take a typing test, you have had firsthand experience with *situational performance measures*. Broadly stated, a **situational performance measure** is a procedure that allows for observation and evaluation of an individual under a standard set of circumstances. A situational performance measure typically involves performance of some specific task under actual or simulated conditions. The road test you took to obtain your driver's license was a situational performance measure that entailed an evaluation of your driving skills in a real car on a real road in real traffic. On the other hand, situational performance measures used to assess the skills of prospective space-traveling astronauts are done in rocket simulators in laboratories firmly planted on Mother Earth. What all the situational performance measures have in common is that the construct they measure is thought to be more accurately assessed by examining behavior directly than by asking subjects to describe their behavior. In some cases, subjects may be motivated to misrepresent themselves, as when asked about moral behavior. In other situations, subjects may simply not know how they will respond under particular circumstances, as in a stress test.

The **leaderless group technique** is a situational assessment procedure wherein several people are organized into a group for the purpose of carrying out a task as an observer records information related to individual group members' initiative, cooperation, leadership, and related variables. All group members typically know they are being evaluated and that their behavior is being observed and recorded. Purposely vague instructions are typically provided to the group, and no one is placed in the position of leadership or authority. The group determines how it will accomplish the task and who will be responsible for what duties. The leaderless group situation provides an opportunity to observe the degree of cooperation exhibited by each individual group member and the extent to which each individual is able to function as part of a team.

The leaderless group technique has been employed in military and industrial settings. Its use in the military developed out of attempts by the U.S. Office of Strategic Services (OSS, 1948) to assess leadership as well as other personality traits. The procedure was designed to aid in the establishment of cohesive military units—cockpit crews, tank crews, and so forth—in which members would work together well and each could make a significant contribution. Similarly, the procedure finds application in industrial and organizational settings in the identification of people who work well together and individuals with superior managerial skills and "executive potential."

The self-managed work-group approach challenges traditional conceptions of manager and worker. How does one manage a group that is supposed to manage itself? One approach is to try to identify *unleaders,* who act primarily as facilitators in the workplace and are able to balance a hands-off management style with a style that is more directive when necessary (Manz & Simms, 1984).

> **JUST THINK . . .**
>
> You are a management consultant to a major corporation with an assignment: Create a situational performance measure designed to identify an *unleader.* Briefly outline your plan.

Role play   The technique of **role play,** or acting an improvised or partially improvised part in a simulated situation, can be used in teaching, therapy, and assessment. Police departments, for example, routinely prepare rookies for emergencies by having them play roles, such as an officer confronted by a criminal holding a hostage at gunpoint. Part of the prospective police officer's final exam may be successful performance on a role-playing task. A therapist might use role play to help a feuding couple avoid harmful shouting matches and learn more effective methods of conflict resolution. That same couple's successful resolution of role-played issues may be one of a therapist's criteria for terminating therapy.

A large and growing literature exists on role play as a method of assessment. In general, role play can provide a relatively inexpensive, highly adaptable means of assessing various behavior "potentials." We cautiously say "potentials" because of the uncertainty that role-played behavior will be elicited in a naturalistic situation (Kern et al., 1983; Kolotkin & Wielkiewicz, 1984). Bellack et al. (1990) employed role play for both evaluative and instructional purposes with psychiatric inpatients who were being prepared for independent living. While acknowledging the benefits of role play in assessing patients' readiness to return to the community, these authors cautioned that "the ultimate validity criterion for any laboratory- or clinic-based assessment is unobtrusive observation of the target behavior in the community" (p. 253).

> **JUST THINK . . .**
>
> Describe a referral for evaluation that would ideally lend itself to the use of role play as a tool of assessment.

Psychophysiological methods   The search for clues to understanding and predicting human behavior has led researchers to the study of physiological indices such as heart rate and blood pressure. These and other indices are known to be influenced by psychological factors—hence the term **psychophysiological** to describe these variables as well as the methods used to study them. Whether these methods are properly regarded as *behavioral* in nature is debatable. Still, these techniques do tend to be associated with behaviorally oriented clinicians and researchers.

Perhaps the best known of all psychophysiological methods used by psychologists is *biofeedback*. **Biofeedback** is a generic term that may be defined broadly as a class of psychophysiological assessment techniques designed to gauge, display, and record a continuous monitoring of selected biological processes such as pulse and blood pressure. Depending on how biofeedback instrumentation is designed, many different biological processes, such as respiration rate, electrical resistance of the skin, and brain waves, may be monitored and "fed back" to the assessee via visual displays, such as lights and scales, or auditory stimuli, such as bells and buzzers.

The use of biofeedback with humans was inspired by reports that animals given rewards (and hence feedback) for the emission of certain involuntary responses (such as heart rate) could successfully modify those responses (Miller, 1969). Early experimentation with humans demonstrated a capacity to produce certain types of brain waves on command (Kamiya, 1962, 1968). Since that time, biofeedback has been used in a wide range of therapeutic and assessment-related applications (French et al., 1997; Hazlett et al., 1997; Hermann et al., 1997; Zhang et al., 1997).

The **plethysmograph** is an instrument that records changes in the volume of a part of the body arising from variations in blood supply. Investigators have used this device to explore changes in blood flow as a dependent variable. For example, Kelly (1966) found significant differences in the blood supplies of normal, anxiety-ridden, and psychoneurotic groups (the anxiety group having the highest mean) by using a plethysmograph to measure blood supply in the forearm.

A **penile plethysmograph** is also an instrument designed to measure changes in blood flow, but more specifically blood flow to the penis. Because the volume of blood in the penis increases with male sexual arousal, the penile plethysmograph has found application in the assessment of male sexual offenders. In one study, subjects who were convicted rapists demonstrated more sexual arousal to descriptions of rape and less arousal to consenting-sex stories than did control subjects (Quinsey et al., 1984). Offenders who continue to deny deviant sexual object choices may be confronted with the findings from such studies as a means of compelling them to speak more openly about their thoughts and behavior (Abel et al., 1986). **Phallometric data,** as it is referred to, also has treatment and program evaluation applications. In one such type of application, the offender—a rapist, a child molester, an exhibitionist, or some other sexual offender—is exposed to visual and/or auditory stimuli depicting scenes of normal and deviant behavior while penile tumescence is simultaneously gauged.

In the public eye, the best-known of all psychophysiological measurement tools is what is commonly referred to as a *lie detector* or **polygraph** (literally, "more than one graph"). Although not commonly associated with psychological assessment, the lie detection industry, given the frequency with which such tests are administered and the potential consequences of the tests, may be characterized as "one of the most important branches of applied psychology" (Lykken, 1981, p. 4). Based on the assumption that detectable physical changes occur when an individual lies, the polygraph provides a continuous written record (variously referred to as a *tracing*, a *graph*, a *chart*, or a *polygram*) of several physiological indices (typically respiration, galvanic skin response, and blood volume/pulse rate) as an interviewer and instrument operator (known as a *polygrapher* or *polygraphist*) asks the assessee a series of *yes/no* questions. Judgments of the truthfulness of the responses are made either informally by surveying the charts or more formally by means of a scoring system.

The reliability of judgments made by polygraphers is a matter of controversy (Iacono & Lykken, 1997). Different methods of conducting polygraphic examinations exist (Lykken, 1981), and polygraphic equipment is not standardized (Abrams, 1977; Skolnick, 1961). A problem with the method is a high false-positive rate for lying. The procedure "may label more than 50% of the innocent subjects as guilty" (Kleinmuntz & Szucko, 1984, p. 774). In light of the judgments polygraphers are called upon to make, education, training, and background requirements seem minimal. After as few as six weeks of training, one may qualify as a polygrapher. From the available psychometric and related data, it seems reasonable to conclude that the promise of a machine purporting to detect dishonesty remains to be fulfilled (Alpher & Blanton, 1985).

> **JUST THINK . . .**
>
> Polygraph evidence is not admissible in most courts, yet law enforcement agencies and the military continue to use it as a tool of evaluation. Your thoughts?

Unobtrusive measures A type of measure quite different from any we have discussed so far is the *nonreactive* or **unobtrusive** variety (Webb et al., 1966). In many instances, an unobtrusive measure is a telling physical trace or record. In one study, it was garbage—literally (Cote et al., 1985). Due to their nature, unobtrusive measures do not necessarily require the presence or cooperation of respondents when measurements are being conducted. In a now-classic book that was almost entitled *The Bullfighter's Beard*,[8] Webb et al. (1966) listed numerous examples of unobtrusive measures, including the following:

- The popularity of a museum exhibit can be measured by examination of the erosion of the floor around it relative to the erosion around other exhibits.

---

8. Webb et al. (1966) explained that the provocative, if uncommunicative, title *The Bullfighter's Beard* was a "title drawn from the observation that toreadors' beards are longer on the day of the fight than on any other day. No one seems to know if the toreador's beard really grows faster that day because of anxiety or if he simply stands further away from the blade, shaking razor in hand. Either way, there were not enough American aficionados to get the point" (p. v). The title they finally settled on was *Unobtrusive Measures: Nonreactive Research in the Social Sciences.*

- The amount of whiskey consumption in a town can be measured by counting the number of empty bottles in trashcans.
- The degree of fear induced by a ghost-story-telling session can be measured by noting the shrinking diameter of a circle of seated children.

More recently, wrappers left on trays at fast-food restaurants were used to estimate the caloric intake of restaurant patrons (Stice et al., 2004). In another innovative use of a "telling record," researchers used college yearbook photos to study the relationship between positive emotional expression and other variables, such as personality and life outcome (see this chapter's *Close-up*).

JUST THINK . . .

Stice et al. (2004) devised several unobtrusive measures to estimate the caloric intake of dieters; however, they were unable to devise an ethically acceptable way to gauge caloric intake in the home. Can you think of a way to accomplish this objective?

Issues in Behavioral Assessment

The psychometric soundness of tools of behavioral assessment can be evaluated, but how best to do that can become something of a debate. More specifically, questions arise as to the appropriateness of various models of measurement. You may recall from Chapter 5 that classical test theory and generalizability theory conceptualize test score variation in somewhat different ways. In generalizability theory, rather than trying to estimate a single true score, consideration is given to how test scores would be expected to shift across situations as a result of changes in the characteristic being measured. It is for this and related reasons that generalizability theory seems particularly applicable in behavioral assessment, as opposed to the measurement of personality traits. Behavior changes across situations, necessitating an approach to reliability that can account for those changes. By contrast, personality traits are presumed by many to be relatively stable across situations. Personality traits are therefore presumed to be more appropriately measured by instruments with assumptions consistent with the true score model.

JUST THINK . . .

Webb et al. (1966) argued that unobtrusive measures can usefully complement other research techniques such as interviews and questionnaires. What unobtrusive measure could conceivably be used to complement a questionnaire on student study habits?

Regardless of whether behavioral measures are evaluated in accordance with classical test theory, generalizability theory, or something else (such as a Skinnerian experimental analysis), it would seem there are some things on which everyone can agree. One is that there must be an acceptable level of inter-rater reliability among behavior observers or raters. A potential source of error in behavioral ratings may arise in the situation where a dissimilarity in two or more of the observed behaviors or other things being rated leads to a more favorable or unfavorable rating than would have been made had the dissimilarity not existed (Maurer & Alexander, 1991). A behavioral rating may be excessively positive (or negative) because a prior rating was excessively negative (or positive). This source of error is referred to as a **contrast effect** (Figure 12–9).

Contrast effects have been observed in interviews (Schuh, 1978), in behavioral diaries and checklists (Maurer et al., 1993), in laboratory-based performance evaluations (Smither et al., 1988), and in field performance evaluations (Ivancevich, 1983). In one study of employment interviews, as much as 80% of the total variance was thought to be due to contrast effects (Wexley et al., 1972).

To combat potential contrast effects and other types of rating error, rigorous training of raters is necessary. However, such training may be costly in terms of time and

Personality, Life Outcomes, and College Yearbook Photos

Few people would be shocked to learn that individual differences in emotion are associated with differences in personality. Yet it will probably surprise many to learn that interpersonal differences in emotion may well have a pervasive effect on the course of one's life. In one study, it was observed that a tendency to express uncontrolled anger in early childhood was associated with ill temper across the lifespan and with several negative life outcomes, such as lower educational attainment, lower-status jobs, erratic work patterns, lower military rank, and divorce (Caspi et al., 1987). Suggestive findings such as these have prompted other investigators to wonder about the possible effects of positive emotions on personality and life outcomes.

Positive emotions have many beneficial effects, ranging from the broadening of thoughts and action repertoires (Cunningham, 1988; Frederickson, 1998; Isen, 1987) to the facilitation of the approach of other people (Berry & Hansen, 1996; Frijda & Mesquita, 1994; Ruch, 1993). A smile may send the message that one is friendly and nonthreatening (Henley & LaFrance, 1984; Keating et al., 1981) and may lead to positive attributions about one's sociability, friendliness, likeability, and stability (Borkenau & Liebler, 1992; Frank et al., 1993; Matsumoto & Kudoh, 1993). On the basis of such findings and related research, Harker and Keltner (2001) hypothesized that positive emotional expression would predict higher levels of well-being across adulthood. They tested the hypothesis by examining the relationship of individual differences in positive emotional expression to personality and other variables.

A measure of positive emotional expression was obtained by coding judges' ratings of college yearbook photographs of women who participated in a longitudinal research project (Helson, 1967; Helson et al., 1984). These coded judgments were analyzed with respect to personality data on file (such as the subjects' responses to the Adjective Check List at ages 21, 27, 43, and 52) and life outcome data (including well-being as measured by the California Psychological Inventory, marital status, and the Marital Tensions Checklist).

Consistent with the researchers' hypothesis, positive emotional expression as evidenced in the college yearbook photos was found to correlate positively with life outcomes such as marital satisfaction and sense of personal well-being. This was the case even when the possible confounding influences of physical attractiveness or social desirability in responding were controlled for in the analysis of the data. The researchers cautioned, however, that the measure of

Is there a relationship between emotion expressed in college yearbook photos and personality and life outcomes? According to one study, the answer is yes. Researchers found that positive emotional expression in women's college photos predicted favorable outcomes in marriage and personal well-being up to 30 years later.

emotional expression used in the study (the yearbook photo) consisted of a single instance of very limited behavior. They urged future researchers to consider the use of different measures of emotional expression obtained in different contexts. The researchers also cautioned that their findings are limited to research with women. Smiling may have different implications for the lives of men (Stoppard & Gruchy, 1993). In fact, smiling was negatively correlated with positive outcomes for a sample of male cadets at West Point (Mueller & Mazur, 1996).

This thought-provoking study was, according to Harker and Keltner (2001), "one of the first to document that individual differences in expression relate to personality and may be stable aspects of personality" (p. 121).

Figure 12–9
The Contrast Effect at the Rink

Figure skating judges, like other behavior raters, are only human. Skaters who give performances worthy of extremely high marks may not always get what they deserve, simply because the skater who performed just before they did excelled by contrast. Ratings may be more favorable when the performance just prior to theirs was very poor. Due to a contrast effect, the points earned by a skater in a figure-skating performance may depend to some degree on the quality of the performance of the skater who skated just before.

labor. For example, teaching professionals how to use the behavior observation and coding system of the Marital Interaction Coding System took "two to three months of weekly instruction and practice to learn how to use its 32 codes" (Fredman & Sherman, 1987, p. 28). Another approach to minimizing error and improving inter-rater reliability among behavioral raters is to employ a **composite judgment,** which is, in essence, an averaging of multiple judgments.

Some types of observer bias cannot practically or readily be remedied. For example, in behavioral observation involving the use of video equipment, it would on many occasions be advantageous if multiple cameras and recorders could be used to cover various angles of the ongoing action, to get close-ups, and so forth. The economic practicality of the situation (let alone other factors, such as the number of hours required to watch footage from multiple views) is that more than one camera in a fixed position recording the action is seldom feasible. The camera is in a sense biased in that one fixed position, because in many instances it is recording information that may be quite different from the information that would have been obtained had it been placed in another position— or if multiple recordings were being made.

As we have already noted in the context of self-monitoring, reactivity is another possible issue with regard to behavioral assessment. This term refers to the fact that people react differently in experimental as opposed to natural situations. Microphones, cameras, and one-way mirrors may themselves alter the behavior of persons being observed. For example, some patients under videotaped observation may attempt to minimize the amount of psychopathology they are willing to record for posterity. Others under the same conditions may attempt to exaggerate it. One possible solution to the problem of reactivity is the use of hidden observers or clandestine recording techniques, although such methods raise serious ethical issues. Many times, all that is required to solve the problem of reactivity is an adaptation period. People being observed may adjust to the idea and begin to behave in their typical ways. Most clinicians are aware from personal experience that a tape recorder in the therapy room might put off some patients at first, but in only a matter of minutes the chances are good that it will be ignored.

A Perspective

More than a half-century ago, Theodor Reik's influential book *Listening with the Third Ear* intrigued clinicians with the possibilities of evaluation and intervention by means of skilled interviewing, active listening, and artful, depth-oriented interpretation. In one vignette, a female therapy patient recounted a visit to the dentist that entailed an injection and a tooth extraction. While speaking, she remarked on a book in Reik's bookcase that was "standing on its head"—to which Reik responded, "But why did you not tell me that you had had an abortion?" (Reik, 1948, p. 263). Reflecting on this dazzling exhibition of clinical intuition, Masling (1997) wrote, "We would all have liked to have had Reik's magic touch, the ability to discern what is hidden and secret, to serve as oracle" (p. 259).

Historically, society has called upon mental health professionals to make diagnostic judgments and intervention recommendations, often on the basis of relatively little information. Early on, psychological tests, particularly in the area of personality assessment, promised to empower clinicians—mere mortals—to play the oracular role society imposed and expected. Soon, two very different philosophies of test design and use emerged. The clinical approach relied heavily on the clinician's judgment and intuition and was characterized by a lack of preset and uniformly applied rules for drawing clinical conclusions and making predictions. By contrast, the statistical or actuarial approach relied heavily on standardization, norms, and preset, uniformly applied rules and procedures. Duels between various members of these two camps were common for many years and have been reviewed in detail elsewhere (Marchese, 1992).

It seems fair to say that in those situations where data are insufficient to formulate rules for decision making and prediction, the clinical approach wins out over the actuarial. For the most part, however, it is the actuarial approach that has been most enthusiastically embraced by contemporary practitioners. This is so for a number of reasons, chief among them a passionate desire to make assessment more a science than an art. And that desire may stem from the fact that most of us are not oracles. Without good tools, it is difficult if not impossible to spontaneously and consistently see through to what Reik (1952) characterized as the "secret self." Even with good tools, it's a challenge.

The actuarial approach permits hypotheses and predictions that have been found useful to retain, whereas untenable hypotheses and predictions may be quickly discovered and discarded (Masling, 1997). Of course, in many instances, skill in clinical assessment can be conceptualized as an internalized, less formal, and more creative version of the actuarial approach.

The actuarial approach to personality assessment is increasingly common. Even projective instruments, once the bastion of the "old school" clinical approach, are increasingly published with norms and subsequently researched using rigorous statistical methods. There have even been efforts—very respectable efforts—to apply sophisticated IRT models to, of all things, TAT data (Tuerlinckx, 2002). But academicians have by and large remained unimpressed: "In academic psychology the climate of opinion about projective tests continues as though nothing has changed and clinicians were still reading tea leaves" (Masling, 1997, p. 263).

If the oracle-like, clinical orientation is characterized as the *third ear approach,* we might characterize the contemporary orientation as a *van Gogh approach;* in a sense, an ear has been dispatched. The day of the all-knowing oracle has passed. Today, it is incumbent upon the responsible clinician to rely on norms, inferential statistics, and related essentials of the actuarial approach. Sound clinical judgment is still desirable, if not mandatory. However, it is required less for the purpose of making off-the-cuff interpretations and predictions and more for the purpose of organizing and interpreting information from different tools of assessment. More on that point as we move to Chapter 13, Clinical and Counseling Assessment.

Self-Assessment

Test your understanding of elements of this chapter by seeing if you can explain each of the following terms, expressions, and abbreviations:

analogue study
analogue behavioral observation
apperceive
behavioral assessment
behavioral observation
biofeedback
composite judgment
contrast effect
Exner's comprehensive system
figure drawing test
free association
functional analysis
HIT
inquiry

leaderless group technique
Murrayan concepts of need, press, and thema
objective methods of personality assessment
penile plethysmograph
percept
phallometric data
plethysmograph
polygraph
projective hypothesis
projective method
psychophysiological (assessment methods)

reactivity
role play
Rorschach inquiry
Rorschach scoring system
Rorschach test
self-monitoring
sentence completion stem
situational performance measure
TAT
testing the limits (on the Rorschach)
timeline followback methodology
unobtrusive measure
word association test

Web Watch

Check out the following Web sites for more information about topics discussed in this chapter.

The Rorschach
www.phil.gu.se/fu/ro.html

www.deltabravo.net/custody/rorschach.htm

http://skepdic.com/inkblot.html

Holtzman Inkblot Technique
www.cps.nova.edu/~cpphelp/HIT.html

The TAT
www.ehendrick.org/healthy/002188.htm

www.pearsonassessments.com/tests/tat.htm

http://web.utk.edu/~wmorgan/tat/tattxt.htm

Online projective tests (usual cautions apply)
http://similarminds.com/word

Projective techniques
www.wermany.org/reading/projections.htm

Psychophysiological techniques: the penile plethysmograph
http://skepdic.com/penilep.html

Projective drawings: How valid are the interpretations of these drawings?
www.psychpage.com/projective/p roj_draw _notes.html

The leaderless group
www.people.vcu.edu/~rsleeth/Tasktips99L .html#THE GROUP DECISION

The contrast effect
http://changingminds.org/explanations/theories/ perceptual_contrast.htm

13

Clinical and Counseling Assessment

Clinical psychology is that branch of psychology that has as its primary focus the prevention, diagnosis, and treatment of abnormal behavior. Clinical psychologists receive training in psychological assessment and psychotherapy and are employed in hospitals, public and private mental health centers, independent practice, and academia. Like clinical psychology, **counseling psychology** is a branch of psychology that is concerned with the prevention, diagnosis, and treatment of abnormal behavior. Clinical psychologists tend to focus their research and treatment efforts on the more severe forms of behavior pathology, whereas counseling psychologists focus more on everyday problems such as marital and family communication problems, career decisions, and difficulties with school study habits. Members of both professions strive to foster personal growth in their clients. The tools employed in the process of assessment overlap considerably.

All the tests and measures we have covered so far—intelligence, personality, self-concept, cognitive style—are appropriate to discuss in this chapter, for all have potential application in clinical and counseling contexts. Other specialized instruments might be covered here as well, such as tools designed to assess workplace-related variables. In an introductory text such as this, however, choices must be made as to coverage and organization.

In the previous two chapters, a variety of approaches to the assessment of personality and behavior were introduced. In this chapter, we look at various tools of psychological assessment in the context of clinical and counseling applications and touch on various issues related to their use. Along the way, you'll find important information regarding *culturally informed assessment:* what is meant by this term and some strategies for its achievement. The chapter concludes with a discussion of issues relating to clinical versus actuarial assessment. After reading that discussion, you'll be better prepared to decide whether the title (and subject matter) of this chapter should be changed in the future to something like "Actuarial Assessment."

An Overview

Clinical assessment may be undertaken for various reasons. For the clinical psychologist working in a hospital, clinic, or other clinical setting, tools of assessment are frequently used to clarify the psychological problem, make a diagnosis, and/or design a treatment plan. "Does this patient have a mental disorder?" and "If so, what is the diagnosis?" are typical questions that require answers. In many cases, tools of assessment, including an interview, a test, and case history data, can provide those answers. Let's briefly explore how these tools can be used in clinical settings.

Before or after interviewing a patient, a clinician may administer tests such as a Wechsler intelligence test and the MMPI-2 to obtain estimates of the patient's intellectual functioning and level of psychopathology. The data derived may provide the clinician with initial hypotheses about the nature of the individual's difficulties, which will then guide the interview. Alternatively, test data can confirm or refute hypotheses made on the basis of the clinical interview. Interview and test data will be supplemented with case history data, especially if the patient will not or cannot cooperate. The clinician may interview people who know the patient, such as family members, co-workers, and friends, and obtain records relevant to the case.

♦ JUST THINK . . .

Clinicians approach assessment in different ways. Some prefer little more than a test referral to begin with (so that their findings will not be shaped in any way by others' impressions or case history data), while other clinicians prefer to obtain as much information as they can prior to interviewing and administering any tests. Your preference?

"What is this person's current level of functioning? How does it compare with that of other people of the same age?" Consider the example of an individual who is suspected of suffering from dementia caused by Alzheimer's disease. The patient has experienced a steady and progressive loss of cognitive skills over a period of months. A diagnosis of dementia may involve tracking the individual's performance with repeated administrations of tests of cognitive ability, including memory. If dementia is present, a progressive decline in test performance will be noted. Periodic testing with various instruments may also provide information about the kinds of activities the patient should be advised to pursue, as well as the kinds of activities the patient should be encouraged to curtail or give up entirely. Ideally, case history data will provide some way to estimate the patient's level of **premorbid** (meaning "before illness or disorder") **functioning.**

"What type of treatment shall this patient be offered?" Tools of assessment can help guide decisions relating to treatment. Patients found to be high in intelligence, for example, tend to make good candidates for insight-oriented methods that require high levels of abstract ability. A person who complains of being depressed may be asked periodically to complete a measure of depression. If such a person is an inpatient, trends in the depth of depression as measured by the instrument may contribute to critical decisions regarding level of supervision within the institution, strength of medication administered, and date of discharge.

"How can this person's personality best be described?" Gaining an understanding of the individual need not focus on psychopathology. People who do not have any mental disorder sometimes seek psychotherapy for personal growth or support in coping with a difficult set of life circumstances. In such instances, interviews and personality tests geared more to the normal testtaker might be employed.

Researchers may raise a wide variety of other assessment-related questions, including "Which treatment approach is most effective?" or "What kind of client tends to benefit most from a particular kind of treatment?" A researcher may believe, for example, that people with a field-dependent cognitive style would be most likely to benefit from a cognitive-behavioral approach to treatment, and people with a field-independent cognitive style would be most likely to benefit from a humanistic approach to treatment. The researcher would use a variety of assessment tools to combine subjects into treatment groups and then to measure outcome in psychotherapy.

Counseling psychologists who do employment counseling may use a wide variety of assessment tools to help determine not only what occupations a person might enjoy but also which occupations would be sufficiently challenging but not overwhelming. School psychologists and counseling psychologists working in a school setting may assist students with a wide variety of problems, including those related to studying. Here, behavioral measures, including self-monitoring, might be employed to better understand exactly how, when, and where the student engages in study behavior. The answer to related questions such as "Why am I not doing well in school?" may in part be found in diagnostic educational tests, such as those designed to identify problem areas in reading and reading comprehension. Another part of the answer may be obtained through other tools of assessment, including the interview, which may focus on aspects of the student's motivation and other life circumstances.

JUST THINK . . .

Cite another example or two to illustrate how a tool of assessment could be used in a clinical or counseling setting.

Clinical Assessment and Managed Care

The majority of all health care in the United States is delivered through a managed-care system (Sanchez & Turner, 2003). For this reason, any overview of contemporary clinical assessment would be incomplete without reference to managed care and the profound effect its widespread institution has had on clinical assessment. In general, **managed care** may be defined as a health care system wherein the products and services provided to patients by a network of participating health care providers are mediated by an administrative agency of the insurer that works to keep costs down by fixing schedules of reimbursement to the providers.

Managed care first became a national reality with the passage into law of the HMO Act of 1973, which provided federal funding for it. Subsequent amendments to that act, as well as the skyrocketing cost of health care, created a fertile environment for managed care. Managed care companies have been unwilling to allocate scarce health care dollars to psychological assessment services. Consequently, despite compelling evidence of the effectiveness of assessment services in health care settings (Kubiszyn et al., 2000), such services have been drastically curtailed (Cushman & Guilford, 2000; Eisman et al., 2000). Payment-based restrictions on time and test selection can create conflicts of interest on the part of test users (Lezak, 2002). To a large degree, both the fate of clinical assessment in health care settings and the nature of the practice of assessment have been linked to the dictates of economic reality and third-party decisions regarding managed care (Piotrowski et al., 1998).

JUST THINK . . .

Argue the case that managed care can be good for the assessment enterprise.

A key function of clinical assessment, in or out of a managed care environment, is the diagnosis of mental disorders. Our overview continues with a focus on this aspect of clinical assessment.

The Diagnosis of Mental Disorders

Frequently, an objective of clinical assessment is to diagnose mental disorders. The reference source used for making such diagnoses is the current version of the American Psychiatric Association's *Diagnostic and Statistical Manual (DSM)*, which presently is the **DSM-IV-TR** (where IV stands for "fourth edition," and TR stands for "text revision"). DSM-IV was published in 1994, and its revision was published in 2000. DSM-IV-TR names and describes all known mental disorders and even includes a category called *Conditions not attributable to a mental disorder that are a focus of attention or treatment.* A DSM-IV-TR diagnosis immediately conveys a great deal of descriptive information about the nature of the behavioral deviance, deficits, or excesses in the diagnosed person.

Some clinical psychologists, most vocally the behaviorally-oriented clinicians, have expressed dissatisfaction with DSM-IV-TR on many grounds. Perhaps their chief concern is that the manual is firmly rooted in the medical model. Patterns of thinking and behavior are not described in DSM-IV-TR as just that—patterns of thinking and behavior—but rather in ways akin to describing diseases. This diagnostic system has also been criticized for being relatively unreliable. Different clinicians interviewing the same patient may well come up with different diagnoses. Further, even when all clinicians concur on a diagnosis, the DSM-IV-TR provides no guidance as to what method of treatment will be optimally effective. From a cultural perspective, the DSM-IV-TR may have been built on a foundation with insufficient sensitivity to certain cultures, especially with regard to the discussion of dissociative disorders (Lewis-Fernandez, 1998).

JUST THINK . . .

Should a diagnostic manual provide clinicians with guidance as to what method of treatment will be optimally effective?

Proponents of DSM-IV-TR believe that this diagnostic system is useful because of the wealth of information conveyed by a psychiatric diagnosis. They argue that perfect interdiagnostician reliability cannot be achieved, because of the nature of the subject matter. In response to the medical model criticism, DSM-IV-TR supporters maintain that the diagnostic system is useful whether or not any particular diagnostic category is actually a disease. Each of the disorders listed is associated with pain, suffering, or disability. The classification system, it is argued, provides useful subject headings under which practitioners can search for (or add to) the research literature with respect to the different diagnostic categories.

In DSM-IV-TR, diagnoses are coded according to five *axes* (dimensions). The types of disorders subsumed under each axis are as follows:

Axis I: Disorders of infancy, childhood, and adolescence; dementias such as those caused by Alzheimer's disease; disorders arising out of drug use; mood and anxiety disorders; and schizophrenia. Also included here are conditions that may be the focus of treatment (such as academic or social problems) but are not attributable to mental disorder.

Axis II: Mental retardation and personality disorders.

Axis III: Physical conditions that may affect mental functioning—from migraine headaches to allergies—are included here.

Axis IV: Different problems or sources of stress may occur in an individual's life at any given time. Financial, legal, marital, occupational, or other problems may precipitate behavior ranging from starting to smoke after having quit to attempting suicide. The presence of such problems is noted on this axis.

Axis V: This axis calls for a global rating of overall functioning. At the high end of this scale are ratings indicative of no symptoms and everyday concerns. At the low end of this scale are ratings indicative of people who are a clear and present danger to themselves or others and must therefore be confined in a secure facility.

DSM-IV-TR diagnoses are descriptive and atheoretical. This is appropriate for an authoritative reference work designed to provide common language for clinicians and researchers with varied theoretical orientations toward the etiology and treatment of mental disorders (Widiger & Clark, 2000). The first two axes contain all the diagnostic categories of mental disorders, and the remaining three axes provide additional information regarding an individual's level of functioning and current life situation. Multiple diagnoses are possible. An individual may be diagnosed, for example, as exhibiting behavior indicative of disorders listed on both Axis I and Axis II.

At this writing, the fifth edition of the DSM is scheduled to be published in the near future. In an effort to address critics of DSM-IV-TR, a variety of intriguing issues related to categorizing mental disorders have been raised (Kupfer et al., 2002). Perhaps one of the most basic questions is, "What is a disorder?" This deceptively simple question has generated heated debate (Clark, 1999; Spitzer, 1999). The third edition of the DSM was the first edition of that manual to contain a definition of mental disorder, and the definition it offered was criticized by many. As an alternative, Jerome C. Wakefield (1992a) conceptualized mental disorder as a "harmful dysfunction." For Wakefield, a disorder is a harmful failure of internal mechanisms to perform their naturally selected functions. Wakefield's position is an **evolutionary view of mental disorder** because the internal mechanisms that break down or fail are viewed as having been acquired through the Darwinian process of natural selection. For Wakefield, the attribution of disorder entails two things: (1) a scientific judgment that such an evolutionary failure exists, and (2) a value judgment that this failure is harmful to the individual (Wakefield, 1992b).

In contrast to the evolutionary view of disorder are myriad other views. Klein (1999) argued that "proper evolutionary function" is not known and that behavior labeled "disordered" may be the product of various involuntary causes (such as disease) or even voluntary causes (as role-playing or malingering). Others have weighed in on this controversial issue by illuminating the role of culture (Kirmayer & Young, 1999) and by championing alternative vantage points, such as focusing on the issue at the level of the neuron (Richters & Hinshaw, 1999). Some have offered that the concept of disorder is so broad that it need not have any defining properties (Lilienfeld & Marino, 1995, 1999).

JUST THINK . . .

So, what *is* a disorder?

Regardless of how disorder is defined, a key tool for identifying it is the interview. And if Jonathan Shedler has his way, disorder will be identified by patients themselves using a handheld computer. Shedler (2000) developed a diagnostic tool designed for self-administration by patients of primary care physicians. The patients are posed questions on the built-in display and then respond yes or no on the keyboard. The physician may obtain a computer-generated report of the findings, including specific DSM diagnoses. Of course, interviews with patients can still be conducted the old-fashioned way, and it is to that variety of dialogue that we now turn.

The Interview

Except in rare circumstances, such as when an assessee is totally noncommunicative, an interview is likely to be part of every clinician's or counselor's individual assessment. In a clinical situation, for example, an interview may be conducted to arrive at a diagnosis, to pinpoint areas that must be addressed in psychotherapy, or to determine whether an individual will harm himself or others. In a typical counseling application, an interview is conducted to help the interviewee learn more about him- or herself, the better to make a career or other life choice. Usually conducted face to face, interviewers learn about interviewees not only from *what* they say but also from *how* they say it and from how they present themselves during the interview.

Often, an interview will guide decisions about what else needs to be done to assess an individual. If symptoms or complaints are described by the interviewee in a vague or inconsistent manner, a test designed to screen in a general way for psychopathology may be indicated. If an interviewee complains of memory problems, a standardized memory test may be administered. If the interviewee is unable to describe the frequency with which a particular problem occurs, a period of self-monitoring may be in order. Interviews are frequently used early on in independent practice settings to solidify a

therapeutic contract, an agreement between client and therapist setting forth goals, expectations, and mutual obligations with regard to a course of therapy.

Seasoned interviewers endeavor to create a positive, accepting climate in which to conduct the interview. They may use open-ended questions initially and then closed questions to obtain specific information. The effective interviewer conveys understanding to the interviewee verbally or nonverbally. Ways of conveying that understanding include attentive posture and facial expression, as well as frequent statements acknowledging or summarizing what the interviewee is trying to say. Sometimes interviewers attempt to convey attentiveness by head nodding and vocalizations such as "um-hmm." However, here the interviewer must exercise caution. Such vocalizations and head nodding have been observed to act as reinforcers that increase the emission of certain interviewee verbalizations (Greenspoon, 1955). For example, if a therapist said "um-hmm" every time an interviewee brought up material related to the subject of mother, then—other things being equal—the interviewee might spend more time talking about mother than if not reinforced for bringing up that topic.

Many different types of interviews exist; the *tone* of one interview may differ markedly from another as a function of the purpose of the interview. Let's now look at different types of interviews.

Types of Interviews

Interviews may be typed with respect to a number of different variables. One such variable is *content.* The content of some interviews, such as a general, getting-to-know-you interview, can be wide ranging. By contrast, other interviews focus narrowly on particular content. Another variable on which interviews differ is *structure.* A highly structured interview is one in which all the questions asked are prepared in advance. In an interview with little structure, few or no questions are prepared in advance, leaving interviewers the freedom to delve into subject areas as their judgment dictates. An advantage of a structured interview is that it provides a uniform method of exploration and evaluation. A structured interview, much like a test, may therefore be employed as a standardized pre/post measure of outcome. In fact, many research studies to explore the efficacy of a new medication, an approach to therapy, or some other intervention, employ structured interviews as outcome measures.

Many structured interviews are available for use by assessment professionals. For example, the Structured Clinical Interview for Dissociative Disorders (SCID-D) is designed to assist in the diagnosis of dissociative disorders (Steinberg et al., 1993). The Schedule for Affective Disorders and Schizophrenia (SADS; Endicott & Spitzer, 1978) is a standardized interview designed to detect schizophrenia and disorders of affect. The Structured Interview of Reported Symptoms (SIRS; Rogers, 1986; Rogers et al., 1992) is used in efforts to detect malingering.

In addition to content and structure, interviews may differ in *tone.* In one type of interview—not very common—the interviewer intentionally tries to make the interviewee feel stressed. **Stress interview** is the general name applied to any interview where one objective is to place the interviewee in a pressured state for some particular reason. The stress may be induced to test for some aspect of personality (such as aggressiveness or hostility) that might be elicited only under such conditions. Screening for work in the security or intelligence fields might entail stress interviews if a criterion of the job is the ability to remain cool under pressure. The source of the stress varies as a function of the purpose of the evaluation; possible sources may emanate from the interviewer as disapproving facial expressions, critical remarks, condescending reassurances, relentless probing, or seeming incompetence. Other sources of stress may emanate from the "rules of the game," such as unrealistic time limits for complying with demands.

Interviewee *state of consciousness* is another variable related to interview type. Most interviews are conducted with the interviewee in an ordinary, everyday, waking state of consciousness. On occasion, however, a particular situation may call for a very specialized interview in which the state of consciousness of the interviewee is deliberately altered. A **hypnotic interview** is one conducted while the interviewee is under hypnosis. Hypnotic interviews may be conducted as part of a therapeutic assessment or intervention when the interviewee has been an eyewitness to a crime or related situations. In all such cases, the prevailing belief is that the hypnotic state will focus the interviewee's concentration and enhance recall (McConkey & Sheehan, 1996; Reiser, 1980, 1990; Vingoe, 1995).

Critics of hypnotic interviewing suggest that any gains in recall may be offset by losses in accuracy and other possible negative outcomes (Kebbell & Wagstaff, 1998). Hypnotic interview procedures may inadvertently make interviewees more confident of their memories, regardless of their correctness (Dywan & Bowers, 1983; Sheehan et al., 1984). As compared to nonhypnotized interviewees, hypnotized interviewees may be more suggestible to leading questions and thus more vulnerable to distortion of memories (Putnam, 1979; Zelig & Beidleman, 1981). Some researchers believe that hypnosis of witnesses may inadvertently produce memory distortion that is irreversible (Diamond, 1980; Orne, 1979). As a result, witnesses who have been hypnotized to enhance memory may be banned from testifying (Laurence & Perry, 1988; Perry & Laurence, 1990).

An interview procedure designed to retain the best features of a hypnotic interview but minus the hypnotic induction has been developed by Fisher and colleagues (Fisher & Geiselman, 1992; Fisher et al., 1989; Fisher et al., 1987; Mello & Fisher, 1996). In the **cognitive interview,** rapport is established and the interviewee encouraged to use imagery and focused retrieval to recall information. If the interviewee is an eyewitness to a crime, he or she may be asked to shift perspective and describe events from the viewpoint of the perpetrator. Much like what typically occurs in hypnosis, a great deal of control of the interview shifts to the interviewee. And unlike many police interviews, there is an emphasis on open-ended rather than closed questions, and interviewees are allowed to speak without interruption (Kebbell & Wagstaff, 1998).

The **collaborative interview** allows the interviewee wide latitude to interact with the interviewer. It is almost as if the boundary between professional assessor and lay assessee has been diminished, and both are participants working closely together—collaborating—on a common mission of discovery, clarification, and enlightenment. In an initial contact prior to a formal assessment by tests and other means, an interviewee might be invited to help frame objectives. What should be accomplished by the assessment? The interviewee is very much an active participant in collaborative assessment. Descriptions of an essentially collaborative assessment process may be found in the writings of Dana (1982), Finn (1996), Fischer (1994), and others. What they have in common is "empowerment of the person through a participatory, collaborative role in the assessment process" (Allen, 2002, p. 221).

> **JUST THINK . . .**
>
> In what innovative way would you like to participate or collaborate in your own clinical or counseling interview?

Regardless of the specific type of interview conducted, certain "standard" questions are typically raised with regard to the following areas. These questions are followed by additional queries as clinical judgment dictates:

Demographic data: Name, age, sex, religion, number of persons in family, race, occupation, marital status, socioeconomic status, address, telephone numbers.

Reason for referral: Why is this individual requesting or being sent for psychological assessment? Who is the referral source?

Past medical history: What events are significant in this individual's medical history?

Present medical condition: What current medical complaints does this individual have? What medications are currently being used?

Familial medical history: What chronic or familial types of disease are present in the family history?

Past psychological history: What traumatic events has this individual suffered? What psychological problems (such as disorders of mood or disorders of thought content) have troubled this individual?

Past history with medical or psychological professionals: What similar contacts for assessment or intervention has this individual had? Were these contacts satisfactory in the eyes of the assessee? If not, why not?

Current psychological conditions: What psychological problems are currently troubling this person? How long have these problems persisted? What is causing these problems? What are the psychological strengths of this individual?

Throughout the interview, the interviewer may jot down subjective impressions about the interviewee's general appearance (appropriate?), personality (sociable? suspicious? shy?), mood (elated? depressed?), emotional reactivity (appropriate? blunted?), thought content (hallucinations? delusions? obsessions?), speech (normal conversational? slow and rambling? rhyming? singing? shouting?), and judgment (regarding such matters as prior behavior and plans for the future). During the interview, any chance actions by the patient that may be relevant to the purpose of the assessment are noted.[1]

One variety of clinical interview used frequently, especially in medical settings, is the mental status examination.

The mental status examination   A parallel to the general physical examination conducted by a physician is a **mental status examination** conducted by a clinician. This examination, used to screen for intellectual, emotional, and neurological deficits, typically includes questioning or observation with respect to each area discussed in the following list.

Appearance: Are the patient's dress and general appearance appropriate?

Behavior: Is anything remarkably strange about the patient's speech or general behavior during the interview? Does the patient exhibit facial tics, involuntary movements, difficulties in coordination or gait?

Orientation: Is the patient oriented to person? That is, does he know who he is? Is the patient oriented to place? That is, does she know where she is? Is the patient oriented to time? That is, does he or she know the year, the month, and the day?

Memory: How is the patient's memory of recent and long-past events?

---

1. Tangentially we note the experience of the senior author (RJC) while conducting a clinical interview in the Bellevue Hospital Emergency Psychiatric Service. Throughout the intake interview, the patient sporadically blinked his left eye. At one point in the interview, the interviewer said, "I notice that you keep blinking your left eye"—in response to which the interviewee said, "Oh, this . . ." as he proceeded to remove his (glass) eye. Once he regained his breath, the interviewer noted this vignette on the intake sheet.

Sensorium: Are there any problems related to the five senses?

Psychomotor activity: Does there appear to be any abnormal retardation or quickening of motor activity?

State of consciousness: Does consciousness appear to be clear, or is the patient bewildered, confused, or stuporous?

Affect: Is the patient's emotional expression appropriate? For example, does the patient (inappropriately) laugh while discussing the death of an immediate family member?

Mood: Throughout the interview, has the patient generally been angry? Depressed? Anxious? Apprehensive?

Personality: In what terms can the patient best be described? Sensitive? Stubborn? Apprehensive?

Thought content: Is the patient hallucinating—seeing, hearing, or otherwise experiencing things that aren't really there? Is the patient delusional—expressing untrue, unfounded beliefs (such as the delusion that someone follows him or her everywhere)? Does the patient appear to be obsessive—does the patient appear to think the same thoughts over and over again?

Thought processes: Is there under- or overproductivity of ideas? Do ideas seem to come to the patient abnormally slowly or quickly? Is there evidence of loosening of associations? Are the patient's verbal productions rambling or disconnected?

Intellectual resources: What is the estimated intelligence of the interviewee?

Insight: Does the patient realistically appreciate his or her situation and the necessity for professional assistance if such assistance is necessary?

Judgment: How appropriate has the patient's decision making been with regard to past events and future plans?

A mental status examination begins the moment the interviewee enters the room. The examiner takes note of the examinee's appearance, gait, and so forth. **Orientation** is assessed by straightforward questions such as "What is your name?" "Where are you now?" and "What is today's date?" If the patient is indeed oriented to person, place, and time, the assessor may note in the record of the assessment "Oriented × 3" (read "**oriented times 3**").

Different kinds of questions based on the individual examiner's own preferences will be asked, to assess different areas in the examination. For example, to assess intellectual resources, questions may range from those of general information (such as "What is the capital of New York?"), to arithmetic calculations (such as "What is 81 divided by 9?"), to proverb interpretations (such as "What does this saying mean: People who live in glass houses shouldn't throw stones?"). Insight may be assessed, for example, simply by asking the interviewee why he or she is being interviewed. The interviewee who has little or no appreciation of the reason for the interview will indicate little insight. An alternative explanation, however, might be that the interviewee is malingering.

As a result of a mental status examination, a clinician might be better able to diagnose the interviewee, if in fact the purpose of the interview is diagnostic. The outcome of such an examination might be, for example, a decision to hospitalize or not to hospitalize, or a request for a deeper-level psychological or neurological examination.

JUST THINK . . .

A clinical interviewer conducts a mental status examination and determines that the interviewee is extremely depressed, possibly to the point of being a danger to himself. How might this clinical impression be validated?

Psychometric Aspects of the Interview

After an interview, an interviewer usually reaches some conclusions about the interviewee. Those conclusions, like test scores, can be evaluated for their reliability and validity.

If more than one interviewer conducts an interview with the same individual, inter-rater reliability for interview data could be represented by the degree of agreement between the different interviewers' conclusions. One study explored the diagnosis of schizophrenia through two different types of interviews, one structured and one unstructured. Perhaps not surprisingly, Lindstrom et al. (1994) found that more structured interviews yielded higher inter-rater reliability, even though the content of the two types of interviews was similar.

Consistent with the findings of Lindstrom et al. (1994), the inter-rater reliability of interview data may be increased when different interviewers consider specific issues systematically. Systematic and specific consideration of various interview issues can be fostered in various ways. One way involves having interviewers complete a scale rating the interviewee on targeted variables at the conclusion of the interview. In one study, family members were interviewed by several psychologists for the purpose of diagnosing depression. The actual content of the interviews was left to the discretion of the interviewers, although all interviewers completed the same rating scale at the conclusion of the interview. Completion of the post-interview rating scale improved inter-rater reliability (Miller et al., 1994).

In general, when an interview is undertaken for diagnostic purposes, the reliability and validity of the diagnostic conclusions made on the basis of the interview data are likely to increase when the diagnostic criteria are clear and specific. Efforts to increase inter-rater reliability for diagnostic purposes are evident in the third revision of the *Diagnostic and Statistical Manual* (DSM-III), published in 1980. Although its predecessor, DSM-II (1968), provided descriptive information about the disorders listed, the descriptions were inconsistent in specific detail and in some cases could be fairly vague. For example, this is the DSM-II description of paranoid personality:

> This behavioral pattern is characterized by hypersensitivity, rigidity, unwarranted suspicion, jealousy, envy, excessive self-importance, and a tendency to blame others and ascribe evil motives to them. These characteristics often interfere with the patient's ability to maintain satisfactory interpersonal relations. Of course, the presence of suspicion itself does not justify the diagnosis, since suspicion may be warranted in some cases. (American Psychiatric Association, 1968, p. 42)

A description such as this may be helpful in communicating the nature of the disorder, but because of its nonspecificity and openness to interpretation, it is of only minimal value for diagnostic purposes. In an effort to bolster the reliability and validity of psychiatric diagnoses, the DSM-III (American Psychiatric Association, 1980) provided specific diagnostic guidelines, including a specific number of symptoms that had to be present for the diagnosis to be made. The diagnostic criteria for paranoid personality disorder, for example, listed eight ways in which suspicion might be displayed, at least three of which must be present for the diagnosis to be made. It listed four ways in which hypersensitivity might be displayed, two of which had to be present for the diagnosis to be made. It listed four ways in which restricted affect might be displayed, two of which had to be present for the diagnosis to be made (American Psychiatric Association, 1980). This trend toward increased specificity in diagnostic descriptions continued in an interim revision of DSM-III (published in 1987 and referred to as DSM-III-R) as well as in the more recent revisions, DSM-IV (American Psychiatric Association, 1994) and DSM-IV-TR.

Evaluating the consistency of conclusions drawn from two interviews separated by some period of time produces a coefficient of reliability that conceptually parallels a coefficient of test-retest reliability. As an example, consider a study of the reliability of a semi-structured interview for the diagnosis of alcoholism, as well as commonly co-occurring disorders (such as substance dependence, substance abuse, depression, and antisocial personality disorder). Bucholz et al. (1994) found that some disorders (substance dependence and depression) were diagnosed with greater test-retest reliability than were other disorders (substance abuse and antisocial personality disorder).

Criterion validity of conclusions made on the basis of interviews concerns psychometricians as much as the criterion validity of conclusions made on the basis of test data. The degree to which an interviewer's findings or conclusions concur with other test results or other behavioral evidence reflects on the criterion-related validity of the conclusions. Consider in this context a study that compared the accuracy of two different tools of assessment in predicting the behavior of probationers: an objective test and a structured interview. Harris (1994) concluded that the structured interview was much more accurate in predicting the criterion (later behavior of probationers) than was the test. In another study, this one having as a criterion the accurate reporting of the subject's drug use, a paper-and-pencil test was also pitted against an interview. The written test was found to be more criterion-valid than the interview, perhaps because people may be more disposed to admit to illegal drug use in writing than in a face-to-face interview (McElrath, 1994).

An interview is a dynamic interaction between two or more people. On occasion, interviews may seem to develop lives of their own. Ultimately, the nature and form of any interview is determined by many factors, such as

- the interview referral question
- the context and setting of the interview (clinic, prison, practitioner's office, etc.)
- the nature and quality of background information available to the interviewer
- time constraints, if any, as well as any other limiting factors
- the interviewee's previous experience, if any, with similar types of interviews
- the motivation, willingness, and abilities of the interviewee
- the motivation, willingness, and abilities of the interviewer
- cultural aspects of the interview

What do we mean by this last point? Read on.

Cultural Aspects of the Interview

When an interview is conducted in preparation for counseling or psychotherapy, it may be useful to explore a number of culture-related issues. To what extent does the client feel different from other people, and how much of a problem is this? What conflicts, if any, are evident with regard to motivation to assimilate versus commitment to a particular culture? To what extent does the client feel different as an individual vis-à-vis the cultural group with which she or he identifies most? What role, if any, does racism or prejudice play as an obstacle to this client's adjustment? What role, if any, do the dominant culture's standards (such as physical attractiveness) play in this client's adjustment? In what ways have culture-related factors affected this client's feelings of self-worth? What potential exists for cultural loss or feelings of rootlessness and loss of native heritage as a function of efforts to assimilate? Questions regarding physical health may also be appropriate, especially if the client is from a cultural group that has a documented tendency to express emotional distress through physical symptoms (Cheung & Lau, 1982; Kleinman & Lin, 1980).

The misspelled **ADRESSING** is an easy-to-remember acronym that may help the assessor remember various sources of cultural influence when assessing clients. As proposed by Pamela Hays (Hays, 1996; Hays & LeVine, 2001), the letters in ADRESSING stand for *a*ge, *d*isability, *r*eligion, *e*thnicity, *s*ocial status (including variables such as income, occupation, and education), *s*exual orientation, *i*ndigenous heritage, *n*ational origin, and *g*ender. How, for example, might a particular disability affect one's worldview in a particular context? Why might a deeply religious person feel strongly about a particular issue? These are the types of questions that could be raised by considering the ADRESSING acronym in the assessment of clients.

Whether using an interview, a test, or some other tool of assessment with a culturally different assessee, the assessor needs to be aware of ostensibly psychopathological responses that may be fairly commonplace in a particular culture. For example, claims of spirit involvement are not uncommon among some groups of depressed Native Americans (Johnson & Johnson, 1965), as well as others (Matchett, 1972). Diagnostic conclusions and judgments should attempt to distinguish veritable psychological and behavioral problems from behavior that may be deviant by the standards of the dominant culture but customary by the standards of the assessee's culture. To be of maximum value, reports of assessment should go well beyond diagnostic determinations. Reports should provide a richly detailed account of the problem as well as what specific types of interventions are recommended. Throughout the interview, indeed throughout the assessment, the professional serves the best interests of the client with cultural sensitivity. Let's elaborate on this important point before proceeding.

Culturally informed psychological assessment   We may define **culturally informed psychological assessment** as an approach to evaluation that is keenly perceptive of and responsive to issues of acculturation, values, identity, worldview, language, and other culture-related variables as they may impact the evaluation process or the interpretation of resulting data. We offer this definition not as the last word on the subject but rather as a first step designed to promote constructive and scholarly dialogue about what culturally sensitive psychological assessment really is, and all that it can be.

When planning an assessment in which there is some question regarding the projected impact of culture, language, or some related variable on the validity of the assessment, the culturally sensitive assessor can do a number of things. One is to carefully read any existing case history data. Such data may provide answers to key questions regarding the assessee's level of acculturation and other factors useful to know about in advance of any formal assessment. Family, friends, clergy, professionals, and others who know the assessee may be able to provide valuable information about culture-related variables prior to the assessment. In some cases, it may be useful to enlist the aid of a local cultural advisor as preparation for the assessment. One administrative note here: If any such informants are to be used, it will be necessary to have signed permission forms authorizing the exchange of information related to the assessee.

We should also note that assessment experts themselves may disagree on key assessment-related issues regarding individuals who are members of particular groups. Consider, for example, the opinion of two experts regarding one widely used personality test, the MMPI-2. In an article entitled "Culturally Competent MMPI Assessment of Hispanic Populations," Dana (1995, p. 309) advised that "the MMPI-2 is neither better nor worse than [its predecessor] the MMPI for Hispanics." By contrast, Velasquez et al. (1997, p. 111) wrote, *"Counselors should always apply the MMPI-2, and not the MMPI, to Chicano clients"* (emphasis in the original). On the basis of clinical experience, Velasquez et al. (1997) concluded that as compared to the MMPI, the MMPI-2 "lessens the chances of overpathologization of Chicanos" (p. 111).

We might consider factual disagreements such as that cited above as only the tip of the iceberg when it comes to the potential for disagreement about what constitutes culturally competent assessment. Better, and more realistic, we think, to aspire to culturally informed or culturally sensitive psychological assessment. With specific reference to the disagreement cited above, it would be useful to be informed about, or have a sensitivity to, the possibility of overpathologization of test results.

JUST THINK . . .

Is cultural competence a realistic and achievable goal? If so, what are the criteria for achieving it? Is a culturally competent assessor capable of assessing people from any culture, or only the culture in which they are "competent"? Would you consider yourself culturally competent to assess someone from the same culture as yourself?

Prior to the formal assessment, the assessor may consider a screening interview with the assessee, in which rapport is established and various culture-related issues are discussed.

The *Close-up* in Chapter 11 lists some of the questions that could be raised during such an interview. During the formal assessment, the assessor keeps in mind all the cultural information acquired, including any customs, regarding personal space, eye contact, and so forth. After the assessment, the culturally sensitive assessor might reevaluate the data and conclusions for any possible adverse impact of culture-related factors. So, for example, with the cautions of Velasquez et al. (1997) firmly in mind, an assessor who happened to have administered the MMPI and not the MMPI-2 to a Chicano client might revisit the protocol and its interpretation with an eye toward identifying any possible overpathologization.

Translators are frequently used in clinic emergency rooms, crisis intervention cases, and other such situations. Whenever a translator is used, the interviewer must be wary not only of the translation of the words of the interviewee but of their intensity as well (Draguns, 1984). Members of the assessee's family are frequently enlisted to serve as translators, although such a practice may not be desirable under some circumstances. For example, in some cultures a younger person translating the words of an older person, particularly with regard to certain topics (such as sexual matters), may be perceived as very awkward, if not disrespectful (Ho, 1987). Case study and behavioral observation data must be interpreted with sensitivity to the meaning of the historical or behavioral data in a cultural context (Longabaugh, 1980; Williams, 1986). Ultimately, a key aspect of culturally informed psychological assessment entails raising important questions regarding the generalizability and appropriateness of the evaluative measures employed.

JUST THINK . . .

How can culturally informed assessment be taught?

If you just happen to be thinking about the Just Think question just raised, you are probably not alone. Students frequently are curious about how a culturally informed approach to assessment is acquired. Although there are no hard-and-fast rules, our own view is that when it is formally taught, it is done so in the context of a curriculum with three major components: a foundation in basic assessment, a foundation in culture issues in assessment, and supervised training and experience. A more detailed model for this approach is presented in Table 13–1. This model was informed by our reading of descriptions of various existing assessment training curriculums as described by Allen (2002), Hansen (2002), López (2002), and Dana et al. (2002), as well as the writings of Sue and Sue (2003), among others.

Note that in our model a subcomponent of both the Sound Foundation in Cultural Issues in Assessment and the Supervised Training and Experience components of the curriculum is Shifting Cultural Lenses (Kleinman & Kleinman, 1991). The meaning of this term has been explained and illustrated memorably by Steven Regeser López, who

Table 13–1
A Model for Teaching Culturally Informed Psychological Assessment

I. Sound Foundation in General Principles of Assessment

Basic statistics	Scales of measurement Describing data The normal curve Correlation Standard scores Sampling
Basic psychometrics	Standardization Norms Reliability Validity Test development Item analysis Test bias/fairness Interpretation Culture and inference
History of testing and assessment	Overview of the evolution of the assessment enterprise Issues of historical interest to the public Issues of historical interest to the profession
Legal/ethical issues in assessment	Litigation that impacts assessment Legislation that impacts assessment Administrative regulations that impact assessment Prominent ethical issues, including rights of testtakers
Cultural considerations in assessment	Culture and test norms Notions of "culture fair" and "culture free" tests and test items Acculturation and assessment Culture and various tools of assessment Group membership and test interpretation issues Language and assessment Culturally informed psychological assessment
Ability assessment, including IQ testing	Defining intelligence Theories of intelligence Issues regarding the nature of intelligence Cultural issues in ability assessment
Assessment of achievement and aptitude	Defining achievement and aptitude Measuring achievement and aptitude
Personality assessment	Defining personality Theories of personality Development of personality tests Objective methods Projective methods Behavioral methods Cultural issues in personality assessment
Clinical and counseling assessment	Overview Using tools of assessment in clinical and counseling applications Special applications of clinical measures The psychological report Cultural issues in evaluation and interpretation
Neuropsychological assessment	Overview The nervous system and behavior The neuropsychological examination Tools of neuropsychological assessment

Table 13–1
(***continued***)

Assessment in business, organizational, and industrial settings	Overview Screening, selection, classification, and placement Career counseling Productivity, motivation, and attitude Organizational culture Related areas, such as consumer psychology
Assessment of people with disabilities	Overview Assessment and the law Accommodation and assessment Assessment and specific disabilities Disability as a diversity issue

II. Sound Foundation in Cultural Issues in Assessment

Diversity issues	Readings from the relevant literature such as Castro (2003), Hall (1997), Illovsky (2003), Nilsson et al. (2003), and Taylor (2002) Student discussion and role play Self-examination through cultural autobiography
Multicultural assessment	Readings from the relevant literature, such as Hornby (2003), Lopez (1989), Sue & Sue (2003), and Suzuki et al. (2000) Critiquing available psychological reports from multicultural perspective Understanding benefits and limitations of culture-specific tests Understanding cultural sensitivity through readings such as Edwards & Kumru (1999), Hansen et al. (2000), and Lewis-Fernandez & Diaz (2002) Shifting cultural lenses
Collaborative assessment	Readings from the relevant literature, such as Chinman et al. (1999) and Fischer (1994)
Therapeutic assessment	Readings from the relevant literature, such as Finn (1996) and Finn & Tonsager (2002)
Assessment in research	Readings from the relevant literature, such as Okazaki & Sue (1995)
Using community resources	Use of guest speakers to reinforce other learning Cultural advisors as partners in assessment

III. Supervised Training and Experience

Prior to assessment	Consulting a cultural advisor Understanding the referral question Understanding the assessee in terms of culture, language preferences, and other relevant considerations Understanding the clinician's potential biases Evaluating tools of assessment for appropriateness of existing norms Obtaining informed consent for assessment
Conducting an assessment	Understanding cultural aspects of the assessment, including potential issues such as personal space and eye contact Applying a collaborative model Establishing rapport in culturally sensitive and appropriate ways Monitoring one's own multicultural competence
Interpreting data	Shifting cultural lenses Generating and testing alternative hypotheses
Communicating findings	Observing customs Understanding the impact of culture on the process of communicating results
Report writing	Writing with cultural sensitivity to avoid alienating the assessee or perpetuating prejudice

teaches a core course in culturally informed assessment at UCLA. In his course, López (2002) draws on lessons he learned from driving public highways in Mexico, most of which have only two lanes, one in each direction. Frequently, traffic will back up on one lane due to a slow-moving vehicle. Drivers who wish to pass slow-moving vehicles may be assisted by other drivers in front of them, who use their turn signals to indicate when it is safe to pass. A blinking right turn signal indicates that it is *not* safe to pass due to oncoming traffic or visibility issues in the opposing lane. A blinking left turn signal indicates that it is safe to pass. Large trucks may have printed on their rear mudflaps the word *siga* ("continue") by the left turn signal light or *alto* ("stop") by the right one. Besides signaling other drivers when it is safe to pass, turn signals have the same meaning as they do in the United States, as an indication of an intention to turn.

In a class exercise that uses slides of highway scenes as well as close-ups of turn signals, López asks students to interpret the meaning of a blinking turn signal in different traffic scenarios: Does it mean pass, don't pass, or turning? Students quickly appreciate that the meaning of the blinking signal can only be interpreted correctly from cues in a specific context. López next builds on this lesson:

> I then translate this concrete example into more conceptual terms. In discerning the appropriate meaning, one must first entertain both sets of meanings or apply both sets of cultural lenses. Then one collects data to test both ideas. Ultimately, one weights the available evidence and then applies the meaning that appears to be most appropriate. It is important to note that whatever decision is made, there usually exists some degree of uncertainty. By collecting evidence to test the two possible meanings, the psychologist attempts to reduce uncertainty. With multiple assessments over time, greater certainty can be achieved. (2002, pp. 232–233)

The notion of shifting cultural lenses is intimately tied to critical thinking and hypothesis testing. Interview data may suggest, for example, that a client is suffering from some form of psychopathology that entails delusional thinking. A shift in cultural lenses, however, permits the clinician to test an alternative hypothesis: that the observed behavior is culture specific, arising out of long-held family beliefs. The process of culturally informed psychological assessment demands such lense-shifting with all forms of assessment data, including, for example, case history data.

Case History Data

Biographical and related data about an assessee may be obtained by interviewing the assessee and/or significant others in that person's life. Additional sources of case history data include hospital records, school records, military records, employment records, and related documents. All such data are combined in an effort to obtain an understanding of the assessee, including insights into observed behavior patterns.[2] Case history data may be invaluable in helping a therapist develop a meaningful context

---

2. For an example of a case study from the psychology literature, the interested reader is referred to "Socially Reinforced Obsessing: Etiology of a Disorder in a Christian Scientist" (Cohen & Smith, 1976), wherein the authors suggest that a woman's exposure to Christian Science predisposed her to an obsessive disorder. The article stirred some controversy and elicited a number of comments (for example, Coyne, 1976; Halleck, 1976; London, 1976; McLemore & Court, 1977), including one from a representative of the Christian Science Church (Stokes, 1977)—all rebutted by Cohen (1977, 1979, pp. 76–83).

in which to interpret data from other sources, such as interview transcripts and reports of psychological testing.

JUST THINK . . .

How might the contents of an assessee's home video library be a useful source of information in assembling a case history?

Psychological Tests

Clinicians and counselors may have occasion to use many different tests in the course of their practices, and nearly all of the tests we have described could be employed in clinical or counseling assessment. Some tests are designed primarily to be of diagnostic assistance to clinicians. One such test is the Millon Clinical Multiaxial Inventory-III (MCMI-III; Millon et al., 1994), a 175-item true/false test that yields scores related to enduring personality features as well as acute symptoms. As implied in the name of this *multiaxial* test, it can yield information that can assist clinicians in making diagnoses based on the multiaxial DSM.

In addition to tests that are used for general diagnostic purposes, thousands of tests focus on specific traits, states, interests, attitudes, and related variables. Depression is perhaps the most common mental health problem and reason for psychiatric hospitalization. A diagnosis of depression is a most serious matter, as this condition is a key risk factor in suicide. Given the critical importance of depression, many instruments have been developed to measure it and provide insights with respect to it.

Perhaps the most widely used test to measure the severity of depression is the Beck Depression Inventory-II (BD-II; Beck et al., 1996). This is a self-report measure consisting of 21 items, each tapping a specific symptom or attitude associated with depression. For each item, testtakers circle one of four statements that best describes their feelings over the past two weeks. The statements reflect different intensities of feeling and are weighted in their scoring accordingly. Beck et al. (1996) presented data to document their assertion that on average, patients with mood disorders obtain higher scores on the BDI-II than patients with anxiety, adjustment, or other disorders. Additionally, they presented data to support their claim that on average, patients with more serious depressive disorders score higher on the BDI-II than patients with less serious forms of depression. However, because the items are so transparent and the test outcome so easily manipulated by the testtaker, it is usually recommended that the BDI-II be used only with patients who have no known motivation to fake good or fake bad. Further, because the BDI-II contains no validity scales, it is probably advisable to administer it along with other tests that do have validity scales, such as the MMPI-2.

Whether assessment is undertaken for general or more specific diagnostic purposes, it is usually good practice to use more than one tool of assessment to meet the assessment objective. Often, more than one test is administered to an assessee. The phrase used to describe the group of tests administered is *test battery*.

JUST THINK . . .

Why is it usually a good idea not to rely on just one test to make any sort of clinical or counseling decision?

The Psychological Test Battery

If you are a culinary aficionado, or if you are a fan of *Iron Chef* on the Food Network, then you will know that the word *batter* refers to a beaten liquid mixture that typically contains a number of ingredients. Somewhat similar in meaning to this definition of batter is one definition of the word *battery:* an array or grouping of like things to be used together. When psychological assessors speak of a **test battery,** they are referring to a group of tests administered together to gather information about an individual from a variety of instruments.

Personality test battery refers to a group of personality tests. The term *projective test battery* also refers to a group of personality tests, though this term is more specific because it additionally tells us that the battery is confined to projective techniques (such as the Rorschach, the TAT, and figure drawings). In shoptalk among clinicians, if the type of battery referred to is left unspecified, or if the clinician refers to a battery of tests as a **standard battery,** what is usually being referred to is a group of tests including one intelligence test, at least one personality test, and a test designed to screen for neurological deficit (discussed in the following chapter).

Each test in the standard battery provides the clinician with information that goes beyond the specific area the test is designed to tap. Thus, for example, a test of intelligence may yield not only information about intelligence but also information about personality and neurological functioning. Conversely, information about intelligence and neurological functioning can be gleaned from personality test data (and here we refer specifically to projective tests rather than personality inventories). The insistence on using a battery of tests and not a single test was one of the many contributions of psychologist David Rapaport in his now-classic work, *Diagnostic Psychological Testing* (Rapaport et al., 1945–1946). At a time when using a battery of tests might mean using more than one projective test, Rapaport argued that assessment would be incomplete if there weren't "right or wrong answers" to at least one of the tests administered. Here, Rapaport was referring to the need for inclusion of at least one test of intellectual ability.

Special Applications of Clinical Measures

Clinical measures have application in a wide variety of settings, from drug rehabilitation clinics to courts to research on the relationship of adjustment to general health, immune system functioning, and longevity. In what follows, we provide a sample of special applications of clinical measures.

The Assessment of Addiction and Substance Abuse

Assessment for drug addiction and for alcohol and substance abuse has become routine in a number of settings. Whether an individual is seeking outpatient psychotherapy services, being admitted for inpatient services, or even seeking employment, submitting to screening for drug use may be a prerequisite. Such screening can take varied forms, from straightforward physical tests involving the analysis of urine or blood samples to much more imaginative laboratory procedures that involve the analysis of psychophysiological responses (Carter & Tiffany, 1999; Lang et al., 1993; Sayette et al., 2000).

Exploration of personal history with drugs and alcohol may be accomplished by means of questionnaires or face-to-face interviews. However, such direct procedures are highly subject to impression management and all the other potential drawbacks of a self-report instrument. A number of tests and scales have been developed to assist in the assessment of abuse and addiction. The MMPI-2, for example, contains three scales that provide information about substance abuse potential. The oldest of these three scales is the MacAndrew Alcoholism Scale (MacAndrew, 1965), since revised and usually referred to simply as the **MAC-R.** This scale was originally constructed to aid in differentiating alcoholic from nonalcoholic psychiatric patients.

A number of other tests focus on various aspects of drug abuse. The Addiction Potential Scale (APS; Weed et al., 1992) contains 39 items that substance abusers tended to endorse differently from either psychiatric patients or nonclinical samples. The Addiction Acknowledgment Scale (AAS; Weed et al., 1992) contains 13 items that make direct and obvious acknowledgments of substance abuse. The AAS is therefore a much more face-valid scale for substance abuse assessment than either the MAC-R or the APS. This is so because the endorsement of the transparent items of the AAS amounts to an outright admission of drug abuse. By contrast, the MAC-R and the APS "do not measure substance abuse directly but rather measure personality traits that often serve as pathways to substance abuse" (Rouse et al., 1999, p. 106).

> **JUST THINK . . .**
>
> In your opinion, what are some personality traits that "often serve as pathways to substance abuse"?

The Addiction Severity Index (McDermott et al., 1996; McLellan et al., 1980) is one of the most widely used tests in the substance abuse field (Alterman et al., 2000), with applications in intake evaluations and follow-ups as well as the identification of patient subgroups in research. Raters assess severity of addiction in seven problem areas: medical condition, employment functioning, drug use, alcohol use, illegal activity, family/social relations, and psychiatric functioning. Items tap various problems experienced in each of these areas within the past 30 days, as well as lifetime problems. Estimates of the severity of the problems are derived from the scores.

Behavior associated with substance abuse or its potential has also been explored by analogue means, such as role play. The Situational Competency Test (Chaney et al., 1978), the Alcohol Specific Role Play Test (Abrams et al., 1991), and the Cocaine Risk Response Test (Carroll, 1998; Carroll et al., 1999) are all measures that contain audiotaped role-play measures. In the latter test, assessees are asked to orally respond with a description of what they would do under certain conditions—conditions known to prompt cocaine use in regular cocaine users. One scenario has to do with having had a difficult week followed by cravings for cocaine to reward oneself. Another scenario takes place at a party where people are using cocaine in the next room. Assessees are asked to candidly detail their thinking and behavior in response to these and other situations. Of course, the value of the information elicited will vary as a function of many factors, among them the purpose of the assessment and the candor with which assessees respond. One might expect assessees to be straightforward in their responses if they were self-referred for addiction treatment. On the other hand, assessees might be less than straightforward if, for example, they were court-referred on suspicion of probation violation.

Efforts to reduce widespread substance abuse have led researchers to consider how culture may contribute to the problem and how culturally informed intervention may be part of the solution. Using a wide variety of measures, researchers have explored substance abuse in the context of variables such as cultural identity and generational status (Ames & Stacy, 1998; Chappin & Brook, 2001; Duclos, 1999; Kail & DeLaRosa, 1998; Karlsen et al., 1998; Lessinger, 1998; O'Hare & Van Tran, 1998; Pilgrim et al., 1999), religious beliefs (Corwyn & Benda, 2000; Klonoff & Landrine, 1999), and sexual orientation (Kippax et al., 1998). Recovery from drug addiction has itself been conceptualized as a socially mediated process of **reacculturation** that can result in a new sense of identity (Hurst, 1997).

> **JUST THINK . . .**
>
> Why is it useful to conceptualize recovery from drug addiction as reacculturation?

An important ethical concern when assessing substance abusers, especially in research contexts, has to do with obtaining fully informed consent to assessment. McCrady & Bux (1999) noted that substance abusers may be high or intoxicated at the time of consent, and therefore their ability to attend to and comprehend the requirements of the research might be compromised. Further, because their habit may have thrust them into desperate financial straits, any payment offered to substance abusers for participation in a research study may appear coercive. Procedures to maximize comprehension of consent and minimize the appearance of coercion are necessary elements of the consent process.

Forensic Psychological Assessment

The word *forensic* means "pertaining to or employed in legal proceedings," and the term **forensic psychological assessment** can be defined broadly as the theory and application of psychological evaluation and measurement in a legal context. Psychologists, psychiatrists, and other health professionals may be called on by courts, corrections and parole personnel, attorneys, and others involved in the criminal justice system to offer expert opinion. With respect to criminal proceedings, the opinion may, for example, concern an individual's competency to stand trial or his or her criminal responsibility (that is, sanity) at the time a crime is committed. With respect to a civil proceeding, the opinion may have to do with issues as diverse as the extent of emotional distress suffered in a personal injury suit, the suitability of one or the other parent in a custody proceeding, or the testamentary capacity (capacity to make a last will and testament) of a person before death.

Before discussing some of the assessment-related aspects in some of the many areas of forensic psychology, it is important to note that there are major differences between forensic and general clinical practice. Perhaps the biggest difference is that in the forensic situation, the clinician may be the client of a third party (such as a court) and not the assessee. This fact, as well as its implications with respect to issues such as confidentiality, must be made clear to the assessee. Another difference between forensic and general clinical practice is that the patient may have been compelled to undergo assessment. Unlike the typical client seeking therapy, for example, the assessee is not highly motivated to be truthful. Consequently, it is imperative that the assessor rely not only on the assessee's representations but on all available documentation, such as police reports and interviews with persons who may have pertinent knowledge. The mental health professional who performs forensic work would do well to be educated in the language of the law:

> To go into court and render the opinion that a person is not responsible for a crime because he is psychotic is to say nothing of value to the judge or jury. However, to go into the same court and state that a man is not responsible because as a result of a mental disorder, namely, paranoid schizophrenia, "he lacked substantial capacity to conform his behavior to the requirements of the law"—because he was hearing voices that told him he must commit the crime to protect his family from future harm—would be of great value to the judge or jury. It is not because the man had a psychosis that he is not responsible; it is how his illness affected his behavior and his ability to form the necessary criminal intent or to have the *mens rea,* or guilty mind, that is important. (Rappeport, 1982, p. 333)

Forensic assessors are sometimes placed in the role of psychohistorians, especially in cases involving questions of capacity to testify. In such cases, assessors may be called on to offer opinions about people they have never personally interviewed or observed—a situation that seldom if ever arises in nonforensic assessments. Forensic assessment frequently entails rendering opinions about momentous matters such as whether a person is competent to stand trial, criminally responsible, or ready for parole. Some have challenged the role of mental health professionals in these and related matters, citing the unreliability of psychiatric diagnosis and the invalidity of various assessment tools for use with such objectives (Faust & Ziskin, 1988a, 1988b; see also Matarazzo, 1990, for a response). Still, judges, juries, district attorneys, the police, and other members of the criminal justice system rely on mental health professionals to provide them with their best judgments concerning such critical questions. One such question that is raised frequently concerns the prediction of dangerousness (Lally, 2003).

Dangerousness to oneself or others An official determination that a person is dangerous to self or others is legal cause to deprive that individual of liberty. The individual so judged will, on a voluntary or involuntary basis, undergo psychotherapeutic intervention, typically in a secure treatment facility, until such time that he or she is no longer judged to be dangerous. This is so because the state has a compelling duty to protect its citizens from danger. The duty extends to protecting suicidal people, who are presumed to be suffering from mental disorder, from acting on self-destructive impulses. Mental health professionals play a key role in decisions about who is and is not considered dangerous.

The determination of dangerousness is ideally made on the basis of multiple data sources, including interview data, case history data, and formal testing. When dealing with potentially homicidal or suicidal assessees, the professional assessor must have knowledge of the risk factors associated with such violent acts. Risk factors may include a history of previous attempts to commit the act, drug/alcohol abuse, and unemployment. If given an opportunity to interview the potentially dangerous individual, the assessor will typically explore the assessee's ideation, motivation, and imagery associated with the contemplated violence. Additionally, questions will be raised related to the availability and lethality of the method and means by which the violent act would be perpetrated. The assessor will assess how specific and detailed the plan, if any, is. The assessor may also explore the extent to which helping resources such as family, friends, or roommates can prevent violence from occurring. If the assessor determines that a homicide is imminent, the assessor has a legal **duty to warn** the endangered third party—a duty that overrides the privileged communication between psychologist and client. As stated in the landmark 1974 case *Tarasoff v. the Regents of the University of California*, "Protective privilege ends where the public peril begins" (see Cohen, 1979, for elaboration of this and related principles).

Dangerousness manifests itself in sundry ways in varied settings, from the school playground to the post office lobby. Working together, members of the legal and mental health communities strive to keep people reasonably safe from themselves and others while not unduly depriving any citizens of their right to liberty. Toward that end, a rather large literature dealing with the assessment of dangerousness, including suicide, has emerged (see, for example, Baumeister, 1990; Blumenthal & Kupfer, 1990; Catalano et al., 1997; Copas & Tarling, 1986; Gardner et al., 1996; Jobes et al., 1997; Lewinsohn et al., 1996; Lidz et al., 1993; Monahan, 1981; Olweus, 1979; Rice & Harris, 1995; Steadman, 1983; van Praag et al., 1990; Wagner, 1997; Webster et al., 1994), along with a number of tests (Beck et al., 1989; Eyman & Eyman, 1990; Linehan et al., 1983; Patterson et al., 1983; Reynolds, 1987; Rothberg & Geer-Williams, 1992; Williams et al., 1996) and clinical interview guidelines (Sommers-Flanagan & Sommers-Flanagan, 1995; Truant et al., 1991; Wollersheim, 1974).

Despite the best efforts of many scholars, the prediction of dangerousness must be considered more an art than a science at present. Historically, clinicians have not been very accurate in their predictions of dangerousness. On a brighter note, many people and organizations are working to better the odds of successfully predicting dangerousness. As pointed out in this chapter's *Close-up,* among the organizations committed to the application of behavioral science to issues of dangerousness is the U.S. Secret Service.

> **JUST THINK . . .**
>
> During the course of a counseling assessment, a counselor learns that an HIV-infected patient is planning to have unprotected sexual contact with an identified party. Does the counselor have the duty to warn that party?

Assessment of Dangerousness and the Secret Service

The Secret Service is charged by federal law with a number of responsibilities, including investigation of crimes of counterfeiting, forgery, and fraud involving computers and financial institutions. It is perhaps best known for its protective functions and its duty to protect the following people and their families: the president of the United States, the vice president, former presidents and vice presidents, major candidates for or successors to these offices, and visiting foreign heads of state.

Law enforcement agencies have evinced a great deal of interest in terms of how behavioral science, and more specifically knowledge of dangerousness, can be applied in prevention of crime. In Los Angeles, where the stalking of celebrities has been a well-publicized problem, the police department established a threat management unit (Lane, 1992). When members of Congress or their staffs receive threats, the matter may be referred to a similar police unit established by the U.S. Capitol Police. Additionally, "the United States Marshals Service has initiated systematic efforts to formulate a protective investigative function to analyze inappropriate communications to, and to evaluate and manage potential threats against, federal judicial officials" (Coggins et al., 1998, p. 53).

The Secret Service has been exemplary in its efforts to integrate behavioral research and clinical expertise into its policies and practices, including its risk assessment and protective activities. In the course of attempting to prevent a highly specific crime from taking place, some of the things the Service must do are (1) identify and investigate people who may pose a risk to a protectee; (2) make a determination of the level of risk the identified people pose; and (3) implement a case management program for those identified as possibly posing a genuine risk. To meet these and related objectives with maximum effectiveness, the service established a behavioral research program. The head of that program is Margaret Coggins, Ph.D., and much of what we say here about that program is derived from a publication by Coggins and her colleagues (1998).

Charged with duties that entail very specialized assessments of dangerousness on a regular basis, the Secret Service has a history of receiving input from clinical and forensic professionals. In 1980, the agency contracted with the Institute of Medicine to sponsor a conference of clinicians and behavioral scientists addressed to issues such as the prediction of dangerousness, case management of dangerous persons, and agent training needs (Takeuchi et al., 1981). Another conference in 1982 extended the agenda to issues such as the development of an internal research program on the assessment of people who threatened protectees and training for agents in the assessment and management of mentally ill threateners (Institute of Medicine, 1984). The Secret Service's behavioral research program evolved out of these conferences. The research program now studies diverse matters such as risk assessment issues, factors in agent decision making, and attitudes of mental health professionals toward the Secret Service vis-à-vis their effect on the reporting of threats to the Service's protectees. A collaboration between researchers and practitioners was forged in order to achieve the program objectives:

> Special agents and researchers, both internal Secret Service staff and external consultants, work together to identify practical study questions, prioritize areas of inquiry, design study methodologies, collect and analyze data, and disseminate research findings. Agents play a key role in ensuring that relevant investigative, risk assessment, and case management concerns are brought forward for study, and their participation in research design and data collection lends internal credibility to the importance of incorporating study findings into practice. Similarly, research staff and scholars from the academic and scientific communities ensure that principles of scientific integrity guide the research process and are instrumental in protecting the external validity of the data and findings according to rigorous standards of peer review. (Coggins et al., 1998, p. 61)

The case study is a potentially useful tool of assessment and research, particularly in efforts to identify factors related

Competency to stand trial   *Competency* in the legal sense has many different meanings. One may speak, for example, of competence to make a will, enter into a contract, commit a crime, waive constitutional rights, consent to medical treatment . . . the list goes on. Before convicted murderer Gary Gilmore was executed in Utah, he underwent an examination designed to determine whether or not he was competent to be executed. That

The Secret Service relies on research on the assessment of dangerousness in fulfilling its protective mission.

to an individual's potential for violence against a Secret Service protectee. The Secret Service's Exceptional Case Study Project (ECSP) was designed to study persons who have either attacked or approached with lethal means an individual targeted on the basis of public status. Variables selected for study include behavior, thinking, planning, mental status, motivation, and communication patterns. One noteworthy finding from such research could be paraphrased in terms of the aphorism "actions speak louder than words." Indeed, prior behavior has been found to take precedence over threatening statements as a factor related to potential for violence (Vossekuil & Fein, 1997). This finding is consistent with the findings of psychiatrist Park Dietz in his research on individuals who stalk Hollywood celebrities. Dietz et al. (1991) concluded that there was little relation between writing a threatening letter to the celebrity and attempting to physically approach the celebrity. People who wrote such letters were no more or less likely to attempt to approach the celebrity than people who did not make threats.

Behavioral science, and in particular assessment-related research, has much to offer the Secret Service and other organizations involved in law enforcement and crime prevention. This is so despite the fact that the Secret Service's "operational mission always takes precedence over academic or scientific interest" (Coggins et al., 1998, p. 68).

is so because the law mandates that a certain propriety exists with respect to state-ordered executions, and it would not be morally proper to execute insane persons.

Competence to stand trial has to do largely with a defendant's ability to understand the charges against him or her and assist in his or her own defense. As stated in the Supreme Court's ruling in *Dusky v. United States,* a defendant must have "sufficient present

Table 13-2
Georgetown Criteria for Competency to Stand Trial

Factual Items

Defendant's ability to:
1. understand his [or her] current legal situation
2. understand the charges made against him [or her]
3. understand the legal issues and procedures in the case
4. understand the possible dispositions, pleas, and penalties
5. understand the facts relevant to the case
6. identify and locate witnesses

Inferential Items

Defendant's ability to communicate with counsel and to:
7. comprehend instructions and advice
8. make decisions after advice
9. follow testimony for contradictions or errors
10. maintain a collaborative relationship with his [or her] attorney
11. testify if necessary and be cross-examined
12. tolerate stress at the trial or while awaiting trial
13. refrain from irrational behavior during the trial

Source: Bukatman et al. (1971)

ability to consult with his lawyer with a reasonable degree of rational . . . (and) factual understanding of the proceedings against him." This "understand and assist" requirement, as it has come to be called, is in effect an extension of the constitutional prohibition against trials *in absentia;* a defendant must be not only physically present during the trial but mentally present as well.

The competency requirement protects an individual's right to choose and assist counsel, the right to act as a witness on one's own behalf, and the right to confront opposing witnesses. The requirement also increases the probability that the truth of the case will be developed, since the competent defendant is able to monitor continuously the testimony of witnesses and help bring discrepancies in testimony to the attention of the court. In general, persons who are mentally retarded, psychotic, or suffering from a debilitating neurological disorder are persons held to be incompetent to stand trial. However, it cannot be overemphasized that any one of these three diagnoses is not sufficient in itself for a person to be found incompetent. Stated another way: It is possible for a person to be mentally retarded, psychotic, or suffering from a debilitating neurological disorder—or all three—and still be found competent to stand trial. The person will be found to be incompetent if and only if he or she is unable to understand the charges against him or her and is unable to assist in his or her own defense.

A number of instruments have been developed as aids in evaluating whether a defendant meets the understand and assist requirement. For example, researchers at Georgetown University Law School (Bukatman et al., 1971) enumerated 13 criteria of competency to stand trial (Table 13–2). Sample questions used in conjunction with these criteria include the following:

- What is your lawyer's job?
- What is the purpose of the judge?
- What does the jury do?
- What will the prosecutor do?
- What alibi or defense do you think you have now?
- What does "incompetent to stand trial" mean to you?
- Do you think there is any reason why you should be found incompetent?

Table 13–3
Competency Screening Test

1. The lawyer told Bill that _____ .
2. When I go to court, the lawyer will _____ .
3. Jack felt that the judge _____ .
4. When Phil was accused of the crime, he _____ .
5. When I prepare to go to court with my lawyer, _____ .
6. If the jury finds me guilty, I _____ .
7. The way a court trial is decided _____ .
8. When the evidence in George's case was presented to the jury, _____ .
9. When the lawyer questioned his client in court, the client said _____ .
10. If Jack had to try his own case, he _____ .
11. Each time the D.A. asked me a question, I _____ .
12. While listening to the witnesses testify against me, I _____ .
13. When the witness testifying against Harry gave incorrect evidence, he _____ .
14. When Bob disagreed with his lawyer on his defense, he _____ .
15. When I was formally accused of the crime, I thought to myself, _____ .
16. If Ed's lawyer suggests that he plead guilty, he _____ .
17. What concerns Fred most about his lawyer _____ .
18. When they say a man is innocent until proven guilty, _____ .
19. When I think of being sent to prison, I _____ .
20. When Phil thinks of what he is accused of, he _____ .
21. When the [members of the jury hear] my case, they will _____ .
22. If I had a chance to speak to the judge, I _____ .

Source: Lipsitt et al. (1971)

According to Bukatman et al., a thorough competency evaluation would entail answers to such questions "with sufficient information on each point to indicate whether there is, or might be in the future, a problem in that area" (p. 1226).

An alternative measure of competency, the Competency Screening Test (Lipsitt et al., 1971) employs a sentence completion format (Table 13–3) with each of 22 items relating to a legal criterion of competency to stand trial. The test is scored on a 3-point scale ranging from 0 to 2, with appropriate responses scored 2, marginally appropriate responses scored 1, and clearly inappropriate responses scored 0. For example, consider this item: *When I go to court, the lawyer will* _____ ." A 2-point response would be "defend me." Such a response indicates that the assessee has a clear understanding of the lawyer's role. By contrast, a 0-point response might be "have me guillotined," which would be indicative of an inappropriate perception of the lawyer's role. Lipsitt et al. reported the inter-rater reliability among trained scorers of this test to be $r = .93$. They also reported that their test was successful in discriminating seriously disturbed, state-hospitalized men from control groups consisting of students, community adults, club members, and civilly committed hospitalized patients.

Criminal responsibility   "Not guilty by reason of insanity" is a plea to a criminal charge that we have all heard. But stop and think about the meaning of the legal term **insanity** to mental health professionals, and the evaluation procedures by which psychological assessors could identify the insane. The insanity defense has its roots in the idea that only blameworthy persons (that is, those with a criminal mind) should be punished. Possibly exempt from blame, therefore, are children, mental incompetents, and others who may be irresponsible, lack control of their actions, or have no conception that what they are doing may be criminal. As early as the sixteenth century, it was argued in an English court that an offending act should not be considered a felony if the offender had no conception of good and evil. By the eighteenth century, the focus had shifted from good and evil as a criterion for evaluating criminal responsibility to the issue of whether the defendant "doth not know what he is doing no more than . . . a wild beast."

Judicial history was made in nineteenth-century England when in 1843 Daniel M'Naghten was found not guilty by reason of insanity after attempting to assassinate the British prime minister. (He mistakenly shot and killed the prime minister's secretary.) But M'Naghten was acquitted. According to the court, he could not be held accountable for the crime if, "at the time of the committing of the act, the party accused was laboring under such a defect of reason from disease of the mind as not to know the nature and quality of the act he was doing, or if he did know it, that he did not know he was doing what was wrong."

The decision in the *M'Naghten* case has come to be referred to as the *right or wrong test*, or the **M'Naghten standard.** To the present day, this test of sanity is used in England as well as in a number of jurisdictions in the United States. However, a problem with the right or wrong test is that it does not provide for the acquitting of persons who know right from wrong yet still are unable to control impulses to commit criminal acts. In 1954, an opinion written by the United States Court of Appeal for the District of Columbia in the case of *Durham v. United States* held a defendant not to be culpable for criminal action "if his unlawful act was the product of a mental disease or defect" (**the Durham standard**). Still another standard of legal insanity was set forth by the American Law Institute (ALI) in 1956. **The ALI standard** has become one of the most widely used throughout the United States (Weiner, 1980). With slight alterations from one jurisdiction to another, this legal test of sanity provides as follows:

> A person is not responsible for criminal conduct, i.e., insane if, at the time of such conduct, as a result of a mental disease or defect, he lacks substantial capacity either to appreciate the criminality (wrongfulness) of his conduct, or to conform his conduct to the requirements of the law.
>
> As used in this article, the terms "mental disease or defect" do not include an abnormality manifested only by repeated criminal or otherwise antisocial conduct.

In clinical practice, defendants who are mentally retarded, psychotic, or neurologically impaired are likely to be the ones found not guilty by reason of insanity. However, as was the case with considerations of competency to stand trial, the mere fact that a person is judged to be mentally retarded, psychotic, or neurologically impaired is in itself no guarantee that the individual will be found not guilty. Other criteria, such as the ALI standards cited, must be met.

To help determine if the ALI standards are met, a number of instruments such as the Rogers Criminal Responsibility Assessment Scale (RCRAS) have been developed. Psychologist Richard Rogers and his colleagues (Rogers & Cavanaugh, 1980, 1981; Rogers et al., 1981) designed the RCRAS as a systematic and empirical approach to insanity evaluations. This instrument consists of 25 items tapping both psychological and situational variables. The items are scored with respect to five scales: reliability (including malingering), organic factors, psychopathology, cognitive control, and behavioral control. After scoring, the examiner employs a hierarchical decision model to arrive at a decision concerning the assessee's sanity. Validity studies done with this scale (for example, Rogers et al., 1983; Rogers et al., 1984) have shown it to be useful in discriminating between sane and insane patients/defendants.

JUST THINK . . .

Should mental health professionals be involved in the business of determining who is not guilty by reason of insanity?

Readiness for parole or probation Some people convicted of a crime will pay their dues to society and go on to lead fulfilling, productive lives after their incarceration. At the other extreme are career criminals who will violate laws at the first opportunity upon their release—or escape—from prison. Predicting who is ready for parole or probation and what the outcome of such a release might be has proved no easy task. Still, attempts have been made to develop measures useful in parole and probation decisions.

A person with a diagnosis of psychopathy (a **psychopath**) is four times more likely than a nonpsychopath to fail on release from prison (Hart et al., 1988). A classic work by Cleckley (1976) provided a detailed profile of psychopaths. They are people with few inhibitions who may pursue pleasure or money with callous disregard for the welfare of others. Based on a factor-analytic study of Cleckley's description of persons with psychopathy, Robert D. Hare (1980) developed a 22-item Psychopathy Checklist (PCL) that reflects personality characteristics as rated by the assessor (such as callousness, impulsiveness, and empathy), as well as prior history as gleaned from the assessee's records (such as "criminal versatility"). In the revised version of the test, the Revised Psychopathy Checklist (PCL-R; Hare, 1985), two items from the original PCL were omitted because of their relatively low correlation with the rest of the scale, and the scoring criteria for some of the remaining items were modified. Hare et al. (1990) report that the two forms are equivalent.

In one study that employed a maximum-security psychiatric sample, the PCL correctly identified 80% of the violent recidivists (Harris et al., 1989). A version of the PCL specially modified for use with young male offenders produced scores that correlated significantly with variables such as number of conduct disorder symptoms, previous violent offenses, violent recidivism, and violent behavior within the maximum security institution in which the study was conducted (Forth et al., 1990). In another study, psychopathy ratings were found to predict outcome for both temporary absence and parole release. Psychopaths were recommitted four times more frequently than nonpsychopaths (Serin et al., 1990).

Diagnosis and evaluation of emotional injury   **Emotional injury,** or psychological harm or damage, is a term sometimes used synonymously with mental suffering, pain and suffering, and emotional harm. In cases involving charges such as discrimination, harassment, malpractice, stalking, and unlawful termination of employment, psychological assessors may be responsible for evaluating alleged emotional injury. Such an evaluation will be designed to shed light on an individual's functioning prior to and then subsequent to the alleged injury (Melton et al., 1997). The court will evaluate the findings in light of all of the evidence and make a determination regarding whether the alleged injury exists, and if so, the magnitude of the damage.

Many tools of assessment, including the interview, the case study, and psychological tests may be used in the process of evaluating and diagnosing claims of emotional injury. Interviews may be conducted with the person claiming the injury as well as with others who have knowledge relevant to the claim. Case study materials include documents such as physician or therapist records, school records, military records, employment records, and police records. The specific psychological tests used in an emotional injury evaluation will vary with the preferences of the assessor. In one study in which 140 forensic psychologists returned a survey dealing with assessment practices, it was found that no two practitioners routinely used exactly the same combination of tests to assess emotional injury (Boccaccini & Brodsky, 1999). The reasons given for the use of specific tests and test batteries most frequently had to do with established norms, personal clinical experience, the widespread acceptance of the instrument, the research support, and content. Greater consistency in test selection would be desirable. Such consistency could be achieved by studying the incremental

JUST THINK . . .

Why would greater consistency be desirable in instruments used to evaluate emotional injury?

validity each test adds to the task of assessing different types of emotional injury in specific contexts.

Custody Evaluations

As the number of divorces in this country continues to climb, so does the number of custody proceedings. Before the 1920s, it was fairly commonplace for the father to be granted custody of the children (Lamb, 1981). The pendulum swung, however, with the widespread adoption of what was referred to as the "tender years" doctrine and the belief that the child's interest would be best served if the mother were granted custody. But with the coming of age of the dual-career household, the courts have begun to be more egalitarian in their custody decisions (McClure-Butterfield, 1990). Courts have recognized that the best interest of the child may be served by father custody, mother custody, or joint custody. Psychological assessors can assist the court in making such decisions through the use of a **custody evaluation**—a psychological assessment of parents or guardians and their parental capacity, and/or children and their parental needs and preferences, usually undertaken for the purpose of assisting a court in making awards of custody with reports. Ideally, one impartial expert in the mental health field should be responsible for assessing *all* family members and submitting a report to the court (Gardner, 1982). More often than not, however, the husband has his expert, the wife has her expert, and a battle, often bitter in tone, is on (Benjamin & Gollan, 2003).

Evaluation of the parent The evaluation of parental capacity typically entails a detailed interview that focuses primarily on various aspects of child rearing, though tests of intelligence, personality, and adjustment may be employed if questions remain after the interview. The assessor might begin with open-ended questions designed to let the parent ventilate some of his or her feelings, and then proceed to more specific questions tapping a wide variety of areas, including

- the parent's own childhood: happy? abused?
- the parent's own relationship with parents, siblings, peers
- the circumstances that led up to the marriage and the degree of forethought that went into the decision to have (or adopt) children
- the adequacy of prenatal care and attitudes toward the pregnancy
- the parent's description of the child
- the parent's own evaluation of himself or herself as a parent, including strengths and weaknesses
- the parent's evaluation of his or her spouse in terms of strengths and weaknesses as a parent
- the quantity and quality of time spent caring for and playing with children
- the parent's approach to discipline
- the parent's receptivity to the child's peer relationships

During the course of the interview, the assessor may find evidence that the interviewee really does not want custody of the children but is undertaking the custody battle for some other reason. For example, custody may be nothing more than another issue to bargain over with respect to the divorce settlement. Alternatively, for example, a parent might be embarrassed to admit to himself or herself and to observers of the proceedings that he or she really doesn't want custody of the children. Sometimes a parent, emotionally scathed by all that has gone on before the divorce, may be employing the

Figure 13–1
Projective Techniques Used in Custody Evaluation

The picture on the left is from the Children's Apperception Test-H (Bellak & Bellak, 1965), and the one on the right is from The Boys and Girls Book About Divorce *(Gardner, 1971). These, as well as TAT and other pictures used as projective stimuli, may be useful in evaluating children's parental preferences.*

custody battle as a technique of vengeance—to threaten to take away that which is most prized and adored by the spouse. The clinician performing the evaluation must appreciate that such ill-motivated intentions do underlie some custody battles. In the best interest of the children, it is the obligation of the clinician to report such findings.

In certain cases an assessor may deem it desirable to assess any of many variables related to marriage and family life. A wide variety of such instruments is available, including those designed to measure adjustment (Beier & Sternberg, 1977; Epstein et al., 1983; Locke & Wallace, 1959; McCubbin et al., 1985a, 1985b; Spanier, 1976; Spanier & Filsinger, 1983; Udry, 1981), assets (Olson et al., 1985), preferences (Price et al., 1982), intimacy (Waring & Reddon, 1983), jealousy (Bringle et al., 1979), communication (Bienvenu, 1978), feelings (Lowman, 1980), satisfaction (Roach et al., 1981; Snyder, 1981), stability (Booth & Edwards, 1983), trust (Larzelere & Huston, 1980), expectancies (Notarius & Vanzetti, 1983; Sabatelli, 1984), parenting ability (Bavolek, 1984), coping strategies (McCubbin et al., 1985a, 1985b; Straus, 1979), strength of family ties (Bardis, 1975), family interpersonal environment (Kinston et al., 1985; Moos & Moos, 1981; Robin et al., 1990), children's attitudes toward parents (Hudson, 1982), and overall quality of family life (Beavers, 1985; Olson & Barnes, 1985).

Evaluation of the child   The court will be interested in knowing if the child in a custody proceeding has a preference with respect to future living and visitation arrangements. Toward that end, the psychological assessor can be of assistance with a wide variety of tests and techniques. Most authorities agree that the preferences of children under the age of 5 are too unreliable and too influenced by recent experiences to be accorded much weight. However, if intelligence test data indicate that the child who is chronologically 5 years old is functioning at a higher level, then his or her preferences may be accorded greater weight. This is particularly true if the Comprehension subtest score on a Wechsler test is elevated. Some methods that can be useful in assessing a child's parental preference include structured play exercises with dolls that represent the child and other family members, figure drawings of family members followed by storytelling to the drawings, and the use of projective techniques such as the TAT and related tests (Figure 13–1).

Sometimes impromptu innovation on the part of the examiner is required. In performing a custody evaluation on a 5-year-old child, the senior author of this text (RJC) noted that the child seemed to identify very strongly with the main character in *E. T., The Extraterrestrial.* The child had seen the film three times, came into the test session carrying two *E. T.* bubble-gum cards, and identified as "E. T." the picture he drew when instructed to draw a person. To obtain a measure of parental preference, the examiner took four figures and represented them as "E. T.," "E. T.'s mother," "E. T.'s father," and "E. T.'s sister." An empty cardboard box was then labeled a "spaceship," and the child was told that E. T. (stranded on earth and longing to return to his home planet) had the opportunity to go home but that the spaceship had room for only two other passengers. The child boarded his mother and his sister in addition to "E. T." The child told the examiner that E. T.'s father would "wave goodbye."

Specially constructed sentence completion items can also be of value in the assessment of parental preferences. For example, the following items might be useful in examining children's differing perceptions of each parent:

Mothers _____.

If I do something wrong, my father _____.

It is best for children to live with _____.

Fathers _____.

Mommies are bad when _____.

I like to hug _____.

I don't like to hug _____.

Daddies are bad when _____.

The last time I cried _____.

My friends think that my mother _____.

My friends think that my father _____.

The data-gathering process for the evaluation begins the moment the child and the parent(s) come into the office. The assessor takes careful note of the quality of the interaction between the parent(s) and the child. The child will then be interviewed alone and asked about the nature and quality of the relationship. If the child expresses a strong preference for one parent or the other, the assessor must evaluate how meaningful that preference is. For example, a child who sees his rancher father only every other weekend might have a good ol' time on the brief occasions they are together and express a preference for living there—unaware that life in the country would soon become just as routine as life in the city with Mom. If children do not express a preference, insight into their feelings can be obtained by using the tests described earlier, combined with skillful interviewing. Included among the topics for discussion will be the child's physical description of his or her parents as well as his or her living quarters. Questions will be asked about the routine aspects of life (such as "Who makes breakfast for you?"), as well as questions about recreation, parental visitation, parental involvement with their education, their general well-being, and their siblings and friends.

JUST THINK . . .

How might hand puppets be used as a tool of assessment with very young children involved in a custody dispute?

Child Abuse and Neglect

A legal mandate exists in most states for many licensed professionals to report *child abuse* and *child neglect* when they have knowledge of it. The legal definitions of child abuse and child neglect vary from state to state. Typically, definitions of **abuse** refer to the creation of conditions that may give rise to abuse of a child (a person under the state-defined age of majority) by an adult responsible for the care of that person. The abuse may be in the form of (1) the infliction or allowing of infliction of physical injury or emotional impairment that is nonaccidental, (2) the creation or allowing the creation of substantial risk of physical injury or emotional impairment that is nonaccidental, or (3) the committing or allowing of a sexual offense to be committed against a child. Typical definitions of **neglect** refer to a failure on the part of an adult responsible for the care of a child to exercise a minimum degree of care in providing the child with food, clothing, shelter, education, medical care, and supervision.

A number of excellent general sources for the study of child abuse and child neglect are currently available (see, for example, Board of Professional Affairs, 1999; Cicchetti & Carlson, 1989; Ellerstein, 1981; Fischer, 1999; Fontana et al., 1963; Helfer & Kempe, 1988; Kelley, 1988; Reece & Groden, 1985). Resources are also available to assist professionals in recognizing specific forms of child abuse such as head injury (Billmire & Myers, 1985), eye injury (Gammon, 1981), mouth injury (Becker et al., 1978), emotional trauma (Brassard et al., 1986), burns (Alexander et al., 1987; Lung et al., 1977), bites (American Board of Forensic Odontology, 1986), fractures (Worlock et al., 1986), poisoning (Kresel & Lovejoy, 1981), sexual abuse (Adams-Tucker, 1982; Faller, 1988; Friedrich et al., 1986; Sanfilippo et al., 1986; Sebold, 1987), and shaken infant syndrome (Dykes, 1986). What follows are some brief, very general guidelines for the assessment of physical and emotional signs of child abuse.

Physical signs of abuse and neglect   Although psychologists and other mental health professionals without medical credentials typically do not have occasion to physically examine children, a knowledge of physical signs of abuse and neglect is important.

Many signs of abuse take the form of physical injuries. During an evaluation, these injuries may be described by abused children or abusing adults as the result of an accident. The knowledgeable professional needs a working familiarity with the various kinds of injuries that may signal more ominous causes. Consider, for example, the case of injury to the face. In most veritable accidents, only one side of the face is injured. It may therefore be significant if a child evidences injury on both sides of the face—both eyes and both cheeks. Marks on the skin may be telling. Grab marks made by an adult-size hand and marks that form a recognizable pattern (such as the tines of a fork, a cord or rope, or human teeth) may be especially revealing. Burns from a cigarette or lighter may be in evidence as marks on the soles of the feet, the palms of the hands, the back, or the buttocks. Burns from scalding water may be in evidence as a glove-like redness on the hands or feet. Any bone fracture or dislocation should be investigated, as should head injuries, particularly when a patch of hair appears to be missing. In some instances, the head injury may have resulted from being held by the hair.

Physical signs that may or may not indicate neglect include dress that is inappropriate for the season, poor hygiene, and lagging physical development. Physical signs indicative of sexual abuse are not present in the majority of cases. In many instances, there is no penetration or only partial penetration by the abusing adult, and no physical scars. In young children, physical signs that may or may not indicate sexual abuse include difficulty in sitting or walking; itching or reported pain or discomfort of genital areas; stained, bloody, or torn underclothing; and foreign objects in orifices. In older children, the presence of sexually transmitted diseases or a pregnancy may or may not signal child sexual abuse.

Emotional and behavioral signs of abuse and neglect   Emotional and behavioral indicators may reflect something other than child abuse and neglect. Child abuse or neglect is only one of several possible explanations underlying the appearance of such signs. Fear of going home or fear of adults in general and reluctance to remove outer garments may be signs of abuse. Other possible emotional and behavioral signs of abuse include:

- unusual reactions or apprehension in response to other children crying
- low self-esteem
- extreme or inappropriate moods
- aggressiveness
- social withdrawal
- nail biting, thumb sucking, or other habit disorders

Possible emotional and behavioral signs of neglect include frequent lateness to or absence from school, chronic fatigue, and chronic hunger. Age-inappropriate behavior may also be a sign of neglect. Most typically, this is seen as the result of a child taking on many adult roles with younger children due to the absence of a caregiver at home.

Possible emotional and behavioral signs of sexual abuse in children under 8 years of age may include fear of sleeping alone, eating disorders, enuresis, encopresis, sexual acting out, change in school behavior, tantrums, crying spells, sadness, and suicidal thoughts. These signs may also be present in older children, along with other possible signs such as memory problems, emotional numbness, violent fantasies, hyperalertness, self-mutilation, and sexual concerns or preoccupations, which may be accompanied by guilt or shame.

Interviews, behavioral observation, and psychological tests are all used in identifying child abuse. However, professionals disagree about the appropriate tools for such an assessment, particularly when it involves identifying sexual abuse. One technique involves observing children while they play with *anatomically detailed dolls (ADDs)*. **ADDs** are dolls with accurately represented genitalia. Sexually abused children may, on average, engage ADDs in more sexually oriented activities than other children, but differences between groups of abused and nonabused children tend not to be significant. Many nonabused children play in a sexually explicit way with ADDs, so such play is not necessarily diagnostic of sexual abuse (Elliott et al., 1993; Wolfner et al., 1993).

Human-figure drawings are also used to assess sexual and physical abuse, though their accuracy in distinguishing abused from nonabused children is a subject of debate (Burgess et al., 1981; Chantler et al., 1993; Kelley, 1985). Questionnaires designed for administration to a child who may have been abused (Mannarino et al., 1994) or to adults such as teachers or parents who know that child well (Chantler et al., 1993) have been explored, although no well-developed and thoroughly validated instrument yet exists. In short, no widely accepted, reliable, and valid set of techniques for the assessment of sexual abuse is available. Professionals who have occasion to conduct assessments for sexual abuse have been advised to integrate information from many assessment tools and to select those tools on a case-by-case basis.

> **JUST THINK . . .**
>
> What obstacles do test developers face as they attempt to develop psychometrically sound instruments to assess sexual abuse in children?

Issues in reporting child abuse and neglect   Child abuse, when it occurs, is a tragedy. A claim of child abuse when in fact there has been no such abuse is also a tragedy—one that can scar irrevocably an accused but innocent individual for life. It is incumbent on professionals who undertake the weighty obligation of assessing a child for potential abuse not to approach their task with any preconceived notions, because such notions can be conveyed to the child and perceived as the right answer to questions (King & Yuille, 1987; White et al., 1988). Children from the ages of about 2 to 7 are highly suggestible, and their memory is not as well developed as that of older children. It is possible that events that occurred after the alleged incident—including events only referred to in conversations—may be confused with the actual incident (Ceci et al., 1987; Goodman & Reed, 1986; Loftus & Davies, 1984). Related considerations regarding the psychological examination of a child for abuse have been discussed in detail by Weissman (1991). Sensitivity to the rights of all parties in a child abuse proceeding, including the rights of the accused, is critical to making certain that justice is served.

Risk assessment   In an effort to prevent child abuse, test developers have sought to create instruments useful in identifying parents and others who may be at risk for abusing children. The Child Abuse Potential Inventory (CAP; Milner et al., 1986; Milner, 1991) has demonstrated impressive validity in identifying abusers. Another test, the Parenting Stress Index (PSI; Loyd & Abidin, 1985), measures stress associated with the parental role. Parents are asked to reflect on their relationship with one child at a time. Some of the items focus on child characteristics that could engender stress, such as activity level and mood. Other PSI items reflect potentially stressful aspects of the parent's life, such as lack of social support and marital problems (Gresham, 1989). The test's authors report internal consistency reliability coefficients ranging from .89 to .95 for factors and total scores. Test-retest reliability coefficients range from .71 to .82 over three weeks, and .55 to .70 over a one-year interval (Loyd & Abidin, 1985). With respect to the test's validity, parents who physically abuse their children tend to score higher on the PSI than parents who do not (Wantz, 1989).

What are the appropriate uses of measures like the CAP and the PSI? Although positive relationships exist between child abuse and scores on the tests, the tests cannot be used to identify or prosecute child abusers in a legal context (Gresham, 1989). Because child abuse is a low base-rate phenomenon, even the use of highly reliable instruments will produce many false positives. In this instance, a false positive is an erroneous identification of the assessee as an abuser when the assessee is not an abuser. For some parents, high levels of stress as measured by the PSI may indeed lead to physical abuse. However, for most parents they will not. Some parent-child relationships, such as those involving children with disabilities, are inherently stressful (Innocenti et al., 1992; Orr et al., 1993). Still, most parents manage to weather the relationship without inflicting any harm. Some parents who experience high levels of stress as a result of their relationship with a child may themselves be harmed—and stressed even more—to hear from a mental health official that they are at risk for child abuse. For that reason, great caution is called for in interpreting and acting on the results of a test designed to assess risk for child abuse.

On the other hand, high CAP or PSI scores may well point the way to an abusive situation, and they should alert concerned professionals to be watchful for signs of abuse. A second appropriate use of such scores concerns the allocation of resources designed to reduce parenting stress. Parents who score high on the CAP and the PSI could be given priority for placement in a parenting skills class, individualized parent training, child care assistance, and other such programs. If reducing the stress of the parent will reduce the risk of child abuse, everything that can possibly be done to reduce the parental stress should be attempted.

> **JUST THINK . . .**
>
> Other than by administering a psychological test, how else might professionals identify parents who are extremely stressed?

As we have seen throughout this book, there are many different tools of assessment and many different ways the tools can be used. If all of these tools have anything at all in common, it is that their use by a professional will at some time or another culminate in a written report. In clinical and counseling settings, that report is referred to simply as **the psychological report.**

The Psychological Report

A critical component of any testing or assessment procedure is the reporting of the findings. The high reliability or validity of a test or assessment procedure may be cast to the wind if the assessment report is not written in an organized and readable fashion. Of course, what constitutes an organized and readable report will vary as a function of the goal of the assessment and the audience for whom the report is intended. A psychoanalyst's report exploring a patient's unresolved oedipal conflict designed for presentation to the New York Psychoanalytic Society will look and sound very different from a school psychologist's report to a teacher concerning a child's hyperactive behavior in the classroom.

Psychological reports may be as different as the reasons for undertaking the assessment. Reports may vary on a number of variables, such as the extent to which conclusions rely on one or another assessment procedure, and the specificity of recommendations made, if any. Still, some basic elements are common to most clinical reports. We focus our attention on those elements in this chapter's *Everyday Psychometrics*. It should be clear, however, that report writing is a skill necessary in educational, organizational, and other settings—any setting where psychological assessment takes place.

The Barnum Effect

The showman P. T. Barnum is credited with having said, "There's a sucker born every minute." Psychologists, among others, have taken P. T. Barnum's words about the widespread gullibility of people quite seriously. In fact, *Barnum effect* is a term that should be familiar to any psychologist called on to write a psychological report. Before reading on to find out exactly what the Barnum effect is, imagine that you have just completed a computerized personality test and that the printout describing the results reads as follows:

> You have a strong need for other people to like you and for them to admire you. You have a tendency to be critical of yourself. You have a great deal of unused capacity that you have not turned to your advantage. While you have some personality weaknesses, you are generally able to compensate for them. Your sexual adjustment has presented some problems for you. Disciplined and controlled on the outside, you tend to be worrisome and insecure inside. At times you have serious doubts as to whether you have made the right decision or done the right thing. You prefer a certain amount of change and variety and become dissatisfied when hemmed in by restrictions and limitations. You pride yourself on being an independent thinker and do not accept others' opinions without satisfactory proof. You have found it unwise to be too frank in revealing yourself to others. At times you are extraverted, affable, and sociable, while at other times you are introverted, wary, and reserved. Some of your aspirations tend to be pretty unrealistic.

Still imagining that the preceding test results had been formulated specifically for you, please rate the accuracy of the description as it does or does not apply to you personally.

> I feel that the interpretation was:
> excellent
> good
> average
> poor
> very poor

Now that you have completed the exercise, we can say, "Welcome to the ranks of those who have been subject to the Barnum effect." This psychological profile is, as you

Elements of a Typical Report of Psychological Assessment

There is no single, universally accepted style or form for a psychological report. Most assessors develop a style and form that they believe best suits the specific objectives of the assessment. Generally, however, most clinical reports contain the elements listed and briefly discussed below.

Demographic Data

Included here are all or some of the following: the patient's name, address, telephone number, education, occupation, religion, marital status, date of birth, place of birth, ethnic membership, citizenship, date of testing. The examiner's name must also be considered part of the identifying material in the report.

Reason for Referral

Why was this patient referred for psychological assessment? This section of the report may sometimes be as short as one sentence (for example, "Johnny was referred for evaluation to shed light on the question of whether his inattention in class is due to personality, neurological, or other difficulties"). Alternatively, this section of the report may be extended with all relevant background information (for example, "Johnny complained of hearing difficulties in his fourth-grade class, according to a note in his records"). If all relevant background information is not covered in the "Reason for Referral" section of the report, it may be covered in a separate section labeled "Background" or in a section labeled "Findings."

Tests Administered

Here the examiner simply lists the names of the tests that were administered. Thus, for example, this section of the report may be as brief as the following:

- Wechsler Intelligence Scale for Children-IV (1/8/05 1/12/05)
- Bender Visual-Motor Gestalt Test-2 (1/8/05)
- Rorschach Test (1/12/05)
- Thematic Apperception Test (1/12/05)
- Sentence Completion Test (1/8/05)
- Figure drawings (1/8/05)

Note that the date of the test administration has been inserted next to the name of each test administered. This is a good idea under any circumstances and particularly important if testing was executed over the course of a number of days, weeks, or longer. In the sample section above, the WISC-IV was administered over the course of two testing sessions on two days. The Bender-2, the Sentence Completion Test, and figure drawings were administered on 1/8/05; the Rorschach and the Thematic Apperception Test were administered on 1/12/05.

Also in this section, the examiner might place the names and the dates of tests known to have been previously administered to the examinee. If the examiner has a record of the findings (or better yet, the original test protocols) from this prior testing, this information may be integrated into the next section of the report, "Findings."

Findings

Here the examiner reports not only findings (for example, "On the WISC-IV Johnny achieved a Verbal IQ of 100, a Performance IQ of 110, yielding a full-scale IQ of 106") but also all extra-test considerations, such as observations concerning the examinee's motivation ("the examinee did/did not appear to be motivated to do well on the tests"), the examinee's level of fatigue, the nature of the relationship and rapport with the examiner, indices of anxiety, and method of approach to the task. The section labeled "Findings" may begin with a description of the examinee that is detailed enough for the reader of the report almost to visualize him or her. For example:

> John is a 20-year-old college student with brown, shoulder-length, stringy hair and a full beard. He came to the testing wearing a "psychedelic" shirt, cutoff and ragged shorts, and sandals. He sat slouched in his chair for most of the test session, tended to speak only when spoken to, and spoke in a slow, lethargic manner.

Also included in this section is mention of any extraneous variables that might in some way have affected the test results. Was testing in a school interrupted by any event such as a fire drill, an earth tremor, or some other disturbance? Did loud or atypical noise in or out of the test site affect the testtaker's concentration? Did the hospitalized patient receive any visitors just before an evaluation, and could such a visit have affected the findings? Answers to these types of questions may prove invaluable in interpreting assessment data.

(*continued*)

Elements of a Typical Report of Psychological Assessment (*continued*)

The "Findings" section of the report is where all the background material, behavioral observations, and test data are integrated to provide an answer to the referral question. Whether or not the examiner makes reference to the actual test data is a matter of personal preference. Thus, for example, one examiner might simply state, "There is evidence of neurological deficit in this record" and stop there. Another examiner might document exactly why this was being asserted:

> There is evidence of neurological deficit as indicated by the rotation and perseveration errors in the Bender-Gestalt-2 record. Further, on the TAT, this examinee failed to grasp the situation as a whole and simply enumerated single details. Additionally, this examinee had difficulty abstracting—still another index of neurological deficit—as evidenced by the unusually low score on the WISC-IV Similarities subtest.

The "Findings" section should lead logically into the "Recommendations" section.

Recommendations

On the basis of the psychological assessment, with particular attention to factors such as the personal aspects and deficiencies of the examinee, recommendations addressed to ameliorating the presenting problem are given. The recommendation may be for psychotherapy, a consultation with a neurologist, placement in a special class, short-term family therapy addressed to a specific problem—whatever the examiner believes is required to ameliorate the situation is spelled out here.

Summary

The "Summary" section includes in "short form" a statement concerning the reason for referral, the findings, and the recommendation. This section is usually only a paragraph or two, and it should provide a concise statement of who the examinee is, why the examinee was referred for testing, what was found, and what needs to be done.

---

no doubt have noticed, vague and general. The same paragraph (sometimes with slight modifications) has been used in a number of psychological studies (Forer, 1949; Jackson et al., 1982; Merrens & Richards, 1970; Sundberg, 1955; Ulrich et al., 1963), with similar findings: People tend to accept vague and general personality descriptions as uniquely applicable to themselves without realizing that the same description could be applied to just about anyone.

The finding that people tend to accept vague personality descriptions as accurate descriptions of themselves came to be known as the **Barnum effect** after psychologist Paul Meehl's (1956) condemnation of "personality description after the manner of P. T. Barnum."[3] Meehl suggested that the term Barnum effect be used "to stigmatize those pseudo-successful clinical procedures in which personality descriptions from tests are made to fit the patient largely or wholly by virtue of their triviality." Cognizance of this effect and the factors that may heighten or diminish it is necessary if psychological assessors are to avoid making interpretations in the manner of P. T. Barnum.

JUST THINK . . .

Write one paragraph—a vague and general personality description—that could be used to study the Barnum effect. Here's a hint: You may use the daily horoscope column in your local newspaper for assistance in finding the words.

---

3. Meehl credited D. G. Patterson with having first used the term *Barnum effect*. The same phenomenon has also been characterized as the *Aunt Fanny effect*. Tallent (1958) originated this term when he deplored the generality and vagueness that plagued too many psychology reports. For example, of the finding that an assessee had "unconscious hostile urges," Tallent wrote, "so has my Aunt Fanny!"

Clinical Versus Mechanical Prediction

Should clinicians review test results and related assessment data and then draw conclusions, make recommendations, and take actions that are based on their own education, training, and clinical experience? Alternatively, should clinicians review test results and related assessment data and then draw conclusions, make recommendations, and take actions on the basis of known statistical probabilities, much like an actuary or statistician whose occupation is to calculate risks? A debate regarding the respective merits of what has become known as *clinical versus actuarial prediction* or *clinical versus actuarial assessment* began to simmer over a half-century ago with the publication of a monograph on the subject by Paul Meehl (1954; see also Dawes et al., 1989; Garb, 1994; Holt, 1970; Marchese, 1992).[4]

The increasing popularity of computer-assisted psychological assessment (CAPA) and computer-generated test interpretation has resurrected the clinical-versus-actuarial debate. The battleground has shifted to the frontier of new technology and questions about actuarial assessment compared to clinical judgment. Contemporary scholars and practitioners tend not to debate whether clinicians should be using actuary-like methods to make clinical judgments. It is more *au courant* to debate whether clinicians should be using software that uses actuary-like methods to make clinical judgments.

Some clarification and definition of terms may be helpful here. In the context of clinical decision-making, **actuarial assessment** and **actuarial prediction** have been used synonymously to refer to the application of empirically demonstrated statistical rules and probabilities as a determining factor in clinical judgment and actions. As observed by Butcher et al. (2000), *actuarial assessment* is not synonymous with *computerized assessment*. Citing Sines (1966), Butcher et al. (2000, p. 6) noted that "a computer-based test interpretation (CBTI) system is actuarial only if its interpretive output is wholly determined by statistical rules that have been demonstrated empirically to exist between the output and the input data." It is possible for the interpretive output of a CBTI system to be determined by things other than statistical rules. The output may be based, for example, not on any statistical formulas or actuarial calculations but rather on the clinical judgment, opinions, and expertise of the author of the software. *Computerized assessment* in such an instance would amount to a computerized application of clinical opinion; that is, the application of a clinician's (or group of clinicians') judgments, opinions, and expertise to a particular set of data as processed by the computer software.

Clinical prediction refers to the application of a clinician's own training and clinical experience as a determining factor in clinical judgment and actions. Clinical prediction relies on clinical judgment, which Grove et al. (2000) characterized as

> the typical procedure long used by applied psychologists and physicians, in which the judge puts data together using informal, subjective methods. Clinicians differ in how they do this: The very nature of the process tends to preclude precise specification. (p. 19)

Grove et al. (2000) proceeded to compare clinical judgment with what they termed **mechanical prediction,** or the application of empirically demonstrated statistical rules

---

4. Although this debate has traditionally been couched in terms of clinical assessment (or prediction) as compared to statistical or actuarial assessment (or prediction), a parallel debate could pit other applied areas of assessment (including educational, personnel, or organizational assessment, for example) against statistically based methods. At the heart of the debate are questions concerning the utility of a rather subjective approach to assessment that is based on one's training and experience, as compared to a more objective and statistically sophisticated approach that is strictly based on preset rules for analyzing the data.

and probabilities, as well as computer algorithms, to the computer generation of findings and recommendations. These authors reported the results of a meta-analysis of 136 studies that pitted the accuracy of clinical prediction against mechanical prediction. In some studies, the two approaches to assessment seemed to be about equal in accuracy. On average, however, Grove et al. concluded that the mechanical approach was about 10% more accurate than the clinical approach. The clinical approach fared least well when the predictors included clinical interview data. Perhaps this was so because, unlike computer programs, human clinicians make errors in judgment; for example, failing to take account of base rates or other statistical mediators of accurate assessment. The researchers also hinted that the cost of mechanical prediction probably was less than the cost of clinical prediction, since the mechanical route obviated the necessity for highly paid professionals and team meetings.

Several studies have supported the use of statistical prediction over clinical prediction. One reason is that some of the methods used in the comparison research seem to tip the scales in favor of the statistical approach. As Karon (2000) observed, "clinical data" in many of the studies was not defined in terms of qualitative information elicited by a clinician but rather in terms of MMPI or MMPI-2 scores. Perhaps many clinicians remain reluctant to place too much trust in CAPA products because, as Karon (1981) argued, variables in the study of personality, abnormal behavior, and other areas of psychology are truly infinite. Exactly which variables need to be focused on in a particular situation can be a very individual matter. Combine these variables with the many other possible variables that may be operative in a situation requiring clinical judgment (such as an assessee's English-speaking ability, cooperativeness, and cultural background), and the size of the software database needed for accurate prediction begins to mushroom. Given that is the case, many clinicians remain willing to hazard their own clinical judgment rather than rely on preprogrammed interpretations.

Computers have a long and distinguished history as workhorses when it comes to scoring test protocols and organizing test data. Their value when it comes to interpreting data and printing out reports is a bit more controversial. On the positive side, computers reliably apply the decision rules they are programmed to apply. Unlike inter-rater reliability, "inter-computer" reliability is perfect—barring program glitches, power outages, or the like. Computers carry no biases regarding race, social class, gender, or sexual orientation. And unlike some clinicians, they don't fall back on a favored personality theory when in doubt about making a test-related decision. Rather, computers diligently play by the rules with which they are programmed. It is only when those rules are flawed that their output is flawed. And this gives rise to critical questions about the lack of validation or the improper validation of many computer programs.

The present authors share with others (for example, Garb, 2000a, 2000b; Marks, 1999) the view that computers will become increasingly important for psychological assessment. However, for this prophecy to become a reality beneficial to clients, thoughtful solutions to obstacles must continue to be developed (Drasgow & Olson-Buchanan, 1999), and users of assessment-related programs must become more discriminating consumers (Snyder, 2000). Hopefully, users will become better clinicians as well. The development, enhancement, and sharpening of clinical skills ideally will proceed along tracks parallel to the development of new technology. After all, it is in human hands that even the most eloquent computer narratives are placed. It is human judgment that processes and interprets these reports. Ultimately, there is no substitute for clinical judgment, and the optimal combination of actuarial methods and clinical judgment must be identified for all types of predictive enterprises.

JUST THINK . . .

Will clinicians who increasingly rely on computers for test scoring and test interpretation become better or worse clinicians?

Self-Assessment

Test your understanding of elements of this chapter by seeing if you can explain each of the following terms, expressions, and abbreviations:

abuse
actuarial assessment
actuarial prediction
ADRESSING
ALI standard
anatomically detailed doll (ADD)
Barnum effect
clinical prediction
clinical psychology
cognitive interview
collaborative interview
competence to stand trial
counseling psychology
culturally informed psychological assessment
custody evaluation

DSM-IV-TR
Durham standard
duty to warn
emotional and behavioral signs of abuse and neglect
emotional injury
evolutionary view of mental disorder
forensic psychological assessment
hypnotic interview
insanity
interview
MacAndrew Alcoholism Scale (MAC-R)
managed care
mechanical prediction

mental status examination
M'Naghten standard
neglect
orientation
oriented times 3
physical signs of abuse
physical signs of neglect
premorbid functioning
psychological report
psychopath
reacculturation
standard battery
stress interview
test battery
therapeutic contract

Web Watch

Check out the following Web sites for more information about topics discussed in this chapter.

APA Division 12 (Clinical Psychology)
www.apa.org/divisions/div12/homepage.html

APA Division 17 (Counseling Psychology)
www.div17.org

Managed care
www.themcic.com

www.ncpamd.com/mcjokes.htm

www.nepsy.com/leading/0211_ne_reform.html

www.managedcareinfo.com

DSM-IV-TR
www.behavenet.com/capsules/disorders/dsm4TRclassification.htm

www.behavenet.com/capsules/disorders/dsm4tr.htm

The addiction severity index
www.niaaa.nih.gov/publications/asi.htm

Online substance abuse assessment
www.drug-rehabilitation.com/online_assessment.htm

Forensic psychology
www.unl.edu/ap-ls

http://members.optushome.com.au/dwillsh/forensic.htm

The duty to warn
www.ncrel.org/sdrs/areas/issues/envrnmnt/css/cs31k1.htm

A psychopathy checklist
www.swin.edu.au/victims/resources/assessment/personality/psychopathy_checklist.html

Insanity in legal context
http://dictionary.law.com

Child abuse and neglect
http://nccanch.acf.hhs.gov/index.cfm

www.ifapa.org/Brochures/ca_assessment.pdf

www.state.sd.us/social/CPS/Services/signs.htm

http://home.nyc.gov/html/acs/html/getinvolved/abuseprevent_signs.html

Anatomically detailed dolls
www.ipt-forensics.com/library/special_problems5.htm

www.secasa.com.au/index.php/workers/17/41/8

Barnum effect
http://skepdic.com/forer.html

14

Neuropsychological Assessment

The branch of medicine that focuses on the nervous system and its disorders is **neurology.** The branch of psychology that focuses on the relationship between brain functioning and behavior is **neuropsychology.** Formerly a specialty area within clinical psychology, neuropsychology has evolved into a specialty in its own right. Neuropsychologists study the nervous system as it relates to behavior, using various tools, including *neuropsychological assessment.* **Neuropsychological assessment** may be defined as the evaluation of brain and nervous system functioning as it relates to behavior.

In this chapter, we survey some of the tools and procedures used by clinicians and neuropsychologists to screen for and diagnose neuropsychological disorders. We begin with a brief introduction to brain–behavior relationships. This material is presented to lay a foundation for understanding how testtaking, as well as other behavior, can be evaluated to form hypotheses about levels of brain intactness and functioning.

The Nervous System and Behavior

The nervous system is composed of various kinds of **neurons** (nerve cells) and can be divided into the **central nervous system** (consisting of the brain and the spinal cord) and the **peripheral nervous system** (consisting of the neurons that convey messages to and from the rest of the body). Viewed from the top, the large, rounded portion of the brain, (called the cerebrum) can be divided into two sections, or hemispheres.

Some brain–behavior correlates are summarized in Table 14–1. Each of the two cerebral hemispheres receives sensory information from the opposite side of the body and also controls motor responses on the opposite side of the body—a phenomenon termed **contralateral control.** It is due to the brain's contralateral control of the body that an injury to the right side of the brain may result in sensory or motor defects on the left side of the body. The meeting ground of the two hemispheres is the corpus callosum, although one hemisphere, most frequently the left one, is dominant. It is because the left hemisphere is most frequently dominant that most people are right-handed. The dominant hemisphere leads in such activities as reading, writing, arithmetic, and speech. The nondominant hemi-

---

JUST THINK . . .

We take for granted everyday activities such as walking, but imagine the complex mechanics of that simple act with reference to the phenomenon of contralateral control.

Table 14–1
Some Brain–Behavior Characteristics for Selected Nervous System Sites

Site	Characteristic
Temporal lobes	These lobes contain auditory reception areas as well as certain areas for the processing of visual information. Damage to the temporal lobe may affect sound discrimination, recognition, and comprehension; music appreciation; voice recognition; and auditory or visual memory storage.
Occipital lobes	These lobes contain visual reception areas. Damage to this area could result in blindness to all or part of the visual field or deficits in object recognition, visual scanning, visual integration of symbols into wholes, and recall of visual imagery.
Parietal lobes	These lobes contain reception areas for the sense of touch and for the sense of bodily position. Damage to this area may result in deficits in the sense of touch, disorganization, and distorted self-perception.
Frontal lobes	These lobes are integrally involved in ordering information and sorting out stimuli. Concentration and attention, abstract-thinking ability, concept-formation ability, foresight, problem-solving ability, and speech, as well as gross and fine motor ability, may be affected by damage to the frontal lobes.
Thalamus	The thalamus is a kind of communications relay station for all sensory information transmitted to the cerebral cortex. Damage to the thalamus may result in altered states of arousal, memory defects, speech deficits, apathy, and disorientation.
Hypothalamus	The hypothalamus is involved in the regulation of bodily functions such as eating, drinking, body temperature, sexual behavior, and emotion. It is sensitive to changes in environment that call for a "fight or flight" response from the organism. Damage to it may elicit a variety of symptoms ranging from uncontrolled eating or drinking to mild alterations of mood states.
Cerebellum	Together with the pons (another brain site in the area of the brain referred to as the hindbrain), the cerebellum is involved in the regulation of balance, breathing, and posture, among other functions. Damage to the cerebellum may manifest as problems in fine motor control and coordination.
Reticular formation	In the core of the brain stem, the reticular formation contains fibers en route to and from the cortex. Because stimulation to this area can cause a sleeping organism to awaken and an awake organism to become even more alert, it is sometimes referred to as the reticular activating system. Damage to this area can cause the organism to sleep for long periods of time.
Limbic system	Composed of the amygdala, the cingulate cortex, the hippocampus, and the septal areas of the brain, the limbic system is integral to the expression of emotions. Damage to this area may profoundly affect emotional behavior.
Spinal cord	Many reflexes necessary for survival (such as withdrawing from a hot surface) are carried out at the level of the spinal cord. In addition to its role in reflex activity, the spinal cord is integral to the coordination of motor movements. Spinal cord injuries may result in various degrees of paralysis or other motor difficulties.

sphere leads in tasks involving spatial and textural recognition as well as art and music appreciation. In the normal, neurologically intact individual, one hemisphere complements the other.

Neurological Damage and the Concept of Organicity

Modern-day researchers exploring the link between the brain and the body use a number of varied tools and procedures in their work. Beyond the usual tools of psychological assessment (tests, case studies, etc.), investigators employ high-technology imaging equipment, experimentation involving the electrical or chemical stimulation of various human and animal brain sites, experimentation involving surgical alteration of the brain of animal subjects, laboratory testing and field observation of head-trauma victims, and autopsies of normal and abnormal human and animal subjects. Through these varied means, researchers have learned much about healthy and pathological neurological functioning.

Neurological damage may take the form of a lesion in the brain or any other site within the central or peripheral nervous system. A **lesion** is a pathological alteration of tissue, such as that which could result from injury or infection. Neurological lesions may be physical or chemical in nature, and they are characterized as *focal* (relatively circumscribed at one site) or *diffuse* (scattered at various sites). Because different sites of the brain control various functions, focal and diffuse lesions at different sites will manifest themselves in varying behavioral deficits. A partial listing of the technical names for the many varieties of sensory and motor deficits is presented in Table 14–2.

Table 14–2
Technical Names for Various Kinds of Sensory and Motor Deficits

Name	Description of Deficit
acalculia	Inability to perform arithmetic calculations
acopia	Inability to copy geometric designs
agnosia	Deficit in recognizing sensory stimuli (for example, *auditory agnosia* is difficulty in recognizing auditory stimuli)
agraphia	Deficit in writing ability
akinesia	Deficit in motor movements
alexia	Inability to read
amnesia	Loss of memory
amusia	Deficit in ability to produce or appreciate music
anomia	Deficit associated with finding words to name things
anopia	Deficit in sight
anosmia	Deficit in sense of smell
aphasia	Deficit in communication due to impaired speech or writing ability
apraxia	Voluntary movement disorder in the absence of paralysis
ataxia	Deficit in motor ability and muscular coordination

It is possible for a focal lesion to have diffuse ramifications with regard to behavioral deficits. Stated another way, a circumscribed lesion in one area of the brain may affect many different kinds of behaviors. It is possible for a diffuse lesion to affect one or more areas of functioning so severely that it masquerades as a focal lesion. With an awareness of these possibilities, neuropsychologists sometimes "work backward" as they try to determine from outward behavior where neurological lesions, if any, may be.

Neurological assessment may also play a critical role in determining the extent of behavioral impairment that has occurred or can be expected to occur as the result of a neurological disorder or injury. Such diagnostic information is useful not only in designing remediation programs but also in evaluating the consequences of drug treatments, physical training, and other therapy.

JUST THINK . . .

A patient complains of problems maintaining balance. At what site in the brain might a neuropsychologist "work backward" from this complaint and identify a problem? Hint: You may wish to "work backward" yourself and refer back to Table 14–1.

The terms *brain damage, neurological damage,* and *organicity* unfortunately have been used interchangeably in much of the psychological literature. The term *neurological damage* is the most inclusive because it covers not only damage to the brain but also damage to the spinal cord and to all the components of the peripheral nervous system. The use of the term *organicity* derives from the post–World War I research of the German neurologist Kurt Goldstein. Studies of brain-injured soldiers led Goldstein to the conclusion that the factors differentiating organically impaired individuals from normals included the loss of abstraction ability, deficits in reasoning ability, and inflexibility in problem-solving tasks. Accordingly, Goldstein (1927, 1939, 1963a) and his colleagues developed psychological tests that tapped these factors and were designed to help in the diagnosis of *organic brain syndrome,* or **organicity** for short. Although Goldstein's test is now out of print, it is still useful in illustrating some of the types of tasks still used today to screen for neurological deficit (Figure 14–1).

In the tradition of Goldstein and his associates, two German psychologists, Heinz Werner and Alfred Strauss, examined brain–behavior correlates in brain-injured, mentally retarded children (Werner & Strauss, 1941; Strauss & Lehtinen, 1947). Like their predecessors who had worked with brain-injured adults, these investigators attempted to delineate characteristics common to *all* brain-injured people, including children. Al-

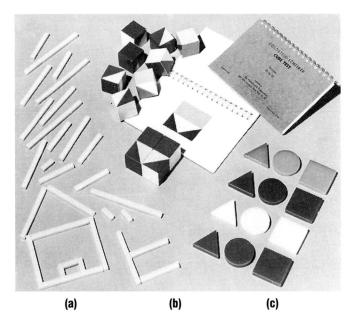

(a)   (b)   (c)

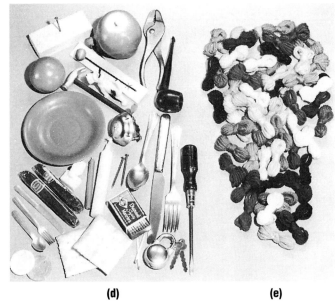

(d)   (e)

Figure 14–1
The Goldstein-Scheerer Tests
of Abstract and Concrete Thinking *

(a) *The Stick Test is a measure of recent memory. The subject's task is to reproduce designs from memory, using sticks.* **(b)** *The Cube Test challenges the subject to replicate with blocks a design printed in a booklet. This subtest was the predecessor of the Block Design task on Wechsler intelligence tests. It is used as a measure of nonverbal abstraction ability.* **(c)** *The Color-Form Sorting Test contains 12 objects, including 4 triangles, 4 circles, and 4 squares (each piece in one of four colors). The objects are presented in a random order, and the subject is instructed to sort according to which belong together. Once they are sorted, the subject is next asked to sort the objects a different way. The subject's flexibility in shifting from one sorting principle to another is noted.* **(d)** *The Object Sorting Test consists of 89 objects, which the subject is required to group. Concrete thinking and organic impairment may be inferred if the subject sorts, for example, by color instead of function.* **(e)** *The Color Sorting Test employs several woolen skeins of varying colors. The task here is to sort the skeins according to a sample sketch displayed by the examiner.*

* The Goldstein-Scheerer Tests of Abstract and Concrete Thinking are now out of print.

though their work led to a better understanding of the behavioral consequences of brain injury in children, it also led to the presumption that all organically impaired children, regardless of the specific nature or site of their impairment, shared a similar pattern of cognitive, behavioral, sensory, and motor deficits. The unitary concept of organicity that emerged from this work in the 1940s prevailed through much of the 1950s. But by then, researchers such as Birch and Diller (1959) were already beginning to question what they termed the "naivete of the concept of 'organicity'":

> It is abundantly clear that "brain damage" and "organicity" are terms which though overlapping are not identities and serve to designate interdependent events. "Brain-damage" refers to the fact of an anatomical destruction, whereas "organicity" represents

one of the varieties of functional consequences which may attend such destruction. (p. 195)

In fact, the view that organicity and brain damage are nonunitary is supported by a number of observations:

- Persons who have identical lesions in the brain may exhibit markedly different symptoms.

- Many interacting factors, such as the patient's premorbid functioning, the site and diffuseness of the lesion, the cause of the lesion, and its rate of spread, may make one organically impaired individual appear clinically quite dissimilar from another.

- Considerable similarity may exist in the symptoms exhibited by persons who have entirely different types of lesions. Further, these different types of lesions may arise from a variety of causes, such as trauma with or without loss of consciousness, infection, nutritional deficiencies, tumor, stroke, neuronal degeneration, toxins, insufficient cardiac output, and a variety of metabolic disturbances.

- Many conditions that are not due to brain damage produce symptoms that mimic those produced by brain damage. For example, an individual who is psychotic, depressed, or simply fatigued may produce data on an examination for organic brain damage that are characteristically diagnostic of neuropsychological impairment.

- Factors other than brain damage (such as psychosis, depression, fatigue) influence the responses of brain-damaged persons. Some types of responses are consequences (rather than correlates) of the brain damage. For example, if brain-injured children as a group tend to be described as more aggressive than normals, this may reflect more on the way such children have been treated by parents, teachers, and peers than on the effect of any lesions.

JUST THINK . . .

Can you think of any other diagnostic labels that are routinely used as though they were unitary but that are really nonunitary? What about the diagnostic label *psychotic*?

- Persons who are in fact brain-damaged are sometimes able to compensate for their deficits to such an extent that some functions are actually taken over by other, more intact parts of the brain.

With this brief introduction to neuropsychology as background, let's look at the neuropsychological examination and the various tools of assessment that may be employed to conduct it.

The Neuropsychological Examination

Clinicians doing routine evaluations may not be neuropsychologists, although they are trained to screen for signs and symptoms of neurological deficit. Neuropsychologists make a distinction between *hard signs* and *soft signs*. A **hard sign** may be defined as an indicator of definite neurological deficit. Abnormal reflex performance is an example of a hard sign. A **soft sign** is an indicator that is merely suggestive of neurological deficit. An example of a soft sign is a 15-point discrepancy between the verbal and performance scales on a Wechsler intelligence test. Signs (hard or soft) and symptoms may present themselves during history taking, as when an assessee reports having lost consciousness on occasion. Areas that require further study may emerge during interviewing, as when the assessee complains of severe, long-lasting headaches. Signs or symptoms may be observed by interviewers during an interview or by examiners during the administration of a test. Signs indicating neuropsychological deficit may be evident in test scores.

In cases in which signs or symptoms lead to a suspicion of neurological deficit, the assessee typically is referred either to a neurologist for a neurological examination or to a neuropsychologist for a neuropsychological evaluation. The objective of the typical neuropsychological evaluation is "to draw inferences about the structural and functional characteristics of a person's brain by evaluating an individual's behavior in defined stimulus-response situations" (Benton, 1994, p. 1).

Many of the tools of neuropsychological assessment are tools with which most psychological assessors are quite familiar, such as the test, the case study, and the interview. Some tools, such as imaging equipment, are modern marvels of technology with workings known to relatively few medical professionals. Our focus is on tools of the more familiar variety, although we will briefly overview some modern marvels as well.

The tools of assessment used in a neuropsychological examination vary as a function of several factors; for example, the purpose of the examination, the neurological intactness of the examinee, and the thoroughness of the examination. In a sense, any routine administration of a psychological test or battery of tests in a clinical setting can also serve the purpose of neuropsychological screening. In the course of assessing intelligence, personality, or other variables, the clinician may be alerted to suspicious findings that signal the need for a deeper neuropsychological examination. Sometimes a patient is referred to a psychologist for screening for neurological problems. In such a case, a battery of tests will typically be administered. This battery at a minimum will consist of an intelligence test, a personality test, and a perceptual-motor/memory test.[1] If suspicious neurological signs are discovered in the course of the evaluation, the examinee is referred for further and more detailed evaluation.

Beyond general screening purposes, an individual might be referred for an in-depth neuropsychological evaluation because of the nature of a specific presenting problem, such as a complaint of loss of memory. A neuropsychological examination might be ordered by a neurologist who seeks to find out more about the cognitive and behavioral consequences of a suspected or known lesion. A neurologist's referral note to a neuropsychologist in such an instance might read:

> JUST THINK . . .
>
> Describe a finding as a result of an intelligence test administration that might prompt an assessor to refer the assessee for a thorough neuropsychological evaluation.

> My examination was negative, but I feel I might be missing something. This patient did have a head injury about six months ago, and he still complains of headaches and slight memory problems for recent events. I found no hard signs, some soft signs such as a right hand tremor (possibly due to anxiety), and a pattern of findings on laboratory tests ranging from negative to equivocal. Please evaluate this patient and let me know whether you find the headaches and other vague complaints to be organic or functional in origin.

In addition to asking whether any observed deficits are **organic** (physically based) or **functional** (psychologically based), the referral note might also ask the neuropsychologist

---

1. We have listed here what we believe to be the minimum amount of testing for an adequate neuropsychological screening. It is, however, not uncommon for some clinicians to administer only a perceptual-motor/memory test, a practice some have cautioned strongly against. See, for example, Bigler & Ehrenfurth (1981) and Kahn & Taft (1983).

other kinds of questions, such as "Is this condition acute or chronic?" "Is this individual ready to go back to school or work?" "What skills require remediation?"

The neuropsychological examination will vary widely as a function of the nature of the referral question. Questions concerning the functional or organic origin of observed behavior will require deeper examination of personality and psychiatric history.

The content and nature of the examination will also vary as a function of the neurological intactness of the assessee. Neuropsychologists assess persons exhibiting a wide range of physical and psychological disabilities. Some, for example, have known visual or auditory deficits, concentration and attention problems, speech and language difficulties, and so forth. Allowance must be made for such deficits, and a way must be found to administer the appropriate tests so that meaningful results can be obtained. Frequently, neuropsychologists will administer preliminary visual, auditory, and other such examinations to ascertain the gross intactness of sensory and motor functioning before proceeding with more specialized tests. An olfactory (sense of smell) deficit, for example, may be symptomatic of a great variety of neurological and nonneurological problems as diverse as Alzheimer's disease (Serby et al., 1991), Parkinson's disease (Serby et al., 1985), and AIDS (Brody et al., 1991). The discovery of such a deficit by means of a test such as the University of Pennsylvania Smell Identification Test (UPSIT; Doty et al., 1984) would be a stimulus for continued diagnostic assessment.

Common to all thorough neuropsychological examinations are a history taking, a mental status examination, and the administration of tests and procedures designed to uncover any problems of neuropsychological functioning. Throughout the examination, the neuropsychologist's knowledge of neuroanatomy, neurochemistry, and neurophysiology are essential for optimal interpretation of the data. In addition to guiding decisions concerning what to test for and how to test for it, such knowledge will also come into play with respect to the decisions concerning *when* to test. Thus, for example, it would be atypical for a neuropsychologist to psychologically test a stroke victim immediately after the stroke has occurred. Because some recovery of function could be expected to spontaneously occur in the weeks and months following the stroke, testing the patient immediately after the stroke would therefore yield an erroneous picture of the extent of the damage.

History Taking, the Case History, and Case Studies

Neuropsychologists pay careful attention to patients' histories as told to them by the patients themselves and as revealed in patients' records. Neuropsychologists also study findings from similar cases, the better to understand their assessees.

The typical neuropsychological examination begins with a careful history taking. Areas of interest to the examiner include the following:

- The medical history of the patient.
- The medical history of the patient's immediate family and other relatives. A sample question here might be "Have you or any of your relatives experienced dizziness, fainting, blackouts, or spasms?"
- The presence or absence of certain **developmental milestones,** a particularly critical part of the history-taking process when examining young children. A list of some of these milestones appears in Table 14–3.
- Psychosocial history, including level of academic achievement and estimated level of intelligence; an estimated level of adjustment at home and at work or school; observations regarding personality (for example, Is this individual hypochondria-

Table 14-3
Some Developmental Milestones

Age	Development
16 weeks	Gets excited, laughs aloud Smiles spontaneously in response to people Anticipates eating at sight of food Sits propped up for 10 to 15 minutes
28 weeks	Smiles and vocalizes to a mirror and pats at mirror image Many vowel sounds Sits unsupported for brief period and then leans on hands Takes solids well When lying on back, places feet to mouth Grasps objects and transfers objects from hand to hand When held standing, supports most of weight
12 months	Walks with only one hand held Says "mamma" and "dada" and perhaps two other words Gives a toy in response to a request or gesture When being dressed, will cooperate Plays "peek-a-boo" games
18 months	Has a vocabulary of some ten words Walks well, seldom falls, can run stiffly Looks at pictures in a book Feeds self, although spills Can pull a toy or hug a doll Can seat self in a small or adult chair Scribbles spontaneously with a crayon or pencil
24 months	Walks up and down stairs alone Runs well, no falling Can build a tower of six or seven blocks Uses personal pronouns ("I" and "you") and speaks a three-word sentence Identifies simple pictures by name and calls self by name Verbalizes needs fairly consistently May be dry at night Can pull on simple garment
36 months	Alternates feet when climbing stairs and jumps from bottom stair Rides a tricycle Can copy a circle and imitate a cross with a crayon or pencil Comprehends and answers questions Feeds self with little spilling May know and repeat a few simple rhymes
48 months	Can dry and wash hands, brushes teeth Laces shoes, dresses and undresses with supervision Can play cooperatively with other children Can draw figure of a person with at least two clear body parts
60 months	Knows and names colors, counts to 10 Skips on both feet Can print a few letters, can draw identifiable pictures

Source: Gesell and Amatruda (1947)

cal?), thought processes, and motivation (Is this person willing and able to respond accurately to these questions?).

- The character, severity, and progress of any history of complaints involving disturbances in sight, hearing, smell, touch, taste, or balance; disturbances in muscle tone, muscle strength, and muscle movement; disturbances in autonomic functions such as breathing, eliminating, and body temperature control; disturbances in speech; disturbances in thought and memory; pain (particularly headache and facial pain); and various types of thought disturbances.

A careful history is critical to the accuracy of the assessment. Consider, for example, a patient who exhibits flat affect, is listless, and doesn't seem to know what day it is or what time it is. Such an individual might be suffering from something neurological in origin (such as a dementia). However, a functional disorder (such as severe depression) might be causing the problem instead. A good history taking will shed light on whether the observed behavior is the result of a genuine dementia or a product of what is referred to as a *pseudodementia* (a condition that presents *as if* it were dementia but is not). Raising a number of history-related questions may prove helpful when evaluating such a patient. For example: How long has the patient been in this condition, and what emotional or neurological trauma may have precipitated it? Does this patient have a personal or family history of depression or other psychiatric disturbance? What factors appear to be operating to maintain the patient in this state?

◆————————————————————

JUST THINK . . .

What else might you like to know about this listless patient with flat affect who doesn't know what day it is or what time it is?

The history-taking interview can help shed light on questions of the organic or functional origin of an observed problem and whether the problem is *progressive* (likely to spread or worsen) or *nonprogressive.* Data from a history-taking interview may also lead the interviewer to suspect that the presenting problem has more to do with malingering than with neuropsychological deficit.

Beyond the history-taking interview, knowledge of an assessee's history is also developed through existing records. Case history files are valuable resources for all psychological assessors, but they are particularly valuable in neuropsychological assessment. In many instances, the referral question concerns the degree of damage that has been sustained relative to a patient's preexisting condition. The assessor must determine the level of the patient's functioning and neuropsychological intactness prior to any trauma, disease, or other disabling factors. In making such a determination of premorbid functioning, the assessor may rely on a wide variety of case history data, from archival records to videotapes made with the family video camera.

In addition to a history-taking interview and historical records in the form of case history data, published case studies on people who have suffered the same or a similar type of neuropsychological deficit may be a source of useful insights. Case study material can provide leads regarding areas of evaluation to explore in depth and can also suggest the course a particular disease or deficit will follow and how observed strengths or weaknesses may change over time. Additionally, case study material can be valuable in formulating plans for therapeutic intervention.

The Interview

A variety of structured interviews and rating forms are available as aids to the neuropsychological screening and evaluation process. Neuropsychological screening devices point the way to further areas of inquiry with more extensive evaluation methods. Such devices can be used economically with members of varied populations who may be at risk for neuropsychological impairment, such as psychiatric patients, the elderly, and alcoholics. Some of these measures, such as the Short Portable Mental Status Questionnaire, are completed by an assessor; others, such as the Neuropsychological Impairment Scale, are self-report instruments.

The Mini-Mental State Exam (Folstein et al., 1975) has more than a quarter-century of history as a clinical and research tool used to screen for cognitive impairment. Factor-analytic research suggests this test measures primarily concentration, language, orientation, memory, and attention (Baños & Franklin, 2003; Jones & Gallo, 2000). Also in the category of brief, structured measures is the 7 Minute Screen, an instrument developed to help identify patients with symptoms characteristic of Alzheimer's disease (Solomon et al., 1998). Tasks on this test tap orientation, verbal fluency, and various aspects of memory. Both the Mini-Mental State Examination and the 7 Minute Screen have value in identifying individuals with previously undetected cognitive impairment (Lawrence et al., 2000). However, neither of these screening instruments should be used for the purpose of diagnosis.

In addition to structured interviews designed for quick screening, there is the more comprehensive neuropsychological mental status examination. Let's take a brief look at it.

The Neuropsychological Mental Status Examination An outline for a general mental status examination was presented in Chapter 13. The neuropsychological mental status examination overlaps the general examination with respect to questions concerning the assessee's consciousness, emotional state, thought content and clarity, memory, sensory perception, performance of action, language, speech, handwriting, and handedness. The mental status examination administered for the express purpose of evaluating neuropsychological functioning may delve more extensively into specific areas of interest. For example, during a routine mental status examination, the examiner might require the examinee to interpret the meaning of only one or two proverbs. On the neuropsychological mental status examination, many proverbs may be presented to obtain a more comprehensive picture of the patient's capacity for abstract thought.

Throughout the mental status examination, as well as other aspects of the evaluation (including history-taking and testing), the clinician observes and takes note of aspects of the assessee's behavior relevant to neuropsychological functioning. For example, the clinician notes the presence of involuntary movements (such as facial tics), locomotion difficulties, and other sensory and motor problems. The clinician may note, for example, that one corner of the mouth is slower to curl than the other when the patient smiles— a finding suggestive of damage to the seventh (facial) cranial nerve. Knowledge of brain–behavior relationships comes in handy in all phases of the evaluation, including the physical examination.

The Physical Examination

Most neuropsychologists perform some kind of physical examination on patients, but the extent of this examination varies widely as a function of the expertise, competence, and confidence of the examiner. Some neuropsychologists have had extensive training in performing physical examinations under the tutelage of neurologists in teaching hospitals. Such psychologists feel confident in performing many of the same **noninvasive procedures** (procedures that do not involve any intrusion into the examinee's body) that neurologists perform as part of their neurological examination. In the course of the following discussion, we list some of these noninvasive procedures. We precede this discussion with the caveat that it is the physician and not the neuropsychologist who is always the final arbiter of medical questions.

In addition to making observations about the examinee's appearance, the examiner may also physically examine the scalp and skull for any unusual enlargements or depressions. Muscles may be inspected for their tone (soft? rigid?), strength (weak or tired?), and size relative to other muscles. With respect to the last point, the examiner might find, for example, that a patient's right biceps is much larger than his left biceps.

Table 14–4
Sample Tests Used to Evaluate Muscle Coordination

Walking-running-skipping

If the examiner has not had a chance to watch the patient walk for any distance, he or she may ask the patient to do so as part of the examination. We tend to take walking for granted; but, neurologically speaking, it is a highly complex activity that involves proper integration of many varied components of the nervous system. Sometimes abnormalities in gait may be due to nonneurological causes; if, for example, a severe case of bunions is suspected as the cause of the difficulty, the examiner may ask the patient to remove his or her shoes and socks so that the feet may be physically inspected. Highly trained examiners are additionally sensitive to subtle abnormalities in, for example, arm movements while the patient walks, runs, or skips.

Standing still (technically, the Romberg test)

The patient is asked to stand still with feet together, head erect, and eyes open. Whether patients have their arms extended straight out or at their sides and whether or not they are wearing shoes or other clothing will be a matter of the examiner's preference. Patients are next instructed to close their eyes. The critical variable is the amount of sway exhibited by the patient once the eyes are closed. Because normal persons may sway somewhat with their eyes closed, experience and training are required to determine when the amount of sway is indicative of pathology.

Nose-finger-nose

The patient's task is to touch her nose with the tip of her index finger, then touch the examiner's finger, and then touch her own nose again. The sequence is repeated many times with each hand. This test, as well as many similar ones (such as the toe-finger test, the finger-nose test, the heel-knee test), is designed to assess, among other things, cerebellar functioning.

Finger wiggle

The examiner models finger wiggling (that is, playing an imaginary piano or typing), and then the patient is asked to wiggle his own fingers. Typically, the nondominant hand cannot be wiggled as quickly as the dominant hand, but it takes a trained eye to pick up a significant difference in rate. The experienced examiner will also look for abnormalities in the precision of the movements and the rhythm of the movements, "mirror movements" (uncontrolled similar movements in the other hand when instructed to wiggle only one), and other abnormal involuntary movements. Like the nose-finger test, finger wiggling supplies information concerning the quality of involuntary movement and muscular coordination. A related task involves tongue wiggling.

Such a finding could indicate muscular dystrophy in the left arm. But it also could reflect the fact that the patient has been working as a shoemaker for the past 40 years—a job in which he has had to constantly hammer nails, thus building up the muscle in his right arm. This patient's case presentation underscores the importance of placing physical findings in historical context; the importance of careful history taking cannot be overstated.

JUST THINK . . .

Do you agree that neuropsychologists should engage in noninvasive physical examinations? Or do you believe that any physical examination is better left to a physician?

In addition to physical examination of the skull and the musculature, simple reflexes may be tested. **Reflexes** are involuntary motor responses to stimuli. Many reflexes have survival value for infants but then disappear as the child grows older. One such reflex is the mastication (chewing) reflex. Stroking the tongue or lips will elicit chewing behavior in the normal infant; however, chewing elicited in the older child or adult indicates neurological deficit. In addition to testing for the presence or absence of various reflexes, the examiner might examine muscle coordination by using measures such as those listed in Table 14–4.

The physical examination aspect of the neuropsychological examination is designed to assess not only the functioning of the brain but aspects of the functioning of the nerves, muscles, and other organs and systems as well. Some procedures used to shed light on the adequacy and functioning of some of the 12 cranial nerves are summarized in Table 14–5. Additional procedures of evaluation and measurement are presented in the remainder of this chapter as we review several more specialized tools of neuropsychological assessment.

Table 14–5

Sample Tests Used by Neurologists to Assess the Intactness of Some of the 12 Cranial Nerves

Cranial Nerve	Test
I (olfactory nerve)	Closing one nostril with a finger, the examiner places some odoriferous substance under the nostril being tested and asks whether the smell is perceived. Subjects who perceive it are next asked to identify it. Failure to perceive an odor when one is presented may indicate lesions of the olfactory nerve, a brain tumor, or other medical conditions. Of course, failure may be due to other factors, such as oppositional tendencies on the part of the patient or intranasal disease, and such factors must be ruled out as causal.
II (optic nerve)	Assessment of the intactness of the second cranial nerve is a highly complicated procedure, for this is a sensory nerve with functions related to visual acuity and peripheral vision. A Snellen eye chart is one of the tools used by the physician in assessing optic nerve function. If the subject at a distance of 20 feet from the chart is able to read the small numbers or letters in the line labeled "20," then the subject is said to have 20/20 vision in the eye being tested. This is only a standard. Although many persons can read only the larger print at higher numbers on the chart (that is, a person who reads the letters on line "40" of the chart would be said to have a distance vision of 20/40), some persons have better than 20/20 vision. An individual who could read the line labeled "15" on the Snellen eye chart would be said to have 20/15 vision.
V (trigeminal nerve)	The trigeminal nerve supplies sensory information from the face, and it supplies motor information to and from the muscles involved in chewing. Information regarding the functioning of this nerve is examined by the use of tests for facial pain (pinpricks are made by the physician), facial sensitivity to different temperatures, and other sensations. Another part of the examination entails having the subject clamp his or her jaw shut. The physician will then feel and inspect the facial muscles for weakness and other abnormalities.
VIII (acoustic nerve)	The acoustic nerve has functions related to the sense of hearing and the sense of balance. Hearing is formally assessed with an audiometer. More frequently, the routine assessment of hearing involves the use of a "dollar watch." Provided the examination room is quiet, an individual with normal hearing should be able to hear a dollar watch ticking at a distance of about 40 inches from each ear (30 inches if the room is not very quiet). Other quick tests of hearing involve placing a vibrating tuning fork on various portions of the skull. Individuals who complain of dizziness, vertigo, disturbances in balance, and so forth may have their vestibular system examined by means of specific tests.

Neuropsychological Tests

A wide variety of tests is used by neuropsychologists as well as others who are charged with finding answers to neuropsychology-related referral questions. Researchers may employ neuropsychological tests to gauge change in mental status or other variables as a result of the administration of medication or the onset of a disease or disorder. Forensic evaluators may employ tests to gain insight into the effect of neuropsychological factors on issues such as criminal responsibility or competency to stand trial.

In what follows, we present only a sample of the many types of tests used in neuropsychological applications.

Tests of general intellectual ability   Tests of intellectual ability, particularly Wechsler tests, occupy a prominent position among the diagnostic tools available to the neuropsychologist. The varied nature of the tasks on the Wechsler scales and the wide variety of responses required make these tests potentially very useful tools for neuropsychological screening. For example, a clue to the existence of a deficit might be brought to light by difficulties in concentration during one of the subtests. Because certain patterns of test response indicate particular deficits, the examiner looks beyond performance on individual tests to a study of the pattern of test scores, a process termed **pattern analysis.** Thus, for example, extremely poor performance on the Block Design and other performance subtests might be telling in a record that contains relatively high scores on all the verbal subtests. In combination with a known pattern of other data, the poor Block Design performance could indicate damage in the right hemisphere.

A number of researchers intent on developing a definitive sign of brain damage have devised various ratios and quotients based on patterns of subtest scores. David Wechsler himself referred to one such pattern, called a **deterioration quotient** or DQ (also referred to by some as a *deterioration index*). However, neither Wechsler's DQ nor any other WAIS-based index has performed satisfactorily enough to be deemed a stand-alone measure of neuropsychological impairment.

We have already noted the need to administer standardized tests in strict conformance with the instructions in the test manual. Yet because of the limited ability of the testtaker, such "by-the-book" test administrations are not always possible or desirable when testing members of the neurologically impaired population. Because of various problems or potential problems (such as the shortened attention span of some neurologically impaired individuals), the experienced examiner may need to modify the test administration to accommodate the testtaker yet yield clinically useful information. The examiner administering a Wechsler scale may deviate from the prescribed order of test administration when administering the test to an individual who becomes fatigued quickly. In such cases, the more taxing subtests will be administered early in the exam. In the interest of shortening the total test administration time, the trained examiner might omit certain subtests that he or she suspects will not provide any information over and above that already obtained. Let us reiterate that such deviations in the administration of standardized tests such as the Wechsler scales can be made—and meaningfully interpreted—by trained and experienced neuropsychologists. For the rest of us, it's by the book!

◆

JUST THINK . . .

Why should deviations from standardized test instructions be made very judiciously, if at all?

Tests to measure the ability to abstract   One symptom commonly associated with neuropsychological deficit, regardless of the site or exact cause of the problem, is inability or lessened ability to think abstractly. One traditional measure of verbal abstraction ability has been the Wechsler Similarities subtest, isolated from the age-appropriate version of the Wechsler intelligence scale. The task in this subtest is to identify how two objects (for instance, a ball and an orange) are alike.

Another type of task used to assess ability to think abstractly is proverb interpretation. For example, interpret the following proverb:

A stitch in time saves nine.

If your interpretation of this proverb conveyed the idea that haste makes waste, then you have evinced an ability to think abstractly. By contrast, some people with neurological deficits might have interpreted that proverb more concretely (that is, with less abstraction). Here is an example of a concrete interpretation: When sewing, take one stitch at a time—it'll save you from having to do it over nine times. This type of response might (or might not, depending on other factors) betray a deficit in abstraction ability. The Proverbs Test, an instrument specifically designed to test abstraction and related ability, contains a number of proverbs along with standardized administration instructions and normative data. In one form of this test, the subject is instructed to write an explanation of the proverb. In another form of the test, this one multiple-choice, each proverb is followed by four choices, three of which may be either common misinterpretations or concrete responses.

Nonverbal tests of abstraction include any of the various sorting tests—tests that require the respondent to sort objects in some logical way. Common to most of the sorting tests are instructions like "Group together all the ones that belong together," followed by questions like "Why did you group those objects together?" Representative of such tests are the Object Sorting Test (refer back to Figure 14–1) and the Color-Form Sorting Test (also known as Weigl's Test), which require testtakers to sort objects of different shapes and colors. Another way sorting tasks are administered is by grouping a few of the stimulus objects together and requiring the testtaker (a) to explain why those objects go together or (b) to select the object that does not belong with the rest.

Figure 14–2
The Tower of Hanoi

This version of the Tower of Hanoi puzzle comes with three pegs and eight rings. The puzzle begins with all of the rings on one of the pegs ordered from the bottom up in decreasing size. To solve the puzzle, all of the rings must be transferred to another peg following three rules: (1) Only one ring may be moved at a time; (2) the ring is moved from one peg to another; and (3) no ring may ever be placed on a smaller one.

The Wisconsin Card Sorting Test-64 Card Version (WCST-64; Kongs et al., 2000) requires the testtaker to sort a pack of 64 cards that contain different geometric figures printed in different colors. The cards are to be sorted according to matching rules that must be inferred and that shift as the test progresses. Successful performance on this test requires several abilities associated with frontal lobe functioning, including concentration, planning, organization, cognitive flexibility in shifting set, working memory, and inhibition of impulsive responding. The test may be useful in screening for neurological impairment with or without suspected injury of the frontal lobe. Caution is suggested when using this or similar tests, as some evidence suggests that the test may erroneously indicate neurological impairment when in reality the testtaker has schizophrenia or a mood disorder (Heinrichs, 1990). It is therefore important for clinicians to rule out alternative explanations for test performance indicative of neurological deficit.

Tests of executive function Sorting tests measure one element of **executive function,** which may be defined as organizing, planning, cognitive flexibility, and inhibition of impulses and related activities associated with the frontal and prefrontal lobes of the brain. One test used to measure executive function is the Tower of Hanoi (Figure 14–2), a puzzle that made its first appearance in Paris in 1883 (Rohl, 1993). It is set up by stacking the rings on one of the pegs, beginning with the largest diameter ring, with no succeeding ring resting on a smaller one. Probably because the appearance of these stacked rings is reminiscent of a pagoda, the puzzle was christened *La Tour de Hanoi.* The Tower of Hanoi, either in solid form for manipulation by hand or adapted for computerized administration in graphic form, has been used by many researchers to measure various aspects of executive function (Aman et al., 1998; Arnett et al., 1997; Butters et al., 1985; Byrnes & Spitz, 1977; Glosser & Goodglass, 1990; Goel & Grafman, 1995; Goldberg et al., 1990; Grafman et al., 1992; Leon-Carrion et al., 1991; Mazzocco et al., 1992; Miller & Ozonoff, 2000; Minsky et al., 1985; Schmand et al., 1992; Spitz et al., 1985).

Performance on mazes is another type of task used to measure executive function. As early as the 1930s, psychologist Stanley D. Porteus became enamored with the potential for psychological assessment of the seemingly simple task of identifying the correct path in a maze and then tracing a line to the endpoint of that maze. This type of task was originally introduced to yield a quantitative estimate of "prudence, forethought,

Figure 14–3
"Where do we go from here, Charly?"

A Porteus–maze-like task is being illustrated by the woman in the white coat to actor Cliff Robertson as "Charly" in the now-classic film of the same name.

mental alertness, and power of sustained attention" (Porteus, 1942). Porteus urged colleagues to use mazes for varied research purposes ranging from the exploration of cultural differences (Porteus, 1933) to the study of social inadequacy (Porteus, 1955) to the study of personality traits by means of qualitative analysis of a testtaker's performance (Porteus, 1942). Today, maze tasks like those in the Porteus Maze Test (Figure 14–3) are used primarily as measures of executive function (Daigneault et al., 1992; Krikorian & Bartok, 1998; Mack & Patterson, 1995). Although useful in measuring such functioning in adults, its utility for that purpose in children has been questioned. Shum et al. (2000) observed no adverse impact on Porteus maze performance of children with traumatic brain injury.

JUST THINK . . .

How might qualitative analysis of performance on a maze task be telling with regard to the testtaker's personality?

Representative items for four other types of tasks that may be used in neuropsychological assessment are illustrated in Figure 14–4. Part (a) illustrates a **trail-making item.** The task is to connect the circles in a logical way. This type of task is thought to tap many abilities, including visual-conceptual, visual-motor, planning, and other cognitive abilities, although exactly which abilities are tapped has been a matter of long-standing debate (Stanczak et al., 1998). The Trail Making Tests in the Halstead-Reitan Neuropsychological Battery (a fixed battery to be discussed shortly) are among the most widely used measures of brain damage (Salthouse et al., 2000; Thompson et al., 1999) and have been employed in a variety of studies (Bassett, 1999; Beckham et al., 1998; Compton et al., 2000; King et al., 2000; Nathan et al., 2001; Ruffolo et al., 2000; Sherrill-Pattison et al., 2000; Wecker et al., 2000).

Figure 14–4
**Sample Items Used
in Neuropsychological Assessment**

(a) The Trail Making Test
The testtaker's task is to connect the dots in
logical fashion.

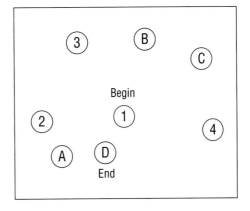

(b) The Field of Search
After being shown a sample stimulus, the testtaker's task is to locate a match as quickly as
possible.

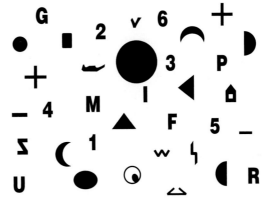

(c) An Identification Task
A task entailing what is referred to as confrontation naming.

(d) A Picture Absurdity
The testtaker answers questions like,
"What's wrong or silly about this picture?"

Illustration (b) in Figure 14–4 is an example of a **field-of-search item.** Shown a sample or target stimulus (usually some sort of shape or design), the testtaker must scan a field of various stimuli to match the sample. This kind of item is usually timed. People with right hemisphere lesions may exhibit deficits in visual scanning ability, and a test of field-of-search ability can be of value in discovering such deficits. Field-of-search ability has strong adaptive value and can have life-or-death consequences for predator and prey. Field-of-search research has found many applications. For example, it helps us to better understand some everyday activities such as driving (Crundall et al., 1998; Duchek et al., 1998; Guerrier et al., 1999; Recarte & Nunes, 2000; Zwahlen et al., 1998) as well as more specialized activities such as piloting aircraft (Seagull & Gopher, 1997) and monitoring air traffic (Remington et al., 2000).

Illustration (c) is an example of a simple line drawing reminiscent of the type of item that appears in instruments such as the Boston Naming Test. The testtaker's task on the Boston (as it is often abbreviated) is **confrontation naming;** that is, naming each stimulus presented. This seemingly simple task entails three component operations: a perceptual component (perceiving the visual features of the stimulus), a semantic component (accessing the underlying conceptual representation or core meaning of whatever is pictured), and a lexical component (accessing and expressing the appropriate name).

JUST THINK . . .

Picture absurdity items have traditionally been found on tests of intelligence or neuro-psychological tests. Describe your own, original, picture absurdity item that you believe could have value in assessing personality.

Difficulty with the naming task could therefore be due to deficits in any or all of these components. Persons who are neurologically compromised as a result of Alzheimer's disease or other dementia typically experience difficulty with naming tasks.

Illustration (d) in Figure 14–4 is what is called a **picture absurdity item.** The pictorial equivalent of a verbal absurdity item, the task here is to identify what is wrong or silly about the picture. It is similar to the picture absurdity items on the Stanford-Binet intelligence test. As with Wechsler-type Comprehension items, this type of item can provide insight into the testtaker's social comprehension and reasoning abilities.

Tests of perceptual, motor, and perceptual-motor functions   The term **perceptual test** is a general reference to any of many instruments and procedures used to evaluate varied aspects of sensory functioning, including aspects of sight, hearing, smell, touch, taste, and balance. Similarly, **motor test** is a general reference to any of many instruments and procedures used to evaluate varied aspects of one's ability and mobility, including the ability to move limbs, eyes, or other parts of the body. The term **perceptual-motor test** is a general reference to any of many instruments and procedures used to evaluate the integration or coordination of perceptual and motor abilities. For example, putting together a jigsaw puzzle taps perceptual-motor ability—more specifically, eye-hand coordination. Thousands of tests have been designed to measure various aspects of perceptual, motor, and perceptual-motor functioning. Some of them you may have heard of long before you decided to take a course in assessment. For example, does *Ishihara* sound familiar? The Ishihara (1964) test is used to screen for color blindness. More specialized—and less well-known—instruments are available if rare forms of color perception deficit are suspected.

Among the tests available for measuring deficit in auditory functioning is the Wepman Auditory Discrimination Test. This brief, easy-to-administer test requires that the examiner read a list of 40 pairs of monosyllabic meaningful words (such as *muss/much*) pronounced with lips covered (not muffled, please) by either a screen or a hand. The examinee's task is to determine whether the two words are same or different. It's quite a straightforward test—provided the examiner isn't suffering from a speech defect, has no heavy accent, and doesn't mutter. The standardization sample for the test repre-

Figure 14–5
Lauretta Bender (1896–1987)

Bender (1970) reflected that the objective in her visual-motor test was not to get a perfect reproduction of the test figures but "a record of perceptual motor experience— a living experience unique and never twice the same, even with the same individual . . ." (p. 30).

sented a broad range within the population, but there is little information available about the reliability and validity of the test. The test manual also fails to outline standardized administration conditions, which are particularly critical for the test given the nature of the stimuli (Pannbacker & Middleton, 1992).

A test designed to assess gross and fine motor skills is the Bruininks-Oseretsky Test of Motor Proficiency. Designed for use with children aged 4½ to 14½, this instrument includes subtests that assess running speed and agility, balance, strength, response speed, and dexterity. On a less serious note, the test's box cover could be used as an informal screening device for reading ability by asking colleagues to pronounce the test's name correctly. A test designed to measure manual dexterity is the Purdue Pegboard Test. Originally developed in the late 1940s as an aid in employee selection, the object is to insert pegs into holes using first one hand, then the other hand, and then both hands. Each of these three segments of the test has a time limit of 30 seconds, and the score is equal to the number of pegs correctly placed. Normative data are available, and it is noteworthy that in a non-brain-injured population, women generally perform slightly better on this task than men do. With brain-injured subjects, this test may help answer questions regarding the lateralization of a lesion.

Perhaps one of the most widely used neuropsychological instruments is the **Bender Visual-Motor Gestalt Test,** usually referred to simply as the Bender-Gestalt or even just "the Bender." As originally conceived by Lauretta Bender (Figure 14–5), the test consisted of nine cards, on each of which was printed one design. The designs had been used by psychologist Max Wertheimer (1923) in his study of the perception of *gestalten* (German for "configurational wholes"). Bender (1938) believed these designs could be used to assess perceptual maturation and neurological impairment. Testtakers were shown each of the cards in turn and instructed "Copy it as best you can." Although there was no time limit, unusually long or short test times were considered to be of diagnostic significance. Average administration time for all nine designs was about five minutes—a fact which also contributed to its wide appeal among test users.

Bender (1938, 1970) intended the test to be scored by means of clinical judgment. It was published with few scoring guidelines and no normative information. Still, a number of quantitative scoring systems for this appealingly simple test soon became available for adult (Brannigan & Brunner, 2002; Hutt, 1985; Pascal & Suttell, 1951; Reichenberg & Raphael, 1992) and child (Koppitz, 1963, 1975; Reichenberg & Raphael, 1992) protocols. A sampling of scoring terminology common to many of these systems is presented in Figure 14–6. In addition, a number of modifications were proposed, such as the addition of a recall phase. After all nine designs had been copied, a blank piece of paper was placed before the testtaker with the instructions "Now please draw all of the designs you can remember." Gobetz (1953) proposed this procedure as a means of testing a hypothesis about differential performance on the Bender as a function of personality. He hypothesized that owing to the pressure of the unexpected second test, subjects diagnosed as neurotic would be able to recall fewer figures on the recall portion of the test than would normal subjects. The recall procedure gained widespread usage, however, not as a means of providing personality-related data but rather as a means of providing additional neuropsychological data.

JUST THINK . . .

Test authors, Lauretta Bender among them, may intend their instrument to be scored and interpreted only on the basis of clinical judgment. But users of tests demand otherwise. Why?

The Bender Visual-Motor Gestalt Test, Second Edition (Bender-Gestalt II; Brannigan & Decker, 2003) added seven new items, extending the range of ability assessed by its predecessor. Four of the items are used exclusively with testtakers from ages 4 years to 7 years 11 months, and three of the new items are used exclusively with testtakers from ages 8 years to 85 or older. A recall phase was built into the test, as were two supplementary tests called the Motor Test and the Perception Test. The supplementary tests were designed to detect deficits in performance or motor skills that would adversely affect performance. The task in the Motor Test is to draw a line between dots without touching borders. The task in the Perception Test is to circle or point to a design that best matches a stimulus design. The test is conducted by administration of a Copy phase (copying designs), a Recall phase (re-creating the designs drawn from memory), the Motor Test, and then the Perception test. The Copy and Recall phases are timed. Specific guidelines for scoring are provided throughout. For example, during the Copy phase, discrepancies between the design on the stimulus card and the assessee's responses are scored as follows:

0 = No resemblance, random drawing, scribbling, lack of design

1 = Slight–vague resemblance

2 = Some–moderate resemblance

3 = Strong–close resemblance, accurate reproduction

4 = Nearly perfect

The Bender-Gestalt-II was standardized on 4,000 individuals from ages 4 to 85+ matched to the 2000 United States Census. Included were members of special populations, including individuals with mental retardation, learning disorders, attention-deficit hyperactivity disorder, autism, Alzheimer's disease, and the gifted. Numerous studies attesting to the reliability and the validity of the test are presented in the test manual. The types of reliability studies reported on were of the test-retest, internal consistency, and inter-rater variety. The validity studies were interpreted as supporting the

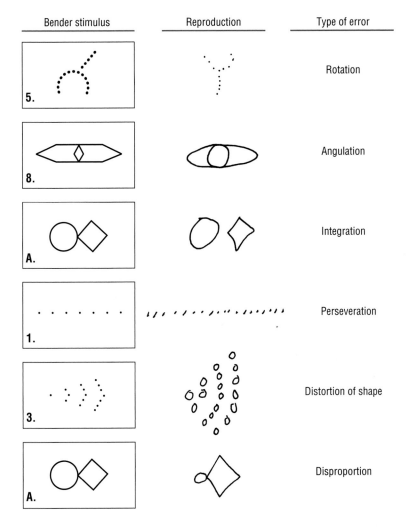

Bender stimulus	Reproduction	Type of error
5.		Rotation
8.		Angulation
A.		Integration
1.		Perseveration
3.		Distortion of shape
A.		Disproportion

Figure 14–6
Sample Errors on the Bender-Gestalt

These types of errors may suggest organic impairment. Not all the illustrated errors are signs of organic impairment at all ages.

view that the test measures what it purports to measure. The test authors concluded that the test

> measures a single underlying construct that is sensitive to maturation and/or development, and scores from the Copy and Recall phases are highly influenced and sensitive to clinical conditions. This dimensionality provides added utility to the test. (Brannigan & Decker, 2003, p. 67)

Of course, as the test authors acknowledged, determinations regarding the psychometric soundness of a new test are an ongoing process. Interested students are advised to check current publications for independent reviews of this test as they are published.

Tests of verbal functioning   Verbal fluency and fluency in writing are sometimes affected by injury to the brain, and there are tests to assess the extent of the deficit in such skills.

In the Controlled Word Association Test (formerly the Verbal Associative Fluency Test), the examiner says a letter of the alphabet, and it is the subject's task to say as many words as he or she can think of that begin with that letter. Each of three trials employs three different letters as a stimulus and lasts one minute; the testtaker's final score on the test reflects the total number of correct words produced, weighted by factors such as the gender, age, and education of the testtaker. Controlled Word Association Test scores are related in the predicted direction to the ability of dementia patients to complete tasks of daily living, such as using the telephone or writing a check (Loewenstein et al., 1992). And although people with dementia tend to do poorly on the test as compared with controls, the differences observed have not been significant enough to justify using the test as an indicator of dementia (Nelson et al., 1993).

The Sequenced Inventory of Communication Development (SICD) is a test designed to assess the development of receptive and expressive communication in children aged 4 months to 4 years. The test contains a number of observation and test procedures designed to assess various aspects of the young child's awareness and understanding. In support of the test's construct validity, two studies showed that chronic middle ear infections in young children produce a delay in language development as measured by the SICD (Friel-Patti & Finitzo, 1990; Wallace et al., 1988).

Not to be confused with *aphagia*, **aphasia** refers to a loss of ability to express oneself or to understand spoken or written language because of some neurological deficit.[2] A number of tests have been developed to measure aspects of aphasia. For example, the Reitan-Indiana Aphasia Screening Test (AST), available in both a child and an adult form, contains a variety of tasks such as naming common objects, following verbal instructions, and writing familiar words. Factor analysis has suggested that these tasks load on two factors: language abilities and coordination involved in writing words or drawing objects (Williams & Shane, 1986). Both forms of the test were designed to be screening devices that can be administered in 15 minutes or less. Used alone as a screening tool (Reitan, 1984a, 1984b; Reitan & Wolfson, 1992) or in combination with other tests (Tramontana & Boyd, 1986), the AST may be of value in distinguishing testtakers who have brain damage from those who do not. For testtakers of Hispanic descent, a more culturally relevant instrument might be the Multilingual Aphasia Examination. Rey et al. (1999) found the published norms to be comparable to their own data using a sample of Hispanic testtakers. They also discussed specific problems encountered in neuropsychological research with Hispanics and suggested guidelines and directions for future research.

Tests of memory Memory is a complex, multifaceted cognitive function that has defied simple explanation. To appreciate just how complex it is, consider the following:

> Humans possess an estimated 1 trillion neurons, plus 70 trillion synaptic connections between them. . . . A single neuron may have as many as 10,000 synapses, but during the process of memory formation perhaps only 12 synapses will be strengthened while another 100 will be weakened. The sum of those changes, multiplied neuron by neuron, creates a weighted circuit that amounts to memory. (Hall, 1998, p. 30)

Different models of memory compete for recognition in the scientific community, and no one model has garnered universal acceptance. For our purposes, a sample model is presented in Figure 14–7—along with the caveat that this relatively simple model, which was pieced together from various sources, is incomplete at best and *not*

---

2. **Aphagia** is a condition in which the ability to eat is lost or diminished.

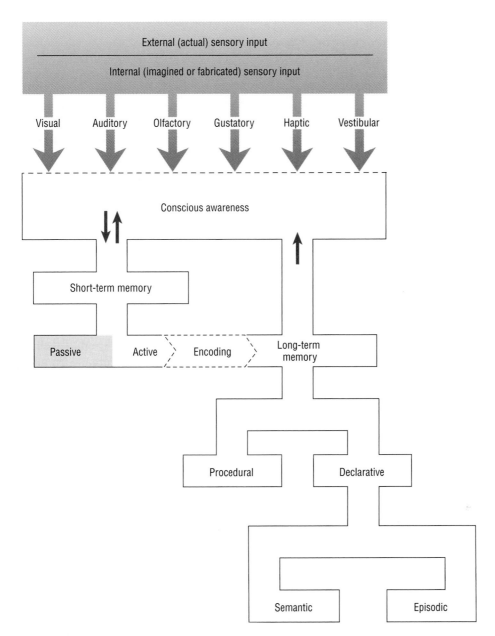

Figure 14–7
A Model of Memory

According to our model, memory results from information processing by the nervous system of external (actual) sensory input, such as sights, sounds, smells, and tastes. Your stored vision of a loved one's face, the song you will never forget, and the smell of freshly mowed grass are examples of memories formed from actual sensory input. Memory of a sort may also result from what one produces internally, in the absence of actual sensation. What one imagines, dreams, and misperceives are all examples of this latter sort of memory. Of course, dominance of imagined or fabricated sorts of memories can become a matter of clinical significance. The line between the sensory input channel and conscious awareness is broken to indicate that not all sensory input automatically makes it into conscious awareness. Attention, concentration, and related factors play a key role in determining which input actually makes it into conscious awareness.

universally accepted. Moreover, the model contains elements that are still very much a matter of debate among contemporary researchers.

Contrary to the popular image of memory as a storehouse of sorts, memory is a very active process, presumed to entail both short-term and long-term processes (Atkinson & Shiffrin, 1968). Incoming information is processed in short-term memory, where it is temporarily stored for as little as seconds or as long as a minute or two. Short-term memory has also been characterized by some researchers as virtually synonymous with *working memory* (Daneman & Carpenter, 1980; Newell, 1973). The more traditional view of short-term memory is as a passive buffer in which information is either transferred to long-term memory or dissipated (that is, forgotten). Our model allows for both passive and active components of short-term memory, with encoding of long-term memory made from the active, "working" component of short-term memory.

In our model, note that the path between short-term memory and conscious awareness is two-way. Stimuli from conscious awareness can be fed into short-term memory, and short-term memory can feed stimuli back into conscious awareness. Note also that the path to long-term memory is illustrated by a broken line—this to indicate that not all information in short-term memory is encoded in long-term memory.

JUST THINK . . .

Visualize some remembered image or event. Now, referring to our model of memory, outline how that memory may have gotten there.

With regard to long-term memory, researchers have distinguished between procedural and declarative memory. **Procedural memory** is memory for things like driving a car, making entries on a keyboard, or riding a bicycle. Most of us can draw on procedural memory with little effort and concentration. **Declarative memory** refers to memory of factual material—such as the differences between procedural and declarative memory. We have compartmentalized the procedural and declarative components of long-term memory for illustrative purposes.

Also illustrated as compartmentalized are what are widely believed to be two components of declarative memory: semantic and episodic memory. **Semantic memory** is, strictly speaking, memory for facts. **Episodic memory** is memory for facts in a particular context or situation. An example of episodic or context-dependent memory might be the recollection of a classmate's name while in class but not at a chance meeting at a social event. Being asked to repeat digits in the context of a memory test is another example of episodic memory because it is linked so intimately to the (testing) context.

As indicated by the one-way pathway from long-term memory to consciousness, information stored in long-term memory is available for retrieval. Whether information so retrieved can be restored directly to long-term memory or must instead be processed again through short-term memory is a matter of debate.

Neuropsychological tests designed to evaluate memory tap different components of memory as outlined in our model. One of the most widely used tests of memory, the Wechsler Memory Scale-III (WMS-III), taps primarily declarative episodic memory. As stated in its technical manual, "The information that is presented is novel and contextually bound by the testing situation and requires the examinee to learn and retrieve information" (Tulsky et al., 1997, p. 3). Much like its predecessor (the WMS-R), the WMS-III is an individually administered memory test designed for use with older adolescents and adults. However, there are many significant differences between the WMS-R and the WMS-III in terms of the test's subtests and scales, norm development, index structure and index scoring, and related factors (see Tulsky et al., 1997).

The WMS-III requires examinees to complete tasks such as retelling a story read aloud, sequencing letters and numbers (similar to the Letter-Number Sequencing task previously described for the WAIS-III), and learning word pairs that are seemingly unrelated. There are also subtests involving the recognition of pictures of faces. Examinees are first presented with an array of target faces. They must then identify which of these

Figure 14–8
Two Tools Used in the Measurement of Tactile Memory

(a) *Four pieces of wire bent into what are in essence "tactile nonsense figures" can be used in a tactile test of immediate memory. Examinees may be instructed to feel one of the figures with their right or left hand (or both hands) and then locate a matching figure.* **(b)** *Shown here is one form of the Seguin-Goddard Formboard. Blindfolded examinees are instructed to fit each of the ten wooden blocks into the appropriate space in the formboard with each hand separately and then with both hands. Afterward, the examinee may be asked to draw the formboard from memory. All responses are timed and scored for accuracy.*

target faces are included among a second array of faces that includes both target and other faces. Optional tests include those involving tasks such as reproduction of designs presented on cards and multitasking (that is, doing more than one thing at a time, such as reciting the alphabet while counting backward from 30).

Factor-analytic studies performed with the WMS-III supported different factor solutions as a function of age group. In general, however, the findings were interpreted by the test developers as supporting three factors tapped by the test: immediate and delayed auditory memory, immediate and delayed visual memory, and working memory.

Two other approaches to memory testing are illustrated in Figure 14–8. In an approach devised by Milner (1971), tactile nonsense figures are employed to measure immediate tactile (or haptic) memory. Another tactile memory test involves an adaptation of the administration of the Seguin-Goddard Formboard. Halstead (1947a) suggested that the formboard could be used to assess tactile memory if examinees were blindfolded during the test and a recall trial added.

One effort to make memory tests more real is to integrate in them tasks that people must perform each day. A computerized test battery developed by Thomas Crook and described by Hostetler (1987) uses a number of real-world tasks (such as telephone dialing and name–face association). The battery has been employed as an outcome measure in studies of the efficacy of various drugs in the treatment of Alzheimer's disease.

> **JUST THINK . . .**
>
> What are some real-world tasks that you would recommend be included on Crook's memory test?

Neuropsychological Test Batteries

On the basis of the mental status examination, the physical examination, and the case history data, the neuropsychologist typically administers a battery of tests for further clinical study. Trained neuropsychologists may administer a pre-packaged **fixed battery** of tests, or they may modify a fixed battery for the case at hand. They may choose to administer a **flexible battery,** consisting of an assortment of instruments hand-picked for some purpose relevant to the unique aspects of the patient and the presenting problem.

The clinician who administers a flexible battery has not only the responsibility of selecting the tests to be used but also the burden of integrating all the findings from each of the individual tests—no simple task, because each test may have been normed on different populations. Another problem inherent in the use of a flexible battery is that the tests administered frequently overlap with respect to some of the functions tested, and the result is some waste in testing and scoring time. Regardless of these and other drawbacks, the preference of most highly trained neuropsychologists traditionally has been to tailor a battery of tests to the specific demands of a particular testing situation. Of course, all of that may change as a result of judicial action (see this chapter's *Close-up*).

Fixed neuropsychological test batteries are designed to comprehensively sample the patient's neuropsychological functioning. The fixed battery is appealing to clinicians, especially clinicians who are relatively new to neuropsychological assessment, because it tends to be less demanding in many ways. Whereas a great deal of expertise and skill is required to fashion a flexible battery that will adequately answer the referral question, a prepackaged battery represents a non-tailor-made but comprehensive alternative. Various tests sampling various areas are included in the battery, and each is supplied with clear scoring methods. One major drawback of the prepackaged tests, however, is that the specific disability of the patient may greatly—and adversely—influence performance on the test. Thus, an individual with a visual impairment, for example, may perform poorly on many of the other subtests of a battery that require certain visual skills.

Perhaps the most widely used fixed neuropsychological test battery is the **Halstead-Reitan Neuropsychological Battery.** Ward C. Halstead (1908–1969) was an experimental psychologist whose interest in the study of brain–behavior correlates led him to establish a laboratory for that purpose at the University of Chicago in 1935. His was the first laboratory of its kind in the world. During the course of 35 years of research, Halstead studied more than 1,100 brain-damaged persons. From his observations, Halstead (1947a, 1947b) derived a series of 27 tests designed to assess the presence or absence of organic brain damage—the Halstead Neurological Test Battery. A student of Halstead's, Ralph M. Reitan, later elaborated on his mentor's findings. In 1955, Reitan published two papers that dealt with the differential intellectual effects of various brain lesion sites (Reitan, 1955a, 1955b). Fourteen years and much research later, Reitan (1969) privately published a book entitled *Manual for Administration of Neuropsychological Test Batteries for Adults and Children*—the forerunner of the Halstead-Reitan Neuropsychological Test Battery (H-R; see also Reitan & Wolfson, 1993).

Administration of the H-R requires a highly trained examiner conversant with the procedures for administering the various subtests (Table 14–6). Even with such an examiner, the test generally requires a full workday to complete. Subtest scores are interpreted not only with respect to what they mean by themselves but also by their relation to scores on other subtests. Appropriate interpretation of the findings requires the eye of a trained neuropsychologist, though H-R computer interpretation software—no substitute for clinical judgment but an aid to it—is available. Scoring yields a number referred to as the Halstead Impairment Index, and an index of .5 or above, the cutoff point, is indicative of a neuropsychological problem. Data on more than 10,000 patients in the standardization sample were used to establish that cutoff point. Normative information

Fixed Versus Flexible Neuropsychological Test Batteries and the Law

Do courts have any preferences regarding the specific tests administered by assessors who function as expert witnesses in litigation? With reference to neuropsychological assessment, does it matter if the assessor administered a fixed or a flexible battery? The ruling of a federal court in *Chapple v. Ganger* is enlightening with regard to such questions. In the *Chapple* case, the court applied the *Daubert* standard with regard to the admission of scientific evidence.

The *Chapple* Case

Chapple originated with an automobile accident in which a 10-year-old boy sustained closed head injuries. The plaintiff claimed that these injuries impaired brain functioning and were permanent, whereas the defendant denied this claim. Three neuropsychological examinations of the boy were undertaken by three different assessors at three different times. The first was conducted by a clinical psychologist, who administered a flexible battery of tests, including the Aphasia Screening Test, the Benton Visual Retention Test, the Knox Cube, the Rey Complex Figure Test, the Seashore Rhythm Test, the Trails Test, and the Wisconsin Card Sorting Test. In addition, the flexible battery included other tests such as Draw a Bicycle, Draw a Clock, Draw a Family, Draw a Person, Category Test, Incomplete Sentences, Lateral Dominance Test, Manual Finger Tapping Test, Peabody Picture Vocabulary Test, subtests of the Woodcock-Johnson, the WISC-R, and the WRAT-R.

The second neuropsychological examination, about a year later, also entailed the administration of a flexible battery, this time by a neuropsychologist. The tests administered were Trails, Sentence Imitation, Word Sequencing and Oral Direction (subtests of the Detroit Test of Learning Aptitude), Taylor Complex Figure Test, Hooper Visual Organization Test, Attention Capacity (a subtest of the Auditory Verbal Learning Test), Sound and Visual Symbol Recall Test, Paragraph Copy Test, Kaufman Brief Intelligence Test, the Individual Achievement Test, and the Wechsler Reading Comprehension and Listening Comprehension Test.

The third neuropsychological examination, commissioned by the defendant and conducted by neuropsychologist Ralph Reitan, entailed an administration of most of the subtests of the Halstead-Reitan Neuropsychological Test Battery for Older Children.

In the two earlier examinations, the findings referred to some degree of brain trauma as a result of the accident, which in turn left the child with some degree of permanent impairment. By contrast, as a result of the third examination, Reitan concluded that the child scored in the normal range on most of the tests in his fixed battery. Reitan did allow, however, for the possibility of some mild impairment attributable to some minor brain dysfunction. Reitan's opinions were formed on the basis of the child's test performance as well as evaluation of case records. The other two psychologists also reviewed the child's records and historical data in coming to their conclusions.

Invoking the *Daubert* standard, the court ruled in favor of the defendant, finding no evidence to support permanent organic brain damage. Although no explicit reference to the value of flexible versus fixed batteries was made, the court seemed to find the results of the fixed battery administration more compelling. The court wrote, "The focus is on the methodology of the experts, and not the conclusions which they generate." In *Chapple,* then, testimony regarding the administration of a fixed battery was accepted by the court as medical evidence, whereas testimony regarding the administration of flexible batteries was not accepted by the court.

The Implications of *Daubert* and *Chapple*

On its face, the implications of *Daubert* seem vague and open to multiple interpretations (Black et al., 1994; Faigman, 1995; Larvie, 1994). However, there may be a lesson to be learned from *Chapple,* at least with regard to the admissibility of evidence obtained as the result of fixed versus flexible neuropsychological batteries. Although administration of flexible batteries is generally accepted in the professional community, a court may look more favorably on conclusions reached as the result of a fixed, standardized battery. The *Chapple* court's decision also suggested that it might accept as evidence results from individual standardized tests, as those test results were used to supplement the findings from a fixed neuropsychological test battery.

Table 14-6
Subtests of the Halstead-Reitan Battery

Category

This is a measure of abstracting ability in which stimulus figures of varying size, shape, number, intensity, color, and location are flashed on an opaque screen. Subjects must determine what principle ties the stimulus figures together (such as color) and indicate their answer among four choices by pressing the appropriate key on a simple keyboard. If the response is correct, a bell rings; if incorrect, a buzzer sounds. The test primarily taps frontal lobe functioning of the brain.

Tactual performance

Blindfolded examinees complete the Seguin-Goddard Formboard (see Figure 14−8) with their dominant and nondominant hands and then with both hands. Time taken to complete each of the tasks is recorded. The formboard is then removed, the blindfold is taken off, and the examinee is given a pencil and paper and asked to draw the formboard from memory. Two scores are computed from the drawing: the memory score, which includes the number of shapes reproduced with a fair amount of accuracy, and the localization score, which is the total number of blocks drawn in the proper relationship to the other blocks and the board. Interpretation of the data includes consideration of the total time to complete this task, the number of figures drawn from memory, and the number of blocks drawn in the proper relationship to the other blocks.

Rhythm

First published as a subtest of the Seashore Test of Musical Talent and subsequently included as a subtest in Halstead's (1947a) original battery, the subject's task here is to discriminate between like and unlike pairs of musical beats. Difficulty with this task has been associated with right temporal brain damage (Milner, 1971).

Speech sounds perception

This test consists of 60 nonsense words administered by means of an audiotape adjusted to the examinee's preferred volume. The task is to discriminate a spoken syllable, selecting from four alternatives presented on a printed form. Performance on this subtest is related to left hemisphere functioning.

Finger-tapping

Originally called the "finger oscillation test," this test of manual dexterity measures the tapping speed of the index finger of each hand on a tapping key. The number of taps from each hand is counted by an automatic counter over five consecutive, 10-second trials with a brief rest period between trials. The total score on this subtest represents the average of the five trials for each hand. A typical, normal score is approximately 50 taps per 10-second period for the dominant hand and 45 taps for the nondominant hand (a 10% faster rate is expected for the dominant hand). Cortical lesions may differentially affect finger-tapping rate of the two hands.

Time sense

The examinee watches the hand of a clock sweep across the clock and then has the task of reproducing that movement from sight. This test taps visual motor skills as well as ability to estimate time span.

Other tests

Also included in the battery is the Trail Making Test (see Figure 14−4), in which the examinee's task is to correctly connect numbered and lettered circles. A strength-of-grip test is also included; strength of grip may be measured informally by a handshake grasp and more scientifically by a dynamometer (in Chapter 3, Figure 3−1).

To determine which eye is the preferred or dominant eye, the Miles ABC Test of Ocular Dominance is administered. Also recommended is the administration of a Wechsler intelligence test, the MMPI (useful in this context for shedding light on questions concerning the possible functional origin of abnormal behavior), and an aphasia screening test adapted from the work of Halstead and Wepman (1959).

Various other sensorimotor tests may also be included. A test called the critical flicker fusion test was once part of this battery but has been discontinued by most examiners. If you have ever been in a disco and watched the action of the strobe light, you can appreciate what is meant by a light that flickers. In the flicker fusion test, an apparatus that emits a flickering light at varying speeds is turned on, and the examinee is instructed to adjust the rate of the flicker until the light appears to be steady or fused.

has also been published with respect to special populations. Cultural factors must also be considered when administering this battery (Evans et al., 2000).

Conducting test-retest reliability studies on the H-R is a prohibitive endeavor in light of the amount of time it may take to complete one administration of the battery, as well as other factors (such as practice effects and effects of memory). Still, the test is generally viewed as reliable. A growing body of literature attests to the validity of the instrument in differentiating brain-damaged subjects from subjects without brain damage, and for assisting in making judgments relative to the severity of a deficit and its possible site (Reitan, 1994; Reitan & Wolfson, 2000). The battery has also been used to identify neuropsychological impairment associated with learning disabilities (Batchelor et al., 1990, 1991), as well as cognitive, perceptual, motor, and behavioral deficits associated with particular neurological lesions (Guilmette & Faust, 1991; Guilmette et al., 1990; Heaton et al., 2001).

Another fixed neuropsychological battery is the Luria-Nebraska Neuropsychological Battery (LNNB). The writings of the Russian neuropsychologist Aleksandr Luria served as the inspiration for a group of standardized tests (Christensen, 1975) that were subsequently revised (Golden et al., 1980, 1985) and became known as the LNNB. In its various published forms, the LNNB contains clinical scales designed to assess cognitive processes and functions. Analysis of scores on these scales may lead to judgments as to whether neuropsychological impairment exists, and if so, the area of the brain that is affected. The LNNB takes about a third of the time it takes to administer the Halstead-Reitan battery. Still, judging by the use of these tests, the Halstead-Reitan remains the battery of choice for experienced neuropsychological assessors. A neuropsychological test battery for children, also derived in part on the basis of Luria's work, is the NEPSY (Korkman et al., 1997), the inspiration for which was detailed by its senior author (Korkman, 1999).

Many published and unpublished neuropsychological test batteries are designed to probe deeply into one area of neuropsychological functioning instead of surveying for possible behavioral deficit in a variety of areas. Test batteries exist that focus on visual, sensory, memory, and communication problems. The Neurosensory Center Comprehensive Examination of Aphasia (NCCEA) is a battery of tests that focuses on communication deficit. The Montreal Neurological Institute Battery is particularly useful to trained neuropsychologists in locating specific kinds of lesions. The Southern California Sensory Integration Tests are a battery designed to assess sensory-integrative and motor functioning in children 4 to 9 years of age.

A neuropsychological battery called the Severe Impairment Battery (SIB; Saxton et al., 1990) is designed for use with severely impaired assessees who might otherwise perform at or near the floor of existing tests. The battery is divided into six subscales: Attention, Orientation, Language, Memory, Visuoperception, and Construction. Another specialized battery is the Cognitive Behavioral Driver's Inventory, which was specifically designed to assist in determining whether individuals with brain damage are capable of driving a motor vehicle (Lambert & Engum, 1992).

> **JUST THINK . . .**
>
> Just for a moment, don the role of a neuropsychologist who spends the better part of many workdays administering a single neuropsychological test battery to a single assessee. What do you like best about your job? What do you like least about your job?

> **JUST THINK . . .**
>
> The Cognitive Behavioral Driver's Inventory is a neuropsychological battery specially designed to help determine whether an assessee should be driving a motor vehicle. What is another specialized neuropsychological battery that needs to be developed?

Other Tools of Neuropsychological Assessment

Perhaps the greatest advances in the field of neuropsychological assessment have come in the form of high technology and the mutually beneficial relationship that has developed between psychologists and medical personnel. For example, recent advances in genetic research have led to exciting suggestive evidence regarding the origins of autism. Mutations in a gene essential to brain development may predict the onset of this debilitating developmental disorder (O'Connor, 2001). Beyond the level of the gene, more "everyday" miracles in diagnosis and treatment are brought about using imaging technology and related technology discussed in this chapter's *Everyday Psychometrics.*

Medical Diagnostic Aids and Neuropsychological Assessment

Data from neuropsychological assessment, combined with data derived from various medical procedures, can in some cases yield a thorough understanding of a neurological problem. For example, certain behavioral indices evident in neuropsychological testing may result in a recommendation to further explore a particular brain site. The suspicion may be confirmed by a diagnostic procedure that yields cross-sectional pictures of the site and clearly reveals the presence of lesions.

The trained neuropsychologist has a working familiarity with the array of medical procedures that may be brought to bear on neuropsychological problems. Here, let's take a closer look at a sample of these procedures. Let's begin with a brief description of the medical procedure and apparatus that is perhaps most familiar to us all, whether from experience in a dentist's chair or elsewhere: the X-ray.

To the radiologist, the X-ray photograph's varying shades convey information about the corresponding density of the tissue through which the X-rays have been passed. With front, side, back, and other X-ray views of the brain and the spinal column, the diagnosis of tumors, lesions, infections, and other abnormalities can frequently be made. There are many different types of neuroradiologic procedures. These range from the simple X-ray of the skull to more complicated procedures. One procedure, called a **cerebral angiogram,** entails the injection of a tracer element into the bloodstream before x-raying the cerebral area.

Perhaps you have also heard or read about another imaging procedure, the **CAT (computerized axial tomography) scan,** also known as a "CT" scan (Figure 1). The CAT scan is superior to traditional X-rays because the structures in the brain may be represented in a systematic series of three-dimensional views, a feature that is extremely important in assessing conditions such as spinal anomalies. The **PET (positron emission tomography) scan** is a tool of nuclear medicine particularly useful in diagnosing biochemical lesions in the brain. Conceptually related to the PET scan is **SPECT (single photon emission computed tomography),** a technology that records the course of a radioactive tracer

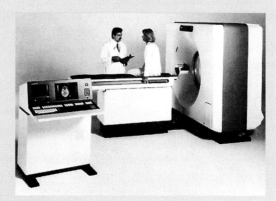

Figure 1
The CT scan is useful in pinpointing the location of tumors, cysts, degenerated tissue, or other abnormalities, and its use may eliminate the need for exploratory surgery or painful diagnostic procedures used in brain or spinal studies.

fluid (iodine), producing exceptionally clear photographs of organs and tissues (Figure 2).

The term *radioisotope scan* or simply **brain scan** describes a procedure that also involves the introduction of radioactive material into the brain through an injection. The cranial surface is then scanned with a special camera to track the flow of the material. Alterations in blood supply to the brain are noted, including alterations that may be associated with disease such as tumors.

The **electroencephalograph (EEG)** is a machine that measures the electrical activity of the brain by means of electrodes pasted to the scalp. EEG activity will vary as a function of age, level of arousal (awake, drowsy, asleep), and other variables in addition to brain abnormalities. Electroencephalography is a safe, painless, noninvasive procedure that can be of significant value in diagnosing and treating seizure and other disorders.

Information about nerve damage and related abnormalities may be obtained by direct electrical stimulation of

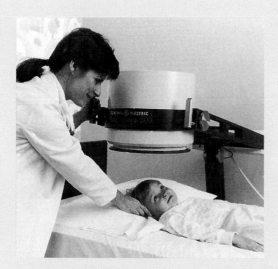

Figure 2

SPECT technology has been found promising in evaluating conditions such as cerebral vascular disease, Alzheimer's disease, and seizure disorders.

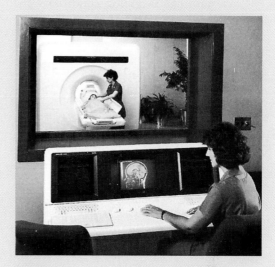

Figure 3

This magnetic resonance system utilizes a magnetic field and radio waves to create detailed images of the body. These and related imaging techniques may be employed not only in the study of neuropsychological functioning but in the study of abnormal behavior as well; see, for example, Kellner et al.'s (1991) study of obsessive-compulsive disorder.

nerves and notation of movement or lack of movement in corresponding muscle tissue. The **electromyograph (EMG)** is a machine that records electrical activity of muscles by means of an electrode inserted directly into the muscle. Abnormalities found in the EMG can be used with other clinical and historical data as an aid in making a final diagnosis. The **echoencephalograph** is a machine that transforms electric energy into sound (sonic) energy. The sonic energy ("echoes") transversing the tissue area under study is then converted back into electric energy and displayed as a printout. This printout is used as an adjunct to other procedures in helping the diagnostician to determine the nature and location of certain types of lesions in the brain. Radio waves in combination with a magnetic field can also be used to create detailed anatomical images, as illustrated in Figure 3.

Laboratory analysis of bodily fluids such as blood and urine can provide clues not only about neurological problems but also non-neurological problems masquerading as neurological problems. Examination of the cerebrospinal fluid for blood and other abnormalities can yield key diagnostic insights. A sample of the fluid is obtained by means of a medical procedure termed a **lumbar puncture,** or spinal tap. This procedure entails inserting a special needle into the widest spinal interspace after a local anesthetic has been applied. In addition to providing information concerning the chemical normality of the fluid, the test lets the diagnostician gauge the normality of the intracranial pressure.

Working together, neuropsychologists and medical professionals can help improve the quality of life of many people with neurological problems.

The tools of neuropsychological assessment, much like many other measuring instruments used by psychologists, can help improve the quality of life of the people who are assessed with them. In the following chapter, we look at how tools of psychological assessment can be modified to accommodate the special needs of people with handicapping conditions. We will also look at many issues regarding the assessment of people with handicapping conditions, including legal issues. Chapter 15 concludes with a provocative discussion of disability as a diversity issue.

Self-Assessment

Test your understanding of elements of this chapter by seeing if you can explain each of the following terms, expressions, and abbreviations:

aphagia
aphasia
Bender Visual-Motor Gestalt Test
brain–behavior relationships
brain damage
brain scan
CAT scan
central nervous system
cerebral angiogram
confrontation naming
contralateral control
declarative memory
deterioration quotient
developmental milestone
echoencephalograph
electroencephalograph (EEG)
electromyograph (EMG)
episodic memory
executive function
field-of-search item

fixed battery
flexible battery
functional
Halstead-Reitan Neuropsychological Battery (H-R)
hard sign
lesion
lumbar puncture
memory tests
motor tests
NEPSY
neurological damage
neurology
neuron
neuropsychological assessment
neuropsychological history
neuropsychological mental status examination
neuropsychological physical examination

neuropsychological tools of assessment
neuropsychology
noninvasive procedures
organic
organicity
pattern analysis
perceptual-motor tests
perceptual tests
peripheral nervous system
PET scan
physical examination
picture absurdity item
procedural memory
reflex
semantic memory
soft sign
SPECT
trail-making item

Web Watch

Check out the following Web sites for more information about topics discussed in this chapter.

APA Division 40 (Neuropsychology)
www.div40.org

www.apa.org/about/division/div40.html

The Halstead-Reitan Neuropsychology Battery
http://web.lemoyne.edu/~hevern/psy448/448documents/hrntb.html

The Tower of Hanoi (interactive)
www.mazeworks.com/hanoi

The Wisconsin Card Sorting Test
www.tvtc.com/publications/testprod.asp?testid=38

The Bender-Gestalt II
www.riverpub.com/products/clinical/bg/home.html

http://assess.nelson.com/test-ind/bender.html

www.pearsonassessments.com/tests/bender.htm

The WMS-III
http://marketplace.psychcorp.com/PsychCorp.com/Cultures/en-US/Products/Product+Detail.htm?CS_ProductID=015-8981-928&CS_Category=Adults&CS_Catalog=TPC-USCatalog

The Mini-Mental Status exam
www.minimental.com

The Auditory Discrimination Test
http://courses.smsu.edu/jjm095f/Red/
WepSPPT4IAX.PDF

The nervous system
http://faculty.washington.edu/chudler/introb.html

http://faculty.washington.edu/chudler/lobe.html

Developmental milestones
www.med.umich.edu/1libr/yourchild/devmile.htm

Aphasia
www.aphasia.org

Neuropsychological aspects of driving ability
www.nanonline.org/nandistance/mtbi/modules/
suppl/driving.html

Neuropsychological aspects of memory
www.crossroadsinstitute.org/memory.html

15

The Assessment of People With Disabilities

After Hurricane Andrew hit south Florida, death, destruction, and a great deal of emotional distress were left in its wake. One who had been traumatized by this natural disaster was Neil Tugg. Tugg was a 40-year-old deaf man who received counseling from the Deaf Services Bureau (DSB) with a counselor proficient in American Sign Language (ASL). Tugg still required counseling after the State of Florida's consulting contract with the DSB had expired, so he was referred to a new provider. The new provider did not have a counselor proficient in ASL, so a translator was used. Citing the Americans with Disabilities Act (ADA), Tugg brought a lawsuit, claiming that "the presence of an interpreter in a therapeutic setting [deprived him of] an equal opportunity to achieve the same results as a hearing individual" (*Tugg v. Towey*, 1994, p. 1001). In the lawsuit, the plaintiffs argued that in addition to—or even in place of—conceptualizing deafness as a medical disability, deafness could be considered a cultural identity. They further intimated that this culturally distinct group, like other culturally distinct groups, could be unjustly stigmatized or discriminated against.

Tugg was adjudicated, and we have more to say about it and the issues it raised later in this chapter. The case, which we may reasonably presume to be illustrative of many other such cases, is dramatic evidence of the aggressiveness with which claims of ADA violations are making their way to the courts. The case also serves as a useful point of departure for thinking about broader issues concerning conceptions of *disability*, the rights of people with disabilities, and more to the point of this chapter, the rights of people with disabilities vis-à-vis psychological assessment.

An Overview

Over a decade ago, it was estimated that as many as one in seven Americans had a disability that interfered with activities of daily living (O'Keefe, 1993). In recent years, society has acknowledged more than ever before the special needs of citizens challenged by physical and/or mental disabilities. The effects of this ever-increasing acknowledgment are visibly evident in things like special access ramps alongside flights of stairs; specially equipped buses designed to accommodate passengers in wheelchairs; large-print newspapers, books, and magazines for the visually impaired; captioned television programming for the hearing impaired; and signing and pantomiming of important

Table 15–1
Two Paradigms for Disability Research

Paradigm 1	Paradigm 2
Is based on a medical model of disability	Is based on a social model or the new paradigm of disability
Is pathology oriented	Shifts to a systemic and societal perspective
Views differences due to disability as deficits or developmental aberrations	Takes a life-span approach
Is usually cross-sectional	Uses concept of "response" to disability as a fluid process
Sees people with disabilities and their families as at high risk for difficulties	Promotes health and resilience
Focuses predominantly on intrapsychic, personal characteristics or intrapersonal variables	Usually focuses on chronic phases of disability
Tends to focus on acute phases of disability onset or exacerbation	Is more likely to be in community settings
Is more likely to be in inpatient or treatment settings	Values disability history and culture
Uses concept of "adjustment" or "adaptation" to disability	Incorporates those being researched into the research process
Uses norms based on able-bodied individuals for comparison	Sees the major problems of disability as social, political, economic, legal
Is about, but rarely by, people with disabilities	Is grounded in the belief that those with disabilities have been denied their civil rights
Perpetuates a we–they model	Seeks remedies in public policy, legislation, and systemic programmatic changes
	Is usually not just about, but by, people with disabilities

Source: Olkin & Pledger (2003)

speeches for the hearing impaired.[1] In general, the trend has been toward altering environments to make individuals with handicapping conditions feel less challenged. This trend is consistent with what is increasingly referred to as a **new paradigm of disability,** also referred to as a *social model of disability* (Pledger, 2003).

Disability Defined

Two paradigms, or models, of disability may be distinguished. The **medical model of disability** conceptualizes disability as a medical condition or deficit that prevents participation in activities. The **social model of disability** includes a medical perspective but focuses more on the environment and factors external to the body as they relate to the disability experience. The U.S. Department of Education (2000) described the new paradigm as "integrative and holistic" and focused on "the whole person functioning in an environmental context" (p. 9). Aspects of the two paradigms have been discussed by Gill et al. (2003), Tate and Pledger (2003), and Melia et al. (2003). Perhaps the most detailed delineation of the two paradigms was made by Olkin and Pledger (2003), this in the context of disability research. Their points are presented in Table 15–1.

The International Classification of Functioning, Disability, and Health, published by the World Health Organization (2001), does take into account environmental and contextual factors in its definition of disability. However, most

JUST THINK . . .

What factors may have contributed to a perceived need to focus more on the full *context* of disabilities, as opposed to medical aspects of disabilities?

---

1. Like the noun *mime,* the verb *to pantomime* has to do with communication by gesturing. As used in the context of psychological testing, pantomime is something that a test administrator might do with an examinee who is deaf or hearing impaired to help convey the meaning of some instruction, question, or response.

definitions of disability as they are written into law here in the United States are written more from a medical than a social perspective.

In 1973, Congress passed the Rehabilitation Act, a law that has been referred to as the "Bill of Rights for Handicapped Citizens" because it addressed many of the special needs of people with disabilities and outlawed job discrimination on the basis of disability by agencies of the federal government and by entities receiving federal funds. This protection was extended to disabled people involved with private companies through the Americans with Disabilities Act of 1990 (Public Law 101-336). Similar protections have been extended to children as well. In 1975, Congress passed Public Law 94-142, the Education for All Handicapped Children Act, mandating appropriate educational assessment and programs to meet the needs of handicapped children aged 3 to 18. This act was amended in 1986 (Public Law 99-457) to extend the age range covered by the law to birth. A 1990 amendment of the same act (Public Law 101-476) specified the broad range of conditions covered by the law: "mental retardation, hearing impairments including deafness, speech or language impairments, visual impairments including blindness, serious emotional disturbance, orthopedic impairments, autism, traumatic brain injury, other health impairments, or specific learning disabilities" (Section 101).

Psychologists assessing individuals with such disabling conditions were obliged by law to "use tests and other assessment materials which have been validated for the purposes for which they are being used" (Department of Health, Education, and Welfare, 1977a, 1977b)—this in the face of a paucity of psychological tests standardized on disabled populations.

The Education for All Handicapped Children Act of 1975 (PL 94-142) was amended some 27 years later by Public Law 105-17 (see this chapter's *Everyday Psychometrics*). Also referred to as the Individuals with Disabilities Education Act Amendments of 1997 (IDEA), this act defined the terms *infant or toddler with a disability* and *child with a disability*. An **infant or toddler with a disability** was defined as

> an individual under 3 years of age who needs early intervention services because the individual (i) is experiencing developmental delays, as measured by appropriate diagnostic instruments and procedures in one or more of the areas of cognitive development, physical development, communication development, social or emotional development, and adaptive development; or (ii) has a diagnosed physical or mental condition which has a high probability of resulting in developmental delay; and . . . may also include, at a State's discretion, at-risk infants and toddlers. (p. 108)

The term **at-risk infants and toddlers** was defined in the act as "an individual under 3 years of age who would be at risk of experiencing a substantial developmental delay if early intervention services were not provided to the individual" (p. 106). The IDEA defined *child with a disability* in two ways: one way with reference to a child in general, and one way for children aged 3 through 9. In general, **child with a disability** refers to a child

> with mental retardation, hearing impairments (including deafness), speech or language impairments, visual impairments (including blindness), serious emotional disturbance . . . orthopedic impairments, autism, traumatic brain injury, other health impairments, or specific learning disabilities. (p. 43)

For a child aged 3 through 9, the term *child with a disability* may, at the discretion of the state or local educational agency, include a child

> experiencing developmental delays, as defined by the State and as measured by appropriate diagnostic instruments and procedures, in one or more of the following areas: physical development, cognitive development, communication development, social or emotional development, or adaptive development. (p. 43)

Public Law 105-17 and Everyday Practice

Public Law (PL) 105-17 is the Individuals with Disabilities Act Amendments of 1997. This act contains a number of provisions that are relevant to the everyday practice of measurement professionals who have occasion to evaluate school-age children. It affects not only the way children are evaluated but the recommendations for intervention made as a result of the evaluation. The provisions of PL 105-17 include requirements concerning the following:

- *A "least restrictive environment" for learning*
  "To the maximum extent appropriate, children with disabilities, including children in public or private institutions or other care facilities, are educated with children who are not disabled, and special classes, separate schooling, or other removal of children with disabilities from the regular educational environment occurs only when the nature or severity of the disability of a child is such that education in regular classes with the use of supplementary aids and services cannot be achieved satisfactorily" (p. 61).

- *An individualized education program*
  "An individualized education program, or an individualized family service plan . . . is developed, reviewed, and revised for each child with a disability" (p. 61).

- *Evaluation materials that are culturally appropriate*
  "Testing and evaluation materials and procedures utilized for the purposes of evaluation and placement of children with disabilities will be selected and administered so as not to be racially or culturally discriminatory. Such materials or procedures shall be provided and administered in the child's native language or mode of communication, unless it is clearly not feasible to do so, and no single procedure shall be the sole criterion for determining an appropriate educational program for a child" (p. 62).

- *Regular state and district-wide performance evaluations, including "alternate assessments" where necessary*
  "Children with disabilities are included in general state and district-wide assessment programs, with appropriate accommodations, where necessary. As appropriate, the State or local educational agency (i) develops guidelines for the participation of children with disabilities in alternate assessments for those children who cannot participate in State and district-wide assessment programs; and (ii) develops and, beginning not later than July 1, 2000, conducts those alternate assessments" (p. 67).

- *Parental involvement in the education of the child, including parental consent for evaluation*
  "The agency proposing to conduct an initial evaluation to determine if the child qualifies as a child with a disability . . . shall obtain an informed consent from the parent of such child before the evaluation is conducted. Parental consent shall not be construed as consent for placement for receipt of special education and related services. . . . If the parents of such child refuse consent for the evaluation, the agency may continue to pursue an evaluation by utilizing the mediation and due process procedures . . . except to the extent inconsistent with State law relating to parental consent" (p. 81).

- *Conduct of evaluations*
  "In conducting the evaluation, the local educational agency shall (A) use a variety of assessment tools and strategies to gather relevant functional and developmental information, including information provided by the parent, that may assist in determining whether the child is a child with a disability and the content of the child's individualized education program, including information related to enabling the child to be involved in and progress in the general curriculum or, for preschool children, to participate in appropriate activities; (B) not use any single procedure as the sole criterion for determining whether a child is a child with a disability or determining an appropriate educational program for the child; and (C) use technically sound instruments that may assess the relative contribution of cognitive and behavioral factors, in addition to physical or developmental factors. . . . Each local educational agency shall ensure that—(A) tests and other evaluation materials used to assess a child under this section—(i) are selected and administered so as not to be discriminatory on a racial or cultural basis; and (ii) are provided and administered in the child's native language or other mode of communication, unless it is clearly not feasible to do so; and (B) any standardized tests that are given to the child—(i) have been validated for the specific purpose for which they are used; (ii) are administered by trained and knowledgeable personnel; and (iii) are administered in accordance with any instructions provided by the producer of such tests; (C) the child is assessed in all areas of suspected disability; and (D) assessment tools and strategies that provide relevant information that directly assists persons in determining the educational needs of the child are provided" (pp. 81–82).

- *Review of existing data*
  "As part of an initial evaluation (if appropriate) and as part of any reevaluation . . . qualified professionals, as appropriate shall (A) review existing evaluation data on the child, including evaluations and information provided by the parents of the child, current classroom-based assessments and observations, and teacher and related service providers' observations; and (B) on

(continued)

Public Law 105-17
and Everyday Practice
(*continued*)

the basis of that review, and input from the child's parents, identify what additional data, if any, are needed to determine— (i) whether the child has a particular category of disability, as described in section 602(3), or, in the case of a reevaluation of a child, whether the child continues to have such a disability; (ii) the present levels of performance and educational needs of the child; (iii) whether the child needs special education and related services, or in the case of a reevaluation of a child, whether the child continues to need special education and related services; and (iv) whether any additions or modifications to the special education and related services are needed to enable the child to meet the measurable annual goals set out in the individualized education program of the child and to participate, as appropriate, in the general curriculum" (pp. 82–83).

- *Determinations of eligibility*
"The determination of whether the child is a child with a disability . . . shall be made by a team of qualified professionals and the parent of the child. . . . In making a determination of eligibility . . . a child shall not be determined to be a child with a disability if the determinant factor for such determination is lack of instruction in reading or math or limited English proficiency" (p. 82).

- *Assessment of infants and toddlers with disabilities and development of individualized family service plans*
"A statewide system . . . shall provide, at a minimum, for each infant or toddler with a disability . . . (1) a multidisciplinary assessment of the unique strengths and needs of the infant or toddler and the identification of services appropriate to meet such needs; (2) a family-directed assessment of the resources, priorities, and concerns of the family and the identification of the supports and services necessary to enhance the family's capacity to meet the developmental needs of the infant or toddler; and (3) a written individualized family service plan developed by a multidisciplinary team, including the parents, as required by subsection (e). (b) Periodic Review.—The individualized family service plan shall be evaluated once a year and the family shall be pro-

vided a review of the plan at 6-month intervals (or more often where appropriate based on infant or toddler and family needs). (c) Promptness After Assessment.—The individualized family service plan shall be developed within a reasonable time after the assessment required by subsection (a)(1) is completed. With the parents' consent, early intervention services may commence prior to the completion of the assessment. (d) Content of Plan.—The individualized family service plan shall be in writing and contain—(1) a statement of the infant's or toddler's present levels of physical development, cognitive development, communication development, social or emotional development, and adaptive development, based on objective criteria; (2) a statement of the family's resources, priorities, and concerns relating to enhancing the development of the family's infant or toddler with a disability; (3) a statement of the major outcomes expected to be achieved for the infant or toddler and the family, and the criteria, procedures, and timelines used to determine the degree to which progress toward achieving the outcomes is being made and whether modifications or revisions of the outcomes or services are necessary; (4) a statement of specific early intervention services necessary to meet the unique needs of the infant or toddler and the family, including the frequency, intensity, and method of delivering services; (5) a statement of the natural environments in which early intervention services shall appropriately be provided, including a justification of the extent, if any, to which the services will not be provided in a natural environment; (6) the projected dates for initiation of services and the anticipated duration of the services; (7) the identification of the service coordinator from the profession most immediately relevant to the infant's or toddler's or family's needs (or who is otherwise qualified to carry out all applicable responsibilities under this part) who will be responsible for the implementation of the plan and coordination with other agencies and persons; and (8) the steps to be taken to support the transition of the toddler with a disability to preschool or other appropriate services" (pp. 111–112).

After reading these definitions as well as this chapter's *Everyday Psychometrics,* you may have concluded that what constitutes a disability is a fairly clear-cut matter. In practice, however, applying such definitions can be less than straightforward. *Disability* itself has been defined in many different ways (Walkup, 2000), and the federal legislation left the states considerable leeway in defining who is disabled and who shall be entitled to services. One source of that leeway is the term *developmental delay*, which may be defined in different ways by different states. We define **developmental delay** as slower-than-expected progress, usually on the basis of age norms, with regard to physical, cognitive, social, emotional, adaptive, or communication-related expression of one's ability or potential.

Even with legal definitions in place, reasonable people as well as knowledgeable professionals may differ as to whether an individual truly fits in a diagnostic category. The process of making official determinations as to who is in need of services in the classroom or accommodation in the workplace may sometimes be the source of heated debate.

Disability defined in school and other settings In everyday practice, the determination of whether a student shall be considered disabled and therefore entitled to special services is made by a multidisciplinary committee, often with the child's parent in attendance. In clear-cut cases of disability (as is the case with blindness, deafness, and so forth), all parties tend to agree on the evaluation as well as plans for intervention. However, many borderline cases also come before committees. These cases often involve mild developmental lags—the significance of which is arguable. Sometimes professionals disagree among themselves about the extent of a disability and whether or not special services are required. For example, on the basis of the very same data about a child described by a teacher as hyperactive and impulsive, some professionals may see exuberance (and thus no need for intervention), whereas other professionals might diagnose attention deficit disorder and see a need for medication and a well-structured program of behavior modification.

Beyond disagreements among professionals, and regardless of the outcome of a committee hearing, some parents want their child to be recognized as having a disability so the child will be entitled to special services. On the other hand, some parents, perhaps because of a fear that their child will be stigmatized, do not want a child so labeled, and they will reject committees' recommendations for special services. Disagreements among professionals, parents, and other parties to decisions regarding special services may arise as a result of differential emphasis given to facts in the case. For this reason, even when there is undisputed acceptance of the facts by all concerned parties, individual committee members and parents may privately accord different emphasis and weight to particular facts. Consequently, the door is left open to conflicting opinions and conclusions.

Professional organizations, state and local agencies, individual professionals involved in assessment and intervention, and members of a group of individuals with a particular disability may have their own ideas about definition, assessment, and intervention. For example, consistent with the new paradigm, many people who are deaf have begun to view deafness not as a disability but rather as a distinct culture within the majority culture. In this context, Deaf (with a capital *D*) culture becomes a diversity issue and not an issue of disability.

Mental retardation is another condition that has had a stormy history in terms of definition, assessment, and classification (Baumeister & Muma, 1975; Lowitzer et al., 1987; Roszkowski & Spreat, 1981; Taylor, 1980; Utley et al., 1987; Wilson & Spitzer, 1969). Even today, experts are divided regarding the extent to which the AAMR (American Association on Mental Retardation) classification system draws on the values of science and professionalism versus advocacy and consumerism (MacMillan et al., 1995).

Another definitional issue, one not touched on in PL 105-17, has to do with what is called a *functional disability*. A **functional disability** may be defined as a condition in

> **JUST THINK . . .**
>
> Assume that the parents and the school personnel in a committee hearing are all honestly trying to address the best interests of the child. What factors could derail those efforts?

which one's ability to perform in some characteristic physical, social, or other way—that is, one's ability to function—has been disrupted. Measures of functional disability first began to appear in the 1930s, primarily for the purpose of assessing compensation for claims of accident and injury (McDowell & Newell, 1987). Since that time, the term *functional disability* and a sister term, *functional assessment,* have been applied in an increasingly wide range of contexts (Bombadier & Tugwell, 1987; Feinstein et al., 1986; Granger & Gresham, 1984; Halpern & Fuherer, 1984; Slater et al., 1974; Spiegel et al., 1988).

Although *functional disability* was once applied primarily to matters concerning one's ability to earn a living, it is now used in sundry contexts ranging from housework to recreation. One may speak, for example, of a "functional social interaction disability" or a "communication disability." As used with reference to disorders of childhood, one may speak of a "functional disability at home" or at school (Walker & Greene, 1991).[2] Various tests and measurement procedures have been developed to assess functional disability in different contexts (see, for example, Brady & Halle, 1997; Desrochers et al., 1997; Neath et al., 1997).

JUST THINK . . .

A psychologist employed as an assessor suffers a functional disability in the workplace. In what ways might that disability manifest itself?

To what extent are functional disabilities considered *real* disabilities? To what extent are schools required to supply services to people with functional disabilities? To what extent must accommodations be made in testing and in other services for people with functional disabilities? Such questions are matters of academic debate among assessment professionals. Conceivably, future legislation, administrative regulations, and court rulings will provide more specific guidelines for the assessment of and intervention in functional disabilities.

Alternate assessment: Some issues   PL 105-17 contains a general mandate for the development and implementation of alternate assessment programs for children who, as a result of a disability, could not otherwise participate in state- and district-wide assessments. The law left open the definition of *alternate assessment* as well as many related questions of definition, procedure, and interpretation. It was left to the states and/or the local school districts to define who requires alternate assessment, how such assessments are conducted, and how meaningful inferences are drawn from the data derived from such assessments.

Alternate assessment is typically accomplished by means of some **accommodation** made to the assessee. The verb *to accommodate* may be defined as "to adapt, adjust, or make suitable." In the context of everyday life, we are all familiar with many varied examples of accommodation. Buses that lower for wheelchair passengers and elevator buttons coded in Braille are two of many such examples. In the context of psychological testing and assessment, there are many different ways people with disabilities can be accommodated. Accommodation may take the form of a modification in the way a test is presented or in the way the assessee responds to the test. Accommodation may mean that one test or measurement procedure is substituted for another. Accommodation may take the form of extended time limits or a change in the physical or interpersonal environment in which a test is administered. Let's take a closer look at these methods of accommodation, as well as some general considerations regarding the appropriateness of various methods for members of different populations.

---

2. Walker and Greene (1991) described the development of the Functional Disability Inventory, a scale to measure functional disability in child-relevant contexts, including home, school, and community. The measure is available in both self-report and parent-report formats.

Assessment and Accommodation

People with disabilities are assessed for exactly the same reasons that people with no disabilities are assessed: to obtain employment, to earn a professional credential, to be screened for psychopathology—the list goes on. People with disabilities may also be assessed for other reasons. They may be assessed for the purpose of evaluating the extent to which their disability affects their ability to carry out activities in some sphere of daily life. Perhaps in combination with such diagnostic evaluations, an assessment may be conducted for the purpose of determining the appropriateness of various interventions ranging from treatment to special services.

Depending on the nature of one's disability and other factors, modifications may have to be made in a test (or measurement procedure) in order for an evaluation to proceed. These accommodations may take many forms. One general type of accommodation has to do with *the form of the test as presented to the testtaker.* In what way has the test been modified from its usual form? For example, a written test may be modified for presentation to a visually impaired testtaker by being set in larger type. The time limits of a speeded test may be extended or suspended when a testtaker's disability impacts the ability to concentrate, move quickly, or otherwise respond within the test's prescribed time limit. A test may have to be shortened or in some cases administered over the course of several sessions. Depending on the nature of the testtaker's disability, some tasks of a test composed of several subtests may have to be omitted. For example, consider a situation in which an individual who has a fine motor disability is assessed with a test of cognitive ability. The test includes a subtest that requires the manipulation of blocks. The assessor might omit the block design subtest and/or substitute an optional test that does not rely on fine motor coordination. An estimate of cognitive ability would then be made from the data on the remaining tests.

Another general type of accommodation has to do with *the way responses to the test are obtained.* How was the response format modified for the purposes of the accommodation? For example, a speech-impaired individual may be accommodated by being allowed to write out responses in an examination that would otherwise be administered orally. Students with learning disabilities may be accommodated by being permitted to read test questions aloud (Fuchs et al., 2000).

Modification of the physical environment in which a test is conducted is yet another general type of accommodation. What changes are necessary in the place or setting of the test? For example, standardized tests usually administered at central locations in group administrations on occasion may be administered individually to a disabled person in his or her home. An extremely obese individual may require accommodation in the form of special furniture for a test. For an individual with a visual deficit, modified lighting may be required.

Modifications of the interpersonal environment in which a test is conducted is another possibility. Beyond the physical environment, the interpersonal environment may also require some modification. Individual testtakers routinely come unaccompanied to test sites. However, depending on the nature of an individual's disability, a helper, translator, or even a guide dog may have to be present during the assessment.

> **JUST THINK . . .**
>
> What types of disabilities may require very special modifications in the interpersonal environment in which a test is conducted?

The demands of a particular situation may require the substitution of one test for another. For example, a young preschooler or school-age child with severe cerebral palsy may not be able to be screened for cognitive deficit with any of the popular instruments used for this purpose. Alternatively, a test such as the Peabody Picture Vocabulary Test (PPVT-III; Dunn &

Dunn, 1997) might be used for such screening because neither an oral nor a pointing response is required from the testtaker. The child would simply have to signal yes or no, in whatever fashion is possible, to indicate to the examiner which of four pictures matches the word spoken by the examiner.

In some situations, an alternative test might be better suited for use with a particular individual owing to the availability of norms for people with the identical disability. In most cases, however, clinical judgment is the key to decisions about if, when, and how an accommodation will be made. A blind person who cannot complete a paper-and-pencil, multiple-choice examination will have to take the test in some type of alternate format. The alternate format might be a Braille administration, a paper-and-pencil administration modified by means of large type, an individually given oral administration, or a computer format with electronically administered (aural) instructions (with responses keyboarded in). Which of these alternate formats shall be employed? Ideally, this question will be answered not on the basis of convenience or the availability of one or another alternate forms, but rather on the basis of an informed consideration of

- what is known about the assessee
- the capabilities of the assessor
- the purpose of the assessment
- the meaning attached to test scores

The capabilities of the assessee   Which of several alternate means of assessment is best tailored to the needs and capabilities of the assessee? Case history data, records of prior assessments, and interviews with friends, family, teachers, and others who know the assessee all can provide a wealth of useful information. In addition, the assessor might pre-interview the assessee to learn about the potential benefits and drawbacks of using any available alternate means of assessment. What an assessor should *not* do is simply presume that a particular alternate method of assessment is equivalent to the original method. In the case of blind assessees, for example, proficiencies in Braille and keyboarding may vary widely. Additionally, some people who are sight impaired are also hearing impaired, thus raising obstacles to the use of methods involving auditory input. No method of alternate assessment is the correct choice for everyone. The unique needs and capabilities of the assessee must be considered on a case-by-case basis.

JUST THINK . . .

From a psychometric perspective, what challenges arise from the fact that no method of alternate assessment is the correct choice for everyone?

The capabilities of the assessor   Early in his career, the senior author (RJC), as part of his clinical psychology internship at Bellevue Hospital in New York City, did a rotation through the children's ward. At that time, the children's ward contained a female patient who was severely disabled as a result of her mother's use of the fertility drug thalidomide. This patient had failed to develop normal limbs and instead had stumps for arms and legs. She delighted in getting a rise out of new visitors to the ward by repeatedly slapping all four of her malformed limbs against them. On one occasion, a researcher visited the ward to conduct an evaluation of this patient, among others. Perhaps not surprisingly, the researcher was somewhat taken aback by the appearance of the patient with the malformed limbs—and horrified to the point of being visibly shaken when she was greeted with the patient's most vigorous, though playful, attack. An outside observer could not help but wonder if the researcher could ever recover enough to develop a rapport with the assessee so that a meaningful evaluation could be conducted.

This vignette is presented to emphasize the fact that in assessments involving individuals with disabilities, the state of mind of the assessor can play a role. We probably would all like to think that we can deal professionally with any assessee we are assigned to evaluate. However, the comfort level of the assessor in a particular assessment situation can affect the results. In this context, it is important to acknowledge that some assessors may feel extremely uncomfortable in the presence of people with certain disabilities. Should an assessee perceive such discomfort on the part of the assessor, the working relationship between the two will be jeopardized, as will the validity of any data obtained. If assessors have concerns about their performance in assessing people with any sort of disability, these concerns should be discussed candidly with a supervisor or a colleague. A course of action that takes into account the needs of both the assessor and the assessee will have to be charted. The assessor may require additional training prior to conducting the assessment, including supervised experience with members of certain populations. Alternatively, the assessor may refer such assessment assignments to another assessor who has had more training and experience with members of a particular population.

The purpose of the assessment Accommodation is appropriate under some circumstances and inappropriate under others. In general, one looks to the purpose of the assessment and the consequences of the accommodation in order to judge the appropriateness of modifying a test to accommodate a person with a disability. For example, modifying a written driving test—or a road test—so a blind person could be tested for a driver's license is clearly inappropriate. For their own as well as the public's safety, the blind are prohibited from driving automobiles. On the other hand, changing the form of most other written tests so that a blind person could take them is another matter entirely. In general, accommodation is simply a way of being true to a social policy that promotes and guarantees equal opportunity for and treatment of all citizens.

Whether a particular disability will significantly affect one's ability to perform, for example, in a particular employment setting is a question debated not only in academic journals but in corporate offices and the courts. One survey of accommodation policies by state found that states tend to offer more accommodations on criterion-referenced tests than on norm-referenced tests (Thurlow et al., 2000). Even when parties agree that some sort of accommodation is appropriate, one side may claim that a particular variety of accommodation goes too far, whereas the other may argue that it does not go far enough. In mediating such disputes, the courts tend to evaluate how reasonable a particular accommodation is, given the circumstances, including the nature of one's duties, the purpose of the assessment, and related variables.

> **JUST THINK . . .**
>
> Describe your own example of another assessment situation that might be an exception to the rule, one in which it might not be prudent to provide any sort of accommodation.

Inferences made from test scores After administering a standardized test, the test user looks to the test manual for guidelines in interpreting the test score. It is in the context of the normative data that scores on standardized tests are imbued with meaning. It is also in the context of normative data that test users can make reasonable inferences and predictions on the basis of scores on standardized tests. But what happens to the meaning of a score on a standardized test when that test has not been administered in the prescribed, standardized fashion? If there are published norms relevant to the modifications or abbreviations made, then a sound basis exists for interpretation of such scores. More often than not, however, when a standardized test is modified, the meaning of the score on that test becomes questionable at best. Test users are left to their own devices with regard to making interpretations from such data.

Interpreting scores from modified standardized tests is an unenviable task. Professional judgment, expertise, and, quite frankly, guesswork can all enter into the process of drawing inferences from scores on modified tests. Still, the inferences will most likely be vulnerable to legitimate challenges. Accordingly, interpreting scores from standardized tests that have been modified is not a task for the timid, the inexperienced, or the professional who lacks the background or training to make an educated guess when necessary.

A burgeoning scholarly literature has focused on various aspects of accommodation, including issues related to general policies (Burns, 1998; Shriner, 2000; Simpson et al., 1999; Thurlow et al., 2000), method of test administration (Calhoon et al., 2000; Danford & Steinfeld, 1999), score comparability (Elliott et al., 2001; Johnson, 2000; Pomplun & Omar, 2000, 2001), and documentation (Schulte et al., 2000). Before a decision about accommodation is made for any individual testtaker, due consideration must be given to issues regarding the meaning of scores derived from modified instruments and the validity of the inferences that can be made from the data derived. After any such accommodation, some notation on the record regarding the nature of the modification of a standardized test may be in order.

Noting accommodations made on the test protocol   It is useful for test users and other consumers of assessment data to be aware of how a standardized test has been modified, if at all, for administration to people with disabilities. However, consumers' need for this information must be balanced against social policies and laws designed to safeguard people with disabilities from discrimination. Accordingly, in assessment situations involving employment, academic, and other matters where some accommodation has been made as a result of the assessee's disability, a note limited to a description of the accommodation, rather than a description of the assessee's disability, is in order. An exception to this is the assessment situation that is specifically focused on the assessee's disability, undertaken for diagnostic or evaluative purposes. Another exception is the case where scores on a particular modification of a test are known to be equivalent to scores on the unmodified version of the test. In that case, there is no need to report details of the modification. Of course, another exception is the particular case wherein such an addendum is prohibited by law or inadvisable according to the standards of a profession.

In the absence of any laws, regulations, or professional standards to the contrary, it seems reasonable to write an addendum to reports of psychological assessment in which a standardized test or measurement procedure was in some way modified to accommodate the special needs of an assessee. The addendum should describe the nature of the change made, the rationale for the change, and any other information relevant to test users who may make inferences from the test scores. The accommodation addendum we are proposing, illustrated in Table 15–2, contains three headings: nature of the accommodation, rationale for the accommodation, and other remarks. The addendum should be attached to and made a part of the psychological report.

> **JUST THINK . . .**
>
> Formulate an argument against writing an accommodation addendum and attaching it to a psychological report.

Disability, Assessment, and the Workplace

The Americans with Disabilities Act of 1990 (ADA) mandated that employers with 15 or more employees not discriminate against people with disabilities in hiring, in access to facilities, and in the terms, conditions, and benefits of employment. As defined in the ADA, a **disability** is a physical or mental impairment that substantially limits one or more of an individual's major life activities. Any psychological disorder, such as mental retardation, organic brain syndrome, mental illness, or specific learning disability, may qualify under the ADA guidelines as a disability. An individual need not even be diagnosed as having such a disability to be protected under the ADA. Rather, the mere per-

Table 15–2
Elements of an Accommodation Addendum

Element of an Accommodation Addendum	Description
Nature of the accommodation	Exactly how was the test or measurement procedure modified or adapted? A sample description might be: *Instead of being administered in a group administration in its usual written (paper-and-pencil) format, the test was administered individually and read to the assessee, who orally responded.*
Rationale for the accommodation	Not to be confused with an entry designed to describe the assessee's disability, *rationale* in this sense refers to the basis for the accommodation vis-à-vis the test manual, the scholarly literature, or other research and clinical experience. Here, test users can explain, preferably with reference to test manuals, published studies, or pilot research, the rationale for the modification of the test. For example, a test user may draw on a study cited in the test manual that has to do with the comparability of test scores when the test is administered in an unmodified way versus an administration with a particular modification. If such sources cannot be drawn on, test users must draw on their own psychometric expertise and judgment to provide the reader of the report with a rationale for the modifications.
Other remarks	This space is for any other noteworthy aspect of the test administration that might affect inferences made from the test score. For many tests administered under accommodated conditions, this section will include a caution regarding interpretations made from the test score.

ception that an individual is disabled may qualify him or her for protection (*Sutton v. United Airlines*, 1999). A **perceived disability case** involves a claim of discrimination by a person who is merely regarded as having an impairment and discriminated against as a result of that perception.

Limitation of a major life activity is a key element of the ADA definition of disability, but exactly what constitutes such a limitation is not defined in the act. Goodman-Delahunty (2000) provides some assistance in this context by noting that a **major life activity** can be presumed to constitute functions such as caring for oneself, performing manual tasks, walking, seeing, hearing, speaking, breathing, learning, sitting, standing, lifting, reading, reaching, reproducing, and working. She pointed out that assessment of whether a substantial impairment exists requires consideration of three factors: (1) the nature and severity of the impairment, (2) the duration or expected duration of the impairment, and (3) the long-term impact of the impairment. If the claimed impairment is not deemed severe or long-term in nature, it may not qualify as a disability. So, for example, in *Pack v. K-Mart* (1999), the plaintiff claimed impairment of the major life activity of sleeping, due to the fact that she was depressed. The court rejected the claim because the sleep problem was controlled by medication, and there was insufficient evidence to prove that the problem was severe, long-term, or permanent.

An employee who is deemed to be a qualified individual with a disability (QUID) is entitled to accommodation in the workplace. Such accommodation typically takes the form of modification of job functions or circumstances (National Council on Disability, 1996). A **QUID** is a disabled employee who meets the employer's standards for education, skill, and other job-related qualifications and who can perform the essential functions of the job with or without accommodation in the workplace. The essential functions of a job are those fundamental duties that cannot be delegated to others and may require specific expertise, knowledge, or skill.

Since the passage of the ADA, more than 20,000 claims have been filed with the federal agency charged with enforcing antidiscrimination laws in employment settings (Wylonis, 1999). Courts have ruled that even prison inmates

JUST THINK . . .

The idea of workers being accommodated in the workplace and students being accommodated in educational settings may engender various sentiments on the part of peers. What types of sentiments might accommodation engender? How might administrators effectively deal with such sentiments?

Expert Testimony

Psychological assessors are routinely called upon to serve as experts in trials. Assessors may serve as experts in many different types of court cases, ranging from claims of disability to claims of incompetency to stand trial.

Assessors working in everyday clinical, counseling, and other settings typically have the best interests of their assessees in mind, and their assessees are confident of that fact. By contrast, assessors acting as expert witnesses may be agents of the court or even legal adversaries. In court-ordered evaluations conducted for trials in the military, a military psychologist is bound to put the objectives and interests of the military ahead of the objectives and interests of the assessee. There are even some professionals—hopefully few—who are hired guns in legal proceedings, most visibly in civil cases involving divorce and child custody and in criminal cases in which insanity is claimed as a defense. Tossing professional ethics to the wind, hired guns conduct evaluations and manipulate data for a price to arrive at the conclusions they were contracted to find. As compared to everyday assessment, then, evaluations conducted for presentation in court may differ in terms of the objectives of the assessment, the nature and tone of the assessment, and ultimately the results.

A landmark case heard by the Supreme Court in June 1993 has implications for the *type* of expert testimony that is admissible in court. The case was *Daubert v. Merrell Dow Pharmaceuticals*. The origins of this case can be traced to Mrs. Daubert's use of the prescription drug Bendectin to relieve nausea during pregnancy. The plaintiffs sued Merrell Dow Pharmaceuticals, the manufacturer of Bendectin, when their children were born with birth defects. Their claim was that Bendectin had caused the defects.

Attorneys for the Dauberts were armed with research that they claimed would prove that Bendectin causes birth defects. However, the trial judge ruled that the research failed to meet the criteria for admissibility. In the end, the judge ruled against the plaintiffs; Merrell Dow was not found to be liable for the birth defects.

The plaintiffs appealed to the next higher court. That court, too, ruled against them and in favor of the defendant,

Merrell Dow. Once again, the plaintiffs appealed, this time to the Supreme Court of the United States. A question before the Supreme Court was whether the judge in the original trial had acted properly by not allowing the plaintiffs' research to be admitted into evidence. To understand whether or not the trial judge acted properly, it is important to understand (1) a ruling that was made in the 1923 case *Frye v. the United States*, and (2) a law subsequently passed by Congress, Rule 702 in the *Federal Rules of Evidence* (FRE, 1975).

In *Frye*, the Court held that scientific research is admissible as evidence when the research study or method enjoys general acceptance. For our purposes, this means that if an expert claims something that most other experts in the same field would agree with, then the testimony can be admitted into evidence. Rule 702 changed that by allowing more experts to testify as to the admissibility of the original expert testimony. In addition to the expert testimony or research that enjoyed general acceptance in the field, other experts could now testify as to the admissibility of research or research methods. An expert might offer an opinion to a jury concerning the acceptability of a research study or method regardless of whether the opinion represented the opinions of other experts. Rule 702 was enacted to assist juries in their fact finding by helping them to understand the issues involved.

Presenting their case before the Supreme Court, the attorneys for the Dauberts argued that Rule 702 had been ignored, wrongly, by the trial judge. The attorneys for the defendant, Merrell Dow Pharmaceuticals, countered that the trial judge had ruled appropriately. They argued that high standards of evidence admissibility were necessary to protect juries from "scientific shamans who, in the guise of their purported expertise, are willing to testify to virtually any conclusion to suit the needs of the litigant with resources sufficient to pay their retainer."

Ultimately, the Supreme Court ruled that the *Daubert* case be retried and the trial judge given wide discretion in deciding what does and does not qualify as scientific evidence. In effect, federal judges were charged with a gatekeeping function. The ruling superseded the long-standing

are entitled to protection from discrimination under the ADA (Clements, 1999). For example, a prison inmate denied access to a motivational boot camp because of a history of hypertension claimed successfully that his rights under the ADA had been violated (*Pennsylvania Department of Corrections v. Yeskey*, 1998). Claims of discrimination on the basis of emotional, neurological, or other psychological impairment constitute about

. . . the Ancients measured facial beauty by the millihelen, *a unit equal to that necessary to launch one ship . . . .*

policy set forth in *Frye,* of admitting into evidence only scientific testimony that had won general acceptance in the scientific community.

In *Daubert,* factors such as general acceptance in the scientific community or publication in a peer-reviewed journal were simply some of many possible factors for judges to consider. Other factors judges might consider included the extent to which a theory or technique had been tested and the extent to which the theory or technique might be subject to error. In essence, the Supreme Court's ruling in *Daubert* gave trial judges a great deal of leeway in deciding what juries could and could not hear.

Subsequently, the Supreme Court has ruled on several other cases which in one way or another clarify or slightly modify its position in *Daubert.* For example, in the case of *General Electric v. Joiner* (1997), the Court emphasized that the trial court had a duty to exclude unreliable expert testimony as evidence. In the case of *Kumho Tire Company v. Carmichael* (1999), the Supreme Court expanded the principles expounded in *Daubert* to include the testimony of *all* experts, whether or not the experts claimed scientific research as a basis for their testimony. Thus, for example, a psychologist's testimony based on personal experience in practice rather than on scientific evidence may be admitted into evidence if the trial judge so chooses (Mark, 1999). Various commentators have speculated on just how *Daubert* and related cases might affect the admissibility of expert testimony in cases involving mental capacity (Frolik, 1999), child custody (Krauss & Sales, 1999), criminal prosecution (Slobogin, 1999), civil litigation (Lipton, 1999), and related matters (Grove & Barden, 1999; Saxe & Ben-Shakhar, 1999; Tenopyr, 1999).

30% of the cases filed with federal agencies, but that proportion may well increase as time goes on (Moss et al., 1999). Whenever a case is litigated in court, each side may retain its own experts with their own opinions as to how the facts should be interpreted. This reality, along with information about the admissability of expert testimony, is the subject of our *Close-up.*

Psychologists and others with expertise in psychological assessment have many possible roles to play with regard to ADA-related claims of discrimination (Blanck & Berven, 1999). One role they can play is to evaluate the knowledge of corporate personnel about provisions of the Americans with Disabilities Act. Hernandez et al. (2003) constructed and validated a measure designed to assess ADA knowledge among public- and private-sector representatives who were responsible for the law's implementation. In an exploratory validity study, public and private representatives scored significantly higher on the test than did a control group of undergraduate students. However, the researchers were not encouraged by the level of ADA knowledge exhibited by the representatives.

Psychological experts may act as advisors to companies that are putting hiring and other policies in place to prevent violations of law. A need exists for such advisors, especially in the design of policies on hiring persons with cognitive or psychological impairments (Scheid, 1999). Psychologists and other assessment professionals may serve as advisors to parties in the claims, or to the courts, regarding the nature and course of claimed disabilities as well as the effects of therapy or other intervention on the claimed disability. On the basis of an evaluation of workplace demands and the individual claimant, a clinician may be able to suggest what constitutes reasonable accommodation in the workplace. On the basis of an evaluation of a job description, an industry consultant may be able to render an educated, third-party opinion on the essential functions of the job. In cases where it is determined that discrimination has taken place, assessment professionals can provide useful input into the question of damages by testifying about the emotional or other injury suffered by the claimant (Goodman-Delahunty & Foote, 1995).

Assessment and Specific Disabilities

A number of special considerations must be taken into account in the individual evaluation of people with disabilities. In general, it is desirable for the assessor to understand the assessee's deficits and strengths with regard to (a) a particular disability, and (b) other areas (for example, language development, socialization skills, and personality in general) that may or may not be related to the primary disability. Such information will be essential in making appropriate accommodations (if any are deemed necessary), selecting appropriate test materials (if the assessor has this discretion), and interpreting interview, test, observational, and related data derived from the assessment. Sources for such information include case files as well as teachers, parents, friends, family members, and others acquainted with the assessee. Information should be obtained from as many different sources as possible. Various sources can help the assessor to better understand the assessee's functioning in different types of situations and under a wide variety of conditions. Exactly which variables to focus on in such pre-assessment activities will of course depend on the objectives of the assessment. What follows are some considerations applicable in many types of assessment situations with people who have sensory, motor, and cognitive disabilities. We begin with some general issues applicable to the assessment of people who are visually impaired.

JUST THINK . . .

Part of the preassessment work that may be required is some familiarization with the culture of a particular disability. Explain.

Visual Disabilities

Vision impairment is a matter not only of what one can see but of what one can do. Vision impairment may negatively impact activities most of us take for granted, such as shopping and preparing meals. For many older Americans in particular, chronic visual impairment is a fact of life. It has been estimated that more than 20% of people 65 or older have suffered severe loss of vision. The percentage of the population affected rises to 25% at age 75 and older (Lighthouse Research Institute, 1995). At any age, this variety of impairment, as with other varieties, can drastically affect one's quality of life. It can also impact one's ability to take tests and undergo other sorts of assessments.

A three-category taxonomy of visual impairment useful relative to testing and assessment was proposed by Bauman (1974). Included in the first category are people for whom vision is of no practical use in testing. The totally blind fall into this classification. Also included in this category are individuals who can differentiate between light and dark or who can distinguish shapes only when those shapes are held between the eyes and the light source. The next category includes people for whom vision is of some assistance in handling large objects, locating test pieces in a work space, or following the hand movements of the examiner during a demonstration, but who cannot read even enlarged print well enough to be tested using printed materials. Such individuals may be tested with materials that do not rely heavily on vision but require a combination of vision and touch. The third category includes people who read print efficiently, although they may need large type, may hold the page very close to their eyes, or may use a magnifier or some other special visual aid.

Accommodation of a visually impaired testtaker may take many different forms, depending, of course, on the nature and extent of the impairment. It may be necessary, for example, to modify the lighting in the room. Some testtakers may require more light, others may be disturbed by excessive light and glare. Some other types of modification are as follows:

- For the partially sighted examinee, writing instruments and written materials should be appropriate for the task. For example, a black felt-tip pen or crayon may be more appropriate than a fine-point ballpoint pen. Similarly, special wide-lined paper may be required.

- In general, persons with impaired vision require more time than nonimpaired individuals. It may take longer to dictate materials to them than for the examinees to read the materials themselves. When the partially sighted person is asked to use residual vision, test fatigue may set in, shown by behavior such as eye rubbing or other extraneous movements. In some instances, testtakers may use different pairs of glasses for different types of tasks. Adequate time must be allowed when testing the visually impaired, and speeded tests may be inappropriate (Nester, 1993).

- Multiple-choice questions, even in Braille, are frowned on by experts in this area because this type of question places an extra burden of concentration on the visually impaired examinee.

- In the introduction to the test, the examinee with a severe visual impairment may need time to touch all the materials he or she will be working with. During testing, more verbal information may be required than for a sighted individual. It is important under any testing conditions to have a quiet testing room that is free of distractions. However, this requirement takes on added importance in the testing of blind or visually impaired people because these individuals may be more distracted by extraneous sounds than are the fully sighted.

- The work space should be relatively compact so that all equipment is within the examinee's grasp. The work space should be well-lit but not so well lit as to cause glare on any stimulus materials that must be read.

- If the test stimulus materials require some reading, and the test is being administered to a partially sighted person, it may be advisable to retype the materials in large type. An administration in Braille may be appropriate; however, relatively few blind individuals read Braille, and relatively few of these read it well.

If an objective of the test is assessment of intellectual ability, many tests and subtests, such as the Verbal scale of a Wechsler test, have been used for purposes of estimation. Some research has called this fairly common practice into question. In one study, children who were blind or severely visually impaired tended to perform about one standard deviation below the mean of sighted children on the Comprehension subtest (Groenveld & Jan, 1992). Although these testtakers' scores were close to the average for sighted children on the Information, Similarities, Vocabulary, and Arithmetic subtests, the study calls attention to the need for norms specifically developed for blind and visually impaired testtakers.

In the area of personality assessment, most existing methods available for use with the sighted can be readily adapted for use with the visually impaired and the blind. Test materials that must be read can be reprinted in large type, read to the examinee, or prerecorded on tape. Even a test such as the Thematic Apperception Test can be administered to a blind person if the blind person hears a description of the card and then proceeds to tell a story about it. A specially developed TAT-like test for the blind is the Sound Test, which contains prerecorded sounds such as footsteps, running water, and music, combined in some instances with verbal interchanges. The examinee's task is to construct a story about such aural stimuli.[3]

Other specially devised personality tests are the Emotional Factors Inventory and the Adolescent Emotional Factors Inventory, two tests that include scales measuring the examinee's adjustment to blindness. The Maxfield-Bucholz Social Competency Scale for Blind Preschool Children is a measure of social competence and adaptive behavior designed for use with blind children from birth to age 6. The scale is administered to a third party such as the parent, guardian, or primary caregiver, and it is designed to explore areas such as the subject's physical development, self-care ability, and social competency.

Tests have also been developed to help the blind and the visually impaired with vocational guidance. Many of the available tests of finger and hand dexterity are used with this population. Available vocational interest inventories are administered to this population in large-print editions, Braille, or other adaptations. One such test, the PRG Interest Inventory, was based entirely on the content of the types of jobs held by and the types of hobbies indulged in by blind respondents. In the test's instructions, examinees are advised to respond as if they had the visual capabilities to handle the description of the various jobs. The instructions were worded this way so that the test would yield a veritable measure of interest as opposed to perceived capability.

Visual impairment may affect the outcome of neuropsychological tests (Kempen et al., 1994), thus prompting a neurologically oriented neuropsychologist to look to the brain for answers about the poor test performance. However, as Kempen et al. (1994) have advised, a simple vision test may be all that is necessary in some cases to answer such questions.

It bears repeating that extreme care must be taken in making inferences from test scores on standardized tests that have been modified to accommodate the testtaker. Even when no test modification has been made, the interpretation of test scores of people with disabilities contains many pitfalls. Based on experiences at the Texas School for the Blind and Visually Impaired, for example, Loftin (1997) cautioned that a number of diagnosed conditions may be directly related to vision deficit, congenital blindness in

---

3. You may recall from Chapter 12 that it was none other than behaviorist B. F. Skinner who created the first instrument used to measure auditory projection.

particular. These conditions include delayed motor milestones, echolalic speech, tangential or egocentric conversations, overidentification with adults, a tendency to be passive in problem solving, and others.

Sensitivity to the needs of a particular population can be developed by work with members of that population in a professional or volunteer capacity. The prospective assessment professional may also wish to read about the experience of other assessment professionals working with members of various populations. Resources in the literature having to do with the assessment of the blind and the visually impaired include Bauman and Kropf (1979), Bradley-Johnson (1994), Bradley-Johnson and Harris (1990), Chase (1986), Drinkwater (1976), Evans (1978), Levack (1991), Loftin (1997), Swallow (1981), Tillman (1973), and Vander Kolk (1977).

> **JUST THINK . . .**
>
> How might an assessor go about developing a culturally informed approach to the assessment of individuals who are blind?

Hearing Disabilities

Hearing impairment may occur at any age for a wide variety of reasons, from disease and infection to prolonged exposure to loud music. It has been estimated that about half the population of the United States age 65 and older has suffered some degree of hearing impairment (Vernon, 1989). Assessees who seem not to comprehend instructions, often ask to have things repeated, intently watch a speaker's lips for cues, and/or behave as if they understand what is being said to them when they do not, should all be suspected of having undiagnosed hearing impairment.

People with impaired hearing differ with respect to variables such as magnitude of hearing loss, age at onset of loss, and consequential effects of the loss on language skills, social adjustment, and other abilities and personality characteristics. From a cultural perspective (to be discussed in greater detail later in this chapter), people with profound hearing loss prior to the age of 3 belong to a different culture from members of the relatively small segment of the deaf population who have experienced a profound loss of hearing in later life (Raifman & Vernon, 1996). The latter group use speech and may perceive themselves as part of the majority culture; by contrast, people who are deaf from an early age use a language that is visual, tend to work with their hands rather than words, and due to their isolation from the majority culture, interact primarily with others who are deaf (Higgins, 1983; Lane, 1992; Padden & Humphries, 1988; Vernon & Andrews, 1990). When a hearing assessor has the task of assessing a nonhearing person, the problem, at least at first glance, is one of communication. Unfortunately, the problem may go well beyond communication and in fact may be better characterized as a culture clash (Phillips, 1996).

For assessees who are hearing impaired and/or did not lose their hearing at an early age, a number of test modification strategies may be employed to facilitate assessor-assessee communication. These strategies include (1) presenting written instructions at a reading level appropriate to the assessee (printed on paper or electronically by means of computer or a special teletype device), (2) amplification of the assessor's voice (through amplification equipment or the assessee's own hearing aid), and (3) using an interpreter proficient in a sign language in which the assessee is proficient.[4] For assessees with early-onset deafness, it is highly recommended that only assessors who are fluent themselves in American Sign Language (ASL) and familiar with the culture be

---

4. One source of information and a directory of certified interpreters is the Registry of Interpreters for the Deaf. Their Web address is http://www.rid.org.

used (Leigh et al., 1996; Raifman & Vernon, 1996). This is essential for reasons related to rapport, communication, and accuracy in interpretation of test findings. To facilitate such examinations, special test materials may be employed. For example, Barbara Brauer, a psychologist who is deaf, developed a videotaped version of an MMPI administration in American Sign Language (Brauer, 1993).

Essential as one or more of the foregoing adaptations may be, there are drawbacks associated with each (Orr et al., 1987). For example, using written communication instead of spoken communication introduces another variable (reading proficiency) into a task where no such variable had existed before. Pantomiming instructions and cues in the absence of explicit directions for doing so in the test manual results in a situation where different pantomimists (that is, different test administrators) may well have different ideas about how to get a point across by gestures. As a result, the standardization of the instructions to examinees will suffer.

The introduction of any interpreter into an assessment situation may diminish the rapport between examiner and examinee. Additionally, a certain amount of error in expressive and receptive translations can also be expected. When translation entails signing, the interpreter's signing skills must be compatible with the assessee's receptive skills. It would be inappropriate, for example, for the interpreter to sign in Coded Sign English (a method of communication more closely linked to the written/verbal expression of people with no hearing impairment) with an assessee more fluent in ASL. Verbal information, especially idioms and proverbs, is not readily amenable to translation into sign, and the assessor must carefully examine test materials in advance with that fact in mind—and appropriately modify the administration materials if need be. Sign language is, in fact, a different language from English, and translations of tests into sign language should be treated with as much care as any foreign-language translation (Nester, 1993).

Performance subtests of Kaufman tests (Gibbins, 1988; Kennedy & Hiltonsmith, 1988; Phelps & Branyan, 1988) and Wechsler tests have been used to gauge the intellectual functioning of people who are deaf and hearing impaired. Jeffrey Braden (1985, 1990, 1992; Maller & Braden, 1993) and Patricia Sullivan (1982) and colleagues (Maller, 1997; Sullivan & Brookhouser, 1996; Sullivan & Burley, 1990; Sullivan & Montoya, 1997; Sullivan & Schulte, 1992) have written extensively on the use of the Wechsler and other tests with people who are deaf or hard of hearing. Sullivan recently urged a reevaluation of the historic taboo against the use of verbal intelligence tests with members of this population. Sullivan and Montoya (1997) argued that the majority of people who are deaf and hard of hearing are now competing with hearing persons in academic as well as employment environments. Face-to-face communication skills and English literacy are typically required for higher-paying jobs (Allen, 1994; Schildroth et al., 1991).

In contrast to tests originally designed for use with the general population, some tests designed to measure cognitive ability were standardized on hearing as well as nonhearing respondents. The Hiskey-Nebraska Test of Learning Aptitude is one such test. Developed for use with children and adolescents ages 3 to 17 by Marshall S. Hiskey (1966), the Hiskey-Nebraska was developed with sensitivity to the needs of testtakers who are deaf or hard of hearing. The test includes pantomine practice exercises as well as a manual replete with helpful guidelines for testing deaf and hard-of-hearing respondents. Although the norms are in need of updating, the test has endured as a useful measure of cognitive ability (Sullivan & Burley, 1990). It has international appeal as the test of choice in clinical and research applications with deaf and hard-of-hearing assessees (see, for example, Collins et al., 1987; Nagyne Rez & Zsoldos, 1991; Qu et al., 1992).

Measures of academic achievement using tests such as the Metropolitan Achievement Test and the Stanford Achievement Tests can be useful because both of these tests have been standardized with members of this population. In general, hearing-impaired and deaf children do not perform as well on such tests as do their hearing peers. This is due not only to their language impairment but also to the lack of curriculum methods developed specifically to meet the educational needs of the deaf. Only 5% of graduates from educational programs for the deaf attain a tenth-grade education; 41% achieve a seventh- or eighth-grade education, and 30% are functionally illiterate.

Tools used for personality assessment with the deaf and hard of hearing, as with other people, include the interview (appropriately modified, such as with signing or amplification), case history evaluation, and tests. In some cases, personality tests that minimize requirements for verbal ability are preferred (Leigh et al., 1996). So, for example, tests involving drawing (such as the Draw A Person and the House-Tree-Person) are frequently used with assessees

JUST THINK . . .

What special challenges does a test developer face when revising a test originally designed for persons with normal hearing for use with a population of deaf individuals?

who are deaf. Personality assessment with children and adults using paper-and-pencil personality tests should be used only if the reading level of the test is known and the assessee is known to be reading at or above that level.

The Rorschach has been recommended for use with only those deaf people known to be above average in intelligence and able to sign fluently (Vernon & Brown, 1964), although clinicians experienced with this special population may be able to use it more routinely (Sachs, 1976). Other projective measures, such as those involving drawings (Johnson, 1989; Ouellette, 1988), the Bender Visual-Motor Gestalt Test used projectively (Gibbins, 1989), and the TAT (Vernon & Brown, 1964), may prove insightful. Cates and Lapham (1991) caution that although the TAT may be useful, deaf children and adolescents may concretely label the cards and then perseverate on themes in an effort to supply the "right" answer:

> A potential difficulty in administering apperception techniques to deaf children and adolescents is a tendency toward response perseveration. For example, if unfamiliar with the task, the deaf student may initially attempt to label the picture. If this response is corrected, the deaf student may then perceive the first story told as the correct response. If the first correct response is a story containing a violent theme, then the deaf client may assume that violence is desired or appropriate in the stories and perseverate on violent themes. The clinician must decide whether to allow the perseveration or restructure the response set of the child or adolescent. The authors generally noted the perseverative phenomenon, then restructured the response set, indicating that each picture may elicit differing themes. (p. 125)

Cates and Lapham (1991) also reported on concrete types of response that may be given on another projective measure, the Hand Test:

> Deaf children and adolescents give a higher frequency of concrete responses to the Hand Test than do their hearing counterparts. For example, in response to the first card—a hand held up, palm outward—the deaf child may initially provide a description of the hand (e.g., "It's a hand, held up. Five fingers.") rather than describe the hand in some form of activity, as requested in the instructions. In the Hand Test scoring system, this type of descriptive response is considered indicative of severe disturbance. The clinician using the Hand Test, then, may wish to administer the test according to standardized procedure, followed by a testing-the-limits procedure, in which the deaf child is urged to provide more appropriate responses. Alternatively, following the first descriptive response, the clinician may wish to reemphasize the instructions, elicit a more appropriate

response, and consider the initial response as training. The deaf subject may also benefit from an inclusion to the standard directions that the hands are not signing. (p. 122)

Behavior checklists and rating scales can prove to be valuable tools of assessment with the deaf (McCoy, 1972). The checklist used most extensively with deaf children and adolescents is the Meadow-Kendall Social-Emotional Assessment Inventory (Meadow et al., 1980), appropriate for use with individuals aged 7 to 21 years. Other such instruments, not necessarily designed especially for the deaf, include the Behavior Problem Checklist (Quay & Peterson, 1967, 1983), the Devereaux Adolescent Behavior Rating Scale (Spivack et al., 1967), the Devereaux Child Behavior Rating Scale (Spivack & Spotts, 1966), the Child Behavior Checklist (Achenbach, 1978), and the Walker Problem Behavior Identification Checklist (Walker, 1976).

As is frequently the case when testing people who are deaf or hard of hearing, appropriate norms for the test employed may be scant or nonexistent. In such circumstances, assessors must draw on their own training and experience—or, if necessary, that of a more experienced and highly trained colleague—in an effort to make reasonable inferences from the resulting data. Where appropriate, conclusions should be supported by multiple sources of data, including case history data, data from behavioral observation, and reports from parents, teachers, therapists, or other caregivers.

Before administering psychological and educational tests to hearing-impaired and deaf testtakers, most psychologists and other test users would profit from education, supervised experience, and training relevant to hearing loss and deafness (Cates & Lapham, 1991; Elliot et al., 1987; Elliott & Carroll, 1997; Pollard, 1993; Weaver & Bradley-Johnson, 1993; Zieziula, 1982). Such specialized preparation is critical if accurate interpretations are to be made from assessment data. Misiaszek et al. (1985) cautioned that mental health professionals who are unfamiliar with the effects of prelingual deafness on personality, communication, cognition, and socialization are prone to make diagnostic errors. People who suffer prelingual deafness may exhibit behavior that seems similar to the concrete and sometimes fragmented behavior patterns typical of people with schizophrenia. Other products of deaf enculturation, such as egocentric and rigid behaviors, may be mistaken for personality disorders. Consideration of such potential pitfalls leads to a general conclusion that cannot be overemphasized in any discussion of assessment with members of a population who have a particular disability: Specialized education, training, and supervised experience is highly desirable if not mandatory.

Visual/Hearing Disabilities

Ten Regional Centers for Deaf-Blind Youth and Adults were created by Congress in 1967 in response to an increase in babies born with multiple handicaps as the result of a rubella epidemic that spread across the United States from 1963 to 1965. The centers were charged with the responsibility of identifying and assessing such children. The assessment of members of this population represents the "most difficult diagnosis task a psychologist can be asked to do" (Vernon et al., 1979, p. 291). The assessor must be particularly wary of diagnostic errors that might lead to the placement of such children in programs for the mentally or emotionally impaired when in fact such programs would be inappropriate for the particular child.

JUST THINK . . .

What preparation do you think is necessary for assessors to be able to effectively avoid mistaking physical disability for emotional impairment?

Few standardized tests are appropriate for use with the deaf-blind. Standardized tests developed for and standardized on individuals with other disabling conditions do not adequately take into account the multiplicity and the pervasiveness of impairments of the deaf-blind. Psychological assessment of the deaf-blind most typically involves assessment of adaptive behavior (discussed later in greater detail) as well as interviews with caregivers and analysis of case history material. One of the few tests designed for use with and standardized on this population is the Callier-Azusa Scale (CAS).

The CAS is a behavior checklist that enables the examiner to compare the subject's development in a number of areas (motor, perceptual, language, daily living skills, and socialization) with typical development for deaf-blind children from birth to 9 years who have received appropriate interventions. The test is useful both in educational program planning and as a posttest to assess behavior change after a specific intervention. Stillman (1974) recommends that more than one rater assess the child's behavior both at home and at school for at least two weeks. Information is usually provided by a parent, the teacher, or some other person having extensive contact with the child. Adequate reliability has been reported with respect to the test's 16 subscales. The test authors also reported that the scale's reliability was not significantly influenced by the child's educational setting or the number of people rating the child (Bennett et al., 1979). Related to validity evidence, Diebold, Curtis, and Dubose (1978) have demonstrated the strong relationship for a sample of 6- to 13-year-old deaf-blind children between systematic observation of daily behavior measures and performance on CAS developmental scales. The 16 subscales of the CAS yield an age-equivalent score rather than IQ, but the conversion table is psychometrically unsound and therefore few professionals use it. Credit for particular items is awarded only if the behavior is "present fully and regularly." Behaviors that are just emerging are not credited. If the deaf-blind child has additional disabilities, such as a motor deficit, specific CAS items can be omitted.

Another standardized test that can be used with the deaf-blind is the Assessment of Development Levels by Observation (ADLO; Wolf-Schein, 1993). As its name implies, the ADLO entails systematic observation of behavior and classification of it by developmental level. Behavior is assessed and classified on variables related to self-help skills, fine and gross motor skills, receptive (listening and understanding) and expressive language, and relationships with adults. Typically, the test is conducted in a setting familiar to the child; an observer evaluates the child playing alone, interacting with familiar and unfamiliar adults, and working with a language specialist. Norms are available for children from birth to 8 years of age.

Motor Disabilities

Motor deficits come in many forms, have many varied causes, and may involve any muscle or muscle group in the body. Paralysis, tremors, involuntary movement, gait difficulties, and problems with volitional movement and speech are some of the many types of motor problems. The cause of the motor problem may be an inherited muscular or neurological difficulty or one acquired as a result of a trauma to the muscle, the brain, or the spinal cord. Other causal factors include the wide range of neuromuscular diseases. Cases of cerebral palsy, for example, are believed to occur at the rate of 1.6 to 5 per 1,000 in the under-21 population. The palsy may be caused by an endocrine imbalance, low blood sugar, anoxia, a high forceps delivery, or any of a variety of other factors occurring before, during, or after birth.

Most of the tests used to assess intellectual functioning rely at least in part on the respondent's ability to manipulate some materials—cards, blocks, beads, and so forth. The test that does not contain such tasks would be criticized by experts as too loaded on verbal as opposed to performance measures of intelligence. Examiners wishing to assess the intelligence of motor-handicapped people will attempt to select an existing test that does not need to be modified in any way for administration to the particular individual being assessed.

If all available tests were to require modification, the test requiring the least modification would be selected. An example of a modification that might be employed when administering a block design task, for example, would require the examiner to physically turn the blocks until the examinee indicates that the rotation of the block is his or her response. The examinee might indicate this with a verbal response or, if there is a speech deficit, with some other response, such as a wink of the eye. On paper-and-pencil tasks that require fine motor coordination, such as tests that involve blackening tiny grids with number two pencils, the motor-handicapped individual might require a writer to enter the responses. The alternative (not to administer any motor tasks to the motor-handicapped examinee) is the approach taken by some examiners. The rationale here is that a verbal test such as the Vocabulary subtest of a Wechsler examination correlates highly with the rest of the examination and may therefore be used as a rough estimate of both verbal and nonverbal intelligence. However, such a procedure provides only a *rough estimate* and is never a good practice if used for placement decisions in the absence of other assessment data.

Psychologists and special educators who assess variables such as the severity of a motor deficit have a number of tests at their disposal. Four test batteries in current use are the Purdue Perceptual-Motor Survey, the Bruininks-Oseretsky Test of Motor Proficiency, the Frostig Movement Skills Test Battery, and the Southern California Sensory Integration Tests. The Purdue is a screening device that provides guidelines for assessing various gross and fine motor functions in children aged 6 to 10 years. The Bruininks-Oseretsky tests gross and fine motor skills as well as general motor proficiency. It is a technically sound test but one that requires (1) a very well-trained examiner to administer and interpret, and (2) extensive space to administer (such as a playground or a specially equipped room). The Frostig is designed to assess sensorimotor development, gross and fine motor coordination, balance, strength, and flexibility in children aged 6 to 12 years. It is popular among many examiners because it is relatively simple to administer, contains a relatively wide range of motor skills sampled, and is easy to score. The Southern California is also a measure of sensory integrative functioning designed for use with children aged 4 to 9 years. However, this time-consuming test must be administered and interpreted by a highly trained examiner.

Other motor skills tests have been developed for use with elderly individuals, including the Physical Disability Index (PDI; Gerety et al., 1993). Designed specifically for frail elderly populations, the PDI assesses strength, balance, mobility, and range of motion.

> **JUST THINK . . .**
>
> What might be some tasks to assess motor ability in the frail elderly? How might the information developed from these tasks be used?

Cognitive Disabilities

The term **cognitive disability** covers a broad spectrum of disabling conditions, including various neurological deficits, learning disabilities, autism, and mental retardation. Elsewhere in this book, we have discussed many issues relative to the assessment of some of these cognitive disabilities. Here we focus on assessment issues related to mental retardation.

Mental retardation and adaptive behavior   Definitions of mental retardation and associated classification systems vary by source. Most definitions make reference to significant subaverage general intellectual functioning existing along with deficits in adaptive behavior, all manifested during the developmental period. **Adaptive behavior** in this context refers to the personal and social effectiveness and appropriateness of one's actions. One's behavior is characterized as adaptive to the extent that one acts or modifies one's behavior consistent with age-appropriate adjustment, social maturity, and personal and social competence (Cain et al., 1963; Doll, 1953; Fullan & Loubser, 1972). In 1905, Alfred Binet made indirect reference to the concept of adaptive behavior when he said "an individual is normal if he is able to conduct his affairs of life without having need of supervision of others, if he is able to work sufficiently . . . to supply his own personal needs" (Binet, quoted in Goddard, 1916).

Traditionally, mental retardation has been diagnosed primarily on the basis of intelligence tests and then classified in terms of one of four categories: mild, moderate, severe, and profound. These categories designate progressively lower measured IQs and are associated with characteristic deficits in adaptive behavior with regard to specific contexts throughout the lifespan. In 1992, a manual published by the American Association on Mental Retardation (AAMR) replaced these four categories with four revised ways of classifying people with mental retardation. AAMR (1992) defined mental retardation as a condition that develops before the age of 18 in which there is significant subaverage intellectual functioning (measured IQ of 75 or less) concurrent with limitations in at least two of ten adaptive skill areas. Adaptive skill areas ranged from leisure to academics to work and included areas such as communication, self-care, and social skills.

Consistent with the new paradigm discussed earlier in this chapter, the revised AAMR classification system emphasized the role of adaptive behavior in the definition of mental retardation by replacing the qualitative labels associated with deficit (*mild, moderate,* and so on) with a qualifier indicative of intensity of support required across various environments. Required intensity of support was categorized as *intermittent* (support required on an as-needed basis), *limited* (time-limited but consistent over time), *extensive* (daily in at least some environments), or *pervasive* (constant support required across environments).

Heavily criticized by many, the 1992 AAMR system was characterized as a "dead manual walking" (Greenspan, 1997). The manual raised a host of new problems in terms of assessing and classifying intelligence, adaptive behavior, and intensities of needed supports (Gresham et al., 1995; Hodapp, 1995), especially with young children (Vig & Jedrysek, 1996). For some, the 1992 manual represented an abandonment of a pragmatic/scientific perspective on mental retardation for one that is primarily political (Matson, 1995). The AAMR's Committee on Terminology and Classification responded to such criticisms by arguing, in part, that a system based on required intensity of supports has more utility than one based on IQ level (Luccas-

> **JUST THINK . . .**
>
> Is the classification system described in the 1992 AAMR aptly characterized as a "dead manual walking"?

son et al., 1996). Still, years after the AAMR recommendations, many descriptions of research subjects in the scholarly literature employ the mild-to-profound classification system.

The diagnosis of mental retardation is typically made on the basis of data from an appropriate measure of intelligence as well as a measure of adaptive behavior. Especially for very young assessees, measures of sensory, motor, and sensorimotor ability are included as part of an evaluation designed to distinguish deficit from developmental delay. If an evaluation of the assessee's understanding of basic concepts is desired, a test such as the Boehm Test of Basic Concepts or the Bracken Basic Concept Scale-Revised may be employed. If autism is suspected or needs to be ruled out, specialized diagnostic instruments, such as the Childhood Autism Rating Scale or the Diagnostic Assessment for the Severely Handicapped-II, may be administered (Matson et al., 1998). An invaluable contribution can be made by the assessee's family in such assessments (Parette & Brotherson, 1996). Ideally, the net result of the assessment will be an understanding of the assessee—not only in terms of scores on standardized tests and standing relative to peers but in terms of his or her unique behavioral deficits and excesses across environments (Desrochers et al., 1997; Harris et al., 1996).

Many standardized measures of adaptive behavior exist, and test users must be aware of the pros and cons of these varied instruments. For example, the AAMR Adaptive Behavior Scale-School:2 (ABS-S:2; Lambert et al., 1993) is something of an anomaly; it was designed to measure typical performance in coping with various environmental demands, but the domains assessed are mismatched with the AAMR's 1992 manual (Stinnett, 1997). Further, although the standardization sample for this measure was quite large, including people with mental retardation ($n = 2,074$) as well as a nonchallenged sample ($n = 1,254$), high-functioning people with mental retardation were underrepresented. The result is the potential for an error in interpretation whereby the adaptive functioning of members of this population is overestimated (Stinnett, 1997).

The Adaptive Behavior Assessment System (ABAS; Harrison & Oakland, 2000) was designed to provide a comprehensive assessment of persons from ages 5 through 89 in areas of adaptive skills specified in the AAMR manual, such as communication, community, home living, work, and health and safety. The instrument, available in English and Spanish, comes in three different forms, one each for parents and teachers (available for ages 5 through 21), and an adult form that may be completed by assessees themselves or by a spouse, a relative, or other caretaker. Scores allow for both evaluation of functioning and pinpointing of strengths and weaknesses. According to the manual, it may also have application in specifying goals for persons with learning disabilities. The test was published relatively recently. A more "classic" approach to assessment of adaptive behavior is embodied in a test referred to simply as "the Vineland."

The Vineland Social Maturity Scale was developed by Edgar A. Doll (1953), then director of research at the Vineland Training School in Vineland, New Jersey. Three decades later, the test was revised and published as the Vineland Adaptive Behavior Scales (VABS; Sparrow et al., 1984a, 1984b). The revised test, like its predecessor, is usually referred to simply as "the Vineland." In the tradition of its predecessor, it emphasizes social competence, which Doll (1953, p. 2) conceived of as "a functional composite of human traits which subserves social usefulness as reflected in self-sufficiency and service to others." The primary use of the Vineland is to assess the adaptive behavior of developmentally disabled individuals.

The revised Vineland is available in three forms: the Survey Form of the Interview Edition, the Expanded Form of the Interview Edition, and the Classroom Edition. The two Interview Edition forms (Sparrow et al., 1984a, 1984b) were designed for use with individuals from birth to age 18 as well as with low-functioning adults. They are both structured interviews undertaken with a parent or some other informant who is very familiar with the assessee. The Survey Form contains 297 items and requires 20 to 60 minutes to administer. The Expanded Form is a more detailed version of the interview that contains 577 items (including the 297 items in the briefer form). It takes between 60 and 90 minutes to administer. The third form of the Vineland, the Classroom Edition (Sparrow et al., 1985), is a 244-item form, completed by a teacher, that focuses primarily on behavior in an academic context. It is designed for use with assessees ranging in age from 3 to 13 years.

All three forms of the test tap the areas, or domains, of daily living, socialization, motor function, and communication. In addition, the two Interview Edition forms contain items relevant to maladaptive behavior. In each domain, the informant is asked to provide information relative to actual behaviors. Skills are broken down into component behaviors so that the level of ability can be specified. For example, in the area of daily living skills, the informant is asked about the individual's ability to put on shoes, including the individual elements of this ability, such as lacing shoes and tying a bowknot. In the area of socialization skills, the informant may be asked about the assessee's table manners, and everything from using a napkin to requesting items on the table.

Normative data are available for all forms of the Vineland. For the Interview Edition, data were gathered on about 4,800 people without disabilities. For the Classroom Edition, approximately three thousand children and adolescents constituted the normative sample. All standardization data were gathered from normative groups that had been drawn nationally and stratified according to the 1980 U.S. census for sex, geographical region, size of community, parents' education, and race and ethnicity. Raw scores on the test are converted into standard scores with a mean of 100 and a standard deviation of 15. Scores are calculated separately for each domain. A total score, called the Adaptive Behavior Composite, incorporates evaluative data from each of the domains. More on psychometric aspects of this test is presented in Cohen (2005).

As in the assessment of members of other populations, education, training, and experience with members of the population of people with mental retardation are essential for understanding and dealing with the special diagnostic questions unique to this population (Silka & Hauser, 1997). In pervasive developmental disorders, multidisciplinary collaboration in the assessment is particularly critical (Volkmar et al., 1996).

Quality of life   In addition to recent increases in interest in the assessment of adaptive behavior, interest has increased in the measurement of variables related to the quality of life of people with mental retardation (Hughes et al., 1995; Rosen et al., 1995) as well as other disabilities (Renwick et al., 1996; Storey, 1997). Researchers have examined sundry variables such as stress, loneliness, sources of satisfaction, and quality of friendships (Rosen et al., 1995; Siperstein et al., 1997). Researchers have sought to understand the needs and desires of parents of intellectually challenged children (Westling, 1996) and have explored how quality-of-life and related issues may vary by age (Mast & Lichtenberg, 2000), disability (Gallagher & MacLachlan, 2000), and culture (Keith et al., 1996). The definition of *quality of life* has varied in different studies. In some research, *quality of life* referred to an observer's judgment of a subject's lifestyle. In other research, this same term referred to a more subjective appraisal of the subject's own life. In the interest of uniformity, Felce (1997) proposed a definition of *quality of life* based in part on an assessment of personal values, life conditions, and personal satisfaction. Alternatively, Storey (1997) acknowledged that the assessment of issues related to quality of life must necessarily be quite broad because the relevant dependent measures change over time and with different populations.

Related to issues of quality of life has been a great deal of research interest in social information processing (Gomez & Hazeldine, 1996), including matters related to sexual activity (Lumley & Miltenberger, 1997; Lumley et al., 1998) and consent to same (Parker & Abramson, 1995). One instrument specifically designed for use in assessing the sexual knowledge and attitudes of the developmentally disabled is the Socio-Sexual Knowledge & Attitudes Test (Wish et al., 1980). Topic areas covered by the instrument include anatomy terminology, menstruation, masturbation, dating, marriage, intimacy, intercourse, pregnancy, childbirth, alcohol and drugs, homosexuality, and venereal disease (Figure 15–1). Because expressive language required by the examinee is minimal— most responses are made by pointing or indicating yes or no. The test is suitable for

JUST THINK . . .

As we consider various quality-of-life issues for assessees, let's also consider these issues as they pertain to assessors. For a professional assessor, what might be the greatest source of satisfaction? The greatest source of stress?

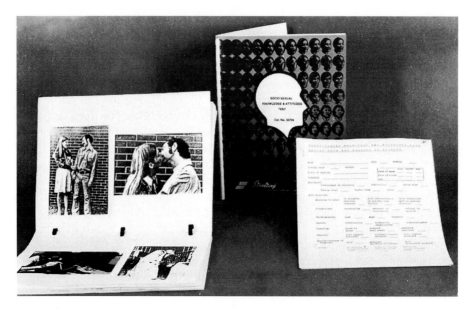

Figure 15–1
The Socio-Sexual Knowledge & Attitudes Test

administration to those with limited language skills or ability. Though the test manual includes normative data on developmentally disabled individuals aged 18 to 42, the intent of the test authors is that the test be used in a criterion-referenced as opposed to a norm-referenced fashion, as a measure of what the individual testtaker knows, believes, or doesn't know. Using a testing-the-limits procedure, it is possible for the examiner to employ some of the pictorial stimuli to explore the examinee's understanding of diseases such as AIDS and concepts such as sexual abuse and sexual harassment.

Biopsychosocial Assessment

A social model of disability demands that psychologists and others who assess individuals with disabilities truly strive to get "the big picture" in full, "wide-screen" context, as opposed to a "cropped" and pathology-focused close-up. Getting this big picture entails using some familiar tools in new ways as well as employing some new tools altogether. This broader approach to assessment is embodied in what has been called *biopsychosocial assessment*. As its name implies, **biopsychosocial assessment** is an approach or model of assessment that includes exploration of relevant biological, psychological, social, cultural, and environmental variables and an evaluation of how such variables, independently or in combination, affect the assessee. For example, in a study that investigated aspects of the disablement process in older adults, researchers explored the role of factors such as self-confidence, intellectual resources, and beliefs regarding how much control people actually have over what happens to them. Among their findings was the fact that a high degree of **fatalism** (the belief that what happens in life is largely out of a person's control) as measured in 1974, was predictive of illness and cognitive difficulties in 1994 (Caplan & Schooler, 2003).

The biopsychosocial approach has been employed by clinicians in realms other than disability evaluation and disability research, although it seems tailor made for the new paradigm. Feldman and Rivas-Vazquez (2003) employed a biopsychosocial approach in their study of the assessment and treatment of social anxiety disorder. They concluded that pharmacotherapy and psychosocial interventions used in combination over the long term offered the best hope for people with this disorder. Keefe et al. (2002) illustrated the value of the biopsychosocial approach in their study of the assessment and treatment of arthritis. For example, they discussed the use of in-depth interviews to identify life changes brought on by a diagnosis of arthritis, as well as coping strategies. In this regard, Blalock et al. (1993) noted that little flexibility in coping behavior was associated with decreased psychosocial functioning. Keefe and colleagues also discussed their use of diary methods as a useful tool for keeping track of a variety of variables ranging from relaxation exercises to a standardized measure of spiritual coping strategies. These researchers tried to see the "big picture" in terms of many other variables such as **self-efficacy** (confidence in one's own ability to accomplish a task) and **social support** (expressions of understanding, acceptance, empathy, love, advice, guidance, care, concern, or trust from friends, family, community caregivers or others in one's social environment).

> **JUST THINK . . .**
>
> Describe what you envision to be some essential elements of a biopsychosocial assessment program for patients suffering from depression.

Integral to a biopsychosocial approach to assessment is an exploration of culture and related issues as these issues may impact on the wellness, adjustment, or illness of an assessee. For this reason, it may be instructive to "shift lenses" and consider disability as a diversity issue.

Disability as a Diversity Issue

It is uncontroversial to assert that "disabilities are part of human diversity" (Leigh et al., 1996, p. 364). It is quite another matter, however, to assert that the members of a group of people who all have the same disability constitute a distinct cultural group. As we noted at the beginning of this chapter, the plaintiffs in *Tugg v. Towey* alleged just that. In *Tugg,* the argument was that people who are deaf constitute a distinct cultural minority, one that may be discriminated against in many of the same ways as other cultural minorities. We conclude this chapter with a brief examination of this assertion as it applies to the population singled out in the lawsuit—deaf individuals—keeping in mind that analogous arguments could be applied to most any population of people who have the same or a similar disability.

Disability, diversity, and culture   Most of the half-million or so people who cannot hear speech well enough to understand it were deaf before they were 3 years old (Schein & Delk, 1974). These people communicate with one another using American Sign Language and have other deaf people as their primary social contacts. As a group, members of this population have in common not only their language but many of their beliefs, attitudes, values, nonverbal behavior, norms, and traditions. In short, they have in common many of the things used to define a distinct cultural group (Dolnick, 1993; Padden, 1980; Paul & Jackson, 1993; Phillips, 1996; Sacks, 1989; Tyler, 1993). In fact, members of this cultural group can be assimilated with relative ease by any of the many deaf communities that exist throughout the country (Jankowski, 1991; Padden & Humphries, 1988). By contrast, members of this group are assimilated by the hearing world only with great effort (Higgins, 1983).

Conceiving members of the deaf population as a distinct cultural minority rather than as people who have the same handicap is useful and therapeutic in the sense that it shifts the focus of attention from deficit to the richness of Deaf culture (Lane, 1992).

Recall that *Deaf* in this context is spelled with a capital *D* to emphasize that the people so described really do share a common culture—as opposed to a medical condition (Padden, 1980; Padden & Humphries, 1988; Woodward, 1972). Members of the Deaf culture tend to be held in high esteem by others who also identify themselves as culturally Deaf (Phillips, 1996). Let's also point out that many members of the culture see themselves as multicultural in that they are members of more than one minority culture. The resulting multicultural issues to be considered in clinical assessment, as well as intervention, can be complex (Akamatsu, 1993–1994; Anderson & Grace, 1991; Christensen & Delgado, 1993; Cohen et al., 1990; Eldredge, 1993; Freeman, 1989; Rodriguez & Santiviago, 1991).

The need for sensitivity   Throughout this book, we have referred to the need for culturally informed assessment and sensitivity in the assessment of people from cultures with which an assessor may have little or no acquaintance. Much of what we have said in this context seems eminently applicable to the assessment of people with disabilities. People from different cultures may view or understand certain experiences in different ways and interpret them against backdrops of widely varying cultural wisdoms. These people may act in ways that seem odd, even pathological, from one's own cultural perspective. For example, in Deaf culture, it is critically important to gain eye contact before communication can proceed—this because communication is very much a visual, not an aural, medium. Consequently, the rules in Deaf culture for attention getting and turn taking in conversation are quite different from the rules for the broader society (Phillips, 1996). Culturally accepted ways of gaining visual attention include firmly tapping the hand of the person with whom one wishes to communicate or, if out of reach, waving one's hand to attract attention. Such behavior may strike a nonaccustomed individual as odd but is very much everyday in Deaf culture.

It is incumbent upon mental health professionals to avoid culture-related pitfalls in assessment and treatment. One such pitfall derives from reflexive adherence to one's own cultural truths while giving insufficient consideration to the world as seen through the eyes of people from diverse backgrounds, including people with disabling conditions.

Self-Assessment

Test your understanding of elements of this chapter by seeing if you can explain each of the following terms, expressions, and abbreviations:

AAMR
accommodation
accommodation by alternate
    assessment
ADA
adaptive behavior
Americans with Disabilities Act
    of 1990
at-risk infant or toddler
    (according to IDEA)
biopsychosocial assessment

child aged 3 through 9 with a disability (according to IDEA)
child with a disability (in general, according to IDEA)
cognitive disability
developmental delay
disability (ADA definition)
disability as a diversity issue
Education for All Handicapped
    Children Act
functional disability

fatalism
hired gun
IDEA
Individuals with Disabilities
    Education Act Amendments
    of 1997
infant or toddler with a disability
intensity of support (in AAMR
    definition)
issues in alternate assessment

major life activity (as implied in ADA)
medical model of disability
new paradigm of disability
perceived disability case
Public Law 94-142
Public Law 99-457
Public Law 101-336
Public Law 101-476
Public Law 105-17
QUID
Rehabilitation Act of 1973
sample accommodations for cognitive disabilities
sample accommodations for hearing disabilities
sample accommodations for motor disabilities
sample accommodations for visual disabilities
self-efficacy
social model of disability
social support
the Vineland

Web Watch

Check out the following Web sites for more information about topics discussed in this chapter.

Rehabilitation Act
www.section508.gov

IDEA
www.ed.gov/offices/OSERS/Policy/IDEA/index.html

www.ideapractices.org

The Americans with Disabilities Act of 1990
www.usdoj.gov/crt/ada/adahom1.htm

AAMR
www.aamr.org

Callier-Azusa Scale
www.callier.utdallas.edu/scale.html

www.winfssi.com/history.html

Developmental delay
www.devdelay.org

www.med.umich.edu/1libr/yourchild/devdel.htm

New Freedom Initiative
www.whitehouse.gov/news/freedominitiative/freedominitiative.html

QUID
www.wierlaw.com/glossary%20employment%20law.htm#americansdisabilities

16

Assessment, Careers, and Business

What do you want to be when you grow up?

It seems just yesterday that we were asked that question. For some of us, it really *was* just yesterday.

Questions and concerns about career choice are not uncommon among college students and others contemplating a transition from student to member of the workforce (Collins, 1998). And such questions and concerns are by no means limited to people initially contemplating the world of work. Millions of Americans already established in careers are contemplating career changes (Heppner et al., 1994).

Professionals involved in career counseling have hundreds of tools at their disposal to help their clients identify what work they might succeed at and enjoy doing. In this chapter, we look at some of those tools, as well as a wide variety of related instruments and procedures. You may be intrigued by some of the measures we discuss for use in the career choice process. If that's the case, we encourage you to obtain firsthand experience with them. Later in the chapter, many of the measures we discuss are designed for use by businesses or other organizations in the service of various organizational objectives.

Let's begin with a look at some of the types of instruments used to assist in career choice and career transition.

> **JUST THINK . . .**
>
> How do you think most people decide on their careers? What factors entered (or will enter) into your own career decision?

Career Choice and Career Transition

A whole world of tests is available to help in various phases of career choice. There are tests to survey interests, aptitudes, skills, or special talents. There are tests to measure attitudes toward work, confidence in one's skills, assumptions about careers, perceptions regarding career barriers, even dysfunctional career thoughts.. There is an instrument designed to measure psychological resources of adults in career transition (Heppner, 1998), and one to identify students who are undecided about career objectives (Larson & Majors, 1998). Variables thought to be important in occupational choice range from

Figure 16–1
It's Not Just a Job, It's an Adventure!

Had Orin Scrivello, D.D.S. (Steve Martin) in the comedy Little Shop of Horrors *taken an interest survey, the results might have been quite bizarre. As a child, young Orin's interests leaned toward bashing the heads of pussycats, shooting puppies with a BB gun, and poisoning guppies. He was able to put what his mother described as his "natural tendencies" to use in gainful employment: He became a dentist.*

whether one is a "people person" (Roe & Klos, 1969) to whether a particular work environment brings out the best in a particular worker (Moos, 1986).

Historically, one variable considered closely related to occupational fulfillment and success is personal interests. It stands to reason that what intrigues, engages, and engrosses would be good to work at. In fact, an individual's interests may be sufficiently solidified by age 15 so as to be useful in course and career planning (Care, 1996). Further, evidence suggests that these interests will be fairly stable over time (Savickas & Spokane, 1999). So, what are some measures of interest, and how are they used by assessment professionals?

Measures of Interest

Assuming that interest in one's work promotes better performance, greater productivity, and greater job satisfaction, both employers and prospective employees should have much to gain from methods that can help individuals identify their interests and jobs tailored to those interests. Using such methods, individuals can discover, for example, whether their interests lie in commanding a starship and "seeking new worlds and exploring new civilizations," or more along the lines of dentistry (Figure 16–1).

Employers can use information about their employees' interest patterns to formulate job descriptions and attract new personnel. For example, a company could design an employment campaign emphasizing job security, if job security were found to be the chief interest of the successful workers currently holding similar jobs. Although there are many instruments designed to measure interests, our discussion focuses on the one with the longest history of continuous use, the Strong Interest Inventory (SII).

◆

JUST THINK . . .

Visualize an employer's "want ad" that begins "Wanted: Employees interested in _____." Fill in the blank with each and every one of your own interests. Next, list the possible positions for which this employer might be advertising.

The Strong Interest Inventory One of the first measures of interest was published in 1907 by psychologist G. Stanley Hall. His questionnaire was designed to assess children's interest in various recreational pursuits. It was not until the early 1920s that Edward K. Strong, Jr., inspired by a seminar he attended on the measurement of interest, began a program of systematic investigation in this area. His efforts culminated in a 420-item test originally called the Strong Vocational Interest Blank (SVIB).

Originally designed for use with men only, the SVIB was published with a test manual by Stanford University Press in 1928 and then revised in 1938. In 1935, a 410-item SVIB for women was published, along with a test manual. The women's SVIB was revised in 1946. Both the men's and the women's SVIB were again revised in the mid-1960s. Amid concern about sex-specific forms of the test in the late 1960s and early 1970s (McArthur, 1992), a merged form was published in 1974. Developed under the direction of David P. Campbell, the merged form was called the Strong-Campbell Interest Inventory (SCII). The test was revised in 1985 and again in 1994. Today, the test is called the Strong Interest Inventory (SII; Strong et al., 1985; Harmon et al., 1994). Although one form is used for both men and women, gender differences in patterns of interest can be expected (Fouad, 2002), as can gender differences in expressed confidence and self-efficacy in various areas (Rottinghaus et al., 2003).

Strong's recipe for test construction was empirical and straightforward: (1) Select hundreds of items that could conceivably distinguish the interests of a person by that person's occupation; (2) administer this rough cut of the test to several hundred people selected as representative of certain occupations or professions; (3) sort out which items seemed of interest to persons by occupational group, and discard items with no discriminative ability; and (4) construct a final version of the test that would yield scores describing how an examinee's pattern of interest corresponded to those of people actually employed in various occupations and professions. With such a test, college students majoring in psychology, for example, could see how closely their interests paralleled those of working psychologists. Presumably, if an individual's interests closely match psychologists' (in contrast to the interests of, say, tow truck operators), that individual would probably enjoy the work of a psychologist.

Test items, all written in multiple-choice format, probe personal preferences for school subjects, occupations, amusement, activities, and other variables. Respondents are also asked to describe themselves with statements (such as "win friends easily") by indicating *yes, no,* or *uncertain.* Each protocol is computer scored and interpreted, yielding information on the testtaker's personal style, basic interests, and other data useful in determining how similar or dissimilar the respondent's interests are to those of people holding a variety of jobs.

The standardization sample for the 1994 revision included an occupational reference group consisting of adults employed in 50 different occupations, and a general reference group. To qualify for membership in the occupational reference group, respondents must have reported that they liked their work and had been employed at it for at least three years. The general reference group served as a kind of control group, selected to represent men and women in general. Minorities were represented in both the occupational and general reference groups. One study of the criterion-related validity of the SII across racial-ethnic groups supported the use of the test with respondents from diverse cultural backgrounds, particularly college-educated respondents (Lattimore & Borgen, 1999). In general, the test is psychometrically sound.

JUST THINK . . .

Are people interested in things they do well? Or do people develop abilities in areas that interest them?

How well do interest measures predict the kind of work in which individuals will be successful and happy? In general, interest and aptitude measures correlate in a range of about .40 to .72 (Lam et al., 1993). In one of the few studies examining the accuracy with which interest and aptitude tests predict future job performance and satisfaction, Bizot and Goldman (1993) identified people who had been tested in high school with measures of vocational interest and aptitude. Eight years later, these individuals reported on their satisfaction with their jobs, even permitting the researchers to contact their employers for information about the quality of their work.

The researchers found that when a good match existed between a subject's aptitude in high school and the level of his or her current job, performance was likely to be evaluated positively by the employer. When a poor match existed between a subject's aptitude as measured in high school and current job level, a poor performance rating by the employer was more likely. The extent to which employees were satisfied with their jobs was not related to aptitudes as measured in high school. As for predictive validity, the interest tests administered in high school predicted neither job performance nor job satisfaction eight years later. The results of this and related studies (for example, Jagger et al., 1992) sound a caution to counselors regarding overreliance on interest inventories. Still, this genre of test seems to bring a dimension to vocational counseling not provided by many other tests.

Other interest inventories   In addition to the SII, many other interest inventories are now in widespread use, and there is overlap in what they measure (Savickas et al. 2002). The Self-Directed Search explores interests within the context of Holland's (1997) theory of vocational personality types and work environments. According to that theory, vocational choice is an expression of one of six personality types: Realistic, Investigative, Artistic, Social, Enterprising, or Conventional (variously shortened to RIASEC and **Big Six**). Interestingly, in one study of high school students who completed both a paper-and-pencil and online version of the Self-Directed Search, the Realistic, Social, and Enterprising scales were found to be higher for the online administration, whereas the three other scales were not statistically different (Barak & Cohen, 2002). This finding might prompt further exploration of possible differences between online and paper-and-pencil administration of interest inventories.

The Minnesota Vocational Interest Inventory is an empirically keyed instrument designed to compare respondents' interest patterns with those of persons employed in a variety of nonprofessional occupations (such as stock clerks, painters, printers, truck drivers). A number of interest tests designed for use with people who do not read well use drawings and other visual media such as slides and filmstrips (Elksnin & Elksnin, 1993). A listing of various measures of interest is presented in Table 16–1.

Some research suggests that measures of interest may have more utility, meaning, or validity when used in combination with other measures such as measures of confidence and self-efficacy (Chartrand et al., 2002; Rottinghaus et al., 2003), personality (Larson & Borgen, 2002; Staggs et al., 2003), or a portfolio project (Larkin et al., 2002). In fact, the trend is toward unifying many of these constructs, as noted by Spokane and Decker (1999): "It is increasingly apparent that interests, personality, self-efficacy, and other

Table 16–1
Some Measures of Interest

Test	Description
Campbell Interest and Skill Survey	Developed by David Campbell, who revised the Strong Interest Inventory, this instrument focuses on occupations that require four or more years of postsecondary education. In addition to assessing interests, it is designed to provide an estimate of the individual's confidence in performing various occupational activities.
Career Interest Inventory	Designed for use with students in grades 7 through 12 as well as adults, this test introduces testtakers to the world of occupational and educational alternatives. In addition to career-related interests, the test taps interest in school subjects and school-related activities.
Guidance Information System (GIS 3.0)	Available only on disk or CD-ROM, this combination assessment instrument and information retrieval system contains a number of components ranging from information on colleges to information on the types of jobs college majors in different areas tend to get. The interest assessment component of the system is called the Career Decision-Making System. After probing the assessee's interests, interest scores are calculated, and the system provides lists of suggested careers and occupations to explore.
Jackson Vocational Interest Survey	This is a forced-choice measure of interests as they relate to 26 work roles (what one does at work) and 8 work styles (the type of work environment preferred, usually related to one's personal values). Designed for use with high school and college students, the test yields scores on ten Holland-like themes, as well as validity-related indices. The development of this test has been described in detail by Jackson (1977; Jackson & Williams, 1975).
Kuder Occupational Interest Survey (KOIS)	This classic interest-measuring instrument is an outgrowth of the Kuder Preference Survey, which was originally published in 1939. Each item presents testtakers with three choices of activity, and their task is to select their most and least preferred choices. Scores are reported in terms of magnitude of interest in various occupational categories. The test has been criticized for its lack of predictive validity, an assertion that has been addressed by the test's author and his colleagues (Kuder et al. 1998; Zytowski, 1996).
Reading-Free Vocational Interest Inventory (R-FVII)	Designed for use with people 10 years of age and older with learning disabilities, mental retardation, or other special needs, this test measures vocational likes and dislikes using pictures of people at work in different occupations. For each item, respondents select one of three drawings depicting the preferred job task. The protocol yields scores on 11 occupational categories that represent types of occupations at which members of special populations might be employed.
Self-Directed Search-Form R	Developed by John L. Holland, this is a self-administered, self-scored, and self-interpreted interest inventory appropriate for use by individuals 12 years of age and older. Form-R (1994) contains updated norms. Testtakers complete a booklet in which they are asked questions about various interest-related areas, including activities, aspirations, and competencies.

variants of personality and vocational self-concept may be facets of a unified set of complex underlying traits" (p. 230).

Recently, a group of researchers took the well-worn interest construct and "kicked it up a notch" by discussing it in terms of *passion* (Vallerand et al., 2003). They distinguished between two types, *obsessive passion* and *harmonious passion*. Both types were conceived of as deriving from internal pressure to engage in activity one likes. However, whereas harmonious passion was seen as promoting healthy adaptation, obsessive passion was seen as derailing it. Obsessive passion leads to rigid persistence, which in turn produces negative affect. It will be interesting to see the extent to which *passion* enters the vocabulary of career development researchers in the future.

Measures of Ability and Aptitude

As we saw in Chapter 10, achievement, ability, and aptitude tests measure prior learning to some degree, but they differ in the uses to which the test data will be put. Beyond that, aptitude tests may tap a greater amount of informal learning than achievement tests. Achievement tests may be more limited and focused than aptitude tests.

Figure 16–2
The O'Connor Tweezer Dexterity Test

Ability and aptitude measures vary widely in topics covered, specificity of coverage, and other variables. The Wonderlic Personnel Test measures mental ability in a general sense. This brief (12-minute) test includes items that assess spatial skill, abstract thought, and mathematical skill. The test may be useful in screening individuals for jobs that require both fluid and crystallized intellectual abilities (Bell et al., 2002).

The Bennet Mechanical Comprehension Test is a widely used paper-and-pencil measure of a testtaker's ability to understand the relationship between physical forces and various tools (for example, pulleys and gears) as well as other common objects (carts, steps, and seesaws). Other mechanical tests, such as the Hand-Tool Dexterity Test, blur the lines among aptitude, achievement, and performance tests by requiring the testtaker actually to take apart, reassemble, or otherwise manipulate materials, usually in a prescribed sequence within a time limit. If a job consists mainly of securing tiny transistors into the inner workings of an electronic appliance or game, then the employer's focus of interest might well be on prospective employees' perceptual-motor abilities, finger dexterity, and related variables. In such an instance, the O'Connor Tweezer Dexterity Test might be the instrument of choice (Figure 16–2). This test requires the examinee to insert brass pins into a metal plate using a pair of tweezers.

A number of other tests are designed to measure specific aptitudes for a wide variety of occupational fields. For the professions, a number of psychometrically sophisticated assessment programs exist to screen or select applicants by means of aptitude tests. An extensive list of these tests, such as the Medical College Admissions Test (MCAT), was presented in Chapter 10. For a while, one of the most widely used aptitude tests was the General Aptitude Test Battery (GATB). A description of that test, as well as the controversy surrounding it, follows.

> **JUST THINK . . .**
>
> What types of "real-world" tasks might be on a new aptitude test designed to select candidates for admission to a graduate program in psychological testing and assessment?

The General Aptitude Test Battery   The United States Employment Service (USES) developed the General Aptitude Test Battery (GATB) and first put it into use in 1947 after extensive research and development. The GATB (pronounced like "Gatsby" without the *s*) is available for use by state employment services as well as other agencies and organizations, such as school districts and nonprofit organizations, that have obtained official permission from the government to administer the test. The GATB is a tool used to identify aptitudes for occupations, and it is a test just about anyone of working age can take. The test is administered regularly at local state offices (referred to by names such as the Job Service, Employment Security Commission, and Labor Security Commission) to people who want the agency to help find them a job. It may also be administered to people who are unemployed and have been referred by a state office of unemployment, or to employees of a company that has requested such aptitude assessment.

If you are curious about your own aptitude for work in fields as diverse as psychology, education, and plumbing, you may want to visit your local state employment office and sample the GATB yourself. Be prepared to sit for an examination that will take about three hours if you take the entire test. The GATB consists of 12 timed tests that measure nine aptitudes that in turn can be divided into three composite aptitudes. About half the time will be spent on psychomotor tasks and the other half on paper-and-pencil tasks. In some instances, depending on factors such as the reason for the assessment, only selected tests of the battery will be administered. The version of the test used to selectively measure aptitudes for a specific line of work is referred to as a Special Aptitude Test Battery, or SATB. SATB data may also be isolated for study from other test data when the entire test is taken.

The GATB has evolved from a test with multiple cutoffs to one that employs regression and *validity generalization* for making recommendations based on test results. The rationale and process by which the GATB has made this evolution has been described by John E. Hunter (1980, 1986), Frank Schmidt, and their associates (Hunter & Schmidt, 1983; Hunter et al., 1982; Hunter & Hunter, 1984); validity generalization is the subject of our chapter *Close-up.*

In the past, recommendations with respect to aptitude for a particular job had been made on the basis of GATB validity studies bearing on specific jobs. For example, if there existed 500 job descriptions covering 500 jobs for which scores on the GATB were to be applied, there would be 500 individual validation studies with the GATB—one validation study for each individual job, typically with a relatively small sample size (many of these single studies containing only 76 subjects on average). Further, there were no validation studies for the other 12,000-plus jobs in the American economy (according to the *Dictionary of Occupational Titles* published by the United States Department of Labor, 1977).

Using meta-analysis to cumulate results across a number of validation studies and statistically correct for error such as sampling error, Hunter demonstrated that all the jobs could be categorized within five families of jobs, based on the *worker function codes* of the *Dictionary of Occupational Titles.* The five families of jobs are (1) Setting Up, (2) Feeding and Off-Bearing, (3) Synthesizing and Coordinating, (4) Analyzing, Compiling, and Computing, and (5) Copying and Comparing. Regression equations for each of the families were then developed; using these equations, Hunter found that recommendations for individual testtakers could be generalized to various jobs.

In the late 1980s, the GATB became a center of controversy when it became public knowledge that the test had been race-normed. Discussed in Chapter 4, race-norming refers to the process of adjusting scores to show an individual testtaker's standing within his or her own racial group. With the race-normed GATB, high scorers who were categorized within certain groups according to race were recommended for employment.

Validity Generalization and the GATB

Can a test validated for use in personnel selection for one occupation also be valid for use in personnel selection for another occupation? Must the validation of a test used in personnel selection be situation specific? Stated more generally, can validity evidence for a test meaningfully be applied to situations other than those in which the evidence was obtained? These are the types of questions raised when validity generalization is discussed.

As applied to employment-related decision making on the basis of test scores achieved on the General Aptitude Test Battery (GATB), *validity generalization* refers to the fact that the same test-score data may be predictive of aptitude for all jobs; the implication is that if a test is validated for a few jobs selected from a much larger cluster of jobs—each requiring similar skills at approximately the same level of complexity—the test is valid for all jobs in that cluster. For example, if a validation study conclusively indicated that GATB scores are predictive of aptitude for (and ultimately proficiency in) the occupation of assembler in an aircraft assembly plant, an entirely new validation study may not be needed to apply such data to the occupation of assembler in a shipbuilding plant; if the type and level of skill required in the two occupations can be shown to be sufficiently similar, it may be that the same or similar procedures used to select aircraft assemblers can profitably be used to select assemblers of ships.

Validity generalization (VG) as applied to personnel selection using the GATB makes unnecessary the burden of conducting a separate validation study with the test for every one of the more than 12,000 jobs in the American economy. The application of VG to GATB scores also enables GATB users to supply employers with more precise information about testtakers. To understand why this is so, let's begin by consulting the pie chart in Figure 1.

Note that the inner circle of the chart lists the 12 tests in the General Aptitude Test Battery and the next ring of the circle lists eight aptitudes derived from the 12 tests. Not illustrated here is a ninth aptitude, General Learning Ability, which is derived from scores on the Vocabulary, Arithmetic Reasoning, and Three-Dimensional Space tests. A brief description of each of the eight aptitudes measured by the GATB follows:

- *Verbal Aptitude* (V): Understanding the meaning of words and their relationships and using words effectively are two of the abilities tapped here. V is measured by Test 4.

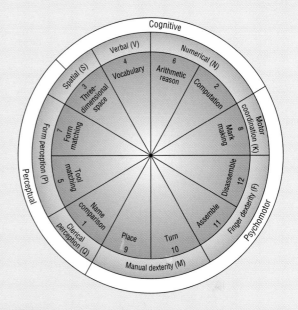

Figure 1
Aptitudes Measured by the General Aptitude Test Battery

- *Numerical Aptitude* (N): N is measured by tasks requiring the quick performance of arithmetic operations. It is measured by Tests 2 and 6.

- *Spatial Aptitude* (S): The ability to visualize and mentally manipulate geometric forms is tapped here. S is measured by Test 3.

- *Form Perception* (P): Attention to detail, including the ability to discriminate slight differences in shapes, shading, lengths, and widths, as well as the ability to perceive pertinent detail, is measured. P is measured by Tests 5 and 7.

- *Clerical Perception* (Q): Attention to detail in written or tabular material, as well as the ability to proofread words and numbers and to avoid perceptual errors in arithmetic computation, is tapped here. Q is measured by Test 1.

- *Motor Coordination* (K): This test taps the ability to quickly make precise movements that require eye-hand coordination. K is measured by Test 8.

- *Finger Dexterity* (F): This test taps the ability to quickly manipulate small objects with the fingers. F is measured by Tests 11 and 12.

- *Manual Dexterity* (M): The ability to work with one's hands in placing and turning motions is measured here. M is measured by Tests 9 and 10.

(*continued*)

Validity Generalization and the GATB
(*continued*)

In the outermost ring of the diagram, note that the three composite aptitudes can be derived from the nine specific aptitudes: a Cognitive composite, a Perceptual composite, and a Psychomotor composite. The nine aptitudes that compose the three composite aptitudes may be summarized as follows:

The Nine GATB Aptitudes		The Three Composite Scores
G	General Learning Ability (also referred to as *intelligence*)	
V	Verbal Aptitude	Cognitive
N	Numerical Aptitude	
S	Spatial Aptitude	
P	Form Perception	Perceptual
Q	Clerical Perception	
K	Motor Coordination	
F	Finger Dexterity	Psychomotor
M	Manual Dexterity	

Traditionally—before the advent of VG—testtakers who sat for the GATB might subsequently receive counseling about their performance in each of the nine aptitude areas. Further, they might have been informed (1) how their own pattern of GATB scores compared with patterns of aptitude (referred to as Occupational Aptitude Patterns, or OAPs) deemed necessary for proficiency in various occupations, and (2) how they performed with respect to any of the 467 constellations of a Special Aptitude Test Battery (SATB) that could potentially be extracted from a GATB protocol. VG provides additional information useful in advising prospective employers and counseling prospective employees, including more precise data on a testtaker's performance with respect to OAPs, as well as scores (usually expressed in percentiles) with respect to the five job families.

Research (Hunter, 1982) has indicated that the three composite aptitudes can be used to validly predict job proficiency for all jobs in the United States economy. All jobs may be categorized according to five job families, and the aptitude required for each of these families can be described with respect to various contributions of the three composite GATB scores. For example, Job Family 1 (Set-up Jobs) is 59% Cognitive, 30% Perceptual, and 11% Psychomotor.

GATB scoring is done by computer, as is weighting of scores to determine suitability for employment in each of the five job families.

Proponents of VG as applied to use with the GATB list the following advantages:

1. *The decreased emphasis on multiple cutoffs as a selection strategy has advantages for both prospective employers and prospective employees.* In a multiple cutoff selection model, a prospective employee would have to achieve certain minimum GATB scores in each of the aptitudes deemed critical for proficiency in a given occupation; failure to meet the minimal cutting score in these aptitudes would mean elimination from the candidate pool for that occupation. Using VG, a potential benefit for the prospective employee is that the requirement of a minimum cutting score on any specific aptitude is eliminated. For employers, VG encourages the use of a top-down hiring policy, one in which the best-qualified people (as measured by the GATB) are offered jobs first.

2. *Research has suggested that the relationship between aptitude test scores and job performance is linear (Waldman & Avolio, 1989), a relationship statistically better suited to VG than to the multiple cutoff selection model.* The nature of the relationship between scores on a valid test of aptitude and ratings of job performance is illustrated in Figure 2. Given that such a relationship exists, Hunter (1980, 1982) notes that from a technical standpoint, linear data are better suited to analysis using a VG model than using a model with multiple cutoffs.

3. *More precise information can be reported to employers regarding a testtaker's relative standing in the continuum of aptitude test scores.* Consider in this context Figure 3, and let's suppose that an established and validated cutoff score for selection in a particular occupation using this hypothetical test of aptitude is 155. Examinee X and Examinee Y both meet the cutoff requirement, but Examinee Y is probably better qualified for the job—we say "probably" because there may be exceptions to this general rule, depending on variables such as the actual demands of the specific job. Although the score for Examinee X falls below the median score for all testtakers, the score for Examinee Y lies at the high end of the distribution of scores. All other factors being equal, which individual would you prefer to hire if you owned the company? Using a simple cutoff procedure, no distinction with respect to aptitude score would have been made between Examinee X and Examinee Y, provided both scores met the cutoff criterion.

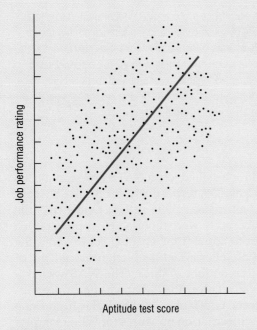

Figure 2
The Linear Relationship Between Aptitude Test Scores and Job Performance Ratings

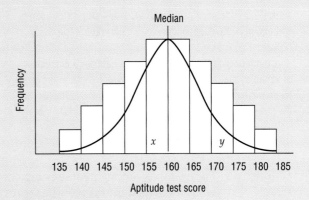

Figure 3
Results of a Hypothetical Aptitude Test

4. *VG better assists employers in their efforts to hire qualified employees.* Studies such as one conducted at the Philip Morris Company suggest that a significant increase in the rate of training success can be expected for employees hired using a selection procedure that uses VG, as compared with employees hired by other means (Warmke, 1984).

Is VG the answer to all personnel selection problems? Not at all. VG is simply one rationale for justifiably avoiding the time and expense of conducting a separate validation study for every single test with every possible group of test-takers under every possible set of circumstances—too often with too few subjects to achieve meaningful findings. Note, however, that with the convenience of VG come many concerns about the efficacy of the procedures employed. And although we have devoted a fair amount of time to acquainting you with this important concept in the personnel selection literature, it is equally important for you to be aware that a number of technical issues with respect to VG are currently being debated in the professional literature.

You will recall that in the development of VG as applied to personnel selection, Hunter and his colleagues used a process called meta-analysis to cumulate findings across a number of studies. One important aspect of this work involved statistically correcting for the small sample sizes that occurred in the studies analyzed. The types of procedures used in such a process, and the types of interpretations that legitimately can be made as a result, have been the subject of a number of critical analyses of VG. The amount of unexplained variance that remains even after statistical corrections for differences in sample size (Cascio, 1987), the unknown influence of a potential restriction-of-range problem with respect to subject self-selection (Cronbach, 1984), objections about using employer ratings as a criterion (Burke, 1984), and the fact that alternative models may explain variation in validity coefficients as well as the cross-situational consistency model (James et al., 1986) are some of the technical issues that have been raised with respect to the use of VG (see also Zedeck & Cascio, 1984). With specific reference to VG as applied to use with the GATB, one might inquire further: What problems arise when more than 12,000 occupations are grouped into five job families? Is it really meaningful to place an occupation such as truck driver in the same job family as secretary?

Clearly, much remains to be learned about how VG can most effectively be brought to bear on problems related to personnel testing. Difficult questions—some psychometric, others that relate more to societal values—will have to be

(continued)

Validity Generalization and the GATB
(*continued*)

addressed. A detailed critique of VG beginning with its logic and ending with its application can be found in Murphy (2003).

Compounding the task of fairly evaluating VG is a litany of variables that are neither psychometric in nature nor directly related to values. Included here are such variables as the strength of the economy, the size of the available labor pool, the experience of the available labor pool, the general desirability of specific jobs, and the salaries offered for various kinds of work. Whether one looks favorably or not at the government's experimentation with VG in personnel selection, it seems reasonable to assume that there is much to be learned in the process, and the field of personnel selection may ultimately profit from the experience.

For example, among people being considered for a skilled job, a GATB raw score of 300 was "translated into percentile scores of 79, 62, and 38, respectively, for Blacks, Hispanics, and others" (Gottfredson, 1994, p. 966). Only percentile scores and not raw scores were reported to employers.

In an attempt to address the ensuing controversy, the U.S. Department of Labor asked the National Academy of Sciences (NAS) to conduct a study. The NAS issued a report (Hartigan & Wigdor, 1989) that was generally supportive of race-norming. The NAS noted that the GATB appeared to suffer from slope bias such that the test correlated more highly with criterion measures for White samples (.19) than for Black samples (.12). Intercept bias was also present, with the result that the performance of Blacks would be more favorably predicted relative to the performance of Whites if the same regression line were used for both groups. The NAS found race-norming to be a reasonable method of correcting for the bias of the test.

The NAS report also addressed more general issues concerning the utility of the GATB as a predictor of job performance. Using a database of 755 studies, the NAS noted that the GATB correlated approximately .22 with criteria such as supervisory ratings. Others have estimated the test's validity to be .20 (Vevea et al., 1993) and .21 (Waldman & Avolio, 1989). These relatively small coefficients were viewed by the NAS as modest but acceptable. To understand why they were considered acceptable, recall from Chapter 6 that criterion validity is limited by the reliability of the measures. Although the GATB has adequate test-retest reliability (around .81), the likely poor reliability of supervisory ratings may depress the GATB's validity coefficient. Such depression of a validity coefficient could be expected to occur for any test designed to predict job performance that is validated against supervisors' ratings (Hartigan & Wigdor, 1989). Of course, even predictors with modest criterion validity can improve personnel selection decisions. Thus, despite the low criterion validity coefficients, the GATB is widely viewed as a valid means of selecting employees.

The NAS recommendation to continue the practice of race-norming the test may have done more to fan the flames of controversy than to quell them. In July 1990, the Department of Labor proposed a two-year suspension in the use of the GATB, during which time the efficacy of the test and its scoring procedures would be further researched. The legality of the practice of race-norming had also become a heated topic of debate by that time (Baydoun & Neuman, 1992; Delahunty, 1988). The question of

JUST THINK . . .

What are the pros and cons of race-norming an aptitude test?

whether race-norming of the GATB should continue became moot after Congress passed the Civil Rights Act of 1991, a law that made the practice of race-norming illegal.

Today, the GATB is still in use by the U.S. Employment Service. However, reports to employers are no longer race-normed. The raw scores of people from all racial groups are now converted to interpretable standard scores using the same norms. In addition to its potential applied value, the GATB remains a valuable resource for researchers in areas such as theory validation (see, for example, Farrell & McDaniel, 2001).

A driving passion—of the *harmonious* variety, we trust—has led those who conduct research in employment-related areas to search for predictors beyond interests and aptitude. Perhaps the long sought answers can be found in constructs such as *personality trait* or *personality type.*

Measures of Personality

Just thinking about the questions raised in our *Just Think . . .* feature compels one to consider the role of personality in career choice. When researchers consider such questions, they may seek answers in a study that includes the administration of a personality test. Although there are many personality tests, some will be more appropriate for the task at hand than others. For example, the MMPI-2, widely used in clinical settings, may have limited application in the context of career counseling. Other personality tests may be preferred, such as the Guilford-Zimmerman Temperament Survey and the Edwards Personal Preference Schedule, perhaps because the measurements they yield tend to be better related to the specific variables under study. Today, two of the most widely used personality tests in the workplace are the NEO PI-R (previously described in Chapter 11 and discussed at length in the companion workbook to this text) and the Myers-Briggs Type Indicator (MBTI). We discuss the MBTI, a tool for developing information on psychological type, after a brief discussion of studies that approach career- and occupation-related questions at the level of the trait.

Measuring personality traits Personality assessment in the context of employment-related research or counseling might begin with the administration of a test designed to measure Costa and McCrae's (1992c) Big Five, Tellegen's (1985) **Big Three,** Holland's *Big Six,* or some other (Big, Little, or Nothing-So-Special) number of traits or types according to a particular conceptualization of personality.[1] The researchers will then analyze the personality test data as they compare to other job- or career-related variables. A sampling of such "other job- or career-related variables" from the research literature would include

- managerial potential (Lillibridge & Williams, 1992) and leadership ability (Judge & Bono, 2000)
- on-the-job performance motivation (Judge & Ilies, 2002)
- absence, lateness, and supervisory performance ratings (Conte & Jacobs, 2003),

---

1. Holland (1999) made clear that for him, interest inventories *are* personality inventories. For this reason, it is appropriate to mention Holland's work in discussing interest or personality assessment as an aid to career counseling.

- job satisfaction (Furnham et al., 2002)
- career success (Seibert & Kraimer, 2001)
- the degree to which an organization is attractive to applicants (Lievens et al., 2001)
- the degree to which activities in sales jobs are attractive to applicants (Stevens & Macintosh, 2003)

Most of the research cited above employed Costa and McCrae's (1992c) NEO PI-R. In fact, this test probably is the most widely used today. There are, however, more specialized types of instruments that also fall under the general heading of personality test. For example, we may speak of an **integrity test,** specifically designed to predict employee theft, honesty, adherence to established procedures, and/or potential for violence. Such narrowly defined personality tests used in the context of employment-related research and practice have been characterized as *criterion-focused occupational personality scales,* COPS for short (Ones & Viswesvaran, 2001).

Integrity tests may be used to screen new employees as well as to keep honest those already hired. The use of such tests has increased dramatically with the passage of legislation prohibiting the use of polygraphs (lie detectors) in most employment settings. The trend is away from lengthy paper-and-pencil questionnaires toward measures that can be administered quickly and efficiently electronically. One such measure is the Applicant Potential Inventory (API), which can be administered by computer (online or offline), telephone, and fax. Jones et al. (2002) described the development of this test as well as research designed to explore its psychometric soundness.

Sackett et al. (1989) dichotomized integrity tests into *overt integrity tests* (which may straightforwardly ask the examinee questions like "Do you always tell the truth?"), and *personality-based measures,* which resemble in many ways objective personality inventories such as the MMPI. Items on the latter type of test may be far more subtle than on the former. Also, responses to items on the personality-based measures are less likely to be interpreted on the basis of the face validity of the item and more likely to be interpreted with reference to the responses of groups of people known to have or lack integrity, as defined by the particular test.

Whether integrity tests measure what they purport to measure is debatable. Reviews of the validity of such measures have ranged from mixed (APA, 1991; Sackett & Harris, 1984; Sackett et al., 1989) to positive (DePaulo, 1994; Honts, 1994; Sackett, 1994; Saxe, 1994). Perhaps the fairest conclusion from this literature is that when the test has been professionally developed, it stands an excellent chance of meeting acceptable standards of validity. *Model Guidelines for Preemployment Integrity Testing Programs,* a document developed by the Association of Personnel Test Publishers (APTP, 1990), addresses many of the issues surrounding integrity tests, including issues relating to test development, administration, scoring, interpretation, confidentiality, public statements regarding the tests, and test-marketing practices. Specific guidelines in these areas are provided, and the responsibilities of test users and publishers are discussed (see Jones et al., 1990, for an overview).

Beyond issues regarding the validity of integrity tests lie broader questions about various aspects of the use of such tests (Camara & Schneider, 1994). For example, is privacy invaded when a prospective employee is asked to sit for such a test? Can such tests be used to support discrimination practices? Should such tests be used alone or in combination with other measurement procedures as a basis for granting or denying employment? Interestingly, White (1984) suggests that pre-employment honesty testing may induce negative work-related attitudes. Having to undergo such a test may be interpreted by prospective employees as evidence of high levels of employee theft—paradoxically resulting in a new and higher norm of stealing by employees.

Figure 16–3
A Mother-Daughter Team of Test Developers

Katharine Cook Briggs (left) and Isabel Briggs Myers (right) created the Myers-Briggs Type Indicator.
Katharine developed an interest in individual differences in 1915 upon being introduced to her future
son-in-law, Clarence Myers. For Katharine, Clarence seemed different in fundamental ways from other
members of the Briggs family. Owing in part to a desire to better understand these differences, Katharine
created a category of psychological types. Years later, Isabel would put her mother's ideas to the test—
literally.

Measuring personality types   How could anyone have foreseen in 1915 that the prospect
of having Clarence Myers as a son-in-law would eventually lead Katharine Cook Briggs
(Figure 16–3) down a path that would culminate in the creation of an enduring measure
of personality type?

From a psychometric perspective, the test has earned mixed reviews. A meta-
analysis of published studies did indicate that the test and its scales tended to be internally consistent and stable over time, although some variations were observed (Capraro
& Capraro, 2002). Still, many assessment professionals have expressed serious concerns
about the MBTI on psychometric and related grounds (Arnau et al., 2003; Girelli & Stake,
1993; Harvey & Murry, 1994; Lorr, 1991; Martin & Bartol, 1986; Pittenger, 1993; Vacha-
Haase & Thompson, 2002; Zumbo & Taylor, 1993). Regardless of such criticism, the test
remains very popular, especially among counselors and organizational consultants. References to it in the recent literature, for example, show it being used to derive profiles of
typical workers in various occupations, such as software engineers (Capretz, 2003), and
to validate a new pre-employment measure of "job fit" (Piotrowski & Armstrong, 2002).
In other sorts of applications, it has been used to explore phenomena as diverse as suicidality (Janowsky et al., 2002), celebrity worship (McCarley & Escoto, 2003), and effective

Isabel Briggs Myers and her mother, Katharine Cook Briggs, two women with no
formal training in psychology or assessment, were inspired by the writings of Carl Jung
(1923) and his ideas about different psychological types. In part, that inspiration was instrumental in the creation of the MBTI (Myers & Briggs, 1943/1962), a test used to classify assessees by psychological type and to shed light on "basic differences in the ways
human beings take in information and make decisions" (McCaulley, 2000, p. 117).

teaching of gifted students (Mills, 2003). A more detailed description of the MBTI can be found in the companion workbook to this textbook (Cohen, 2005) as well as in many published articles (see, for example, Furnham et al., 2003; McCaulley, 2000, 2002; Myers & Carskadon, 2002).

Before leaving the subject of personality assessment in the world of work, let's mention an intriguing line of research that raised the question "Does the emotional disposition of children have anything to do with how satisfied they are with their jobs as adults?" If you think the question itself is somewhat surprising, hold on to your hats when we tell you that the answer to the question (a resounding *yes*) is even more surprising. Using data from three separate longitudinal studies, Staw et al. (1986) found that dispositional data obtained in infancy predicted job-related attitudes over a time span of some 50 years. Although the interpretation of the data in this study has been questioned, it generally has received support from other researchers (Arvey et al., 1989; House et al., 1996; Judge et al., 2000; Motowidlo, 1996). It may be that one's temperament mediates emotionally significant events, including those at work, which in turn influence one's level of job satisfaction (Weiss & Cropanzano, 1996).

JUST THINK . . .

From the perspective of an employer, might there be a "down side" to seeking one specific *type* of employee for a particular position?

Findings such as these have critics. More generally, the use of personality tests in any employment-related context has critics (see, for example, Ghiselli, 1973; Hollenbeck & Whitener, 1988; Kinslinger, 1966; Schmitt et al., 1984). Still, the majority of researchers in this area believe that valuable job- and career-related information can be developed through the study of the assessment of personality (Fontanna, 2000).

Other Measures

Numerous other tools of assessment may be used in career planning and pre-employment contexts, even though not specifically designed for that purpose. For example, the Checklist of Adaptive Living Skills (CALS; Morreau & Bruininks, 1991) surveys the life skills needed to make a successful transition from school to work. Organized into four broad domains (Personal Living Skills, Home Living Skills, Community Living Skills, and Employment Skills), this test evaluates 794 life skills. The checklist is designed for use with assessees of any age. According to the manual, the individual completing the checklist must have had the opportunity to observe the assessee for at least three months in natural settings. Assessees are judged to be *independent* with regard to a specific skill if they perform the task with good quality at least 75% of the time when needed and without reminder. This criterion-based instrument may be particularly useful in career and pre-employment counseling with members of special populations.

Researchers are interested in the role of culture in various aspects of assessment for employment (Blustein & Ellis, 2000; Hofstede, 1998; Leong & Hartung, 2000; Ponterotto et al., 2000; Rotundo & Sackett, 1999; Ryan et al., 2000; Sandoval et al., 1998; Subich, 1996). According to Meyers (1994), the fact that a new job can sometimes result in a kind of "culture shock" prompted the creation of an instrument called the Cross-Cultural Adaptability Inventory (CCAI; Kelley & Meyers, 1992). The CCAI is a self-administered and self-scored instrument designed to provide information on the testtaker's ability to adapt to other cultures. Testtakers respond to 50 items written in a 6-point Likert format. The test yields information about one's readiness to adapt to new situations, tolerate ambiguity, maintain one's personal identity in new surroundings, and interact with people from other cultures. The report is organized into information with regard to four factors thought to be relevant to cross-cultural adaptability: Emotional Resilience, Flexibility/Openness, Perceptual Acuity, and Personal Autonomy. The test may hold value in evaluating readiness to take a job or to be relocated overseas.

Table 16–2
Sample Questions Derived From Students' Beliefs and Assumptions

- What background, both educational and professional, is needed to enter this field?
- Briefly describe your career path and the steps you took to get here.
- What do you do on a typical day?
- In what industries and companies would such careers and jobs exist, or what industries and companies would be best for this career?
- What are the sources of stress in your job?
- If you could, what would you change about your job?
- How does one get started or break into this career or job?
- What kind of lifestyle does such a career or job provide or allow?
- What are the compensation range and benefits for this career or job?
- How often are you required to travel, and for what reasons do you travel?
- Would this type of career or job typically require relocation?
- Do you enjoy your work?
- What advancement opportunities are there for individuals in this field?
- Do you find your job or career satisfying and challenging?
- What special skills are required for a position like yours?
- What is the average number of hours worked in a typical work week?
- What types of skills are necessary to be successful in _____?
- What should I do or where should I go to acquire these needed skills?
- What is the most challenging aspect of your job?
- What is the most satisfying aspect of your job? What is the least satisfying aspect of your job?
- How would this career impact one's family?
- How important are grades?
- How is your performance evaluated?
- How does your career affect your life outside of work? Spouse? Social? Spiritual?
- What is the job market like in this particular professional area? What do you think it will be like 5–10 years from now?
- What recommendations would you make to me? What would you do if you were me?
- If you were me, who else would you suggest that I talk to? Why would you suggest that person? May I use your name in contacting that person?
- Describe your typical work week.

Source: Laker (2002). Reprinted by permission.

Perhaps one of the most important instruments of assessment relevant to a career decision can be a questionnaire devised by assessees themselves, one that is *not* designed for administration to a prospective employee. Rather, it is written by the assessee and designed for administration to a person established in the career the assessee is contemplating. Laker (2002) proposed that students contemplating career choice think of more than one career they would like to enter. Students should next identify resource persons already in those careers who can address the students' beliefs and assumptions about the nature of work life in that career. Such resource people can be identified by informal means such as "asking around," as well as more formally by the use of a reference work such as the *Encyclopedia of Associations* (Hunt, 2002). Find the association the desired resource person belongs to, and contact the association for help in identifying someone local who is willing to assist. In preparation for the meeting, students list their beliefs and assumptions about the career and then translate that list into questions, such as those presented in Table 16–2.

All the tools of assessment we have discussed up to this point have application not only in career entry but also in career transition. One test specifically designed for use with people contemplating a career change is the Career Transitions Inventory (CTI; Heppner et al., 1994). The purpose of this test is to assess psychological resources during the process of career transition. For the purposes of the test, *career transition* was operationally defined as *task change* (a shift to other types of tasks but essentially the same job), *position change* (a shift in jobs with the same employer), or *occupation change* (a shift in duties and work settings). The test authors presented evidence for the test's reliability as well as evidence they described as "promising" for the construct validity of this instrument.

Career transition is one variety of what could be referred to as *exit strategy* for a person in a particular career or business. Another type of exit strategy is retirement. The decision to retire is momentous and multifaceted—and one that has also been explored by means of instruments of assessment. A retirement decision should not be made on the basis of a single criterion such as global satisfaction or financial security (Parnes & Less, 1985). To persons considering retirement, counselors may offer assistance in the form of probing interviews, as well as the administration of various measures that assess life satisfaction, goal-directedness, leisure satisfaction, and interpersonal support. More specifically, the Goal Instability Scale (Robbins & Patton, 1985), the Life Satisfaction Index A (Neugarten et al., 1961), the Leisure Satisfaction Scale (Beard & Ragheb, 1980), and the Interpersonal Support Evaluations List (Cohen et al., 1985) are some of the instruments that may provide valuable data. Floyd et al. (1992) developed the Retirement Satisfaction Inventory to help assess adjustment to retirement.

JUST THINK . . .

How might data from personality tests be useful in counseling an individual who is contemplating retirement?

Tests and other tools of assessment may be used by businesses and other organizations to assist in staffing and other personnel-related decisions. Some of the issues in such decision making are discussed following.

Screening, Selection, Classification, and Placement

In the context of employment, **screening** refers to a relatively superficial process of evaluation based on certain minimal standards, criteria, or requirements. For example, a municipal fire department may screen for certain minimal requirements for height, weight, physical health, physical strength, and cognitive ability for admission to a training program for firefighters. The government may use a group-administered test of intelligence to screen out people unsuited for military service or to identify intellectually gifted recruits for special assignments.

Selection refers to a process whereby each person evaluated for a position will be either accepted or rejected for that position. By contrast, **classification** does not imply acceptance or rejection but rather a rating, categorization, or "pigeonholing" with respect to two or more criteria. The military, for example, classifies personnel with respect to security clearance on the basis of variables such as rank, personal history of political activity, and known associations. As a result of such evaluations, one individual might be granted access to documents labeled *Secret,* whereas another individual might be granted access to documents labeled *Top Secret.*

Like classification, *placement* need not carry any implication of acceptance or rejection. **Placement** is a disposition, transfer, or assignment to a group or category that may be made on the basis of one criterion. If, for example, you took a college-level course while still in high school, the score you earned on the advanced placement test in that subject area may have been the sole criterion used to place you in an appropriate section of that college course upon your acceptance to college.

Businesses, academic institutions, the military, and other organizations regularly screen, select, classify, or place individuals. A wide array of tests can be used as aids to decision making. Measures of ability, aptitude, interest, and personality may all be of value, depending on the demands of the particular decision. In the high-profile world of

Table 16–3
Checklist for an Application Form Item

1. Is the item necessary for identifying the applicant?
2. Is it necessary for screening out those who are ineligible under the company's basic hiring policies?
3. Does it help to decide whether the candidate is qualified?
4. Is it based on analysis of the job or jobs for which applicants will be selected?
5. Has it been pretested on the company's employees and found to correlate with success?
6. Will the information be used? How?
7. Is the application form the proper place to ask for it?
8. To what extent will answers duplicate information to be obtained at another step in the selection procedure—for example, through interviews, tests, or medical examinations?
9. Is the information needed for selection at all, or should it be obtained at induction or even later?
10. Is it probable that the applicants' replies will be reliable?
11. Does the question violate any applicable federal or state legislation?

Source: Ahern (1949)

professional sports, where selection errors can be extremely costly, psychological tests may be used to help assess whether a new draft choice player will live up to his or her potential (Gardner, 2001). Of course, for more everyday types of employment decision making, and especially at the pre-employment stage, some of the most common tools of assessment include the letter of application and the résumé, the job application form, the letter of recommendation, and the interview.

The Résumé and the Letter of Application

There is no single, standard résumé; résumés can be "as unique as the individuals they represent" (Cohen, 1994, p. 394). Typically, information related to one's work objectives, qualifications, education, and experience is included on a résumé. A companion cover letter to a résumé, called a letter of application, lets a job applicant demonstrate motivation, businesslike writing skills, and his or her unique personality. Neither a résumé nor a letter of application is likely to be the sole vehicle through which employment is secured. At best, both of these documents are stepping-stones to personal interviews or other evaluation situations. On the other hand, the employer, the personnel psychologist, or some other individual reading the applicant's résumé and cover letter may use these documents as a basis for rejecting an application. The cover letter and the résumé may be analyzed for details such as quality of written communication, perceived sincerity, and appropriateness of the applicant's objectives, education, motivation, and prior experience with regard to the available position. From the perspective of the evaluator, much the same is true of another common tool of assessment in employment settings, the application form.

The Application Form

Application forms may be thought of as biographical sketches that supply employers with information pertinent to the acceptability of job candidates. In addition to demographic information (such as name, address, and telephone number), pertinent details about other areas, such as educational background, military service, and previous work experience, may be requested. Some classic questions relevant to a traditional application form are presented in Table 16–3. The guiding philosophy is that each item in the form be relevant to consideration for employment. The application form is a highly useful tool for quick screening in numerous settings.

Letters of Recommendation

Another tool useful in the preliminary screening of applicants is the letter of recommendation (Arvey, 1979; Glueck, 1978). Such letters may be a unique source of detailed information about the applicant's past performance, the quality of the applicant's relationships with peers, and so forth. Of course, such letters are not without their drawbacks. It is no secret that applicants solicit letters from those they believe will say only positive things about them. Another possible drawback to letters of recommendation is the variance in the observational and writing skills of the letter writers.

JUST THINK . . .

Put yourself in the position of an employer. Now discuss how much "weight" you assign letters of recommendation relative to test data and other information about the applicant. Explain the basis of your "weightings."

In research that employed application files for admission to graduate school in psychology, it was found that an applicant might variously be described as "analytically oriented, reserved, and highly motivated" or "free-spirited, imaginative, and outgoing," depending on the letter writer's perspective. As the authors of that study pointed out, "Although favorable recommendations may be intended in both cases, the details of and bases for such recommendations are varied" (Baxter et al., 1981, p. 300). Efforts to minimize the drawbacks inherent in the open-ended letter of recommendation have sometimes taken the form of "questionnaires of recommendation" wherein former employers, professors, and other letter writers respond to structured questions concerning the applicant's prior performance. Some questionnaires employ a forced-choice format designed to force respondents to make negative as well as positive statements about the applicant.

Although originally written to provide a prospective employer with an opinion about an applicant, some letters of reference now serve the function of an archival record—one that provides a glimpse of an unfortunate chapter of American history and the prevailing prejudices of an era. Winston (1996, 1998) documented how letters of reference written by prominent psychologists in the United States for Jewish psychology students and psychologists during the 1920s through the 1950s followed a common practice of identifying the job candidates as Jews. The letters went on to disclose whether or not, in the letter-writers' opinion, the candidate evidenced the "objectionable traits" thought to characterize Jews. These letters support a compelling argument that although American history tends to treat anti-Semitism as a problem from which European immigrants fled, negative stereotypes associated with being Jewish were very much a part of the cultural landscape in the United States.

Interviews

Interviews, be they individual or group in nature, provide an occasion for the face-to-face exchange of information. Like other interviews, the employment interview may fall anywhere on a continuum from highly structured, with uniform questions being asked to all, to highly unstructured, with the questions left largely to the interviewer's discretion. As with other interviews, too, the interviewer's biases and prejudices may creep into the evaluation and influence the outcome. Other factors, such as the order of interviewing, might also affect outcomes by reason of contrast effects. For example, an average applicant may appear better or less qualified, depending on whether the preceding candidate was particularly poor or outstanding. Factors that may affect the outcome of an employment interview, according to Schmitt (1976), include the backgrounds, attitudes, motivations, perceptions, expectations, knowledge about the job, and interview behavior of both the interviewer and the interviewee. Situational factors, such as the nature of the job market, may also affect the outcome of the interview.

Research on the psychometric soundness of the interview as a tool of assessment in employment settings has yielded a very mixed picture. A number of studies seem to indicate that structure in an interview can contribute to the predictive value of an interview—but only to a point. There comes a point when adding additional structure to an interview no longer increases the validity of this tool of assessment (Huffcutt & Arthur, 1994).

Portfolio Assessment

In the context of industrial/organizational assessment, portfolio assessment entails an evaluation of an individual's work sample for the purpose of making some screening, selection, classification, or placement decision. A video journalist applying for a position at a new television station may present a portfolio of video clips, including rehearsal footage and outtakes. An art director for a magazine may present a portfolio of art to a prospective employer, including rough drafts and notes about how to solve a particular design-related problem. In portfolio assessment, the assessor may have the opportunity (1) to evaluate many work samples created by the assessee, (2) to obtain some understanding of the assessee's work-related thought processes and habits through an analysis of the materials from rough draft to finished form, and (3) to question the assessee further regarding various aspects of his or her work-related thinking and habits. The result may be a more complete picture of the prospective employee at work in the new setting than might otherwise be available.

> **JUST THINK . . .**
>
> What are some things that a portfolio *fails* to tell an employer about a prospective employee?

Performance Tests

As its name implies, a performance test requires assessees to demonstrate certain skills or abilities under a specified set of circumstances. The typical objective of such an exercise is to obtain a *job-related performance sample.* For example, a word-processing test as a prerequisite for employment as a word processor provides a prospective employer with a job-related performance sample.

Boundaries between performance, achievement, and aptitude tests are often blurred, especially when the work sample entails taking a standardized test of skill or ability. For example, the Seashore Bennett Stenographic Proficiency Test is a standardized measure of stenographic competence. The test materials include a recording in which a voice dictates a series of letters and manuscripts that the assessee must transcribe in shorthand and then type. The recorded directions provide a uniform clarity of voice and rate of dictation. The test protocol may well be viewed as an achievement test, an aptitude test, or a performance sample, depending upon the context of its use.

One widely used instrument designed to measure clerical aptitude and skills is the Minnesota Clerical Test (MCT). The MCT comprises two subtests, Number Comparison and Name Comparison. Each subtest contains 200 items, with each item consisting of either a pair of names or a pair of numbers (depending upon the subtest) to be compared. For each item, the assessee's task is to check whether the two names (or numbers) in the pair are the same or different. A score is obtained simply by subtracting the number of incorrect responses from the number of correct ones. Because speed and accuracy in clerical work are important to so many employers, this deceptively simple test has been used for decades as an effective screening tool in the workplace. Not only can it be administered and scored quickly and easily, but also the pattern of the testtakers' errors or omissions on this timed test may suggest whether the testtaker values speed over accuracy or vice versa.

Figure 16–4
Games Psychologists Play

Psychologists have long recognized the value of game-like situations in the process of evaluating prospective personnel. A task referred to as the "Manufacturing Problem" was used as part of the AT&T Management Progress Study conducted in 1957. The assessee's task here is to collaborate with others in buying parts and manufacturing a "product."

More sophisticated varieties of performance assessment are regularly employed in the field of aviation, in the training of pilots (Retzlaff & Gibertini, 1988) and air traffic controllers (Ackerman & Kanfer, 1993). In this context, computer simulations and commercially available video games have a long history of use (Kennedy et al., 1982). Computer simulations permit assessors to evaluate assessees' response to a standardized set of tasks and to precisely monitor the time of response. As technology ever becomes more sophisticated, the virtual reality of simulations continues to improve.

The kind of special equipment necessary for performance tests varies widely. For a simulation involving a manufacturing problem, for example, all that may be necessary are tinkertoy parts (Figure 16–4). During World War II, the assessment staff of the Office of Strategic Services (OSS) was charged with selecting personnel to serve as American secret agents, saboteurs, propaganda experts, and other such job titles for assignments overseas. In addition to interviews, personality tests, and other paper-and-pencil tests, the OSS administered situational performance tests. Today, the Israelis, among other military powers, use similar methods. For example, the optimal composition of a three-person crew performing tasks in a military field setting might be determined on the basis of field testing as well as by tests of ability and motivation (Tziner &Eden, 1985).

◆ **JUST THINK . . .**

In general, what types of performance assessments lend themselves more to a virtual reality context than to "real-life" reality?

A commonly used performance test in the assessment of business leadership ability is the **leaderless group technique.** Communication skills, problem-solving ability, the ability to cope with stress, and other skills can also be assessed economically by a group exercise in which the participants' task is to work together in the solution of some problem or the achievement of some goal. As group members interact, the assessors make judgments with respect to questions such as "Who is the leader?" and "What role do other members play in this group?" The answers to such questions will no doubt figure into decisions concerning the individual assessee's future position in the organization.

Another performance test frequently used to assess managerial ability, organizational skills, and leadership potential is the **in-basket technique.** This technique simulates the way a manager or an executive deals with his or her in-basket filled with mail, memos, announcements, and various other notices and directives. Assessees are instructed that they have only a limited amount of time, usually two or three hours, to deal with all the items in the basket (more commonly a manila envelope). Through posttest interviews and an examination of the way the assessee handled the materials, assessors can make judgments concerning variables such as organizing and planning, problem solving, decision making, creativity, leadership, and written communication skills.

The assessment center   A widely used tool in selection, classification, and placement is the **assessment center.** Although it sounds as if it might be a place, the term actually denotes an organizationally standardized procedure for evaluation involving multiple assessment techniques such as paper-and-pencil tests and situational performance tests. The assessment center concept had its origins in the writings of Henry Murray and his associates (1938). Assessment center activities were pioneered by military organizations both in the United States and abroad (Thornton & Byham, 1982).

In 1956, the first application of the idea in an industrial setting occurred with the initiation of the Management Progress Study (MPS) at American Telephone and Telegraph (Bray, 1964). MPS was to be a longitudinal study that would follow the lives of over four hundred telephone company management and nonmanagement personnel. Participants attended a three-and-a-half-day assessment center in which they were interviewed for two hours. They then took a number of paper-and-pencil tests designed to shed light on cognitive abilities and personality (for example, the School and College Ability Test and the Edwards Personal Preference Schedule) and participated in individual and group situational exercises (such as the in-basket test and a leaderless group). Additionally, projective tests such as the Thematic Apperception Test and the Sentence Completion Test were administered. All the data on each of the assessees were integrated at a meeting of the assessors, at which judgments on a number of dimensions were made. The dimensions, grouped by area, are listed in Table 16–4.

The use of the assessment center method has mushroomed, with some two thousand or more business organizations relying on some form of it for selection, classification, placement, promotion, career training, and early identification of leadership potential (Gaugler et al., 1987). The method has been subject to numerous studies concerning its validity, and the consensus is that the method has much to recommend it (B. Cohen et al., 1977; Gaugler et al., 1987; Hunter & Hunter, 1984; McEvoy & Beatty, 1989; Schmitt et al., 1984).

Physical Tests

A lifeguard who is visually impaired is seriously compromised in his or her ability to perform the job. A wine taster with damaged tastebuds is of little value to a vintner. An aircraft pilot who has lost the use of his or her arms . . . the point is clear: Physical

Table 16–4
Original Management Progress Study Dimensions

Area	Dimension
Administrative skills	Organizing and planning—How effectively can this person organize work, and how well does he or she plan ahead?
	Decision making—How ready is this person to make decisions, and how good are the decisions made?
	Creativity—How likely is this person to solve a management problem in a novel way?
Interpersonal skills	Leadership skills—How effectively can this person lead a group to accomplish a task without arousing hostility?
	Oral communication skills—How well would this person present an oral report to a small conference group on a subject he or she knew well?
	Behavior flexibility—How readily can this person, when motivated, modify his or her behavior to reach a goal? How able is this person to change roles or style of behavior to accomplish objectives?
	Personal impact—How forceful and likable an early impression does this person make?
	Social objectivity—How free is this person from prejudices against racial, ethnic, socioeconomic, educational, and other social groups?
	Perceptions of threshold social cues—How readily does this person perceive minimal cues in the behavior of others?
Cognitive skills	General mental ability—How able is this person in the functions measured by tests of intelligence, scholastic aptitude, and learning ability?
	Range of interests—To what extent is this person interested in a variety of fields of activity such as science, politics, sports, music, art?
	Written communication skill—How well would this person compose a communicative and formally correct memorandum on a subject he or she knew well? How well written are memos and reports likely to be?
Stability of performance	Tolerance of uncertainty—To what extent will this person's work performance stand up under uncertain or unstructured conditions?
	Resistance to stress—To what extent will this person's work performance stand up in the face of personal stress?
Work motivation	Primacy of work—To what extent does this person find satisfactions from work more important than satisfactions in other areas of life?
	Inner work standards—To what extent will this person want to do a good job, even if a less good one is acceptable to the boss and others?
	Energy—How continuously can this person sustain a high level of work activity?
	Self-objectivity—How realistic a view does this person have of his or her own assets and liabilities, and how much insight into his or her own motives?
Career orientation	Need for advancement—To what extent does this person need to be promoted significantly earlier than his or her peers? To what extent are further promotions needed for career satisfaction?
	Need for security—How strongly does this person want a secure job?
	Ability to delay gratification—To what extent will this person be willing to wait patiently for advancement if confident advancement will come?
	Realism of expectations—To what extent do this person's expectations about his or her work life with the company conform to what is likely to be true?
	Bell System value orientation—To what extent has this person incorporated Bell System values such as service, friendliness, justice of company position on earnings, rates, wages?
Dependency	Need for superior approval—To what extent does this person need warmth and nurturant support from immediate supervisors?
	Need for peer approval—To what extent does this person need warmth and acceptance from peers and subordinates?
	Goal flexibility—To what extent is this person likely to reorient his or her life toward a different goal?

Source: Bray (1982)

requirements of a job must be taken into consideration when screening, selecting, classifying, and placing applicants. Depending on the specific requirements of the job, a number of physical subtests may be used. Thus, for example, for a job in which a number of components of vision are critical, a test of visual acuity might be administered along with tests of visual efficiency, stereopsis (distance/depth perception), and color blindness.

General physical fitness is required in many jobs, such as police work, where successful candidates might one day have to chase a fleeing suspect on foot or defend themselves against a suspect resisting arrest. The tests used in assessing such fitness might include a complete physical examination, tests of physical strength, and a performance test that meets some determined criterion with respect to running speed and running agility. Tasks like vaulting some object, stepping through tires, and going through a window frame would be included to simulate running on difficult terrain.

In some instances, an employer's setting certain physical requirements for employment are so reasonable and so necessary that they would readily be upheld by any court if challenged. Other physical requirements for employment, however, may fall into a gray area. In general, the law favors physical standards that are both nondiscriminatory and job related.

Also included under the heading of physical tests are tests of sensory intactness/impairment, including tests to measure color blindness, visual acuity, visual depth perception, and auditory acuity. These types of tests are routinely employed in industrial settings in which the ability to perceive color or the possession of reasonably good eyesight or hearing is essential to the job. Additionally, physical techniques have been applied in the assessment of integrity and honesty, as is the case with the polygraph and drug testing.

> **JUST THINK . . .**
>
> "A police officer must meet certain minimum height requirements." Your thoughts?

Drug testing   Beyond concerns about traditional physical, emotional, and cognitive job requirements lies great concern about employee drug use. Personnel and human resource managers are increasingly seeking assurance that the people they hire and the staff they currently employ do not and will not use illegal drugs. The dollar amounts vary by source, but estimates of corporate losses in the workplace due directly or indirectly to employee drug or alcohol use run into the tens of billions of dollars. Revenue may be lost because of injury to people or animals, damage to products and the environment, or employee absenteeism, tardiness, or sick leave. And no dollar amount can be attached to the tragic loss of life that may result from a drug- or alcohol-related mishap.

Testing for drug use is a growing practice in corporate America, with upwards of one-half of all major companies conducting drug testing in some form. Applicants for employment may be tested during the selection process. Employees typically will be tested only if drug use is suspected. Random drug testing is relatively unusual in private companies, although it is common in government agencies and in the military.

Methods of drug testing vary. One method, the Immunoassay Test, employs the subject's urine to determine the presence or absence of drugs in the body by identifying the metabolized by-products of the drug (metabolites). Although widely used in workplace settings, the test can be criticized for its inability to specify the precise amount of the drug that was taken, when it was taken, and which of several possible drugs in a particular category was taken. Further, there is no way to estimate the degree of impairment that occurred in response to the drug. The Gas Chromatography/Mass Spectrometry (GCMS) Test also examines metabolites in urine to determine the presence or absence of drugs, but it can more accurately specify which drug was used. GCMS technology cannot, however, pinpoint the time at which the drug was taken or the degree of impairment that occurred as a consequence.

> **JUST THINK . . .**
>
> Generally speaking, is random drug testing in the workplace a good thing?

Many employees object to drug testing as a condition of employment and have argued that such testing violates their constitutional rights to privacy and freedom from unreasonable search and seizure. In the course of legal proceedings, a question that emerges frequently is the validity of drug testing. The consequences of **false positives** (an individual tests positively for drug use when in reality there has been no drug use) and **false negatives** (an individual tests negatively for drug use when in reality there has been drug use) in such cases can be momentous. A false positive may result in, among other things, the loss of one's livelihood. A false negative may result in an impaired person working in a position of responsibility and placing others at risk.

Modern laboratory techniques tend to be relatively accurate in detecting telltale metabolites. Error rates are generally well under 2% (West & Ackerman, 1993). However, laboratory techniques may not always be used correctly. By one estimate, fully 93% of laboratories that do drug testing fail to meet standards designed to reduce human error (Comer, 1993). Error may also occur in the interpretation of results. Metabolites may be identified accurately, but whether they originated in the abuse of some illicit drug or in some over-the-counter medication cannot always be determined. To help prevent such confusion, administrators of the urine test typically ask the subject to compile a list of any medications currently being taken. However, not all subjects are willing or able to remember all medications they may have taken. Further, some employees are reluctant to report some prescription medications they may have taken to treat conditions to which any possible social stigma may be attached, such as depression or epilepsy. Additionally, some foods may also produce metabolites that mimic the metabolites of some illegal drugs. For example, metabolites of opiates will be detected following the subject's ingestion of (perfectly legal) poppy seeds (West & Ackerman, 1993).

Another question related to the validity of drug tests concerns the degree to which drugs identified through testing actually affect job performance. Some drugs leave the body very slowly. For example, a person may test positive for marijuana use up to a month after the last exposure to it. Thus, the residue of the drug remains long after any discernible impairment from having taken the drug. By contrast, cocaine leaves the body in only three days. It is possible for a habitual cocaine user to be off the drug for three days, be highly impaired as a result of cocaine withdrawal, yet still test negative for drug use. Thus, neither a positive nor a negative finding with regard to a drug test necessarily means that behavior has or has not been impaired by drug use (Comer, 1993).

An alternative to drug testing involves using performance tests to directly examine impairment. For example, sophisticated video game-style tests of coordination, judgment, and reaction time are available to compare current performance with baseline performance as established on earlier tests. The advantages of these performance tests over drug testing include a more direct assessment of impairment, fewer ethical concerns regarding invasion of privacy, and immediate information about impairment. The latter advantage is particularly vital in preventing potentially impaired individuals from hurting themselves or others. Organizations using such electronic tests have reported greater employee satisfaction and fewer accidents (Comer, 1993).

Productivity, Motivation, Attitude, and Organizational Culture

Beyond their use in pre-employment counseling and in the screening, selection, classification, and placement of personnel, various tools of assessment are used to accomplish various goals in the workplace. Let's briefly survey some of these varied uses of tools of assessment with reference to measures of cognitive ability, productivity, motivation, and organizational culture.

Measures of Cognitive Ability

Selection decisions regarding personnel, as well as other types of selection decisions such as those regarding professional licensure or acceptance for academic training, are often based, at least in part, on performance on tests that tap acquired knowledge as well as various cognitive skills and abilities. In general, cognitive-based tests are popular tools of selection because they have been shown to be valid predictors of future performance (Schmidt & Hunter, 1998). However, along with that impressive track record come a number of potential considerations with regard to diversity issues.

Personnel selection and diversity issues The continued use of tests that tap primarily cognitive abilities and skills for screening, selection, classification, and placement has become controversial. This controversy stems from a well-documented body of evidence that points to consistent group differences on cognitive ability tests. For example, on average, Asians tend to score higher than Whites on mathematical and quantitative ability measures, while Whites score higher than Asians on measures of comprehension and verbal ability. On average, Whites also tend to score higher on cognitive ability tests than Blacks and Hispanics. Given that the test scores may differ on average by as much as one standard deviation (Sackett et al., 2001), such differences may have great impact on who gets what job or who is admitted to an institution of higher learning; average differences between groups on tests of cognitive ability may contribute to limiting diversity in employment settings, in the professions, and in access to education and training.

It is in society's interest to promote diversity in employment settings, in the professions, and in access to education and training. Toward that end, diversity has, in the past, been encouraged by various means. One approach entailed the use of cut scores on tests defined on the basis of group membership. However, there has been a general trend away from efforts that entail preferential treatment of any group with regard to test scores. This trend is evident in legislation, court actions, and public referenda. For example, the Civil Rights Act of 1991 made it illegal for employers to adjust test scores as a function of group membership. In 1996, Proposition 209 was passed in California, prohibiting the use of group membership as a basis for any selection decision in that state. In that same year, a federal court ruled that race was not a relevant criterion in selecting university applicants (*Hopwood v. State of Texas*, 1996). In the state of Washington, voters approved legislation that banned the use of race as a criterion in college admissions, contracting, and hiring (Verhovek & Ayres, 1998).

How may diversity in the workplace and other settings be achieved while still using tests known to be good predictors of performance and while not building into the selection criteria a preference for any group? Although no single answer to this complex question is likely to satisfy all concerned, there are jobs waiting to be filled and seats waiting to be occupied at educational and training institutions; some strategy for balancing the various interests must be found. Sackett et al. (2001) proposed that employers and other users of cognitive ability tests use video- and computer-based formats for administering such tests, as well as any other format that may minimize verbal content and the demand for testtakers' verbal skills and abilities. They also recommended other strategies, such as greater reliance on relevant job or life experience as selection criteria. However, Sackett et al. (2001) also advised that "subgroup differences are not simply artifacts of paper-and-pencil technologies" (p. 316), and it is incumbent upon society at large to effectively address such extra-test issues.

> **JUST THINK . . .**
>
> In what general ways can society at large best address such extra-test issues?

Productivity

Productivity may be defined simply as output or value yielded relative to work effort made. The term is used here in its broadest sense, equally applicable to workers who make products and workers who provide services. If a business endeavor is to succeed, monitoring output with the ultimate goal of maximizing output is essential. Measures of productivity help to define not only where a business is but also what it needs to do to get where it wants to be. A manufacturer of television sets, for example, might find that the people who manufacture the housing are working at optimal efficiency but the people responsible for installing the picture tubes in the cabinets are working at one-half the expected efficiency. A productivity evaluation can help identify the factors responsible for the sagging performance of the picture-tube installers.

Using techniques such as supervisor ratings, interviews with employees, and undercover employees planted in the picture-tube workshop, management might determine what—or who in particular—is responsible for the unsatisfactory performance. Perhaps the most common method of evaluating worker productivity or performance is through the use of rating and ranking procedures by superiors in the organization. One type of ranking procedure used when large numbers of employees are assessed is the **forced distribution technique.** This procedure involves distributing a predetermined number or percentage of assessees into various categories that describe performance (such as *unsatisfactory, poor, fair, average, good, superior*). Another index of on-the-job performance is number of absences within a given period. It typically reflects more poorly on an employee if he or she is absent on, say, 20 separate occasions than on 20 consecutive dates as the result of illness.

JUST THINK . . .

What might be the long-range consequences of using evaluation techniques that rely on the use of "undercover employees" in a manufacturing setting?

The **critical incidents technique** (Flanagan & Burns, 1955) involves the supervisor recording positive and negative employee behaviors. The supervisor catalogues the notations according to various categories (for example, *dependability* or *initiative*) for ready reference when an evaluation needs to be made. Some evidence suggests that a honeymoon period of about three months occurs when a new worker starts a job and that supervisory ratings will more truly reflect the worker at the conclusion of that period.

Peer ratings or evaluations by other workers at the same level have proved to be a valuable method of identifying talent among employees. Although peers have a tendency to rate their counterparts higher than these people would be rated by superiors, the information obtained from the ratings and rankings of peers can be highly predictive of future performance. For example, one study involved 117 inexperienced life insurance agents who attended a three-week training class. At the conclusion of the course, the budding insurance agents were asked to list the three best people in their class with respect to each of 12 situations. From these data, a composite score was obtained for each of the 117 agents. After one year, these peer ratings and three other variables were correlated with job tenure (number of weeks on the job) and with production (number of dollars' worth of insurance sold). As can be seen from Table 16–5, peer ratings had the highest validity in all of the categories. By contrast, a near zero correlation was obtained between final course grade and all categories.

JUST THINK . . .

Suppose your instructor initiated a peer rating system as the sole determinant of your grade in your measurement class. Would such a system be better than the one in place?

Is there a down side to peer ratings? Most definitely. Even when peer ratings are carried out anonymously, a person being rated may feel as if some suspected peer rated him or her too low. The reaction of that individual in turn may be to rate that suspected peer extremely low in retaliation. Also, peers do not always have a basis for judging the criteria that the rating scale asks them to judge. But that typically does not stop a rater in the workplace from rating a peer. Instead of rating the peer on the criteria listed on

Table 16–5
Peer Ratings and Performance of Life Insurance Salespeople

	Job Tenure		Production	
	6 months	1 year	6 months	1 year
Peer rating	.18*	.29[†]	.29[†]	.30[†]
Age	.18*	.24[†]	.06	.09
Starting salary	.01	.03	.13	.26[†]
Final course grade	.02	.06	−.02	.02

Source: Mayfield (1972)

*$p = .05$ (one-tailed test)

[†]$p = .01$ (one-tailed test)

the questionnaire, the rater might use a private "What has this person done for me lately?" criterion to respond to the rating scale.

In many organizations, people work in teams. In an organizational or workplace context, a **team** may be defined as two or more people who interact interdependently toward a common and valued goal, who have each been assigned specific roles or functions to perform. For a sales team, the division of labor may simply reflect division of sales territories. In the creation of complicated software, the division of labor may involve the assignment of tasks that are too complicated for any one individual. The operation of a cruise ship or military vessel requires a trained team due to the multitude of things that must be done if the ship is to sail. To achieve greater productivity, organizations ask questions such as "What does the team know?" and "How does the collective knowledge of the team differ qualitatively from the individual knowledge and expertise of each of the team members?" Addressing these and related questions, a literature exploring different ways of measuring team knowledge has begun to emerge (see, for example, Cannon-Bowers et al., 1998; Cooke et al., 2000; Salas et al., 1998).

Motivation

Why do some people skip lunch, work overtime, and take home work nightly, whereas others strive to do as little as possible and live a life of leisure at work? At a practical level, light may be shed on such questions using assessment instruments that tap the values of the assessee. Dealing with a population of unskilled personnel may require specially devised techniques. Champagne (1969) responded to the challenge of knowing little about what might appeal to rural, unskilled people in attempts to attract them to work, so he devised a motivational questionnaire. As illustrated by the three items in Figure 16–5, the questionnaire used a paired comparison (forced-choice) format that required the subject to make choices relative to 12 factors used by companies to entice employment applications: fair pay, steady job, vacations and holidays with pay, job extras such as pensions and sick benefits, a fair boss, interesting work, good working conditions, chance for promotion, a job close to home, working with friends and neighbors, nice people to work with, and praise for good work.

The job-seeking factor found to be most important in Champagne's sample of 349 male and female, rural, unskilled subjects was *steady job*. The least important factor was found to be *working with friends and neighbors*. *Praise for good work* was a close runner-up for least important. In interpreting the findings, Champagne cautioned that "the factors reported here relate to the job-seeking behavior of the unskilled and are not measures of how to retain and motivate the unskilled once employed. . . . What prompts a person to

Figure 16–5
Studying Values With the Unskilled

Champagne (1969) used test items such as those pictured in a recruitment study with a rural, unskilled population.

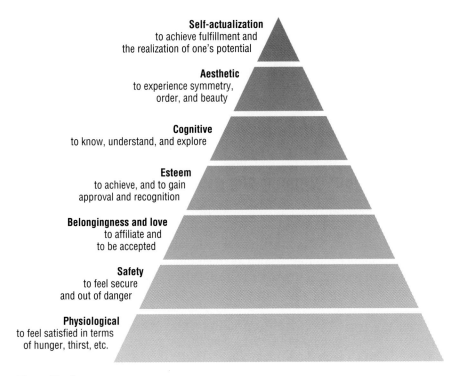

Figure 16–6
Maslow's Hierarchy of Needs (adapted from Maslow, 1970)

accept a job is not necessarily the same as what prompts a person to retain a job or do well in it" (p. 268).

On a theoretical level, an abundance of theories seek to delineate the specific needs, attitudes, social influences, and other factors that might account for differences in motivation. For example, Vroom (1964) proposed an expectancy theory of motivation, which essentially holds that employees expend energy in ways designed to achieve the outcome they want; the greater the expectancy that an action will achieve a certain outcome, the more energy will be expended to achieve that outcome. Maslow (1943, 1970) constructed a theoretical hierarchy of human needs (Figure 16–6) and proposed that as one category of need is met, people move on to satisfy the next category of need.

JUST THINK . . .

What motivates you to do what you do? How could that motivation best be measured?

Employers who subscribe to Maslow's theory would seek to identify (1) the need level required of the employee by the job and (2) the current need level of the prospective employee. Alderfer (1972) proposed an alternative need theory of motivation, one that was not hierarchical. Whereas Maslow saw the satisfaction of one need leading to the satisfaction of the next need in the hierarchy, Alderfer proposed that once a need is satisfied, the organism may strive to satisfy it to an even greater degree. The Alderfer theory also provides that frustrating one need might channel energy into the achievement of a need at another level.

In a widely cited program that undertook to define the characteristics of achievement motivation, McClelland (1961) used as his measure of that motivation stories written under special instructions about TAT and TAT-like pictures. McClelland described the individual with a high need for achievement as one who prefers a task that is neither too simple nor extremely difficult, something with moderate, not extreme, risks. A situation with little or no risk will not lead to feelings of accomplishment if the individual succeeds. On the other hand, an extremely high-risk situation may not lead to feelings of accomplishment because of the high probability of failure. Persons with high need for achievement enjoy taking responsibility for their actions because they desire the credit and recognition for their accomplishments. Such individuals also desire information about their performance to constantly improve their output. Other researchers also used TAT-like pictures and their own specially devised scoring systems to study related areas of human motivation such as the fear of failure (Birney et al., 1969; Cohen & Houston, 1975; Cohen & Parker, 1974; Cohen & Teevan, 1974, 1975; Cohen et al., 1975) and the fear of success (Horner, 1973).

Motivation may be conceptualized as stemming from incentives that are either primarily internal or primarily external in origin. Another way of stating this is to speak of *intrinsic motivation* and *extrinsic motivation*. In **intrinsic motivation,** the primary force driving the individual stems from things such as the individual's involvement in work or satisfaction with work products. In **extrinsic motivation,** the primary force driving the individual stems from rewards, such as salary and bonuses, or from constraints, such as job loss.

A scale designed to assess aspects of intrinsic and extrinsic motivation is the Work Preference Inventory (WPI; Amabile et al., 1994). The WPI contains 30 items rated on a 4-point scale based on how much the testtaker believes the item to be self-descriptive. Factor analysis indicates that the test does appear to tap two distinct factors: intrinsic and extrinsic motivation. Each of these two factors may be divided into two subfactors. The intrinsic motivation factor may be divided into one subfactor that has to do with the challenge of the work tasks and another factor that has to do with the enjoyment of work. The extrinsic motivation factor may be divided into one subfactor that has to do with compensation for work and another factor that has to do with external influences such as recognition of one's work by others. The WPI has been shown to be internally consistent and to correlate in the predicted direction with behavioral and other questionnaire measures of motivation.

In some instances, it seems as if the motivation to perform a particular job becomes markedly reduced compared to previous levels. Such is the case with a phenomenon referred to as *burnout.*

Burnout and its measurement   *Burnout* is an occupational health problem associated with cumulative occupational stress (Shirom, 2003). **Burnout** has been defined as "a psychological syndrome of emotional exhaustion, depersonalization, and reduced personal accomplishment that can occur among individuals who work with other people in some capacity" (Maslach et al., 1997, p. 192). In this definition, *emotional exhaustion* refers to an inability to give of oneself emotionally to others, and *depersonalization* refers to distancing other people and even developing cynical attitudes toward them. The potential consequences of burnout range from deterioration in service provided, to absenteeism and job turnover. The potential effects of burnout on a worker suffering from it range from insomnia to alcohol and drug use.

The most widely used measure of burnout is the Maslach Burnout Inventory (MBI), Third Edition (Maslach et al., 1996). Developed by Christina Maslach and her colleagues, this test contains 22 items divided into three subscales: Emotional Exhaustion (nine items), Depersonalization (five items), and Personal Accomplishment (eight items). Testtakers respond on a scale ranging from 0 (*never*) to 6 (*every day*) to items like this one from the Exhaustion scale: *Working all day is really a strain for me.* The MBI manual contains data relevant to the psychometric soundness of the tests. Included is a discussion of discriminant validity in which burnout is conceptually distinguished from similar concepts such as depression and job dissatisfaction.

Using instruments such as the MBI, researchers have found that some occupations seem to be subject to higher levels of burnout than others. For example, personnel in nursing (Happell et al., 2003) and related fields, including staff in residential homes caring for the elderly (Evers et al., 2002) and children (Decker et al., 2002), seem subject to high levels of stress and burnout. Exactly why is not known.

JUST THINK . . .

Why might it be critically important for some employers to know if their employees are burning out? Besides a test, how else might burnout be gauged?

In one study that employed student support services personnel as subjects, as well as a measure of job satisfaction, it was found that low levels of job satisfaction led to high levels of the emotional exhaustion component of burnout (Brewer & Clippard, 2002).

Attitude

An **attitude** may be defined formally as a presumably learned disposition to react in some characteristic manner to a particular stimulus. The stimulus may be an object, a group, an institution—virtually anything. Later in this chapter, we discuss how attitudes toward goods and services are measured. More immediately, however, we focus on workplace-related attitudes. Although attitudes do not necessarily predict behavior (Tittle & Hill, 1967; Wicker, 1969), there has been great interest in measuring the attitudes of employers and employees toward each other as well as toward numerous variables in the workplace. Much research has been done, for example, on the subject of job satisfaction.

Job satisfaction Compared with dissatisfied workers, satisfied workers in the workplace are believed to be more productive (Petty et al., 1984), more consistent in work output (Locke, 1976), less likely to complain (Burke, 1970; Locke, 1976), and less likely to be absent from work or to be replaced (Herzberg et al., 1957; Vroom, 1964). Although these assumptions are somewhat controversial (Iaffaldano & Muchinsky, 1985) and should probably be considered on a case-by-case basis, employers, employees, researchers, and consultants have maintained a long-standing interest in the measurement of job satisfaction. Traditionally, **job satisfaction** has been defined as "a pleasurable or positive emotional state resulting from the appraisal of one's job or job experiences" (Locke, 1976, p. 300).

One diagnostic measure of job satisfaction (or in this case, dissatisfaction) entails video-recording an employee at work and then playing back the video for the employee on a computer-assisted setup (Johansson & Forsman, 2001). The employee clicks on virtual controls to indicate when an unsatisfactory situation arises, and a window of questions automatically opens. According to data from studies of manual workers, analysis of the responses can be useful in creating a more satisfactory work environment (Johansson & Forsman, 2001).

Of course, contemporary measures of job satisfaction may focus on other elements of the job, including cognitive evaluations of the work (Organ & Near, 1985) and the work schedule (Baltes et al., 1999; Barnett & Gareis, 2000), perceived sources of stress (Brown & Peterson, 1993; Vagg & Spielberger, 1998), various aspects of well-being (Daniels, 2000), and mismatches between an employee's cultural background and the prevailing organizational culture (Aycan et al., 2000; Early et al., 1999; Parkes et al.,

Table 16-6

Consequences of Organizational Commitment Level for Individual Employees and the Organization

	Level of Organizational Commitment		
	Low	**Moderate**	**High**
The Individual Employee	Potentially positive consequences for opportunity for expression of originality and innovation, but an overall negative effect on career advancement opportunities	Enhanced feeling of belongingness and security, along with doubts about the opportunity for advancement	Greater opportunity for advancement and compensation for efforts, along with less opportunity for personal growth and potential for stress in family relationships
The Organization	Absenteeism, tardiness, workforce turnover, and poor quality of work	As compared with low commitment, less absenteeism, tardiness, turnover, and better quality of work, as well as increased level of job satisfaction	Potential for high productivity, but sometimes accompanied by lack of critical/ethical review of employee behavior and by reduced organizational flexibility

2001). In addition to job satisfaction, other job-related constructs that have attracted the attention of theorists and assessment professionals include job involvement, work centrality, organizational socialization, and organizational commitment (Caught et al., 2000; Nystedt et al., 1999; Paullay et al., 1994; Taormina & Bauer, 2000). Before focusing on the broader construct of organizational culture, let's briefly take a closer look at the concept of organizational commitment.

Organizational commitment Organizational commitment has been defined as "the strength of an individual's identification with and involvement in a particular organization" (Porter et al., 1974, p. 604). This "strength" has been conceptualized and measured in ways that emphasize both its attitudinal and behavioral components (Mathieu & Zajac, 1990). In general, **organizational commitment** refers to a person's feelings of loyalty to, identification with, and involvement in an organization. Presumed correlates of high and low organizational commitment as observed by Randall (1987) are summarized in Table 16-6. The most widely used measure of this construct is the Organizational Commitment Questionnaire (OCQ; Porter et al., 1974), a 15-item Likert scale wherein respondents express their commitment-related attitudes toward an organization. Despite its widespread use for over a quarter-century, however, there is relatively little evidence to support its construct validity (Bozeman & Perrewe, 2001).

As you might expect, the measurement of attitude extends far beyond the workplace. For example, politicians seeking reelection may monitor the attitudes of their constituencies on various issues. We will revisit the subject of attitude measurement in somewhat greater detail when we survey measurement in the area of consumer psychology. However, before leaving the world of work and organizations, let's look at the measurement of organizational culture.

Organizational Culture

Organizational culture, or corporate culture, as it is known when applied to a company or corporation, has been defined in many ways. For our purposes, we will define **organizational culture** after Cohen (2001) as the totality of socially transmitted behavior patterns characteristic of a particular organization or company, including the structure of the organization and the roles within it, the leadership style, the prevailing values, norms, sanctions, and support mechanisms, as well as the past traditions and folklore, methods of enculturation, and characteristic ways of interacting with people and institutions outside of the culture (such as customers, suppliers, the competition, government agencies, and the general public).

Much like different social groups at different times throughout history, organizations and corporations have developed distinctive cultures. They have distinctive ceremonies, rights, and privileges—formal as well as informal—tied to success and advancement, as well as various types of sanctions tied to failure (Trice & Beyer, 1984). Organizational cultures have observable artifacts, which may be in the form of an annual report or a videotape of the office Christmas party. Organizational cultures also typically have sets of core values or beliefs that guide the actions of the organization as well as the direction in which it moves.

Just as the term *culture* is traditionally applied to a group of people who share a particular way of life, the term *organizational culture* applies to a *way of work*. An organizational culture provides a way of coping with internal and external challenges and demands. And just as conflicts between ways of thinking and doing things can cause conflicts between groups of people, so conflicts between organizational cultures may develop. Such conflicts are perhaps most evident when a company with one type of corporate culture acquires or merges with a company that has a very different corporate culture (Brannen & Salk, 2000; Veiga et al., 2000). Any effort to remedy such a clash in corporate cultures must be preceded by sober study and understanding of the cultures involved.

Perhaps because the concept of organizational culture is so multifaceted, obtaining a measure of it is no simple feat. To appreciate just how complex is the task of describing an organizational culture, consider how you would describe any other type of culture—American culture, NASCAR culture, or antiquing culture.

As a qualitative research consultant to many companies, the senior author of this textbook was presented with the challenge of assessing several organizational cultures. Because no satisfactory measure existed for conducting such an assessment, he created an instrument to do so; that instrument is the subject of this chapter's *Everyday Psychometrics.*

JUST THINK . . .

Describe in detail a particular culture you know well. What difficulties do you encounter in trying to capture this culture in a description?

Other Applications of Tools of Assessment

Psychometric expertise is applied in a wide variety of industrial, organizational, and business-related settings. For example, experimental and engineering psychologists use a variety of assessment tools in their ergonomic (work-related) and human factors research as they help develop the plans for everything from household items (Hsu & Peng, 1993) to components for automobiles (Chira-Chavala & Yoo, 1994) and aircraft (Begault, 1993). These researchers may use custom-designed measurement instruments, standardized tests, or both in their efforts to better understand human response to specific equipment or instrumentation in a particular work environment.

Another business-related area in which tests and other tools of assessment are used extensively is consumer psychology.

Assessment of Corporate and Organizational Culture

Corporations and other organizations have shown growing interest in self-examination and self-improvement. The Discussion of Organizational Culture (DOC; Cohen, 2001) was devised to assist in those efforts. This interview and discussion guide, designed for administration by a trained interviewer or focus-group moderator, is divided into 10 discussion topics. The questions under each discussion topic explore various aspects of organizational culture. Beginning with "First Impressions" and proceeding through other topics that tap content related to the physical space, prevailing values, and other areas, the objective is to develop a sense of what is unique about the culture at a particular company or organization. Diagnostic insights useful in determining where and how the corporate or organizational culture may be improved can be derived from such data. Space limitations preclude the publication of all ten parts of this comprehensive discussion guide. However, a sense of the types of questions raised for discussion can be gleaned from just the first few parts, reprinted here.

Discussion of Organizational Culture (DOC; Cohen, 2001)*

I. First Impressions
1. What does it mean to be an employee of this corporation? (*Note:* Substitute terminology as appropriate throughout. For example, this question might be rephrased as "What does it mean to be a volunteer at this organization?" or "What does it mean to be an 'IBMer'?")
2. a. How is working here the same as working anyplace else?
   b. How is working here different from working anyplace else?
   c. What makes working here special?
3. a. How does working here make you feel part of a team?
   b. How does working here let you shine as an individual?
4. a. What is obvious about this company to any visitor who has ever taken a tour of it?
   b. What is obvious about this company only to you?
5. In general, how would you describe the compatibility of personnel at this company and the jobs they are assigned to do?
   a. How much role ambiguity exists in job descriptions?
   b. If such role ambiguity exists, how do you and others deal with it?

II. The Physical Space
1. In general terms, describe the physical space of this company.
2. Comment specifically on the physical space with reference to:
   a. the grounds
   b. parking spaces

Consumer Psychology

Consumer psychology is that branch of social psychology that deals primarily with the development, advertising, and marketing of products and services. As is true of almost all other specialty areas in psychology, some consumer psychologists work exclusively in academia, some work in applied settings, and many do both (Tybout & Artz, 1994). In both applied and research studies, consumer psychologists can be found working closely with professionals in fields such as marketing and advertising to help answer questions such as the following:

- Does a market exist for this new product?
- Does a market exist for this new use of an existing product?
- Exactly who, with respect to age, sex, race, social class, and other demographic variables, constitutes the market for this product?

c. the general "feel" of the exteriors and interiors

d. the offices

e. the dining areas

f. the restrooms

g. the storage facilities

h. other aspects of the physical space

3. a. Overall, what works about the physical space?

   b. What does not work about it, and how can it be improved?

4. What does the way that space is laid out here tell you about this company?

III. Corporate Structure and Roles

1. Describe the administrative structure of this company, including a brief description of who reports to whom.

   a. What works about this structure?

   b. What does not work about this structure?

   c. What is unique about this structure?

   d. What does this structure tell you about this company?

2. Describe the roles associated with key job titles in the organizational structure.

   a. Is there ambiguity in roles, or do employees have a clear idea of their function in the company?

b. Are there any roles within the company that seem antiquated or unnecessary?

c. Do any roles need to be created within the company? Strengthened? Better defined?

d. Describe your own role in the company and how you fit into the "grand scheme" of things.

e. How might your role be improved for your own personal benefit?

f. How might your role be improved for the benefit of the company?

3. What can one tell about this company by analyzing

   a. its annual reports

   b. its company records

   c. the type of information that it makes public

   d. the type of information it maintains as private

   e. the products or services it provides

   f. the way it provides those products or services

   g. the corporate vision as articulated by senior management

- How can the targeted consumer population be made aware of this product in a cost-effective way?

- How can the targeted consumer population be persuaded to purchase this product in the most cost-effective way?

- What is the best way to package this product?[2]

One area of interest shared by the consumer psychologist and psychologists in other specialty areas is the measurement of attitudes. For the consumer psychologist, however, the attitude of interest might be one toward a particular product or concept.

---

2. Questions concerning packaging and how to make a product stand out on the shelf have been referred to as issues of *shelf esteem* by consumer psychologists with a sense of humor.

The Measurement of Attitudes

Attitudes formed about products, services, or brand names are a frequent focus of interest in consumer attitude research. Attitude is typically measured by self-report, using tests and questionnaires. A limitation of this approach is that people differ in their ability to be introspective and in their level of self-awareness. People also differ in the extent to which they are willing to be candid about their attitudes. In some instances, the use of an attitude measure in essence may create an attitude where none existed before. In such studies, the attitude measured may be viewed as an artifact of the measurement procedure (Sandelands & Larson, 1985).

Questionnaires and other self-report instruments designed to measure consumer attitudes are developed in ways similar to those previously described for psychological tests in general (see Chapter 7). A more detailed description of the preparation of measures of attitude can be found in the now-classic work *The Measurement of Attitude* (Thurstone & Chave, 1929). A monograph entitled "A Technique for the Measurement of Attitudes" (Likert, 1932) provided researchers with a simple procedure for constructing an instrument for measuring attitudes. Essentially, this procedure consists of listing statements (either favorable or unfavorable) that reflect a particular attitude. These statements are then administered to a group of respondents whose responses are analyzed to identify the most discriminating statements—items that best discriminate people at different points on the hypothetical continuum—which are then included in the final scale. Each statement included in the final scale is accompanied by a 5-point continuum of alternative responses. Such a scale may range, for example, from *strongly agree* to *strongly disagree*. Scoring is accomplished by assigning numerical weights of 1 through 5 to each category such that 5 represents the strongest favorable response and 1 reflects the least favorable response.

Measures of attitude found in the psychological literature run the gamut from instruments devised solely for research and testing of academic, theoretical formulations, to scales with wide-ranging, real-world applications. In the latter context, we might find sophisticated industrial/organizational measures designed to gauge workers' attitudes toward their work, or scales designed to measure the general public's attitudes toward some politician or issue. The Self-Help Agency Satisfaction Scale, for example, designed to gauge self-help agency clients' satisfaction with aspects of the support they receive (Segal et al., 2000), is representative of measures designed to measure consumer satisfaction with a product or service. Attitude scales with applied utility may also be found in the educational psychology literature. Consider in this context measures such as the Study Attitudes and Methods Survey (a scale designed to assess study habits) and the Minnesota Teacher Attitude Survey (a scale designed to assess student-teacher relations).

To help answer questions such as those listed on pages 554–555, consumer psychologists may rely on a variety of methods used individually or in combination. These methods include surveys, "motivation research" as it is referred to by marketing professionals, and behavioral observation.

Surveys In consumer psychology, a **survey** is a fixed list of questions administered to a selected sample of persons for the purpose of learning about consumers' attitudes, beliefs, opinions, and/or behavior with regard to the targeted products, services, or advertising. There are many different ways to conduct a survey, and these various methods all have specific pros and cons in terms of study design and data interpretation (Johnson et al., 2000; Lavrakas, 1998; Massey, 2000; Schwartz et al., 1998; Visser et al., 2000). One specialized type of survey, the **poll,** is much like an instrument to record votes and usually contains questions that can be answered with a simple *yes/no* or *for/against* response. Politicians, news organizations, and special interest organizations may retain researchers who conduct polls (pollsters) to gauge public opinion about controversial issues.

Surveys and polls may be conducted by means of face-to-face, online, and telephone interviews, as well as by mail. The personal interaction of the face-to-face interview helps ensure that questions are understood and adequate clarification of queries is provided. Another advantage of this survey method is the ability to present interviewees with stimuli (such as products) that they can hold in their hands and evaluate. However, the face-to-face approach may also introduce bias into the study, as some respondents act to manage favorable impressions or seek to provide responses they believe the interviewer would like to hear. The face-to-face approach may not be the best when the topic discussed is particularly sensitive or when responses may be embarrassing or otherwise place the respondent in a bad light (Midanik et al., 2001). The face-to-face approach is also labor intensive and therefore can be quite costly when it comes to selecting, training, and employing interviewers.

Surveying by face-to-face interview is a very common method of survey research, and it can be conducted almost anywhere—on a commuter bus or ferry, at a ball game, or near an election polling station. A common site for face-to-face survey research on consumer products is the shopping mall. *Mall intercept studies,* as they are called, can be conducted by interviewers with clipboards who approach shoppers. The shopper may be asked to participate in a survey by answering some questions right then and there or may be led to a booth or room where a more extended interview takes place. Another face-to-face survey method, this one more popular with political pollsters, is the door-to-door approach. Here an entire neighborhood may be polled by knocking on the doors of individual households and soliciting responses to the questionnaire.

> **JUST THINK . . .**
>
> Have you ever participated in a consumer survey of any kind? Whether or not you have, what are your recommendations for improving the process and the quality of the data obtained?

Online, telephone, and mail surveys do not necessarily require personal contact between the researcher and respondent and in many instances may reduce the biases associated with personal interaction. Further, survey methods conducted in the absence of face-to-face interaction tend to be more cost effective due to automation of process components, the need for fewer personnel and less training, and the possibility of executing the entire study from a central location. The online survey holds great potential due to its easy access and feedback potential (Kaye & Johnson, 1999) and can be particularly useful for learning about various aspects of online behavior, such as purchasing (Li et al., 1999) and teamwork (Levesque et al., 2001), as well as self-improvement (Mueller et al., 2000) and deviant online behavior (Greenfield, 1999; Houston et al., 2001; Young et al., 1999). However, unsolicited online surveys are viewed by many as unwanted e-mail or spam, and such perceptions may result not only in low response rates but also in a sense that one's privacy has been violated (Cho & LaRose, 1999). Researchers may also feel a certain degree of doubt regarding whether or not respondents actually are who they say they are. In this regard, there is no substitute for a face-to-face interview complete with identity verification.

The telephone survey offers a number of advantages, but it does suffer from some limitations. Generally, the amount of information that can be obtained by telephone is less than what can be obtained by personal interview or mail. It is not possible to show respondents visual stimuli over the phone. In addition, bias may be introduced if telephone directories are used for identifying respondents. As many as 40 percent of all telephones in some cities are not listed. Since the institution of a national Do Not Call list in

2003, most telephone solicitations cannot be made by random dialing. The primary disadvantage of phone surveys is that they are viewed by many as an unwelcome annoyance and an invasion of privacy.

A mail survey may be the most appropriate survey method when the survey questionnaire is particularly long and will require some time to complete. In general, mail surveys tend to be relatively low in cost because they do not require the services of a trained interviewer and can provide large amounts of information. They are also well suited for obtaining information about which respondents may be sensitive or shy in a face-to-face or even a telephone interview. They are ideal for posing questions that require the use of records or consultation with others (such as family members) for an answer. Note also that much of what we say about mail surveys also applies to electronic mail surveys or surveys conducted by means of fax machines.

The major disadvantages of mail questionnaires are (1) the possibility of no response at all from the intended recipient of the survey (for whatever reason—the survey was never delivered, or it was thrown out as junk mail as soon as it arrived); (2) the possibility of response from someone (perhaps a family member) who was not the intended recipient of the survey; and (3) the possibility of a late—and hence useless for tabulation purposes—response. If large numbers of people fail to respond to a mail questionnaire, it is impossible to determine whether those individuals who did respond are representative of those who did not. People may not respond to a mail questionnaire for many different reasons, and various techniques ranging from incentives to follow-up mailings have been suggested for dealing with various types of nonresponse (Furse & Stewart, 1984).

It is possible to combine the various survey methods to obtain the advantages of each. For example, the survey researcher might mail a lengthy questionnaire to potential respondents and then obtain responses by telephone. Alternatively, those individuals not returning their responses by mail might be contacted by telephone or in person.

Many commercial research firms maintain a list of a large number of people or families who have agreed to respond to questionnaires that are sent to them. The people who make up this list are referred to as a **consumer panel.** In return for their participation, panel members may receive incentives such as cash and free samples of all the products about which they are asked to respond in surveys. One special type of panel is called a **diary panel.** Respondents on such a panel must keep detailed records of their behavior. For example, they may be required to keep a record of products they purchased, coupons they used, or radio stations they listened to while in the car. There are also specialized panels that serve to monitor segments of the market, political attitudes, or other variables.

Survey research may employ a wide variety of item types. One approach to item writing, particularly popular for surveys administered in writing, is referred to as the **semantic differential technique** (Osgood et al., 1957). Originally developed as a clinical tool for defining the meaning of concepts and relating concepts to one another in a "semantic space," the technique entails graphically placing a pair of bipolar adjectives (such as *good/bad* or *strong/weak*) on a 7-point scale such as this one:

GOOD _____ / _____ / _____ / _____ / _____ / _____ / _____ BAD

Respondents are instructed to place a mark on this continuum that corresponds to their judgment or rating. In research involving certain consumer applications, the bipolar adjectives may be replaced by descriptive expressions more consistent with the research objectives. For example, in rating a new cola-flavored soft drink, the phrase *just another cola* might be at one end of the rating continuum and *a very special beverage* might be at the other.

As with any research, care must be exercised in interpreting the results of a survey. Both the quantity and the quality of the data may vary from survey to survey. Response rates may differ, questions may be asked in different forms, and data collection procedures may vary from one survey to another (Henry, 1984). Ultimately, the utility of any conclusions rests on the integrity of the data and the analytic procedures used.

Occasions arise when research questions cannot be answered through a survey or a poll. Consumers may simply lack the insight to be accurate informants. As an example, consider the hypothetical case of Ralph, who smokes a hypothetical brand of cigarettes we will call "Cowboy." When asked why he chose to smoke Cowboy brand cigarettes, Ralph might reply "taste." In reality, however, Ralph may have begun smoking Cowboy because the advertising for this brand appealed to Ralph's image of himself as an independent, macho type. The reality matters not that Ralph is employed as a clerk at a bridal boutique and bears little resemblance to the Cowboy image portrayed in the advertising.

Consumers may also be unwilling or reluctant to respond to some survey or poll questions. Suppose, for example, that the manufacturers of Cowboy cigarettes wished to know where on the product's packaging the Surgeon General's warning could be placed so that it would be *least* likely to be read. How many consumers would be willing to entertain such a question? Indeed, what would even posing such a question do for the public image of the product? It can be seen that if this hypothetical company were interested in obtaining an answer to such a question, it would have to do so through other means, such as motivation research.

> **JUST THINK . . .**
>
> What is another type of question that consumers may be unwilling or reluctant to respond to in a survey or a poll? What means could a consumer psychologist use to obtain an answer to this question?

Motivation Research Methods

Motivation research in consumer psychology and marketing is so named because it typically involves analyzing motives for consumer behavior and attitudes. **Motivation research methods** include individual interviews and focus groups. These two qualitative research methods are used to examine in depth the reactions of consumers representative of the group of people who use a particular product or service. Unlike quantitative research, which typically involves large numbers of subjects and elaborate statistical analyses, qualitative research typically involves few respondents and little or no statistical analysis. The emphasis in the latter type of research is not on quantity (of subjects or of data) but on the qualities of whatever is under study. Qualitative research often provides the data from which to develop hypotheses that may then be tested with larger numbers of consumers. Qualitative research also has diagnostic value. The best way to obtain highly detailed information about what a consumer likes and dislikes about a product, a store, or an advertisement is to use qualitative research.

A **focus group** is a group interview led by a trained, independent moderator who, ideally, has a knowledge of group discussion facilitation techniques and group dynamics.[3] As their name implies, *focus groups* are designed to *focus* group discussion on something—such as a particular commercial, a concept for a new product, or packaging

---

3. Focus group moderators vary greatly in training and experience. Ideally a focus group moderator should be independent so that he or she can dispassionately discuss the topics with some distance and perspective. Contrary to this caveat, some advertising agencies maintain an in-house focus group moderator staff to test the advertising produced by the agency. Critics of this practice have likened it to assigning wolves to guard the henhouse.

for a new product. Focus groups have examined everything from the choice to purchase organically grown rather than conventionally grown produce (Hammitt, 1990) to issues surrounding the purchase of condoms by college students (Mays et al., 1993).

Focus groups usually consist of 6 to 12 participants who may have been recruited off the floor of a shopping mall or selected in advance to meet some preset qualifications for participation. The usual objective here is for the members of the group to represent in some way the population of targeted consumers for the product or service. Thus, for example, only beer drinkers (defined, for example, as males who drink at least two six-packs per week and females who drink at least one six-pack per week) might be solicited for participation in a focus group designed to explore attributes of a new brand of beer—including such variables as its taste, its packaging, its advertising. Another attribute of beer not known to most consumers is what is referred to in the industry as its *bar call,* a reference to the ease with which one could order the brew in a bar. Because of the high costs associated with introducing a new product and advertising a new or established product, professionally conducted focus groups, complete with a representative sampling of the targeted consumer population, are a valuable tool in market research.

Depending on the requirements of the moderator's client (an advertiser, a manufacturer, etc.), the group discussion can be relatively structured (with a number of points to be covered) or relatively unstructured (with few points to be covered exhaustively). After establishing a rapport with the group, the moderator may, for example, show some advertising or a product to the group and then pose a general question (such as "What did you think of the beer commercial?") to be followed up by more specific kinds of questions (such as "Were the people in that commercial the kind of people you would like to have a beer with?"). The responses of the group members may build on those of other group members, and the result of the free-flowing discussion may be new information, new perspectives, or some previously overlooked problems with the advertising or product.

Focus groups typically last from one to two hours and are usually conducted in rooms (either conference rooms or living rooms) equipped with one-way mirrors (from which the client's staff may observe the proceedings) and audio or video equipment so that a record of the group session will be preserved. Aside from being an active listener and an individual who is careful not to suggest answers to questions or draw conclusions for the respondents, the moderator's duties include (1) following a discussion guide (usually created by the moderator in consultation with the client) and keeping the discussion on the topic; (2) drawing out silent group members so that everyone is heard from; (3) limiting the response time of group members who might dominate the group discussion; and (4) writing a report that not only provides a summary of the group discussion but also offers psychological or marketing insights to the client.

Technology may be employed in focus groups so that second-by-second reaction to stimulus materials such as commercials can be monitored. Cohen described the advantages (1985) and limitations (1987) of a technique whereby respondents watching television commercials pressed a calculator-like keypad to indicate how positive or negative they were feeling on a moment-to-moment basis while watching television. The response could then be visually displayed as a graph and played back for the respondent, who could be asked about the reasons for the spontaneous response.

Focus groups are widely employed in consumer research to

- generate hypotheses that can be further tested quantitatively
- generate information for designing or modifying consumer questionnaires
- provide general background information about a product category

- provide impressions of new product concepts for which little information is available
- obtain new ideas about older products
- generate ideas for product development or names for existing products
- interpret the results of previously obtained quantitative results

In general, the focus group is a highly useful technique for exploratory research, a technique that can be a valuable springboard to more comprehensive quantitative studies. Because so few respondents are typically involved in such groups, the findings from them cannot automatically be thought of as representative of the larger population. Still, many a client (including advertising agency creative staff) has received inspiration from the words spoken by ordinary consumers on the other side of a one-way mirror.

Widely used in consumer research, the focus group is a qualitative research tool used by researchers with varied objectives. Focus groups have been used to explore such topics as adolescent perceptions of smoking imagery in films (McCool et al., 2001), sources of stress in caregivers (Ducharme et al., 2001), ethical dilemmas among medical students (Hicks et al., 2001), influences on meat consumption (Lea & Worsley, 2001), behavior related to feminine hygiene (Lichtenstein & Nansel, 2000), positive by-products of struggles with chemical dependency (McMillen et al., 2001), and the needs of persons who are at risk for suicide (Pullen & Gow, 2000). Most major test developers employ focus groups with test users as part of the test development and test revision process.

> **JUST THINK . . .**
>
> For what type of research questions would a focus group probably not be advisable?

Focus groups provide a forum for open-ended probing of thoughts, which ideally stimulates dialogue and discussion among the participants. Although the open-ended nature of the experience is a strength, the lack of any systematic framework for exploring human motivation is not. No two focus group moderators charged with answering the same questions may approach their task in quite the same way. Addressing this issue, Cohen (1999) proposed a *dimensional* approach to qualitative research. This approach attempts to apply the overlapping psychological modalities or dimensions found so important by clinician Arnold Lazarus (1973, 1989) in his multimodal diagnostic and therapeutic efforts (Lazarus, 1973, 1989) to nonclinical objectives in qualitative research. Specifically, **dimensional qualitative research** is an approach to qualitative research that seeks to ensure that a study is comprehensive and systematic from a psychological perspective, by guiding the study design and proposed questions for discussion on the basis of "BASIC ID" dimensions. BASIC ID is an acronym for the key dimensions in Lazarus's approach to diagnosis and intervention. The letters stand for *behavior, affect, sensation, imagery, cognition, interpersonal relations*, and *drugs*. Cohen's adaptation of Lazarus's work adds an eighth dimension, a sociocultural one, thus adding an *s* to the acronym and changing it to its plural form (BASIC IDS). Reflecting on this approach, Cohen wrote,

> The dimensions of the BASIC IDS can provide a uniform yet systematic framework for exploration and intervention, yet be flexible enough to allow for the implementation of new techniques and innovation. Anchored in logic, it is an approach that is accessible by nonpsychologists who seek to become more knowledgeable in the ways that psychology can be applied in marketing contexts. . . . Regardless of the specific framework adopted by a researcher, it seems high time to acknowledge that we are all feeling, sensing, behaving, imagining, thinking, socially relating, and biochemical beings who are products of our culture. Once this acknowledgment is made, and once we strive to routinely and systematically account for such variables in marketing research, we can begin

to appreciate the added value psychologists bring to qualitative research with consumers in a marketing context. (1999, p. 365)

Behavioral observation   In October 1982, the sales of pain relievers such as aspirin, Bufferin, Anacin, and Excedrin rose sharply. Was this rise in sales due to the effectiveness of the advertising campaigns for these products? No. The sales rose sharply in 1982 when it was learned that seven people had died from ingesting Tylenol capsules laced with cyanide. As Tylenol, the pain reliever with the largest share of the market, was withdrawn from the shelves of stores nationwide, there was a corresponding rise in the sale of alternative preparations. A similar phenomenon occurred in 1986.

Just think what would have happened had market researchers based their judgments concerning the effectiveness of an ad campaign for an over-the-counter pain reliever on sales figures alone during the period of the Tylenol scare. No doubt the data easily could have led to a misinterpretation of what actually occurred. How might market researchers add a quality control component to their research methods? One way is by using multiple methods, such as behavioral observation in addition to survey methods.

It is not unusual for market researchers to station behavioral observers in stores to monitor what really prompts a consumer to buy this or that product at the point of choice. Such an observer at a store selling pain relievers in October 1982 might have observed, for example, a conversation with the clerk about the best alternative to Tylenol. Behavioral observers in a supermarket who studied the purchasing habits of people buying breakfast cereal concluded that children accompanying the purchaser requested or demanded a specific brand of cereal (Atkin, 1978). Hence, it would be wise for breakfast cereal manufacturers to gear their advertising to children, not the adult consumer.

JUST THINK . . .

From your own informal experience, what other types of purchases are probably guided more by input from children than from adults? How could consumer psychologists best test your beliefs regarding this purchase decision?

Other methods   A number of other methods and tools may be brought to bear on marketing and advertising questions. Consumer psychologists sometimes employ projective tests—existing as well as custom designed—as an aid in answering the questions raised by their clients. Special instrumentation, including tachistoscopes and electroencephalographs, have also been used in efforts to uncover consumer motivation. Special computer programs may be used to derive brand names for new products. Thus, for example, when Honda wished to position a new line of its cars as "advanced precision automobiles," a company specializing in the naming of new products conducted a computer search of over 6,900 English-language morphemes to locate word roots that mean or imply "advanced precision." The applicable morphemes were then computer combined in ways the phonetic rules of English would allow. From the resulting list, the best word (that is, one that has visibility among other printed words, one that will be recognizable as a brand name, and so forth) was then selected. In this case, that word was *Acura* (Brewer, 1987).

Literature reviews are another method available to consumer psychologists. A literature review might suggest, for example, that certain sounds or imagery in a particular brand tend to be more popular with consumers than other sounds or imagery (Figure 16–7). Schloss (1981) observed that the sound of the letter *K* was represented better than six times more often than would be expected by chance in the 200 top brand-name products (such as Sanka, Quaker, Nabisco—and, we might add, Acura). Schloss went on to speculate about the ability of this as well as other sounds of words to elicit emotional reactions as opposed to rational ones.

Figure 16–7
What's in a Name?

"What's in a name? A rose by any other name would smell as sweet." Sentiments such as this may be touching to read and beautiful to behold when spoken by talented actors on Broadway. However, they wouldn't have taken William Shakespeare very far on Madison Avenue. The name given to a product is an important part of what is referred to as the "marketing mix": the way a product is positioned, marketed, and promoted in the marketplace. The ad shown, reproduced from a 1927 magazine, touts the benefits of a toothbrush with the name Pro-phy-lac-tic. The creator of this brand name no doubt wished to position this toothbrush as being particularly useful in preventing disease. However, the word prophylactic *(defined as "protective") became more identified in the public's mind with condoms, a fact that could not have helped the longevity of this brand of toothbrush in the marketplace. Today, researchers use a variety of methods, including word association, to create brand names.*

And speaking of eliciting reactions, it is we, Ron Cohen and Mark Swerdlik, who must now pause to *just think* and wonder: What reaction will be elicited from you as the realization sets in that you have come to the end of our textbook? Your reaction could range from *extreme sorrow* (you wish there were more pages to turn) to *unbridled ecstasy* (party time!). Whatever, we want you to know that we consider it an honor and a privilege to have helped introduce you to the world of measurement in psychology and education. You have our best wishes for success in your academic and professional development. And who knows? Maybe it will be you and your work that we will present to students in the future in a succeeding edition of *Psychological Testing and Assessment*.

Self-Assessment

Test your understanding of elements of this chapter by seeing if you can explain each of the following terms, expressions, and abbreviations:

ability and aptitude measures
assessment in career counseling
assessment center
attitude
Big Six
Big Three
burnout
classification
consumer panel
consumer psychology
critical incidents technique
diary panel
dimensional qualitative
   research
drug test
extrinsic motivation

false negative
false positive
focus group
forced distribution technique
GATB
in-basket technique
integrity test
interest measures
intrinsic motivation
job satisfaction
leaderless group technique
MBTI
motivation research methods
organizational commitment
organizational culture
performance test

personality assessment and the
   workplace
physical test
placement
poll
portfolio assessment
pre-employment assessment
productivity
race norming
screening
selection
semantic differential technique
SII
survey
team

Web Watch

Check out the following Web sites for more information about topics discussed in this chapter.

Strong Interest Inventory
www.cpp.com/products/strong/index.asp

www.discoveryourpersonality.com/Strong.html

O'Connor Tweezer Dexterity Test
www.brandymd.com/hair_restoration_assistants.cfm

The General Aptitude Test Battery
157.182.15.43/courses/620/units/unit%202/620GATB.htm

Minnesota Clerical Test
www.behavioraldynamicsphil.com/ped052.htm

Vocational assessment (general)
www.yorku.ca/psycentr/tests/voc.html

Burnout
www.aafp.org/fpm/970400fm/lead.html

www.cpp.com/detail/detailprod.asp?pc=35

www.career-lifeskills.com/products_services/atpr/corpcultdev/cpp-34500.htm

Semantic differential technique
www.cultsock.ndirect.co.uk/MUHome/cshtml/
introductory/semdif.html

Consumer psychology
http://fisher.osu.edu/marketing/scp

www.consumerpsychologist.com

www.wcupa.edu/_ACADEMICS/sch_cas.psy/
Career_Paths/Consumer/Career05.htm

**Abstracts of current articles published
in *Psychology & Marketing***
www.wiley.com/WileyCDA/WileyTitle/
productCd-MAR.html

References

Abel, G. G., Rouleau, J., & Cunningham-Rathner, J. (1986). Sexually aggressive behavior. In W. J. Curran, A. L. McGarry, & S. Shah (Eds.), *Forensic psychiatry and psychology: Perspectives and standards for interdisciplinary practice* (pp. 289–314). Philadelphia: Davis.

Abeles, N., & Barlev, A. (1999). End of life decisions and assisted suicide. *Professional Psychology: Research and Practice, 30,* 229–234.

Abidin, R. R. (1990). *Parenting stress index* (3rd ed.). Odessa, FL: Psychological Assessment Resources.

Abrams, D. B., Binkoff, J. A., Zwick, W. R., et al. (1991). Alcohol abusers' and social drinkers' responses to alcohol-relevant and general situations. *Journal of Studies on Alcohol, 52,* 409–414.

Abrams, S. (1977). *A polygraph handbook for attorneys.* Lexington, MA: Heath.

Achenbach, T. M. (1978). *Child Behavior Profile.* Bethesda, MD: Laboratory of Developmental Psychology, National Institutes of Mental Health.

Achenbach, T. M. (1981). A junior MMPI? *Journal of Personality Assessment, 45,* 332–333.

Achenbach, T. M. (1993). Implications of Multiaxial Empirically Based Assessment for behavior therapy with children. *Behavior Therapy, 24,* 91–116.

Achenbach, T. M., McConaughy, S. H., & Howell, C. T. (1987). Child/adolescent behavioral and emotional problems: Implications of cross-informant correlations for situational specificity. *Psychological Bulletin, 101,* 213–232.

Ackerman, M. J. (1995). *Clinician's guide to child custody evaluations.* New York: Wiley-Interscience.

Ackerman, P. L., & Heggestad, E. D. (1997). Intelligence, personality, and interests: Evidence for overlapping traits. *Psychological Bulletin, 121,* 219–245.

Ackerman, P. L., & Kanfer, R. (1993). Integrating laboratory and field study for improving selection: Development of a battery for predicting air traffic controller success. *Journal of Applied Psychology, 78,* 413–432.

Acklin, M. W. (1995). Avoiding Rorschach dichotomies: Integrating Rorschach interpretation. *Journal of Personality Assessment, 64,* 235–238.

Acklin, M. W. (1996). Personality assessment and managed care. *Journal of Personality Assessment, 66,* 194–201.

Acklin, M. W. (1997). Swimming with sharks. *Journal of Personality Assessment, 69,* 448–451.

Adams, K. M. (1984). Luria left in the lurch: Unfulfilled promises are not valid tests. *Journal of Clinical Neuropsychology, 6,* 455–458.

Adams, K. M. (2000). Practical and ethical issues pertaining to test revisions. *Psychological Assessment, 12,* 281–286.

Adams-Tucker, C. (1982). Proximate effects of sexual abuse in childhood: A report on 28 children. *American Journal of Psychiatry, 139,* 1252–1256.

Addeo, R. R., Greene, A. F., & Geisser, M. E. (1994). Construct validity of the Robson Self-Esteem Questionnaire in a sample of college students. *Educational and Psychological Measurement, 54,* 439–446.

Adelman, S. A., Fletcher, K. E., Bahnassi, A., & Munetz, M. R. (1991). The Scale for Treatment Integration of the Dually Diagnosed (STIDD): An instrument for assessing intervention strategies in the pharmacotherapy of mentally ill substance abusers. *Drug and Alcohol Dependence, 27,* 35–42.

Adler, A. (1927/1965). *Understanding human nature.* Greenwich, CT: Fawcett.

Adler, A. (1933/1964). *Social interest: A challenge to mankind.* New York: Capricorn.

Adler, T. (1990). Does the "new" MMPI beat the "classic"? *APA Monitor, 20,* (4), 18–19.

Administration on Aging. (1999). *Profile of older Americans.* Washington, DC: Author.

Ahern, E. (1949). *Handbook of personnel forms and records.* New York: American Management Association.

Aikman, K. G., Belter, R. W., & Finch, A. J. (1992). Human figure drawings: Validity in assessing intellectual level and academic achievement. *Journal of Clinical Psychology, 48,* 114–120.

Airasian, P. W., Madaus, G. F., & Pedulla, J. J. (1979). *Minimal competency testing.* Englewood Cliffs, NJ: Educational Technology Publications.

Akamatsu, C. T. (1993–1994). The view from within and without: Conducting research on deaf Asian-Americans. *Journal of the American Deafness and Rehabilitation Association, 27,* 12–16.

Alderfer, C. (1972). *Existence, relatedness and growth: Human needs in organizational settings.* New York: Free Press.

Alderson, J. C., Krahnke, K. J., & Stansfield, C. W. (1987). *Reviews of English language proficiency tests.* Washington, DC: TESOL.

Alessandri, S. M., Bendersky, M., & Lewis, M. (1998). Cognitive functioning in 8- to 18-month-old drug-exposed infants. *Developmental Psychology, 34,* 565–573.

Alexander, R. C., Surrell, J. A., & Cohle, S. D. (1987). Microwave oven burns in children: An unusual manifestation of child abuse. *Pediatrics, 79,* 255–260.

Allen, J. (2002). Assessment training for practice in American Indian and Alaska native settings. *Journal of Personality Assessment, 79,* 216–225.

Allen, M. J., & Yen, W. M. (1979). *Introduction to measurement theory.* Monterey, CA: Brooks/Cole.

Allen, N. J., & Meyer, J. P. (1990). The measurement and antecedents of affective, continuance, and normative commitment to the organization. *Journal of Occupational Psychology, 63,* 1–18.

Allen, R., Wasserman, G. A., & Seidman, S. (1990). Children with congenital anomalies: The preschool period. *Journal of Pediatric Psychology, 15,* 327–345.

Allen, T. E. (1994). *Who are the deaf and hard-of-hearing students leaving high school and entering postsecondary education?* (pp. 1–16). U.S. Office of Special Education and Rehabilitative Services: Pelavin Research Institute.

Allport, G. W. (1937). *Personality: A psychological interpretation.* New York: Holt.

Allport, G. W., & Odbert, H. S. (1936). Trait-names: A psycho-lexical study. *Psychological Monographs, 47* (Whole No. 211).

Allport, G. W., Vernon, P. E., & Lindzey, G. (1951). *Study of values* (rev. ed.). Boston: Houghton Mifflin.

Allred, L. J., & Harris, W. G. (1984). *The nonequivalence of computerized and conventional administrations of the Adjective Checklist.* Unpublished manuscript, Johns Hopkins University, Baltimore.

Alpher, V. S., & Blanton, R. L. (1985). The accuracy of lie detection: Why lie tests based on the polygraph should not be admitted into evidence today. *Law & Psychology Review, 9*, 67–75.

Alterman, A. I., McDermott, P. A., Cook, T. G., et al. (2000). Generalizability of the clinical dimensions of the Addiction Severity Index to nonopioid-dependent patients. *Psychology of Addictive Behaviors, 14*, 287–294.

Amabile, T. M., Hill, K. G., Hennessey, B. A., & Tighe, E. M. (1994). The Work Preference Inventory: Assessing intrinsic and extrinsic motivational orientations. *Journal of Personality and Social Psychology, 66*, 950–967.

Amada, G. (1996). You can't please all of the people all of the time: Normative institutional resistances to college psychological services. *Journal of College Student Psychotherapy, 10*, 45–63.

Aman, C. J., Roberts, R. J., & Pennington, B. F. (1998). A neuropsychological examination of the underlying deficit in attention deficit hyperactivity disorder: Frontal lobe versus right parietal lobe theories. *Developmental Psychology, 34*, 956–969.

Ambrosini, P. J., Metz, C., Bianchi, M. D., Rabinovich, H., & Undie, A. (1991). Concurrent validity and psychometric properties of the Beck Depression Inventory in outpatient adolescents. *Journal of the American Academy of Child and Adolescent Psychiatry, 30*, 51–57.

American Association on Mental Retardation. (1992). *Mental retardation: Definition, classification, and systems of supports* (9th ed.). Washington, DC: Author.

American Board of Forensic Odontology, Inc. (1986). Guidelines for analysis of bite marks in forensic investigation. *Journal of the American Dental Association, 12*, 383–386.

American Educational Research Association, American Psychological Association, & National Council on Measurement in Education. (1999). *Standards for educational and psychological testing*. Washington, DC: Author.

American Law Institute. (1956). *Model penal code*. Tentative Draft Number 4.

American Psychiatric Association. (1968). *Diagnostic and statistical manual of mental disorders* (2nd ed.). Washington, DC: Author.

American Psychiatric Association. (1980). *Diagnostic and statistical manual of mental disorders* (3rd ed.). Washington, DC: Author.

American Psychiatric Association. (1987). *Diagnostic and statistical manual of mental disorders* (3rd ed., rev.). Washington, DC: Author.

American Psychiatric Association. (1994). *Diagnostic and statistical manual of mental disorders* (4th ed.). Washington, DC: Author.

American Psychiatric Association. (2000). *Diagnostic and statistical manual of mental disorders* (4th ed.; text rev.). Washington, DC: Author.

American Psychiatric Association. (2001). *Diagnostic and statistical manual of mental disorders* (4th ed.; text rev.). [CD-ROM (Windows)]. Washington, DC: Author.

American Psychological Association. (1953). *Ethical standards of psychologists*. Washington, DC: Author.

American Psychological Association. (1954). *Technical recommendations for psychological tests and diagnostic techniques*. Washington, DC: Author.

American Psychological Association. (1967). *Casebook on ethical standards of psychologists*. Washington, DC: Author.

American Psychological Association. (1981). Ethical principles of psychologists. *American Psychologist, 36*, 633–638.

American Psychological Association. (1985). *Standards for educational and psychological testing*. Washington, DC: Author.

American Psychological Association. (1987). *Casebook on ethical principles of psychologists*. Washington, DC: Author.

American Psychological Association. (1991). *Questionnaires used in the prediction of trustworthiness in pre-employment selection decisions: An APA Task Force report*. Washington, DC: Author.

American Psychological Association. (1992). Ethical principles of psychologists and code of conduct. *American Psychologist, 47*, 1597–1611.

American Psychological Association. (1993, January). Call for book proposals for test instruments. *APA Monitor, 24*, 12.

American Psychological Association. (1996). *Standards for psychological tests*. Washington, DC: Author.

American Psychological Association, Committee on Professional Practice and Standards. (1994a). Guidelines for child custody evaluations in divorce proceedings. *American Psychologist, 49*, 677–680.

American Psychological Association. (1994b). C. H. Lawshe. *American Psychologist, 49*, 549–551.

American Psychological Association. (1995). *Finding information about psychological tests*. Washington, DC: Author.

American Psychological Association. (1996). *Affirmative action: Who benefits?* Washington, DC: Author.

American Psychological Association. (2002). Ethical principles of psychologists and code of conduct. *American Psychologist, 57*, 1060–1073.

American Psychological Association. (2003). Guidelines on multicultural education, training, research, practice, organizational change for psychologists. *American Psychologist, 58*, 377–402.

Ames, S. L., & Stacy, A. W. (1998). Implicit cognition in the prediction of substance use among drug offenders. *Psychology of Addictive Behaviors, 12*, 272–281.

Amrine, M. (Ed.). (1965). Special issue. *American Psychologist, 20*, 857–991.

Anderson, G., & Grace, C. (1991). The Black deaf adolescent: A diverse and underserved population. *Volta Review, 93*, 73–86.

Anderson, J. W. (1990). The life of Henry A. Murray: 1893–1988. In A. I. Rabin, R. A. Zucker, R. A. Emmons, & S. Frank (Eds.), *Studying persons and lives* (pp. 304–333). New York: Springer.

Anderson, W. P. (1995). Ethnic and cross-cultural differences on the MMPI-2. In J. C. Duckworth & W. P. Anderson (Eds.), *MMPI and MMPI-2: Interpretation manual for counselors and clinicians* (4th ed.; pp. 439–460). Bristol, PA: Accelerated Development.

Andrew, G., Hartwell, S. W., Hutt, M. L., & Walton, R. E. (1953). *The Michigan Picture Test*. Chicago: Science Research Associates.

Angoff, W. H. (1962). Scales with nonmeaningful origins and units of measurement. *Educational and Psychological Measurement, 22*, 27–34.

Angoff, W. H. (1964). Technical problems of obtaining equivalent scores on tests. *Educational and Psychological Measurement, 1*, 11–13.

Angoff, W. H. (1966). Can useful general-purpose equivalency tables be prepared for different college admissions tests? In A. Anastasi (Ed.), *Testing problems in perspective* (pp. 251–264). Washington, DC: American Council on Education.

Angoff, W. H. (1971). Scales, norms, and equivalent scores. In R. L. Thorndike (Ed.), *Educational measurement* (2nd ed.). Washington, DC: American Council on Education.

Appelbaum, P., & Grisso, T. (1995a). The MacArthur Treatment Competence Study: I. Mental illness and competence to consent to treatment. *Law and Human Behavior, 19*, 105–126.

Appelbaum, P., & Grisso, T. (1995b). The MacArthur Treatment Competence Study: III. Abilities of patients to consent to psychiatric and medical treatments. *Law and Human Behavior, 19,* 149–174.

Arbisi, P. A., Ben-Porath, Y. S., & McNulty, J. (2002). A comparison of MMPI-2 validity in African American and Caucasian psychiatric inpatients. *Psychological Assessment, 14,* 3–15.

Arnau, R. C., Green, B. A., Rosen, D. H., et al. (2003). Are Jungian preferences really categorical? *Personality & Individual Differences, 34,* 233–251.

Arnett, P. A., Rao, S. M., Grafman, J., et al. (1997). Executive functions in multiple sclerosis: An analysis of temporal ordering, semantic encoding, and planning abilities. *Neuropsychology, 11,* 535–544.

Arnold, D. S., O'Leary, S. G., Wolff, L. S., & Acker, M. M. (1993). The Parenting Scale: A measure of dysfunctional parenting in discipline situations. *Psychological Assessment, 5,* 137–144.

Aronow, E., & Reznikoff, M. (1976). *Rorschach content interpretation.* Orlando, FL: Grune & Stratton.

Aronow, E., & Reznikoff, M. (1983). *A Rorschach introduction: Content and perceptual approaches.* Orlando, FL: Grune & Stratton.

Aronow, E., Reznikoff, M., & Moreland, K. L. (1995). The Rorschach: Projective technique or psychometric test? *Journal of Personality Assessment, 64,* 213–228.

Arvey, R. D. (1979). *Fairness in selecting employees.* Reading, MA: Addison-Wesley.

Arvey, R. D., Bouchard, T. J., Segal, N. L., & Abraham, L. M. (1989). Job satisfaction: Environmental and genetic components. *Journal of Applied Psychology, 74,* 187–192.

Asch, S. E. (1951). Effects of group pressure upon the modification and distortion of judgment. In H. Guetzkow (Ed.), *Groups, leadership, and men.* Pittsburgh, PA: Carnegie.

Asch, S. E. (1955). Opinions and social pressure. *Scientific American, 193,* 33–35.

Asch, S. E. (1957a). Studies of independence and conformity. A minority of one against a unanimous majority. *Psychological Monographs, 70* (9, Whole No. 416).

Asch, S. E. (1957b). An experimental investigation of group influence. In Walter Reed Army Institute of Research (Ed.), *Symposium on preventive and social psychiatry.* Washington, DC: U.S. Government Printing Office.

Association of Personnel Test Publishers (APTP). (1990). Model guidelines for preemployment integrity testing programs. Washington, DC: APTP.

ASVAB 18/19 Counselor Manual: The ASVAB career exploration program. (1995). Washington, DC: U.S. Department of Defense.

Atkin, C. K. (1978). Observation of parent–child interaction in supermarket decision making. *Journal of Marketing, 42,* 41–45.

Atkinson, J. W. (1981). Studying personality in the context of an advanced motivational psychology. *American Psychologist, 36,* 117–128.

Atkinson, R. C., & Shiffrin, R. M. (1968). A proposed system and its control processes. In K. W. Spence & J. T. Spence (Eds.), *The psychology of learning and motivation: Advances in research and theory* (Vol. 2; pp. 82–90). Oxford: Oxford University Press.

Aycan, Z., Kanungo, R. N., Mendonca, M., et al. (2000). Impact of culture on human resource management practices: A 10-country comparison. *Applied Psychology: An International Review, 49,* 192–221.

Ayres, R. R., & Cooley, E. J. (1986). Sequential versus simultaneous processing on the K-ABC: Validity in predicting learning success. *Journal of Psychoeducational Assessment, 4,* 211–220.

Baker, E. L., O'Neill, H. F., & Linn, R. L. (1993). Policy and validity prospects for performance-based assessment. *American Psychologist, 48,* 1210–1218.

Baldwin, A. L., Kalhorn, J., & Breese, F. H. (1945). Patterns of parent behavior. *Psychological Monographs, 58* (Whole No. 268).

Baldwin, J. A. (1984). African self-consciousness and the mental health of African-Americans. *Journal of Black Studies, 15,* 177–194.

Baldwin, J. A., & Bell, Y. R. (1985). The African Self-Consciousness Scale: An Africentric personality questionnaire. *Western Journal of Black Studies, 9*(2), 65–68.

Ball, J. D., Archer, R. P., Gordon, R. A., & French, J. (1991). Rorschach depression indices with children and adolescents: Concurrent validity findings. *Journal of Personality Assessment, 57,* 465–476.

Ball, T. S., & Bernardoni, L. C. (1953). The application of an auditory apperception test to clinical diagnosis. *Journal of Clinical Psychology, 9,* 54–58.

Baltes, B. B., Briggs, T. E., Huff, J. W., et al. (1999). Flexible and compressed workweek schedules: A meta-analysis of their effects on work-related criteria. *Journal of Applied Psychology, 84,* 496–513.

Bank, A. L., MacNeill, S. E., & Lichtenberg, P. A. (2000). Cross validation of the MacNeill-Lichtenberg Decision Tree triaging mental health problems in geriatric rehabilitation patients. *Rehabilitation Psychology, 45,* 193–204.

Baños, J. H., & Franklin, L. M. (2003). Factor structure of the Mini-Mental State Examination in adult psychiatric inpatients. *Psychological Assessment, 14,* 397–400.

Barak, A., & Cohen, L. (2002). Empirical examination of an online version of the Self-Directed Search. *Journal of Career Assessment, 10,* 387–400.

Barden, R. C., Ford, M. E., Jensen, A. G., Rogers-Salyer, M., & Salyer, K. E. (1989). Effects of craniofacial deformity in infancy on the quality of mother-infant interactions. *Child Development, 60,* 819–824.

Bardis, P. D. (1975). The Borromean family. *Social Science, 50,* 144–158.

Bardos, A. N. (1993). Human figure drawings: Abusing the abused. *School Psychology Quarterly, 8,* 177–181.

Barends, A., Westen, D., Leigh, J., Silbert, D., & Byers, S. (1990). Assessing affect-tone of relationship paradigms from TAT and interview data. *Psychological Assessment, 2,* 329–332.

Barker, R. (1963). On the nature of the environment. *Journal of Social Issues, 19,* 17–38.

Barko, N. (1993, August). What's your child's emotional IQ? *Working Mother, 16,* 33–35.

Barnett, L. A., Far, J. M., Mauss, A. L., & Miller, J. A. (1996). Changing perceptions of peer norms as a drinking reduction program for college students. *Journal of Alcohol & Drug Education, 41*(2), 39–62.

Barnett, R. C., & Gareis, K. C. (2000). Reduced hours, job-role quality, and life satisfaction among married women physicians with children. *Psychology of Women Quarterly, 24,* 358–364.

Baron, J., & Norman, M. F. (1992). SATs, achievement tests, and high-school class rank as predictors of college performance. *Educational and Psychological Measurement, 52,* 1047–1055.

Bartholomew, D. (1996a). "Metaphor taken as math: Indeterminacy in the factor analysis model": Comment. *Multivariate Behavioral Research, 31,* 551–554.

Bartholomew, D. (1996b). Response to Dr. Maraun's first reply to discussion of his paper. *Multivariate Behavioral Research, 31,* 631–636.

Barton, K. A., Blanchard, E. B., & Veazy, C. (1999). Self-monitoring as an assessment strategy in behavioral medicine. *Psychological Assessment, 11,* 490–497.

Bartram, D., Beaumont, J. G., Cornford, T., & Dann, P. L. (1987). Recommendations for the design of software for computer based assessment: Summary statement. *Bulletin of the British Psychological Society, 40,* 86–87.

Bass, B. M. (1956). Development of a structured disguised personality test. *Journal of Applied Psychology, 40,* 393–397.

Bass, B. M. (1957). Validity studies of proverbs personality test. *Journal of Applied Psychology, 41,* 158–160.

Bass, B. M. (1958). Famous Sayings Test: General manual. *Psychological Reports, 4,* Monograph Number 6.

Bassett, S. S. (1999). Attention: Neuropsychological predictor of competency in Alzheimer's disease. *Journal of Geriatric Psychiatry and Neurology, 12,* 200–205.

Batchelor, E., Jr., Sowles, G., Dean, R. S., & Fischer, W. (1991). Construct validity of the Halstead-Reitan Neuropsychological Battery for children with learning disorders. *Journal of Psychoeducational Assessment, 9,* 16–31.

Batchelor, E. S., Gray, J. W., & Dean, R. S. (1990). Empirical testing of a cognitive model to account for neuropsychological functioning underlying arithmetic problem solving. *Journal of Learning Disabilities, 23*(1), 38–42.

Batson, D. C. (1975). Attribution as a mediator of bias in helping. *Journal of Personality and Social Psychology, 32,* 455–466.

Baughman, E. E., & Dahlstrom, W. B. (1968). *Negro and white children: A psychological study in the rural South.* New York: Academic Press.

Bauman, M. K. (1974). Blind and partially sighted. In M. V. Wisland (Ed.), *Psychoeducational diagnosis of exceptional children* (pp. 159–189). Springfield, IL: Charles C Thomas.

Bauman, M. K., & Kropf, C. A. (1979). Psychological tests used with blind and visually handicapped persons. *School Psychology Digest, 8,* 257–270.

Baumeister, A. A., & Muma, J. R. (1975). On defining mental retardation. *Journal of Special Education, 9,* 293–306.

Baumeister, R. F. (1990). Suicide as escape from self. *Psychological Review, 97,* 90–113.

Baumrind, D. (1993). The average expectable environment is not good enough: A response to Scarr. *Child Development, 64,* 1299–1317.

Bavolek, S. J. (1984). *Handbook for the Adult-Adolescent Parenting Inventory.* Eau Claire, WI: Family Development Associates.

Baxter, J. C., Brock, B., Hill, P. C., & Rozelle, R. M. (1981). Letters of recommendation: A question of value. *Journal of Applied Psychology, 66,* 296–301.

Baydoun, R. B., & Neuman, G. A. (1992). The future of the General Aptitude Test Battery (GATB) for use in public and private testing. *Journal of Business and Psychology, 7,* 81–91.

Bayley, N. (1955). On the growth of intelligence. *American Psychologist, 10,* 805–818.

Bayley, N. (1959). Value and limitations of infant testing. *Children, 5,* 129–133.

Bayley, N. (1969). *Bayley Scales of Infant Development: Birth to Two Years.* New York: Psychological Corporation.

Bayley, N. (1993). *Bayley Scales of Infant Development (2nd Edition) Manual.* San Antonio, TX: Psychological Corporation.

Beard, J. G., & Ragheb, M. G. (1980). Measuring leisure satisfaction. *Journal of Leisure Research, 12,* 20–33.

Beavers, R. (1985). *Manual of Beavers-Timberlawn Family Evaluation Scale and Family Style Evaluation.* Dallas, TX: Southwest Family Institute.

Beck, A. T., Brown, G., & Steer, R. A. (1989). Prediction of eventual suicide in psychiatric inpatients by clinical ratings of hopelessness. *Journal of Consulting and Clinical Psychology, 57,* 309–310.

Beck, A. T., Rush, A. J., Shaw, B. F., & Emery, G. (1979). *Cognitive therapy for depression.* New York: Guilford.

Beck, A. T., & Steer, R. A. (1993). *Beck Depression Inventory manual.* San Antonio, TX: Psychological Corporation.

Beck, A. T., Steer, R. A., & Brown, G. K. (1996). *Manual for the Beck Depression Inventory, 2nd ed.* San Antonio, TX: Psychological Corporation.

Beck, A. T., & Stein, D. (1961). *Development of a self-concept test.* Unpublished manuscript, University of Pennsylvania School of Medicine, Center for Cognitive Therapy, Philadelphia.

Beck, A. T., Ward, C. H., Mendelson, M., Mock, J., & Erbaugh, J. (1961). An inventory for measuring depression. *Archives of General Psychiatry, 4,* 561–571.

Beck, S. J. (1944). *Rorschach's test: Vol. 1. Basic processes.* New York: Grune & Stratton.

Beck, S. J. (1945). *Rorschach's test: Vol. 2. A variety of personality pictures.* New York: Grune & Stratton.

Beck, S. J. (1952). *Rorschach's test: Vol. 3. Advances in interpretation.* New York: Grune & Stratton.

Beck, S. J. (1960). *The Rorschach experiment.* New York: Grune & Stratton.

Becker, H. A., Needleman, H. L., & Kotelchuck, M. (1978). Child abuse and dentistry: Orificial trauma and its recognition by dentists. *Journal of the American Dental Association, 97*(1), 24–28.

Becker, K. A. (2003). *History of the Stanford-Binet intelligence scales: Content and psychometrics.* (Stanford-Binet Intelligence Scales, Fifth Edition, Assessment Service Bulletin No. 1). Itasca, IL: Riverside Publishing.

Beckham, J. C., Crawford, A. L., & Feldman, M. E. (1998). Trail Making Test performance in Vietnam combat veterans with and without posttraumatic stress disorder. *Journal of Traumatic Stress, 11,* 811–819.

Beebe, S. A., Casey, R., & Pinto-Martin, J. (1993). Association of reported infant crying and maternal parenting stress. *Clinical Pediatrics, 32,* 15–19.

Begault, D. R. (1993). Head-up auditory displays for traffic collision avoidance advisories: A preliminary investigation. *Human Factors, 35,* 707–717.

Beier, E. G., & Sternberg, D. P. (1977). Marital communication. *Journal of Communication, 27,* 92–100.

Beier, M. E., & Ackerman, P. L. (2003). Determinants of health knowledge: An investigation of age, gender, abilities, personality, and interests. *Journal of Personality & Social Psychology, 84,* 439–447.

Bell, N. L., Matthews, T. D., Lassiter, K. S., & Leverett, J. P. (2002). Validity of the Wonderlic Personnel Test as a measure of fluid or crystallized intelligence: Implications for career assessment. *North American Journal of Psychology, 4,* 113–120.

Bellack, A. S., & Hersen, M. (Eds.). (1988). *Behavioral assessment: A practical guide* (3rd ed.). Elmsford, NY: Pergamon.

Bellack, A. S., Morrison, R. L., Mueser, K. T., Wade, J. H., & Sayers, S. L. (1990). Role play for assessing the social competence of psychiatric patients. *Psychological Assessment, 2,* 248–255.

Bellak, L. (1971). *The TAT and CAT in clinical use* (2nd ed.). New York: Grune & Stratton.

Bellak, L., & Bellak, S. (1965). *The CAT-H—A human modification.* Larchmont, NY: C.P.S.

Bellak, L., & Bellak, S. S. (1973). *Senior Apperception Technique.* New York: C.P.S.

Benbow, C. P., & Stanley, J. C. (1996). Inequity in equity: How "equity" can lead to inequity for high-potential students. *Psychology, Public Policy, and Law, 2,* 249–292.

Bender, L. (1938). A visual-motor gestalt test and its clinical use. *American Orthopsychiatric Association Research Monographs*, No. 3.

Bender, L. (1970). The visual-motor gestalt test in the diagnosis of learning disabilities. *Journal of Special Education, 4,* 29–39.

Benedict, R. H., Schretlen, D., & Bobholz, J. H. (1992). Concurrent validity of three WAIS-R short forms in psychiatric inpatients. *Psychological Assessment, 4,* 322–328.

Benjamin, G. A. H., & Gollan, J. K. (2003*). Family evaluation in custody litigation: Reducing risks of ethical infractions and malpractice.* Washington, DC: APA Books.

Bennett, F., Hughes, A., & Hughes, H. (1979). Assessment techniques for deaf-blind children. *Exceptional Children, 45,* 287–288.

Ben-Porath, Y. S. (1990). Cross-cultural assessment of personality: The case for replicatory factor analysis. In J. N. Butcher & C. D. Spielberger (Eds.), *Advances in personality assessment* (Vol. 8; pp. 1–26). Hillsdale, NJ: Erlbaum.

Ben-Porath, Y. S., & Waller, N. G. (1992). Five big issues in clinical personality assessment: A rejoinder to Costa and McCrae. *Psychological Assessment, 4,* 23–25.

Benton, A. L. (1994). Neuropsychological assessment. *Annual Review of Psychology, 45,* 1–25.

Berk, R. A. (Ed.). (1982). *Handbook of methods for detecting test bias.* Baltimore: Johns Hopkins University.

Berkowitz, L., & Frodi, A. (1979). Reactions to a child's mistakes as affected by her/his looks and speech. *Social Psychology Quarterly, 42,* 420–425.

Bernardin, H. J. (1978). Effects of rater training on leniency and halo errors in student ratings of instructors. *Journal of Applied Psychology, 63,* 301–308.

Bernhardt, G. R., Cole, D. J., & Ryan, C. W. (1993). Improving career decision making with adults: Use of portfolios. *Journal of Employment Counseling, 30,* 67–72.

Bernstein, L. (1956). The examiner as an inhibiting factor in clinical testing. *Journal of Consulting Psychology, 20,* 287–290.

Berry, D. S., & Hansen, J. S. (1996). Positive affect, negative affect, and social interaction. *Journal of Personality and Social Psychology, 71,* 796–809.

Besetsny, L. K., Ree, M. J., & Earles, J. A. (1993). Special test for computer programmers? Not needed: The predictive efficiency of the Electronic Data Processing Test for a sample of Air Force recruits. *Educational and Psychological Measurement, 53,* 507–511.

Bienvenu, M. J., Sr. (1978). *A counselor's guide to accompany a Marital Communication Inventory.* Saluda, NC: Family Life.

Bigler, E. D., & Ehrenfurth, J. W. (1981). The continued inappropriate singular use of the Bender Visual Motor Gestalt Test. *Professional Psychology, 12,* 562–569.

Billmire, M. G., & Myers, P. A. (1985). Serious head injury in infants: Accident or abuse? *Pediatrics, 75,* 341–342.

Binet, A., & Henri, V. (1895a). La psychologie individuelle. *L'Année Psychologique, 2,* 411–465.

Binet, A., & Henri, V. (1895b). La mémoire des mots. *L'Année Psychologique, 1,* 1–23.

Binet, A., & Henri, V. (1895c). La mémoire des phrases. *L'Année Psychologique, 1,* 24–59.

Binet, A., & Simon, T. (1905). Méthodes nouvelles pour le diagnostic du niveau intellectuel des anormaux. *L'Année Psychologique, 11,* 191–244.

Binet, A., & Simon, T. (1908). La developpement de l'intelligence chez les enfants [The development of intelligence in children] (E. S. Kite, Trans.). In J. J. Jenkins & D. G. Paterson (reprint Eds.), *Studies in individual differences: The search for intelligence* (pp. 90–96). New York: Appleton-Century-Crofts. (Reprinted in 1961)

Birch, H. G., & Diller, L. (1959). Rorschach signs of "organicity": A physiological basis for perceptual disturbances. *Journal of Projective Techniques, 23,* 184–197.

Birney, R. C., Burdick, H., & Teevan, R. C. (1969). *Fear of failure.* New York: Van Nostrand Reinhold.

Birren, J. E. (1968). Increments and decrements in the intellectual status of the aged. *Psychiatric Research Reports, 23,* 207–214.

Birren, J. E., & Schaie, K. W. (1985). *Handbook of psychology of aging* (2nd ed.). New York: Van Nostrand Reinhold.

Bizot, E. B., & Goldman, S. H. (1993). Prediction of satisfactoriness and satisfaction: An 8-year follow up. Special issue: The theory of work adjustment. *Journal of Vocational Behavior, 43,* 19–29.

Black, B., Ayala, F., & Saffran-Brinks, C. (1994). Science and the law in the wake of *Daubert:* A new search for scientific knowledge. *Texas Law Review, 72,* 715–802.

Black, H. (1963). *They shall not pass.* New York: Morrow.

Black, H. C. (1979). *Black's law dictionary* (rev. ed.). St. Paul, MN: West.

Black, M., Schuler, M., & Nair, P. (1993). Prenatal drug exposure: Neurodevelopment outcome and parenting environment. *Journal of Pediatric Psychology, 18,* 605–620.

Blalock, S. J., Devellis, B. M., Holt, K., & Hahn, P. M. (1993). Coping with rheumatoid arthritis: Is one problem the same as another? *Health Education Quarterly, 20,* 119–132.

Blanck, P. D., & Berven, H. M. (1999). Evidence of disability after *Daubert. Psychology, Public Policy, and Law, 5,* 16–40.

Bloom, A. S., Allard, A. M., Zelko, F. A. J., Brill, W. J., Topinka, C. W., & Pfohl, W. (1988). Differential validity of the K-ABC for lower functioning preschool children versus those of higher ability. *American Journal of Mental Retardation, 93*(3), 273–277.

Blum, G. S. (1950). *The Blacky pictures: A technique for the exploration of personality dynamics.* New York: Psychological Corporation.

Blum, M. L., & Naylor, J. C. (1968). *Industrial psychology: Its theoretical and social foundations* (rev. ed.). New York: Harper & Row.

Blumenthal, S. J., & Kupfer, D. J. (Eds.). (1990). *Suicide over the life cycle: Risk factors, assessment, and treatment of suicidal patients.* Washington, DC: American Psychiatric Press.

Blustein, D. L., & Ellis, M. V. (2000). The cultural context of career assessment. *Journal of Career Assessment, 8,* 379–390.

Board of Professional Affairs, Committee on Professional Practice & Standards, Practice Directorate, American Psychological Association. (1999). Guidelines for psychological evaluations in child protection matters. *American Psychologist, 54,* 586–593.

Boccaccini, M. T., & Brodsky, S. L. (1999). Diagnostic test usage by forensic psychologists in emotional injury cases. *Professional Psychology: Research and Practice, 30,* 253–259.

Bock, R. D., & Jones, L. V. (1968). *The measurement and prediction of judgment and choice.* San Francisco: Holden-Day.

Bombadier, C., & Tugwell, P. (1987). Methodological considerations in functional assessment. *Journal of Rheumatology, 14,* 6–10.

Bond, G. B., & Fox, C. M. (2001). *Applying the Rasch model: Fundamental measurement in human science.* Mahwah, N.J.: Erlbaum.

Bond, G. G., Aiken, L. S., & Somerville, S. C. (1992). The health belief model and adolescents with insulin-dependent diabetes mellitus. *Health Psychology, 11,* 190–198.

Bond, M. H., & Forgas, J. P. (1984). Linking person perception to behavior intention across cultures: The role of cultural collectivism. *Journal of Cross-Cultural Psychology, 1,* 185–216.

Bond, R., & Smith, P. B. (1996). Culture and conformity. A meta-analysis of studies using Asch's line judgment task. *Psychological Bulletin, 119,* 111–137.

Boone, D. E. (1991). Item-reduction vs. subtest-reduction short forms on the WAIS-R with psychiatric inpatients. *Journal of Clinical Psychology, 47,* 271–276.

Booth, A., & Edwards, J. (1983). Measuring marital instability. *Journal of Marriage and the Family, 45,* 387–393.

Boring, E. G. (1923, June 6). Intelligence as the tests test it. *New Republic,* pp. 35–37.

Boring, E. G. (1950). *A history of experimental psychology* (rev. ed.). New York: Appleton-Century-Crofts.

Borkenau, P., & Liebler, A. (1992). Trait inferences: Sources of validity at zero acquaintance. *Journal of Personality and Social Psychology, 62,* 645–657.

Bornstein, P. H., Hamilton, S. B., & Bornstein, M. T. (1986). Self-monitoring procedures. In A. R. Ciminero, C. S. Calhoun, & H. E. Adams (Eds.), *Handbook of behavioral assessment* (pp. 176–222). New York: Wiley.

Bornstein, R. F. (1998). Interpersonal dependency and physical illness: A meta-analytic review of retrospective and prospective studies. *Journal of Research in Personality, 32,* 480–497.

Bornstein, R. F. (1999). Criterion validity of objective and projective dependency tests: A meta-analytic assessment of behavioral prediction. *Psychological Assessment, 11,* 48–57.

Bornstein, R. F., Rossner, S. C., Hill, E. L., & Stepanian, M. L. (1994). Face validity and fakability of objective and projective measures of dependency. *Journal of Personality Assessment, 63,* 363–386.

Bove, C. F., Sobal, J., & Rauschenbach, B. S. (2003). Food choices among newly married couples: Convergence, conflict, individualism, and projects. *Appetite, 40,* 25–41.

Boyle, J. P. (1987). Intelligence, reasoning, and language proficiency. *Modern Language Journal, 71,* 277–288.

Bozeman, D. P., & Perrewe, P. L. (2001). The effect of item content overlap on Organizational Commitment Questionnaire–turnover cognitions relationships. *Journal of Applied Psychology, 86,* 161–173.

Bracken, B. A. (1985). A critical review of the Kaufman Assessment Battery for Children (K-ABC). *School Psychology Review, 14,* 21–36.

Bracken, B. A., & Barona, A. (1991). State of the art procedures for translating, validating, and using psychoeducational tests in cross-cultural assessment. *School Psychology International, 12,* 119–132.

Braden, J. P. (1985). *Deafness, deprivation, and IQ.* New York: Plenum.

Braden, J. P. (1990). Do deaf persons have a characteristic psychometric profile on the Wechsler Performance Scales? *Journal of Psychoeducational Assessment, 8,* 518–526.

Braden, J. P. (1992). Intellectual assessment of deaf and hard-of-hearing people: A quantitative and qualitative research synthesis. *School Psychology Review, 21,* 82–84.

Bradley, J. P., Nicol, A. A., Charbonneau, D., & Meyer, J. P. (2002). Personality correlates of leadership development in Canadian Forces officer candidates. *Canadian Journal of Behavioural Science, 34,* 92–103.

Bradley-Johnson, S. (1994). *Psychoeducational assessment of students who are visually impaired or blind: Infancy through high school.* Austin, TX: PRO-ED.

Bradley-Johnson, S., & Harris, S. (1990). Best practices in working with students with a visual loss. In A. Thomas & J. Grimes (Eds.), *Best practices in school psychology II* (pp. 871–885). Washington, DC: National Association of School Psychologists.

Brady, N. C., & Halle, J. W. (1997). Functional analysis of communicative behaviors. *Focus on Autism and Other Developmental Disabilities, 12*(2), 95–104.

Braginsky, B. M., Braginsky, D. D., & Ring, K. (1969). *Methods of madness.* New York: Holt, Rinehart & Winston.

Brannen, M. Y., & Salk, J. E. (2000). Partnering across borders: Negotiating organizational culture in a German-Japanese joint venture. *Human Relations, 53,* 451–487.

Brannigan, G. G., & Brunner, N. A. (2002). *Guide to the qualitative scoring system for the modified version of the Bender-Gestalt test.* Springfield, IL: Charles C Thomas.

Brannigan, G. G., & Decker, S. L. (2003). *Bender Visual-Motor Gestalt Test Second Edition, Examiner's Manual.* Itasca, IL: Riverside Publishing.

Brassard, M., et al. (Eds.). (1986). *The psychological maltreatment of children and youth.* Elmsford, NY: Pergamon.

Brauer, B. (1993). Adequacy of a translation of the MMPI into American Sign Language for use with deaf individuals: Linguistic equivalency issues. *Rehabilitation Psychology, 38,* 247–259.

Bray, D. W. (1964). The management progress study. *American Psychologist, 19,* 419–429.

Bray, D. W. (1982). The assessment center and the study of lives. *American Psychologist, 37,* 180–189.

Bresolin, M. J., Jr. (1984). A comparative study of computer administration of the Minnesota Multiphasic Personality Inventory in an inpatient psychiatric setting. *Dissertation Abstracts International, 46,* 295B. (University Microfilms No. 85–06, 377).

Brewer, E. W., & Clippard, L. F. (2002). Burnout and job satisfaction among student support services personnel. *Human Resource Development Quarterly, 13,* 169–186.

Brewer, S. (1987, January 11). A perfect package, yes, but how 'bout the name? *Journal-News* (Rockland County, NY), pp. H-1, H-18.

Bricklin, B. (1984). *The Bricklin Perceptual Scales: Child-Perception-of-Parents-Series.* Furlong, PA: Village.

Bringle, R., Roach, S., Andler, C., & Evenbeck, S. (1979). Measuring the intensity of jealous reactions. *Catalogue of Selected Documents in Psychology, 9,* 23–24.

Brittain, H. L. (1907). A study in imagination. *Pedagogical Seminary, 14,* 137–207.

Brody, D., Serby, M., Etienne, N., & Kalkstein, D. C. (1991). Olfactory identification deficits in HIV infection. *American Journal of Psychiatry, 148,* 248–250.

Brody, M. L., Walsh, B. T., & Devlin, M. J. (1994). Binge eating disorder: Reliability and validity of a new diagnostic category. *Journal of Consulting and Clinical Psychology, 62,* 381–386.

Brody, N. (1972). *Personality: Research and theory.* New York: Academic Press.

Brodzinsky, D. M. (1993). On the use and misuse of psychological testing in child custody evaluations. *Professional Psychology: Research and Practice, 24,* 213–219.

Brogden, H. E. (1946). On the interpretation of the correlation coefficient as a measure of predictive efficiency. *Journal of Educational Psychology, 37,* 65–76.

Brogden, H. E. (1949). When tests pay off. *Personnel Psychology, 2,* 171–183.

Brotemarkle, R. A. (1947). Clinical psychology, 1896–1946. *Journal of Consulting and Clinical Psychology, 11,* 1–4.

Brown, D. C. (1994). Subgroup norming: Legitimate testing practice or reverse discrimination. *American Psychologist, 49,* 927–928.

Brown, G., Nicassio, P. W., & Wallston, K. A. (1989). Pain coping strategies and depression in rheumatoid arthritis. *Journal of Consulting and Clinical Psychology, 57,* 652–657.

Brown, J. M. (1984). Imagery coping strategies in the treatment of migraine. *Pain, 18,* 157–167.

Brown, R. D. (1972). The relationship of parental perceptions of university life and their characterizations of their college sons and daughters. *Educational and Psychological Measurement, 32,* 365–375.

Brown, R. T., Reynolds, C. R., & Whitaker, J. S. (1999). Bias in mental testing since *Bias in Mental Testing. School Psychology Quarterly, 14,* 208–238.

Brown, S. P., & Peterson, R. A. (1993). Antecedents and consequences of salesperson job satisfaction: Meta-analysis and assessment of causal effects. *Journal of Marketing Research, 30,* 63–77.

Browning, D. L. (1987). Ego development, authoritarianism, and social status: An investigation of the incremental validity of Loevinger's Sentence Completion Test (Short Form). *Journal of Personality and Social Psychology, 53,* 113–118.

Bryer, J. B., Martines, K. A., & Dignan, M. A. (1990). Millon Clinical Multiaxial Inventory Alcohol Abuse and Drug Abuse scales and the identification of substance-abuse patients. *Psychological Assessment, 2,* 438–441.

Bucholz, K. K., Cadoret, R., Cloninger, C. R., & Dinwiddie, S. H. (1994). A new, semi-structured psychiatric interview for use in genetic linkage studies: A report on the reliability of the SSAGA. *Journal of Studies on Alcohol, 55,* 149–158.

Buck, J. N. (1948). The H-T-P technique: A qualitative and quantitative scoring manual. *Journal of Clinical Psychology, 4,* 317–396.

Buck, J. N. (1950). *Administration and interpretation of the H-T-P test: Proceedings of the H-T-P workshop at Veterans Administration Hospital, Richmond, Virginia.* Beverly Hills, CA: Western Psychological Services.

Buckle, M. B., & Holt, N. F. (1951). Comparison of Rorschach and Behn Inkblots. *Journal of Projective Techniques, 15,* 486–493.

Buckner, F., & Firestone, M. (2000). "Where the public peril begins": 25 years after *Tarasoff. Journal of Legal Medicine, 21,* 187–222.

Bucofsky, D. (1971). Any learning skills taught in the high school? *Journal of Reading, 15*(3), 195–198.

Bukatman, B. A., Foy, J. L., & De Grazia, E. (1971). What is competency to stand trial? *American Journal of Psychiatry, 127,* 1225–1229.

Burger, J. M., Horita, M., Kinoshita, L., et al. (1997). Effects of time on the norm of reciprocity. *Basic and Applied Social Psychology, 19,* 91–100.

Burgess, A. W., McCausland, M. P., & Wolbert, W. A. (1981, February). Children's drawings as indicators of sexual trauma. *Perspectives in Psychiatric Care, 19,* 50–58.

Burisch, M. (1984). Approaches to personality inventory construction: A comparison of merits. *American Psychologist, 39,* 214–227.

Burke, M. J. (1984). Validity generalization: A review and critique of the correlation model. *Personnel Psychology, 37,* 93–115.

Burke, R. J. (1970). Occupational and life strains, satisfactions, and mental health. *Journal of Business Administration, 1,* 35–41.

Burns, A., Jacoby, R., & Levy, R. (1991). Progression of cognitive impairment in Alzheimer's disease. *Journal of the American Geriatrics Society, 39,* 39–45.

Burns, E. (1998). *Test accommodations for students with disabilities.* Springfield, IL: Charles C Thomas.

Burns, R. C., & Kaufman, S. H. (1970). *Kinetic Family Drawings (K-F-D): An introduction to understanding through kinetic drawings.* New York: Brunner/Mazel.

Burns, R. C., & Kaufman, S. H. (1972). *Actions, styles, and symbols in Kinetic Family Drawings (K-F-D).* New York: Brunner/Mazel.

Buros, O. K. (1938). *The 1938 mental measurements yearbook.* New Brunswick, NJ: Rutgers University Press.

Buros, O. K. (1968). The story behind the mental measurements yearbooks. *Measurement and Evaluation in Guidance, 1*(2), 86–95.

Burstein, A. G. (1972). Review of the Wechsler Adult Intelligence Scale. In O. K. Buros (Ed.), *The seventh mental measurements yearbook* (pp. 786–788). Highland Park, NJ: Gryphon.

Burwen, L. S., & Campbell, D. T. (1957). The generality of attitudes toward authority and nonauthority figures. *Journal of Abnormal and Social Psychology, 54,* 24–31.

Bushard, P., & Howard, D. A. (Eds.). (1994). *Resource guide for custody evaluators: A handbook for parenting evaluations.* Madison, WI: Association for Family and Conciliation Courts.

Bushman, B. J., & Cantor, J. (2003). Media ratings for violence and sex: Implications for policymakers and parents. *American Psychologist, 58,* 130–141.

Bushman, B. J., & Wells, G. L. (1998). Trait aggressiveness and hockey penalties: Predicting hot tempers on the ice. *Journal of Applied Psychology, 83,* 969–974.

Butcher, J. N. (1987). The use of computers in psychological assessment: An overview of practices and issues. In J. N. Butcher (Ed.), *Computerized psychological assessment: A practitioner's guide* (pp. 3–14). New York: Basic.

Butcher, J. N. (1990). *MMPI-2 in psychological treatment.* New York: Oxford University Press.

Butcher, J. N. (1994). Psychological assessment by computer: Potential gains and problems to avoid. *Psychiatric Annals, 24,* 20–24.

Butcher, J. N. (2000). Revising psychological tests: Lessons learned from the revision of the MMPI. *Psychological Assessment, 12,* 263–271.

Butcher, J. N. (2003). Discontinuities, side steps, and finding a proper place: An autobiographical account. *Journal of Personality Assessment, 80,* 223–236.

Butcher, J. N., & Han, K. (1995). Development of an MMPI-2 scale to assess the presentation of self in a superlative manner: The S Scale. In J. N. Butcher & C. D. Spielberger (Eds.), *Advances in personality assessment* (Vol. 10; pp. 25–50). Hillsdale, NJ: Erlbaum.

Butcher, J. N., Perry, J. N., & Atlis, M. M. (2000). Validity and utility of computer-based test interpretation. *Psychological Assessment, 12,* 6–18.

Butcher, J. N., Williams, C. L., Graham, J. R., et al. (1992). *Minnesota Multiphasic Personality Inventory-Adolescent (MMPI-A): Manual for administration, scoring, and interpretation.* Minneapolis: University of Minnesota Press.

Butters, N., Wolfe, J., Martone, M., et al. (1985). Memory disorders associated with Huntington's disease: Verbal recall, verbal recognition and procedural memory. *Neuropsychologia, 23,* 729–743.

Byrne, D. (1974). *An introduction to personality* (2nd ed.). Englewood Cliffs, NJ: Prentice-Hall.

Byrnes, M. M., & Spitz, H. H. (1977). Performance of retarded adolescents and non-retarded children on the Tower of Hanoi problem. *American Journal of Mental Deficiency, 81,* 561–569.

Cain, L. F., Levine, S., & Elsey, F. F. (1963). *Cain-Levine Social Competency Scale.* Palo Alto, CA: Consulting Psychologists Press.

Calhoon, M. B., Fuchs, L. S., & Hamlett, C. L. (2000). Effects of computer-based test accommodations on mathematics performance assessments for secondary students with learning disabilities. *Learning Disability Quarterly, 23,* 271–282.

Callahan, J. (1994). The ethics of assisted suicide. *Health and Social Work, 19,* 237–244.

Callero, P. L. (1992). The meaning of self-in-role: A modified measure of role-identity. *Social Forces, 71,* 485–501.

Camara, W. J., Nathan, J. S., & Puente, A. E. (2000). Psychological test usage: Implications in professional psychology. *Professional Psychology: Research and Practice, 31,* 141–154.

Camara, W. J., & Schneider, D. L. (1994). Integrity tests: Facts and unresolved issues. *American Psychologist, 49,* 112–119.

Camilli, G., & Shepard, L. A. (1985). A computer program to aid the detection of biased test items. *Educational & Psychological Measurement, 45,* 595–600.

Campbell, D. P. (1971). *Handbook for the Strong Vocational Interest Blank.* Palo Alto, CA: Stanford University Press.

Campbell, D. P. (1972). The practical problems of revising an established psychological test. In J. N. Butcher (Ed.), *Objective personality assessment: Changing perspectives* (pp. 117–130). New York: Academic Press.

Campbell, D. T., & Fiske, D. W. (1959). Convergent and discriminant validation by the multitrait-multimethod matrix. *Psychological Bulletin, 56,* 81–105.

Campos, L. P. (1989). Adverse impact, unfairness, and bias in the psychological screening of Hispanic peace officers. *Hispanic Journal of Behavioral Sciences, 11,* 122–135.

Cannon-Bowers, J. A., Salas, E., Blickensderfer, E., & Bowers, C. A. (1998). The impact of cross-training and workload on team functioning: A replication and extension of initial findings. *Human Factors, 40,* 92–101.

Caplan, L. J., & Schooler, C. (2003). The roles of fatalism, self-confidence, and intellectual resources in the disablement process in older adults. *Psychology and Aging, 18,* 551–561.

Capraro, R. M., & Capraro, M. M. (2002). Myers-Briggs Type Indicator score reliability across studies: A meta-analytic reliability generalization study. *Educational & Psychological Measurement, 62,* 590–602.

Capretz, L. F. (2003). Personality types in software engineering. *International Journal of Human-Computer Studies, 58,* 207–214.

Care, E. (1996). The structure of interests related to college course destinations. *Journal of Career Assessment, 4,* 77–89.

Carey, M. P., Faulstich, M. E., Gresham, F. M., Ruggerio, L., & Enyart, P. (1987). Children's Depression Inventory: Construct and discriminant validity across clinical and non-referred (control) populations. *Journal of Consulting and Clinical Psychology, 55,* 755–761.

Carey, N. B. (1994). Computer predictors of mechanical job performance: Marine Corps findings. *Military Psychology, 6,* 1–30.

Carmichael, L. (1927). A further study of the development of behavior in vertebrates experimentally removed from the influence of external stimulation. *Psychological Review, 34,* 34–47.

Carroll, J. B. (1985, May). Domains of cognitive ability. Symposium: Current theories and findings on cognitive abilities. Los Angeles: AAAS.

Carroll, J. B. (1993). *Human cognitive abilities: A survey of factor-analytic studies.* Cambridge, England: Cambridge University Press.

Carroll, J. B. (1997). The three-stratum theory of cognitive abilities. In D. P. Flanagan et al. (Eds.), *Contemporary intellectual assessment: Theories, tests, and issues* (pp. 122–130). New York: Guilford.

Carroll, K. M. (1998). *A cognitive-behavioral approach: Treating cocaine addiction.* NIH Publication No. 98-4308. Rockville, MD: National Institute on Drug Abuse.

Carroll, K. M., Nich, C., Frankforter, T. L., & Bisighini, R. M. (1999). Do patients change in the ways we intend? Assessing acquisition of coping skills among cocaine-dependent patients. *Psychological Assessment, 11,* 77–85.

Carter, B. L., & Tiffany, S. T. (1999). Meta-analysis of cue reactivity in addiction research. *Addiction, 94,* 327–340.

Caruso, J. C. (2000). Reliability generalization of the NEO personality scales. *Educational and Psychological Measurement, 60,* 236–254.

Carver, R. P. (1968/1969). Designing an aural aptitude test for Negroes: An experiment that failed. *College Board Review, 70,* 10–14.

Carver, R. P. (1969). Use of a recently developed listening comprehension test to investigate the effect of disadvantagement upon verbal proficiency. *American Educational Research Journal, 6,* 263–270.

Cascio, W. F. (1987). *Applied psychology in personnel management* (3rd ed.). Englewood Cliffs, NJ: Prentice-Hall.

Cascio, W. F., Outtz, J., Zedeck, S., & Goldstein, I. L. (1991). Statistical implications of six methods of test score use in personnel selection. *Personnel Psychology, 4,* 233–264.

Caspi, A., Begg, D., Dickson, N., et al. (1997). Personality differences predict health-risk behaviors in young adulthood: Evidence from a longitudinal study. *Journal of Personality and Social Psychology, 73,* 1052–1063.

Caspi, A., Elder, G., & Bem, D. J. (1987). Moving against the world: Life-course patterns of explosive children. *Developmental Psychology, 23,* 308–313.

Cassel, R. N. (1958). *The leadership q-sort test: A test of leadership values.* Murfreesboro, TN: Psychometric Affiliates.

Castro, V. S. (2003). *Acculturation and psychological adaptation.* Westport, CT: Praeger.

Catalano, R., Novaco, R., & McConnell, W. (1997). A model of the net effect of job loss on violence. *Journal of Personality and Social Psychology, 72,* 1440–1447.

Cates, J. A., & Lapham, R. F. (1991). Personality assessment of the prelingual, profoundly deaf child or adolescent. *Journal of Personality Assessment, 56,* 118–129.

Cattell, H. E. P. (1996). The original big five: A historical perspective. *European Review of Applied Psychology, 46,* 5–14.

Cattell, J. M. (1887). Experiments on the association of ideas. *Mind, 12,* 68–74.

Cattell, J. M., & Bryant, S. (1889). Mental association investigated by experiment. *Mind, 14,* 230–250.

Cattell, P. (1940). *Cattell Infant Intelligence Scale.* New York: Psychological Corporation.

Cattell, R. B. (1940). A culture free intelligence test, Part I. *Journal of Educational Psychology, 31,* 161–179.

Cattell, R. B. (1941). Some theoretical issues in adult intelligence testing. *Psychological Bulletin, 38,* 592.

Cattell, R. B. (1946). *The description and measurement of personality.* New York: Harcourt, Brace & World.

Cattell, R. B. (1947). Confirmation and clarification of the primary personality factors. *Psychometrika, 12,* 197–220.

Cattell, R. B. (1948a). The primary personality factors in the realm of objective tests. *Journal of Personality, 16,* 459–487.

Cattell, R. B. (1948b). The primary personality factors in women compared with those in men. *British Journal of Psychology, Statistical Section, 1,* 114–130.

Cattell, R. B. (1950). *Personality: A systematic theoretical and factual study.* New York: McGraw-Hill.

Cattell, R. B. (1957). *Personality and motivation, structure and measurement.* Yonkers, NY: World Book.

Cattell, R. B. (1965). *The scientific analysis of personality.* Baltimore: Penguin.

Cattell, R. B. (1971). *Abilities: Their structure, growth, and action.* Boston: Houghton Mifflin.

Cattell, R. B., Cattell, A. K. S., & Cattell, H. E. P. (1993). *16 PF, Fifth Edition.* Champaign, IL: Institute for Personality and Ability Testing.

Cattell, R. B., & Horn, J. L. (1978). A check on the theory of fluid and crystallized intelligence with description of new subtest design. *Journal of Educational Measurement, 15,* 139–164.

Cattell, R. B., & Krug, S. E. (1986). The number of factors in the 16 PF: A review of the evidence with special emphasis on methodological problems. *Educational and Psychological Measurement, 46,* 509–522.

Caught, K., Shadur, M. A., & Rodwell, J. J. (2000). The measurement artifact in the Organizational Commitment Questionnaire. *Psychological Reports, 87,* 777–788.

Ceci, S. J., Ross, D. F., & Toglia, M. P. (1987). Suggestibility of children's memory: Psycholegal implications. *Journal of Experimental Psychology, 116,* 38–49.

Celis, W., III. (1994, December 16). Computer admissions test found to be ripe for abuse. *New York Times,* pp. A1, A32.

Cerney, M. S. (1984). One last response to the Rorschach test: A second chance to reveal oneself. *Journal of Personality Assessment, 48,* 338–344.

Champagne, J. E. (1969). Job recruitment of the unskilled. *Personnel Journal, 48,* 259–268.

Chan, K.-Y., Drasgow, F., & Sawin, L. L. (1999). What is the shelf life of a test? The effect of time on the psychometrics of a cognitive ability test battery. *Journal of Applied Psychology, 84,* 610–619.

Chance, N. A. (1965). Acculturation, self-identification, and personality adjustment. *American Anthropologist, 67,* 372–393.

Chaney, E. F., O'Leary, M. R., & Marlatt, G. A. (1978). Skill training with problem drinkers. *Journal of Consulting and Clinical Psychology, 46,* 1092–1104.

Chantler, L., Pelco, L., & Mertin, P. (1993). The psychological evaluation of child sexual abuse using the Louisville Behavior Checklist and human figure drawing. *Child Abuse and Neglect, 17,* 271–279.

Chaplin, W. F., John, O. P., & Goldberg, L. R. (1988). Conceptions of state and traits: Dimensional attributes with ideals as prototypes. *Journal of Personality and Social Psychology, 54,* 541–557.

Chapman, J. C. (1921). *Trade tests.* New York: Holt.

Chapman, L., & Chapman, J. (1967). Genesis of popular but erroneous psychodiagnostic observations. *Journal of Abnormal Psychology, 72,* 193–204.

Chappin, S. R., & Brook, J. S. (2001). The influence of generational status and psychosocial variables on marijuana use among Black and Puerto Rican adolescents. *Hispanic Journal of Behavioral Sciences, 23,* 22–36.

Chartrand, J. M., Borgen, F. H., Betz, N. E., & Donnay, D. (2002). Using the Strong Interest Inventory and the Skills Confidence Inventory to explain career goals. *Journal of Career Assessment, 10,* 169–189.

Chase, J. (1986). Application of assessment techniques to the totally blind. In P. Lazarus & S. Storchart (Eds.), *Psychoeducational evaluation of children and adolescents with low incidence handicaps.* New York: Grune & Stratton.

Chase, S., & Schlink, F. J. (1927). *Your money's worth: A study in the waste of the consumer's dollar.* New York: Macmillan.

Chess, S., & Thomas, A. (1973). Temperament in the normal infant. In J. C. Westman (Ed.), *Individual differences in children.* New York: Wiley.

Cheung, F. M., & Lau, B. (1982). Situational variations of help-seeking behavior among Chinese patients. *Comprehensive Psychiatry, 23,* 252–262.

Chinman, M. J., Allende, M., Weingarten, R., et al. (1999). On the road to collaborative treatment planning: Consumer and provider perspectives. *Journal of Behavioral Health Services & Research, 26,* 211–218.

Chinoy, E. (1967). *Society: An introduction to sociology.* New York: Random House.

Chira-Chavala, T., & Yoo, S. M. (1994). Potential safety benefits on intelligence cruise control systems. *Accident Analysis & Prevention, 26,* 135–146.

Cho, H., & LaRose, R. (1999). Privacy issues in Internet surveys. *Social Science Computer Review, 17,* 421–434.

Christensen, A. L. (1975). *Luria's neuropsychological investigation.* New York: Spectrum.

Christensen, K. M., & Delgado, G. L. (1993). *Multicultural issues in deafness.* White Plains, NY: Longman.

Christiansen, A. J., Weibe, J. S., Smith, T. W., & Turner, C. W. (1994). Predictors of survival among hemodialysis patients: Effects of perceived family support. *Health Psychology, 13,* 521–525.

Church, A. T., & Burke, P. J. (1994). Exploratory and confirmatory tests of the Big Five and Tellegen's three- and four-dimensional models. *Journal of Personality and Social Psychology, 66,* 93–114.

Cicchetti, D., & Carlson, V. (Eds.). (1989). *Child maltreatment: Theory and research on the causes and consequences of child abuse and neglect.* New York: Cambridge University Press.

Clarizio, H. F. (1989). *Assessment and treatment of depression in children and adolescents.* Brandon, VT: Clinical Psychological Publishing.

Clark, B. (1979). *Growing up gifted.* Columbus, OH: Merrill.

Clark, B. (1988). *Growing up gifted* (3rd ed.). Columbus, OH: Merrill.

Clark, L. A. (1999). Introduction to the special section on the concept of disorder. *Journal of Abnormal Psychology, 108,* 371–373.

Cleckley, H. (1976). *The mask of sanity* (5th ed.). St. Louis, MO: Mosby.

Clements, C. B. (1999). Psychology, attitude shifts, and prison growth. *American Psychologist, 54,* 785–786.

Cloninger, C. R., Przybeck, T. R., & Svrakis, D. M. (1991). The Tridimensional Personality Questionnaire: U.S. normative data. *Psychological Reports, 69,* 1047–1057.

Code of Fair Testing Practices in Education. (1988). Washington, DC: Joint Committee on Testing Practices.

Coggins, M. H., Pynchon, M. R., & Dvoskin, J. A. (1998). Integrating research and practice in federal law enforcement: Secret Service applications of behavioral science expertise to protect the president. *Behavioral Sciences and the Law, 16,* 51–70.

Cohen, B. M., Moses, J. L., & Byham, W. C. (1977). *The validity of assessment centers: A literature review* (rev. ed.; monograph no. 2). Pittsburgh, PA: Development Dimensions.

Cohen, F., & Lazarus, R. S. (1973). Active coping processes, coping dispositions, and recovery from surgery. *Psychosomatic Medicine, 35,* 375–389.

Cohen, J. (1952a). A factor-analytically based rationale for the Wechsler-Bellevue. *Journal of Consulting Psychology, 16,* 272–277.

Cohen, J. (1952b). Factors underlying Wechsler-Bellevue performance of three neuropsychiatric groups. *Journal of Abnormal and School Psychology, 47,* 359–364.

Cohen, J. (1957a). The factorial structure of the WAIS between early adulthood and old age. *Journal of Consulting Psychology, 21,* 283–290.

Cohen, J. (1957b). A factor-analytically based rationale for the Wechsler Adult Intelligence Scale. *Journal of Consulting Psychology, 21,* 451–457.

Cohen, O., Fischgrund, J., & Redding, R. (1990). Deaf children from ethnic, linguistic, and racial minority backgrounds: An overview. *American Annals of the Deaf, 135,* 67–73.

Cohen, R. J. (1977). Socially reinforced obsessing: A reply. *Journal of Consulting and Clinical Psychology, 45,* 1166–1171.

Cohen, R. J. (1979). *Malpractice: A guide for mental health professionals.* New York: Free Press.

Cohen, R. J. (1985). Computer-enhanced qualitative research. *Journal of Advertising Research, 25*(3), 48–52.

Cohen, R. J. (1987). Overview of emerging evaluative and diagnostic methods technologies. In *Proceedings of the fourth annual Advertising Research Foundation workshop: Broadening the horizons of copy research.* New York: Advertising Research Foundation.

Cohen, R. J. (1994). *Psychology & adjustment: Values, culture, and change.* Boston: Allyn & Bacon.

Cohen, R. J. (1999a). *Exercises in psychological testing and assessment.* Mountain View, CA: Mayfield.

Cohen, R. J. (1999b). What qualitative research can be. *Psychology & Marketing, 16,* 351–368.

Cohen, R. J. (2001). *Discussion of Organizational Culture* (DOC). Jamaica, NY: Author.

Cohen, R. J. (2005). *Exercises in psychological testing and assessment.* San Francisco: McGraw-Hill.

Cohen, R. J., Becker, R. E., & Teevan, R. C. (1975). Perceived somatic reaction to stress and hostile press. *Psychological Reports, 37,* 676–678.

Cohen, R. J., & Houston, D. R. (1975). Fear of failure and rigidity in problem solving. *Perceptual and Motor Skills, 40,* 930.

Cohen, R. J., Montague, P., Nathanson, L. S., & Swerdlik, M. E. (1988). *Psychological testing: An introduction to tests and measurement.* Mountain View, CA: Mayfield.

Cohen, R. J., & Parker, C. (1974). Fear of failure and death. *Psychological Reports, 34,* 54.

Cohen, R. J., & Smith, F. J. (1976). Socially reinforced obsessing: Etiology of a disorder in a Christian Scientist. *Journal of Consulting and Clinical Psychology, 44,* 142–144.

Cohen, R. J., & Teevan, R. C. (1974). Fear of failure and impression management: An exploratory study. *Psychological Reports, 35,* 1332.

Cohen, R. J., & Teevan, R. C. (1975). Philosophies of human nature and hostile press. *Psychological Reports, 37,* 460–462.

Cohen, S., Nermelstein, R., Karmack, T., & Hoberman, H. (1985). Measuring the functional components of social support. In I. G. Sarason & B. Sarason (Eds.), *Social support: Theory, research, and practice* (pp. 73–94). Dordrecht, Netherlands: Martinus Nijhoff.

Cole, S. T., & Hunter, M. (1971). Pattern analysis of WISC scores achieved by culturally disadvantaged children. *Psychological Reports, 20,* 191–194.

Collins, J. K., Jupp, J. J., Maberly, G. F., et al. (1987). An exploratory study of the intellectual functioning of neurological and myxoedematous cretins in China. *Australia & New Zealand Journal of Developmental Disabilities, 13,* 13–20.

Collins, L. M. (1996). Is reliability obsolete? A commentary on "Are simple gain scores obsolete?" *Applied Psychological Measurement, 20,* 289–292.

Collins, M. (1998, Spring). Great expectations: What students have to say about the process and practice of launching a career. *Journal of Career Planning and Placement,* 41–47.

Comer, D. R. (1993). Workplace drug testing reconsidered. *Journal of Managerial Issues, 5,* 517–531.

Commons, M. (1985, April). How novelty produces continuity in cognitive development within a domain and accounts for unequal development across domains. Toronto: SRCD, Ontario, Canada.

Compton, D. M., Bachman, L. D., Brand, D., & Avet, T. L. (2000). Age-associated changes in cognitive function in highly educated adults: Emerging myths and realities. *International Journal of Geriatric Psychiatry, 15,* 75–85.

Comrey, A. L. (1992). *A first course in factor analysis.* Hillsdale, NJ: Erlbaum.

Cone, J. D. (1977). The relevance of reliability and validity for behavioral assessment. *Behavior Therapy, 8,* 411–426.

Cone, J. D. (1981). Psychometric considerations. In M. Hersen & A. S. Bellack (Eds.), *Behavioral assessment: A practical handbook* (2nd ed.). New York: Pergamon.

Cone, J. D. (1986). Idiographic, nomothetic, and related perspectives in behavioral assessment. In R. O. Nelson & S. C. Hayes (Eds.), *Conceptual foundations of behavioral assessment.* New York: Guilford.

Cone, J. D. (1987). Behavioral assessment: Some things old, some things new, some things borrowed? *Behavioral Assessment, 9,* 1–4.

Cone, J. D. (1999). Introduction to the special section on self-monitoring: A major assessment method in clinical psychology. *Psychological Assessment, 11,* 411–414.

Conger, A. J. (1985). Kappa reliabilities for continuing behaviors and events. *Educational and Psychological Measurement, 45,* 861–868.

Connolly, J. (1976). Life events before myocardial infarction. *Journal of Human Stress, 3,* 3–17.

Conte, J. M., & Jacobs, R. R. (2003). Validity evidence linking polychronicity and Big Five personality dimensions to absence, lateness, and supervisory performance ratings. *Human Performance, 16,* 107–129.

Cooke, N. J., Salas, E., Cannon-Bowers, J. A., & Stout, R. J. (2000). Measuring team knowledge. *Human Factors, 42,* 151–173.

Cooper, A. (1981). A basic TAT set for adolescent males. *Journal of Clinical Psychology, 37*(2), 411–414.

Copas, J. B., & Tarling, R. (1986). Some methodological issues in making predictions. In A. Blumstein et al. (Eds.), *Criminal careers and "career criminals"* (pp. 291–313). Washington, DC: National Academy.

Corish, C. D., Richard, B., & Brown, S. (1989). Missed medication doses in rheumatoid arthritis patients: Intentional and unintentional reasons. *Arthritis Care and Research, 2,* 3–9.

Cornell, D. G. (1985). External validation of the Personality Inventory for Children—Comment on Lachar, Gdowski, and Snyder. *Journal of Consulting and Clinical Psychology, 53,* 273–274.

Corwyn, R. F., & Benda, B. B. (2000). Religiosity and church attendance: The effects on use of "hard drugs" controlling for sociodemographic and theoretical factors. *International Journal for the Psychology of Religion, 10,* 241–258.

Costa, P. T., Jr., & McCrae, R. R. (1985). *The NEO Personality Inventory manual.* Odessa, FL: Psychological Assessment Resources.

Costa, P. T., Jr., & McCrae, R. R. (1986). Major contributions to personality psychology. In S. Modgil & C. Modgil (Eds.), *Hans Eysenck: Consensus and controversy* (pp. 63–72, 86, 87). Barcombe Lewes, Sussex, England: Falmer.

Costa, P. T., Jr., & McCrae, R. R. (1987). On the need for longitudinal evidence and multiple measures in behavior-genetics studies of adult personality. *Behavioral and Brain Sciences, 10,* 22–23.

Costa, P. T., Jr., & McCrae, R. R. (1992a). Four ways five factors are basic. *Personality and Individual Differences, 13,* 653–665.

Costa, P. T., Jr., & McCrae, R. R. (1992b). Reply to Eysenck. *Personality and Individual Differences, 13,* 861–865.

Costa, P. T., Jr., & McCrae, R. R. (1992c). *Revised NEO Personality Inventory (NEO-PI-R) and NEO Five-Factor Inventory (NEO-FFI) professional manual.* Odessa, FL: Psychological Assessment Resources.

Costa, P. T., Jr., & McCrae, R. R. (1997). Stability and change in personality assessment: The Revised NEO Personality

Inventory in the year 2000. *Journal of Personality Assessment, 68,* 86–94.

Cote, J. A., McCullough, J., & Reilly, M. (1985). Effects of unexpected situations on behavior-intention differences: A garbology analysis. *Journal of Consumer Research, 12,* 188–194.

Cotton, P. (1992). Women's health initiative leads way as research begins to fill gender gaps. *Journal of the American Medical Association, 267*(4), 469–470, 473.

Coyne, J. C. (1976). The place of informed consent in ethical dilemmas. *Journal of Consulting and Clinical Psychology, 44,* 1015–1017.

Cramer, P. (1991). *The development of defense mechanisms: Theory, research, and assessment.* New York: Springer-Verlag.

Cramer, P. (1996). *Storytelling, narrative, and the Thematic Apperception Test.* New York: Guilford.

Crèvecoeur, M. G. St. J. de (1951). What is an American letter? In H. S. Commager (Ed.), *Living ideas in America.* New York: Harper. (Originally published in *Letters from an American farmer,* 1762)

Crick, N. R. (1997). Engagement in gender normative versus nonnormative forms of aggression: Links to social-psychological adjustment. *Developmental Psychology, 33,* 610–617.

Crick, N. R., Bigbee, M. A., & Howes, C. (1996). Gender differences in children's normative beliefs about aggression: How do I hurt thee? Let me count the ways. *Child Development, 67,* 1003–1014.

Crocker, L., Llabre, M., & Miller, M. D. (1988). The generalizability of content validity ratings. *Journal of Educational Measurement, 25,* 287–299.

Cronbach, L. J. (1949). Statistical methods applied to Rorschach scores: A review. *Psychological Bulletin, 46,* 393–429.

Cronbach, L. J. (1951). Coefficient alpha and the internal structure of tests. *Psychometrika, 16,* 297–334.

Cronbach, L. J. (1970). *Essentials of psychological testing* (3rd ed.). New York: Harper & Row.

Cronbach, L. J. (1975). Five decades of public controversy over mental testing. *American Psychologist, 30,* 1–13.

Cronbach, L. J. (1984). *Essentials of psychological testing* (4th ed.). New York: Harper & Row.

Cronbach, L. J., & Gleser, G. C. (1957). *Psychological tests and personnel decisions.* Champaign, IL: University of Illinois.

Cronbach, L. J., & Gleser, G. C. (1965). *Psychological tests and personnel decisions* (2nd ed.). Urbana: University of Illinois.

Cronbach, L. J., Gleser, G. C., Nanda, H., & Rajaratnam, N. (1972). *The dependability of behavioral measurement: Theory of generalizability for scores and profiles.* New York: Wiley.

Crosby, F. J., Iyer, A., Clayton, S., & Downing, R. A. (2003). Affirmative action: Psychological data and the policy debates. *American Psychologist, 58,* 93–115.

Cross, T. L., Coleman, L. J., & Stewart, R. A. (1993). The social cognition of gifted adolescents: An exploration of the stigma of the giftedness paradigm. *Roeper Review, 16,* 37–40.

Cross, T. L., Coleman, L. J., & Terhaar-Yonkers, M. (1991). The social cognition of gifted adolescents in schools: Managing the stigma of giftedness. *Journal for the Education of the Gifted, 15,* 44–55.

Crowne, D. P., & Marlowe, D. (1964). *The approval motive: Studies in evaluative dependence.* New York: Wiley.

Crundall, D. E., Underwood, G., & Chapman, P. R. (1998). How much do drivers see? The effects of demand on visual search strategies in novice and experienced drivers. In G. Underwood (Ed.), *Eye guidance in reading and scene perception* (pp. 395–417). Oxford, England: Elsevier.

Cuellar, I., Harris, I. C., & Jasso, R. (1980). An acculturation scale for Mexican American normal and clinical populations. *Hispanic Journal of Behavioral Science, 2,* 199–217.

Cundick, B. P. (1976). Measures of intelligence on Southwest Indian students. *Journal of Social Psychology, 81,* 151–156.

Cunningham, M. R. (1988). What do you do when you're happy or blue? Mood, expectancies, and behavioral interests. *Motivation and Emotion, 12,* 309–331.

Cureton, E. E. (1957). The upper and lower twenty-seven percent rule. *Psychometrika, 22,* 293–296.

Cushman, P., & Guilford, P. (2000). Will managed care change our way of being? *American Psychologist, 55,* 985–996.

Dahlstrom, W. G. (1995). Pigeons, people, and pigeon holes. *Journal of Personality Assessment, 64,* 2–20.

Dahlstrom, W. G., & Dahlstrom, L. E. (Eds.). (1980). *Basic readings on the MMPI: A new selection on personality measurement.* Minneapolis: University of Minnesota.

Dahlstrom, W. G., & Welsh, G. S. (1960). *An MMPI handbook: A guide to use in clinical practice and research.* Minneapolis: University of Minnesota.

Dahlstrom, W. G., Welsh, G. S., & Dahlstrom, L. E. (1972). *An MMPI handbook: Vol. 1. Clinical interpretation.* Minneapolis: University of Minnesota.

Daigneault, S., Braun, C. M. J., & Whitaker, H. A. (1992). Early effects of normal aging on perseverative and nonperseverative prefrontal measures. *Developmental Neuropsychology, 8,* 99–114.

Dana, R. H. (1982). *A human science model for personality assessment with projective techniques.* Springfield, IL: Charles C Thomas.

Dana, R. H. (1995). Culturally competent MMPI assessment of Hispanic populations. *Hispanic Journal of Behavioral Sciences, 17,* 305–319.

Dana, R. H., Aguilar-Kitibutr, A., Diaz-Vivar, N., & Vetter, H. (2002). A teaching model for multicultural assessment: Psychological report contents and cultural competence. *Journal of Personality, 79,* 207–215.

Dana, R. H., & Whatley, P. R. (1991). When does a difference make a difference? MMPI scores and African-Americans. *Journal of Clinical Psychology, 47,* 400–406.

Daneman, M., & Carpenter, P. A. (1980). Individual differences in working memory and reading. *Journal of Verbal Learning and Verbal Behavior, 19,* 450–466.

Danford, G. S., & Steinfeld, E. (1999). Measuring the influences of physical environments on the behaviors of people with impairments. In E. Steinfeld & G. S. Danford (Eds.), *Enabling environments: Measuring the impact of environment on disability and rehabilitation* (pp. 111–137). New York: Kluwer Academic/Plenum.

Daniels, K. (2000). Measures of five aspects of affective well-being at work. *Human Relations, 53,* 275–294.

Darwin, C. (1859). *On the origin of species by means of natural selection.* London: Murray.

Das, J. P. (1972). Patterns of cognitive ability in nonretarded and retarded children. *American Journal of Mental Deficiency, 77,* 6–12.

Das, J. P., Kirby, J., & Jarman, R. F. (1975). Simultaneous and successive synthesis: An alternative model for cognitive abilities. *Psychological Bulletin, 82,* 87–103.

Daubert v. Merrell Dow Pharmaceuticals, 113 S. Ct. 2786 (1993).

Davids, A., & Murray, H. A. (1955). Preliminary appraisal of an auditory projective technique for studying personality and cognition. *American Journal of Orthopsychiatry, 25,* 543–554.

Davidson, H. A. (1949). Malingered psychosis. *Bulletin of the Menninger Clinic, 13,* 157–163.

Davidson, T. N., Bowden, L., & Tholen, D. (1979). Social support as a moderator of burn rehabilitation. *Archives of Physical Medicine and Rehabilitation, 60,* 556.

Davies, M., Stankov, L., & Roberts, R. D. (1998). Emotional intelligence: In search of an elusive construct. *Journal of Personality and Social Psychology, 75,* 989–1015.

Davies, P. L., & Gavin, W. J. (1994). Comparison of individual and group/consultation treatment methods for preschool children with developmental delays. *American Journal of Occupational Therapy, 48,* 155–161.

Davis, G. A. (1989). Testing for creative potential. *Contemporary Educational Psychology, 14,* 257–274.

Davison, G. C., Vogel, R. S., & Coffman, S. G. (1997). Think-aloud approaches to cognitive assessment and the articulated thoughts in simulated situations paradigm. *Journal of Consulting and Clinical Psychology, 65,* 950–958.

Dawes, R. M., Faust, D., & Meehl, P. E. (1989, March 31). Clinical versus actuarial judgment. *Science, 243,* 1668–1674.

Day, D. V., & Silverman, S. B. (1989). Personality and job performance: Evidence of incremental validity. *Personnel Psychology, 42,* 25–36.

Decker, J. T., Bailey, T. L., & Westergaard, N. (2002). Burnout among childcare workers. *Residential Treatment for Children & Youth, 19*(4), 61–77.

Delahunty, R. J. (1988). Perspectives on within-group scoring. *Journal of Vocational Behavior, 33,* 463–477.

Deloria, D. J. (1985). Review of the Miller Assessment for Preschoolers. In J. V. Mitchell, Jr. (Ed.), *The ninth mental measurements yearbook.* Lincoln: Buros Institute of Mental Measurements, University of Nebraska.

DeMulder, E. K., Denham, S., Schmidt, M., & Mitchell, J. (2000). Q-sort assessment of attachment security during the preschool years: Links from home to school. *Developmental Psychology, 36,* 274–282.

Dennis, W., & Dennis, M. G. (1940). The effect of cradling practice upon the onset of walking in Hopi children. *Journal of Genetic Psychology, 56,* 77–86.

Department of Health, Education, and Welfare. (1977a). Nondiscrimination on basis of handicap: Implementation of Section 504 of the Rehabilitation Act of 1973. *Federal Register, 42*(86), 22676–22702.

Department of Health, Education, and Welfare. (1977b). Education of Handicapped Children: Implementation of Part B of the Education of the Handicapped Act. *Federal Register, 42*(163), 42474–42518.

DePaulo, B. M. (1994). Spotting lies: Can humans learn to do better? *Current Directions in Psychological Science, 3,* 83–86.

Desrochers, M. N., Hile, M. G., & Williams-Mosely, T. L. (1997). Survey of functional assessment procedures used with individuals who display mental retardation and severe problem behaviors. *American Journal on Mental Retardation, 101,* 535–546.

Detterman, D. K. (1986). Qualitative integration: The last word? In R. J. Sternberg & D. K. Detterman (Eds.), *What is intelligence?* (pp. 163–166). Norwood, NJ: Ablex.

Devlin, B., Daniels, M., & Roeder, K. (1997). The heritability of IQ. *Nature, 388,* 468–471.

Diamond, B. L. (1980). Inherent problems in the use of pretrial hypnosis on a prospective witness. *California Law Review, 68,* 313–349.

Dickson, C. R. (1975). Role of assessment in behavior therapy. In P. McReynolds (Ed.), *Advances in psychological assessment* (Vol. 3). San Francisco: Jossey-Bass.

Diebold, M. H., Curtis, W. S., & DuBose, R. F. (1978). Developmental scales versus observational measures for deaf-blind children. *Exceptional Children, 44,* 275–278.

Dietz, P. E., Matthews, D. B., Van Duyne, C., et al. (1991). Threatening and otherwise inappropriate letters to Hollywood celebrities. *Journal of Forensic Sciences, 36,* 185–209.

Dimock, P. H., & Cormier, P. (1991). The effects of format differences and computer experience on performance and anxiety on a computer-administered test. *Measurement and Evaluation in Counseling and Development, 24,* 119–126.

Dion, K. K. (1979). Physical attractiveness and evaluation of children's transgressions. *Journal of Personality and Social Psychology, 24,* 207–213.

Dipboye, R. L. (1992). *Selection interviews: Process perspectives.* Cincinnati, OH: South-Western Publishing.

Diven, K. (1937). Certain determinants in the conditioning of anxiety reactions. *Journal of Psychology, 3,* 291–308.

Dixon, M., Wang, S., Calvin, J., et al. (2002). The panel interview: A review of empirical research and guidelines for practice. *Public Personnel Management, 31,* 397–428.

Dohrenwend, B. P., & Shrout, P. E. (1985). Hassles in the conceptualization and measurement of life stresses variables. *American Psychologist, 40,* 780–785.

Doll, E. A. (1917). A brief Binet-Simon scale. *Psychological Clinic, 11,* 197–211, 254–261.

Doll, E. A. (1953). *Measurement of social competence: A manual for the Vineland Social Maturity Scale.* Circle Pines, MN: American Guidance Service.

Dolnick, E. (1993). Deafness as culture. *Atlantic, 272*(3), 37–53.

Donahue, E. M., Robins, R. W., Roberts, B. W., & John, O. P. (1993). The divided self: Concurrent and longitudinal effects of psychological adjustment and social roles on self-concept differentiation. *Journal of Personality and Social Psychology, 64,* 834–846.

Donders, J. (1992). Validity of the Kaufman Assessment Battery for Children when employed with children with traumatic brain injury. *Journal of Clinical Psychology, 48,* 225–230.

Dosajh, N. L. (1996). Projective techniques with particular reference to inkblot tests. *Journal of Projective Psychology and Mental Health, 3,* 59–68.

Doty, R. L., Shaman, P., & Dann, M. (1984). Development of the University of Pennsylvania Smell Identification Test: A standard microencapsulated test of olfactory dysfunction. *Physiological Behavior, 32,* 489–502.

Dougherty, T. M., & Haith, M. M. (1997). Infant expectations and reaction time as predictors of childhood speed of processing C and IQ. *Developmental Psychology, 33,* 146–155.

Douglas, A. (1993). *Translate this darkness: The life of Christiana Morgan.* New York: Simon & Schuster.

Draguns, J. G. (1984). Assessing mental health and disorder across cultures. In P. Pedersen, N. Sartorius, & A. J. Marsella (Eds.), *Mental health services: The cross-cultural context* (pp. 31–57). Beverly Hills, CA: Sage.

Drasgow, F., & Olson-Buchanan, J. B. (Eds.). (1999). *Innovations in computerized assessment.* Mahwah, NJ: Erlbaum.

Dreger, R. M., & Miller, K. S. (1960). Comparative studies of Negroes and Whites in the U.S. *Psychological Bulletin, 51,* 361–402.

Drinkwater, M. J. (1976). Psychological evaluation of visually handicapped children. *Massachusetts School Psychologists Association Newsletter, 6.*

Drotar, D., Olness, K., & Wiznitzer, M., et al. (1999). Neurodevelopmental outcomes of Ugandan infants with HIV infection: An application of growth curve analysis. *Health Psychology, 18,* 114–121.

DuBois, P. H. (1966). A test-dominated society: China 1115 B.C.–1905 A.D. In A. Anastasi (Ed.), *Testing problems in perspective* (pp. 29–36). Washington, DC: American Council on Education.

DuBois, P. H. (1970). *A history of psychological testing.* Boston: Allyn & Bacon.

Ducharme, F., Levesque, L., Gendron, M., & Legault, A. (2001). Development process and qualitative evaluation of a program to promote the mental health of family caregivers. *Clinical Nursing Research, 10,* 182–201.

Duchek, J. M., Hunt, L., Ball, K., et al. (1998). Attention and driving performance in Alzheimer's disease. *Journal of*

Gerontology: Series B: Psychological Science & Social Sciences, 53B(2), 130–141.

Duclos, C. W. (1999). Factors associated with alcohol, drug, and mental health service utilization among a sample of American Indian adolescent detainees. *Dissertation Abstracts International, Section B: The Sciences & Engineering, 40*(4-B), 1524.

Dudycha, G. J. (1936). An objective study of punctuality in relation to personality and achievement. *Archives of Psychology, 204,* 1–319.

Dugdale, R. (1877). *The Jukes: A study in crime, pauperism, disease, and heredity.* New York: Putnam.

Duncker, K. (1945). On problem solving. *Psychological Monographs, 5,* 1–13.

Dunham, R. B., Grube, J. A., & Castaneda, M. B. (1994). Organizational commitment: The utility of an integrative definition. *Journal of Applied Psychology, 79,* 370–380.

Dunn, L. M., & Dunn, L. M. (1997). *Examiner's manual for the PPVT-III, Peabody Picture Vocabulary Test, Third Edition.* Circle Pines, MN: American Guidance Service.

Dwyer, C. A. (1996). Cut scores and testing: Statistics, judgment, truth, and error. *Psychological Assessment, 8,* 360–362.

Dykes, L. (1986). The whiplash shaken infant syndrome: What has been learned? *Child Abuse and Neglect, 10,* 211.

Dywan, J., & Bowers, K. (1983). The use of hypnosis to enhance recall. *Science, 22,* 184–185.

Earles, J. A., & Ree, M. J. (1992). The predictive validity of the ASVAB for training grades. *Educational and Psychological Measurement, 52,* 721–725.

Early, P. C., Gibson, C. B., & Chen, C. C. (1999). "How did I do?" versus "How did we do?": Cultural contrasts of performance feedback use and self-efficacy. *Journal of Cross-Cultural Psychology, 30,* 594–619.

Eccles, J. S. (1987). Gender roles and women's achievement-related decisions. *Psychology of Women Quarterly, 11,* 135–171.

Edwards, A. L. (1953). *Edwards Personal Preference Schedule.* New York: Psychological Corporation.

Edwards, A. L. (1957a). *Techniques of attitude scale construction.* New York: Appleton-Century-Crofts.

Edwards, A. L. (1957b). *The social desirability variable in personality assessment and research.* New York: Dryden.

Edwards, A. L. (1966). Relationship between probability of endorsement and social desirability scale value for a set of 2,824 personality statements. *Journal of Applied Psychology, 50,* 238–239.

Edwards, A. L., & Walsh, J. A. (1964). Response sets in standard and experimental personality scales. *American Education Research Journal, 1,* 52–60.

Edwards, C. P., & Kumru, A. (1999). Culturally sensitive assessment. *Child and Adolescent Psychiatric Clinics of North America, 8,* 409–424.

Eichler, R. M. (1951). A comparison of the Rorschach and Behn-Rorschach inkblot tests. *Journal of Consulting Psychology, 15,* 185–189.

Eisenberg, N., Guthrie, I. K., Cumberland, A., et al. (2002). Prosocial development in early adulthood: A longitudinal study. *Journal of Personality & Social Psychology, 82,* 993–1006.

Eisman, E. J., Dies, R. R., Finn, S. E., et al. (2000). Problems and limitations in using psychological assessment in the contemporary health care delivery system. *Professional Psychology: Research and Practice, 31,* 131–140.

Elder, G. H., Van Nguyen, T., & Caspi, A. (1985). Linking family hardship to children's lives. *Child Development, 56,* 361–375.

Eldredge, N. (1993). Culturally affirmative counseling with American Indians who are deaf. *Journal of the American Deafness and Rehabilitation Association, 26,* 1–18.

Elksnin, L. K., & Elksnin, N. (1993). A review of picture interest inventories: Implications for vocational assessment of students with disabilities. *Journal of Psychoeducational Assessment, 11,* 323–336.

Ellerstein, N. S. (Ed.). (1981). *Child abuse and neglect: A medical reference.* New York: Wiley.

Elliot, H., Glass, L., & Evans, J. (Eds.). (1987). *Mental health assessment of deaf clients: A practical manual.* Boston: Little, Brown.

Elliott, A. N., O'Donohue, W. T., & Nickerson, M. A. (1993). The use of sexually anatomically detailed dolls in the assessment of sexual abuse. *Clinical Psychology Review, 13,* 207–221.

Elliott, C. D. (1990a). *The Differential Ability Scales.* San Antonio, TX: Psychological Corporation.

Elliott, C. D. (1990b). *Technical handbook: The Differential Ability Scales.* San Antonio, TX: Psychological Corporation.

Elliott, S. N. (1988). Acceptability of behavioral treatments in educational settings. In J. C. Witt, S. N. Elliott, & F. M. Greshma (Eds.), *The handbook of behavior therapy education* (pp. 121–150). New York: Plenum.

Elliott, S. N., Katochwill, T. R., & McKevitt, B. C. (2001). Experimental analysis of the effects of testing accommodations on the scores of students with and without disabilities. *Journal of School Psychology, 39,* 3–24.

Elliott, T. R., & Carroll, M. N. (1997). Issues in psychological assessment for rehabilitation services. Paper presented at the annual convention of the American Psychological Association, August, Chicago.

Embretson, S. E. (1996). The new rules of measurement. *Psychological Assessment, 8,* 341–349.

Endicott, J., & Spitzer, R. L. (1978). A diagnostic interview: The Schedule for Affective Disorders and Schizophrenia. *Archives of General Psychiatry, 35,* 837–844.

Engin, A., Wallbrown, F., & Brown, D. (1976). The dimensions of reading attitude for children in the intermediate grades. *Psychology in the Schools, 13*(3), 309–316.

Epstein, J. L., & McPartland, J. M. (1978). *The Quality of School Life Scale administration and technical manual.* Boston: Houghton Mifflin.

Epstein, N., Baldwin, L., & Bishop, S. (1983). The McMaster Family Assessment Device. *Journal of Marital and Family Therapy, 9,* 171–180.

Erdelyi, M. H. (1974). A new look at the new look: Perceptual defense and vigilance. *Psychological Review, 81,* 1–25.

Evan, W. M., & Miller, J. R. (1969). Differential effects of response bias of computer vs. conventional administration of a social science questionnaire. *Behavioral Science, 14,* 216–227.

Evans, J. D., et al. (2000). Cross-cultural applications of the Halstead-Reitan batteries. In E. Fletcher-Janzen et al. (Eds.), *Handbook of cross-cultural neuropsychology* (pp. 287–303). New York: Kluwer Academic/Plenum.

Evans, M. (1978). Unbiased assessment of locally low incidence handicapped children. *IRRC practitioners talk to practitioners.* Springfield, IL: Illinois Regional Resource Center.

Evers, W., Tomic, W., & Brouwers, A. (2002). Aggressive behavior and burnout among staff of homes for the elderly. *International Journal of Mental Health Nursing, 11,* 2–9.

Exner, J. E. (1962). A comparison of human figure drawings of psychoneurotics, character disturbances, normals, and subjects experiencing experimentally induced fears. *Journal of Projective Techniques, 26,* 292–317.

Exner, J. E. (1969). *The Rorschach systems.* New York: Grune & Stratton.

Exner, J. E. (1974). *The Rorschach: A comprehensive system.* New York: Wiley.

Exner, J. E. (1978). *The Rorschach: A comprehensive system: Vol. 2. Current research and advanced interpretations.* New York: Wiley-Interscience.

Exner, J. E. (1983). Rorschach assessment. In I. B. Weiner (Ed.), *Methods in clinical psychology* (2nd ed.). New York: Wiley.

Exner, J. E. (1986). *The Rorschach: A comprehensive system: Vol. 1. Basic foundations* (2nd ed.). New York: Wiley.

Exner, J. E. (1989). Searching for projection in the Rorschach. *Journal of Personality Assessment, 53,* 520–536.

Exner, J. E. (1990). *Workbook for the comprehensive system* (3rd ed.). Asheville, NC: Rorschach Workshops.

Exner, J. E. (1993). *The Rorschach: A comprehensive system: Vol. 2. Interpretations.* New York: Wiley.

Exner, J. E., Jr. (1991). *The Rorschach: A comprehensive system: Vol. 2. Interpretation* (2nd ed.). New York: Wiley.

Exner, J. E., Jr. (1993). *The Rorschach: A comprehensive system: Vol. 1. Basic foundations* (3rd ed.). New York: Wiley.

Exner, J. E., Jr. (1997). Critical bits and the Rorschach response process. *Journal of Personality Assessment, 67,* 464–477.

Exner, J. E., & Weiner, I. B. (1982). *The Rorschach: A comprehensive system: Vol. 3. Assessment of children and adolescents.* New York: Wiley.

Exner, J. E., & Weiner, I. B. (1995). *The Rorschach: A comprehensive system: Vol. 3. Assessment of children and adolescents* (2nd ed.). New York: Wiley.

Eyde, L. D., Kowal, D. M., & Fishburne, F. J., Jr. (1990). The validity of computer-based test interpretations of the MMPI. In S. Wise & T. B. Gutkin (Eds.), *The computer as adjunct to the decision-making process.* Lincoln: Buros Institute of Mental Measurements, University of Nebraska.

Eyde, L. D., Moreland, K. L., Robertson, G. J., Primoff, E. S., & Most, R. B. (1988). Test user qualifications: A data-based approach to promoting good test use. *Issues in Scientific Psychology: Report of the Test User Qualifications Working Group of the Joint Committee on Testing Practices.* Washington, DC: American Psychological Association.

Eyman, J. R., & Eyman, S. K. (1990). Suicide risk and assessment instruments. In P. Cimbolic & D. A. Jobes (Eds.), *Youth suicide: Issues, assessment, and intervention* (pp. 9–32). Springfield, IL: Charles C Thomas.

Eysenck, H. J. (1961). The effects of psychotherapy. In H. J. Eysenck (Ed.), *Handbook of abnormal psychology: An experimental approach* (pp. 697–725). New York: Basic.

Eysenck, H. J. (1967). Intelligence assessment: A theoretical and experimental approach. *British Journal of Educational Psychology, 37,* 81–98.

Eysenck, H. J. (1985). Can personality study ever be scientific? *Journal of Social Behavior and Personality, 1,* 3–19.

Eysenck, H. J. (1991). Dimensions of personality: 16, 5, or 3?—Criteria for a taxonomic paradigm. *Personality and Individual Differences, 12,* 773–790.

Faigman, D. L. (1995). The evidentiary status of social science under *Daubert:* Is it "scientific," "technical," or "other" knowledge? *Psychology, Public Policy, and Law, 1,* 960–979.

Faller, K. C. (1988). *Child sexual abuse.* New York: Columbia University.

Farrell, A. D. (1986). The microcomputer as a tool for behavioral assessment. *Behavior Therapist, 1,* 16–17.

Farrell, J. N., & McDaniel, M. A. (2001). The stability of validity coefficients over time: Ackerman's (1988) model and the General Aptitude Test Battery. *Journal of Applied Psychology, 86,* 60–79.

Farrenkopf, T., & Bryan, J. (1999). Psychological consultation under Oregon's 1994 Death With Dignity Act: Ethics and procedures. *Professional Psychology: Research and Practice, 30,* 245–249.

Faust, D. S., & Ziskin, J. (1988a). The expert witness in psychology and psychiatry. *Science, 241,* 31–35.

Faust, D. S., & Ziskin, J. (1988b). Response to Fowler and Matarrazo. *Science, 242,* 1143–1144.

Federal Rules of Evidence. (1975). Eagan, MN: West Group Publishing.

Feinstein, A. R., Josephy, B. R., & Wells, C. K. (1986). Scientific and clinical problems in indexes of functional disability. *Annals of Internal Medicine, 105,* 413–520.

Felce, D. (1997). Defining and applying the concept of quality of life. *Journal of Intellectual and Research, 41,* 126–135.

Feldman, L. B., & Rivas-Vazquez, R. (2003). Assessment and treatment of social anxiety disorder. *Professional Psychology: Research and Practice, 34,* 396–405.

Fenn, D. S., & Ganzini, L. (1999). Attitudes of Oregon psychologists toward physician-assisted suicide and the Oregon Death With Dignity Act. *Professional Psychology: Research and Practice, 30,* 235–244.

Ferguson, R. L., & Novick, M. R. (1973). Implementation of a Bayesian system for decision analysis in a program of individually prescribed instruction. *ACT Research Report,* Number 60.

Field, T. M., & Vega-Lahr, N. (1984). Early interactions between infants with cranio-facial anomalies and their mothers. *Infant Behavior and Development, 7,* 527–530.

Filsinger, E. (1983). A machine-aided marital observation technique: The Dyadic Interaction Scoring Code. *Journal of Marriage and the Family, 2,* 623–632.

Finding information about psychological tests. (1995). Washington, DC: American Psychological Association, Science Directorate.

Finkelhor, D., & Dziuba-Leatherman, J. (1994). Victimization of children. *American Psychologist, 49,* 173–183.

Finn, S. E. (1996). *Using the MMPI-2 as a therapeutic intervention.* Minneapolis: University of Minnesota Press.

Finn, S. E. (2003). Therapeutic assessment of a man with "ADD." *Journal of Personality Assessment, 80,* 115–129.

Finn, S. E., & Martin, H. (1997). Therapeutic assessment with the MMPI-2 in managed health care. In J. N. Butcher (Ed.), *Objective psychological assessment in managed health care: A practitioner's guide* (pp. 131–152). New York: Oxford University Press.

Finn, S. E., & Tonsager, M. E. (2002). How therapeutic assessment became humanistic. *Humanistic Psychologist, 30(1-2),* 10–22.

Fischer, C. T. (1978). Collaborative psychological assessment. In C. T. Fischer & S. L. Brodsky (Eds.), *Client participation in human services: The Prometheus principle* (pp. 41–61). New Brunswick, NJ: Transaction.

Fischer, C. T. (1994). *Individualizing psychological assessment.* Hillsdale, NJ: Erlbaum.

Fischer, C. T. (2004). In what sense is collaborative psychological assessment collaborative? Some distinctions. *SPA Exchange, 16(1),* 14–15.

Fischer, H. (1999). Exemptions from child abuse reporting. *American Psychologist, 54,* 145.

Fisher, R. P., & Geiselman, R. E. (1992). *Memory-enhancing techniques for investigative interviewing.* Springfield, IL: Charles C Thomas.

Fisher, R. P., Geiselman, R. E., & Amador, M. (1989). Field test of the cognitive interview: Enhancing the recollection of actual victims and witnesses of crime. *Journal of Applied Psychology, 74,* 722–727.

Fisher, R. P., Geiselman, R. E., Raymond, D. S., et al. (1987). Enhancing enhanced eyewitness memory: Refining the cognitive interview. *Journal of Police Science & Administration, 15,* 291–297.

Fiske, D. W. (1967). The subjects react to tests. *American Psychologist, 22,* 287–296.

Fitts, W. H. (1965). *Manual for the Tennessee Self-Concept Scale.* Nashville: Counselor Recordings and Tests.

Fitzgibbons, D. J., & Shearn, C. R. (1972). Concepts of schizophrenia among mental health professionals: A factor-analytic study. *Journal of Consulting and Clinical Psychology, 38,* 288–295.

Flanagan, D. P., & McGrew, K. S. (1997). A cross-battery approach to assessing and interpreting cognitive abilities: Narrowing the gap between practice and cognitive science. In D. P. Flanagan, J. L. Genshaft, & P. L. Harrison (Eds.), *Contemporary intellectual assessment: Theories, tests, and issues* (pp. 314–325). New York: Guilford.

Flanagan, J. C. (1938). Review of *Measuring Intelligence* by Terman and Merrill. *Harvard Educational Review, 8,* 130–133.

Flanagan, J. C., & Burns, R. K. (1955). The employee business record: A new appraisal and development tool. *Harvard Business Review, 33*(5), 99–102.

Flowers, J. H. (1982). Some simple Apple II software for the collection and analysis of observational data. *Behavior Research Methods and Instrumentation, 14,* 241–249.

Floyd, F. J., Haynes, S. N., Doll, E. R., et al. (1992). Assessing retirement satisfaction and perceptions of retirement experiences. *Psychology and Aging, 7,* 609–621.

Floyd, F. J., & Widaman, K. F. (1995). Factor analysis in the development and refinement of clinical assessment instruments. *Psychological Assessment, 7,* 286–299.

Floyd, R. G., Evans, J. J., & McGrew, K. S. (2003). Relations between measures of Cattell-Horn-Carroll (CHC) cognitive abilities and mathematics achievement across the school-age years. *Psychology in the Schools, 40,* 155–171.

Flynn, J. R. (1984). The mean IQ of Americans: Massive gains 1932 to 1978. *Psychological Bulletin, 95,* 29–51.

Flynn, J. R. (1988). Massive IQ gains in 14 nations: What IQ tests really measure. *Psychological Bulletin, 101,* 171–191.

Flynn, J. R. (1991). *Asian-Americans: Achievement beyond IQ.* Hillsdale, NJ: Erlbaum.

Flynn, J. R. (2000). The hidden history of IQ and special education: Can the problems be solved? *Psychology, Public Policy, and Law, 6,* 191–198.

Foerster, L. M., & Little Soldier, D. (1974). Open education and native American values. *Educational Leadership, 32,* 41–45.

Folstein, M. F., Folstein, S. E., & McHugh, P. R. (1975). "Mini-Mental State": A practical method for grading the cognitive state of patients for the clinician. *Journal of Psychiatric Research, 12,* 189–198.

Fontana, V. J., Donovan, D., & Wong, R. J. (1963, December 8). The maltreatment syndrome in children. *New England Journal of Medicine, 269,* 1389–1394.

Fontanna, D. (2000). *Personality in the workplace.* Lewiston, NY: Macmillan Press.

Forer, B. R. (1949). The fallacy of personal validation: A classroom demonstration of gullibility. *Journal of Abnormal and Social Psychology, 44,* 118–123.

Forrest, D. W. (1974). *Francis Galton: The life and works of a Victorian genius.* New York: Taplinger.

Forth, A. E., Hart, S. D., & Hare, R. D. (1990). Assessment of psychopathy in male young offenders. *Psychological Assessment, 2,* 342–344.

Foster, S. L., Laverty-Finch, C., Gizzo, D. P., & Osantowski, J. (1999). Practical issues in self-observation. *Psychological Assessment, 11,* 426–438.

Fouad, N. A. (2002). Cross-cultural differences in vocational interests: Between-group differences on the Strong Interest Inventory. *Journal of Counseling Psychology, 49,* 282–289.

Fouad, N. A., & Dancer, L. S. (1992). Cross-cultural structure of interests: Mexico and the United States. *Journal of Vocational Behavior, 40,* 129–143.

Fowler, D. R., Finkelstein, A., & Penk, W. (1986). *Measuring treatment responses by computer interview.* Paper presented at the 94th annual meeting of the American Psychological Association, Washington, DC.

Franco, J. N. (1983). An acculturation scale for Mexican-American children. *Journal of General Psychology, 108,* 175–181.

Frank, E., & Brandstaetter, V. (2002). Approach versus avoidance: Different types of commitment in intimate relationships. *Journal of Personality & Social Psychology, 82,* 208–221.

Frank, L. K. (1939). Projective methods for the study of personality. *Journal of Psychology, 8,* 389–413.

Frank, M. G., Ekman, P., & Friesen, W. V. (1993). Behavioral markers and recognizability of the smile of enjoyment. *Journal of Personality and Social Psychology, 64,* 83–93.

Frantz, D., & Nordheimer, J. (1997, September 28). Giant of exam business keeps quiet on cheating. *New York Times,* pp. A1, A32.

Frederickson, B. L. (1998). What good are positive emotions? *Review of General Psychology, 2,* 300–319.

Fredman, N., & Sherman, R. (1987). *Handbook of measurements for marriage & family therapy.* New York: Brunner/Mazel.

Freeman, S. T. (1989). Cultural and linguistic bias in mental health evaluations of deaf people. *Rehabilitation Psychology, 34,* 51–63.

French, C. C., & Beaumont, J. G. (1991). The Differential Aptitude Test (Language Usage and Spelling): A clinical study of a computerized form. *Current Psychology: Research and Reviews, 10,* 31–48.

French, D. J., Gauthier, J. G., Roberge, C., et al. (1997). Self-efficacy in the thermal biofeedback treatment of migraine sufferers. *Behavior Therapy, 28,* 109–125.

French, J. L. (Ed.). (1964). *Educating the gifted.* New York: Holt, Rinehart & Winston.

Freud, S. (1913/1959). Further recommendations in the technique of psychoanalysis. In E. Jones (Ed.) and J. Riviere (Trans.), *Collected papers* (Vol. 2). New York: Basic.

Freund, K. (1963). A laboratory method for diagnosing predominance of homosexual and heterosexual erotic interest in the male. *Behavior Research and Therapy, 1,* 85–93.

Freund, K., Sedlacek, E., & Knob, K. (1965). A simple transducer for mechanical plethysmography of the male genital. *Journal of Experimental Analysis of Behavior, 8,* 169–170.

Friedman, M., & Rosenman, R. H. (1974). *Type A behavior and your heart.* New York: Knopf.

Friedrich, W. N., Urquiza, A. J., & Beike, R. (1986). Behavioral problems in sexually abused young children. *Journal of Pediatric Psychiatry, 11,* 47–57.

Friedrich, W. N., Fisher, J. L., Dittner, C. A., et al. (2001). Child Sexual Behavior Inventory: Normative, psychiatric, and sexual abuse comparisons. *Child Maltreatment: Journal of the American Professional Society on the Abuse of Children, 6,* 37–49.

Friel-Patti, S., & Finitzo, T. (1990). Language learning in a prospective study of otitis media with effusion in the first two years of life. *Journal of Speech and Hearing Research, 33,* 188–194.

Frijda, N. H., & Mesquita, B. (1994). The social roles and functions of emotions. In S. Kitayama & H. R. Markus (Eds.), *Emotion and Culture: Empirical studies of mutual influence* (pp. 51–87). Washington, DC: American Psychological Association.

Frolik, L. A. (1999). Science, common sense, and the determination of mental capacity. *Psychology, Public Policy, and Law, 5,* 41–58.

Frumkin, R. M. (1997). Significant neglected sociocultural and physical factors affecting intelligence. *American Psychologist, 52,* 76–77.

Frye v. United States, 293 Fed. 1013 (D.C. Cir. 1923).

Fuchs, L. S., Fuchs, D., Eaton, S. B., et al. (2000). Using objective data sources to enhance teacher judgments about test accommodations. *Exceptional Children, 67,* 67–81.

Fullan, M., & Loubser, J. (1972). Education and adaptive capacity. *Sociology of Education, 45,* 271–287.

Fullard, W., McDevitt, S. C., & Carey, W. B. (1984). Assessing temperament in one- to three-year-old children. *Journal of Pediatric Psychology, 9,* 205–217.

Furnham, A., Moutafi, J., & Crump, J. (2003). The relationship between the revised NEO-Personality Inventory and the Myers-Briggs Type Indicator. *Social Behavior & Personality, 31,* 577–584.

Furnham, A., Petrides, K. V., Jackson, C. J., & Cotter, T. (2002). Do personality factors predict job satisfaction? *Personality & Individual Differences, 33,* 1325–1342.

Furse, D. H., & Stewart, D. W. (1984). Manipulating dissonance to improve mail survey response. *Psychology & Marketing, 1,* 71–84.

Gaither, G. A., & Sellbom, M. (2003). The Sexual Sensation Seeking Scale: Reliability and validity within a heterosexual college student sample. *Journal of Personality Assessment, 81,* 157–167.

Gallagher, J. J. (1966). *Research summary on gifted child education.* Springfield, IL: State Department of Public Instruction.

Gallagher, P., & MacLachlan, M. (2000). Development and psychometric evaluation of the Trinity Amputation and Prosthesis Experience Scales. *Rehabilitation Psychology, 45,* 130–154.

Galton, F. (1869). *Hereditary genius.* London: Macmillan. (Re-published in 1892)

Galton, F. (1874). *English men of science.* New York: Appleton.

Galton, F. (1879). Psychometric experiments. *Brain, 2,* 149–162.

Galton, F. (1883). *Inquiries into human faculty and its development.* London: Macmillan.

Gammon, J. A. (1981). Ophthalmic manifestations of child abuse. In N. S. Ellerstein (Ed.), *Child abuse and neglect: A medical reference* (pp. 121–139). New York: Wiley.

Ganellen, R. J. (1996). Comparing the diagnostic efficiency of the MMPI, MCMI-II, and Rorschach: A review. *Journal of Personality Assessment, 67,* 219–243.

Gann, M. K., & Davison, G. C. (1997). *Cognitive assessment of reactance using the articulated thoughts in simulated situations paradigm.* Unpublished manuscript, University of Southern California, Los Angeles.

Garb, H. N. (1994). Toward a second generation of statistical prediction rules in psychodiagnosis and personality assessment. *Computers in Human Behavior, 11,* 313–324.

Garb, H. N. (2000a). Introduction to the special section on the use of computers for making judgments and decisions. *Psychological Assessment, 12,* 3–5.

Garb, H. N. (2000b). Computers will become increasingly important for psychological assessment: Not that there's anything wrong with that! *Psychological Assessment, 12,* 31–39.

Garcia, M., & Lega, L. I. (1979). Development of a Cuban Ethnic Identity Questionnaire. *Hispanic Journal of Behavioral Sciences, 1,* 247–261.

Gardner, F. L. (2001). Applied sport psychology in professional sports: The team psychologist. *Professional Psychology: Research and Practice, 32,* 34–39.

Gardner, H. (1983). *Frames of mind: The theory of multiple intelligences.* New York: Basic.

Gardner, H. (1994). Multiple intelligences theory. In R. J. Sternberg, (Ed.), *Encyclopedia of human intelligence* (pp. 740–742). New York: Macmillan.

Gardner, R. A. (1971). *The boys' and girls' book about divorce.* New York: Bantam.

Gardner, R. A. (1982). *Family evaluation in child custody litigation.* Cresskill, NJ: Creative Therapeutics.

Gardner, W., Lidz, C. W., Mulvey, E. P., & Shaw, E. C. (1996). Clinical versus actuarial prediction of violence in patients with mental illnesses. *Journal of Consulting and Clinical Psychology, 64,* 602–609.

Garfield, S. L., & Eron, L. D. (1948). Interpreting mood and activity in TAT stories. *Journal of Abnormal and Social Psychology, 43,* 338–345.

Garrett, H. E., & Schneck, M. R. (1933). *Psychological tests, methods and results.* New York: Harper.

Gaugler, B. B., Rosenthal, D. B., Thornton, G. C., III, & Bentson, C. (1987). Meta-analysis of assessment center validity. *Journal of Applied Psychology, 72,* 493–511.

Gavzer, B. (1990, May 27). Should you tell all? *Parade Magazine,* pp. 4–7.

General Electric Co. v. Joiner, 118 S. Ct. 512 (1997).

Gerety, M. B., Mulrow, C. D., Tuley, M. R., Hazuda, H. P., Lichtenstein, M. J., Bohannon, R., Kanten, D. N., O'Neil, M. B., & Gorton, A. (1993). Development and validation of a physical performance instrument for the functionally impaired elderly: The Physical Disability Index (PDI). *Journal of Gerontology, 48,* M33–M38.

Gerry, M. H. (1973). Cultural myopia: The need for a corrective lens. *Journal of School Psychology, 11,* 307–315.

Gesell, A. (1945). *The embryology of behavior. The beginnings of the human mind.* New York: Harper.

Gesell, A. (1954).The ontogenesis of infant behavior. In L. Carmichael (Ed.), *Manual of child psychology.* New York: Wiley.

Gesell, A., & Amatruda, C. S. (1947). *Development diagnosis: Normal and abnormal child development* (2nd ed.). New York: Harper & Row.

Gesell, A., & Thompson, H. (1929). Learning and growth in identical twin infants. *Genetic Psychology Monographs, 6,* 1–124.

Gesell, A., et al. (1940). *The first five years of life.* New York: Harper.

Ghiselli, E. E. (1973). The variety of aptitude tests in personnel selection. *Personnel Psychology, 26,* 461–477.

Ghiselli, E. E., & Barthol, R. P. (1953). The validity of personality inventories in the selection of employees. *Journal of Applied Psychology, 38,* 18–20.

Ghiselli, E. E., Campbell, J. P., & Zedeck, S. (1981). *Measurement theory for the behavioral sciences.* San Francisco: Freeman.

Gibbins, S. (1988, April). *Use of the K-ABC and WISC-R with deaf children.* Paper presented at the Annual Meeting of the National Association of School Psychologists, Chicago.

Gibbins, S. (1989). The provision of school psychological assessment services for the hearing impaired: A national survey. *Volta Review, 91,* 95–103.

Gill, C. J., Kewman, D. G., & Brannon, R. W. (2003). Transforming psychological practice and society: Policies that reflect the new paradigm. *American Psychologist, 58,* 305–312.

Girelli, S. A., & Stake, J. E. (1993). Bipolarity in Jungian type theory and the Myers-Briggs Type Indicator. *Journal of Personality Assessment, 60,* 290–301.

Glaser, R., & Nitko, A. J. (1971). Measurement in learning and instruction. In R. L. Thorndike (Ed.), *Educational measurement* (2nd ed.). Washington, DC: American Council on Education.

Glassbrenner, J. (1998). Continuity across contexts: Prison, women's counseling center, and home. In L. Handler (Chair), *Conducting assessments in clients' homes: Contexts, surprises, dilemmas, opportunities.* Symposium presented at the Society for Personality Assessment 1998 Midwinter Meeting, February 20.

Glazer, W. M., Kramer, R., Montgomery, J. S., & Myers, L. (1991). Use of medical necessity scales in concurrent review of psychiatric inpatient care. *Hospital and Community Psychiatry, 42,* 1199–1200.

Glosser, G., & Goodglass, H. (1990). Disorders in executive control functions among aphasic and other brain-damaged patients. *Journal of Clinical and Experimental Neuropsychology, 12,* 485–501.

Gluck, M. R. (1955). The relationship between hostility in the TAT and behavioral hostility. *Journal of Projective Techniques, 19,* 21–26.

Glueck, W. F. (1978). *Personnel: A diagnostic approach.* Dallas, TX: Business Publications.

Gobetz, W. A. (1953). Quantification, standardization, and validation of the Bender-Gestalt test on normal and neurotic adults. *Psychological Monographs, 67,* No. 6.

Goddard, H. H. (1908). The Binet and Simon tests of intellectual capacity. *Training School, 5,* 3–9.

Goddard, H. H. (1910). A measuring scale of intelligence. *Training School, 6,* 146–155.

Goddard, H. H. (1912). *The Kallikak family.* New York: Macmillan.

Goddard, H. H. (1913). The Binet tests in relation to immigration. *Journal of Psycho-Asthenics, 18,* 105–107.

Goddard, H. H. (1916). *Feeblemindedness.* New York: Macmillan.

Goddard, H. H. (1917). Mental tests and the immigrant. *Journal of Delinquency, 2,* 243–277.

Goel, V., & Grafman, J. (1995). Are the frontal lobes implicated in "planning" functions? Interpreting data from the Tower of Hanoi. *Neuropsychologia, 33,* 623–642.

Goffman, E. (1963). *Behavior in public places.* Glencoe, IL: Free Press.

Gokhale, D. V., & Kullback, S. (1978). *The information in contingency tables.* New York: Marcel Dekker.

Gold, D. P., Andres, D., Etezadi, J., et al. (1995). Structural equation model of intellectual change and continuity and predictors of intelligence in older men. *Psychology & Aging, 10,* 294–303.

Goldberg, L. R. (1993). The structure of phenotypic personality traits. *American Psychologist, 48,* 26–34.

Goldberg, T. E., Gold, J. M., Greenberg, R., Griffin, S., Schulz, S. C., Pickar, D., Kleinman, J. E., & Weinberger, D. R. (1993). Contrasts between patients with affective disorders and patients with schizophrenia on a neuropsychological test battery. *American Journal of Psychiatry, 150,* 1355–1362.

Goldberg, T. E., Saint-Cyr, J. A., & Weinberger, D. R. (1990). Assessment of procedural learning and problem solving in schizophrenic patients by Tower of Hanoi type tasks. *Journal of Neuropsychiatry, 2,* 165–173.

Golden, C. J., Hammeke, T. A., & Purisch, A. D. (1980). *The Luria-Nebraska Neuropsychological Battery: Manual.* Los Angeles: Western Psychological Services.

Golden, C. J., Purisch, A. D., & Hammeke, T. A. (1985). *Luria-Nebraska Neuropsychological Battery: Forms I and II, manual.* Los Angeles: Western Psychological Services.

Goldfried, M. R., & Davison, G. C. (1976). *Clinical behavior therapy.* New York: Holt, Rinehart & Winston.

Goldfried, M. R., Stricker, G., & Winer, I. B. (1971). *Rorschach handbook of clinical and research applications.* Englewood Cliffs, NJ: Prentice-Hall.

Golding, S. L. (1975). Flies in the ointment: Methodological problems in the analysis of the percentage of variance due to persons and situations. *Psychological Bulletin, 82,* 278–288.

Goldman, B. A., & Mitchell, D. F. (Eds.) (1997). *Directory of unpublished experimental measures (Vol. 7).* Dubuque, IA: W. C. Brown.

Goldstein, K. (1927). Die lokalisation in her grosshin rinde. *Handb. norm. pathol. psychologie.* Berlin: J. Springer.

Goldstein, K. (1939). *The organism.* New York: American Book.

Goldstein, K. (1963a). *The organism.* Boston: Beacon.

Goldstein, K. (1963b). The modifications of behavior consequent to cerebral lesions. *Psychiatric Quarterly, 10,* 586–610.

Gomez, R., & Hazeldine, P. (1996). Social information processing in mild mentally retarded children. *Research in Developmental Disabilities, 17,* 217–227.

Good, R. H., Chowdhri, S., Katz, L., Vollman, M., & Creek, R. (1989, March). *Effect of matching instruction and simultaneous/sequential processing strength.* Paper presented at the Annual Meeting of the National Association of School Psychologists, Boston.

Good, R. H., & Lane, S. (1988). *Confirmatory factor analysis of the K-ABC and WISC-R: Hierarchical models.* Paper presented at the Annual Meeting of the American Psychological Association, Atlanta.

Good, R. H., Vollmer, M., Creek, R. J., & Katz, L. (1993). Treatment utility of the Kaufman Assessment Battery for Children: Effects of matching instruction and student processing strength. *School Psychology Review, 22,* 8–26.

Goodman, G. S., & Reed, R. S. (1986). Age differences in eyewitness testimony. *Law and Human Behavior, 10,* 317–332.

Goodman-Delahunty, J. (2000). Psychological impairment under the Americans with Disabilities Act: Legal guidelines. *Professional Psychology: Research and Practice, 31,* 197–205.

Goodman-Delahunty, J., & Foote, W. E. (1995). Compensation for pain, suffering and other psychological injuries: The impact of *Daubert* on employment discrimination claims. *Behavioral Sciences and the Law, 13,* 183–206.

Gopaul-McNicol, S. (1993). *Working with West Indian families.* New York: Guilford.

Gorsuch, R. L. (1997). Exploratory factor analysis: Its role in item analysis. *Journal of Personality Assessment, 68,* 532–560.

Gottfredson, L. S. (1988). Reconsidering fairness: A matter of social and ethical priorities. *Journal of Vocational Behavior, 33,* 293–319.

Gottfredson, L. S. (1994). The science and politics of race-norming. *American Psychologist, 49,* 955–963.

Gottfredson, L. S. (2000). Skills gaps, not tests, make racial proportionality impossible. *Psychology, Public Policy, and Law, 6,* 129–143.

Gottfried, A. W. (Ed.). (1984). *Home environment and early cognitive development: Longitudinal research.* New York: Academic Press.

Gottfried, A. W., Gottfried, A. E., Bathurst, K., & Guerin, D. W. (1994). *Gifted IQ: Early developmental aspects.* New York: Plenum.

Gough, H. G. (1960). The Adjective Check List as a personality assessment research technique. *Psychological Reports, 6,* 107–122.

Gough, H. G. (1962). Clinical versus statistical prediction in psychology. In L. Postman (Ed.), *Psychology in the making: Histories of selected research problems* (pp. 526–584). New York: Knopf.

Gough, H. G., & Heilbrun, A. B., Jr. (1980). *The Adjective Checklist manual (Revised).* Palo Alto, CA: Consulting Psychologists Press.

Grafman, J., Litvan, I., Massaquoi, S., & Stewart, M. (1992). Cognitive planning deficit in patients with cerebellar atrophy. *Neurology, 42,* 1493–1496.

Graham, J. R. (1990). *MMPI-2: Assessing personality and psychopathology.* New York: Oxford University.

Granger, C. V., & Gresham, G. E. (Eds.). (1984). *Functional assessment in rehabilitation medicine.* Baltimore: Williams & Wilkins.

Greaud, V. A., & Green, B. F. (1986). Equivalence of conventional and computer presentation of speed tests. *Applied Psychological Measurement, 10,* 23–34.

Green, A. (1986). True and false allegations of sexual abuse in child custody disputes. *Journal of the American Academy of Child Psychology, 25,* 449–456.

Green, B. F. (1984). *Computer-based ability testing.* Paper delivered at the 91st annual meeting of the American Psychological Association, Toronto, Ontario, Canada.

Green, S. B. (2003). A coefficient alpha for test-retest data. *Psychological Methods, 8,* 88–101.

Greene, R. L. (1987). Ethnicity and MMPI performance: A review. *Journal of Consulting and Clinical Psychology, 55,* 497–512.

Greenfield, D. N. (1999). Psychological characteristics of compulsive Internet use: A preliminary analysis. *CyberPsychology & Behavior, 2,* 403–412.

Greenlaw, P. S., & Jensen, S. S. (1996). Race-norming and the Civil Rights Act of 1991. *Public Personnel Management, 25,* 13–24.

Greenspan, S. (1997). Dead manual walking? Why the AAMR definition needs redoing. *Education & Training in Mental Retardation & Developmental Disabilities, 32,* 179–190.

Greenspoon, J. (1955). The reinforcing effect of two spoken sounds on the frequency of two responses. *American Journal of Psychology, 68,* 409–416.

Greenspoon, J., & Gersten, C. D. (1967). A new look at psychological testing: Psychological testing from the standpoint of a behaviorist. *American Psychologist, 22,* 848–853.

Gregoire, J. (1999). Emerging standards for test applications in the French-speaking countries of Europe. *European Journal of Psychological Assessment, 15,* 158–164.

Gresham, F. M. (1989). Review of the Parenting Stress Index. In J. C. Conoley & J. J. Kramer (Eds.), *The tenth mental measurements yearbook.* Lincoln: Buros Institute of Mental Measurements, University of Nebraska.

Gresham, F. M., MacMillan, D. L., & Siperstein, G. N. (1995). Critical analysis of the 1992 AAMR definition: Implications for school psychology. *School Psychology Quarterly, 10*(1), 1–19.

Grey, R. J., & Kipnis, D. (1976). Untangling the performance appraisal dilemma: The influence of perceived organizational context on evaluative processes. *Journal of Applied Psychology, 61,* 329–335.

Griffith, L. (1997). Surviving no-frills mental health care: The future of psychological assessment. *Journal of Practical Psychiatry and Behavioral Health, 3,* 255–258.

Grisso, T. (1986). *Evaluating competencies: Forensic assessments and instruments.* New York: Plenum.

Groeger, J. A., & Chapman, P. R. (1997). Normative influences on decisions to offend. *Applied Psychology: An International Review, 46,* 265–285.

Groenveld, M., & Jan, J. E. (1992). Intelligence profiles of low vision and blind children. *Journal of Visual Impairment and Blindness, 86,* 68–71.

Grossman, I., Mednitsky, S., Dennis, B., & Scharff, L. (1993). Validation of an "amazingly" short form of the WAIS-R for a clinically depressed sample. *Journal of Psychoeducational Assessment, 11,* 173–181.

Grove, W. M., & Barden, R. C. (1999). Protecting the integrity of the legal system: The admissibility of testimony from mental health experts under *Dauberg/Kumho* analyses. *Psychology, Public Policy, and Law, 5,* 224–242.

Grove, W. M., Zald, D. H., Lebow, B. S., et al. (2000). Clinical versus mechanical prediction: A meta-analysis. *Psychological Assessment, 12,* 19–30.

Guastello, S. J., & Rieke, M. L. (1990). The Barnum Effect and the validity of computer-based test interpretations: The Human Resource Development Report. *Psychological Assessment, 2,* 186–190.

Guerrier, J. H., Manivannan, P., & Nair, S. N. (1999). The role of working memory, field dependence, visual search, and reaction time in the left turn performance of older female drivers. *Applied Ergonomics, 30,* 109–119.

Guilford, J. P. (1954). A factor analytic study across the domains of reasoning, creativity, and evaluation. I. Hypothesis and description of tests. *Reports from the psychology laboratory.* Los Angeles: University of Southern California.

Guilford, J. P. (1959). *Personality.* New York: McGraw-Hill.

Guilford, J. P. (1967). *The nature of human intelligence.* New York: McGraw-Hill.

Guilford, J. P., et al. (1974). *Structure-of-Intellect Abilities.* Orange, CA: Sheridan Psychological Services.

Guilmette, T. J., & Faust, D. (1991). Characteristics of neuropsychologists who prefer the Halstead-Reitan Battery or the Luria-Nebraska Neuropsychological Battery. *Professional Psychology: Research and Practice, 22*(1), 80–83.

Guilmette, T. J., Faust, D., Hart, K., & Arkes, H. R. (1990). A national survey of psychologists who offer neuropsychological services. *Archives of Clinical Neuropsychology, 5,* 373–392.

Guion, R. M. (1980). On trinitarian doctrines of validity. *Professional Psychology, 11,* 385–398.

Gulliksen, H., & Messick, S. (Eds.). (1960). *Psychological scaling: Theory and applications.* New York: Wiley, 1960.

Guttman, L. (1947). The Cornell technique for scale and intensity analysis. *Educational and Psychological Measurement, 7,* 247–280.

Guttman, L. A. (1944a). A basis for scaling qualitative data. *American Sociological Review, 9,* 139–150.

Guttman, L. A. (1944b). A basis for scaling qualitative data. *American Sociological Review, 9,* 179–190.

Haaga, D. A., Davison, G. C., McDermut, W., Hillis, S. L., & Twomey, H. B. (1993). "State of mind" analysis of the articulated thoughts of ex-smokers. *Cognitive Therapy and Research, 17,* 427–439.

Hadaway, N., & Marek-Schroer, M. F. (1992). Multidimensional assessment of the gifted minority student. *Roeper Review, 15,* 73–77.

Haensly, P. A., & Torrance, E. P. (1990). Assessment of creativity in children and adolescents. In C. R. Reynolds & R. W. Kamphaus (Eds.), *Handbook of psychological and educational assessment of children: Intelligence & achievement* (pp. 697–722). New York: Guilford.

Hafemeister, T. L. (2001, February). Ninth Circuit rejects immunity from liability for mental health evaluations. *Monitor on Psychology, 32.*

Haidt, J., Rosenberg, E., & Horn, H. (2003). Differentiating differences: Moral diversity is not like other kinds. *Journal of Applied Social Psychology, 33,* 1–36.

Haier, R. J. (1993). Cerebral glucose metabolism and intelligence. In P. A. Vernon (Ed.), *Biological approaches to the study of human intelligence* (pp. 317–332). Norwood, NJ: Ablex.

Haines, M., & Spear, S. F. (1996). Changing the perception of the norm: A strategy to decrease binge drinking among college students. *Journal of American College Health, 45*(3), 134–140.

Haley, K., & Lee, M. (Eds.). (1998). *The Oregon Death With Dignity Act: A guidebook for health care providers.* Portland, OR: Oregon Health Sciences University, Center for Ethics in Health Care.

Hall, C. I. J. (1997). Cultural malpractice: The growing obsolescence of psychology with the changing U.S. population. *American Psychologist, 52,* 642–651.

Hall, C. S., & Lindzey, G. (1970). *Theories of personality.* New York: Wiley.

Hall, J. A., & Rosenthal, R. (1995). Interpreting and evaluating meta-analysis. *Evaluation and the Health Professions, 18,* 393–407.

Hall, S. S. (1998, February 15). Our memories, our selves. *New York Times Magazine,* pp. 26–33, 49, 56–57.

Halleck, S. L. (1976). Discussion of "Socially Reinforced Obsessing." *Journal of Consulting and Clinical Psychology, 44,* 146–147.

Halpern, A. S., & Fuherer, M. J. (Eds.). (1984). *Functional assessment in rehabilitation.* Baltimore: Paul H. Brookes.

Halpern, D. F. (1997). Sex differences in intelligence: Implications for education. *American Psychologist, 52,* 1901–1102.

Halpern, D. F. (2000). Validity, fairness, and group differences: Tough questions for selection testing. *Psychology, Public Policy, & Law, 6,* 56–62.

Halpern, F. (1958). Child case study. In E. F. Hammer (Ed.), *The clinical application of projective drawings* (pp. 113–129). Springfield, IL: Charles C Thomas.

Halstead, W. C. (1947a). *Brain and intelligence.* Chicago: University of Chicago.

Halstead, W. C. (1947b). *Brain and intelligence: A quantitative study of the frontal lobes.* Chicago: University of Chicago.

Halstead, W. C., & Wepman, J. M. (1959). The Halstead-Wepman Aphasia Screening Test. *Journal of Speech and Hearing Disorders, 14,* 9–15.

Hambleton, R. K., & Jurgensen, C. (1990). Criterion-referenced assessment of school achievement. In C. R. Reynolds & R. W. Kamphaus (Eds.), *Handbook of psychological and educational assessment of children: Intelligence & achievement* (pp. 456–476). New York: Guilford.

Hamera, E., & Brown, C. E. (2000). Developing a context-based performance measure for persons with schizophrenia: The test of grocery shopping skills. *American Journal of Occupational Therapy, 54,* 20–25.

Hammer, E. F. (1958). *The clinical application of projective drawings.* Springfield, IL: Charles C Thomas.

Hammer, E. F. (1981). Projective drawings. In A. I. Rabin (Ed.), *Assessment with projective techniques: A concise introduction* (pp. 151–185). New York: Springer.

Hammitt, J. K. (1990). Risk perceptions and food choice: An exploratory analysis of organic—versus conventional—produce buyers. *Risk Analysis, 10,* 367–374.

Handler, L. (1996). John Exner and the book that started it all: A review of *The Rorschach Systems. Journal of Personality Assessment, 66,* 441–471.

Handler, L. (2001). Assessment of men: Personality assessment goes to war by the Office of Strategic Services Assessment Staff. *Journal of Personality Assessment, 76,* 558–578.

Haney, W. (1981). Validity, vaudeville, and values: A short history of social concerns over standardized testing. *American Psychologist, 36,* 1021–1034.

Haney, W., & Madaus, G. F. (1978). Making sense of the competency testing movement. *Harvard Educational Review, 48,* 462–484.

Hansen, J. C. (1987). Cross-cultural research on vocational interests. *Measurement and Evaluation in Counseling and Development, 19,* 163–176.

Hansen, N. D. (2002). Teaching cultural sensitivity in psychological assessment: A modular approach used in a distance education program. *Journal of Personality, 79,* 200–206.

Hansen, N. D., Pepitone-Arreola-Rockwell, F., & Greene, A. F. (2000). Multicultural competence: Criteria and case examples. *Professional Psychology: Research and Practice, 31,* 652–660.

Happell, B., Pinikahana, J., & Martin, T. (2003). Stress and burnout in forensic psychiatric nursing. *Stress & Health, 19,* 63–68.

Hare, R. D. (1980). A research scale for the assessment of psychopathy in criminal populations. *Personality and Individual Differences, 1,* 111–119.

Hare, R. D. (1985). *The Psychopathy Checklist.* Unpublished manuscript. University of British Columbia, Vancouver, Canada.

Hare, R. D., Harpur, A. R., Hakstian, A. R., Forth, A. E., Hart, S. D., & Newman, J. P. (1990). The Revised Psychopathy Checklist: Reliability and Factor Structure. *Psychological Assessment, 2,* 338–341.

Harker, L., & Keltner, D. (2001). Expressions of positive emotion in women's college yearbook pictures and their relationship to personality and life outcomes across adulthood. *Journal of Personality and Social Psychology, 80,* 112–124.

Harmon, L. W., Hansen, J. C., Borgen, F. H., & Hammer, A. L. (1994). *Strong Interest Inventory: Applications and technical guide.* Palo Alto, CA: Consulting Psychologists Press.

Harris, D. (1963). *Children's drawings as measures of intellectual maturity.* New York: Harcourt Brace Jovanovich.

Harris, G. T., Rice, M. E., & Cormier, C. A. (1989). Violent recidivism among psychopaths and non-psychopaths treated in a therapeutic community. *Penetanguishene Mental Health Centre Research Report VI* (No. 181). Penetanguishene, Ontario, Canada: Penetanguishene Mental Health Centre.

Harris, P. M. (1994). Client management classification and prediction of probation outcome. *Crime and Delinquency, 40,* 154–174.

Harris, S. L., Delmolino, L., & Glasberg, B. A. (1996). Psychological and behavioral assessment in mental retardation. *Child & Adolescent Psychiatric Clinics of North America, 5,* 797–808.

Harrison, P., & Oakland, T. (2000). *Adaptive Behavior Assessment System.* San Antonio, TX: Psychological Corporation.

Harrison, P. L. (1990). *AGS Early Screening Profiles.* Circle Pines, MN: American Guidance Service.

Hart, B., & Risley, T. R. (1992). American parenting of language-learning children: Persisting differences in family-child interactions observed in natural home environments. *Developmental Psychology, 28,* 1096–1105.

Hart, R. R., & Goldstein, M. A. (1985). Computer-assisted psychological assessment. *Computers in Human Services, 1,* 69–75.

Hart, S. D., Kropp, P. R., & Hare, R. D. (1988). Performance of male psychopaths following conditional release from prison. *Journal of Consulting and Clinical Psychology, 56,* 227–232.

Hart, V. (1992). Review of the Infant Mullen Scales of Early Development. In J. J. Kramer & J. C. Conoley (Eds.), *The eleventh mental measurements yearbook.* Lincoln: Buros Institute of Mental Measurements, University of Nebraska.

Hartigan, J. A., & Wigdor, A. K. (1989). *Fairness in employment testing: Validity generalization, minority issues, and the General Aptitude Test Battery.* Washington, DC: National Academy.

Hartman, D. E. (1986a). On the use of clinical psychology software: Practical, legal, and ethical concerns. *Professional Psychology: Research and Practice, 17,* 462–465.

Hartman, D. E. (1986b). Artificial intelligence or artificial psychologist? Conceptual issues in clinical microcomputer use. *Professional Psychology: Research and Practice, 17,* 528–534.

Hartmann, D. P., Roper, B. L., & Bradford, D. C. (1979). Some relationships between behavioral and traditional assessment. *Journal of Behavioral Assessment, 1,* 3–21.

Hartmann, E., Sunde, T., Kristensen, W., & Martinussen, M. (2003). Psychological measures as predictors of military training performance. *Journal of Personality Assessment, 80,* 87–98.

Hartshorne, H., & May, M. A. (1928). *Studies in the nature of character. Vol. 1: Studies in deceit.* New York: Macmillan.

Harvey, R. J., & Murry, W. D. (1994). Scoring the Myers-Briggs Type Indicator: Empirical comparison of preference score versus latent-trait methods. *Journal of Personality Assessment, 62,* 116–129.

Hassler, M., & Gupta, D. (1993). Functional brain organization, handedness, and immune vulnerability in musicians and nonmusicians. *Neuropsychologia, 31,* 655–660.

Hathaway, S. R., & McKinley, J. C. (1940). A multiphasic personality schedule (Minnesota): 1. Construction of the schedule. *Journal of Psychology, 10,* 249–254.

Hathaway, S. R., & McKinley, J. C. (1942). A multiphasic personality schedule (Minnesota): III. The measurement of symptomatic depression. *Journal of Psychology, 14,* 73–84.

Hathaway, S. R., & McKinley, J. C. (1943). *The Minnesota Multiphasic Personality Inventory* (rev. ed.). Minneapolis: University of Minnesota.

Hathaway, S. R., & McKinley, J. C. (1951). *The MMPI manual.* New York: Psychological Corporation.

Hayden, D. C., Frulong, M. J., & Linnemeyer, S. (1988). A comparison of the Kaufman Assessment Battery for Children and the Stanford-Binet IV for the assessment of gifted children. *Psychology in the Schools, 25,* 239–243.

Hayes, S. C. (1999). Comparison of the Kaufman Brief Intelligence Test and the Matrix Analogies Test-Short Form in an adolescent forensic population. *Psychological Assessment, 11,* 108–110.

Haynes, R. B., Taylor, D. W., & Sackett, D. L. (Eds.). (1979). *Compliance in health care.* Baltimore: Johns Hopkins University.

Haynes, S. N. (2001a). Introduction to the special section on clinical applications of analogue behavioral observation. *Psychological Assessment, 13,* 3–4.

Haynes, S. N. (2001b). Clinical applications of analogue behavioral observation: Dimensions of psychometric evaluation. *Psychological Assessment, 13,* 73–85.

Haynes, S. N., Follingstad, D. R., & Sullivan, J. (1979). Assessment of marital satisfaction and interaction. *Journal of Consulting and Clinical Psychology, 47,* 789–791.

Haynes, S. N., Jensen, B. J., Wise, E., & Sherman, D. (1981). The marital intake interview: A multimethod criterion validity assessment. *Journal of Consulting and Clinical Psychology, 49,* 379–387.

Hays, P. A. (1996). Culturally responsive assessment with diverse older clients. *Professional Psychology: Research and Practice, 27,* 188–193.

Hays, P. A., & LeVine, P. (2001). *Addressing cultural complexities in practice: A framework for clinicians and counselors.* Washington, DC: American Psychological Association.

Hazlett, R. L., Falkin, S., Lawhorn, W., Friedman, E., & Haynes, S. N. (1997). Cardiovascular reactivity to a naturally occurring stressor: Development and psychometric evaluation of psychophysiological assessment procedure. *Journal of Behavioral Medicine, 20,* 551–571.

Heaton, R. K., Temkin, N., Dikmen, S., et al. (2001). Detecting change: A comparison of three neuropsychological methods, using normal and clinical samples. *Archives of Clinical Neuropsychology, 16,* 75–91.

Hedges, C. (1997, November 25). In Bosnia's schools, 3 ways never to learn from history. *New York Times,* pp. A1, A4.

Heinrichs, R. W. (1990). Variables associated with Wisconsin Card Sorting Test performance in neuropsychiatric patients referred for assessment. *Neuropsychiatry, Neuropsychology, and Behavioral Neurology, 3,* 107–112.

Heinze, M. C., & Grisso, T. (1996). Review of instruments assessing parenting competencies used in child custody evaluations. *Behavioral Sciences and the Law, 14,* 293–313.

Helfer, R. E., & Kempe, R. S. (Eds.). (1988). *The battered child* (4th ed.). Chicago: University of Chicago Press.

Helson, R. (1967). Personality characteristics and developmental history of creative college women. *Genetic Psychology Monographs, 76,* 205–256.

Helson, R., Mitchell, V., & Moane, G. (1984). Personality and patterns of adherence and nonadherence to the social clock. *Journal of Personality and Social Psychology, 46,* 1079–1096.

Henk, W. A. (1993). New directions in reading assessment. *Reading and Writing Quarterly: Overcoming Learning Difficulties, 9,* 103–120.

Henley, N. M., & LaFrance, M. (1984). Gender as culture: Difference in dominance in nonverbal behavior. In A. Wolfgang (Ed.), *Nonverbal behavior: Perspectives, applications, intercultural insights* (pp. 351–371). Lewiston, NY: Hogrefe & Huber.

Henry, E. M., & Rotter, J. B. (1956). Situational influences on Rorschach responses. *Journal of Consulting Psychology, 20,* 457–462.

Henry, J. D. (1984). Syndicated public opinion polls: Some thoughts for consideration. *Journal of Advertising Research, 24,* I-5–I-8.

Henry, W. E. (1956). *The analysis of fantasy.* New York: Wiley.

Henson, R. K. (2001). Understanding internal consistency reliability estimates: A conceptual primer on coefficient alpha. *Measurement and Evaluation in Counseling and Development, 34,* 177–189.

Heppner, M. J. (1998). The Career Transitions Inventory: Measuring internal resources in adulthood. *Journal of Career Assessment, 6,* 135–145.

Heppner, M. J., Multon, K. D., & Johnston, J. A. (1994). Assessing psychological resources during career change: Development of the Career Transitions Inventory. *Journal of Vocational Behavior, 44,* 55–74.

Herlihy, B. (1977). Watch out, IQ myth: Here comes another debunker. *Phi Delta Kappan, 59,* 298.

Hermann, C., Blanchard, E. B., & Flor, H. (1997). Biofeedback treatment for pediatric migraine: Prediction of treatment outcome. *Journal of Consulting and Clinical Psychology, 65,* 611–616.

Hernandez, B., Keys, C., & Balcazar, F. (2003). The Americans wth Disabilities Act Knowledge Survey: Strong psychometrics and weak knowledge. *Rehabilitation Psychology, 48,* 93–99.

Herrnstein, R., & Murray, C. (1994). *The bell curve.* New York: Free Press.

Herzberg, F., Mausner, B., Peterson, R. O., & Capwell, D. F. (1957). Job attitudes: Review of research and opinion. *Journal of Applied Psychology, 63,* 596–601.

Hess, E. H. (1965). Attitude and pupil size. *Scientific American, 212,* 46–54.

Hetherington, E. M., & Parke, R. D. (1993). *Child psychology: A contemporary viewpoint* (4th ed.). New York: McGraw-Hill.

Heyman, R. E. (2001). Observation of couple conflicts: Clinical assessment applications, stubborn truths, and shaky foundations. *Psychological Assessment, 13,* 5–35.

Hibbard, S. (2003). A critique of Lilienfeld et al.'s (2000) "The scientific status of projective techniques." *Journal of Personality Assessment, 80,* 260–271.

Hibbard, S., Farmer, L., Wells, C., et al., (1994). Validation of Cramer's defense mechanism manual for the TAT. *Journal of Personality Assessment, 63,* 197–210.

Hicks, L. K., Lin, Y., Robertson, D. W., et al. (2001). Understanding the clinical dilemmas that shape medical students' ethical development: Questionnaire survey and focus group study. *British Medical Journal, 322,* 709–710.

Higgins, P. C. (1983). *Outsiders in a hearing world.* Beverly Hills, CA: Sage.

Hill, P. C., & Pargament, K. I. (2003). Advances in the conceptualization and measurement of religion and spirituality: Implications for physical and mental health research. *American Psychologist, 58,* 64–74.

Hiller, J. B., Rosenthal, R., Bornstein, R. F., & Brunell-Neuleib, S. (1999). A comparative meta-analysis of Rorschach and MMPI validity. *Psychological Assessment, 11,* 278–296.

Hills, D. A. (1985). Prediction of effectiveness in leaderless group discussions with the Adjective Check List. *Journal of Applied Psychology, 15,* 443–447.

Hines, M., Chiu, L., McAdams, L. A., Bentler, M. P., & Lipcamon, J. (1992). Cognition and the corpus callosum: Verbal fluency, visuospatial ability, language lateralization related to midsagittal surface areas of the corpus callosum. *Behavioral Neuroscience, 106,* 3–14.

Hinkle, J. S. (1994). Counselors and cross-cultural assessment: A practical guide to information and training. *Measurement and Evaluation in Counseling and Development, 27,* 103–115.

Hinrichsen, J. J., & Bradley, L. A. (1974). Situational determinants of personal validation of general personality interpretations: A re-examination. *Journal of Personality Assessment, 38,* 530–534.

Hirsch, J. (1997). Some history of heredity-vs-environment, genetic inferiority at Harvard(?), and *The* (incredible) *bell curve. Genetics, 99,* 207–224.

Hiscox, M. D. (1983). *A balance sheet for educational item banking.* Paper presented at the annual meeting of the National Council for Measurement in Education, Montreal, Canada.

Hiscox, M. D., & Brzezinski, E. (1980). *A guide to item banking in education.* Portland, OR: Northwest Regional Educational Laboratory, Assessment and Education Division.

Hishinuma, E. S., Andrade, N. N., Johnson, R. C., et al. (2000). Psychometric properties of the Hawaiian Culture Scale-Adolescent Version. *Psychological Assessment, 12,* 140–157.

Hishinuma, E. S., & Yamakawa, R. (1993). Construct and criterion-related validity of the WISC-III for exceptional students and those who are "at risk." In B. A. Bracken (Ed.), *Monograph series, Advances in psychoeducational assessment: Wechsler Intelligence Scale for Children, Third Edition; Journal of Psychoeducational Assessment* (pp. 94–104). Brandon, VT: Clinical Psychology Publishing.

Hiskey, M. S. (1966). *Hiskey-Nebraska Test of Learning Aptitude.* Lincoln: Union College.

Ho, M. K. (1987). *Family therapy with ethnic minorities.* Newbury Park, CA: Sage.

Hodapp, R. M. (1995). Definitions in mental retardation: Effects on research, practice, and perceptions. *School Psychology Quarterly, 10*(1), 24–28.

Hofer, P. J., & Green, B. F. (1985). The challenge of competence and creativity in computerized psychological testing. *Journal of Consulting and Clinical Psychology, 53,* 826–838.

Hoffman, B. (1962). *The tyranny of testing.* New York: Crowell-Collier.

Hoffman, K. I., & Lundberg, G. D. (1976). A comparison of computer monitored group tests and paper-and-pencil tests. *Educational and Psychological Measurement, 36,* 791–809.

Hofstede, G. (1998). Attitudes, values, and organizational culture: Disentangling the concepts. *Organization Studies, 19,* 477–493.

Holahan, C., & Sears, R. (1995). *The gifted group in later maturity.* Stanford, CA: Stanford University Press.

Holden, G. W., & Edwards, L. A. (1989). Parental attitudes toward child rearing: Instruments, issues, and implications. *Psychological Bulletin, 106,* 29–58.

Holland, A. (1980). *Communicative abilities in daily living: A test of functional communication for aphasic adults.* Baltimore: University Park.

Holland, J. L. (1973). *Making vocational choices.* Englewood Cliffs, NJ: Prentice-Hall.

Holland, J. L. (1985). *Manual for the vocational preference inventory.* Odessa, FL: Psychological Assessment Resources.

Holland, J. L. (1997). *Making vocational choices: A theory of vocational personalities and work environments* (3rd ed.). Odessa, FL: Psychological Assessment Resources.

Holland, J. L. (1999a). *Making vocational choices: A theory of vocational personalities and work environments* (3rd ed.). Odessa, FL: Psychological Assessent Resources.

Holland, J. L. (1999b). Why interest inventories are also personality inventories. In M. L. Savickas & A. R. Spokane (Eds.), *Vocational interests: Meaning, measurement, and counseling use* (87–101). Palo Alto, CA: Davies-Black Publishing.

Holland, J. L., Powell, A. B., & Fritzsche, B. A. (1994). *The Self-Directed Search (SDS) professional user's guide—1994 edition.* Odessa, FL: Psychological Assessment Resources.

Holland, W. R. (1960). Language barrier as an educational problem of Spanish-speaking children. *Exceptional Children, 27,* 42–47.

Hollander, E. P., & Willis, R. H. (1967). Some current issues in the psychology of conformity and nonconformity. *Psychological Bulletin, 68,* 62–76.

Hollenbeck, J. R., & Whitener, E. M. (1988). Reclaiming personality traits for personal selection: Self-esteem as an illustrative case. *Journal of Management, 14,* 81–91.

Hollingshead, A. B., & Redlich, F. C. (1958). *Social class and mental illness: A community study.* New York: Wiley.

Holmstrom, R. W., Silber, D. E., & Karp, S. A. (1990). Development of the Apperceptive Personality Test. *Journal of Personality Assessment, 54,* 252–264.

Holt, R. R. (1958). Clinical and statistical prediction: A reformulation and some new data. *Journal of Abnormal and Social Psychology, 56,* 1–12.

Holt, R. R. (1970). Yet another look at clinical and statistical prediction: Or, is clinical psychology worthwhile? *American Psychologist, 25,* 337–349.

Holt, R. R. (1971). *Assessing personality.* New York: Harcourt Brace Jovanovich.

Holt, R. R. (1978). *Methods in clinical psychology: Vol. 2. Prediction and research.* New York: Plenum.

Holtzman, W. H. (1993). An unjustified, sweeping indictment by Motta et al. of human figure drawings for assessing psychological functioning. *School Psychology Quarterly, 8,* 189–190.

Holtzman, W. H., Thorpe, J. S., Swartz, J. D., & Herron, E. W. (1961). *Inkblot perception and personality: Holtzman Inkblot Technique.* Austin: University of Texas Press.

Honaker, L. M. (1988). The equivalency of computerized and conventional MMPI administration: A review. *Clinical Psychology Review, 8,* 561–577.

Honaker, L. M. (1990, August). Recommended guidelines for computer equivalency research (or everything you should know about computer administration but will be disappointed if you ask). In W. J. Camara (Chair), *The state of computer-based testing and interpretation: Consensus or chaos?* Symposium conducted at the Annual Convention of the American Psychological Association, Boston.

Honaker, L. M., & Fowler, R. D. (1990). Computer-assisted psychological assessment. In G. Goldstein & M. Hersen

(Eds.), *Handbook of psychological assessment* (2nd ed., pp. 521–546). New York: Pergamon.

Honts, C. R. (1994). Psychophysiological detection of deception. *Current Directions in Psychological Science, 3,* 77–82.

Honzik, M. P. (1967). Environmental correlates of mental growth: Prediction from the family setting at 21 months. *Child Development, 38,* 337–364.

Hopkins, K. D., & Glass, G. V. (1978). *Basic statistics for the behavioral sciences.* Englewood Cliffs, NJ: Prentice-Hall.

Hopwood v. State of Texas, 78 F.3d 932, 948 (5th Cir. 1996).

Horn, J. (1988). Thinking about human abilities. In J. R. Nesselroade & R. B. Cattell (Eds.), *Handbook of multivariate psychology.* New York: Plenum.

Horn, J. L. (1968). Organization of abilities and the development of intelligence. *Psychological Review, 75,* 242–259.

Horn, J. L. (1985). Remodeling old theories of intelligence: GF-Gc theory. In B. B. Wolman (Ed.), *Handbook of intelligence* (pp. 267–300). New York: Wiley.

Horn, J. L. (1988). Thinking about human abilities. In J. R. Nesselroade & R. B. Cattell (Eds.), *Handbook of multivariate psychology* (rev. ed., pp. 645–685). New York: Academic Press.

Horn, J. L. (1989). Cognitive diversity: A framework for learning. In P. L. Ackerman et al. (Eds.), *Learning and individual differences* (pp. 61–116). New York: W. H. Freeman.

Horn, J. L. (1991). Measurement of intellectual capabilities: A review of theory. In K. S. McGrew et al. (Eds.), *Woodcock-Johnson technical manual* (pp. 197–232). Chicago: Riverside.

Horn, J. L. (1994). Theory of fluid and crystallized intelligence. In R. J. Sternberg (Ed.), *Encyclopedia of human intelligence* (pp. 443–451).

Horn, J. L., & Cattell, R. B. (1966). Refinement and test of the theory of fluid and crystallized intelligence. *Journal of Educational Psychology, 57,* 253–270.

Horn, J. L., & Cattell, R. B. (1967). Age differences in fluid and crystallized intelligence. *Acta Psychologica, 26,* 107–129.

Horn, J. L., & Hofer, S. M. (1992). Major abilities and development in the adult period. In R. J. Sternberg & C. A. Berg (Eds.), *Intellectual development* (pp. 44–99). Boston, MA: Cambridge University Press.

Hornby, R. (1993). *Cultural competence for human service providers.* Rosebud, SD: Sinte Gleska University Press.

Horner, M. S. (1973). A psychological barrier to achievement in women: The motive to avoid success. In D. C. McClelland & R. S. Steele (Eds.), *Human motivation* (pp. 222–230). Morristown, NJ: General Learning.

Horowitz, R., & Murphy, L. B. (1938). Projective methods in the psychological study of children. *Journal of Experimental Education, 7,* 133–140.

Hostetler, A. J. (1987). Try to remember. *APA Monitor, 18*(5), 18.

House, R. J., Shane, S. A., & Herold, D. M. (1996). Rumors of the death of dispositional research are vastly exaggerated. *Academy of Management Review, 20,* 203–224.

Houston, T. K., Cooper, L. A., Vu, H., et al. (2001). Screening the public for depression through the Internet. *Psychiatric Services, 52,* 362–367.

Howard, M. N. (1991). The neutral expert: A plausible threat to justice. *Criminal Law Review.*

Howe Chief, E. (1940). An assimilation study of Indian girls. *Journal of Social Psychology, 11,* 19–30.

Hsu, S-H, & Peng, Y. (1993). Control/display relationship of the four-burner stove: A re-examination. *Human Factors, 35,* 745–749.

Hudson, W. W. (1982). *The clinical measurement package: A field manual.* Chicago: Dorsey.

Huesmann, L. R., & Guerra, N. G. (1997). Children's normative beliefs about aggression and aggressive behavior. *Journal of Personality and Social Psychology, 72,* 408–419.

Huffcutt, A. I., & Arthur, Jr., W. (1994). Hunter and Hunter (1984) revisited: Interview validity for entry-level jobs. *Journal of Applied Psychology, 79,* 184–190.

Hughes, C., Hwang, B., Kim, J.-H., et al. (1995). Quality of life in applied research: A review and analysis of empirical measures. *American Journal on Mental Retardation, 99,* 623–641.

Hull, C. L. (1922). *Aptitude testing.* Yonkers, NY: World Book.

Hulse, W. G. (1951). The emotionally disturbed child draws his family. *Quarterly Journal of Child Behavior, 3,* 151–174.

Hulse, W. G. (1952). Childhood conflict expressed through family drawings. *Quarterly Journal of Child Behavior, 16,* 152–174.

Humphreys, L. G. (1996). Linear dependence of gain scores on their components imposes constraints on their use and interpretation: Comment on "Are simple gain scores obsolete?" *Applied Psychological Measurement, 20,* 293–294.

Hunsley, J., & Bailey, J. M. (1999). The clinical utility of the Rorschach: Unfulfilled promises and an uncertain future. *Psychological Assessment, 11,* 266–277.

Hunt, J. McV. (1961). *Intelligence and experience.* New York: Ronald.

Hunt, K. N. (2002). *Encyclopedia of associations.* Farmington Hills, MI: Gale Group.

Hunter, J. E. (1980). *Validity generalization for 12,000 jobs: An application of synthetic validity and validity generalization to the General Aptitude Test Battery (GATB).* Washington, DC: U.S. Employment Service, Department of Labor.

Hunter, J. E. (1982). *The dimensionality of the General Aptitude Test Battery and the dominance of general factors over specific factors in the prediction of job performance.* Washington, DC: U.S. Employment Service, Department of Labor.

Hunter, J. E. (1986). Cognitive ability, cognitive aptitudes, job knowledge, and job performance. *Journal of Vocational Behavior, 29,* 340–362.

Hunter, J. E., & Hunter, R. (1984). Validity and utility of alternate predictors of job performance. *Psychological Bulletin, 96,* 72–98.

Hunter, J. E., & Schmidt, F. L. (1976). A critical analysis of the statistical and ethical implications of various definitions of "test bias." *Psychological Bulletin, 83,* 1053–1071.

Hunter, J. E., & Schmidt, F. L. (1981). Fitting people into jobs: The impact of personal selection on normal productivity. In M. D. Dunnette & E. A. Fleishman (Eds.), *Human performance and productivity: Vol. 1. Human capability assessment.* Hillsdale, NJ: Erlbaum.

Hunter, J. E., & Schmidt, F. L. (1983). Quantifying the effects of psychological interventions on employee job performance and work-force productivity. *American Psychologist, 38,* 473–478.

Hunter, J. E., & Schmidt, F. L. (1990). *Methods of meta-analysis.* Newbury Park, CA: Sage.

Hunter, J. E., Schmidt, F. L., & Jackson, G. B. (1982). *Meta-analysis: Cumulating research findings across studies.* Beverly Hills, CA: Sage.

Hunter, M. S. (1992). The Women's Health Questionnaire: A measure of mid-aged women's perceptions of their emotional and physical health. *Psychology and Health, 7,* 45–54.

Hurlburt, R. T. (1997). Randomly sampling thinking in the natural environment. *Journal of Consulting and Clinical Psychology, 65,* 941–949.

Hurst, N. H. (1997). A narrative analysis of identity change in treated substance abusers. *Dissertation Abstracts International, Section B: The Sciences & Engineering, 58*(4-B), 2124.

Hutt, M. L. (1985). *The Hutt adaptation of the Bender-Gestalt Test* (4th ed.). Orlando, FL: Grune & Stratton.

Iacono, W. G., & Lykken, D. T. (1997). The validity of the lie detector: Two surveys of scientific opinion. *Journal of Applied Psychology, 82,* 425–433.

Iaffaldano, M. T., & Muchinsky, P. M. (1985). Job satisfaction and job performance: A meta-analysis. *Psychological Bulletin, 97,* 251–273.

Illovsky, M. E. (2003). Mental health professionals, minorities, and the poor. New York: Brunner-Routledge.

Ilyin, D. (1976). *The Ilyin oral interview.* Rowley, MA: Newbury House.

Impara, J. C., & Plake, B. S. (Eds.). (1998). *The thirteenth mental measurements yearbook.* Lincoln: Buros Institute of Mental Measurements, University of Nebraska.

Innocenti, M. S., Huh, K., & Boyce, G. C. (1992). Families of children with disabilities: Normative data and other considerations on parenting stress. *Topics in Early Childhood Special Education, 12,* 403–427.

Institute for Juvenile Research. (1937). *Child guidance procedures, methods and techniques employed at the Institute for Juvenile Research.* New York: Appleton-Century.

Institute of Medicine. (1984). *Research and training for the Secret Service: Behavioral science and mental health perspectives: A report of the Institute of Medicine* (IOM Publication No. IOM-84–01). Washington, DC: National Academy Press.

International Test Commission. (1993). *Technical standards for translating tests and establishing test score equivalence.* Amherst, MA: Author. (Available from Dr. Ronald Hambleton, School of Education, University of Massachusetts, Amherst, MA 01003).

Ironson, G. H., & Subkoviak, M. J. (1979). A comparison of several methods of assessing item bias. *Journal of Educational Measurement, 16,* 209–225.

Irvine, S. H., & Berry, J. W. (Eds.). (1983). *Human assessment and cultural factors.* New York: Plenum.

Isen, A. M. (1987). Positive affect, cognitive processes, and social behavior. *Advances in Experimental Social Psychology, 20,* 203–253.

Ishihara, S. (1964). *Tests for color blindness* (11th ed.). Tokyo: Kanehara Shuppan.

Ivancevich, J. M. (1983). Contrast effects in performance evaluation and reward practices. *Academy of Management Journal, 26,* 465–476.

Ivnik, R. J., Malec, J. F., Smith, G. E., Tangalos, E. G., Petersen, R. C., Kokmen, E., & Kurland, L. T. (1992). Mayo's older American normative studies: WAIS-R norms for ages 56–97. *Clinical Neuropsychologist, 6*(Suppl.), 1–30.

Ivnik, R. J., Smith, G. E., Malec, J. F., Petersen, R. C., & Tangalos, E. G. (1995). Long-term stability and intercorrelations of cognitive abilities in older persons. *Psychological Assessment, 7,* 155–161.

Jackson, C. L., & LePine, J. A. (2003). Peer responses to a team's weakest link: A test and extension of LePine and Van Dyne's model. *Journal of Applied Psychology, 88,* 459–475.

Jackson, D. E., O'Dell, J. W., & Olson, D. (1982). Acceptance of bogus personality interpretations: Face validity reconsidered. *Journal of Clinical Psychology, 38,* 588–592.

Jackson, D. N. (1964). Desirability judgments as a method of personality assessment. *Educational and Psychological Measurement, 24,* 223–238.

Jackson, D. N. (1977). *Jackson Vocational Interest Survey manual.* Port Huron, MI: Research Psychologists.

Jackson, D. N. (1986). *Computer-based personality testing.* Washington, DC: Scientific Affairs Office, American Psychological Association.

Jackson, D. N., & Messick, S. (1962). Response styles and the assessment of psychopathology. In S. Messick & J. Ross (Eds.), *Measurement in personality and cognition.* New York: Wiley.

Jackson, D. N., & Williams, D. R. (1975). Occupational classification in terms of interest patterns. *Journal of Vocational Behavior, 6,* 269–280.

Jackson, J. F. (1993). Human behavioral genetics, Scarr's theory, and her views on interventions: A critical review and commentary on their implications for African American children. *Child Development, 64,* 1318–1332.

Jackson, J. L. (1999). Psychometric considerations in self-monitoring assessment. *Psychological Assessment, 11,* 439–447.

Jacobs, J. (1970). Are we being misled by fifty years of research on our gifted children? *Gifted Child Quarterly, 14,* 120–123.

Jacobsen, M. E. (1999). Arousing the sleeping giant: Giftedness in adult psychotherapy. *Roeper Review, 22,* 36–41.

Jacob-Timm, S., & Hartshorne, T. (1998). *Ethics and law for school psychologists* (3rd ed.). New York: Wiley.

Jaffee v. Redmond. (1996). 518 U.S. 1; 116 S. Ct. (1923).

Jagger, L., Neukrug, E., & McAuliffe, G. (1992). Congruence between personality traits and chosen occupation as a predictor of job satisfaction for people with disabilities. *Rehabilitation Counseling Bulletin, 36,* 53–60.

Jagim, R. D., Wittman, W. D., & Noll, J. O. (1978). Mental health professionals' attitudes towards confidentiality, privilege, and third-party disclosure. *Professional Psychology, 9,* 458–466.

James, L. R., Demaree, R. G., & Mulaik, S. A. (1986). A note on validity generalization procedures. *Journal of Applied Psychology, 71,* 440–450.

James, L. R., Demaree, R. G., & Wolf, G. (1984). Estimating within-group interrater reliability with and without response bias. *Journal of Applied Psychology, 69,* 85–98.

Janis, I. L. (1972). *Victims of groupthink.* Boston: Houghton Mifflin.

Jankowski, K. (1991). On communicating with deaf people. In L. A. Samovar & R. E. Belmont (Eds.), *Intercultural communication: A reader.* (6th ed., pp. 142–150). Belmont, CA: Wadsworth.

Janowsky, D. S., Morter, S., & Hong, L. (2002). Relationship of Myers-Briggs Type Indicator personality characteristics to suicidality in affective disorder patients. *Journal of Pediatric Research, 36,* 33–39.

Jay, M. (2002). *Cracking the GRE Psychology Test* (6th ed.). New York: Princeton Review.

Jenkins, C. D., Zyzanski, S. J., & Rosenman, R. H. (1979). *Jenkins Activity Survey: Manual.* San Antonio, TX: Psychological Corporation.

Jennings, B. (1991). Active euthanasia and forgoing life-sustaining treatment: Can we hold the line? *Journal of Pain, 6,* 312–316.

Jensen, A. R. (1965). A review of the Rorschach. In O. K. Buros (Ed.), *The sixth mental measurements yearbook* (pp. 501–509). Lincoln: Buros Institute of Mental Measurement, University of Nebraska.

Jensen, A. R. (1969). How much can we boost IQ and scholastic achievement? *Harvard Educational Review, 39,* 1–123.

Jensen, A. R. (1980). *Bias in mental testing.* New York: Free Press.

Jensen, A. R. (2000). Testing: The dilemma of group differences. *Psychology, Public Policy, and Law, 6,* 121–127.

Jobes, D. A., Jacoby, A. M., Cimbolic, P., & Hustead, L. A. T. (1997). Assessment and treatment of suicidal clients in a university. *Journal of Consulting Psychology, 44,* 368–377.

Johansson, H. J., & Forsman, M. (2001). Identification and analysis of unsatisfactory psychosocial work situations: A participatory approach employing video-computer interaction. *Applied Ergonomics, 32,* 23–29.

Johnson, D. L., & Johnson, C. A. (1965). Totally discouraged: A depressive syndrome of the Dakota Sioux. *Psychiatric Research Review, 2,* 141–143.

Johnson, E. S. (2000). The effects of accommodation on performance assessments. *Remedial and Special Education, 21,* 261–267.

Johnson, G. S. (1989). Emotional indicators in the human figure drawings of hearing-impaired children: A small sample validation study. *American Annals of the Deaf, 134,* 205–208.

Johnson, J. A., & Ostendorf, F. (1993). Clarification of the five-factor model with the abridged big five dimensional circumplex. *Journal of Personality and Social Psychology, 65,* 563–576.

Johnson, L. C., Beaton, R., Murphy, S., & Pike, K. (2000). Sampling bias and other methodological threats to the validity of health survey research. *International Journal of Stress Management, 7,* 247–267.

Johnson, L. J., Cook, M. J., & Kullman, A. J. (1992). An examination of the concurrent validity of the Battelle Developmental Inventory as compared with the Vineland Adaptive Scales and the Bayley Scales of Infant Development. *Journal of Early Intervention, 16,* 353–359.

Johnson, R. C. (1963). Similarity in IQ of separated identical twins as related to length of time spent in same environment. *Child Development, 34,* 745–749.

Joiner, T. E., Jr., & Schmidt, K. L. (1997). Drawing conclusions—or not—from drawings. *Journal of Personality Assessment, 69,* 476–481.

Joiner, T. E., Jr., Schmidt, K. L., & Barnett, J. (1996). Size, detail, and line heaviness in children's drawings as correlates of emotional distress: (More) negative evidence. *Journal of Personality Assessment, 67,* 127–141.

Joiner, T. E., Jr., & Walker, R. L. (2002). Construct validity of a measure of acculturative stress in African Americans. *Psychological Assessment, 14,* 462–466.

Jolles, J. (1952). *A catalogue for the qualitative interpretation of the H-T-P.* Los Angeles: Western Psychological Services.

Jones, J. W., Arnold, D., & Harris, W. G. (1990). Introduction to the Model Guidelines for Preemployment Integrity Testing. *Journal of Business and Psychology, 4,* 525–532.

Jones, J. W., Brasher, E. E., & Huff, J. W. (2002). Innovations in integrity-based personnel selection: Building a technology-friendly assessment. *International Journal of Selection and Assessment, 10,* 87–97.

Jones, P., & Rodgers, B. (1993). Estimating premorbid IQ in schizophrenia. *British Journal of Psychiatry, 162,* 273–274.

Jones, R. N., & Gallo, J. J. (2000). Dimensions of the Mini-Mental State Examination among community-dwelling older adults. *Psychological Medicine, 30,* 605–618.

Jones, S., Guy, A., & Omrod, J. A. (2003). A Q-methodological study of hearing voices: A preliminary exploration of voice hearers' understanding of their experiences. *Psychology & Psychotherapy: Theory, Research and Practice, 76,* 189–209.

Jones, S. E. (2001, February). Ethics Code Draft published for comment. *APA Monitor, 32.*

Judge, T. A., & Bono, J. E. (2000). Five-factor model of personality and transformational leadership. *Journal of Applied Psychology, 85,* 751–765.

Judge, T. A., Bono, J. E., & Locke, E. A. (2000). Personality and job satisfaction: The mediating role of job characteristics. *Journal of Applied Psychology, 85,* 237–249.

Judge, T. A., Heller, D., & Mount, M. K. (2002). Five-factor model of personality and job satisfaction: A meta-analysis. *Journal of Applied Psychology, 87,* 530–541.

Judge, T. A., & Ilies, R. (2002). Relationship of personality to performance motivation: A meta-analytic review. *Journal of Applied Psychology, 87,* 797–807.

Jung, C. G. (1910). The association method. *American Journal of Psychology, 21,* 219–269.

Jung, C. G. (1923). *Psychological types.* London: Routledge & Kegan Paul.

Juni, S. (1996). Review of the revised NEO Personality Inventory. In J. C. Conoley & J. C. Impara (Eds.), *The twelfth mental measurements yearbook* (pp. 863–868). Lincoln: Buros Institute of Mental Measurements, University of Nebraska.

Kagan, J. (1956). The measurement of overt aggression from fantasy. *Journal of Abnormal and Social Psychology, 52,* 390–393.

Kahn, M., & Taft, G. (1983). The application of the standard of care doctrine to psychological testing. *Behavioral Sciences and the Law, 1,* 71–84.

Kail, B. L., & DeLaRosa, M. (1998). Challenges to treating the elderly Latino substance abuser: A not so hidden research agenda. *Journal of Gerontological Social Work, 30,* 128–141.

Kaiser, H. F. (1958). A modified stanine scale. *Journal of Experimental Education, 26,* 261.

Kaiser, H. F., & Michael, W. B. (1975). Domain validity and generalizability. *Educational and Psychological Measurement, 35,* 31–35.

Kalat, J. W., & Matlin, M. W. (2000). The GRE Psychology Test: A useful but poorly understood test. *Teaching of Psychology, 27,* 24–27.

Kamin, L. J. (1974). *The science and politics of IQ.* New York: Wiley.

Kamiya, J. (1962). *Conditional discrimination of the EEG alpha rhythm in humans.* Paper presented at the annual meeting of the Western Psychological Association, April.

Kamiya, J. (1968). Conscious control of brain waves. *Psychology Today, 1*(11), 56–60.

Kamphaus, R. W., Petoskey, M. D., & Rowe, E. W. (2000). Current trends in psychological testing of children. *Professional Psychology: Research and Practice, 31,* 155–164.

Kamphaus, R. W., & Pleiss, K. L. (1993). Comment on "The use and abuse of human figure drawings." *School Psychology Quarterly, 8,* 187–188.

Kanaya, T., Scullin, M. H., & Ceci, S. J. (2003). The Flynn effect and U. S. policies: The impact of rising IQ scores on American society via mental retardation diagnoses. *American Psychologist, 58,* 778–790.

Karlsen, S., Rogers, A., & McCarthy, M. (1998). Social environment and substance misuse: A study of ethnic variations among inner London adolescents. *Ethnicity & Health, 3,* 265–273.

Karon, B. P. (1981). The Thematic Apperception Test (TAT). In A. I. Rabin (Ed.), *Assessment with projective techniques: A concise introduction* (pp. 85–120). New York: Springer.

Karon, B. P. (2000). The clinical interpretation of the Thematic Apperception Test, Rorschach, and other clinical data: A reexamination of statistical versus clinical prediction. *Professional Psychology: Research and Practice, 31,* 230–233.

Karp, S. A., Holmstrom, R. W., & Silber, D. E. (1990). *Apperceptive Personality Test Manual* (Version 2.0). Orland Park, IL: International Diagnostic Systems, Inc.

Katz, R. C., Santman, J., & Lonero, P. (1994). Findings on the Revised Morally Debatable Behaviors Scale. *Journal of Psychology, 128,* 15–21.

Katz, W. F., Curtiss, S., & Tallal, P. (1992). Rapid automatized naming and gesture by normal and language-impaired children. *Brain and Language, 43,* 623–641.

Kaufman, A. S. (1990). *Assessing adolescent and adult intelligence.* Needham Heights, MA: Allyn & Bacon.

Kaufman, A. S. (1993). Joint exploratory factor analysis of the Kaufman Battery for Children and the Kaufman Adolescent and Adult Intelligence Test for 11- and 12-year-olds. *Journal of Clinical Child Psychology, 22,* 355–364.

Kaufman, A. S. (1994a). *Intelligent testing with the WISC-R.* New York: Wiley.

Kaufman, A. S. (1994b). *Intelligent testing with the WISC-III.* New York: Wiley.

Kaufman, A. S., Ishkuma, T., & Kaufman-Packer, J. L. (1991). Amazingly short forms of the WAIS-R. *Journal of Psychoeducational Assessment, 9,* 4–15.

Kaufman, A. S., & Kaufman, N. L. (1983a). *Kaufman Assessment Battery for Children (K-ABC): Administration and scoring manual.* Circle Pines, MN: American Guidance Service.

Kaufman, A. S., & Kaufman, N. L. (1983b). *Kaufman Assessment Battery for Children (K-ABC) interpretative manual.* Circle Pines, MN: American Guidance Service.

Kaufman, A. S., & Kaufman, N. L. (1990). *Kaufman Brief Intelligence Test (K-BIT): Manual.* Circle Pines, MN: American Guidance Service.

Kaufman, A. S., & Kaufman, N. L. (1993). *Kaufman Adolescent and Adult Intelligence Test (KAIT): Manual.* Circle Pines, MN: American Guidance Service.

Kaufman, A. S., Kaufman, N. L., & Goldsmith, B. (1984). *Kaufman Sequential or Simultaneous (K-SOS).* Circle Pines, MN: American Guidance Service.

Kaufman, A. S., & Lichtenberger, E. O. (1999). *Essentials of WAIS-III assessment.* New York: Wiley.

Kaufman, A. S., & McLean, J. E. (1986). K-ABC/WISC-R factor analysis for a learning-disabled population. *Journal of Learning Disabilities, 19,* 145–153.

Kaufman, A. S., & McLean, J. E. (1987). Joint factor analysis of the K-ABC and WISC-R with normal children. *Journal of School Psychiatry, 25,* 105–118.

Kaufman, A. S., Reynolds, C. R., & McLean, J. E. (1989). Age and WAIS-R intelligence in a national sample of adults in the 20- to 74-year age range: A cross-sectional analysis with educational level controlled. *Intelligence, 13,* 235–253.

Kavale, K. A. (1995). Meta-analysis at 20: Retrospect and prospect. *Evaluation and the Health Professionals, 18,* 349–369.

Kaye, B. K., & Johnson, T. J. (1999). Taming the cyber frontier: Techniques for improving online surveys. *Social Science Computer Review, 17,* 323–337.

Keating, C. F., Mazur, A., Segall, M. H., et al. (1981). Culture and the perception of social dominance from facial expression. *Journal of Personality and Social Psychology, 40,* 615–626.

Kebbell, M. R., & Wagstaff, G. F. (1998). Hypnotic interviewing: The best way to interview eyewitnesses? *Behavioral Sciences & the Law, 16,* 115–129.

Keefe, F. J., Smith, S. J., Buffington, A. L. H., Gibson, J., Studts, J. L., & Caldwell, D. S. (2002). Recent advances and future directions in the biopsychosocial assessment and treatment of arthritis. *Journal of Consulting and Clinical Psychology, 70,* 640–655.

Kehoe, J. F., & Tenopyr, M. L. (1994). Adjustment in assessment scores and their usage: A taxonomy and evaluation of methods. *Psychological Assessment, 6,* 291–303.

Keiser, R. E., & Prather, E. N. (1990). What is the TAT? A review of ten years of research. *Journal of Personality Assessment, 55,* 800–803.

Keith, K. D., Heal, L. W., & Schalock, R. L. (1996). Cross-cultural measurement of critical quality of life concepts. *Journal of Intellectual and Disability Research, 21,* 273–293.

Keith, T. Z. (1985). Questioning the K-ABC: What does it measure? *School Psychology Review, 1,* 21–36.

Keith, T. Z., & Kranzler, J. H. (1999). The absence of structural fidelity precludes construct validity: Rejoinder to Naglieri on what the Cognitive Assessment System does and does not measure. *School Psychology Review, 28,* 117–144.

Keith, T. Z., & Novak, C. G. (1987). Joint factor structure of the WISC-R and K-ABC for referred school children. *Journal of Psychoeducational Assessment, 5(4),* 370–386.

Keith, T. Z., Powell, A. L., & Powell, L. R. (2001). Review of Wechsler Abbreviated Scale of Intelligence. In B. S. Plake & J. C. Impara (Eds.), *The fourteenth mental measurements yearbook* (pp. 1329–1331). Lincoln: University of Nebraska Press.

Keith, T. Z., & Witta, L. (1997). Hierarchical and cross-age confirmatory factor analysis of the WISC-III: What does it measure? *School Psychology Quarterly, 12,* 80–107.

Kelley, C., & Meyers, J. (1992). *Cross-Cultural Adaptability Inventory.* Minneapolis, MN: NCS Assessments.

Kelley, S. J. (1985). Drawings: Critical communications for the sexually abused child. *Pediatric Nursing, 11,* 421–426.

Kelley, S. J. (1988). Physical abuse of children: Recognition and reporting. *Journal of Emergency Nursing, 14(2),* 82–90.

Kelley, T. L. (1927). *Interpretation of educational measurements.* Yonkers, NY: World Book.

Kelley, T. L. (1939). The selection of upper and lower groups for the validation of test items. *Journal of Educational Psychology, 30,* 17–24.

Kellner, C. H., Jolley, R. R., Holgate, R. C., et al. (1991). Brain MRI in obsessive-compulsive disorder. *Psychiatric Research, 36,* 45–49.

Kelly, D. H. (1966). Measurement of anxiety by forearm blood flow. *British Journal of Psychiatry, 112,* 789–798.

Kelly, E. J. (1985). The personality of chess players. *Journal of Personality Assessment, 49,* 282–284.

Kempen, J. H., Kritchevsky, M., & Feldman, S. T. (1994). Effect of visual impairment on neuropsychological test performance. *Journal of Clinical and Experimental Neuropsychology, 16,* 223–231.

Kendall, P. C., Williams, L., Pechacek, T. F., Graham, L. E., Shisslak, C., & Herzof, N. (1979). Cognitive-behavioral and patient education interventions in cardiac catheterization procedures: The Palo Alto Medical Psychology Project. *Journal of Consulting and Clinical Psychology, 47,* 48–59.

Kennedy, M. H., & Hiltonsmith, R. W. (1988). Relationships among the K-ABC Nonverbal Scale, the Pictorial Test of Intelligence and the Hiskey-Nebraska Test of Learning Aptitude for speech- and language-disabled preschool children. *Journal of Psychoeducational Assessment, 6(1),* 49–54.

Kennedy, R. S., Bittner, A. C., Harbeson, M., & Jones, M. B. (1982). Television computer games: A "new look" in performance testing. *Aviation, Space and Environmental Medicine, 53,* 49–53.

Kent, G. H., & Rosanoff, A. J. (1910). A study of association in insanity. *American Journal of Insanity, 67,* 37–96, 317–390.

Kent, N., & Davis, D. R. (1957). Discipline in the home and intellectual development. *British Journal of Medical Psychology, 30,* 27–33.

Kerlinger, F. N. (1973). *Foundations of behavioral research* (2nd ed.). New York: Holt.

Kern, J. M., Miller, C., & Eggers, J. (1983). Enhancing the validity of role-play tests: A comparison of three role-play methodologies. *Behavior Therapy, 14,* 482–492.

Khan, S. B., Alvi, S. A., Shaukat, N., & Hussain, M. A. (1990). A study of the validity of Holland's theory in a non-Western culture. *Journal of Vocational Behavior, 36,* 132–146.

Kim, B. S. K., Atkinson, D. R., & Yang, P. H. (1999). The Asian Values Scale: Development, factor analysis, validation, and reliability. *Journal of Counseling Psychology, 46,* 342–352.

King, D. A., Conwell, Y., Cox, C., et al. (2000). A neuropsychological comparison of depressed suicide attempters and nonattempters. *Journal of Neuropsychiatry and Clinical Neurosciences, 12,* 64–70.

King, M. A., & Yuille, J. C. (1987). Suggestibility and the child witness. In S. J. Ceci, M. P. Toglia, & D. F. Ross (Eds.), *Children's eyewitness testimony.* New York: Springer-Verlag.

Kinslinger, H. J. (1966). Application of projective techniques in personnel psychology since 1940. *Psychological Bulletin, 66*, 134–149.

Kinston, W., Loader, P., & Miller, L. (1985). *Clinical assessment of family health.* London: Hospital for Sick Children, Family Studies Group.

Kippax, S., Campbell, D., Van de Ven, P., et al. (1998). Cultures of sexual adventurism as markers of HIV seroconversion: A case control study in a cohort of Sydney gay men. *AIDS Care, 10*, 677–688.

Kirmayer, L. J., & Young, A. (1999). Culture and context in the evolutionary concept of mental disorder. *Journal of Abnormal Psychology, 108*, 446–452.

Klanderman, J. W., Perney, J., & Kroeschell, Z. B. (1985). Comparison of the K-ABC and WISC-R for LD children. *Journal of Learning Disabilities, 18*, 524–527.

Klein, D. F. (1999). Harmful dysfunction, disorder, disease, illness, and evolution. *Journal of Abnormal Psychology, 108*, 421–429.

Kleinman, A., & Kleinman, J. (1991). Suffering and its professional transformation: Toward an ethnography of interpersonal experience. *Culture, Psychiatry and Medicine, 15*, 275–301.

Kleinman, A. M., & Lin, T. Y. (1980). Introduction. In A. M. Kleinman & T. Y. Lin (Eds.), *Normal and abnormal behavior in Chinese cultures* (pp. 1–6). Dordrecht, Netherlands: Reidel.

Kleinmuntz, B., & Szucko, J. J. (1984). Lie detection in ancient and modern times: A call for contemporary scientific study. *American Psychologist, 39*, 766–776.

Kline, R. B., & Lachar, D. (1992). Evaluation of age, sex, and race bias in the Personality Inventory for Children (PIC). *Psychological Assessment, 4*, 333–339.

Kline, R. B., Lachar, D., & Boersma, D. C. (1993). Identification of special education needs with the Personality Inventory for Children (PIC): A hierarchical classification model. *Psychological Assessment, 5*, 307–316.

Kline, R. B., Lachar, D., & Gdowski, C. L. (1992). Clinical validity of a Personality Inventory for Children (PIC) profile typology. *Psychological Assessment, 58*, 591–605.

Kline, R. B., Lachar, D., & Sprague, D. J. (1985). The Personality Inventory for Children (PIC): An unbiased predictor of cognitive and academic status. *Journal of Pediatric Psychology, 10*, 461–477.

Kline, R. B., Snyder, J., Guilmette, S., & Castellanos, M. (1993). External validity of the Profile Variability Index for the K-ABC, Stanford-Binet, and WISC-R: Another cul-de-sac. *Journal of Learning Disabilities, 26*, 557–567.

Klinger, E. (1978). Modes of normal conscious flow. In K. S. Pope & J. L. Singer (Eds.), *The stream of consciousness: Scientific investigations into the flow of human experience* (pp. 225–258). New York: Plenum.

Klonoff, E. A., & Landrine, H. (1999). Acculturation and alcohol use among Blacks: The benefits of remaining culturally traditional. *Western Journal of Black Studies, 23*, 211–216.

Klopfer, B., Ainsworth, M., Klopfer, W., & Holt, R. R. (1954). *Developments in the Rorschach technique: Vol. 1. Technique and theory.* Yonkers-on-Hudson, NY: World.

Klopfer, B., & Davidson, H. (1962). *The Rorschach technique: An introductory manual.* New York: Harcourt.

Kluckhohn, F. R. (1954). Dominant and variant value orientations. In C. Kluckhohn & H. A. Murray (Eds.), *Personality in nature, society, and culture* (pp. 342–358). New York: Knopf.

Kluckhohn, F. R. (1960). A method for eliciting value orientations. *Anthropological Linguistics, 2*(2), 1–23.

Kluckhohn, F. R., & Strodtbeck, F. L. (1961). *Variations in value orientations.* Homewood, IL: Dorsey.

Knapp, R. R. (1960). The effects of time limits on the intelligence test performance of Mexican and American subjects. *Journal of Educational Psychology, 51*, 14–20.

Knoff, H. M. (1990a). Evaluation of projective drawings. In C. R. Reynolds and T. B. Gutkin (Eds.), *Handbook of school psychology* (2nd ed., pp. 898–946). New York: Wiley.

Knoff, H. M. (1990b). Review of Children's Depression Inventory. In J. J. Kramer & J. C. Conoley (Eds.), *The supplement to the tenth mental measurements yearbook* (pp. 48–50). Lincoln: The Buros Institute of Mental Measurements, University of Nebraska.

Knoff, H. M., & Prout, H. T. (1985). *The Kinetic Drawing System: Family and School.* Los Angeles: Western Psychological Services.

Knowles, E. S., & Condon, C. A. (2000). Does the rose still smell as sweet? Item variability across test forms and revisions. *Psychological Assessment, 12*, 245–252.

Kobak, K. A., Reynolds, W. M., & Greist, J. H. (1993). Development and validation of a computer administered version of the Hamilton Anxiety Scale. *Psychological Assessment, 5*, 487–492.

Kolotkin, R. A., & Wielkiewicz, R. M. (1984). Effects of situational demand in the role-play assessment of assertive behavior. *Journal of Behavioral Assessment, 6*, 59–70.

Kongs, S. K., Thompson, L. L., Iverson, G. L., & Heaton, R. K. (2000). *Wisconsin Card Sorting Test-64 Card Version (WCST-64).* Odessa, FL: Psychological Assessment Resources.

Koppitz, E. M. (1963). *The Bender-Gestalt Test for young children.* New York: Grune & Stratton.

Koppitz, E. M. (1975). *The Bender-Gestalt Test for young children* (Vol. 2). New York: Grune & Stratton.

Korchin, S. J., & Schuldberg, D. (1981). The future of clinical assessment. *American Psychologist, 36*, 1147–1158.

Korkman, M. (1999). Applying Luria's diagnostic principles in the neuropsychological assessment of children. *Neuropsychology Review, 9*, 89–105.

Korkman, M., Kirk, U., & Kemp, S. (1997). *NEPSY.* San Antonio, TX: Psychological Corporation.

Korman, A. K. (1988). *The outsiders: Jews and corporate America.* Lexington, MA: Lexington.

Koson, D., Kitchen, C., Kochen, M., & Stodolsky, D. (1970). Psychological testing by computer: Effect on response bias. *Educational and Psychological Measurement, 30*, 803–810.

Kraepelin, E. (1892). *Uber die Beeinflussing einfacher psychischer Vorgange durch einige Arzneimittel.* Jena, Germany: Fischer.

Kraepelin, E. (1895). Der psychologische versuch in der psychiatrie. *Psychologische Arbeiten, 1*, 1–91.

Kraepelin, E. (1896). Der psychologische versuch in der psychiatrie. *Psychologische Arbeiten, 1*, 1–91.

Kranzler, G., & Moursund, J. (1999). *Statistics for the terrified* (2nd ed.). Upper Saddle River, NJ: Prentice-Hall.

Kranzler, J. H., & Keith, T. Z. (1999). Independent confirmatory factor analysis of the Cognitive Assessment System (CAS): What does the CAS measure? *School Psychology Review, 28*, 117–144.

Krauss, D. A., & Sales, B. D. (1999). The problem of "helpfulness" in applying *Daubert* to expert testimony: Child custody determinations in family law as an exemplar. *Psychology, Public Policy, and Law, 5*, 78–99.

Krauss, M. W. (1993). Child-related and parenting stress: Similarities and differences between mothers and fathers of children with disabilities. *American Journal on Mental Retardation, 97*, 393–404.

Kresel, J. J., & Lovejoy, F. H. (1981). Poisonings and child abuse. In N. S. Ellerstein (Ed.), *Child abuse and neglect: A medical reference* (pp. 307–313). New York: Wiley.

Krikorian, R., & Bartok, J. A. (1998). Developmental data for the Porteus Maze Test. *Clinical Neuropsychologist, 12,* 305–310.

Krohn, E. J., & Lamp, R. E. (1989). Concurrent validity of the K-ABC and Stanford-Binet—Fourth Edition for Head Start Children. *Journal of School Psychology, 27*(1), 59–67.

Krohn, E. J., Lamp, R. E., & Phelps, C. G. (1988). Validity of the K-ABC for a black preschool population. *Psychology in the Schools, 25,* 15–21.

Kronholz, J. (1998, February 12). As states end racial preferences, pressure rises to drop SAT to maintain minority enrollment. *Wall Street Journal,* p. A24.

Kubiszyn, T. W., Meyer, G. J., Finn, S. E., et al. (2000). Empirical support for psychological assessment in clinical health care settings. *Professional Psychology: Research and Practice, 31,* 119–130.

Kuder, F., Diamond, E. E., & Zytowski, D. G. (1998). Differentiation as fundamental validity for criterion-group and scaled interest inventories. *Educational and Psychological Measurement, 58,* 38–41.

Kuder, G. F. (1979). *Kuder Occupational Interest Survey, Revised: General manual.* Chicago: Science Research Associates.

Kuder, G. F., & Richardson, M. W. (1937). The theory of the estimation of reliability. *Psychometrika, 2,* 151–160.

Kuhlmann, F. (1912). A revision of the Binet-Simon system for measuring the intelligence of children. *Journal of Psycho-Asthenics Monograph Supplement, 1*(1), 1–41.

Kumho Tire Co. Ltd. v. Carmichael, 119 S. Ct. 1167 (1999).

Kuncel, N. R., Hezlett, S. A., & Ones, D. S. (2001). A comprehensive meta-analysis of the predictive validity of the Graduate Record Examinations: Implications for graduate student selection and performance. *Psychological Bulletin, 127,* 162–181.

Kupfer, D. J., First, M. B., & Regier, D. A. (Eds.) (2002). *A research agenda for DSM-V.* Washington, DC: American Psychiatric Association.

Lachar, D. (1982). *Personality Inventory for Children (PIC): Revised format manual supplement.* Los Angeles: Western Psychological Services.

Lachar, D., Gdowski, C. L., & Snyder, D. K. (1985). Consistency of maternal report and the Personality Inventory for Children: Always useful and sometimes sufficient—Reply to Cornell. *Journal of Consulting and Clinical Psychology, 53,* 275–276.

Lachar, D., & Gruber, C. P. (2001). *The Personality Inventory for Children, Second Edition (PIC-2).* Los Angeles: Western Psychological Services.

Lachar, D., Kline, R. B., & Boersma, D. C. (1986). The Personality Inventory for Children: Approaches to actuarial interpretation in clinic and school settings. In H. M. Knoff (Ed.), *The psychological assessment of child and adolescent personality* (pp. 273–308). New York: Guilford.

Lachar, D., & Wirt, R. D. (1981). A data-based analysis of the psychometric performance of the Personality Inventory for Children (PIC): An alternative to the Achenbach review. *Journal of Personality Assessment, 45,* 614–616.

Lacks, P. (1999). *Bender-Gestalt screening for brain dysfunction.* New York: Wiley.

LaCombe, J. A., Kline, R. B., Lachar, D., Butkus, M., & Hillman, S. B. (1991). Case history correlates of a Personality Inventory for Children (PIC) profile typology. *Psychological Assessment, 3,* 678–687.

Lah, M. I. (1989). New validity, normative, and scoring data for the Rotter Incomplete Sentences Blank. *Journal of Personality Assessment, 53,* 607–620.

Laidlaw, T. M. (1999). Designer testing: Using subjects' personal vocabulary to produce individualised tests. *Personality and Individual Differences, 27,* 1197–1207.

Laker, D. R. (2002). The career wheel: An exercise for exploring and validating one's career choices. *Journal of Employment Counseling, 39,* 61–72.

Lally, S. J. (2003). What tests are acceptable for use in forensic evaluations? A survey of experts. *Professional Psychology: Research & Practice, 34,* 491–498.

Lam, C. S., Chan, F., Hilburger, J., Heimburger, M., Hill, V., & Kaplan, S. (1993). Canonical relationships between vocational interests and aptitudes. *Vocational Evaluation and Work Adjustment Bulletin, 26,* 155–160.

Lamb, M. E. (Ed.). (1981). *The role of the father in child development* (2nd ed.). New York: Wiley.

Lambert, E. W., & Engum, E. S. (1992). Construct validity of the Cognitive Behavioral Driver's Inventory: Age, diagnosis, and driving ability. *Journal of Cognitive Rehabilitation, 10,* 32–45.

Lambert, N., Nihira, K., & Leland, H. (1993). *AAMR Adaptive Behavior Scale-School-Second Edition: Examiner's manual.* Austin, TX: PRO-ED.

Lamp, R. E., & Krohn, E. J. (1990). Stability of the Stanford-Binet Fourth Edition and K-ABC for young black and white children from low-income families. *Journal of Psychoeducational Assessment, 8,* 139–149.

Lamp, R. E., & Krohn, E. J. (2001). A longitudinal predictive validity investigation of the SB:FE and K-ABC with at-risk children. *Journal of Psychoeducational Assessment, 19,* 334–349.

Landrum, M. S., & Ward, S. B. (1993). Behavioral assessment of gifted learners. *Journal of Behavioral Education, 3,* 211–215.

Landy, F. J. (1986). Stamp collecting versus science. *American Psychologist, 41,* 1183–1192.

Landy, F. J., & Farr, J. H. (1980). Performance rating. *Psychological Bulletin, 87,* 72–107.

Lane, H. (1992). *The mask of benevolence: Disabling the deaf community.* New York: Vintage.

Lane, J. C. (1992, August). Threat management fills void in police services. *Police Chief,* pp. 27–29, 31.

Lang, P. J., Greenwald, M. K., Bradley, M. M., & Hamm, A. O. (1993). Looking at pictures: Affective, facial, visceral, and behavioral reactions. *Psychophysiology, 30,* 261–273.

Langer, E. J., & Abelson, R. P. (1974). A patient by any other name: Clinician group difference in labeling bias. *Journal of Consulting and Clinical Psychology, 42,* 4–9.

Langlois, J. H., Ritter, J. M., Casey, R. J., & Sawin, D. B. (1995). Infant attractiveness predicts maternal behaviors and attitudes. *Developmental Psychology, 31,* 464–472.

Lanyon, R. I. (1984). Personality assessment. *Annual Review of Psychology, 35,* 667–701.

Lanyon, R. I. (1993a). Assessment of truthfulness in accusations of child molestation. *American Journal of Forensic Psychology, 11,* 29–44.

Lanyon, R. I. (1993b). Development of scales to assess specific deception strategies on the Psychological Screening Inventory. *Psychological Assessment, 5,* 324–329.

Larkin, J. E., Pines, H. A., & Bechtel, K. M. (2002). Facilitating students' career development in psychology courses: A portfolio project. *Teaching of Psychology, 29,* 207–210.

Larson, L. M., & Borgen, F. H. (2002). Convergence of vocational interests and personality: Examples in an adolescent gifted sample. *Journal of Vocational Behavior, 60,* 91–112.

Larson, L. M., & Majors, M. S. (1998). Applications of the Coping with Career Indecision instrument with adolescents. *Journal of Career Assessment, 6,* 163–179.

Larson, L. M., Rottinghaus, P. J., & Borgen, F. H. (2002). Meta-analyses of big six interests and big five personality factors. *Journal of Vocational Behavior, 61,* 217–239.

La Rue, A., & Watson, J. (1998). Psychological assessment of older adults. *Professional Psychology: Research and Practice, 29,* 5–14.

Larvie, V. (1994). Evidence—Admissability of scientific evidence in federal courts—The Supreme Court decides Frye is dead and the Federal Rules of Evidence provide the standard, but is there a skeleton in the closet? *Daubert v. Pharmaceuticals,* 113 S. Ct. 2786. *Land & Water Review, 29,* 275–309.

Larzelere, R., & Huston, T. (1980). The Dyadic Trust Scale: Toward understanding interpersonal trust in close relationships. *Journal of Marriage and the Family, 43,* 595–604.

Latimer, E. J. (1991). Ethical decision-making in the care of the dying and its applications to clinical practice. *Journal of Pain and Symptom Management, 6,* 329–336.

Lattimore, R. R., & Borgen, F. H. (1999). Validity of the 1994 Strong Interest Inventory with racial and ethnic groups in the United States. *Journal of Counseling Psychology, 46,* 185–195.

Laurence, J. R., & Perry, C. W. (1988). *Hypnosis, will, and memory.* New York: Guilford.

Lavin, M. (1992). The Hopkins Competency Assessment Test: A brief method for evaluating patients' capacity to give informed consent. *Hospital and Community Psychiatry, 646,* 132–136.

Lavrakas, P. J. (1998). Methods for sampling and interviewing in telephone surveys. In L. Bickman & D. J. Rog (Eds.), *Handbook of applied social research methods* (pp. 429–472). Thousand Oaks, CA: Sage.

Lawlor, J. (1990, September 27). Loopholes found in truth tests. *USA Today,* p. D-1.

Lawrence, B. S. (1996). Organizational age norms: Why is it so hard to know one when you see one? *Gerontologist, 36,* 209–220.

Lawrence, J., Davidoff, D. A., Katt-Lloyd, D., et al. (2000). A pilot program of community-based screening for memory impairment. *Journal of the American Geriatrics Society, 48,* 854–855.

Lawshe, C. H. (1975). A quantitative approach to content validity. *Personnel Psychology, 28,* 563–575.

Lazarus, A. A. (1973). Multimodal behavior therapy: Treating the BASIC ID. *Journal of Nervous and Mental Disease, 156,* 404–411.

Lazarus, A. A. (1989). *The practice of multimodal therapy.* Baltimore: Johns Hopkins University Press.

Lea, E., & Worsley, A. (2001). Influences on meat consumption in Australia. *Appetite, 36,* 127–136.

Leahy, A. (1932). A study of certain selective factors influencing prediction of the mental status of adopted children or adopted children in nature-nurture research. *Journal of Genetic Psychology, 41,* 294–329.

Leahy, A. M. (1935). Nature-nurture and intelligence. *Genetic Psychology Monographs, 17,* 241–306.

Lee, S. D. (1968). *Social class bias in the diagnosis of mental illness.* Unpublished doctoral dissertation, University of Oklahoma.

Lee, S.-J., & Tedeschi, J. T. (1996). Effects of norms and norm-violations on inhibition and instigation of aggression. *Aggressive Behavior, 22,* 17–25.

Leigh, I. W., Corbett, C. A., Gutman, V., & Moore, D. A. (1996). Providing psychological services to deaf individuals: A response to new perceptions of diversity. *Professional Psychology: Research and Practice, 27,* 364–371.

Leon-Carrion, J., et al. (1991). The computerized Tower of Hanoi: A new form of administration and suggestions for interpretation. *Perceptual and Motor Skills, 73,* 63–66.

Leong, F. T., & Hartung, P. J. (2000). Cross-cultural career assessment: Review and prospects for the new millennium. *Journal of Career Assessment, 8,* 391–401.

Lerner, B. (1980). *Minimum competence, maximum choice: Second chance legislation.* New York: Irvington.

Lerner, B. (1981). The minimum competence testing movement: Social, scientific, and legal implications. *American Psychologist, 36,* 1056–1066.

Lerner, P. M. (1991). *Psychoanalytic theory and the Rorschach.* New York: Analytic.

Lerner, P. M. (1996a). Current perspectives on psychoanalytic Rorschach assessment. *Journal of Personality Assessment, 67,* 450–461.

Lerner, P. M. (1996b). The interpretive process in Rorschach testing. *Journal of Personality Assessment, 67,* 494–500.

Lesser, G. S., Fifer, G., & Clark, D. H. (1965). Mental abilities of children from different social-class and cultural groups. *Monographs of the Society for Research in Child Development, 30* (Serial No. 102).

Lessinger, L. H. (1998). The relationship between cultural identity and MMPI-2 scores of Mexican-American substance abuse patients. *Dissertation Abstracts International, Section B: The Sciences & Engineering, 59*(2-B), 877.

Levack, N. (1991). *Low vision: A resource guide with adaptations for students with visual impairments.* Austin: Texas School for the Blind and Visually Impaired.

Levesque, L. L., Wilson, J. M., & Wholey, D. R. (2001). Cognitive divergence and shared mental models in software development project teams. *Journal of Organizational Behavior, 22,* 135–144.

Levine, E., & Padilla, A. (1980). *Crossing cultures in therapy.* Monterey, CA: Brooks/Cole.

Levy-Shiff, R., Dimitrovsky, L., Shulman, S., & Har-Even, D. (1998). Cognitive appraisals, coping strategies, and support resources as correlates of parenting and infant development. *Developmental Psychology, 34,* 1417–1427.

Lewinsohn, P. M., Rohde, P., & Seeley, J. R. (1996). Adolescent suicidal ideation and attempts: Prevalence, risk factors and clinical implications. *Clinical Psychology: Science and Practice, 3,* 25–46.

Lewis-Fernandez, R. (1998). A cultural critique of the DSM-IV dissociative disorders section. *Transcultural Psychiatry, 35,* 387–400.

Lewis-Fernandez, R., & Diaz, N. (2002). The cultural formulation: A method for assessing cultural factors affecting the clinical encounter. *Psychiatric Quarterly, 73,* 271–295.

Lezak, M. D. (2002). Responsive assessment and the freedom to think for ourselves. *Rehabilitation Psychology, 47,* 339–353.

Li, H., Kuo, C., & Russel, M. G. (1999). The impact of perceived channel utilities, shopping orientations, and demographics on the consumer's online buying behavior. *Journal of Computer-Mediated Communication, 5*(2).

Li, J. (2003). The core of Confucian learning. *American Psychologist, 58,* 146–147.

Libby, W. (1908). The imagination of adolescents. *American Journal of Psychology, 19,* 249–252.

Lichtenstein, B., & Nansel, T. R. (2000). Women's douching practices and related attitudes: Findings from four focus groups. *Women and Health, 31,* 117–131.

Lichtenstein, D., Dreger, R. M., & Cattell, R. B. (1986). Factor structure and standardization of the Preschool Personality Questionnaire. *Journal of Social Behavior and Personality, 1,* 165–181.

Lidz, C. S. (1987). Historical perspectives. In C. S. Lidz (Ed.), *Dynamic assessment: An interactional approach to evaluating learning potential* (pp. 288–326). New York: Guilford.

Lidz, C. S. (1991). *Practitioner's guide to dynamic assessment.* New York: Guilford.

Lidz, C. S. (1996). Dynamic assessment and the legacy of L. S. Vygotsky. *School Psychology International, 16,* 143–154.

Lidz, C. W., Mulvey, E. P., & Gardner, W. (1993). The accuracy of predictions of violence to others. *Journal of the American Medical Association, 269,* 1007–1011.

Lievens, F., Decaesteker, C., & Christoph, C. P. (2001). Organizational attractiveness for prospective applicants. *Applied Psychology: An International Review, 50,* 30–51.

Lighthouse Research Institute. (1995). *The Lighthouse National Survey on Vision Loss.* New York: The Lighthouse, Inc.

Likert, R. (1932). A technique for the measurement of attitudes. *Archives of Psychology,* Number 140.

Lilienfeld, S. O., & Marino, L. (1995). Mental disorder as a Roschian concept: A critique of Wakefield's "harmful dysfunction" analysis. *Journal of Abnormal Psychology, 104,* 411–420.

Lilienfeld, S. O., & Marino, L. (1999). Essentialism revisited: Evolutionary theory and the concept of mental disorder. *Journal of Abnormal Psychology, 108,* 400–411.

Lilienfeld, S. O., Wood, J. M., & Garb, H. N. (2000). The scientific status of projective techniques. *Psychological Science in the Public Interest, 1(2),* 27–66.

Lillibridge, J. R., & Williams, K. J. (1992). Another look at personality and managerial potential: Application of the five-factor model. In K. Kelley (Ed.), *Issues, theory, and research in industrial/organizational psychology: Advances in psychology, 82* (pp. 91–115). Oxford, England: North-Holland.

Lim, J., & Butcher, J. N. (1996). Detection of faking on the MMPI-2: Differentiation among faking-bad, denial, and claiming extreme virtue. *Journal of Personality Assessment, 67,* 1–25.

Lindell, M. K., Brandt, C. J., & Whitney, D. J. (1999). A revised index of interrater agreement for multi-item ratings of a single target. *Applied Psychological Measurement, 23,* 127–135.

Lindgren, B. (1983, August). N or N–1? [Letter to the editor]. *American Statistician,* p. 52.

Lindskog, C. O., & Smith, J. V. (2001). Review of Wechsler Abbreviated Scale of Intelligence. In B. S. Plake & J. C. Impara (Eds.), *The fourteenth mental measurements yearbook* (pp. 1331–1332). Lincoln: University of Nebraska Press.

Lindstrom, E., Wieselgren, I. M., & von Knorring, L. (1994). Interrater reliability of the Structured Clinical Interview for the Positive and Negative Syndrome Scale for schizophrenia. *Acta Psychiatrica Scandinavica, 89,* 192–195.

Linehan, M. M., Goodstein, J. L., Nielsen, S. L., & Chiles, J. A. (1983). Reasons for staying alive when you are thinking of killing yourself: The Reasons for Living Inventory. *Journal of Consulting and Clinical Psychology, 51,* 276–286.

Lippmann, W. (1922, October). The mental age of Americans. *New Republic.*

Lipsitt, P. D., Lelos, D., & McGarry, A. L. (1971). Competency for trial: A screening instrument. *American Journal of Psychiatry, 128,* 105–109.

Lipton, J. P. (1999). The use and acceptance of social science evidence in business litigation after *Daubert. Psychology, Public Policy, and Law, 5,* 59–77.

Locke, E. A. (1976). The nature and causes of job satisfaction. In M. D. Dunnette (Ed.), *Handbook of industrial and organizational psychology.* Chicago: Rand McNally.

Locke, H. J., & Wallace, K. M. (1959). Short marital adjustment and prediction tests: Their reliability and validity. *Marriage and Family Living, 21,* 251–255.

Loevinger, J. (1966). The meaning and measurement of ego development. *American Psychologist, 21,* 195–206.

Loevinger, J., & Ossorio, A. G. (1958). Evaluation of therapy by self-report: A paradox. *American Psychologist, 13,* 366.

Loevinger, J., Wessler, R., & Redmore, C. (1970). *Measuring ego development: Vol. 1. Construction and use of a sentence completion test. Vol. 2. Scoring manual for women and girls.* San Francisco: Jossey-Bass.

Loewenstein, D. A., Rubert, M. P., Berkowitz-Zimmer, N., Guterman, A., Morgan, R., & Hayden, S. (1992). Neuropsychological test performance and prediction of functional capacities in dementia. *Behavior, Health, and Aging, 2,* 149–158.

Loftin, M. (1997). Critical factors in assessment of students with visual impairments. *RE:view, 28,* 149–159.

Loftus, E. F., & Davies, G. M. (1984). Distortions in the memory of children. *Journal of Social Issues, 40,* 51–67.

Lohman, D. F. (1989). Human intelligence: An introduction to advances in theory and research. *Review of Educational Research, 59,* 333–373.

London, P. (1976). Psychotherapy for religious neuroses? Comments on Cohen and Smith. *Journal of Consulting and Clinical Psychology, 44,* 145–147.

Longabaugh, R. (1980). The systematic observation of behavior in naturalistic settings. In H. C. Triandis & J. W. Berry (Eds.), *Handbook of cross-cultural psychology: Vol. 2. Methodology* (pp. 57–126). Boston: Allyn & Bacon.

Lonner, W. J. (1985). Issues in testing and assessment in cross-cultural counseling. *Counseling Psychologist, 13,* 599–614.

López, S. (1988). The empirical basis of ethnocultural and linguistic bias in mental health evaluations of Hispanics. *American Psychologist, 42,* 228–234.

López, S., & Hernandez, P. (1987). When culture is considered in the evaluation and treatment of Hispanic patients. *Psychotherapy, 24,* 120–127.

López, S. R. (1989). Patient variable biases in clinical judgment: A conceptual overview and methodological considerations. *Psychological Bulletin, 106,* 184–203.

López, S. R. (2000). Teaching culturally informed psychological assessment. In R. H. Dana (Ed.), *Handbook of cross-cultural and multicultural personality assessment* (pp. 669–687). Mahwah, NJ: Erlbaum.

López, S. R. (2002). Teaching culturally informed psychological assessment: Conceptual issues and demonstrations. *Journal of Personality, 79,* 226–234.

Lord, F. M. (1980). *Applications of item response theory to practical testing problems.* Hillsdale, NJ: Erlbaum.

Lorr, M. (1991). An empirical evaluation of the MBTI typology. *Personality and Individual Differences, 12,* 1141–1145.

Lovejoy, M. C., Weis, R., O'Hare, E., & Rubin, E. (1999). Development and initial validation of the Parent Behavior Inventory. *Psychological Assessment, 11,* 534–545.

Lowitzer, A. C., Utley, C. A., & Baumeister, A. A. (1987). AAMD's 1983 Classification in Mental Retardation as utilized by state mental retardation/developmental disabilities agencies. *Mental Retardation, 25,* 287–291.

Lowman, J. C. (1980). Measurement of family affective structure. *Journal of Personality Assessment, 44,* 130–141.

Loyd, B. H., & Abidin, R. R. (1985). Revision of the Parenting Stress Index. *Journal of Pediatric Psychology, 10,* 169–177.

Lubin, B., Wallis, R. R., & Paine, C. (1971). Patterns of psychological test usage in the United States: 1935–1969. *Professional Psychology, 2,* 70–74.

Luckasson, R., Schalock, R. L., Snell, M. E., & Spitalnik, D. M. (1996). The 1992 AAMR definition and preschool children: Response from the Committee on Terminology and Classification. *Mental Retardation, 34,* 247–253.

Lukin, M. E., Dowd, E. T., Plake, B. S., & Kraft, R. G. (1985). Comparing computerized versus traditional psychological assessment. *Computers in Human Behavior, 1,* 49–58.

Lumley, V. A., & Miltenberger, R. G. (1997). Sexual abuse prevention for persons with mental retardation. *American Journal on Mental Retardation, 101,* 459–472.

Lumley, V. A., Miltenberger, R. G., Long, E. S., Rapp, J. T., & Roberts, J. A. (1998). Evaluation of a sexual abuse prevention program for adults with mental retardation. *Journal of Applied Behavior Analysis, 31,* 91–101.

Lung, R. J., Miller, S. H., Davis, T. S., & Graham, W. P. (1977). Recognizing burn injuries as abuse. *American Family Physician, 15,* 134–135.

Luria, A. R. (1966a). *Human brain and psychological processes.* New York: Harper & Row.

Luria, A. R. (1966b). *Higher cortical functions in man.* New York: Basic.

Luria, A. R. (1970, March). The functional organization of the brain. *Scientific American, 222,* 66–78.

Luria, A. R. (1973). *The working brain: An introduction to neuropsychology.* New York: Basic.

Luria, A. R. (1980). *Higher cortical functions in man* (2nd ed.). New York: Basic.

Lutey, C., & Copeland, E. P. (1982). Cognitive assessment of the school-age child. In C. R. Reynolds & T. B. Gutkin (Eds.), *The handbook of school psychology.* New York: Wiley.

Lykken, D. T. (1981). *A tremor in the blood: Uses and abuses of the lie detector.* New York: McGraw-Hill.

Lyman, H. B. (1972). Review of the Wechsler Adult Intelligence Scale. In O. K. Buros (Ed.), *The seventh mental measurements yearbook* (pp. 788–790). Highland Park, NJ: Gryphon.

Lynn, R. (1997). Direct evidence for a genetic basis for black–white differences in IQ. *American Psychologist, 5,* 73–74.

Lyons, J. A., & Scotti, J. R. (1994). Comparability of two administration formats of the Keane Posttraumatic Stress Disorder Scale. *Psychological Assessment, 6,* 209–211.

MacAndrew, C. (1965). The differentiation of male alcoholic outpatients from nonalcoholic psychiatric outpatients by means of the MMPI. *Quarterly Journal of Studies on Alcohol, 26,* 238–246.

Machover, K. (1949). *Personality projection in the drawing of the human figure: A method of personality investigation.* Springfield, IL: Charles C Thomas.

Mack, J. L., & Patterson, M. B. (1995). Executive dysfunction and Alzheimer's disease: Performance on a test of planning ability—the Porteus Maze Test. *Neuropsychology, 9,* 556–564.

Macmillan, D. L., Gresham, F. M., & Siperstein, G. N. (1995). Heightened concerns over the 1992 AAMR definition: Advocacy versus precision. *American Journal on Mental Retardation, 100,* 87–95.

Macmillan, D. L., & Meyers, C. E. (1980). Larry P.: An education interpretation. *School Psychology Review, 9,* 136–148.

Mael, F. A. (1991). Career constraints of observant Jews. *Career Development Quarterly, 39,* 341–349.

Magnello, M. E., & Spies, C. J. (1984). Francis Galton: Historical antecedents of the correlation calculus. In B. Laver (Chair), *History of mental measurement: Correlation, quantification, and institutionalization.* Paper session presented at the 92nd annual convention of the American Psychological Association, Toronto, Ontario, Canada.

Maher, L. (1996). Hidden in the light: Occupational norms among crack-using street-level sex workers. *Journal of Drug Issues, 26,* 143–173.

Malec, J. F., Ivnik, R. J., & Smith, G. E. (1993). *Neuropsychology and normal aging.* In R. W. Parks, R. F. Zec, & R. S. Wilson (Eds.), *Neuropsychology of Alzheimer's disease and other dementias* (pp. 81–111). New York: Oxford University Press.

Malgady, R. G., Costantino, G., & Rogler, L. H. (1984). Development of a Thematic Apperception Test (TEMAS) for urban Hispanic children. *Journal of Consulting and Clinical Psychology, 52,* 986–996.

Malgady, R. G., Rogler, L. H., & Constantino, G. (1987). Ethnocultural and linguistic bias in mental health evaluations of Hispanics. *American Psychologist, 42,* 228–234.

Maller, S. J. (1997). Deafness and WISC-III item difficulty: Invariance and fit. *Journal of School Psychology, 35,* 299–314.

Maller, S. J., & Braden, J. P. (1993). The construct and criterion-related validity of the WISC-III with deaf adolescents. *Journal of Psychoeducational Assessment, WISC-III Monograph,* 105–113.

Malone, P. S., Brounstein, P J., van Brock, A., & Shaywitz, S. S. (1991). Components of IQ scores across levels of measured ability. *Journal of Applied Social Psychology, 21,* 15–28.

Maloney, M. P., & Ward, M. P. (1976). *Psychological assessment.* New York: Oxford University Press.

Mannarino, A. P., Cohen, J. A., & Berman, S. R. (1994). The Children's Attributions and Perceptions Scale: A new measure of sexual-abuse related factors. *Journal of Clinical Child Psychology, 23,* 204–211.

Manz, C. C., & Sims, H. P. (1984). Searching for the "unleader": Organizational member views on leading self-managed groups. *Human Relations, 37,* 409–424.

Maraist, C. C., & Russell, M. T. (2002). 16PF Fifth Edition norm supplement. Champaign, IL: Institute for Personality and Ability Testing.

Maranell, G. M. (1974). *Scaling: A sourcebook for behavioral scientists.* Chicago: Aldine.

Maraun, M. D. (1996a). Metaphor taken as math: Indeterminacy in the factor analysis model. *Multivariate Behavioral Research, 31,* 517–538.

Maraun, M. D. (1996b). Meaning and mythology in the factor analysis model. *Multivariate Behavioral Research, 31,* 603–616.

Maraun, M. D. (1996c). The claims of factor analysis. *Multivariate Behavioral Research, 31,* 673–689.

Marchese, M. C. (1992). Clinical versus actuarial prediction: A review of the literature. *Perceptual and Motor Skills, 75,* 583–594.

Mardell-Czudnowski, C., & Goldenberg, D. S. (1998). *Developmental Indicators for the Assessment of Learning—3* (DIAL-3). Circle Pines, MN: American Guidance Service.

Mardell-Czudnowski, C. D., & Goldenberg, D. S. (1983, 1990). *Developmental Indicators for the Assessment of Learning—Revised.* Circle Pines, MN: American Guidance Service.

Mark, M. M. (1999). Social science evidence in the courtroom: *Daubert* and beyond? *Psychology, Public Policy, and Law, 5,* 175–193.

Marks, I. (1999). Computer aids to mental health care. *Canadian Journal of Psychiatry, 44,* 548–555.

Marquette, B. W. (1976). *Limitations on the generalizability of adult competency across all situations.* Paper presented at the annual meeting of the Western Psychological Association, Los Angeles.

Martens, M. P., Cox, R. H., Beck, N. C., & Heppner, P. P. (2003). Measuring motives for intercollegiate athlete alcohol use: A confirmatory factor analysis of the Drinking Motives Measure. *Psychological Assessment, 15,* 235–239.

Martin, D. C., & Bartol, K. M. (1986). Holland's Vocational Preference Inventory and the Myers-Briggs Type Indicator as predictors of vocational choice among Master's of Business Administration. *Journal of Vocational Behavior, 29,* 51–65.

Marx, E. (1998). Sibling antagonism transformed during assessment in the home. In L. Handler (Chair), *Conducting assessments in clients' homes: Contexts, surprises, dilemmas, opportunities.* Symposium presented at the Society for Personality Assessment 1998 Midwinter Meeting, February 20.

Maslach, C., Jackson, S. E., & Leiter, M. P. (1996). *The Maslach Burnout Inventory* (3rd ed.). Palo Alto, CA: Consulting Psychologists Press.

Maslach, C., Jackson, S. E., & Leiter, M. P. (1997). The Maslach Burnout Inventory. In C. P. Zalaquett & R. J. Wood (Eds.), *Evaluating stress: A book of resources* (3rd ed., pp. 191–218). Lanham, MD: Scarecrow.

Masling, J. (1960). The influence of situational and interpersonal variables in projective testing. *Psychological Bulletin, 57*, 65–85.

Masling, J. (1965). Differential indoctrination of examiners and Rorschach responses. *Journal of Consulting Psychology, 29*, 198–201.

Masling, J. M. (1997). On the nature and utility of projective tests and objective tests. *Journal of Personality Assessment, 69*, 257–270.

Maslow, A. H. (1943). A theory of motivation. *Psychological Review, 50*, 370–396.

Maslow, A. H. (1970). *Motivation and personality* (2nd ed.). New York: Harper & Row.

Massey, D. S. (2000). When surveys fail: An alternative for data collection. In A. A. Stone et al. (Eds.), *The science of self-report: Implications for research and practice* (pp. 145–160). Mahwah, NJ: Erlbaum.

Massil, H. (1995). Postpartum sexual function: What is the norm? *Sexual and Marital Therapy, 10*, 263–276.

Mast, B. T., & Lichtenberg, P. A. (2000). Assessment of functional abilities among geriatric patients: A MIMIC model of the functional independence measure. *Rehabilitation Psychology, 45*, 49–64.

Masuda, M., Matsumoto, G. H., & Meredith, G. M. (1970). Ethnic identity in three generations of Japanese Americans. *Journal of Social Psychology, 81*, 199–207.

Matarazzo, J. D. (1972). *Wechsler's measurement and appraisal of adult intelligence* (5th ed.) Baltimore: Williams & Wilkins.

Matarazzo, J. D. (1990). Psychological assessment versus psychological testing: Validation from Binet to the school, clinic, and courtroom. *American Psychologist, 45*, 999–1017.

Matarazzo, J. D., & Wiens, A. N. (1977). Black Intelligence Test of Cultural Homogeneity and Wechsler Adult Intelligence Scale scores of black and white police applicants. *Journal of Applied Psychology, 62*, 57–63.

Matchett, W. F. (1972). Repeated hallucinatory experiences as part of the mourning process. *Psychiatry, 35*, 185–194.

Mathieu, J. E., & Zajac, D. M. (1990). A review and meta-analysis of the antecedents, correlates, and consequences of organizational commitment. *Psychological Bulletin, 108*, 171–194.

Matson, J. L. (1995). Comments on Gresham, MacMillan, and Siperstein's paper "Critical analysis of the 1992 AAMR definition: Implications for school psychology." *School Psychology Quarterly, 10*(1), 20–23.

Matson, J. L., Smiroldo, B. B., & Hastings, T. L. (1998). Validity of the Autism/Pervasive Developmental Disorder subscale of the Diagnostic Assessment for the Severely Handicapped-II. *Journal of Autism & Developmental Disorders, 28*, 77–81.

Matsumoto, D., & Kudoh, T. (1993). American-Japanese cultural differences in attributions of personality based on smiles. *Journal of Nonverbal Behavior, 17*, 231–243.

Matsumoto, G. M., Meredith, G. M., & Masuda, M. (1970). Ethnic identification: Honolulu and Seattle Japanese-Americans. *Journal of Cross-Cultural Psychology, 1*, 63–76.

Maurer, T. J., & Alexander, R. A. (1991). Contrast effects in behavioral measurement: An investigation of alternative process explanations. *Journal of Applied Psychology, 76*, 3–10.

Maurer, T. J., Palmer, J. K., & Ashe, D. K. (1993). Diaries, checklists, evaluations, and contrast effects in measurement of behavior. *Journal of Applied Psychology, 78*, 226–231.

Mayfield, E. C. (1972). Value of peer nominations in predicting life insurance sales performance. *Journal of Applied Psychology, 56*, 319–323.

Mays, V. M., Cochran, S. D., Hamilton, E., & Miller, N. (1993). Just cover up: Barriers to heterosexual and gay young adults' use of condoms. *Health Values: The Journal of Health Behavior, Education, and Promotion, 17*, 41–47.

Mazzocco, M. M. M., Hagerman, R. J., & Pennington, B. F. (1992). Problem-solving limitations among cytogenetically expressing Fragile X women. *American Journal of Medical Genetics, 43*, 78–86.

McArthur, C. (1992). Rumblings of a distant drum. *Journal of Counseling and Development, 70*, 517–519.

McArthur, D. S., & Roberts, G. E. (1982). *Roberts Apperception Test for Children manual.* Los Angeles: Western Psychological Services.

McBride, B. A. (1989). Stress and fathers' parental competence: Implications for family life and parent educators. *Family Relations, 38*, 385–389.

McCall, W. A. (1922). *How to measure in education.* New York: Macmillan.

McCall, W. A. (1939). *Measurement.* New York: Macmillan.

McCarley, N. G., & Escoto, C. A. (2003). Celebrity worship and psychological type. *North American Journal of Psychology, 5*, 117–120.

McCaulley, M. H. (2000). Myers-Briggs Type Indicator: A bridge between counseling and consulting. *Consulting Psychology Journal: Practice and Research, 52*, 117–132.

McCaulley, M. H. (2002). Autobiography: Mary H. McCaulley. *Journal of Psychological Type, 61*, 51–59.

McClelland, D. C. (1951). *Personality.* New York: Holt-Dryden.

McClelland, D. C. (1961). *The achieving society.* Princeton, NJ: Van Nostrand.

McCloskey, G. W. (1989, March). *The K-ABC sequential simultaneous information processing model and classroom intervention: A report—the Dade County Classroom research study.* Paper presented at the Annual Meeting of the National Association of School Psychologists, Boston.

McClure-Butterfield, P. (1990). Issues in child custody evaluation and testimony. In C. R. Reynolds & R. W. Kamphaus (Eds.), *Handbook of psychological and educational assessment of children: Personality, behavior and context* (pp. 576–588). New York: Guilford.

McConkey, K. M., & Sheehan, P. W. (1996). *Hypnosis, memory, and behavior in criminal investigation.* New York: Guilford.

McCool, J. P., Cameron, L. D., & Petrie, K. J. (2001). Adolescent perceptions of smoking imagery in film. *Social Science & Medicine, 52*, 1577–1587.

McCoy, G. F. (1972). *Diagnostic evaluation and educational programming for hearing impaired children.* Springfield, IL: Office of the Illinois Superintendent of Public Instruction.

McCrady, B. S., & Bux, D. A. (1999). Ethical issues of informed consent with substance abusers. *Journal of Consulting and Clinical Psychology, 67*, 186–193.

McCrae, R. R., & Costa, P. T., Jr. (1983). Social desirability and scales: More substance than style. *Journal of Consulting and Clinical Psychology, 51*, 882–888.

McCrae, R. R., Costa, P. T., Jr., Dahlstrom, W. G., Barefoot, J. C., Siegler, I. C., & Williams, R. B., Jr. (1989). A caution on the use of the MMPI K-correction in research on psychosomatic medicine. *Psychosomatic Medicine, 51*, 58–65.

McCrae, R. R., Costa, P. T., Jr., Del Pilar, G. H., Rolland, J.-P., & Parker, W. D. (1998). Cross-cultural assessment of the five-factor model: The Revised NEO Personality Inventory. *Journal of Cross-Cultural Psychology, 29*, 171–188.

McCrae, R. R., Costa, P. T., Jr., Terracciano, A., et al. (2002). Personality trait development from age 12 to age 18: Longitudinal, cross-sectional and cross-cultural analyses. *Journal of Personality & Social Psychology, 83*, 1456–1468.

McCubbin, H., Larsen, A., & Olson, D. (1985a). F-COPES: Family Crisis Oriented Personal Evaluation Scales. In D. H. Olson, H. I. McCubbin, H. L. Barnes, A. S. Larsen,

M. Muxen, & M. Wilson (Eds.), *Family inventories* (rev. ed.). St. Paul: Family Social Science, University of Minnesota.

McCubbin, H. I., Patterson, J. M., & Wilson, L. R. (1985b). FILE: Family Inventory of Life Events and Changes. In D. H. Olson, H. I. McCubbin, H. L. Barnes, A. S. Larsen, M. Muxen, & M. Wilson (Eds.), *Family inventories* (rev. ed.). St. Paul: Family Social Science, University of Minnesota.

McCusker, P. J. (1994). Validation of Kaufman, Ishikuma, Kaufman-Packer's Wechsler Adult Intelligence Scale— Revised short forms on a clinical sample. *Psychological Assessment, 6,* 246–248.

McDermott, P. A., Alterman, A. I., Brown, L., et al. (1996). Construct refinement and confirmation for the Addiction Severity Index. *Psychological Assessment, 8,* 182–189.

McDevitt, S. C., & Carey, W. B. (1978). The measurement of temperament in 3- to 7-year-old children. *Journal of Child Psychology & Psychiatry & Allied Disciplines, 19,* 245–253.

McDonald, R. P. (1996a). Latent traits and the possibility of motion. *Multivariate Behavioral Research, 31,* 593–601.

McDonald, R. P. (1996b). Consensus emerges: A matter of interpretation. *Multivariate Behavioral Research, 31,* 663–672.

McDonald, W. J. (1993). Focus group research dynamics and reporting: An examination of research objectives and moderator influences. *Journal of the Academy of Marketing Science, 21,* 161–168.

McDowell, C., & Acklin, M. W. (1996). Standardizing procedures for calculating Rorschach interrater reliability: Conceptual and empirical foundations. *Journal of Personality Assessment, 66,* 308–320.

McDowell, I., & Newell, C. (1987). *Measuring health: A guide to rating scales and questionnaires.* New York: Oxford University Press.

McElrath, K. (1994). A comparison of two methods for examining inmates' self-reported drug use. *International Journal of the Addictions, 29,* 517–524.

McElwain, B. A. (1998). On seeing Beth at home and in a different light. In L. Handler (Chair), *Conducting assessments in clients' homes: Contexts, surprises, dilemmas, opportunities.* Symposium presented at the Society for Personality Assessment 1998 Midwinter Meeting, February 20.

McEvoy, G. M., & Beatty, R. W. (1989). Assessment centers and subordinate appraisals of managers: A seven-year examination of predictive validity. *Personnel Psychology, 42,* 37–52.

McGaghie, W. C. (2002, September 4). Assessing readiness for medical education: Evolution of the Medical College Admission Test. *Journal of the American Medical Association, 288,* p. 1085.

McGrath, R. E., Pogge, D. L., & Stokes, J. M. (2002). Incremental validity of selected MMPI-A content scales in an inpatient setting. *Psychological Assessment, 14,* 401–409.

McGrew, K. S. (1997). Analysis of the major intelligence batteries according to a proposed comprehensive *Gf-Gc* framework. In D. P. Flanagan, J. L. Genshaft, & P. L. Harrison (Eds.), *Contemporary intellectual assessment: Theories, tests, and issues* (pp. 151–180). New York: Guilford.

McGrew, K. S., & Flanagan, D. P. (1998). *The intelligence test desk reference: Gf-Gc cross-battery assessment.* Boston: Allyn & Bacon.

McGue, M. (1997). The democracy of the genes. *Nature, 388,* 417–418.

McGurk, F. J. (1975). Race differences—twenty years later. *Homo, 26,* 219–239.

McKinley, J. C., & Hathaway, S. R. (1940). A multiphasic schedule (Minnesota): II. A differential study of hypochondriases. *Journal of Psychology, 10,* 255–268.

McKinley, J. C., & Hathaway, S. R. (1944). The MMPI: V. Hysteria, hypomania, and psychopathic deviate. *Journal of Applied Psychology, 28,* 153–174.

McLellan, A. T., Luborsky, L., Woody, G. E., & O'Brien, C. P. (1980). An improved diagnostic evaluation instrument for substance abuse patients. *Journal of Nervous and Mental Disease, 168,* 26–33.

McLemore, C. W., & Court, J. H. (1977). Religion and psychotherapy—ethics, civil liberties, and clinical savvy: A critique. *Journal of Consulting and Clinical Psychology, 45,* 1172–1175.

McMillen, C., Howard, M. O., Nower, L., & Chung, S. (2001). Positive by-products of the struggle with chemical dependency. *Journal of Substance Abuse Treatment, 20,* 69–79.

McNeish, T. J., & Naglieri, J. A. (1993). Identification of individuals with serious emotional disturbance using the Draw A Person: Screening Procedure for Emotional Disturbance. *Journal of Special Education, 27,* 115–121.

McNemar, Q. (1964). Lost: Our intelligence. Why? *American Psychologist, 19,* 871–882.

McNemar, Q. (1975). On so-called test bias. *American Psychologist, 30,* 848–851.

McReynolds, P. (1987). Lightner Witmer: Little-known founder of clinical psychology. *American Psychologist, 42,* 849–858.

McReynolds, P., & Ludwig, K. (1984). Christian Thomasius and the origin of psychological rating scales. *ISIS, 75,* 546–553.

Mead, M. (1978). *Culture and commitment: The new relationship between the generations in the 1970s* (Rev. ed.). New York: Columbia University Press.

Meadow, K. P., Karchmer, M. A., Petersen, L. M., & Rudner, L. (1980). *Meadow-Kendall Social-Emotional Assessment Inventory.* Washington, DC: Gallaudet University.

Meadows, G., Turner, T., Campbell, L., Lewis, S. W., Reveley, M. A., & Murray, R. M. (1991). Assessing schizophrenia in adults with mental retardation: A comparative study. *British Journal of Psychiatry, 158,* 103–105.

Mednick, S. A. (1962). The associative basis of the creative process. *Psychological Review, 69,* 220–232.

Mednick, S. A., Higgins, J., & Kirschenbaum, J. (1975). *Psychology.* New York: Wiley.

Medvec, V. H., Madey, S. F., & Gilovich, T. (1995). When less is more: Counterfactual thinking and satisfaction among Olympic medalists. *Journal of Personality and Social Psychology, 69,* 603–610.

Medvec, V. H., & Savitsky, K. (1997). When doing better means feeling worse: The efforts of categorical cutoff points on counterfactual thinking and satisfaction. *Journal of Personality and Social Psychology, 72,* 1284–1296.

Meehl, P. E. (1951). *Research results for counselors.* St. Paul, MN: State Department of Education.

Meehl, P. E. (1954). *Clinical versus statistical prediction: A theoretical analysis and a review of the evidence.* Minneapolis: University of Minnesota.

Meehl, P. E. (1956). Wanted: A good cookbook. *American Psychologist, 11,* 263–272.

Mehl, M. R., & Pennebaker, J. W. (2003). The sounds of social life: A psychometric analysis of students' daily social environments and natural conversations. *Journal of Personality and Social Psychology, 84,* 857–870.

Meier, S. T. (1984). The construct validity of burnout. *Journal of Occupational Psychology, 57,* 211–219.

Meier, S. T. (1991). Tests of the construct validity of occupational stress measures with college students: Failure to support discriminant validity. *Journal of Counseling Psychology, 38,* 91–97.

Melchert, T. P., & Patterson, M. M. (1999). Duty to warn and interventions with HIV-positive clients. *Professional Psychology: Research and Practice, 30,* 180–186.

Melia, R. P., Pledger, C., & Wilson, R. (2003). Disability and rehabilitation research: Opportunities for participation, collaboration, and extramural funding for psychologists. *American Psychologist, 58,* 285–288.

Mellenbergh, G. J. (1994). Generalized linear item response theory. *Psychological Bulletin, 115,* 300–307.

Mello, E. W., & Fisher, R. P. (1996). Enhancing older adult eyewitness memory with the cognitive interview. *Applied Cognitive Psychology, 10,* 403–418.

Melton, G., Petrila, J., Poythress, N. G., & Slobogin, C. (1997). *Psychological evaluations for the courts: A handbook for mental health professionals and lawyers* (2nd ed.). New York: Guilford.

Melton, G. B. (1989). Review of the Child Abuse Protection Inventory, Form VI. In J. C. Conoley & J. J. Kramer (Eds.), *The tenth mental measurements yearbook.* Lincoln: Buros Institute of Mental Measurements, University of Nebraska.

Melton, G. B., & Limber, S. (1989). Psychologists' involvement in cases of child maltreatment. *American Psychologist, 44,* 1225–1233.

Mendoza, R. H. (1989). An empirical scale to measure type and degree of acculturation in Mexican-American adolescents and adults. *Journal of Cross-Cultural Psychology, 20,* 372–385.

Menninger, K. A. (1953). *The human mind* (3rd ed.). New York: Knopf.

Mercer, J. R. (1976). A system of multicultural pluralistic assessment (SOMPA). In *Proceedings: With bias toward none.* Lexington: Coordinating Office for Regional Resource Centers, University of Kentucky.

Merrens, M. R., & Richards, W. S. (1970). Acceptance of generalized versus "bona fide" personality interpretation. *Psychological Reports, 27,* 691–694.

Mershon, B., & Gorsuch, R. L. (1988). Number of factors in the personality sphere: Does increase in factors increase predictability of real-life criteria? *Journal of Personality and Social Psychology, 55,* 675–680.

Messick, S. (1995). Validity of psychological assessment. *American Psychologist, 50,* 741–749.

Meyer, G. J., & Handler, L. (1997). The ability of the Rorschach to predict subsequent outcome: Meta-analysis of the Rorschach Prognostic Rating Scale. *Journal of Personality Assessment, 69,* 1–38.

Meyers, J. (1994, January/February). Assessing cross-cultural adaptability with the CCAI. *San Diego Psychological Association Newsletter, 3*(1 & 2).

Micceri, T. (1989). The unicorn, the normal curve and other improbable creatures. *Psychological Bulletin, 105,* 156–166.

Midanik, L. T., Greenfield, T. K., & Rogers, J. D. (2001). Reports of alcohol-related harm: Telephone versus face-to-face interviews. *Journal of Studies on Alcohol, 62,* 74–78.

Miller, I. W., Kabacoff, R. I., Epstein, N. B., & Bishop, D. S. (1994). The development of a clinical rating scale for the McMaster Model of Family Functioning. *Family Process, 33,* 53–69.

Miller, J. N., & Ozonoff, S. (2000). The external validity of Asperger disorder: Lack of evidence from the domain of neuropsychology. *Journal of Abnormal Psychology, 109,* 227–238.

Miller, N. E. (1969). Learning of visceral and glandular responses. *Science, 163,* 434–445.

Millman, J., & Arter, J. A. (1984). Issues in item banking. *Journal of Educational Measurement, 21,* 315–330.

Millon, T., Millon, C., & Davis, R. (1994). *MCMI-III manual: Millon Clinical Multiaxial Inventory-III.* Minneapolis, MN: National Computer Systems.

Mills, C. J. (2003). Characteristics of effective teachers of gifted students: Teacher background and personality styles of students. *Gifted Child Quarterly, 47,* 272–282.

Milner, B. (1971). Interhemispheric differences in the localization of psychological processes in man. *British Medical Bulletin, 27,* 272–277.

Milner, J. (1989). Additional cross-validation of the Child Abuse Potential Inventory. *Psychological Assessment, 1,* 219–223.

Milner, J. S. (1986). *The Child Abuse Potential Inventory: Manual* (2nd ed.). Webster, NC: Psytec Corporation.

Milner, J. S. (1989). Applications of the Child Abuse Potential Inventory. *Journal of Clinical Psychology, 45,* 450–454.

Milner, J. S. (1991). Additional issues in child abuse assessment. *American Psychologist, 46,* 82–84.

Milner, J. S., Gold, R. G., & Wimberley, R. C. (1986). Prediction and explanation of child abuse: Cross-validation of the Child Abuse Protection Inventory. *Journal of Consulting and Clinical Psychology, 54,* 865–866.

Minsky, S. K., Spitz, H. H., & Bessellieu, C. L. (1985). Maintenance and transfer of training by mentally retarded young adults on the Tower of Hanoi problem. *American Journal of Mental Deficiency, 90,* 190–197.

Minton, H. L. (1988). *Lewis M. Terman: Pioneer in psychological testing.* New York: New York University Press.

Mirka, G. A., Kelaher, D. P., Nay, T., & Lawrence, B. M. (2000). Continuous assessment of back stress (CABS): A new method to quantify low-back stress in jobs with variable biomechanical demands. *Human Factors, 42,* 209–225.

Mischel, W. (1968). *Personality and assessment.* New York: Wiley.

Mischel, W. (1973). Toward a cognitive social learning reconceptualization of personality. *Psychological Review, 80,* 252–283.

Mischel, W. (1977). On the future of personality measurement. *American Psychologist, 32,* 246–254.

Mischel, W. (1979). On the interface of cognition and personality: Beyond the person-situation debate. *American Psychologist, 34,* 740–754.

Misiaszek, J., Dooling, J., Gieseke, M., Melman, H., Misiaszek, J. G., & Jorgensen, K. (1985). Diagnostic considerations in deaf patients. *Comprehensive Psychiatry, 26,* 513–521.

Mitchell, J. (1999). *Measurement in psychology: Critical history of a methodological concept.* New York: Cambridge University Press.

Mitchell, J. V., Jr. (Ed.). (1985). *The ninth mental measurements yearbook.* Lincoln: Buros Institute of Mental Measurements, University of Nebraska.

Mitchell, J. V., Jr. (1986). Measurement in the larger context: Critical current issues. *Professional Psychology: Research and Practice, 17,* 544–550.

Moffitt, T. E., Caspi, A., Krueger, R. F., et al. (1997). Do partners agree about abuse in their relationship? A psychometric evaluation of interpartner agreement. *Psychological Assessment, 9,* 47–56.

Moffitt, T. E., Gabrielli, W. F., Mednick, S. A., & Schulsinger, F. (1981). Socioeconomic status, IQ, and delinquency. *Journal of Abnormal Psychology, 90,* 152–156.

Monahan, J. (1981). *The clinical prediction of violent behavior.* Washington, DC: U.S. Government Printing Office.

Montague, M. (1993). Middle school students' mathematical problem solving: An analysis of think-aloud protocols. *Learning Disability Quarterly, 16,* 19–32.

Montgomery, G. T., & Orozco, S. (1985). Mexican Americans' performance on the MMPI as a function of level of acculturation. *Journal of Clinical Psychology, 41,* 203–212.

Moore, M. S., & McLaughlin, L. (1992). Assessment of the preschool child with visual impairment. In E. Vasquez Nutall, I. Romero, & J. Kalesnik (Eds.), *Assessing and screening pre-schoolers: Psychological and educational dimensions* (pp. 345–368). Boston: Allyn & Bacon.

Moos, R. H. (1986). *Work Environment Scale* (2nd ed.). Palo Alto, CA: Consulting Psychologists Press.

Moos, R. H., & Moos, B. S. (1981). *Family Environment Scale manual.* Palo Alto, CA: Consulting Psychologists Press.

Moos, R. H., & Moos, B. S. (1994). *Family environment manual: Development, applications, research.* Palo Alto, CA: Consulting Psychologists Press.

Moreland, K. L. (1985). Validation of computer-based test interpretations: Problems and prospects. *Journal of Consulting and Clinical Psychology, 53,* 816–825.

Moreland, K. L. (1986). An introduction to the problem of test user qualifications. In R. B. Most (Chair), *Test purchaser qualifications: Present practice, professional needs, and a proposed system.* Symposium presented at the 94th annual convention of the American Psychological Association, Washington, DC.

Moreland, K. L. (1987). Computerized psychological assessment: What's available. In J. N. Butcher (Ed.), *Computerized psychological assessment: A practitioner's guide* (pp. 26–49). New York: Basic.

Moreland, K. L., Eyde, L. D., Robertson, G. J., Primoff, E. S., & Most, R. B. (1995a). Assessment of test user qualifications: A research-based measurement procedure. *American Psychologist, 50,* 14–23.

Moreland, K. L., Reznikoff, M., & Aronow, E. (1995b). Integrating Rorschach interpretation by *carefully* placing *more* of your eggs in the content basket. *Journal of Personality Assessment, 64,* 239–242.

Morgan, C. D. (1938). Thematic Apperception Test. In H. A. Murray (Ed.), *Explorations in personality: A clinical and experimental study of fifty men of college age* (pp. 673–680). New York: Oxford University Press.

Morgan, C. D., & Murray, H. A. (1935). A method for investigating fantasies: The Thematic Apperception Test. *Archives of Neurology and Psychiatry, 34,* 289–306.

Morgan, C. D., & Murray, H. A. (1938). Thematic Apperception Test. In H. A. Murray (Ed.), *Explorations in personality: A clinical and experimental study of fifty men of college age* (pp. 530–545). New York: Oxford University Press.

Morgan, W. G. (1995). Origin and history of Thematic Apperception Test images. *Journal of Personality Assessment, 65,* 237–254.

Mori, L. T., & Armendariz, G. M. (2001). Analogue assessment of child behavior problems. *Psychological Assessment, 13,* 36–45.

Morreau, L. E., & Bruininks, R. H. (1991). *Checklist of Adaptive Living Skills.* Itasca, IL: Riverside.

Moses, S. (1991). Major revision of SAT goes into effect in 1994. *APA Monitor, 22*(1), 35.

Mosier, C. I. (1947). A critical examination of the concepts of face validity. *Educational and Psychological Measurement, 7,* 191–206.

Moss, K., Ullman, M., Johnsen, M. C., et al. (1999). Different paths to justice: The ADA, employment, and administrative enforcement by the EEOC and FEPAs. *Behavioral Sciences and the Law, 17,* 29–46.

Motowidlo, S. J. (1996). Orientation toward the job and organization. In K. R. Murphy (Ed.), *Individual differences and behavior in organizations* (pp. 20–175). San Francisco: Jossey-Bass.

Motta, R. W., Little, S. G., & Tobin, M. I. (1993a). The use and abuse of human figure drawings. *School Psychology Quarterly, 8,* 162–169.

Motta, R. W., Little, S. G., & Tobin, M. I. (1993b). A picture is worth less than a thousand words: Response to reviewers. *School Psychology Quarterly, 8,* 197–199.

Mueller, C. G. (1949). Numerical transformations in the analysis of experimental data. *Psychological Bulletin, 46,* 198–223.

Mueller, J. H., Jacobsen, D. M., & Schwarzer, R. (2000). What are computers good for? A case study in online research. In M. H. Birnbaum (Ed.), *Psychological experiments on the Internet* (pp. 195–216). San Diego, CA: Academic Press.

Mueller, U., & Mazur, A. (1996). Facial dominance in *homo sapiens* as honest signaling of male quality. *Behavioral Ecology, 8,* 569–579.

Mulaik, S. A. (1996a). On Maraun's deconstructing of factor indeterminacy with constructed factors. *Multivariate Behavioral Research, 31,* 579–592.

Mulaik, S. A. (1996b). Factor analysis is not just a model in pure mathematics. *Multivariate Behavioral Research, 31,* 655–661.

Mulvey, E. P., & Lidz, C. W. (1984). Clinical considerations in the prediction of dangerousness in mental patients. *Clinical Psychology Review, 4,* 379–401.

Murguia, A., Zea, M. C., Reisen, C. A., & Peterson, R. A. (2000). The development of the Cultural Health Attributions Questionnaire (CHAQ). *Cultural Diversity and Ethnic Minority Psychology, 6,* 268–283.

Murphy, G. E. (1984). The prediction of suicide: Why is it so difficult? *American Journal of Psychotherapy, 38,* 341–349.

Murphy, K. R. (Ed.). (2003). *Validity generalization: A critical review.* Mahwah, NJ: Erlbaum.

Murphy, L. L., Conoley, J. C., & Impara, J. C. (1994). *Tests in print IV: An index to tests, test reviews, and the literature on specific tests.* Lincoln: Buros Institute of Mental Measurements, University of Nebraska.

Murphy, L. L., Plake, B. S., Impara, J. C., & Spies, R. A. (Eds.), (2002). *Tests in print VI.* Lincoln: University of Nebraska Press.

Murphy-Berman, V. (1994). A conceptual framework for thinking about risk assessment and case management in child protective service. *Child Abuse and Neglect, 18,* 193–201.

Murray, H. A. (1943). *Thematic Apperception Test manual.* Cambridge, MA: Harvard University.

Murray, H. A., et al. (1938). *Explorations in personality.* Cambridge, MA: Harvard University.

Murray, H. A., & MacKinnon, D. W. (1946). Assessment of OSS personnel. *Journal of Consulting Psychology, 10,* 76–80.

Murstein, B. I., & Mathes, S. (1996). Projection on projective techniques = pathology: The problem that is not being addressed. *Journal of Personality Assessment, 66,* 337–349.

Murstein, B. I. (1961). Assumptions, adaptation level, and projective techniques. *Perceptual and Motor Skills, 12,* 107–125.

Mussen, P. H., & Naylor, H. K. (1954). The relationship between overt and fantasy aggression. *Journal of Abnormal and Social Psychology, 49,* 235–240.

Mussen, P. H., & Scodel, A. (1955). The effects of sexual stimulation under varying conditions on TAT sexual responsiveness. *Journal of Consulting and Clinical Psychology, 19,* 90.

Myers, I. B. (1962). *The Myers-Briggs Type Indicator: Manual.* Palo Alto, CA: Consulting Psychologists Press.

Myers, I. B., & Briggs, K. C. (1943/1962). *The Myers-Briggs Type Indicator.* Palo Alto, CA: Consulting Psychologists Press.

Myers, K. D., & Carskadon, T. G. (2002). Eminent interview: Katharine Downing Myers. *Journal of Psychological Type, 61,* 43–49.

Nagle, R. J., & Bell, N. L. (1993). Validation of Stanford-Binet Intelligence Scale: Fourth Edition Abbreviated Batteries with college students. *Psychology in the Schools, 30,* 227–231.

Naglieri, J. A. (1985a). Use of the WISC-R and K-ABC with learning disabled, borderline mentally retarded, and normal children. *Psychology in the Schools, 22,* 133–141.

Naglieri, J. A. (1985b). Normal children's performance on the McCarthy Scales, Kaufman Assessment Battery and Peabody Individual Achievement Test. *Journal of Psychoeducational Assessment, 3,* 123–129.

Naglieri, J. A. (1989). A cognitive processing theory for the measurement of intelligence. *Educational Psychologist, 24,* 185–206.

Naglieri, J. A. (1990). *Das-Naglieri Cognitive Assessment System.* Paper presented at the conference "Intelligence: Theories and Practice," Memphis, TN.

Naglieri, J. A. (1993). Human figure drawings in perspective. *School Psychology Quarterly, 8,* 170–176.

Naglieri, J. A. (1997). IQ: Knowns and unknowns, hits and misses. *American Psychologist, 52,* 75–76.

Naglieri, J. A., & Anderson, D. F. (1985). Comparison of the WISC-R and K-ABC with gifted students. *Journal of Psychoeducational Assessment, 3,* 175–179.

Naglieri, J. A., & Das, J. P. (1988). Planning-arousal-simultaneous-successive (PASS): A model for assessment. *Journal of School Psychology, 26,* 35–48.

Naglieri, J. A., & Das, J. P. (1997). *Das-Naglieri Cognitive Assessment System: Interpretive handbook.* Itasca, IL: Riverside.

Naglieri, J. A., McNeish, T. J., & Bardos, A. N. (1991). *Draw A Person: Screening Procedure for Emotional Disturbance—Examiner's manual.* Austin, TX: PRO-ED.

Nagyne Rez, I., & Zsoldos, M. (1991). Issues of diagnosis of learning problems in patients with impaired hearing on the basis of observations gained during the application of the Hiskey-Nebraska Test of Learning Aptitude. *Magyar Pszichologiai Szemle, 47,* 393–402.

Nathan, J., Wilkinson, D., Stammers, S., & Low, L. (2001). The role of tests of frontal executive function in the detection of mild dementia. *International Journal of Geriatric Psychiatry, 16,* 18–26.

National Association of School Psychologists. (2000). *Professional conduct manual* (4th ed.). Washington, DC: Author.

National Council on Disability. (1996). *Cognitive impairments and the application of Title I of the Americans with Disabilities Act.* Washington, DC: Author.

National Joint Committee on Learning Disabilities. (1985). *Learning disabilities and the preschool child: A position paper of the National Joint Committee on Learning Disabilities.* Baltimore: Author.

Naylor, J. C., & Shine, L. C. (1965). A table for determining the increase in mean criterion score obtained by using a selection device. *Journal of Industrial Psychology, 3,* 33–42.

Neagoe, A. D. (2000). Abducted by aliens: A case study. *Psychiatry, 63,* 202–207.

Neale, E. L., & Rosale, M. L. (1993). What can art therapists learn from projective drawing techniques for children? A review of the literature. *The Arts in Psychotherapy, 20,* 37–49.

Neath, J., Bellini, J., & Bolton, B. (1997). Dimensions of the Functional Assessment Inventory for five disability groups. *Rehabilitation Psychology, 42,* 183–207.

Needham, J. (1959). *A history of embryology.* New York: Abelard-Schuman.

Neisser, U. (1979). The concept of intelligence. *Intelligence, 3,* 217–227.

Neisser, U., Boodoo, G., Bouchard, T. J., Jr., et al. (1996). Intelligence: Knowns and unknowns. *American Psychologist, 51,* 77–101.

Nellis, L., & Gridley, B. E. (1994). Review of the Bayley Scales of Infant Development—Second Edition. *Journal of School Psychology, 32,* 201–209.

Nelson, C. A., Wewerka, S., Thomas, K. M., et al. (2000). Neurocognitive sequelae of infants of diabetic mothers. *Behavioral Neuroscience, 114,* 950–956.

Nelson, D. V., Harper, R. G., Kotik-Harper, D., & Kirby, H. B. (1993). Brief neuropsychologic differentiation of demented versus depressed elderly inpatients. *General Hospital Psychiatry, 15,* 409–416.

Nelson, L. D. (1994). Introduction to the special section on normative assessment. *Psychological Assessment, 4,* 283.

Nelson, R. O., Hay, L. R., & Hay, W. M. (1977). Comment on Cone's "The relevance of reliability and validity for behavior assessment." *Behavior Therapy, 8,* 427–430.

Nester, M. A. (1993). Psychometric testing and reasonable accommodation for persons with disabilities. *Rehabilitation Psychology, 38,* 75–85.

Nettelbeck, T., & Rabbit, P. M. A. (1992). Aging, cognitive performance, and mental speed. *Intelligence, 16,* 189–205.

Neugarten, B., Havighurst, R. J., & Tobin, S. (1961). The measurement of life satisfaction. *Journal of Gerontology, 16,* 134–143.

Newborg, J., Stock, J. R., Wnek, L., et al. (1984). *Battelle Developmental Inventory.* Allen, TX: DLM Teaching Resources.

Newcomb, T. M. (1929). *Consistency of certain extrovert-introvert behavior patterns in 51 problem boys.* New York: Columbia University Bureau of Publications.

Newell, A. (1973). Production systems: Models of control structures. In W. G. Chase (Ed.), *Visual information processing* (pp. 463–526). New York: Academic Press.

Newman, H. H., Freeman, F. N., & Holzinger, K. J. (1937). *Twins.* Chicago: University of Chicago.

Nilsson, J. E., Berkel, L. A., Flores, L. Y., et al. (2003). An 11-year review of *Professional Psychology: Research and Practice:* Content and sample analysis with an emphasis on diversity. *Professional Psychology: Research and Practice, 34,* 611–616.

Norton, P. J., & Hope, D. A. (2001). Analogue observational methods in the assessment of social functioning in adults. *Psychological Assessment, 13,* 59–72.

Notarius, C., & Markman, H. (1981). Couples Interaction Scoring System. In E. Filsinger & R. Lewis, (Eds.), *Assessing marriage: New behavioral approaches.* Beverly Hills, CA: Sage.

Notarius, C. I., & Vanzetti, N. A. (1983). The Marital Agendas Protocol. In E. Filsinger (Ed.), *Marriage and family assessment: A sourcebook for family therapy.* Beverly Hills, CA: Sage.

Novick, M. R., & Lewis, C. (1967). Coefficient alpha and the reliability of composite measurements. *Psychometrika, 32,* 1–13.

Nunnally, J. C. (1967). *Psychometric theory.* New York: McGraw-Hill.

Nunnally, J. C. (1978). *Psychometric theory* (2nd ed.). New York: McGraw-Hill.

Nyborg, H., & Jensen, A. R. (2000). Black–white differences on various psychometric tests: Spearman's hypothesis tested on American armed services veterans. *Personality and Individual Differences, 28,* 593–599.

Nystedt, L., Sjoeberg, A., & Haegglund, G. (1999). Discriminant validation of measures of organizational commitment, job involvement, and job satisfaction among Swedish army officers. *Scandinavian Journal of Psychology, 40,* 49–55.

O'Boyle, M. W., Gill, H. S., Benbow, C. P., & Alexander, J. E. (1994). Concurrent finger-tapping in mathematically gifted males: Evidence for enhanced right hemispheric involvement during linguistic processing. *Cortex, 30,* 519–526.

O'Connor, E. (2001, February). Researchers pinpoint potential cause of autism. *Monitor on Psychology, 32*(2), 13.

Oden, M. H. (1968). The fulfillment of promise: 40-year follow-up of the Terman gifted group. *Genetic Psychology Monographs, 77,* 3–93.

O'Donnell, W. E., DeSoto, C. B., & DeSoto, J. L. (1993). Validity and reliability of the Revised Neuropsychological Impairment Scales (NIS). *Journal of Clinical Psychology, 49,* 372–382.

O'Donnell, W. E., DeSoto, C. B., DeSoto, J. L., & Reynolds, D. M. (1993). *The Neuropsychological Impairment Scale (NIS) manual.* Los Angeles: Western Psychological Services.

O'Hare, T., & Van Tran, T. (1998). Substance abuse among Southeast Asians in the U.S.: Implications for practice and research. *Social Work in Health Care, 26,* 69–80.

Okazaki, S., & Sue, S. (1995). Methodological issues in assessment research with ethnic minorities. *Psychological Assessment, 7,* 367–375.

Okazaki, S., & Sue, S. (2000). Implications of test revisions for assessment with Asian Americans. *Psychological Assessment, 12,* 272–280.

O'Keefe, J. (1993). Disability, discrimination, and the Americans with Disabilities Act. *Consulting Psychology Journal, 45*(2), 3–9.

O'Leary, K. D., & Arias, I. (1988). Assessing agreement of reports of spouse abuse. In G. T. Hotaling, D. Finkelhor, J. T. Kirkpatrick, & M. A. Straus (Eds.), *Family abuse and its consequences* (pp. 218–227). Newbury Park, CA: Sage.

Olkin, R., & Pledger, C. (2003). Can disability studies and psychology join hands? *American Psychologist, 58,* 296–304.

Olson, D. H., & Barnes, H. L. (1985). Quality of life. In D. H. Olson, H. I. McCubbin, H. L. Barnes, A. S. Larsen, M. Muxen, & M. Wilson (Eds.), *Family inventories* (rev. ed.). St. Paul: Family Social Science, University of Minnesota.

Olson, D. H., Larsen, A. S., & McCubbin, H. I. (1985). Family strengths. In D. H. Olson, H. I. McCubbin, H. L. Barnes, A. S. Larsen, M. Muxen, & M. Wilson (Eds.), *Family inventories* (rev. ed.). St. Paul: Family Social Science, University of Minnesota.

Olweus, D. (1979). Stability of aggressive reaction patterns in males: A review. *Psychological Bulletin, 86,* 852–875.

Ones, D. S., & Viswesvaran, C. (2001). Integrity tests and other criterion-focused occupational personality scales (COPS) used in personnel selection. *International Journal of Selection and Assessment, 9,* 31–39.

Oregon Death With Dignity Act, 2 Ore. Rev. Stat. §§127.800-127.897 (1997).

Organ, D. W., & Near, J. P. (1985). Cognition versus affect in measures of job satisfaction. *International Journal of Psychology, 20,* 241–253.

Orne, M. T. (1979). The use and misuse of hypnosis in court. *International Journal of Clinical and Experimental Hypnosis, 27,* 311–341.

Orr, D. B., & Graham, W. R. (1968). Development of a listening comprehension test to identify educational potential among disadvantaged junior high school students. *American Educational Researcher Journal, 5,* 167–180.

Orr, F. C., DeMatteo, A., Heller, B., Lee, M., & Nguyen, M. (1987). Psychological assessment. In H. Elliott, L. Glass, & J. W. Evans (Eds.), *Mental health assessment of deaf clients* (pp. 93–106). Boston: Little, Brown.

Orr, R. R., Cameron, S. J., Dobson, L. A., & Day, D. M. (1993). Age-related changes in stress experienced by families with a child who has developmental delays. *Mental Retardation, 31,* 171–176.

Osberg, T. M., & Poland, D. L. (2002). Comparative accuracy of the MMPI-2 and the MMPI-A in the diagnosis of psychopathology in 18-year-olds. *Psychological Assessment, 14,* 164–169.

Osgood, C. E., Suci, G. J., & Tannenbaum, P. H. (1957). *The measurement of meaning.* Urbana: University of Illinois.

Osipow, S. H., & Reed, R. (1985). Decision-making style and career indecision in college students. *Journal of Vocational Behavior, 27,* 368–373.

OSS Assessment Staff. (1948). *Assessment of men: Selection of personnel for the Office of Strategic Service.* New York: Rinehart.

Ouellette, S. E. (1988). The use of projective drawing techniques in the personality assessment of prelingually deafened young adults: A pilot study. *American Annals of the Deaf, 133,* 212–217.

Outtz, J. (1994, June). Cited in T. DeAngelis, New tests allow takers to tackle real-life problems. *APA Monitor, 25,* 14.

Ozer, D. J. (1985). Correlation and the coefficient of determination. *Psychological Bulletin, 97,* 307–315.

Ozonoff, S. (1995). Reliability and validity of the Wisconsin Card Sorting Test in studies of autism. *Neuropsychology, 9,* 491–500.

Pack v. K-Mart. 166 F.3d, 1300 (10th Cir. 1999).

Padden, C. (1980). The deaf community and the culture of deaf people. In C. Baker & R. Battison (Eds.), *Sign language and the deaf community* (pp. 89–103). Washington, DC: National Association of the Deaf.

Padden, C., & Humphries, T. (1988). *Deaf in America: Voices from a culture.* Cambridge, MA: Harvard University.

Padilla, A. M., Wagatsuma, Y., & Lindholm, K. J. (1985). Acculturation and personality as predictors of stress in Japanese and Japanese Americans. *Journal of Social Psychology, 125,* 295–305.

Palmore, E. (Ed.). (1970). *Normal aging.* Durham, NC: Duke University Press.

Panell, R. C., & Laabs, G. J. (1979). Construction of a criterion-referenced, diagnostic test for an individualized instruction program. *Journal of Applied Psychology, 64,* 255–261.

Pannbacker, M., & Middleton, G. (1992). Review of Wepman's Auditory Discrimination Test, Second Edition. In J. J. Kramer & J. C. Conoley (Eds.), *The eleventh mental measurements yearbook.* Lincoln: Buros Institute of Mental Measurements, University of Nebraska.

Panter, A. T., Swygert, K. A., Dahlstrom, W. G., & Tanaka, J. S. (1997). Factor analytic approaches to personality item-level data. *Journal of Personality Assessment, 68,* 561–589.

Paolo, A. M., & Ryan, J. J. (1991). Application of WAIS-R short forms to persons 75 years of age and older. *Journal of Psychoeducational Assessment, 9,* 345–352.

Parette, H. P., & Brotherson, M. J. (1996). Family participation in assistive technology assessment for young children with mental retardation and developmental disabilities. *Education & Training in Mental Retardation & Developmental Disabilities, 31,* 29–43.

Parke, R. D., Hymel, S., Power, T., & Tinsley, B. (1977, November). Fathers and risk: A hospital-based model of intervention. In D. B. Sawin (Chair), *Symposium on psychosocial risks during infancy.* Austin: University of Texas at Austin.

Parke, R. D., & Sawin, D. B. (1975, April). *Infant characteristics and behavior as elicitors of maternal and paternal responsivity in the newborn period.* Paper presented at the meetings of the Society for Research in Child Development, Denver, CO.

Parker, T., & Abramson, P. R. (1995). The law hath not been dead: Protecting adults with mental retardation from sexual abuse and violation of their sexual freedom. *Mental Retardation, 33,* 257–263.

Parkes, L. P., Bochner, S., & Schneider, S. K. (2001). Person-organisation fit across cultures: An empirical investigation of individualism and collectivism. *Applied Psychology: An International Review, 50,* 81–108.

Parnes, H. S., & Less, L. J. (1985). Introduction and overview. In H. S. Parnes, J. E. Crowley, R. J. Haurin, et al. (Eds.), *Retirement among American men.* Lexington, MA: Lexington Books.

Pascal, G. R., & Suttell, B. J. (1951). *The Bender-Gestalt Test: Quantification and validity for adults.* New York: Grune & Stratton.

Pascoe, C. J. (2003). Multiple masculinities? Teenage boys talk about jocks and gender. *American Behavioral Scientist, 46,* 1423–1438.

Patterson, W. M., Dohn, H. H., Bird, J., & Patterson, G. A. (1983). Evaluation of suicidal patients: The SAD PERSONS scale. *Psychosomatics, 24,* 343–349.

Paul, G. L. (1987). *The time-sample behavioral checklist: Observational assessment instrumentation for service and research.* Champaign, IL: Research Press.

Paul, V., & Jackson, D. W. (1993). *Toward a psychology of deafness.* Boston: Allyn & Bacon.

Paulhus, D. L. (1984). Two-component models of socially desirable responding. *Journal of Personality and Social Psychology, 46,* 598–609.

Paulhus, D. L. (1986). Self-deception and impression management in test responses. In A. Angleitner & J. S. Wiggins (Eds.), *Personality assessment via questionnaire* (pp. 142–165). New York: Springer.

Paulhus, D. L. (1990). Measurement and control of response bias. In J. P. Robinson, P. R. Shaver, & L. Wrightsman (Eds.), *Measures of personality and social-psychological attitudes* (pp. 17–59). San Diego, CA: Academic Press.

Paulhus, D. L., & Levitt, K. (1987). Desirable response triggered by affect: Automatic egotism? *Journal of Personality and Social Psychology, 52,* 245–259.

Paulhus, D. L., & Reid, D. B. (1991). Enhancement and denial in socially desirable responding. *Journal of Personality and Social Psychology, 60,* 307–317.

Paullay, I. M., Alliger, G. M., & Stone-Romero, E. F. (1994). Construct validation of two instruments designed to measure job involvement and work centrality. *Journal of Applied Psychology, 79,* 224–228.

Pearson, K., & Moul, M. (1925). The problem of alien immigration of Great Britain illustrated by an examination of Russian and Polish Jewish children. *Annals of Eugenics, 1,* 5–127.

Pennsylvania Department of Corrections v. Yeskey, 118 F.3d, 168 (1998).

Perez, J. A., Dasi, F., & Lucas, A. (1997). Length overestimation bias as a product of normative pressure arising from anthropocentric vs. geocentric representations of length. *Swiss Journal of Psychology, 56,* 243–255.

Perry, C., & Laurence, J. R. (1990). Hypnosis with a criminal defendant and a crime witness: Two recent related cases. *International Journal of Clinical and Experimental Hypnosis, 38,* 266–282.

Petersen, N. S., & Novick, M. R. (1976). An evaluation of some models for culture-fair selection. *Journal of Educational Measurement, 13,* 3–29.

Peterson, C. A. (1997). *The twelfth mental measurements yearbook:* Testing the tests. *Journal of Personality Assessment, 68,* 717–719.

Petrie, K., & Chamberlain, K. (1985). The predictive validity of the Zung Index of Potential Suicide. *Journal of Personality Assessment, 49,* 100–102.

Petty, M. M., McGhee, G. W., & Cavender, J. W. (1984). A meta-analysis of the relationships between individual job satisfaction and individual performance. *Academy of Management Review, 9,* 712–721.

Phelps, L., & Branyon, B. (1988). Correlations among the Hiskey, K-ABC Nonverbal Scale, Leiter, and WISC-R Performance Scale with public school deaf children. *Journal of Psychoeducational Assessment, 6,* 354–358.

Phillips, B. A. (1996). Bringing culture to the forefront: Formulating diagnostic impressions of deaf and hard-of-hearing people at times of medical crisis. *Professional Psychology: Research and Practice, 27,* 137–144.

Piaget, J. (1954). *The construction of reality on the child.* New York: Basic.

Piaget, J. (1971). *Biology and knowledge.* Chicago: University of Chicago.

Piedmont, R. L., & McCrae, R. R. (1996). *Are validity scales valid in volunteer samples? Evidence from self-reports and observer ratings.* Unpublished manuscript, Loyola College, Maryland.

Piedmont, R. L., McCrae, R. R., Riemann, R., & Angleitner, A. (2000). On the invalidity of validity scales: Evidence from self-reports and observer ratings in volunteer samples. *Journal of Personality and Social Psychology, 78,* 582–593.

Pilgrim, C., Luo, Q., Urberg, K. A., & Fang, X. (1999). Influence of peers, parents, and individual characteristics on adolescent drug use in two cultures. *Merrill-Palmer Quarterly, 45,* 85–107.

Pintner, R. (1931). *Intelligence testing.* New York: Holt.

Piotrowski, C., & Armstrong, T. (2002). Convergent validity of the KeyPoint pre-employment measure with the MBTI. *Psychology & Education: An Interdisciplinary Journal, 39,* 49–50.

Piotrowski, C., Belter, R. W., & Keller, J. W. (1998). The impact of "managed care" on the practice of psychological testing: Preliminary findings. *Journal of Personality Assessment, 70,* 441–446.

Piotrowski, Z. (1957). *Perceptanalysis.* New York: Macmillan.

Pittenger, D. J. (1993). The utility of the Myers-Briggs Type Indicator. *Review of Educational Research, 63,* 467–488.

Plake, B. S., Impara, J. C., & Spies, R. A. (Eds.). (2003). *The fifteenth mental measurements yearbook.* Lincoln: Buros Institute of Mental Measurements, University of Nebraska.

Pledger, C. (2003). Discourse on disability and rehabilitation issues: Opportunities for psychology. *American Psychologist, 58,* 279–284.

Plucker, J. A., & Levy, J. J. (2001). The downside of being talented. *American Psychologist, 56,* 75–76.

Polizzi, D. (1998). Contested space: Assessment in the home and the combative marriage. In L. Handler (Chair), *Conducting assessments in clients' homes: Contexts, surprises, dilemmas, opportunities.* Symposium presented at the Society for Personality Assessment 1998 Midwinter Meeting, February 20.

Pollard, R. Q. (1993). 100 years in psychology and deafness: A centennial retrospective. *Journal of the American Deafness & Rehabilitation Association, 26,* 32–46.

Pomplun, M., & Omar, M. H. (2000). Score comparability of a state mathematics assessment across students with and without reading accommodations. *Journal of Applied Psychology, 85,* 21–29.

Pomplun, M., & Omar, M. H. (2001). Score comparability of a state reading assessment across selected groups of students with disabilities. *Structural Equation Modeling, 8,* 257–274.

Ponterotto, J. G., Rivera, L., & Sueyoshi, L. A. (2000). The Career-in-Culture interview: A semi-structured protocol for the cross-cultural intake interview. *Career Development Quarterly, 49,* 85–96.

Porter, L. W., Steers, R. W., Mowday, R. T., & Boulian, P. V. (1974). Organizational commitment, job satisfaction, and turnover among psychiatric technicians. *Journal of Applied Psychology, 59,* 603–609.

Porteus, S. D. (1933). *The Maze Test and mental differences.* Vineland, NJ: Smith Printing & Publishing.

Porteus, S. D. (1942). *Qualitative performance in the Maze Test.* San Antonio, TX: Psychological Corporation.

Porteus, S. D. (1955). *The Maze Test: Recent advances.* Palo Alto, CA: Pacific Books.

Powell, D. H. (1994). *Profiles in cognitive aging.* Cambridge, MA: Harvard University Press.

Preston, R. (1961). Improving the item validity of study habits inventories. *Educational and Psychological Measurement, 21,* 129–131.

Price, G., Dunn, R., & Dunn, K. (1982). *Productivity Environmental Survey manual.* Lawrence, KS: Price Systems.

Prince, R. J., & Guastello, S. J. (1990). The Barnum Effect in a computerized Rorschach interpretation system. *Journal of Psychology: Interdisciplinary and Applied, 124,* 217–222.

Procedures for evaluating specific learning disabilities. (1977). *Federal Register,* December 29, Part III.

Prout, H. T., & Phillips, P. D. (1974). A clinical note: The kinetic school drawing. *Psychology in the Schools, 11,* 303–396.

Psychological Corporation, The. (1992a). *Wechsler Individual Achievement Test.* San Antonio, TX: Author.

Psychological Corporation, The. (1992b). *Wechsler Individual Achievement Test manual.* San Antonio, TX: Author.

Psychological Corporation, The. (2001). *Wechsler Individual Achievement Test-Second Edition.* San Antonio, TX: Author.

Pullen, L., & Gow, K. (2000). University students elaborate on what young persons "at risk of suicide" need from listeners. *Journal of Applied Health Behaviour, 2,* 32–39.

Putnam, W. H. (1979). Hypnosis and distortions in eyewitness memory. *International Journal of Clinical and Experimental Hypnosis, 27,* 437–448.

Q and A on balancing the SAT scores. (1994). New York: College Board.

Qu, C., Zhang, P., Zheng, R., et al. (1992). An examination of the IQs of 319 hearing-impaired students in 5 cities in China. *Chinese Mental Health Journal, 6,* 219–221.

Quay, H. C., & Peterson, C. (1983). *Manual for the Revised Behavior Problem Checklist.* Coral Gables, FL: Authors.

Quay, H. C., & Peterson, D. R. (1967). *Behavior Problem Checklist.* Champaign: University of Illinois Press.

Quill, T. E., Cassel, C. K., & Meier, D. E. (1992). Care of the hopelessly ill: Proposed clinical criteria for physician-assisted suicide. *New England Journal of Medicine, 327,* 1380–1384.

Quinsey, V. L., Chaplin, T. C., & Upfold, D. (1984). Sexual arousal to nonsexual violence and sadomasochistic themes among rapists and nonsex-offenders. *Journal of Consulting and Clinical Psychology, 52,* 651–657.

Raifman, L. J., & Vernon, M. (1996). Important implications for psychologists of the Americans with Disabilities Act: Case in point, the patient who is deaf. *Professional Psychology: Research and Practice, 27,* 372–377.

Raju, N. S., Drasgow, F., & Slinde, J. A. (1993). An empirical comparison of the area methods, Lord's chi-square test, and the Mantel-Haenszel technique for assessing differential item functioning. *Educational and Psychological Measurement, 53,* 301–314.

Ramirez, M., III. (1984). Assessing and understanding biculturalism-multiculturalism in Mexican-American adults. In J. L. Martinez, Jr., & R. H. Mendoza (Eds.), *Chicano psychology* (pp. 77–94). Orlando, FL: Academic Press.

Randall, A., Fairbanks, M. M., & Kennedy, M. L. (1986). Using think-aloud protocols diagnostically with college readers. *Reading Research & Instruction, 25,* 240–253.

Randall, D. M. (1987). Commitment and the organization: The organization man revisited. *Academy of Management Review, 12,* 460–471.

Randolph, C., Mohr, E., & Chase, T. N. (1993). Assessment of intellectual function in dementing disorders: Validity of WAIS-R short forms for patients with Alzheimer's, Huntington's, and Parkinson's disease. *Journal of Clinical and Experimental Neuropsychology, 15,* 743–753.

Ranseen, J. D., & Humphries, L. L. (1992). The intellectual functioning of eating disorder patients. *Journal of the American Academy of Child and Adolescent Psychiatry, 31,* 844–846.

Rapaport, D. (1946–1967). Principles underlying nonprojective tests of personality. In M. M. Gill (Ed.), *David Rapaport: Collected papers.* New York: Basic.

Rapaport, D., Gill, M. M., & Schafer, R. (1945–1946). *Diagnostic psychological testing* (2 vols.). Chicago: Year Book.

Rapaport, D., Gill, M. M., & Schafer, R. (1968). In R. R. Holt (Ed.), *Diagnostic psychological testing* (rev. ed.). New York: International Universities.

Raphael, S., & Halpert, L. H. (1999). *Graduate Record Examination: Psychology.* New York: Arco Publishing.

Rappeport, J. R. (1982). Differences between forensic and general psychiatry. *American Journal of Psychiatry, 139,* 331–334.

Raven, J. C. (1976). *Standard Progressive Matrices.* Oxford: Oxford Psychologists.

Raz, S., Glogowski-Kawamoto, B., Yu, A. W., et al. (1998). The effects of perinatal hypoxic risk on developmental outcome in early and middle childhood: A twin study. *Neuropsychology, 12,* 459–467.

Razran, G. (1961). The observable unconscious and the inferable conscious in current Soviet psychophysiology: Introceptive conditioning, semantic conditioning, and the orienting reflex. *Psychological Review, 68,* 81–147.

Recarte, M. A., & Nunes, L. M. (2000). Effects of verbal and spatial-imagery tasks on eye fixations while driving. *Journal of Experimental Psychology: Applied, 6,* 31–43.

Reckase, M. D. (1996). Test construction in the 1990s: Recent approaches every psychologist should know. *Psychological Assessment, 8,* 354–359.

Ree, M. J., & Earles, J. A. (1990). *Differential validity of a differential aptitude test* (Rpt 89-59). Texas: Brooks Air Force Base.

Reece, R. N., & Groden, M. A. (1985). Recognition of non-accidental injury. *Pediatric Clinics of North America, 32,* 41–60.

Reed, T. E. (1997). "The genetic hypothesis": It was not tested but it could have been. *American Psychologist, 52,* 77–78.

Reed, T. E., & Jensen, A. R. (1992). Conduction velocity in a brain nerve pathway of normal adults correlates with intelligence level. *Intelligence, 16,* 259–272.

Reed, T. E., & Jensen, A. R. (1993). Choice reaction time and visual pathway conduction velocity both correlate with intelligence but appear not to correlate with each other: Implications for information processing. *Intelligence, 17,* 191–203.

Reeder, G. D., Maccow, G. C., Shaw, S. R., Swerdlik, M. E., Horton, C. B., & Foster, P. (1997). School psychologists and full-service schools: Partnerships with medical, mental health, and social services. *School Psychology Review, 26,* 603–621.

Reichenberg, N., & Raphael, A. J. (1992). *Advanced psychodiagnostic interpretation of the Bender-Gestalt Test: Adults and children.* Westport, CT: Praeger.

Reik, T. (1948). *Listening with the third ear.* New York: Farrar, Straus.

Reik, T. (1952). *The secret self.* New York: Grove.

Reimers, T. M., Wacker, D. P., & Koeppel, G. (1987). Acceptability of behavioral treatments: A review of the literature. *School Psychology Review, 16,* 212–227.

Reinehr, R. C. (1969). Therapist and patient perceptions of hospitalized alcoholics. *Journal of Clinical Psychology, 25,* 443–445.

Reise, S. P., & Henson, J. M. (2003). A discussion of modern versus traditional psychometrics as applied to personality assessment scales. *Journal of Personality Assessment, 81,* 93–103.

Reise, S. P., Waller, N. G., & Comrey, A. L. (2000). Factor analysis and scale revision. *Psychological Assessment, 12,* 287–297.

Reiser, M. (1980). *Handbook of investigative hypnosis.* Los Angeles: Lehi.

Reiser, M. (1990). Investigative hypnosis. In D. C. Raskin (Ed.), *Psychological methods in criminal investigation evidence* (pp. 151–190). New York: Springer.

Reitan, R. (1994, July). *Child neuropsychology and learning disabilities.* Advanced Workshop, Los Angeles.

Reitan, R. M. (1955a). An investigation of the validity of Halstead's measures of biological intelligence. *Archives of Neurology and Psychiatry, 73,* 28–35.

Reitan, R. M. (1955b). Certain differential effects of left and right cerebral lesions in human adults. *Journal of Comparative and Physiological Psychology, 48,* 474–477.

Reitan, R. M. (1969). *Manual for administration of neuropsychological test batteries for adults and children.* Indianapolis: Author.

Reitan, R. M. (1984a). *Aphasia and sensory-perceptual disorders in adults.* South Tucson, AZ: Neuropsychology Press.

Reitan, R. M. (1984b). *Aphasia and sensory-perceptual disorders in children.* South Tucson, AZ: Neuropsychology Press.

Reitan, R. M. (1994). Ward Halstead's contributions to neuropsychology and the Halstead-Reitan Neuropsychological Test Battery. *Journal of Clinical Psychology, 50,* 47–70.

Reitan, R. M., & Wolfson, D. (1990). A consideration of the comparability of the WAIS and WAIS-R. *Clinical Neuropsychologist, 4,* 80–85.

Reitan, R. M., & Wolfson, D. (1992). A short screening examination for impaired brain functions in early school-age children. *Clinical Neuropsychologist, 6,* 287–294.

Reitan, R. M., & Wolfson, D. (1993). *The Halstead-Reitan Neuropsychological Test Battery: Theory and clinical interpretation* (2nd ed.). Tucson, AZ: Neuropsychology Press.

Reitan, R. M., & Wolfson, D. (2000). The neuropsychological similarities of mild and more severe head injury. *Archives of Clinical Neuropsychology, 15,* 433–442.

Remington, R. W., Johnston, J. C., Ruthruff, E., et al. (2000). Visual search in complex displays: Factors affecting conflict detection by air traffic controllers. *Visual Cognition, 7,* 769–784.

Renwick, R., et al. (Eds.). (1996). *Quality of life in health promotion and rehabilitation: Conceptual approaches, issues, and applications.* Thousand Oaks, CA: Sage.

Retzlaff, P. D., & Gibertini, M. (1988). Objective psychological testing of U.S. Air Force officers in pilot training. *Aviation, Space, and Environmental Medicine, 59,* 661–663.

Rey, G. J., Feldman, E., Rivas-Vazquez, R., et al. (1999). Neuropsychological test development and normative data on Hispanics. *Archives of Clinical Neuropsychology, 14,* 593–601.

Reynolds, C. E., & Brown, R. T. (Eds.). (1984). *Perspectives on bias in mental testing.* New York: Plenum.

Reynolds, C. R., Sanchez, S., & Wilson, V. L. (1996). Normative tables for calculating the WISC-III Performance and Full Scale IQs when Symbol Search is substituted for Coding. *Psychological Assessment, 8,* 378–382.

Reynolds, W. M. (1987). *Suicidal Ideation Questionnaire.* Odessa, FL: Psychological Assessment Resources.

Rezmovic, V. (1977). The effects of computerized experimentation on response variance. *Behavior Research Methods and Instrumentation, 9,* 144–147.

Reznikoff, M., & Tomblen, D. (1956). The use of human figure drawings in the diagnosis of organic pathology. *Journal of Consulting Psychology, 20,* 467–470.

Rice, M. E., & Harris, G. T. (1995). Violent recidivism: Assessing predictive validity. *Journal of Consulting and Clinical Psychology, 63,* 737–748.

Richardson, M. W., & Kuder, G. F. (1939). The calculation of test reliability based upon the method of rational equivalence. *Journal of Educational Psychology, 30,* 681–687.

Richman, J. (1988). The case against rational suicide. *Suicide & Life-Threatening Behavior, 18,* 285–289.

Richters, J. E., & Hinshaw, S. (1999). The abduction of disorder in psychiatry. *Journal of Abnormal Psychology, 108,* 438–445.

Rierdan, J., & Koff, E. (1981). Sexual ambiguity in children's human figure drawings. *Journal of Personality Assessment, 45,* 256–257.

Riethmiller, R. J., & Handler, L. (1997a). Problematic methods and unwarranted conclusions in DAP research: Suggestions for improved research procedures. *Journal of Personality Assessment, 69,* 459–475.

Riethmiller, R. J., & Handler, L. (1997b). The great figure drawing controversy: The integration of research and clinical practice. *Journal of Personality Assessment, 69,* 488–496.

Riggs, D. S., Murphy, C. M., & O'Leary, K. D. (1989). Intentional falsification in reports of interpartner aggression. *Journal of Interpersonal Violence, 4,* 220–232.

Ritson, B., & Forest, A. (1970). The simulation of psychosis: A contemporary presentation. *British Journal of Medical Psychology, 43,* 31–37.

Ritzler, B. (1995). Putting your eggs in the content analysis basket: A response to Aronow, Reznikoff and Moreland. *Journal of Personality Assessment, 64,* 229–234.

Ritzler, B. A., Sharkey, K. J., & Chudy, J. F. (1980). A comprehensive projective alternative to the TAT. *Journal of Personality Assessment, 44,* 358–362.

Riverside Publishing. (2001). *Report Writer for the WJ III.* Itasca, IL: Author.

Roach, R. J., Frazier, L. P., & Bowden, S. R. (1981). The Marital Satisfaction Scale: Development of a measure for intervention research. *Journal of Marriage and the Family, 21,* 251–255.

Roback, A. A. (1961). *History of psychology and psychiatry.* New York: Philosophical Library.

Robbins, S. B., & Patton, M. J. (1985). Self-psychology and career development: Construction of the Superiority and Goal Instability Scales. *Journal of Counseling Psychology, 32,* 221–231.

Roberts, B. W., & DelVecchio, W. F. (2000). The rank-order consistency of personality traits from childhood to old age: A quantitative review of longitudinal studies. *Psychological Bulletin, 126,* 3–25.

Roberts, M. W. (2001). Clinic observations of structured parent-child interaction designed to evaluate externalizing disorders. *Psychological Assessment, 13,* 46–58.

Roberts, R. N., & Magrab, P. R. (1991). Psychologists' role in a family-centered approach to practice, training, and research with young children. *American Psychologist, 46,* 144–148.

Robertson, G. J. (1990). A practical model for test development. In C. R. Reynolds & R. W. Kamphaus (Eds.), *Handbook of psychological and educational assessment of children: Intelligence & achievement* (pp. 62–85). New York: Guilford.

Robin, A. L., Koepke, T., & Moye, A. (1990). Multidimensional assessment of parent-adolescent relations. *Psychological Assessment, 2,* 451–459.

Robinson, F. G. (1992). *Love's story untold: The life of Henry A. Murray.* Cambridge, MA: Harvard University.

Robinson, N. M., Zigler, E., & Gallagher, J. J. (2000). Two tails of the normal curve: Similarities and differences in the study of mental retardation and giftedness. *American Psychologist, 55,* 1413–1424.

Rodriguez, O., & Santiviago, M. (1991). Hispanic deaf adolescents: A multicultural minority. *Volta Review, 93,* 89–97.

Roe, A., & Klos, D. (1969). Occupational classification. *Counseling Psychologist, 1,* 84–92.

Rogers, C. R. (1959). A theory of therapy, personality, and interpersonal relationships, as developed in the client-centered framework In S. Koch (Ed.), *Psychology: A study of a science* (Vol. 3, pp. 184–256). New York: McGraw-Hill.

Rogers, L. S., Knauss, J., & Hammond, K. R. (1951). Predicting continuation in therapy by means of the Rorschach Test. *Journal of Consulting Psychology, 15,* 368–371.

Rogers, R. (1986). *Structured interview of reported symptoms (SIRS).* Unpublished scale. Toronto: Clarke Institute of Psychiatry.

Rogers, R., Bagby, R. M., & Dickens, S. E. (1992). *Structured Interview of Reported Symptoms (SIRS) and professional manual.* Odessa, FL: Psychological Assessment Resources.

Rogers, R., & Cavanaugh, J. L. (1980). Differences in psychological variables between criminally responsible and insane patients: A preliminary study. *American Journal of Forensic Psychiatry, 1,* 29–37.

Rogers, R., & Cavanaugh, J. L. (1981). Rogers Criminal Responsibility Assessment Scales. *Illinois Medical Journal, 160,* 164–169.

Rogers, R., Dolmetsch, R., & Cavanaugh, J. L. (1981). An empirical approach to insanity evaluations. *Journal of Clinical Psychology, 37,* 683–687.

Rogers, R., Seman, W., & Wasyliw, D. E. (1983). The RCRAS and legal insanity: A cross validation study. *Journal of Clinical Psychology, 39,* 554–559.

Rogers, R., Wasyliw, D. E., & Cavanaugh, J. L. (1984). Evaluating insanity: A study of construct validity. *Law & Human Behavior, 8,* 293–303.

Rogler, L. H. (2002). Historical generations and psychology: The case of the Great Depression and World War II. *American Psychologist, 57,* 1013–1023.

Rohl, J. S. (1993). The Tower of Hanoi. Supplementary information supplied with *Jarrah Wooden Tower of Hanoi.* Mt. Lawley, Australia: Built-Rite Sales.

Rohner, R. P. (1984). Toward a conception of culture for cross-cultural psychology. *Journal of Cross-Cultural Psychology, 15,* 111–138.

Roid, G. H. (2003a). *Stanford-Binet Intelligence Scales, Fifth Edition.* Itasca, IL: Riverside Publishing.

Roid, G. H. (2003b). *Stanford-Binet Intelligence Scales, Fifth Edition, Technical manual.* Itasca, IL: Riverside Publishing.

Roid, G. H. (2003c). *Stanford-Binet Intelligence Scales, Fifth Edition, Examiner's manual.* Itasca, IL: Riverside Publishing.

Roid, G. H., Woodcock, R. W., & McGrew, K. S. (1997). *Factor analysis of the Stanford-Binet L and M forms.* Unpublished paper. Itasca, IL: Riverside Publishing.

Rokeach, M. (1973). *The nature of human values.* New York: Free Press.

Romanczyk, R. G. (1986). *Clinical utilization of microcomputer technology.* New York: Pergamon.

Romano, J. (1994, November 7). Do drunken drivers get railroaded? *New York Times,* pp. NNJ1, NNJ19.

Rome, H. P., Mataya, P., Pearson, J. S., Swenson, W., & Brannick, T. L. (1965). Automatic personality assessment. In R. W. Stacey & B. Waxman (Eds.), *Computers in biomedical research* (Vol. 1, pp. 505–524). New York: Academic Press.

Ronan, G. G., Date, A. L., & Weisbrod, M. (1995). Personal problem-solving scoring of the TAT: Sensitivity to training. *Journal of Personality Assessment, 64,* 119–131.

Rorer, L. G. (1965). The great response-style myth. *Psychological Bulletin, 63,* 129–156.

Rorschach, H. (1921/1942). *Psycho-diagnostics: A diagnostic test based on perception* (P. Lemkau & B. Kronenburg, Trans.). Berne: Huber. (First German edition: 1921. Distributed in the United States by Grune & Stratton.)

Rorschach, H., & Oberholzer, E. (1923). The application of the interpretation of form to psychoanalysis. *Journal of Nervous and Mental Diseases, 60,* 225–248, 359–379.

Rosen, J. (1998, February 23/March 2). Damage control. *New Yorker, 74,* 64–68.

Rosen, M., Simon, E. W., & McKinsey, L. (1995). Subjective measure of quality of life. *Mental Retardation, 33,* 31–34.

Rosenman, R. H., Brand, R. J., Jenkins, C. D., Friedman, M., Straus, R., & Wurm, M. (1975). Coronary heart disease in the Western Collaborative Group Study: Final followup experience of 8½ years. *Journal of the American Medical Association, 233,* 872–877.

Rosenzweig, S. (1945). The picture-association method and its application in a study of reactions to frustration. *Journal of Personality, 14,* 3–23.

Rosenzweig, S. (1978). *The Rosenzweig Picture Frustration (P-F) Study: Basic manual.* St. Louis, MO: Rana House.

Rossini, E. D., & Moretti, R. J. (1997). Thematic Apperception Test (TAT) interpretation: Practice recommendations from a survey of clinical psychology doctoral programs accredited by the American Psychological Association. *Professional Psychology, 28,* 393–398.

Roszkowski, M. J., & Spreat, S. (1981). A comparison of the psychometric and clinical methods of determining level of mental retardation. *Applied Research in Mental Retardation, 2,* 359–366.

Rothberg, J. M., & Geer-Williams, C. (1992). A comparison and review of suicide prediction scales. In R. W. Maris et al. (Eds.), *Assessment and prediction of suicide* (pp. 202–217). New York: Guilford.

Rotter, J. B. (1966). Generalized expectancies for internal versus external control of reinforcement. *Psychological Monographs, 80* (Whole Number 609).

Rotter, J. B., Lah, M. I., & Rafferty, J. E. (1992). *Rotter Incomplete Sentences Blank manual.* San Antonio, TX: Psychological Corporation.

Rotter, J. B., & Rafferty, J. E. (1950). *The manual for the Rotter Incomplete Sentences Blank.* New York: Psychological Corporation.

Rottinghaus, P. J., Betz, N. E., & Borgen, F. H. (2003). Validity of parallel measures of vocational interests and confidence. *Journal of Career Assessment, 11,* 355–378.

Rotton, J., & Kelly, I. W. (1985). Much ado about the full moon: A meta-analysis of lunar-lunacy research. *Psychological Bulletin, 97,* 286–306.

Rotundo, M., & Sackett, P. R. (1999). Effect of rater race on conclusions regarding differential prediction in cognitive ability tests. *Journal of Applied Psychology, 84,* 815–822.

Rouse, S. V., Butcher, J. N., & Miller, K. B. (1999). Assessment of substance abuse in psychotherapy clients: The effectiveness of MMPI-2 substance abuse scales. *Psychological Assessment, 11,* 101–107.

Routh, D. K., & King, K. W. (1972). Social class bias in clinical judgment. *Journal of Consulting and Clinical Psychology, 38,* 202–207.

Roy, P. (1962). The measurement of assimilation: The Spokane Indians. *American Journal of Sociology, 67,* 541–551.

Rozeboom, W. W. (1996a). What might common factors be? *Multivariate Behavioral Research, 31,* 555–570.

Rozeboom, W. W. (1996b). Factor-indeterminacy issues are not linguistic confusions. *Multivariate Behavioral Research, 31,* 637–650.

Ruch, G. M. (1925). Minimum essentials in reporting data on standard tests. *Journal of Educational Research, 12,* 349–358.

Ruch, G. M. (1933). Recent developments in statistical procedures. *Review of Educational Research, 3,* 33–40.

Ruch, W. (1993). Exhilaration and humor. In M. Lewis & J. M. Haviland (Eds.), *Handbook of emotions* (pp. 605–616). New York: Guilford.

Ruffolo, L. F., Guilmette, T. J., & Grant, W. W. (2000). Comparison of time and error rates on the Trail Making Test among patients with head injuries, experimental malingerers, patients with suspect effort on testing, and normal controls. *Clinical Neuropsychologist, 14,* 223–230.

Russell, J. S. (1984). A review of fair employment cases in the field of training. *Personnel Psychology, 37,* 261–276.

Russo, D. C., Bird, B. L., & Masek, B. J. (1980). Assessment issues in behavioral medicine. *Behavioral Assessment, 2,* 1–18.

Rutherford, A. (2003). B. F. Skinner and the auditory inkblot: The rise and fall of the verbal summator as a projective technique. *History of Psychology, 6,* 362–378.

Ryan, A. M., Sacco, J. M., McFarland, L. A., & Kriska, S. D. (2000). Applicant self-selection: Correlates of withdrawal from a multiple hurdle process. *Journal of Applied Psychology, 85,* 163–169.

Ryan, J. J., Paolo, A. M., & Brungardt, T. M. (1990). Standardization of the Wechsler Adult Intelligence Scale—Revised for persons 75 years and older. *Psychological Assessment, 2,* 404–411.

Ryan, J. J., & Ward, L. C. (1999). Validity, reliability, and standard errors of measurement for two seven-subtest short forms of the Wechsler Adult Intelligence Scale-III. *Psychological Assessment, 11,* 207–211.

Sabatelli, R. M. (1984). The Marital Comparison Level Index: A measure for assessing outcomes relative to expectations. *Journal of Marriage and the Family, 46,* 651–662.

Sachs, B. B. (1976). Some views of a deaf Rorschacher on the personality of deaf individuals. *Hearing Rehabilitation Quarterly, 2,* 13–14.

Sackett, P. R. (1994). Integrity testing for personnel selection. *Current Directions in Psychological Science, 3,* 73–76.

Sackett, P. R., Burris, L. R., & Callahan, C. (1989). Integrity testing for personnel selection: An update. *Personnel Psychology, 42,* 491–529.

Sackett, P. R., & Harris, M. M. (1984). Honesty testing for personnel selection: A review and critique. *Personnel Psychology, 37,* 221–245.

Sackett, P. R., Schmitt, N., Ellingson, J. E., & Kabin, M. B. (2001). High-stakes testing in employment, credentialing, and higher education: Prospects in a post-affirmative action world. *American Psychologist, 56,* 302–318.

Sackett, P. R., & Wilk, S. L. (1994). Within-group norming and other forms of score adjustment in preemployment testing. *American Psychologist, 49,* 929–954.

Sacks, E. (1952). Intelligence scores as a function of experimentally established social relationships between child and examiner. *Journal of Abnormal and Social Psychology, 47,* 354–358.

Sacks, O. (1989). *Seeing voices: A journey into the world of the deaf.* Berkeley: University of California.

Salas, E., Cannon-Bowers, J. A., Church-Payne, S., & Smith-Jentsch, K. A. (1998). Teams and teamwork in the military. In C. Cronin (Ed.), *Military psychology: An introduction* (pp. 71–87). Needham Heights, MA: Simon & Schuster.

Salthouse, T. A., Toth, J., Daniels, K., et al. (2000). Effects of aging on efficiency of task switching in a variant of the Trail Making Test. *Neuropsychology, 14,* 102–111.

Salvia, J., & Hritcko, T. (1984). The K-ABC and ability training. *Journal of Special Education, 18,* 345–356.

Samuda, R. J. (1982). *Psychological testing of American minorities: Issues and consequences.* New York: Harper & Row.

Sanchez, L. M., & Turner, S. M. (2003). Practicing psychology in the era of managed care. *American Psychologist, 58,* 116–129.

Sandelands, L. E., & Larson, J. R. (1985). When measurement causes task attitudes: A note from the laboratory. *Journal of Applied Psychology, 70,* 116–121.

Sandoval, J. (1995). Review of the Wechsler Intelligence Scale for Children, Third Edition. In J. C. Conoley & J. C. Impara (Eds.), *The twelfth mental measurements yearbook.*

Lincoln: Buros Institute of Measurements, University of Nebraska.

Sandoval, J., et al. (Eds.). (1998). *Test interpretation and diversity: Achieving equity in assessment.* Washington, DC: American Psychological Association.

Sandoval, J., Antunez-Bellatin, M., & Lewis, S. (2002). Using the DAS nonverbal scales with Spanish-speaking children: Translation and validation. *California School Psychologist, 7,* 7–25.

Sanfilippo, J., et al. (1986). Identifying the sexually molested preadolescent girl. *Pediatric Annals, 15,* 621–624.

Sattler, J. M. (1991). How good are federal judges in detecting differences in item difficulty on intelligence tests for ethnic groups? *Psychological Assessment, 3,* 125–129.

Sattler, J. M. (1992). *Assessment of children: WISC-III and WPPSI-R supplement.* San Diego: Author.

Saunders, E. A. (1991). Rorschach indicators of chronic childhood sexual abuse in female borderline inpatients. *Bulletin of the Menninger Clinic, 55,* 48–65.

Savickas, M. L., Alexander, D. E., Osipow, S. H., & Wolf, F. M. (1985). Measuring specialty indecision among career-decided students. *Journal of Vocational Behavior, 27,* 356–357.

Savickas, M. L., & Spokane, A. R. (Eds.). (1999). *Vocational interests: Meaning, measurement, and counseling use.* Palo Alto, CA: Davies-Black Publishing.

Savickas, M. L., Taber, B. J., & Spokane, A. R. (2002). Convergent and discriminant validity of five interest inventories. *Journal of Vocational Behavior, 61,* 139–184.

Saxe, L. (1994). Detection of deception: Polygraph and integrity tests. *Current Directions in Psychological Science, 3,* 69–73.

Saxe, L., & Ben-Shakhar, G. (1999). Admissibility of polygraph tests: The application of scientific standards post-*Daubert. Psychology, Public Policy, and Law, 5,* 203–223.

Saxton, J., McGonigle-Gibson, K. L., Swihart, A. A., Miller, V. J., & Boller, F. (1990). Assessment of the severely impaired patient: Description and validation of a new neuropsychological test battery. *Psychological Assessment, 2,* 298–303.

Sayer, A. G., Willett, J. B., & Perrin, E. C. (1993). Measuring understanding of illness causality in healthy children and in children with chronic illness: A construct validation. *Journal of Applied Developmental Psychology, 14,* 11–36.

Sayette, M. A., Shiffman, S., Tiffany, S. T., et al. (2000). The measurement of drug craving. *Addiction, 93*(Suppl. 2), S189–S210.

Scarr, S. (1992). Developmental theories for the 1990s: Development and individual differences. *Child Development, 63,* 1–19.

Scarr, S. (1993). Biological and cultural diversity: The legacy of Darwin for development. *Child Development, 64,* 1333–1353.

Schaie, K. W. (1978). External validity in the assessment of intellectual development in adulthood. *Journal of Gerontology, 33,* 695–701.

Scheid, T. L. (1999). Employment of individuals with mental disabilities: Business response to the ADA's challenge. *Behavioral Sciences and the Law, 17,* 73–91.

Schein, J. D., & Delk, M. T., Jr. (1974). *The deaf population in the United States.* Silver Springs, MD: National Association for the Deaf.

Schildroth, A., Rawlings, B., & Allen, T. (1991). Deaf students in transition: Education and employment issues for deaf adolescents. In O. Cohen & G. Long (Eds.), Selected issues in adolescence and deafness [Special issue]. *Volta Review, 93*(5), 41–53.

Schloss, I. (1981). Chicken and pickles. *Journal of Advertising Research, 21,* 47–49.

Schmand, B., Brand, N., & Kuipers, T. (1992). Procedural learning of cognitive and motor skills in psychotic patients. *Schizophrenia Research, 8*, 157–170.

Schmidt, F. L. (1988). The problem of group differences in ability scores in employment selection. *Journal of Vocational Behavior, 33*, 272–292.

Schmidt, F. L., & Hunter, J. E. (1974). Racial and ethnic bias in psychological tests: Divergent implications of two definitions of test bias. *American Psychologist, 29*, 1–8.

Schmidt, F. L., & Hunter, J. E. (1992). Development of a causal model of processes determining job performance. *Current Directions in Psychological Science, 1*, 89–92.

Schmidt, F. L., & Hunter, J. E. (1998). The validity and utility of selection methods in personnel psychology: Practical and theoretical implications of 85 years of research findings. *Psychological Bulletin, 124*, 262–274.

Schmidt, F. L., Hunter, J. E., McKenzie, R. C., & Muldrow, T. W. (1979). Impact of valid selection procedures on work force productivity. *Journal of Applied Psychology, 64*, 609–626.

Schmidt, F. L., Hunter, J. E., Outerbridge, A. N., & Trattner, M. H. (1986). The economic impact of job selection methods on size, productivity, and payroll costs of the federal work force: An empirically based demonstration. *Personnel Psychology, 32*, 1–29.

Schmitt, N. (1976). Social and situational determinants of interview decisions: Implications for the employment interview. *Personnel Psychology, 29*, 79–101.

Schmitt, N., Gooding, R., Noe, R., & Kirsch, M. (1984). Meta-analysis of validity studies published between 1964 and 1982 and the investigation of study characteristics. *Personnel Psychology, 37*, 407–422.

Schneider, B. (1987). The people make the place. *Personnel Psychology, 40*, 437–453.

Schneider, M. F. (1989). *Children's Apperceptive Story-telling Test.* Austin, TX: PRO-ED.

Schönemann, P. H. (1996a). The psychopathology of factor indeterminacy. *Multivariate Behavioral Research, 31*, 571–577.

Schönemann, P. H. (1996b). Syllogisms of factor indeterminacy. *Multivariate Behavioral Research, 31*, 651–654.

Schoop, L. H., Herrman, T. D., Johnstone, B., Callahan, C. D., & Roudebush, I. S. (2001). Two abbreviated versions of the Wechsler Adult Intelligence Scale-III: Validation among persons with traumatic brain injury. *Rehabilitation Psychology, 46*, 279–287.

Schouten, P. G. W., & Kirkpatrick, L. A. (1993). Questions and concerns about the Miller Assessment for Preschoolers. *Occupational Therapy Journal of Research, 13*, 7–28.

Schuh, A. J. (1978). Contrast effect in the interview. *Bulletin of the Psychonomic Society, 11*, 195–196.

Schuler, M. E., Nair, P., & Harrington, D. (2003). Developmental outcome of drug-exposed children through 30 months: A comparison of Bayley and Bayley-II. *Psychological Assessment, 15*, 435–438.

Schulte, A. A., Gilbertson, E., Kratochwil, T. R. (2000). Educators' perceptions and documentation of testing accommodations for students with disabilities. *Special Services in the Schools, 16*, 35–56.

Schultz, B. M., Dixon, E. B., Lindenberger, J. C., & Ruther, N. J. (1989). *Solomon's sword: A practical guide to conducting child custody evaluations.* San Francisco: Jossey-Bass.

Schwartz, L. A. (1932). Social situation pictures in the psychiatric interview. *American Journal of Orthopsychiatry, 2*, 124–132.

Schwartz, N., Groves, R. M., & Schuman, H. (1998). Survey methods. In D. T. Gilbert et al. (Eds.), *The handbook of social psychology* (4th ed., Vol. 1, pp. 143–179). New York: McGraw-Hill.

Scott, L. H. (1981). Measuring intelligence with the Goodenough-Harris Drawing Test. *Psychological Bulletin, 89*, 483–505.

Seagull, F. J., & Gopher, D. (1997). Training head movement in visual scanning: An embedded approach to the development of piloting skills with helmet-mounted displays. *Journal of Experimental Psychology: Applied, 3*, 163–180.

Sears, R. R. (1977). Sources of life satisfaction of the Terman gifted men. *American Psychologist, 32*, 119–281.

Seashore, C. E. (1938). *Psychology of music.* New York: McGraw-Hill.

Sebold, J. (1987). Indicators of child sexual abuse in males. *Social Casework, 68*, 75–80.

Segal, S. P., Redman, D., & Silverman, C. (2000). Measuring clients' satisfaction with self-help agencies. *Psychiatric Services, 51*, 1148–1152.

Seibert, S. E., & Kraimer, M. L. (2001). The five-factor model of personality and career success. *Journal of Vocational Behavior, 58*, 1–21.

Serby, M., Corwin, J., Conrad, P., et al. (1985). Olfactory dysfunction in Alzheimer's disease and Parkinson's disease. *American Journal of Psychiatry, 142*, 781–782.

Serby, M., Larson, P., & Kalkstein, D. (1991). The nature and course of olfactory deficits in Alzheimer's disease. *American Journal of Psychiatry, 148*, 357–360.

Serin, R. C., Peters, R. DeV., & Barbaree, H. E. (1990). Predictors of psychopathy and release outcome in a criminal population. *Psychological Assessment, 2*, 419–422.

Serpell, R. (1979). How specific are perceptual skills? A cross-cultural study of pattern reproduction. *British Journal of Psychology, 70*, 365–380.

Sevig, T. D., Highlen, P. S., & Adams, E. M. (2000). Development and validation of the Self-Identity Inventory (SII): A multicultural identity development instrument. *Cultural Diversity and Ethnic Minority Psychology, 6*, 168–182.

Shah, S. A. (1969). Privileged communications, confidentiality, and privacy: Privileged communications. *Professional Psychology, 1*, 56–59.

Shakow, D., & Rosenzweig, S. (1940). The use of the tautophone ("verbal summator") as an auditory apperceptive test for the study of personality. *Character and Personality, 8*, 216–226.

Shapiro, E. S., & Skinner, C. H. (1990). Principles of behavior assessment. In C. R. Reynolds & R. W. Kamphaus (Eds.), *Handbook of psychological and educational assessment of children: Personality, behavior & context* (pp. 343–363). New York: Guilford.

Shavelson, R. J., Webb, N. M., & Rowley, G. L. (1989). Generalizability theory. *American Psychologist, 44*, 922–932.

Shaw, S. R., Swerdlik, M. E., & Laurent, J. (1993). Review of the WISC-III. In B. A. Bracken (Ed.), *Monograph series, Advances in psychoeducational assessment: Wechsler Intelligence Scale for Children, Third Edition: Journal of Psychoeducational Assessment* (pp. 151–159). Brandon, VT: Clinical Psychology Publishing.

Shaywitz, B. A., Shaywitz, S. E., Pugh, K. R., et al. (1995). Sex differences in the functional organization of the brain for language. *Nature, 373*, 607–609.

Shedler, J. (2000). The Shedler QPD Panel (Quick Psych-Diagnostics Panel): A psychiatric "lab test" for primary care. In M. E. Maruish (Ed.), *Handbook of psychological assessment in primary care settings* (pp. 277–296). Mahwah, NJ: Erlbaum.

Sheehan, P. W., Grigg, L., & McCann, T. (1984). Memory distortion following exposure to false information in hypnosis. *Journal of Abnormal Psychology, 93*, 259–296.

Sheffield, D., Biles, P. L., Orom, H., Maixner, W., & Sheps, D. S. (2000). Race and sex differences in cutaneous pain perception. *Psychosomatic Medicine, 62*, 517–523.

Shell, R. W. (1980). Psychiatric testimony: Science or fortune telling? *Barrister, 7,* 6–12.

Shepard, L. A. (1983). The role of measurement in educational policy: Lessons from the identification of learning disabilities. *Journal of Special Education, 14,* 79–91.

Sherrill-Pattison, S., Donders, J., & Thompson, E. (2000). Influence of demographic variables on neuropsychological test performance after traumatic brain injury. *Clinical Neuropsychologist, 14,* 496–503.

Shiffman, S., Hufford, M., Hickcox, M., et al. (1997). Remember that? A comparison of real-time versus retrospective recall of smoking lapses. *Journal of Consulting and Clinical Psychology, 65,* 292–300.

Shirom, A. (2003). Job-related burnout: A review. In J. C. Quick & L. E. Tetrick (Eds.), *Handbook of occupational health psychology* (pp. 245–264). Washington, DC: American Psychological Association.

Shneidman, E. S. (1952). Manual for the Make a Picture Story Method. *Projective Techniques Monographs, 2.*

Shneidman, E. S. (1958). Some relationships between thematic and drawing materials. In E. F. Hammer (Ed.), *The clinical applications of projective drawings* (pp. 296–307). Springfield, IL: Charles C Thomas.

Shock, N. W., Greulich, R. C., Andres, R., et al. (1984). *Normal human aging: The Baltimore longitudinal study of aging* (NIH Publication No. 84–2450). Washington, DC: U.S. Government Printing Office.

Shockley, W. (1971). Models, mathematics, and the moral obligation to diagnose the origin of Negro IQ deficits. *Review of Educational Research, 41,* 369–377.

Shriner, J. G. (2000). Legal perspectives on school outcomes assessment for students with disabilities. *Journal of Special Education, 33,* 232–239.

Shuey, A. M. (1966). *The testing of Negro intelligence* (2nd ed.). New York: Social Science.

Shum, D., Short, L., Tunstall, J., et al. (2000). Performance of children with traumatic brain injury on a 4-disk version of the Tower of London and the Porteus Maze. *Brain & Cognition, 44,* 59–62.

Shuman, D. W., & Sales, B. D. (1999). The impact of *Daubert* and its progeny on the admissibility of behavioral and social science evidence. *Psychology, Public Policy, and Law, 5,* 3–15.

Siegler, R. S., & Richards, D. (1980). The development of intelligence. In R. S. Sternberg (Chair), *People's conception of the nature of intelligence.* Symposium presented at the 88th annual convention of the American Psychological Association, Montreal, Canada.

Silka, V. R., & Hauser, M. J. (1997). Psychiatric assessment of the person with mental retardation. *Psychiatric Annals, 27*(3), 162–169.

Silverstein, A. B. (1990). Short forms of individual intelligence tests. *Psychological Assessment, 2,* 3–11.

Silverstein, M. L., & Nelson, L. D. (2000). Clinical and research implications of revising psychological tests. *Psychological Assessment, 12,* 298–303.

Simpson, R. (1970). Study of the comparability of the WISC and WAIS. *Journal of Consulting and Clinical Psychology, 2,* 156–158.

Simpson, R. L., Griswold, D. E., & Myles, B. S. (1999). Educators' assessment accommodation preferences for students with autism. *Focus on Autism and Other Developmental Disabilities, 14*(4), 212–219, 230.

Sines, J. O. (1966). Actuarial methods in personality assessment. In B. A. Maher (Ed.), *Progress in experimental personality research* (Vol. 3, pp. 133–193). New York: Academic Press.

Siperstein, G. N., Leffert, J. S., & Wenz-Gross, M. (1997). The quality of friendships between children with and without learning problems. *American Journal on Mental Retardation, 102,* 111–125.

Sivec, H. J., Lynn, S. J., & Garske, J. P. (1994). The effect of somatoform disorders and paranoid psychotic role-related dissimulations as a response set on the MMPI-2. *Assessment, 1,* 69–81.

Skafte, D. (1985). *Child custody evaluations: A practical guide.* Beverly Hills, CA: Sage.

Skinner, B. F. (1979). *The shaping of a behaviorist.* New York: Knopf.

Skinner, H. A., & Allen, B. A. (1983). Does the computer make a difference? Computerized versus face-to-face versus self-report assessment of alcohol, drug, and tobacco use. *Journal of Consulting and Clinical Psychology, 51,* 267–275.

Skinner, H. A., & Pakula, A. (1986). Challenge of computers in psychological assessment. *Professional Psychology: Research and Practice, 17,* 44–50.

Skolnick, J. H. (1961). Scientific theory and scientific evidence: An analysis of lie detection. *Yale Law Journal, 70,* 694–728.

Slakter, M. J., Crehan, K. D., & Koehler, R. A. (1975). Longitudinal studies of risk taking on objective examinations. *Educational and Psychological Measurement, 35,* 97–105.

Slate, J. R., Jones, C. H., Murray, R. A., & Coulter, C. (1993). Evidence that practitioners err in administering and scoring the WAIS-R. *Measurement and Evaluation in Counseling and Development, 25,* 156–161.

Slater, S. B., Vukmanovic, C., Macukanovic, P., Prvulovic, T., & Cutler, J. L. (1974). The definition and measurement of disability. *Social Science and Medicine, 8,* 305–308.

Slay, D. K. (1984). A portable Halstead-Reitan Category Test. *Journal of Clinical Psychology, 40,* 1023–1027.

Slobogin, C. (1999). The admissibility of behavioral science information in criminal trials: From primitivism to *Daubert* to Voice. *Psychology, Public Policy, and Law, 5,* 100–119.

Smith, D. E. (1986). Training programs for performance appraisal: A review. *Academy of Management Review, 11,* 22–40.

Smith, D. K. (1985). *Test use and perceived competency: A survey of school psychologists.* Unpublished manuscript, University of Wisconsin–River Falls, School Psychology Program.

Smith, D. K., Bolin, J. A., & Stovall, D. R. (1988). K-ABC stability in a preschool sample: A longitudinal study. *Journal of Psychoeducational Assessment, 6,* 396–403.

Smith, D. K., & Knudtson, L. S. (1990). *K-ABC and S-B:FE relationships in an at-risk preschool sample.* Paper presented at the Annual Meeting of the American Psychological Association, Boston.

Smith, D. K., Lasee, M. J., & McCloskey, G. M. (1990). *Test-retest reliability of the AGS Early Screening Profiles.* Paper presented at the Annual Meeting of the National Association of School Psychologists, San Francisco.

Smith, D. K., & Lyon, M. A. (1987). *Children with learning difficulties: Differences in ability patterns as a function of placement.* Paper presented at the Annual Meeting of the American Educational Research Association, Washington, DC. (ERIC Document Reproduction Service No. ED 285 317).

Smith, D. K., St. Martin, M. E., & Lyon, M. A. (1989). A validity study of the Stanford-Binet Fourth Edition with students with learning disabilities. *Journal of Learning Disabilities, 22,* 260–261.

Smith, G. E., Ivnik, R. J., Malec, J. F., Kokmen, E., Tangalos, E. G., & Kurland, L. T. (1992). Mayo's older Americans normative studies (MOANS): Factor structure of a core battery. *Psychological Assessment, 4,* 382–390.

Smith, G. T., McCarthy, D. M., & Anderson, K. G. (2000). On the sins of short form development. *Psychological Assessment, 12,* 102–111.

Smith, M. (1948). Cautions concerning the use of the Taylor-Russell tables in employee selection. *Journal of Applied Psychology, 32,* 595–600.

Smith, R. E. (1963). Examination by computer. *Behavioral Science, 8,* 76–79.

Smith, R. G., & Iwata, B. A. (1997). Antecedent influences on behavior disorders. *Journal of Applied Behavior Analysis, 30,* 343–375.

Smith, T., Smith, B. L., Bramlett, R. K., & Hicks, N. (2000). WISC-III stability over a three-year period in students with learning disabilities. *Research in the Schools, 7,* 37–41.

Smith, T. C., Matthews, N., Smith, B., & Kennedy, S. (1993). Subtest scatter and Kaufman regroupings on the WISC-R in non-learning-disabled and learning-disabled children. *Psychology in the Schools, 30,* 24–28.

Smith, T. T., Myers-Jennings, C., & Coleman, T. (2000). Assessment of language skills in rural preschool children. *Communication Disorders Quarterly, 21,* 98–113.

Smither, J. W., Reilly, R. R., & Buda, R. (1988). Effect of prior performance information on ratings of present performance: Contrast versus assimilation revisited. *Journal of Applied Psychology, 73,* 487–496.

Smither, R., & Rodriguez-Giegling, M. (1982). Personality, demographics, and acculturation of Vietnamese and Nicaraguan refugees to the United States. *International Journal of Psychology, 17,* 19–25.

Snowden, L. R., & Hines, A. M. (1999). A scale to assess African American acculturation. *Journal of Black Psychology, 25,* 36–47.

Snyder, C. R., Shenkel, R. J., & Lowery, C. R. (1977). Acceptance of personality interpretations: The "Barnum effect" and beyond. *Journal of Consulting and Clinical Psychology, 45,* 104–114.

Snyder, C. R., Shenkel, R. J., & Schmidt, A. (1976). Effect of role perspective and client psychiatric history on locus of problem. *Journal of Consulting and Clinical Psychology, 44,* 467–472.

Snyder, D. K. (1981). *Marital Satisfaction Inventory (MSI) manual.* Los Angeles: Western Psychological Services.

Snyder, D. K. (2000). Computer-assisted judgment: Defining strengths and liabilities. *Psychological Assessment, 12,* 52–60.

Snyder, D. K., Widiger, T. A., & Hoover, D. W. (1990). Methodological considerations in validating computer-based test interpretations: Controlling for response bias. *Psychological Assessment, 2,* 470–477.

Snyder, P., Lawson, S., Thompson, B., Stricklin, S., & Sexton, D. (1993). Evaluating the psychometric integrity of instruments used in early intervention research: The Battelle Developmental Inventory. *Topics in Early Childhood Special Education, 32,* 273–280.

Sobell, L. C., & Sobell, M. B. (1992). Timeline followback: A technique for assessing self-reported alcohol consumption. In R. Z. Litten & J. P. Allen (Eds.), *Measuring alcohol consumption* (pp. 41–71). Totowa, NJ: Humana Press.

Sobell, L. C., & Sobell, M. B. (2000). Alcohol timeline followback (TLFB). In American Psychiatric Association (Ed.), *Handbook of psychiatric measures* (pp. 477–479).

Sodowsky, G. R., & Carey, J. C. (1988). Relationships between acculturation-related demographics and cultural attitudes of an Asian-Indian immigrant group. *Journal of Multicultural Counseling and Development, 16*(July), 117–136.

Sokal, M. M. (1991). Psyche Cattell (1893–1989). *American Psychologist, 46,* 72.

Solomon, I. L., & Starr, B. D. (1968). *The School Apperception Method.* New York: Springer.

Solomon, P. R., Hirschoff, A., Kelly, B., et al. (1998). A 7-minute neurocognitive screening battery highly sensitive to Alzheimer's disease. *Archives of Neurology, 55,* 349–355.

Sommers-Flanagan, J., & Sommers-Flanagan, R. (1995). Intake interviewing with suicidal patients: A systematic approach. *Professional Psychology: Research and Practice, 26,* 41–47.

Sontag, L. W., Baker, C. T., & Nelson, V. L. (1958). Personality as a determinant of performance. *American Journal of Orthopsychiatry, 25,* 555–562.

Spanier, G. (1976). Measuring dyadic adjustment: New scales for assessing the quality of marriage and similar dyads. *Journal of Marriage and the Family, 38,* 15–28.

Spanier, G. B., & Filsinger, E. (1983). The Dyadic Adjustment Scale. In E. Filsinger (Ed.), *Marriage and family assessment.* Beverly Hills, CA: Sage.

Sparrow, S. S., Balla, D. A., & Cicchetti, D. V. (1984a). *Vineland Adaptive Behavior Scales, Interview Edition: Expanded form manual.* Circle Pines, MN: American Guidance Service.

Sparrow, S. S., Balla, D. A., & Cicchetti, D. V. (1984b). *Vineland Adaptive Behavior Scales, Interview Edition: Survey form manual.* Circle Pines, MN: American Guidance Service.

Sparrow, S. S., Balla, D. A., & Cicchetti, D. V. (1985). *Vineland Adaptive Behavior Scales, Classroom Edition manual.* Circle Pines, MN: American Guidance Service.

Spearman, C. (1927). *The abilities of man: Their nature and measurement.* New York: Macmillan.

Spearman, C. E. (1904). "General intelligence" objectively determined and measured. *American Journal of Psychiatry, 15,* 201–293.

Spearman, C. E. (1930–1936). Autobiography. In C. Murchison (Ed.), *A history of psychology in autobiography* (3 vols.). Worcester, MA: Clark University Press.

Speth, E. B. (1992). *Test-retest reliabilities of Bricklin Perceptual Scales.* Unpublished doctoral dissertation, Hahneman University Graduate School, Philadelphia.

Spiegel, J. S., Leake, B., Spiegel, T. M., et al. (1988). What are we measuring? An examination of self-reported functional status measures. *Arthritis and Rheumatism, 31,* 721–728.

Spielberger, C. D., et al. (1980). *Test Anxiety Inventory: Preliminary professional manual.* Palo Alto, CA: Consulting Psychologists Press.

Spitz, H. H., Minsky, S. K., & Bessellieu, C. L. (1985). Influence of planning time and first-move strategy on Tower of Hanoi problem-solving performance of mentally retarded young adults and non-retarded children. *American Journal of Mental Deficiency, 90,* 46–56.

Spitzer, R. L. (1999). Harmful dysfunction and the *DSM* definition of mental disorder. *Journal of Abnormal Psychology, 108,* 430–432.

Spivack, G., & Spotts, J. (1966). *Devereux Child Behavior Rating Scale manual.* Devon, PA: Devereux Foundation.

Spivack, G., Spotts, J., & Haimes, P. E. (1967). *Devereux Adolescent Behavior Rating Scale.* Devon, PA: Devereux Foundation.

Spokane, A. R., & Decker, A. R. (1999). Expressed and measured interests. In M. L. Savickas & A. R. Spokane (Eds.), *Vocational interests: Meaning, measurement, and counseling use* (pp. 211–233). Palo Alto, CA: Davies-Black Publishing.

Spranger, E. (1928). *Types of men* (P. J. W. Pigors, Trans.). Halle, Germany: Niemeyer.

Spreen, O., & Benton, A. L. (1965). Comparative studies of some psychological tests for cerebral damage. *Journal of Nervous and Mental Disease, 140,* 323–333.

Spruill, J., & May, J. (1988). The mentally retarded offender: Prevalence rates based on individual versus group intelligence tests. *Criminal Justice and Behavior, 15,* 484–491.

Spruill, J. A. (1993). Secondary assessment: Structuring the transition process. *Learning Disabilities Research & Practice, 8*, 127–132.

Staggs, G. D., Larson, L. M., & Borgen, F. H. (2003). Convergence of specific factors in vocational interests and personality. *Journal of Career Assessment, 11*, 243–261.

Stahl, P. M. (1995). *Conducting child custody evaluations.* Thousand Oaks, CA: Sage.

Stanczak, D. E., Lynch, M. D., McNeil, C. K., & Brown, B. (1998). The Expanded Trail Making Test: Rationale, development, and psychometric properties. *Archives of Clinical Neuropsychology, 13*, 473–487.

Stanford Special Report, Number 9. (1992). Bias control. San Antonio, TX: Psychological Corporation/Harcourt Brace Jovanovich.

Stanley, J. C. (1971). Reliability. In R. L. Thorndike (Ed.), *Educational measurement* (2nd ed.). Washington, DC: American Council on Education.

Starch, D., & Elliot, E. C. (1912). Reliability of grading of high school work in English. *School Review, 20*, 442–457.

Staw, B. M., Bell, N. E., & Clausen, J. A. (1986). The dispositional approach to job attitudes: A lifetime longitudinal test. *Administrative Science Quarterly, 31*, 56–77.

Steadman, H. J. (1983). Predicting dangerousness among the mentally ill: Art, magic, and science. *International Journal of Law and Psychiatry, 6*, 381–390.

Stedman, J. M., Hatch, J. P., & Schoenfeld, L. S. (2000). Pre-internship preparation in psychological testing and psychotherapy: What internship directors say they expect. *Professional Psychology: Research and Practice, 31*, 321–326.

Steiger, J. H. (1996a). Dispelling some myths about factor indeterminacy. *Multivariate Behavioral Research, 31*, 539–550.

Steiger, J. H. (1996b). Coming full circle in the history of factor indeterminacy. *Multivariate Behavioral Research, 31*, 617–630.

Steinberg, M., Cicchetti, D., Buchanan, J., & Hall, P. (1993). Clinical assessment of dissociative symptoms and disorders: The Structured Clinical Interview for DSM-IV Dissociative Disorders (SCID-D). *Dissociation: Progress in Dissociative Disorders, 6*, 3–15.

Stephens, J. J. (1992). Assessing ethnic minorities. *SPA Exchange, 2*(1), 4–6.

Stephenson, W. (1953). *The study of behavior: Q-technique and its methodology.* Chicago: University of Chicago.

Sternberg, R. J. (1981). The nature of intelligence. *New York Education Quarterly, 12*(3), 10–17.

Sternberg, R. J. (1982, April). Who's intelligent? *Psychology Today,* pp. 30–33, 35–36, 38–39.

Sternberg, R. J. (1985). *Beyond IQ: A triarchic theory of human intelligence.* Cambridge: Cambridge University Press.

Sternberg, R. J. (1986). Intelligence is mental self-government. In R. J. Sternberg & D. K. Detterman (Eds.), *What is intelligence?* (pp. 141–148). Norwood, NJ: Ablex.

Sternberg, R. J. (1994). PRSVL: An integrative framework for understanding mind in context. In R. J. Sternberg & R. K. Wagner (Eds.), *Mind in context* (pp. 218–232). Cambridge: Cambridge University Press.

Sternberg, R. J. (1997). Managerial intelligence. *Journal of Management, 23*, 475–493.

Sternberg, R. J., & Berg, C. A. (1986). Quantitative integration: Definitions of intelligence: A comparison of the 1921 and 1986 symposia. In R. J. Sternberg & D. K. Detterman (Eds.), *What is intelligence?* (pp. 155–162). Norwood, NJ: Ablex.

Sternberg, R. J., Conway, B. E., Ketron, J. L., & Bernstein, M. (1981). People's conceptions of intelligence. *Journal of Personality and Social Psychology, 41*, 37–55.

Sternberg, R. J., & Detterman, D. K. (Eds.). (1986). *What is intelligence?* Norwood, NJ: Ablex.

Sternberg, R. J., Lautrey, J., & Lubart, T. I. (Eds.). (2003). *Models of intelligence.* Washington, DC: APA Books.

Stevens, C. D., & Macintosh, G. (2003). Personality and attractiveness of activities within sales jobs. *Journal of Personal Selling & Sales Management, 23*, 23–37.

Stice, E., Fisher, M., & Lowe, M. R. (2004). Are dietary restraint scales valid measures of acute dietary restriction? Unobtrusive observational data suggest not. *Psychological Assessment, 16*, 51–59.

Stillman, R. (1974). *Assessment of deaf-blind children: The Callier-Azusa Scale.* Paper presented at the Intercom '74, Hyannis, MA.

Stinnett, T. A. (1997). "AAMR Adaptive Behavior Scale-School: 2" Test review. *Journal of Psychoeducational Assessment, 15*, 361–372.

Stokes, J. B. (1977). Comment on "Socially reinforced obsessing: Etiology of a disorder in a Christian Scientist." *Journal of Consulting and Clinical Psychology, 45*, 1164–1165.

Stone, A. A. (1986). Vermont adopts *Tarasoff:* A real barn-burner. *American Journal of Psychiatry, 143*, 352–355.

Stone, B. J. (1992). Prediction of achievement by Asian-American and White children. *Journal of School Psychology, 30*, 91–99.

Stone, D. R. (1950). A recorded auditory apperception test as a new projective technique. *Journal of Psychology, 29*, 349–353.

Stoppard, J. M., & Gruchy, C. D. G. (1993). Gender, context, and expression of positive emotion. *Personality and Social Psychology Bulletin, 19*, 143–150.

Storandt, M. (1994). General principles of assessment of older adults. In M. Storandt & G. R. VandenBos (Eds.), *Neuro-psychological assessment of dementia and depression in older adults: A clinician's guide* (pp. 7–32). Washington, DC: American Psychological Association.

Storey, K. (1997). Quality of life issues in social skills assessment of persons with disabilities. *Education and Training in Mental Retardation and Developmental Disabilities, 32*, 197–200.

Stout, C. E., Levant, R. F., Reed, G. M., & Murphy, M. J. (2001). Contracts: A primer for psychologists. *Professional Psychology: Research and Practice, 32*, 89–91.

Straus, M. A. (1979). Measuring intrafamily conflict and violence: The Conflict Tactics (CT) Scales. *Journal of Marriage and the Family, 41*, 75–85.

Strauss, A. A., & Lehtinen, L. E. (1947). *Psychopathology and education of the brain injured child.* New York: Grune & Stratton.

Strauss, E., Ottfried, S., & Hunter, M. (2000). Implications of test revisions for research. *Psychological Assessment, 12*, 237–244.

Streiner, D. L. (2003a). Being inconsistent about consistency: When coefficient alpha does and doesn't matter. *Journal of Personality Assessment, 80*, 217–222.

Streiner, D. L. (2003b). Starting at the beginning: An introduction to coefficient alpha and internal consistency. *Journal of Personality Assessment, 80*, 99–103.

Stricker, G., & Gold, J. R. (1999). The Rorschach: Toward a nomothetically based, idiographically applicable configurational model. *Psychological Assessment, 11*, 240–250.

Stricker, G., & Healey, B. J. (1990). Projective assessment of object relations: A review of the empirical literature. *Psychological Assessment, 2*, 219–230.

Strong, E. K., Jr., Hansen, J. C., & Campbell, D. C. (1985). *Strong Vocational Interest Blank. Revised edition of Form T325, Strong-Campbell Interest Inventory.* Stanford, CA: Stanford University. (Distributed by Consulting Psychologists Press)

Sturges, J. W. (1998). Practical use of technology in professional practice. *Professional Psychology: Research and Practice, 29,* 183–188.

Subich, L. M. (1996). Addressing diversity in the process of career assessment. In M. L. Savickas & W. B. Walsh (Eds.), *Handbook of career counseling: Theory and practice* (pp. 277–289). Palo Alto, CA: Davies-Black.

Suczek, R. F., & Klopfer, W. G. (1952). Interpretation of the Bender-Gestalt Test: The associative value of the figures. *American Journal of Orthopsychiatry, 22,* 62–75.

Sue, D. W., & Sue, D. (2003). *Counseling the culturally diverse: Theory and practice* (4th ed.). New York: Wiley.

Sugarman, A. (1991). Where's the beef? Putting personality back into personality assessment. *Journal of Personality Assessment, 56,* 130–144.

Suinn, R. M., Rickard-Figueroa, K., Lew, S., & Vigil, S. (1987). The Suinn-Lew Asian Self-Identity Acculturation Scale: An initial report. *Educational and Psychological Measurement, 47,* 401–407.

Sullivan, H. S. (1953). *The interpersonal theory of psychiatry.* New York: Norton.

Sullivan, P. M. (1982). Administration modifications on the WISC-R Performance Scale with different categories of deaf children. *American Annals of the Deaf, 127,* 780–788.

Sullivan, P. M., & Brookhouser, P. E. (Eds.). (1996). *Proceedings of the Fourth Annual Conference on the Habilitation and Rehabilitation of Hearing Impaired Adolescents.* Boys Town, NE: Boys Town.

Sullivan, P. M., & Burley, S. K. (1990). Mental testing of the deaf child. In C. Reynolds & R. Kamphaus (Eds.), *Handbook of psychological and educational assessment of children* (pp. 761–788). New York: Guilford.

Sullivan, P. M., & Montoya, L. A. (1997). Factor analysis of the WISC-III with deaf and hard-of-hearing children. *Psychological Assessment, 9,* 317–321.

Sullivan, P. M., & Schulte, L. E. (1992). Factor analysis of WISC-R with deaf and hard-of-hearing children. *Psychological Assessment, 4,* 537–540.

Sundberg, N. D. (1955). The acceptability of "fake" versus "bona fide" personality test interpretations. *Journal of Abnormal and Social Psychology, 50,* 145–147.

Sundberg, N. D., & Gonzales, L. R. (1981). Cross-cultural and cross-ethnic assessment: Overview and issues. In P. McReynolds (Ed.), *Advances in psychological assessment* (Vol. 5, pp. 460–541). San Francisco: Jossey-Bass.

Sundberg, N. D., & Tyler, L. E. (1962). *Clinical psychology.* New York: Appleton-Century-Crofts.

Super, C. M. (1983). Cultural variation in the meaning and uses of children's "intelligence." In J. B. Deregowski, S. Dziurawiec, & R. C. Annis (Eds.), *Explorations in cross-cultural psychology.* Lisse, Netherlands: Swets & Zeitlinger.

Sutton v. United Airlines. 527 U.S. 471, 119 S. Ct. 213 (1999).

Sutton-Simon, K., & Goldfried, M. R. (1979). Faulty thinking patterns in two types of anxiety. *Cognitive Therapy and Research, 3,* 193–203.

Suzuki, L. A., Ponterotto, J. G., & Meller, P. J. (Eds.). (2000). *Handbook of multicultural assessment* (2nd ed.). San Francisco: Jossey-Bass.

Swallow, R. (1981). Fifty assessment instruments commonly used with blind and partially seeing individuals. *Journal of Visual Impairment and Blindness, 75,* 65–72.

Swanson, J. L. (1992). The structure of vocational interests for African-American college students. *Journal of Vocational Behavior, 40,* 144–157.

Sweet, J. J., Moberg, P. J., & Tovian, S. M. (1990). Evaluation of Wechsler Adult Intelligence Scale—Revised premorbid IQ formulas in clinical populations. *Psychological Assessment, 2,* 41–44.

Swensen, C. H. (1968). Empirical evaluations of human figure drawings: 1957–1966. *Psychological Bulletin, 70,* 20–44.

Swerdlik, M. E. (1985). Review of Brigance Diagnostic Comprehensive Inventory of Basic Skills. In J. V. Mitchell, Jr. (Ed.), *The ninth mental measurements yearbook* (pp. 214–215). Lincoln: Buros Institute of Mental Measurements, University of Nebraska.

Swerdlik, M. E. (1992). Review of the Otis-Lennon School Ability Test. In J. J. Kramer & J. C. Conoley (Eds.), *The eleventh mental measurements yearbook.* Lincoln: Buros Institute of Mental Measurements, University of Nebraska.

Swerdlik, M. E., & Dornback, F. (1988, April). *An interpretation guide to the fourth edition of the Stanford-Binet Intelligence Scale.* Paper presented at the annual meeting of the National Association of School Psychologists, Chicago.

Swift, J. W. (1944). Reliability of Rorschach scoring categories with pre-school children. *Child Development, 15,* 207–216.

Sylvester, R. H. (1913). Clinical psychology adversely criticized. *Psychological Clinic, 7,* 182–188.

Symonds, P. M. (1949). *Adolescent fantasy: An investigation of the picture-story method of personality study.* New York: Columbia University.

Takeuchi, J., Solomon, F., & Menninger, W. W. (Eds.). (1981). *Behavioral science and the Secret Service: Toward the prevention of assassination.* Washington, DC: National Academy.

Tallent, N. (1958). On individualizing the psychologist's clinical evaluation. *Journal of Clinical Psychology, 114,* 243–244.

Tamkin, A. S., & Kunce, J. T. (1985). A comparison of three neuropsychological tests: The Weigl, Hooper and Benton. *Journal of Clinical Psychology, 41,* 660–664.

Tan, U. (1993). Normal distribution of hand preference and its bimodality. *International Journal of Neuroscience, 68,* 61–65.

Taormina, R. J., & Bauer, T. N. (2000). Organizational socialization in two cultures: Results from the United States and Hong Kong. *International Journal of Organizational Analysis, 8,* 262–289.

Tate, D. G., & Pledger, C. (2003). An integrative conceptual framework of disability: New directions for research. *American Psychologist, 58,* 289–295.

Taylor, D. M. (2002). *The quest for identity: From minority groups to Generation Xers.* Westport, CT: Praeger.

Taylor, H. C., & Russell, J. T. (1939). The relationship of validity coefficients to the practical effectiveness of tests in selection. *Journal of Applied Psychology, 23,* 565–578.

Taylor, L. B. (1979). Psychological assessment of neurosurgical patients. In T. Rasmussen & R. Marino (Eds.), *Functional neurosurgery.* New York: Raven.

Taylor, R. L. (1980). Use of the AAMD classification system: A review of recent research. *American Journal of Mental Deficiency, 85,* 116–119.

Teague, W. (State Superintendent of Education). (1983). *Basic competency education: Reading, language, mathematics specifications for the Alabama High School Graduation Examination* (Bulletin No. 4). Montgomery: Alabama State Department of Education.

Tein, J.-Y., Sandler, I. N., & Zautra, A. J. (2000). Stressful life events, psychological distress, coping, and parenting of divorced mothers: A longitudinal study. *Journal of Family Psychology, 14,* 27–41.

Tellegen, A. (1985). Structures of mood and personality and their relevance to assessing anxiety with an emphasis on self-report. In A. H. Tuma & J. D. Master (Eds.), *Anxiety and the anxiety disorders* (pp. 681–706). Hillsdale, NJ: Erlbaum.

Tellegen, A., & Ben-Porath, Y. S. (1992). The new uniform *T* scores for the MMPI-2: Rationale, derivation, and appraisal. *Psychological Assessment, 4,* 145–155.

Tenopyr, M. L. (1999). A scientist-practitioner's viewpoint on the admissibility of behavioral and social scientific information. *Psychology, Public Policy, and Law, 5,* 194–202.

Teplin, S. W., et al. (1991). Neurodevelopmental health, and growth status at age 6 years of children with birth weights less than 1001 grams. *Journal of Pediatrics, 118,* 768–777.

Terman, L. M., et al. (1925). *The mental and physical traits of a thousand gifted children: Vol. 1. Genetic studies of genius.* Stanford, CA: Stanford University.

Terman, L. M., & Miles, C. C. (1936). *Sex and personality: Studies in masculinity and femininity.* New York: McGraw-Hill.

Tharinger, D. J., & Stark, K. (1990). A qualitative versus quantitative approach to evaluating the Draw-A-Person and Kinetic Family Drawing: A study of mood- and anxiety-disorder children. *Psychological Assessment, 2,* 365–375.

Thomas, A. D., & Dudek, S. Z. (1985). Interpersonal affect in Thematic Apperception Test responses: A scoring system. *Journal of Personality Assessment, 49,* 30–36.

Thompson, A. E. (1986). An object relational theory of affect maturity: Applications to the Thematic Apperception Test. In M. Kissen (Ed.), *Assessing object relations phenomena* (pp. 207–224). Madison, CT: International Universities.

Thompson, C. (1949). The Thompson modification of the Thematic Apperception Test. *Journal of Projective Techniques, 13,* 469–478.

Thompson, J. K., & Smolak, L. (Eds.). (2001). *Body image, eating disorders, and obesity in youth: Assessment, prevention, and treatment.* Washington, DC: APA Books.

Thompson, J. K. & Thompson, C. M. (1986). Body size distortion and self-esteem in asymptomatic, normal weight males and females. *International Journal of Eating Disorders, 5,* 1061–1068.

Thompson, J. M., & Sones, R. (1973). *The Education Apperception Test.* Los Angeles: Western Psychological Services.

Thompson, M. D., Scott, J. G., & Dickson, S. W. (1999). Clinical utility of the Trail Making Test practice time. *Clinical Neuropsychologist, 13,* 450–455.

Thompson, R. J., Gustafson, K. E., Meghdadpour, S., & Harrell, E. S. (1992). The role of biomedical and psychosocial processes in the intellectual and academic functioning of children and adolescents with cystic fibrosis. *Journal of Clinical Psychology, 48,* 3–10.

Thorndike, E. L., et al. (1921). Intelligence and its measurement: A symposium. *Journal of Educational Psychology, 12,* 123–147, 195–216.

Thorndike, E. L., Bregman, E. O., Cobb, M. V., Woodward, E., & the staff of the Division of Psychology of the Institute of Educational Research of Teachers College, Columbia University. (1927). *The measurement of intelligence.* New York: Bureau of Publications, Teachers College, Columbia University.

Thorndike, E. L., Lay, W., & Dean, P. R. (1909). The relation of accuracy in sensory discrimination to general intelligence. *American Journal of Psychology, 20,* 364–369.

Thorndike, R. (1985). Reliability. *Journal of Counseling & Development, 63,* 528–530.

Thorndike, R. L. (1971). Concepts of cultural fairness. *Journal of Educational Measurement, 8,* 63–70.

Thorndike, R. L., Hagan, E. P., & Sattler, J. P. (1986). *Technical manual for the Stanford-Binet Intelligence Scale, Fourth Edition.* Chicago: Riverside.

Thornton, G. C., & Byham, W. C. (1982). *Assessment centers and managerial performance.* New York: Academic Press.

Thurlow, M. L., House, A. L., Scott, D. L., & Ysseldyke, J. E. (2000). Students with disabilities in large-scale assessments: State participation and accommodation policies. *Journal of Special Education, 34,* 154–163.

Thurstone, L. L. (1925). A method of scaling psychological and educational tests. *Journal of Educational Psychology, 16,* 433–451.

Thurstone, L. L. (1927). A law of comparative judgment. *Psychological Review, 34,* 273–286.

Thurstone, L. L. (1929). Theory of attitude measurement. *Psychological Bulletin, 36,* 222–241.

Thurstone, L. L. (1931). *Multiple-factor analysis.* Chicago: University of Chicago Press.

Thurstone, L. L. (1935). *The vectors of mind.* Chicago: University of Chicago Press.

Thurstone, L. L. (1938). Primary mental abilities. *Psychometric Monographs,* No. 1. Chicago: University of Chicago Press.

Thurstone, L. L. (1947). *Multiple factor analysis.* Chicago: University of Chicago.

Thurstone, L. L. (1959). *The measurement of values.* Chicago: University of Chicago.

Thurstone, L. L., & Chave, E. J. (1929). *The measurement of attitude.* Chicago: University of Chicago.

Tillman, M. H. (1973). Intelligence scale for the blind: A review with implications for research. *Journal of School Psychology, 11,* 80–87.

Timbrook, R. E., & Graham, J. R. (1994). Ethnic differences on the MMPI-2? *Psychological Assessment, 6,* 212–217.

Tinsley, H. E. A., & Weiss, D. J. (1975). Interrater reliability and agreement of subjective judgments. *Journal of Counseling Psychology, 22,* 358–376.

Tittle, C. R., & Hill, R. J. (1967). Attitude measurement and prediction of behavior: An evaluation of conditions and measurement techniques. *Sociometry, 30,* 199–213.

Torrance, E. P. (1966). *Torrance Tests of Creative Thinking.* Bensenville, IL: Scholastic Testing Service.

Torrance, E. P. (1987a). *Guidelines for administration and scoring/Comments on using the Torrance Tests of Creative Thinking.* Bensenville, IL: Scholastic Testing Service.

Torrance, E. P. (1987b). *Survey of the uses of the Torrance Tests of Creative Thinking.* Bensenville, IL: Scholastic Testing Service.

Touliatos, J., Perlmutter, B. F., & Strauss, M. A. (1991). *Handbook of family measurements.* Newbury Park, CA: Sage.

Tramontana, M. G., & Boyd, T. A. (1986). Psychometric screening of neuropsychological abnormality in older children. *International Journal of Clinical Neuropsychology, 8,* 53–59.

Trautscholdt, M. (1883). Experimentelle unterschungen uber die association der vorstellungen. *Philosophische Studien, 1,* 213–250.

Trice, H. M., & Beyer, J. M. (1984). Studying organizational cultures through rites and ceremonies. *Academy of Management Review, 9,* 653–669.

Trimble, M. R. (Ed.). (1986). *New brain imaging techniques and psychopharmacology.* Oxford: Oxford University.

Truant, G. S., O'Reilly, R., & Donaldson, L. (1991). How psychiatrists weigh risk factors when assessing suicide risk. *Suicide and Life-Threatening Behavior, 21,* 106–114.

Tryon, R. C. (1957). Reliability and behavior domain validity: Reformulation and historical critique. *Psychological Bulletin, 54,* 229–249.

Tuerlinckx, F., De Boeck, P., & Lens, W. (2002). Measuring needs with the Thematic Apperception Test: A psychometric study. *Journal of Personality and Social Psychology, 82,* 448–461.

Tugg v. Towey (1994, July 19). *National Disability Law Reporter, 5,* 999–1005.

Tulchin, S. H. (1939). The clinical training of psychologists and allied specialists. *Journal of Consulting Psychology, 3,* 105–112.

Tulsky, D., Zhu, J., & Ledbetter, M. F. (Project directors). (1997). *WAIS-III, WMS-III Technical manual.* San Antonio, TX: Psychological Corporation.

Tulsky, D. S., & Ledbetter, M. F. (2000). Updating to the WAIS-III and WMS-III: Considerations for research and clinical practice. *Psychological Assessment, 12,* 253–262.

Tuttle, F. B., & Becker, A. (1980). *Characteristics and identification of gifted and talented students.* Washington, DC: National Education Association.

Tybout, A. M., & Artz, N. (1994). Consumer psychology. *Annual Review of Psychology, 45,* 131–169.

Tyler, L. E. (1961). Research explorations in the realm of choice. *Journal of Counseling Psychology, 8,* 195–202.

Tyler, L. E. (1965). *The psychology of human differences* (3rd ed.). New York: Appleton-Century-Crofts.

Tyler, R. S. (1993). Cochlear implants and the deaf culture. *American Journal of Audiology, 2,* 26–32.

Tyler, R. W. (1978). *The Florida accountability program: An evaluation of its educational soundness and implementation.* Washington, DC: National Education Association.

Tziner, A., & Eden, D. (1985). Effects of crew composition on crew performance: Does the whole equal the sum of its parts? *Journal of Applied Psychology, 70,* 85–93.

Udry, J. R. (1981). Marital alternatives and marital disruption. *Journal of Marriage and the Family, 43,* 889–897.

Ulrich, R. E., Stachnik, T. J., & Stainton, N. R. (1963). Student acceptance of generalized personality interpretations. *Psychological Reports, 13,* 831–834.

University of Minnesota. (1984). *User's guide for the Minnesota Report: Personal Selection System.* Minneapolis: National Computer Systems.

U.S. Department of Education, Office of Special Education and Rehabilitative Services, National Institute on Disability and Rehabilitation Research. (2000). *Long range plan: 1999–2003.* Washington, DC: Author.

Utley, C. A., Lowitzer, A. C., & Baumeister, A. A. (1987). A comparison of the AAMD's definition, eligibility criteria, and classification schemes with state departments of education guidelines. *Education and Training in Mental Retardation, 22*(1), 35–43.

Vacha-Haase, T., & Thompson, B. (2002). Alternative ways of measuring counselees' Jungian psychological-type preferences. *Journal of Counseling & Development, 80,* 173–179.

Vagg, P. R., & Spielberger, C. D. (1998). Occupational stress: Measuring job pressure and organizational support in the workplace. *Journal of Occupational Health Psychology, 3,* 294–305.

Vale, C. D., & Keller, L. S. (1987). Developing expert computer systems to interpret psychological tests. In J. N. Butcher (Ed.), *Computerized psychological assessment: A practitioner's guide* (pp. 64–83). New York: Basic.

Vale, C. D., Keller, L. S., & Bentz, V. J. (1986). Development and validation of a computerized interpretation system for personnel tests. *Personnel Psychology, 39,* 525–542.

Vallerand, R. J., Blanchard, C., Mageau, G. A., et al. (2003). Les passions de l'âme: On obsessive and harmonious passion. *Journal of Personality and Social Psychology, 85,* 756–767.

Vander Kolk, C. J. (1977). Intelligence testing for visually impaired persons. *Journal of Visual Impairment & Blindness, 71,* 158–163.

Van der Merwe, A. B., & Theron, P. A. (1947). A new method of measuring emotional stability. *Journal of General Psychology, 37,* 109–124.

Vanderwood, M. L., McGrew, K. S., Flanagan, D. P., & Keith, T. Z. (2001). The contribution of general and specific cognitive abilities to reading achievement. *Learning and Individual Differences, 13,* 159–188.

van Praag, H. M., Plutchik, R., & Apter, A. (Eds.). (1990). *Violence and suicidality: Perspectives in clinical and psychobiological research* (pp. 37–65). New York: Brunner/Mazel.

Varon, E. J. (1936). Alfred Binet's concept of intelligence. *Psychological Review, 43,* 32–49.

Veiga, J., Lubatkin, M., Calori, R., & Very, P. (2000). Measuring organizational culture clashes: A two-nation post-hoc analysis of a cultural compatibility index. *Human Relations, 53,* 539–557.

Velasquez, R. J., Gonzales, M., Butcher, J. N., et al. (1997). Use of the MMPI-2 with Chicanos: Strategies for counselors. *Journal of Multicultural Counseling and Development, 25,* 107–120.

Velden, M. (1997). The heritability of intelligence: Neither known nor unknown. *American Psychologist, 52,* 72–73.

Verhovek, S. H., & Ayres, B. D., Jr. (1998, November 4). The 1998 elections: The nation—referendums. *New York Times,* p. B2.

Vernon, M. (1989). Assessment of persons with hearing disabilities. In T. Hunt & C. J. Lindley (Eds.), Testing older adults: A reference guide for geropsychological assessments (pp. 150–162). Austin, TX: PRO-ED.

Vernon, M., & Andrews, J. E., Jr. (1990). *Psychology of deafness: Understanding deaf and hard-of-hearing people.* New York: Longman.

Vernon, M., Blair, R., & Lotz, S. (1979). Psychological evaluation and testing of children who are deaf-blind. *School Psychology Digest, 8,* 291–295.

Vernon, M., & Brown, D. W. (1964). A guide to psychological tests and testing procedures in the evaluation of deaf and hard-of-hearing children. *Journal of Speech and Hearing Disorders, 29,* 414–423.

Vernon, P. A. (1993). *Biological approaches to the study of human intelligence.* Norwood, NJ: Ablex.

Vernon, P. E. (1950). *The structure of human abilities.* New York: Wiley.

Vernon, P. E. (1964). *Personality assessment: A critical survey.* New York: Wiley.

Vevea, J. L., Clements, N. C., & Hedges, L. V. (1993). Assess the effects of selection bias on validity data for the General Aptitude Test Battery. *Journal of Applied Psychology, 78,* 981–987.

Vig, S., & Jedrysek, E. (1996). Application of the 1992 AAMR definition: Issues for preschool children. *Mental Retardation, 34,* 244–246.

Viglione, D. J. (1999). A review of recent research addressing the utility of the Rorschach. *Psychological Assessment, 11,* 251–265.

Vingoe, F. J. (1995). Beliefs of British law and medical students compared to expert criterion group on forensic hypnosis. *Contemporary Hypnosis, 12,* 173–187.

Visser, P. S., Krosnick, J. A., & Lavrakas, P. J. (2000). Survey research. In H. T. Reis & C. M. Judd (Eds.), *Handbook of research methods in social and personality psychology* (pp. 223–252). New York: Cambridge University Press.

Volkmar, F. R., Klin, A., Marans, W., & Cohen, D. J. (1996). The pervasive developmental disorders: Diagnosis and assessment. *Child & Adolescent Psychiatric Clinics of North America, 5,* 963–977.

von Knorring, L., & Lindstrom, E. (1992). The Swedish version of the Positive and Negative Syndrome Scale (PANSS) for schizophrenia: Construct validity and interrater reliability. *Acta Psychiatrica Scandinavica, 86,* 463–468.

von Wolff, C. (1732). *Psychologia empirica.*

von Wolff, C. (1734). *Psychologia rationalis.*

Vossekuil, B., & Fein, R. A. (1997). *Final report: Secret Service Exceptional Case Study Project.* Washington, DC: U.S. Secret Service, Intelligence Division.

Vroom, V. H. (1964). *Work and motivation.* New York: Wiley.

Vygotsky, L. S. (1978). *Mind in society: The development of higher psychological processes.* Cambridge, MA: Harvard University.

Waddell, D. D. (1980). The Stanford-Binet: An evaluation of the technical data available since the 1972 restandardization. *Journal of School Psychology, 18,* 203–209.

Waehler, C. A. (1997). Drawing bridges between science and practice. *Journal of Personality Assessment, 69,* 482–487.

Wagner, B. M. (1997). Family risk factors for child and adolescent suicidal behavior. *Psychological Bulletin, 121,* 246–298.

Wagner, E. E. (1983). *The Hand Test.* Los Angeles: Western Psychological Services.

Wainer, H. (1990). *Computerized adaptive testing: A primer.* Hillsdale, NJ: Erlbaum.

Wakefield, J. C. (1992a). Disorder as harmful dysfunction: A conceptual critique of DSM-III-R's definition of mental disorder. *Psychological Review, 99,* 232–247.

Wakefield, J. C. (1992b). The concept of mental disorder: On the boundary between biological facts and social values. *American Psychologist, 47,* 373–388.

Wald, A. (1947). *Sequential analysis.* New York: Wiley.

Wald, A. (1950). *Statistical decision function.* New York: Wiley.

Waldman, D. A., & Avolio, B. J. (1989). Homogeneity of test validity. *Journal of Applied Psychology, 74,* 371–374.

Walker, H. M. (1976). *Walker Problem Behavior Identification Checklist.* Los Angeles: Western Psychological Services.

Walker, L. S., & Greene, J. W. (1991). The Functional Disability Inventory: Measuring a neglected dimension of child health status. *Journal of Pediatric Psychology, 16,* 39–58.

Walkup, J. (2000). Disability, health care, and public policy. *Rehabilitation Psychology, 45,* 409–422.

Wallace, I. F., Gravel, J. S., McCarton, C. M., & Ruben, R. J. (1988). Otitis media and language development at 1 year of age. *Journal of Speech and Hearing Disorders, 53,* 245–251.

Waller, N. G., & Zavala, J. D. (1993). Evaluating the big five. *Psychological Inquiry, 4,* 131–135.

Wallston, K. A., Wallston, B. S., & DeVellis, R. (1978). Development of the Multidimensional Health Locus of Control (MHLC) Scales. *Health Education Monographs, 6,* 160–170.

Wantz, R. A. (1989). Review of the Parenting Stress Index. In J. C. Conoley & J. J. Kramer (Eds.), *The tenth mental measurements yearbook.* Lincoln: Buros Institute of Mental Measurements, University of Nebraska.

Ward, P. B., McConaghy, N., & Catts, S. V. (1991). Word association and measures of psychosis proneness in university students. *Personality and Individual Differences, 12,* 473–480.

Waring, E. M., & Reddon, J. (1983). The measurement of intimacy in marriage: The Waring Questionnaire. *Journal of Clinical Psychology, 39,* 53–57.

Warmke, D. L. (1984). *Successful implementation of the "new" GATB in entry-level selection.* Presentation at the American Society for Personnel Administrators Region 4 Conference, October 15, Norfolk, VA.

Watkins, C. E., Jr. (1986). Validity and usefulness of WAIS-R, WISC-R, and WPPSI short forms. *Professional Psychology: Research and Practice, 17,* 36–43.

Watkins, C. E., Jr., Campbell, V. L., Nieberding, R., & Hallmark, R. (1995). Contemporary practice of psychological assessment by clinical psychologists. *Professional Psychology: Research and Practice, 26,* 54–60.

Watkins, E. O. (1976). *Watkins Bender-Gestalt Scoring System.* Novato, CA: Academic Therapy.

Watson, C. G. (1967). Relationship of distortion to DAP diagnostic accuracy among psychologists at three levels of sophistication. *Journal of Consulting Psychology, 31,* 142–146.

Watson, C. G., Felling, J., & Maceacherr, D. G. (1967). Objective draw-a-person scales: An attempted cross-validation. *Journal of Clinical Psychology, 23,* 382–386.

Watson, C. G., Thomas, D., & Anderson, P. E. D. (1992). Do computer-administered Minnesota Multiphasic Personality Inventories underestimate booklet-based scores? *Journal of Clinical Psychology, 48,* 744–748.

Weaver, C. B., & Bradley-Johnson, S. (1993). A national survey of school psychological services for deaf and hard-of-hearing students. *American Annals of the Deaf, 138,* 267–274.

Webb, E. J., Campbell, D. T., Schwartz, R. D., & Sechrest, L. (1966). *Unobtrusive measures: Nonreactive research in the social sciences.* Chicago: Rand McNally.

Webster, C. D., Harris, G. T., Rice, M. E., Cormier, C., & Quinsey, V. L. (1994). *The violence prediction scheme.* Ontario, Canada: University of Toronto Centre of Criminology.

Wechsler, D. (1939). *The measurement of adult intelligence.* Baltimore: Williams & Wilkins.

Wechsler, D. (1944). *The measurement of adult intelligence* (3rd ed.). Baltimore: Williams & Wilkins.

Wechsler, D. (1955). *Manual for the Wechsler Adult Intelligence Scale.* New York: The Psychological Corporation.

Wechsler, D. (1958). *The measurement and appraisal of adult intelligence* (4th ed.). Baltimore: Williams & Wilkins.

Wechsler, D. (1967). *Manual for the Wechsler Preschool and Primary Scale of Intelligence.* New York: The Psychological Corporation.

Wechsler, D. (1974). *Manual for the Wechsler Intelligence Scale for Children—Revised.* New York: The Psychological Corporation.

Wechsler, D. (1975). Intelligence defined and undefined: A relativistic appraisal. *American Psychologist, 30,* 135–139.

Wechsler, D. (1981). *Manual for the Wechsler Adult Intelligence Scale—Revised.* New York: The Psychological Corporation.

Wechsler, D. (1991). *Manual for the Wechsler Intelligence Scale for Children—Third Edition.* San Antonio, TX: The Psychological Corporation.

Wechsler, D. (1997). *Wechsler Adult Intelligence Scale—Third Edition.* San Antonio, TX: The Psychological Corporation.

Wechsler, D. (2002). *Wechsler Preschool and Primary Scale of Intelligence—Third edition (WPPSI-III), Technical and interpretive manual.* San Antonio, TX: The Psychological Corporation.

Wechsler, D. (2003). *Wechsler Intelligence Scale for Children—Fourth edition (WISC-IV), Technical and interpretive manual.* San Antonio, TX: The Psychological Corporation.

Wecker, N. S., Kramer, J. H., Wisniewski, A., et al. (2000). Age effects on executive ability. *Neuropsychology, 14,* 409–414.

Weed, N. C., Butcher, J. N., McKenna, T., & Ben-Porath, Y. S. (1992). New measures for assessing alcohol and drug abuse with the MMPI-2: The APS and AAS. *Journal of Personality Assessment, 58,* 389–404.

Weiner, B. A. (1980). Not guilty by reason of insanity: A sane approach. *Chicago Kent Law Review, 56,* 1057–1085.

Weiner, I. B. (1966). *Psychodiagnosis in schizophrenia.* New York: Wiley.

Weiner, I. B. (1997). Current status of the Rorschach Inkblot Method. *Journal of Personality Assessment, 68,* 5–19.

Weir, R. F. (1992). The morality of physician-assisted suicide. *Law, Medicine and Health Care, 20,* 116–126.

Weiss, D. J. (1985). Adaptive testing by computer. *Journal of Consulting and Clinical Psychology, 53,* 774–789.

Weiss, D. J., & Davison, M. L. (1981). Test theory and methods. *Annual Review of Psychology, 32,* 629–658.

Weiss, D. J., & Vale, C. D. (1987). Computerized adaptive testing for measuring abilities and other psychological variables. In J. N. Butcher (Ed.), *Computerized psychological assessment: A practitioner's guide* (pp. 325–343). New York: Basic.

Weiss, D. S., Zilberg, N. J., & Genevro, J. L. (1989). Psychometric properties of Loevinger's Sentence Completion Test in an adult psychiatric outpatient sample. *Journal of Personality Assessment, 53,* 478–486.

Weiss, H. M., & Cropanzano, R. (1996). Affective events theory: A theoretical discussion of the structure, causes, and consequences of affective experiences at work. *Research in Organizational Behavior, 18,* 1–74.

Weiss, R., & Summers, K. (1983). Marital Interaction Coding System III. In E. Filsinger (Ed.), *Marriage and family assessment: A sourcebook of family therapy.* Beverly Hills, CA: Sage.

Weisse, D. E. (1990). Gifted adolescents and suicide. *School Counselor, 37,* 351–358.

Weissman, H. N. (1991). Forensic psychological examination of the child witness in cases of alleged sexual abuse. *American Journal of Orthopsychiatry, 6,* 48–58.

Welsh, G. S. (1948). An extension of Hathaway's MMPI profile coding system. *Journal of Consulting Psychology, 12,* 343–344.

Welsh, G. S. (1956). Factor dimensions A and R. In G. S. Welsh & W. G. Dahlstrom (Eds.), *Basic readings on the MMPI in psychology and medicine* (pp. 264–281). Minneapolis: University of Minnesota.

Welsh, G. S., & Dahlstrom, W. G. (Eds.). (1956). *Basic readings on the MMPI in psychology and medicine.* Minneapolis: University of Minnesota.

Welsh, J. R., Kucinkas, S. K., & Curran, L. T. (1990). *Armed Services Vocational Aptitude Battery (ASVAB): Integrative review of validity studies* (Rpt 90-22). San Antonio, TX: Operational Technologies Corp.

Werner, H., & Strauss, A. A. (1941). Pathology of figure-background relation in the child. *Journal of Abnormal and Social Psychology, 36,* 236–248.

Wertheimer, M. (1923). Untersuchungen zur Lehre von der Gestalt. *Psychologische Forschung* [Studies in the theory of Gestalt Psychology. *Psychology for Schools*], *4,* 301–303. Translated by Don Cantor in R. J. Herrnstein & E. G. Boring (1965), *A sourcebook in the history of psychology.* Cambridge, MA: Harvard University.

Wesman, A. G. (1968). Intelligent testing. *American Psychologist, 23,* 267–274.

West, L. J., & Ackerman, D. L. (1993). The drug-testing controversy. *Journal of Drug Issues, 23,* 579–595.

Westen, D., Barends, A., Leigh, J., Mendel, M., & Silbert, D. (1988). *Manual for coding dimensions of object relations and social cognition from interview data.* Unpublished manuscript, University of Michigan, Ann Arbor.

Westen, D., Silk, K. R., Lohr, N., & Kerber, K. (1985). *Object relations and social cognition: TAT scoring manual.* Unpublished manuscript, University of Michigan, Ann Arbor.

Westling, D. L. (1996). What do parents of children with moderate and severe mental disabilities want? *Education and Training in Mental Retardation and Developmental Disabilities, 31,* 86–114.

Wexley, K. N., Yukl, G. A., Kovacs, S. Z., & Sanders, R. E. (1972). Importance of contrast effects in employment interviews. *Journal of Applied Psychology, 56,* 45–48.

White, B. L. (1971). *Human infants: Experience and psychological development.* Englewood Cliffs, NJ: Prentice-Hall.

White, D. M., Clements, C. B., & Fowler, R. D. (1985). A comparison of computer administration with standard administration of the MMPI. *Computers in Human Behavior, 1,* 153–162.

White, J. A., Davison, G. C., Haaga, D. A. F., & White, K. L. (1992). Cognitive bias in the articulated thoughts of depressed and nondepressed psychiatric patients. *Journal of Nervous and Mental Disease, 180,* 77–81.

White, L. T. (1984). Attitudinal consequences of the pre-employment polygraph examination. *Journal of Applied Social Psychology, 14,* 364–374.

White, R. W., Sanford, R. N., Murray, H. A., & Bellak, L. (1941, September). *Morgan-Murray Thematic Apperception Test: Manual of directions* [mimeograph]. Cambridge, MA: Harvard Psychological Clinic.

White, S., Santilli, G., & Quinn, K. (1988). Child evaluator's roles in child sexual abuse assessments. In E. B. Nicholson & J. Bulkley (Eds.), *Sexual abuse allegations in custody and visitation cases: A resource book for judges and court personnel* (pp. 94–105). Washington, DC: American Bar Association.

Whitworth, R. H. (1984). Review of Halstead-Reitan Neuropsychological Battery and allied procedures. In D. J. Keyser & R. C. Sweetland (Eds.), *Test critiques* (Vol. 1, pp. 305–314). Kansas City, MO: Test Corporation of America.

Whitworth, R. H., & Unterbrink, C. (1994). Comparison of MMPI-2 clinical and content scales administered to Hispanic and Anglo-Americans. *Hispanic Journal of Behavioral Sciences, 16,* 255–264.

Wicker, A. W. (1969). Attitudes versus actions: The relationship of verbal and overt behavioral responses to attitude objects. *Journal of Social Issues, 25,* 41–78.

Wickes, T. A., Jr. (1956). Examiner influences in a testing situation. *Journal of Consulting Psychology, 20,* 23–26.

Widiger, T. A., & Clark, L. A. (2000). Toward DSM-V and the classification of psychopathology. *Psychological Bulletin, 126,* 946–963.

Wienstock, J., Whelan, J. P., & Meyers, A. W. (2004). Behavioral assessment of gambling: An application of the time-line followback method. *Psychological Assessment, 16,* 72–80.

Wigdor, A. K., & Garner, W. R. (1982). *Ability testing: Uses, consequences, and controversies.* Washington, DC: National Academy.

Wiggins, N. (1966). Individual viewpoints of social desirability. *Psychological Bulletin, 66,* 68–77.

Wilcox, R., & Krasnoff, A. (1967). Influence of test-taking attitudes on personality inventory scores. *Journal of Consulting Psychology, 31,* 185–194.

Wilkinson, G. S. (1993). *Wide Range Achievement Test-3.* Wilmington, DE: Wide Range, Inc.

Williams, A. D. (2000). Fixed versus flexible batteries. In R. J. McCaffrey et al. (Eds.), *The practice of forensic neuropsychology: Meeting challenges in the courtroom* (pp. 57–70). New York: Plenum.

Williams, C. L. (1986). Mental health assessment of refugees. In C. L. Williams & J. Westermeyer (Eds.), *Refugee mental health in resettlement countries* (pp. 175–188). New York: Hemisphere.

Williams, J. M., & Shane, B. (1986). The Reitan-Indiana Aphasia Screening Test: Scoring and factor analysis. *Journal of Clinical Psychology, 42,* 156–160.

Williams, R. (1975). The BITCH-100: A culture-specific test. *Journal of Afro-American Issues, 3,* 103–116.

Williams, R. H., & Zimmerman, D. W. (1996a). Are simple gains obsolete? *Applied Psychological Measurement, 20,* 59–69.

Williams, R. H., & Zimmerman, D. W. (1996b). Are simple gain scores obsolete? Commentary on the commentaries of Collins and Humphreys. *Applied Psychological Measurement, 20,* 295–297.

Williams, S. K., Jr. (1978). The Vocational Card Sort: A tool for vocational exploration. *Vocational Guidance Quarterly, 26,* 237–243.

Williams, T. O., Jr., & Eaves, R. C. (2001). Exploratory and confirmatory factor analysis of the Woodcock Reading Mastery Tests-Revised with special education students. *Psychology in the Schools, 38,* 561–567.

Williams, T. Y., Boyd, J. C., Cascardi, M. A., & Poythress, N. (1996). Factor structure and convergent validity of the Aggression Questionnaire in an offender population. *Psychological Assessment, 8*, 398–403.

Wilmer, H. A., & Husni, M. (1951, December). An auditory sound association technique. *Science, 114*, 621–622.

Wilson, G. G., & Vitousek, K. M. (1999). Self-monitoring in the assessment of eating disorders. *Psychological Assessment, 11*, 480–489.

Wilson, P. T., & Spitzer, R. L. (1969). A comparison of three current classification systems for mental retardation. *American Journal of Mental Deficiency, 74*, 428–435.

Wilson, S. L., Thompson, J. A., & Wylie, G. (1982). Automated psychological testing for the severely physically handicapped. *International Journal of Man-Machine Studies, 17*, 291–296.

Winner, E. (1996). *Gifted children: Myths and realities.* New York: Basic.

Winner, E. (2000). The origins and ends of giftedness. *American Psychologist, 55*, 159–169.

Winston, A. S. (1996). "As his name indicates": R. S. Woodworth's letters of reference and employment for Jewish psychologists in the 1930s. *Journal of the History of the Behavioral Sciences, 32*, 30–43.

Winston, A. S. (1998). "The defects of his race": E. G. Boring and antisemitism in American psychology, 1923–1953. *History of Psychology, 1*, 27–51.

Wirt, R. D., Lachar, D., Klinedinst, J. K., & Seat, P. D. (1984). *Multidimensional description of child personality: A manual for the Personality Inventory for Children.* (1984 revision by David Lachar.) Los Angeles: Western Psychological Services.

Wish, J., McCombs, K. F., & Edmonson, B. (1980). *Socio-Sexual Knowledge & Attitudes Test.* Chicago: Stoelting.

Witkin, H. A., & Berry, J. W. (1975). Psychological differentiation in cross-cultural perspective. *Journal of Cross-Cultural Psychology, 6*, 4–87.

Witkin, H. A., Dyk, R. B., Faterson, H. F., Goodenough, D. R., & Karp, S. A. (1962). *Psychological differentiation.* New York: Wiley.

Witkin, H. A., & Goodenough, D. R. (1977). Field dependence and interpersonal behavior. *Psychological Bulletin, 84*, 661–689.

Witkin, H. A., & Goodenough, D. R. (1981). *Cognitive styles: Essence and origins* (Psychological Issues Monograph 51). New York: International Universities.

Witkin, H. A., Lewis, H. B., Hertzman, M., Machover, K., Meissner, P. B., & Wapner, S. (1954). *Personality through perception: An experimental and clinical study.* New York: Harper.

Witmer, L. (1907). Clinical psychology. *Psychological Clinic, 1*, 1–9.

Witt, J. C., & Elliott, S. N. (1985). Acceptability of classroom management strategies. In T. R. Kratochwill (Ed.), *Advances in school psychology, Vol. 4* (pp. 251–288). Hillsdale, NJ: Erlbaum.

Witty, P. (1940). Some considerations in the education of gifted children. *Educational Administration and Supervision, 26*, 512–521.

Wober, M. (1974). Towards an understanding of the Kiganda concept of intelligence. In J. W. Berry & P. R. Dasen (Eds.), *Culture and cognition: Readings in cross-cultural psychology* (pp. 261–280). London: Methuen.

Wolfner, G., Fause, D., & Dawes, R. M. (1993). The use of anatomically detailed dolls in sexual abuse evaluations: The state of the science. *Applied and Preventive Psychology, 2*, 1–11.

Wolfram, W. A. (1971). Social dialects from a linguistic perspective: Assumptions, current research, and future directions. In R. Shuy (Ed.), *Social dialects and interdisciplinary perspectives.* Washington, DC: Center for Applied Linguistics.

Wolf-Schein, E. G. (1993). Assessing the "untestable" client: ADLO. *Developmental Disabilities Bulletin, 21*, 52–70.

Wollersheim, J. P. (1974). The assessment of suicide potential via interview methods. *Psychotherapy, 11*, 222–225.

Wong-Rieger, D., & Quintana, D. (1987). Comparative acculturation of Southeast Asians and Hispanic immigrants and sojourners. *Journal of Cross-Cultural Psychology, 18*, 145–162.

Woodcock, R. W. (1990). Theoretical foundations of the WJ-R measures of cognitive ability. *Journal of Psychoeducational Assessment, 8*, 231–258.

Woodcock, R. W. (1997). The Woodcock-Johnson Tests of Cognitive Ability—Revised. In D. P. Flanagan, J. L. Genshaft, & P. L. Harrison (Eds.), *Contemporary intellectual assessment: Theories, tests, and issues* (pp. 230–246). New York: Guilford.

Woodcock, R. W., & Mather, N. (1989). *WJ-R Tests of Cognitive Ability—Standard and Supplemental Batteries: Examiner's manual.* In R. W. Woodcock & M. B. Johnson, *Woodcock-Johnson Psychoeducational Battery—Revised.* Allen, TX: DLM Teaching Resources.

Woodcock, R. W., & Mather, N. (1989, 1990). *WJ-R Tests of Achievement: Examiner's manual.* In R. W. Woodcock & M. B. Johnson, *Woodcock-Johnson Psychoeducational Battery—Revised.* Allen, TX: DLM Teaching Resources.

Woodcock, R. W., McGrew, K. S., & Mather, N. (2000). *Woodcock-Johnson III.* Itasca, IL: Riverside Publishing.

Woodward, J. (1972). Implications for sociolinguistics research among the deaf. *Sign Language Studies, 1*, 1–7.

Woodworth, R. S. (1917). *Personal Data Sheet.* Chicago: Stoelting.

Worchel, F. F., & Dupree, J. L. (1990). Projective story-telling techniques. In C. R. Reynolds & R. W. Kamphaus (Eds.), *Handbook of psychological and educational assessment of children: Personality, behavior, & context* (pp. 70–88). New York: Guilford.

World Health Organization. (2001). *International classification of functioning, disability, and health.* Geneva, Switzerland: Author.

Worlock, P., et al. (1986). Patterns of fractures in accidental and non-accidental injury in children. *British Medical Journal, 293*, 100–103.

Wright, B. D., & Stone, M. H. (1979). *Best test design: Rasch measurement.* Chicago: Mesa.

Wylonis, L. (1999). Psychiatric disability, employment, and the Americans with Disabilities Act. *Psychiatric Clinics of North America, 22*, 147–158.

Yao, E. L. (1979). The assimilation of contemporary Chinese immigrants. *Journal of Psychology, 101*, 107–113.

Yarnitsky, D., Sprecher, E., Zaslansky, R., & Hemli, J. A. (1995). Heat pain thresholds: Normative data and repeatability. *Pain, 60*, 329–332.

Yerkes, R. M. (Ed.). (1921). *Psychological examining in the United States Army: Memoirs of the National Academy of Sciences* (Vol. 15). Washington, DC: Government Printing Office.

Yin, P., & Fan, X. (2000). Assessing the reliability of Beck Depression Inventory scores: Reliability generalization across studies. *Educational and Psychological Measurement, 60*, 201–223.

Young, K. S., Pistner, M., O'Mara, J., & Buchanan, J. (1999). Cyber disorders: The mental health concern for the new millennium. *CyberPsychology & Behavior, 2*, 475–479.

Younger, J. B. (1991). A model of parenting stress. *Research on Nursing and Health, 14*, 197–204.

Youngjohn, J. R., & Crook, T. H., III. (1993). Stability of everyday memory in age-associated memory impairment: A longitudinal study. *Neuropsychology, 7*, 406–416.

Yussen, S. R., & Kane, P. T. (1980). *Children's conception of intelligence.* Madison report for the project on studies of instructional programming for the individual student, University of Wisconsin, Technical Report #546.

Zedeck, S., & Cascio, W. F. (1984). Psychological issues in personnel decisions. *Annual Review of Psychology, 35,* 461–518.

Zelig, M., & Beidleman, W. B. (1981). Investigative hypnosis: A word of caution. *International Journal of Clinical and Experimental Hypnosis, 29,* 401–412.

Zhang, L.-M., Yu, L.-S., Wang, K.-N., et al. (1997). The psychophysiological assessment method for pilot's professional reliability. *Aviation, Space, & Environmental Medicine, 68,* 368–372.

Zieziula, F. R. (Ed.). (1982). *Assessment of hearing-impaired people.* Washington, DC: Gallaudet College.

Zimmerman, I. L., & Woo-Sam, J. M. (1978). Intelligence testing today: Relevance to the school age child. In L. Oettinger (Ed.), *Psychologists and the school age child with MBD/LD.* New York: Grune & Stratton.

Zubin, J. (1939, November 20). Letter to B. F. Skinner. (B. F. Skinner Papers, Harvard University Archives, Cambridge, MA).

Zubin, J., Eron, L. D., & Schumer, F. (1965). *An experimental approach to projective techniques.* New York: Wiley.

Zucker, S. (1985). *MSCA/K-ABC with high risk pre-schoolers.* Paper presented at the Annual Meeting of the National Association of School Psychologists, Las Vegas.

Zucker, S., & Copeland, E. P. (1987). *K-ABC/McCarthy Scale performance among three groups of "at-risk" pre-schoolers.* Paper presented at the Annual Meeting of the National Association of School Psychologists, Las Vegas.

Zuckerman, M. (1979). Traits, states, situations, and uncertainty. *Journal of Behavioral Assessment, 1,* 43–54.

Zuckerman, M. (1990). Some dubious premises in research and theory on racial differences. *American Psychologist, 45,* 1297–1303.

Zumbo, B. D., & Taylor, S. V. (1993). The construct validity of the Extraversion subscales of the Myers-Briggs Type Indicator. *Canadian Journal of Behavioural Science, 25,* 590–604.

Zuniga, M. E. (1988). Assessment issues with Chicanas: Practice implications. *Psychotherapy, 25,* 288–293.

Zwahlen, H. T., Schnell, T., Liu, A., et al. (1998). Driver's visual search behaviour. In A. G. Gale et al. (Eds.), *Vision in vehicles-VI* (pp. 3–40). Oxford, England: Elsevier.

Zweigenhaft, R. L. (1984). *Who gets to the top? Executive suite discrimination in the eighties.* New York: American Jewish Committee Institute of Human Relations.

Zytowski, D. G. (1996). Three decades of interest inventory results: A case study. *Career Development Quarterly, 45,* 141–148.

Credits

Chapter 1—P. 7, Fig. 1–1: © Jason Childs/STL/Newsport. P. 9, Fig. 1–2: © AP/Wide World Photos. P. 11, Fig. 1–3: © 2001 Ronald Jay Cohen; all rights reserved. P. 14, Fig. 1–4: Courtesy of Gary A. Mirka, Department of Industrial Engineering, North Carolina State University. P. 17, Fig. 1–5: Courtesy National Archives. P. 19: PG-13 graphic reprinted by permission of the Motion Picture Association of America. P. 24–25, Fig. 1–6: (top left) © Tom Stewart/CORBIS; (middle left) © 2001 Ronald Jay Cohen; all rights reserved; (bottom left) © David Linton; (top right) © 1940 Meier Art Judgment Test, The University of Iowa, Iowa City, IA; bottom right, courtesy Sammons Preston Rolyan. P. 27, Fig. 1–7: Courtesy of the Buros Center for Testing.

Chapter 2—P. 32, Fig. 2–1: © Maynard Williams/NGS Image Collection. P. 34, Fig. 2–2; left, Archives of the History of American Psychology, The University of Akron; right, courtesy of Hudson Cattell. P. 39, Fig. 2–3: © Brown Brothers. P. 46, Fig. 2–4: © AP/Wide World Photos. P. 51: © Jason Reed/CORBIS. P. 55: © Bettmann/CORBIS.

Chapter 3—P. 67, Fig. 3–1: Courtesy Stoelting Co., Wood Dale, IL.

Chapter 4—P. 93, Fig. 4–1: © AP/Wide World Photos. P. 116, Fig. 4–2: University College, London. P. 119, Fig. 4–3: Archives of the History of American Psychology, The University of Akron.

Chapter 5—P. 143: Courtesy of Nancy Bayley. P. 147: © A. Ramey/PhotoEdit.

Chapter 6—P. 161, Table 6–1: From C. H. Lawshe, "A Quantitative Approach to Content Validity," *Personnel Psychology* (1975) 28, 563–575. Reprinted with permission from *Personnel Psychology*. P. 162: Fig. 6–1: (left and right) © Bettmann/CORBIS. P. 168, Fig. 6–2, and p. 169, Table 6–2: From *The Manual of Differential Aptitude Tests: Fifth Edition, Forms S & T,* copyright © 1973, 1974 by The Psychological Corporation, a Harcourt Assessment Company; reproduced by permission. All rights reserved. "Differential Aptitude Tests" and "DAT" are registered trademarks of The Psychological Corporation, registered in the United States of America and/or other jurisdictions. P. 169, Fig. 6–3: From *Test Service Bulletin,* "How Effective Are Your Tests?" The Psychological Corporation, San Antonio, TX. Reproduced by permission of the publisher.

Chapter 7—P. 194, Fig. 7–2: Courtesy of University of North Carolina at Chapel Hill, L. L. Thurstone Psychometric Laboratory. Pp. 207–209: From J. Millman and J. A. Arter, 1984, "Issues in Item Banking," *Journal of Educational Measurement,* 21, 315–330; copyright © 1984 by the National Council on Measurement Education. Reprinted with permission. P. 214, Fig. 7–4: From *Introduction to Measurement Theory, First Edition,* by M. J. Allen and W. M. Yen, Brooks/Cole, 1979. Reprinted with permission of Brooks/Cole Publishing Company, Pacific Grove, CA. P. 215, Fig. 7–5: From *Introduction to Measurement Theory, First Edition,* by M. J. Allen and W. M. Yen, Brooks/Cole, 1979. P. 218, Fig. 7–6: From *Measurement Theory for the Behavioral Sciences* by Edwin E. Ghiselli, John P. Campbell, and Sheldon Zedeck. Copyright © 1981 by W. H. Freeman and Company. Used with permission.

Chapter 8—P. 240, Fig. 8–2: © William Bachman/Photo Researchers. P. 243, Fig. 8–3: Reproduced with permission of the author from Well, *Assessment and Management of Developmental Changes and Problems in Children, Second Edition,* C. V. Mosby, 1981. P. 247, Fig. 8–4: © The Granger Collection, Ltd. P. 249, Fig. 8–5: © Wally McNamee/CORBIS. P. 252: © E! Networks. P. 259: © 2001 Ronald Jay Cohen; all rights reserved.

Chapter 9—Pp. 266–267, Table 9–1: Copyright © 2003 by The Riverside Publishing Company. All rights reserved. Reproduced from the *Stanford-Binet Intelligence Scales, Fifth Edition,* Assessment Service Bulletin #1 by Kirk A. Becker. No part of this work may be reproduced or transmitted in any form or by any means, electronic or mechanical, including photocopying and recording, or by any information storage or retrieval system without the proper written permission of The Riverside Publishing Company unless such copying is expressly permitted by federal copyright law. Address inquiries to Contracts and Permissions Department, The Riverside Publishing Company, 425 Spring Lake Drive, Itasca, IL 60143-2079. P. 271, Fig. 9–1: © 2004 Ronald Jay Cohen. Photo by Angel G. Morales with special thanks to Terence Ramnarine and "les zombies," Ricky Ilermont and Ulrick Pierre. P. 277, Fig. 9–2: Simulated items similar to those in the Wechsler Adult Intelligence Scale: Third Edition. Copyright © 1997 by The Psychological Corporation, a Harcourt Assessment Company. Reproduced by permission. All rights reserved. "Wechsler Adult Intelligence Scale" and "WAIS" are trademarks of The Psychological Corporation from the *Catalog for Psychological Assessment and Intervention Products,* 1998. Copyright © 1998 by The Psychological Corporation, a Harcourt Assessment Company. Reproduced by permission. All rights reserved. P. 281, Fig. 9–3: From *WISC-IV Technical Manual,* The Psychological Corporation, a Harcourt Assessment Company.

Chapter 10—P. 302: © Annie Griffiths Belt/CORBIS. P. 304, Fig. 10–1: Courtesy Mark E. Swerdlik. P. 323, Table 10–3: Reprinted with permission from A. S. Kaufman, N. L. Kaufman, B. Z. Goldsmith, *Sequential or Simultaneous (K-SOS),* 1984, with modifications. Circle Pines, MN: American Guidance Service.

Chapter 11—P. 338, Fig. 11–1: © Jeff Diedrich. P. 349, Fig. 11–3: Courtesy of Sublogic Corporation, Champaign, IL. P. 367, Fig. 11–4: Courtesy of Dr. James Butcher.

Chapter 12—P. 379, Fig. 12–1: © Hans Huber Publishers, Bern. P. 385, Fig. 12–4: Courtesy of Harvard University News Office. P. 386, Fig. 12–5: Courtesy Henry A. Murray. P. 395, Fig. 12–7: © Bettmann/CORBIS. P. 404, Table 12–5: From D. B. Hartmann, B. L. Roper, and D. C. Bradford, "Differences Between Behavioral and Traditional Approaches to Psychological Assessment," in *Journal of Behavioral Assessment,* 1979. Reprinted by permission. Pp. 408–409, text and photo: Courtesy of Supervised Lifestyles Health, Inc. P. 415: © 2001 by Shirley Eberson. All rights reserved. May not be reproduced without permission. P. 416, Fig. 12–9: © Paul J. Sutton/Duomo/CORBIS.

Chapter 13—P. 441: © Rick Wilkins/Reuters/TimePix/Getty Images. P. 442, Table 13–2: From B. A. Bukatman, J. L. Foy, and E. DeGrazia, "Georgetown Criteria for Competency to Stand Trial," *American Journal of Psychiatry,* 1971, 127:9, March. Copyright © 1971 The American Psychiatric Association. Reprinted by permission. P. 443, Table 13–2: From P. D. Lipsitt, D. Lelos, and A. L. McGarry, "Competency for Trial: A Screening Instrument," *American Journal of Psychiatry,* 1971, 128, 105–109. Copyright © 1971 Paul D. Lipsitt and David Lelos. Used with permission of the authors. P. 447, Fig. 13–1: (left) CAT-H card reproduced by permission of the publisher, CPS, Inc., Larchmont, NY; (right) Reproduced by permission of Jason Arnoson, Inc.

Chapter 14—P. 461, Fig. 14–1: Goldstein-Scheerer Tests of Abstract and Concrete Thinking. © 1945, renewed 1972 by The Psychological Corporation. Reproduced by permission. P. 471, Fig. 14–2: © 2001 Ronald Jay Cohen; all rights reserved. P. 472, Fig. 14–3: © Archive Photos/Getty News Service. P. 473, Fig. 14–4(b):"Field of Search" items from Warren and Ekert, *Frontal Granular Cortex and Behavior,* McGraw-Hill. Reprinted with permission of The McGraw-Hill Companies. P. 475, Fig. 14–5: Courtesy Dr. Peter Schilder. P. 477, Fig. 14–6: From "Use of the Visual Motor Gestalt Test in the Diagnosis of Learning Disabilities" by Lauretta Bender, 1970, *The Journal of Special Education,* 4(1), 29–39. Copyright © 1970 by PRO-ED, Inc. Reprinted by permission. P. 481, Fig. 14–8: Courtesy Stoelting Co., Wood Dale, IL. Pp. 486–487, Figs. 1, 2, and 3: Courtesy General Electric Medical Systems.

Chapter 15—P. 491, Table 15–1: From R. Olkin and C. Pledger, "Can Disability Studies and Psychology Join Hands?" from *American Psychologist,* Vol. 58, No. 4, April 203, p. 301. Copyright © 2003 by the American Psychological Association. Reprinted with permission. P. 516, Fig. 15–1: Courtesy Stoelting Co, Wood Dale, IL.

Chapter 16—P. 525, Fig. 16–2: Courtesy Lafayette Instrument Co. P. 533, Fig. 16–3: Courtesy of the Center for Applications of Psychological Type, Inc. P. 535, Table 16–2: From Dennis R. Laker, "The Career Wheel," in *Journal of Employment Counseling,* June 2002, p. 71. Reprinted by permission of American Counseling Association and the author. P. 540, Fig. 16–4: Courtesy of Dr. Douglas Bray. P. 542, Table 16–4, from D. W. Bray, *American Psychologist,* 1982, 37, 180–189, Table 2 p. 184. Copyright © 1982 by the American Psychological Association. Reprinted with permission. P. 548, Fig. 16–5, from J. E. Champagne, "Job Recruitment of the Unskilled," *Personnel Journal,* 48, 259–268. Copyright © 1968 ACA. Reprinted with permission. No further reproduction authorized without written permission of the American Counseling Association.

Name Index

Abel, G. G., 413
Abeles, N., 55
Abelson, R. P., 401
Abidin, R. R., 101, 451
Abrams, D. B., 437
Abrams, S., 413
Abramson, P. R., 515
Achenbach, T. M., 343, 345, 510
Ackerman, D. L., 544
Ackerman, M. J., 100
Ackerman, P. L., 254, 340, 540
Acklin, M. W., 380, 382, 383
Adams, K. M., 227
Adams-Tucker, C., 449
Addeo, R. R., 84
Adelman, S. A., 84
Administration on Aging, 21
Ahern, E., 537
Aikman, K. G., 291
Airasian, P. W., 309
Akamatsu, C. T., 518
Alderfer, C., 549
Alessandri, S. M., 144
Alexander, R. A., 414
Alexander, R. C., 449
Allen, J., 425, 431
Allen, M. J., 216, 220
Allen, N. J., 303
Allen, T. E., 508
Allport, Gordon W., 92, 93, 336, 337, 353, 358, 372
Alpher, V. S., 413
Alterman, A. I., 437
Amabile, T. M., 84, 550
Aman, C. J., 471
Ambrosini, P. J., 164
American Association on Mental Retardation (AAMR), 513
American Board of Forensic Odontology, 449
American Educational Research Institute (AERA), 52, 175
American Psychiatric Association, 151, 428
American Psychological Association (APA), 16, 44, 57, 100, 127, 175, 226
Ames, S. L., 437
Amrine, M., 47
Anderson, G., 518
Anderson, W. P., 345
Andrew, G., 389
Andrews, J. E., Jr., 507
Angoff, W. H., 109
Arbisi, P. A., 369
Arias, I., 132

Armendariz, G. M., 410–411
Armstrong, T., 533
Arnau, R. C., 533
Arnett, P. A., 471
Arnold, D. S., 305
Arnow, E., 380
Arter, J. A., 209
Arthur, W., Jr., 539
Artz, N., 554
Arvey, R. D., 534, 538
Asch, Solomon, 125–126
Association of Personnel Test Publishers (APTP), 532
Atkin, C. K., 562
Atkinson, J. W., 134
Atkinson, R. C., 480
Avolio, B. J., 528, 530
Aycan, Z., 551
Ayres, B. D., Jr., 545
Ayres, R. R., 322

Bailey, J. M., 383
Baker, E. L., 330
Baldwin, A. L., 255
Baldwin, J. A., 371
Ball, T. S., 395
Baltes, B. B., 551
Bank, A. L., 228
Baños, J. H., 467
Barak, A., 523
Barden, R. C., 303, 503
Bardis, P. D., 447
Bardos, A. N., 290
Barends, A., 389
Barker, R., 337
Barlev, A., 55
Barnes, H. L., 447
Barnett, R. C., 551
Baron, J., 315
Bartholomew, D., 180
Bartok, J. A., 472
Bartol, K. M., 533
Barton, K. A., 409
Bassett, S. S., 472
Batchelor, E. S., Jr., 485
Batson, D. C., 401
Bauer, T. N., 552
Baughman, E. E., 255
Bauman, M. K., 505, 507
Baumeister, A. A., 495
Baumeister, R. F., 439
Baumrind, D., 255
Bavolek, S. J., 447
Baxter, J. C., 538
Baydoun, R. B., 530
Bayley, Nancy, 143
Beard, J. G., 536
Beatty, R. W., 541
Beavers, R., 447

Beck, A. T., 164, 341, 435, 439
Beck, S. J., 380
Becker, A., 253
Becker, H. A., 449
Becker, K. A., 265, 267
Beckham, J. C., 472
Beebe, S. A., 101
Begault, D. R., 553
Beidleman, W. B., 425
Beier, E. G., 447
Beier, M. E., 340
Bell, N. L., 285, 525
Bell, Y. R., 371
Bellack, A. S., 406, 412
Bellak, L., 389, 447
Bellak, S., 389, 447
Benbow, C. P., 44
Benda, B. B., 437
Bender, Lauretta, 475
Benedict, R. H., 284
Benjamin, G. A. H., 446
Bennett, F., 511
Ben-Porath, Y. S., 354, 366
Ben-Shakhar, G., 503
Benton, A. L., 463
Berg, C. A., 262
Berk, R. A., 181
Berkowitz, L., 303
Bernardoni, L. C., 395
Bernhardt, G. R., 330
Bernstein, L., 401
Berry, D. S., 415
Berry, J. W., 345
Berven, H. M., 504
Besetsny, L. K., 295
Beyer, J. M., 553
Bienvenu, M. J., Sr., 447
Bigler, E. D., 463n
Billmire, M. G., 449
Binet, Alfred, 35, 65, 235, 256, 318, 513
Birch, H. G., 461–462
Birney, R. C., 550
Birren, J. E., 250
Bizot, E. B., 523
Black, B., 483
Black, H. C., 156
Black, M., 101
Blalock, S. J., 517
Blanck, P. D., 504
Blanton, R. L., 413
Blum, G. S., 348, 389
Blum, M. L., 171
Blumenthal, S. J., 439
Blustein, D. L., 534
Board of Professional Affairs, 449
Boccaccini, M. T., 445
Bock, R. D., 194
Bolin, J. A., 250

Bombadier, C., 496
Bond, G. B., 219
Bond, R., 126
Bono, J. E., 531
Boone, D. E., 284
Booth, A., 447
Borgen, F. H., 523
Boring, Edwin G., 34, 234
Borkenau, P., 415
Bornstein, P. H., 409
Bornstein, R. F., 158, 383
Bove, C. F., 9
Bowers, K., 425
Boyd, T. A., 478
The Boys and Girls Book About Divorce (Gardner), 447
Bozeman, D. P., 552
Bracken, B. A., 322
Braden, Jeffrey P., 508
Bradford, D. C., 404
Bradley, J. P., 341
Bradley-Johnson, S., 507, 510
Brady, N. C., 496
Braginsky, B. M., 346
Brandstaetter, V., 340
Brannen, M. Y., 553
Brannigan, G. G., 476, 477
Branyon, B., 508
Brassard, M., 449
Brauer, B., 508
Bray, D. W., 2, 541, 542
Brewer, E. W., 551
Brewer, S., 562
Bricklin, B., 101
Briggs, Katharine Cook, 339, 533
Bringle, R., 447
Brittain, H. L., 384
Brodsky, S. L., 445
Brody, D., 464
Brody, N., 400
Brodzinsky, D. M., 101
Brogden, H. E., 171
Brook, J. S., 437
Brookhouser, P. E., 508
Brotemarkle, R. A., 35
Brotherson, M. J., 514
Brown, C. E., 11
Brown, D. C., 186
Brown, D. W., 509
Brown, R. D., 352
Brown, R. T., 181, 183
Brown, S. P., 551
Browning, D. L., 393
Bruininks, R. H., 534
Brunner, N. A., 476
Bryan, J., 55
Bryant, S., 391
Bucholz, K. K., 429
Buck, J. N., 290, 397, 398

Walker, H. M., 510
Walker, L. S., 496
Walker, R. L., 371
Walkup, J., 494
Wallace, I. F., 478
Wallace, K. M., 179, 447
Waller, N. G., 354, 358
Wallston, K. A., 347
Walsh, J. A., 401
Wantz, R. A., 451
Ward, L. C., 285
Ward, M. P., 2, 3
Ward, P. B., 393
Waring, E. M., 447
Warmke, D. L., 529
Watkins, C. E., Jr., 285
Watson, C. G., 398
Weaver, C. B., 510
Webb, E. J., 413–414
Webster, C. D., 439
Wechsler, David, 3, 38, 85, 104, 105, 229–230, 235, 244, 254, 273, 276, 278, 279–280, 282, 284
Wecker, N. S., 472
Weed, N. C., 436, 437
Weiner, B. A., 444
Weiner, I. B., 380, 382, 383–384
Weinstock, 405
Weir, R. F., 55
Weiss, D. J., 160, 205
Weiss, D. S., 393
Weiss, H. M., 534

Weiss, R., 407
Weisse, D. E., 253
Weissman, H. N., 451
Wells, G. L., 338
Welsh, G. S., 361, 365
Welsh, J. R., 295
Werner, Heinz, 460
Wertheimer, Max, 475–476
Wesman, A. G., 244, 250
West, L. J., 544
Westen, D., 387
Westling, D. L., 515
Wexley, K. N., 414
Whatley, P. R., 355
White, B. L., 254
White, J. A., 224
White, L. T., 532
White, R. W., 385
White, S., 450
Whitener, E. M., 534
Whitworth, R. H., 355, 369
Wicker, A. W., 551
Wickes, T. A., Jr., 401
Widaman, K. F., 180
Widiger, T. A., 422
Wielkiewicz, R. M., 412
Wiens, A. N., 260
Wigdor, A. K., 44, 530
Wiggins, N., 363–364
Wilcox, R., 401
Wilk, S. L., 186
Wilkinson, G. S., 306
Williams, C. L., 431
Williams, D. R., 524

Williams, J. M., 478
Williams, K. J., 531
Williams, R., 260
Williams, R. H., 132
Williams, T. Y., 439
Willis, R. H., 337
Wilmer, H. A., 395
Wilson, G. G., 409
Wilson, P. T., 495
Wilson, S. L., 14
Winner, E., 251
Winston, A. S., 538
Wirt, R. D., 343, 343n
Wish, J., 515
Witkin, Herman A., 24
Witmer, Lightner, 35
Witty, P., 252
Wober, M., 255
Wolfner, G., 450
Wolfram, W. A., 40
Wolf-Schein, E. G., 511
Wolfson, D., 227, 478, 482, 485
Wollersheim, J. P., 439
Wong-Rieger, D., 371
Woodcock, R. W., 327
Woodward, J., 518
Woodworth, R. S., 356, 362
Woo-Sam, J. M., 282
Worchel, F. F., 389
World Health Organization (WHO), 491
Worlock, P., 449

Worsley, A., 561
Wylonis, L., 501

Yamakawa, R., 278
Yao, E. L., 371
Yen, W. M., 216, 220
Yerkes, R. M., 291
Yin, P., 140
Yoo, S. M., 553
Young, A., 423
Young, K. S., 557
Younger, J. B., 101
Youngjohn, J. R., 250
Yuille, J. C., 450
Yussen, S. R., 234

Zajac, D. M., 552
Zavala, J. D., 358
Zedeck, S., 529
Zelig, M., 425
Zhang, L.-M., 412
Zieziula, F. R., 510
Zimmerman, D. W., 132
Zimmerman, I. L., 282
Ziskin, J., 438
Zsoldos, M., 508
Zubin, Joseph, 395
Zuckerman, M., 93, 255, 402
Zumbo, B. D., 533
Zuniga, M. E., 374
Zwahlen, H. T., 474
Zweigenhaft, R. L., 43
Zytowski, D. G., 524

ALI standard: *(continued)* the person lacked substantial capacity either to appreciate the criminality of the conduct or to conform the conduct to the requirements of the law; contrast with the *Durham standard* and the *M'Naghten standard,* 444

Allen v. District of Columbia, 48

Allied Health Professions Admission Test (AHPAT), 319

"All-in-one" tests, 306

Alpha. *See* **Coefficient alpha**

Alternate assessment: An evaluative or diagnostic procedure or process that varies from the usual, customary, or standardized way a measurement is derived, either by some special accommodation made to the assessee or by alternative methods designed to measure the same variable(s), 4–5, 496

Alternate forms: Different versions of the same test or measure; contrast with *parallel forms,* 134

Alternate-forms reliability: An estimate of the extent to which item sampling and other error have affected scores on two versions of the same test; contrast with *parallel forms reliability,* 133–134, 144

Alternate item, 265

American Association for Measurement and Evaluation in Counseling and Development, 53

American Association on Mental Retardation (AAMR), 495, 513, 514

American Board of Assessment Psychology (ABAP), 22–23, 53

American Board of Professional Psychology (ABPP), 22

American College Testing Program, 310

American Educational Research Institute (AERA), 16, 52–53

American Men of Science, 34, 35

American Psychiatric Association, 55

American Psychological Association (APA), 16
   on ethical issues, 49, 52–53, 55, 57–58
   on intelligence, 261
   online databases, 27–28

American Sign Language (ASL), 507–508

American Speech-Language-Hearing Association, 53

Americans with Disabilities Act (PL 101-336) (1990), 48, 490, 492, 500–501, 504

Analogue approaches, 410–412, 437

Analogue behavioral observation: The observation of a person or persons in an environment designed to increase the assessor's chance of observing targeted behaviors and interactions, 410

Analogue study: Research or behavioral intervention that replicates a variable or variables in ways that are similar to or analogous to the real variables the experimenter wishes to study; for example, a laboratory study designed to research a phobia of snakes in the wild, 410–411

Anatomically detailed doll (ADD): A human figure in doll form with accurately represented genitalia, typically used to assist in the evaluation of sexually abused children, 450

Anchoring, 110

Anchor protocol: A test answer sheet developed by a test publisher to check the accuracy of examiners' scoring, 230, 284

Anti-Semitism, 538

APA: American Psychological Association. In other sources, particularly medical texts, this may refer to the American Psychiatric Association. *See* American Psychiatric Association; American Psychological Association

APAT (Accounting Program Admission Test), 319

Apgar, Virginia, 302

Apgar number, 302

Aphagia: A condition in which the ability to eat is lost or diminished

Aphasia: A loss of ability to express oneself or to understand spoken or written language due to a neurological deficit, 478

API (Applicant Potential Inventory), 532

Apperceive: To perceive in terms of past perceptions (from this verb, the noun apperception is derived), 386

Apperceptive Personality Test (APT), 391

Applicant Potential Inventory (API), 532

Application forms, 537

Applied Measurement in Education, 27

APS (Addiction Potential Scale), 436–437

APT (Apperceptive Personality Test), 391

Aptitude test: A test that usually focuses more on informal as opposed to formal learning experiences and is designed to measure both learning and inborn potential for the purpose of making predictions about the testtaker's future performance; also referred to as a *prognostic test* and, especially with young children, a *readiness test,* 311–318, 319, 524–531

Arithmetic mean: Also referred to simply as the *mean,* a measure of central tendency derived by calculating an average of all scores in a distribution, 74, 75

Armed Forces Qualification Test (AFQT), 294–295

Armed Services Vocational Aptitude Battery (ASVAB), 292, 293–294

Army Alpha test, 291–292

Army Beta test, 291–292

Army General Classification Test (AGCT), 292

Asian Indian Acculturation, 371

Asian Values Scale, 371

ASL (American Sign Language), 507–508

Assessee characteristics, 341–345, 404. *See also* Testtakers

Assessment center: An organizationally standardized procedure for evaluation involving multiple assessment techniques, 2, 541

Assessment of Development Levels by Observation (ADLO), 511

Assessment of Men (OSS), 2

Assimilation: In Piagetian theory, one of two basic mental operations through which humans learn, this one involving the active organization of new information into what is already perceived, known, and thought; contrast with *accommodation,* 236

Assimilation Measure for Spokane Indians, 371

Assisted suicide, 54, 55–56

AST (Reitan-Indiana Aphasia Screening Test), 478

ASVAB (Armed Services Vocational Aptitude Battery), 292, 293–294

At risk: Defined in different ways by different school districts, but in general, a reference to functioning that is deficient and possibly in need of intervention, 301, 492

At-risk infant or toddler: According to IDEA, a child under 3 years of age who would be in danger of experiencing a substantial developmental delay if early intervention services were not provided, 492

Attention deficit hyperactivity disorder (ADHD), 300–301

Attitude: A presumably learned disposition to react in some characteristic manner to a particular stimulus, 332–333, 551–552, 556–559

Auditory Apperception Test, 395

Auditory functioning, 474–475

Aunt Fanny effect. *See* **Barnum effect**

Authentic assessment: Also known as performance-based assessment, evaluation on relevant, meaningful tasks that may be conducted to examine learning of academic subject matter but that demonstrates the student's transfer of that study to real-world activities, 330–331

Autism, 513

Average. *See* **Mode**

Average deviation: A measure of variability derived by summing the absolute value of all the scores in a distribution and dividing by the total number of scores, 78–79

Azzageddi test, 395

Bar graph: A graphic illustration of data wherein numbers indicative of frequency are set on the vertical axis, categories are set on the horizontal axis, and the rectangle bars that describe the data are typically noncontiguous, 70, 71

Barnum effect: The consequence of one's belief that a vague personality description truly describes oneself, when in reality that description may apply to almost anyone; sometimes referred to as the "Aunt Fanny effect," because the same personality might be applied to anyone's Aunt Fanny, 452, 454

Basal level: A stage in a test achieved by a testtaker by meeting some preset criterion to continue to be tested, for example, responding correctly to two consecutive items on an ability test that contains increasingly difficult items may establish a "base" from which to continue testing; contrast with *ceiling level,* 271

BAS (British Ability Scales), 324

Base rate: An index, usually expressed as a proportion, of the extent to which a particular trait, behavior, characteristic, or attribute exists in a population, 167, 171, 172–173

BASIC ID/S, 561–562

Bayley, Nancy, 143

Bayley Scales of Infant Development (BSID), 143–144

BDI (Beck Depression Inventory), 164, 435

Beck Depression Inventory (BDI), 164, 435

Beck Self-Concept Test, 341–342

Behavioral assessment: An approach to evaluation based on the analysis of samples of behavior, including the antecedents and consequences of the behavior, 402–416
   analogue approaches, 410–412, 437
   assessees, 404
   behavioral observation, 10–11, 402, 407–409, 410–411, 431, 562
   issues in, 414, 416
   and psychometrics, 406–407
   psychophysiological methods, 412–413
   purposes of, 405–406
   self-monitoring, 402, 408–410
   test users, 404–405
   vs. traditional assessment, 402–404
   unobtrusive measures, 413–414, 415

Behavioral observation: Monitoring the actions of others or oneself by visual or electronic means while recording quantitative and/or qualitative information regarding the actions, typically for diagnostic or related purposes and either to design intervention or to measure the outcome of an intervention, 10–11, 402, 407–409, 410–411, 431, 562

Behavior Problem Checklist, 510

Behn-Rorschach, 383

The Bell Curve (Herrnstein & Murray), 261

Bell-shaped curve. *See* **Normal curve**

Bender, Lauretta, 475

Bender-Gestalt test: A widely used screening tool for neuropsychological deficit that entails copying designs; also referred to simply as "the Bender"; developed by Lauretta Bender, M.D., 475–477

Bender Visual-Motor Gestalt Test, 509

Bennet Mechanical Comprehension Test, 525

Bias: As applied to tests, a factor inherent within a test that systematically prevents accurate, impartial measurement
   and aptitude tests, 530
   and behavioral assessment, 416
   and graphs, 73
   and item analysis, 221–222
   and panel interviews, 8
   and personality assessment, 344
   and reliability, 147
   and validity, 181
   See also **Fairness**

Big Five model of personality, 358–359, 369–370, 531

Big Six vocational personality types, 357, 369, 523, 531

Big Three personality factors, 531

Bimodal distribution: A distribution in which the central tendency consists of two scores occurring an equal number of times, both the most frequently occurring scores in the distribution, 76

Binary-choice item, 204

Binet, Alfred
   and cultural issues, 256
   and intelligence testing, 1, 35, 38, 265
   and ordinal scales, 65
   on personality, 254
   on theories of intelligence, 235, 244

Binet-Simon Scale, 265, 285

Biofeedback, 15, 412

Biopsychosocial assessment, 516–517

BITCH (Black Intelligence Test of Cultural Homogeneity), 257, 260

Black Intelligence Test of Cultural Homogeneity (BITCH), 257, 260

Blacky Pictures Test, 348, 389

Blindness. *See* Visual disabilities

Blueprinting, 159

Board interviews. *See* Panel interviews

Boehm Test of Basic Concepts, 513

Boston Naming Test, 474

BPS (Bricklin Perceptual Scales), 101

Bracken Basic Concept Scale-Revised, 513

Brain, 458–459

Brain scans, 486

Branched testing. *See* **Adaptive testing**

Brand names, 562, 563

Brauer, Barbara, 508

Breathalyzer tests, 147

Bricklin Perceptual Scales (BPS), 101

Briggs, Katharine Cook, 533

British Ability Scales (BAS), 324

Bruininks-Oseretsky Test of Motor Proficiency, 475, 512

BSID (Bayley Scales of Infant Development), 143–144

Burnout: A psychological syndrome of emotional exhaustion, depersonalization, and reduced personal accomplishment, 550–551

Buros, Oscar Krisen, 26, 27, 46

Buros Institute of Mental Measurements, 26, 27

Business-related assessment, 22
   consumer psychology, 554–563
   Web resources, 564–565
   See also Career counseling; Employment assessment

Butcher, James, 367

California Achievement Tests, 307

California Psychological Inventory (CPI), 347, 415

California Test of Mental Maturity, 295

Callier-Azusa Scale (CAS), 511

CALS (Checklist of Adaptive Living Skills), 534

Campbell, David P., 522, 524

Campbell Interest and Skill Survey, 524

CAPA. *See* Computer-assisted psychological assessment

CAP (Child Abuse Potential Inventory), 172–173, 451

Career counseling, 339, 520–536
   aptitude tests, 524–531
   and clinical/counseling assessment, 420–421
   cultural issues, 369, 534
   interest measures, 521–524
   personality assessment, 531–534
   and theory, 357

Career Interest Inventory, 524

Career transition, 535–536

Career Transitions Inventory (CTI), 535–536

Carroll model of cognitive abilities. *See* **Three-stratum theory of cognitive abilities**

CAS (Callier-Azusa Scale), 511

Case history data: Records, transcripts, and other accounts in written, pictorial, or other form, in any media, that preserve archival information, official and informal accounts, and other data and items relevant to an assessee, 10, 431, 434–435

Case studies, 10. *See also* **Case history data**

Codes of professional ethics, 45

Coefficient alpha: Also referred to as Cronbach's alpha and *alpha,* a statistic widely employed in test construction and used to assist in deriving an estimate of reliability; more technically, it is equal to the mean of all split-half reliabilities, 138, 139–140

Coefficient of correlation: Symbolized by *r,* an index of the strength of the linear relationship between two continuous variables expressed as a number that can range from −1 to +1. Although different statistics may be used to calculate a coefficient of correlation, the most frequently used is the Pearson *r,* 114

Coefficient of determination: A value indicating how much variance is shared by two variables being calculated. This value is obtained by squaring the obtained correlation coefficient, multiplying by 100, and expressing the result as a percentage; the percentage indicates the amount of variance accounted for by the correlation coefficient, 117

Coefficient of equivalence: An estimate of parallel-forms reliability or alternate-forms reliability, 134

Coefficient of generalizability: In generalizability theory, an index of the influence that particular facets have on a test score, 149

Coefficient of stability: An estimate of test-retest reliability obtained during time intervals of six months or longer, 133

Coefficient of validity. *See* **Validity coefficient**

Cognitive Abilities Test, 295

Cognitive Assessment System (CAS), 242, 286

Cognitive Behavioral Driver's Inventory, 485

Cognitive disability: A general reference to a broad spectrum of disabling conditions, including various neurological deficits, learning disabilities, autism, and mental retardation, 495, 512–516

Cognitive interview: A type of hypnotic interview without the hypnotic induction; the interviewee is encouraged to use imagery and focused retrieval to recall information, 425

Collaborative Drawing Technique, 398

Collaborative interview, 425

Collaborative psychological assessment, 4

College Entrance Examination Board, 308

College Level Examination Program (CLEP), 308, 310

Comparative scaling: In test development, a method of developing ordinal scales through the use of a sorting task that entails judging a stimulus in comparison with every other stimulus used on the test, 199

Competence to stand trial: Understanding the charges against one and being able to assist in one's own defense, 440–443

Competency Screening Test, 442

Completion item, 204

Composite judgment, 416

Computer-assisted education, 113

Computer-assisted psychological assessment (CAPA), 12–14, 15
and clinical/counseling assessment, 455
ethical issues, 54, 57
and test development, 205–210

Computer-generated psychological reports, 13

Computerized adaptive testing (CAT): An interactive, computer-administered testtaking process wherein items presented to the testtaker are based in part on the testtaker's performance on previous items, 205–206

Computerized axial tomography (CAT) scan, 486

Computer simulations, 540

Concurrent validity: A form of criterion-related validity that is an index of the degree to which a test score is related to some criterion measure obtained at the same time (concurrently), 163, 164

Confidence interval: A range or band of test scores that is likely to contain the "true score," 151–152

Confidential information: Communication between a professional and a client, along with other data obtained by the professional in the course of a professional relationship that the professional has an ethical obligation not to disclose; contrast with *privileged information,* 58–59

Confidentiality: The ethical obligation of professionals to keep confidential all communications made or entrusted to them in confidence. Professionals may be compelled to disclose such confidential communications under court order or other extraordinary conditions, such as when such communications refer to a third party in imminent danger; contrast with *privacy right,* 58–59

Configural interpretation, 364

Confirmatory factor analysis (CFA): A class of mathematical procedures employed when a factor structure that has been explicitly hypothesized is tested for its fit with the observed relationships between the variables, 180, 238n, 289–290

Confrontation naming: Identifying a pictured stimulus in a neuropsychological context, such as in response to administration of items in the Boston Naming Test, 473, 474

Confucius, 31

Connors Rating Scales-Revised (CRS-R), 301

Co-norming: The test norming process conducted on two or more tests using the same sample of testtakers; when used to validate all of the tests being normed, this process may also be referred to as *co-validation,* 109n, 228

Construct: An informed, scientific idea developed or generated to describe or explain behavior; some examples of constructs include "intelligence," "personality," "anxiety," and "job satisfaction," 93, 175

Constructed-response format: A form of test item requiring the testtaker to construct or create a response, as opposed to simply selecting a response. Items on essay examinations, fill-in-the-blank, and short-answer tests are examples of items in a constructed-response format; contrast with *selected-response format,* 202

Construct validity: A judgment about the appropriateness of inferences drawn from test scores regarding individual standings on a variable called a construct, 175–180, 195–196, 278

Consultative report: A type of interpretive report designed to provide expert and detailed analysis of test data that almost mimics the work of an expert consultant, 13

Consumer panel: A sample of respondents selected by demographic and other criteria, who have contracted with a consumer or marketing research firm to respond on a periodic basis to surveys, questionnaires, and related research instruments regarding various products, services, and/or advertising or other promotional efforts, 558

Consumer psychology: The branch of social psychology dealing primarily with the development, advertising, and marketing of products and services, 554–563
attitudes, 556–559
motivation research, 559–563

Content, 6
cultural issues, 42
and error variance, 130, 134
and personality assessment, 345–346, 356
and validity, 99, 159–162, 195

Content-referenced testing and assessment, 113. *See also* **Criterion-referenced testing and assessment**

Content sampling: Also referred to as *item sampling,* the variety of the subject matter contained in the items; frequently referred to in the context of the variation between individual test items in a test or between test items in two or more tests, 130, 134

Content validity: A judgment regarding how adequately a test or other tool of measurement samples behavior representative of the universe of behavior it was designed to sample, 159–162, 195

Content validity ratio (CVR): A formula developed by C. H. Lawshe used to gauge agreement among raters regarding how essential an individual test item is for inclusion in a test, 160

Contextual cues, 126

Continuous scales, 63, 64

Contralateral control: Phenomenon resulting from the fact that each of the two cerebral hemispheres receives sensory information from the opposite side of the body and also controls motor responses on the opposite side of the body; understanding of this phenomenon is necessary in understanding brain-behavior relationships and in diagnosing neuropsychological deficits, 458–459

Contrast effect: A potential source of error in behavioral ratings when a dissimilarity in the observed behaviors or other things being rated leads to a more or less favorable rating than would have been made had the dissimilarity not existed, 414, 416

Control group: (1) In an experiment, the untreated group; (2) in test development by means of empirical criterion keying, a group of testtakers, typically randomly selected, who do not share the shared characteristic of members of the standardization sample, 361–362

Controlled Word Association Test, 478

Convenience sampling. *See* **Incidental sampling**

Convergent evidence: With reference to construct validity, data from other measurement instruments designed to measure the same or a similar construct as the test being construct-validated, which all point to the same judgment or conclusion with regard to a test or other tool of measurement; contrast with *discriminant evidence,* 179

Convergent thinking, 297

Convergent validity: Data indicating that a test measures the same construct as another test purporting to measure the same construct, 179n

Cooperative Achievement Test, 308

COPS (criterion-focused occupational personality scales), 532

Core subtest, 280

Correlation: An expression of the degree and direction of correspondence between two things, when each thing is continuous in nature, 114–125
  and graphs, 118–122
  Pearson r, 115–118, 139–140, 165
  regression, 122–125, 181–182, 183
  Spearman's rho, 118, 176
  and validity, 166, 176

Correlation coefficient. *See* **Coefficient of correlation**

Counseling assessment. *See* Clinical/counseling assessment

Counseling psychology, 419

Couples Interaction Coding System, 407

Courts. *See* **Forensic psychological assessment**

Co-validation: The test validation process conducted on two or more tests using the same sample of testtakers; when used in conjunction with the creation of norms or the revision of existing norms, this process may also be referred to as *co-norming,* 228–229

CPI (California Psychological Inventory), 347, 415

Cracking the GRE Psychology, 317

Cranial nerves, 469

Creativity, 131, 296–298, 330

Credentialing, 22–23, 53, 193

Criminal justice system. *See* **Forensic psychological assessment**

Criminal responsibility, 443–444

Criterion: The standard against which a test or a test score is evaluated; this standard may take many forms, including a specific behavior or set of behaviors, 110, 163–164, 359. *See also* **Criterion group; Criterion-referenced testing and assessment**

Criterion contamination: A state in which a criterion measure is itself based, in whole or in part, on a predictor measure, 163–164

Criterion-focused occupational personality scales (COPS), 532

Criterion group: A reference group of testtakers who share characteristics and whose responses to test items serve as a standard by which items will be included or discarded from the final version of a scale; the shared characteristic of the criterion group will vary as a function of the nature and scope of the test being developed, 359–361

Criterion-referenced testing and assessment: Also referred to as *domain-referenced testing and assessment* and *content-referenced testing and assessment,* a method of evaluation and a way of deriving meaning from test scores by evaluating an individual's score with reference to a set standard (or criterion); contrast with *norm-referenced testing and assessment,* 110, 113–114, 145–146, 192–193

Criterion-related validity: A judgment regarding how adequately a score or index on a test or other tool of measurement can be used to infer an individual's most probable standing on some measure of interest (the criterion), 163–176
  and classroom tests, 195
  of clinical/counseling assessment, 429
  concurrent validity, 164
  and criterion characteristics, 163–164
  and decision theory, 171–175
  and expectancy data, 166–171
  and incremental validity, 166
  and item analysis, 215
  and validity coefficient, 165–166
  Wechsler Adult Intelligence Scale, 278

Criterion validity. *See* **Criterion-related validity**

Critical incidents technique: In workplace settings, a procedure that entails recording employee behavior evaluated as positive or negative by a supervisor or other rater, 546

Critical mass, 50

Cronbach, Lee, 250

Crook, Thomas, 481

Cross-battery assessment: Evaluation that employs tests from different test batteries and entails interpretation of data from specified tests to provide a comprehensive assessment, 241

Cross-Cultural Adaptability Inventory (CCAI), 534

Cross-validation: A revalidation on a sample of testtakers other than the testtakers on whom test performance was originally found to be a valid predictor of some criterion, 226, 228

CRS-R (Connors Rating Scales-Revised), 301

CRUST (Cultural/Regional Uppercrust Savvy Test), 259

Crystallized intelligence: In Cattell's two-factor theory of intelligence, acquired skills and knowledge that are very much dependent on formal and informal education; contrast with *fluid intelligence,* 239

CTI (Career Transitions Inventory), 535–536

Cuban Behavioral Identity Questionnaire, 371

Cultural Health Attributions Questionnaire, 371

Cultural issues, 37–44
  acculturation, 370–373
  and career counseling, 369, 534

Dimensional qualitative research: An adaptation of Lazarus's multimodal clinical approach for use in qualitative research applications, designed to ensure that the research is comprehensive and systematic from a psychological perspective and guided by discussion questions based on the seven modalities (or dimensions) named in Lazarus's model, which are summarized by the acronym BASIC ID (behavior, affect, sensation, imagery, cognition, interpersonal relations, and drugs). Cohen's adaptation of Lazarus's work adds an eighth dimension, sociocultural, changing the acronym to BASIC IDS, 561–562

Directory of Unpublished Experimental Measures (Goldman & Mitchell), 28

Direct (positive) correlations, 114–115, 120

Disabilities, people with, 490–519
    and accommodation, 496–500, 501, 505–506, 507–508, 511–512
    and alternate assessment, 4–5, 496
    biopsychosocial assessment, 516–517
    cognitive disabilities, 512–516
    cultural issues, 507, 517–518
    definitions, 491–492, 494–496, 500–501
    ethical issues, 53–54
    hearing disabilities, 495, 507–510
    motor disabilities, 511–512
    and preschool assessment, 300–301
    and psychological assessment tools, 14
    visual disabilities, 504–507
    visual/hearing disabilities, 510–511
    Web resources, 519
    and workplace discrimination, 500–504

Disability: As defined in the Americans with Disabilities Act of 1990, a physical or mental impairment that substantially limits one or more of the major life activities of an individual, 491–495. *See also* Disabilities, people with

Discrete scales, 63

Discriminant evidence: With reference to construct validity, data from a test or other measurement instrument showing little relationship between test scores or other variables with which the scores on the test being construct-validated should not theoretically be correlated; contrast with *convergent evidence,* 179

Discrimination, 43, 185. *See also* Cultural issues; Group membership; Race

Discussion of Organizational Culture (DOC), 554–555

Disequilibrium, 236

Distribution: In a psychometric context, a set of test scores arrayed for recording or study, 68, 69–70, 72
    and measures of central tendency, 74–77
    and measures of variability, 77–81
    normal curve, 70, 80, 83–86
    normalizing, 89, 90

Divergent thinking, 297

Diversity issues. *See* Cultural issues

DMM (Drinking Motives Measure), 23

DOC (Discussion of Organizational Culture), 554–555

Domain-referenced testing and assessment, 113. *See also* **Criterion-referenced testing and assessment**

Domain sampling: (1) A sample of behaviors from all possible behaviors that could be indicative of a particular construct; (2) a sample of test items from all possible items that could be used to measure a particular construct, 95n, 146, 148. *See also* **Generalizability theory**

Do Not Call list, 557–558

DQ. *See* **Deterioration quotient**

Draw A Person: Screening Procedure for Emotional Disturbance (DAP: SPED), 398

Draw A Person (DAP) test, 397

Drawing-based projective tests, 290–291, 395–399, 450, 509

Drinking Motives Measure (DMM), 23

Drug testing, 543–544

DSM-IV-TR: Abbreviation for *Diagnostic and Statistical Manual of Mental Disorders, Fourth Edition, Text Revision,* published in May 2000, a slightly modified version of DSM-IV, which was published in 1994. *See Diagnostic and Statistical Manual of Mental Disorders IV*

Dual easel format, 304

Durham standard: A standard of legal insanity in *Durham v. United States* wherein the defendant was not found culpable for criminal action if his unlawful act was the product of a mental disease or defect; contrast with *ALI standard* and *M'Naghten standard,* 444

Durrell Analysis of Reading Test, 320

Dusky v. United States, 441–442

Duty to warn: A legally mandated obligation to advise an endangered third party of their peril that may override patient privilege. Therapists and assessors may have a legal duty to warn when a client expresses intent to hurt a third party in any way, ranging from physical violence to disease transmission, 59, 439

Dynamic characteristics, 142, 144

Dynamic psychological assessment, 4

Dynamometer, 67

Easel format, 304

Eating disorders, 24

Echoencephalograph, 487

ECSP (Exceptional Case Study Project), 441

Educational and Psychological Measurement, 27

Educational assessment, 20–21, 305–334
    achievement tests, 20, 305–311, 312, 509
    aptitude tests, 311–318, 319
    authentic assessment, 330–331
    and bias, 182–183
    classroom tests, 195–196
    and clinical/counseling assessment, 421
    and content validity, 159
    and criterion-referenced testing, 193
    diagnostic tests, 318–321
    and grade norms, 107–108
    group intelligence tests, 295–296
    and item branching, 206, 210
    peer appraisal, 331–332
    performance assessment, 329–330
    portfolios, 330
    psychoeducational assessment, 241
    psychoeducational test batteries, 298, 321–329
    stanine scoring in, 88
    Web resources, 333–334

Educational Resources Information Center (ERIC), 27

Educational Testing Service (ETS), 28

Education Apperception Test, 389

Education for All Handicapped Children Act Amendments (PL 99-457), 300, 492

Education for All Handicapped Children Act (PL 94-142), 48, 300, 306, 492

Edwards Personal Preference Schedule (EPPS), 210–211, 350, 531

EEG (electroencephalograph), 486

EEOC (Equal Employment Opportunity Commission), 47–48

Elaboration, 297

Elderly people, 512

Electroencephalograph (EEG), 486

Electromyograph (EMG), 487

Embedded-figure tests, 351

EMG (electromyograph), 487

Emotional injury: A term sometimes used synonymously with *mental suffering, emotional harm,* and *pain and suffering,* to convey psychological damage, 445–446

Emotional intelligence: A popularization of aspects of Gardner's theory of multiple intelligences, with emphasis on the notions of interpersonal and intrapersonal intelligence, 239

Empirical criterion keying: The process of using criterion groups to develop test items, wherein the scoring or keying of items has been demonstrated empirically to differentiate among groups of test-takers, 359–361

Employment assessment, 22, 537–553
and application materials, 537–538
attitude, 551–552
and cognitive ability measures, 544–545
and content validity, 159–160
and group membership, 43
integrity tests, 532
interviews, 538–539
legal issues, 47, 49, 160
motivation, 547–551
organizational culture, 552–553, 554–555
and people with disabilities, 500–504
performance tests, 539–541, 542, 544
physical tests, 541–544
portfolios, 539
and predictive validity, 167–171, 173–175
productivity, 545–547
and reliability, 150, 154
See also Career counseling
Encyclopedia of Associations (Hunt), 535
End-of-major outcomes assessment, 308
English Men of Science (Galton), 247
English proficiency tests, 308
Entertainment industry ratings, 19
Entrance Examination for Schools of Nursing (RNEE), 319
Episodic memory, 480
EPPS (Edwards Personal Preference Schedule), 210–211, 350, 531
Equal Employment Opportunity Commission (EEOC), 47–48
Equipercentile method: A procedure for comparing scores on two or more tests, as in the creation of national anchor norms, which entails the calculating of percentile norms for each test and identifying the score on each test that corresponds to the percentile, 108–109
Equivalence coefficient. See **Coefficient of equivalence**
ERIC (Educational Resources Information Center), 27
Error: Collectively, all of the factors other than what a test purports to measure that contribute to scores on the test; error is a variable in all testing and assessment, 63–64, 96–97
and drug testing, 543–544
and regression, 123–124
and reliability, 129, 140
and self-report measures, 342–343, 354, 362–363
and validity scales, 354–355
See also **Error variance; Reliability**
Error of central tendency: Less than accurate rating or evaluation by a rater or judge due to that rater's general tendency to make ratings at or near the midpoint of the scale; contrast with *generosity error* and *severity error*, 184, 343
Error variance: In the true score model, the component of variance attrib-

utable to random sources irrelevant to the trait or ability the test purports to measure in an observed score or distribution of scores. Common sources of error variance include those related to test construction (including item or content sampling), test administration, and test scoring and interpretation, 96–97, 130–132, 141–142
Essay item, 204–205
Estimated true score transformations, 183
Ethical issues
assisted suicide, 54, 55–56
computer-assisted psychological assessment, 54, 57
deception, 57–58, 178
people with disabilities, 53–54
professional guidelines, 49, 52, 57
public opinion, 45–47
and substance abuse, 437–438
testtaker rights, 57–60
test-user qualifications, 52–53
See also **Fairness**
Ethical Principles of Psychologists and Code of Conduct (APA), 57–58
Ethical Standards for the Distribution of Psychological Tests and Diagnostic Aids (APA), 52
Ethics: A body of principles of right, proper, or good conduct; contrast with *laws*, 45. See also Ethical issues
Ethnic Identity Questionnaire, 371
ETS (Educational Testing Service), 28
Eugenics, 38, 247–248
Evaluative information: Test or other data used to make judgments such as class placement, pass/fail, and admit/reject decisions; contrast with *diagnostic information*, 42, 318
Event (frequency) recording, 405
Evolutionary theory, 32–33, 423
Evolutionary view of mental disorder: The view that an attribution of mental disorder requires both a scientific judgment (from an evolutionary perspective) that there exists a failure of function, and a value judgment (from the perspective of social values) that the failure is harmful to the individual, 423
Exceptional Case Study Project (ECSP), 441
Executive functions: In neuropsychology, organizing, planning, cognitive flexibility, inhibition of impulses, and other activities associated with the frontal and prefrontal lobes of the brain, 471–472
Exit strategies, 536
Expectancy chart: Graphic representation of an expectancy table, 167
Expectancy data: Information, usually in the form of an expectancy table, illustrating the likelihood that an individual testtaker will score within some interval of scores on a criterion measure, 166–171

Expectancy table: Information presented in tabular form illustrating the likelihood that an individual testtaker will score within some interval of scores on a criterion measure, 167–171
Expectancy theory of motivation, 549
Experimental psychology, 33–34
Expert panel: In the test development process, a group of people knowledgeable about the subject matter being tested and/or the population for whom the test was designed who can provide input to improve the test's content, fairness, and other related ways, 224, 261
Expert testimony, 502–503, 504
Exploratory factor analysis: A class of mathematical procedures employed to estimate factors, extract factors, or decide how many factors to retain, 180, 238n, 289
Extended scoring report: A type of scoring report that provides not only a listing of scores but statistical data as well, 13
Extra-test behavior, 272–273
Extrinsic motivation: A state in which the primary force driving an individual comes from external sources (such as a salary or bonus) and external constraints (such as job loss), 550

Facet: In generalizability theory, variables of interest in the universe including, for example, the number of items in the test, the amount of training the test scorers have had, and the purpose of the test administration, 148
Face validity: A judgment regarding how well a test or other tool of measurement measures what it purports to measure, based solely on "appearances" such as the content of the test's items, 158
Factor analysis: A class of mathematical procedures, frequently employed as data reduction methods, designed to identify variables on which people may differ (or factors). In measurement, two types of factor analysis are common, exploratory factor analysis and confirmatory factor analysis, 119, 194
and intelligence testing, 268, 270, 286
and inter-item consistency, 214
overview, 180, 287–290
and personality assessment, 357–358
and theories of intelligence, 236–241, 245
Factor loading: In factor analysis, a metaphor suggesting that test (or an individual test item) carries a certain amount of one or more abilities which, in turn, has a determining influence on the test

ICC. *See* **Item-characteristic curve**

Identification: (1) A process by which an individual assumes a pattern of behavior that is characteristic of other people; (2) thoughts, feelings, or behavior on the part of one person that resonates in some familiar way with the experiences of another person, 374

Identity: A set of cognitive and behavioral characteristics by which individuals define themselves as members of a particular group; one's sense of self, 374

Idiographic approach: An approach to assessment characterized by efforts to learn about each individual's unique constellation of personality traits, with no attempt to characterize each person according to any particular set of traits; contrast with *nomothetic*, 353

Illness Causality Scale, 220

Immigration, 39, 308

Immunoassay Test, 543

Impression management: Attempting to manipulate others' opinions and impressions through the selective exposure of some information, including false information, usually coupled with the suppression of other information; in responding to self-report measures of personality, psychopathology, or achievement, impression management may be synonymous with attempts to "fake good" or "fake bad," 342, 346

In-basket technique, 541

Incidental sampling: Also referred to as *convenience sampling*, the process of arbitrarily selecting some people to be part of a sample because they are readily available, not because they are most representative of the population being studied, 104

Incremental validity: Used in conjunction with *predictive validity*, an index of the explanatory power of additional predictors over and above the predictors already in use, 166

Indian Assimilation Scale, 371

Individuals with Disabilities Education Act (IDEA) Amendments (PL 105-17)
  and achievement tests, 307
  on alternate assessment, 4–5, 496
  on definitions of disability, 492, 493–494
  overview, 48
  and preschool assessment, 300

Infant assessment, 302–303. *See also* Preschool assessment

Infant or toddler with a disability: According to IDEA, a child under 3 years of age who needs early intervention service because of developmental delays or a diagnosed physical or mental condition that has a high probability of resulting in developmental delay. See *at-risk infants and toddlers* (according to IDEA), as they may also be included at a state's discretion, 492

Inference: A logical result or a deduction in a reasoning process, 125–127, 156. *See also* **Correlation;** Interpretation

Inflation of range: Also referred to as *inflation of variance,* a reference to a phenomenon associated with reliability estimates wherein the variance of either variable in a correlational analysis is inflated by the sampling procedure used and the resulting correlation coefficient tends to be higher as a consequence; contrast with *restriction of range,* 144–145, 165

Inflation of variance. *See* **Inflation of range**

Informal evaluation: A typically non-systematic, relatively brief, and "off-the-record" assessment leading to the formation of an opinion or attitude, conducted by any person in any way for any reason, in an unofficial context and not subject to the same ethics or standards as evaluation by a professional; contrast with *formal evaluation,* 20–21, 303

Information-processing theories, 236, 241–242, 322, 323

Informed consent: Permission to proceed with a (typically) diagnostic, evaluative, or therapeutic service on the basis of knowledge about the service and its risks and potential benefits, 57–58

Inkblot tests, 37, 226, 379–384

Inquiry: A typical element of Rorschach test administration; following the initial presentation of all ten cards, the assessor asks specific questions designed, among other things, to determine what about each card led to the assessee's perceptions, 381

Insanity: A legal term denoting an inability to tell right from wrong, a lack of control, or a state of other mental incompetence or disorder sufficient to prevent that person from standing trial, being judged guilty, or entering into a contract or other legal relationship, 443–444

Institutional settings, 11. *See also* Clinical/counseling assessment; Educational assessment; **Forensic psychological assessment**

Instrumental values: Guiding principles in the attainment of some objective; for example, honesty and ambition, 373

Integrative report: A form of interpretive report of psychological assessment, usually computer-generated, in which data from behavioral, medical, administrative, and/or other sources are integrated; contrast with *scoring report* and *interpretive report,* 13

Integrity test: A screening instrument designed to predict who will and will not be an honest employee, 532

Intelligence: A simple yet controversial term that has been defined in many ways, such as: a multifaceted capacity that manifests itself in different ways across the life span but in general includes the abilities and capacities to acquire and apply knowledge, to reason effectively and logically, to exhibit sound judgment, to be perceptive, intuitive, mentally alert, and able to find the right words and thoughts with facility, and to be able to cope with and adjust to new situations and new types of problems, 232–242
  and Differential Ability Scales, 324
  and factor analysis, 236–241, 245
  and family environment, 254–255
  and gender, 254
  giftedness, 250–251, 252–253
  historical perspective, 234–236, 237
  information-processing theories, 236, 241–242, 322, 323
  introductory definition, 232–233
  nature/nurture issues, 246–249
  and personality, 254
  public views, 233–234
  recent debates, 261–262
  stability of, 250–251
  Web resources, 263
  See also Intelligence testing

Intelligence testing, 243–246, 264–299
  and age norms, 107
  cultural issues, 30, 38, 39–40, 255–261, 279
  error variance in, 131
  Flynn effect, 251, 254
  and giftedness, 252–253
  historical perspective, 35–36, 39
  infants, 304–305
  Kaufman tests, 286
  military, 291–295
  and neuropsychological assessment, 469–470
  and normal curve, 84, 85
  normative sampling, 104–105
  and ordinal scales, 65
  and people with disabilities, 506, 508
  reliability, 151–152
  scoring, 131–132
  short forms, 284–285
  specific intellectual abilities, 296–298
  standard scores in, 88–89
  task types, 243–244
  and theories of intelligence, 244–246, 278, 279–280, 282

Web resources, 298–299

Wechsler Abbreviated Scale of Intelligence, 285–286

Wechsler Adult Intelligence Scale, 35–36, 151–152, 260, 275–279, 284–285, 469–470

Wechsler Intelligence Scale for Children, 38, 39–40, 104–105, 229–230, 279–282

Wechsler Preschool and Primary Scale of Intelligence, 282–284, 302

Wechsler tests overview, 273–275

See also Stanford-Binet Intelligence Scales

Interactionism: The belief that heredity and environment interact to influence the development of one's mental capacity and abilities, 236, 249

Intercept: In the equation for a regression line, $Y = a + bX$, the letter a, which stands for a constant indicating where the line crosses the vertical or Y-axis, 122

Intercept bias: Refers to the point at which a regression line intercepts the Y-axis; refers to a test or measurement procedure systematically underpredicting or overpredicting the performance of members of a group; contrast with *slope bias,* 182, 530

Intercultural Contact and Western Identification Scales, 371

Interest, measures of, 521–524

Inter-item (internal) consistency. *See* **Internal consistency**

Internal consistency: Also referred to as *inter-item consistency,* an estimate of how consistently the items of a test measure a single construct obtained from a single administration of a single form of the test and the measurement of the degree of correlation among all of the test items, 134–140, 141, 145, 148, 214, 388

The International Classification of Functioning, Disability, and Health (WHO), 491

Internet testing sites, 54, 57

Interpersonal intelligence: In Gardner's theory of multiple intelligences, the ability to understand other people, what motivates them, how they work, and how to work cooperatively with them; contrast with *intrapersonal intelligence,* 239

Interpersonal Support Evaluations List, 536

Interpretation, 6, 8

computer-assisted, 12

and consumer psychology, 559

and error variance, 131–132

intelligence testing, 272–273

and people with disabilities, 499–500, 506–507

personality assessment, 352–353, 364–365

and validity, 99

See also **Scoring**

Interpreters, 507, 508

Interpretive report: A formal or official computer-generated account of test performance, presented in both numeric and narrative form and including an explanation of the findings; the three varieties of interpretive report are descriptive, screening, and consultative; contrast with *scoring report* and *integrative report,* 13

Interquartile range: An ordinal statistic of variability equal to the difference between the third and first quartile points in a distribution that has been divided into quartiles, 78

Inter-rater reliability. *See* **Inter-scorer reliability**

Inter-scorer reliability: Also referred to as inter-rater reliability, observer reliability, judge reliability, and scorer reliability, an estimate of the degree of agreement or consistency between two or more scorers (or judges or raters or observers), 140, 143–144, 147

of behavioral assessment, 414, 416

of clinical/counseling assessment, 428

and computers, 456

of projective methods, 383

Interval recording, 405

Interval scale: A system of measurement in which all things measured can be rank-ordered, where the rank-ordering contains equal intervals, every unit on the scale is equal to every other unit on the scale, and there is no absolute zero point; mathematical operations may not be performed on interval-level data because of the absence of a true or absolute zero point, 66, 67–68

Interview: A tool of assessment in which information is gathered through direct, reciprocal communication, 423–434

and consumer psychology, 557

cultural issues, 429–434

and employment assessment, 538–539

and neuropsychological assessment, 466–467

overview, 8–10

and psychometrics, 428–429

types of, 424–427

Intrapersonal intelligence: In Gardner's theory of multiple intelligences, a capacity to form accurate self-perceptions, to discriminate accurately between emotions, and to be able to draw upon one's emotions as a means of understanding and an effective guide, 239

Intrinsic motivation: A state in which the primary force driving an indi-

vidual comes from within, such as personal satisfaction with one's work; contrast with *extrinsic motivation,* 550

Inverse (negative) correlations, 115, 121

Ipsative scoring: An approach to test scoring and interpretation wherein the testtaker's responses and the presumed strength of a measured trait are interpreted relative to the measured strength of other traits for that testtaker; contrast with *class scoring* and *cumulative scoring,* 210–211, 353

IQ (intelligence quotient), 267. *See also* Intelligence testing

IRT. *See* **Item response theory**

Ishihara test, 474

Item analysis: A general term to describe various procedures, usually statistical, designed to explore how individual test items work as compared to other items in the test and in the context of the whole test; item analyses may be conducted, for example, to explore the level of difficulty of individual items on an achievement test or the reliability of a personality test; contrast with *qualitative item analysis,* 212–225

and bias, 221–222

and guessing, 220–221

item-characteristic curves, 217–219, 221–222

item-difficulty index, 212–213

item-discrimination index, 215–217

item-reliability index, 214

and item response theory, 219–220

item-validity index, 214–215

qualitative methods, 222–225

and speed tests, 222

and test homogeneity, 177

Item bank: A collection of questions to be used in the construction of tests, 205, 207–209

Item branching: In computerized adaptive testing, the individualized presentation of test items drawn from an item bank based on the testtaker's previous responses, 206, 210

Item-characteristic curve (ICC): A graphic representation of item difficulty and discrimination, 217–219, 221–222

Item-difficulty index: In achievement or ability testing and other contexts in which responses are keyed correct, a statistic indicating how many testtakers responded correctly to an item. In theory, this index may range from zero (no testtaker responded with the answer keyed correct) to x, where x is the total number of items on the test; in contexts where the nature of the test is such that responses are not keyed correct, this same statistic

SVIB (Strong Vocational Interest Blank), 12, 522

Tail: The area on the normal curve between 2 and 3 standard deviations above the mean, and the area on the normal curve between -2 and -3 standard deviations below the mean; a normal curve has two tails, 84–86

Tailored testing. *See* **Adaptive testing**

Tarasoff v. Regents of the University of California, 48, 59, 439

TAT (Thematic Apperception Test), 226, 384–389, 391, 506, 509

Tautophone, 394

Taylor-Russell tables, 167, 169–171

Teaching item, 270

Team: Two or more people acting interdependently toward a common goal, who have each been assigned specific roles or functions, 547

Technical Recommendations for Achievement Tests (NEA), 52

Technical Recommendations for Psychological Tests and Diagnostic Tests (APA), 52

Telephone interviews, 8

Telephone surveys, 557–558

Teleprocessing: Computerized scoring, interpretation, or other conversion of raw test data sent over telephone lines by modem from a test site to a central location for computer processing; contrast with *central processing* and *local processing,* 13

Tellegen's Big Three personality factors, 531

TEMAS, 389

Temperament: With reference to personality assessments of infants, the distinguishing manner of the child's observable actions and reactions, 254, 534

Temporal lobes, 459

Tennessee Self-Concept Scale, 342

Terman, Lewis M., 248, 250–251, 265

Terminal values: Guiding principles and a mode of behavior that are an end-point objective; for example, "a comfortable life" and "an exciting life"; contrast with *instrumental values,* 373

"Termites": Humorous reference to gifted children who participated in Lewis M. Terman's study of intelligence initiated in 1916, 250

Test: A measuring device or procedure, 5–8. *See also* **Psychological testing**

Test battery: A selection of tests and assessment procedures typically composed of tests designed to measure different variables but having a common objective; for example, an intelligence test, a personality test, and a neuropsychological test might be used to obtain

a general psychological profile of an individual, 137n, 435–436, 482–485

psychoeducational, 298, 321–329

Test catalogues, 26

Test composite: A test score or index derived from the combination and/or mathematical transformation of one or more test scores, 268

Test conceptualization, 190–194

Test development, 16, 190–231

classroom tests, 195–196

and computer-assisted assessment, 205–210

conceptualization, 190–194

content-oriented approach, 356

and content validity, 159

and criterion groups, 359–362

cultural issues in, 40, 261

data reduction methods, 357–359

and error variance, 130

and item format, 202–205, 206

and item pool, 201–202, 226

Minnesota Multiphasic Personality Inventory, 361–369

and normal curve, 90

normative sampling, 105–106

process overview, 190, 191

scaling, 194, 196–201

scoring items, 210–211

standardization, 102

test revision, 225–230

test tryout, 211–212

and theory, 356–357

Web resources, 231

See also **Item analysis**

Test environment, 131, 497

Test evaluation, 100–102

Test heterogeneity: Also simply *heterogeneity,* the extent to which individual test items do not measure a single construct but instead measure different factors; contrast with *test homogeneity,* and reliability, 136, 137, 142

Test homogeneity: Also simply *homogeneity,* the extent to which individual test items measure a single construct; contrast with *test heterogeneity,* 137, 142, 143, 176–177

Testing the limits: (1) In ability testing, the continued administration of test items beyond the level at which the test manual dictates discontinuance; usually conducted only when the examiner has reason to believe an examinee can "pass" the higher-level items; (2) in the administration of the Rorschach test, an optional interview after the initial inquiry, in which the examiner asks questions designed to yield additional insights into the assessee's thought processes and personality, 271n, 381, 516

Test interpretation. *See* Interpretation

Test manuals, 26

Test of Grocery Shopping Skills, 11

Test publishers, 28. *See also* Test development

Test-retest reliability: An estimate of reliability obtained by correlating pairs of scores from the same people on two different administrations of the same test, 101, 132–133, 134, 139, 143, 269, 429

Test revision, 225–230, 365–369

Tests, 5–8. *See also* **Psychological testing**

Tests in Microfiche, 28

Tests in Print (Murphy et al.), 26

Testtakers, 18

and error variance, 96

extra-test behavior, 272–273

and face validity, 158

and qualitative item analysis, 222–224

rights of, 57–60

Test tryout, 211–212

Test users

behavioral assessment, 404–405

and error variance, 96–97

and local norms, 109

and local validity studies, 157

overview, 16–18

and people with disabilities, 498–499

qualifications of, 52–53

and validity, 165–166

See also **Inter-scorer reliability**

Test utility theory, 171. *See also* Decision theory

Texas School for the Blind and Visually Impaired, 506

Thalamus, 459

Thema: In the personality theory of Henry Murray, a unit of interaction between need and press, 387

Thematic Apperception Test (TAT), 226, 384–389, 391, 506, 509

Theories of Personality (Hall & Lindzey), 335–336

Therapeutic contract, 424

Therapeutic psychological assessment, 4

"Think aloud" test administration: A method of qualitative item analysis requiring examinees to verbalize their thoughts as they take a test; useful in understanding how individual items function in a test and how testtakers interpret or misinterpret the meaning of individual items, 224

Thorndike, E. L., 88, 245, 278

Thorndike's multifactor theory of intelligence, 245, 278

Three-stratum theory of cognitive abilities: John B. Carroll's conception of mental abilities and processing classified by three levels or strata with *g* at the broadest level, followed by eight abilities or processes at the second level and a number of more narrowly defined abilities and processes at the third, 239–240, 245

Notes

Notes

Notes

Notes

Notes

Notes

Notes

Notes

Notes

Notes

Notes

(continued from inside front cover)

1931

L. L. Thurstone publishes *Multiple Factor Analysis*, a landmark work that will have the effect of focusing research attention on cognitive abilities.

1935

Christiana D. Morgan and Henry A. Murray collaborate on what was originally called the *Morgan-Murray Thematic Apperception Test*. This tool of personality assessment entails showing pictures to assessees who are prompted to make up stories in response to them. The final version of the test would be published in 1943 with authorship credited to "Henry A. Murray, Ph.D., and the Staff of the Harvard Psychological Clinic."

1938

Mental testing is becoming big business. According to the *1938 Mental Measurements Yearbook*, at least 4,000 different psychological tests are in print. One test published this year comes with a monograph entitled "A Visual Motor Gestalt Test and Its Clinical Use." This, of course, is what has come to be known simply as the Bender-Gestalt test authored by physician Lauretta Bender. In its original form, the test consists of nine designs which the assessee copies. The Bender-Gestalt II would be published in 2003.

1939

Revise the above figure to at least 4,001. Working at Bellevue Hospital in New York City, David Wechsler introduces the *Wechsler-Bellevue Intelligence Scale*, designed to measure adult intelligence. This test would subsequently be revised several times, and from it would be developed a children's test, as well as a preschooler's test. Today, various Wechsler tests are the most popular instruments used to measure the intelligence of children and adults.

1940

World War II prompts an accelerated need for a means to screen military recruits. Also at about this time, psychologist Starke R. Hathaway and psychiatrist/neurologist John Charnley McKinley collaborate on the development of a new personality test they call the Minnesota Multiphasic Personality Inventory (MMPI).

1941

Raymond B. Cattell, with the benefit of factor analysis as a statistical tool, introduces a theory of intelligence based on two general factors he calls *fluid intelligence* and *crystallized intelligence*.

1942

Once again, a world war accelerates the need for psychometrically-sound tools to screen thousands of recruits.

1945

With its emphasis on the administration and clinical interpretation of various tests in a coordinated battery, *Diagnostic Psychological Testing*, by David Rapaport, Roy Schafer, and Merton Gill, represents a milestone in clinical assessment. Criticism centers on the clinical emphasis of the book, with too little statistical rigor.

1951

Test expert Lee Cronbach introduces *coefficient alpha* to measure test reliability. Cronbach's formula is a modification of KR-20 (Kuder and Richardson's twentieth formula). Conceptually, Cronbach's *alpha* calculates the mean of all possible split-half test correlations, corrected by the Spearman-Brown formula.

1954

The first edition of Anne Anastasi's textbook, *Psychological Testing,* is published. The book presents a test-focused perspective on measurement. Also this year, the Swiss psychologist Jean Piaget publishes an original and influential work on the development of cognition in children.

1956

Bernard I. Murstein publishes "The Projection of Hostility on the Rorschach and as a Result of Ego Threat," beginning what will become a long series of articles over many years in which he shares with colleagues critical thinking with regard to projective methods.

1957

Long before "the Donald" would be featured in the television reality show *The Apprentice*, another Donald, psychologist Donald Super, sensitizes us to how personality and career choice can have reciprocal effects. In *The Psychology of Careers,* Super proposes a theory of careers that he then researches over the next three decades.

1961

Based on the same underlying premise as the Rorschach, the Holtzman Inkblot Technique (HIT) is published. What distinguishes the HIT, however, is that it is designed to be a psychometrically sound projective instrument with two parallel forms. The test still has its proponents, primarily in research, but clinicians who employ inkblot tests decidedly prefer the Rorschach.

1962

The beginnings of the practical application of biofeedback can be traced back to this year, when research provides evidence that human subjects are able to produce certain types of brain waves on command. A year later, published research describes the use of the penile plethysmograph as a diagnostic tool for male erotic interest. Biofeedback instrumentation is now available in various forms to monitor many different variables, such as muscle tension and skin temperature.

1963

Stanley Milgram publishes "Behavioral Study of Obedience" and makes a momentous contribution to psychology. The experimental procedure and measurement methods arouse questioning on ethical grounds